COMPARATIVE COGNITION

COMPARATIVE COGNITION

Experimental Explorations of Animal Intelligence

Edited by

Edward A. Wasserman
Thomas R. Zentall

OXFORD
UNIVERSITY PRESS

2006

OXFORD
UNIVERSITY PRESS

Oxford University Press, Inc., publishes works that further
Oxford University's objective of excellence
in research, scholarship, and education.

Oxford New York
Auckland Cape Town Dar es Salaam Hong Kong Karachi
Kuala Lumpur Madrid Melbourne Mexico City Nairobi
New Delhi Shanghai Taipei Toronto

With offices in
Argentina Austria Brazil Chile Czech Republic France Greece
Guatemala Hungary Italy Japan Poland Portugal Singapore
South Korea Switzerland Thailand Turkey Ukraine Vietnam

Published by Oxford University Press, Inc.
198 Madison Avenue, New York, New York, 10016

www.oup.com

Library of Congress Cataloging-in-Publication Data
Comparative cognition : experimental explorations of animal intelligence / edited by
Edward A. Wasserman, Thomas R. Zentall.
p. cm.
Includes bibliographical references.
ISBN-13 978-0-19-516765-8
ISBN 0-19-516765-1
1. Animal intelligence. 2. Psychology, Comparative. 3. Cognition in animals.
I. Wasserman, Edward A. II. Zentall, Thomas R.
QL785.C535 2006
591.5'13—dc22 2005051558

9 8 7 6 5 4 3 2 1

Printed in the United States of America on acid-free paper

Preface

In 1978, Hulse, Fowler, and Honig published an edited volume entitled, *Cognitive Processes in Animal Behavior*. That book represented a true landmark in the scientific study of animal intelligence, freeing interest in complex behavior and learning from the grasp of the rigid theoretical strictures of behaviorism that had prevailed during the previous four decades.

With that volume, a new field was born: comparative cognition. At last, the study of the cognitive capacities of animals other than humans could emerge as a worthwhile scientific enterprise. No less rigorous than purely behavioristic investigations, studies of animal intelligence spanned such wide-ranging topics as: perception, spatial learning and memory, timing and numerical competence, categorization and conceptualization, problem solving, rule learning, and creativity.

In the ensuing 28 years, the field of comparative cognition has grown and thrived. Animals from bees to bonobos have been studied by psychological scientists in their quest to understand the evolution and function of intelligence. Most psychological society meetings (e.g., American Psychological Association, American Psychological Society, Psychonomic Society) hold one or more sessions on comparative cognition. A new scientific society has even been formed: the Comparative Cognition Society, which holds its own yearly meeting, the Conference on Comparative Cognition (CO3). And unprecedented public interest in the field has arisen.

The present volume arose as the result of the kind invitation of Catharine Carlin, cognitive psychology editor at Oxford University Press. Her support and enthusiasm has led us to solicit the present 34 chapters on comparative cognition, authored by leading experts in the field. Not only will readers be treated to a full tour of research on a broad range of topics in a variety of species, but the research will have been conducted by workers from four continents. Comparative cognition is truly an international undertaking.

We have organized the book into topical sections to bring together the work of several researchers studying related issues. But the reader should feel free to move from chapter to chapter as interests dictate.

Reference

Hulse, S. H., Fowler, H., & Honig, W. K. (Eds.). (1978). *Cognitive processes in animal behavior*. Hillsdale, NJ: Erlbaum.

Contents

Contributors xi

Comparative Cognition: A Natural Science Approach to the Study of Animal Intelligence 3
Edward A. Wasserman and Thomas R. Zentall

I. Perception and Illusion

1. Grouping and Segmentation of Visual Objects by Baboons (*Papio papio*) and Humans (*Homo sapiens*) 15
Joël Fagot and Isabelle Barbet

2. Seeing What Is Not There: Illusion, Completion, and Spatiotemporal Boundary Formation in Comparative Perspective 29
Kazuo Fujita

3. The Cognitive Chicken: Visual and Spatial Cognition in a Nonmammalian Brain 53
Giorgio Vallortigara

4. The Comparative Psychology of Absolute Pitch 71
Ronald G. Weisman, Mitchel T. Williams, Jerome S. Cohen, Milan G. Njegovan, and Christopher B. Sturdy

II. Attention and Search

5. Reaction-Time Explorations of Visual Perception, Attention, and Decision in Pigeons 89
Donald S. Blough

6. Selective Attention, Priming, and Foraging Behavior 106
Alan C. Kamil and Alan B. Bond

7. Attention as It Is Manifest Across Species 127
David A. Washburn and Lauren A. Taglialatela

III. Memory Processes

8. The Questions of Temporal and Spatial Displacement in Animal Cognition 145
William A. Roberts

9. Memory Processing 164
Anthony A. Wright

IV. Spatial Cognition

10. Arthropod Navigation: Ants, Bees, Crabs, Spiders Finding Their Way 189
Ken Cheng

11. Comparative Spatial Cognition: Processes in Landmark- and Surface-Based Place Finding 210
Marcia L. Spetch and Debbie M. Kelly

12. Properties of Time-Place Learning 229
Christina M. Thorpe and Donald M. Wilkie

V. Timing and Counting

13. Behavioristic, Cognitive, Biological, and Quantitative Explanations of Timing 249
Russell M. Church

14. Sensitivity to Time: Implications for the Representation of Time 270
Jonathon D. Crystal

15. Time and Number: Learning, Psychophysics, Stimulus Control, and Retention 285
J. Gregor Fetterman

VI. Conceptualization and Categorization

16. Relational Discrimination Learning in Pigeons 307
Robert G. Cook and Edward A. Wasserman

17. A Modified Feature Theory as an Account of Pigeon Visual Categorization 325
Ludwig Huber and Ulrike Aust

18. Category Structure and Typicality Effects 343
Masako Jitsumori

19. Similarity and Difference in the Conceptual Systems of Primates: The Unobservability Hypothesis 363
Jennifer Vonk and Daniel J. Povinelli

20. Rule Learning, Memorization Strategies, Switching Attention Between Local and Global Levels of Perception, and Optimality in Avian Visual Categorization 388
Charles P. Shimp, Walter T. Herbranson, Thane Fremouw, and Alyson L. Froehlich

21. Responses and Acquired Equivalence Classes 405
Peter J. Urcuioli

VII. Pattern Learning

22. Spatial Patterns: Behavioral Control and Cognitive Representation 425
Michael F. Brown

23. The Structure of Sequential Behavior 439
Stephen B. Fountain

24. Truly Random Operant Responding: Results and Reasons 459
Greg Jensen, Claire Miller, and Allen Neuringer

25. The Simultaneous Chain: A New Look at Serially Organized Behavior 481
Herbert Terrace

VIII. Tool Fabrication and Use

26. Cognitive Adaptations for Tool-Related Behavior in New Caledonian Crows 515
Alex Kacelnik, Jackie Chappell, Ben Kenward, and Alex A. S. Weir

27. What Is Challenging About Tool Use? The Capuchin's Perspective 529
Elisabetta Visalberghi and Dorothy Fragaszy

IX. Problem Solving and Behavioral Flexibility

28. Intelligences and Brains: An Evolutionary Bird's Eye View 555
Juan D. Delius and Julia A. M. Delius

29. How Do Dolphins Solve Problems? 580
Stan A. Kuczaj II and Rachel Thames Walker

30. The Comparative Cognition of Caching 602
S. R. De Kort, S. Tebbich, J. M. Dally, N. J. Emery, and N. S. Clayton

31. The Neural Basis of Cognitive Flexibility in Birds 619
Shigeru Watanabe

X. Social Cognition Processes

32. Chimpanzee Social Cognition in Early Life: Comparative–Developmental Perspective 639
Masaki Tomonaga, Masako Myowa-Yamakoshi, Yuu Mizuno, Sanae Okamoto, Masami K. Yamaguchi, Daisuke Kosugi, Kim A. Bard, Masayuki Tanaka, and Tetsuro Matsuzawa

33. Stimuli Signaling Rewards That Follow a Less-Preferred Event Are Themselves Preferred: Implications for Cognitive Dissonance 651
Thomas R. Zentall, Tricia S. Clement, Andrea M. Friedrich, and Kelly A. DiGian

Postscript: An Essay on the Study of Cognition in Animals 668
Stewart H. Hulse

Author Index 679

Subject Index 694

Contributors

ULRIKE AUST
Institute of Zoology, University of Vienna, Austria

ISABELLE BARBET
CNRS, Institut de Neurosciences Cognitives de la Méditerranée, France

KIM A. BARD
Department of Psychology, University of Portsmouth, UK

DONALD S. BLOUGH
Department of Psychology, Brown University, USA

ALAN B. BOND
School of Biological Sciences, Nebraska Behavioral Biology Group, University of Nebraska, Lincoln, USA

MICHAEL F. BROWN
Department of Psychology, Villanova University, USA

JACKIE CHAPPELL
Department of Zoology, University of Oxford, UK

KEN CHENG
Department of Psychology, Macquarie University, Australia

RUSSELL M. CHURCH
Department of Psychology, Brown University, USA

N. S. CLAYTON
Department of Experimental Psychology, University of Cambridge, UK

TRICIA S. CLEMENT
Department of Biological Sciences, Stanford University, USA

JEROME S. COHEN
Department of Psychology, University of Windsor, Canada

ROBERT G. COOK
Department of Psychology, Tufts University, USA

JONATHON D. CRYSTAL
Department of Psychology, University of Georgia, USA

J. M. DALLY
Department of Experimental Psychology, University of Cambridge, UK

S. R. DE KORT
Department of Experimental Psychology, University of Cambridge, UK

JUAN D. DELIUS
Experimental Psychology Unit, University of Konstanz, Germany

JULIA A. M. DELIUS
Center for Lifespan Psychology, Max Planck Institute for Human Development, Berlin, Germany

KELLY A. DIGIAN
Department of Psychology, Rutgers University, USA

N. J. EMERY
Department of Experimental Psychology, University of Cambridge, UK

JOËL FAGOT
CNRS, Institut de Neurosciences Cognitives de la Méditerranée, France

J. GREGOR FETTERMAN
Department of Psychology, Indiana University, Purdue University, Indianapolis, USA

STEPHEN B. FOUNTAIN
Department of Psychology, Kent State University, USA

DOROTHY FRAGASZY
Department of Psychology, University of Georgia, USA

THANE FREMOUW
Department of Psychology, University of Maine, USA

ANDREA M. FRIEDRICH
Department of Psychology, University of Kentucky, USA

ALYSON L. FROEHLICH
Department of Psychology, University of Utah, USA

KAZUO FUJITA
Graduate School of Letters, Kyoto University, Japan

WALTER T. HERBRANSON
Department of Psychology, Whitman College, USA

LUDWIG HUBER
Institute of Zoology, University of Vienna, Austria

STEWART H. HULSE
Department of Psychological and Brain Sciences, Johns Hopkins University, USA

GREG JENSEN
Department of Psychology, Reed College, USA

MASAKO JITSUMORI
Department of Cognitive and Information Sciences, Chiba University, Japan

ALEX KACELNIK
Department of Zoology, University of Oxford, UK

ALAN C. KAMIL
School of Biological Sciences, Nebraska Behavioral Biology Group and Department of Psychology, University of Nebraska, USA

DEBBIE M. KELLY
School of Biological Sciences, University of Nebraska–Lincoln, USA

BEN KENWARD
Department of Zoology, University of Oxford, UK

DAISUKE KOSUGI
Department of Psychology, Kyoto University and Japan Society for the Promotion of Science, Japan

Stan A. Kuczaj II
Department of Psychology, University of Southern Mississippi, USA

Tetsuro Matsuzawa
Primate Research Institute, Kyoto University, Japan

Claire Miller
Department of Psychology, Reed College, USA

Yuu Mizuno
University of Shiga Prefecture, Japan

Masako Myowa-Yamakoshi
Primate Research Institute, Kyoto University, Japan

Allen Neuringer
Department of Psychology, Reed College, USA

Milan G. Njegovan
Department of Psychology, University of Alberta, Canada

Sanae Okamoto
Graduate School of Environmental Studies, Nagoya University, Japan

Daniel J. Povinelli
Cognitive Evolution Group, Center for Child Studies, University of Louisiana at Lafayette, USA

William A. Roberts
Department of Psychology, University of Western Ontario, Canada

Charles P. Shimp
Department of Psychology, University of Utah, USA

Marcia L. Spetch
Department of Psychology, University of Alberta, Canada

Christopher B. Sturdy
Department of Psychology, University of Alberta, Canada

Lauren A. Taglialatela
Department of Psychology, Georgia State University, USA

Masayuki Tanaka
Primate Research Institute, Kyoto University, Japan

S. Tebbich
Department of Experimental Psychology, University of Cambridge, UK

Herbert Terrace
Department of Psychology, Columbia University and New York State Psychiatric Institute, USA

Christina M. Thorpe
Department of Psychology, University of British Columbia, Canada

Masaki Tomonaga
Primate Research Institute, Kyoto University, Japan

Peter J. Urcuioli
Department of Psychology, Purdue University, USA

Giorgio Vallortigara
Dipartimento di Psicologia, Università degli Studi di Trieste, Italy

Elisabetta Visalberghi
Istituto di Scienze e Tecnologie della Cognizione, CNR, Italy

Jennifer Vonk
Cognitive Evolution Group, Center for Child Studies, University of Louisiana at Lafayette, USA

Rachel Thames Walker
Department of Psychology, University of Southern Mississippi, USA

David A. Washburn
Department of Psychology, Georgia State University, USA

EDWARD A. WASSERMAN
Department of Psychology, University of Iowa, USA

SHIGERU WATANABE
Department of Psychology, Keio University, Japan

ALEX A. S. WEIR
Department of Zoology, University of Oxford, UK

RONALD G. WEISMAN
Department of Psychology, Queen's University, Canada

DONALD M. WILKIE
Department of Psychology, University of British Columbia, Canada

MITCHEL T. WILLIAMS
Department of Psychology, University of Windsor, Canada

ANTHONY A. WRIGHT
Neurobiology and Anatomy, University of Texas Medical School at Houston, USA

MASAMI K. YAMAGUCHI
Department of Psychology, Chuo University, Japan

THOMAS R. ZENTALL
Department of Psychology, University of Kentucky, USA

COMPARATIVE COGNITION

Comparative Cognition: A Natural Science Approach to the Study of Animal Intelligence

EDWARD A. WASSERMAN AND THOMAS R. ZENTALL

1A. At first, the allure is weak; there is a vague yearning and a mild agitation. Ultimately, the strength of the desire grows irresistible; its head turns sharply and it skitters across the uneven floor to caress the object of its affection with consummate rapture.

1B. A coin is drawn toward a magnet.

2A. A grim sense of foreboding wells up in the prey as the jaws of the predator draw near. Then, jagged teeth tear deeply into the succulent tissues of the defenseless prey. Excruciating pain sears through its flesh until the predator's canines pierce the prey's heart.

2B. A boy eats an artichoke.

3A. The slight chill gradually becomes a wintry frost. Decisive action is initiated with the clear goal of returning the ambient temperature to a balmy radiance.

3B. A thermostat activates a furnace.

Scientific descriptions and explanations of natural happenings are supposed to be objective, materialistic, and mechanistic, as is the case for some of the above accounts (labeled B) of three everyday events. In other of the above overdramatized accounts (labeled A) of the same events, the proffered mentalistic interpretations appear to be gratuitous, if not downright preposterous, given our current understanding of metals, vegetables, and machines.

Mentalistic explanations of behavior and cognition in human and nonhuman animals may be equally needless; after careful experimental scrutiny, these mentalistic accounts too may seem ridiculous. Natural science has, indeed, succeeded in supplanting superstition and religion as explanations for countless other worldly events—from eclipses and the tides to infectious diseases and the circulation of the blood.

What, then, is the relevance of mentalism to the present volume that is concerned with the intelligence of nonhuman animals? Quite simply, mentalistic accounts of animal behavior and cognition were proposed early in the history of comparative psychology by none other than Charles Darwin (1871/1920). After the rise of behaviorism, mentalism fell out of favor.

Surprisingly, mentalistic accounts have assumed contemporary significance due to the writings of the late D. R. Griffin, founder of the school of inquiry called *cognitive ethology*, whose prime aim is to analyze the possible conscious thoughts and experiences of nonhuman animals (see Griffin, 1976, for the first announcement of the field; see Mason, 1976, for the first critical appraisal of the field; see Griffin, 1992, for a more recent statement of the agenda of cognitive ethology and a review of the behavioral evidence that workers in the field adduce in support of this approach; and see Yoerg, 1992, and Yoerg & Kamil, 1991, for comprehensive critiques of the writings of cognitive ethologists). At least one of its most ardent supporters considers the main accomplishment of cognitive ethology to be that the very ideas of animal thinking and consciousness have gone from being "heretical" to "respectable" (Jolly, 1991).

Putting aside the matter of respectability, we wish to take the present opportunity to place cognitive ethology into logical and methodological perspective as well as to lobby on behalf of what we and others believe may be a preferable alternative to this mentalistic movement in behavioral science. The other scientific school—what current workers call *comparative cognition*—counts among its growing members most of the contributors to the current volume.

Our introductory chapter therefore discusses a series of central issues in the study of cognition that separate these two prominent approaches to the comparative study of human and animal cognition. After reviewing this chapter, the reader should be better able to appreciate the nature of these approaches and the notable disparities between them (also see Wasserman, 1993, 1997). This deeper appreciation should further help readers to understand the methodological and theoretical positions espoused by the authors of the collected chapters.

CENTRAL ISSUES IN THE COMPARATIVE STUDY OF COGNITION

Definitional and Observational Concerns

Few things set the animal world so dramatically apart from the rest of nature as does cognition—an animal's ability to remember the past, to choose in the present, and to plan for the future. To the best of our knowledge, the human and nonhuman animals on our planet are the only living beings that evidence cognition. (The continually controversial case of cognition and the inanimate digital computer will not concern us here; see Blakemore & Greenfield, 1987, for a discussion of this issue.)

Despite the remarkable capacity, intricacy, and flexibility of adaptive behavior, cognition is not a magical or supernatural power; it is the natural product of the biological activity of the brain (see the chapters by Delius & Delius [chapter 28] and Watanabe [chapter 31], this volume). Elucidating the workings of the brain is undoubtedly one of the most daunting challenges ever undertaken by the human species. The current excitement that is being generated by discoveries in the field of neuroscience testifies to the importance of this matter.

Unlike the operation of other bodily systems (like respiration), whose activity is usually *directly* observed in the *isolated* responses of *particular* organs (like the lungs), cognition is usually *indirectly* evidenced through the *diverse* responses of many *different* effectors, generally the skeletal muscles (although emerging methods in neuroscience herald the advent of more *direct* measures of brain activity). Hence, a youngster may sing, hum, or whistle a tune; play it on a piano, xylophone, or trumpet; tap out its rhythm with a stick on a drum; or write out its score with a pen on a sheet of paper. All of these various behaviors divulge her musical knowledge (for more on the substitutability of different behaviors to achieve a common end, see Rachlin, 1992, and Tolman, 1932). Therefore, although the core of cognition lies in the activity of the brain, we usually learn of cognition via what the early comparative psychologist Romanes (1883/1977) dubbed "behavioral ambassadors" (Wasserman, 1984).

Unequivocal distinctions between cognition and simpler Pavlovian and instrumental learning processes, as well as other behavioral or physiological processes like reflex action, maturation, fatigue, and motivation, are devilishly difficult to devise. There is often spirited disagreement among researchers on the merits of these distinctions, as when workers try to explain the occurrence and integration of elaborate behavior patterns like courtship rituals.

Many cognitive processes may be behaviorally indistinguishable from simpler learning processes. For example, one may learn and remember a telephone number, say 987-2468, by repeatedly saying the number aloud (i.e., learning by rote), considered by many theorists to represent a simple learning process. Alternatively, one may notice that the telephone number contains digit patterns like the descending serial order 9-8-7 and the even-number sequence 2-4-6-8, a cognitive process. Unless clear evidence is provided that a more complex cognitive process has been used, C. Lloyd Morgan's famous canon of parsimony obliges us to assume that it has not; we must then conclude that a simpler learning process can account for the learning.

The challenge then is to identify flexible behavior that cannot be accounted for by simpler learning mechanisms. Thus, a cognitive process is one that does not merely result from the repetition of a behavior or from the repeated pairing of a stimulus with reinforcement. Cognitive processes often involve emergent (untrained) relations. Furthermore, because simple learning is assumed to generalize to physically similar stimuli or contexts, in order to qualify as a cognitive process, the emergent relations cannot involve stimuli or relations that are physically similar to those that were explicitly trained.

For example, if one wanted to show that a pigeon had the concept of identity, then one might train a pigeon to match red and green hues (i.e., to select red rather than green when the initial stimulus is red, but to select green rather than red when the initial stimulus is green). If one later tested the pigeon with orange and teal stimuli and one found good transfer, then one could not assume that the concept of identity had been demonstrated because orange is similar to red and teal is similar to green. On the other hand, if one tested the pigeons with stimuli that were not differentially similar to the training stimuli (e.g., black-and-white shapes such as circle and square), then evidence of good transfer might suggest that an untrained relation had emerged (i.e., that the concept of identity had been demonstrated; see Cook & Wasserman, chapter 16, this volume). Thus, the demonstration of cognitive behavior implies that simpler learning processes cannot account for the demonstrated actions.

Studying the Generality of Cognition

Humans are far from unique in exhibiting cognition. Comparable investigative methods have disclosed that nonhuman animals also exhibit complex and flexible behaviors that most observers would confidently conclude disclose cognition, if members of our own species had displayed the same behaviors in the same circumstances. One of Darwin's enduring legacies is his provocative proposal of *mental continuity* between human and nonhuman animals: "The difference in mind between man and the higher animals, great as it is, certainly is one of degree and not of kind" (1871/1920, p. 128).

More infamous was Darwin's penchant to infer a wide variety of cognitive and emotional functions—including, love, memory, attention, curiosity, imitation, and reason—from numerous anecdotes related by pet owners, naturalists, and zookeepers. These anecdotists were not always impartial observers or careful recorders of either the behavior in question or the conditions that promoted the behavior. As interesting and suggestive as these anecdotes were to Darwin, they could not stand the stringent tests of scientific scrutiny, for they were of dubious objectivity and reliability. The anecdotal method simply would not do to establish a science of comparative cognition. A new and different approach was needed to study the generality of cognition.

Comparative Cognition: A Natural Science Approach

Uncovering similarities and differences between human and animal behavior is a prime concern of the field of comparative psychology. The subfield of comparative psychology that is expressly concerned with cognitive processes in human and nonhuman behavior is called *comparative cognition.*

In contrast to Darwin's naive reliance on anecdotal evidence of questionable veracity and replicability, comparative psychologists now use investigative methods that are wholly objective in order to study advanced behavior and cognition in nonhuman animals. Precise control over relevant factors and systematic variation in pertinent organic and environmental parameters encourages researchers in the field to adhere closely to the experimental method.

As most students of behavior are aware, I. P. Pavlov, in Russia, and E. L. Thorndike, in the United States, devised highly reliable and objective techniques for studying learning in nonhuman animals. Much of the progress in the experimental study of comparative cognition has been due to the creative application or modification of their two basic methods.

In addition, respect for Morgan's canon of parsimony tempers the tendency for workers in the field of comparative cognition to invoke overly elaborate interpretations of the behavioral evidence, as Darwin and his early followers were prone to do. As Yoerg and Kamil (1991) echoed a century after Morgan advanced his canon, "we should be circumspect in our evaluation of the level or complexity of explanation the evidence demands" (p. 277).

Experimental Locale

Rare or remarkable natural behaviors by animals often provide the impetus for careful experimental investigations in laboratory settings (for compelling examples of this strategy in the study of food storage and recovery by birds, see Balda & Kamil, 1989, and De Kort, Tebbich, Dally, Emery, & Clayton, chapter 30, this volume). Movement from the field to the laboratory is often necessary if the biological mechanisms controlling the behavior are to be properly pinpointed and if rival interpretations of the behavior are to be systematically explored and convincingly eliminated (Kacelnik, Chappell, Kenward, & Weir, chapter 26, this volume; Yoerg & Kamil, 1991). Appropriately designed field experiments are also a most enlightening brand of investigation (see Cheng, chapter 10, this volume).

At other times, the scientific objective is to discover whether some human cognitive feat can be exhibited by nonhuman animals (this approach is exemplified by the studies of conceptual behavior by pigeons that have been reviewed and analyzed by Wasserman & Astley, 1994, as well as by the research on directed forgetting in nonhumans that has been reviewed by Roper & Zentall, 1993). Such demonstrations not only speak to the species generality of the cognitive process in question but also provide essential empirical information for understanding the possible evolutionary origins of cognition. Most workers have found the laboratory to be a particularly suitable venue for probing the cognitive limits of nonhuman behavior, due to the ease of varying situational variables and recording behavioral responses.

Zentall (1993), in particular, has examined the longstanding interest in exploring the limits of animal intelligence and the problems posed by naturalistic study alone. He concluded that it is not unreasonable to expect that evidence of cognitive behavior will be found in an "unnatural" laboratory setting, despite the fact that animals may exhibit little sign of cognitive behavior when they are observed in their natural environment. Zentall suggested that laboratory experimentation is especially useful because it may be the only way to elicit latent cognitive strategies whose use results in higher levels of, or more efficient, behavior. It may be necessary to expose an animal to artificial procedures both to rule out explanations of behavior in terms of simple learning principles and to induce the animal to deploy advanced cognitive abilities.

Hence, the laboratory studies of animal behavior that are conducted by comparative psychologists are not substitutes for, but complements to, the careful naturalistic observations of field biologists and ecologists. What we learn in one setting must inform our understanding of what we observe in the other (Riley, Brown, & Yoerg, 1986).

Cognition and Unobservables

Because cognition is not itself directly observable, the field of comparative cognition must (with great reluctance, it should be noted) refer to *unobservables* in the description and explanation of behavior (more about this issue can be found in Honig, 1978; Mackenzie, 1977; Riley et al., 1986, Wasserman, 1981, 1982, 1983; and Zuriff, 1985). Many of the unobservables that are used in the field of comparative cognition are of the same "functional" sort as those that are commonly invoked by chemists and physicists (also see Pribram, 1978).

For example, the term *memory* describes those cases when an organism's present behavior is a function of a past stimulus: an animal is thus said to remember a light if it responds differently to the light on its first and second occasions (see the chapters by Roberts [chapter 8] and Wright [chapter 9], this volume). In a parallel way, a capacitor can be said to have *stored* charge when the same current applied to it on a second occasion leads to a smaller increase in electrical potential than occurred on a first occasion, thereby yielding a lawful functional relation between applied current and stored charge. Similar functional considerations guide the deployment of the cognitive construct of attention (see Blough [chapter 5] and Washburn & Taglialatela [chapter 7], this volume).

Although interpretive dangers attend the study of cognition in nonhuman animals, there are safeguards to those dangers. One of the founders of modern research on comparative cognition, W. K. Honig, assessed the merits of this approach in the following way: "The analysis is plausible because it places cognitive process and cognitive behavior within the framework of a functional and experimental analysis of behavior. . . . There is nothing magical or mysterious about the relevant experimental or criterion behaviors, and thus processes remain within the realm of *behavioral* identification and analysis. We do not need a new kind of psychology to deal with cognitive events" (1978, p. 11).

Other unobservables are of a distinctly different, mentalistic nature and are scrupulously avoided by natural scientists—whether they are psychologists or physicists. These mentalistic notions spring from our own private experience and they are further shaped by an enculturation process that is strongly rooted in Cartesian dualism and "folk" psychology (Michel, 1991, offers an incisive analysis of the fruitlessness of folk psychological theory as it has been applied to both human and nonhuman animals). Such mentalistic ideas are well represented by three of the accounts that began this introduction.

Sometimes, however, aspects of ideas that began as vague mentalistic thoughts based on subjective experience can be operationalized and empirically studied—at least within a limited framework. An example is the study of "theory of mind."

If *you* have a theory of mind, then you should be capable of understanding what *others* may or may not know. This notion does not require that you have the ability to read the mind of another person, just that you understand that for someone to know something, some experience with it is required.

When studied in children, theory of mind may take the form of the following scenario: two children, Sally and Billy, are shown the contents of two covered boxes: one is empty, whereas the other contains a small toy. Sally is then asked to leave the room and the experimenter moves the toy to the other box. The experimenter then asks Billy, "When Sally comes back into the room and I ask her, 'Where is the toy?', what will she say?"

When tested in this way, young children, who presumably do not have theory of mind, indicate the veridical (changed) location of the toy. Older children, however, understand that Sally did not see the toy being moved and therefore Sally should believe that the toy is where it was originally. Older children can therefore infer what Sally knows and does not know. In this case, language provides an important tool for the study of cognitive behavior in humans, but carefully designed experiments may allow researchers similar access to cognitive processes, analogous to theory of mind, in nonverbal animals (see Premack & Woodruff, 1978, and Vonk & Povinelli, chapter 19, this volume).

Cognition and Mentalism

Especially when mentalistic notions are applied to other living beings, they suggest the *analogous* experience of some private thought or feeling (for an early discussion of mentalistic inference via this anthropomorphic analogy, see Romanes, 1883/1977; for a more recent discussion of anthropomorphism in behavioral science, see Kennedy, 1992). For instance, a rat that is placed into a cold environment will learn to press a lever that briefly activates a heat lamp. Some individuals might say that the rat does so because it "feels" cold, because it "wants" warmth, and because it "knows" that pressing the lever will produce heat. But, it is crucial to realize that any "feeling," "wanting," and "knowing" are not necessarily in the rat but may reside in the person projecting onto the rat his or her own private experiences. Nothing in the rat's behavior demands that we use these mentalistic terms, a point that can forcefully be made by considering the similar behavior of a thermostat: a human-made device that we staunchly believe is quite unable to think or to feel as we do.

Of course, the use of mentalistic terms is common in everyday speech and in some circles of scientific and philosophical discourse. Its ubiquity suggests that this explanatory style may be innate (Humphrey, 1978). But, it may be learned; children are frequently instructed by their elders that "the cat wants to have its head rubbed," that "mom's car didn't feel like starting today," or that "nature abhors a vacuum." Whatever its provenance (for further conjectures on the origins of mentalism, see Kennedy, 1992, and Povinelli, 1993), many individuals believe that mentalism is not a sound basis for a natural science of cognition—whether of humans or of other animals. These theorists consider that mentalism is a prescientific mode of explanation that may hamper progress in the behavioral and brain sciences (for more on this view, see Kennedy, 1992; Skinner, 1977, 1985; and Hulse, Postscript, this volume).

These points notwithstanding, mentalism is not a theoretical affliction that affects only the softheaded among us. No less than the Nobel Laureate physiologist Ivan P. Pavlov once adopted a mentalistic approach to understanding the conditioned reflexes that he and his co-workers discovered in their studies of canine digestion.

The beginning of that story is familiar enough: Pavlov and his Russian colleagues serendipitously observed that hungry dogs salivated not only to food in the mouth but also to stimuli that were repeatedly paired with food, like the familiar sight of the experimenter entering the room holding a bowl of food. The end of the story is also well known: Pavlov vigorously insisted that natural scientific laws of association formation could be experimentally established that linked—via the dog's neural machinery—temporally contiguous stimuli, like the sight of the food bowl with food in the mouth.

What is missing from most textbooks is an account of the extraordinary difficulty that Pavlov and his collaborators had in deciding just how to go about investigating and interpreting their groundbreaking observations. In the 1928 book chronicling his first 25 years of conditioning research, "Lectures on Conditioned Reflexes," Pavlov describes this fascinating story as involving two opposite paths to comprehending conditioned reflexes: the mentalistic approach and the scientific approach.

According to the mentalistic approach, we should be mainly interested in the internal or subjective world of the dog rather than in its overt actions. This approach assumes that the internal world of the dog—its thoughts, its feelings, and its desires (if it has any)—is analogous to our own. Pavlov and his colleagues actually entertained this approach prior to 1903 in order to understand the then-called "psychical" secretions of their dogs to signals for food.

Using the mentalistic approach, the researchers tried to explain their findings by "fancying the subjective condition" of their dogs. Unfortunately, all that came from these many musings were endless controversies and unverifiable personal opinions. This interpretive breakdown forced the researchers to abandon what Pavlov suspected was an inborn inclination for people to adopt a mentalistic interpretation and to promote a less familiar, but more productive objective approach. This analytical transition from mentalistic interpretation to a natural science approach was not an easy one to make; indeed, Pavlov described the process as involving persistent deliberation and considerable interpersonal dispute.

From a different perspective, other authors have argued on behalf of mentalism as a bountiful source of fresh hypotheses for proper scientific scrutiny. Famous among those authors was Tolman (1938), who wrote, "I, in my future work intend to go ahead imagining how, *if I were a rat*, I would behave" (p. 24; further discussion of this proposal can be found in Burghardt, 1985, and Kennedy, 1992). As long as mentalistic musings are used purely heuristically, like the fanciful flights that are said to have inspired August Kekule's hypothesization of the benzene ring, they may be beneficial; they are, in this case, unproblematic. The problem is that too many workers pursue mentalism to its more troublesome extremes.

Mentalism and Cognitive Ethology

Several cognitive ethologists have contended that our private experience is so profound and salient that to exclude it from a scientific analysis is to leave out a necessary ingredient to a "complete" understanding of cognition and behavior (see Feigl, 1967, p. 138, for a recounting of Einstein's colorful comments on the matter). Cognitive ethologists have further claimed that, although we presently lack the critical methodological tools for directly assaying consciousness in other organisms, these techniques may be on the immediate horizon. We must, they implore, not close *our* minds to the possible development of such "windows" into *others'* minds (Ristau, 1991).

Personal experience is indeed basic and striking; it was utterly undeniable to René Descartes (1641/1988). Yet, experience is inherently *private*. As Lubinski and Thompson (1993) have observed, "experiential phenomena are directly accessible via one road, a road on which only one person travels" (p. 668) (also see Baum, 1993). Because of the impossibility of independent observers ever agreeing on the experiential "facts" at issue, many theorists have suggested that private experience simply falls outside of the ken of natural science—a positively *public* business. The development of objective "windows" into others' minds is thus better considered to be the stuff of science fiction than of science fact. It is extraordinarily unlikely that any behavioral, introspective, or physiological methods will ever allow us to experience the thoughts and feelings of another organism—human or nonhuman.

Critically, cognitive ethologists' fascination with interspecific communication (see Kuczaj & Walker, chapter 29, this volume) as such an objective window is probably not the royal road to shared private experience: "Asking another [organism] what it is thinking may give you another piece of behavior, but it will never give you direct access to its mental state" (Laasko, 1993). Let us not forget Wittgenstein's famous (1953) aphorism, "If a lion could talk, we could not understand him." Appeal to the eventual development of objective mental "windows" appears to be, at best, wishful thinking and, at worst, an obstacle to real progress in the scientific analysis of complex behavior and cognition. "If the history of other sciences can be a guide, the study of animal behavior will progress only to the extent that we can devise techniques and metaphors that avoid imputation of human mental phenomena to animals which result from metaphoric extensions of our folk psychology" (Michel, 1991, p. 268). To many past and present workers in the field of comparative cognition, what is generally called operational behaviorism (Zuriff, 1985) provides those progressive techniques and metaphors.

Simply put, the notion of "windows" into others' minds appears to be misguided. Behaviors—be they simple or complex, be they verbal or nonverbal, be they those of human or nonhuman animals—are purely the product of biological mechanisms. When we infer private experiences in others from their public behaviors, we are not using a metaphorical "window" at all, but rather a "mirror." We see *ourselves* in the behavior of *others*. Even more perilously, we see our *inner* selves reflected in the *outward* behavior of others. It is, of course, reassuring to see ourselves when we look into a mirror; to see someone or something else would be most discombobulating. We may thus be comforted that other animals seem pretty much like us when we describe and interpret their behavior in terms of our own private experience.

Our tendency to infer mental states in animals may be an extension of our ability to project onto other humans our own mental states. We infer what their mental state would be if we were to behave similarly under similar circumstances. Such inferences may have practical value in our social relations with other humans. For example, we express our sorrow to a friend who has lost a parent or who has been involved in an accident. But, we should not confuse any possible social function of assuming similar mental states between ourselves and others (sympathy or empathy) with an objective understanding of those states. When we express sympathy, it does not much matter if we are wrong; our expression of concern alone is appreciated because others are grateful for our thoughts. In those cases, the assumption of a common mental or emotional state may play a social role, but that state itself is not the subject of science. When we make assumptions about the similarity of our own mental states to those of other animals, this vision may be so distorted by the lens of mentalism that a clear view of the animal mind can never be gained—and that is our true quest.

Finally, we might well ask what cognitive ethologists hope to gain by postulating the existence of conscious experience in animals other than a possibly false sense of completeness in treating both the "inner" and "outer" aspects of behavior (see Romanes, 1883/1977, for more on this distinction). Griffin's answer is that, if animals do indeed have mental experience, then that experience may "affect the animals' behavior, welfare, and biological fitness" (1978, p. 528). However, understanding any possible functional significance of mental experience must surely await the collection of convincing empirical evidence of that experience and the delineation of the mechanisms of its proximate causation. Many critics fear that this wait will be endless.

Might it not be better to pursue a purely objective analysis of behavior and cognition, one that judiciously avoids such treacherous concepts as mind and consciousness and that follows the proven path of natural science? This course of action was precisely what the early behaviorist H. S. Jennings proposed when he observed that "apart from their relation to the problem of consciousness . . . the objective processes in behavior are of the highest interest in themselves. . . . [W]e need a knowledge of the laws controlling them, of the same sort as our knowledge of the laws of metabolism" (1904/1976, p. v).

THE AGENDA OF COMPARATIVE COGNITION

The myriad behaviors of humans and other animals persuade us that they remember the past, they choose in the present, and they plan for the future. On what behavioral, situational, and historical grounds do we make these cognitive inferences? What are the behavioral and biological mechanisms of remembering, choosing, and planning? Are humans special among all other animals in their processes of cognition? What, if anything, does language add to an animal's ability to adapt to changing conditions of survival? These are some of the truly crucial, exciting, and answerable questions for a science of comparative cognition; these and other intriguing issues are carefully considered in the 34 chapters that follow.

The experimental study of animal intelligence should greatly advance our understanding of behavioral adaptation and its evolution in the animal kingdom. Perhaps we should simply get on with this task and leave mentalistic speculations to philosophers, whose theories of mind and conjectures about consciousness need not be bound by the constraints of natural science. We do need a science of comparative cognition. But, that field "should not be loosely slung in a net of mentalistic verbiage. Rather, it should be defined as the rigorous, wholly scientific study of cognition in an ethological and ecological context" (Yoerg & Kamil, 1991, p. 278).

References

Balda, R. P., & Kamil, A. C. (1989). A comparative study of cache recovery by three corvid species. *Animal Behaviour, 38,* 486–495.

Baum, W. M. (1993). The status of private events in behavior analysis. *Behavioral and Brain Sciences, 16,* 644.

Blakemore, C., & Greenfield, S. (Eds.) (1987). *Mindwaves: Thoughts on intelligence, identity and consciousness.* Oxford: Basil Blackwell.

Burghardt, G. M. (1985). Animal awareness: Current perceptions and historical perspective. *American Psychologist, 40,* 905–919.

Darwin, C. (1871/1920). *The descent of man; and selection in relation to sex* (2nd ed.). New York: D. Appleton and Company.

Descartes, R. (1641/1998). Meditations on First Philosophy. In *Meditations and other metaphysical writings* (translated by D. Clarke). London: Penguin.

Feigl, H. (1967). *The mental and the physical.* Minneapolis: University of Minnesota Press.

Griffin, D. R. (1976). *The question of animal awareness: Evolutionary continuity of mental experience.* New York: The Rockefeller University Press.

Griffin, D. R. (1978). Prospects for a cognitive ethology. *Behavioral and Brain Sciences, 4,* 527–538.

Griffin, D. R. (1992). *Animal minds.* Chicago: University of Chicago Press.

Honig, W. K. (1978). On the conceptual nature of cognitive terms: An initial essay. In S. H. Hulse, H. Fowler, & W. K. Honig (Eds.), *Cognitive processes in animal behavior* (pp. 1–14). Hillsdale, NJ: Erlbaum.

Humphrey, N. K. (1978). Nature's psychologists. *New Scientist, 29,* 900–904.

Jennings, H. S. (1904/1976). *Behavior of the lower organisms.* Bloomington: Indiana University Press.

Jolly, A. (1991). Conscious chimpanzees? A review of recent literature. In C. A. Ristau (Ed.), *Cognitive ethology: The minds of other animals* (pp. 231–252). Hillsdale, NJ: Erlbaum.

Kennedy, J. S. (1992). *The new anthropomorphism.* Cambridge: Cambridge University Press.

Laasko, A. (1993). Pigeons and the problem of other minds. *Behavioral and Brain Sciences, 16,* 652–653.

Lubinski, D., & Thompson, T. (1993). Species and individual differences in communication based on private states. *Behavioral and Brain Sciences, 16,* 627–680.

Mackenzie, B. D. (1977). *Behaviourism and the limits of scientific method.* Atlantic Highlands, NJ: Humanities Press.

Mason, W. A. (1976). Windows on other minds. *Science, 194,* 930–931.

Michel, G. F. (1991). Human psychology and the minds of other animals. In C. A. Ristau (Ed.), *Cognitive ethology: The minds of other animals* (pp. 253–272). Hillsdale, NJ: Erlbaum.

Pavlov, I. P. (1928). *Lectures on conditioned reflexes.* New York: International.

Povinelli, D. J. (1993). Reconstructing the evolution of mind. *American Psychologist, 48,* 493-509.

Premack, D., & Woodruff, G. (1978). Does the chimpanzee have a theory of mind? *Behavioral and Brain Sciences, 4,* 515–526.

Pribram, K. H. (1978). Consciousness, classified and declassified. *Behavioral and Brain Sciences, 4,* 590–592.

Rachlin, H. (1992). Teleological behaviorism. *American Psychologist, 47,* 1371–1382.

Riley, D. A., Brown, M. F., & Yoerg, S. I. (1986). Understanding animal cognition. In T. J. Knapp & L. C. Robertson (Eds.), *Approaches to cognition: Contrasts and controversies* (pp. 111–136). Hillsdale, NJ: Erlbaum.

Ristau, C. A. (Ed.). (1991). *Cognitive ethology: The minds of other animals.* Hillsdale, NJ: Erlbaum.

Romanes, G. J. (1883/1977). *Animal intelligence.* Washington, DC: United Publications of America.

Roper, K. L., & Zentall, T. R. (1993). Directed forgetting in animals. *Psychological Bulletin, 113,* 513–532.

Skinner, B. F. (1977). Why I am not a cognitive psychologist. *Behaviorism, 5,* 1–10.

Skinner, B. F. (1985). Cognitive science and behaviorism. *British Journal of Psychology, 76,* 291–301.

Tolman, E. C. (1932). *Purposive behavior in animals and men.* New York: Appleton-Century-Crofts.

Tolman, E. C. (1938). The determiners of behavior at a choice point. *Psychological Review, 45,* 1–41.

Wasserman, E. A. (1981). Comparative psychology returns: A review of Hulse, Fowler, and Honig's *Cognitive processes in animal behavior. Journal of the Experimental Analysis of Behavior, 35,* 243–257.

Wasserman, E. A. (1982). Further remarks on the role of cognition in the comparative analysis of behavior. *Journal of the Experimental Analysis of Behavior, 38,* 211–216.

Wasserman, E. A. (1983). Is cognitive psychology behavioral? *Psychological Record, 33,* 6–11.

Wasserman, E. A. (1984). Animal intelligence: Understanding the minds of animals through their behavioral "ambassadors." In H. L. Roitblat, T. G. Bever, & H. S. Terrace (Eds.), *Animal cognition* (pp. 45–60). Hillsdale, NJ: Erlbaum.

Wasserman, E. A. (1993). Comparative cognition: Beginning the second century of the study of animal intelligence. *Psychological Bulletin, 113,* 211–228.

Wasserman, E. A. (1997). Animal cognition: Past, present, and future. *Journal of Experimental Psychology: Animal Behavior Processes, 23,* 123–125.

Wasserman, E. A., & Astley, S. L. (1994). A behavioral analysis of concepts: Its application to pigeons and children. In D. L. Medin (Ed.), *Psychology of learning and motivation.* San Diego, CA: Academic Press.

Wittgenstein, L. (1953). *Philosophical investigations.* Oxford: Basil Blackwell.

Yoerg, S. I. (1992). Mentalist imputations. *Science, 258,* 830–831.

Yoerg, S. I., & Kamil, A. C. (1991). Integrating cognitive ethology with cognitive psychology. In C. A. Ristau (Ed.), *Cognitive ethology: The minds of other animals* (pp. 273–289). Hillsdale, NJ: Erlbaum.

Zentall, T. R. (1993). Animal cognition: An approach to the study of animal behavior. In T. R. Zentall (Ed.), *Animal cognition: A tribute to Donald A. Riley* (pp. 3–15). Hillsdale, NJ: Erlbaum.

Zuriff, G. E. (1985). *Behaviorism: A conceptual reconstruction.* New York: Columbia University Press.

I

PERCEPTION AND ILLUSION

1

Grouping and Segmentation of Visual Objects by Baboons (*Papio papio*) and Humans (*Homo sapiens*)

JOËL FAGOT AND ISABELLE BARBET

The study of primate cognition has enjoyed a long history, since the early work of pioneers such as Robert Yerkes, Wolfgang Köhler, Kinji Imanichi, and others. Two cornerstones have supported this longstanding interest in the study of primate cognition. The first one is that nonhuman primates are phylogenetically closely related to our own species. Because of our relatedness to other primates, the study of primate cognition provides direct information on the origins of our cognitive system and its evolution, from nonhuman primates to humans. The second cornerstone supporting the comparative study of primate cognition is the fact that only humans have spoken language. Nonhuman primate species certainly have complex systems of communication, but these systems do not rely on spoken language. Consequently, central to comparative psychology is the idea that documentation of the intelligence of nonhuman primates offers direct input on what a cognitive system can be in the absence of language and, thus, on aspects of human cognition that are language dependent.

Early investigations of primate cognition largely focused on the study of higher cognitive functions. Tool use, representation of the self, concept formation, abstract reasoning, and the ability to solve complex social or nonsocial problems are examples of scientific issues that have attracted much interest in the scientific community. Surprisingly, and in parallel with the emergence of cognitive neuroscience, it is only during the past two decades that comparative psychologists have directed their interest to even more fundamental issues, which can be synthesized by the following question: "What do primates perceive in the world?" Or, stated differently, "Is their perceptual world the same as ours?" Indeed, students of human perception have well documented that perception does not solely depend on the characteristics of sensory inputs. Perception results from the interaction of bottom-up and top-down processes and therefore also depends on factors such as attention, expectation, personal history, memory, and cognitive abilities. Consequently, the effects of top-down processes on perception make it very unlikely that animals live in the same perceptual world as we do and, when placed in experimental contexts, necessarily process the same dimensions of the stimuli as we do.

In our laboratory, we conducted a series of experiments that were aimed at delineating the visual world of primates. Two lines of research on baboons are presented in this chapter. The first one explores the processes of perceptual grouping. We demonstrate that, in comparison to humans when similarly tested, baboons barely group spatially separated elements into a single percept. The second one addresses the issue of depth perception. We show that baboons perceive depth when presented with pictorial depth cues, but we also highlight human–baboon differences in the processing

Figure 1.1. View of a baboon manipulating a joystick.

of occlusion cues as indicators of depth. Implications of such perceptual differences are discussed in the final section of this chapter.

SUBJECTS AND GENERAL PROCEDURE

Our research was conducted on a group of Guinea baboons (*Papio papio*) maintained in the animal facility in Marseille. For several reasons, baboons are very well suited for the study of visual cognition from a comparative human–nonhuman primate perspective. First, baboons belong to the Cercopithecoidea (Old World monkeys) superfamily. Like primate species even more closely related to humans, this group of primates has a visual system that shares important properties with that of humans. Like humans, Cercopithecoidea primates are trichromates, have approximately the same spectral sensitivity as do humans (de Valois & de Valois, 1990), and share with humans the ability to detect fine visual details (Fobes & King, 1982). Even more interestingly, baboons live in open fields. They are short-grass savannah primates (Altman & Altman, 1970) and consequently strongly rely on vision for daily activities and social communication. Probably as a consequence of their living conditions, baboons evolved a more elongated visual field than forest primate species (Kobayashi & Koshima, 2001) and a more elongated retina (Fischer & Kirby, 1991), facilitating the comparison with humans, who are an open-field species with a similarly elongated visual field. Finally, baboons are highly active and manipulative animals. Precision grip is easy in baboons due to a complete opposition between the thumb and index finger (Napier & Napier, 1967). Manipulative skills associated with precision grip allow delicate manual actions in experimental contexts.

All of the baboons in the laboratory were originally wild-caught. They joined the research center in 1987 at the age of 1 year, and they have been continuously tested since then with computerized operant conditioning tasks involving joystick manipulation. In practice, these socially housed baboons are tested in an experimental enclosure (68 cm × 50 cm × 72 cm) while facing an analog joystick, a metal touch pad, and a 14-in color monitor driven by a Pentium IV personal computer (see figure 1.1; for a technical description, see Vauclair & Fagot, 1994). Because operant conditioning procedures are used, an automatic dispenser is installed outside the cage for the delivery of 190-mg food pellets into the enclosure in accordance with the prevailing reinforcement contingencies.

A major problem in visual cognition studies often is to ensure that the attention of the subject is captured by the stimulus on each trial. A behavioral procedure was developed to achieve that goal: Whatever the testing procedure, the baboon is systematically required to touch the metal pad to initiate a trial. Once done, a fixation point appears on the screen along with a cursor. Manipulation of the joystick induces isomorphic displacements of the cursor on the monitor; the baboon then has to manipulate the joystick to place the cursor on a fixation stimulus, triggering the display of the experimental stimuli. Video recording of eye fixation indicated that this procedure is highly effective in capturing a baboon's attention to the fixation stimulus (Wilde, Vauclair, & Fagot, 1994).

Multiple procedures were developed and used with our baboons over several years to study perceptual/cognitive phenomena. As a consequence of intensive training and testing, all of the baboons in the laboratory are now familiar with the go–no-go task, the two-alternative forced-choice (2AFC) discrimination task, the visual search task, and variations of identity and conditional matching tasks. Combining these different procedures is common in our research. Direct human–baboon comparisons are also regularly conducted, using human volunteers tested with the same joystick task as used by the baboons.

PERCEPTUAL GROUPING AND ATTENTION TO GLOBAL AND LOCAL STIMULUS LEVELS

Global/Local Precedence Effects

Objects have a hierarchical structure. They are composed of parts and subparts. The following research on perceptual grouping and global/local processing in animals was conducted to determine whether animals decompose objects into wholes and parts as we do and whether they pay attention to the same components of objects as we do.

In the late 1970s, Navon (1977) proposed that the visual perception of objects proceeds from an initial analysis at the global level (i.e., whole) prior to the analysis of the more local details (i.e., parts). Experimental support for this hypothesis, called the *global precedence hypothesis*, is extensive in human literature (e.g., Lamb & Robertson, 1988; Lamb, Robertson, & Knight, 1990), at least when the stimuli are not overly large (Martin, 1979). Such support mainly derives from presenting discriminative stimuli structured in a clear two-level hierarchy, such as a large letter (e.g., a large H) constructed from appropriately positioned smaller letters (e.g., small Ss). Two main effects supporting the global precedence hypothesis typically emerge when humans are cued to identify the global or local level of such stimuli (Navon, 1977). The first, called *global advantage*, is revealed by shorter response times for identification of the global letter compared with the local letters. The second, called *global-to-local interference,* is disclosed by faster identification of the local letters when the two stimulus levels represent the same letter (consistent stimuli) than when they represent two different letters (inconsistent stimuli).

Very little attention had been paid to this issue of global/local processing in the animal literature prior to our work. In the first study, Horel (1994) showed that cooling the inferotemporal cortex of macaques hampered their ability to process the local level of a hierarchical form, but it had no such effect at the global level. In another study, Hopkins (1997) reported a right visual field (i.e., left hemispheric) advantage in chimpanzees for processing hierarchical forms at the local level but no significant advantage for processing at the global level. We thus conducted several experiments to investigate whether the global-precedence hypothesis also applies to baboons. The experiments summarized next are reported in detail by Fagot and Deruelle (1997), Deruelle and Fagot (1997), and Fagot, Tomonaga, and Deruelle (2001).

Baboons ($N = 8$) were tested with Navon's type of two-level structured hierarchical stimuli in the context of a matching-to-sample task (see Fagot & Deruelle, 1997, Experiment 2). Examples of the experimental stimuli are shown in figure 1.2; they were large geometrical shapes (4.7×4.7 degrees of visual angle), such as a large circle, square, diamond, and cross, made up of small circles, squares, diamonds, and crosses (0.6 degree of visual angle). Each matching-to-sample trial proceeded as follows: after the eye fixation period, the baboon was presented a 120-ms hierarchical sample stimulus. It was then presented with two comparison stimuli. One of the comparison stimuli shared one stimulus

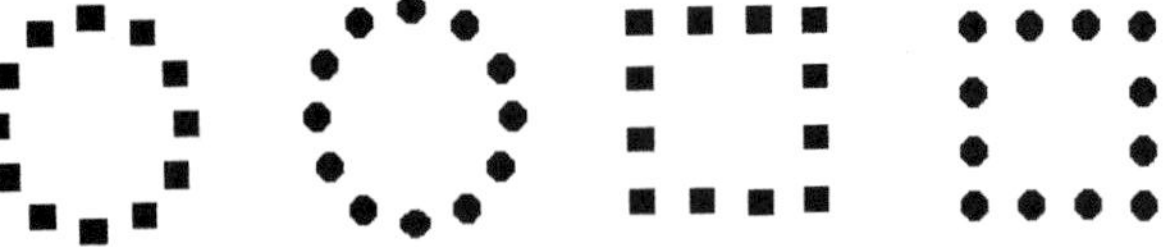

Figure 1.2. Examples of the compound form stimuli used with baboons.

level with the sample, whereas the other one was completely different from the sample at both stimulus levels. To receive a food pellet, the baboon had to manipulate the joystick and select (with the cursor) the form sharing one stimulus level with the sample. Of course, test sessions involved both local trials, in which S+ matched the sample at the local stimulus level, and global trials, in which the S+ matched the sample at the global stimulus level. For comparative purposes, and to ascertain that our stimuli were adequate to reveal global precedence, humans ($N = 14$) were also tested. The procedure used with humans was the same as with baboons, except that the monitor and joystick were placed on a table at which human subjects were seated.

A clear-cut human–baboon difference emerged in both accuracy scores (figure 1.3a) and response times (figure 1.3b). First, only humans showed a global advantage (i.e., their accuracy scores were reliably greater and their response times were reliably shorter for global trials compared with local trials); baboons, by contrast, exhibited reliably greater accuracy scores and shorter response times for local trials compared with global trials. Second, only humans showed a global-to-local interference effect, as revealed by higher performance on local consistent trials compared with local inconsistent trials (figure 1.3c). In other words, humans exhibited the two effects predicted by the global precedence hypothesis: the *global advantage* and the *global-to-local inference* effect. By contrast, baboons showed an advantage for local trials and no global-to-local interference.

Attention to Global and Local Stimulus Properties

The next experiment was conducted in an effort to better understand why only humans showed global precedence. In line with the studies of humans by Saarinen (1994) and Enns and Kingstone (1995), we introduced a visual search task to verify the nature of the attentional mechanisms recruited by humans and baboons when they process at the global and local levels of hierarchical stimuli.

After the eye fixation procedure had been completed, the eight baboons perceived a go or a no-go display containing a varying number of compound stimuli, either 4, 8, or 12. On no-go trials, all of the stimuli constituting the display were identical to one another at the local and global levels: they were either a large circle consisting of eight small squares or a large square consisting of eight small circles. One compound stimulus (the target) was different from the other stimuli (the distractors) on go trials. For those trials, the difference between the target and the distractors was at either the global or the local level. To be rewarded on go trials, baboons had to move the joystick as fast as possible when a target was detected; 3 s was allowed for target detection. Refraining from responding for 3 s on no-go trials was similarly reinforced. Again, the results were compared with those obtained with humans ($N = 8$) tested with the same monitor, joystick, and procedure as baboons.

Our attention was focused on response time differences for go trials as a function of species, stimulus level (global versus local), and display size. For humans, response times were significantly shorter on average for global trials (mean = 421 ms) than for local trials (mean = 470 ms), thus replicating the global advantage. Again, our findings indicated a local advantage in baboons, with response times for local trials (mean = 466 ms) being significantly shorter than for global trials (mean = 510 ms). Even more importantly, there was a significant interaction of the three manipulated factors. Post-hoc trend analyses showed that the baboons' response times on global trials increased linearly with display size (linearity accounted for 99% of the variance). By contrast, the response times on local trials were not statistically affected by display size (92% of the variance; not significant). There

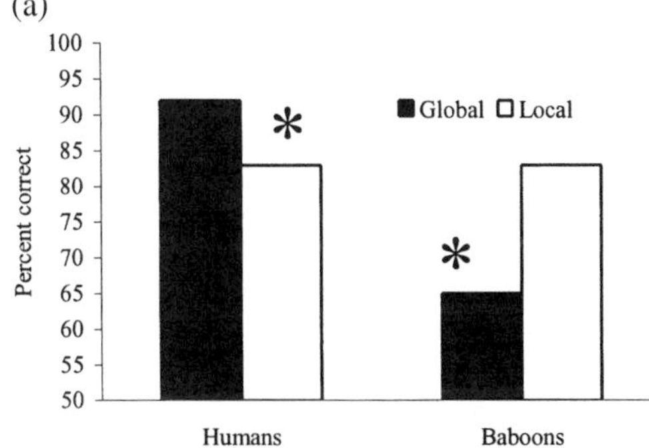

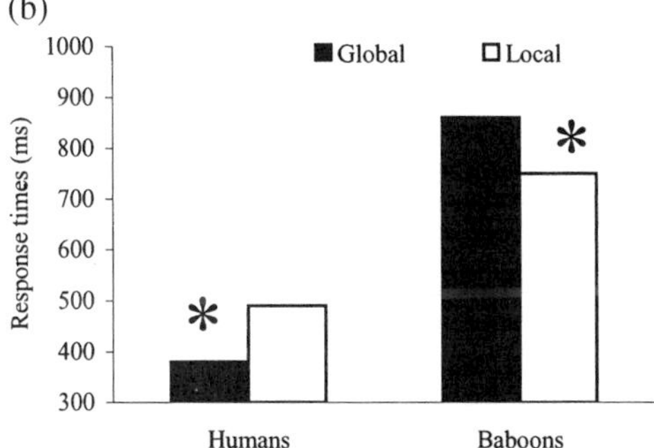

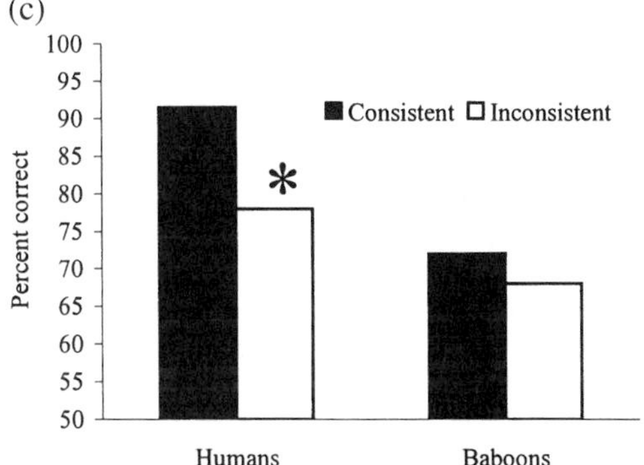

Figure 1.3. (*a*) Average accuracy scores achieved by humans and baboons on global and local trials; (*b*) average correct response latencies for humans and baboons on global and local trials; (*c*) average accuracy scores obtained on consistent and inconsistent local trials.

was no reliable effect of display size in humans, whatever the stimulus level considered (linearity accounted for less than 90% of the variance; not significant).

Treisman and Gelade (1980) proposed that a flat search slope in visual search experiments reflects parallel processing of the information contained in the display. Very few attentional resources would be recruited in that case. By contrast, a linear relation between the size of the display and response times would be a sign of serial search, during which the subjects sequentially pay attention to the various items in the displays. With reference to Treisman and Gelade's theory (1980), our results are straightforward. First, our two species used parallel search strategies recruiting little attentional resources when they had to detect the local target on our test trials. By contrast, baboons used an attention-demanding serial search to detect global shape variations, whereas humans detected the global target by way of a parallel search strategy. The two species thus responded on the global trials in two different ways, although the stimuli presented to the two species were physically similar and the testing conditions were identical.

Local Precedence or Global Disadvantage?

One interesting aspect of Navon's hierarchical stimuli is that the local elements are coherent entities because they are small, continuous shapes (such as a small square). The global structure of the stimuli is by contrast much less coherent, mostly because these stimuli are made of spatially disconnected local elements. Compared with the perception of the local elements, the perception of the whole structure of the compound forms implies an additional operation, in which the local elements are grouped into a single percept. Because only baboons adopted a serial search strategy to detect the global target, the hypothesis arises that the baboons are not deficient in processing at the global stimulus level per se but that they have greater difficulty than humans in grouping the local elements into a coherent whole. In other words, the baboons do not experience a local *advantage* but rather a global *disadvantage* induced by the imperative to group the local elements. This hypothesis was tested in the next experiment.

The same visual task as before was used to test this idea. However, we independently manipulated two novel factors: the overall size of the global shapes (2 or 4 degrees of visual angle) and their density (8 or 16 local elements; see figure 1.4). Three test conditions were given to humans ($N = 8$) and baboons ($N = 8$); the large/dense condition

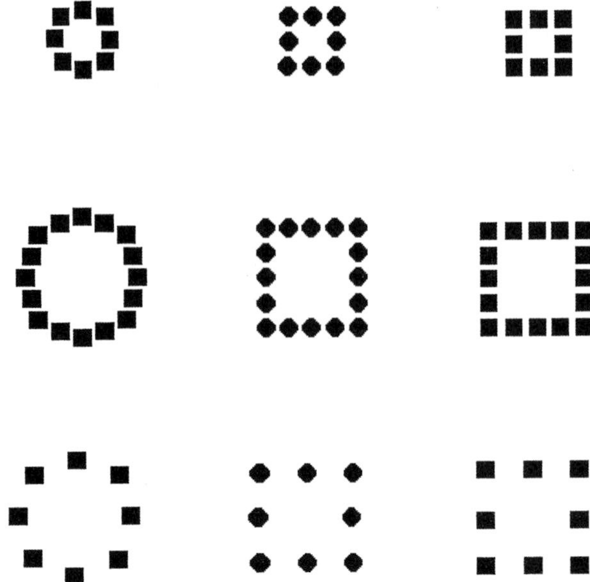

Figure 1.4. Stimuli used in testing the effect of stimulus size and stimulus density.

(4 degrees, 16 local elements), the large/sparse condition (4 degrees, 8 local elements), and the small/dense condition (2 degrees, 8 local elements). Note that the interelement distance remained identical in the large/dense and small/dense conditions. In this experiment, the display size was set to three, six, or nine stimuli.

Comparison across conditions could not be performed for correct response times, because the baboons evidenced very poor performance in the large/sparse condition. The analysis was thus restricted to accuracy scores, which indicated significantly poorer performance on average on the large/sparse trials (mean = 58% correct) than on the large/dense (mean = 94.5%) and small/dense (mean = 91.2%) trials. There was no reliable statistical difference between the final two test conditions, suggesting that variations in global size did not affect processing. Even more interesting findings were obtained when display size was introduced as a factor in the analyses. In this case, the baboons showed a linear relation between the number of errors and display size on the large/sparse trials (linearity accounted for 99% of the variance). By contrast, linearity never accounted for a significant portion of the variance in the other test conditions (small/dense and large/dense stimuli) by either humans or baboons. It can thus be concluded that the significant search slope obtained in baboons when they have to detect global targets on large/sparse trials is a direct consequence of the grouping process that perception of the global target implies. Baboons appear to be much more sensitive than humans to the separation between the local elements; in comparable test situations, baboons are not as proficient as humans in overcoming spatial separation between the elemental features of the stimuli to perceive a coherent whole.

We thus conclude that differences between humans and baboons do not concern the ability to perceive the overall structure of objects, hierarchical or not, or to pay attention to that structure. These differences are more likely to reflect some deficiencies of baboons (compared with humans) to group spatially independent elemental features into a coherent whole.

Convergent Findings and Conclusions

Several papers have been published on global/local processing in animals, similar in procedure to our studies (pigeons: Cook, 2001; Fremouw, Herbranson, & Shimp, 1998; capuchins: Spinozzi, de Lillo, & Truppa, 2003; macaques: Hopkins & Washburn, 2000; Tanaka & Fujita, 2000; and chimpanzees: Fagot & Tomonaga, 1999; Fagot et al.,

2001; Hopkins & Washburn, 2000). Considered together, these publications confirm that animals can successfully process the two levels of hierarchical stimuli, but they do not consistently reveal a local precedence effect.

Thus, in agreement with our initial report, some experiments showed local precedence in pigeons (Cook, 2001), capuchins (Spinozzi et al., 2003), and chimpanzees (Fagot & Tomonaga, 1999; Fagot et al., 2001), in particular with large/sparse stimuli (Fagot & Tomonaga, 1999; Spinozzi et al., 2003). By contrast, a global precedence effect was reported in macaques (Tanaka & Fujita, 2000) and chimpanzees (Hopkins & Washburn, 2000).

In Tanaka and Fujita's study (2000), their macaques made very few discrimination errors (less than 5%), although the task was a highly difficult one, involving stimuli that were mirror images of each other at both the global and local stimulus levels. The reduced number of errors, in addition to the apparent difficulty of the task, led us assume that the macaques were overtrained in this experiment. Unfortunately, the effects of training on global/local advantages cannot be evaluated due to a lack of details as to the training procedure and the number of training trials given to each subject. As for Hopkins and Washburn's study (2000), it is noteworthy that the authors used very dense stimuli for the discrimination. We assume that global precedence occurred in this study because of the reduced need for grouping across short interelement distances.

Despite inconsistencies in global versus local precedence effects, the existing literature strongly supports the idea that, when a local advantage emerges in an animal species, this effect results from perceptual grouping deficiencies. For example, Spinozzi et al. (2003) searched for an effect of stimulus density on precedence effects in capuchin monkeys. They reported a local advantage in these primates, which was mostly evident when large/sparse stimuli were used. Similarly, using a visual search task, we also reported that chimpanzees exhibit a reliable local advantage in the processing of hierarchical stimuli (Fagot & Tomonaga, 1999). This advantage, however, turned into a global advantage when the gaps that separated the local elements were filled by line segments, thus favoring the grouping of these elements into a coherent whole.

Additional evidence of a deficit in perceptual grouping was obtained from research in which proximity grouping was studied in animals by way of grids. A reduced capacity for perceptual grouping, in comparison to humans, was obtained by Kurylo, van Nest, and Knepper (1997) in working with hooded rats. A deficit in perceptual grouping was also obtained in a more visual species, the Australian sea lion (Burke, Everingham, Rogers, Hinton, & Hall-Aspand, 2001). Although more studies would be useful to confirm the generality of the phenomenon, animals of several species do indeed appear to have difficulties overcoming gap barriers in perceptual grouping.

PERCEPTION OF PICTORIAL DEPTH

One important function of our visual system is the ability to perceive and to process depth. Processing depth is critical for survival and is highly adaptive. At least two main sources of depth information are available to primates when perceiving a visual scene. First, depth information about the distance of objects arises from factors that depend on the state of the eyes themselves, such as accommodation and convergence. Second, depth can be derived from an analysis of the optical input. An important source of depth information comes from so-called monocular pictorial cues, such as gradient, shading, or occlusion cues, which remain available in absence of motion and thus are potentially available in still images (see Palmer, 1999).

For comparative psychologists, one interesting case of depth perception occurs when subjects (animals or humans) perceive pictorial representations of three-dimensional scenes or objects. Consider what is a two-dimensional image. Two of the three dimensions of the visual world are explicitly available in such images—width and height—but information about the third dimension—depth—is highly ambiguous and contradictory in such pictorial images. On the one hand, images are flat objects. Reflection of the surface of the image, as well as motion and stereoscopic cues, suggests that this image is flat. On the other hand, pictorial depth cues, which provide at least some indication of how objects are organized in depth, remain in the image. For instance, if an object is partly masked by another object, then it suggests that the occluded object is more distant from the observer than the occluding object. Images are thus equivocal stimuli: they are flat objects suggesting depth. Considering these attributes of pictorial representations, the questions arise as to how animals process depth information from pictorial images and if they perceive them as do we humans.

How baboons process pictorial depth was studied in two complementary ways in our laboratory. We first verified that baboons experience the corridor illusion, a special case of a size illusion induced in humans by the perception of pictorial depth cues. We then verified the role of occlusion cues as inducers of depth perception in baboons (Barbet & Fagot, 2002; Deruelle, Barbet, Dépy, & Fagot, 2000).

The Corridor Illusion

When viewing figure 1.5, we generally judge the sizes of the two persons to be unequal: The person in the lower portion of the picture appears to be smaller than the person in the upper portion of the picture. This appearance is an illusion; the two people are exactly the same size, as can be confirmed by measuring them with a ruler. This illusion, called the *corridor illusion*, is interesting for our purpose because it is induced by the various depth cues contained by the hallway background. Indeed, if the background is removed or replaced by a picture of a flat surface, then the illusion disappears and the two people appear to be of the same size.

The theoretical explanation of the corridor illusion is that the illusory image deceives the size constancy system, a mechanism by which the sizes of visual objects look constant, regardless of their absolute distance from the observer (and thus independent of variations in their retinal size). In the case of the corridor illusion, our visual system assumes that the background person is the larger one because the two people have the same visual size but appear to be located at different distances from the viewer. The following study demonstrated that baboons also experience the corridor illusion when presented with the stimuli shown in figure 1.5. This result provides evidence that baboons can gain depth information from pictorial depth cues available in two-dimensional images.

A procedure based on the go–no-go paradigm was designed to test the corridor illusion in

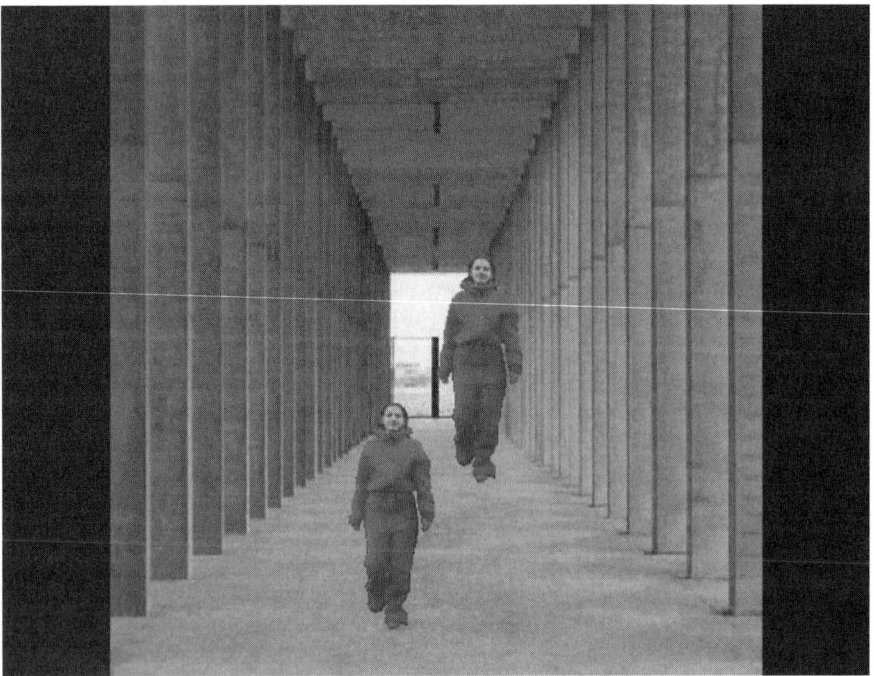

Figure 1.5. Illustration of the stimuli used to assess the corridor illusion in baboons. The two human forms in this figure have the same veridical size.

baboons. After eye gaze had been fixed on the screen, the baboons perceived an image containing two people of either equal or unequal veridical sizes. To be rewarded, they had to move the joystick during a response period of 3 s when the sizes of the two people were unequal and to refrain from moving the joystick during those 3 s when their sizes were equal.

During training, the background images were devoid of depth cues; they were pictures of textured flat surfaces or wallpaper. The testing procedure was begun after the baboons met a training criterion of 80% or greater correct during training sessions with flat backgrounds. Four kinds of backgrounds were introduced after the training criterion was met. They were photographic images of real corridors and their control images, which were scrambled by dividing the corridor picture into 240 four-pixel squares and rearranging them randomly on the surface of the image. The two other types of backgrounds were novel pictures of two-dimensional surfaces, such as wallpaper showing textures or floors devoid of depth cues, and their corresponding control scrambled images.

If baboons perceive the corridor illusion, then when the two people have the same veridical size in the images, the baboons should exhibit more go (i.e., "different") responses with the corridor background than with the other three kinds of backgrounds; that is just what we observed. In the first block of test trials, the frequency of go responses was reliably higher for the three-dimensional corridor pictures (45%) than for the three other kinds of backgrounds (corridor scramble, 21.2%; two-dimensional background, 17.5%; scramble of two-dimensional background, 8.8%). The same finding was replicated in the second block of test trials (corridor, 56.2%; corridor scramble, 8.7%; two-dimensional background, 18.7%; scramble of the two-dimensional background, 12.5%).

Another result was also expected, if baboons experience the corridor illusion: Presentation of a corridor background should facilitate detection of size differences on go trials when the larger person is shown above the smaller one. This expected effect was not obtained from the analysis of accuracy scores, but it was obtained when response times were considered. Thus, response times were reliably faster with the corridor backgrounds (mean, 796 ms) than with their scrambled versions (mean = 935 ms, $p < .05$). There were no reliable differences between response times obtained with

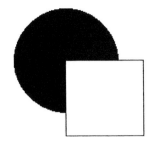

Figure 1.6. Stimulus display inducing amodal completion in humans.

two-dimensional backgrounds (mean = 814 ms) and their scrambled controls (mean = 774 ms). These findings therefore converge with those obtained on no-go trials. All confirmed that the use of three-dimensional backgrounds altered size judgments in our baboons. Moreover, these findings are consistent with the idea that the baboons are sensitive to the corridor illusion. Because the corridor illusion reflects deception of the size constancy system by background pictorial depth cues, we conclude from this study that baboons (and presumably other animals, too) can derive depth information from pictorial depth cues.

Occlusion as a Cue to Depth

One particularly salient pictorial cue suggesting depth is occlusion (Palmer, 1999) (see figure 1.6 for an illustration). Like most humans (e.g., Rensink & Enns, 1998), you probably spontaneously perceive a square in front of a circle rather than a square adjacent to a three-quarter-circle. If so, then your visual system has segmented the two-dimensional visual display to interpret it as a three-dimensional display—a circle *behind* a square. In this case, depth is inferred because the visible junctions between the objects are coherent with what would be seen if a square occluded one part of a circle.

Whether animals perceive occluded shapes as complete (i.e., amodal completion), as do humans, has been studied in a number of behavioral studies. However, the results are inconsistent. Some studies suggest that animals can complete invisible objects (Forkman, 1998; Forkman & Vallortigara, 1999; Kanizsa, Renzi, Compostela, & Guerani, 1993; Lea, Slater, & Ryan, 1996), whereas others fail to demonstrate completion (Cerella, 1980; Fujita, 2000; Sekuler, Lee, & Shettleworth, 1996). Differences across studies might come into play because

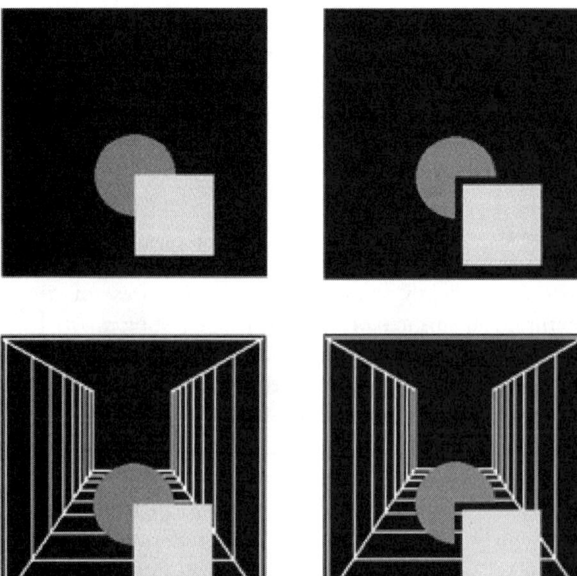

Figure 1.7. (*Top*) Occluded and amputated test stimuli used with baboons. (*Bottom*) The same stimuli shown on a background depicting depth by way of perspective lines.

researchers have tested very different species—mice, pigeons, chicks, and hens—that may have evolved their own peculiar modes of visual processing. Behavioral differences may also indicate that the stimuli used in these studies contained different kinds of pictorial depth cues that were probably not equally efficient in affording the impression of depth. The stimuli used by Sekuler et al. (1996), for instance, contained only junction cues to induce depth perception, whereas those of Forkman and Vallortigara (1999) contained both junction cues and background perspective as possible sources of depth information.

Occlusion Is Not Inferred From Junction Cues

Several experiments were conducted in our laboratory on visual completion in baboons. We report only the most critical ones here, published by Deruelle et al. (2000, Experiment 5) and Fagot, Barbet, Parron, and Deruelle (in press). In the first experiment, after eye gaze was fixated on the screen, baboons were initially trained to select a circle on the screen and to avoid the amputated stimulus, a three-quarter circle. The circle and the amputated stimulus were presented side by side with their left/right location randomly determined. After an 80% criterion was met on training trials, subjects were presented with the two compound stimuli shown in figure 1.7, which were displayed as a 2AFC. One of these stimuli can be interpreted as a full circle partially occluded by a square. It will be referred to as the occluded test stimulus. An amputated circle shown adjacent to the square represented the other test stimulus. This other stimulus will be referred as the amputated test stimulus. Note that these two test stimuli were visually similar, as they both contained the same elements, but only the occluded test stimulus contained the junction cues leading (in humans) to the perception of an occluded circle. Our hypothesis was that, if baboons experience amodal completion on test trials, then they should exhibit a reliable preference for the occluded shape.

The results disconfirmed our hypothesis. As shown in figure 1.8 (empty bars), there was not a single baboon that showed a statistically significant preference for the occluded stimulus. Note that our results were replicated in several experiments, using occluded shapes defined only by junction cues, and with a go–no-go procedure rather than with a 2AFC procedure (see Deruelle et al., 2000).

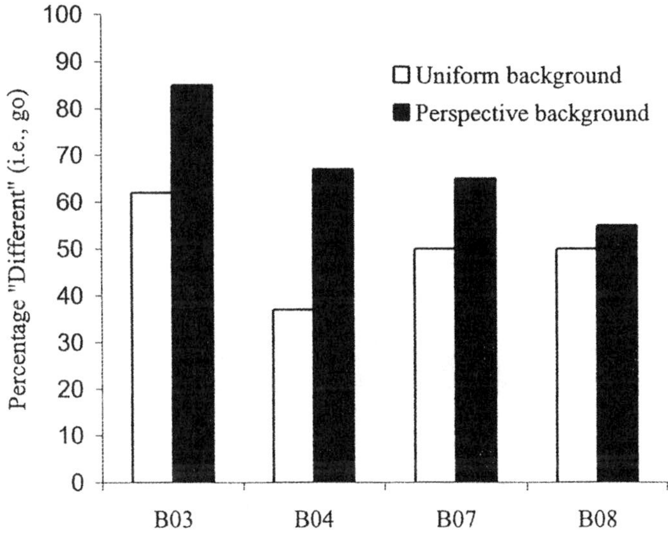

Figure 1.8. Percentage of go (i.e., different) responses obtained by each subject tested for amodal completion. All baboons provided more go responses when the stimuli were shown on a background containing perspective lines than when the background was uniformly black.

Completion Induced by Background Depth Cues

Two studies on hens suggest that these animals complete visual objects when the stimuli contain contextual information suggesting depth in addition to the junction cues (Forkman, 1998; Forkman & Vallortigara, 1999). Would baboons also show amodal completion if they were now tested with the same stimuli as before but with contextual background containing depth cues?

To test this new hypothesis, baboons ($N = 4$) were retested with the same 2AFC procedure as before but with the stimuli shown in bottom portion of figure 1.7. The results clearly indicated that use of the background depth cues altered the baboons' judgments. The baboons now selected the occluded stimulus on 67.5 percent of the trials (see figure 1.8, black bars). Preference for the occluded stimulus was reliable for three of the four baboons, by chi-square tests ($p < .05$).[1]

The immediate conclusion is thus that perception of the corridor background alters the processing of the to-be-completed image. The results indicated that baboons did not perceive the to-be-completed stimuli as complete in the first experiment, but they did so in the second experiment when the forms were shown on a background receding in depth.

Role of Junction Cues and Reliability, Compared With Humans

In the human literature, although theoretical interpretations of completion processes vary, authors agree that the presence of junction cues exerts a strong influence on completion processes (e.g., Rubin, 2001). When the contour of an object is occluded by another object, the contours typically form intersections known as T junctions. The continuous contour (the horizontal bar of the T) delineates the border of the object whose surface occludes the other edge (the stem of the T). Such T junctions exert the greatest control on amodal completion, when the edges leading to discontinuities can be related to each other—that is, when they can be connected with minimally curved line segments (Kellman & Shipley, 1991; Palmer, 1999).

Why baboons did not complete our stimuli in absence of a depth background remains uncertain at this point. One possible reason is that the T junctions available in the display were not properly treated as indicators of depth, thus hampering the necessary segmentation processes necessary for amodal completion. This account is unlikely because baboons would not have been able to complete the visual form with the corridor background if T junctions were not properly processed as depth cues. It is more likely that baboons correctly processed the junction cues as the border of two objects, but they were unable to identify the T junctions as belonging to the same (occluded) objects. If this hypothesis is correct, then baboons' difficulty in perceiving the occluded object would have the same basis as their difficulty in perceiving the global structure of hierarchical stimuli (Navon, 1977). That is, this difficulty would result from a diminished capacity for perceptual grouping. We can further hypothesize that the use of the corridor background facilitated depth processing and induced greater attention to the global aspects of the stimuli. Attention to the global aspects of the stimuli may have helped the baboons to identify the T junctions of the display and thus to detect the (amodal) continuities of the disconnected contours. We will conduct experiments to test this hypothesis.

CONCLUDING REMARKS

Two aspects of visual information processing in baboons were addressed here. The first is the ability to perceive the global structure of hierarchical visual objects (Navon, 1977). A local precedence effect was observed in baboons, in contrast to humans, who showed a global precedence effect. Experiments further revealed that local precedence in baboons is a direct consequence of their difficulty in overcoming the separation between the local elements, a necessary process for perceiving the whole.

The second aspect of visual information processing is depth perception. We have demonstrated that baboons perceive the corridor illusion. Perception of the corridor illusion reveals that these animals gain depth information from the pictorial cues available in the image background. Baboons, however, failed to perceive occluded objects as complete when the to-be-completed objects were shown on a uniformly black background. We hypothesized that this mode of processing results from baboons' diminished capacity (in comparison to humans) to group the junctions of cues in order to complete the missing segments of the occluded objects. When a corridor background was added to the display, the background depth cues triggered the processing of depth and induced additional attention to the global aspects of the forms, permitting completion of the occluded objects.

Taken together, our research findings question the efficiency of grouping mechanisms (in particular, grouping by proximity) in baboons, and by extension in other animals (e.g., Burke et al., 2001; Kurylo et al., 1997). Very likely, a diminished capacity for proximity grouping retards the recognition of both pictorial and real objects (see Kurylo et al., 1997). Note, however, that grouping by proximity is only one of the grouping mechanisms used by humans; it is possible that the process of unit formation leading to object recognition in animals relies more on the analysis of other grouping cues such as similarity, alignment, or common fate (e.g., Koffka, 1935) than on proximity cues. However, it is impossible to estimate the importance of these other grouping mechanisms, because they have not been systematically examined by comparative psychologists. Studies involving these other grouping mechanisms by comparative psychologists, in association with neuroscientists, would be useful to better understand the perceptual world of animals.

It can be hypothesized that failures of proximity grouping not only interfere with the recognition of objects but also affect perception of the abstract relations among objects. It has been amply demonstrated that animals do process spatial relations such as above/below (Dépy, Fagot, & Vauclair, 1999) and in/out (Herrnstein, Vaughan, Mumford, & Kosslyn, 1989) but that the processing of such relations is quite difficult and far from being spontaneous and immediate. Deficiencies in grouping mechanisms may be key factors that explain why such relations are so difficult to establish in animals.

The difficulties that animal have in processing nonspatial abstract relations (e.g., same/different relations), in comparison to humans, are also well documented (e.g., Fagot, Wasserman, & Young, 2001). Psychologists often attribute these difficulties to the fact that animals do not have language and thus lack the necessary cognitive codes to describe these relations (e.g., Premack, 1983). Another tempting hypothesis is that animals cannot perceptually group objects into a single cognitive unit to determine if these objects are the same as or different from one another. Delineating the perceptual world of animals is probably one of the major avenues leading to a better understanding of their cognitive power.

Note

1. The test procedure ensured that completion with the corridor background was not a consequence of test order in training, due to test order (see Fagot et al., in press).

References

Altman, S. A., & Altman, J. (1970). *Baboon ecology*. Chicago: The University of Chicago Press.

Barbet, I., & Fagot, J. (2002). Perception of the corridor illusion by baboons. *Behavioural Brain Research, 132*, 111–115.

Burke, D., Everingham, P., Rogers, T., Hinton, M., & Hall-Aspland, S. (2001). Perceptual grouping in two visually reliant species: Humans (*Homo sapiens*) and Australian sea lions (*Neophoca cinerea*). *Perception, 30*, 1093–1106.

Cerella, J. (1980). The pigeon's analysis of pictures. *Pattern Recognition, 12*, 1–6.

Cook, R. G. (2001). Avian visual cognition. Retrieved August 27, 2005, from http://www.pigeon.psy.tufts.edu/avc/.

Dépy, D., Fagot, J., & Vauclair, J. (1999). Processing of above-below categorical spatial relations by baboons (*Papio papio*). *Behavioral Processes, 48*, 1–9.

Deruelle, C., Barbet, I., Dépy, D., & Fagot, J. (2000). Perception of partly occluded figures by baboons (*Papio papio*). *Perception, 29*, 1483–1497.

Deruelle, C., & Fagot, J. (1997). Hemispheric lateralization and global precedence effects in the processing of visual stimuli by humans and baboons. *Laterality, 2*, 233–246.

de Valois, R. L., & de Valois, K. K. (1990). *Spatial vision*. Oxford: Oxford University Press.

Enns, J. T., & Kingstone, A. (1995). Access to global and local properties in visual search four compound stimuli. *Psychological Science, 6*, 283–291.

Fagot, J., Barbet, I., Parron, C., & Deruelle, C. (in press). Amodal completion by baboons (*Papio papio*): Contribution of background depth cues. *Primates*.

Fagot, J., & Deruelle, C. (1997). Processing of global and local visual information and hemispheric specialization in humans (*Homo sapiens*) and baboons (*Papio papio*). *Journal of Experimental Psychology: Human Perception and Performance, 23*, 429–442.

Fagot, J., & Tomonaga, M. (1999). Comparative assessment of global-local processing in humans (*Homo sapiens*) and chimpanzees (*Pan troglodytes*): Use of a visual search task with compound stimuli. *Journal of Comparative Psychology, 113*, 3–12.

Fagot, J., Tomonaga, M., & Deruelle, C. (2001). Processing of the global and local dimensions of visual hierarchical stimuli by humans (*Homo sapiens*), chimpanzees (*Pan troglodytes*) and baboons (*Papio-papio*). In T. Matsuzawa (Ed.), *Primate origins of human cognition and behavior* (pp. 87–103). Tokyo: Springer.

Fagot, J., Wasserman, E., & Young, M. (2001). Discriminating the relation between relations: The role of entropy in abstract conceptualization by baboons and humans. *Journal of Experimental Psychology: Animal Behavior Processes, 27*, 316–328.

Fischer, Q. S., & Kirby, M. A. (1991). Number and distribution of retinal ganglion cells in anubis baboons. *Brain Behaviour and Evolution, 37*, 189–203.

Fobes, J. L., & King, J. E. (1982). Vision: The dominant primate modality. In J. L. Fobes & J. E. King (Eds.), *Primate behavior* (pp. 219–243). New York: Academic Press.

Forkman, B. (1998). Hens use occlusion to judge depth in a two-dimensional picture. *Perception, 27*, 861–867.

Forkman, B., & Vallortigara, G. (1999). Minimization of modal contours: An essential cross-species strategy in disambiguating relative depth. *Animal Cognition, 2*, 181–185.

Fremouw, T., Herbranson, W. T., & Shimp, C. P. (1998). Priming of attention to local and global levels of visual analysis. *Journal of Experimental Psychology: Animal Behavior Processes, 24*, 278–290.

Fujita, K. (2000). What you see is different from what I see: Species differences in visual perception. In T. Matsuzawa (Ed.), *Primate origin of human cognition and behavior* (pp. 28–54). Springer: Tokyo.

Herrnstein, R. J., Vaughan, W., Jr., Mumford, D. B., & Kosslyn, S. M. (1989). Teaching pigeons an abstract relational rule: Insideness. *Perception & Psychophysics, 46*, 56–64.

Hopkins, W. D. (1997). Hemispheric specialization for local and global processing of hierarchical visual stimuli in chimpanzees (*Pan troglodytes*). *Neuropsychologia, 35*, 343–348.

Hopkins, W. D., & Washburn, D. (2002). Matching visual stimuli on the basis of global and local features by chimpanzees (*Pan troglodytes*) and rhesus monkeys (*Macaca mulatta*). *Animal Cognition, 5*, 27–31.

Horel, J. A. (1994). Local and global perception examined by reversible suppression of temporal cortex with cold. *Behavioural Brain Research, 65*, 157–164.

Kanizsa, G., Renzi, P., Conte, S., Compostela, C., & Guerani, L. (1993). Amodal completion in mouse vision. *Perception, 22*, 713–721.

Kellman, P. J., & Shipley, T. F. (1991). A theory of visual interpolation in object perception. *Cognitive Psychology, 23*, 141–221.

Kobayashi, H., & Koshima, S. (2001). Evolution of the human eye as a device for communication. In T. Matsuzawa (Ed.), *Primate origins of human cognition and behavior* (pp. 383–401). Tokyo: Springer.

Koffka, K. (1935). *Principles of Gestalt psychology*. New York: Harcourt, Brace and World.

Kurylo, D. D., van Nest, J., & Knepper, B. (1997). Characteristics of perceptual grouping in rats. *Journal of Comparative Psychology, 111*, 126–134.

Lamb, M. R., & Robertson, L. C. (1988). The processing of hierarchical stimuli: Effects of retinal locus, locational uncertainty and stimulus identity. *Perception and Psychophysics, 44*, 172–181.

Lamb, M. R., Robertson, L. C., & Knight, R. T. (1990). Component mechanisms underlying the processing of hierarchically organized patterns: Inferences from patients with unilateral cortical lesions. *Journal of Experimental Psychology: Learning, Memory and Cognition, 16*, 471–483.

Lea, S. E. G., Slater, A. M., & Ryan, C. M. E. (1996). Perception of object unity in chicks: A comparison with the human infant. *Infant Behavior and Development, 19*, 501–504.

Martin, M. (1979). Local and global processing: The role of sparsity. *Memory and Cognition, 7*, 476–484.

Napier, J. R., & Napier, P. H. (1967). *A handbook of living primates*. New York: Academic Press.

Navon, D. (1977). Forest before the tree: The precedence of global feature in visual perception. *Cognitive Psychology, 9*, 353–383.

Palmer, S. E. (1999). *Vision science: Photons to phenomenology*. Cambridge, MA: MIT Press.

Premack, D. (1983). The codes of man and beast. *The Behavioral and Brain Sciences, 6*, 125–137.

Rensink, R. A., & Enns, J. T. (1998). Early completion of occluded objects. *Vision Research, 38*, 2489–2505.

Rubin, N. (2001). The role of junctions in surface completion and contour matching. *Perception, 30*, 339–366.

Saarinen, J. (1994). Visual search for global and local stimulus features. *Perception, 23*, 237–243.

Sekuler, A. B., Lee, J. A. J., & Shettleworth, S. J. (1996). Pigeons do not complete partly occluded figures. *Perception, 25*, 1109–1120.

Spinozzi, G., de Lillo, C., & Truppa, V. (2003). Global and local processing of hierarchical visual stimuli in tufted capuchin monkeys (*Cebus apella*). *Journal of Comparative Psychology, 117*, 15–23.

Tanaka, H., & Fujita, I. (2000). Global and local processing of visual patterns in macaque monkeys. *Neuroreport, 11*, 2881–2884.

Treisman, A., & Gelade, G. (1980). A feature integration theory of attention. *Cognitive Psychology, 12*, 97–136.

Vauclair, J., & Fagot, J. (1994). A joystick system for the study of hemispheric asymmetries in nonhuman primates. In J. R. Anderson, J. J. Roeder, B. Thierry, & N. Herrenschmidt (Eds.), *Current primatology: Behavioral neuroscience, physiology and reproduction* (pp. 69–75). Strasbourg: Presses de l'Université Louis Pasteur.

Wilde, J., Vauclair, J., & Fagot, J. (1994). Eye movements in baboons performing a matching-to-sample task presented in a divided-field format. *Behavioural Brain Research, 63*, 61–70.

2

Seeing What Is Not There: Illusion, Completion, and Spatiotemporal Boundary Formation in Comparative Perspective

KAZUO FUJITA

Our perceptual world is often quite different from what it is physically. Size constancy is a good example: When a dog rushes around us, its image on our retina repeatedly enlarges and shrinks, but we do not perceive corresponding changes in its size. We sometimes even perceive something that is not present, like Kanizsa's triangle (Kanizsa, 1979) (figure 2.1a). Dissociation of the physical world from the perceptual world is ever present. Such dissociation supposedly occurs because we process sensory information with a variety of constraints that usually help us to recognize the external object. When the constraints are inappropriate in the current context, we perceive illusions like the ones seen in psychology textbooks. Natural selection has probably favored such information processing with a variety of constraints to enhance prompt processing of sensory information. Thus, the dissociation of the physical world from the perceptual world is in all probability a solution that our perceptual system uses to adapt to the challenges of the environment.

Do nonhumans perceive their environments the way that we do? From the argument just given, similar dissociation would be expected in nonhumans, possibly in an enhanced manner because of the smaller size of their brains; more constraints may be required to process complicated information with less developed neural systems. However, we still do not know very much about how the perceptual systems of nonhumans function. Investigating the perceptual processes of a variety of species seems important to understand how this critical aspect of cognition has evolved.

In this chapter, I discuss three aspects of visual perception in primates and birds. The first is the Ponzo illusion (figure 2.1b)—we perceive the object located near the apex of the inverted V to be larger than that located farther from the apex. The second is amodal completion—we complete the portion of a figure that is partly occluded by another to perceive an intact figure. The third is spatiotemporal boundary formation—we perceive a boundary of a figure that is never explicitly presented from fragmentary information.

PONZO ILLUSION

Geometric illusions were noticed by early comparative psychologists, and there have been several reports of many different visual illusions in a variety of nonhuman species. For example, Dominguez (1954) demonstrated that monkeys experienced a horizontal-vertical illusion, in which vertical lines are perceived as longer than horizontal lines of the same length. Dominguez (1954) and Harris (1968) showed that monkeys perceived a breadth-of-rectangles illusion, in which rectangles are judged to be taller than squares of the same height. Benhar and Samuel (1982) reported that anubis baboons perceived a Zöllner illusion, in which parallel lines

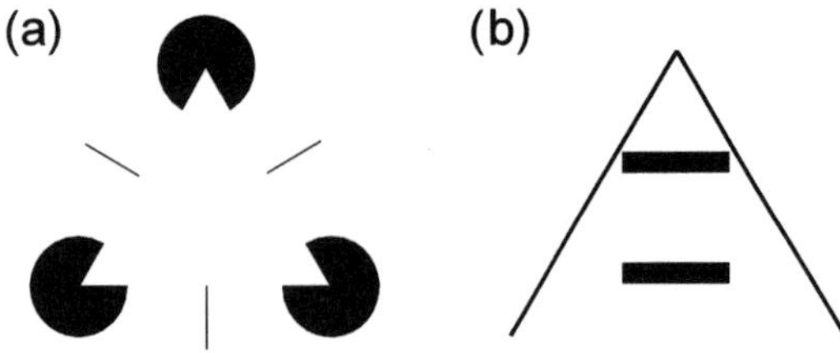

Figure 2.1. Examples of dissociation between perception and physical reality. (*a*) Kanizsa's triangle. We perceive a white triangle. (*b*) Ponzo illusion. The bar above looks longer than the one below.

are perceived to be nonparallel due to numbers of transverse short lines. Bayne and Davis (1983) showed that rhesus monkeys perceived a variation of the Ponzo illusion. Malott, Malott, and Pokrzywinski (1967) and Malott and Malott (1970) reported suggestive evidence that pigeons perceived a Müller-Lyer illusion. Thus, perception of a variety of visual illusions may be widespread in the animal kingdom.

However, none of the previous studies systematically compared the illusory perception between different species including humans or compared the effects of figural parameters on the illusion among species. Thus, it is not well documented whether such illusory perception is homologous or analogous to corresponding human perceptions. In a series of studies, we systematically compared primates and pigeons.

Illusory Perception by Pigeons

Our first demonstration was that pigeons had difficulty in simultaneously discriminating the length of two vertical bars if the shorter one was placed closer to the apex of the converging context lines (Fujita, Blough, & Blough, 1991). The birds showed good discrimination if the lines were parallel or if the longer one was placed nearer the apex. These results are most easily interpreted as showing that the pigeons perceived the bar closer to the apex to be subjectively longer than the bar farther from the apex (see figure 2.1b).

In later experiments in the same series, we used a successive discrimination of bar length. Pigeons were trained to peck at a rectangular box on one side of the viewing screen when they saw the horizontal target bar to be shorter than a predetermined length as the sample and at the box on the other side of the viewing screen when they saw the bar to

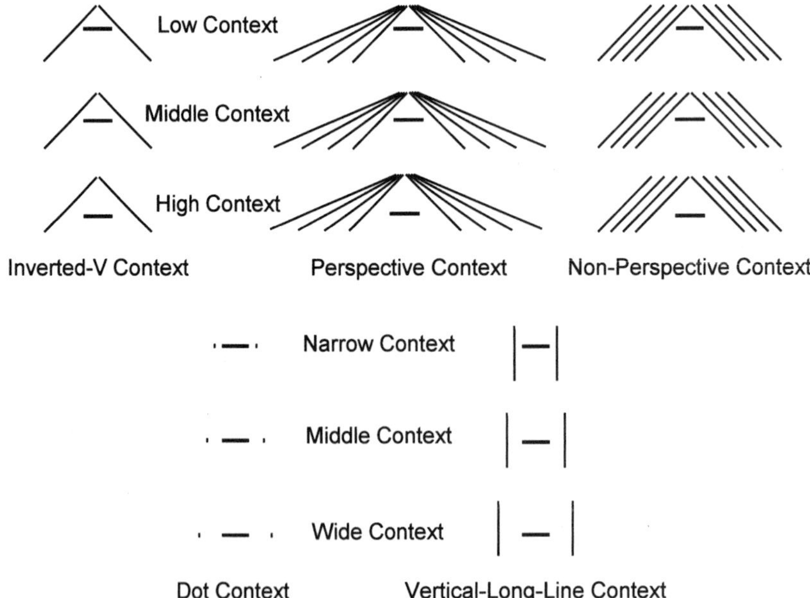

Figure 2.2. Stimuli used in the series of Ponzo experiments with pigeons and primates. (From "What You See Is Different From What I See: Species Differences in Visual Perception," by K. Fujita, 2001b, in *Primate Origins of Human Cognition and Behavior*, edited by T. Matsuzawa, p. 35. Copyright 2001 by Springer-Verlag Tokyo. Reprinted with permission.)

be longer than a predetermined length. The pigeons were thus asked to classify bars of various lengths into "long" and "short" categories based on their absolute length. After the pigeons learned this discrimination, they were tested with bars located at three different distances from the apex of the converging lines, using all-reinforced probe trials in which any choice of "long" or "short" was nondifferentially reinforced. The pigeons' classification was biased toward "long" when the bar was near the apex and "short" when it was far from the apex. These results were also consistent with the idea that pigeons perceived the Ponzo illusion.

Thus, we obtained converging evidence for pigeons' perception of the Ponzo illusion in two different procedures. In our next study, we asked how the magnitude of the illusion would be influenced by the inclination of the converging lines (Fujita, Blough, & Blough, 1993). The inclination is 90 degrees for parallel lines, smaller than 90 degrees for upward-converging lines, and larger than 90 degrees for downward-converging lines. We used inverted-V lines having seven different inclinations from 54.6 degrees (converging upward) to 125.4 degrees (converging downward). The magnitude of the illusion was the largest for both 54.6 and 125.4 degrees, and the data for the upward converging contexts and the downward converging contexts closely mirrored one another. The magnitude of the illusion changed linearly against the ratio of the bar to the gap between the bar and the context line. In humans, upward converging contexts are more powerful in inducing the illusion (Brislin, 1974; Leibowitz, Brislin, Perlmutter, & Hennessy, 1969). Thus, there was a slight suggestion that the sensitivity to the orientation of the illusory figure may be different between the species, although it is not clear that this particular procedure was sensitive enough to detect a slight difference in the magnitude of the illusion.

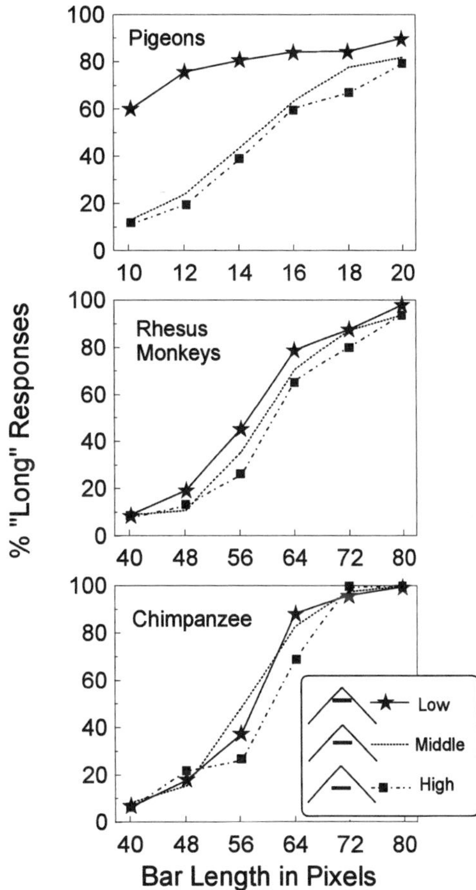

Figure 2.3. Comparison of the Ponzo illusion for pigeons, rhesus monkeys, and chimpanzees. The horizontal axis is the length of the target bars, and the vertical axis is the proportion of subjects' responses to the "long" key. All species show a bias toward "long" for low context figures in which the target bar is located closer to the apex of the inverted-V context. (Redrawn based on Fujita et al., 1993, and Fujita, 1997.)

Illusory Perception by Nonhuman Primates

I next tested two nonhuman primate species: rhesus monkeys and chimpanzees (Fujita, 1997). The procedure was the same as that used in my pigeon studies. That is, the monkeys and chimpanzees were first trained to classify the horizontal target bars according to their absolute length and then were tested with the bars located either nearer to or farther from the apex of the converging context.

I used the three stimuli at the top left, Inverted-V in figure 2.2. The inclination of the context line was 45 degrees. Training was conducted with the middle context stimuli. Later, the subjects were tested with all the three context locations: high, middle, and low. Figure 2.3 shows the results from two rhesus monkeys and one chimpanzee. The data from five pigeons in Fujita et al. (1993) for the same type of context lines having the most similar inclination (54.6 degrees) are also shown for comparison.

All three species showed a bias toward "long" for the target bars placed nearer the apex (labeled Low Context) than for those farther from the apex

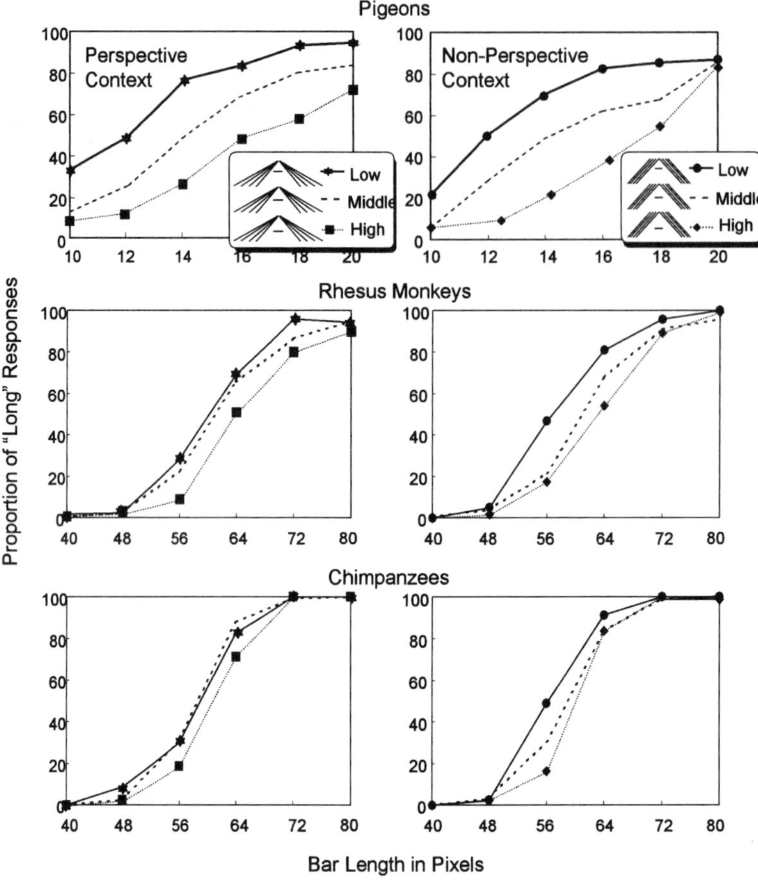

Figure 2.4. Ponzo illusion with line-drawn contexts providing stronger perspective (*left:* Perspective Context) and weaker perspective (*right:* Non-Perspective Context) in pigeons, rhesus monkeys, and chimpanzees. Other details are as in figure 2.3. In no species was there a significant difference in the magnitude of the illusion between the different types of contexts. (Redrawn based on Fujita et al., 1991, and Fujita, 1997.)

(labeled High Context). Thus, all three species clearly perceived the Ponzo illusion. However, the magnitude of the illusion was much larger in pigeons than in the two primate species. Optical blur theory, proposed by Chiang (1968) and Coren (1969), states that the blurred image produced by the low-frequency processing channel in the visual system accounts for assimilatory illusions such as the Ponzo. That is, blurred images of the target bars may assimilate with the context lines nearby. Thus, species more dependent on low-frequency information may be more strongly susceptible to the Ponzo illusion. This theory might explain the species difference, but this account may not be particularly plausible if we take into account the pigeons' good visual acuity (Hodos, 1993). This difference is likely to be at least partly due to a difference in neural systems between primates and birds; primates have cortex-based vision, whereas birds have tectum-based vision. The generality of this difference across species and across illusory figures should be examined further.

Effects of Line-Drawn Perspective

I also compared the strength of the perspective impression induced by the context lines. Perspective implied by context has been suggested to be a factor inducing a variety of visual illusions such as the Ponzo, Müller-Lyer, and Poggendorff illusions (Gillam, 1971; Gregory, 1963; Leibowitz et al.,

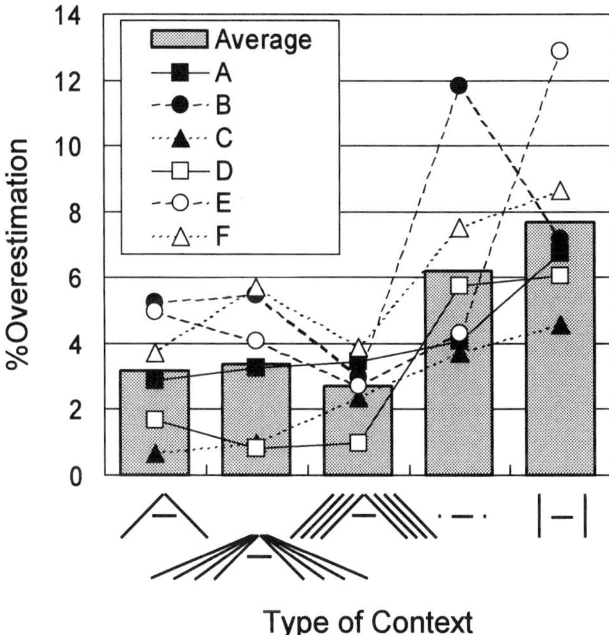

Figure 2.5. The magnitude of the Ponzo illusion under five different line-drawn conditions in human subjects. Line graphs show each individual; the histogram shows the average. (Redrawn based on Fujita, 1997.)

1969). Although this classic notion has been disputed (Fineman & Carlson, 1973; Georgeson & Blakemore, 1973; Humphrey & Morgan, 1965; Newman & Newman, 1974), an effect of perspective could explain illusory perception in nonhumans.

I prepared the two types of context shown in the top middle and top right of figure 2.2. One was labeled Perspective Context, and the other, Non-Perspective Context. Both had the same innermost lines, but in the former, all of the lines were converging, and in the latter, they were parallel.

All of the three species—pigeons, rhesus monkeys, and chimpanzees—clearly perceived the illusion, but in no species was there a strong difference in the magnitude of the illusion between perspective and nonperspective contexts (Fujita, 1997; Fujita et al., 1991) (figure 2.4). The stronger perspective given by the converging lines had no material effect on this illusion.

Humans were also tested in basically the same procedure (Fujita, 1997). The five types of stimuli shown in figure 2.2 (inverted V, perspective, nonperspective, dot, and vertical long line) appeared in the same session and the subjects received 15 independent titration schedules (five types of contexts × three locations of contexts) running simultaneously. The length of the target bar was shortened when the subject reported "long" on two consecutive trials of the same stimulus pattern, and vice versa. As seen in figure 2.5, the magnitude of the illusion did not change among the simple inverted-V context and the perspective and nonperspective contexts. Thus, the perspective suggested by the line-drawn context proved at most to be a minor factor to induce the illusion produced in this series of experiments.

Effects of Photographic Perspective

In humans, the Ponzo illusion is enhanced when the background context is a perspective photograph such as a railway. This effect was compared between rhesus monkeys and humans (Fujita, 1996). I prepared the following four types of stimuli. The first was the inverted-V figure superimposed on a perspective photograph of a highway. The second was the same inverted-V figures on the top-bottom reversed photograph. The third was the isolated target bar on the upright photograph, that is, with no line-drawn context. The last was the isolated target bar on the reversed photograph. The monkeys were trained and tested on the same procedure as before, and human subjects were tested in the titration procedure described earlier together with the basic inverted-V context.

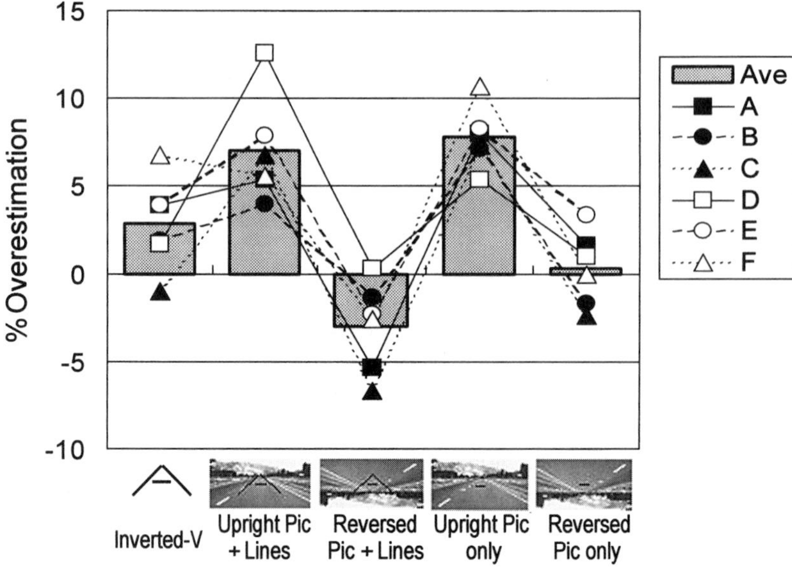

Figure 2.6. Magnitude of the Ponzo illusion under different types of photographic contexts in human subjects. Subjects perceived a strong illusion whenever there was an upright photograph providing perspective. (Redrawn based on Fujita, 1996.)

Figure 2.6 shows the data obtained from six humans. As is clear, the illusion was enhanced for the two stimuli having the upright photograph regardless of the presence or absence of the line-drawn context. Little illusion was observed for the stimuli having the inverted photograph alone. Given the fact that humans show only a small illusion in the inverted-V context, the effect of photographic perspective appears to have overshadowed the effect of the line-drawn context.

Figure 2.7 shows the results from two rhesus monkeys. The monkeys showed the strongest illusion for the first two stimuli having the line-drawn context (top two panels). However, the monkeys also showed a smaller illusion for the third stimulus having the isolated target on the upright photograph (bottom left panel). Contrary to the data for humans, these results suggest that, in monkeys, the effect of the line-drawn context was so strong that it overshadowed the effect of the photographic context.

Overall, both factors, the line-drawn context and the photographic perspective, appeared to induce the illusion. The former is stronger in monkeys, whereas the latter is stronger in humans.

Effects of Short Lines Rather Than Converging Lines

Humans perceive a similar illusion when small dots or short lines replace the converging lines (see figure 2.2, bottom left). I found that this effect is actually stronger than the illusion induced by the converging lines (see figure 2.5). This possibility was tested together with the perspective and nonperspective contexts described in "Effects of Line-Drawn Perspective." The magnitude of the illusion was doubly large for the dot context and the vertical long-line context than for the other three.

Rhesus monkeys and chimpanzees were tested with the stimuli shown in the bottom left panel (dot context) in figure 2.2, using the same procedure described above. Figure 2.8 shows the results from these two species. Surprisingly, rhesus monkeys showed no illusion in the dot context. Chimpanzees still see the illusion in this type of context, but the magnitude of the illusion is not different from that of the inverted-V context tested in the same session. Thus, there is a systematic change in the effect of dots located at both ends of the target bar as we go from primate species to species: no

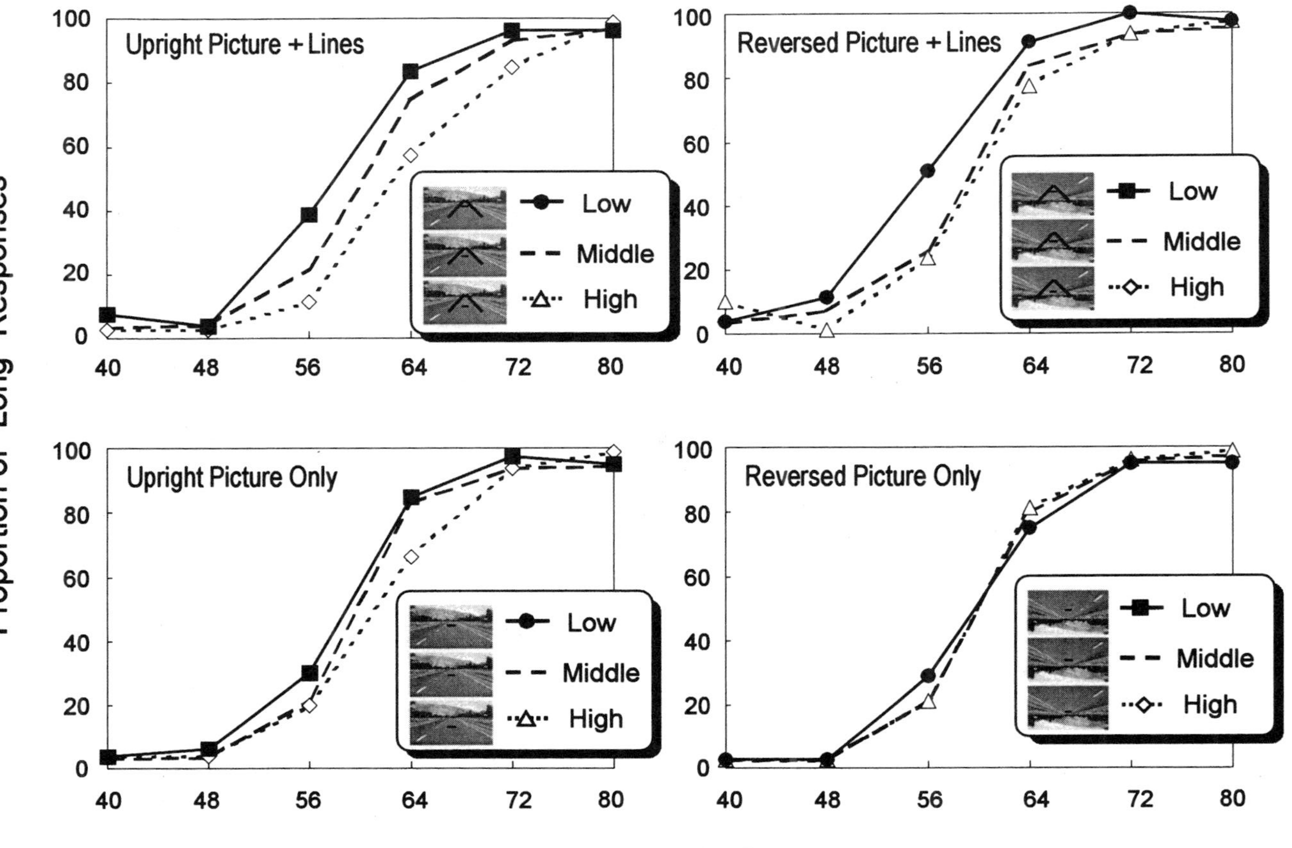

Figure 2.7. Effects of photographic perspective on the Ponzo illusion in rhesus monkeys. Other details are as in figure 2.3. Although an upright photograph induces illusion (*bottom left*), the effect is overshadowed by the line-drawn contexts (*top two panels*). (Redrawn based on Fujita, 1996.)

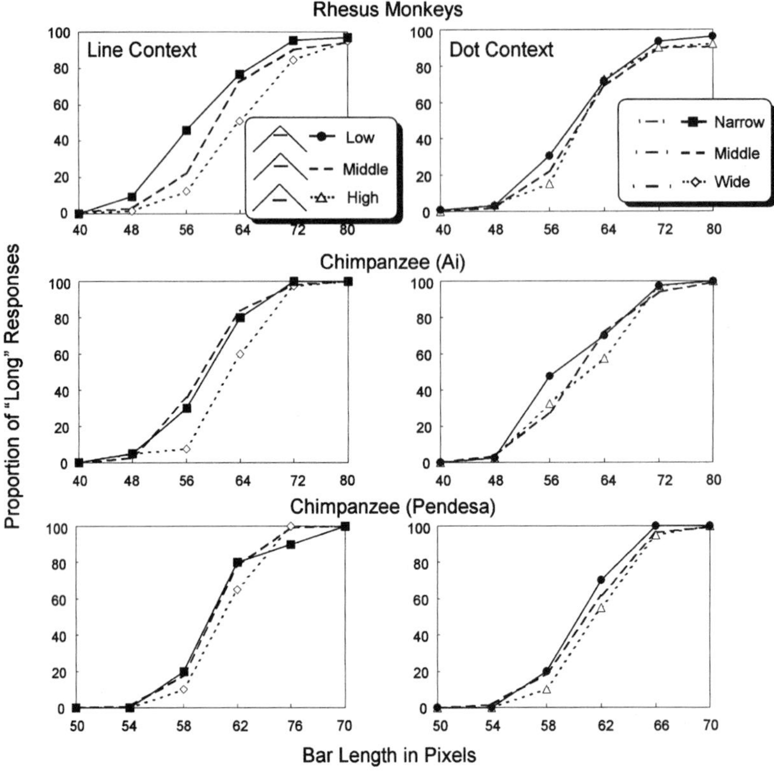

Figure 2.8. Ponzo illusion with the line context (*left:* Inverted-V) and the dot context (*right*) in rhesus monkeys and chimpanzees. Other details are as in figure 2.3. There is a large species difference in the effects of the dot context between rhesus monkeys, chimpanzees, and humans (shown in figure 2.5). (Redrawn based on Fujita, 1997.)

effect in rhesus monkeys, some effect comparable to converging lines in chimpanzees, and an effect that is much stronger than the converging lines in humans.

A plausible source of these perceptual differences has not yet been identified. One possibility may be a species difference in the spatial anisotropy of interaction among figural elements. Visual illusions can be viewed as a consequence of the interaction among figural elements. Such interaction may be stronger among elements oriented in one direction than in a different direction. In the case of the dot context, the illusion is expected only when there is strong interaction between the target and the dot placed horizontally. For monkeys, the interaction may be stronger among vertically arranged elements.

To test this possibility, the same rhesus monkeys and chimpanzees received the same test using the stimuli rotated 90 degrees to the right (Fujita, 2001b). The results were mixed. One of the rhesus monkeys showed some illusion in the vertically arranged dot context, whereas the other showed no sign of illusory perception in this context. One chimpanzee showed a strong illusion in this orientation, but the other chimpanzee showed no illusion. Thus, this hypothesis has received little support.

Ponzo Illusion: Summary

This series of comparative experiments on the perception of the Ponzo illusion revealed both similarities and differences among the species tested. Figure 2.9 summarizes the obtained results (Fujita, 2001b). Clearly, all of the species tested here (pigeons, rhesus monkeys, chimpanzees, and humans) perceive the Ponzo illusion. However, effects of the variables contributing to this illusion are far from

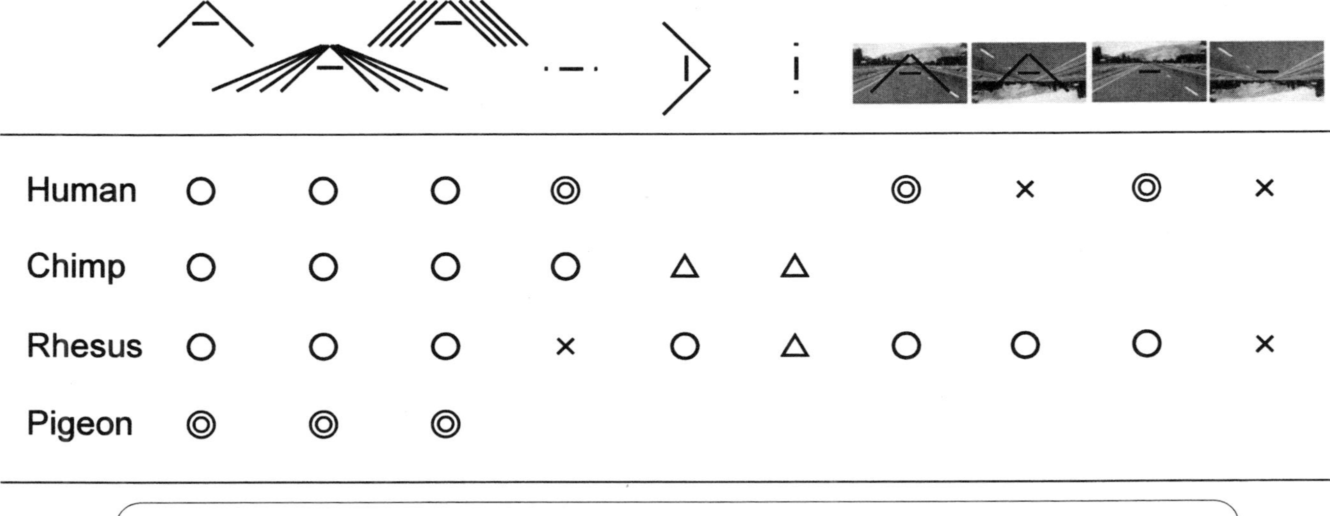

Human ○ ○ ○ ◎ ◎ × ◎ ×
Chimp ○ ○ ○ ○ △ △
Rhesus ○ ○ ○ × ○ △ ○ ○ ○ ×
Pigeon ◎ ◎ ◎
◎ : Strong Illusion
○ : Moderate Illusion
× : No Illusion
△ : Not Clear / Individual Difference

Figure 2.9. Summary of the series of studies on the perception of the Ponzo illusion. (From "What You See Is Different From What I See: Species Differences in Visual Perception," by K. Fujita, 2001b, in *Primate Origins of Human Cognition and Behavior*, edited by T. Matsuzawa, p. 44. Copyright 2001 by Springer-Verlag Tokyo. Reprinted with permission.)

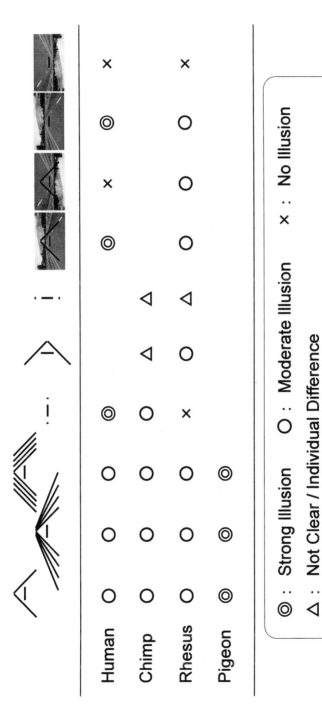

homogeneous among these species. More species must be tested in a comparative manner and with a variety of parameters to sketch how this illusory perception has evolved and what kinds of ecological and phylogenetic constraints contribute to the current way in which the species perceive the environment. However, from the data obtained so far, neocortices may not necessarily contribute to these visual illusions, because pigeons clearly perceived a version of Ponzo illusion. Thus, perception of some types of visual illusions may be traced back at least to the common ancestor of mammals and avians.

AMODAL COMPLETION

Objects are often partly hidden by other objects. Under these conditions, all that we can obtain through our eyes will be incomplete information about such occluded objects. However, we have little difficulty recognizing intact but occluded objects. It may be that we routinely complete the missing information.

Kanizsa (1979) proposed two types of completion process: modal completion and amodal completion. Modal completion is a process in which observers actually experience the completed image; this completed image is difficult to differentiate from reality. For example, in Kanizsa's famous triangle figure (see figure 2.1a), observers cannot believe that there is no real triangle before they inspect the figure very carefully. Amodal completion is a process in which observers not only perceive the completed image but also perceive a noncompleted image or even an irregularly completed image.

For example, if you observe the figure in the top left panel of figure 2.10, you may be most likely to perceive a triangle placed on a disk (top right); at other times, you may perceive a Pac-Man biting a triangle (bottom left) or even an irregular contour behind the triangle (bottom right). Amodal completion represents a perceptual decision of the most plausible solution to the stimuli presented. How the visual system calculates the solution remains controversial (e.g., Albert, 2001), but what should be considered is that the solution is likely to fit the necessary agendas of the species in the prevailing context. Thus, amodal completion may be a useful phenomenon with which to examine how perceptual systems have evolved to adapt to the environment.

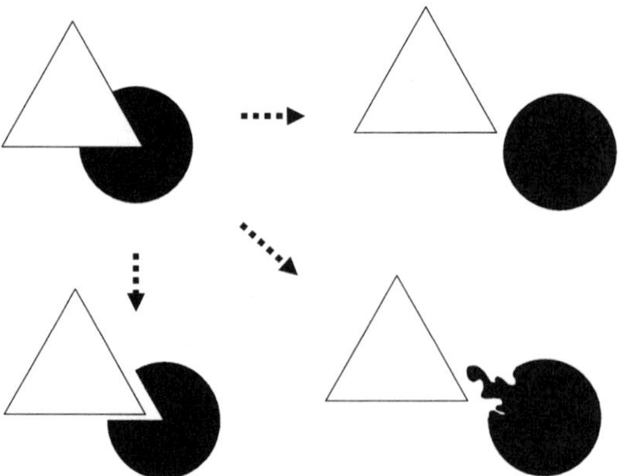

Figure 2.10. An example showing that amodal completion is a most plausible solution based on sensory input.

Perception of Object Unity in Nonhuman Primates

When 4-month-old human infants are habituated to two aligned rods moving in concert behind an occluder, the infants are surprised to see the two rods without the occluder. This result suggests that infants perceive the rods behind the occluder as a single rod (perception of object unity: Kellman & Spelke, 1983). Thus, this process of perceptual completion develops early in humans.

We asked whether nonhuman primates also perceive object unity. First, we tested a female chimpanzee (Sato, Kanazawa, & Fujita, 1997). She was trained on a 0-delay matching-to-sample task using a diagonal rod and a pair of short diagonal rods aligned on the cathode ray tube (CRT) monitor (figure 2.11, top). The sample moved from left to right at a constant speed. The comparison stimuli were stationary. She immediately performed almost perfectly on this task. Then, we presented the sample with a horizontal belt occluding the central portion of the sample on all-reinforced probe test trials (figure 2.11, synchronized condition). In this case, the two types of sample rods were nondiscriminable. The chimpanzee consistently matched this occluded sample to the unitary rod. In two control conditions, in which the bottom portion of the stimulus was either stationary or moved in the other direction (figure 2.11, fixed and opposite), her choice was the pair of the separate rods. It is clear that this chimpanzee perceived object unity. More recent studies on several primate species have consistently

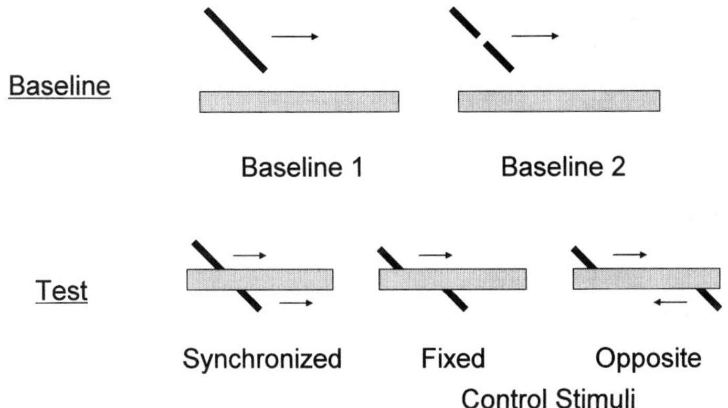

Figure 2.11. Baseline (*top*) and test stimuli (*bottom*) used in studying the perception of object unity in a chimpanzee (Sato et al., 1997) and pigeons (Ushitani et al., 2001). The question was: Which stimulus, a unitary rod or separated rods, would the subjects match to the unidentifiable test stimulus as the sample in the presence of the occluder?

obtained similar results with a variety of procedures and stimuli (Guinea baboons: Deruelle, Barbet, Dépy, & Fagot, 2000; tufted capuchin monkeys: Fujita, 2000; squirrel monkeys: Nagasaka & Osada, 2000; Japanese monkeys: Sugita, 1999).

Human infants develop this completion ability in at least three stages. In the first stage, 4-month-old infants simply recognize the unity of two visible portions as long as they move in concert. The infants do not take the edges of the two portions into account and thus recognize no more than mere connectedness. This process, in which common motion specifies unity, is called an *edge-insensitive process* (Kellman, 1996). In the second stage, 6-month-old infants recognize the unity of two portions without common motion but with relatable edges. This process is called an *edge-sensitive process*. However, infants do not complete the occluded portion as human adults would do. Craton (1996) demonstrated that 6-month-old infants were not surprised when they saw an irregular contour behind the occluder as long as they were connected, whereas 8-month-old infants were surprised. Thus, the interpolation of contours in some specified form requires 2 additional months after the infants start to follow the relatability rules. This stage may be called *smooth interpolation*.

Sato, Kanazawa, and Fujita (1997) tested the same chimpanzee with stationary stimuli. The vernier (alignment) gap between the top and bottom portions was systematically changed. The chimpanzee's choice of the unitary rod was the highest for the stimuli having no vernier gap (i.e., nicely aligned) but decreased as the size of the gap increased. Thus, the completion process for the chimpanzee was clearly edge sensitive.

I further tested which rule nonhuman primates would follow when they completed occluded figures. The subjects were capuchin monkeys. I prepared the four stimuli in figure 2.12a. The top and the bottom portions of three of the stimuli are connected, but only one of them (straight) has a smooth contour; the other two stimuli (irregular and rectangle) have irregularly connected contours. Each was distinguishable in the central part of the stimuli.

Two monkeys were trained to match these four stimuli on a four-choice 0-delay matching-to-sample task. After they showed high accuracies, the subjects were tested with the samples having a red occluding belt at the center of the stimulus (figure 2.12b). Under these conditions, the four stimuli were indistinguishable. The red belt was placed off center in two control conditions (figure 2.12c). Under these conditions, the stimuli were distinguishable from each other. These test stimuli were presented on all-reinforced probe trials. The choice stimuli were always intact. The first test involved the sample figures moving left and right. The second test involved stationary sample figures.

Figure 2.13 shows the monkeys' choice of each of the four stimuli for the center-occluded samples. The left panel is for moving samples and the right is for stationary ones. Both monkeys consistently chose the straight bar over the others for both moving and stationary samples. For control stimuli, the monkeys' choice was almost as accurate as baseline trials. These results suggest that capuchin monkeys did not simply perceive object unity but also judged the occluded contour most likely to be completed by a straight line. This completion process evidenced by the monkeys is more like the one

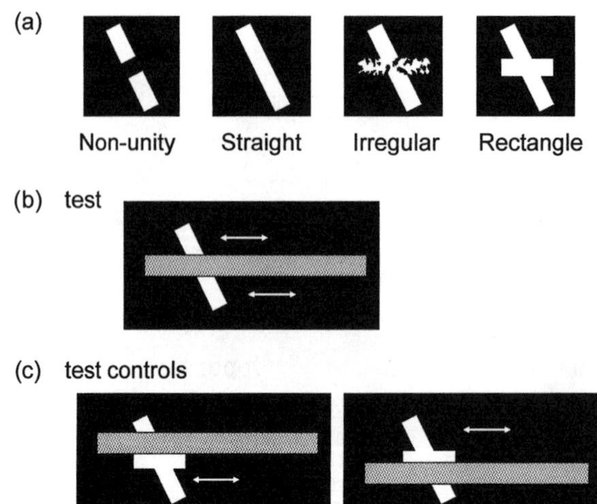

Figure 2.12. Stimuli used in the first study on the completion of occluded contour in capuchin monkeys: (*a*) stimuli used in matching training, (*b*) test stimulus, and (*c*) control stimuli.

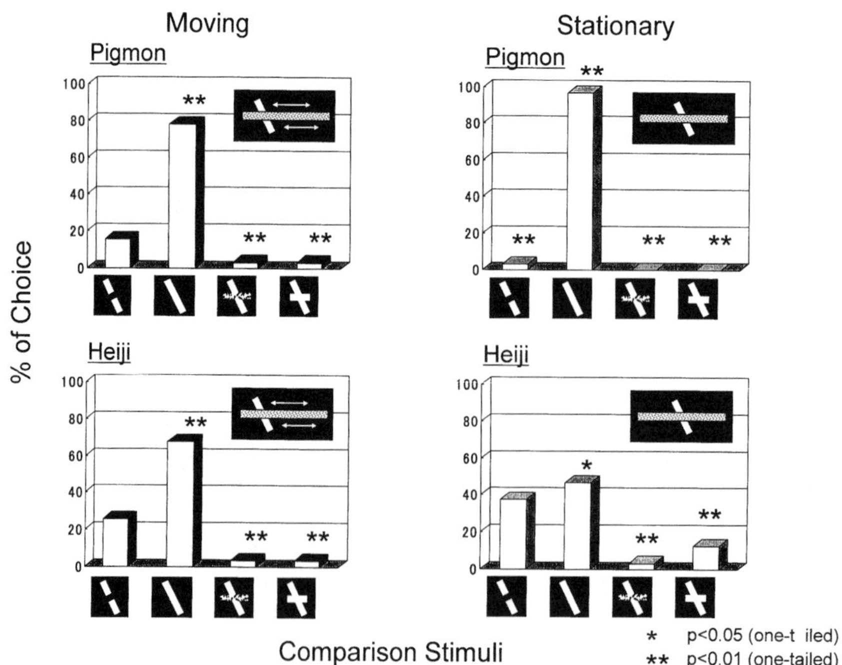

Figure 2.13. Completion of occluded contour by each of two capuchin monkeys. The vertical axis shows the proportion of the choice of each stimulus shown along the abscissa. The test sample stimuli are shown in each graph. The left panels are for moving samples, and the right panels are for stationary samples. Asterisks designate statistically significant deviations from chance.

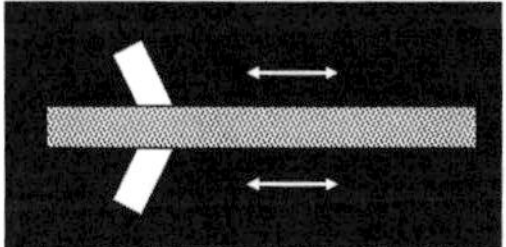

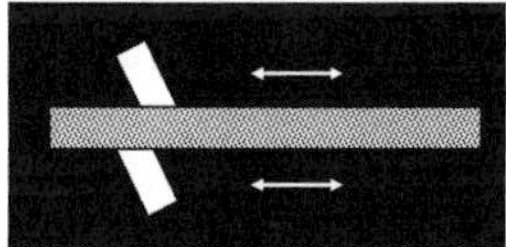

Figure 2.14. Stimuli used to test the relatability rule in completing contour for capuchin monkeys: (*a*) two sets of stimuli used in training and (*b*) test stimuli for each set of training stimuli.

shown by human infants older than 8 months than by younger infants.

What Determines Completion by Monkeys?

I next asked whether capuchin monkeys obey the same rules that humans follow when connecting two edges. Kellman and Shipley (1991) suggested that humans tend to connect the two edges by a monotonically curved line only if the extensions of the two edges make an obtuse angle. To test this hypothesis, I prepared the two sets of stimuli shown in figure 2.14a. One set of stimuli contained those having relatable edges, according to Kellman and Shipley (1991), and the other contained nonrelatable edges. When the monkeys were tested with the relatable samples with the occluding belt at the center, they overwhelmingly chose the connected figure. In contrast, when the monkeys were tested with the nonrelatable samples, they switched to choose the disconnected figure. The results were virtually the same for both moving and stationary samples. Thus, the monkeys completed only the relatable edges, just like humans, regardless of the presence or absence of common motion.

Next, I tested whether the monkeys would follow the regularity rule when they completed occluded contours. I prepared the four figures having zigzag contours shown in figure 2.15. As before, three of the four figures were connected rods, but only one of them had a regular contour. When the monkeys were tested with moving samples, both subjects matched the stimuli having the occluding belt at the center to the unitary zigzag. However, when they were tested with stationary samples, one of the monkeys chose the nonunitary zigzag. Thus, the capuchin monkeys basically followed the regularity rule like humans, but there was some interaction of this rule with the presence or absence of common motion of the two visible parts.

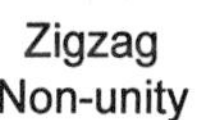

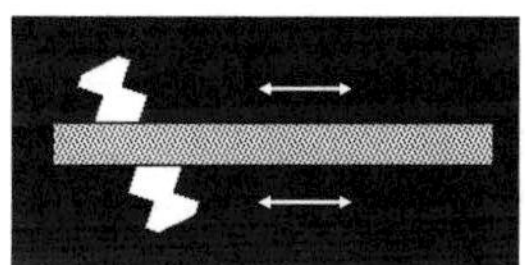

Figure 2.15. Stimuli used to test the overall regularity rule in contour completion for capuchin monkeys: (*a*) training stimuli and (*b*) test stimulus.

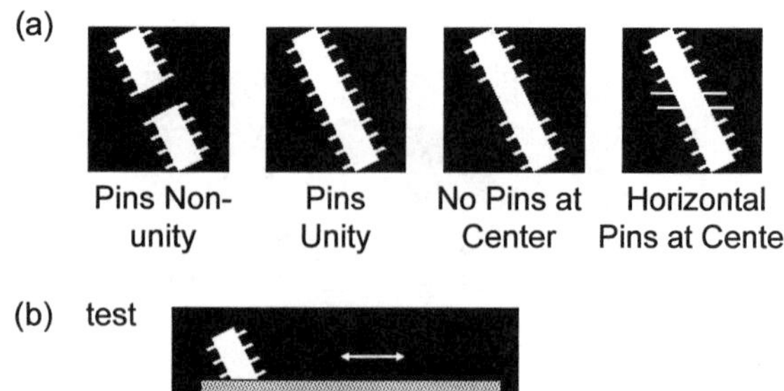

Figure 2.16. The second set of stimuli to test the overall regularity rule in contour completion in capuchin monkeys: (*a*) training stimuli and (*b*) test stimulus.

The last question that I asked concerned how the monkeys would behave if the local and global cues for completion contradicted one another. I prepared the four stimuli depicted in figure 2.16. Note that although the global rule specifies a regularly pinned rod when the central portion is occluded, the local rule specifies no pins at the center (the third stimulus).

Although one monkey attained 85% correct matching, the matching accuracy for the second monkey remained at about 50%. The successful monkey was tested with the sample having the occluding belt at the center, as in the previous experiments. He matched the partly occluded samples to the regularly pinned rod. Thus, the global rule was more dominant than the local rule for completion.

The dominance of the global aspect of the stimulus was not consistent with the local precedence effect demonstrated in baboons and chimpanzees by Deruelle and Fagot (1998) and Fagot and Tomonaga (1999). This difference may be due to the species and/or procedures used. But, regardless of the cause, this result shows that the global aspects of visual stimuli sometimes control figure recognition in nonhuman primates.

Adult humans were also tested with a slightly different procedure. They received a 10-choice matching task. The samples were always center occluded. Among the 10 intact choice stimuli were all of the stimuli theoretically matchable from the partly occluded sample. The obtained results were almost the same as those obtained from capuchin monkeys for both moving and stationary samples. This result suggests that many of the rules governing visual completion are probably shared between humans and capuchin monkeys. Although data from other nonhuman primates are needed before we conclude that this similarity is due to homology, this similarity may suggest that these perceptual rules can be traced back to the common ancestor of humans and New World monkeys.

The Pigeon Problem

In contrast to nonhuman primates, pigeons have repeatedly been reported not to complete partly occluded figures in studies using a variety of stimuli and procedures (Cerella, 1980; Sekuler, Lee, & Shettleworth, 1996; Shimizu, 1998; Watanabe & Furuya, 1997). We tested whether pigeons perceive object unity in basically the same procedure as we used to test the chimpanzee and the capuchin monkeys (Ushitani, Fujita, & Yamanaka, 2001). That is, pigeons were first trained to match a complete rod and a pair of separated rods, and then they were tested with the sample having the occluding belt on it. We expected that pigeons might complete the occluded portion of the figures if the visible components moved in concert. The results were, however, completely different from what we obtained with nonhuman primates. Pigeons tended to choose separated rods for the moving sample that the chimpanzee matched to the unitary rod.

We suspected that choosing separated rods might be reasonable because the size and the shape of the portion of the stimulus above and below the occluding belt remained unchanged as they moved. Thus, we replaced the horizontal occluding belt with a diagonal belt (figure 2.17a). In doing this, the size and the shape of the visible portion changed as they moved. The result was, however, negative again. Both pigeons consistently chose the separated rods for this modified stimulus.

It is possible that the speed and the magnitude of the change in shape and size of the visible portions

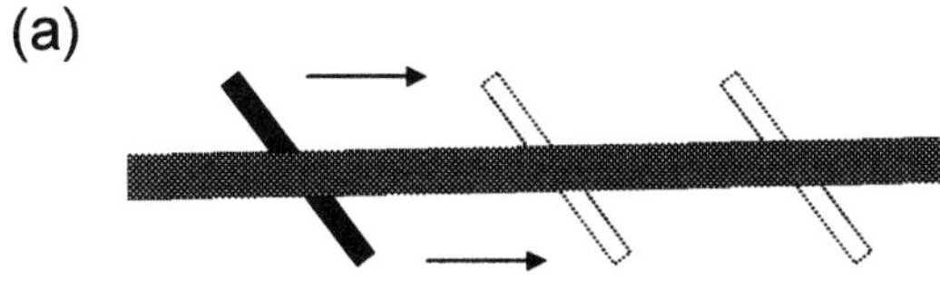

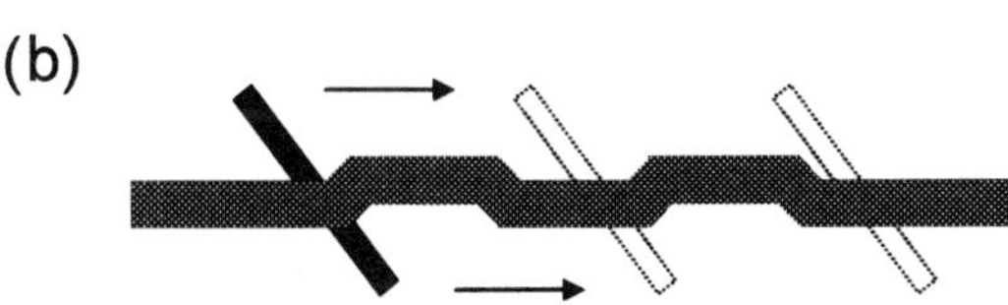

Figure 2.17. Diagonal (*a*) and zigzag (*b*) occluding surfaces to test pigeons' perception of object unity. For these stimuli, the top and the bottom visible portions change their size and shape as they move.

might have been too small for the pigeons to recognize. Thus, we replaced the diagonal belt with a zigzag-shaped belt (figure 2.17b). In this case, the size and shape of the visible portions should change abruptly as they move along the belt. Nevertheless, one of the two pigeons showed a complete position bias and the other pigeon still chose separated rods.

In our next experiment (Ushitani & Fujita, 2005), we changed the geometric stimuli to more naturalistic ones: photographs of food and nonfood objects. Pigeons were trained to peck at all of the photographs of grains but at none of the nonfood items, such as screw nuts presented simultaneously. Then, the pigeons were tested with photographs of these items that were either truncated or occluded by a feather. We hypothesized that if pigeons completed occluded photographs, then they would peck at intact food first, occluded food second, and truncated food last, if at all. The result was, however, that the pigeons pecked at the truncated food earlier than at the occluded food. This result suggests that pigeons may not complete even naturalistic stimuli.

Actually, a similar failure was previously reported by Watanabe and Furuya (1997). In their study, pigeons performed a go–no-go discrimination of a photograph of a partly occluded pigeon from a photograph of the occluder. In testing, the pigeons pecked at a photograph of a truncated pigeon as well as one of an intact pigeon. The pigeon's responses were found to be completely determined by the presence of any physical component. No evidence of completion was obtained.

One problem with all of the studies on pigeons just described is that, in these studies, subjects were expected to complete the occluded portion in the way that humans do. For example, in our study on object unity, choosing a straight rod was deemed to demonstrate pigeons' object completion. However, it is not obvious that pigeons should complete objects in the same way as do humans. We have seen that capuchin monkeys do, but pigeons may not. Thus, we should devise a procedure in which the shape of the completed contours is not specified.

A hint of such a procedure comes from Kanizsa's (1979) illusion. When a small box is placed adjacent to a larger rectangle, humans overestimate the size of the box (see figure 2.18, right, where the lower box appears to be slightly larger than the upper box). Kanizsa interpreted this illusion as a consequence of perceptual completion. That is, we perceive the small box touching the rectangle as partly hidden by the rectangle. Therefore, we automatically complete the "occluded" part of the small box. This illusion is useful because it does not specify with what shape the observer completes the occluded part.

Fujita (2001a) trained pigeons and rhesus monkeys in the bar length discrimination task used in the Ponzo study described earlier. That is, the animals classified bars of a variety of lengths into "long" and "short" categories. During training, a large gray rectangle was placed at a fixed distance from the black target bar. On all-reinforced probe trials, test stimuli appeared with the same gray rectangle located at varied distances from the black target bar. In one condition, the distance was 0—that is, touching.

Figure 2.19 shows the results. Rhesus monkeys showed a consistent bias, reporting "long" for the target bar touching the rectangle more often than in the other conditions. That is, the monkeys

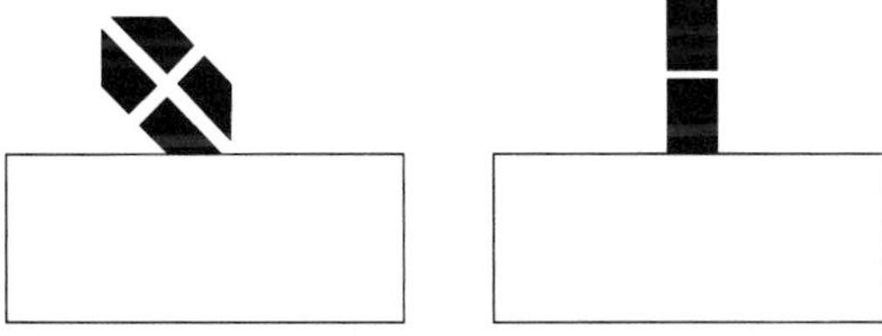

Figure 2.18. Two illusory figures shown in Kanizsa (1979). Small figures touching the rectangle typically appear larger (or longer) than the others.

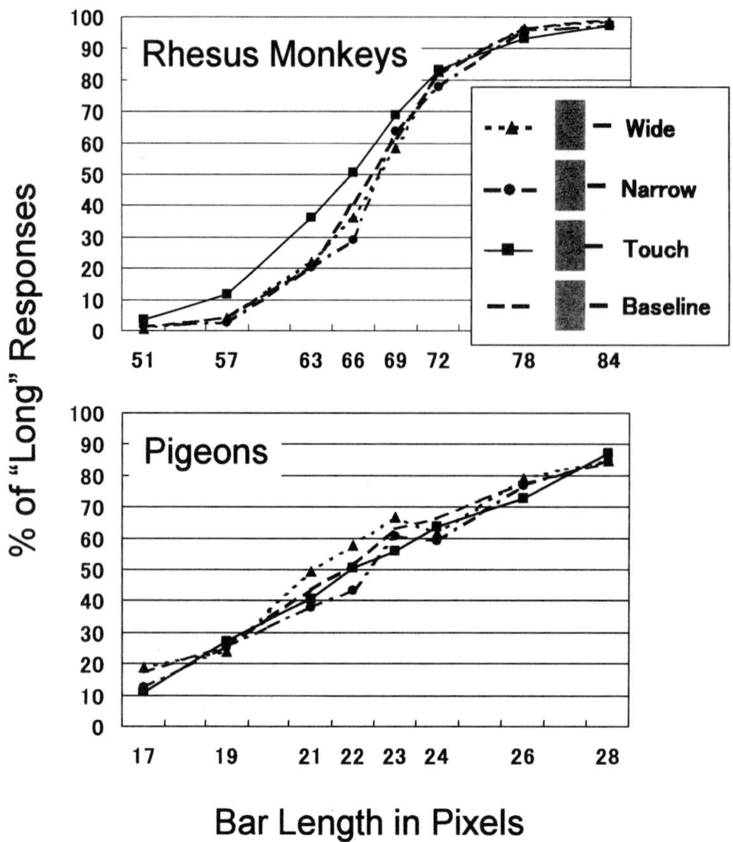

Figure 2.19. Proportion of subjects' responses to the "long" key (vertical axis) as a function of the length of the target bar (horizontal axis) in rhesus monkeys and pigeons. Monkeys show a bias toward "long" when the bar touches the gray rectangle like the ones shown in figure 2.18, whereas pigeons do not. (Redrawn based on Fujita, 2001a.)

perceived the same illusion as do humans. In contrast, pigeons showed no such bias. Pigeons do not seem to perceive continuation of the target bar behind the rectangle. This negative result suggests that pigeons do not perceive the occluding relationship between figural components.

Summary of Perceptual Completion in Nonhumans

Figure 2.20 summarizes what has been obtained from a series of comparative studies on perceptual completion. As it shows, we have not yet found substantial differences among primate species. Thus, it is likely that the completion processes in primates are homologously related.

On the other hand, pigeons show no evidence for completion. This could be because pigeons lack a neocortex. Sugita (1999) has found neurons in V1 of Japanese monkeys that are plausibly related to object unity perception. However, domestic chicks have been found to complete objects in two separate studies (Lea, Slater, & Ryan, 1996; Regolin & Vallortigara, 1995). Therefore, the neocortex does not appear to be indispensable for performing visual completion. These studies used a social procedure, namely, imprinting. It is possible that pigeons may complete objects in such social situations. However, Shimizu (1998) failed to obtain positive results for completion in the context of courtship. Pigeons may not have evolved to complete fragmentary information. This point is discussed later.

Most of the data in this literature, including our own, come from primates and a few birds. Mice are the only nonprimate mammal so far tested to show evidence of completion. Many more species, in particular species from different taxa, should be

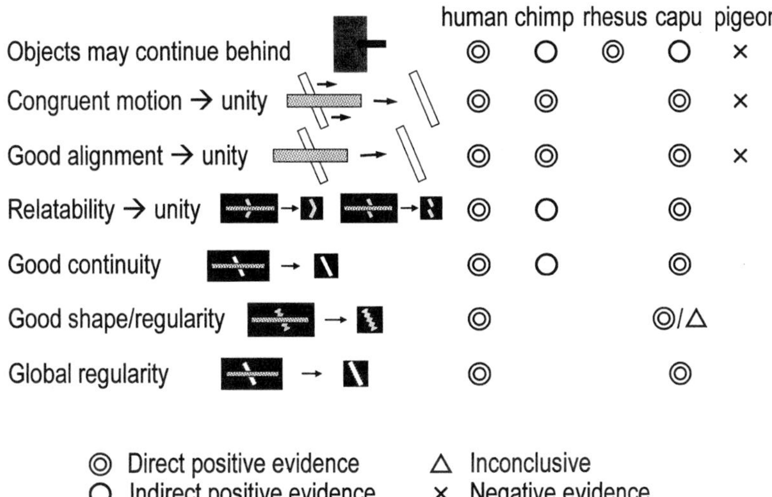

Figure 2.20. Summary of the results of the series of studies on amodal completion in five species.

tested to learn how this perceptual process may have evolved.

SPATIOTEMPORAL BOUNDARY FORMATION

When we look into dense shrubbery while we are stationary, it is difficult for us to recognize a house behind. However, once we start to walk, we can recognize the house easily. In this case, each frame we obtain from our sensory system may contain no more than a collection of tiny fractions of the wall of a house, which is not enough to recognize something meaningful. Nevertheless, once we see different frames in sequence, we immediately recognize the house. The human visual system integrates information over time to draw a plausible solution to the series of visual inputs.

An experimental demonstration of this process is called spatiotemporal boundary formation (Shipley & Kellman, 1994). Figure 2.21 schematically shows what it is like. Subjects are shown a random dot array. Some attribute of the dots, color in this example, inside an imaginary figure placed on this random dot array is different from that of the other dots outside of the imaginary figure. When this imaginary figure is stationary, it is difficult for humans to tell the shape of the figure, especially when the dot array is sparse. However, once the imaginary figure moves and the color of the dots correspondingly changes, humans easily recognize the figure. This situation is like a colored tile moving around behind a randomly punched opaque board.

Shipley and Kellman (1994) have shown that this integration of spatial information over time occurs only for a limited temporal window. That is, when the stimulus is presented as a sequence of independent frames on the monitor, the duration of each frame should be as short as 10 to 30 ms.

We asked whether chimpanzees also perceptually integrate such spatiotemporal information over time. We also examined whether there are any substantial differences in this process between humans and chimpanzees.

First, two chimpanzees were trained using a touch-screen monitor to match five solid red

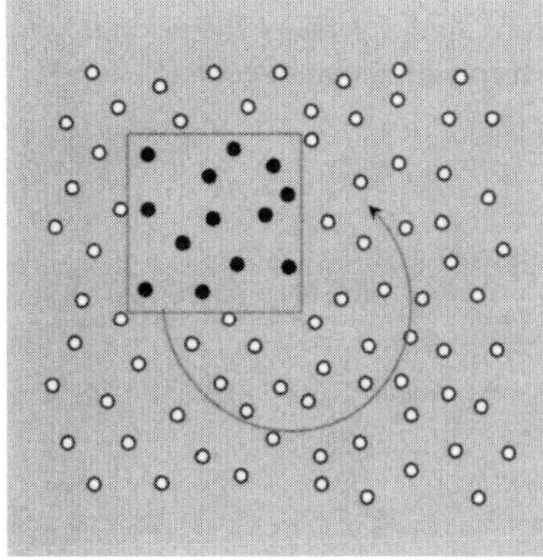

Figure 2.21. A schematic representation of spatiotemporal boundary formation.

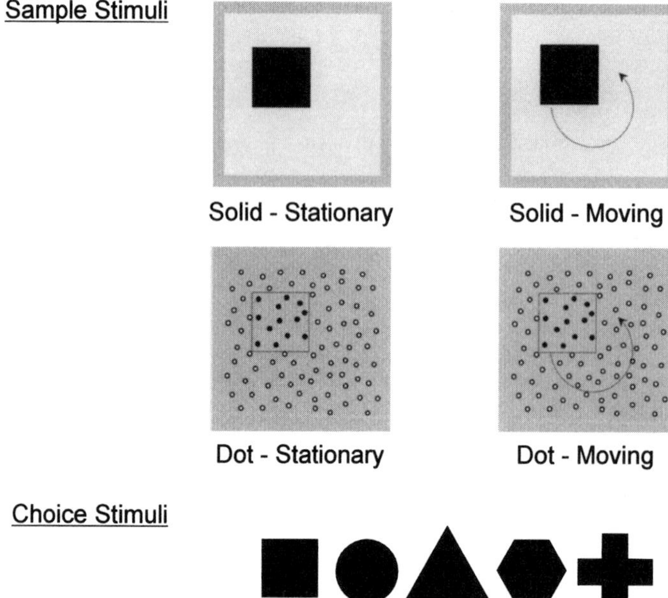

Figure 2.22. Sample (*top two rows*) and choice stimuli (*bottom*) used for the matching-to-sample task in the study of spatiotemporal boundary formation in chimpanzees.

geometrical figures of the same surface size shown in figure 2.22. The samples were placed on a large white square. On half of the trials, the sample figure revolved at a speed of 2 s per cycle (180 degrees/s), whereas on the remaining half of the trials it was stationary at a random location on the orbit of the revolving sample. The comparison stimuli were always stationary. Both chimpanzees quickly solved this five-choice matching-to-sample task.

Then, the background square was changed to a random dot array. The background dots were white and the dots inside the sample figure were red. On half of the trials, the sample figure revolved; thus, the cluster of red dots changed both its envelope shape and its location as the sample figure moved. On the remaining half of the trials, the sample figure remained stationary at a randomly chosen location on the orbit of the moving sample.

The density of the random dots changed from dense (48 dots per row/column) to sparse as sessions repeated. The sparsest density was determined to be the density at which the chimpanzee no longer responded because of the difficulty of the task. In practice, we stopped decreasing the density when the subjects showed accuracies lower than 50% for two consecutive sessions. This series was repeated five times but with different revolving speeds and frame durations: (1) 30 frames/s and 180 degrees/s, (2) 15 frames/s and 180 degrees/s, (3) 8 frames/s and 180 degrees/s, (4) 15 frames/s and 90 degrees/s, and (5) 8 frames/s and 45 degrees/s. Finally, the chimpanzees were returned to the first condition: that is, 30 frames/s and 180 degrees/s.

Figure 2.23 shows the accuracies of the two subjects in the first condition as a function of dot density. The leftmost point in each graph denotes solid samples. There is no difference in accuracy for solid samples between moving and stationary stimuli. On the other hand, the accuracies for samples made of dots were higher for moving samples than for stationary ones. That is, the chimpanzees better recognized the sample figure made of dots when they moved than when they were stationary. This result demonstrates that chimpanzees integrate spatiotemporal information presented over time as do humans. It should be noted that in no frame did the dot-made samples show their actual contours. Thus, this result represents a perception of the contour that is absent from what was actually presented.

The benefit of motion was different in magnitude across conditions. Figure 2.24 shows the difference in accuracy between moving and stationary conditions. The largest benefit came from the first condition in which the frame duration was the shortest (30 ms) and the moving speed was the fastest (180 degrees/s). The smallest benefit was from the third condition in which the frame duration was the longest (125 ms) and the same moving speed held as in the first condition.

When we tested humans using a similar procedure, they performed the five-choice matching-to-

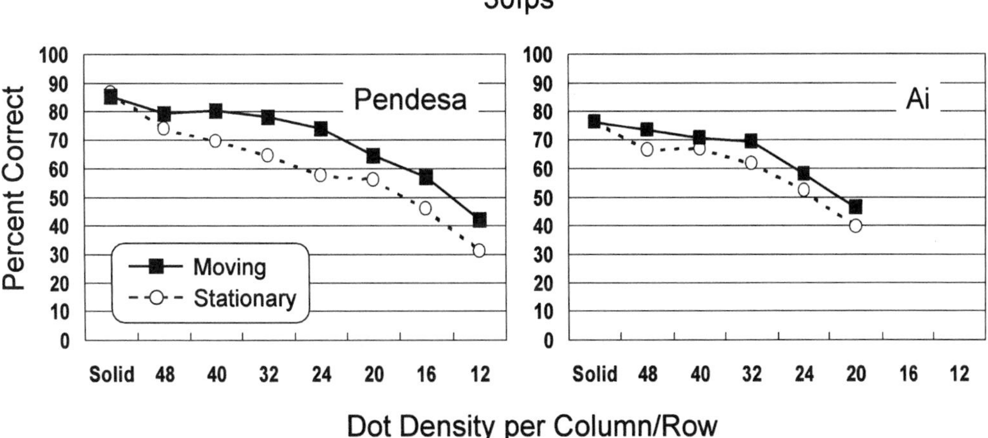

Figure 2.23. Matching accuracy of two chimpanzees for moving and stationary samples made of random dots. Horizontal axis shows the density of dots per column/row. Solid means unobscured geometric figure. Both subjects showed higher matching accuracy for moving samples made of dots than stationary ones (see figure 2.22).

sample task with slightly different parameters: (1) 32 frames/s and 180 degrees/s, (2) 16 frames/s and 180 degrees/s, (3) 8 frames/s and 180 degrees/s, (4) 64 frames/s and 90 degrees/s, and (5) 128 frames/s and 45 degrees/s. The first three conditions closely corresponded to those used for chimpanzees, but the last two conditions were new. The dot density was 32, 24, and 16 per column and row. All combinations of these parameters were mixed within a session as were stationary samples.

Seven of the 10 humans consistently benefited from the moving stimuli. Figure 2.25a shows the average increase in accuracy for each condition from stationary samples. The data are clearly comparable to what was obtained with chimpanzees: namely, among the three conditions of 180 degrees/s speed common to both species, the largest benefit came from 32 frames/s (31 ms/frame) and the smallest benefit from 8 frames/s (125 ms). Thus, given the revolving speed fixed at 180 degrees/s,

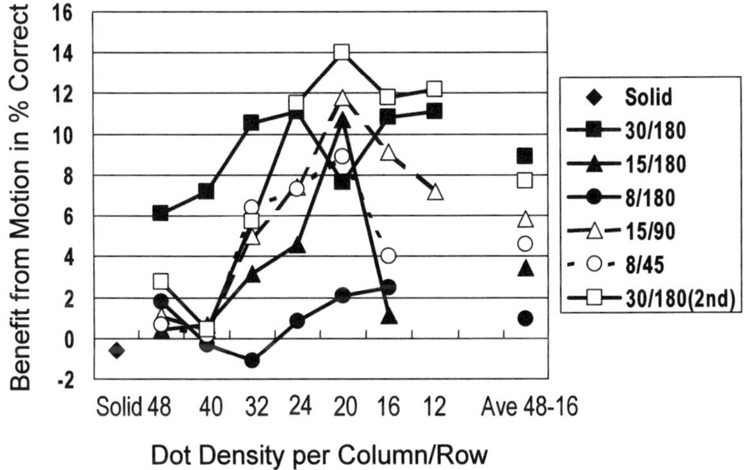

Figure 2.24. Benefit from motion in recognizing figures made of dots in chimpanzees. Horizontal axis shows the density of dots per column/row, and the vertical axis is the difference in matching accuracy between moving and stationary samples.

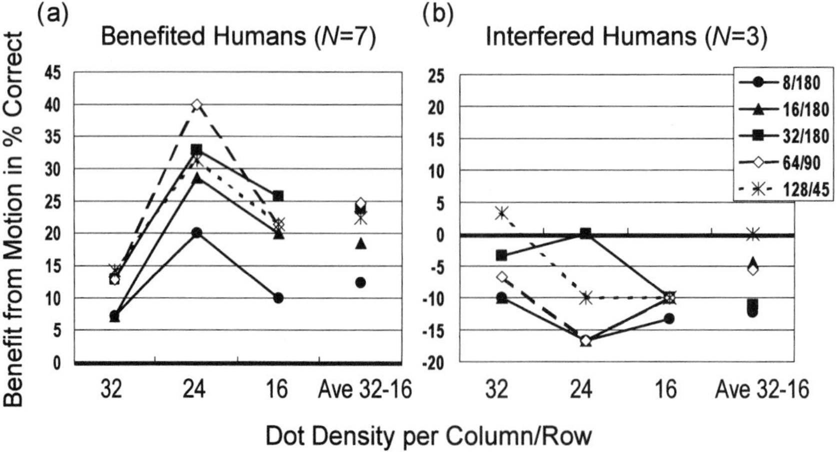

Figure 2.25. Benefit from motion in recognizing figures made of dots in humans: (*a*) data from subjects who received benefit from motion and (*b*) data from subjects who received interference from motion. Other details are as in figure 2.24.

these two species of primates both received a benefit that increased as the frame duration shortened. For still shorter frame durations of 15 ms (64 frames/s) and 8 ms (128 frames/s), the degree of benefit did not change. These results in humans were consistent with those of Shipley and Kellman (1994).

What is interesting in this study is that 3 of 10 human subjects who were tested showed consistent decreases in accuracy with moving samples. Figure 2.25b shows the average benefit (loss, actually) of these three subjects. This result suggests that there may be large individual differences in the ability to integrate spatiotemporal information. The reason why motion proved to be interfering for these subjects is not evident from the questionnaire that we administered after the session. The characteristics of the perceptual system that could give rise to such individual difference should be studied further.

We thus showed that chimpanzees and humans may share a common process in integrating spatiotemporal information. Other species should be tested to reveal how this process may have evolved.

CONCLUSIONS

We have analyzed three perceptual phenomena—the Ponzo illusion, amodal completion, and spatiotemporal boundary formation—in primates and birds. In doing so, we have found similarities across a variety of species and surprising differences in some cases.

First, we found that all four species tested—namely, pigeons, rhesus monkeys, chimpanzees, and humans—perceive the Ponzo illusion. The perspective strength of the line-drawn context stimuli did not affect the magnitude of the illusion in any species. On the other hand, we found other factors that affected the strength of the Ponzo illusion. (a) The magnitude of the illusion is much larger in pigeons than in primates. (b) A type of context, the dot context, induces the illusion more strongly in humans than the more typically used line context; on the other hand, the dot context induces an illusion of comparable strength to the line context for chimpanzees, and it induces no illusion at all for rhesus monkeys. (c) The relative strength of photographic perspective and the line-drawn context in inducing the illusion was different for rhesus monkeys and humans.

These results suggest that the Ponzo illusion is not necessarily a product of neocortical information processing. We are still not sure whether the Ponzo illusion in pigeons is homologous with that in primates. However, this kind of illusion may be a byproduct of efficient judgment of object size. That is, identification of objects may be facilitated given there is size invariance. Judgment of size not only by the size of the retinal image but also by simultaneously considering size in relation to other environmental objects may help organisms better recognize target objects. Therefore, illusions like the Ponzo could result from visual systems having different hardware implementation but sharing the same computational algorithm.

Other performance differences across primate species seem to be differences in quantity. The effects of dot context changes and the effects of photographic perspective are not critically different between humans and monkeys. These results suggest that the parameters controlling the Ponzo illusion are common but different in relative strength among different species of primates. The Ponzo illusion is likely to be homologously related among primates.

On the other hand, the process of amodal completion was completely different between primates and pigeons. Actually, pigeons are the only species found not to complete objects among the variety of species tested: namely, chimpanzees (Sato et al., 1997); rhesus monkeys (Fujita, 2001a); Guinea baboons (Deruelle et al., 2000); Japanese monkeys (Sugita, 1999); capuchin monkeys (Fujita, 2000, 2004); squirrel monkeys (Nagasaka & Osada, 2000); mice (Kanizsa, Renzi, Conte, Compostela, & Guerani, 1993); domestic chicks (Lea et al., 1996; Regolin & Vallortigara, 1995); Bengalese finches (Okanoya & Takahashi, 2000), and pigeons (Cerella, 1980; Sekuler et al., 1996; Ushitani & Fujita, 2005; Ushitani, Fujita, & Yamanaka, 2001; Watanabe & Furuya, 1997).

Completion of partly occluded objects seems, in general, to be adaptive for animals with well-developed neural systems to recognize objects; thus, it is reasonable to assume that this process is widespread among animals. In this sense, the failure of pigeons seems peculiar considering the variety of intelligent behaviors demonstrated in this species (e.g., Herrnstein & Loveland, 1964; Wasserman & Bhatt, 1992; Zentall, Clement, Bhatt, & Allen, 2001).

Of course, pigeons may complete objects in other situations. In fact, when DiPietro, Wasserman, and Young (2002) trained pigeons to discriminate the stimuli on "top" of the occluder, the birds' discrimination performance to the same stimuli "behind" the occluder improved. Although this result does not necessarily mean that pigeons completed the occluded portion, a more careful training procedure might reveal the ability for completion in pigeons. Another possibility is that pigeons may complete three-dimensional stimuli. However, even if they do so, then it does not account for the large difference between pigeons and the many other species that completed two-dimensional stimuli.

Thus, it seems that pigeons may have evolved with a visual system that does not actively complete occluded stimuli. It should be noted that pigeons live heavily on grains. Grains are small and abundant; thus, it may be that there is little need for them to look for hidden or partly hidden seeds. Completion, in theory, requires more processing time; therefore, it may be adaptive for pigeons not to complete stimuli, at least not in the feeding context commonly used to test pigeons. It is interesting to note that chicks have been shown to complete occluded objects; these birds also forage on grains but in addition they eat worms and other small prey that may hide themselves behind objects.

However, pigeons may not complete even in a social situation. As noted earlier, male pigeons made the courtship display when the bottom half of the videotaped females on the monitor was occluded by the cardboard, but they courted very little when the top half was occluded (Shimizu, 1998). Thus, the pigeons simply displayed toward the head of females. Similar local processing was also reported in other studies (Cerella, 1977; Watanabe, 2001).

Finally, I have shown for the first time that chimpanzees perceive figures by integrating visual information presented over time as do humans. This is a process in which the visual system calculates a plausible solution from a series of obscure bits of visual information. Each frame resulting from a set of visual inputs sampled at a given time may not always be sufficient to identify an object. By integrating such insufficient information, organisms may better recognize external stimuli. We still do not know how widespread this efficient perceptual process is or how it may have evolved. Comparative studies with animals from a variety of taxa would be helpful in this regard.

We have also found that the integration process is limited to short temporal windows in humans and chimpanzees. This fact may suggest that the integration process is likely to be homologous between the species. However, before reaching this conclusion, we have to explore the possible differential effects of parameters contributing to spatiotemporal boundary formation and we should do this for many species. One parameter that may affect this perception is the critical flicker frequency of the species. Pigeons again are most interesting subjects to study because they may have much higher critical flicker frequencies (Powell, 1967) than primates.

In summary, the studies described here show how rich and varied the perceptual processes of animal species may be. A most important lesson from this research is that human perception is simply one of a variety of perceptual systems that has evolved among different species. We are apt to regard our perception, or the way we see the world, as the single best way or the ultimate solution provided by ever-advancing evolution. However, our perceptual system is simply adapted to the way we humans live. It might be easy to imagine the difficulty that we would have with pigeon-like brains (of a larger size), but the reverse may be also true. Pigeons might function best with the brains with which they evolved.

Acknowledgments Preparation of this chapter was supported by Grants-in-Aid for Scientific Research 13410026 and 14651020 from Ministry of Education, Culture, Sports, Science, and Technology (MEXT) to the author. It was also supported by the 21st Century Center of Excellence (COE) Program, MEXT, D-10 to Kyoto University.

The author also acknowledges with thanks that the capuchin monkeys used in this series of studies were provided by the Cooperation Research Program from the Primate Research Institute, Kyoto University, with Tetsuro Matsuzawa as the counterpart. Studies with humans on completion and spatiotemporal boundary formation were conducted in collaboration with Dr. Anne Giersch, University of Louis Pasteur, with a support from the Kyoto-ULP international exchange program. The author also wishes to thank Tetsuro Matsuzawa and Toyomi Matsuno, Primate Research Institute, for their help in testing chimpanzees for the spatiotemporal formation study.

References

Albert, M. K. (2001). Surface perception and the generic view principle. *Trends in Cognitive Sciences, 15,* 197–203.

Bayne, K. A. L., & Davis, R. T. (1983). Susceptibility of rhesus monkeys (*Macaca mulatta*) to the Ponzo illusion. *Bulletin of the Psychonomic Society, 21,* 476–478.

Benhar, E., & Samuel, D. (1982). Visual illusions in the baboon (*Papio anubis*). *Animal Learning & Behavior, 10,* 115–118.

Brislin, R. W. (1974). The Ponzo illusion: Additional cues, age, orientation, and culture. *Journal of Cross Cultural Psychology, 5,* 139–161.

Cerella, J. (1977). Absence of perspective processing in the pigeon. *Pattern Recognition, 9,* 65–68.

Cerella, J. (1980). The pigeon's analysis of pictures. *Pattern Recognition, 12,* 1–6.

Chiang, C. (1968). A new theory to explain geometrical illusions produced by crossing lines. *Perception & Psychophysics, 3,* 174–176.

Coren, S. (1969). The influence of optical aberrations on the magnitude of the Poggendorff illusion. *Perception & Psychophysics, 6,* 185–186.

Craton, L. G. (1996). The development of perceptual completion abilities: Infants' perception of stationary, partially occluded objects. *Child Development, 67,* 890–904.

Deruelle, C., Barbet, I., Dépy, D., & Fagot, J. (2000). Perception of partly occluded figures by baboons (*Papio papio*). *Perception, 29,* 1483–1497.

Deruelle, C., & Fagot, J. (1998). Visual search for global/local stimulus features in humans and baboons. *Psychonomic Bulletin & Review, 5,* 476–481.

DiPietro, N., Wasserman, E. A., & Young, M. E. (2002). Effects of occlusion on pigeons' visual object recognition. *Perception, 31,* 1299–1312.

Dominguez, K. E. (1954). A study of visual illusions in the monkey. *Journal of Genetic Psychology, 85,* 105–127.

Fagot, J., & Tomonaga, M. (1999). Global and local processing in humans (*Homo sapiens*) and chimpanzees (*Pan troglodytes*): Use of a visual search task with compound stimuli. *Journal of Comparative Psychology, 113,* 3–12.

Fineman, M. B., & Carlson, J. (1973). A comparison of the Ponzo illusion with a textural analogue. *Perception & Psychophysics, 14,* 31–33.

Fujita, K. (1996). Linear perspective and the Ponzo illusion: A comparison between rhesus monkeys and humans. *Japanese Psychological Research, 38,* 136–145.

Fujita, K. (1997). Perception of the Ponzo illusion by rhesus monkeys, chimpanzees, and humans: Similarity and difference in the three primate species. *Perception & Psychophysics, 59,* 284–292.

Fujita. K. (2000). Recognition of figures by nonhuman primates (in Japanese). *Japan Scientific Monthly, 53,* 1074–1081.

Fujita, K. (2001a). Perceptual completion in rhesus monkeys (*Macaca mulatta*) and pigeons (*Columba livia*). *Perception & Psychophysics, 63,* 115–125.

Fujita, K. (2001b). What you see is different from what I see: Species differences in visual perception. In T. Matsuzawa (Ed.), *Primate origins of human cognition and behavior* (pp. 29–54). New York: Springer-Verlag.

Fujita, K. (2004). How do nonhuman animals perceptually integrate figural fragments? *Japanese Psychological Research, 46,* 154–169.

Fujita, K., Blough, D. S., & Blough, P. M. (1991). Pigeons see the Ponzo illusion. *Animal Learning & Behavior, 19,* 283–293.

Fujita, K., Blough, D. S., & Blough, P. M. (1993). Effects of the inclination of context lines on perception of the Ponzo illusion by pigeons. *Animal Learning & Behavior, 21,* 29–34.

Georgeson, M. A., & Blakemore, C. (1973). Apparent depth and the Mueller-Lyer illusion. *Perception, 2,* 225–234.

Gillam, B. (1971). A depth processing theory of the Poggendorff illusion. *Perception & Psychophysics, 10,* 211–216.

Gregory, R. L. (1963). Distortion of visual space as inappropriate constancy scaling. *Nature, 199,* 678–680.

Harris, A. V. (1968). Perception of the horizontal-vertical illusion by stumptail monkeys. *Radford Review, 22,* 61–72.

Herrnstein, R. J., & Loveland, D. H. (1964). Complex visual concept in the pigeon. *Science, 146,* 549–551.

Hodos, W. (1993). The visual capabilities of birds. In H. P. Ziegler & H.-J. Bischof (Eds.), *Vision, brain, and behavior in birds* (pp. 63–76). Cambridge, MA: MIT Press.

Humphrey, N. K., & Morgan, M. J. (1965). Constancy and the geometric illusions. *Nature, 206,* 744–745.

Kanizsa, G. (1979). *Organization in vision: Essays on Gestalt perception.* New York: Praeger Publishers.

Kanizsa, G., Renzi, P., Conte, S., Compostela, C., & Guerani, L. (1993). Amodal completion in mouse vision. *Perception, 22,* 713–721.

Kellman, P. J. (1996). The origins of object perception. In R. Gelman & T. K.-F. Au (Eds.), *Perceptual and cognitive development* (pp. 3–48). New York: Academic Press.

Kellman, P. J., & Shipley, T. F. (1991). A theory of visual interpolation in object perception. *Cognitive Psychology, 23,* 141–221.

Kellman, P. J., & Spelke, E. S. (1983). Perception of partly occluded objects in infancy. *Cognitive Psychology, 15,* 483–524.

Lea, S. E. G., Slater, A. M., & Ryan, C. M. E. (1996). Perception of object unity in chicks: A comparison with the human infant. *Infant Behavior and Development, 19,* 501–504.

Leibowitz, H., Brislin, R., Perlmutter, L., & Hennessy, R. (1969). Ponzo perspective illusions as a manifestation of space perception. *Science, 166,* 1174–1176.

Malott, R. W., & Malott, M. K. (1970). Perception and stimulus generalization. In W. C. Stebbins (Ed.), *Animal psychophysics* (pp. 363–400). New York, Plenum Press.

Malott, R. W., Malott, M. K., & Pokrzywinski, J. (1967). The effects of outward-pointing arrowheads on the Mueller-Lyer illusion in pigeons. *Psychonomic Science, 9,* 55–56.

Nagasaka, Y., & Osada, Y. (2000). Subjective contours, amodal completion, and transparency in animals. *The Japanese Journal of Animal Psychology, 50,* 61–73. (in Japanese with English summary)

Newman, C. V., & Newman, B. M. (1974). The Ponzo illusion in pictures with and without suggested depth. *American Journal of Psychology, 87,* 511–516.

Okanoya, K., & Takahashi, M. (2000). Ecological approach to visual completion. In *Reports of the Grant-in-Aid for Scientific Research for Priority Area* (pp. 34–41). (in Japanese)

Powell, R. W. (1967). The pulse-to-cycle fraction as a determinant of critical flicker fusion in the pigeon. *Psychological Record, 17,* 151–160.

Regolin, L., & Vallortigara, G. (1995). Perception of partly occluded objects by young chicks. *Perception & Psychophysics, 57,* 971–976.

Sato, A., Kanazawa, S., & Fujita, K. (1997). Perception of object unity in a chimpanzee (*Pan troglodytes*). *Japanese Psychological Research, 39,* 191–199.

Sekuler, A. B., Lee, J. A. J., & Shettleworth, S. J. (1996). Pigeons do not complete partly occluded figures. *Perception, 25,* 1109–1120.

Shimizu, T. (1998). Conspecific recognition in pigeons (*Columba livia*) using dynamic video images. *Behaviour, 135,* 43–53.

Shipley, T., & Kellman, P. J. (1994). Spatiotemporal boundary formation: Boundary, form, and motion perception from transformations of surface elements. *Journal of Experimental Psychology: General, 123,* 3–20.

Sugita, Y. (1999). Grouping of image fragments in primary visual cortex. *Nature, 401,* 269–272.

Ushitani, T., & Fujita, K. (2005). Pigeons do not perceptually complete partly occluded photos of food: An ecological approach to the "pigeon problem." *Behavioural Processes, 69,* 67–78.

Ushitani, T., Fujita, K., & Yamanaka, R. (2001). Do pigeons (*Columba livia*) perceive object unity? *Animal Cognition, 4,* 153–161.

Wasserman, E., & Bhatt, R. S. (1992). Conceptualization of natural and artificial stimuli by pigeons. In W. K. Honig & J. Fetterman (Eds.), *Cognitive aspects of stimulus control* (pp. 203–223). Hillsdale, NJ: Lawrence Erlbaum.

Watanabe, S. (2001). Discrimination of cartoons and photographs in pigeons: Effect of scrambling of elements. *Behavioural Processes, 53,* 3–9.

Watanabe, S., & Furuya, I. (1997). Video display for study of avian visual cognition: From psychophysics to sign language. *International Journal of Comparative Psychology, 10,* 111–127.

Zentall, T. R., Clement, T. S., Bhatt, R. S., & Allen, J. (2001). Episodic-like memory in pigeons. *Psychonomic Bulletin & Review, 8,* 685–690.

3

The Cognitive Chicken: Visual and Spatial Cognition in a Nonmammalian Brain

GIORGIO VALLORTIGARA

A GENERAL AND PERSONAL INTRODUCTION

Since the 1960s, research on animal cognition has gained increased visibility and importance within psychology, partly as a result of the so-called cognitive revolution (Gardner, 1987) and partly because of some events that have occurred within the tradition of the psychology of animal learning (e.g., the emergence of evidence for constraints on learning) and of other events that occurred outside of, and sometimes in opposition to, such a tradition (e.g., the rise and development of classical ethology in Europe). Although all of these developments favored a more "liberal" interpretation of animal behavior, most of the research on animal cognition has been (and still is) quite mammal centered. It is true that an enormous amount of work has been carried out using the pigeon; but this species is typically regarded as a sort of laboratory companion of the rat in experimental psychology, rather than a representative of a different class. Truly comparative research has been usually carried out within different, more ethologically oriented traditions, looking at specific (and sometimes highly developed) abilities of nonmammals, such as hoarding in food-storing birds (e.g., Clayton, 1998; Shettleworth, 1990) or homing in pigeons (e.g., Bingman, Gagliardo, Hough, Ioalé, Kahn, & Siegel, 2005).

I believe, however, that the cognitive abilities of species outside of mammalian classes may prove useful and insightful to the study of animal intelligence. In Europe, particularly within the tradition of Gestalt psychology (see, e.g., Herz, 1926, 1928, 1935) or in the work of zoologists somewhat influenced by the Gestalt tradition (e.g., Koehler, 1950), studies of the intelligence of birds and fish (and even nonvertebrate species such as insects) have been quite common. Interestingly, the kinds of cognitive problems that have been investigated within this tradition have been quite different from those typically studied in the psychology of learning and have included, for instance, detour behavior, perceptual organization, problem solving, and number concepts.

After World War II, the Gestalt research tradition largely disappeared and the remaining followers of Gestalt psychology (concentrated in a few universities in Germany, the northeast of Italy, and Japan) concerned themselves mainly with studies of human visual perception. I was fortunate to be trained in this tradition and to have turned (or re-turned) to animal research from human perceptual psychology. In this chapter, I describe some of the work that I have carried out with my collaborators in the past 15 years using nonmammalian species (mainly the domestic chicken) and address issues that were largely inspired by the European Gestalt tradition, rather than by the psychology of animal learning,

Figure 3.1. The halos of the Apostles depicted from the back seem to be localized in front of them, rather than behind them, an example of the strength of "amodal" completion. (By Giotto, "Cappella degli Scrovegni," Padua, Italy.)

which has provided the typical background of most contemporary comparative psychology.

RECOGNIZING PARTLY OCCLUDED OBJECTS

Let us begin with a basic problem in vision. Visually guided behavior must constantly deal with the problem of "incompletedness," because our visual environment is mostly composed of opaque objects that may well overlap and partly hide each other. In our visual experience, when an object is partially concealed by an obstacle, we do not perceive only the pieces or fragments of that object: the parts that are directly visible usually suffice for recognition of the whole object. Although previous knowledge and memory may sometimes play a part in this recognition, it has convincingly been shown that they are secondary to a more fundamental perceptual process of "amodal" completion (Michotte, 1963; Michotte, Thines, & Crabbe, 1964), which depends on detecting certain configurational relationships in visual scenes, such as the alignment of visible parts and similarities in their colors and textures (Grossberg & Mingolla, 1985).

Partial occlusion sometimes poses a serious representational problem to visual artists. Figure 3.1 shows part of the famous fresco in the "Cappella degli Scrovegni" in Padua, painted by Giotto. The halo of Jesus and the Apostles produces the impression of a complete disc behind the head when the subjects are seen in front view. The problem arises with the Apostles who are observed from the back: if you represent a complete halo, then you have to cover the head of the Saints, which is somewhat blasphemous. But, even the solution adopted by Giotto is imperfect: the Apostles seem to be dazzled by a complete Sun, placed just a few centimeters from their faces. (Alternatively, some people experience a loss of the circular shape of the halo, which becomes a sort of U-shaped ring around the Apostles' heads.)

Do other animals perceive the completion of visual objects in the way that we do? The problem with studying nonhuman species is that we cannot ask them directly whether they perceive completion of partly occluded objects; some sort of nonverbal trick is needed to reveal this information. Most studies with birds have used conditioning procedures and the pigeon as a model. For example, after training pigeons to respond to a triangle,

Cerella (1980) found that responses to an amputated triangle (i.e., lacking a piece) exceeded those to a partially occluded triangle. He also reported that after learning to discriminate figures of Charlie Brown from other Peanuts characters, although pigeons responded to pictures representing only parts of Charlie Brown's figure, they also emitted many responses to random mixtures of these parts. These results seem to suggest that pigeons perceive complex stimuli as an assembly of local features and that responses to partly occluded objects depend only on the visual information remaining after fragmentation of the stimulus.

Mammals, like mice, seem to behave quite differently from pigeons in similar tests. Kanizsa, Renzi, Conte, Compostela, and Guerani (1993) trained mice to discriminate between complete and amputated disks. After reaching a learning criterion, the mice performed test trials in which outlined rectangles were either exactly juxtaposed or only placed close to the missing sectors of the disks in order to produce or not produce the impression (to a human observer) of an occlusion of the missing sectors by the rectangles. Mice responded in these tests as if they were experiencing completion of the partly occluded disks; pigeons, in contrast, responded on the basis of local, visible features and failed to complete (Sekuler, Lee, & Shettleworth, 1996) or even perceive continuation of the figure behind the occluder (Fujita, 2001).

Apparently, the visual world of pigeons consists only of fragments, single unstructured pieces of actual retinal stimulation. A very strange visual world, no? However, things may not be so clear-cut, because evidence has been obtained in other studies with pigeons that global relations among component parts can be critical in discriminative control. For example, using naturalistic stimuli rather than figures of Charlie Brown, it has been shown that pigeons do not respond only to local features. Watanabe and Ito (1991) trained pigeons to discriminate color slides of different individuals and then tested them with the full face, separate parts, and randomly connected parts of the original stimuli. In this case, pigeons emitted very few responses to scrambled figures. Similarly, Wasserman, Kirkpatrick-Steger, Van Hamme, and Biederman (1993) found that scrambling the component parts of complex objects reduced pigeons' discrimination, indicative of at least partial control by the spatial configuration of the component parts (see also Kirkpatrick, 2001; Towe, 1954). These somewhat contrasting results suggest that pigeons can perceive and discriminate complex stimuli based on either the local parts or the global configuration, much like humans—a point to which I shall return.

Some years ago, we tried to develop a different method to investigate the recognition of partly occluded objects in birds. We reasoned that filial imprinting—the learning process through which the young of some animals (usually of precocial species) come to recognize an object by simply being exposed to it for a certain time—might be an ecologically more valid context than conditioning to study the problem. In the natural environment, the mother hen and the chicks' companions are often likely to be partially concealed by vegetation; it is important for the chick not to lose contact with them even when only parts of its mother and social fellows are directly visible.

We took advantage of the fact that imprinting can occur even with artificial objects. Soon after hatching, chicks were reared with a red triangle, which thus became their "mother." At test, chicks were presented with different versions of their mother (figure 3.2) located at the opposite ends of a test cage, and we measured the chicks' time spent near and their choice of the two versions of the mother. The two versions look quite different to people. Although, overall, there is the same amount of black and red areas, in one case, we perceive a complete triangle that is, by accident, partly covered by a bar. In the other case, we perceive a completely different figure: an amputated triangle or two pieces with a small triangle and a small trapezoidal shape. We found that chicks indeed behaved as humans might do so in the same situation—they chose the partly occluded triangle.

Obviously, several control experiments were needed to demonstrate that this observation provides evidence that chicks do complete partly occluded objects (see Regolin & Vallortigara, 1995, for more details). For example, in one experiment (see figure 3.3), we reared chicks with a partly occluded triangle. At test, they preferred a complete triangle to an amputated one and they did so despite the fact that the partly occluded triangle was more similar, physically, to the amputated triangle than to the complete one. Furthermore, it is not that the chicks' choices depended on a preference for the stimulus with the more extended red area; in the reverse condition, chicks reared with an amputated triangle preferred the amputated triangle over the complete triangle at test.

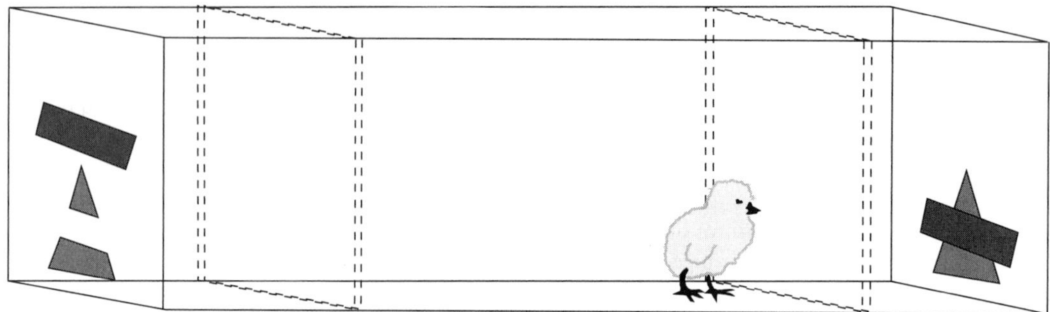

Figure 3.2. Chicks imprinted on a complete triangle were later tested for choice between a partly occluded and an amputated triangle. The chicks preferred the partly occluded triangle, thus suggesting that they complete partly occluded objects. (See text for explanation.)

It is interesting to compare chicks' abilities with those of newborn human infants. Human newborns provide scientists with the same type of challenge offered by nonhuman species: We cannot simply ask them what they are perceiving; we must use some tricks to obtain such an answer. A technique used by developmental scientists is a procedure called habituation/dishabituation (Kellman & Spelke, 1983).

For instance, infants are habituated to a rod that moves back and forth behind a central occluder, so that only the top and bottom of the rod are visible. After habituation has occurred, babies are shown either of two stimuli without the occluder: one is a complete rod and the other consists of the top and bottom parts of the rod, with a gap where the occluder had been. Surprise (as measured by longer looking times) when viewing the complete rod would indicate that this display is novel and that the infants did not see a complete rod during the habituation trials, whereas surprise when viewing the rod pieces is taken to indicate that the infants had perceived object unity. It takes about 4 to 7 months, depending on details of procedure, for human infants to show evidence of completion of partly occluded objects (Kellman &

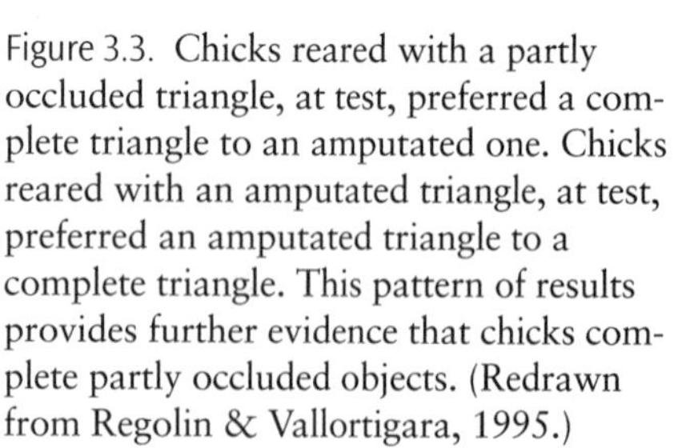

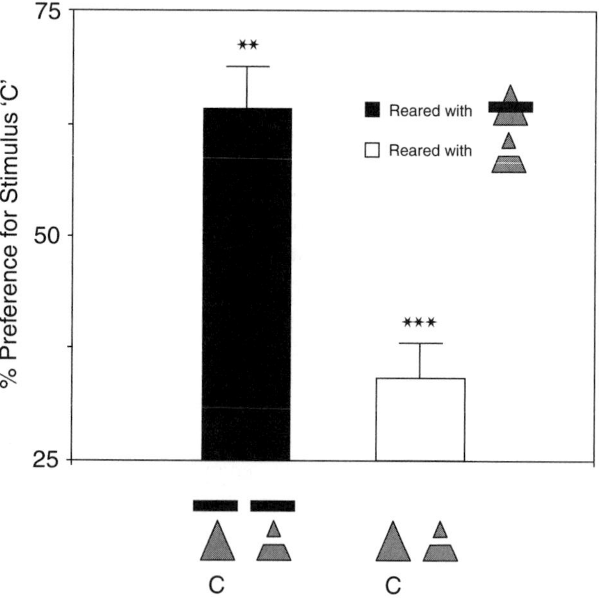

Figure 3.3. Chicks reared with a partly occluded triangle, at test, preferred a complete triangle to an amputated one. Chicks reared with an amputated triangle, at test, preferred an amputated triangle to a complete triangle. This pattern of results provides further evidence that chicks complete partly occluded objects. (Redrawn from Regolin & Vallortigara, 1995.)

Arterberry, 1998). Chicks do that soon after hatching; Lea, Slater, and Ryan (1996) duplicated our imprinting results using the same type of stimuli used with newborn infants. As expected, they found that, at test, chicks imprinted on a complete rod preferred the complete rod to the fragmented rod, whereas chicks imprinted on the fragmented rod preferred the fragmented to the complete rod. In the crucial condition, however, chicks imprinted on a partly occluded rod preferred the complete rod to the fragmented rod.

The difference between the species in developmental time-course is not surprising. Recognition of a partly occluded mother would be useful when you can move by yourself to rejoin her in order to reinstate social contact; this is the case for the highly precocial young chick but not for highly altricial species like the human newborn. The emergence of recognition of partly occluded objects can be delayed in our species, allowing the nervous system extra time for neural development.

What about other avian species? Standardized tests of object permanence include, for the initial stages of its development (specifically, stage 3), tasks in which the animal has to respond to partly occluded objects. Psittacine birds, such as parrots and parakeets (Funk, 1996; Pepperberg & Funk, 1990), mynahs (Plowright, Reid, & Kilian, 1998), and magpies (Pollok, Prior, & Güntürkün, 2000), pass these tests easily (as well as much more advanced stages of object permanence). Interestingly, pigeons, in contrast, lose interest in food when it becomes invisible behind a screen (Plowright et al., 1998).

Could it be that the difference between chicks and pigeons resides in the use of a more ecologically valid procedure (filial imprinting) and/or age differences? This conclusion is unlikely because evidence has been obtained for completion in adult hens using conditioning procedures (Forkman, 1998). As well, recent work by DiPietro, Wasserman, and Young (2002) shows that pigeons can recognize partly occluded objects but only if special training is provided that may help pigeons to distinguish the object from the occluder. This result suggests that pigeons probably can perceive amodal completion but that this may not be their "natural" way to analyze visual scenes. My point becomes clearer when we consider a phenomenon that is strictly related to amodal completion—the perception of subjective contours.

In figure 3.4, the perception of the subjective triangle is associated with the impression that the interrupted circles continue and are completed behind the illusory triangle. It has been suggested that a single unit-formation process underlies the formation of "subjective" contours and "amodal" completion (Shipley & Kellman, 1992). If so, then we can predict that those species that perceive subjective contours should also manifest completion of partly occluded objects and vice versa.

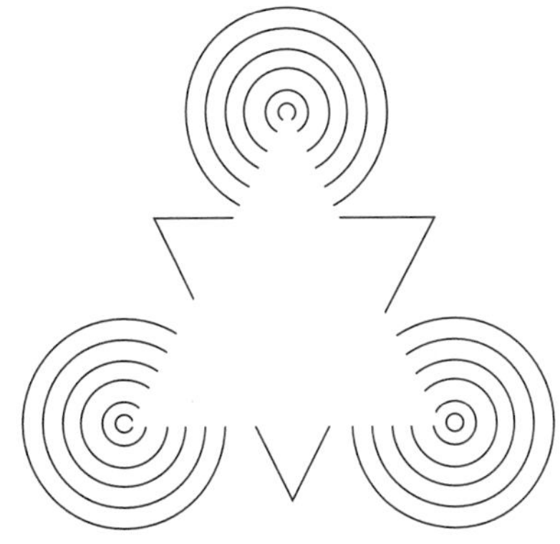

Figure 3.4. An example of subjective contours: the Kanizsa triangle (Kanizsa, 1979). Some species of birds, including the domestic chick, have been shown to perceive subjective contours (see text).

Evidence indicates that a number of mammalian species do perceive subjective contours (e.g., cats: Bravo, Blake, & Morrison, 1988; and monkeys: Peterhans & von der Heydt, 1989). In birds, young chickens (about 2 weeks old) have been shown to perceive subjective contours (Zanforlin, 1981), which would agree with evidence for completion of partly occluded objects in this species. Barn owls have also been shown to perceive subjective contours (Nieder & Wagner, 1999).

But what about pigeons? In a study on subjective contours with Kanizsa's triangles and squares, Prior and Güntürkün (1999) were able to demonstrate that 4 of 14 pigeons that they tested reacted to the test stimuli as if they were seeing subjective contours. Control tests suggested that the pigeons responding to subjective contours were attending to the "global" pattern of the stimuli, whereas the pigeons not responding to subjective contours were attending to extracted elements of the stimuli.

Perception of subjective contours is closely linked to amodal completion. In natural situations, in which objects occlude one another, boundaries may vanish and interpolation mechanisms are sometimes needed to reconstruct contours that are absent from the retinal images. The fact that only pigeons attending to the more global aspects of the stimulation responded to subjective contours suggests that such individual variability in attending globally or locally to visual scenes can explain why pigeons fail in amodal completion tests that are effective in other species (see Sekuler et al., 1996). It is as if, for pigeons, a "featural" style of analysis is more natural than a global one, although pigeons can apparently switch to such a global style of analysis with some effort. Thus, pigeons appear to be able to respond to amodal completion but only if they are strongly encouraged to do so (e.g., DiPietro et al., 2002).

It is important to stress that the possibility of such a switch is inherent to our own visual perception. We can, with some effort, turn to a featural, mosaic-like perception of a visual scene, in which we look at fragments of partly occluded objects without completing them (visual artists, because of training and perhaps natural inclination, do this routinely). There is also evidence that such a mosaic stage normally occurs during very early phases of visual processing (see Sekuler & Palmer, 1992) and in human infants before 4 to 7 months of age.

Why should there be such a striking species difference in the relative importance of the two strategies of perceptual analysis, and what mechanisms could underlie the major reliance on one or another strategy? As to the first issue, Fujita (2001) observed that pigeons are grain eaters; grain is a type of food that is usually abundant and does not require the animal to search behind obstacles. Fowl, in contrast, engage in finding and eating worms and insects that often hide under leaves or soil and may be only partly visible. Thus, there could be ecological differences favoring perception based on response to parts or on reconstruction of the whole objects, on the basis of their parts. I would add here that finding food that moves (prey) or that does not move (grain) can also be crucial in this respect (although looking for grains in grass may also require the recognition of occluded objects and it is unknown whether birds in these cases tend to respond only to parts).

As to the issue of mechanisms, it is interesting to observe in experiments using conditioning procedures, such as those performed with pigeons, that the stimuli fall into the frontal binocular visual field of the animals, a portion of the visual field that is mainly represented within the tectofugal pathway in pigeons (Güntürkün & Hahmann, 1999; Hellmann & Güntürkün, 1999). The frontal visual field seems to be specialized for (myopic) foraging for food on the ground, whereas the lateral visual field seems to be specialized for predator detection and flight control. Near-sighted acuity would favor examination of fine stimulus details and may be responsible for the local advantages observed in most experiments that used frontal presentations of visual stimuli; the lateral visual fields, in contrast, may be more concerned with the larger-scale integration of scene and flight control information (Martinoya, Rivaud, & Bloch, 1984), thus showing more sensitivity to global information (see also Cook, 2001).

Unlike the case of pigeons (Hodos, Macko, & Bessette, 1984), lesions to the thalamofugal visual system markedly affect chicks' performance on tasks that rely on frontal viewing (Deng & Rogers, 1997; 1998a, 1998b). This observation suggests that, unlike in pigeons, the frontal field is represented within the thalamofugal system in chicks.

We recently hypothesized that these differences could be also associated with brain asymmetry. Research using temporary occlusion of one eye, which takes advantage of complete decussation of optic nerve fibers and of large segregation of function between the hemispheres in the avian brain (see Andrew, 1991; Rogers, 1995; Vallortigara, 2000; Vallortigara, Cozzutti, Tommasi, & Rogers, 2001; Vallortigara, Zanforlin, & Pasti, 1999), has revealed that the right eye (which sends input mainly to the left hemisphere) is dominant in pigeons' visual discrimination learning (Güntürkün, 1997) and presumably favors a featural strategy of analysis of visual scenes. Chicks, in contrast, have shown a more balanced and complementary use of the two eyes, with the left eye (and right hemisphere) being dominant when more global strategies of analysis are needed (such as in spatial analyses; see Vallortigara [2000] for a review).

We recently put these ideas to a test (Regolin, Marconato, Tommasi, & Vallortigara, 2001; Regolin, Marconato, & Vallortigara, 2004). In the first experiment, three separate groups of newly hatched chicks were imprinted (in a binocular condition): (1) on a red cardboard square partly occluded by a superimposed black bar, (2) on the complete red square, or (3) on an amputated version of the red square (consisting of the two visible parts of the occluded square with a missing central part). At test, each chick was presented with a pair of stimuli located at opposite ends of a test cage: a complete square and an amputated one. Chicks could freely approach either stimulus.

When tested with only their left eye uncovered, chicks behaved very much like binocular chicks would do, choosing the complete stimulus (the square). In contrast, when tested with only their right eye uncovered, chicks tended to choose the amputated square. These findings suggest that, in the chick, the neural structures fed by the left eye (mainly located in the right hemisphere) are more inclined to perform a "global" analysis of visual scenes, whereas those fed by the right eye (mainly located in the left hemisphere) seem to be more inclined to perform a "featural" analysis of visual scenes. Interestingly, even in humans, the right hemisphere seems to play a more important role in amodal completion (Corballis, Fendrich, Shapley, & Gazzaniga, 1999).

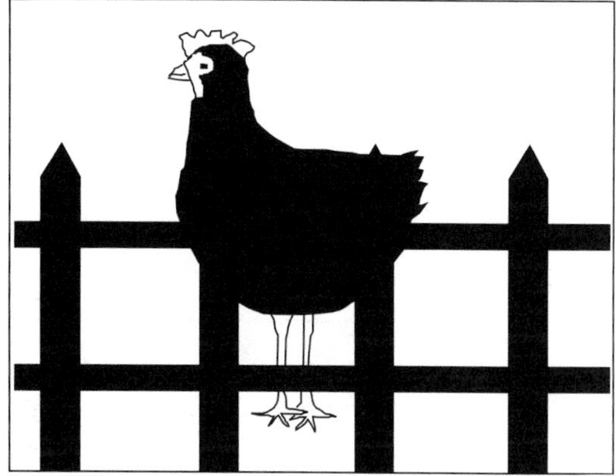

Figure 3.5. The hen appears to be standing in front of the fence in the region of the trunk, but if one inspects the region of the legs, then it appears as though standing behind the fence. Domestic hens seem to be susceptible to this sort of illusion (see text).

ESTABLISHING THE DIRECTION OF VISUAL OCCLUSION

Another basic computational problem in perceiving occlusion deals with establishing the direction of depth stratification (i.e., determining which surface is in front and which is behind). Usually, when two objects differ in color, brightness, or texture, humans solve occlusion indeterminacy by determining, on the basis of contour collinearity, what boundaries belong with each other and thereby allowing the formation of modal (occluding) and amodal (occluded) contours (Michotte, 1963). However, humans can perceive unconnected and depth-stratified surfaces even in chromatically homogeneous patterns.

Consider figure 3.5. Although it would be possible, in principle, to perceive a peculiar, but unitary object, the hen appears as being *behind* the fence when the region of the legs is inspected (because of the differences in color that specify the direction of occlusion), whereas it appears to be in *front* of the fence when the region of the upper part of the body is inspected.

The reason that larger surfaces (such as the trunk of the hen) tend to be seen modally as being in front of, rather than behind, might depend on the geometrical property that overlapping objects in which larger surfaces are closer present shorter occluding boundaries than when smaller surfaces are closer. Shorter modal (occluding) contours are needed to account for the occlusive effect of the hen on the fence, whereas larger modal contours would be needed to account for the occlusive effect of the fence on the upper body of the hen.

This "rule," according to which the visual system tends to minimize the formation of interpolated modal contours, was first described by Petter (1956) and has been confirmed in several studies of human visual perception (Shipley & Kellman, 1992; Singh, Hoffman, & Albert, 1999; Tommasi, Bressan, & Vallortigara, 1995). It should be noted that Petter's rule is independent of the empirical depth cue of relative size (Tommasi et al., 1995) and can be made to play against information based on other depth cues, thereby generating intriguing visual paradoxes such as the hen/fence illusion (see Kanizsa, 1979, for further examples).

Recently, we wondered whether Petter's rule reflected a geometrical regularity that is incorporated into the design of all vertebrate brains or whether it is limited to the human visual system (see Forkman & Vallortigara, 1999). We presented domestic hens with two chromatically identical patterns, a diamond and a ladder, shown on a computer touchscreen (see figure 3.6). Hens were reinforced for pecking at the pattern that was higher up on a grid that provided pictorial depth information (i.e., on the pattern that to a human appears as being farther away). Every 10th trial was a nonrewarded probe trial with the two patterns partially overlapping. In the absence of other cues, depth stratification can

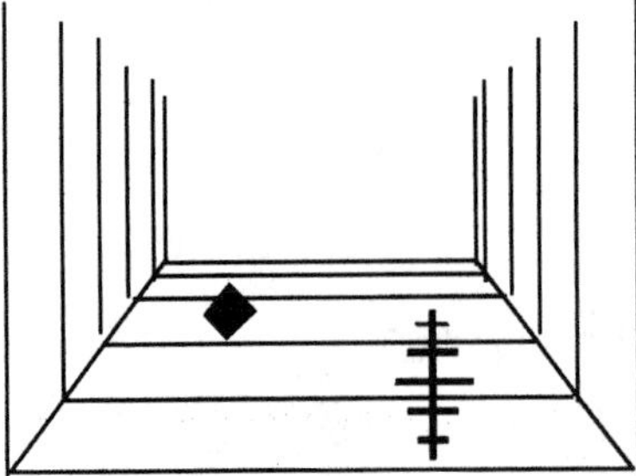
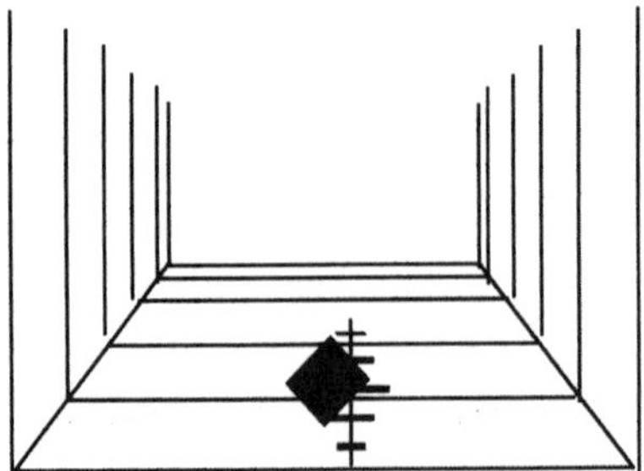

Figure 3.6. Schematic representation of Forkman and Vallortigara's (1999) experiments to investigate how hens disambiguate relative depth in chromatically homogeneous patterns. During rewarded trials, the two stimuli, the ladder and the diamond, never overlapped (*left*); during the probe trials (*right*), they partially overlapped (see text). During the probe trials, the touch-sensitive area was defined as that part of the touch-sensitive area of each symbol that did not overlap with that of the other symbol.

occur on the basis of a minimization of interpolated occluding contours. In humans, the diamond is usually perceived to be in front of the ladder because shorter interpolated contours are needed to account for the occlusive effect of the diamond on the ladder. The hens pecked more often at the ladder during the probe trial. These findings suggest that there may be quite general visual constraints that are related to the geometrical and physical properties of the world and that must be incorporated in the design of any efficient biological visual system (see also Vallortigara & Tommasi, 2002).

REPRESENTING COMPLETELY OCCLUDED OBJECTS

Under certain conditions, objects are not simply partly occluded by other objects but rather are entirely covered by other objects; thus, they are completely unavailable to direct sensory experience. In this case, an internal representation of the unseen objects is needed to guide behavior.

This problem has been traditionally investigated within the Piagetian framework of "object permanence." According to Piaget (1953), human object permanence develops in stages. In stage 1, children do not search for an object that they have seen disappear. In stage 2, they track the object's movement. In stage 3, children recover a partly occluded object. In stage 4, they recover a fully occluded object. In stage 5, children can retrieve an object that has been hidden successively in several locations (i.e., hidden, exposed, and rehidden several times). Finally, in stage 6, they can master invisible displacements (e.g., an object is hidden in a container, the container is moved behind an occluding device, the object is transferred to this second device, the children are shown that the first container is empty, and the children successfully infer where the object now resides).

Several comparative studies have been conducted within the Piagetian framework. However, extreme caution in interpreting their results is needed. For instance, some early studies (Etienne, 1973) reported that young domestic chicks apparently did not recover a fully occluded object (stage 4). More recently, however, we have shown that simple modifications of the behavioral procedure can dramatically improve animals' performance (see Regolin, Vallortigara, & Zanforlin, 1995a).

As in Etienne's (1973) experiments, we presented chicks with a goal-object that was made to disappear behind one of two screens opposite each other. Chicks searched at random behind either screen when the goal-object was a palatable prey (i.e., a mealworm), as originally found by Etienne (1973). However, chicks were also able to choose the correct screen when the goal-object was a "social" partner (i.e., a red ball on which they had been imprinted). Moreover, chicks also appeared to make use of the directional cue provided by the movement of the prey when they were tested in the presence of a cagemate. These results suggest that the previous failure to obtain detour behavior with the double screen, using the prey as a target, was not due to a cognitive limitation but rather to the evocation of fear responses to the novel environment that interfered with the correct execution of the spatial task.

Further work into detour behavior has shown that 2-day-old chicks master some, but not all,

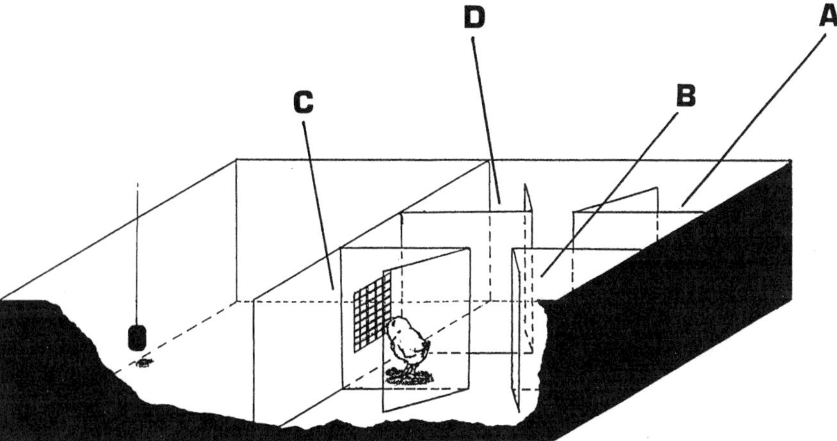

Figure 3.7. Schematic representation of the experimental apparatus used to study the representation of hidden objects in chicks. The imprinting stimulus is visible behind the small window-grid barrier. Two symmetrical apertures, placed at the midline of the corridor, allowed the chick to pass around the barrier. After entering the apertures, the chick is faced with a choice between a correct and an incorrect compartment (A, B are incorrect compartments; C, D are correct compartments). (After Regolin et al., 1994.)

aspects of stage 4 of object permanence (see Regolin, Vallortigara, & Zanforlin, 1994, 1995b; Vallortigara & Regolin, 2002; and see also Campbell, 1988, for similar evidence in adult hens). For instance, although chicks do have an object concept that maintains a representation of the object in the absence of direct sensory cues, it seems that they are not able to predict the resting position of an imprinted ball from its direction of movement prior to occlusion (Freire & Nicol, 1997, 1999). It is not yet clear whether this finding reflects a basic cognitive limitation or an adaptation to ecological demands (for instance, when prey or other interesting objects hide themselves behind an occluder, it is more likely that they will reappear, after some time, in the same location where they were seen to disappear rather than at the other side of the occluder; see Haskell & Forkman, 1997).

One problem with the classic Piagetian or other object-permanence tests is that they provide evidence that animals represent and maintain something in memory, but little can be deduced as to the precise nature of this. Consider the case of the detour problem. Some years ago, we tested the representational abilities of young chicks in the task shown in figure 3.7. Chicks could observe an imprinting object (a small red plastic ball) through a window, but in order to rejoin their "mother," they had to make a detour, using one or another of the two symmetrical apertures that allowed them to go outside of the corridor. We knew from previous work that chicks can learn to make a detour (Regolin et al., 1994), but we were interested in what happens the first time that a chick loses sight of its mother. If the chick moves randomly in the environment when the ball is no longer available to direct perception, then no straightforward conclusion can be drawn because the chick might have the ability to represent the object but lack any ability to discover its position (admittedly, a more economic and conservative tenet would be to deny possession of both capacities). On the other hand, if the chick moves nonrandomly and shows the ability to orient toward the disappeared goal, choosing the C-D rather than the A-B compartments, then some sort of mental representation of the goal can be ascribed to the animal. We found that 18 of the 20 animals tested chose the correct compartments C-D. However, does this provide any evidence that chicks do "represent" the ball in much the same way as we would do in similar circumstances? Obviously not, for the only specific aspect that needs to be represented here is the spatial location of the object. Nothing can be said about other properties of the object, such as its color or shape. But, of course, these other aspects are open to experimental investigation.

One interesting procedure that may be used to investigate other aspects of animals' representations exploits the observation that prior feeding with one type of food selectively reduces the value of that food (see Hetherington & Rolls, 1996). In a series of experiments, we fed 5-day-old chicks in an enclosure with two food-plates, each with a different type of food (see Cozzutti & Vallortigara, 2001). The food was devalued by prefeeding with one of the food types. When tested with food that was displaced, the chicks moved to the location previously occupied by the nondevalued food. Similar results have been reported even for adult hens (Forkman, 2000; and see Clayton & Dickinson, 1999a, 1999b, for evidence in corvids). This result suggests that these birds can remember the contents of food caches apart from their positions (i.e., that they are able to conjoin "where" and "what" information to form "declarative-like" memories).

DELAYING MEMORIES

The notion that objects are separate entities that continue to exist when out of sight of the observer is relevant when considering that these "represented" objects serve to guide the course of action. When a prey has disappeared from sight, the predator can maintain a representation of its continuing presence for some time and thus actively search for it. But, how long can the representation be maintained? This issue has been investigated using the so-called delayed response problem (Hunter, 1913). However, very little is known about delayed responding in avian species. Studies on object permanence in birds (discussed earlier) did not address the issue of delay. Obviously, the so-called matching-to-sample task is derived from the delayed response problem and has been largely used with pigeons and other avian species. However, the delays used are typically very short (on the order of seconds, see Foster, Temple, MacKenzie, Demello, & Poling, 1995, for evidence in hens).

We trained 5-day-old chicks to follow an imprinted object (a small red ball with which they had been reared) that was moving slowly in a large arena, until it disappeared behind an opaque screen (see Vallortigara, Regolin, Rigoni, and Zanforlin, 1998). At test, each chick was initially confined in a transparent cage, from which it could see and track the ball while moving toward, and then behind, one of two screens. The screens could be either identical or they could differ in color and pattern. Immediately after the disappearance of the ball (or with a certain delay), the chick was released and was allowed to search for the imprinted object behind either screen. Results showed that the chicks could take into account the directional cue provided by the ball's movement and its concealment, up to a delay period of about 180 s, regardless of the perceptual characteristics of the two screens. If an opaque partition was positioned in front of the transparent cage immediately after the ball had disappeared so that, throughout the delay, neither the goal-object nor the two screens were visible, then chicks were still capable of remembering and choosing the correct screen, although for a much shorter period (about 60 s). A 1-min delay is quite comparable to the retention intervals observed in primates under similar testing conditions (Fletcher, 1965; Wu, Sacket, & Gunderson, 1986).

It is possible to claim that the chicks simply learned to associate the proximity of the ball to a screen as a cue to direct approach responses toward that screen. Nevertheless, in order to solve the problem, the chicks needed to maintain some representation of the position of the correct screen and to continuously update the content of the representation from trial to trial on the basis of the directional cues provided by the movement of the ball, particularly in the condition in which the screens were not visible. In mammals, such "on-line" maintenance of information during short temporal intervals is usually described as "working memory" and is believed to be represented in the neural circuitry of the prefrontal cortex (Fuster, 1989; Goldman-Rakic, 1987). Involvement of the prefrontal cortex in Piagetian object-permanence tasks has been suggested in both humans and monkeys (Diamond & Goldman-Rakic, 1989). Interestingly, there is evidence that a region resembling the mammalian prefrontal cortex exists in the avian telencephalon—a semilunar area in the caudalmost part of the forebrain, called the neostriatum caudolaterale (NCL) (see Mogensen & Divac, 1982).

In pigeons, it has been shown that temporary receptor blocking of D_1 receptors (the dopamine receptor subtype in the mammalian prefrontal cortex) in the NCL has an important effect on working memory (Güntürkün & Durstewitz, 2001). Moreover, neurons in the NCL have been found that respond selectively during the delay period of a working memory task, and they show activity patterns that are identical to those described for delay cells in the primate prefrontal cortex (Kalt, Diekamp, & Güntürkün, 1999).

Preliminary results obtained in my laboratory also suggest that lesioning of chicks' NCL severely

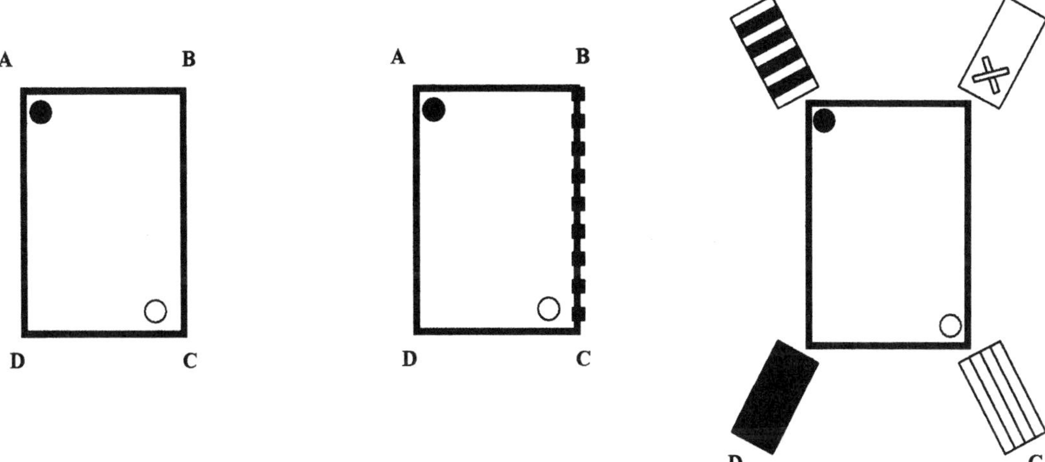

Figure 3.8. Schematic representation of the test apparatus used to investigate geometrical representations. The animal could find food (or other desired targets) in the rectangular enclosure at, say, corner A. In one version of the test (*left*), all walls were white and the task for the animal was to distinguish between corners A, C and corners B, D using purely geometrical information (corner A and its rotational equivalent, corner C, are in fact indistinguishable on the basis of purely geometrical information but can be distinguished from corners B and D, which, in turn, are geometrically equivalent and cannot be distinguished from each other). In another version of the task (*middle*), one wall (indicated by the dotted line) was colored differently (with some species, panels with different features and colors were positioned in the four corners instead of using a colored wall as nongeometrical information, see rightmost figure). The animal in this case could disambiguate the two geometrically equivalent corners A and C using the nongeometrical information provided by the colored wall (or by the panels).

impairs performance in the delayed response task at delays of 30 s or longer but not in the absence of a delay (Pagni, Gagliardo, Chiandetti, Diekamp, Güntürkün, & Vallortigara, unpublished data). Thus, although the anatomical structure of the avian NCL is very different from the primate neocortical architecture of the prefrontal cortex, the neuronal mechanisms that have evolved to master analogous cognitive demands may be similar.

MAKING "NATURAL GEOMETRY"

Quite sophisticated spatial cognition can be observed in nonmammalian vertebrate brains, even in those species that do not show the amazing abilities at retrieving large numbers of hidden items that are exhibited by food-storing birds. Direct comparisons with mammals in similar tasks, however, have rarely been performed. One interesting exception are tests on the "geometric sense of space" (Cheng, 1986; Gallistel, 1990).

When disoriented in an environment with a distinctive geometry—such as a rectangular-shaped arena (figure 3.8a), animals can (partially) reorient themselves, even in the absence of any extra-arena cues, by simply using the geometry of the environment. Suppose that a food target is located at corner A and then is made to disappear. Following passive disorientation (i.e., being turned slowly without viewing the environment) and in the presence of only proximal corner cues, the animals should choose at random among the four corners. But, in fact, partial disambiguation of the problem is possible: Corner A (the food location) appears in the same geometrical relation to the shape of the environment as corner C. Thus, geometrical information alone, which cannot unambiguously differentiate between corners A and C, is sufficient to distinguish between corners A-C and corners B-D.

Several species of animals been shown to be able to reorient using this "purely geometrical" information (birds: Kelly, Spetch, & Heth, 1998; Vallortigara, Zanforlin, & Pasti, 1990; primates:

Deipolyi, Santos, & Hauser, 2001; Gouteux, Thinus-Blanc, & Vauclair, 2001; fish: Sovrano, Bisazza, & Vallortigara, 2002). Interestingly, however, it has been reported that human infants (Hermer & Spelke, 1994) and adult rats (Cheng, 1986) fail to reorient using nongeometrical information, such as a distinctive differently colored wall in the rectangular cage, despite the fact this featural information would allow fully successful reorientation (see figure 3.8b).

These findings have been interpreted to suggest that spatial reorientation depends on an encapsulated, task-specific mechanism or "geometrical module" (Cheng, 1986; Cheng & Gallistel, 1984; see also Fodor, 1983). The module encodes only the geometrical properties of the arrangement of surfaces as surfaces. In the case of the spatial reorientation task in the rectangular environment, for instance, the geometrical module would use only "metric properties" (i.e., the distinction between a long and a short wall) and what is known in geometry as "sense" (i.e., the distinction between right and left). Use of geometrical information for spatial reorientation makes sense ecologically. The large-scale shape of the landscape does not change across seasons, whereas there are important seasonal changes in the nongeometrical properties of the landscape (e.g., the appearance of grass and vegetation, snowfall and melting, and so on).

Human adults, in contrast to young children and rats, easily solve the distinctive-color-wall version of the reorientation task in the rectangular environment (i.e., when both geometrical and nongeometrical information are available; see Hermer & Spelke, 1994), suggesting that the most striking limitations of the geometrical module can be overcome during human development. Hermer and Spelke (1994; 1996) thus suggested that the performance of human adults, compared with that of rats and human infants, indicates that some representational systems become more accessible and flexible over development and evolution. These authors suggested that language, and more specifically spatial language, may provide the medium for representing conjunctions of geometrical and nongeometrical properties in the environment (Hermer-Vasquez, Spelke, & Katsnelson, 1999). Indeed, the ability to orient correctly in the distinctive blue-wall task (Hermer & Spelke, 1994) correlated with the ability of children to produce and use phrases involving "left" and "right" together with "blue" and "white" when describing the locations of hidden objects (MacWhinney, 1991).

It could be that human beings conjoin geometrical and nongeometrical information using language as a medium (Spelke, 2003), but this seems not to be the case for nonhuman animals. We found, in fact, that young chickens (Vallortigara et al., 1990; Vallortigara, Pagni, & Sovrano, 2004) can easily combine geometrical and nongeometrical information (see also Kelly et al., 1998, for similar results in pigeons). The performance of chicks in these tasks, in which they were able to identify the correct location conjoining geometrical and nongeometrical information, is therefore identical to that of human adults and clearly surpasses that of rats or human infants. We recently found that that even fish (*Xenotoca eiseni*) reorient themselves by conjoining geometrical and nongeometrical information in the rectangular arena task (Sovrano, Bisazza, & Vallortigara, 2003, 2005; Vallortigara & Sovrano, 2002; Vallortigara, Feruglio, & Sovrano, 2005).

Research carried out in my laboratory has further explored the capabilities of encoding geometrical information in the chick's brain. We found that chicks can learn to localize the central position of a closed environment in the absence of any external cues (Tommasi, Vallortigara, & Zanforlin, 1997). After several days of training, during which food-deprived chicks were allowed to eat food that was progressively buried deeper under sawdust in the center of the floor of an arena, they developed a ground-scratching strategy to uncover the food and eat it. With training, the chicks became more accurate in finding food so that when they were eventually tested in the absence of any food, their pattern of ground scratching was limited to the central area. We also showed that chicks were able to generalize to arenas of different shapes. For instance, when trained to find the center in a square-shaped arena and then tested in a triangular or circular one of nearly the same size, the chicks searched in the central region of the novel arena.

We have also shown that when the environmental change involved a substantial modification in the size of the arena, as is the case for the transition from a square-shaped arena to an arena of the same shape, but of a larger size, the scratching bouts of chicks in the test (larger) arena were localized in two regions: in the actual center of the test arena and also at a distance from the walls that was equal to the distance from the walls to the center in the training (smaller) arena (see figure 3.9). Apparently, two behavioral strategies seem to be available to the chicks: (a) encoding a goal location in terms of absolute distance and direction from the walls and

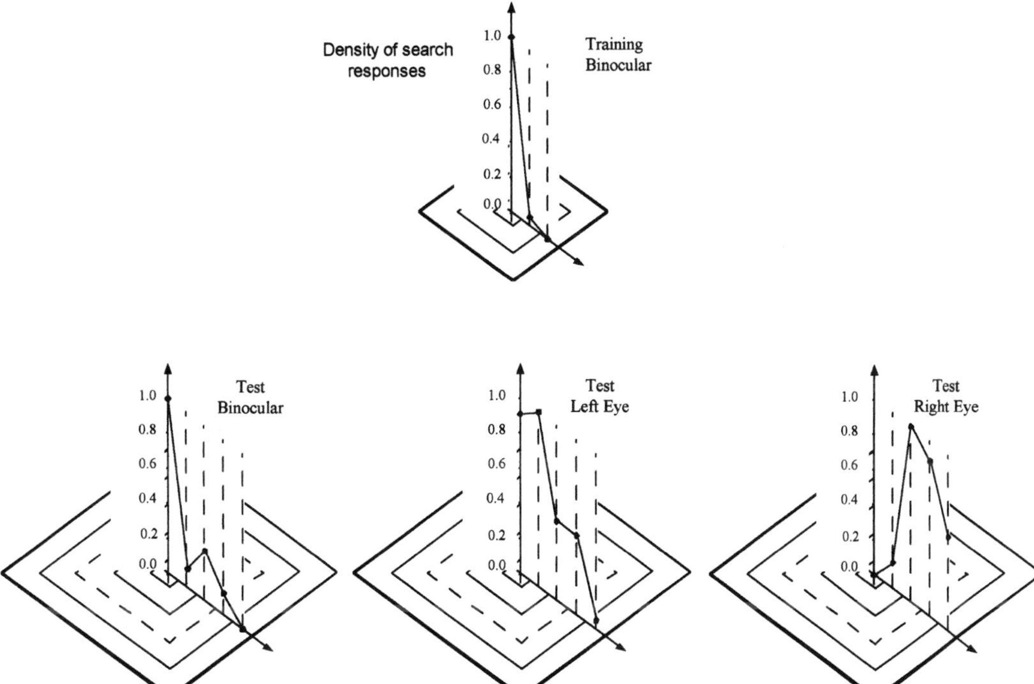

Figure 3.9. Amount of searching behavior as a function of the distance from the center during training in the small enclosure in binocular chicks (*top*) and during test in a larger enclosure of the same shape in binocular (*bottom left*), left-eyed (*bottom middle*), and right-eyed (*bottom right*) chicks. As can be seen, during test, binocular and left-eyed chicks showed one peak located in the center of the large enclosure and another peak located at a distance from the walls corresponding to the previously learned distance from the center in the training (small) enclosure. Right-eyed chicks, in contrast, showed only one peak located at the distance from the walls corresponding to the previously learned distance from the center in the training (small) enclosure. (After Tommasi & Vallortigara, 2001.)

(b) encoding a goal location in terms of the ratios of distances from the walls independent of their absolute values. As can be seen in figure 3.9, chicks showed one peak located in the center of the large enclosure and another peak located at a distance from the walls corresponding to the previously learned distance from the center in the training (small) enclosure. Tests carried out under monocular viewing (after binocular training) revealed striking asymmetries of brain function: encoding of absolute distance being predominantly attended to by the left hemisphere and encoding of relative distance being predominantly attended to by the right hemisphere (see figure 3.9; Tommasi & Vallortigara, 2001).

When training was performed in the presence of a conspicuous landmark (e.g., a red cylinder) located at the center of the arena, animals searched in the central location, even after the removal of the landmark. Apparently, domestic chicks seem to be able to use the geometrical relationships among the walls of the arena as well, although they were not explicitly trained to do so. Furthermore, marked changes in the height of the walls of the arena produced some displacement in the spatial location of searching behavior, suggesting that the chicks also used the angular size of the walls to estimate distances within the arena.

These results provide evidence that chicks encode information about the absolute and relative distance of the food from the walls of the arena and that they encode this large-scale spatial information even when the orientation of a single landmark alone would suffice for food localization. Encoding of large-scale information using the shape of the arena seems to be based on hippocampal function: Lesions to the hippocampus rendered chicks unable to find the center of the arena in the absence of the landmark or to follow the landmark when it was displaced from the center of the arena to another location (Tommasi, Gagliardo, Andrew, & Vallortigara, 2003).

Previously, similar studies on spatial localization in pigeons using expansion tests provided somewhat different results. Spetch and her colleagues, using both naturalistic settings (Spetch et al., 1997) and a touch-screen procedure (Spetch, Cheng, & MacDonald, 1996), compared pigeons' and humans' search for an unmarked goal located in the middle of a square array of four identical landmarks. Humans searched in the middle of expanded arrays, whereas pigeons preserved distance and direction relative to a single landmark. I believe that the difference in performance between chicks (and humans) and pigeons reflects the fact that encoding based on arrays of discrete landmarks is different from encoding the shape of a test environment based on extended surfaces (see also Pearce et al., 2001) and may have different neural substrates (see, for evidence, Vallortigara et al., 2004). Recent research carried out by Gray, Spetch, Kelly, and Nguyen (2004) seems to confirm that searching based on surfaces of an enclosure is different from searching based on an array of discrete landmarks: When tested in the center localization task in a closed arena, rather than with an array of discrete landmarks, pigeons showed both relative and absolute encoding when tested in expanded arenas, exactly as did chicks in the tasks that we investigated.

CONCLUSIONS

For a long time, the domestic chick has been recognized in comparative psychology as providing ideal material for the study of early learning (Spalding, 1873). More recently, the chick has become a reference model for the investigation of the neurobiological basis of certain forms of learning such as imprinting (Horn, 1998) and passive avoidance (Rose, 2000), and it has become the most used vertebrate species for investigation of lateralization of brain functions (Andrew, 1991; Andrew & Rogers, 2002; Rogers, 1996; Vallortigara et al., 1999). Several features of the chick model have facilitated neurobiological research, the most important being the fact that the chick's experience can be precisely controlled both in the embryo and immediately after hatching and that at an early stage of its life, the chick is capable of highly organized patterns of behavior, making very early learning accessible to investigation.

The brief survey reported here shows that chicks possess quite remarkable cognitive abilities that can be revealed using as tools those forms of early learning that have been the concern of classic ethologists and early comparative psychologists. This evidence, together with reasonable knowledge of the chick's neuroanatomy (Rogers, 1995), can allow investigators of the brain–mind relationship to proceed a step further, moving from investigation of the neural basis of simple basic learning abilities (imprinting, passive avoidance learning) to cognitive phenomena that have direct counterparts in humans, such as completion of partly occluded objects, biological motion perception (Regolin, Tommasi, & Vallortigara, 2000), and object and spatial representations (Vallortigara, 2002, 2004). Some recent work by the group headed by Toshiya Matsushima in Japan has provided remarkable evidence from single-unit recordings in the unanesthetized chick on the neural machinery that may underlie the chick's anticipation of forthcoming events, particularly the quality/quantity and temporal proximity of rewards (Matsushima, Izawa, Aoki, & Yanagihara, 2003; Aoki, Izawa, Yanagihara, & Matsushima, 2003). In the next few years, we can thus expect new recruits among both neurobiologists and comparative psychologists who are attracted to comparative cognitive research by the many possibilities offered by the humble chick. Certainly, it will be increasingly difficult to seriously consider the expression "chicken brain" as an insult.

References

Andrew, R. J. (1991). The chick in experiment: Techniques and tests. General. In R. J. Andrew (Ed.), *Neural and behavioural plasticity* (pp. 6–11). Oxford: Oxford University Press.

Aoki, N., Izawa, E., Yanagihara, S., & Matsushima, T. (2003). Neural correlates of memorized associations and cued movements in archistriatum of the domestic chick. *European Journal of Neuroscience, 17,* 1935–1946.

Bingman, V. P., Gagliardo, A., Hough, G. E., Ioalé, P., Kahn, M., & Siegel, J. J. (2005). The avian hippocampus: Homing in pigeons and the memory representation of large-scale space. *Integrative and Comparative Biology, 45,* 555–564.

Bravo, M., Blake, R., & Morrison, S. (1988). Cats see subjective contours. *Vision Research, 28,* 861–865.

Campbell, D. (1988). Object permanence in the domestic hen (*Gallus domesticus*). Honors dissertation, University of Edinburgh.

Cerella, J. (1980). The pigeon's analysis of pictures. *Pattern Recognition, 12,* 1–6.

Cheng, K. (1986). A purely geometric module in the rat's spatial representation. *Cognition, 23,* 149–178.

Clayton, N. S. (1998). Memory and the hippocampus in food-storing birds: A comparative approach. *Neuropharmacology, 37,* 441–452.

Clayton, N. S., & Dickinson, A. D. (1999a). Memory for the content of caches by scrub jays (*Aphelocoma coerulescens*). *Journal of Experimental Psychology: Animal Behavior Processes, 25,* 82–91.

Clayton, N. S., & Dickinson, A. D. (1999b). Motivational control of caching behaviour in the scrub jay *Aphelocoma coerulescens. Animal Behaviour, 57,* 435–444.

Cook, R. G. (2001). Hierarchical stimulus processing by pigeons. In R. G. Cook (Ed.), *Avian visual cognition.* Retrieved August 29, 2005, from http://www.pigeon.psy.tufts.edu/avc/cook/.

Corballis, P. M., Fendrich, R., Shapley, R., & Gazzaniga, M. (1999). Illusory contour perception and amodal boundary completion: Evidence of a dissociation following callosotomy. *Journal of Cognitive Neuroscience, 11,* 459–466.

Cozzutti, C., & Vallortigara, G. (2001). Hemispheric memories for the content and position of food caches in the domestic chick. *Behavioral Neuroscience, 115,* 305–313.

Deipolyi, A., Santos, L., & Hauser, M. D. (2001). The role of landmarks in cotton-top tamarin spatial foraging: Evidence for geometric and non-geometric features. *Animal Cognition, 4,* 99–108.

Deng, C., & Rogers, L. J. (1997). Differential contributions of the two visual pathways to functional lateralization in chicks. *Behavioural Brain Research, 87,* 173–182.

Deng, C., & Rogers, L. J. (1998a). Bilaterally projecting neurons in the two visual pathways of chicks. *Brain Research, 794,* 281–290.

Deng, C., & Rogers, L. J. (1998b). Organisation of the tectorotundal and SP/IPS-rotundal projections in the chick. *Journal of Comparative Neurology, 394,* 171–185.

Diamond, A., & Goldman-Rakic, P. S. (1989). Comparison of human infants and infant rhesus monkeys on Piaget's AB task: Evidence for dependence on dorsolateral prefrontal cortex. *Experimental Brain Research, 74,* 24–40.

DiPietro, N. T., Wasserman, E. A., & Young, M. E. (2002). Effects of occlusion on pigeons' visual object recognition. *Perception, 31,* 1299–1312.

Dumas, C., & Wilkie, D. M. (1995). Object permanence in ring doves. *Journal of Comparative Psychology, 109,* 142–150.

Etienne, A. S. (1973). Searching behaviour towards a disappearing prey in the domestic chick as affected by preliminary experience. *Animal Behaviour, 21,* 749–761.

Fodor, J. A. (1983). *The modularity of mind. An essay on faculty psychology,* Cambridge, MA: MIT Press.

Forkman, B. (1998). Hens use occlusion to judge depth in a two-dimensional picture. *Perception, 27,* 861–867.

Forkman, B. (2000). Domestic hens have declarative representations. *Animal Cognition, 3,* 135–137.

Forkman, B., & Vallortigara, G. (1999). Minimization of modal contours: An essential cross species strategy in disambiguating relative depth. *Animal Cognition, 4,* 181–185.

Foster, T. M., Temple, W., MacKenzie, C., Demello, L. R., & Poling, A. (1995). Delayed matching-to-sample performance of hens. Effects of sample duration and response requirements during the sample. *Journal of Experimental Analysis of Behavior, 64,* 19–31.

Freire, F., & Nicol, C. J. (1997). Object permanence in chicks: Predicting the position of an occluded imprinted object. Abstracts of the ASAB Meeting Biological Aspects of Learning, St Andrews, Scotland, July 1–4, 1997, p. 21.

Freire, F., & Nicol, C. J. (1999). Effect of experience of occlusion events on the domestic chick's strategy for locating a concealed imprinting object. *Animal Behaviour, 58,* 593–599.

Fujita, K. (2001). Perceptual completion in rhesus monkeys (*Macaca mulatta*) and pigeons (*Columba livia*). *Perception and Psychophysics, 63,* 115–125.

Funk, M. S. (1996). Development of object permanence in the New Zealand parakeet (*Cyanoramphus auriceps*). *Animal Learning and Behavior, 24,* 375–383.

Fuster, J. M. (1989). *The prefrontal cortex* (2nd ed.). New York: Raven Press.

Gallistel, C. R. (1990). *The organization of learning.* Cambridge, MA: MIT Press.

Gardner, H. (1987). *The mind's new science. A history of the cognitive revolution.* New York: Basic Books.

Goldman-Rakic, P. S. (1987). Development of cortical circuitry and cognitive function. *Child Development, 58,* 601–622.

Gouteux, S., Thinus-Blanc, C., & Vauclair, J. (2001). Rhesus monkeys use geometric and non-geometric information during a reorientation task. *Journal of Experimental Psychology: General, 130,* 505–519.

Gray, E. R., Spetch, M. L., Kelly, D. M., & Nguyen, A. (2004). Searching in the centre: Pigeons encode relative distance from walls of an enclosure. *Journal of Comparative Psychology, 118,* 113–117.

Grossberg, S., & Mingolla, E. (1985). Neural dynamics of form perception: Boundary completion, illusory figures, and neon colour spreading. *Psychological Review, 92,* 173–211.

Güntürkün, O. (1997). Avian visual lateralization: A review. *Neuroreport, 8,* 3–11.

Güntürkün, O., & Durstewitz, D. (2001). Multimodal areas of the avian forebrain—Blueprints for cognition? In G. Roth & M. Wulliman (Eds.), *Evolution of the brain and cognition* (pp. 431–450). New York: Wiley.

Güntürkün, O., & Hahmann, U. (1999). Functional subdivisions of the ascending visual pathways in the pigeon. *Behavioural Brain Research, 98,* 193–201.

Haskell, M., & Forkman, B. (1997). An investigation into object permanence in the domestic hen. Abstracts of the ASAB Meeting Biological Aspects of Learning, St Andrews, Scotland, July 1–4, 1997, p. 22.

Hellmann, B., & Güntürkün, O. (1999). Visual field specific heterogeneity within the tectofugal projection of the pigeon. *European Journal of Neuroscience, 11,* 1–18.

Hermer, L., & Spelke, E. S. (1994). A geometric process for spatial reorientation in young children. *Nature, 370,* 57–59.

Hermer, L., & Spelke, E. S. (1996). Modularity and development: The case of spatial reorientation. *Cognition, 61,* 195–232.

Hermer-Vasquez, L., Spelke, E. S., & Katsnelson, A. S. (1999). Sources of flexibility in human cognition: Dual-task studies of space and language. *Cognitive Psychology, 39,* 3–36.

Herz, M. (1926). Beobachtugen an gefangenen Rabenvögeln. *Psychologische Forschung, 8,* 336–397.

Herz, M. (1928). Wahrnehmungspsychologische Untersuchungen am Eichelhäher. *Zeitschrift für vergleichende Physiologie, 7,* 144–194.

Herz, M. (1935). Die Untersuchungen über den Formensinn der Honigbiene. *Naturwissenschaften, 23,* 618–624.

Hetherington, M. M., & Rolls, B. J. (1996). Sensory-specific satiety: Theoretical issues and central characteristics. In E. D. Capaldi (Ed.), *Why we eat what we eat* (pp. 267–290). Washington, DC: American Psychological Association.

Hodos, W., Macko, K. A., & Bessette, B. B. (1984). Near-field acuity changes after visual system lesions in pigeons. II. Telencephalon. *Behavioural Brain Research, 13,* 15–30.

Horn, G. (1998). Visual imprinting and the neural mechanisms of recognition memory. *Trends in Neurosciences, 21,* 300–305.

Hunter, W. S. (1913). The delayed reaction in animals and children. *Behavior Monographs, 2,* 1–86.

Kalt, T., Diekamp, B., & Güntürkün, O. (1999). Single unit activity during a go/nogo task in the "prefrontal cortex" of the pigeon. *Brain Research, 839,* 263–278.

Kanizsa, G. (1979). *Organization in vision.* New York: Praeger.

Kanizsa, G., Renzi, P., Conte, S., Compostela, C., & Guerani, L. (1993). Amodal completion in mouse vision. *Perception, 22,* 713–722.

Kellman, P. J., & Arterberry, M. E. (1998). *The cradle of knowledge.* Cambridge, MA: MIT Press.

Kellman, P. J., & Spelke, E. S. (1983). Perception of partly occluded objects in infancy. *Cognitive Psychology, 15,* 483–524.

Kelly, D. M., Spetch, M. L., & Heth, C. D. (1998). Pigeons' (*Columba livia*) encoding of geometric and featural properties of a spatial environment. *Journal of Comparative Psychology, 112,* 259–269.

Kirkpatrick, K. (2001). Object recognition. In R. G. Cook (Ed.), *Avian visual cognition.* Retrieved August 29, 2005, from http://www.pigeon.psy.tufts.edu./avc/kirkpatrick/.

Koehler, O. (1950). The ability of birds to count. *Bulletin of Animal Behaviour, 9,* 41–45.

Kozlowski, L. T., & Cutting, J. E. (1977). Recognising the sex of a walker from a dynamic point-light display. *Perception and Psychophysics, 21,* 575–580.

Lea, S. E. G., Slater, A. M., & Ryan, C. M. E. (1996). Perception of object unity in chicks: A comparison with the human infant. *Infant Behaviour and Development, 19,* 501–504.

MacWhinney, B. (1991). *The CHILDES project: Tools for analyzing talk.* Hillsdale, NJ: Erlbaum.

Martinoya, C., Rivaud, S., & Bloch, S. (1984). Comparing frontal and lateral viewing in pigeons: II. Velocity thresholds for movement discrimination. *Behavioural Brain Research, 8,* 375–385.

Matsushima, T., Izawa, E.-I., Aoki, N., & Yanagihara, S. (2003). The mind through chick eyes: Memory, cognition and anticipation. *Zoological Science, 20,* 395–408.

Michotte, A. (1963). *The perception of causality.* New York: Basic Books.

Michotte, A. Thines, G., & Crabbe, G. (1964). *Les Complements Amodaux des Structures Perceptives (Amodal Completion of Perceptual Structures)* (Studia Psychologica). Louvain: Publications Universitaires de Louvain. (in French)

Mogensen, J., & Divac, I. (1982). The prefrontal "cortex" in the pigeon. Behavioral evidence. *Brain Behavior Evolution, 21,* 60–66.

Nieder, A., & Wagner, H. (1999). Perception and neuronal coding of subjective contours in the owl. *Nature Neuroscience, 2,* 660–663.

Pearce, J. M., Ward-Robinson, J., Good, M., Fussell, C., & Aydin, A. (2001). Influence of a beacon on spatial learning based on the shape of the test environment. *Journal of Experimental Psychology: Animal Behavior Processes, 27,* 329–344.

Pepperberg, I. M., & Funk, M. S. (1990). Object permanence in four species of psittacine birds: An African Grey parrot (*Psittacus erithacus*), an Illiger mini macaw (*Ara maracana*), a parakeet (*Melopsittacus undulatus*), and a cockatiel (*Nymphicus hollandicus*). *Animal Learning and Behavior, 18,* 97–108.

Peterhans, E., & von der Heydt, R. (1989). Mechanisms of contour perception in monkey visual cortex: II. Contours bridging gaps. *Journal of Neuroscience, 9,* 1749–1763.

Petter, G. (1956). Nuove ricerche sperimentali sulla totalizzazione percettiva. *Rivista di Psicologia, 50,* 213–227.

Piaget, J. (1953). *Origin of intelligence in the child.* London: Routledge & Kegan Paul.

Plowright, C. M. S., Reid, S., & Kilian, T. (1998). Finding hidden food: Behavior on visible displacement tasks by mynahs (*Gracula religiosa*) and pigeons (*Columba livia*). *Journal of Comparative Psychology, 112,* 13–25.

Pollok, B., Prior, H., & Güntürkün, O. (2000). Development of object permanence in food-storing magpies (*Pica pica*). *Journal of Comparative Psychology, 114,* 148–157.

Prior, H., & Güntürkün, O. (1999). Patterns of visual lateralization in pigeons: Seeing what is there and beyond. *Perception, 28(suppl),* 22.

Regolin, L., Marconato, F., Tommasi, L., & Vallortigara, G. (2001). Do chicks complete partly occluded objects only with their right hemisphere? *Behavioural Pharmacology, 12(suppl 1),* S82. From the First Joint Meeting of the European Brain and Behaviour Society and European Behavioural Pharmacology Society, Marseilles, France, September 8–12, 2001.

Regolin, L., Marconato, F., & Vallortigara, G. (2004). Hemispheric differences in the recognition of partly occluded objects by newly-hatched domestic chicks (*Gallus gallus*). *Animal Cognition, 7,* 162–170.

Regolin, L., Tommasi, L., & Vallortigara, G. (2000). Visual perception of biological motion in newly hatched chicks as revealed by an imprinting procedure. *Animal Cognition, 3,* 53–60.

Regolin, L., Vallortigara, G., & Zanforlin, M. (1994). Perceptual and motivational aspects of detour behaviour in young chicks. *Animal Behaviour, 47,* 123–131.

Regolin, L., Vallortigara, G., & Zanforlin, M. (1995a). Detour behaviour in the domestic chick: Searching for a disappearing prey or a disappearing social partner. *Animal Behaviour, 50,* 203–211.

Regolin, L., Vallortigara, G., & Zanforlin, M. (1995b). Object and spatial representations in detour problems by chicks. *Animal Behaviour, 49,* 195–199.

Rogers, L. J. (1995). *The development of brain and behaviour in the chicken.* Wallingford, UK: CAB International.

Rogers, L. J. (1996). Behavioral, structural and neurochemical asymmetries in the avian brain: A model system for studying visual development and processing. *Neuroscience and Biobehavioral Reviews, 20,* 487–503.

Rogers, L. J., & Andrew, R. J. (2002). *Comparative vertebrate lateralization.* Cambridge: Cambridge University Press.

Rolls, B. J. (1990). The role of sensory-specific satiety in food intake and food selection. In E. D. Capaldi & T. L. Powley (Eds.), *Taste, experience and feeding* (pp. 197–209). Washington, DC: American Psychological Association.

Rose, S. P. R. (2000). God's organism? The chick as a model system for memory studies. *Learning and Memory, 7,* 1–17.

Sekuler, A. B., Lee, J. A. J., & Shettleworth, S. J. (1996). Pigeons do not complete partly occluded figures. *Perception, 25,* 1109–1120.

Sekuler, A. B., & Palmer, S. E. (1992). Perception of partly occluded objects: A microgenetic analysis. *Journal of Experimental Psychology: General, 121,* 95–111.

Shettleworth, S. J. (1990). Spatial memory in food-storing birds. *Philosophical Transactions of the Royal Society (Biology), 329,* 143–151.

Shipley, T. F., & Kellman, P. J. (1992). Strength of visual interpolation depends on the ratio of physically specified to total edge length. *Perception and Psychophysics, 52,* 97–106.

Singh, M., Hoffman, D., & Albert, M. (1999). Contour completion and relative depth: Petter's rule and support ratio. *Psychological Science, 10,* 423–428.

Sovrano, V. A., Bisazza, A., & Vallortigara, G. (2003). Modularity and spatial reorientation in a simple mind: Encoding of geometric and nongeometric properties of a spatial environment by fish. *Cognition, 85,* 51–59.

Sovrano, V. A., Bisazza, A., & Vallortigara, G. (2003). Modularity as a fish views it: Conjoining geometric and nongeometric information for spatial reorientation. *Journal of Experimental Psychology: Animal Behavior Processes, 29,* 199–210.

Sovrano, V. A., Bisazza, A., & Vallortigara, G. (2005). Animals' use of landmarks and metric information to reorient: Effects of the size of the experimental space. *Cognition, 97,* 121–133.

Spalding, D. A. (1873). Instinct; with original observations on young animals. *Macmillans Magazine, 27,* 282–293.

Spelke, E. S. (2003). What makes us smart? Core knowledge and natural language. In D. Gentner & S. Goldin-Meadow (Eds.), *Language in mind. Advances in the study of language and thought* (pp. 277–311). Cambridge, MA: MIT Press.

Spetch, M. L., Cheng, K., & MacDonald, S. E. (1996). Learning the configuration of a landmark array: I. Touch-screen studies with pigeons and humans. *Journal of Comparative Psychology, 110,* 55–68.

Spetch, M. L., Cheng, K., MacDonald, S. E., Linkenhoker, B.A., Kelly, D. M., & Doerkson, S. (1997). Learning the configuration of a landmark array in pigeons and humans. II. Generality across search tasks. *Journal of Comparative Psychology, 111,* 14–24.

Tommasi, L., Bressan, P., & Vallortigara, G. (1995). Solving occlusion indeterminacy in chromatically homogeneous patterns. *Perception, 24,* 391–403.

Tommasi, L., Gagliardo, A., Andrew, R. J., & Vallortigara, G. (2003). Separate processing mechanisms for encoding geometric and landmark information in the avian brain. *European Journal of Neuroscience, 17,* 1695–1702.

Tommasi, L., & Vallortigara, G. (2000). Searching for the centre: Spatial cognition in the domestic chick. *Journal of Experimental Psychology: Animal Behavior Processes, 26,* 477–486.

Tommasi, L., & Vallortigara, G. (2001). Encoding of geometric and landmark information in the left and right hemispheres of the avian brain. *Behavioral Neuroscience, 115,* 602–613.

Tommasi, L., Vallortigara, G., & Zanforlin, M. (1997). Young chickens learn to localize the centre of a spatial environment. *Journal of Comparative Physiology A, 180, 567–572.*

Towe, A. L. (1954). A study of figural equivalence in the pigeon. *Journal of Comparative and Physiological Psychology, 47,* 283–287.

Vallortigara, G. (2000). Comparative neuropsychology of the dual brain: A stroll through left and right animals' perceptual worlds. *Brain and Language, 73,* 189–219.

Vallortigara, G. (2002). Other minds, other brains. Comparative cognition and consciousness. In *Proceedings of the International Symposium Exploring Consciousness: Humanities, Natural Sciences, Religion* (pp. 61–79). Milan: Fondazione Carlo Erba.

Vallortigara, G. (2004). Visual cognition and representation in birds and primates. In L. J. Rogers & G. Kaplan (Eds.), *Vertebrate comparative cognition: Are primates special?* (pp. 57–94). New York: Kluwer Academic/Plenum Publishers.

Vallortigara, G., Cozzutti, C., Tommasi, L., & Rogers, L. J. (2001). How birds use their eyes: Opposite left-right specialisation for the lateral and frontal visual hemifield in the domestic chick. *Current Biology, 11,* 29–33.

Vallortigara, G., Feruglio, M., & Sovrano, V. A. (2005). Reorientation by geometric and landmark information in environments of different spatial size. *Developmental Science, 8,* 393–401.

Vallortigara, G., Pagni, P., & Sovrano, V. A. (2004). Separate geometric and non-geometric modules for spatial reorientation: Evidence from a lopsided animal brain. *Journal of Cognitive Neuroscience, 16,* 390–400.

Vallortigara, G., & Regolin, L. (2002). Facing an obstacle: Lateralization of object and spatial cognition. In R. J. Andrew & L. J. Rogers (Eds.), *Comparative vertebrate lateralization* (pp. 383–444). Cambridge: Cambridge University Press.

Vallortigara, G., Regolin, L., Rigoni, M., & Zanforlin, M. (1998). Delayed search for a concealed imprinted object in the domestic chick. *Animal Cognition, 1,* 17–24.

Vallortigara, G., Rogers, L. J., & Bisazza, A. (1999). Possible evolutionary origins of cognitive brain lateralization. *Brain Research Reviews, 30,* 164–175.

Vallortigara, G., & Sovrano, V. A. (2002). Conjoining information from different modules: A comparative perspective. *Behavioral Brain Sciences, 25,* 701–702.

Vallortigara, G., & Tommasi, L. (2001). Minimization of modal contours: An instance of an evolutionary internalized geometric regularity? *Brain and Behavioral Sciences, 24,* 706–707.

Vallortigara, G., Zanforlin, M., & Pasti, G. (1990). Geometric modules in animal's spatial representation: A test with chicks. *Journal of Comparative Psychology, 104,* 248–254.

Wasserman, E. A., Kirkpatrick-Steger, K., Van Hamme, L. J., & Biederman, I. (1993). Pigeons are sensitive to the spatial organization of complex visual stimuli. *Psychological Science, 4,* 336–341.

Watanabe, S., & Ito, Y. (1991). Discrimination of individuals in pigeons. *Bird Behaviour, 9,* 20–29.

Wu, H. M., Sackett, G. P., & Gunderson, V. M. (1986). Social stimuli as incentives for delayed response performance by infant Pigtailed macaques (*Macaca nemestrina*). *Primates, 27,* 229–236.

Zanforlin, M. (1981). Visual perception of complex forms (anomalous surfaces) in chicks. *Italian Journal of Psychology, 8,* 1–16.

4

The Comparative Psychology of Absolute Pitch

RONALD G. WEISMAN, MITCHEL T. WILLIAMS, JEROME S. COHEN, MILAN G. NJEGOVAN, AND CHRISTOPHER B. STURDY

Absolute pitch (AP) is the ability to identify, classify, and memorize pitches without an external referent. Musical AP adds the further requirement of pitch naming in the notation of Western music. Here, the authors consider the more general kind of AP, without the requirement of note naming. They report several operant experiments in which two species of mammals (humans and rats), three species of songbirds (zebra finches, white-throated sparrows, and black-capped chickadees), and one species of parrot (budgerigars) discriminated and categorized individual tones or ranges of tones correlated with reward and nonreward. As the discriminations became more difficult, the avian species, which learn their vocalizations, maintained highly accurate AP, but the mammals slipped from lackluster to nonexistent AP. The findings illustrate Darwin's hypothesis (*The Descent of Man*, 1874) that continuity in mental abilities underlies differences among species.

ABSOLUTE PITCH PERCEPTION IN HUMANS AND SONGBIRDS

Absolute pitch (AP) perception refers to the ability to identify, classify, and memorize pitches without the use of an external reference pitch. Theorists of music perception and cognition have added a second defining task: to accurately name pitches using the notation of modern Western music (see Krumhansl, 2000; Takeuchi & Hulse, 1993). Thus, possessors of *musical AP* can name the note and octave of a musical sound with an accuracy of 50% to 95% depending on the reference study and its methods (Miyazaki, 1988). There is much speculation about the origin and functions of AP; most hypotheses center on the developing perception of young musicians (Takeuchi & Hulse, 1993). Here, we present a fresh approach to understanding AP based on a comparative analysis across species of birds and mammals.

In preparing this chapter, we began our comparative analysis by separating general AP from musical AP. Musical AP requires note naming. *General AP* (Weisman, Njegovan, Williams, Cohen, & Sturdy, 2004), or simply AP, requires only accurate discrimination or production of pitches without a current external referent. We have excluded note naming from the definition of general AP because naming puts objectionable limitations on who can possess AP. Only humans (*Homo sapiens*) have vocabularies sufficient to name large numbers of events and only musicians have the training to name the several dozen musical pitches by note and octave.

Consider an example from visual perception: If color naming were required to demonstrate color vision, then only humans (and perhaps only some interior decorators among humans) could qualify; yet, everyone knows that chimpanzees and pigeons (*Pan troglodytes* and *Columba livia*), for example, also see colors. In a similar way, we show that other animals, the oscines, for example, have robust and accurate AP.

Musical AP is easy to uncouple from general AP in humans. Musical AP is rare: Only about 1 in 10,000 people in the general population possess it (Profita & Bidder, 1988), suggesting that musical AP may be a maladaptive trait. A hallmark of maladaptive traits is that natural selection has greatly reduced their occurrence in the population (Fisher, 1930). Further evidence that musical AP may be maladaptive is that it does not make people better musicians; in fact, it seems to makes them worse musicians by interfering with relative pitch processing (see Miyazaki, 1992, 1995; Ward, 1963). Finally, musical AP is unwholesome: It is considerably more probable among musicians diagnosed with Williams syndrome, a developmental disability (Lenhoff, Perales, & Hickok, 2001), and autism spectrum disorder, an even more severe developmental disability (Bonnel et al., 2003), than among otherwise normal musicians. Taken together, this evidence suggests that musical AP is an unfortunate side effect of early and intense musical training in individuals in whom unwholesome obsessive-compulsive issues are developing.

In contrast to musical AP, general AP appears to be common, helpful, and wholesome. For example, the fundamental spectral frequencies in male and female voices and in infant alarm calls form nonoverlapping pitch ranges (Bakan, 1987); most humans can accurately sort the pitches of male, female, and infant voices (e.g., Weisman et al., 1998). Halpern (1989) found that humans consistently sang familiar songs beginning at the same frequency over two testing days. Also, Levitin (1994) demonstrated that humans without musical training could match the original frequencies in recorded popular music. Using procedures similar to those of Halpern (1989), Deutsch, Henthorn, and Dolson (1999) found that speakers of a tone language (either Mandarin or Vietnamese) consistently produced several tones associated with their language at the same frequency over two testing days. In these examples, humans required little or no musical training to accurately sort and reproduce pitches. That much of this evidence depends on pitch production should not be seen as problematic; there is no evidence of motor memory for voiced pitch production without pitch memory (Ward, 1999).

Two final points on general AP in humans should be made. First, the biological usefulness of the ability to accurately sort males from females and both sexes as adults from helpless infants at a distance and to accurately pronounce the sounds in human languages requires no further explanation. Second, that general AP is common among humans argues against it having an unwholesome association with any neurological disorder.

Our main objection to equating general AP with musical AP is that musical AP excludes, by definition, the remarkable ability of songbirds (oscines) to classify and memorize the pitches in their songs. The *Passeriformes* suborder *oscines*, the true songbirds, are distinguished from other perching birds (order *Passeriformes*) by the more complex morphology of their sound producing organ, the syrinx (Larsen & Goller, 2003), and by brain structures associated with their extraordinary ability while young to learn song from adult conspecifics (see Ball & Hulse, 1998, for a review). Birdsong is communication used, typically, by adult males to defend their breeding territories and to attract females. Birdsong serves the biologically important functions of promoting sex and reducing violence among conspecific oscines. Song serves the equally important function of isolating oscine species from one another; as such it is (almost certainly) a determinant of the vast proliferation of the Oscines suborder (only one suborder among many avian suborders and orders). Some 5,000 species, or about half of all avian species, are oscines (Monroe & Sibley, 1997).

The case for the importance of highly accurate general AP in songbirds comes from bioacoustics measurement studies and song playback experiments conducted in the field. Bioacoustics research reveals that the least variable acoustic features of birdsong are the frequencies of its notes (Brooks & Falls, 1975; Nelson, 1988; Nowicki, Mitani, Nelson, & Marler, 1989). In many species, the note frequencies sung by individual birds are constant from occasion to occasion. In all species studied so far, song notes are sung within relatively narrow, species-typical frequency ranges, described by confidence intervals about mean note frequencies; each of these frequency ranges spans less than an octave (see Nelson, 1989a).

Nelson (1989a) used a discriminant analysis to determine which song features differentiate field sparrow (*Spizella pusilla*) and chipping sparrow (*Spizella passerina*) songs from the songs of 12 other oscine species. He found that maximum and minimum frequencies were among the most accurate single features, with maximum frequency being important to both species in classifying songs as conspecific or heterospecific.

Studies that play recorded songs to males defending territories in the wild have repeatedly observed close approach and frequent song in response to the playback of normal conspecific songs and little response to the playback of conspecific songs that were pitch-shifted outside the normal frequency range of conspecific song (e.g., Falls, 1962). Playback of a well-established neighbor's song engenders little territorial response unless the location, pitch, or another important characteristic of the song is altered (Brooks & Falls, 1975).

Nelson (1989b) has provided an elegant example of the conjoint discrimination of the specific frequency of a neighbor's song and the frequency range of conspecific songs in field sparrows. When Nelson played a neighbor's song at its normal pitch (and from its normal direction), as expected, he observed little territorial response. Then, when he decreased the pitch of the playback of the neighbor's song (still within the frequency range of conspecific songs), he found a marked increase in territorial response. When he further decreased the pitch of the neighbor's song to outside the range of conspecific songs (the range is taken here to be $M \pm 2$ to 3 *SD*s), he found that the territorial response fell to the same level as to heterospecific songs. In summary, evidence from the field shows that songbirds can use AP both to sort neighbors' from strangers' songs and to sort conspecifics' songs from heterospecifics' songs.

COMPARATIVE EVIDENCE FROM LABORATORY ABSOLUTE PITCH TASKS

Bioacoustics measurement studies and playback experiments conducted in the field have provided conclusive evidence of the importance of AP to songbirds. The main purpose of this chapter was to compare the AP abilities of several avian and mammalian species. A second purpose was to use the results of these comparisons to examine Darwin's (1874) famous hypothesis about the continuity of mental abilities across species.

Relative pitch (RP) refers to the ability to use relationships between frequencies, such as, constant frequency ratios, sometimes called pitch intervals, to identify and classify sequences of pitches. In the course of their studies of RP perception in songbirds, Hulse, Cynx, and Humpal (1984; see also Hulse, Page, & Braaten, 1990) developed laboratory operant discrimination procedures that have provided good, but indirect, evidence of AP in songbirds. Also, MacDougall-Shackleton and Hulse (1996), using similar procedures, found good evidence of concurrent RP and AP in European starlings (*Sturnus vulgaris*). However, the procedures of these experiments provide no direct measure of the accuracy of AP. Over the past decade, we (e.g., Njegovan, Ito, Mewhort, & Weisman, 1994; Weisman et al., 1998) have developed and tested a suite of operant discrimination tasks that provide direct and comparable measures of AP across several species of birds and mammals, including both songbirds and humans. The songbird species in much of our work has been the zebra finch (*Taeniopygia guttata*); this species is native to Australia, is easily bred in the laboratory, and is among the most commonly studied avian species.

In this chapter, we report progress in testing alternative comparative hypotheses about the origins and prevalence of AP in birds and mammals. The first hypothesis corresponds to conventional wisdom about AP: Humans mostly possess weak, lackluster AP, probably because of interference from RP, whereas all other species of mammals and birds have highly accurate AP similar to that observed here in zebra finches. The second hypothesis is that all mammals and many birds have weak AP; only zebra finches and possibly all songbirds have highly accurate AP, developed perhaps in the course of acquiring the unusual ability to learn to produce conspecific vocalizations. Variations on these hypotheses also deserve testing. For example, a third hypothesis is that avian species have highly accurate AP and, in general, mammals have weak AP. The reasoning behind the third hypothesis is that accurate AP may have preceded and determined oscine and other avian adaptations in the use of auditory communication.

Absolute Pitch Across Avian and Mammalian Species

The operant go–no-go discrimination tests of AP described here rewarded responses to multiple pure tone stimuli, the S+s, and extinguished responses to many other pure tone stimuli, the S–s. That is, S+ tones and S– tones were, respectively, the discriminative stimuli that signaled reward and nonreward for responding. For songbirds, the responses were alighting and briefly remaining on a perch to hear a sine-wave tone (randomly selected from those presented in the discrimination and played once) and then flying or hopping to the feeder to obtain food. For humans, the responses were pressing the left button to hear the tone and pressing the right button to obtain competitive and noncompetitive monetary rewards. For rats (*Rattus norvegicus*), the responses were lever pressing to hear the tone and poking their heads into the feeder to obtain food. In short, hungry birds and rats were rewarded with food for approaching a feeder, and hungry musicians were rewarded with money for pressing a button after some tones but not others. In addition to the instructions implicit in the operant discrimination task, humans had explicit instruction and a brief interactive tutorial in the rules for each discrimination task. The tones, their correlations with reward and nonreward, and the species of the animals doing the discriminating were the principal independent variables in the AP tests described later.

Table 4.1 Frequencies of S+ (Rewarded) and S– (Unrewarded) Tones in the 359–1,633 Hz and 1,200–5,459 Hz Spectral Regions for the Three Frequency-Range Discrimination Groups

Reward Status	Lower Region (Hz)	Higher Region (Hz)
S–	359	1,200
S–	381	1,272
S–	403	1,348
S–	428	1,429
S–	453	1,515
S–	480	1,606
S–	509	1,702
S–	540	1,804
S+	572	1,913
S+	607	2,027
S+	643	2,149
S+	681	2,278
S+	722	2,415
S+	766	2,560
S+	812	2,713
S+	860	2,876
S+	912	3,048
S+	967	3,231
S–	1,025	3,425
S–	1,086	3,631
S–	1,151	3,849
S–	1,220	4,079
S–	1,294	4,324
S–	1,371	4,584
S–	1,454	4,859
S–	1,541	5,150
S–	1,633	5,459

Easy and More Difficult Three-Range Discriminations In the first set of AP tests reported here, subjects learned discriminations among three ranges of tones, with individual tones separated by 6% in frequency, in the 359- to 1633-Hz and 1200- to 5459-Hz spectral regions (see table 4.1, but see Weisman et al., 1998, 2004, for full reports of the methods and results). Responses in the high and low ranges were not rewarded, but those in the middle range were rewarded. In figure 4.1, results for zebra finches, humans, and rats are compared with those expected from a perfect tone sorter: 0% response to tones in the S– ranges and 100% response to tones in the S+ ranges. In their final session, zebra finches discriminated the nine middle (S+) range tones with precision, approaching the feeder little to adjacent tones in the upper and lower (S–) frequency ranges. Humans and rats responded much more to the adjacent S– tones. Clearly, these results indicate a quantitative advantage of zebra finches over humans and rats in the three-range discrimination.

In a second set of AP tests, discriminations were again among three ranges of tones, but individual tones were separated one from the next by a fixed 120 Hz, from 2,000 Hz to 5,120. This was a more difficult discrimination because the percentage change between tones decreased with frequency from 6% in the lower S– range, to 3.6% in the middle S+ range, to 2.4% in the upper S– range (see table 4.2 and Njegovan et al., 1994, for a full report of the methods and results). In figure 4.2, results are compared for zebra finches and humans with those for a perfect sorter. As in the easier three-range task, zebra finches discriminated more accurately than humans. However, in this more difficult discrimination, humans fell even farther behind songbirds by responding more to S– tones in both the lower and upper ranges than in the easier discrimination.

Discriminating Among 27 Individual Tones In a third set of AP tests, the spectral region and separations between tones were the same as those used in the second set of tests, but instead of discriminating between frequency ranges, zebra finches and

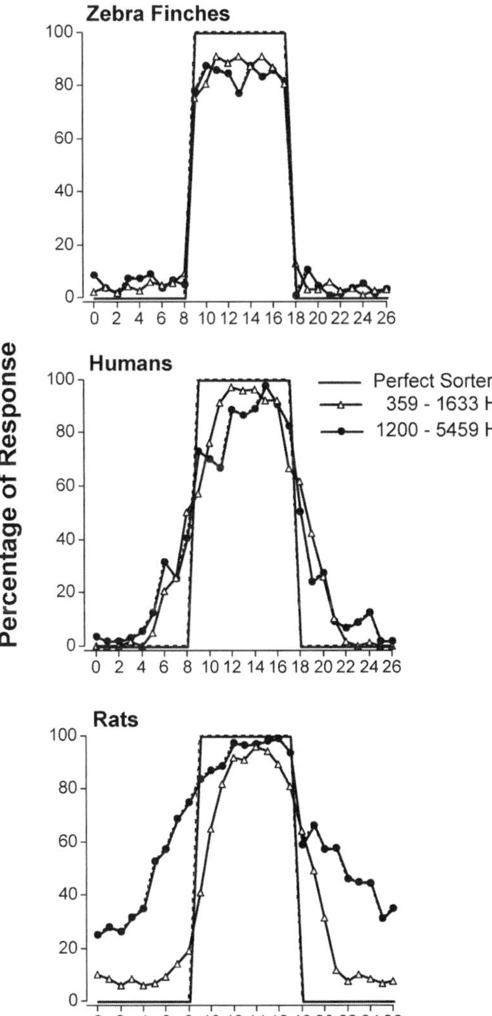

Figure 4.1. Mean percentages of responses in a three-range operant discrimination task, with tones separated in frequency by 6%, from 359 Hz and 1,200 Hz, by zebra finches, humans, and rats. The dashed lines show the performance of a perfect sorter, responding at 100% to all tones in the (S+) middle frequency range, and at 0% to all tones in the S– lower and upper frequency ranges. Discrimination by zebra finches approached that of a perfect sorter with discrete changes in the percentage of response to tones in the S+ and S– ranges. Humans and rats discriminated the middle range from the upper and lower ranges, but the change in responding between ranges was continuous. Also, responding in humans and rats was skewed toward the higher frequency tones in both spectral regions.

Table 4.2 Frequencies of Tones Used as S+ and S– Tones in the Three-Range and Distributed S+ Discrimination Groups

Frequency (Hz)	*Discrimination Group*	
	Three-Range	Distributed
2,000	S–	S–
2,120	S–	S–
2,240	S–	S+
2,360	S–	S–
2,480	S–	S–
2,600	S–	S+
2,720	S–	S–
2,840	S–	S–
2,960	S–	S+
3,080	S+	S–
3,200	S+	S–
3,320	S+	S+
3,440	S+	S–
3,560	S+	S–
3,680	S+	S+
3,800	S+	S–
3,920	S+	S–
4,040	S+	S+
4,160	S–	S–
4,280	S–	S–
4,400	S–	S+
4,520	S–	S–
4,640	S–	S–
4,760	S–	S+
4,880	S–	S–
5,000	S–	S–
5,120	S–	S+

humans had to respond differently to nine individual S+ tones that were distributed among 18 S– tones (see table 4.2 and Njegovan et al., 1994, for a full report of the methods and results). In the two three-range tasks, zebra finches and humans were trained for 5,000 to 7,000 trials. In the distributed S+ task, both species had 15,000 to 20,000 trials.

In the distributed S+ task, as in the two previous AP tests, zebra finches discriminated more accurately than humans (see figure 4.3). Humans fell even further behind songbirds by responding less to the S+ tones and more to the S– tones. Although humans did show some weak ability to discriminate the S+ tones from the S– tones (about 8% more responding to S+ than to S– tones), the difference in favor of the S+ tones was not statistically significant. We estimate that either twice the number of humans or twice the number of trials would be necessary to detect significant discrimination of distributed S+ tones by humans. In contrast, zebra

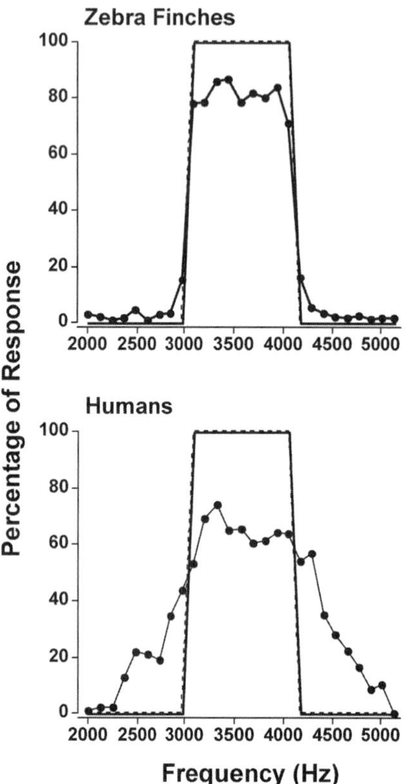

Figure 4.2. Mean percentages of responses in a three-range operant discrimination, with tones separated in frequency by 120 Hz, from 2,000 Hz and 5,120 Hz, by zebra finches and humans. The dashed lines show the performance of a perfect sorter, responding at 100% to all tones in the (S+) middle frequency range, and at 0% to all tones in the S– lower and upper frequency ranges. Discrimination by zebra finches approached that of a perfect sorter with nearly discrete changes in the percentage of response to tones in the S+ and S– ranges. Humans discriminated the middle range from the upper and lower ranges, but the change in responding between ranges was continuous and uneven. Responding in the S– ranges in humans was skewed toward the higher-frequency S– tones.

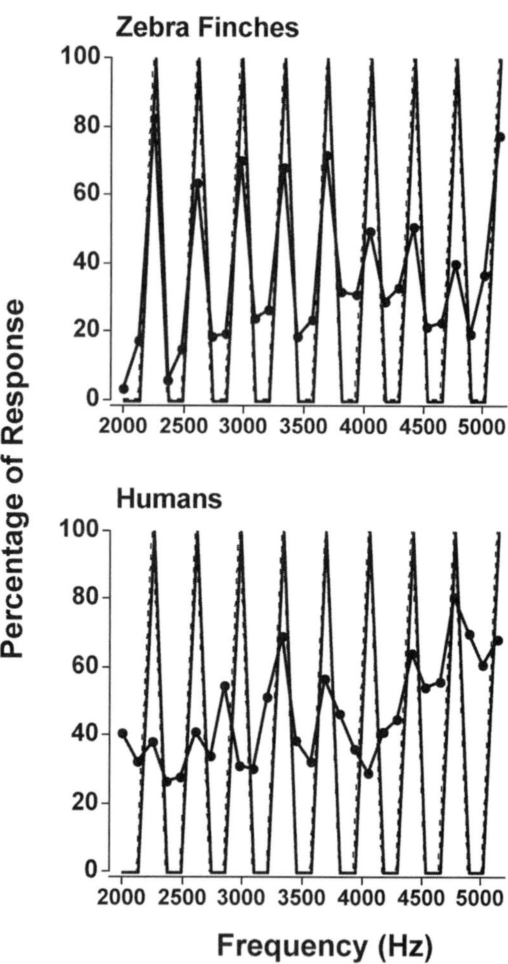

Figure 4.3. Mean percentages of responses in a distributed discrimination between 9 S+ tones interspersed among 18 S– tones separated in frequency by 120 Hz, from 2,000 Hz and 5,120 Hz, by zebra finches and humans. The dashed lines show the performance of a perfect sorter, responding at 100% to all the S+ tones and at 0% to all the S– tones. After 15,000 to 20,000 trials, zebra finches responded about 40% more to the S+ tones. Humans responded only 8% more to the S+ tones, which was not significantly different from responding to the S– tones. Zebra finches can memorize the multiple individual tones correlated with reward and nonreward much more effectively than humans.

finches responded about 40% more to S+ than to S– tones, a large and highly significant difference. In the distributed S+ task, the two lowest frequency tones were S– tones and the highest frequency tone was an S+; this design feature may have led to some anchor effects in both species. In zebra finches, the two lowest frequency tones were among the best-discriminated S-s, and in humans, responding increased with frequency over the spectrum of test tones.

Eight-Range Discriminations In the fourth set of AP tests, the spectral range and separations among tones were similar to those in the second and third tests, but, instead of three ranges, or nine distributed S+ tones, zebra finches, humans, and rats discriminated eight frequency ranges of five adjacent tones each (see table 4.3 and Weisman et al. 1998, 2004, for full reports of the methods and results). In these eight-range discriminations, we counterbalanced whether the lowest frequency tones were S+ tones (and the highest tones S– tones) or the reverse. Subjects were each given 8,000 to 10,000 training trials. As in the three previous AP tests and as shown in figure 4.4, zebra finches approximated the performance of a perfect sorter. However, zebra finches did respond slightly more to some S– tones adjacent to the S+ ranges and slightly less to some S+ tones adjacent to the S– ranges in the eight-range task than in the three-range task. These results suggest that zebra finches found the eight-range task more difficult than the three-range tasks. Also, zebra finches showed weak anchor effects in the eight-range tasks: That is, they responded slightly more in the first S+ range and slightly less in the last S– range in the S+ first condition, whereas responding had the opposite trend in the S– first condition.

Humans and rats fell farther and more dramatically behind songbirds in the eight-range AP task (see figure 4.4). In rats, we needed to include a test in extinction (no reward for S+ tones) to unmask significant but weak discrimination of the S+ ranges (see Hearst, 1987, for a previous use of extinction to reveal discrimination). Humans and rats showed similar emphatic anchor effects. In the S+ first discrimination, both species showed a linear decline in responding from the first (S+) range to the eighth (S–) range. In the S– first discrimination, based on a reversal in the correlation of reward with frequency, both humans and rats showed the opposite linear trend in responding.

The pattern of discrimination in the eight-range task differed fundamentally between songbirds on the one side and humans and rats on the other, but performances by humans and rats were similar even in the details of their meager discriminations. In zebra finches, the eight-range discrimination was almost completely determined by the alternation of S+ and S– frequency ranges and only mildly influenced by anchor effects of the first and last ranges. In humans and rats, the eight-range discrimination was little influenced by the alternation of S+ and S– ranges and dominated by anchor effects of the first and last ranges. A similar pattern of results was obtained in the distributed S+ task. Zebra finches discriminated the S+ from the S– tones, whereas mainly the anchor effects of nonreward and reward associated with the first and last tones influenced humans.

Discriminating Among 27 Two-Tone Sequences Finally, we refer briefly to performance in an AP control for the demonstration of RP in humans and two species of songbirds: zebra finches and black-capped chickadees (*Poecile atricapilla*) (see Njegovan & Weisman, 1997; Weisman, Njegovan, & Ito, 1994, for a full report of the methods and results). The proper control for an RP-based discrimination of two-tone S+ sequences with a common frequency ratio from two-tone S– sequences with different ratios is a pseudo-ratio discrimination. In the experiments cited here, the pseudo-ratio discrimination presented 27 sequences consisting of two 440-ms sine-wave tones each and spanning the frequency region from 2,500 to 5,400 Hz. Nine randomly chosen sequences were S+s and the 18 remaining two-tone sequences were S–s. To discriminate accurately, subjects needed to memorize the 54 individual notes and their orders in the 27 two-note sequences used in the pseudo-ratio task.

Table 4.3 Frequencies of S+ (Responses Reinforced) and S– (Responses Unreinforced) Tones in the S– First S+ First Frequency-Range Discrimination Groups

Frequency Range	S– First Group	S+ First Group	Frequency (Hz)				
1	S–	S+	980	1,100	1,220	1,340	1,460
2	S+	S–	1,580	1,700	1,820	1,940	2,060
3	S–	S+	2,180	2,300	2,420	2,540	2,660
4	S+	S–	2,780	2,900	3,020	3,140	3,260
5	S–	S+	3,380	3,500	3,620	3,740	3,860
6	S+	S–	3,980	4,100	4,220	4,340	4,460
7	S–	S+	4,580	4,700	4,820	4,940	5,060
8	S+	S–	5,180	5,300	5,420	5,540	5,660

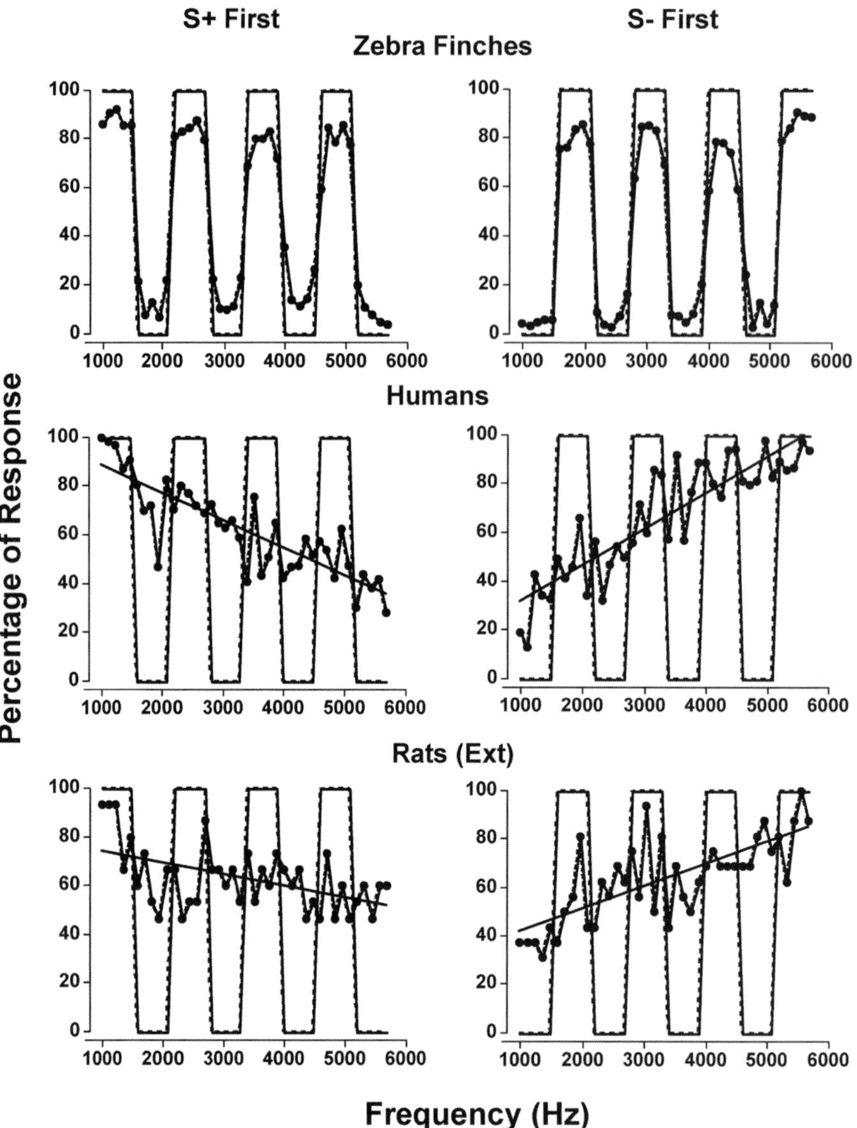

Figure 4.4. Mean percentages of responses in the eight-range task during the final discrimination session for zebra finches and humans and during an extinction session for rats. The dashed line shows the ideal performance of a perfect sorter responding at 100% to all tones in the S+ ranges and at 0% to all tones in the S– ranges. Discrimination by zebra finches was precise and accurate, approximating that of a perfect sorter. Discrimination by humans and rats was nonexistent, except that both species anchored their discriminations on the first and last ranges of the task, with responding falling off from the first S+ range to the last S– range in the S+ first condition and rising from the first S– range to the last S+ range in S– first condition. Linear equations fit to the results for humans and rats ranged from $r = -0.52$ to $r = -0.85$ for the S+ first condition and from $r = 0.70$ to $r = 0.88$ for the S– first condition.

According to this analysis, the 54-tone pseudo-ratio task is at least twice as difficult as the 27-tone three-frequency-range task, presented earlier, because it requires AP for twice as many tones. Both zebra finches and chickadees eventually learned the pseudo-ratio task (in 10,000 to 18,000 trials), reliably discriminating a mean of 5.5 of the 9 S+ two-tone sequences from the 18 S– tone sequences. Only one of four humans memorized any of the pseudo-ratio S+ tone sequences. The results suggest that the pseudo-ratio memorization task was just barely within the AP of songbirds and out of reach for the AP of humans.

Conclusions We believe that the above results justify our comparative approach to AP. In particular, eliminating note naming in favor of a more general definition allowed us to uncover the lackluster AP of humans and rats and the amazingly accurate AP of songbirds. Our comparative analysis continues. Thus far, we have not completed as many comparisons between rats and humans as between songbirds and humans. We would like to have information from rats in a reference task, say timing, using the same methodology as in the frequency range discriminations to provide a positive control for our finding of weak AP in rats. Of course, there is already evidence that rats time events about as well as humans and songbirds (see Church & Gibbon, 1982; Weisman et al., 1999), but comparisons using just the methods we report here would ensure that we have not inadvertently chosen discrimination procedures that are unfavorable to rats. Even without evidence from a positive control, it is clear that AP in humans and rats shares several common features: a steep decline in AP as the task increases in difficulty, positive skewing in the three-range task, and anchor effects in the distributed S+ and eight-range discriminations.

D'Amato and Salmon (1982, 1984) suggested that rats and monkeys (*Cebus apella*) have strong AP. The flaw here is that D'Amato and Salmon's methods are similar to those of Hulse, Cynx, and Humpal (1984) in that they reveal that rats and monkeys have AP but not how much AP they possess. We used methods explicitly designed to measure AP; these methods do confirm that rats have AP, but our extensive, quantitative comparisons with songbirds reveal that rats and humans share weak, lackluster, AP. This evidence leads us to ask about the quality of general AP in humans who possess musical AP. Given that musical AP possessors are not accurate at identifying pitches between the notes in Western music (Rakowski, 1972), we suspect that general AP, when it is measured in our discrimination tasks, will not be much improved by skill at note naming.

Some researchers have wondered why most humans do not possess musical AP (e.g., Deutsch, Henthorm, & Dolson, 1999). Cognitive psychologists have suggested that the acquisition of language and delayed music training might be causes of poor AP in humans (e.g., Krumhansl, 2000). Interestingly, AP is much admired among musicians; we logged onto a dozen Web sites promising to help musicians develop musical AP (for a fee, of course). What all of these researchers, musicians, and entrepreneurs alike seem to have missed is the probable reason humans are poor AP processors: Humans are mammals and it appears likely that most mammals (among them, humans and rats) share lackluster AP. Of course, more mammals must be tested before we can claim with high confidence that mammals in general are poor at AP. We think bats and dogs would be interesting test species. Still, humans and rats are not near relatives, so minimal AP for only these two mammalian species is unlikely.

Absolute Pitch Across Avian Species

We have compared zebra finches (and a few black-capped chickadees) as representative oscines with humans and rats as representative mammals. Here, we present the results of eight-range discriminations from another oscine species, white-throated sparrows (*Zonotrichia albicollis*), and a species from another avian order that learns its calls, the *Psittaciformes* or parrots, represented by budgerigars (*Mellopsittacus undulatus*). All the birds were tested in the S+ first, eight-range discrimination (see Weisman et al., 2004). Figure 4.5 illustrates two findings about frequency-range discriminations in birds. Female zebra finches responded more to higher frequency S+ ranges than female white-throated sparrows. Male parrots and songbirds (specifically, zebra finches and budgerigars) were highly similar and accurate in their responses to tones in all eight-frequency ranges.

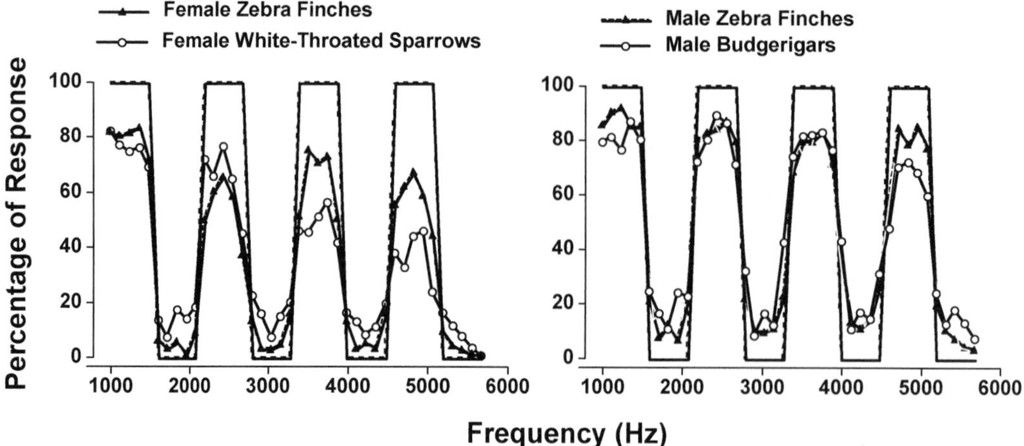

Figure 4.5. Mean percentages of responses by female zebra finches and female white-throated sparrows (*left*) and male zebra finches and male budgerigars (*right*) in the S+ first version of the eight-range task. The dashed line shows the ideal performance of a perfect sorter responding at 100% to all tones in the S+ ranges and at 0% to all tones in the S– ranges. Females responded less than males and white-throated sparrow females responded less than zebra finch females to tones in the higher frequency S+ ranges. Zebra finch and budgerigar males' responding approximated that of a perfect sorter.

In the comparisons between songbirds and mammals already described, inferring the accuracy of discrimination from the percentages of response to tones in the S+ and S– ranges was straightforward: zebra finches always responded more to the S+ tones and less the S– tones (more like the perfect sorter) than did either humans or rats. In comparisons between female zebra finches and white-throated sparrows, it is unclear whether the differences in responding reflect differences in discrimination.

Discrimination of S+ From S– Tones The discrimination ratio (responses to S+/total responses to S+ and S–) is often used to provide an overall measure of discrimination. In several experiments, we have found the discrimination ratio to be an indifferent measure of discrimination among large numbers of S+s and S–s, as in the present research. For example, a bird could achieve a high discrimination ratio without mastering the perceptual task by responding to only a few of the many S+ tones and by responding little to other S+ and S– tones. To provide a more useful measure of how many of the S+ tones were well discriminated from the S– tones (i.e., how well a bird performed in the perceptual task), we followed Weisman et al. (1994) in adapting the two-tailed 95% confidence interval (CI) from sampling statistics (Sokal & Rohlf, 1981). In this adaptation, the 95% CI was calculated from the mean (*M*) and standard deviation (*SD*) of the percentages of response to the S– tones during the final 1,000 trials of training. In the absence of a true difference between responding to an individual S+ tone and responding across the distribution of S– tones, the response to 19 of 20 S+ tones should be included in the 95% CI (equals $M \pm 1.96$ *SD*s) of the S– tones (Sokal & Rohlf, 1981). In other words, when responding to an individual S+ tone exceeds the 95% CI for the S– tones, there is statistical evidence that the S+ tone was well discriminated. Figure 4.6 shows the number of S+ tones with percentages of response >1.96 *SD*s above the mean percentage of response to the 20 S– tones. Female zebra finches and female white-throated sparrows discriminated similar and large numbers of S+ tones. In a separate comparison, each male zebra finch and each male budgerigar discriminated all 20 S+ tones.

Conclusions Taken together, the percentages of responses and the number of S+ tones >95% CI (see figures 4.5 and 4.6) suggest that female oscines may be biased against responding to higher-frequency S+ tones but they discriminate eight frequency ranges about as well as male

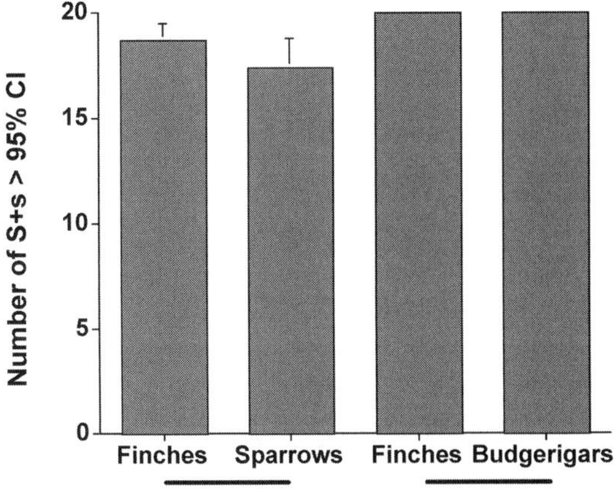

Figure 4.6. The number of S+ tones for which the percentage of responses was more than 1.96 *SD*s (the 95% confidence interval) above the mean percentage of responses to the 20 S– tones during the final 1,000 trials of the eight-range test of AP in female zebra finches and white-throated sparrows in one comparison and male zebra finches and budgerigars in a second comparison. A perfect sorter would score 20 S+s >1.96 CI. Female finches and sparrows responded similarly and accurately. Male finches and budgerigars discriminated all 20 S+s >95% CI.

oscines and budgerigars. Clearly, the most interesting finding is highly accurate AP for both songbirds (oscine passeriform) and parrots (psittaciformes) in these challenging eight-frequency-range discriminations.

The generality of accurate AP across oscines and parrots prompts us to propose further investigations of AP across a wider range of avian species. That oscines (Baptista, 1996) and parrots (Farabaugh & Dooling, 1996) learn their vocalizations may be a limitation on the generality of highly accurate AP among avian species. Whether only avian species that learn their vocalizations or whether all birds have accurate AP is a question for future research.

Absolute Pitch and Experience

In oscines, experience with male conspecifics is critical to the development of normal song (Baptista, 1996). Males reared in isolation from adult males and their songs sing only aberrant songs (Volman & Khanna, 1995). In two studies, we have determined that isolate rearing also impairs the development of RP and AP (Njegovan & Weisman, 1995; Sturdy, Phillmore, Sartor, & Weisman, 2001). We present a summary of comparisons between normally reared and isolate reared male and female zebra finches in the S+ first version of the eight-range AP task in figure 4.7 (see Sturdy et al., 2001). The new finding here was that isolate males and females showed an exaggerated version of the pattern of responding shown by normal females (i.e., fewer responses to tones in the higher frequency S+ regions). In other words, the primary effect of isolation from adult males may have been to feminize male isolate AP.

Discrimination of S+ From S– Tones As in the study of AP across avian species, we used the number of S+ tones >95% CI as a measure of the discriminability of S+ tone ranges. Figure 4.8 shows the mean number (of 20) of S+ tones with percentages of response higher than 1.96 *SD*s above the mean percentage of response for the 20 S– tones. Normally reared males and females discriminated 20 and 19 S+ tones, respectively; isolate reared males and females discriminated significantly fewer, but still sizable numbers of S+s: 15 and 14 tones, respectively.

Conclusions We found differences between the eight-range discriminations of male and female zebra finches. Males responded much more to tones in the higher three S+ frequency ranges and slightly more to tones in the lower three S– frequency ranges than normal females. Isolate males and females showed an exaggerated version of the pattern of responding shown by normal females. Not all of these changes in the pattern of responding over frequency ranges signaled poorer AP. Normal females responded less to higher frequency S+ tones but discriminated these tones as about well as males. Isolate males and females responded still less to higher frequency S+ tones; that decrease in responding did signal significantly reduced AP in isolates. Although isolates had reduced AP relative to normally reared songbirds, even isolate zebra finches had much more accurate AP than humans in sorting the 40 tones into eight ranges.

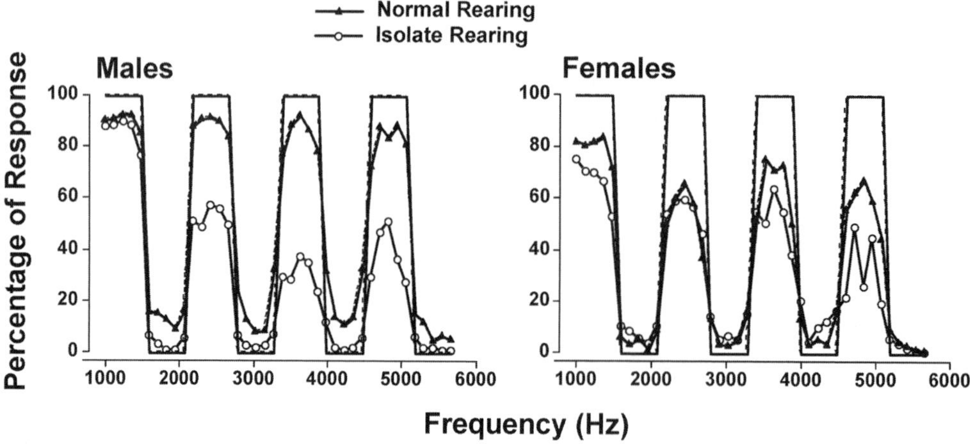

Figure 4.7. Mean percentages of response by normally reared and isolate reared, male and female zebra finches in the eight-range task. The dashed line shows the ideal performance of a perfect sorter responding at 100% to all tones in the S+ ranges and at 0% to all tones in the S– ranges. Normally reared females and isolate males and females responded less than normally reared males to tones in the higher S+ frequency ranges.

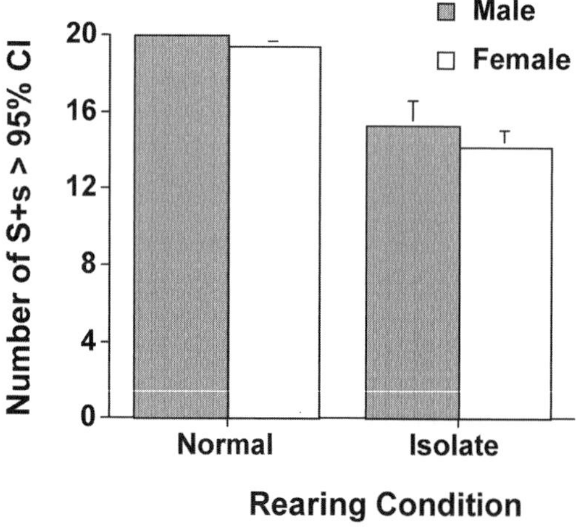

Figure 4.8. The number of S+ tones for which the percentage of responses was more than 1.96 *SD*s (the 95% confidence interval) above the mean percentage of responses to the 20 S– tones during the final 1,000 trials of the eight-range test of AP in male and female normally reared and isolate reared zebra finches. A perfect sorter would score 20 S+s >1.96 CIs. Isolate birds discriminated fewer S+ tones than normally reared zebra finches.

RESOLVING METHODOLOGICAL ISSUES IN COMPARATIVE COGNITION

We need to consider the possibility that our AP comparisons between humans and zebra finches are the product of an inappropriate methodology. For example, we trained with sine wave (pure) tones. Should we have instead trained with complex, harmonic-laden tones? Early in the study of musical AP, researchers tested with complex piano tones, but Abraham (1901, as cited by Ward, 1999) pointed out the confounding effects of timbre differences, inharmonic partials, and myriad other extraneous cues present in piano notes as well as notes from other musical instruments (for the confirming evidence, see Miyazaki, 1988). Ward (1999) derisively labeled experiments with complex tones tests of absolute piano, rather than tests of AP. Here, we chose to avoid complex acoustic cues that might complicate the study of pitch memory in AP.

Our findings rule out strong AP in rats to at least 5 kHz. Humans hear and produce frequencies in communication to at least 6 kHz, and songbirds hear and produce songs and calls to at least 7 kHz (e.g., Okanoya & Dooling, 1987). Remarkably, rats have a range of hearing from 250 Hz to beyond 40 kHz at 70 dB (Kelly & Masterton, 1977). We chose to make comparisons at frequencies more relevant to songbird and human than to rat communication. In favor of this choice, (a) it unlikely that humans can extract pitch information from frequencies over 6 kHz (Ward & Burns, 1982). (b) Rats do hear and discriminate sine wave tones (Kelly & Masterton, 1977) and conspecific infant separation calls (Michelsson, Christensson, Rothganger, & Winberg, 1996) in the spectral regions where we have tested AP in humans and songbirds.

The auditory memories of rats and other mammals should be studied further. For example, we propose studies of AP using some of the higher frequencies rats produce in communication (see Knutson, Burgdorf, & Panksepp, 2002; White & Barfield, 1987). Also, testing in other mammalian orders will help us determine whether, and then perhaps why, weak AP is general among mammals.

We suggest that comparative research with widely separated species is a useful, even exciting, companion to research with closely related species. However, caution is necessary in comparisons among distantly related species because of differences in responsiveness and motivation. Also, differences in apparatus and procedure between tests in distantly related species are often unavoidable. For example, songbirds can fly from a perch to a feeder, whereas humans have no wings. By contrast, humans can push buttons with their fingers to hear tones, but songbirds have no fingers. A comparative psychology dependent on rote similarity between the responses and rewards used in contrasts among species would hardly be worth the effort. In our experiments, button pushing and flying are comparable responses and pure tones are comparable stimuli across species, because in independent tests, termed positive controls, humans pressing buttons for monetary reinforcers and songbirds flying to feeders for food reinforcers are similar at sorting sine wave tones by temporal duration (Weisman et al., 1999) and sine wave tone pairs by relative pitch (Weisman et al., 1994). Hence, it is perfectly clear that humans and songbirds can hear and discriminate quantitative aspects of pure tones using button pushing and flight, respectively, as responses, because they do so in independent tests. Equally important, in the present tests of AP, humans and rats were able (but less able than songbirds) to sort pure tones in the three-range discrimination.

WHAT DOES AVIAN AUDITORY PSYCHOPHYSICS TELLS US ABOUT AVIAN ABSOLUTE PITCH?

Science is most often cumulative. One might have thought that comparative data on songbird and parrot hearing (e.g., Okanoya & Dooling, 1987) would have helped researchers to predict the vast superiority of these avian species over humans in their AP abilities. AP appears to be critical to the everyday recognition of oscine and parrot vocalizations by conspecifics, so surely research on the psychophysics of auditory perception should have alerted us to important differences between mammalian and avian auditory perception. Unfortunately, over 20 years of avian auditory psychophysics research (see Dooling, Lohr, & Dent, 2000) has proved to be of little value in predicting or explaining the results of bioacoustics research, playback experiments in the field, or the results of comparative laboratory studies of AP.

For example, painstaking research on Weber fractions for pitch change revealed that songbirds detect about a 1% change in pitch (Dooling et al., 2000), whereas it is well known that humans can detect perhaps a 0.25% pitch change. These findings could lead one to the mistaken conclusion that humans are better AP perceivers than songbirds when, in fact, just the opposite is true.

ABSOLUTE PITCH AND CONTINUITY OF THE SPECIES

The science of comparative psychology owes its first claim to scientific legitimacy to Charles Darwin. We modernize Darwin's famous claim from *The Descent of Man* (1874): Everyone who accepts the principle of evolution must see that the mental powers of higher animals are the same in kind as those of humans but differ only in degree. Darwin provided a rough scale for differences among species in mental abilities, when he concluded that there is a greater difference in degree of mental powers between one of the species of lower fishes and one of the species of higher apes than between an ape and a human. Clearly, these are the hypotheses that launched our science.

Evidence in support of Darwin's hypotheses has accumulated (as in the chapters of this book) for over 125 years. Still, it has always been difficult to provide clear, demonstrable examples in support of Darwin's (1874) concept of the continuity of mental abilities across species.

Here, in the study of AP, we have discovered some wonderful examples of continuity. Viewing the results of the eight-range discrimination task (see figure 4.4) on their own, it is difficult to imagine continuity between the paltry general AP of humans and the superior AP of songbirds. Gifted and expert, the songbirds appear to have evolved on another planet from the struggling humans. It is only by viewing the results from the eight-range task in the context of the results from the three-range tasks (see figures 4.2 and 4.3) that continuity emerges: Oscine and mammalian AP differ not in kind but only in degree.

Darwin, again in *The Descent of Man* (1874), observed that humans and songbirds share an instinct to learn their vocalizations. He compared the first attempts of young male songbirds to sing with the first attempts of human infants to babble; he observed that songbirds and humans continue to practice and learn their vocalizations during development. Today, we would describe the evolution of communication in humans and songbirds as convergent (in vocal learning and auditory perception). From the evidence presented here, it seems clear that the main perceptual bases of the communication systems of songbirds and humans differ: The amazing AP perception of songbirds is high in importance to the development of song, whereas the poorer AP of humans is lower in importance to the development of language and music.

Comparative psychologists and animal behaviorists subscribe to the continuity of mental abilities over species. In their rebellion against behaviorism, modern cognitive psychologists, in contrast, have concocted a litany of discontinuities in favor of human mental powers over those of other species. In an especially relevant example, musical AP was taken to be a superiority of a few gifted musicians over other humans and certainly over other species. We have shown here that superiority in the pitch memory that underlies AP belongs not to musicians but to species that have not shared a common ancestor with humans for about 150 million years. We believe that our results are a telling argument in favor of the comparative approach. No research program based on a single species or even a single group of related species could have uncovered the continuities we have observed in AP.

Acknowledgments This research was supported by grants from the Natural Science and Engineering Council of Canada to Ronald Weisman, Jerome Cohen, and Christopher Sturdy. We thank Laura-Lee Balkwill and Joseph Tramblay for their assistance with the manuscript.

We dedicate this chapter to Jack King, zoologist and animal behaviorist, in his 82nd year. Some 40 years ago at Michigan State University, Professor King was the first author's teacher and mentor in the comparative method.

References

Bakan, R. J. (1987). *Clinical measurement of speech and voice.* New York: Little, Brown.

Ball, G. F., & Hulse, S. H. (1998). Birdsong. *American Psychologist, 53*, 37–58.

Baptista, L. F. (1996). Nature and its nurturing in avian vocal development. In D. E. Kroodsma & E. H. Miller (Eds.), *Ecology and evolution of acoustic communication in birds* (pp. 39–60). Ithaca, NY: Cornell University Press.

Bonnel, A., Mottron, L., Peretz, I., Trudel, M., Gallun, E., & Bonnel, A. (2003). Enhanced pitch sensitivity in individuals with autism: A signal detection analysis. *Journal of Cognitive Neuroscience, 15*, 226–235.

Brooks, R. J., & Falls, J. B. (1975). Individual recognition by song in white-throated sparrows: III. Song features used in individual recognition. *Canadian Journal of Zoology, 53*, 1749–1761.

Church, R. M., & Gibbon, J. (1982). Temporal generalization. *Journal of Experimental Psychology: Animal Behavior Processes, 8*, 165–186.

D'Amato, M. R., & Salmon, D. P. (1982). Tune discrimination in monkeys (*Cebus apella*) and in rats. *Animal Learning & Behavior, 10*, 126–134.

D'Amato, M. R., & Salmon, D. P. (1984). Processing of complex auditory stimuli (tunes) by rats and monkeys (*Cebus apella*). *Animal Learning & Behavior, 12*, 184–194.

Darwin, C. (1874). *The descent of man; and selection in relation to sex* (2nd ed.). Amherst, NY: Prometheus.

Deutsch, D., Henthorn, T., & Dolson, M. (1999). Absolute pitch is demonstrated in speakers of tone languages. *Journal of the Acoustical Society of America, 106*, 2264.

Dooling, R. J., Lohr, B., & Dent, M. L. (2000). Hearing in birds and reptiles. In R. J. Dooling, R. R. Fay, & A. N. Popper (Eds.), *Comparative hearing: Birds and reptiles* (pp. 308–359). New York: Springer-Verlag.

Falls, J. B. (1962). Properties of bird song eliciting responses from territorial males. *Proceedings of the XIII International Ornithological Congress, 13*, 259–271.

Farabaugh, S. E., & Dooling, R. J. (1996). Acoustic communication in parrots: Laboratory and field studies of budgerigars, *Melopsittacus undulatus*. In D. E. Kroodsma & E. H. Miller (Eds.), *Ecology and evolution of acoustic communication in birds* (pp. 97– 116). Ithaca, NY: Cornell University Press.

Fisher, R. A. (1930). *The genetical theory of natural selection*. Oxford: Clarendon.

Halpern, A. R. (1989). Memory for the absolute pitch of familiar songs. *Memory & Cognition, 17*, 572–581.

Hearst, E. (1987). Extinction reveals stimulus control: Latent learning of feature-negative discriminations in pigeons. *Journal of Experimental Psychology: Animal Behavior Processes, 13*, 52–64.

Hulse, S. H., Cynx, J., & Humpal, J. (1984). Absolute and relative pitch discrimination in serial pitch perception by birds. *Journal of Experimental Psychology: General, 113*, 38–54.

Hulse, S. H., Page, S. C., & Braaten, R. F. (1990). Frequency range size and the frequency range constraint in auditory perception by European starlings (*Sturnus vulgaris*). *Animal Learning & Behavior, 18*, 238–245.

Kelly, J. B., & Masterton, B. (1977). Auditory sensitivity of the albino rat. *Journal of Comparative and Physiological Psychology, 19*, 930–936.

Knutson, B., Burgdorf, J., & Panksepp, J. (2002). Ultrasonic vocalizations as indices of affective states in rats. *Psychological Bulletin, 128*, 961–977.

Krumhansl, C. L. (2000). Rhythm and pitch in music cognition. *Psychological Bulletin, 126*, 159–179.

Larsen, O. N., & Goller, F. (2002). Direct observation of syringeal muscle function in songbirds and a parrot. *Journal of Experimental Biology, 205*, 25–35.

Lenhoff, H. M., Perales, O., & Hickok, G. 2001. Absolute pitch in Williams syndrome. *Music Perception, 18*, 491–503.

Levitin, D. (1994). Absolute memory for musical pitch: Evidence from the production of learned melodies. *Perception & Psychophysics, 56*, 414–423.

MacDougall-Shackleton, S. A., & Hulse, S. H. (1996). Concurrent absolute and relative pitch processing by European starlings, (*Sturnus vulgaris*). *Journal of Comparative Psychology, 110*, 139–146.

Michelsson, K., Christensson, K., Rothganger, H., & Winberg, J. (1996). Crying in separated and non-separated newborns: Sound spectrographic analysis. *Acta Paediatratrics, 85*, 471–475.

Miyazaki, K. (1988). Musical pitch identification by absolute pitch possessors. *Perception & Psychophysics, 44*, 501–512.

Miyazaki, K. (1992). Perception of musical intervals by absolute pitch possessors. *Music Perception, 9*, 413–426.

Miyazaki, K. (1995). Perception of relative pitch with different references: Some absolute-pitch listeners can't tell musical interval names. *Perception & Psychophysics, 57*, 962–970.

Monroe, B. L., Jr., & Sibley, C. G. (1997). *A world checklist of birds*. New Haven,CT: Yale University Press.

Nelson, D. A. (1988). Feature weighting in species song recognition by the field sparrow, *Spizella pusilla*. *Behaviour, 106*, 158–181.

Nelson, D. A. (1989a). The importance of invariant and distinctive features in species recognition of bird song. *Condor, 91*, 120–130.

Nelson, D. A. (1989b). Song frequency as a cue for recognition of species and individuals in the field sparrow (*Spizella pusilla*). *Journal of Comparative Psychology, 103*, 171–176.

Njegovan, M., Ito, S., Mewhort, D., & Weisman, R. (1994). Classification of frequencies into ranges by songbirds and humans. *Journal of Experimental Psychology: Animal Behavior Processes, 21*, 33–42.

Njegovan, M., & Weisman, R. (1997). Pitch discrimination in field and isolation-reared black-capped chickadees (*Parus atricapillus*). *Journal of Comparative Psychology, 111*, 294–301.

Nowicki, S., Mitani, J. C., Nelson, D. A., & Marler, P. (1989). The communicative significance of tonality in birdsongs: Responses to songs produced in helium. *Bioacoustics, 2*, 35–46.

Okanoya, K., & Dooling, R. J. (1987). Hearing in passerine and psittacine birds: A comparative study of absolute and masked auditory thresholds. *Journal of Comparative Psychology, 101*, 7–15.

Profita, J., & Bidder, T. G. (1988). Perfect pitch. *American Journal of Medical Genetics, 29*, 763–771.

Rakowski, A. (1972). Direct comparison of absolute and relative pitch. In F. A. Bilsen (Ed.), *Symposium on hearing theory* (pp. 105–108). Eindhoven, the Netherlands: Instituut voor Perceptie Underzoek.

Sokal, R. R., & Rohlf, F. J. (1981). *Biometry*. New York: Freeman.

Sturdy, C. B., Phillmore, L. S., Sartor, J. J., & Weisman, R. G. (2001). Reduced social contact causes auditory perceptual deficits in zebra finches, *Taeniopygia guttata*. *Animal Behaviour, 62*, 1207–1218.

Takeuchi, A. H., & Hulse, S. H. (1993). Absolute pitch. *Psychological Bulletin, 113*, 345–361.

Volman, S. F., & Khanna, H. (1995). Convergence of untutored song in group-reared zebra finches (*Taeniopygia guttata*). *Journal of Comparative Psychology, 109,* 211–221.

Ward, W. D. (1963). Absolute pitch: Part II. *Sound, 2,* 33–41.

Ward, W. D. (1999). Absolute pitch. In D. Deutsch (Ed.), *The psychology of music* (pp. 265–298). New York: Academic Press.

Ward, W. D., & Burns, E. M. (1982). Absolute pitch. In D. Deutsch (Ed.), *The psychology of music* (pp. 431–451). New York: Academic Press.

Weisman, R., Brownlie, L., Olthof, A., Njegovan, M., Sturdy, C., & Newhort, D. (1999). Timing and classifying brief acoustic stimuli by songbirds and humans. *Journal of Experimental Psychology: Animal Behavior Processes, 25,* 139–152.

Weisman, R., Njegovan, M., & Ito, S. (1994). Frequency ratio discrimination by zebra finches (*Taeniopygia guttata*) and humans (*Homo sapiens*). *Journal of Comparative Psychology, 108,* 363–372.

Weisman, R., Njegovan, M., Sturdy, C., Phillmore, L., Coyle, J., & Mewhort, D. (1998). Frequency range discriminations: Special and general abilities in zebra finches (*Taeniopygia guttata*) and humans (*Homo sapiens*). *Journal of Comparative Psychology, 112,* 244–258.

Weisman, R. G., Njegovan, M. D., Williams, M. T., Cohen, J. S., & Sturdy, C. B. (2004). A behavior analysis of absolute pitch: Sex, experience, and species. *Behavioural Processes, 66,* 289–307.

White, N. R., & Barfield, R. J. (1987). Role of the ultrasonic vocalization of the female rat (*Rattus norvegicus*) in sexual behavior. *Journal of Comparative Psychology, 101,* 73–81.

II

ATTENTION AND SEARCH

5

Reaction-Time Explorations of Visual Perception, Attention, and Decision in Pigeons

DONALD S. BLOUGH

This chapter is about some of the perceptual and decision processes that guide pigeons through their interactions with the environment. To study such processes, my colleagues and I have used methods that are, on the whole, rather simple. Our pigeons work day after day on discrimination tasks too boring for humans to contemplate, producing reams of data that yield functional relations sufficiently detailed to support quantitative analysis. Some of the most interesting relations and analyses have come from experiments using response latencies, or reaction times (RTs), as their main behavioral measure; I have restricted this discussion to those experiments and results. Part of my purpose in doing so is to advertise the utility of RTs for explicating psychological processes in animals. This utility is evident in many studies of human perception and cognition; the experiments described here are sometimes similar to experiments with humans, and it is often informative to compare the results of the two.

RT is defined here as the duration of an interval beginning with the onset of a visual stimulus and ending with a pigeon's peck directed at that stimulus. In most of the experiments described here, the stimuli were small computer-generated forms that appeared on a display screen in an operant chamber. When pecks to such a target are followed by food, birds peck at the target with high probability and great persistence, even when food is delivered on fewer than 10% of the target presentations. This procedure makes possible experimental sessions of 1,000 or more trials, which yield enough data to define the frequency distributions of RTs that contribute to some of the more interesting results summarized later.

The RT measure has some useful properties that are not shared by other common behavioral measures. Perhaps the most important is that an RT must somehow reflect the duration of processes that generate a response; it may be possible to reason back from patterns of RTs to identify some characteristics of those underlying processes (Luce, 1986; Van Zandt, 2002). This inference is helped by the fact that a single response generates a quantity, not just a "count," and this quantity is more useful because time is both continuous and additive. Thus, for example, if two processes of durations A and B occur independently and sequentially, then their total elapsed time is A + B. This simple fact is the basis for a whole cottage industry in the area of human cognition, surfacing notably in models of processing in visual and memory search (cf. Sternberg, 1998); it also plays a role in the interpretation of some of the data described here.

As I mentioned, I and others in our laboratory have used RTs to help clarify some of the processes that control discriminative responding. To do so, we have manipulated several kinds of variables, which may be roughly sorted into those having to do with sensory, perception, attention, and incentive processes. The accounts of these manipulations build on one another to some extent, because analysis of one problem or set of variables often opens the way to a somewhat deeper and more detailed investigation of a related problem. From time to time, I also mention a link, actual or potential, between research with pigeons and related research with humans; each informs the other, whether the relevant findings are similar or different.

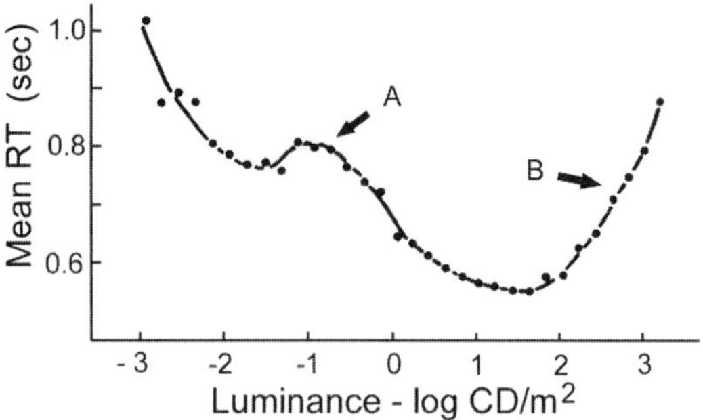

Figure 5.1. Reaction time (RT) as a function of stimulus luminance, averaged over three birds. The left cusp is presumed to reflect scotopic function, the right photopic. The rise at point A may indicate inhibitory rod-cone interaction; the rise to the right (B) is unexplained. See text. (Data from P. M. Blough & D. S. Blough, 1978.)

REACTION TIMES AND VISUAL PROCESSES

More than one may realize, the interpretation of an animal's behavior depends on understanding its sensory capacities and its unique perceptual skills. If we thought that a dog could discriminate colors as humans do, we might set it an impossible memory task; if we did not know it can hear things that we cannot, we might endow it with magical powers. Here, I summarize an experiment that may contribute to our understanding of the pigeon's visual system. In a small way, the experiment also illustrates that researchers interested in a specific process often choose to study a species in which that process is particularly evident or accessible.

The experiment measured the relationship between RT and the intensity of a stimulus light (P. M. Blough & D. S. Blough, 1978). This relationship attracted our attention largely because although sensory thresholds are relatively easy to measure in animals, psychophysical measures of suprathreshold sensory processes are relatively scarce. Magnitude estimates, for example, are not easy to extract from animals, but they might be replaced by an RT measure (e.g., Stebbins, 1966). In humans, RT generally decreases with increasing stimulus intensity (e.g., Cattell, 1886); we sought to quantify this relationship in pigeons. The results of our experiment were more complex than we expected and, because the effect of stimulus intensity is usually thought to occur early in the stream of perceptual processing, the results may reflect interesting and little-known interactions at the retinal level.

To explore the RT–intensity relation in pigeons, we used a standard operant chamber fitted with an external system that could project spots of white light onto the back of a response key. The chamber was dark, and the pigeons began their work after 45 min of dark adaptation. A stimulus spot appeared on a response key about every 20 s; single pecks to this spot were rewarded on an intermittent schedule. Spot luminance was randomized within each session, and luminance spanned different ranges in different sessions. The total intensity range covered a bit more than 6 log units; the least intense lights were visible only to a dark-adapted eye (D. S. Blough, 1956).

Some of the results of the experiment appear in figure 5.1, which shows the mean RTs of three birds. As intensity increased, starting from the dimmest lights at left, mean RT declined at first as expected, but then it rose somewhat at about −1 log Cd/m^2 (at point A in the figure), declined again, and then rose rapidly (figure 5.1, point B). In keeping with earlier threshold determinations (D. S. Blough, 1956) and RT observations in humans, we suggested that the pigeon's scotopic (rod) system determined RTs to the left of point A, whereas the photopic (cone) system determined the RTs to the brighter lights to the right.

If our idea of the contributions of scotopic and photopic systems is correct, then the curious rise in RTs at point A in figure 5.1 may occur where the two systems are about equally sensitive. This observation discloses in a new way, at suprathreshold intensities, a phenomenon that had earlier been found to occur at the absolute threshold (D. S. Blough, 1958). In both cases, the rise suggests an inhibitory interaction between rod and cone systems. This finding may apply to humans as well. After I observed the effect in pigeon threshold data, the phenomenon was discovered in humans, although it is considerably less obvious there (Jenness, 1993; Wooten & Butler, 1976). (Incidentally, this is the only case I know in which a visual phenomenon was first discovered through animal psychophysics and later confirmed in humans.) The steep rise in the RTs with bright lights (point B in figure 5.1) was also a surprise. This rise precludes any direct use of RT for magnitude estimation in pigeons, and its source remains to be determined, so far as I know. It could be a visual phenomenon, possibly involving an early stage in a light-adaptation mechanism or a startle reaction competing with the keypeck response.

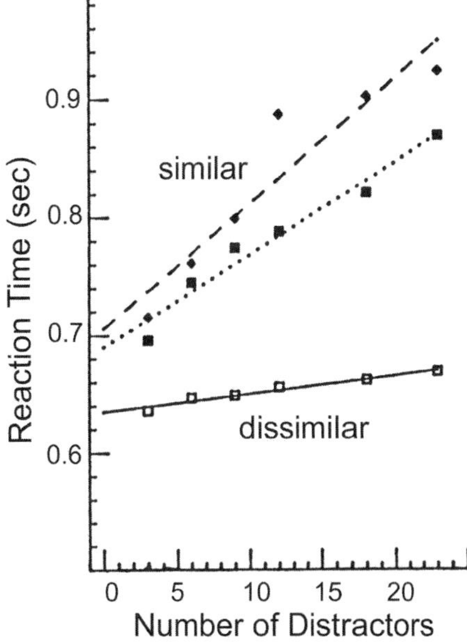

Figure 5.2. Reaction time (RT)/display-size functions showing the mean search RTs from six birds. The birds searched for a black triangle among either open squares (*bottom curve*), black squares (*middle curve*), or black diamonds (*top curve*). (Data from Blough & Blough, 1990.)

CONTRIBUTIONS FROM VISUAL SEARCH EXPERIMENTS

Visual search is a particularly attractive way to study discriminative processes. Those who study human perception and cognition have used search to answer a surprising variety of questions about perception, attention, and pattern recognition; to a growing extent, the same can be said for those working with animals. It is hard to avoid the impression that pigeons *like* to search, and, if so, we have pleased a great many birds in recent years. I next describe some of the results we have found.

In these studies, the pigeon subject viewed a computer monitor on which a small target form appeared briefly, usually in the midst of other small forms called distractors. Pecks to the target brought food on some percentage of trials. Over the many brief trials in an experimental session, the target varied in location; an infrared detector system enabled the computer to determine the location of the peck and the time between display onset and the first peck to the screen, which defined the search RT.

Reaction Time/Display-Size Functions

Certain basic data provide a foundation for a good deal of other research that uses the search method. Among these are data that describe the effect of two variables, both of which are involved in many search tasks and have a powerful effect on search speed. The first variable is "display size": In a scene or display containing many objects, finding a specific target takes longer the more irrelevant items ("distractors") are present. The second variable is similarity: A search takes longer the more similar the target is to the distractors. The impact of these variables is typically displayed as a graph of mean search RT plotted as a function of display size, with separate functions for different target-distractor similarities.

Figure 5.2 shows RT/display-size functions produced by pigeons searching among simple forms. In this case, the target was a black triangle that appeared in a random location. Background distractors were scattered across the display in such a way that the total area to be searched was unaffected by the number of visible items. Within a given display, all of the distractors were the same, but on some trials they were open squares; on others, black squares; and on still others, black diamonds. One can see that two of the three curves in figure 5.2 rise steeply with number of distractors, whereas the third function is almost horizontal. This pattern illustrates the finding that the similarity of the target to its surrounding distractors modifies the RT/display-size relationship. The slope of this function rises as target–distractor similarity increases; in this case, open squares represent low similarity, black squares represent intermediate similarity, and black diamonds represent high similarity of the distractors to the black triangle target.

A horizontal display-size function is most likely when the target differs in a striking way from the distractors, for example, a red target among green distractors. In this case, the target is said to have a "distinctive feature"; the lowest curve in figure 5.2 (a black target among white distractors) comes close to this condition. Viewing such a display, a human subject has the impression that true search is unnecessary because the target "pops out" from the background of distractors. To account for this pop-out phenomenon, theorists have suggested that, for such a distinctive target, the visual scene can be processed all at once, in parallel (e.g., Treisman & Gelade, 1980). If, instead, the target and distractors are more similar, then the rising display-size function suggests serial processing, that is, a search carried out by looking at the distractors one at a time until the target is found. The more similar the target is to the distractors, the more time that must be taken with each item, so the curve rises more steeply with increasing similarity.

Modern research with humans suggests that the perceptual events involved in search are more complicated than the simple dichotomy between serial and parallel processing just described (e.g., Wolfe, 1998). Nonetheless, it is interesting to find that these fundamental functions with pigeons are hardly distinguishable from those with humans (e.g., D. S. Blough, 1979; P. M. Blough, 1989, 1991; D.S. Blough & P. M. Blough, 1997). As in research with humans, these functions merit further analysis, which is exemplified in the next sections of this chapter.

Search Asymmetry

As just described, when one changes the similarity of a target to other items within view or the number of items on display, one finds that search speed in pigeons varies in much the same way as it does in humans. These relationships have been the starting point for a number of lines of research that explore the nature of recognition and attention. One of these concerns the definition of "features" as distinctive aspects of forms and the role of features in the identification of objects. The following study examined this matter in pigeons; it also provides an instance in which data from pigeon subjects may cause us to reexamine the meaning of data from experiments with humans.

The phenomenon of interest here is related to observations of "pop out" in search. As I suggested, when a search target is distinguished from distractors by a distinctive feature, the RT/display-size function is relatively flat—the target "pops out." But, what is a "distinctive feature"? The answer to this question may seem obvious to a viewer but it eludes a strict expression. One way to approach the question is to reverse the statement that a distinctive feature causes a target to pop out; one can say, instead, that if a target pops out, then it contains a distinctive feature. More formally, by this definition, a target is said to contain a distinctive feature if, on a given background, its display-size function is relatively flat. This idea came in part from the theoretical notion of parallel processing; because a flat display-size function suggests that the pattern recognition system is looking everywhere at once, it may have "feature detectors" spread across the visual field that support pop out of the target.

The phenomenon of search asymmetry shows how these ideas can be rather neatly tested. In the typical experiment on search asymmetry, subjects look for a target hidden somewhere in a field of identical distractors. This target is made to differ from the distractors in a well-defined way, by either the presence or absence of a putative feature. In a common example, an "O" serves as the basic form, and a tail, which turns the form into a "Q," serves as the part to be tested as a distinctive feature. On some trials, the subject tries to find a target "Q" on a field of "Os"; on other trials, the target is an "O" on a field of "Qs." If the target contains a feature that is absent from the distractors, then it will tend to pop out and yield a flat display-size function. However, if the distractors have the feature and the target does not, then no pop out occurs and the display-size function increases with the number of distractors in the background. This difference in RT/display-size functions defines a "search asymmetry." In the case of O and Q, the function is flat (in humans) when Q is displayed on a field of Os, but it rises when O is displayed on Qs. This asymmetry marks the tail as a distinctive feature.

Susan Allan and I (Allan & Blough, 1989) explored possible search asymmetries in the pigeon's perception of simple forms and compared the

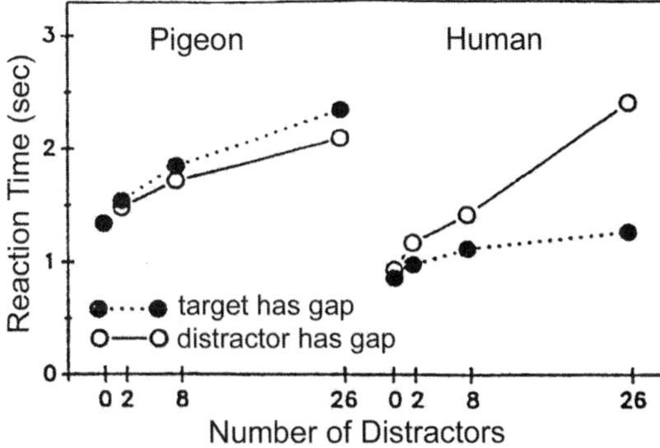

Figure 5.3. Results of comparable search asymmetry tests with pigeons and humans. In this example, a target triangle contained a gap and the distractors were complete triangles or vice versa. Note that the asymmetry for pigeons, such as it is, is in the opposite direction from that for humans. (From "Form Perception and Attention in Pigeons," by D. S. Blough and P. M. Blough, 1997, *Animal Learning and Behavior, 25*, figure 3. Copyright 1997 by The Psychonomic Society. Reprinted with permission.)

results with parallel tests on human participants. The tests used several form pairs, each of which differed in one aspect that was a likely candidate for "feature" status. Both members of each pair included a basic form, such as a triangle, which could be modified by the presence of a break, or gap, in the perimeter or by the presence or absence of a line segment laid across part of the form. Human participants yielded RT/display-size functions confirming our expectations: They produced strong asymmetries, with relatively flat display-size functions for targets containing the line or gap, and rising functions when the gap or line was carried by the distractors.

Pigeons tested for asymmetries with the same sets of forms gave quite different results. In their case, the display-size functions all had a considerable positive slope; these functions were similar whether the target or the distractors carried the gap or line. Figure 5.3 compares the results for pigeons and humans, using as an example the data from displays consisting of small triangles with or without a gap in the side. In the human data to the right, one can see the typical asymmetry result: a relatively flat function when the target contained the gap, but a relatively steep function when the distractors contained the gap. This difference is absent in the pigeon curves, which rise about equally for both configurations, with a small difference in the opposite direction.

There are several possible interpretations of this difference between the asymmetry data of pigeons and humans. Assuming that the results from these few test forms reflect a consistent difference, we might tend to ascribe the disparity to species differences in perceptual processing. Bird brains are, after all, quite unlike human brains, and it has often been assumed that feature detectors are "prewired" into the form processing system. However, considerable evidence suggests extensive cross-species commonality in pattern perception, not least the very similar ways in which pigeons and humans classify small line forms, such as alphabetic letters, which are much like the forms used here (D. S. Blough, 1982, 1985).

As an alternative to a species difference, one might consider the possible role of experience in generating feature detectors. Perhaps features are not "prewired" after all but rather achieve a special status by virtue of the gigantic number of perceptual encounters animals (and humans) have had with their visual environments. In the experiment cited, the pigeons had a great deal of training with the forms that were tested; the humans had little training on these specific forms, but human overlearning of the not-too-dissimilar forms involved in reading might play an important role. Although some work on the matter has been done with human subjects (e.g., Treisman, Vieira, & Hayes, 1992), the role of experience remains largely unresolved. Because relevant perceptual experience is hard to control in humans, further progress on this matter might come from research with pigeons and other animals in which perceptual experience can be controlled prior to experimental tests.

Attention, Expectation, and Search Reaction Times

Neither humans nor animals respond to all aspects of their environment at once; a species that failed to attend to stimuli crucial for survival would probably not be here for us to study. Such attentional focus is guided by distinctive cues and other aspects of the visual scene; in fact, attentional guidance by stimulus factors is one way to interpret the RT/display-size and search asymmetry functions discussed earlier. But other, less-immediate variables also control attention. In particular, a searcher

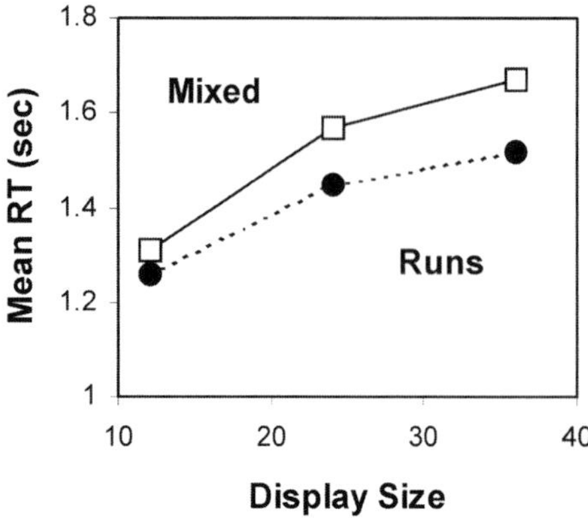

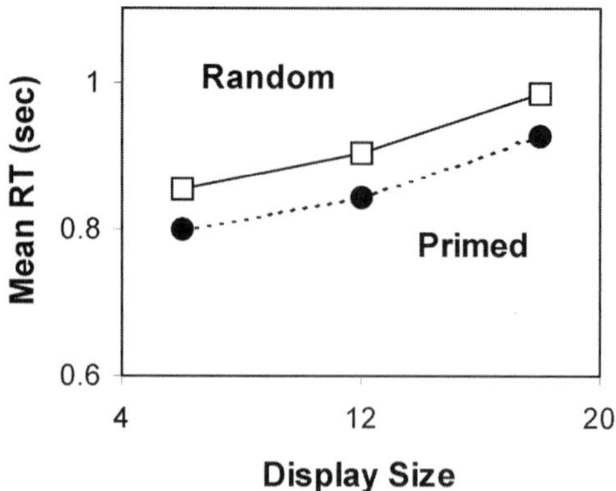

Figure 5.4. Reaction time (RT)/display-size functions showing the facilitating effects of two sources of information on the detection of a target letter. *Left,* In the "runs" condition, the target was signaled by a preceding series of trials with the same target, whereas in the "mixed" condition, the targets appeared randomly. (Data from P. M. Blough, 1991.) *Right,* In the "primed" condition, each target was signaled by preceding the search display with a unique colored frame, whereas in the "random" condition, the frame color was uncorrelated with the subsequent target. (Data from P. M. Blough, 1989, Experiment 1.)

is often influenced by advance information as to what object might, or might not, appear at a given time. Tinbergen (1960) initiated much of the research on this question in animals when he reported that birds tend to overselect abundant prey items in patches where they are concealed. Tinbergen attributed this overselection to a "search-image" induced by repeated encounters with the abundant item. Pietrewicz and Kamil (e.g., 1979), Bond (1983), and others developed an attentional account of the search-image, which has been followed up in our laboratory by P. M. Blough (e.g., 1989, 1991).

It is useful to distinguish two sources of prior information that may lead a searcher to expect the appearance of a particular target. In line with Tinbergen's observations, one of these sources is the recent repeated or frequent appearance of the target that is about to appear. Pietrewicz and Kamil (1979) experimentally confirmed the effect of this variable in blue jays by showing that repeated exposure to images of a single variety of moth enhanced the blue jay's detection of that variety.

P. M. Blough tested the same phenomenon using computer-generated search displays with letters of the alphabet as targets (1991). She found that pigeons' search RTs were shorter after a run of trials with the same target letter than during equivalent sequences in which alternative targets appeared in random order. Figure 5.4 (left) displays this effect as a pair of RT/display-size functions. The targets were relatively difficult to detect, so RT rose with the number of items in the display, as we have already seen. More important here, mean RT was lower at each display size for targets appearing repeatedly in runs than it was for the same targets appearing unpredictably in mixed sequences.

Information about an upcoming target need not come from previous targets; instead, an upcoming target may be signaled by some other stimulus that has often preceded that target in the past. Such a signal is said to have a "priming effect" that facilitates search for the target. In one experiment that demonstrated this priming effect with pigeons (P. M. Blough, 1989), birds were trained to search for either the letter "A" or the letter "L" surrounded by distractors chosen at random from other alphabetic letters and numbers. For the primed condition, the border of the display screen signaled the upcoming target: White borders always preceded an "A" target and black borders always preceded an "L" target. For an unprimed control condition, a striped border preceded displays that contained, at random, either "A" or an "L." Figure 5.4 (right) shows the results of this priming test in the form of RT/display-size functions. It is clear that signaling the target reduced RT at the tested display sizes, relative to RTs from the ambiguous cue condition.

Thus, in pigeons as in humans, stimuli that predict which targets are likely to appear can facilitate visual search. It is interesting to note, by comparing figures 5.2 and 5.4, that the facilitation of search by such prior information is similar to the facilitation of search by a decrease in target–distractor similarity. A later experiment indicated that this correspondence extends to the effects of these variables on the shape of RT distributions (D. S. Blough, 2000). Thus, perhaps, expectancy makes a perceptual object stand out in the same way that a distinctive feature does. These results, together with other attentional data, motivated a further analysis of the search-image, which I summarize in the next section.

What "Is" the Search-Image?

We saw here that prior information about a target can speed target detection, whether the information comes from recent experiences with the target or from a signal that predicts a target. How is this facilitation accomplished? As I mentioned, it is sometimes said that prior information activates a "representation" or, especially in research with animals, a search-image of the target. These terms tempt us to conjure up a little picture in the head. I hope that we can resist that temptation, but we may harbor other hidden assumptions. One of these assumptions might be that each perceptual object has a unique mental representation that equally serves any cognitive function involving that object. More specifically, we might ask, If "expectation" implies an activated representation, is this representation the same as the one that underlies object recognition?

This seemingly difficult representation question may become more tractable if we observe that objects usually have perceptually separable aspects and that these might function differently in different cognitive tasks (e.g., D. S. Blough, 1989b; Tversky, 1977). Thus, we are led to restate our question as follows: Are the (assumed) representational aspects that guide detection of a primed target the same as those that guide recognition of the target?

A recent experiment of mine explored this question, with a view to separating the expectation and recognition functions of the hypothetical representation (D. S. Blough, 2002). I began from observations such as those described earlier here showing that pigeons, like humans, find expected objects more quickly than they do unexpected objects. This relationship was used to test the expectation function. I combined this notion with the idea that a generalization gradient may be used to measure "recognition," that is, the extent to which test items are perceived to match a preestablished internal representation (D. S. Blough, 2001). If the "expectation" of a particular target facilitated search to some other stimuli and these other stimuli were also "recognized" as similar according to a generalization test, then the same representation could be involved in both.

Two experiments implemented these ideas. One experiment tested to see how much a priming stimulus that facilitated detection of one target would facilitate detection of other test items. The other experiment tested ordinary stimulus generalization from the same target to the same set of test items. In both experiments, pigeons searched for gratings made of light and dark bars. There were eight such gratings, which differed in spatial frequency and orientation (figure 5.5). The search procedure was much like that described earlier, except that there were no distracting objects on the display screen. Instead, a single grating target appeared alone on every trial, but this target was so dim that it was barely visible; the average luminance of the bars was the same as the luminance of the background on which the target appeared.

Any one of the gratings might appear on any trial, but in the first experiment, a distinctive cue came on briefly just before the target appeared. This cue was used to control expectation. A bright green block preceded one particular grating, so it was a valid cue for this "primed target," but it was an invalid cue when it preceded any other target on rare probe trials. A nonpredictive black-and-white bull's-eye preceded all of the other targets, except, again, on rare probe trials. Different targets were chosen as the primed target for different groups of subjects, but the results are combined in the summary presented here. Pecks to all targets were reinforced equally, regardless of the preceding cue.

The main aim of this experiment was to compare RTs to targets following the nonpredictive bull's-eye cue with RTs to targets following the green block, which was a valid cue for the primed target and invalid otherwise. This comparison was summarized by the ratio of bull's-eye RTs to green block RTs for each target. If the green block speeded search, as would be expected for the primed target, then this ratio should be above 1.0. If the green block slowed search, as might happen when the green block was invalid, then the ratio should be below 1.0.

Figure 5.5. The set of grating targets used in the "search-image" experiment. During each search trial, one of these appeared at very low contrast somewhere on the display screen. Note the separable aspects of spatial frequency and orientation. (From "Measuring the Search Image: Expectation, Detection, and Recognition in Pigeon Visual Search," by D. S. Blough, 2002, *Journal of Experimental Psychology: Animal Behavior Processes, 28*, figure 1. Copyright 2002 by American Psychological Association. Reprinted with permission.)

Figure 5.6 (left) shows these ratios for each of the targets. On the abscissa is the distance of the test targets from the primed target in spatial frequency steps. The ratio for the primed target itself, at the top left, is well above 1.0, showing the expected facilitation effect. The graph also shows that facilitation generalized somewhat to targets of the same orientation just one spatial-frequency step away from the primed target. However, search speed was relatively slow to all gratings with an orientation at right angles to the orientation of the primed target, as shown by the lower curve in figure 5.6 (left).

At this point, one might think that generalization of the priming effect was governed, like ordinary generalization, by the relative similarity among the targets as seen by the bird. Thus, to a pigeon, targets that differ in orientation may be

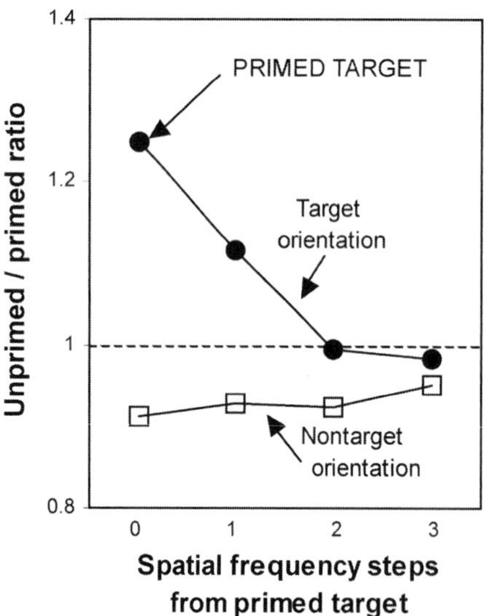

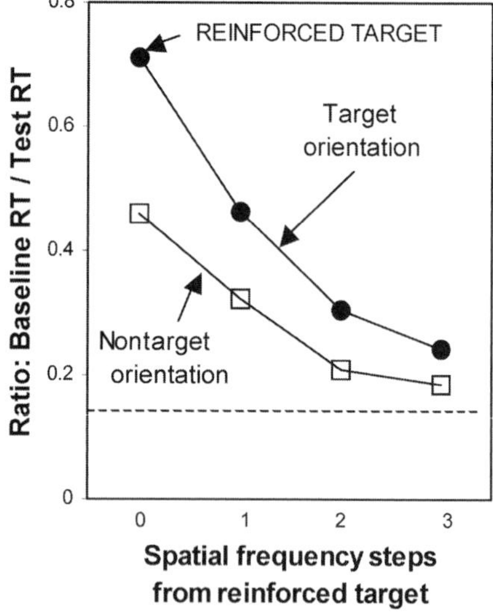

Figure 5.6. A comparison of generalization of priming and generalization of recognition in the "search-image" experiment. The targets were the gratings shown in figure 5.5. *Left*, A signal correlated with the target facilitated search to that target and, to some degree, gratings of the same orientation (*upper curve*), but not gratings differing 90 degrees in orientation (*lower curve*). *Right*, Responding generalized to gratings similar to the reinforced target in either spatial frequency or in orientation. In comparing the left and right panels, notice especially the position of the leftmost point in the lower function. (From "Measuring the Search Image: Expectation, Detection, and Recognition in Pigeon Visual Search," by D. S. Blough, 2002, *Journal of Experimental Psychology: Animal Behavior Processes, 28*, figure 4. Copyright 2002 by American Psychological Association. Reprinted with permission.)

quite dissimilar to each other; that is why priming failed to generalize between orientations. This interpretation is essentially the same as the idea that the functional representation for priming is the same as that for recognition. To see if this was the case, the second experiment tested intertarget similarity in a more direct and familiar way, by generalization from a reinforced stimulus.

This second experiment used much the same procedure as the first, except that the predisplay cues were omitted. The same eight gratings, equally dim, appeared in random sequence, first during baseline sessions in which all received equal reinforcement and then in test sessions in which only one was followed by reinforcement. The reinforced target was the one that had been the primed target in the first experiment; no other reinforcement was delivered. This procedure continued for each bird until responding to the nonreinforced targets had fallen enough to generate a gradient of response to the several stimuli.

Figure 5.6 (right) shows the response gradients to the stimuli in the second experiment. The data are normalized by using as a response measure the ratio of RTs during baseline to RTs during the test. (Failure to respond was counted as a 10-s RT, the maximum trial length. This score set the lower asymptote of these curves.) The key thing to notice here is the manner in which generalization of the effect of expecting a certain target (figure 5.6, left) differs from the ordinary generalization gradient that presumably reflects the similarity of the targets to the reinforced target (figure 5.6, right). The difference is particularly evident in the position of the leftmost point in each of the lower curves, which represents the relative speed of response to the target with the same spatial frequency as the primed or reinforced target but of different orientation. The height of this point in the data from the second experiment (figure 5.6, right) suggests that it represents one of the two targets that are most similar to the reinforced target. However, the same point from the first experiment (figure 5.6, left) is so low that it represents the target most differently affected by the priming cue, compared with the primed target.

What do these results tell us about the nature of the search-image? They suggest that the information about orientation carried by the search-image was crucial to its role in facilitating target detection, with spatial frequency playing a lesser role. In contrast, the generalization results of Experiment 2 display a more equal contribution of orientation and spatial frequency to recognition of the reinforced target. This finding might serve to redirect our thinking about the nature of the attentional priming process. Perhaps the notion of search-image, which suggests a representation of the appearance of the object as a whole, is less useful than the older metaphor of attentional "tuning," here suggesting a sensitization to aspects of a target that are most helpful to detecting that target under particular circumstances. Indeed, the notion that separate features have distinct effects was evident in the account of search asymmetry above; it plays a key role in the attentional theories that have grown up around the human visual search literature (e.g. Treisman & Gelade, 1980).

WHAT REACTION TIME DISTRIBUTIONS SHOW ABOUT DISCRIMINATIVE PROCESSES

Researchers almost always present RT measurements as averages, but such summary statistics often conceal information that deserves further study. Indeed, frequency distributions of RTs have revealed significant aspects of discriminative processing that are not visible in mean RTs or in other measures such as response probability. A fruitful tactic in this sort of analysis has been to find mathematical functions that closely mimic RT distributions, in particular, functions with parameters that can be linked in a reasonable way to hypotheses about the underlying mental processes. That tactic was also followed in most of the research I summarize here. The results have suggested some interesting things about what is going on in a pigeon's head when it makes a discriminative response; they also exemplify the way in which the relative shapes of RT distributions may help us characterize these controlling processes.

Some of the data shown here came from straightforward discrimination procedures in which only a single target appeared on any trial, but there were several potential targets differing in their association with reinforcement. Other data came from experiments that used the search procedure described above, in which a target appeared on a field of distractors and pecks to the target were reinforced. In either case, frequency distributions were constructed by sorting RTs according to their eliciting stimuli and then sorting them again by length into bins of 0.1-s duration or less.

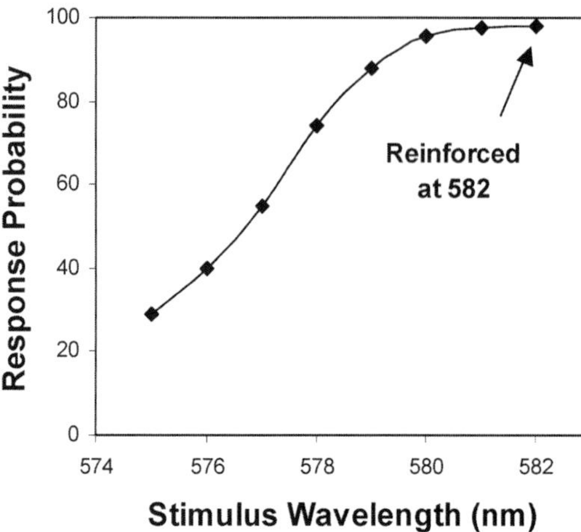

Figure 5.7. Results of a trialwise successive wavelength discrimination in one bird. Only responses to 582 nm were reinforced. (Data from D. S. Blough, 1978.)

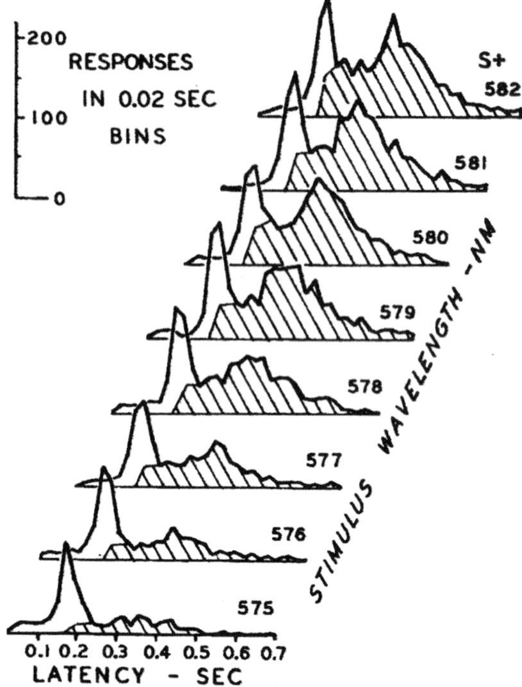

Figure 5.8. The data displayed in figure 5.7 are here distributed by reaction time (RT). There are two kinds of responses: rapid ones controlled only by stimulus onset (white peak to the left) and slower ones controlled by stimulus wavelength. Note, however, that wavelength affects only the probability of the latter responses, not the shape of their RT distributions (see text). (From "Reaction Times of Pigeons on a Wavelength Discrimination Task," by D. S. Blough, 1978, *Journal of the Experimental Analysis of Behavior, 30*, p. 167. Copyright 1978 by *Journal of the Experimental Analysis of Behavior*. Reprinted with permission.)

Reaction Time Distributions and Control by Stimulus Onset

What can RT distributions can tell us about the nature of a stimulus discrimination that response probabilities cannot? An answer to this question is illustrated by the results of an experiment on wavelength discrimination in pigeons (D. S. Blough, 1978). In that study, different wavelengths of light were projected on the pigeon's response key, one on each of many brief trials. A number of slightly different wavelengths appeared in random order. Pecks at only one wavelength, 582 nm, yielded reinforcement, so, after prolonged training, the birds responded to 582 nm on almost every trial and less often for wavelengths differing from that value.

If we look at the probability with which the pigeons responded to the various wavelengths, we see the expected gradient of discriminative control. Figure 5.7 shows this gradient for one bird; it peaks near 100% at the reinforced wavelength and falls to about 24% at the most extreme wavelength. There seems to be nothing unusual about this result. If asked why the function does not fall closer to zero at the lowest wavelength, one would probably reply that the wavelength range was insufficient: The bird was simply unable to discriminate wavelengths more accurately over this narrow range.

However, this reduction of the data to response probabilities yields a misleading picture; RT distributions tell a different story. Figure 5.8 shows an RT distribution corresponding to each point in the gradient of figure 5.7. It seems clear that the distributions have two separate parts: (1) an early peak that changes little with wavelength and (2) a broad later distribution that maintains an approximately constant shape, but that rises as wavelength approaches the reinforced value. The second distribution is shaded to highlight this difference.

This pattern of RT distributions across wavelength strongly suggests two sources of stimulus control, which do not combine to control individual responses but rather exert their effects on different trials. It appears that, on some trials, responses were triggered by stimulus onset, giving the first RT peak. On these trials, it is as if the pigeon pecked as soon as it saw the stimulus, without waiting to decide whether it was the positive wavelength; such responses by humans have been called "fast guesses" (e.g., Luce, 1966). On the remaining trials, stimulus wavelength did control responding; in the shaded distributions of figure 5.8, there are many responses to the S+ and few to the stimuli most different from the S+. The shaded distributions are also interesting because wavelength affected the number of these responses but not their RTs, which were distributed about the same way at each wavelength. In short, stimulus onset controlled one class of responses, whereas wavelength controlled the number of responses in a second class; nevertheless, the mean RT within each response class was approximately constant.

This account exemplifies several contributions of RT distributions to an understanding of discriminative responding. First, they revealed a duality of stimulus control that was lost in data reduced to simple response probabilities. Second, they emphasized the idea that different aspects of a stimulus may control response on different occasions, even within the same procedure. This shifting control can be interpreted as shifting attention from one stimulus aspect to another; such shifts are seen in other contexts as well (e.g., D. S. Blough, 1993). Third, the distributions permitted a tentative identification of the controlling aspects: namely, stimulus onset and stimulus wavelength. Elsewhere, I discuss these aspects of the data in greater depth (D. S. Blough, 1978, 2004).

Finally, these data call attention to a crucial dichotomy among RT distributions. Those in figure 5.8 are heterogeneous; each is really two distributions mixed together, as far as the controlling variables are concerned. Were it not the case that the two classes of RTs are so different in length, interpreting these distributions would be extremely difficult, if not impossible. Because of this difficulty, one seeks procedures that yield homogeneous RT distributions, in which almost all responses are controlled by the same combination of factors. With such distributions, it may still be possible to distinguish the contribution of different variables, but in this case, the different variables combine to control each response, rather than controlling different responses. We next consider such a case.

Reaction Time Distributions and Control by Target-Distractor Similarity

Few issues in psychology can be addressed without mention of stimulus similarity, and this is especially true in the case of stimulus discrimination. We have already seen that visual search is an effective tool for studying discriminative processes, and data presented earlier here showed that the similarity between targets and distractors is reflected in the speed of search (figure 5.2). We next consider how RT distributions from search tasks contribute to a more detailed analysis of the similarity-speed relationship. In my experiments on this matter (D. S. Blough, 1988, 1989a, 2000), the procedure was like that described here, in which the searcher looks among many items for a target that is somewhat difficult to find, so that it is never so salient that it "pops out" from among the distractor items.

There are several ways that target-distractor similarity might work to affect search speed, but probably the most obvious hypothesis is that once a search display is in view, similarity affects the moment-to-moment probability of detecting the target. This hypothesis is open to test by way of a potential correspondence between an obtained distribution of search RTs and a particular probability density function, the exponential decay function. The equation for this distribution is $Pr(t) = exp(-\lambda t)$, where t is the length of the interval up until the time of an event and λ is the decay constant. An example of the exponential function appears in figure 5.9 (top).

The exponential is useful here because it describes the frequency of intervals that start at a fixed time and end randomly, with a constant probability of ending at any given moment. This seems an appropriate model of search for a randomly placed target that has a fixed probability of being found at any given moment. If so, then a change in the decay constant of the exponential would reflect a changed probability of finding a target, as might be caused by changing the similarity between target and distractors.

Although the exponential appears to be a plausible model for the search process, it is obviously not the whole story. The graph of the exponential in figure 5.9 does not resemble an RT distribution; its use alone does not allow for events, other than search itself, that intervene between stimulus onset

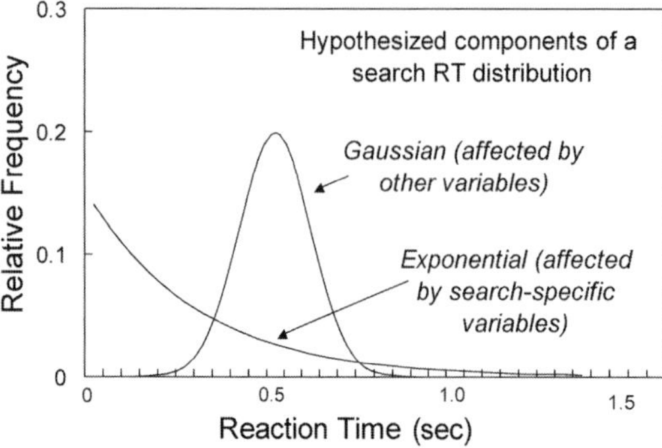

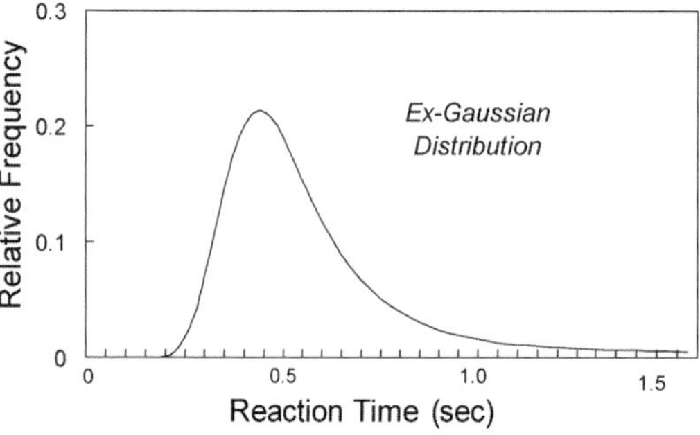

Figure 5.9. Mathematical functions that are useful in modeling search reaction times (RTs). *Top*, The exponential function may represent the distribution of times taken to find a randomly placed target. The normal (Gaussian) function may represent the sum of times taken by the other processes involved in making a discriminative response. *Bottom*, If each RT is the sum of two intervals, one from each the distributions in the *top panel*, the ex-Gaussian represents the resulting RT distribution; it is computed as the convolution of the exponential and the Gaussian distributions.

and response. This consideration suggests that a complete model of search should include at least two components: one for the search time just considered and the other for miscellaneous things such as neural transmission and motor response times. Here, I (and others, cf. Luce, 1986) have used the Gaussian, or normal, distribution to represent the sum of these other durations; figure 5.9 (top) shows an example of this familiar distribution.

We thus arrive at a mathematical representation of search RTs, which arises if each RT is the sum of two values drawn at random: one from the exponential distribution and the other from the Gaussian. The resulting distribution, dubbed the "ex-Gaussian," appears in figure 5.9 (bottom). Its specific form depends on three parameters: the decay constant of the exponential plus the mean and variance of the Gaussian. This function has been used extensively in modeling human RT distributions from sensory and cognitive tasks (cf. Luce, 1986; Van Zandt, 2002). Several visual search experiments have shown that the ex-Gaussian provides a very good fit of pigeon RT distributions (D. S. Blough, 1988, 1989, 1992).

We now return to the initial hypothesis: that target-distractor similarity affects search RT by controlling the momentary probability of target detection. The good fit of search RT distributions by the ex-Gaussian is not yet strong support for the hypothesis. Among other things, several mathematical functions unrelated to this hypothesis provide equally good fits (D. S. Blough, 2004; Luce, 1986; Van Zandt, 2002). A more convincing case for the stated hypothesis would tie RTs directly to the exponential decay constant that is supposed to represent detection probability.

Consideration of some experimental findings shows how this tie between the exponential constant and detection probability can be confirmed. In one experiment (D. S. Blough, 1988, Experiment 2), pigeons searched for a small target that differed only in size from the surrounding distractors. Three of the resulting RT distributions appear in figure 5.10. The size difference between the target and the distractors was small for the top distribution ("High T-D similarity") and was progressively larger for the other two distributions. The actual data are represented by points. The curves are fits of the ex-Gaussian to the points.

The treatment of the fitting parameters was most important: the same Gaussian parameters were used for all three data sets (and other sets not shown here), only the decay constant of the exponential was allowed to change. This finding provides rather strong support for the hypothesis that target-distractor similarity uniquely affected the momentary probability of target detection.

The rather straightforward result just described led to a more general statement of the relation between the probability of detecting a target and target-distractor similarity. Starting with RTs from a large number of target-distractor differences, I used multidimensional scaling to quantify the similarities between the stimuli and showed that RT declines as an exponential decay function of psychological distance, the inverse of

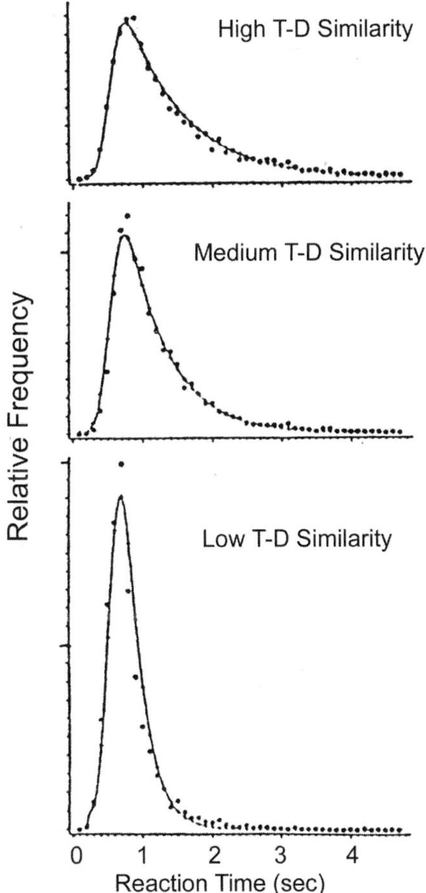

Figure 5.10. Reaction time (RT) distributions of responses emitted in a search task, with three different levels of similarity between the target (T) and the surrounding distractors (D). The points represent data from three pigeons; the lines are fits of these data by the ex-Gaussian depicted in figure 5.9. The same Gaussian parameters were used for all the fits; only the exponential decay constant changed from one to another. (Data from D. S. Blough, 1988.)

similarity. Because, as we just saw, RT is directly related to the probability of detecting a target, this finding leads to a more general statement: the probability of detecting a target increases as an exponential function of the psychological distance between a target and its surrounding distractors. The result is analogous, within its restricted domain, to the exponential relation between psychological distance and the probability of generalization between stimuli stated by Roger Shepard (cf. D. S. Blough, 1988; Shepard, 1987). The result may help guide the construction of process models of detection and recognition.

Reaction Time Distributions and Control by Incentive Value

Incentive seems to be quite a different sort of variable from the display and attentional variables considered earlier. The commonly accepted distinction between these sorts of variables is familiar from signal detection theory, which gives a recipe for separating the effects on response emission and choice of sensory variables, on the one hand, and decision variables, on the other hand (e.g., Green & Swets, 1966; Macmillan & Creelman, 1991). Our analysis thus far has looked into examples of the first class of variables. I now briefly discuss an RT analysis of an incentive effect, which presumably falls into the second class.

Two experiments were designed to determine the effect of incentive variation on RTs and to compare it with the better-known effects of similarity (D. S. Blough, 2004). In a trialwise go–no-go procedure, pigeons pecked at a small bright spot that appeared on many brief trials; the spot varied in hue. Incentive was manipulated by changing the percentage of trials on which a peck to particular target color yielded food reinforcement. Similarity was varied by changing the hue in small steps. The overall results were quite clear: Incentive affected RTs greatly and response probability very little, whereas similarity affected RTs very little and response probability greatly. The RT distributions changed little with similarity; they looked much like those in figure 5.8. However, changes in the RT distributions with incentive showed a new pattern that called for a new mathematical treatment. Having already considered similarity at length, I will limit the remaining discussion to these incentive-based data and their analysis.

Three RT distributions from the experiment just described appear in figure 5.11. The data points represent the average scores from six birds. Each curve came from a different reinforcement condition, which ranged from reinforcement on 100% of trials for the leftmost curve to 2.5% for the rightmost. At first glance, these curves look much like those in figure 5.10, which were based on different target-distractor similarities in search. This resemblance leads one to wonder whether the ex-Gaussian model that fit the data in figure 5.10

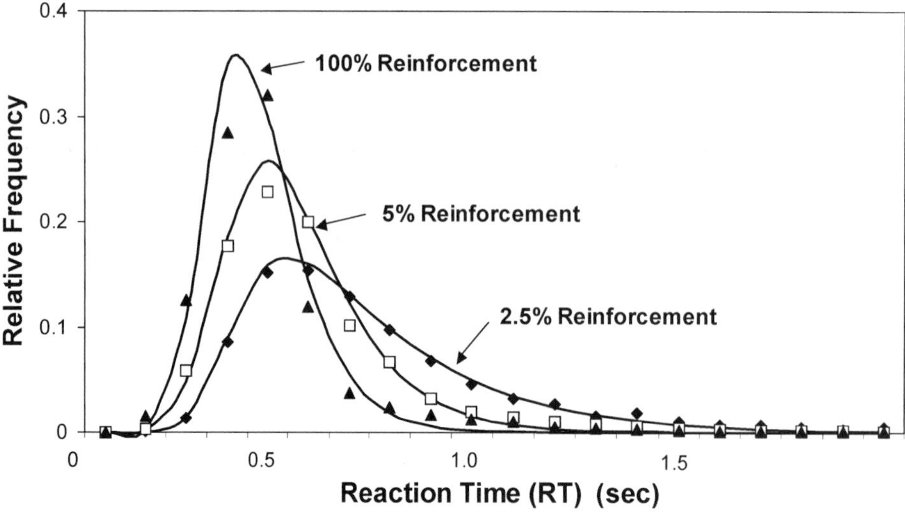

Figure 5.11. Reaction time (RT) distributions from three reinforcement conditions of the "incentive" experiment. The points represent the average of data across birds; the curves represent the average of fits of the shifted Wald distribution to each bird's data. Three parameters were adjusted to fit the 2.5% data; the fits of the other two distributions were derived from that fit by changing a single parameter, which represented the speed of the accumulation shown graphically in figure 5.12. (From "Reaction-Time Signatures of Discriminative Processes: Differential Effects of Stimulus Similarity and Incentive," by D. S. Blough, 2004, *Learning & Behavior, 32*, p. 169. Copyright 2004 by The Psychonomic Society. Reprinted with permission.)

might work with the incentive data as well. The answer is "no." It is true that, as before, one can fit each of the incentive-based curves quite well with an ex-Gaussian function. But, unlike the search data in figure 5.10, these curves cannot all be fit by simply changing the decay constant of the exponential component. Rather, to fit them all, changes in one or both of the Gaussian parameters are also necessary. Thus, by the analysis above, a change in incentive cannot be said to operate by changing by a fixed amount the moment-to-moment probability of response emission.

It is not really surprising that the ex-Gaussian model failed to account for the new incentive data, as that model was supposed to represent a perceptual effect on target detection. An incentive effect would seem to require a different notion of the underlying process. In my discussion of the incentive results (D. S. Blough, 2004), I suggested that the underlying process might correspond to the random walk, or diffusion, model shown in figure 5.12. Like the ex-Gaussian function, the diffusion model has been used extensively in the analysis of human cognitive processes (cf. Luce, 1986; Van Zandt, 2002).

According to the diffusion model, stimulus onset triggers the growth of some quantity in steps of random size until a threshold is reached, at which point a response occurs. When the threshold is crossed, an RT is recorded; many such crossing times yield an RT distribution, as figure 5.12 suggests. Incentive might affect this RT distribution either by changing the level of the threshold (low for strong incentive, high for weak incentive) or by changing the speed with which the accumulation builds toward the threshold. Further analysis enables us to distinguish these possibilities.

The RT distributions that the diffusion model generates can be fit by another fairly common probability density function called the Wald function, if we assume that the accumulation occurs in random increments with a Gaussian distribution (D. S. Blough, 2004; Luce, 1986). The Wald function has just two parameters: these are algebraically related to the mean and standard deviation of the Gaussian function that governs the speed of accumulation. However, in order to fit the incentive RT distributions, I added a third parameter, which controlled the length of a short delay between stimulus onset

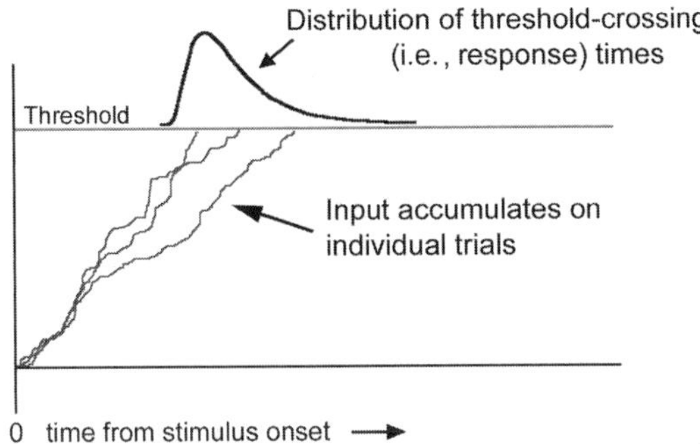

Figure 5.12. Diagram of a diffusion process that could account for incentive-based reaction time (RT) distributions such as those shown in figure 5.11. The distribution of threshold crossing times is described by a Wald density function. The data suggested that the rate of accumulation varies as a function of the rate of reinforcement associated with a stimulus. (From "Reaction-Time Signatures of Discriminative Processes: Differential Effects of Stimulus Similarity and Incentive," by D. S. Blough, 2004, *Learning & Behavior, 32*, p. 168. Copyright 2004 by The Psychonomic Society. Reprinted with permission.)

and the start of accumulation, thus shifting the Wald density function along the time axis.

Assessing the diffusion model thus became a matter of fitting the shifted Wald function to the RT distributions collected under incentive variation. To begin with, I fit the data of each bird from the 2.5% reinforcement condition, allowing all three parameters to vary. The continuous curve through the data points in figure 5.11 represents the average of those fits; it shows a good correspondence between the data and the fitting function. However, as with tests of the ex-Gaussian, the diffusion model would not be strongly tested if fits to the other incentive functions each required adjustment of all of the Wald parameters. Rather, after a fit of one function, fits of the other functions should be done by changing a single parameter that could be linked to the incentive.

In line with this procedure, I next used the parameters determined for the 2.5% curve to fit the data from the 5% and 100% conditions, holding two of those parameters constant and allowing one to change. But, which should be the variable parameter? To many readers, the obvious answer is probably "the threshold" (see figure 5.12), because the threshold seems to correspond with the notion of an adjustable response criterion, which is familiar from detection theory and other decision models. However, when I tried fitting all of the incentive functions by adjusting only the threshold, the outcome was unsatisfactory; the best fits were rather far from the data points. On the other hand, when only the accumulation speed was allowed to vary from fit to fit, the fits were much closer to the data and they seemed to represent the shape of the distributions quite well. These fits, for which only accumulation speed varied from function to function, appear as the continuous curves through the 100% and 5% data points in figure 5.11.

The upshot of this analysis is, then, that the limited data available so far support the hypothesis that incentive acts on RT by influencing the speed of an accumulative process. This result can guide a deeper theoretical analysis of discriminative processes and it connects with other research in significant ways. For example, the idea that decisions arise from the accumulation from sensory or memory sources is already widely embraced (e.g., Ratcliff, 1978). In addition, the idea that the speed of sampling from memory is affected by incentive has already been suggested (Gibbon, 1995).

CONCLUDING COMMENT

This chapter has covered a considerable range of experiments, all concerned in one way or another with what goes on in a pigeon's head when it discriminates objects in the visual world. The experiments are also linked by their common use of RT measurements to uncover those discriminative processes. To briefly review, the chapter began with evidence that pigeon RT-intensity data differ in two interesting ways from comparable human data and that at least one of these differences may expand on evidence for a retinal rod–cone interaction that was first discovered in pigeons and later confirmed in humans. The discussion then moved to higher-level processes that are reflected in the speed with which a searcher discovers a concealed target. In search, a linear rise in RT with the number of items in a display is consistent with a serial processing strategy in both pigeons and humans, but results on search asymmetry suggest that distinctive features may differ across species or, equally interesting, that features may be developed through experience.

The discussion then focused on attention, one of the most common applications of the search method. I summarized evidence for two kinds of attentional influence on pigeon search RTs and how one of these was used to compare the pigeon's search-image with a representation controlling recognition. Finally, the pigeon's discriminative response was dissected by comparing RT distributions. In each of three cases, RT distributions suggested the presence of events or processes that were essentially invisible to analysis using only mean RTs. One was the idea that two kinds of control can be mixed in a seemingly simple hue discrimination. A second was the finding that target-distractor similarity appears primarily to affect the momentary probability of target detection in search. A third was evidence that variations in the incentive value of a stimulus influence RT by affecting the speed of an underlying accumulative process.

At present, these findings are much like pieces of a large puzzle that, put together, would reflect a full understanding of discriminative processes in the pigeon. Additional pieces are supplied in many of the other chapters in this book. The whole picture and, one may hope, even the individual pieces can have implications for related processes in other species, including humans. At present, some of the pigeon results go beyond comparable work with humans; many are quite consonant with such work, and some suggest provocative differences in the way humans and pigeons process visual information.

Acknowledgments Preparation of this chapter was supported in part by grant MH61782 from the National Institutes of Health.

References

Allan, S. E., & Blough, D. S. (1989). Feature-based search asymmetries in pigeons and humans. *Perception and Psychophysics, 46*, 456–464.

Blough, D. S. (1956). Dark adaptation in the pigeon. *Journal of Comparative and Physiological Psychology, 49*, 425–430.

Blough, D. S. (1958). Rise in the pigeon's threshold with a red test stimulus during dark adaptation. *Journal of the Optical Society of America, 48*, 724.

Blough, D. S. (1978). Reaction times of pigeons on a wavelength discrimination task. *Journal of the Experimental Analysis of Behavior, 30*, 133–137.

Blough, D. S. (1979). Effects of the number and form of stimuli on visual search in the pigeon. *Journal of Experimental Psychology: Animal Behavior Processes, 5*, 211–223.

Blough, D. S. (1982). Pigeon perception of letters of the alphabet. *Science, 218*, 397–398.

Blough, D. S. (1985). Discrimination of letters and random dot patterns by pigeons and humans. *Journal of Experimental Psychology: Animal Behavior Processes, 11*, 261–280.

Blough, D. S. (1988). Quantitative relations between visual search speed and target-distractor similarity. *Perception & Psychophysics, 43*, 57–71.

Blough, D. S. (1989a). Contrast as seen in visual search reaction times. *Journal of the Experimental Analysis of Behavior, 52*, 199–211.

Blough, D. S. (1989b). Features of forms in pigeon perception. In W. Honig & G. Fetterman (Eds.), *Cognitive aspects of stimulus control* (pp. 263–277). Hillsdale, NJ: Erlbaum.

Blough, D. S. (1993). Reaction time drifts identify objects of attention in pigeon visual search. *Journal of Experimental Psychology: Animal Behavior Processes, 19*, 107–120.

Blough, D. S. (2000). Effects of priming, discriminability and reinforcement on reaction-time components in pigeon visual search. *Journal of Experimental Psychology: Animal Behavior Processes, 26*, 50–63.

Blough, D. S. (2001). The perception of similarity. In R. G. Cook (Ed.), *Avian visual cognition.* [On-line]. Retrieved November 28, 2005, from http://www.pigeon.psy.tufts.edu/avc/toc.htm.

Blough, D. S. (2002). Measuring the search image: Expectation, detection, and recognition in pigeon visual search. *Journal of Experimental Psychology: Animal Behavior Processes, 28*, 397–405.

Blough, D. S. (2004). Reaction-time signatures of discriminative processes: Differential effects of stimulus similarity and incentive. *Learning & Behavior, 32*, 157–171

Blough, D. S., & Blough, P. M. (1990). Reaction-time assessments of visual perception in pigeons. In M. Berkley & W. Stebbins (Eds.), *Comparative perception* (pp. 245–276). New York: Wiley.

Blough, D. S., & Blough, P. M. (1997). Form perception and attention in pigeons. *Animal Learning and Behavior, 25*, 1–20.

Blough, P. M. (1989). Attentional priming and visual search in pigeons. *Journal of Experimental Psychology: Animal Behavior Processes, 15*, 358–365.

Blough, P. M. (1991). Selective attention and search images in pigeons. *Journal of Experimental Psychology: Animal Behavior Processes, 17*, 292–298.

Blough, P. M., & Blough, D. S. (1978). The reaction-time/luminance relationship for pigeons to lights of different spectral compositions. *Perception & Psychophysics, 23*, 468–474.

Bond, A. B. (1983). Visual search and selection of natural stimuli in the pigeon: The attention threshold hypothesis. *Journal of Experimental Psychology: Animal Behavior Processes, 9*, 292–306.

Cattell, J. (1886). The influence of the intensity of the stimulus on the length of the reaction time. *Brain, 8*, 512–515.

Gibbon, J. (1995). Dynamics of time matching: Arousal makes better seem worse. *Psychonomic Bulletin & Review, 2*, 208–215.

Green, D. M., & Swets, J. A. (1966). *Signal detection theory and psychophysics.* New York: Wiley.

Jenness, J. W. (1993). Blough's effect measured in humans: A rise in the cone-mediated detection threshold during dark adaptation. *Dissertation Abstracts International, 53*, 5479.

Julesz, B. (1981). Textons, the elements of texture perception and their interactions. *Nature, 290*, 91–97.

Luce, R. D. (1986). *Response times: Their role in inferring elementary mental organization.* New York: Oxford University Press.

Mackintosh, N. J. (1983). *Conditioning and associative learning.* New York: Oxford.

Macmillan, N. A. (2002). Signal detection theory. In H. Pashler & J. Wixted (Eds.), *Stevens' handbook of experimental psychology, Volume 4: Methodology in experimental psychology*, 3rd ed. (pp. 43–90). New York: Wiley.

Pietrewicz, A. T., & Kamil, A. C. (1979). Search image formation in the blue jay *Cyanocitta cristata*). *Science, 204*, 1332–1333.

Ratcliff, R. (1978). A theory of memory retrieval. *Psychological Review, 85*, 59–108.

Roberts, S. (1987). Evidence for distinct serial processes in animals: The multiplicative-factors method. *Animal Learning & Behavior, 15*, 135–173.

Shepard, R. N. (1987). Toward a universal law of generalization for psychological science. *Science, 237*, 1317–1323.

Stebbins, W. C. (1966). Auditory reaction time and the derivation of equal loudness contours for the monkey. *Journal of the Experimental Analysis of Behavior, 9*, 135–142.

Sternberg, S. (1998). Discovering mental processing stages: The method of additive factors. In D. Scarborough & S. Sternberg (Eds.), *Invitation to cognitive science, Vol. 4: Methods, models, and conceptual issues* (pp. 703–863). Cambridge, MA: MIT Press.

Tinbergen, L. (1960). The natural control of insects in pine woods: I. Factors influencing the intensity of predation by songbirds. *Archives Neelandaises de Zoologie, 13*, 265–343.

Treisman, A., & Gelade, G. (1980). A feature-integration theory of attention. *Cognitive Psychology, 12*, 97–136.

Treisman, A., Vieira, A., & Hayes, A. (1992). Automaticity and pre-attentive processing. *American Journal of Psychology, 105*, 341–362.

Tversky, A. (1977). Features of similarity. *Psychological Review, 84*, 327–352.

Van Zandt, T. (2002). Analysis of response time distributions. In H. Pashler & J. Wixted (Eds.), *Stevens' handbook of experimental psychology, Volume 4: Methodology in experimental psychology* (3rd ed.) (pp. 461–516). New York: Wiley.

Wooten, B. R., & Butler, T. W. (1978). Possible rod-cone interaction in dark adaptation. *Journal of the Optical Society of America, 66*, 1429–1430.

Wolfe, J. M. (1998). What can 1 million trials tell us about visual search? *Psychological Science, 9*, 33–39.

6

Selective Attention, Priming, and Foraging Behavior

ALAN C. KAMIL AND ALAN B. BOND

Animals selectively filter and transform their sensory input, increasing the accuracy with which some stimuli are detected and effectively ignoring others. This filtering process, collectively referred to as "selective attention," takes place at a variety of different levels in the nervous system. It was described in considerable detail by William James over a century ago (James, 1890/1950) and has been a principal focus of research in cognitive psychology for nearly 50 years (Parasuraman & Davies, 1984; Pashler, 1998; Richards, 1998). Investigations of selective attention have also been central to the study of animal cognition, where the process of attention has been considered to play an important role in a variety of behavioral paradigms (e.g., Mackintosh, 1975; Riley & Roitblat, 1978).

Most attention research, particularly in the realm of visual search, has been directed to the nature of the filtering processes applied to relatively simple, geometrical stimuli (reviewed in Humphreys & Bruce, 1989). Such stimuli can easily be varied along independent physical dimensions, allowing the relationship between targets and distractors to be controlled with considerable precision (e.g., Treisman & Gelade, 1980). However, the role of selective attention in determining responses to more complex visual stimuli, of the sort that organisms regularly deal with in the course of their normal behavioral routines, has been less explored. This neglect is of particular concern because, in the absence of artificial limitations on search time, simple geometrical stimuli do not place a sufficient demand on information processing capacity to demonstrate selective attention effects (Riley & Leith, 1976).

In addition to their use of simple geometrical stimuli, most attention studies in animals have used tasks with no clear, direct connection to the perceptual world of the species under study. There is, however, substantial literature suggesting that selective attention may play a significant role in nature, particularly in predator–prey interactions. A review of this literature, integrating it with more customary work on attentional psychology, raises questions of considerable interest to both psychologists and biologists. For psychologists, naturalistic experimental methods using more complex, multidimensional stimuli cast light on additional, unanticipated aspects of attentional processes in animals. For biologists, selective attention has long been considered a primary cognitive mechanism underlying the well-known tendency of visually searching predators to concentrate their attacks on relatively common prey types. As a consequence, the circumstances under which selective attention occurs and the magnitude of the enhancement in detection accuracy that results can have significant ecological and evolutionary effects. Our goal in this chapter, therefore, is to integrate data and hypotheses from both the ecological and the cognitive perspectives. When these two groups of literature are considered together, a variety of parallels emerge, parallels that lay the groundwork for a unified account of attentional phenomena in animals.

FORAGING BEHAVIOR AND SELECTIVE ATTENTION

Studies of foraging behavior have commonly noted that animals tend to take prey in nonrandom sequences, resulting in much longer "runs" of a single prey type than would be expected by chance. Such concentrated foraging on one food type at a time has been demonstrated across a broad range of vertebrate and invertebrate species, including wood pigeons foraging for seeds on the ground (Murton, 1971), bumblebees feeding on different species of flower (Heinrich, Mudge, & Deringis, 1977), and insectivorous woodland birds searching for moth larvae (Royama, 1970; Tinbergen, 1960). Nonrandom prey sequences can result from passive factors, such as heterogeneity in the spatial distribution of food types or changes in food accessibility with density, but predators also exhibit dynamic, active selection biases, in which they switch from one prey to another in response to changes in relative abundance and availability (Murdoch, 1969; Murdoch & Oaten, 1974).

One defining feature of an active selection bias is a characteristic form of relationship between the availability of a particular prey type in the environment and the frequency with which it occurs in the predator's diet. Predators that take prey items as they encounter them, without differentiating among types, exhibit a monotonic, uninflected relationship between diet and prey abundance. Holling (1966) termed this a "Type II" functional response and noted that it is broadly characteristic of invertebrate predators. Active selection biases, on the other hand, produce a sigmoid diet function: Rarer prey types are taken less frequently than would be expected by chance, whereas more common types are taken disproportionately often, a pattern that Holling (1965) termed a "Type III" functional response.

Biologists have long been fascinated by sigmoid diet functions, as they exhibit stabilizing dynamics, known as "apostatic selection" (Clarke, 1962), which can directly contribute to the generation and maintenance of diversity in prey populations (Allen & Clarke, 1968; Clarke, 1962, 1969; Murdoch & Oaten, 1974; reviewed in Allen, 1988). Sigmoid diet functions can result from a number of different psychological mechanisms (Bond, 1983; Bond & Riley 1991), but the most interesting possibilities from the perspective of cognitive psychology are two proposed mechanisms that have a bearing on the role of attentional processes in foraging behavior. These are hunting by searching image (Tinbergen, 1960) and hunting by expectation (Royama, 1970).

Tinbergen (1960) first suggested the searching image hypothesis to account for the pattern of predation by European tits on insects in pine woodlands. By recording the prey items that foraging birds brought to their nestlings while simultaneously quantifying the actual relative abundance of these insect species in the environment, Tinbergen was able to examine the relationship between the relative density of insects in the woods and the relative frequency of those insects in the diets of the birds on a day-to-day basis. The most common prey species were taken by the tits in a sigmoid pattern that suggested an active selection bias. Tinbergen's collection technique also allowed him to record the sequences in which prey were captured. He found that insectivorous birds tended to bring prey items to the nest in sequential runs of the same type, suggesting that at any given moment the birds were searching for only one kind of prey (Bond, 1983; Dawkins, 1971; Langley, 1996). On the basis of these data, Tinbergen hypothesized that the birds were filtering out alternative stimuli and limiting their search to the visual features characteristic of a single prey type, thereby increasing their ability to detect that prey type and reducing the detectability of alternative prey types. In essence, Tinbergen was proposing that the selection bias was attributable to selective attention (Langley, 1996).

In a subsequent test of this hypothesis, Croze (1970), in a series of ingenious studies with carrion crows, obtained what is still probably the best evidence for searching image in free-ranging animals. The crows were trained to come to a beach and search for painted seashells that covered food rewards. The shells had been made quite cryptic by painting them the same colors as the sand and rocks on the beach. In one of his experiments, Croze used three different colors of shell, which he called morphs. Each day, he laid out 27 of these shells on the beach, scattered among the pebbles and flotsam in a relatively randomized pattern. On some days, the shells comprised a "monomorphic" population in which all of them were the same color (counterbalanced across days). In the other, "trimorphic" condition, all three morphs were equally represented.

Croze predicted that during trimorphic days, individual crows would take the prey in runs of a single type. He reasoned that when three morphs were present, the first detection of one of the prey by a crow would result in the formation of a searching image for that shell type, and this would precipitate a run of detections of that type. This did not occur; there were no more runs during trimorphic days than would be expected by chance. However, the crows were more successful at finding monomorphic prey than trimorphic prey. Croze speculated (post hoc) that this difference could result from formation of a searching image for the prey present during monomorphic, but not trimorphic conditions, if several consecutive experiences with a prey type are necessary to adopt a searching image. It is possible that if Croze could have controlled the order within which morphs were encountered during trimorphic conditions, he would have obtained more convincing evidence for improvements in detection with successive encounters with the same prey type.

A number of other naturalistic experiments have been conducted to test the searching image hypothesis, generally involving simultaneous presentation of multiple targets of two disparate types. Several studies have obtained results that were clearly consistent with the hypothesis, in that subjects took stimuli in nonrandom sequences, producing runs of a single stimulus type. Dawkins (1971) presented chicks with an array of grains of rice that were dyed either green or orange and were presented on backgrounds of painted stones that either matched or contrasted the grain colors. She observed the chicks ate the grains in significantly longer sequential runs than would have been expected by chance, and subsequent probe experiments suggested that the birds were alternately cuing either to the shape of cryptic grains or to the color contrast of conspicuous ones. In an experiment involving human subjects manually sorting colored wooden beads, Bond (1982) found that subjects spontaneously chose to sort items in nonrandom sequences, that the speed and accuracy of the sort were increased at longer run lengths, and that the effect of sorting sequence was enhanced when the beads were harder to discriminate.

Most other multiple target studies have not tracked the sequence of items taken but have instead manipulated the relative numbers of targets of the two types. Although much of the early research in this area was flawed by lack of proper controls (Bond, 1983; Krebs, 1973), later, better-designed studies have demonstrated clear active selection biases when animals are allowed to select among a mixture of targets of several different types (reviewed in Allen, 1988). The most striking and consistent finding of these studies has been that active selection biases are most apparent when the targets are cryptic and difficult to detect, implicating a perceptually based process (Bond, 1983; Cooper, 1984; Cooper & Allen, 1994; Reid & Shettleworth, 1992). In an extension of Bond's (1983) study of pigeons searching for cryptic, real grains, Langley, Riley, Bond, and Goel (1996) were able to show not just that selection biases were only displayed under cryptic conditions but also that they could be "set" by prior trials on either cryptic or conspicuous targets and that the bias setting was lost if a 3-min delay was interpolated between setting and testing trials, suggesting that the bias was transitory. Taken as a whole, these naturalistic, multiple target studies supported Tinbergen's searching image hypothesis, although because the sequence of stimuli experienced by the animals could not be fully controlled, the results could not exclude alternative, nonattentional explanations.

The primary alternative to the searching image hypothesis that can also account for nonrandom prey sequences and sigmoid diet functions in free-ranging predators is known as "hunting by expectation" (Krebs, 1973; Royama, 1970). In many cases, different types of food or prey tend to be found in different areas or microhabitats. For example, in a field experiment with great tits during the breeding season, Royama (1970) found that the birds appeared to use specific locations where their preferred prey was most often found. He observed that succeeding periods during the breeding season were each characterized by particular prey types being brought to the nest and that most of these prey inhabited distinctively different microhabitats within the environment. Early in the season, the tits focused hunting mainly on oak foliage, then switched to blackthorn, hawthorn, and ash trees during the middle of the season, and finally to ground vegetation at the end of the breeding season.

These data suggested that the great tits tracked prey availability and used environmental cues (presumably some combination of visual and spatial stimuli) to concentrate their search in the most profitable areas at each stage of the breeding season. In other words, the birds showed hunting by expectation, appearing to form an association between particular areas and particular reward rates. Other studies have reported similar findings from a variety of settings, including patch selection and responses to leaf damage in insectivorous birds (Heinrich & Collins, 1983; Kono, Reid, & Kamil, 1998; Real, Ianazzi, Kamil, & Heinrich, 1984; Smith & Dawkins, 1971; Smith & Sweatmen, 1974). Getty and Pulliam (1991, 1993) conducted a detailed aviary study of the foraging behavior of white-throated sparrows on small cryptic or conspicuous seeds and found clear indications that the birds selected habitat patches based on their expected detection rates, with diet composition changing accordingly.

If prey types differ strongly from one another in their relative densities across microhabitats, hunting by expectation will readily produce sigmoid diet functions and nonrandom prey sequences. Suppose that foragers regularly sample their environment to learn which microhabitat is the most profitable and then subsequently concentrate their hunting in that area. If the microhabitat was characterized by a single prey type, that prey type will be taken more often than would be expected from its overall density in the foraging environment. When the given microhabitat becomes less profitable, birds might be expected to switch to another one, characterized by a different suite of prey items. The result would be that prey would tend to be taken in runs of a single type, much as Tinbergen (1960) observed. Thus, hunting by either expectation or searching image could have accounted for Tinbergen's field results, as well as those from other studies of free-flying birds (e.g., Allen & Clarke, 1968; Royama, 1970). As was the case with multiple-target studies of searching image, a higher degree of experimental control was required, especially with respect to the sequence of prey types experienced by the predator, to distinguish unequivocally among these possible alternative mechanisms. Progress in the field effectively demanded the use of operant techniques.

OPERANT TECHNIQUES AND FORAGING BEHAVIOR

One of the earliest areas of animal cognition research in which the interests of psychologists and biologists coalesced was in the study of foraging behavior (see reviews in Kamil, Krebs, & Pulliam, 1987; Kamil & Sargent, 1981; Stephens & Krebs, 1986). For example, diet selection theory (Macarthur & Pianka, 1966) predicted that choice among different food types should depend on both their caloric reward and their relative availability, a prediction that was confirmed in operant studies by Krebs, Ryan, and Charnov (1974) and by Fantino (1987). The marginal value theorem (Charnov, 1976) predicted that the time a forager should spend investigating a food patch should be a function of the time required to travel between food patches, a prediction confirmed by Krebs, Erichsen, Webber, and Charnov (1977) and Kamil, Lindstrom, and Peters (1985). Risk-sensitive foraging theory (Caraco, 1980) predicted that the responses of foragers to variations in food reward should depend on their energy budget, a prediction confirmed by Caraco, Martindale, and Whitham (1980) and Caraco (1981).

One of the most successful applications of operant procedures to an issue arising from the study of foraging behavior was a test of the searching image hypothesis. The crucial prediction of Tinbergen's (1960) hypothesis was that a series of successive encounters with a single prey type would, of itself, improve the predator's subsequent ability to detect that prey type. Although experimental designs in which multiple stimuli were presented simultaneously could produce results that were consistent with searching image, their inability to control the order in which prey types were encountered prevented a direct test of Tinbergen's primary prediction. Pietrewicz and Kamil (1977, 1979, 1981) were, therefore, led to develop a technique, loosely based on Herrnstein and Loveland's (1964) procedures for operant learning of concepts, which was designed to simulate the problem of hunting for cryptic prey. The species chosen for this research was the blue jay (*Cyanocitta cristata*). These birds commonly forage for a broad range of prey items, many of which are quite cryptic, whose presence may be cued by a range of different environmental stimuli (Husband & Shimizu, 2001; Meyer, 1977; Sargent, 1976; Tarvin & Woolfenden, 1999). The procedures originally developed were based on the natural predator—prey system of blue jays visually hunting for *Catocala* moths on tree trunks. Field data (reviewed by Sargent, 1976) show that jays are frequent predators on these moths, which are very cryptic when resting during the daytime on the bark of trees such as oaks, white birches, or maples.

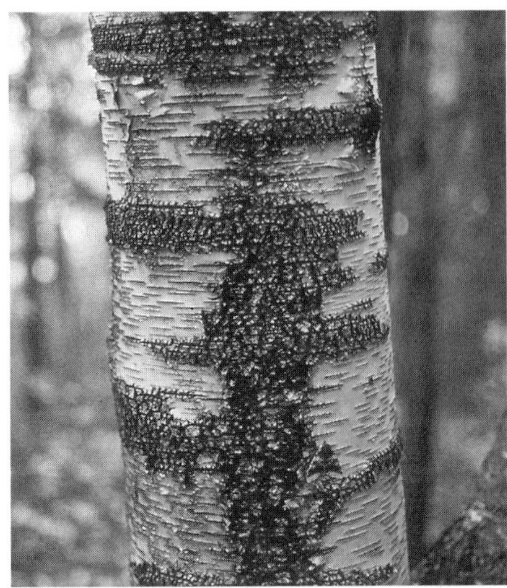

Figure 6.1. A *Catocala relicta* moth, resting head-up on a white birch tree. The moth is located on the lower right of the tree trunk.

Pietrewicz and Kamil (1977, 1979) trained blue jays to search projected images for *Catocala* that had been photographed on tree trunks at a range of camera distances (figure 6.1). Half of the images included moths; half did not. The jays were rewarded for pecking at images that included moths but not for pecking at images without moths. The birds proved very adept at this task, reliably detecting moths that were highly cryptic to human observers while accurately rejecting images without moths. Pietrewicz and Kamil (1979) used several of the many species of moths in the genus in generating their images, allowing them to conduct a critical test of the searching image hypothesis. Highly experienced blue jays were trained to detect two species of moth that were disparate in appearance: *Catocala relicta,* a black and white moth that normally rests on birch trees, and *C. retecta,* a gray, brown, and black moth that normally rests on oak trees. In the middle of sessions during which the two moth types appeared in random order (intermixed with empty slides with no moths), there was a critical sequence of 12 trials—half positive and half negative. In the experimental conditions, the six positive slides each portrayed the same moth type, whereas in the control conditions, the positive slides were half relicta and half retecta, in random order. With this design, the experimental and control conditions were identical except for the ordering of the prey types.

The results clearly supported the searching image hypothesis. When the jays encountered the same type of moth several times in a row during the runs condition, the probability of detecting the moth increased. In addition, the accuracy of the jays in correctly rejecting images without moths also improved in the runs condition. No such changes were observed in the control condition. This provided strong evidence for an improvement in the detectability of a cryptic prey type with successive encounters with that same type. Similar effects have since been obtained in operant studies with pigeons, using cryptic seeds (Bond & Riley, 1991; Langley, 1996) or alphanumeric characters (P. M. Blough, 1989, 1991) as targets, and the results have been repeatedly confirmed in experiments in blue jays, using more precise control over the relationship between the target stimuli and the background (Bond & Kamil, 1998, 1999, 2002; Dukas & Kamil, 2000, 2001).

These findings have firmly established the existence of the searching image effect. It is reasonable to conclude that the increase in detection of a prey type when several exemplars of that type are encountered in succession is at least one of the factors that contributes to the observation that visual predators often take prey, especially cryptic prey, in runs. It is also worth noting that these results are consistent with the results of many studies of natural foraging behavior. In particular, they support Croze's explanation for his failure to obtain clear evidence for searching images in his trimorphic condition. Blue jays generally seem to require several sequential presentations of a particular moth type before their detection significantly improves (although the number of required encounters may depend on the difficulty of the detection task: Bond & Kamil, 2002). If carrion crows also require multiple successive encounters, then Croze's trimorphic condition would not have provided long enough runs of a single prey type to elicit searching image effects. This example demonstrates how laboratory research can help inform research carried out under natural (but less well-controlled) conditions.

The initial operant studies did not, however, establish the mechanism responsible for the increase in search accuracy. In fact, several alternative explanations for the effect have been put forward. Tinbergen (1960) originally suggested an attention-like process, a notion strongly supported by P. M. Blough (1989, 1991) and Langley (1996).

Others have suggested that changes in the rate of visual search (Guilford & Dawkins, 1987) or forgetting during the interval between successive prey stimuli (Plaisted & Mackintosh, 1995) might produce the apparent increase in detection. We return to this issue later in this chapter.

ATTENTION, PRIMING, AND SEARCHING IMAGE

The phenomena of hunting by expectation and of searching image each suggest independent contexts in which selective attention may play an important role during visual search for cryptic targets. When the operant literature on selective attention is examined from this perspective, each of these naturalistically based phenomena has an operant analogue, based on the procedure used to prime an attentional state. Priming has usually been defined as the pretrial activation of a representation of the target (Posner & Snyder, 1975). It was initially identified as an important factor facilitating visual search in experiments with human subjects, where it has been shown that pretrial cues that predict the identity or location of the subsequent target facilitate visual search (Beller, 1971; Eriksen & Hoffman, 1972). There are two priming procedures that have been used in the animal literature. In the first, an arbitrary cue (or symbol) is associated with one of several potentially available targets, accurately predicting the subsequent occurrence of that target. This has been referred to as "symbolic" or "associative" priming (P. M. Blough, 1989), and it might be expected to occur as a consequence of hunting by expectation. In the second procedure, attention is primed by presenting the same target many times in succession, a process that is often called "sequential" priming (P. M. Blough, 1989; P. M. Blough & Lacourse, 1994). This appears to correspond to the presumed mechanism of searching image.

Sequential and Associative Priming

Based on the searching image literature, P. M. Blough (1989) hypothesized that priming might be expected to improve the performance of pigeons that were searching for targets that were difficult to detect. She used a procedure in which the birds searched for two distinctive alphanumeric targets displayed among other similar distractor characters on a computer monitor. Each trial included one target of one of the two types, and trials were terminated by three pecks delivered to one of the on-screen characters. Responses directed at targets were rewarded; if the pigeon mistakenly pecked a distractor, the trial was unrewarded and was subsequently repeated (repeats were omitted from data analyses). Although these procedures differ significantly from natural foraging situations, particularly in the presence of a target in every display, they offer excellent control over many relevant parameters, including the number of possible targets and distractors, the presence of priming stimuli, and the order of target types.

P. M. Blough took full advantage of these possibilities in a series of studies (P. M. Blough, 1989, 1991, 1992, 1996; P. M. Blough & Lacourse, 1994; Vreven & Blough, 1998). Here, we emphasize those results that bear most directly on two issues: the differences and/or similarities between different priming procedures and the role of attentional processes in each type of priming. P. M. Blough (1989) tested for effects of sequential and associative priming separately. Her first two experiments established that each type of priming occurred with the procedures she had developed. During these experiments, each trial could contain either of two possible targets: for example, A or L. To test for associative priming, Blough used three cues, one of which preceded each trial. One cue invariably preceded targets that contained A, another invariably preceded trials that contained L, and the third was followed equally often by A and L trials. Targets were detected more rapidly following the predictive cues than following the nonpredictive cue, although the proportion of correct detections was not affected by cue type. To test for sequential priming, targets were presented in sequential runs of a single target type. In this case, significant effects on both search time and accuracy were found, although the effect on accuracy appeared greater and more consistent.

In her third and fourth experiments, P. M. Blough (1989) tested more specifically for whether the effects of associative priming were attentional in nature. She found that following a normally informative prime with the nonprimed target resulted in particularly poor detection of that target and that this effect disappeared if the target was presented alone (with no distractors). These findings supported the hypothesis that the effects of associative priming were due to an attentional process, in that a limited capacity attention model (Broadbent, 1958, 1971; Kahneman, 1973) assumes that the detectability of a given target type can only be increased at the cost of a reduction in performance on other targets. P. M. Blough (1991) extended these findings, comparing the effects of several variables on associative and sequential priming. Intertrial interval (ITI) had little effect on sequential priming, but associative priming was more variable and less robust when ITIs were relatively long. Increases in the number of target types improved search during sequential priming but not during associative priming. Blough attributed some of these differences to the different associative demands of the two types of priming and suggested that both types of priming may elicit a similar attentional process.

Priming and Selective Attention

What is meant by an attentional process in this context? The strongest form of an attentional account of searching image was effectively articulated by Langley (1996). She conceived of visual search as a process of matching sensory input against a cognitive representation of the sought-for target, a representation that through experience has come to incorporate all of the salient features that enable discrimination of the target from the background. In this view, selective attention is a process of "activation" of this representation, bringing it to the cognitive foreground and installing it as the current attentional filter. This view implies that any cue that is predictive of a particular target type—spatial position, recent experience, or even another, arbitrary associated stimulus—will cause activation of the same attentional state. The hypothesis is attractive, but Langley's (1996) results did not compel its adoption, and other studies appear more consistent with an expectancy-based interpretation of sequential priming. P. M. Blough and Lacourse (1994) compared sequential priming with priming based on spatial location and concluded that stimulus-driven factors, such as activation of something like an eidetic image, played little role in sequential priming.

The most conservative, empirically verifiable definition of attention derives from the notion of a limited information processing capacity. According to this definition, selective attention is demonstrated when a condition enhances detection of the primed target and simultaneously interferes with detection of alternative targets. By this definition, there is clear evidence for attention in both sequential and associative priming. In the case of sequential priming, for example, P. M. Blough (1989) demonstrated that "miscuing" after a run of a single target resulted in high search times in pigeons searching for alphanumeric characters among distractors. Reid and Shettleworth (1992) reported similar data for pigeons searching for cryptic seeds, and Bond and Kamil (1999) also found that, after a run of one type of cryptic digital moth, detection of another type was reduced (see also Bond & Kamil, 2002; Bond & Riley, 1991; Dukas & Kamil, 2000, 2001). In the case of associative priming, P. M. Blough (1989) found that response times increased significantly when an associative prime for one target was followed by a different, unexpected target. D. S. Blough (2002) reported similar results when the targets were gratings of different frequency and orientation.

There is strong evidence in favor of interpreting sequential priming or searching image effects as manifestations of an underlying attentional process and the effects of multiple successive encounters with a single prey type are now commonly attributed to selective attention (e.g., Bond & Kamil, 2002; Dukas, 2002; Dukas & Kamil, 2000, 2001; Langley, 1996). Alternative interpretations of the searching image literature have, however, been advanced in the literature. The most broadly cited of these is the argument proposed by Guilford and Dawkins (1987) that changes in search rate could account for many of the findings attributed to searching image.

The effects of variation in the rate of movement of a visual predator through the environment were originally developed in a series of experiments by Gendron and Staddon on the foraging behavior of bobwhite quail (Gendron, 1986; Gendron & Staddon, 1983, 1984). Gendron and Staddon produced a simple mathematical model, essentially based on a speed/accuracy tradeoff, that demonstrated that for any specific food stimulus, there was an optimal rate of search through the environment that would maximize the rate at which that stimulus was detected. Conspicuous stimuli are detected more readily at greater distances, so they can be searched for more rapidly; difficult, cryptic stimuli, on the other hand, require the bird to slow down and scan its surroundings more thoroughly. This original model was substantially confirmed and greatly expanded in subsequent work by Getty and

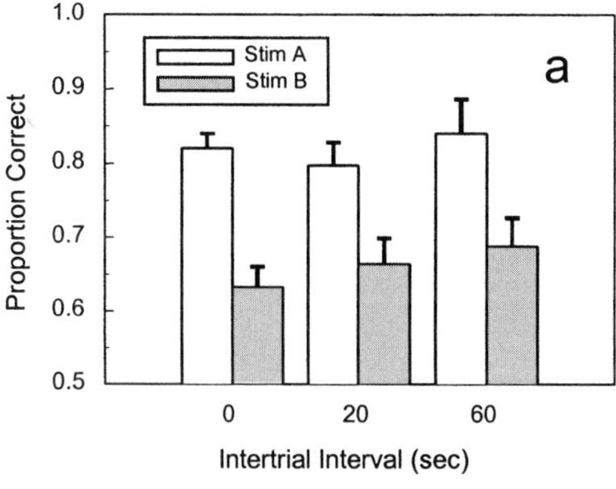

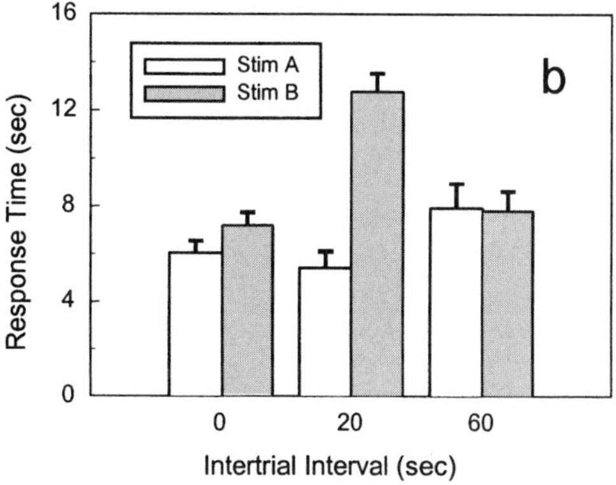

Figure 6.2. The effects of varying intertrial interval during a run of the same prey type (moth A or B) on probability of detection (*a*) and the time required to detect the moth (*b*). Error bars are 1 standard error of the mean. (Redrawn from Cink, 2002.)

Pulliam (Getty, Kamil, & Real, 1987; Getty & Pulliam, 1991, 1993).

Given Gendron's results, Guilford and Dawkins (1987) noted that when two or more prey items that differed in crypticity were present in the environment, repeated encounters with more cryptic items would cause the predator to reduce its search rate to optimize the frequency of detection, while encounters with more conspicuous prey would have the opposite effect. They argued that all of the results (as of 1987, at least) that had been interpreted as evidence of searching image could as readily be seen as consequences of changes in search rate. Subsequent research has demonstrated that their assertions were wholly without merit. In quite different preparations, both Bond and Riley (1991) and Reid and Shettleworth (1992) were able to find indications of independent effects of both search rate and searching image. Improvements in target detection following a run have also been demonstrated in the absence of search rate changes or under conditions in which no change of search rate would be expected (P. M. Blough, 1989, 1992; Bond & Kamil, 1999; Langley, 1996).

But the most compelling argument against Guilford and Dawkins (1987) is that optimization of search rate does not result in sigmoid diet functions. Gendron and Staddon's (1983, 1984) models produce uninflected, Type II functional responses, a result that has since been confirmed by Getty and Pulliam (1993). Fluctuations in the proportion of particular prey types in the diet are passive consequences of changes in search rate, and the Guilford and Dawkins (1987) model cannot, therefore, account for perceptually based, active selection biases (Bond, 1983; Cooper, 1984; Cooper & Allen, 1994; Reid & Shettleworth, 1992).

More recently, Plaisted (1997; Plaisted & Mackintosh, 1995) suggested a forgetting model to account for the results of operant tests of searching image. She pointed out that when targets are presented in runs, the average interval between successive appearances of that target is shorter than when targets of two types are intermixed. In support of her hypothesis, Plaisted cited data showing that pigeons searching for cryptic targets showed clear forgetting effects when the time interval between successive presentations (the "interstimulus" interval) was directly manipulated. However, the intervals she used were relatively short compared with those used in searching image research in other preparations, and the results of several subsequent experiments indicate that interstimulus intervals may play a relatively minor role in operant studies of searching image.

Two direct tests of the Plaisted hypothesis have been conducted in our laboratory in experiments in which jays hunted for cryptic digital moths. In the first (Bond & Kamil, 1999), a post hoc analysis of detection data showed that the interstimulus interval had little effect on detection of cryptic digital moths by blue jays. In fact, the effects of interstimulus interval on response time were in the direction opposite from that predicted by Plaisted and Mackintosh (1995). In another study in our laboratory, Cink (2002) directly manipulated the interstimulus interval in detection trials using cryptic digital moths and blue jays. The jays were trained to detect two types of moths and were given runs of a single type embedded in long sessions. The moths differed somewhat in their crypticity; one was detected with a probability value of about .65, and the other with a probability value of .85. Cink inserted ITIs of 0, 20, or 60 s between the eighth and ninth moths in a run of the same type. He found that runs led to a significant increase in detection probability but no change in the time required to find a moth. There were no significant effects of the ITI on accuracy on the runs trial following the ITI insertion. In fact, mean probability of detection actually increased with longer ITIs. There were some effects on search time, but their magnitude was small, and, again, the direction of the effect was not as predicted by the Plaisted model. For the prey type that was most difficult to detect, search time was longest after the 20-s ITI (figure 6.2). Thus, there is little evidence from operant studies of blue jays to support the interstimulus interval interpretation of searching image effects.

INTERACTIONS BETWEEN ASSOCIATIVE AND SEQUENTIAL PRIMING

To summarize, two naturally occurring foraging patterns, hunting by expectation and searching image, are related to two phenomena studied under laboratory conditions, associative priming and sequential priming. There is good evidence that each type of priming enlists an attentional process. Because there are many similarities between the results of sequential and of associative priming, the two procedures are often assumed to elicit the same process. For example, D. S. Blough (2002) performed a clever and informative set of experiments designed to separate detection and recognition processes. He obtained generalization gradients on trials during which an associative prime was present, which he compared to gradients when no informative prime was present, as well as to gradients obtained following reinforcement of a single stimulus. Although he never presented runs of a single target, he entitled his paper "Measuring the searching image . . . ," apparently reflecting this assumption of the equivalence of an underlying process between the different types of priming.

However, there are clear suggestions in the literature of differences between sequential and associative priming (e.g., P. M. Blough, 1991), and this question deserves further study. One approach might be to conduct experiments in which the interactions between associative and sequential priming are studied by making both types of priming available simultaneously. From a naturalistic viewpoint, it seems likely that both types of priming are often available to a foraging animal. If a forager has learned that the most common prey type is available in a specific microhabitat, then the cues associated with that habitat will provide a basis for associative priming. And, once it is hunting in the chosen microhabitat, the forager is likely to encounter the same prey type many times in succession, providing a basis for sequential priming (Kono et al., 1998).

From a mechanistic point of view, the effects of combining both types of priming might be quite informative. If both types elicit the same attentional process, as suggested by P. M. Blough (1989, 1991) and Langley (1996), then providing both types of priming simultaneously might be no more effective than providing either one alone. On the other hand, if detection is improved when both types of priming are available, then two possibilities suggest themselves. Either the same attentional process is elicited by either type of priming but is somehow strengthened when both types are presented together, or the two modes of priming elicit separable cognitive processes.

Most research modeled on natural foraging systems has concentrated on sequential priming produced by runs of single target types (e.g., Bond & Kamil, 1999; Bond & Riley, 1991; Kono et al., 1998; Langley, 1996; Pietrewicz & Kamil, 1979). In contrast, most studies of associative priming have involved a search for simpler stimuli, especially alphanumeric targets. These tasks differ along several dimensions. Tasks based on the detection of cryptic food items require the targets to be differentiated from backgrounds of similar appearance. As D. S. Blough (2002) pointed out, tasks that require the segregation of a coherent target from a random background may have different characteristics from tasks in which a target must be selected from many visible, coherent forms. Until recently, no studies of associative priming had been conducted in which the subjects were required to search for complex naturalistic stimuli on a matching background.

As the first in a series of experiments designed to investigate the interactions between associative

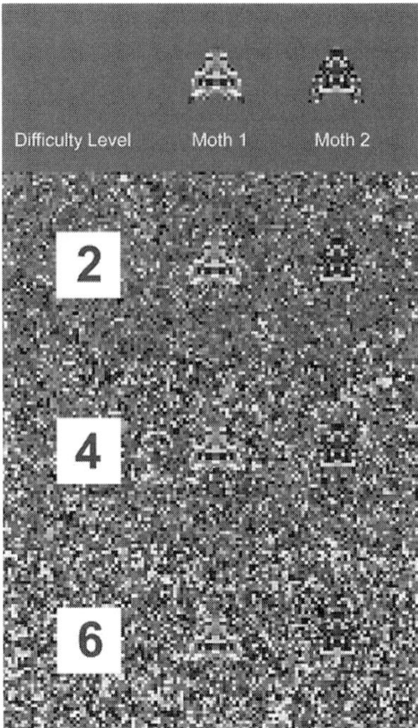

Figure 6.3. The two digital moths used by Belik (2002), on three different backgrounds of increasing crypticity, top to bottom. (From *Effects of Two Different Types of Priming on Visual Search in the Blue Jay* (*Cyanocitta cristata*), by M. Belik, 2002, Unpublished doctoral dissertation, University of Nebraska, Lincoln. Reprinted with permission of the author.)

and sequential priming, Belik (2002), working in our laboratory, decided to determine whether associative priming had an effect on blue jays that were searching for cryptic digital moths. In her first set of experiments, she trained jays to find each of two distinctly different moths (figure 6.3) displayed on a homogeneous, fractal background on which they were moderately cryptic, using the digital moths developed by Bond and Kamil (1998, 1999). There were two priming stimuli that predicted which moth would be presented in the following trial and two uninformative control stimuli that did not. Each trial began with the presentation of one of these four priming stimuli as a "start" key, and the bird had to peck the stimulus repeatedly to produce the display containing the moths. Each priming stimulus was followed by its designated target on a cryptic background, whereas each uninformative control stimulus was followed equally often by each of the two targets. After training, the birds detected target moths more accurately following primes than following control stimuli, learning to associate the priming stimuli with the appropriate digital moths. This provided the first well-controlled demonstration of associative priming with targets based on background-matching prey.

In a second experiment using the same birds, Belik (2002) then introduced sequential priming in a 2×2 factorial design. A series of test trials was embedded within in each daily session. In a control series, neither associative nor sequential priming was provided; the two targets were intermixed in random order and the stimuli on the start key were not informative. In associative-only series, only associative primes were provided; the two targets were sequentially intermixed, but each was reliably signaled by the appropriate associative prime. In sequential-only series, only sequential priming was present. All of the targets in the series were of the same type, but no associative prime was presented. Finally, in associative plus sequential series, both types of priming were present. All of the trials in a series were of a single target type preceded by the appropriate associative prime.

Belik (2002) reasoned that if the two types of priming elicit the same attentional process, then providing both types of priming simultaneously might be no more effective than either one alone. On the other hand, if the multiply primed series produced greater effects than either associative or sequential series alone, then this outcome would suggest that the two modes of priming elicited separable cognitive processes. The results were, however, more complex than she originally envisioned. Introduction of the sequential primes in the factorial design caused the previous associative priming effects to disappear: Neither associative nor sequential primes were superior to control treatments when presented alone, but birds performed more accurately when both types of primes were present than under any other conditions (figure 6.4). It appeared that the combination of associative and sequential priming in a single block of trials somehow interfered with the associative priming obtained in the previous stage of the experiment. The failure to find any effect of sequential priming alone suggests that interference also affected performance during runs with no associative cue.

To test this possibility, Belik (2002) returned the jays to a third experiment, consisting again of a

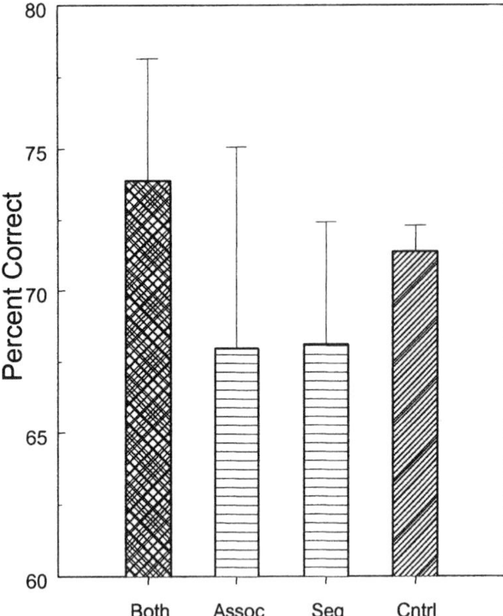

Figure 6.4. Mean percentage correct as a function of the type of priming present. Jays detected the most moths when both sequential and associative primes were available. However, they performed worse with either sequential or associative priming alone than they did under control conditions, when no priming was available. (Redrawn from Belik, 2002.)

series of sessions of associative-only treatments without any sequential patterning. The initial associative priming effect then reappeared, providing support for the notion that the two modes of priming may interfere with one another when they are presented in intermixed sessions to a single subject. This inference is also consistent with the results from Dukas and Kamil (2001), in which there were no costs of switching when cues provided by the background distractors accurately predicted which target type was present.

In another series of experiments, Belik (2002) examined the effects of sequential and associative priming with targets that differed in shape as well as in pattern and with backgrounds that consisted of collections of distractor elements (similar to Dukas & Kamil, 2000). In this experiment, both sequential and associative priming produced some improvement in the detection of very cryptic targets (detected on only 40% to 50% of trials); the best performance was again evident only when both types of priming were present. One interpretation of these results is that recent prior experience with alternative priming modes interferes to some degree with subsequent elicitation of an attentional state using only a single mode.

BACKGROUND MATCHING

One of the ways in which hunting by expectation might commonly be cued in nature is by the characteristics of the background being searched. For example, many palatable insects prefer to rest on substrates on which they are difficult to detect (e.g., *Catocala* moths: Sargent, 1976), so that the preferred background would differ for different species. This possibility is supported by the results of a study of background cuing by Dukas and Kamil (2001). Two targets that were disparate in appearance were presented on different backgrounds, so that the appearance of the background predicted which prey type might be present. By alternating trial types in rapid succession over the course of a session, jays were forced to switch between these different targets. There was little cost to this switching, in that the accuracy and speed of visual search were largely unaffected by whether the shifts were frequent or rare. This pattern of results suggests that the associative cues provided by the background may have facilitated a rapid and efficient switching of attention between the prey types.

This hypothesis was supported by the results of another experiment (Dukas & Kamil, 2001) in which the two targets were presented on the same background, one on which they were equally difficult to detect. Under these conditions, blue jays had to search simultaneously for both cryptic targets, and their overall rate of target detection was reduced by 25%; dividing attentional resources between difficult tasks reduced performance compared with focusing full attention on a single task. The reduction in switching costs when the jays were given an associative cue by the differing backgrounds suggests an attentional priming effect by the different backgrounds.

In contrast, an earlier study on background cuing by Kono et al. (1998) produced paradoxical effects. Jays were trained to search projected photographic images for two moths: *C. relicta,* a black and white moth normally found on white birch trees, and *C. retecta,* a brownish gray and black species commonly found on oaks. During the experiment, relicta was always displayed on birches, retecta on oaks. Each displayed image included two trees, either both birch, both oak, or one birch and one oak. The birch and oak displays were predictive of which moth might be present; the oak/birch combination was not, as either relicta or retecta (each on its appropriate background) sometimes occurred in this set of images. The results were clear, if puzzling. When runs of a single prey type were presented, the runs had significant effects only when the tree background was predictive of the moth. In addition, there was no evidence that the associative cue provided by the background served as an effective prime; the birds showed no general effect of consistent versus inconsistent background on search accuracy.

At the time, we interpreted these results as demonstrating that the inconsistent background (birch and oak in the same display) somehow interfered with sequential priming. In light of Belik's (2002) results, however, these data could well be another example of an interaction between different types of priming in a within-subjects design. As in Belik's study, only sessions in which both sequential and associative priming cues were present (runs of a single prey type plus a background that predicted prey type) resulted in significant improvement in detection. These results provide further evidence that there may be important interactions of associative and sequential priming.

The results of the studies reviewed in the last two sections of this chapter clearly indicate that further study of the mechanisms leading to sequential and associative priming is needed. We believe that this research also demonstrates the benefits that can accrue to those interested in the cognitive capacities of animals to pursue research that is informed by knowledge of the problems that animals face in nature. Cognition plays an important role in nature, affecting interactions within and between species in many different contexts, ranging from predator–prey interactions and foraging behavior to the acquisition and use of social knowledge (e.g., Balda, Pepperberg & Kamil, 1998). Conversely, if cognition plays an important role in nature, then students of nature must also become students of cognition. In the concluding section of this chapter, we review some of our research that has taken methods and ideas from the study of animal cognition and applied them to questions of interest to evolutionary biologists.

BIOLOGICAL AND EVOLUTIONARY IMPLICATIONS

The Costs of Selective Attention

One factor that is often ignored in discussions of cognitive evolution is the potential costs of cognitive abilities, a disregard that is probably attributable to lack of knowledge. It is clear that it is expensive to produce and maintain nervous tissue, and to the degree that additional cognitive abilities require additional neural circuitry, the metabolic costs involved could potentially be substantial. Attwell and Laughlin (2001) recently estimated the energetic cost of signaling-related energy use in mammalian brain tissue at approximately 30 μmol of ATP/g of tissue/min, which is approximately equal to the energy use by human leg muscles while running a marathon. They also found that a very large percentage of total energy use by the brain is caused by the costs of generating action potentials: To generate an action potential in a single neuron, 1.16 billion Na^+ ions must be pumped across the cell membrane, requiring 384 million molecules of ATP.

The high cost of neural tissue has important implications for the evolution of cognitive abilities. If a trait is costly to develop and/or maintain, it follows that organisms that exhibit the trait must obtain considerable, compensatory benefits from its possession. Consider, for example, vision in cave-dwelling fishes. As a general rule, vision is a highly beneficial trait for fishes, but it is also clearly expensive to develop and maintain both the eye itself and the neural tissue that supports vision, suggesting that vision would be lost quickly in fish that inhabited an environment in which the usual benefits of vision were not available. This loss is exactly what has occurred independently in many different lineages of cave fish. In fact, recent evidence suggests that, even in the case of a single genus, *Astyanax*, blindness has evolved independently in isolated populations from different caves in Mexico and the southwestern United States (Wilkens & Strecker, 2003). Analogous considerations of the likely costs of cognitive abilities thus suggest that such abilities must confer consistent, substantial benefits on those individual organisms that possess them if they are to be retained over successive generations of evolution. No cognitive ability would be favored by natural and/or sexual selection, if it did not provide substantial, immediate benefits to the individual.

In the case of selective attention, there are additional potential costs, in that, for example, foragers searching for difficult, cryptic food items must devote proportionately more of their attention to food finding and thus may be less likely to notice peripheral stimuli. This peripheral disregard might then render them more susceptible to attack from approaching predators. This hypothesis is supported by data from several naturalistic studies during which reactions to model predators were less likely when foragers were engaged in a more challenging foraging task (Krause & Godin, 1996; Milinski & Heller, 1978). However, these experiments did not directly control or measure attentional focus, and are therefore subject to alternative interpretations.

Dukas and Kamil (2000) developed a novel approach to directly assessing attentional costs, using an adaptation of our operant prey detection procedures. When blue jays were trained to detect targets that could occur either at the center or in the periphery of a visual display, birds that were searching for central cryptic targets were only one third as likely to detect interpolated trials with peripheral targets as were birds that were searching for central conspicuous targets. The two experimental treatments (easy versus difficult central detection) involved the same background and distractor elements, the same level of conspicuousness of the peripheral targets, and the same frequencies of target appearance within the visual field. The difficult central detection treatment required the bird to dedicate more attention to the center of the visual field, resulting in a reduced frequency of detecting the peripheral targets than during the easy central detection treatment. This experiment thus supports the hypothesis that attending to difficult to find food items carries with it the cost of failing to detect important stimuli, such as those emanating from a predator or social competitor.

The Generation and Maintenance of Phenotypic Diversity

One of the most fundamental issues in biological evolution is concerned with the mechanisms that contribute to generating biodiversity. Density-dependent processes, which select against more abundant forms and in favor of forms that are rarer, presumably play an important role in encouraging development and maintenance of diversity. Apostatic selection, in which a predator concentrates its predation on the most common prey, has long been proposed as a primary example of such density-dependent selection. Many studies have demonstrated such "overselection" by predators, at least to the degree of showing that predators take a larger proportion of the most abundant item in a field of multiple targets (reviewed earlier in this chapter). This does not actually suffice as a demonstration of apostatic selection, however. To maintain diversity, predators would have to cease searching for previously common prey once they became rare, thereby giving the prey a chance to recover. Likewise, they would have to initiate searching for previously rare and ignored prey types when they had increased to some appropriate level of abundance.

A full test of the hypothesis needed to include these features of the dynamic interaction of predators and prey populations, the "switching" process that was actually responsible for producing stable diversity. Dynamic predator–prey interactions were, however, very difficult to emulate in laboratory studies. Based on our earlier operant work, we developed what has proved to be a very successful approach that allows repeatable, laboratory investigations of the selective effects of predation on prey appearance. This "virtual ecology" technique has been used with considerable success to examine the evolutionary origins of cryptic pattern polymorphism (Bond & Kamil, 1998, 2002; Kamil & Bond, 2001, 2002).

Digital moths were first used to test the prediction that frequency-dependent predation, in and of itself, can maintain a balanced polymorphism (Bond & Kamil, 1998). We created a virtual prey population with equal numbers of each of three distinctive morphs and exposed them to daily predation by blue jays. Detected moths were considered "killed" and were subsequently removed from the population. Moths that were overlooked were allowed to breed, bringing the population up to its previous level the following day. Each day thus constituted a generation. Our only experimental intervention was to set the initial numbers of the morphs. In essence, the population of digital moths was a set of asexually reproducing clones of invariant appearance. The number of each morph in each generation was brought up to a constant size based on the relative numbers of surviving individuals in the preceding generation. This design is effectively a "coexistence" experiment (Kassen,

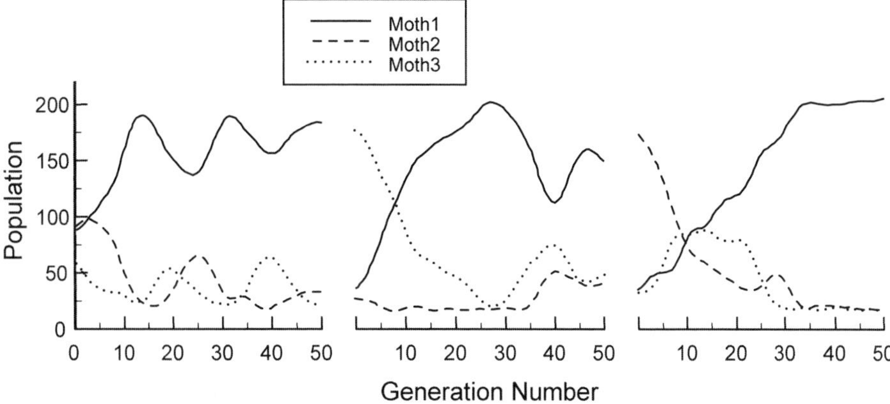

Figure 6.5. Population numbers of three prey morphs in three successive replications of our virtual prey procedure. Curves were smoothed with weighted least squares, using an eight-generation window. (Redrawn from Bond & Kamil, 1998).

2002), in which the population dynamics of the different morphs and their asymptotic levels of abundance are the principal dependent variables.

In all three replications, each of which continued for 50 generations, the numbers of the three morphs rapidly achieved a characteristic equilibrium that was independent of initial relative abundances and resistant to perturbation (figure 6.5). Additional analyses demonstrated that the equilibrium was a consequence of apostatic selection. One of the morphs happened to be somewhat more difficult to detect than the other two; whatever the starting numbers of the three morphs, this one increased within the population. However, as it increased, the probability of its detection by the blue jays increased, which resulted in the numbers of that morph decreasing, along with the probability of detection. The result was a dynamic, oscillatory equilibrium, maintained entirely by apostatic selection. These experiments constituted the first direct demonstration of the dynamic relationship between searching image, apostatic selection, and prey population stability (Allen, 1988; Cooper and Allen, 1994).

Bond and Kamil (1998) also tested the effects of apostatic selection on novel morphs. We twice introduced small numbers of a new prey type into the population. In each case, they were not initially detected by the jays, and their abundance rapidly increased. In one case, the jays ultimately took notice of the new morph and drove its numbers down, establishing a new equilibrium state. In the second case, the new morph was exceedingly cryptic, most of the jays never learned to detect it, and its numbers increased until it dominated the population (figure 6.6). Overall, these results indicated that virtual ecology can be used to study how predator behavior influences prey population dynamics. To extend these procedures to address the evolution of prey appearance, however, we needed to develop a virtual moth genome that would specify digital moth phenotypes.

This genome incorporates many salient features of the developmental genetics of lepidopteran wing patterns (Brakefield et al., 1996; Carroll et al., 1994; Nijhout, 1991; Robinson, 1971), including loci that code for individual patches of pattern elements, loci that produce global changes in wing brightness or contrast without modifying pattern elements, and linkage mechanisms that protect favorable genetic combinations from being lost during recombination. As in real moths, phenotypic characters are polygenic. The genome is divided into nine linkage groups, each of which contains two patch loci and a regulatory locus that include genes for brightness, contrast, and crossing-over probability. Recombination in this system helps to ensure that deleterious patterns are rapidly removed from the population. To preserve integrated pattern features from being broken up by recombination, crossing-over only takes place between linkage groups, and the probability of a cross-over is determined by the combined values of the recombination probability regulators above and below the exchange point. Mutation takes place in bitwise

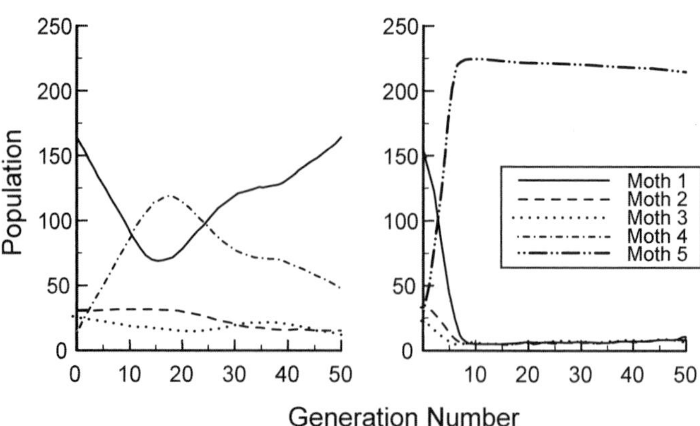

Figure 6.6. Population numbers of four morphs when one was a new morph, first introduced during generation 1. Curves were smoothed with weighted least squares, using an eight-generation window. Replication 4 (*left*), included moths 1 to 3 from previous replications and novel moth 4; replication 5 (*right*) included moths 1 to 3 and novel moth 5. (Redrawn from Bond & Kamil, 1998.)

fashion: The algorithm searches down the genome string and, with a fixed, low probability, randomly selects bits to be toggled. We used Gray code for interpreting gene values, which minimizes the coded distance between adjacent integers and reduces the average phenotypic effects of any single mutation (Bäck, 1996; Mars, Chen, & Namibar, 1996).

In the first study using this genome (Bond & Kamil, 2002), we created a parental population of 200 moths with moderate genetic variance and subjected their phenotypes to predation by jays. The speed and accuracy with which each moth was detected determined its fitness—its probability of reproduction. Detected moths had a significantly reduced likelihood of being chosen as parents, and moths that took longer to detect had a higher probability of breeding than those that were detected quickly. Based on these fitness values, pairs of individuals were chosen to breed using a linear ranking algorithm (Bäck, 1996; Mars et al., 1996). Each pair produced one offspring that was a recombined product of the two parental genotypes. Once the progeny genomes had been obtained, they were passed through a mutation step, with mutation probability of about three events per genome per pairing. Breeding and mutation steps were repeated 200 times, producing the next generation. The previous generation was then discarded, and the new moths were exposed to another round of predation trials. We repeated this experiment three times, each time beginning from the same initial parental population and allowing the jays to determine moth-breeding success for 100 successive progeny generations. This design, in which moth genomes evolve in response to jay predation, is essentially a classic selection experiment (Kassen, 2002). The effects of selection within experimental lines are contrasted to those in control lineages with differing selective regimens.

Our primary interests were whether the moths would show consistent directional selection for increased crypticity and whether the prey population would increase in phenotypic variance, as would be expected from the operation of frequency-dependent, apostatic selection. We developed an empirical measure of crypticity, based on suggestions by Endler (1984, 1990), that compared the distribution of pixel values in the moth with those of the surrounding background. Phenotypic diversity was measured by mean phenotypic distance between each of the individuals in the population and the prototypic "medoid" individual (Kaufman & Rousseeuw, 1990).

To test whether observed changes in crypticity and phenotypic variance in the experimental lines were meaningful, the results were contrasted to those from two sets of control lineages. In both control treatments, we used the same population size, initial parental population, backgrounds, and mutation rate as in the experimental treatment. The first control was for drift, random changes in the genome due to mutation and recombination. In these nonselected lineages, however, the moths were not presented to the jays; instead, the probability of being chosen to breed was uniform across the moth population, regardless of phenotype. This methodology provided a control for the occurrence of directional selection for crypticity in the experimental treatments. For example, if our parental population happened to be more or less cryptic than the "average random" moth produced by the genotype, then random reproduction would produce

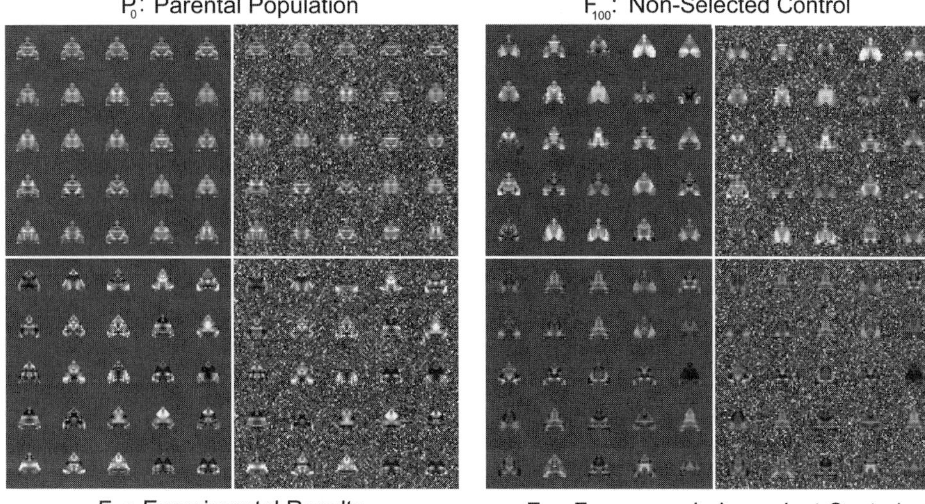

Figure 6.7. Each of the four panels shows 25 randomly selected moths from a different population. Within each panel, the same moths are shown on a plain gray background (*left*) and on a cryptic background (*right*). *Top left,* Moths from the parental generation, before any selection. *Bottom left,* Moths from a population that experienced 100 generations of selection by blue jays. *Top right,* Moths from a population that experienced 100 generations of genetic drift, without selection. *Bottom right,* Moths from a population that experienced 100 generations of selection by "virtual jays," simulated jays without selective attention. (Redrawn from Bond & Kamil, 2002.)

some changes in crypticity, as a kind of regression toward the mean.

The second control was designed to assess our primary hypothesis—that frequency-dependent selection promotes increased phenotypic diversity. The drift control was not adequate for testing this hypothesis because there are more possible phenotypes than there are phenotypes that are cryptic. Random drift, in and of itself, is expected to result in some increase in variability, so we needed a control that would constrain random drift with the need to appear cryptic. In order to accomplish this aim, our second control involved lineages in which selection was independent of the frequency of particular phenotypes but was otherwise similar in intensity and direction to those produced in the experimental lines. For these control lineages, we determined the functional relationship between detection and crypticity for the jays, averaging over all of the results in the experimental lines. This function was then used to determine the probability of a moth's being chosen to breed. That is, the crypticity of each moth was calculated on the basis of its resemblance to the background, and then a look-up table was used to determine the probability of detection for that moth. That probability of detection was then used to determine the probability of reproduction and the next generation produced by the same algorithm used in the other lineages. In essence, this control was a simulated blue jay that hunted without any density dependence. The detection performance of the simulated jay was determined solely by the degree of resemblance of each moth to the background but was unaffected by any recent experience with moths of differing appearance.

The results were striking and unequivocal for both crypticity and variability (figures 6.7 to 6.9). Over successive generations, the experimental moths evolved to become significantly harder to detect, indicating strong directional selection for increased crypticity. Selection in favor of individuals that resemble the background has been invoked as the probable cause of cryptic coloration in prey species for over a century (Poulton, 1890), and there have been numerous demonstrations that predators preferentially feed on more conspicuous prey items (Cott, 1957; Endler, 1978; Robinson, 1969). Our study is, however, the only work other than Endler's (1980) research on color-pattern

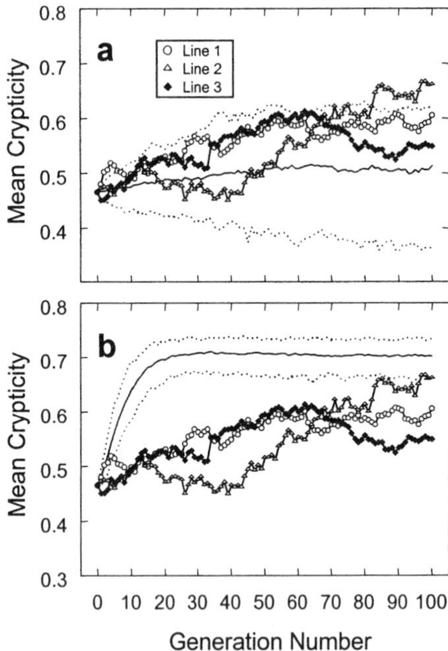

Figure 6.8. Changes in mean crypticity across successive generations in the three experimental lines (plotted with symbols), contrasted with the distribution of values from the two sets of control lines. Nonselected lines form the control group (*a*); the control in (*b*) was produced by frequency-independent selection for crypticity based on parameters derived from global aspects of the jays' behavior. Graphs display medians (solid lines) and 95% confidence limits (dotted lines) from 200 replicate control lines. Crypticity increased across generations to some degree in all three treatments; the increase was greatest for the frequency-independent controls and least for the nonselected lines. Parameters derived from global aspects of the jays' behavior. (Redrawn from Bond & Kamil, 2002.)

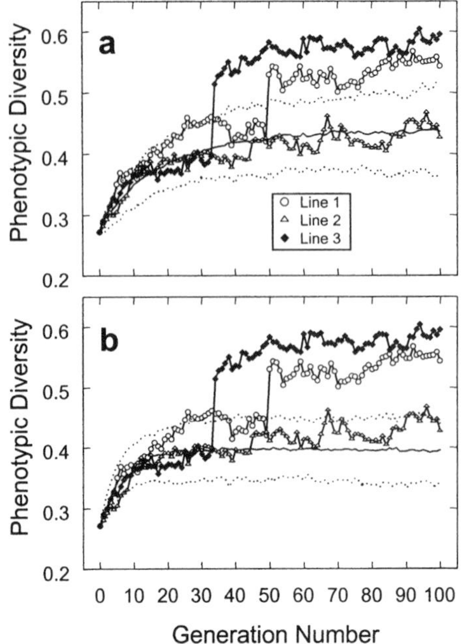

Figure 6.9. Changes in phenotypic variance across successive generations. Graphs display medians (solid lines) and 95% confidence limits (dotted lines) from 200 replicate control lines. Phenotypic variance increased to some degree in all three treatments, but the increase was greater in the experimental lines than in the controls. Experimental lines 1 and 3 each exhibited an abrupt shift to a higher level of phenotypic variance at some point in the course of selection trials. (Redrawn from Bond & Kamil, 2002.)

selection in guppies that has shown significant directional selection by predators over multiple successive prey generations compared with a nonselected control. But the most important finding was that the experimental lines (figure 6.7) showed significantly greater phenotypic variance than either control (figures 6.8 and 6.9), demonstrating that frequency-dependent selection by visual predators can, by itself, promote high phenotypic diversity in prey species. Finally, and most crucially from the perspective of this chapter, additional analyses of the pattern of variation in detection as a function of prey sequences showed that the primary selective effect was due to jays overlooking atypical cryptic moths. These results thus constitute the most elegant and unequivocal evidence of searching image in the literature and the only demonstration of searching images in which the target stimuli were continuously varying.

CONCLUSIONS

We have chosen to approach the study of animal cognition in an integrative fashion, combining the methodology and insights of experimental psychology and evolutionary biology. This combination can be extraordinarily fruitful, yielding novel perspectives that can be applied broadly to the study of learning and memory in animals. In our own work, we have applied it to spatial cognition (e.g., Kamil & Cheng, 2001) and transitive inference (Bond, Kamil, & Balda, 2003; Paz-y-Miño, Bond, Kamil, & Balda, 2004), as well as to selective attention. One of our goals in this chapter has been to demonstrate how this integrative approach can lead to innovative and exciting research. Considerations of how foraging animals might use selective attention while searching for cryptic prey have resulted in interesting questions that focus on the mechanisms of selective attention. The field research of Tinbergen (1960) and others, for instance, gave rise to the concept of the searching image and the study of sequential priming. More recently, considerations of how attentional processes might be integrated in nature gave rise to new questions about sequential and associative priming (Belik, 2002).

One special point we would like to emphasize for experimental psychologists is the enormous contribution that the concepts and methods of experimental psychology can bring to important biological questions. Evolutionary biology has sometimes been criticized for generating just-so stories (e.g., Gould & Lewontin, 1979), post hoc explanations of findings. But the primary difference between a just-so story and a scientific hypothesis is the availability of an empirical test. Untestable hypotheses are just stories. Let someone figure out a way to test an apparently untestable explanation for a phenomenon, however, and a magical transformation occurs: just-so story becomes scientific hypothesis. As our work on the costs of selective attention and on the effects of attentional processes on the evolution of the appearance of prey demonstrates, the ideas and methods of psychology can be used to empirically test many evolutionary ideas, particularly those in which the decisions of one organism have effects on another, through either natural or sexual selection.

Acknowledgments The research reported in this chapter has been supported by multiple grants from the National Science Foundation and the National Institute of Mental Health, most recently IBN-0234441 (NSF) and MH68426 (NIMH).

References

Allen, J. A. (1988). Frequency-dependent selection by predators. *Philosophical Transactions of the Royal Society of London B, 319*, 485–503.

Allen, J. A., & Clarke, B. (1968). Evidence for apostatic selection in wild passerines. *Nature, 220*, 501–502.

Attwell, D., & Laughlin, S. B. (2001). An energy budget for signaling in the grey matter of the brain. *Journal of Cerebral Blood Flow and Metabolism, 21*, 1133–1145.

Bäck, T. (1996). *Evolutionary algorithms in theory and practice.* New York: Oxford University Press.

Balda, R., Pepperberg, I., & Kamil, A. C. (1998). *Animal cognition in nature.* New York: Academic Press.

Belik, M. (2002). *Effects of two different types of priming on visual search in the blue jay (Cyanocitta cristata).* Unpublished doctoral dissertation, University of Nebraska, Lincoln.

Beller, H. K. (1971). Priming: Effects of advance information on matching. *Journal of Experimental Psychology, 57*, 976–982.

Blough, D. S. (2002). Measuring the search image: Expectation, detection, and recognition in pigeon visual search. *Journal of Experimental Psychology: Animal Behavior Processes, 28*, 397–405.

Blough, P. M. (1989). Attentional priming and search images in pigeons. *Journal of Experimental Psychology: Animal Behavior Processes, 15*, 211–223.

Blough, P. M. (1991). Selective attention and search images in pigeons. *Journal of Experimental Psychology: Animal Behavior Processes, 17*, 292–298.

Blough, P. M. (1992). Detectability and choice during visual search: Joint effects of sequential priming and discriminability. *Animal Learning and Behavior, 20*, 293–300.

Blough, P. M. (1996). Priming during multiple-target search: The cumulative effects of relative target frequency. *Animal Learning and Behavior, 24*, 394–400.

Blough, P. M., & Lacourse, D. M. (1994). Sequential priming in visual search: Contributions of stimulus-driven facilitation and learned expectancies. *Animal Learning and Behavior, 22*, 275–281.

Bond, A. B. (1982). The bead game: Response strategies in free assortment. *Human Factors, 24*, 101–110.

Bond, A. B. (1983). Visual search and selection of natural stimuli in the pigeon: The attention threshold hypothesis. *Journal of Experimental Psychology: Animal Behavior Processes, 9*, 292–306.

Bond, A. B., & Kamil, A. C. (1998). Apostatic selection by blue jays produces balanced polymorphism in virtual prey. *Nature, 395*, 594–596.

Bond, A. B., & Kamil, A. C. (1999). Searching image in blue jays: Facilitation and interference in sequential priming. *Animal Learning and Behavior, 27,* 461–471.

Bond, A. B., & Kamil, A. C. (2002). Visual predators select for crypticity and polymorphism in virtual prey. *Nature, 415,* 609–614.

Bond, A. B., Kamil, A. C., & Balda, R. P. (2003). Social complexity and transitive inference in corvids. *Animal Behaviour, 65,* 479–487.

Bond, A. B., & Riley, D. A. (1991). Searching image in the pigeon: A test of three hypothetical mechanisms. *Ethology, 87,* 203–224.

Brakefield, P. M., Gates, J., Keyes, D., Kesbeke, F., Wijngaarden, P. J., Monteiro, A., et al. (1996). Development, plasticity and evolution of butterfly eyespot patterns. *Nature, 384,* 236–242.

Broadbent, D. E. (1958). *Perception and communication.* London: Pergamon.

Broadbent, D. E. (1971). *Decision and stress.* New York: Academic Press.

Caraco, T. (1980). On foraging time allocation in a stochastic environment. *Ecology, 61,* 119–128.

Caraco, T. (1981). Energy budgets, risk and foraging preferences in dark-eyed juncos (*Junco hyemalis*). *Behavioral Ecology and Sociobiology, 8,* 213–217.

Caraco, T., Martindale, S., & Whitham, T. S. (1980). An empirical demonstration of risk-sensitive foraging preferences. *Animal Behaviour, 28,* 820–830.

Carroll, S. B., Gates, J., Paddock, S. W., Panganiban, G. E. F., Selegue, J. E., & Williams, J. A. (1994). Pattern formation and eyespot determination in butterfly wings. *Science, 265,* 109–114.

Charnov, E. L. (1976). Optimal foraging: The marginal value theorem. *Theoretical Population Biology, 9,* 129–136.

Cink, C. (2002). *Factors influencing the use of searching images by blue jays hunting for cryptic prey.* Unpublished doctoral dissertation, University of Nebraska, Lincoln.

Clarke, B. C. (1962). Balanced polymorphism and the diversity of sympatric species. In D. Nichols (Ed.), *Taxonomy and geography* (pp. 47–70). Oxford: Systematics Association.

Clarke, B. C. (1969). The evidence for apostatic selection. *Heredity, 24,* 347–352.

Cooper, J. M. (1984). Apostatic selection on prey that match the background. *Biological Journal of the Linnaean Society, 23,* 221–228.

Cooper, J. M., & Allen, J. A. (1994). Selection by wild birds on artificial dimorphic prey on varied backgrounds. *Biological Journal of the Linnaean Society, 51,* 433–446.

Cott, H. B. (1957). *Adaptive coloration in animals.* London: Methuen.

Croze, H. J. (1970). Searching image in carrion crows. *Zeitschrift für Tierpsychologie Supplement, 5,* 1–85.

Dawkins, M. (1971). Shifts in "attention" in chicks during feeding. *Animal Behaviour, 19,* 575–582.

Dukas, R. (2002). Behavioural and ecological consequences of limited attention. *Philosophical Transactions of the Royal Society of London B, 357,* 1539–1547.

Dukas, R., & Kamil, A. C. (2000). The cost of limited attention in blue jays. *Behavioral Ecology, 11,* 502–506.

Dukas, R., & Kamil, A. C. (2001). Limited attention: The constraint underlying search image. *Behavioral Ecology, 12,* 192–199.

Endler, J. A. (1978). A predator's view of animal color patterns. *Evolutionary Biology, 11,* 319–364.

Endler, J. A. (1980). Natural selection on color patterns in *Poecilia reticulata. Evolution, 34,* 76–91.

Endler, J. A. (1984). Progressive background matching in moths, and a quantitative measure of crypsis. *Biological Journal of the Linnaean Society, 22,* 187–231.

Endler, J. A. (1990). On the measurement and classification of colour in studies of animal colour patterns. *Biological Journal of the Linnaean Society, 41,* 315–352.

Eriksen, C. W., & Hoffmann, J. E. (1972). Some characteristics of selective attention in visual perception determined by vocal reaction time. *Perception and Psychophysics, 11,* 169–171.

Fantino, E. (1987). Operant conditioning simulations of foraging and the delay-reduction hypothesis. In A. C. Kamil, J. R. Krebs, & H. R. Pulliam (Eds.), *Foraging behavior* (pp. 193–214). New York: Plenum.

Gendron, R. P. (1986). Searching for cryptic prey: Evidence for optimal search rates and the formation of search images in quail. *Animal Behaviour, 34,* 898–912.

Gendron, R. P., & Staddon, J. E. R. (1983). Searching for cryptic prey: The effect of search rate. *American Naturalist, 121,* 172–186.

Gendron, R. P., & Staddon, J. E. R. (1984). A laboratory simulation of foraging behavior: The effect of search rate on the probability of detecting prey. *American Naturalist, 124,* 407–415.

Getty, T., Kamil, A. C., & Real, P. G. (1987). Signal detection theory and foraging for cryptic or mimetic prey. In A. C. Kamil, J. R. Krebs, & H. R. Pulliam (Eds.), *Foraging behavior* (pp. 525–548). New York: Plenum.

Getty, T., & Pulliam, H. R. (1991). Random prey detection with pause-travel search. *American Naturalist, 138,* 1459–1477.

Getty, T., & Pulliam, H. R. (1993). Search and prey detection by foraging sparrows. *Ecology, 74,* 734–742.

Gould, S. J., & Lewontin, R. C. (1979). The spandrels of San Marco and the Panglossian paradigm: A critique of the adaptionist programme. *Proceedings of the Royal Society of London, 205,* 581–598.

Guilford, T., & Dawkins, M. S. (1987). Search images not proven: A reappraisal of recent evidence. *Animal Behaviour, 35*, 1838–1845.

Heinrich, B., & Collins, S. L. (1983). Caterpillar leaf damage and the game of hide-and-seek with birds. *Ecology, 64*, 592–602.

Heinrich, B., Mudge, P., & Deringis, P. (1977). A laboratory analysis of flower constancy in foraging bumblebees: *Bombus ternarius* and *B. terricola*. *Behavioral Ecology, 2*, 247–266.

Herrnstein, R. J., & Loveland, D. H. (1964). Complex visual concepts in the pigeon. *Science, 146*, 549–551.

Holling, C. S. (1965). The functional response of predators to prey density and its role in mimicry and population regulation. *Memoirs of the Entomological Society of Canada, 45*, 1–60.

Holling, C. S. (1966). The functional response of invertebrate predators to prey density. *Memoirs of the Entomological Society of Canada, 48*, 3–86.

Humphreys, G. W., & Bruce, V. (1989). *Visual cognition: Computational, experimental, and neuropsychological perspectives*. Hillsdale, NJ: Lawrence Erlbaum.

Husband, S., & Shimizu, T. (2001). Evolution of the avian visual system. In R. G. Cook (Ed.), *Avian visual cognition*. Retrieved August 30, 2005, from http://www.pigeon.psy.tufts.edu/avc/husband/default.htm

James, W. (1950). *Principles of psychology*, Vol. I (pp. 402–458). New York: Dover Publications (original work published 1890).

Kahneman, D. (1973). *Attention and effort*. Englewood Cliffs, NJ: Prentice-Hall.

Kamil, A. C., & Bond, A. B. (2001). The evolution of virtual ecology. In L. A. Dugatkin (Ed.), *Model systems in behavioral ecology* (pp. 288–310). Princeton, NJ: Princeton University Press.

Kamil, A. C., & Bond, A. B. (2002). Cognition as an independent variable: Virtual ecology. In M. Bekoff, C. Allen, & G. Burghart (Eds.), *The cognitive animal: Empirical and theoretical perspectives on animal cognition* (pp. 143–149). Cambridge, MA: MIT Press.

Kamil, A. C., & Cheng, K. 2001. Way-finding and landmarks: The multiple-bearings hypothesis. *Journal of Experimental Biology, 204*, 103–113.

Kamil, A. C., Krebs, J. R., & Pulliam, H. R. (1987). *Foraging behavior*. New York: Plenum.

Kamil, A. C., Lindstrom, F., & Peters, J. (1985). Foraging for cryptic prey by blue jays. I. The effects of travel time. *Animal Behaviour, 33*, 1068–1079.

Kamil, A. C., & Sargent, T. D. (1981). *Foraging behavior: Ecological, ethological and psychological approaches*. New York: Garland Press.

Kassen, R. (2002). The experimental evolution of specialists, generalists, and the maintenance of diversity. *Journal of Evolutionary Biology, 15*, 173–190.

Kaufman, L., & Rousseeuw, P. J. (1990). *Finding groups in data: An introduction to cluster analysis*. New York: Wiley.

Kono, H., Reid, P. J., & Kamil, A. C. (1998). The effects of background cuing on prey detection. *Animal Behaviour, 56*, 963–972.

Krause, J., & Godin, J. G. J. 1996. Influence of prey foraging posture on flight behavior and predation risk: Predators take advantage of unwary prey. *Behavioral Ecology, 7*, 264–271.

Krebs, J. R. (1973). Behavioral aspects of predation. In P. P. G. Bateson & P. H. Klopfer (Eds.), *Perspectives in ethology*, Vol. 1 (pp. 73–111). New York: Plenum.

Krebs, J. R., Erichsen, J. T., Webber, M. I., & Charnov, E. L. (1977). Optimal prey selectiion in the great tit (*Parus major*). *Animal Behaviour, 25*, 30–38.

Krebs, J. R., Ryan, J. C., & Charnov, E. L. (1974). Hunting by expectation or optimal foraging? A study of patch use by chickadees. *Animal Behaviour, 22*, 953–964.

Langley, C. M. (1996). Search images: Selective attention to specific visual features of prey. *Journal of Experimental Psychology-Animal Behavior Processes, 22*, 152–163.

Langley, C. M., Riley, D. A., Bond, A. B., & Goel, N. (1996). Visual search for natural grains in pigeons (*Columba livia*): Search images and selective attention. *Journal of Experimental, Psychology: Animal Behavior Processes, 22*, 139–151.

Macarthur, R. H., & Pianka, E. R. (1966). On optimal use of a patchy environment. *American Naturalist, 100*, 603–609.

Mackintosh, N. J. (1975). A theory of attention: Variations in the associability of stimuli with reinforcement. *Psychological Review, 82*, 276–298.

Mars, P., Chen, J. R., & Namibar, R. (1996). *Learning algorithms: Theory and applications in signal processing, control and communications*. New York: CRC Press.

Meyer, D. B. C. (1977). The avian eye and its adaptations. In F. Crescitelli (Ed.), *The visual system of vertebrates: Handbook of sensory physiology*, Vol. VII (pp. 549–611). Berlin: Springer-Verlag.

Milinski, M., & Heller, R. (1978). Influence of a predator on the optimal foraging behavior of sticklebacks (*Gasterosteus aculeatus*). *Nature, 275*, 642–644.

Murdoch, W. W. (1969). Switching in general predators: Experiments on predator specificity and stability of prey populations. *Ecological Monographs, 39*, 335–354.

Murdoch, W. W., & Oaten, A. (1974). Predation and population stability. *Advances in Ecological Research, 9*, 1–131.

Murton, R. K. (1971). The significance of a specific search image in the feeding behavior of the wood-pigeon. *Behaviour, 40*, 10–42.

Nijhout, H. F. (1991). *The development and evolution of butterfly wing patterns.* Washington, DC: Smithsonian Institution.

Parasuraman, R., & Davies, D. R. (Eds.) (1984). *Varieties of attention.* New York: Academic Press.

Pashler, H. E. (1998). *The psychology of attention.* Cambridge, MA: MIT Press.

Paz-y-Miño, C. G., Bond, A. B., Kamil, A. C., & Balda, R. P. (2004). Pinyon jays use transitive inference to predict social dominance. *Nature, 430,* 778–781.

Pietrewicz, A. T., & Kamil, A. C. (1977). Visual detection of cryptic prey by blue jays (*Cyanocitta cristata*). *Science, 195,* 580–582.

Pietrewicz, A. T., & Kamil, A. C. (1979). Search image formation in the blue jay (*Cyanocitta cristata*). *Science, 204,* 1332–1333.

Pietrewicz, A. T., & Kamil, A. C. (1981). Search images and the detection of cryptic prey: An operant approach. In A. C. Kamil & T. D. Sargent (Eds.), *Foraging behavior: Ecological, ethological and psychological approaches* (pp. 311–332*)*. New York: Garland.

Plaisted, K. (1997). The effect of interstimulus interval on the discrimination of cryptic targets. *Journal of Experimental Psychology: Animal Behavior Processes, 23,* 248–259.

Plaisted, K.C., & Mackintosh, N. J. (1995). Visual search for cryptic stimuli in pigeons: Implications for the search image and search rate hypotheses. *Animal Behaviour, 50,* 1219–1232.

Posner, M. I., & Snyder, C. R. R. (1975). Facilitation and inhibition in the processing of signals. In P. M. R. S. Dornic (Ed.), *Attention and performance, V* (pp. 669–682). San Diego, CA: Academic Press.

Poulton, E. B. (1890). *The colours of animals: Their meaning and use, especially considered in the case of insects.* New York: Appleton.

Real, P. G., Ianazzi, R., Kamil, A. C., & Heinrich, B. (1984). Discrimination and generalization of leaf damage by blue jays. *Animal Learning and Behavior, 12,* 202–208.

Reid, P. J., & Shettleworth, S. J. (1992). Detection of cryptic prey: Search image or search rate? *Journal of Experimental Psychology; Animal Behavior Processes, 18*, 273–286.

Richards, J. E. (Ed.). (1998). *Cognitive neuroscience of attention.* Mahwah, NJ: Lawrence Erlbaum.

Riley, D. A., & Leith, C. R. (1976). Multidimensional psychophysics and selective attention in animals. *Psychological Bulletin, 83*, 138–160.

Riley, D. A., & Roitblat, H. L. (1978). Selective attention and related cognitive processes in pigeons. In S. H. Hulse, H. Fowler, & W. K. Honig (Eds.), *Cognitive processes in animal behavior* (pp. 249–276). Hillsdale, NJ: Lawrence Erlbaum.

Robinson, M. H. (1969). Defenses against visually hunting predators. *Evolutionary Biology, 3,* 225–259.

Robinson, R. (1971). *Lepidopteran genetics.* Oxford: Pergamon Press.

Royama, T. (1970). Factors governing the hunting behavior and selection of food by the great tit (*Parus major L.*). *Journal of Animal Ecology, 39*, 619–668.

Sargent, T. D. (1976). *Legion of night.* Amherst, MA: University of Massachusetts Press.

Smith, J. N. M., & Dawkins, R. (1971). The hunting behavior of individual great tits in relation to spatial variations in their food density. *Animal Behaviour, 19*, 695–706.

Smith, J. N. M., & Sweatman, H. P. A. (1974). Food searching behavior of tit mice in patchy environments. *Ecology, 55*, 1216–1232.

Stephens, D. W., & Krebs, J. R. (1986). *Foraging theory.* Princeton, NJ: Princeton University Press.

Tarvin, K. A., & Woolfenden, G. E. (1999). *Blue jay* (*Cyanocitta cristata*). In A. Poole & F. Gill (Eds.), *The birds of North America, No. 469.* Philadelphia, PA: The Birds of North America, Inc.

Tinbergen, L. (1960). The natural control of insects in pinewoods. 1. Factors influencing the intensity of predation by songbirds. *Archives Néerlandaises de Zoologie, 13*, 265–343.

Treisman, A., & Gelade, G. (1980). A feature-integration theory of attention. *Cognitive Psychology, 12*, 97–136.

Vreven, D., & Blough, P. M. (1998). Searching for one or many targets: Effects of extended experience on the runs advantage. *Journal of Experimental Psychology: Animal Behavior Processes, 24*, 98–105.

Wilkens, H., & Strecker, U. (2003). Convergent evolution of the cavefish *Astyanax* (Characidae, Teleostei): Genetic evidence from reduced eye-size and pigmentation. *Biological Journal of the Linnean Society, 80*, 545–554.

7

Attention as It Is Manifest Across Species

DAVID A. WASHBURN AND LAUREN A. TAGLIALATELA

Attention was among the first topics of study in psychology. It was given prominent treatment in the seminal writings of Paulhan (see Woodruff, 1938), Wundt (see Blumenthal, 1980), and James (1890). The discipline's founders suggested that attention was pivotal to perception, consciousness, and will. Titchener (1908) even went so far as to argue that an individual's merit as a psychologist would be measured by that individual's understanding of attention.

These historical observations notwithstanding, one can make the case that the construct of attention is more central and more important in contemporary theory than at any other time in the history of psychology. Attention remains associated with the selection of which stimulus to process or of which response to execute, with the intensity of mental effort (concentration), with orienting, scanning, or searching behaviors, and with alertness and readiness to respond (including vigilance). In the cognitive theories of today, attention also plays a critical role in—and may in fact be synonymous with—perception (e.g., Treisman & Gelade, 1980), working memory (Kane, Bleckley, Conway, & Engle, 2001; Kane & Engle, 2003), and the collection of mental abilities subsumed under the rubric "executive function" (e.g., Morris, 1996). Consequently, virtually every behavior that is enacted or experienced is influenced at least in part by attention, broadly conceived in this way. If Wundt's prophesy that associationistic laws would be replaced by more powerful laws of attention (Blumenthal, 1980) has yet to be fulfilled, it is nevertheless true that associationistic language has been supplanted largely by theoretical appeals to attention.

This state of affairs characterizes contemporary research on comparative cognition as well, albeit to a lesser extent. Almost three decades ago, Riley and Roitblat (1978) acknowledged that it was controversial whether the construct of attention was even necessary for explaining an animal's performance in discrimination-learning tasks (see also Mackintosh, 1975). Thanks in large measure to the careful work by Riley and many others (e.g., D. S. Blough, 1969; Brown, Cook, Lamb, & Riley, 1984; Chatlosh & Wasserman, 1993; Leith & Maki, 1975; Mackintosh, 1965; Riley & Leith, 1976), we now consider it established that attention is part of the cognitive machinery that pigeons, rats, monkeys, and other animals deploy in processing stimuli into behavioral responses. Nonhuman animals, like humans, attend. They orient to some stimuli but not to others. Only some of the available response cues come to control behavior (in behaviorist terms) or become selected as salient for subsequent processing (in cognitive terms). Theories of attention—in contrast to "theories of human attention" or "theories of animal attention"—and of the relation of attention to other cognitive abilities must be able to account for these examples of selection, mental effort, and alertness, as well as those from human experience. Hence, it is important to build frameworks that accurately describe attention as it is manifest across species, paradigms, and contexts.

Accordingly, attention has been studied with monkeys, apes, pigeons, and other nonhuman animals. Nevertheless, this comparative literature differs from the human-attention literature both in the volume of studies and in the nature of the tasks that have been used. The number of studies with humans on attention is vast. PsycINFO lists more than 23,000 citations with "attention" as a keyword, the corresponding literature for nonhuman animals being only about 3% that size (although, of course, there are many studies that are about attention even though the word itself was not indicated specifically as a key concept). One would be hard pressed to summarize even the many excellent review papers of the attention literature (e.g., Berlyne, 1975; Broadbent, 1982; Egeth & Yantis, 1997; Johnston & Dark, 1986; Kinchla, 1992; Posner, 1982), let alone to summarize the human-attention literature itself. These reviews reveal a long list of experimental paradigms used to test attention in humans, including dichotic listening, visual search, cuing and antisaccade cuing, flanker, Stroop color-naming (and its many variants), rapid serial visual presentation, psychological refractory period (or attention switching), shadowing, signal detection (including vigilance), and dual-task methodologies.

In contrast, studies on attention with nonhuman animals have tended to feature variations of a paradigm quite unlike those used with humans, at least until recently. Animals, particularly pigeons and rats, have often been tested under conditions that produce selective stimulus control, such as discrimination learning or matching tests with simple versus compound stimuli, to determine whether attending to one stimulus dimension (e.g., shape) compromises responding on the basis of the other dimension (e.g., color). This is the procedure emphasized in the review by Riley and Roitblat (1978) and again 15 years later by Chatlosh and Wasserman (1993). That same year, this experimental method (or specifically the difference between the methods used to study attention in animals versus humans) was cited as one of the factors that limit neuropsychological studies of attention with animals (Olton, Pang, Merkel, & Egeth, 1993).

The purpose of this point is not to disparage the significance of the paradigms of selective stimulus control or the empirical phenomena such as blocking (Kamin, 1968) that are associated with them; as noted, these methods have served and continue to serve an important role in comparative cognition. Rather, we intend only to highlight one of the reasons that the animal-cognitive and human-cognitive investigations of attention have remained separate. Fortunately, the methods used to study animal attention have become more homologous to those used with humans over recent years, particularly with the advent of computer-based test apparatus (e.g., Rumbaugh, Richardson, Washburn, Savage-Rumbaugh, & Hopkins, 1989). Thus, both behavioral and neuropsychological research with animals is increasingly characterized by "animal friendly" versions of classic paradigms developed for testing human adults and children. Consequently, in the present chapter, we identify seven principles that emerge across the cognitive and comparative literatures. Specifically, what rule-like generalizations can be made about attention as it is manifest across species?

1. ONLY A SUBSET OF SIMULTANEOUS STIMULUS EVENTS ARE (AND CAN BE) PROCESSED INTO BEHAVIOR

The need to postulate attention as a mediating construct is predicated on the finding that organisms are limited in the information they process. If we could fully process all available input or simultaneously execute all required responses, then selection would be unnecessary. However, sensory stimulation of all types results in neural activity without being necessarily reflected in behavior. As one reads the words on this page, sounds are reaching the ears, smells are stimulating the nose, nerve cells in the skin are firing, and so forth without resulting in awareness, without overwhelming the reader with a dizzying array of distractions, and typically without manifesting an influence on behavior. People do not process all of the information that is available to them, and apparently they cannot process all of the information that is sensed.

The predominant finding from attention studies in the 1950s and 1960s, in which participants were asked to shadow (repeat aloud as they were hearing) a message played through headphones to one ear while a second message was played to the other ear, is that people were quite unable to report virtually anything from the unshadowed message. It appears that attending to one channel resulted in the filtering out or ignoring of other sources of input. People could report only the most general physical characteristics of the unattended message, failing to report words that were repeated many times in the unattended channel or even whether the unattended message was in English. Subsequent research did reveal exceptions to this rule (e.g., salient stimuli like one's own name or highly primed content might be detected in the unattended message), raising questions about how early in processing this attentional bottleneck occurred. However, the basic capacity limitations in human cognition—the inability to process all available information and the need to select a subset from the stimulus array for processing—were never overturned.

Nonhuman animals similarly receive much more stimulation than they can and do process. The aforementioned selective-stimulus-control paradigms illustrate this point. For example, D. S. Blough (1969) trained pigeons in a discrimination-learning format using two-dimensional compound stimuli, each composed of a visual element (light wavelength) and an auditory element (tone frequency). He found that conditions that elicited attention to one dimension resulted in better discriminative performance on that dimension but poorer performance on the unattended dimension.

Gottselig, Wasserman, and Young (2001) extended this finding to four-dimensional compound stimuli (using brightness, size, orientation, and shape as the manipulated dimensions). Each time a new dimension was added to the discrimination training that pigeons received (e.g., small + black + triangle in any orientation reinforced), performance was compromised on the most recently learned dimension of the prior phase (small + black of any shape or orientation reinforced). This finding, like others before it (e.g., D. S. Blough, 1969; see also reviews in Riley, 1984; Roberts, 1997; Roitblat, 1987; Trabasso & Bower, 1968), supports the "inverse hypothesis" (Thomas, 1970); this postulate suggests that as more attention is allocated to one stimulus or response, less attention is available to process other simultaneous inputs or outputs. This assumption, termed "the principle of complementarity" in the human-attention literature (Norman & Bobrow, 1975), was central to the logic of the dual-task research paradigm that dominated cognitive psychology in the 1970s and 1980s. Because attention is a limited resource (or limited-capacity channel or whatever metaphor one prefers for capturing the notion of capacity limitations), only a subset of stimuli becomes fully processed, and the remainder is either processed only partially by any remaining unassigned attention or is ignored altogether.

2. SOME STIMULI ARE DIFFICULT OR IMPOSSIBLE TO IGNORE, AND SEEM TO INFLUENCE BEHAVIOR EVEN WHEN IT IS NOT ADVANTAGEOUS TO DO SO

Although it is impossible to process all of the available information, some stimuli are more likely to be processed than are others; that is, some stimulus conditions appear to force themselves on the organism, to elicit subsequent processing, and to capture attention. A number of perceptual conditions appear to be prepotent in this way. Humans and other animals orient toward movement and toward sudden changes in intensity or appearance. Attention is reflexive in these instances; it appears to be captured by the stimulus event, whether or not it is advantageous for behavior. Movement in the hallway that distracts students who are taking an examination illustrates this principle. The rat that stops lever pressing when there is a loud noise outside the operant chamber similarly exemplifies the principle.

Attention that is elicited by stimuli in this way need not be deleterious to performance. Nealis, Harlow, and Suomi (1977) tested rhesus monkeys on two-choice discrimination-learning problems, in which pairs of novel stimuli were presented and the animals had to learn which stimulus was associated with reward. That is, selection of one stimulus was reinforced but no reward followed selection of the other item; however, there was no way for the monkey to know on the first presentation of the two objects, which one had been designated arbitrarily as the to-be-rewarded item. Nealis and colleagues found that the monkeys learned faster when the stimuli moved than when they remained stationary, even though the movement provided no additional information about which object should be selected.

This movement effect was replicated with additional monkeys that picked from novel pairs of computer-graphic images by manipulating a joystick to control a cursor on a computer screen

(Washburn, 1993; Washburn, Hopkins, & Rumbaugh, 1989). Monkeys learned two-choice discrimination problems, matching-to-sample, and delayed matching-to-sample faster when the stimuli moved on the screen than when stimuli remained stationary. These studies eliminated potential explanations like presentation duration, positional confounds, and even the perceptual predisposition to orient toward movement. Rather, the data suggested that stimulus movement elicited a shift in attention to the discriminanda and that learning benefited from this cognitive effort.

Humans also showed better learning and better retention when stimuli moved compared with when stimuli remained stationary (Washburn, 1994, 2003). As in the research with the monkeys, human participants had to move the cursor to contact computerized images; the images were either easy to touch because they were stationary or were difficult to touch because they had to be "chased and caught" on the screen. For example, undergraduates learning a foreign-language vocabulary used the joystick to touch a Russian word that either moved on the screen or remained in its randomly selected position (Washburn, 2003). When the sample word was touched, two English alternatives appeared on the screen and the participant tried to pick the word that corresponded to the Russian term. Those Russian words that moved when they were introduced were learned significantly faster and remembered significantly better than those words that remained stationary. Again, nonattentional explanations could not account for this finding. Despite the fact that participants did not report paying any more attention to the moving than to the stationary stimuli, these data indicated that attention was elicited by stimulus movement. Thus, for both human and nonhuman animals, attention can be captured by potent environmental events.

3. IN THE ABSENCE OF CHANGE, ATTENTION IS INHIBITED

With repeated presentations of the same stimulus, an organism will habituate or decline its orientation and response to that stimulus. This is why the ticking of a loud clock or the pressure of a new pair of shoes does not bother us forever. So long as the stimulation is constant, we will come not to notice it. But, if the ticking suddenly stops, if the pressure of the new shoes suddenly changes to pain, then we will dishabituate and attend again. Hence, the sudden absence of a familiar stimulus can elicit an attentional shift.

Habituation and dishabituation are not particularly cognitive mechanisms. One need not try to habituate (although frequently we wish we *could* ignore background noises). Indeed, these processes may not even require a brain, as Grau (2002) has shown habituation in spinalized rats. However, habituation and dishabituation are low-level mechanisms that control attention. Just as an organism will orient to sudden change or movement in the environment, attention tends to deselect or drift away from stimuli that do not change (or, probably more accurately, that do not provide new information). Thus, humans and other animals are attracted to novelty and stimulation but are biased against attending to the familiar and unchanging. This bias against "been there, done that" stimuli is evident in babies and in nonhuman animals, thus providing the basis for the preferential-looking and habituation-dishabituation methodologies that are so popular for studying perception by infants of many species (e.g., Bard, Street, McCrary, & Boothe, 1995; Spelke, 1985; Teller, 1983; West & Young, 2002).

It is this tendency to deselect stimulus options that contain scant information and that change little (i.e., that are boring) that anchors the vigilance literature. In the animal-behavior domain, "vigilance" is typically used to refer to predator wariness or to the monitoring of conspecifics for social cues. Perhaps this is an appropriate parallel with the way "vigilance" is used in the human cognitive literature, as the signature vigilance task is something like a radar operator staring at the display for many hours without a single target but maintaining attention so that a rapid response can be made if the enemy does appear.

More specifically, vigilance effects are those changes in performance that result from time-on-task, particularly under conditions in which the rate of target stimulus presentation is very low. Across time, a decline in the accuracy and an increase in the latency of target detection—a vigilance decrement—is predictable, and the slope and cyclicity of this decrement vary systematically with variables such as signal-to-noise ratio, stimulus rate, and motivation. Vigilance research has a rich history and represents an active part of both the human experimental and applied cognitive literatures (see reviews by Ballard, 1996; Davies & Tune, 1969; Parasuraman & Davies, 1976; Parasuraman, Warm, & See, 1998; See, Howe, Warm, & Dember, 1995). The ability to remain alert and vigilant—that is, to sustain attention in direct opposition to the tendency to habituate to boring tasks—has been shown to be orthogonal to other attentional abilities like selection and scanning (for psychometric evidence, see Mirsky, 1996; for neuropsychological evidence, see Posner & Raichle, 1994).

The comparative-cognition literature holds far fewer studies of vigilance in this sense of the term. Although the nonhuman projects are few in number, they indicate that monkeys (Krasnegor & Brady, 1972), rats (Bushnell, 1999), and other animals (Dukas & Clark, 1995) are able to monitor a stimulus display for infrequent signals across intervals that require the animals to remain vigilant. Additional research in this area will not only provide animal models of human vigilance but also forge links between these cognitive conceptions of vigilance and the social watch-keeping that has been more extensively studied. Moreover, and reflecting the theme of the present chapter, such research will provide important information about sustained attention itself, however it is manifest across species, and the nature of the control of that attention.

4. STIMULI CAN COME TO ELICIT ATTENTION VIA EXPERIENCE

The preceding principles attest to the limits of cognitive processing (both for humans and for other animals) and two of the mechanisms used to cope with these limitations: a bias to attend to novelty, movement, or change and a bias to habituate to static, uninformative, repetitive stimuli. In explicating these points, however, we have hinted already that there is more to attention; that is, sometimes we do remain vigilant or attend to stimuli that are not jumping about and shouting "Look at me!" Not only is attention captured by abrupt changes in the stimulus array, but familiar stimuli can gain the potency to elicit shifts of attention. Hence, a stimulus can come—by habit, by "contention scheduling" (which is the mechanism described by Cooper & Shallice, 2000, for the control of automatic behaviors), and by priming—to control what is processed into behavior.

Consider the attention test that is perhaps the most familiar and robust in all of cognitive psychology: the Stroop color-word task. Participants are required to name the color of words, but they find it extremely difficult to ignore the meaning of the word even though reading is not necessary, or even useful, for the task. For example, participants might be shown the words "BOOK, BLUE, SIGN, PINK" with the words displayed in red, blue, black, and green, respectively. The participant's task is to respond "Red, blue, black, green" but responses are likely to be slowed and less accurate on incongruous trials (the word PINK printed in green) than on baseline trials, in which the words are not color words (e.g., BOOK, SIGN). Furthermore, responses are likely to be relatively fast and more accurate on congruous trials (BLUE printed in blue) than on the baseline and incongruous trials.

In the years since Stroop's (1935) original report of this finding, so-called Stroop effects have been replicated and extended many times. McLeod (1991) reviewed the extensive Stroop literature, summarizing about 400 of the more than 700 Stroop-like studies. Granted that the effect is curious and easy to produce, what could motivate hundreds of studies on this phenomenon? We believe that the Stroop task has fascinated so many researchers because it shows how attention can be controlled, even to the detriment of task performance and against the intentions of the participant, by well-ingrained habits (in this case, the highly practiced habit of reading words). This effect is particularly noteworthy because color is such a strong, prepotent cue and color-naming is certainly a more basic skill than color-word reading. Indeed, we become so good at processing the meaning of words that we cannot avoid doing so, even though it now impairs performance to do so!

Similarly, numeric versions of the Stroop task have been used with humans, for example, requiring participants to report the number of stimuli (e.g., there are three stimuli in each of these arrays—"3 3 3," "X X X," and "5 5 5"—but the last array would probably produce more errors and slower responses). These findings are interesting because although nonhuman primates cannot read color words, they can learn the values associated with numeric symbols (Washburn & Rumbaugh, 1991). In a relative numerousness task, rhesus monkeys learned to select the larger of a pair of Arabic numerals (e.g., 7 versus 4), because of the fact that they would receive a proportional number of rewards depending on which numeral was selected (e.g., seven pellets were dispensed if the 7 was touched, but four pellets were dispensed if the 4 was touched). In other words, the monkeys had to learn the relative values of the numerals simply on the basis of the relative number of pellets that were associated with each. Even with novel pairings of numerals, the monkeys responded accurately at levels significantly greater than chance.

This relative numerousness task was modified to allow Stroop-like comparisons of congruous trials, incongruous trials, and baseline trials (Washburn, 1994). On a baseline trial, rhesus monkeys were given options between arrays of letters (e.g., four As versus two Ds), where the task required picking the array with more elements (four As) and the identities of the stimuli were irrelevant. On congruous trials, the array with more elements also had the element with the larger numerical value (e.g., two 1s versus seven 2s). On incongruous trials, the larger of the two numerals was in the smaller of the two arrays (e.g., five 3s versus four 8s). Note that the identities of the elements on all trial types were completely irrelevant to the task and were at least as likely to impair performance as to improve it. Nevertheless, the numerical meaning of the Arabic symbols did influence performance, both for humans and for monkeys. Human adults and monkeys alike responded most slowly on incongruous trials and fastest on congruous trials. Further, rhesus monkeys showed reliable Stroop-like interference and facilitation in the accuracy of responding as well. Even though the undergraduates and monkeys should have attended only to the number of items, they were incapable of ignoring the identity of the items.

Similar Stroop-like effects have been replicated with chimpanzees (Biro & Matsuzawa, 2002) and have also been reported for monkeys in a task in which color, shape, and motion provided the incongruous or congruous cue information (Lauwereyns et al., 2000). Unlike the stimulus movement effects discussed earlier, Stroop effects like these do not stem from an attention capture by prepotent environmental events; rather, Stroop effects are caused by strength of association (Washburn, 1994). It is the habit of reading words or interpreting numeric symbols that causes competition between the potential responses. These semantic cues get selected for processing by prior learning, not by choice or by basic dishabituation.

Cognitive psychologists, the present authors included, have long bristled at the language of the experimental analysis of behavior. There is no question that behavior is changed by respondent and operant conditioning (although other emergent forms of behavior change are also possible; Rumbaugh & Washburn, 2003). However, the terminology of stimulus control, with its implication that behavior is responsive to contingencies rather than being purposive and willful, would seem to be contradictory to the cognitive perspective of organisms as active seekers and processors of information. That said, cognitive theories of attention and executive function frequently acknowledge mechanisms like contention scheduling (Cooper & Shallice, 2000; Shallice, 1994), automaticity (e.g., Logan, 1997; Logan & Compton, 1998; Pashler, 1994), and priming (Johnston & Dark, 1986; Kinchla, 1992) that are quite consistent with the idea of stimulus control. Baddeley's (1990) highly influential model of working memory, for example, endorsed Norman and Shallice's (1980) model of cognitive control in which behavior under familiar and routine circumstances is determined by contention scheduling. In other words, novel or dangerous situations may require supervisory attentional control (or the central executive), according to Baddeley, but routine stimulus processing is accomplished by contention schedules, by stimulus–response associations, and by stimulus control. Similarly, automaticity is defined as a state of low attention demand in which behavior is executed in a highly routine manner under highly practiced circumstances. Priming is a condition in which particular stimuli activate the processing of other strongly associated stimuli. Thus, priming is a mechanism that serves to aim attention on information that is related to whatever has recently been the subject of attention. With contention scheduling and priming and automaticity, the organism's history—and specifically the habits that have developed to respond in particular ways to specific stimuli—determines what stimuli will be processed. Note also that with contention scheduling, automaticity, priming, and the like, attention is being biased by the organism's history in a way ("attend to the familiar and experienced") that directly conflicts with the tendencies to habituate to the familiar and to orient to the novel, as discussed earlier.

Priming effects have been reported in studies with nonhuman animals, although these studies (like complementary studies from the human literature) are typically focused on memory rather than on attention. D. S. Blough and P. M. Blough (1997) discussed the role of priming in visual search by pigeons, providing one source of evidence for the argument that priming can control attention. Rhesus monkeys have also shown priming effects (i.e., facilitated performance as a function of the attended stimuli from a previous trial) and "negative priming effects" (i.e., compromised performance as a function of which stimulus was attended to on a previous trial; see Kane, May, Hasher, & Rahhal, 1997; May, Kane, & Hasher, 1995) in a variety of computer-based tests (Washburn & Kane, 1999). Negative priming effects such as these are thought to reflect the cost on Trial N of inhibiting stimuli on Trial N – 1, although other interpretations have been advanced. These effects were first reported for nonhuman animals by Honey and colleagues (Honey, Good, &Manser, 1998; Honey, Hall, & Bonardi, 1993) with rats and by Taffe (1996) with rhesus monkeys. Like the repetition-priming and semantic-priming effects that have been reported both for humans and for nonhuman animals, these findings show that experience and association exert control over attention.

5. ATTENTION IS BOTH AN EFFECT AND A CAUSE OF SELECTION FOR PROCESSING

In their excellent review of the attention literature, which serves as both a stylistic inspiration and a substantive foundation for the present chapter, Johnston and Dark (1986) classified attention theories into two groups: cause theories and effect theories (see also Fernandez-Duque & Johnson, 2002). Cause theorists are those who contend that attention is the process by which one selects stimuli for processing; that is, attention determines which stimuli will be processed. Attention dictates which possible response will be executed. Most of the influential theories of attention, at least since the latter half of the 1950s and the renaissance of cognitive psychology, have been cause theories. Attention is how we filter some stimuli while allowing others through the bottleneck of perception (Broadbent, 1958). Attention is an attenuator that allows us to adjust the signal-to-noise ratio of some stimuli relative to others (Treisman, 1964). Attention is a limited-supply resource that we can dole out or allocate flexibly, but not infinitely, determining which of multiple simultaneous tasks or operations is performed well (Kahneman, 1973). Attention is a spotlight that we scan and focus on some stimuli, leaving others unprocessed and in the dark (Cowan, 1988; Posner, 1980). Attention is a gate or a window that opens briefly to allow stimuli to access visual short-term memory (Reeves & Sperling, 1986). Attention causes selection for processing.

Other researchers, including Johnston and Dark (1986) themselves, embrace effect theories of attention. According to effect theorists, attention is a consequence of selection or the state of affairs that exists because of selection for processing. That is, we cannot process all available stimuli (Principle 1, earlier), and we have basic perceptual mechanisms whereby some stimuli and not others get perceived (Principles 2, 3, and 4); consequently, that subset of stimuli that does get processed can be said to have been attended to. Neisser (1976) provides an influential voice for this perspective, arguing that attention is not something we use but rather something that we do. Much like the task of apple picking, Neisser contends, attention is simply the skill of picking out some stimuli to be processed. According to this view, there is no more need to filter or to inhibit the unattended information in perception than there is to suppress some apples in order to pick others.

Other strong statements along these lines can be found in James (1890), whom Johnston and Dark (1986) list in the effect theory camp. James noted that, "Everyone knows what attention is. It is the taking possession by the mind, in clear and vivid form, of one out of what seem several simultaneously possible objects or trains of thought" (pp. 402–403). James himself asked, "Is voluntary attention a resultant or a force?" (p. 447) and concluded, "As regards immediate sensorial attention hardly any one is tempted to regard it as anything but an effect" (p. 448) and "Derived attention, where there is no voluntary effort, seems also most plausibly to be a mere effect" (p. 449). According to James, we do not fix our eyes or our thoughts on a topic in order to attend to it. "The fixing *is* the attention" (p. 450, emphasis his).

Conversely, James (1890) identified himself as sympathetic to the cause theories in this debate (p. 448, footnote). It is this spirit that is reflected in familiar statements like, "My experience is what I *agree* to attend to. Only those items which I notice shape my mind" (p. 402). Having built the most cogent case for effect theory that he could, James defended both the possibility and the utility of effortful attention as a causal force in cognition.

Was he simply waffling on a position, or worse, defying both empirical evidence and logical parsimony to cling to an unscientific belief in willful attention? We think not. Rather, we conclude that the duality of James's arguments reflects, in fact, the duality of the control of attention. Attention is not cause or effect, but rather it is both. Under some circumstances, selection for processing appears to be the result of environmental cues or of experiential constraints. Stimuli control responding, either through natural predispositions or acquired associations. Under other conditions, however, attention appears to defy stimulus control. In these instances, attending is accomplished only with effort and conscious control. In these instances, as James picturesquely described it (p. 453), voluntary attention is the star of cognition and the laws of association and stimulation are merely supporting players.

Evidence of effortful attention that defies control by local stimulus–response associations is abundant. True, incongruous cues that have great associative strength (like word meanings) influence performance in the Stroop color-word task, but performance is not dominated by this strength of association. Participants do report the ink color despite these competing cues, and if then asked, they can switch back and forth between response cues. Similarly, the monkeys in the Washburn (1994) study were influenced by the irrelevant stimulus cues, but they nonetheless did perform the Stroop-like task accurately. Similarly, sudden changes or movements in the environment might elicit an involuntary shift of attention, but humans and nonhuman animals are able to arrest this shift and to keep attending to the relevant cues in order to perform a task.

The distinction between attention that is reflexive, associative, and automatic on the one hand and attention that is causal, controlled, and effortful on the other is evident in visual search research. In the visual search paradigm, participants are instructed to scan a stimulus array such as a matrix of letters and to indicate as quickly and as accurately as possible whether a target item is in the display. In some variations of the procedure, the participant also reveals the location of the target. Since being described by Neisser and his colleagues in empirical studies (e.g., Neisser, 1963) and in his classic book *Cognitive Psychology* (Neisser, 1967), the visual search paradigm has been used in thousands of experiments to study the scanning or spatial movement of visual attention and the stimulus characteristics that result in parallel versus serial searches.

Of course, such a large corpus of studies cannot be reviewed adequately in the present chapter; however, several main findings are paradigmatic. First, the time to locate a target tends to increase as the number of items in the search array increases; this result is known as the set-size effect. Target location time increases with set size and is accompanied both by overt evidence (e.g., eye movements) and by self-reports of controlled, effortful serial search. Notably however, this effect is dependent on the similarity between the target item (e.g., a single letter F, in random position) and the items that constitute the search set (e.g., some number of Es, Ls, Ts, and Hs in random order). This result contrasts with the second general finding: Time to locate the target is independent of set size if the target is perceptually dissimilar to the nontargets (e.g., an F embedded in a matrix of O, C, and Q letters); this result is known as the pop-out effect. A target letter will appear effortlessly and immediately, the figure against an unprocessed background, irrespective of the number of letters in the search array. Third, even difficult searches can be accomplished without set-size effects or effortful searching if they follow particular types of practice. This principle originated in a pair of influential papers on the distinction between automatic and controlled processing (Schneider & Shiffrin, 1977; Shiffrin & Schneider, 1977).

These researchers studied the increase in search time as a function of the number of targets as well as the number of distractors. For example, it takes longer to determine whether there is an F or an E in the array than to decide whether there is just an F. Participants practiced under conditions termed "consistent mapping" in which the target and nontarget items were the same on each trial, or under conditions called "varied mapping" in which the target stimulus on one trial might have been a nontarget stimulus on a previous trial. Participants were able to search for any of four target items about as quickly as they could search for a single target in the consistent mapping condition, but no attenuation of the set-size effect was seen in the varied mapping condition. These findings, and the basic distinction between attention that is automatic and attention that seems volitionally controlled, have been replicated numerous times.

The visual search paradigm has also been used extensively with nonhuman animals, replicating these general findings from the human-attention literature. Donald and Patricia Blough, working both independently and together, have led this comparative research on visual search, extensively studying the performance of pigeons under a variety of conditions (e.g., D. S. Blough, 1977, 1989, 2002; D. S. Blough & P. M. Blough, 1997; P. M. Blough, 1984, 1991). Many of these studies served to identify the features that contribute to pop-out effects for pigeons and how this set of fundamental perceptual elements differs from those that produce reliable pop-out effects for humans and nonhuman primates (e.g., D. S. Blough, 1992). Such studies reveal species similarities and differences in perception and pattern recognition but are not particularly focused on the role or control of attention.

Other studies within these research programs have established the interaction between priming and attention in the search task, for instance, by cuing the birds in advance of a trial about the target's identity (e.g., P. M. Blough, 1989, 1996). Importantly, the characteristics of target detection are influenced by advance information about the target, whether that information comes from priming cues or from knowledge about target probability. Across these experiments, it is clear that (1) under some conditions pigeons (like humans—although not necessarily in the same stimulus conditions as humans) find target stimuli in the array automatically, (2) sometimes pigeons direct visual attention in time-consuming, controlled, serial search for the targets, and (3) one can alter the degree to which attention is automatic or controlled, as reflected in the shape of search curves (i.e., response latency as a function of number of items in the search array), by manipulating stimulus characteristics, the bird's expectations, and the bird's advance knowledge or motivation.

Similar results have been suggested by Tomonaga (e.g., 1993a, 1993b, 1995, 1997, 2001). Using variations of the matching-to-sample procedure, Tomonaga (1993b) reported that chimpanzees show longer target-location times as the number of alternatives increases, with a significant shallowing of this set-size effect when the target and nontarget differed by the same perceptual features that generate pop-out effects for humans. Tomonaga (1993a, 2001) also studied search asymmetries (see also D. S. Blough, 1992); an interesting observation was that the time required to find a target stimulus embedded in nontarget letters (e.g., to find a C hidden amidst 29 Os) is different from the time required to conduct the opposite search (i.e., find an O positioned randomly in an array of 29 Cs). These results attest to the visual features that are salient in eliciting attention and driving perception, but they are less informative about the interplay between automatic and controlled attention.

However, as was done with pigeons and humans, Tomonaga also investigated the effects of precuing on performance. In his study, Tomonaga (1997) cued either the correct or incorrect locations in which a target would appear. As is seen when humans are presented with cues of various validity (e.g., Fan, McCandliss, Sommer, Raz, & Posner, 2002; Jonides & Mack, 1984), there are benefits in terms of response time and accuracy to receiving valid cues, but there are substantial costs in these same terms if cues prove to be invalid. Tomonaga (1997) interpreted these findings to reflect a dissociation between the types of priming, but these types appear to map onto the "automatic attention versus controlled attention" distinction discussed here.

The costs of invalid cues have indeed launched a separate, highly active line of research. Under some conditions, invalid cues will set up a phenomenon called "inhibition of return," which works like a spatial version of negative priming in that participants are slower to return to spatial locations that had previously been invalidly cued (Posner, Rafal, Choate, & Vaughan, 1985). Inhibition of return has been demonstrated in human adults and infants (e.g., Clohessy, Posner, Rothbart, & Vecera, 1991; Rayner, Juhasz, Ashby, & Clifton, 2003) and in nonhuman animals (Bichot & Schall, 2002; Dorris, Klein, Everling, & Munoz, 2002). The phenomenon is interesting because it reveals a dissociation between exogenous sources of attentional control: environmental constraints (i.e., shifts that are elicited by peripheral cues, consistent with Principle 2 in the present chapter) and associative constraints (i.e., inhibition that results from an unrewarded shift of attention to the cued position, consistent with Principle 3). Overcoming these influences on attention, that is, ignoring invalid cues or searching in an inhibited location, implies also the third, endogenously controlled attention endorsed by James (1890) and described in the present section.

6. ATTENTION AT ANY MOMENT IN TIME IS CONTROLLED BY THE INTERACTION OF ENVIRONMENTAL CONSTRAINTS, EXPERIENTIAL CONSTRAINTS, AND EXECUTIVE CONSTRAINTS

Of course, terms like "endogenously controlled" and "executive constraints" are highly loaded and have a controversial role in psychological science. They beg the question, "Who is doing the controlling?" and would seem to open doors through which dualism and the homunculus are welcome to enter. It is indeed a nettlesome issue and one that troubled our professional ancestors as well as our contemporary theorists.

Baddeley (2002), for instance, addressed the criticism that his central executive (or supervisory attentional system, to use Norman and Shallice's [1980] term) is a homunculus by endorsing Attneave's (1960) view that a homunculus is acceptable so long as it serves merely as a reminder of what functions remain to be explained. Thus, we acknowledge that this construct of controlled attention is effortful and is shaped by intentions, purposes, and similar executive factors. Further, we acknowledge that these executive constraints may well turn out to be instantiated as a network of higher-order, emergent relations that themselves reflect native predispositions and lifelong experiences. Until the nature of intention is explained, however, we join others in using terms like "executive control of attention" to reflect both the phenomenon and the phenomenology that sometimes people (and other animals) choose what they will attend to, despite constraints that might dictate otherwise. We focus on a lecture (or a chapter) even when it boring, even when there are distractions all around us, and even when the contingencies suggest that rich rewards are otherwise available. Attention is not just reflexive and associative; it can also be purposive.

Could these three sources of influence over attention be pitted against one another in a single experiment? That is, is it possible to identify, for example in the response–time curves reflecting visual search performance, that attention is sometimes reflexive and elicited, sometimes associative and automatic, and sometimes effortful and controlled? One possibility is suggested by a study in which pop-out stimuli were presented in a search array but in which these stimuli were not the target stimuli (Theeuwes & Burger, 1998). For example, the participants might be required to search for a green E embedded in an array of green letters but where there was also a single red letter (e.g., an F) to elicit a shift of attention. Humans were able to ignore these singleton nontargets only when instructions were provided about both the color of the target and the color of the singleton.

Rhesus monkeys and undergraduate students were tested on a similar task in which search arrays were presented under various conditions. All participants, regardless of species, were tested with a computerized apparatus and a joystick for responses (see Rumbaugh et al., 1989). Unlike previous comparative studies of visual search, as discussed, which required animals to touch the target stimulus within the search array and thus risked introducing motor confounds into the chronometrical data, a go–no-go task similar to what is typically used in visual search research with humans was used in the present experiment. The monkeys and humans moved the joystick down to initiate a trial, whereupon an array of letters appeared on the screen. If the target letter was in the array, then the participants were required to move the joystick handle up as quickly as possible but in any case within 5 s. Absence of a response within 5 s (i.e., if the target was not in the array or if the participant did not find the target) was recorded as a "no target" response. Thus, the task recorded the accuracy of responses (hits, misses, and false alarms) and the latency of responses across conditions.

Participants were tested in conditions that allowed for manipulation of the strength of environmental constraints on attention, of experiential (or associative) constraints on attention, and of executive (or controlled) constraints on attention. Of these many conditions, several are particularly relevant for the present discussion. In the baseline condition, participants searched for a target letter embedded in similar nontarget letters (e.g., determine whether an F was among an array of E, L, or T stimuli). On some of the trials, one of the nontarget stimuli would appear in a different color (e.g., find the black F in an array of black E, L, and T letters, with a single red E also in the array); this was termed the "elicited" condition, as this pop-out nontarget should elicit attention away from the actual target and thus slow responding.

On most trials, the identity of this singleton nontarget was unrelated to the target stimulus on the previous trial. On other "elicited" trials, however, the singleton nontarget was the same stimulus that had been the target letter on the previous two trials. In this way, the singleton was not only distinctive by virtue of color but also was primed by association with the previous trials. Responses in this "primed" condition were predicted to be even slower and less accurate than the unprimed "elicited" trials.

Finally, some of the trials were preceded by information about what the target and nontarget stimuli would be. This list of stimuli appeared on the trial-initiation screen and disappeared when the joystick handle was moved downward to start the trial. It seemed reasonable to predict that search times on these "informed" trials would be shorter than for the "elicited" and "primed" trials, where no information was provided. Indeed, it was anticipated that "informed" response times would be comparable to those in the baseline condition (i.e., trials without a singleton nontarget).

Regardless of the conditions just described, 50% of the trials were "target present" trials in which the target stimulus did appear within the search array. Set sizes of 5, 10, 20, and 30 letters were used, balanced across conditions. These data were analyzed to provide answers to the following three questions.

1. Did pop-out nontargets elicit a shift of attention? For human participants, target detection in the baseline condition averaged 995 ms. When one of the nontarget stimuli was a color different from the other letters (the "elicited" condition), mean response time increased significantly to 1,131 ms ($p < .01$). Similarly, response times for the monkeys increased from 824 ms to 1,092 ms (baseline to elicited, respectively; $p < .05$) when a singleton distractor was present. The monkeys additionally showed a decline in accuracy for the elicited versus the baseline conditions (80% versus 93%, respectively; $p < .05$). For both species, novelty in the visual array (in the form of pop-out nontarget stimuli) clearly did elicit attention.
2. Did priming a nontarget stimulus impede target detection? When the singleton nontarget on a trial had been the target stimulus for the two previous trials, response time increased from 1,131 ms to 1,191 ms ($p < .05$) for human participants. Monkeys also showed additive inhibition from the priming of singleton nontargets, with longer responses (1,120 ms) and reduced accuracy (69%) in the "primed" condition ($p < .05$ and $p < .01$, respectively). For both species, attention was influenced by recent stimulus-response associative history.
3. Did instructions facilitate target detection? When the undergraduate students were informed about the identities of the target and nontarget stimuli, including the singleton nontarget, performance was improved (mean = 1,028 ms, $p < .01$) relative to the "elicited" and "primed" conditions. This result replicates the findings of Theeuwes and Burger (1998). Note that performance did not return to baseline levels. Analysis of the rate of attention scanning through the array of stimuli (i.e., the set-size slopes that reflect time to detect the target, by condition, as a function of the number of items in the array) indicated that human participants were able to scan at about same rate with or without the pop-out nontarget but only if they were instructed in advance as to the identity of the singleton and the target. Even then, however, there appeared to be a "set-up cost" (reflected in the y-intercept of the set-size slope) to controlled attention that is revealed in the overall response–time differences. Thus, students who knew the identity of the stimuli in advance could control their visual search to prevent the singleton from capturing attention by virtue of novelty or priming. Nonetheless, there was some response latency cost to this executive control of attention.

A different pattern of results was evident for the rhesus monkeys. The instructions provided in this condition did little to improve responding (mean = 1,032) relative to the "elicited" condition and may have actually compromised performance further in the "primed" condition (mean = 1,133 ms), although neither difference was statistically reliable ($p > .10$). Accuracy was similarly affected by instructions. Although performance in the "elicited" condition was improved when the animals were informed about the stimuli in advance of a trial (85%, $p < .05$), no significant change was observed when instructions preceded the "primed" trials

(70%, $p > .10$). This finding that rhesus monkeys may be less able, compared with humans, to control attention endogenously is consistent with the results from other studies (Washburn, 1994, 2002).

It thus appears that the attention of monkeys and of humans is influenced by environmental conditions (e.g., novelty, movement, suddenness), experiential contingencies (e.g., priming, conditioning), and executive considerations (intentions, motivations, instructions). For monkeys, however, the environmental and experiential factors appear to be particularly potent, whereas the executive constraints are less influential over the control of attention.

7. ATTENTION IS NOT LITERALLY A FILTER, A BOTTLENECK, AN ATTENUATOR, A RESOURCE, A SPOTLIGHT, A GATE, AND SO FORTH; HOWEVER, IT HAS ATTRIBUTES THAT ARE CAPTURED BY EACH OF THESE AND OTHER METAPHORS

This paraphrase of a lecture point by one of our favorite cognitive professors serves as an important reminder that attention is a complex construct that has eluded exhaustive explanation despite extensive research for many decades. The principal findings that have been summarized in this chapter serve primarily to highlight many of the questions that remain about attention as it is inferred across species.

One reason why the study of attention has been so difficult is that the term itself is a category label that corresponds to a heterogeneous collection of skills and mental abilities. It is increasingly evident from experimental evidence, from psychometric evidence (e.g., Putney & Washburn, 2004), and from neuropsychological evidence (e.g., Posner & Raichle, 1994) that attention is a multidimensional construct consisting of at least three separable factors: focusing or selectivity, scanning or orienting, and sustaining or alerting. Focused attention (i.e., concentration, mental effort) is clearly related to scanned attention (i.e., searching, switching) and sustained attention (i.e., vigilance), but these are not the same cognitive processes any more than attention is the same as perception or memory, despite the obvious interrelation among the constructs. (Note that there appears not to be a "divided attention" factor, despite the wealth of research on flexible allocation of attention to multiple, simultaneous inputs. It appears that "attention sharing" is accomplished by focusing, sustaining, and scanning or shifting.)

For the present review, the purpose of this point is to note that nonhuman animals, like humans, have produced evidence for all three aspects of attention. Tasks like Stroop that require executive intervention to resolve response competition reflect the attention-focusing factor in humans, and animals have also shown Stroop-like effects suggesting this factor. Visual search and similar tasks that tap the scanning component of attention have also been used across species. Vigilance tasks have been less frequently used with nonhuman animals, but nonetheless there is a growing literature from humans and animals on alertness or readiness to respond and its relation to performance. Future studies should be designed not just to examine attention generically but also to identify the factors of attention, the control of attention, and the functions of attention as it is manifest across species.

Acknowledgments Preparation of this chapter was supported by grant HD-38051 from the National Institute of Child Health and Human Development to Georgia State University.

We thank Jonathan Gulledge, Duane Rumbaugh, James Pate, and R. Thompson Putney (to whom we attribute Principle 7) for their contributions to the work reviewed here.

References

Attneave, F. (1960). In defence of homunculi. In W. Rosenblith (Ed.), *Sensory communication* (pp. 777–782). Cambridge, MA: MIT Press.

Baddeley, A. D. (1990). *Human memory: Theory and practice.* Hillsdale, NJ: Lawrence Erlbaum.

Baddeley, A. D. (2002). Is working memory still working? *European Psychologist, 7*, 85–97.

Ballard, J. C. (1996). Computerized assessment of sustained attention: A review of factors affecting vigilance performance. Journal of Clinical & Experimental Neuropsychology, 18, 843–863.

Bard, K. A., Street, E. A., McCrary, C., & Boothe, R. G. (1995). Development of visual acuity in infant chimpanzees. *Infant Behavior and Development, 18*, 225–232.

Berlyne, D. E. (1975). Behaviourism? Cognitive theory? Humanistic psychology? To Hull with them all. *Canadian Psychological Review, 16*, 69–80.

Bichot, N. P., & Schall, J. D. (2002). Priming in macaque frontal cortex during popout visual search: Feature-based facilitation and location-based inhibition of return. *Journal of Neuroscience, 22*, 4675–4685.

Biro, D., & Matsuzawa, T. (2002, November). Numerical Stroop in a chimpanzee: Evidence of a symbolic distance effect. Joint International Symposium of COE2/SAGA5, Nagoya, Japan.

Blough, D. S. (1969). Attention shifts in a maintained discrimination. *Science, 166*, 125–126.

Blough, D. S. (1977). Visual search in the pigeon: Hunt and peck method. *Science, 196*, 1013–1014.

Blough, D. S. (1989). Odd-item search in pigeons: Display size and transfer effects. *Journal of Experimental Psychology: Animal Behavior Processes, 15*, 14–22.

Blough, D. S. (1992). Features of forms in pigeon perception. In W. K. Honig & J. G. Fetterman (Eds.), *Cognitive aspects of stimulus control* (pp. 264–277). Hillsdale, NJ: Lawrence Erlbaum.

Blough, D. S. (2002). Measuring the search image: Expectation, detection and recognition in pigeon visual search. *Journal of Experimental Psychology, 28*, 397–405.

Blough, P. M. (1984). Visual search in pigeons: Effects of memory set size and display variables. *Perception & Psychophysics, 35*, 344–352.

Blough, P. M. (1989). Attentional priming and visual search in pigeons. *Journal of Experimental Psychology: Animal Behavior Processes, 15*, 358–365.

Blough, P. M. (1991). Selective attention and search images in pigeons. *Journal of Experimental Psychology: Animal Behavior Processes, 17*, 292–298.

Blough, P. M. (1996). Priming during multiple-target search: The cumulative effects of relative target frequency. *Animal Learning & Behavior, 24*, 394–400.

Blough, D. S., & Blough, P. M. (1997). Form perception and attention in pigeons. *Animal Learning & Behavior, 25*, 1–20.

Blumenthal, A. L. (1980). Wilhelm Wundt and early American psychology: A clash of cultures. In R. W. Rieber (Ed.), *Wilhelm Wundt and the making of a scientific psychology* (pp. 117–135). New York: Plenum Press.

Broadbent, D. E. (1958). *Perception and communication*. London: Pergamon Press.

Broadbent, D. E. (1982). Task combination and selective intake of information. *Acta Psychologica, 50*, 253–290.

Brown, M. F., Cook. R. G., Lamb, M. R., & Riley, D. A. (1984). The relation between response and attentional shifts in pigeon compound matching-to-sample performance. *Animal Learning & Behavior, 12*, 41–49.

Bushnell, P. J. (1999). Detection of visual signals by rats: Effects of signal intensity, event rate, and task type. *Behavioural Processes, 46*, 141–150.

Chatlosh, D. L., & Wasserman, E. A. (1993). Multidimensional stimulus control in pigeons: Selective attention and other issues. In T. R. Zentall (Ed.), *Animal cognition: A tribute to Donald A. Riley* (pp. 271–292). Hillsdale, NJ: Lawrence Erlbaum.

Clohessy, A. B., Posner, M. I., Rothbart, M. K., & Vecera, S. P. (1991). The development of inhibition of return in early infancy. *Journal of Cognitive Neuroscience, 3*, 345–350.

Cooper, R., & Shallice, T. (2000). Contention scheduling and the control of routine activities. *Cognitive Neuropsychology, 17*, 297– 338.

Cowan, N. (1988). Evolving conceptions of memory storage, selective attention, and their mutual constraints within the human information-processing system. *Psychological Bulletin, 104*, 163–191.

Davies, D. R., & Tune, G. S. (1969). *Human vigilance behavior*. Oxford: American Elsevier.

Dorris, M. C., Klein, R. M., Everling, S., & Munoz, D. P. (2002). Contribution of the primate superior colliculus to inhibition of return. *Journal of Cognitive Neuroscience, 14*, 1256–1263.

Dukas, R., & Clark, C. W. (1995). Sustained vigilance and animal performance. *Animal Behaviour, 49*, 1259–1267.

Egeth, H. E., & Yantis, S. (1997). Visual attention: Control, representation, and time course. *Annual Review of Psychology, 48*, 269–297.

Fan, J., McCandliss, B. D., Sommer, T., Raz, A., & Posner, M. I. (2002). Testing the efficiency and independence of attentional networks. *Journal of Cognitive Neurosciences, 14*, 340–347.

Fernandez-Duque, D., & Johnson, M. L. (2002). Cause and effect theories of attention: The role of conceptual metaphors. *Review of General Psychology, 6*, 153–165.

Gottselig, J. M., Wasserman, E. A., & Young, M. E. (2001). Attentional trade-offs in pigeons learning to discriminate newly relevant visual stimulus dimensions. *Learning and Motivation, 32*, 240–253.

Grau, J. W. (2002). Learning and memory without a brain. In M. Bekoff & C. Allen (Eds.), *The cognitive animal: Empirical and theoretical perspectives on animal cognition* (pp. 77–87). Cambridge, MA: MIT Press.

Honey, R. C., Good, M., & Manser, K. L. (1998). Negative priming in associative learning: Evidence from a serial-habituation procedure. *Journal of Experimental Psychology: Animal Behavior Processes, 24*, 229–237.

Honey, R. C., Hall, G., & Bonardi, C. (1993). Negative priming in associative learning: Evidence from a serial-conditioning procedure. *Journal of Experimental Psychology: Animal Behavior Processes, 19*, 90–97.

James, W. (1890). *Principles of psychology*. New York: Dover.

Johnston, W. A., & Dark, V. J. (1986). Selective attention. *Annual Review of Psychology, 37*, 43–75.

Jonides, J., & Mack, R. (1984). On the cost and benefit of cost and benefit. *Psychological Bulletin, 96*, 29–44.

Kahneman, D. (1973). *Attention and effort*. Englewood Cliffs, NJ: Prentice-Hall.

Kamin, L. J. (1968). Attention-like processes in classical conditioning. In M. R. Jones (Ed.), *Miami Symposium on the Prediction of Behavior: Aversive Stimulation* (pp. 9–32). Miami, FL: University of Miami Press.

Kane, M. J., Bleckley, M. K., Conway, A. R. A., & Engle, R. A. (2001). A controlled-attention view of working-memory capacity. *Journal of Experimental Psychology: General, 130*, 169–183.

Kane, M. J., & Engle, R. A. (2003). Working-memory capacity and the control of attention: The contributions of goal neglect, response attention, and task set to Stroop interference. *Journal of Experimental Psychology: General, 132*, 47–70.

Kane, M. J., May, C. P., Hasher, L., & Rahhal, T. (1997). Dual mechanisms of negative priming. *Journal of Experimental Psychology: Human Perception & Performance, 23*, 632–650.

Kinchla, R. A. (1992). Attention. *Annual Review of Psychology, 43*, 711–742.

Krasnegor, N. A., & Brady, J. V. (1972). Signal frequency and shock probability as determinants of prolonged vigilance performance in rhesus monkeys. *Journal of the Experimental Analysis of Behavior, 17*, 113–118.

Lauwereyns, J., Koizumi, M., Sakagami, M., Hikosaka, O., Kobayashi, S., & Tsutsui, K. (2000). Interference from irrelevant features on visual discrimination by macaques (*Macaca mulatta*): A behavioral analogue of the human Stroop effect. *Journal of Experimental Psychology: Animal Behavior Processes, 26*, 352–357.

Leith, C. R., & Maki, W. S. (1975). Attention shifts during matching-to-sample performance in pigeons. *Animal Learning & Behavior, 3*, 85–89.

Logan, G. (1997). Automaticity and reading: Perspectives from the instance theory of automatization. *Reading & Writing Quarterly: Overcoming Learning Difficulties, 13*, 123–146.

Logan, G., & Compton, B. J. (1998). Attention and automaticity. In R. D. Wright (Ed.), *Visual attention: Vancouver studies in cognitive science*, Vol. 8 (pp. 108–131). New York: Oxford University Press.

Mackintosh, N. J. (1965). Selective attention in animal discrimination learning. *Psychological Bulletin, 64*, 124–150.

Mackintosh, N. J. (1975). A theory of attention: Variations in the associability of stimuli with reinforcement. *Psychological Review, 82*, 276–298.

May, C. P., Kane, M. J., & Hasher, L. (1995). Determinants of negative priming. *Psychological Bulletin, 118*, 35–54.

McLeod, C. M. (1991). Half a century of research on the Stroop effect: An integrative review. *Psychological Bulletin, 109*, 163–203.

Mirskly, A. F. (1996). Disorders of attention: A neuropsychological perspective. In R. G. Reid & N. A. Krasnegor (Eds.), *Attention, memory, and executive function* (pp. 71–95). Baltimore: Paul M. Brookes.

Morris, R. D. (1996). Relationships and distinctions among the concepts of attention, memory, and executive function: A developmental perspective. In G. R. Lyon & N. A. Krasnegor (Eds.), *Attention, memory and executive function* (pp. 11–16). Baltimore: Paul M. Brookes.

Nealis, P. M., Harlow, H. F., & Suomi, S. J. (1977). The effects of stimulus movement on discrimination learning by rhesus monkeys. *Bulletin of the Psychonomic Society, 10*, 161–164.

Neisser, U. (1967). *Cognitive psychology*. East Norwalk, CT: Appleton-Century-Crofts.

Norman, D. A., & Bobrow, D. G. (1975). On data-limited and resource-limited processes. *Cognitive Psychology, 7*, 44–64.

Norman, D. A., & Shallice, T. (1980). *Attention to action: Willed and automatic control of behaviour*. Centre for Human Information Processing (Technical Report #99). San Diego, CA: University of California, San Diego.

Olton, D. S., Pang, K., Merkel, F., & Egeth, H. (1993). Attention: Neurocognitive analysis. In T. R. Zentall (Ed.), *Animal cognition: A tribute to Donald A. Riley* (pp. 239–249). Hillsdale, NJ: Lawrence Erlbaum.

Parasuraman, R., & Davies, D. R. (1976). Decision theory analysis of response latencies in vigilance. *Journal of Experimental Psychology: Human Perception & Performance, 2*, 578–590.

Parasuraman, R., Warm, J. S., & See, J. E. (1998). Brain systems and vigilance. In R. Parasuraman (Ed.), *The attentive brain* (pp. 221–256). Cambridge, MA: MIT Press.

Pashler, H. (1994). Dual-task interference in simple tasks: Data and theory. *Psychological Bulletin, 116*, 220–244.

Posner, M. I. (1980). Orienting of attention. *Quarterly Journal of Experimental Psychology, 32*, 3–25.

Posner, M. I. (1982). Cumulative development of attentional theory. *American Psychologist, 37*, 168–179.

Posner, M. I., Rafal, R. D., Choate, L. S., & Vaughan, J. (1985). Inhibition of return: Neural basis and function. *Cognitive Neuropsychology, 2*, 211–228.

Posner, M. I., & Raichle, M. E. (1994). *Images of mind*. New York: Scientific American Library/Scientific American Books.

Putney, R. T., & Washburn, D. A. (2004). Factors of attention: A review of psychometric studies. Submitted for publication.

Rayner, K., Juhasz, B., Ashby, J., & Clifton, C. Jr. (2003). Inhibition of saccade return in reading. *Vision Research, 43*, 1027–1034.

Reeves, A., & Sperling, G. (1986). Attention gating in short-term visual memory. *Psychological Review, 93*, 180–206.

Riley, D. A. (1984). Do pigeons decompose stimulus compounds? In H. L. Roitblat, T. G. Bever, & H. S. Terrace (Eds.), *Animal cognition* (pp. 333–350). Hillsdale, NJ: Lawrence Erlbaum.

Riley, D. A., & Leith, C. R. (1976). Multidimensional psychophysics and selective attention in animals. *Psychological Bulletin, 83*, 138–160.

Riley, D. A., & Roitblat, H. L. (1978). Selective attention and related cognitive processes in pigeons. In S. H. Hulse, H. Fowler, & W. K. Honig (Eds.), *Cognitive processes in animal behavior* (pp. 249–276). Hillsdale, NJ: Lawrence Erlbaum.

Roberts, W. A. (1997). *Principles of animal cognition*. Boston: McGraw-Hill.

Roitblat, H. L. (1987). *Introduction to comparative cognition*. New York: W. H. Freeman.

Rumbaugh, D. M., Richardson, W. K., Washburn, D. A., Savage-Rumbaugh, E. S., & Hopkins, W. D. (1989). Rhesus monkeys (*Macaca mulatta*), video tasks, and implications for stimulus response spatial contiguity. *Journal of Comparative Psychology, 103*, 32–38.

Rumbaugh, D. M., & Washburn, D. A. (2003). *The intelligence of apes and other rational beings*. New Haven, CT: Yale University Press.

Schneider, W., & Shiffrin, R. M. (1977). Controlled and automatic human information processing: I. Detection, search, and attention. *Psychological Review, 84*, 1–66.

See, J. E., Howe, S. R., Warm, J. S., & Dember, W. N. (1995). Meta-analysis of the sensitivity decrement in vigilance. *Psychological Bulletin, 117*, 230–249.

Shiffrin, R. M., & Schneider, W. (1977). Controlled and automatic human information processing: II. Perceptual learning, automatic attending, and general theory. *Psychological Review, 84*, 127–190.

Shallice, T. (1994). Multiple levels of control processes. In C. Umilta & M. Moscovitch (Eds.), *Attention and performance 15: Conscious and nonconscious information processing. Attention and performance series* (pp. 395–420). Cambridge, MA: MIT Press.

Spelke, E. S. (1985). Preferential-looking methods as tools for the study of cognition in infants. In G. Gotleib & N. A. Krasnegor (Eds.), *Measurement of audition and vision in the first year of postnatal life: A methodological overview* (pp. 323–363). Westport, CT: Ablex Publishing.

Stroop, J. R. (1935). Studies of interference in serial verbal reactions. *Journal of Experimental Psychology, 18*, 643–662.

Taffe, M. A. (1996). The contribution of cholinergic and dopaminergic systems to delayed response and selective attention in the macaque (Doctoral dissertation, University of California, San Diego, 1996). *Dissertation Abstracts International: Section B: The Sciences and Engineering, 57*, 754.

Teller, D. Y. (1983). Measurement of visual acuity in human and monkey infants: The interface between laboratory and clinic. *Behavioural Brain Research, 10*, 15–23.

Theeuwes, J., & Burger, R. (1998). Attentional control during visual search: The effect of irrelevant singletons. *Journal of Experimental Psychology: Human Perception and Performance, 24*, 1342–1353.

Thomas, D. R. (1970). Stimulus selection, attention and related matters. In J. J. Reynierse (Ed.), *Current issues in animal learning*. Lincoln, NE: University of Nebraska Press.

Titchener, E. B. (1908). *Lectures on the elementary psychology of feeling and attention*. New York: MacMillan.

Tomonaga, M. (1993a). A search for search asymmetry in chimpanzees (*Pan troglodytes*). *Perceptual and Motor Skills, 76*(3, Pt 2), 1287–1295.

Tomonaga, M. (1993b). Use of multiple-alternative matching-to-sample in the study of visual search in a chimpanzee (*Pan troglodytes*). *Journal of Comparative Psychology, 107*(1), 75–83.

Tomonaga, M. (1995). Visual search by chimpanzees (*Pan troglodytes*): Assessment of controlling relations. *Journal of the Experimental Analysis of Behavior, 63*(2), 175–186.

Tomonaga, M. (1997). Precuing the target location in visual searching by a chimpanzee (*Pan troglodytes*): Effects of precue validity. *Japanese Psychological Research, 39*(3), 200–211.

Tomonaga, M. (2001). Investigating visual perception and cognition in chimpanzees (*Pan troglodytes*) through visual search and related tasks: From basic to complex processes.

In T. Matsuzawa (Ed.), *Primate origins of human cognition and behavior* (pp. 55–86). New York: Springer-Verlag.

Trabasso, T., & Bower, G. H. (1968). *Attention in learning*. New York: Wiley.

Treisman, A. M. (1964). Monitoring and storage of irrelevant messages in selective attention. *Journal of Verbal Learning and Verbal Behavior*, *3*, 449–459.

Treisman, A. M., & Gelade, G. (1980). A feature-integration theory of attention. *Cognitive Psychology*, *12*, 97–136.

Washburn, D. A. (1993). The stimulus movement effect: Allocation of attention or artifact? *Journal of Experimental Psychology: Animal Behavior Processes*, *19*, 380–390.

Washburn, D. A. (1994). Stroop-like effects for monkeys and humans: Processing speed or strength of association? *Psychological Science*, *5*, 375–379.

Washburn, D. A. (2003). The games psychologists play (and the data they provide). *Behavior Research Methods, Instruments and Computers*, *35*, 185–193.

Washburn, D. A., Hopkins, W. D., & Rumbaugh, D. M. (1989). Video-task assessment of learning and memory in macaques (*Macaca mulatta*): Effects of stimulus movement on performance. *Journal of Experimental Psychology: Animal Behavior Processes*, *15*, 393–400.

Washburn, D. A., & Kane, M. J. (1999, March). *Negative priming in macaques*. Paper presented at the meeting of the Eastern Psychological Association, Baltimore, MD.

Washburn, D. A., & Rumbaugh, D. M. (1991). Ordinal judgments of numerical symbols by macaques (*Macaca mulatta*). *Psychological Science*, 2, 190–193.

West, R. E., & Young, R. J. (2002). Do domestic dogs show any evidence of being able to count? *Animal Cognition*, *5*, 183–186.

Woodruff, R. S. (1938). *Experimental Psychology*. New York: Henry Holt and Company.

III

MEMORY PROCESSES

8

The Questions of Temporal and Spatial Displacement in Animal Cognition

WILLIAM A. ROBERTS

Still, thou art blest compar'd wi' me!
Only the present toucheth thee,
But Och! I backward cast my e'e
On prospects drear!
An' forward, tho' I canna' see
I guess an' fear!
—Robert Burns, "To a Mouse"

Human language and cognition are often described as having the property of displacement. Displacement may be both temporal and spatial. Thus, we may think or communicate about events that occurred at some time in the past or that will occur at some time in the future. This ability is referred to as *cognitive time travel*, and memories of personal events that occurred at specific times in the past are referred to as *episodic memories*. People also can think or communicate about places distant from their current location, and we might call this *cognitive spatial travel*. Thus, although I live in North America, I may contemplate what is happening in Europe or Asia.

The human brain then can symbolically represent its own existence both within a linear temporal dimension that extends into a past and into a future from the present moment and within a three-dimensional spatial framework that may extend into outer space.

The question I wish to discuss is whether these displacement abilities of humans can be found in animals. With regard to the temporal displacement question, I have advanced the hypothesis that animals are "stuck in time" (W. A. Roberts, 2002). The *stuck-in-time hypothesis* suggests, as does Robbie Burns's quote, that animals live largely in a cognitive present with no sense of a past or future. The validity of this hypothesis can be evaluated against existing relevant research, and it can generate ideas for further research. A parallel "stuck-in-space" hypothesis may be advanced regarding spatial displacement. Is it possible that animals have no representation of space as extending outward from their current location? Data on spatial navigation in animals may be evaluated against this hypothesis.

In this chapter, it is my intention first to review some of the evidence on the stuck-in-time hypothesis, concerning both the possibility of episodic memory in animals and the anticipation of future events. I then discuss some recent research from my laboratory that was generated by this hypothesis and by relevant work from other laboratories. In the second part of the chapter, I discuss evidence bearing on the issue of spatial displacement in animals.

TEMPORAL DISPLACEMENT

Tulving (1972, 1983, 1984) originally pointed to the distinction between human episodic and semantic memory. *Episodic memory* was defined as memory for personal episodes that could be located at a specific time and place. *Semantic* or *reference memory*, on the other hand, was memory for facts about the world, such as mathematical operations, geography, and vocabulary, which had no personal temporal or spatial reference points. Tulving (1983) specifically restricted episodic memory to humans when he said, "Remembering past events is a universally familiar experience. It is also a uniquely human one" (p. 1). Although Tulving had suggested a major qualitative difference in the contents of memory between humans and animals, his position remained uncontested for a number of years.

Recently, however, the question of episodic memory in animals is receiving considerable attention. Suddendorf and Corbalis (1997) reviewed the evidence from nonhuman primates and concluded that there was little evidence for episodic memory or more generally for cognitive time travel. W. A. Roberts (2002) extended the scope of this inquiry to animals in general and concluded that the bulk of the evidence failed to support cognitive time travel in animals. In contrast to these reviews, Clayton and Dickinson have carried out a number of experiments with scrub jays, which they suggest show clear evidence of "episodic-like memory" (Clayton & Dickinson, 1998, 1999; Clayton, Yu, & Dickinson, 2001; Griffiths, Dickinson, & Clayton, 1999). The following section reviews the evidence for episodic memory in animals.

Evidence on the Question of Episodic Memory in Animals

W. A. Roberts (2002) argued that in order for animals to have episodic memory, they would need to have a sense of time; that is, they would need to represent time as a dimension with specific markers along that dimension that date personal episodes. Early humans undoubtedly used natural phenomena such as position of the sun, phase of the moon, and season of the year to track time. With the development of time technology in the form of calendars and clocks, time keeping became more precise until modern humans are exquisitely aware of time throughout the day. Further, people remember past events as occurring at a particular time by inferring or reconstructing their time of occurrence within a rich temporal framework for time past (Friedman, 1993). Because animals presumably do not have access to such time technology, how could they have a sense of time?

One possibility is that animals might count the number of times natural or unnatural events occurred and use number of events as a time marker. Thus, a wild animal might remember that it caught a particular prey or was chased by a particular predator three day-night cycles ago. A laboratory animal might remember that it was tested in a maze five comings and goings of the experimenter ago. These are measurements of elapsed time and would indicate how long ago a particular event occurred. They would not fix an event at a particular point within a temporal dimension with a beginning point. Such a dimension would be necessary for an animal to specify *when* an event occurred, as opposed to *how long ago* it occurred.

In some ways, animals are quite sensitive to time. Animals can accurately discriminate time of day. Thus, oyster catchers learn to fly to mussel beds at precisely the time of day when the low tide exposes the mussels (Daan & Koene, 1981), and pigeons congregate at noon at a particular outdoor location where people eat lunch (Wilkie et al., 1996). In the laboratory, both garden warblers (Biebach, Gordijn, & Krebs, 1989) and pigeons (Saksida & Wilkie, 1994) learned to go to different locations at different times of day to obtain food. Time-place learning then seems to occur readily in animals. What is the discriminative cue that allows animals to accurately detect time of day?

The most commonly offered explanation is that animals use internal circadian clocks. Changes in internal neural and hormonal states throughout the daily 24-hr cycle provide internal cues to which an animal is sensitive and that can be associated with place of food delivery. However, sensitivity to time of day through internal oscillators in no way requires a sense of extended time.

Numerous experiments performed in the past 25 years or so show that animals are excellent interval timers. In time discrimination experiments, a rat or pigeon learns easily to press one bar or to peck a key of one particular color after a light has been on for 2 s but to press another bar or to peck another color after the light has been on for 8 s. In time estimation experiments, animals are trained on fixed interval (FI) schedules of reinforcement. After a light or sound signal begins, a rat or a pigeon may be able to earn a reward by responding only after a certain length of time has elapsed. In an FI 30-s schedule, for example, only bar presses or key pecks made 30 s after a light or a sound signal began would yield a reward. Animals become very sensitive to this contingency and learn to respond only during a period preceding the end of the FI.

To obtain a precise measure of an animal's expected time of reward, S. Roberts (1981) used the peak procedure. Once rats had been trained to press a bar to obtain reward after 20 s following onset of one cue (light) and after 40 s following onset of another cue (sound), empty trials were introduced as occasional probe tests. On an empty trial, the light or sound cue began the trial and continued for up to 100 s with no reward given for pressing the bar. When Roberts plotted rate of bar pressing against time bins over the course of a number of empty trials, he found Gaussian-shaped curves whose peaks corresponded very closely to the length of the FI signaled by the light or the sound cue. In other words, rats were quite accurately estimating the duration of the FI. Since Roberts's experiment, the peak procedure has been used many times to show accurate interval timing in rats and pigeons.

An important point here is that interval timing again does not require a sense or concept of time. Several theories account for interval timing, and they all have in common the development of an internal process that begins when the interval starts and that triggers an internal sensor when the end of the interval approaches or is reached.

Scalar-timing theory has been the most studied account of interval timing in animals (Church, Meck, & Gibbon, 1994; Gibbon, 1977, 1991). It holds that time is represented as the accumulation of pulses transmitted from a pacemaker and stored in reference memory. A time switch closes when a cue signaling the beginning of an interval occurs and opens when the cue terminates. Pulse totals stored in reference memory serve as criteria for timing subsequent intervals. An internal comparator tracks the difference between a criterion number of pulses retrieved from reference memory and the number of pulses currently accumulating in a working memory. When the working memory value approaches the criterion value, a threshold is crossed and this triggers the initiation of responding. On an empty trial in the peak procedure, responding is held to cease when the pulses accumulating in working memory exceed the criterion by the threshold amount. The time estimate is taken as the midpoint of the response period and closely approximates the length of the reinforced FI. This mechanism allows intervals to be precisely timed at any time during a day, but it does not indicate a point within a time dimension such as a day or a period involving several days.

Memory for the Order of Events It is difficult to study episodic memory in animals because we cannot directly query them about personal episodes. However, because episodes are ordered in time, we may conduct experiments to find out if animals remember the order in which events occurred. Memory for the order of events is usually studied in two ways. One way has been to study working memory for different orders of stimuli. An animal may be presented with two stimuli in the orders AB or BA. On an immediate working memory test for stimulus order, the animal may have to respond to test stimuli for reward in the same or opposite order as they were presented or may have to respond differentially to some new test stimuli for reward depending on whether the order was AB or BA (Devine, Burke, & Rohack, 1979; MacDonald, 1993; Parker, 1984; Weisman, Wasserman, Dodd, & Larew, 1980). Although pigeons and monkeys showed varying degrees of success at this task, animals may not have responded based on memory for the temporal order of events. An alternative is that they used differences in the strengths of the memory traces for the stimuli in the sample sequence as the critical information on which to base their response (W. A. Roberts, 2002). In particular, MacDonald (1993) varied the presentation time of different items in a sequence and found that it affected judgments of order in exactly the ways predicted by a memory-trace model.

The second way in which memory for order has been studied has been to train animals to respond to a set of stimuli in a fixed order. Pigeons and monkeys have been trained to reproduce orders containing as many as five stimuli (D'Amato & Colombo, 1988, 1989; Terrace, 1983, 1987, 1991). Even these reference memory experiments do not conclusively lead to the conclusion that animals can remember a temporal sequence. A first point is that it is not easy for either pigeons or monkeys to learn to reproduce an extended order of stimuli. Training begins with a single pair of stimuli, and single stimuli are gradually added to the chain as learning

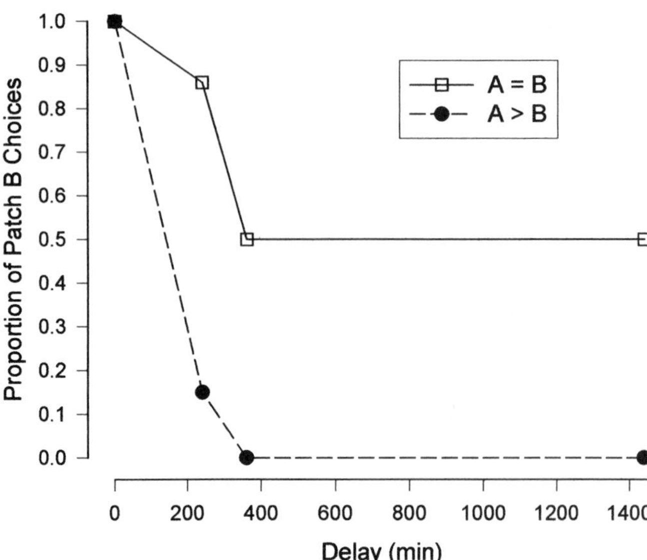

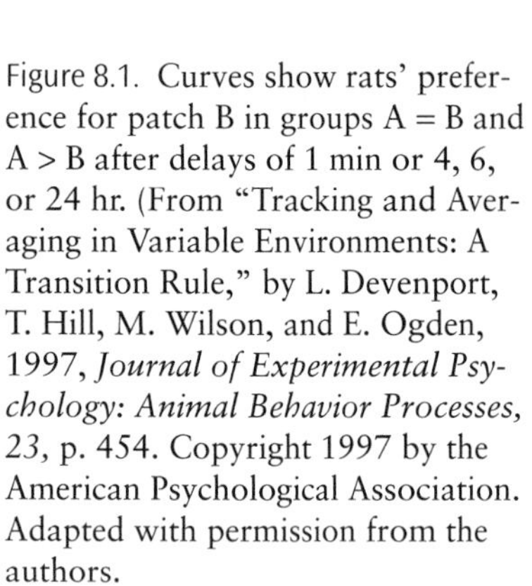
Figure 8.1. Curves show rats' preference for patch B in groups A = B and A > B after delays of 1 min or 4, 6, or 24 hr. (From "Tracking and Averaging in Variable Environments: A Transition Rule," by L. Devenport, T. Hill, M. Wilson, and E. Ogden, 1997, *Journal of Experimental Psychology: Animal Behavior Processes, 23*, p. 454. Copyright 1997 by the American Psychological Association. Adapted with permission from the authors.

progresses. Animals typically require a hundred or more sessions to learn to accurately produce a four- or five-item sequence. A second point is that production of a learned stimulus sequence does not necessarily mean that an animal has learned a temporal representation of that sequence. Based on tests with subsets of two or three stimuli from a list, Terrace (1991) concluded that pigeons had not learned an overall representation of the sequence. Rather, pigeons had learned rules about which stimulus to peck first and which stimulus to peck last. These rules, combined with some inter-item associations, allowed pigeons to successfully produce an ordered sequence. Tests with monkeys did suggest that they represented the entire list of stimuli, but Chen, Swartz, and Terrace (1997) concluded that they could have accomplished this with a spatial map and not a temporal one.

Another relevant well-known phenomenon that may involve more extended memory for order is spontaneous recovery. It was first discovered by Pavlov (1927) and refers to the observation that an extinguished conditioned response seems to spontaneously reappear when a conditioned stimulus (CS) is presented hours after the end of extinction trials. Although there are several accounts of spontaneous recovery based on different mechanisms, one account suggests that animals form two memories: one for a period in which an unconditioned stimulus (US) follows the CS and one for a period in which the US does not follow the CS. The animal has learned to respond on the basis of the events that are most recent and thus currently occupy its working memory. With the passage of time, however, neither event occupies working memory. The stuck-in-time hypothesis argues that because these events were not assigned to particular points along a time dimension, the animal will have no memory of which occurred last. The animal may then respond to the CS, showing spontaneous recovery, because the presence of a memory for the US after the CS indicates some probability that the US may occur.

Recent experiments by Devenport, Hill, Wilson, and Ogden (1997) on rats' memory for food locations seem to support this position. Rats foraged for food in two patches, defined as food cups placed in two different locations, patch A and patch B. On an initial foraging opportunity, group A = B found 24 food pellets in patch A and nothing in patch B. On a second bout of foraging, they found nothing in patch A and 24 pellets in patch B. Another group of rats, group A > B, initially found 40 pellets in patch A and nothing in patch B; on their second foraging opportunity, they found nothing in patch A and 8 pellets in patch B. Both groups then were divided into subgroups that were given opportunities to choose freely between patch A and patch B either 1 min or 4, 6, or 24 hr after the last bout of foraging.

Figure 8.1 shows the results as proportion of patch B choices plotted against delay. All the rats in both subgroups tested after 1 min went to patch B; these rats therefore returned to the patch in which they had most recently found food. As the delay increased, however, rats came to choose between patches based on the food encountered on both foraging bouts. Thus, after 6 and 24 hr, A = B subgroups chose each patch equally often, but A > B subgroups always chose patch A. If rats had no memory for the order in which these patches had been searched with differential consequences, then these results are understandable. If rats in group A > B, for example, only remembered that A yielded 40 pellets and B nothing on one occasion and that A yielded nothing while B yielded 8 pellets on another occasion, then the best bet would be to return to the higher yielding patch A.

The Clayton and Dickinson Experiments Although the Devenport et al. (1997) experiments suggest the absence of memory in rats for when a particular quantity of food was found at a distinctive spatial location, spatial foraging experiments with scrub jays suggest just the opposite. In the basic demonstration, scrub jays showed differential preference for recovery of foods depending on the time that had elapsed since the foods were hoarded. In laboratory experiments, scrub jays cached preferred but perishable wax worms in a tray in one spatial location and less preferred but not perishable peanuts in a tray in a different spatial location. When jays were allowed to search for food 4 hours later, they visited the tray where worms had been cached. If the recovery test was given 128 hours (5 days) later, however, scrub jays searched for food in the peanut tray (Clayton & Dickinson, 1998, 1999).

Several facts are important to know about these experiments. The birds tested had been given prior training in which they could learn that worms, but not peanuts, decay over 5 days but not 4 hr. Tests were carried out with food removed from the trays where it had been cached, ruling out the use of odor cues. Finally, jays still showed these food recovery preferences even when worms and peanuts were cached at different locations within the same trays.

More recently, Clayton et al. (2001) extended this procedure by using a third food—crickets. On different trials, scrub jays cached either peanuts and worms or peanuts and crickets in different places. Birds were allowed to search for their caches after 4, 28, or 100 hr. After 4 hr, caches of all three foods contained fresh items. After 28 hr, decayed worms were found at worm sites, but fresh crickets were found at cricket sites. After 100 hr, both worms and crickets were decayed. Scrub jays searched preferentially for worms or crickets after 4 hr. After 28 hr, they searched for crickets before peanuts, but preferred peanuts to worms. After 100 hr, birds went to peanut caches before either worm or cricket caches. It seems clear from these experiments that scrub jays were quite sensitive to the time periods over which different foods decayed. Griffiths et al. (1999) argue that these experiments show episodic-like memory for three components of hidden food: *what, where,* and *when*. It is particularly the idea that jays remembered when they cached a particular food that suggests episodic-like memory. As an alternative interpretation, W. A. Roberts (2002) suggested that memories of caching different foods in different locations may have different strengths because their durations vary and that birds could be using memory strength as a cue for the decay state of different foods. Thus, birds might learn that a weak memory of cached worms means decayed worms.

A Search for Episodic Memory in Rats If we assume that episodic memory has been shown in scrub jays, then the interesting question arises as to whether it should also be found in other animals. An ecological approach to this question suggests that this ability might have evolved in birds that cache and retrieve food as a mechanism to prevent them from delaying too long before recovering perishable foods (Clayton, Bussey, & Dickinson, 2003). Other animals that hoard food for later consumption then might also have evolved episodic memory. Although *Rattus norvegicus* does not scatter hoard and recover food, many of its rodent relatives do (Vander Wall, 1990). Furthermore, food carrying and hoarding have been found in a number of experiments with laboratory rats (Bindra, 1948; Morgan, 1947; Wallace, 1979). Given these considerations, we have carried out some experiments in our laboratory to look for evidence of episodic memory in rats. All of these experiments have involved the radial maze (Olton & Samuelson, 1976) and thus memory for when different events occurred at different spatial locations.

W. A. Roberts and S. Roberts (2002) tested 10 hooded rats in an enclosed (walled) gray eight-arm radial maze. Eight arms, each 82 cm long and 10.5 cm wide, branched off a circular central area

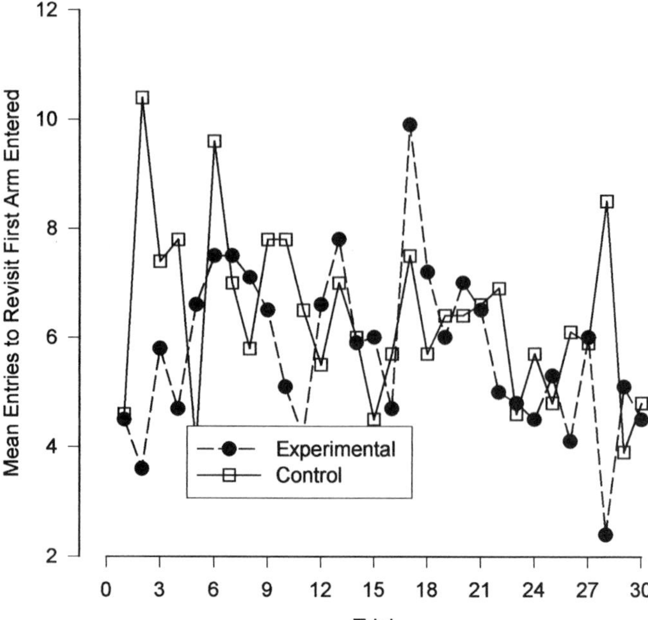

Figure 8.2. The number of arm entries taken by rats in experimental and control groups to revisit the first arm entered on a trial plotted over 30 trials. (From "Two Tests of the Stuck-in-Time Hypothesis," by W. A. Roberts and S. Roberts, 2002, *The Journal of General Psychology, 129*, 422. Copyright 2002 by the Helen Dwight Reid Educational Foundation. Reprinted with permission.)

that was 31 cm wide. At the end of each arm were two sequential goal chambers. Each chamber was 15 cm long and contained a goal cup near the back wall. The entrance to the first chamber was covered with a black curtain that the rats were trained to push through. The back wall of the first chamber was a solid guillotine door that could be raised by the experimenter to allow the rats to enter the second chamber.

Experimental and control groups, each containing five rats, were tested on the maze. After preliminary training, both groups were tested for 30 trials, with one trial given per day. At the beginning of each trial, the maze was prepared for the experimental group by placing one food item (one quarter of a piece of Frosted Cheerios breakfast cereal) in the first goal compartment on each arm. Ten pieces of food were placed into the second goal compartment of each arm. The maze was prepared for the control group by placing one piece of food in each of the goal compartments on each arm. The procedure for testing rats in both groups was the same. A rat was placed in the center of the maze with all arms available for entrance, and rats could freely enter the arms in any order. The experimenter recorded arm entrances and performed one operation during the trial. For whichever arm a rat chose to enter first, the experimenter raised the door between the first and second goal chambers in that arm immediately after the rats had departed and returned to the center of the maze. Thus, a rat that returned to the first arm entered in the experimental group would hit the jackpot of 10 food items. A control rat that reentered the first arm chosen, however, would obtain only one food item, no more than it would get by entering any previously unentered arm.

The logic of this experiment is as follows. If a rat remembers when it went to different locations in space (episodic memory for where and when), then it should be able to remember the first arm it visited. If rats in the experimental group can further learn the rule that return to the first arm visited will yield the jackpot reward, then they should reenter the first arm visited sooner than control rats who only get one food item for reentering the first arm visited. The general tendency of rats on radial mazes is not to revisit an arm until a number of other arms have been visited. Thus, the question here is: Can the experimental rats use episodic memory to short circuit that tendency in order to gain a large reward? The prediction based on the hypothesis that rats have episodic memory is that the experimental group, but not the control group, will show a decrease in the number of arms entered before reentering the first entered arm.

The results are shown in figure 8.2, which plots the mean arm entries required to revisit the first arm entered over 30 trials. Although the curves show considerable variability across trials, the mean number of entries is about 6.0. Most important, there is no clear difference between the experimental and control groups, and neither group shows a significant downward trend over trials. An analysis of variance (ANOVA) performed on these data showed no significant effects of groups, trials, or groups × trials. This experiment then yielded no evidence of episodic memory in rats.

It might be argued that this experiment was too demanding on rat cognition. Perhaps rats did remember when different arms were entered and which one was entered first, but they did not associate it with the jackpot reward. Perhaps an experiment that more closely approximates those performed by Clayton and Dickinson with scrub jays would yield better evidence of episodic memory in rats.

In our laboratory, we developed a procedure for studying memory for cached food in rats (Bird, Roberts, Abroms, Kit, & Crupi, 2003). An eight-arm maze was used that contained enclosed, darkened boxes at the end of each arm. Rats were trained to carry pieces of cheese from the center of the maze to these boxes. On training trials, rats were allowed to carry four pieces of cheese to four different boxes. After a rat entered the enclosed box carrying its piece of cheese, the experimenter opened the box; removed the rat, leaving the cheese in the box; and returned the rat to the center to carry the next piece of cheese. After the fourth piece was carried to a box, the experimenter returned the rat to its home cage for 45 min. The rat then was placed back on the center of the maze and allowed to choose freely among all eight arms.

Figure 8.3 shows the acquisition of accurate food recovery behavior in two groups of rats. The retention score plotted against blocks of 2 days varies between −1.0 and +1.0, with 0 as a chance score and +1.0 representing entry into all of the arms where food was cached before any arms where food was not cached. It can be seen that rats quickly learned to return to cache locations and ultimately reached a plateau of about 0.8. Notice that performance does not differ between forced and free groups. The free group was allowed to cache in any four arms freely chosen by the rat. Caching in the forced group was controlled by the experimenter, who opened one door at a time to allow a rat to enter four arms that were randomly chosen. Thus, the rats' accuracy was not based on hoarding on and returning to favored arms. A final point is that the arms on which food was cached changed on each trial. Therefore, rats showed excellent *working memory* for locations to which they had to return, unlike the more usual radial maze task in which animals must choose previously unentered arms for reward.

Because we had developed a task in which rats cached and retrieved food, we proceeded to study the question of memory for when food was hoarded using the Clayton and Dickinson paradigm. Two groups of rats were allowed to hoard two pieces of a preferred food (cheese) and two pieces of a less preferred food (pretzel). Previous studies had shown that rats both hoarded and retrieved pieces of cheese before pieces of pretzel. The preferred pieces of cheese could be degraded by soaking them in bitter quinine; rats refused to eat cheese soaked in quinine. On different trials, both groups were allowed to search for cached food on the arms of the maze either 1 or 25 hr after caching the food items. In one group (1-hr degrade), the edible cheese found in boxes at end of the arms where they had cached it was replaced with degraded pieces of cheese at the 1-hr test; on 24-hr tests, however, the cheese found was fresh. In the other group, the temporal contingencies were reversed. In the 25-hr degrade group, the cheese found after 1 hr was edible, but the cheese found after 25 hr was degraded. Fresh edible pretzels were available in the boxes where they had been cached on all tests. The experiment lasted for 20 trials at each retention interval for each group.

Overall working memory performance for return to arms where food was cached was not as high in this experiment as that shown in figure 8.3. Nevertheless, both groups showed better-than-chance return to cached food locations. The data most relevant to the episodic memory hypothesis are shown in figure 8.4. Among the four arms containing cached food, the mean rank of entry into arms containing cheese is shown for each group at the retention interval when cheese was degraded and when it was not degraded. Evidence for memory of when foods were cached would appear as higher ranks at the retention interval when cheese degraded than at the retention interval when cheese did not degrade. In the case of the 1-hr degrade group, the data go in the opposite direction to the hypothesis; over the last three blocks of four

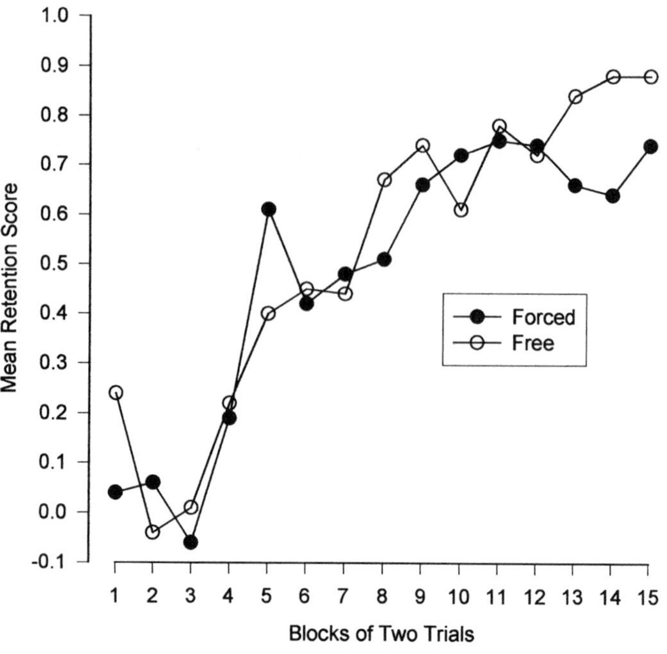

Figure 8.3. Mean retention scores plotted over blocks of two trials. (From "Spatial Memory for Food Hidden by Rats (*Rattus norvegicus*) on the Radial Maze: Studies of Memory of Where, What, and When," by L. R. Bird, W. A. Roberts, B. Abroms, K. A. Kit, and C. Crupi, 2003, *Journal of Comparative Psychology, 117,* 179. Copyright 2003 by the American Psychological Association. Reprinted with permission.)

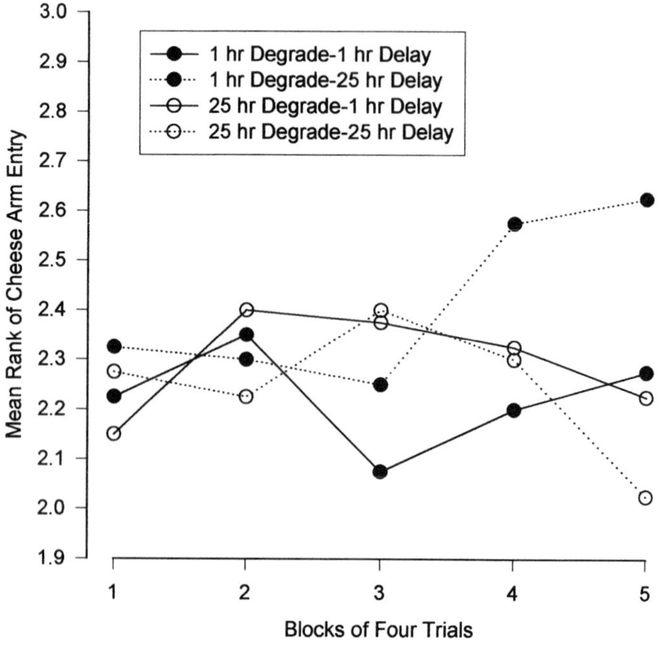

Figure 8.4. Mean rank of entry into arms containing cheese plotted over blocks of four trials for 1-hr and 25-hr degrade groups, each tested on different trials after 1-hr and 25-hr delays. (From "Spatial Memory for Food Hidden by Rats (*Rattus norvegicus*) on the Radial Maze: Studies of Memory of Where, What, and When," by L. R. Bird, W. A. Roberts, B. Abroms, K. A. Kit, and C. Crupi, 2003, *Journal of Comparative Psychology, 117,* 185. Copyright 2003 by the American Psychological Association. Reprinted with permission.)

trials, rats went to the cheese arms sooner after 1 hr than after 25 hr, and this difference was significant, $t(4) = 7.38$. In the 25-hr degrade group, there was no significant difference between mean ranks of visits to cheese arms after 1 hr and 25 hr, $t < 1.00$.

These findings reveal a resounding failure to replicate the scrub jay findings in rats. Two characteristics of this experiment suggest that every effort was made to find an effect. First, groups were tested in which the preferred food degraded at both short and long delays before recovery. Neither delay yielded any evidence for episodic memory. Second, rats in each group were tested for 20 trials at each delay, for a total of 40 trials. The failure to find any suggestion of memory for when food was hoarded may mean that there is a major difference between species; scrub jays may have evolved episodic memory, whereas rats have not. Of course, it is difficult to prove the null hypothesis in the case of rats, and it may be that more sensitive tests carried out under different conditions will reveal evidence of episodic memory in rats or other rodents. The findings from the two experiments reported here, however, encourage a healthy skepticism about the generality of episodic memory in animals.

Evidence Concerning Animals' Ability to Anticipate Future Events

It might be argued that studies of Pavlovian and instrumental learning show evidence of anticipatory processes in animals. An animal in a Pavlovian experiment responds to a CS as it would to a forthcoming US. The *differential-outcomes effect* in instrumental discrimination learning may be seen to imply prospective processing. In a traditional matching-to-sample experiment, a pigeon is rewarded with the *same* reward for choosing a red comparison stimulus after seeing a red sample stimulus and for choosing a green comparison stimulus after seeing a green sample stimulus. In the differential-outcomes procedure, a different reward (reward A) is delivered for choosing a red comparison stimulus after a red sample stimulus from the reward (reward B) delivered for choosing a green comparison stimulus after a green sample stimulus. The effect of differential outcomes is to speed the rate of learning to match the sample and to raise the level of retention of the sample stimulus on delayed comparison stimuli tests, relative to training and testing with the same reward following both samples (Peterson, Wheeler, & Armstrong, 1978).

A favored theoretical account of the differential outcomes effect is that pigeons learn to anticipate reward A or B when the appropriate sample is presented (as the US may be anticipated when the CS is presented) and use this information to cue choice between the matching and nonmatching comparison stimuli. However, these phenomena do not require an animal to project a future event. Through repeated pairing of a CS with a US or of a sample with a particular outcome, the CS or sample may elicit a representation of the US or outcome, which in turn acts as a cue for the appropriate conditioned response or matching response.

Memory experiments with rats on a radial maze (Cook, Brown, & Riley, 1985) and with pigeons in a five-key operant chamber (Zentall, Steirn, & Jackson-Smith, 1990) led these investigators to argue that animals showed both retrospective and prospective strategies. In tasks in which rats had to enter different arms and pigeons had to peck different keys sequentially, time delays were interpolated between responses made early, in the middle, or late in the sequence of responses. It was found that both species showed the highest level of errors when the delay was placed near the middle of the series of choices. This finding was explained by arguing that animals using a strategy of retrospection or remembering which choices had already been made until the memory load became heavy and then switching to a prospective strategy of remembering which choices were still to be made. It was argued that the switch from a retrospective to a prospective strategy occurred near the center of the series of choices; thus, memory was most disrupted by placing a delay in the center. These interesting findings suggest that rats and pigeons may partition their responses into those made and those not yet made, but they do not demand that animals planned a series of choices into the future. Another type of experiment concerned with animals' ability to anticipate future events sets up two choices: one in which an animal may earn an immediate small reward and one in which it may earn a delayed larger reward. In *self-control* experiments, for example, animals often have been given a choice between a stimulus that yields 2 s of access to food reward after a 0.1-s delay and another stimulus that yields 6 s of access to food reward after a 6-s delay (Logue, 1988; Rachlin & Green, 1972). The typical finding with rats and pigeons tested with these outcomes is preference for the immediate, smaller reward (Mazur & Logue, 1978; Tobin, Chelonis, & Logue, 1993). By contrast, human subjects tested in this procedure show self-control by preferring to choose the stimulus that leads to delayed, larger reward (King & Logue, 1987; Logue, Pena-Correal, Rodriguez, & Kabela, 1986). Based on these findings, Logue (1988) suggested that animals may have a very small time window over which they can integrate events and that "if the time window is indeed very short in nonhuman subjects then, functionally, such a subject's choice in a self-control paradigm is between a smaller reinforcer now or no reinforcer at all" (p. 676).

Similar experiments on the *time horizon* have been performed by Timberlake and his colleagues (Lucas, Timberlake, Gawley, & Drew, 1990; Timberlake, 1984; Timberlake, Gawley, & Lucas 1987, 1988). As an example of this kind of experiment, Timberlake et al. (1987) provided rat subjects with two bars in two different locations (patches). At the beginning of a session, only one bar led to food delivery when pressed. This bar yielded food on a progressive ratio schedule, one in which the number of presses required for food increased by one after each reward. At some time after the start of the session, the second bar was enabled and delivered reward consistently for only one press. Thus, if a rat could learn to wait for the second bar to become active, then it could earn more food for much less effort. The delay of activation of the second bar was varied over 4, 8, 16, 32, 64, and 120 min. Up to 16 min, rats responded more slowly on the delayed-activation bar than did control rats for which the second bar was not activated. Beyond this delay, rate of responding on the second bar was equal. However, the degree of suppression was small; even at the shortest 4-min delay, rats worked at a rate that was seven times higher than the price necessary for reward in the delayed patch. Timberlake et al. concluded that "the laboratory data most strongly support the view that animals have a rather short time period over which they behave effectively with respect to temporally separated feeding alternatives" (p. 307).

Findings from self-control and time-horizon experiments then generally suggest that rats and pigeons have a very short view of the future. These experiments were carried out in Skinner boxes with alternative responses to adjacent bars or keys. W. A. Roberts and S. Roberts (2002) looked at the possibility rats could learn to anticipate a future event when there were several alternative responses that were more spatially distributed. Two groups of rats were trained on the enclosed eight-arm radial maze with double-compartment goal boxes previously described for studying episodic memory. In this experiment, one arm of the maze was made distinctive by its odor and texture; almond extract was placed on the arm, and its floor was lined with coarse-grain sandpaper. Before a trial began, one food item was placed into the first goal compartment on every arm of the maze for all subjects in the experimental and control groups. For experimental subjects, 10 more food items were placed into the second goal compartment only on the distinctive arm. For control subjects, only one food item was placed into the second goal compartment of the distinctive arm. Rats in both groups were allowed to freely choose arms on each trial. The experimenter recorded arm choices and performed a simple operation contingent on a rat's behavior. If a rat delayed entering the distinctive arm for four choices, then the door separating the first and second goal compartments was raised. Thus, an experimental rat that delayed entry into the distinctive arm could earn $10 + 1 = 11$ food items, whereas a control rat that delayed entry could earn only $1 + 1 = 2$ food items. Rats in the experimental group could earn the jackpot if they could show self-control and delay choice of the distinctive arm. To do so, however, would require anticipation of a future, delayed payoff. One advantage that this task has over the traditional self-control experiment from the rat's point of view is that it can earn food by entering arms while it delays entrance into the distinctive arm.

Figure 8.5 shows the probability of delayed entry into the novel arm plotted over blocks of three daily trials for experimental and control groups. Evidence that rats had learned to delay entrance into the distinctive arm would be shown by a drop in the curves over blocks: a steeper drop would be expected in the experimental group than in the control group. Those effects clearly do not appear in the figure. An ANOVA yielded no significant effects of groups, blocks, or the groups × blocks interaction. The mean probability of delayed entry into the distinctive arm over 30 trials of training was .41 in the control group and .40 in the experimental group. Once again, our findings with rats failed to yield much evidence of cognitive time

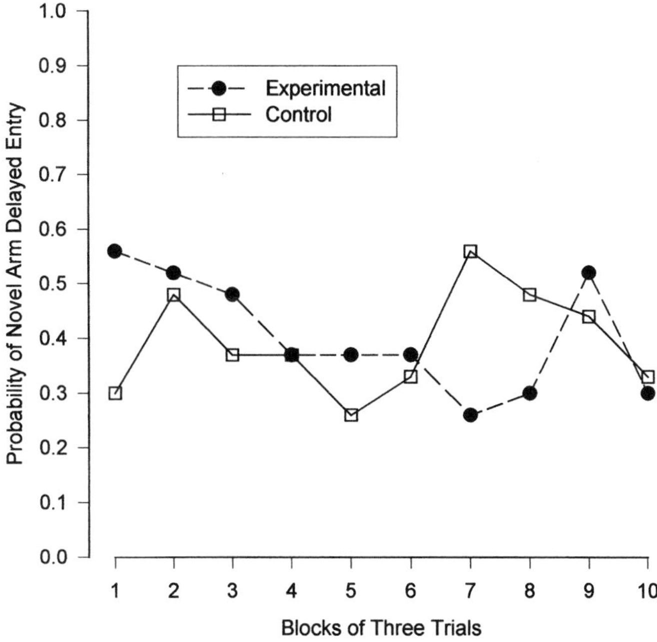

Figure 8.5. The probability of delayed entry into the novel (jackpot) arm by experimental and control groups plotted over 10 three-trial blocks. (From "Two Tests of the Stuck-in-Time Hypothesis," by W. A. Roberts and S. Roberts, 2002, *The Journal of General Psychology, 129,* 424. Copyright 2002 by the Helen Dwight Reid Educational Foundation. Reprinted with permission.)

travel, in this case, the ability to anticipate future events.

Although the focus of memory research with scrub jays has been on episodic-like memory, one study has addressed the issue of forward time travel. Emery and Clayton (2001) allowed scrub jays to cache and recache food items under different conditions. One group of scrub jays had previously pilfered other scrub jays' caches, whereas another group had not had this experience. Both groups then cached worms under a condition in which they were observed by another scrub jay or were given privacy (no observer). When the jays recovered these caches 3 hr later, the birds that had previously pilfered food recached more worms when they had been observed caching than when they had cached in privacy. The jays who had not pilfered before did not show differential recaching between the observed and privacy conditions. A further interesting finding was that jays that had pilfered and been observed caching now recached significantly more often in new sites than in old sites; this new site preference was not found when these jays cached in private and was not found under any conditions in the group that had not previously pilfered.

Emery and Clayton (2001) suggest that these findings may show forward mental time travel in scrub jays that had previously pilfered other scrub jays' caches. These birds could have integrated two memories to predict a future occurrence. One memory was that of being a pilferer; by extension, the bird could reason that other scrub jays, too, could be pilferers. When this memory was combined with the memory that its own caching behavior had been observed by another scrub jay, it could anticipate that its own caches would be pilfered unless they were moved to a new site, presumably unknown to the previous observer.

Although Emery and Clayton (2001) do not discuss theory of mind in their article, their reasoning seems to suggest that scrub jays are imputing certain knowledge and motives to another scrub jay and thus anticipating its behavior several hours into the future. There is an alternative explanation, however, of the scrub jays' behavior. It is possible that the behavior observed was more instinctual or genetically programmed than intentional. That is, scrub jays may be programmed to recache more frequently and in new sites if they have certain experiences, such as pilfering and being observed caching by a conspecific. Birds may do this rather automatically without any anticipation of its future consequences.

One way to test these alternative explanations is to set up consequences to the bird's behavior that should lead to its modification if the behavior is based on intentional planning. Suppose that a scrub jay that recaches food in a new site when observed caching by another scrub jay now finds that its recached food has always been pilfered or is allowed to watch another scrub jay pilfer its recached food. Would such repeated consequences eliminate recaching behavior or would it continue to recache? Little change should occur if the behavior is instinctually driven, but the birds should modify their recaching behavior if it is based on future planning.

A relevant observation was made in our food caching and recovery experiments with rats (Bird et al., 2003). In one experiment, rats were allowed to cache pieces of cheese and to return to cache sites over 12 daily trials. On each trial, however, the cached food was pilfered. Thus, when the rat returned to the box at the end of an arm where it had carried food 45 min earlier, no food was found. One might expect, based both on traditional operant experiments on extinction and on the idea that rats would relate their behavior to its outcome, that both caching and food retrieval behaviors would extinguish or weaken. Surprisingly, rats continued to cache food without hesitancy and to accurately return to cache sites over all 12 trials of the experiment. It was argued that these findings are best explained by assuming that caching and recovery were driven by a biologically prepared response to the circumstances presented and not by anticipation of future access to hoarded food (W. A. Roberts, 2002).

COGNITIVE SPATIAL DISPLACEMENT

To address the issue of cognitive spatial displacement in animals, we have to ask the question of whether animals have a concept of space. Do animals understand that space extends beyond their current location to other locations outside their view? Do they represent the relationships between other locations and their current location? Do they realize that important objects may be found or important events may take place in locations they cannot immediately sense? Or, are animals stuck in space, as they may be stuck in time?

Many people may consider the stuck-in-space hypothesis disproved by a number of observations. We know that many species of animals migrate over vast distances, that pets seem to know the layout of the house or neighborhood and laboratory animals can be trained to travel complex routes in a maze. Yet, much of animal navigation behavior may be explained by mechanisms other than cognitive spatial displacement. Even in the absence of vision or other sensory cues, an animal may travel directly home after a tortuous journey that takes it some distance away. Return along a vector aimed directly at its home base is accomplished by *dead reckoning* or the use of internal vestibular and kinesthetic information to track distance and changes in angular direction of travel (Etienne, Berlie, Georgakopoulos, & Maurer, 1998). Migrating birds accurately travel to winter and summer homes by use of genetically programmed sun, magnetic, and star compasses (Berthold, 1998). Homing pigeons return to their roost when released long distances away by homing on magnetic, sun, and odor cues (Bingman, 1998). It has been suggested that laboratory rats may show complex maze behavior by responding only to a sequence of *local views* (Leonard & McNaughton, 1990; McNaughton, 1988). Thus, given an initial local view at the start of a maze, a rat learns to respond in a certain way; this response leads to the next local view and the appropriate response to it, and so forth until the goal is reached. None of these mechanisms requires that an animal have an understanding of or an appreciation for space that extends beyond its currently experienced location.

The Cognitive Map

The issue of cognitive spatial displacement leads us back to a long debated issue in animal cognition, the question of the *cognitive map* (for reviews, see Pearce, 1997; Poucet, 1993; W. A. Roberts, 2001; Shettleworth, 1998). Tolman (1948) introduced the term to account for the spatial behavior of rats in many of his maze studies; he suggested that "something like a field map of the environment gets established in the rat's brain" (p. 192). Tolman suggested that cognitive maps can be broad and comprehensive, something like a human topological map, or narrow and strip-like, perhaps the type of map suggested by McNaughton's local-view hypothesis. A similar distinction was made later by O'Keefe and Nadel (1978) in their influential book *The Hippocampus as a Cognitive Map*. Narrow and limited routes that animals traveled by response to local views were learned by a *taxon system* in the brain. Comprehensive and global cognitive maps were learned by the *locale system* of the hippocampus. Maps were built up slowly through exploration and allowed animals to respond flexibly to spatial navigation problems.

Latent Learning Experiments

Early evidence for cognitive maps in rats was found in *latent learning* experiments. In the classic experiments of Blodgett (1929) and Tolman and Honzik, 1930), rats were allowed to explore a complex multichoice maze for a number of daily trials, with no food reward available in the maze. When experimental rats then encountered food in the goal box on test trials, their error rate and time to complete the maze dropped dramatically compared with a control group given no reward. It was argued that rats had established a cognitive map of the maze through initial exploration without reward. When one location in the maze was valenced by the presence of food, rats used the cognitive map to rapidly return to that location. From a more contemporary point of view, one might worry that animals perhaps were following some extra-maze cue associated with the reward.

In a particularly well-designed test of latent learning, Seward (1949) used a T-maze that contained end boxes that were differentiated in brightness (black and white) or in texture (floors containing hardware cloth or sponge rubber). Rats could not see the end boxes from the choice point because they were turned at right angles to the choice alley of the maze. Rats were allowed to explore the maze with no reinforcer present for 3 days. On the fourth day, rats were allowed to explore the maze for a few minutes and then were isolated for 25 min. The rat then was placed into one end box (half of the rats were in one end box and the other half were in the other end box) and allowed to eat rat chow for 1 min. The rat then was lifted out of the end box and placed into the start box: it could then run down the stem of the maze and choose freely between the right or left arm. Of the 16 rats tested in the brightness condition, 81.25% chose the alley leading to the end box where they had been fed. In the texture condition, 93.75% of the 16 rats went in the correct direction. These findings are particularly relevant to the question of cognitive spatial displacement, as they suggest that rats in one location (start alley of the maze) could represent the contents of other locations in space (the end boxes). Although Seward covered the maze with hardware cloth and cheese cloth and used dim illumination to prevent rats from seeing out of the maze, he worried that "it is conceivable that during maze exploration these views of some differential cue might have acquired stimulus equivalence for the animal and thus, between them, mediated a choice in the direction of food" (p. 180).

As a control experiment, rats given exploration with differentiated end boxes were then given their direct feeding in one end box detached from the maze and placed directly behind the start box. When tested, rats now made the correct choice on only 54% of the trials, a value that did not differ significantly from chance. Seward noted that in fact "one rat tried to climb the back wall of the starting box" (p. 181). These observations suggest that his rats in fact were using extra-maze cues to follow the location of food. If this experiment were repeated with more contemporary controls for extra-maze cues and dead reckoning, then the findings might be very illuminating with respect to the question of cognitive spatial displacement.

Shortcut Experiments

Tolman as well as O'Keefe and Nadel emphasized the flexible nature of the cognitive map, meaning that it could be used to plot novel routes through space. Several experiments have tested this idea by seeing whether animals would use shortcuts never traveled before when given the opportunity. In another well-known experiment from Tolman's laboratory (Tolman, Ritchie, & Kalish, 1946), rats were trained to travel from a circular platform to a goal containing food by an indirect route. On a test trial, they were placed on the circular platform with alleys radiating in all directions, some leading directly to the goal location. The question was whether the rat would go in the direction of its old indirect route or take an alley that led directly to the goal (a shortcut). Rats did prefer alleys that led in the direction of the goal. However, the experiment had an unfortunate confound. A light bulb had been suspended over the goal throughout the experiment. Thus, rats may have simply approached the light as a beacon associated with food and not have inferred a shortcut based on a cognitive map.

In an experiment performed by Chapuis and Varlet (1987), Alsatian dogs were tested outdoors in a meadow. From a starting point, point D, a dog was led to point A and shown a piece of meat hidden in the grass. The dog was returned to point D and then led to point B, where it was shown a second piece of hidden meat. It was then returned to point D, where its leash was removed, and it was free to search for the meat. Most dogs went directly to point A (the shortest path to meat). The important question was where the dogs now would travel. They could return to point D and then take the previously traveled path to meat at point B, or they could take a shortcut by going directly from point A to point B. All of the dogs tested took paths that approximated a direct path from point A to point B. Control tests showed that the dogs were not using the odor of the hidden meat to guide their route.

Unfortunately, a problem similar to that encountered in the Tolman et al. (1946) experiment arises with the Chapuis and Varlet (1987) experiment as a demonstration of cognitive spatial displacement. Bennett (1996) has pointed out that dogs may have seen unique landmarks near points A and B and associated meat with these landmarks. Rocks, trees, buildings, etc. might then serve as beacons associated with reward that an animal could approach and appear to be taking a shortcut. In fact, this problem also plagues attempts to show cognitive mapping in bees (Dyer, 1991; Gould, 1986). As was the case with latent learning, the question of shortcuts in animals requires experiments in which all alternative accounts, particularly the use of cues or landmarks near the goal, have been eliminated through control procedures. Experiments now being carried out in my laboratory are designed to see if rats can form a cognitive map using only the internal geometry of a maze. By eliminating access to extra-maze cues, rotating the maze, and disorienting the rat before each trial, only relationships between locations within the maze can be learned.

Topological Maps?

As a simple task that shows the flexibility of the human brain, I ask students to draw a top view of their home or apartment. Students immediately begin to draw and in short order produce a reasonably accurate blueprint of their living space. I then ask them how they did it, and the ensuing discussion leads to the point they were able to take their experiences of two-dimensional exploration of their living quarters and convert them into a top view they had never seen before. Thus, humans can readily create and read topological maps, and this ability shows clear evidence of cognitive spatial displacement.

Are animals capable of forming topological maps? Something like this seemed to be implied in Tolman's (1948) suggestion that a field map gets established in the rat's brain. A surprising experiment reported by Dallal and Meck (1990, Experiment 3) encouraged the possibility that rats could form a topological map of a radial maze. On a 12-arm radial maze, the same eight arms (chosen at random by the experimenter) contained food over repeated trials. That rats formed reference memory for the eight rewarded arms was shown by the acquisition of preference for entering these arms before the unbaited arms. The rats then were divided into two subgroups, called the reversal group and the nonreversal group. Both groups were taken to a new room, different in structure and extra-maze cues from the training room, where they had to find food on a new 12-arm radial maze. For the nonreversal group, the pattern of arm locations was exactly the same as that encountered in the first room. For the reversal group, a new random pattern of rewarded arms was used. The important finding reported was that the nonreversal group learned to preferentially enter the rewarded arms much faster than the reversal group. The implication of this finding is that rats had learned the overall pattern of rewards in the first room and then transferred that pattern to the new maze in the second room. Remember that extra-maze cues were of no value in the transfer between mazes, because these cues were completely different in the two rooms.

We were intrigued by this finding and wished to further study this ability in rats (Olthof, Sutton, Slumskie, D'Addetta, & Roberts, 1999). We chose to do an initial experiment in which the maze was rotated within the same room. Rats were trained to find food on six arms of a 12-arm radial maze. They were then divided into two groups: a rotated pattern group and a random control group. For the rotated group, the same pattern of rewarded arms was used but it had been rotated 180° from its original position relative to the training room. For the control group, a new set of six randomly chosen arms contained food.

Performance in stage 1 acquisition is shown for both groups in figure 8.6 (top left). The mean arms

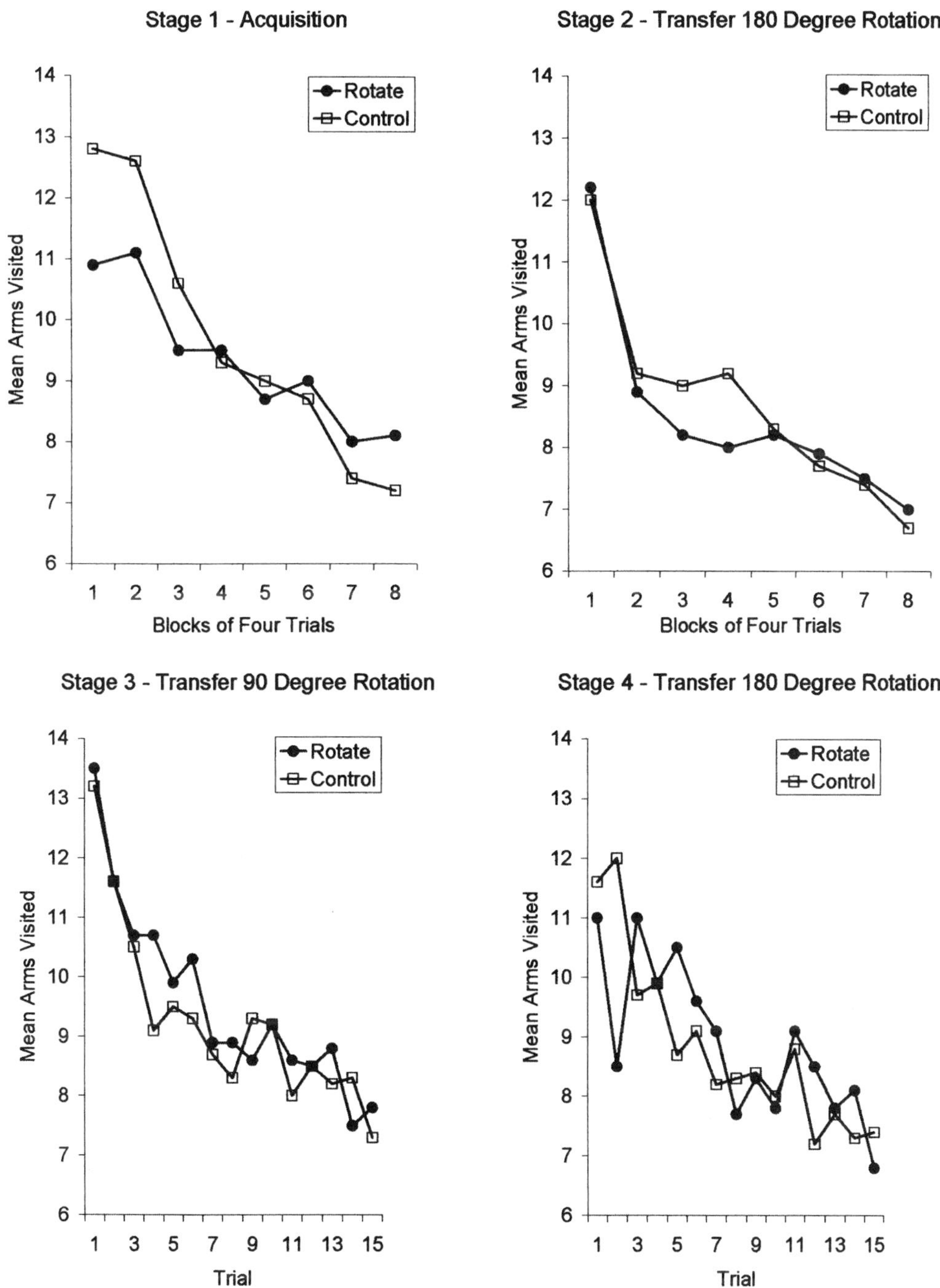

Figure 8.6. Learning curves for the rotate and control groups during initial pattern acquisition and three stages of pattern rotation. (From "In Search of the Cognitive May: Can Rats Learn an Abstract Pattern of Rewarded Arms on the Radial Maze?" by A. Olthof, J. E. Sutton, S. V. Slumskie, J. D'Addetta, and W. A. Roberts, 1999, *Journal of Experimental Psychology: Animal Behavior Processes, 25,* 355. Copyright 1999 by the American Psychological Association. Reprinted with permission.)

entered to collect all six rewards is plotted and can be seen to descend over blocks of four trials. Transfer tests are shown in the top right of the figure. No difference appeared between rotate and control groups. To pursue the possibility of positive transfer in the group in which the pattern was maintained, we carried out further tests with the pattern rotated 90° and then another 180°. For the control group, a new random pattern was used at each rotation. It can be seen that no difference appeared between rotation and control groups on any of these tests.

After some further failures to find evidence that rats could benefit from pattern rotation, we carried out a direct replication of the original Dallal and Meck (1990) experiment. Even when the pattern of rewarded arms was transferred to a new testing room, we found no evidence of positive transfer. Our rather extensive experiments then yielded no evidence that rats could learn a topological map of the overall locations of food on a two-dimensional spatial surface.

CONCLUSIONS

The purpose of this chapter was to raise questions about temporal and spatial cognitive displacement in animals. These questions arise within a comparative framework because humans clearly show cognitive displacement in both time and space. Thus, humans remember a rich autobiographical history based on personal episodic memories and can make elaborate plans for behaviors to be carried out in the future. People also can readily conceive of places other than their present location and what may exist or be happening in those places. The question raised here is whether animals share these abstract capacities for cognitive displacement or whether their cognitive worlds are very different. These alternative hypotheses are referred to as the stuck-in-time and stuck-in-space hypotheses. These hypotheses suggest that animals' response to their environment may be based pretty much on the here and now. Although animals can discriminate time of day, keep track of time intervals, and seem to travel purposefully through space, mechanisms other that symbolic representation of other times and other places may be responsible.

The issues raised by these alternative conceptions of cognitive displacement may be very important to the field of comparative cognition. Macphail (1987) has argued that all vertebrates learn in the same way; with the exception of language, humans and animals are not that different in their fundamental modes of learning and cognition. Quite to the contrary, the stuck-in-time and stuck-in-space hypotheses suggest that a fundamental gap may separate people and animals. As an extreme position, it may be argued that the human brain has provided people with the ability to develop rich conceptual cognitive frameworks for both time and space and that no animal brain approaches this level of abstraction. A less extreme alternative is that we may find important species differences in these capacities within animals, as well as between animals and humans. Already, some of the evidence reviewed here suggests the possibility that episodic memory and anticipation of future events might be found in scrub jays but not in rats. Could it be that ecological selective factors may be crucial for the appearance of temporal and spatial cognitive displacement (Clayton et al., 2003)? Food-storing and retrieving corvids and parids are well known for their ability to remember locations of cached food over long periods of time (Balda & Kamil, 1992; Hitchcock & Sherry, 1990). We might well expect that they would perform well on latent learning tests, shortcut tests, and tests of topological mapping carried out with the proper controls. If they did, then it would suggest the interesting possibility that temporal and spatial cognitive displacement are bound together or promoted by common symbolic capacities.

The work already done on these questions of cognitive displacement in time and space provides quite interesting challenges. Are rats and perhaps other rodents fundamentally different from scrub jays, and perhaps other corvids, or have the right experiments just not been performed yet? Are animals in general stuck in time and/or space, or may ecological pockets of cognitive displacement be found? If so, then what are the ecological factors that promote the evolution of these abilities? Little work thus far has been carried out on these questions with primates. Might we expect to find some degree of temporal and spatial displacement in monkeys and apes, our closest animal relatives?

Even after more than 100 years of research on comparative cognition, two widely different views of the relationship between human and animal minds exist: the Cartesian view of a wide gulf between humans and animals and the Darwinian view of continuity between humans and animals. Because time and space are fundamental physical dimensions that all organisms must process in some way, studies of how these dimensions are represented by humans and different species of animals may provide us with some genuine insights into comparative cognitive differences and similarities.

Acknowledgments Support for this preparation of this chapter was provided by a research grant to the author from the Natural Sciences and Engineering Research Council of Canada.

References

Balda, R. P., & Kamil, A. C. (1992). Long-term spatial memory in Clark's nutcracker, *Nucifraga columbiana. Animal Behaviour, 44*, 761–769.

Bennett, A. T. D. (1996). Do animals have cognitive maps? *Journal of Experimental Biology, 199*, 219–224.

Berthold, P. (1998). Spatiotemporal aspects of avian long-distance migration. In S. Healy (Ed.), *Spatial representation in animals* (pp. 103–118). Oxford: Oxford University Press.

Biebach, H., Gordijn, M., & Krebs, J. R. (1989). Time-and-place learning by garden warblers, *Sylvia borin. Animal Behaviour, 37*, 353–360.

Bindra, D. (1948). What makes a rat hoard? *Journal of Comparative and Physiological Psychology, 41*, 397–402.

Bingman, V. P. (1998). Spatial representation and homing pigeon navigation. In S. Healy (Ed.), *Spatial representation in animals* (pp. 69–85). Oxford: Oxford University Press.

Bird, L. R., Roberts, W. A., Abroms, B., Kit, K. A., & Crupi, C. (2003). Spatial memory for food hidden by rats (*Rattus norvegicus*) on the radial maze: Studies of memory for where, what, and when. *Journal of Comparative Psychology, 117*, 176–187.

Blodgett, H. C. (1929). The effect of the introduction of reward upon the maze performance of rats. *University of California Publications in Psychology, 4*, 113–134.

Chapuis, N., & Varlet, C. (1987). Shortcuts by dogs in natural surroundings. *Quarterly Journal of Experimental Psychology, 39B*, 49–64.

Chen, S., Swartz, K. B., & Terrace, H. S. (1997). Knowledge of the ordinal position of list items in rhesus monkeys. *Psychological Science, 8*, 80–86.

Church, R. M., Meck, W. H., & Gibbon, J. (1994). Application of scalar timing theory to individual trials. *Journal of Experimental Psychology: Animal Behavior Processes, 20*, 135–155.

Clayton, N. S., Bussey, T. J., & Dickinson, A. (2003). Can animals recall the past and plan for the future? *Nature Reviews Neuroscience, 4*, 685–691.

Clayton, N. S., & Dickinson, A. (1998). What, where, and when: Episodic-like memory during cache recovery by scrub jays. *Nature, 395*, 272–274.

Clayton, N. S., & Dickinson, A. (1999). Scrub jays (*Aphelocoma coerulescens*) remember the relative time of caching as well as the location and content of their caches. *Journal of Comparative Psychology, 113*, 403–416.

Clayton, N. S., Yu, K. S., & Dickinson, A. (2001). Scrub jays (*Aphelocoma coerulescens*) form integrated memories of the multiple features of caching episodes. *Journal of Experimental Psychology: Animal Behavior Processes, 27*, 17–29.

Cook, R. G., Brown, M. F., & Riley, D. A. (1985). Flexible memory processing by rats: Use of prospective and retrospective information in the radial maze. *Journal of Experimental Psychology: Animal Behavior Processes, 11*, 453–469.

Daan, S., & Koene, P. (1981). On the timing of foraging flights by oystercatchers, *Haematopus ostralegus*, on tidal mudflats. *Netherlands Journal of Sea Research, 15*, 1–22.

Dallal, N. L., & Meck, W. H. (1990). Hierarchical structures: Chunking by food type facilitates spatial memory. *Journal of Experimental Psychology: Animal Behavior Processes, 16*, 69–84.

D'Amato, M. R., & Colombo, M. (1988). Representation of serial order in monkeys (*Cebus apella*). *Journal of Experimental Psychology: Animal Behavior Processes, 14*, 131–139.

D'Amato, M. R., & Colombo, M. (1989). Serial learning with wild card items by monkeys (*Cebus apella*). *Journal of Comparative Psychology, 15*, 252–261.

Devenport, L., Hill, T., Wilson, M., & Ogden, E. (1997). Tracking and averaging in variable environments: A transition rule. *Journal of Experimental Psychology: Animal Behavior Processes, 23*, 450–460.

Devine, J. V., Burke, M. W., & Rohack, J. J. (1979). Stimulus similarity and order as factors in visual short-term memory in nonhuman primates. *Journal of Experimental Psychology: Animal Behavior Processes, 5*, 335–354.

Dyer, F. C. (1991). Bees acquire route-based memories but not cognitive maps in a familiar landscape. *Animal Behaviour, 41*, 239–246.

Emery, N. J., & Clayton, N. S. (2001). Effects of experience and social context on prospective caching strategies by scrub jays. *Nature, 414*, 443–446.

Etienne, A., Berlie, J., Georgakopoulos, J., & Maurer, R. (1998). Role of dead reckoning in navigation. In S. Healy (Ed.), *Spatial representation in animals* (pp. 54–68). Oxford: Oxford University Press.

Friedman, W. J. (1993). Memory for the time of past events. *Psychological Bulletin, 113*, 44–66.

Gibbon, J. (1977). Scalar expectancy theory and Weber's law in animal timing. *Psychological Review, 84*, 279–325.

Gibbon, J. (1991). Origins of scalar timing. *Learning and Motivation, 22*, 3–38.

Gould, J. L. (1986). The locale map of honey bees: Do insects have a cognitive map? *Science, 232*, 861–863.

Griffiths, D., Dickinson, A., & Clayton, N. (1999). Episodic memory: What can animals remember about their past? *Trends in Cognitive Sciences, 3*, 74–80.

Hitchcock, C. L., & Sherry, D. F. (1990). Long-term memory for cache sites in the black-capped chickadee. *Animal Behaviour, 40*, 701–712.

King, G. R., & Logue, A. W. (1987). Choice in a self-control paradigm with human subjects: Effects of changeover delay duration. *Learning and Motivation, 18*, 421–438.

Leonard, B., & McNaughton, B. L. (1990). Spatial representation in the rat: Conceptual, behavioral, and neurophysiological perspectives. In R. P. Kesner & D. S. Olton (Eds.), *Neurobiology of comparative cognition* (pp. 363–422). Hillsdale, NJ: Erlbaum.

Logue, A. W. (1988). Research on self-control: An integrating framework. *Behavioral and Brain Sciences, 11*, 665–709.

Logue, A. W., Pena-Correal, T. E., Rodriguez, M. L., & Kabela, E. (1986). Self-control in adult humans: Variation in positive reinforcer amount and delay. *Journal of the Experimental Analysis of Behavior, 46*, 159–173.

Lucas, G. A., Timberlake, W., Gawley, D. J., & Drew, J. (1990). Anticipation of future food: Suppression and facilitation of saccharin intake depending on the delay and type of future food. *Journal of Experimental Psychology: Animal Behavior Processes, 16*, 169–177.

MacDonald, S. E. (1993). Delayed matching-to-successive-samples in pigeons: Short-term memory for item and order information. *Animal Learning & Behavior, 21*, 59–67.

Macphail, E. M. (1987). The comparative psychology of intelligence. *Behavioral and Brain Sciences, 10*, 645–695.

Mazur, J. E., & Logue, A. W. (1978). Choice in a "self-control" paradigm: Effects of a fading procedure. *Journal of the Experimental Analysis of Behavior, 30*, 11–17.

McNaughton, B. L. (1988). Neuronal mechanisms for spatial computation and information storage. In L. Nadel, L. Cooper, P. Culicover, & R. M. Harnich (Eds.), *Neural connections and mental computations* (pp. 285–350). Cambridge, MA: MIT Press.

Morgan, C. T. (1947). The hoarding instinct. *Psychological Review, 54*, 335–341.

O'Keefe, J., & Nadel, L. (1978). *The hippocampus as a cognitive map*. Oxford: Clarendon Press.

Olthof, A., Sutton, J. E., Slumskie, S. V., D'Addetta, J., & Roberts, W. A. (1999). In search of the cognitive map: Can rats learn an abstract pattern of rewarded arms on the radial maze? *Journal of Experimental Psychology: Animal Behavior Processes, 25*, 352–362.

Olton, D. S., & Samuelson, R. J. (1976). Remembrance of places passed: Spatial memory in rats. *Journal of Experimental Psychology: Animal Behavior Processes, 2*, 97–116.

Parker, B. K. (1984). Reproduction memory of two-event sequences in pigeons. *Journal of the Experimental Analysis of Behavior, 41*, 135–141.

Pavlov, I. P. (1927). *Conditioned reflexes*. Oxford: Oxford University Press.

Pearce, J. M. (1997). *Animal learning and cognition: An introduction*. East Sussex, UK: Psychology Press.

Peterson, G. B., Wheeler, R. L., & Armstrong, G. D. (1978). Expectancies as mediators in the differential-reward conditional discrimination performance of pigeons. *Animal Learning & Behavior, 6*, 279–285.

Poucet, B. (1993). Spatial cognitive maps in animals: New hypotheses on their structure and neural mechanisms. *Psychological Review, 100*, 163–182.

Rachlin, H., & Green, L. (1972). Commitment, choice, and self-control. *Journal of the Experimental Analysis of Behavior, 17*, 15–22.

Roberts, S. (1981). Isolation of an internal clock. *Journal of Experimental Psychology: Animal Behavior Processes, 7*, 242–268.

Roberts, W. A. (2001). Spatial representation and the use of spatial codes in animals. In M. Gattis (Ed.), *Spatial schemas and abstract thought* (pp. 15–44). Cambridge, MA: MIT Press.

Roberts, W. A. (2002). Are animals stuck in time? *Psychological Bulletin, 128*, 473–489.

Roberts, W. A., & Roberts, S. (2002). Two tests of the stuck-in-time hypothesis. *The Journal of General Psychology, 129*, 415–429.

Saksida, L. M., & Wilkie, D. M. (1994). Time-of-day discrimination by pigeons. *Animal Learning & Behavior, 22*, 143–154.

Seward, J. P. (1949). An experimental analysis of latent learning. *Journal of Experimental Psychology, 39*, 177–186.

Shettleworth, S. J. (1998). *Cognition, evolution, and behavior*. Oxford: Oxford University Press.

Suddendorf, T., & Corballis, M. C. (1997). Mental time travel and the evolution of the human mind. *Genetic, Social, and General Psychology Monographs, 123*, 133–167.

Terrace, H. S. (1983). Simultaneous chaining: The problem it poses for traditional chaining theory. In M. L. Commons, R. J. Herrnstein, & A. R. Wagner (Eds.), *Quantitative analyses of behavior: Discriminative processes* (pp. 115–137). Hillsdale, NJ: Erlbaum.

Terrace, H. S. (1987). Chunking by a pigeon in a serial learning task. *Nature, 325*, 149–151.

Terrace, H. S. (1991). Chunking during serial learning by a pigeon. I. Basic evidence. *Journal of Experimental Psychology: Animal Behavior Processes, 17*, 81–93.

Timberlake, W. (1984). A temporal limit on the effect of future food on current performance in an analogue of foraging and welfare. *Journal of the Experimental Analysis of Behavior, 41*, 117–124.

Timberlake, W., Gawley, D. J., & Lucas, G. A. (1987). Time horizons in rats foraging for food in temporally separated patches. *Journal of Experimental Psychology: Animal Behavior Processes, 13*, 302–309.

Timberlake, W., Gawley, D. J., & Lucas, G. A. (1988). Time horizons in rats: The effect of operant control of access to future food. *Journal of the Experimental Analysis of Behavior, 50*, 405–417.

Tobin, H., Chelonis, J. J., & Logue, A. W. (1993). Choice in self-control paradigms using rats. *The Psychological Record, 43*, 441–454.

Tolman, E. C. (1948). Cognitive maps in rats and men. *Psychological Review, 55*, 189–208.

Tolman, E. C., & Honzik, C. H. (1930). Introduction and removal of reward and maze performance in rats. *University of California Publications in Psychology, 4*, 257–275.

Tolman, E. C., Ritchie, B. F., & Kalish, D. (1946). Studies in spatial learning. I. Orientation and the short-cut. *Journal of Experimental Psychology, 36*, 13–24.

Tulving, E. (1972). Episodic and semantic memory. In E. Tulving & W. Donaldson (Eds.), *Organization of memory* (pp. 381–403). San Diego, CA: Academic Press.

Tulving, E. (1983). *Elements of episodic memory*. Oxford: Clarendon Press.

Tulving, E. (1984). Precis of elements of episodic memory. *The Behavioral and Brain Sciences, 7*, 223–238.

Vander Wall, S. B. (1990). *Food hoarding in animals*. Chicago: The University of Chicago Press.

Wallace, R. J. (1979). Novelty and partibility as determinants of hoarding in the albino rat. *Animal Learning & Behavior, 7*, 549–554.

Weisman, R. G., Wasserman, E. A., Dodd, P. W. D., & Larew, M. B. (1980). Representation and retention of two-event sequences in pigeons. *Journal of Experimental Psychology: Animal Behavior Processes, 6*, 312–325.

Wilkie, D. M., Carr, J. A. R., Siegenthaler, A., Lenger, B., Liu, M., & Kwok, M. (1996). Field observations of time-place behaviour in scavenging birds. *Behavioural Processes, 38*, 77–88.

Zentall, T. R., Steirn, J. N., & Jackson-Smith, P. (1990). Memory strategies in pigeons' performance of a radial-arm-maze analog task. *Journal of Experimental Psychology: Animal Behavior Processes, 16*, 358–371.

9

Memory Processing

ANTHONY A. WRIGHT

The focus of this chapter is how animals remember—the processes of animal memory. The memory processes discussed include active processes (e.g., recollection, episodic memory, rehearsal, and familiarity criteria) as well as passive processes (e.g., decay, consolidation, interference, and familiarity). In the first section, Single-Item Memory in Delayed Matching-to-Sample, the issue is raised as to what delay functions tell us about animal memory. In the second section, Memory Processing in Same/Different and List-Memory Tasks, the memory processes of familiarity, recollection, episodic, and identity are discussed in terms of how subjects deal with proactive interference (PI) from previous trials. In the third section, Serial Position Functions and Interference Among List Items, the changing shapes of visual and auditory serial position functions (SPFs) with retention delay are discussed in terms of PI and retroactive interference (RI) among list items. Interference among list items was tested in monkey auditory list memory. Active and passive aspects of interference are discussed.

SINGLE-ITEM MEMORY IN DELAYED MATCHING-TO-SAMPLE

Investigations of animal memory have traditionally studied how long single items can be accurately remembered (e.g., Miles, 1971; Roberts & Grant, 1976). Among the most popular animal memory procedures has been delayed matching-to-sample (DMTS). In DMTS, a sample is presented. Typically, the subject is required to respond to the sample and after doing so the sample is removed. Then, there is a delay interval—the memory interval—followed by the simultaneous presentation of the choices or comparison stimuli. If the subject chooses the comparison that matches the sample, then it receives a reward; otherwise, it receives no reward. Typically, there are two comparison stimuli located to the left and right of the sample. The right versus left position of the correct choice varies randomly from trial to trial, so that the subject cannot orient toward the position where the correct choice will appear and thereby bridge the memory interval as in spatial delayed response tasks (Miles, 1971).

DMTS memory performance is shown in figure 9.1 for (New World) capuchin monkeys (Etkin & D'Amato, 1969), (Old World) macaque monkeys (Moise, 1976; Overman & Doty, 1980), and pigeons (Roberts & Grant, 1976). These experiments were similar in that they used two stimuli. The sample on each trial was one of the two stimuli. After the (memory) delay, the two stimuli simultaneously appeared as the comparisons and one or the other was chosen. At a 0-s delay, when the comparison choices appeared at the same time as the sample was removed, performance was accurate at more than 80% correct. Performance

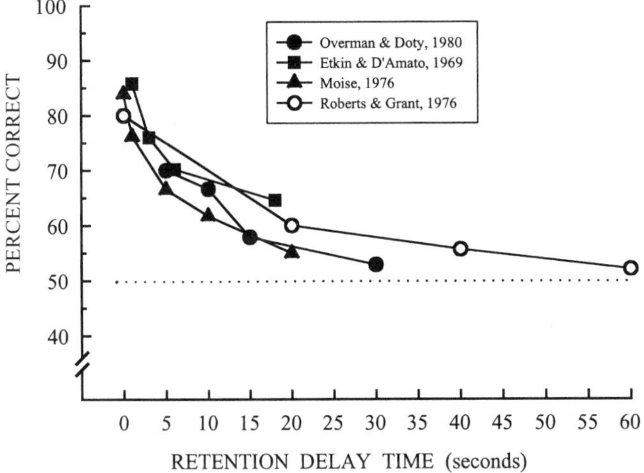

Figure 9.1. Delay functions from three delayed matching-to-sample experiments with monkeys (filled points) and one delayed matching-to-sample experiment with pigeons (unfilled points). The dotted line is located at chance performance.

declined as delay increased. With delays of about 1 min, performance was close to chance (50% correct).

One issue is what these pigeon and monkey DMTS functions say about memory. The answer ultimately depends on one's theoretical persuasion of how memory works in this setting (e.g., encoding, processing, retrieval, etc.) and how the subjects are assumed to perform the DMTS task. As to how subjects perform the DMTS task, one possibility is that the subject considers each comparison stimulus and compares it to its memory trace of the sample stimulus. As to how memory works, one possibility is that the memory trace of the sample fades with time, possibly an exponential decay (cf., Brown, 1958; Peterson & Peterson, 1959; Tulving & Bower, 1974). Decay is, by definition, a passive process (Crowder, 1976). Like most passive processes, decay would likely be a fixed or automatic product of the neural substrate responsible for that species' memory abilities. Accordingly, are we to conclude from these DMTS memory results that decay is complete after a minute or so and that this interval of time is the limit of pigeon and monkey visual memory? If so, then how could pigeons and monkeys survive in the natural environment when they need to remember seasonally changing food sources and hiding places of potential predators? It would seem vital for survival that even brief information about food and danger would need to be remembered for days, weeks, and even months, let alone a minute. Alternatively, if one contends that the retention functions of figure 9.1 do not have anything to do with realistic limits of memory—due to decay or otherwise—then what, if anything, do they say about memory? A consideration of the answer to this and the related questions, I believe, relates to a number of critical issues in animal (and human) memory processing.

As to whether these delay functions reflect anything about the limits of memory, an often overlooked DMTS experiment showed that by using trial-unique stimuli, one can obtain reasonably good memory performance with monkeys even after 24-hr delays (Overman & Doty, 1980). In this study, six macaque monkeys (*Macaca nemestrina*) were trained with 100 slides (35-mm pictures) that were used to make up 50 unique trials each day (trial unique) and were scrambled between days. The results for three different tests are shown in figure 9.2. The lowest function (circles) shows near-chance performance after 30 s for the two-stimuli condition. This is the same (but rescaled) function shown in figure 9.1 and provides a comparison for the other test conditions in this figure. The delay function (hexagons) for the 100-stimuli condition shows a dramatic elevation in performance relative to the two-stimuli condition. Even after a 24-hr delay, performance is better than it was after a 30-s in the two-stimuli condition!

Notwithstanding the dramatic rise in the 100-stimuli delay function, novel-stimulus performance (diamonds) is even better. After a 3-min delay, novel-stimulus performance is still above 80% correct. Even after a 24-hr delay, novel-stimulus performance is above 70% correct. The novel-stimulus

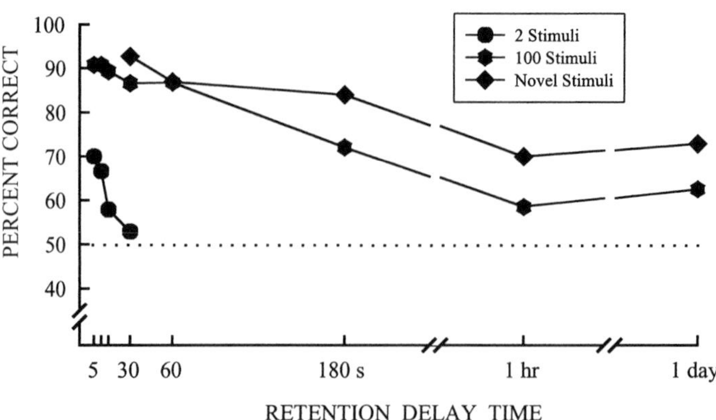

Figure 9.2. Three delay functions from the Overman and Doty (1980) experiment. Results for the two-stimuli condition are the same as those shown in figure 9.1. In the 100-stimuli condition, repetitions of the stimuli were separated by many trials. The novel stimuli had not been seen previously by the monkeys. The dotted line is at chance performance.

test was, of course, a transfer test for concept learning at each delay and shows full concept learning. That novel-stimulus performance was even somewhat more accurate than training-stimulus (i.e., 100-stimulus condition) performance makes sense in light of why the 100-stimulus function might be elevated to such a degree relative to the two-stimuli function.

The flip side of why the 100-stimulus function and novel-stimulus function of figure 9.2 are so elevated is, of course, why the two-stimuli function is so depressed. Consider what the subject faces when it makes a choice in the two-stimuli condition. It is always presented with the same two choices, such as, red and green, on every trial. The subject must decide which one matches the sample seen on that particular trial. The sample (e.g., red), may have been seen several seconds or a half a minute previously, depending on the delay, but also the nonmatching comparison, green in the example, may have been seen quite recently, maybe as the sample on the immediately preceding trial. This past history creates a great deal of confusion. After several trials, both stimuli will have been seen so many times that it is difficult to decide which one is correct (i.e., which is the sample on the current trial). To resolve this confusion, the task becomes: "What was the last one I saw?" or "What was the sample on this particular trial?" This confusion results because of PI from previous trials. *Proactive interference* means that previously seen items interfere with the subject's memory at some later time. It is not so much that the subject does not remember the sample of the current trial; the subject may well remember the current sample, but it may also remember the sample of the previous trial, and the sample on the trial before that, and so on. If the subject remembers all of the samples from all trials very well, then it may have more problems remembering the sample on the current trial than if it remembered previous trial samples less well.

Having said this, we can return to the previous question of what the delay functions of figure 9.1 tell us about memory. What they tell us may have more to do with the adverse effects of PI on memory than anything about the limits of how long something can be remembered. Of course, to make such a distinction one needs to test memory without PI (e.g., novel-stimulus condition in figure 9.2) to assess how PI (e.g., two-stimuli DMTS of figure 9.1) affects memory. Indeed, the results shown in figure 9.1 were selected because two stimuli are the minimum number for an MTS experiment. This turns out to be the condition that produces the maximal amount of PI because the stimuli are most frequently repeated. The functions shown in figure 9.2 represent basically the two ends of the PI spectrum. Thus, the results shown in figure 9.1 say something about memory (i.e., the effects of PI on memory) only when there is a proper baseline to measure such effects (i.e., a test that minimizes PI as in figure 9.2). This issue of PI from previous trials adversely affecting memory performance in the DMTS task is present in virtually all studies of working memory including the Wisconsin General Test Apparatus (WGTA), radial arm maze, seed caching and recovery arenas, and Skinner boxes with same/different and list-memory procedures. The effects of PI can be mitigated to some degree by separating trials (e.g., Grant, 2000; Grant & Roberts, 1973; Hogan, Edwards, & Zentall, 1981; Maki, Moe, & Bierley, 1977; Roberts, 1980), sometimes even by days (e.g.,

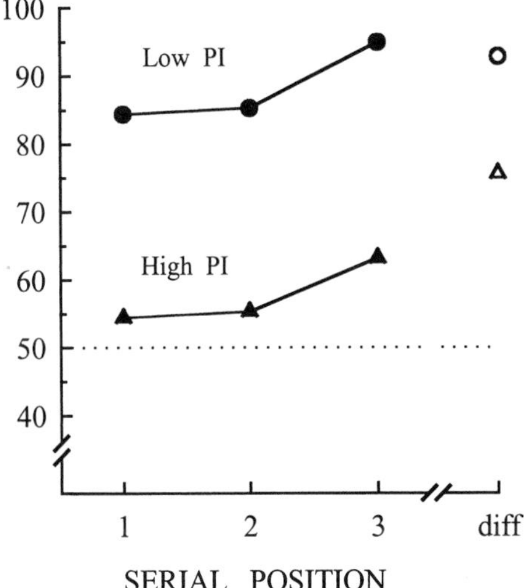

Figure 9.3. A rhesus monkey's three-item list memory results with memory items selected from a 211-item set (Low PI) or a 6-item set (High PI). Serial position 1 was the first list item. The unfilled points (diff) show performance on trials (different) where the test did not match any list item. The dotted line is at chance performance.

Balda & Kamil, 1992), and by increasing sample contact and/or presentation time (e.g., Grant, 1975; Roberts & Grant, 1976). It is unclear at this point what effect concept learning or a lack of concept learning might have on the delay function (or on PI). If the MTS task had been learned by item-specific rules (e.g., learning the configuration of each display pattern with three stimuli, Wright, 1997), then the delay function (and effects of PI) might be expected to be different than if the task had been learned relationally and the abstract concept had been learned. In the Overman and Doty (1980) study, the two-stimuli condition was tested after the 100-stimuli and novel-stimulus conditions; so, it would be reasonable to assume that there was concept learning in all conditions.

MEMORY PROCESSING IN SAME/DIFFERENT AND LIST-MEMORY TASKS

The DMTS procedure is really an awkward task for memory research because there are always two choice stimuli: one correct and one incorrect. Memory accuracy will be affected by how similar and confusable the incorrect stimulus is with the correct stimulus (e.g., two different red flowers). Memory accuracy should also be affected by the presence of the correct stimulus because the subject can compare it to the incorrect stimulus on every trial. For example, PI would make the incorrect stimulus a more likely choice, but the presence of the correct stimulus would allow the subject to choose the one with the stronger memory trace. The PI manipulation might be more effective if the subject had to evaluate the incorrect stimulus by itself. Such is the case in *same/different* (S/D) tasks. In S/D tasks, the correct and incorrect stimuli are not present at the same time; they occur on separate trials. The subject makes each decision in isolation, so to speak. The subject decides whether the test was identical to the sample. If so, the subject makes an (arbitrarily designated) "same" response, or if not, it makes an (arbitrarily designated, but different) "different" response. By eliminating both of these extraneous factors, one should be able to more precisely control and investigate factors contributing to memory processing. Related to the S/D task is the serial probe recognition (SPR) task. Instead of a single memory item presented prior to the test as in delayed S/D tasks, a list of items is presented in SPR tasks prior to the test. If the test is identical to any one of the list items, then the "same" response is correct; otherwise the "different" response is correct. The delayed S/D task is an SPR task but with only one list item.

The powerful effect of PI on SPR performance is shown in figure 9.3. In this SPR task, lists of three items were tested (Sands & Wright, 1980). Three-item lists were used to explore why monkeys in our list-memory task were much more accurate than were monkeys in other list-memory tasks (e.g., Devine & Jones, 1975; Eddy, 1973; Gaffan, 1977). We used the same list length and a similar SPR procedure as had Gaffan (1977), where he obtained 70% correct performance from his monkeys with three-item lists. In our experiment, lists were composed from a set size (pool) of six items, similar to the Gaffan (1977) experiment. This six-item set size was the high-interference condition in our experiment, and we had hypothesized that PI from reusing items may have been responsible for the poorer memory performance in other SPR tasks with monkeys. But, of course, to make this evaluation we had to have a no-interference condition or a low-interference condition for comparison. In our

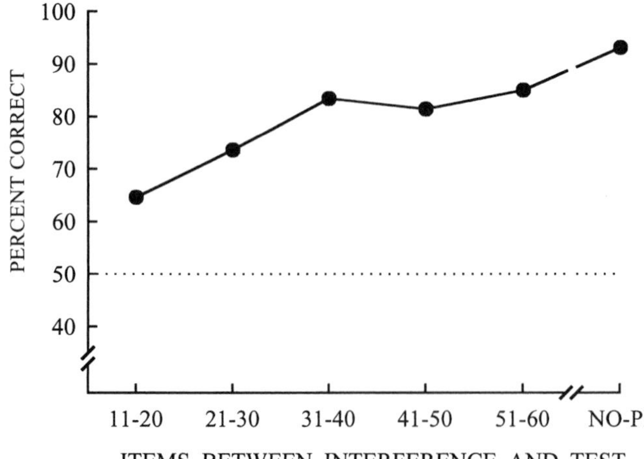

Figure 9.4. A rhesus monkey's 10-item list memory performance as a function of the number of items occurring between a test item on a different trial and its previous presentation. The NO-PI condition is a trial-unique condition. The dotted line is at chance performance.

low-interference condition, lists were composed from a 211-item set of "travel" slides. Items were trial-unique in each daily session. Tests of the two conditions alternated daily. The monkey pushed down on a lever (three-position T pattern) to start trials. List items were presented for 1 s on an upper back-projection screen with a 1-s interstimulus interval (ISI) and a 1-s retention interval. If the probe or test item on a lower screen matched any one of the list items shown in the upper screen, then a "same" response (lever movement to the right) was correct. If the probe matched no list item, then a "different" response (lever movement to the left) was correct. Memory performance was 70% in the high-interference (six-item set) condition (triangles in figure 9.3), identical to that of the Gaffan (1977) experiment and similar to two other experiments also using small set sizes (Devine & Jones, 1975, 65% correct; Eddy, 1973, 72% correct). Recognition performance was 91% in the low-interference condition (circles in figure 9.3). Thus, interference from item repetitions in the high-interference condition lowered performance by a remarkable 26%.

The small set of six items in the high-interference condition of figure 9.3 produced a great deal of PI. The items were reused so frequently and the level of PI was so high (as in the two-stimuli DMTS of figure 9.1) that it would not be possible to determine how far back in time (i.e., number of trials) PI might extend. Although there is abundant evidence from animals and humans that items from an immediately previous trial produce PI (e.g., Bennett, 1975; Grant, 1975; Hogan et al., 1981; Moise, 1976; Roberts, 1980; Roitblat & Scopatz, 1983; Thompson & Herman, 1981; Wickens, Born & Allen, 1963), any determination of the extent of PI needs to be conducted against a low-PI background; otherwise PI saturation will overwhelm a much smaller PI effect that might occur farther back in time. PI builds cumulatively during the session when stimuli are frequently repeated (e.g., Keppel & Underwood, 1962; Olton, 1978; Roberts & Grant, 1976) and rapidly saturates, so that any PI from more than a couple of previous trials will be masked by a PI ceiling effect. Moreover, when PI saturation occurs (i.e., small set sizes), the locus of the PI effect may be difficult to determine.

We conducted a study to systematically explore PI by placing interfering items at different points prior to the target item in a low-PI, 10-item SPR session (Wright, Urcuioli, & Sands, 1986). Forty-eight test sessions (140 trials per session) were conducted. There were 90 trials where the stimuli were trial-unique and thus were free of any PI from items in previous trials. There were 50 PI test trials. On these interference test trials, the interfering item was placed within a previous 10-item list (serial position random) and this item appeared later as the test item on a *different* trial. The critical results are shown in figure 9.4. When the interfering item was in the immediately preceding list, performance was 64%. As separation increased, performance improved. When the separation was five lists, or as many as 60 items, performance was 83%, but it was still 10% less than the 93% correct baseline (trial-unique) performance.

These results point to the locus of the PI effect being the test item on *different* trials where the test does not match any list item. The way PI works is that by seeing the test item earlier, perhaps just in the immediately previous trial, the subject is confused as to whether the test item was in the list being tested or in some previous list. When the PI item is farther separated from the target item (e.g., five lists in the previous experiment), then PI is less, and it is easier to discriminate that the PI item was not in the list being tested. As the interfering item gets closer in time to the test item, then it becomes more difficult to tell whether the test item was in the list being tested or in some previous list. Also, it should be more difficult to tell whether the test item was in the list being tested as the retention delay increases. Possibly a ratio of time intervals, such as the time between presentation of the PI item and test divided by the retention time, will better summarize these PI effects as do time ratios in similar situations (cf., Glenberg, Bradley, Kraus, & Renzaglia, 1983; Winograd, 1971).

Familiarity, Identity, and Episodic Memory

Related to the far-reaching effects of PI is the issue of whether the monkey in figure 9.4 was really relating the probe item to its memory of the matching list item and making an identity judgment or simply making a familiarity judgment. On one hand, what is meant by the terms of *identity* and *familiarity* seems obvious. Considering familiarity, it is clear that with trial-unique stimuli any vague sense of familiarity (e.g., "Have I seen it before?") would work to perform the task accurately. The issue of familiarity versus identity was made popular in animal cognition by David Premack 25 years ago (e.g., Premack, 1978, 1983; Premack & Premack, 1983). In his criticism of delayed S/D behavior (as opposed to simultaneous S/D behavior) as a measure of abstract concept learning, Premack (1983) said, "The animal simply reacts to whether or not it has experienced the item before. Old/new or familiar/unfamiliar would be better tags for this case than same/different" (p. 354).

These same issues of familiarity versus identity apply to all memory and concept-learning tasks (including the S/D, DMTS, and SPR tasks) and all species (including humans). One cannot avoid the issue of familiarity by using delayed nonmatching to sample (DNMS) instead of DMTS (e.g., Gaffan & Weiskrantz, 1980; Mishkin & Delacour, 1975). In DNMS, the subject could use familiarity to identify the matching stimulus (the incorrect choice) and then switch and choose the other (unfamiliar) stimulus. Likewise, using simultaneous instead of delayed S/D does not rule out the use of familiarity and by default "rule in" identity as Premack (1983) would have us believe. In simultaneous S/D, subjects could first look at one stimulus (as they often do) and then look at the other stimulus, thus transforming the simultaneous S/D task into a delayed S/D task.

Use of the terms *familiarity* and *identity* is fashionable in discussions of animal cognition, but their meanings are more apparent than real. These terms, by their very nature, refer to what the subjects are doing in these tasks (e.g., memory processes), but authors and critics using these terms seldom specify what they think (hypothesize) subjects are doing when they make familiarity judgments and how this familiarity process differs from the identity process. This lack of specifying how subjects make familiarity as opposed to identity judgments may be responsible for why these processes have remained untested and just hypotheses—for over 25 years. A recent example would be Mackintosh's (2000) critique of abstract concept learning. While Mackintosh liberally uses terms referring to processes such as *identity, familiarity, relational,* etc., specification of what the subjects are doing when engaged in these processes is largely avoided. This lack of specifying these processes and noting critical differences in such processes makes it impossible to determine what tests and results would show identity concept learning (according to Mackintosh, 2000). Said otherwise, any test or result could be rejected as not measuring up.

Mackintosh (2000), Premack (1978), and others have pointed out that the characteristic distinguishing identity judgments from some other processes is relational processing. Identity judgments are rules based on stimulus relationships. This characteristic of relational processing would distinguish identity from processes that are predominantly item specific such as simple (go/no-go) stimulus discriminations and so-called natural concept learning (i.e., classification and categorization of such things as "tree," "fish," "person," "water," etc.). Nevertheless, beyond this requirement of relational processing, the distinguishing characteristics of identity processing become a little vague. For example, consider familiarity processing—which is where this discussion began. Is familiarity processing item specific or relational? The subject judges some stimulus to be familiar, meaning that this stimulus has been seen before. But is this not a relational judgment, in the strict sense of what is meant by relational processing? So, how is familiarity processing different from identity processing?

Several theories in human cognition have laid claim to distinguishing between familiarity and other forms of memory processing related to identity judgments. Familiarity has been a topic in human memory for at least as long as it has been in animal memory (e.g., Atkinson & Joula, 1974; Mandler, 1980). One difference is that tests have been developed for human familiarity processing. Human subjects have been tested for familiarity, as opposed to "recollection," "controlled memory," or "episodic memory" in so-called dissociation procedures by either instructing participants how to perform the task or by questioning them as to how they actually performed the task. An example of the first type of dissociation procedure (i.e., instructing participants) would be a study by Jacoby (1991). Participants in one group (inclusion group) were instructed to "call an item 'old' if you read it, saw it as an anagram, or heard it." Participants in another group (exclusion group) were instructed to "call an item 'old' only if you heard it" (i.e., exclude it from the "old" category if it was read or seen as an anagram). Jacoby characterized the results by a pair of simultaneous equations, whose solution yielded estimates of familiarity (considered an automatic process) and recollection (a controlled or intentional process). An example of the second type of dissociation procedure (i.e., questioning participants) is the popular remember-know procedure. Participants are asked whether they actually did *remember* (episodic memory) an item or just *know* (semantic memory) that it was presented (e.g., Gardiner & Richardson-Klavehn, 2000; Tulving, 1985). From these two dissociation procedures, terms that correspond roughly to familiarity versus identity as used in this chapter are familiarity versus recollection (e.g., Yonelinas, 2002), automatic versus controlled (e.g., Jacoby, 1991, 1998), and semantic versus episodic (e.g., Tulving, 1972, 2002), respectively. It would probably be fair to say that there is fairly close agreement on the first of these terms—the familiarity term. The second term is more problematic.

There is somewhat less than total agreement among the terms *recollection, controlled memory,* and *episodic memory* and how they might relate to animal memory. Although identity processing in animals should have characteristics in common with recollection and controlled memory, episodic memory is clearly the most problematic when animal memory is concerned. Indeed, some leading memory theorists are skeptical that animals posses episodic memory (e.g., Tulving, 2002). And well they should be. Episodic memory depends, among other things, on conscious (autonoetic) awareness of the past event, like a reliving in memory of the event as it took place (e.g., Baddeley, 2002; Tulving, 1983, 2002). Humans are asked to introspect (their phenomenological experience) and report whether they actually "remembered" the experience of that item being presented or just have a feeling that they "know" it was presented. "Knowing" is just another term for *familiarity*. "Remembering" is the recall of the event itself of being presented with the item (what), on which trial it was presented (when), and in which location (on the computer screen) it was presented (where).

These requirements of "what," "when," and "where" have been demonstrated in a series of clever experiments with scrub jays (e.g., Clayton & Dickinson, 1998, 1999a, 1999b). In one experiment, Clayton and Dickinson (1998) required scrub jays to cache (perishable) wax worms and (nonperishable) peanuts in separate and distinctive halves of two distinctive sand-filled ice-cube trays (2×7 arrays). After a delay of only 4 hr, the jays first recovered the more desirable wax worms. Because the jays had previously learned that wax worms would deteriorate in 124 hr, they first recovered the peanuts after a delay of 124 hr. Reversal of their earlier preference for wax worms means that they remembered "what" (peanuts vs. wax worms), "when" (4 vs. 124 hr), and "where" (which tray side) the foods were stored.

Food caching (and recovery) is perhaps one of the best-suited procedures to demonstrate what, when, and where memories by animals because the subjects generate (by caching) their own memory items. Generating one's own items has been shown to improve memory in humans (see Neath & Surprenant, 2003, for a summary of the generation effect). Clark's nutcrackers, for example, recover more than 30,000 pine seeds buried in some 3,000 cache sites in the forest each year (e.g., Vander Wall, 1982). They remember site locations after snow covers the forest and even burrow at an angle through the snow to arrive at the cache location. The birds use new cache sites ("where") each year and overcome potential confusions (PI) from sites used in previous years, thus demonstrating "when."

So, are these birds using episodic memory to recover their caches? Tulving (2002) is certainly skeptical that they are doing so. The autonoetic requirement makes objective tests of human episodic memory problematic at best, and virtually impossible with nonhuman animals.

Related to issues of episodic, recollection, controlled, or identity processing in animals is whether animals are consciously aware of their memory as are humans (e.g., Jacoby, Toth, & Yonelinas, 1993). The alternative is that they are unaware and are somehow responding on the basis of associative conditioning to combinations of variables that mimic the what, when, and where of episodic memory. As Tulving (2002) said, "They [scrub jays] may just 'know' what kind of food is where, and what state it is in—fresh or rotten—without knowing how or why they know it" (p. 282). This issue is often central in the discussion of how animals perform memory experiments. Strangely, it seldom comes up in the discussion of human memory experiments, but are not humans subject to the same associative learning contingencies as are animals?

There is, however, a recent experiment that I think shows that monkeys have the ability to be consciously aware of their memory (Hampton, 2001). This was a DMTS investigation where rhesus monkeys saw clip-art samples. On each trial, the monkeys touched the sample, had a retention delay, and then decided whether to take a memory test. If they chose to take the memory test, then four choices were presented on the four corners of the monitor and monkeys received a highly desired reward (peanuts) if they made the correct choice. On the other hand, if they declined to take the test, then the monkeys (automatically) received a less-preferred pellet. Occasionally, the monkeys were required to take the test even though they had declined to take it. The monkeys were more accurate when they chose to take the test than when they were required to take the test, and this difference increased with delay. An important aspect of this study was that the monkeys were required to monitor their memory *before* the test was presented, which excludes the possibility of such things as responding on the basis of associative conditioning to a sense of familiarity elicited by recognizing the test stimulus. This study suggests that animals can be aware of their own memory, certainly a necessary condition for what is called episodic, controlled, recollection, and identity processing, and would also bear on conscious control of memory processes such as familiarity.

Testing Familiarity and the Proactive Interference Function

Despite the clever experiments of Clayton and Dickinson, there is very little other evidence as to what animals are doing in most tasks. One could point to pigeons learning a continuous-matching task (e.g., respond if it is old, not if it is new), which has aspects akin to familiarity (Macphail & Reilly, 1989). But this demonstration does not "prove" that familiarity was the basis of this performance or what subjects might be doing in S/D and SPR memory tasks. What are needed are experiments that manipulate the effectiveness of familiarity in performing a particular task and an objective assessment of how subjects use familiarity.

To these ends, I propose that PI could be used to assess the degree to which subjects' memory judgments rely on familiarity. Consider (once more) whether the PI function shown in figure 9.4 implies that this monkey was using familiarity. PI-like familiarity extends back in time, well beyond the current trial. If this monkey were using familiarity to make *same* judgments, then on PI tests it should make errors (e.g., figure 9.4). Thus, judgments based on familiarity should be vulnerable to PI. An important difference between familiarity and PI processes, however, is that, unlike familiarity, PI can be measured in terms of its decrement in relation to interference-free performance. If the monkey of figure 9.4 had been completely indiscriminate with regard to how far back in time he would accept a stimulus as a match (i.e., any degree of familiarity would suffice), then the PI function should have been relatively flat (at 64% correct), extending back across most of the session. Clearly, this was not the case. Thus, if this monkey were using familiarity, then it was graded or relative familiarity—a continuum of familiarity.

Manipulation of the PI function, according to the proposal here, depends on a continuum of familiarity coupled with a familiarity criterion. That is, familiarity has to be at a certain level for accepting a stimulus as a match. It is the familiarity criterion that is manipulated, not familiarity itself (although familiarity could be manipulated by varying the similarity of the lures on *different* trials to "simulate" PI). In considering how PI might be modified, assume that a subject trained extensively with trial-unique stimuli was using a lax familiarity criterion, like the criterion line labeled c (lax) in figure 9.5 (left). Because the subject is trained with trial-unique

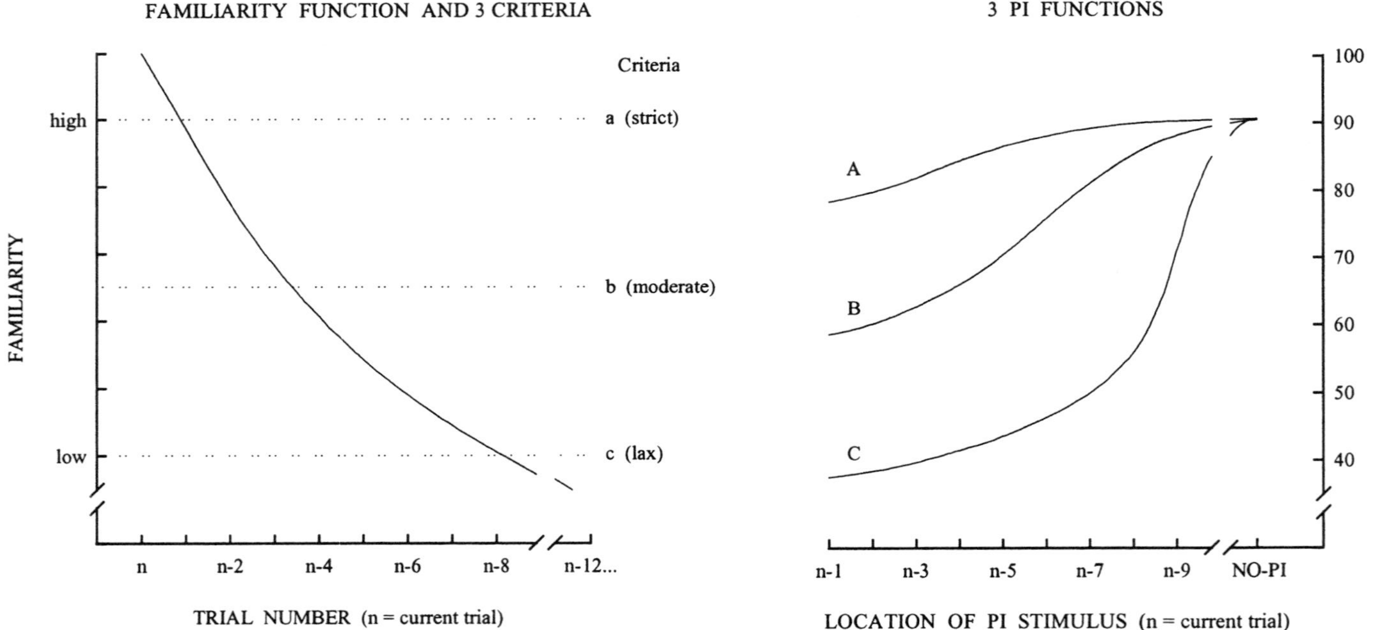

Figure 9.5. *Left*, Hypothetical familiarity (solid line) of an item as a function of how many trials previous, in relation to the current trial (n), the item had been presented. Three hypothetical familiarity criteria (a, b, c) showing high (strict) to low (lax) degrees of familiarity for accepting the test as a match. *Right*, Three hypothetical proactive interference (PI) functions (A, B, C) that might result from the three corresponding familiarity criteria (a, b, c) as a function of how many trials prior to the current trial (n) the interfering (PI) stimulus was presented. The NO-PI condition refers to no interfering stimulus.

stimuli (i.e., no PI), almost any degree of familiarity would serve as the basis for a match as shown by steep PI function—labeled C in figure 9.5 (right). Now consider if the subject had been trained with some stimulus repetitions (e.g., 32-item set) and a moderate amount of PI. Subjects would have to learn to exclude stimuli of low familiarity as matches in order to perform accurately. Learning to exclude stimuli of low familiarity should raise overall performance. The PI function (tested as it was previously) would be expected to rise and might become like that shown for function B in figure 9.5. In signal-detection theory parlance, one can think of a distribution of familiarity effects for the stimuli on the current trial (signal distribution) and a series of "noise" distributions to the left for n – 1, n – 2, etc. As PI is increased, the relative frequency (probability density) of the "noise" distributions will rise and the (likelihood ratio) criterion (i.e., familiarity criterion) will shift to the right as the intersection of the "noise" and "signal" distributions shifts to the right. This rightward shift in the criterion is the adoption of a stricter familiarity criterion. In the limit, after very high PI training (e.g., eight-item set), the familiarity criterion might change to a (strict) and thereby minimize PI like that shown for the A PI function. With such a strict criterion, subjects might be able to exclude most PI stimuli. Nevertheless, there will always be some variability and errors. Errors will be of two types: incorrectly accepting PI stimuli as matches and rejecting true matches of the current-trial items. Errors of the latter type should increase somewhat as the former decrease with stricter familiarity criteria. This change in familiarity criteria should result in a rise in overall performance under high PI conditions where a small set of stimuli is repeated. The interpretation of such a performance change would be a change from a predominantly familiarity process to one more akin to an identity process.

According to the present proposal, the processes of familiarity and identity are thought to be two extremes on a continuum of familiarity effects. For the purposes of investigation, the change on this continuum is the important result, not achieving the end-point states that may be only theoretical limits to be approached. (Other conceptualizations, e.g., those that subscribe to modular memory processes, consider familiarity and identity as distinctly different processes, but see Donaldson, 1996, and Wixted & Stretch, 2004, for related proposals that put familiarity and identity/remember on a continuum of effects.) The proposal made here distinguishes itself from other proposals in that subjects are thought to learn to deal with PI more effectively and to shift their performance on the familiarity continuum. Thus, the effects of familiarity and PI are not thought to be fixed, automatic processes. One can find some support for this position from human and animal memory research. Dissociation tests with humans have shown that humans' familiarity criterion can be modified by changes in stimulus frequency, instructions, or requiring confidence ratings (see Yonelinas, 2002, for a review). This manipulation of humans' familiarity criterion indicates that animals should also be able to vary their familiarity criterion when they are confronted with the appropriate conditions (i.e., high PI conditions).

I know of no direct tests with PI manipulations, but there is some indirect evidence from training animals under high-PI conditions. The rationale for this indirect evidence of PI manipulation is that if PI were unchangeable, then performance should not improve under high-PI training conditions. But it does. One study showed a gradual rise and improvement in the delay function over the course of training one monkey for 30,000 DMTS trials under high-PI (small stimulus set) conditions (D'Amato, 1973). Likewise, pigeons showed better than expected DMTS performance after 15,000 DMTS training trials under high-PI (small stimulus set) conditions (Grant, 1975, 1976; Roberts, 1998, p. 79). A highly trained monkey in my laboratory was switched from a low-PI condition (432-stimuli set) to a high-PI condition (eight-stimuli set). This monkey's long delay (20-s and 30-s) performance gradually improved over 2,000 training trials. Although somewhat indirect, this evidence indicates that animals probably have the ability to ameliorate the effects of PI. Such control over PI (and perhaps a familiarity criterion) has similarities to the controlled and recollection processes of the human dissociation procedures. As Tulving (2002) has said, "Convincing demonstration of the decoupling of what appears a hard-wired connection between fixed behaviour prompted by fixed knowledge would constitute another step in the emancipation of birds, or other animals, as episodic creatures" (p. 283). If animals can develop strategies to combat PI, then familiarity and identity can be shown to be related on the same continuum. There are, however, other interference processes that appear to be more automatic in their effects on memory.

A discussion of these interference processes and how they affect the SPF follows in the next section.

SERIAL POSITION FUNCTIONS AND INTERFERENCE AMONG LIST ITEMS

The experimental study of human memory processing has a long history of using list-memory tasks (Ebbinghaus, 1902; Nipher, 1876). List-memory results are displayed as an SPF, usually showing best memory for items at the beginning (primacy effect) and at the end (recency effect) of each list—a U-shaped SPF. More recently, procedures have been developed to test animal list memory and animals also have shown U-shaped SPFs, including, apes (Buchanan, Gill, & Braggio, 1981), rhesus monkeys (Castro, 1995, 1997; Castro & Larsen, 1992), squirrel monkeys (Roberts & Kraemer, 1981), and rats (Bolhuis & van Kampen, 1988; Harper, McLean, & Dalrymple-Alford, 1993; Kesner & Novak, 1982; Reed, Croft, & Yeomans, 1996).

"Automatic" processes (e.g., decay, interference) play a key role in human list-memory processing (e.g., Crowder, 1976), in addition to any contributions from "controlled" processes (rehearsal, phonological loop, etc.). If anything, automatic processes should play a proportionately larger role in animal list-memory processing. The research of this section is concerned primarily with automatic processes of PI and RI as they determine the shape of the monkey's and pigeon's SPF. A working hypothesis of this section is that interference among list-memory items is primarily an automatic process, in contrast to interference from previous list items, which is thought to have a "controlled" component (i.e., control, in part, by the subjects).

One advantage in using a memory list instead of a single memory item is that interactions among memory items can be studied. These interactions among memory items are some of the most important and interesting processes of memory. A classic example is the dissipation of the recency effect with increases in the retention interval (e.g., Glanzer & Cunitz, 1966; Postman & Phillips, 1965). At the time that this effect was discovered, however, it was thought to support the hypothesis that the recency effect represented a limited-capacity short-term store and, according to the so-called modal model, the recency effect dissipated in the absence of rehearsal (Atkinson & Shiffrin, 1968; Waugh & Norman, 1965). Although the list memory of several animal species has been tested, the SPFs at any single retention delay cannot address the question of whether the animal's recency effect would dissipate with increases in retention interval as it does for humans.

Visual List-Memory Processing

We tested the possibility of dissipation of the recency effect with retention delays with four-item lists (Wright, 1999a; Wright, Santiago, Sands, Kendrick, & Cook, 1985). Because pigeons could not perform adequately with list lengths much longer than four items, we chose this list length to test our other species in order to make direct comparisons. A benefit of using short lists, but one that was not apparent at the time, was that short lists allowed early SPF changes to be observed. Four pictures were presented for 1 s with a 1-s ISI between them in each list. Retention intervals were fixed for a block of 20 trials and two blocks with different retention intervals were tested daily. Four randomized blocks of six retention intervals were tested.

Each individual panel of figure 9.6 shows an SPF for a different retention delay between the end of the list and the test. The functions change systematically with retention interval. At the shortest delay, the SPF is upward sloping, dominated by recency. As the delay is increased, primacy appears, giving the function a U shape, the characteristic shape of SPFs. At the longest delays, recency drops out, producing downward sloping functions dominated by primacy. Rhesus monkeys, capuchin monkeys, and pigeons were tested with travel slide pictures. Humans were tested with kaleidoscope-pattern pictures. The kaleidoscope patterns were distinctly different while at the same time they prevented ceiling effects that would have occurred in humans with travel-slide pictures. The same qualitative pattern of changes in the SPFs occurred for all species; however, the time courses of these changes were different. With regard to the recency effect, these changes took place in about 30 s for rhesus and capuchin monkeys, 10 s for pigeons, and 100 s for humans. With regard to the primacy effect, capuchin monkeys and humans showed development of a primacy effect at the 10-s delay, whereas rhesus and pigeons showed its development at the 1-s delay. These different time courses for different

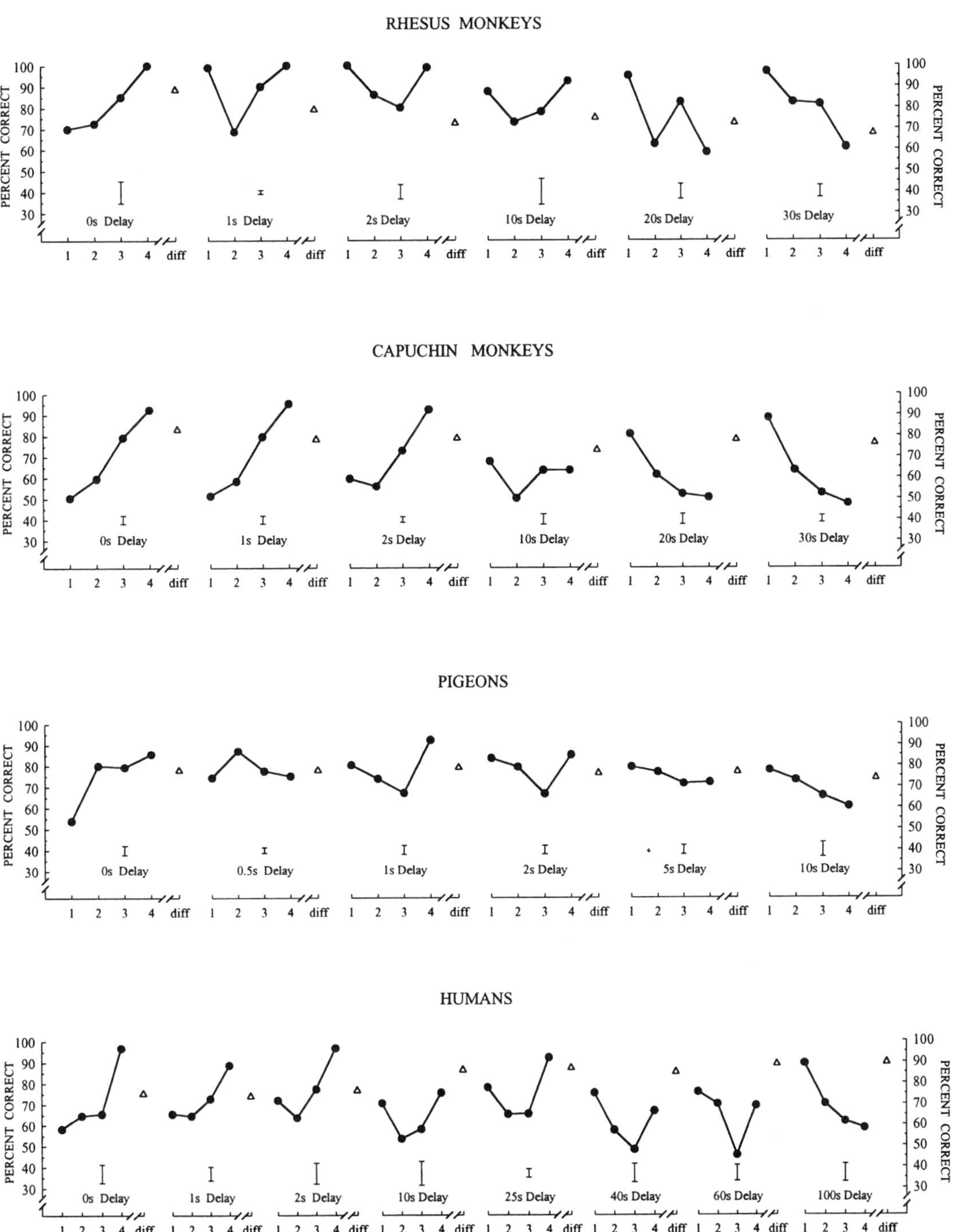

Figure 9.6. Mean serial position functions for rhesus monkeys, capuchin monkeys, pigeons, and humans on four-item visual list memory tests. Serial position 1 was the first list item. The unfilled triangles (diff) show performance on trials (different) where the test did not match any of the list items. Delay is the retention interval between the last list item (position 4) and the test. Error bars are the average standard error of the mean for the four serial positions of each function.

species are quantitative differences. Notwithstanding these different time courses, the similar pattern of SPF changes for the different species shows that their visual memory is qualitatively similar. This qualitative similarity suggests similar processes of visual recognition memory in these species.

Rehearsal and the Visual Primacy Effect

One of the most striking and surprising findings of the results shown in figure 9.6 was that primacy effects were absent initially but then gradually appeared as the retention interval was progressively lengthened. This change was an absolute improvement in memory performance, not just a relative improvement in comparison to the performance at other serial positions. This improving memory is striking because it is counter to the popular opinion that memory fades with time. The primacy effect is memory that grows with time! This improvement in primacy memory had not been shown before because (human) list-memory studies had used much longer list lengths that masked the primacy changes shown in figure 9.6. These primacy changes would have occurred long before presentation of the list was finished. Longer lists do avoid ceiling effects that can occur with short lists, but if the items are difficult to code (e.g., kaleidoscope patterns, Wright et al., 1985; snowflake patterns, Neath, 1993a, 1993b; Neath & Knoedler, 1994; and antique car drawings, Korsnes, 1995; Korsnes & Gilinsky, 1993), then short four-item lists can be used and this early pattern of changes in the primacy effect can be observed in humans without encountering ceiling effects.

Among the theoretical accounts of the SPF's primacy effect, the modal model mentioned previously proposed that participants actively rehearsed items in short-term memory and thereby moved them to long-term memory, resulting in a primacy effect. Although evidence from participants rehearsing overtly provided some early support for rehearsal and the modal model (Rundus, 1971), the primacy effects from animals (i.e., apes, monkeys, rats, and pigeons) would argue against rehearsal being the cause because these animals do not have language and most rehearsal probably depends on language. Furthermore, we tested monkeys with an ISI procedure that has been used to measure human rehearsal. As an example of a human ISI experiment, Intraub (1980) presented humans with lists of 16 pictures with short (110-ms) viewing times and a 0-s ISI. Performance was only slightly above chance. Performance improved as the ISI was lengthened to 5 s and was as accurate as when the picture was presented for 5 s (with a 0-s ISI). The participants used the ISI to rehearse the items and such ISI rehearsal has been shown to be under voluntary control of the participants, not the result of automatic, involuntary physiological effects such as consolidation (e.g., Graefe & Watkins, 1980; Proctor, 1983; Watkins & Graefe, 1981). In our experiment with rhesus monkeys, lists of six travel-slide pictures were tested under different viewing times and ISIs (Cook, Wright, & Sands, 1991). There was no performance increase with increasing ISI (actually a slight decrease) and thus presumably no rehearsal. To determine whether humans rehearse the kaleidoscope pictures in experiments like those of figure 9.6, we tested humans under similar conditions and found no ISI effect and hence probably no rehearsal (Wright et al., 1990). But when humans were taught names for the kaleidoscope pictures, they did rehearse and they showed prominent ISI effects. By manipulating the conditions for rehearsal, this study showed that rehearsal was not instrumental in producing the primacy effect, a result contrary to the modal model.

The dynamically changing SPFs of figure 9.6 appear to be the result of a shifting balance of PI and RI (interference of memory for past items by more recent items) over time. To be sure, there have been numerous proposals that RI and PI produce recency and primacy effects of the serial position curve (e.g., Foucault, 1928; Hull, 1935). The interference caused by RI has traditionally been conceived as akin to extinction in Pavlovian conditioning, complete with spontaneous recovery of inhibited responses (e.g., Postman, Stark, & Fraser, 1968; Underwood, 1948a,b). Paired-associate list-learning experiments (the so-called A-B, A-D procedure) have shown that RI exerts a stronger influence than PI immediately after learning; however, with the passage of time, the influence of PI increases (Crowder, 1976, pp. 229–241). Therefore, the extinguished responses are thought to recover over time and this recovery of the inhibited responses leads to a build-up in PI (e.g., Koppenaal, 1963; Wheeler, 1995). So, from the standpoint of visual memory, an initially strong RI would mean that the last list items would interfere with memory of the first list items and produce the

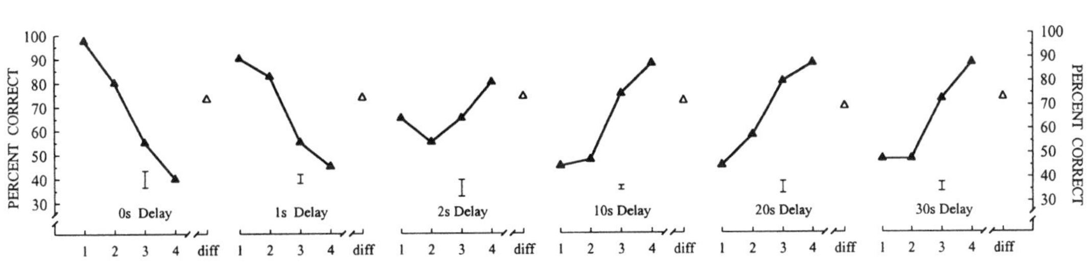

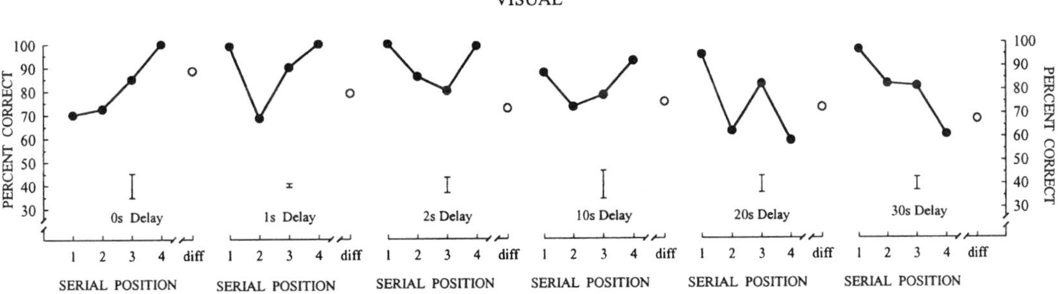

Figure 9.7. Mean rhesus monkey serial position functions for four-item auditory lists in the top panels compared with the rhesus monkey's visual serial position functions from figure 9.6. The unfilled triangles (diff) show performance on different trials. Delay is the retention interval, and error bars are the SEM average for the four serial positions at each delay.

strong recency effects of the visual SPFs. A gradual dissipation of RI would allow the primacy effect to appear, producing the U-shaped visual SPFs. And finally, PI would further strengthen and RI would dissipate, thereby strengthening the primacy effect and weakening the recency effect.

Auditory List-Memory Processing

The results in figure 9.6 cause one to ask whether these SPFs and their changes with retention delay are characteristic of memory in general or are particular to visual memory. Although some quantitative differences might be found between visual and auditory memory (like the "modality" effect in human memory), the question was whether the SPFs from both modalities would show the same general pattern of changes with retention interval. We developed an auditory list-memory task to train rhesus monkeys with four-item auditory lists and compared the test results with the rhesus monkey's visual SPFs (Wright, 1998a).

List sounds were played from a center speaker. On each trial, there were four list sounds selected from a 520-item set of natural/environmental sounds (e.g., steamboat whistle, wood chopping, pig grunts, etc.). Each list sound was played for 2 s with a 1-s ISI. A test sound was then played simultaneously from both side speakers. The same sound always came from both side speakers. If the test sound matched one of the list sounds (*same*), then a touch to the right-side speaker produced 3.5 cc of Tang orange drink. If the test sound matched none of the list sounds (*different*), then a touch to the left-side speaker produced a similar reward. Juice rewards were dispensed adjacent to each side speaker. Daily sessions were typically 32 trials: 16 *same* trials and 16 *different* trials. The intertrial interval (ITI) varied quasi-randomly from 12 s to 27 s. The monkeys' auditory list memory was then tested at the same retention intervals that were used to test visual memory (cf. figure 9.6).

The resulting auditory SPFs are shown in figure 9.7 along with the rhesus' visual SPFs from figure 9.6 for comparison. Auditory SPFs showed a pattern of changes over time that was *opposite* to those for visual memory. On tests immediately after presentation of the list, the SPF showed pure primacy, with best performance on the first item and worst performance on the fourth item. This finding of worst recognition on the last list item, occurring just prior to the test item, is odd and counterintuitive, but it has been replicated in 12 independent experiments under a variety of conditions including random retention intervals and random ITIs (Wright, 1998a, 1999b, 2002; Wright & Roediger, 2003). As the retention interval was increased to around 2 s, the SPF became more typical in shape, a U-shaped curve with primacy and recency effects. At 20- and 30-s retention delays, the SPF reflected pure recency; performance was best on the last item and worst on the first. These SPF changes over 30 s of delay argue that some dynamic process (or set of processes) gives rise to the SPF; its changing shape and interpretive possibilities are discussed in the next section.

How the monkey's auditory SPFs might relate to human auditory memory is unclear. The only two human auditory memory experiments with lists short enough to address this issue showed patterns of SPFs similar to those for visual memory and not like the monkey's auditory memory SPFs (Knoedler, Hellwig, & Neath, 1999, Experiment 3; Surprenant, 2001). One difficulty with human auditory memory experiments is that auditory items "unfold" in time. We have found that humans fragment auditory stimuli and code their distinctive features instead of processing them as a unitary whole. Other evidence suggests that humans may code auditory items in a "visual" format (e.g., Campbell & Dodd, 1980). Another issue is what might be the purpose (e.g., evolutionary value) of opposite-shaped SPFs for visual and auditory memory. An argument can be made (e.g., Wright, 1998b; Wright & Roediger, 2003) for a possible purpose based on associative learning of visual stimuli with food versus auditory stimuli with danger (e.g., Shapiro, Jacobs, & LoLordo, 1980), but such teleological arguments are by nature highly speculative and difficult to test.

Interference Processes in Auditory List Memory

The previous description of a pattern of interference makes sense for the dynamic changes shown for the visual SPFs (figure 9.6), but the monkey's auditory SPFs (figure 9.7) require a different pattern of interference. The switch from a primacy-dominated function to a recency-dominated function for monkey auditory memory is remarkable, because recognition of the fourth (last) item in the sequence shows a dramatic increase over the rather brief retention intervals used. Such recovery of information strongly implicates the presence of interference and spontaneous recovery. This pattern of changes for auditory memory would require that PI should be strong initially and that with increasing delay PI should decrease and RI should increase.

Unlike other proposals that interference accounts for SPFs, we have manipulated interference and obtained evidence that interference does account for the changing pattern of SPFs in five auditory memory experiments with monkeys (Wright, 1998b, 1999b; Wright & Roediger, 2003). In one experiment, separation between the four sounds in each list (2-s presentation times) was increased (from 1 s to 2.5 s). At the short delays, the increased separation decreased the primacy effects (e.g., from 98% to 63% at the 0-s delay). This decrease in primacy was accompanied by an increase in recency (e.g., from 40% to 79% at the 0-s delay). In another experiment, adding 2 s to the middle ISI of the list (i.e., 1 s, 3 s, 1 s for the three ISIs, respectively) produced similar results. The SPF was similar in shape and magnitude to the 2-s SPF of figure 9.7, where all ISIs were 1 s. This is an interesting result because it means that a 2-s delay in the middle of the list can be substituted for a 2-s delay at the end of the list. Because the timing relationships between the last two list items and the test were unchanged, the increased recency effect must be caused by changing interference among list items and not by memory (trace) decay or consolidation during retention delay. Thus, increasing separation between list items reduced interactions and interference among list items—PI in this case. It is of some interest that increasing item separations had little or no effect on the long-delay (e.g., 20-s) SPFs. Item separations do not appear to have the same effect of reducing RI as they do for PI. But, because RI presumably plays its role at longer retention intervals, possibly manipulations of RI through ISI manipulations would depend on the ratio of ISI to the delay time and not the absolute ISI value (cf., Glenberg et al, 1983; Winograd, 1971).

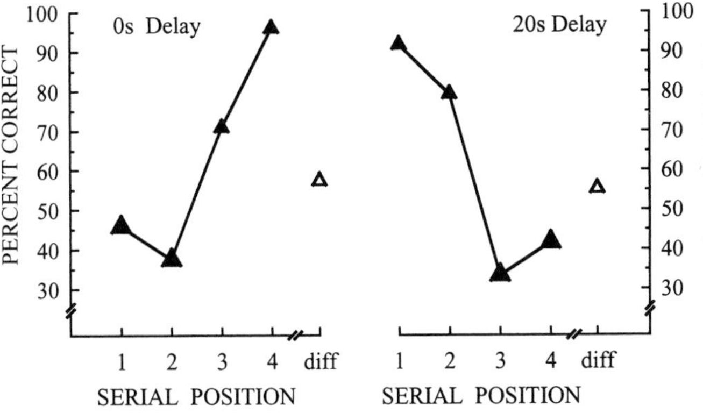

Figure 9.8. *Left*, Mean four-item auditory serial position functions for two rhesus monkeys tested at 0-s delay with the first two list items (large triangles) from a small or difficult-to-remember (DTR) item set and the last two list items (small triangles) from a large or easy-to-remember (ETR) item set. *Right*, Mean auditory serial position functions for the same monkeys tested at 20-s delay with the last two list items (large triangles) from the DTR set and the first two list items (small triangles) from the ETR set.

Another way we manipulated the interactions among memory items was to make some of the list stimuli (either the first two or the last two) more difficult to remember. These difficult-to-remember (DTR) items were created by using a small eight-item set, repeatedly. The monkeys heard these eight sounds hundreds times over several weeks of training prior to this test. The test with the first two list items from this DTR set was to determine whether PI from the first two list items would be reduced and thereby enhance performance to the last two list items. The last two items in this test condition were trial-unique items selected from a much larger 144-item set. Delays of either 0 s or 20 s were tested in this experiment. The short-delay SPF is of most interest because the primacy effect was strongest and presumably PI was strongest at short delays. In another condition of this experiment, the last two list items were from the DTR set and the rationale here was to test whether RI from the last two list items might be reduced and thereby enhance performance for the first two list items. In this case, the long-delay SPF was of most interest because the recency effect was strongest and presumably RI was strongest at long delays. The mean results from these two conditions (the ones of primary interest) are shown in figure 9.8 for two rhesus monkeys. When the first two items were from the DTR set (left panel), memory for them decreased. More important, memory of the last two list items increased relative to the 0-s delay SPF shown in figure 9.7. This result shows that making memory of the first two list items more difficult removed the PI that otherwise would have occurred on the monkeys' memory for the last two list items. In a similar fashion, when the last two items were from the DTR set (right panel), memory for these items decreased. More important, memory of the first two list items in this test at the 20-s delay increased relative to the 20-s delay SPF of figure 9.7. This result shows that making the last two list items DTR removed the RI that otherwise would have interfered with the monkeys' memory for the first two list items. Thus, RI is indeed a major factor controlling performance at long retention intervals.

The last experiment on interference in auditory memory to be discussed provides perhaps the most compelling evidence for PI and RI determining the shape of the monkey's auditory SPFs. In this experiment, we eliminated the first three list items in one condition and compared the resulting single-item memory performance with memory performance where all four list items were presented (Wright & Roediger, 2003). The single-item tests are a control condition to evaluate whether performance changes were due to some process correlated with the sheer passage of time or were the direct result of PI from the earlier items in the list. These predictions perhaps can be best understood by considering the immediate (0-s delay) memory test. If the first three list items interfered (proactively) with the monkey's memory of the last item, then by eliminating the first three items, PI should be eliminated and last-item performance should be elevated. Thus, single-item performance is the baseline condition for comparison to fourth-item performance at all retention intervals because timing parameters are otherwise identical in both conditions. If PI from the first items of the list dissipates with retention interval, as the proposal predicts, then fourth-item performance from four-item lists should rise with retention interval and eventually equal single-item performance.

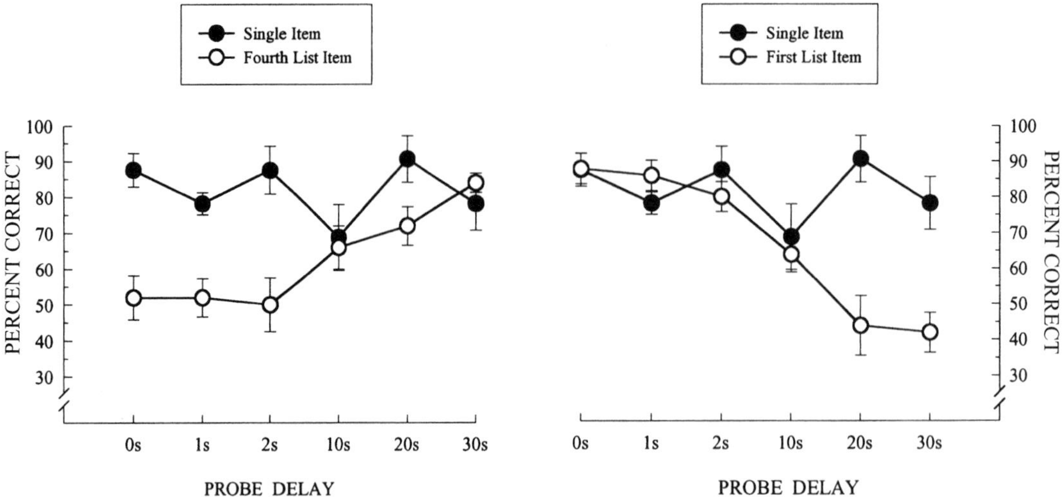

Figure 9.9. Single-item performance compared to the fourth (last) list item performance of four-item lists (*left*) and single-item performance compared with the first list item performance (*right*). Error bars are standard errors of the mean.

SPFs for the four-item lists were similar to those shown in figure 9.7; the critical results from this experiment are shown in figure 9.9. Figure 9.9 (left) shows fourth-item performance compared with mean single-item performance. Single-item performance is much more accurate than fourth-item performance over the shortest three (0-, 1-, and 2-s) retention delays. This large performance difference demonstrates the considerable effect of PI from the first three items on the monkey's memory of the fourth item of the list at these short delays. This is a compelling conclusion, we believe, because otherwise fourth-item performance would be just like single-item performance at these short delays. Fourth-item performance did rise as delay increased and became equivalent to single-item performance at the longest retention intervals, demonstrating that PI from the first three items largely dissipated as retention delay increased. Thus, PI at short delays is thought to be *the* major factor contributing to the shape of the short-delay auditory SPFs.

We also found evidence that RI contributes to the shape of these SPFs at the long retention intervals by showing that RI adversely affects the monkey's memory for the first list items. Figure 9.9 (right) shows performance for the first item of the list compared with the mean single-item performance across delays. In this case, single-item performance is much more accurate than first-item performance over the longest (20- and 30-s) retention intervals. This large performance difference at the longer delays demonstrates the considerable effect of RI at these delays. Although this comparison is not as precise as the previous one because of the additional time from the first item to the test item, it is nevertheless clear that the last three items retroactively interfered with the monkey's memory of the first list item. This interference must hold; otherwise performance would have been just like it was with the single item across all delays. The equivalent performance for the first list item and the single item at the shortest retention intervals demonstrates that RI from the last three items is largely absent at these short retention delays. As the retention delay increases, RI increases and eliminates the primacy effects of the SPFs. Thus, RI at long delays is the second process to explain the shape of these SPFs and is the major factor contributing to the shape of the long-delay auditory SPFs.

There have been, to be sure, accounts other than interference to explain the shape of the SPF. The popular and venerable dual-store models (e.g., modal model) claim that the recency effect represents short-term memory, which decays with time (e.g., Atkinson & Shiffrin, 1968; Gillund & Shiffrin, 1984; Haarmann & Usher, 2001). But the monkey's auditory recency effect cannot represent short-term memory because a recency effect is not present initially; its later appearance is more like a long-term memory effect than like a short-term memory effect. Other accounts of dynamically changing SPFs have included temporal distinctiveness (e.g., Knoedler et al., 1999; Neath, 1993a; Neath & Knoedler, 1994) and storage versus retrieval strength (Bjork, 2001). An item's temporal distinctiveness is thought to change with time, like a receding row of telephone poles, with those in the distance less distinct than those closer (Crowder & Neath, 1991). But, as Bjork (2001) has pointed out, temporal distinctiveness cannot account for absolute (as opposed to relative) memory recovery as shown by the visual primacy effect. To account for absolute recovery, Bjork proposed a storage-strength versus retrieval-strength model. However, Bjork's model depends on learning with repetitions of the same list and would not apply to absolute recovery following a single presentation of each list, like those used to test the monkey's auditory (and visual) memory.

The proposal presented here is that retrieval failure underlying the SPF is the result of interference. The monkey list-memory experiments, particularly the auditory list-memory experiments, provide evidence for interference being instrumental in the changes in the SPF in this item-recognition paradigm. These auditory memory results show that PI is strong just after an auditory list is presented, thereby causing retrieval failure and depressing recognition of the last items. Release from this PI causes an absolute increase in recency and the resulting RI causes retrieval failure of the first items of the list. After 30 s, the shape of the auditory SPF has changed dramatically. With regard to the auditory memory results, we find that no explanation fares as well as interference. For example, one can cast distinctiveness as a result of interference but not the other way around. I cannot think of a way that distinctiveness could increase with delay and account for the absolute performance increases (auditory recency or visual primacy) or a reason why the distinctiveness of auditory and visual lists would be opposite in their properties in monkeys or humans. Whether visual memory will produce complementary interference results is clearly a topic for future research.

In conclusion, I want to say a few words about the relationship between interference from previous trials and interference within the items of a memory list. The evidence is beginning to accumulate that the interference among list items (within-list interference) is different from the interference that builds up across lists (across-list interference). In this latter case, PI, for example, from previous trials (across-list PI) does not prevent the subject from recognizing that the test item had been seen previously. Indeed, it is likely to increase the chances that the subject will recognize the item. But the subject has trouble remembering whether it was in the list being tested or in some previous list (cf. Glenberg, 1987; Gorfein, 1987). By contrast, PI from the first (auditory) list items (within-list PI) does prevent the subject from recognizing the fourth item as heard previously. This effect is due to retrieval failure. It is as if there is a temporary retrieval failure for the fourth list item with recovery after a delay. Additional evidence for the different nature of these two types of interference is that within-list PI (in auditory memory) occurs across diverse items and begins to dissipate in about 2 s in these tasks. Across-list PI, on the other hand, occurs across similar items and identical items and persists for minutes, hours, and even days. If I were to hazard a guess, I would say that the within-list interference effects are more or less automatic, fixed processes, in the Jacoby (e.g., 1998) sense of "automatic" memory processes, certainly in the class of "unwillful" processes in Watkins' (1989) terms. These within-list interference effects adversely affect memory retrieval and certainly do not affect encoding because the visual primacy and auditory recency effects appear after a delay of some seconds. On the other hand, across-list PI is unlikely to be quite such a fixed, immutable, automatic process. Its locus appears to be the decision process itself on a later trial (e.g., the PI test trial) and is likely to be modifiable by the subject (e.g., by changing its familiarity criterion).

Acknowledgments Preparation of this chapter was supported by National Institutes of Health grants DA-10715 and MH61798. The author gratefully acknowledges the helpful comments on this chapter by Jeff Katz, Roddy Roediger, and John Wixted and by editors Ed Wasserman and Tom Zentall.

References

Atkinson, R. C., & Juola, J. F. (1974). Search and decision processes in recognition memory. In D. H. Krantz, R. C. Atkinson, R. D. Luce, & P. Suppes (Eds.), *Contemporary developments in mathematical psychology: Vol. 1. Learning, memory & thinking* (pp. 242–293). San Francisco: Freeman Press.

Atkinson, R. C., & Shiffrin, R. M. (1968). Human memory: A proposed system and its control processes. In K. W. Spence & J. T. Spence (Eds.), *The psychology of learning and motivation,* Vol. 2 (pp. 89–105). New York: Academic Press.

Baddeley, A. (2002). The concept of episodic memory. In A. Baddeley, M. A. Conway, & J. P. Aggleton (Eds.), *Episodic memory* (pp. 1–10). New York: Oxford University Press.

Balda, R. P., & Kamil, A. C. (1992). Long-term spatial memory in Clark's nutcracker, *Nucifraga columbiana. Animal Behavior, 44,* 761–769.

Bennett, R. W. (1975). Proactive interference in short-term memory: Fundamental forgetting processes. *Journal of Verbal Learning and Verbal Behavior, 14,* 123–144.

Bjork, R. A. (2001). Recency and recovery in human memory. In H. L. Roediger III, J. S. Nairne, I. Neath, & A. M. Surprenant (Eds.), *The nature of remembering: Essays in honor of Robert G. Crowder* (pp. 211–232). Washington, DC: American Psychological Association.

Bolhuis, J. J., & van Kampen, H. S. (1988). Serial position curves in spatial memory of rats: primacy and recency effects. *The Quarterly Journal of Experimental Psychology, 40,* 135–149.

Brown, J. (1958). Some tests of the decay theory of immediate memory. *The Quarterly Journal of Experimental Psychology*, 10, 12–21.

Buchanan, J. P., Gill, T. V., & Braggio, J. T. (1981). Serial position and clustering effects in chimpanzee's "free recall." *Memory & Cognition, 9,* 651–660.

Campbell, R., & Dodd, B. (1980). Hearing by eye. *The Quarterly Journal of Experimental Psychology, 32,* 85–99.

Castro, C. A. (1995). Primacy and recency effects in rhesus monkeys (*Macaca mulatta*) using serial probe recognition task: I. Effects of diazepam. *Psychopharmacology, 119,* 421–427.

Castro, C. A. (1997). Primacy and recency effects in rhesus monkeys (*Macaca mulatta*) using a serial probe recognition task: II. Effects of atropine sulfate. *Behavioral Neuroscience,* 111, 676–682.

Castro, C. A., & Larsen, T. (1992). Primacy and recency effects in nonhuman primates. *Journal of Experimental Psychology: Animal Behavior Processes, 18,* 335–340.

Clayton, N. S., & Dickinson, A. (1998). Episodic-like memory during cache recovery by scrub jays. *Nature, 395,* 272–274.

Clayton, N. S., & Dickinson, A. (1999a). Memory for the content of caches by scrub jays (*Aphelocoma coerulescens*). *Journal of Experimental Psychology: Animal Behavior Processes, 25,* 82–91.

Clayton, N. S., & Dickinson, A. (1999b). Scrub jays (*Aphelocoma coerulescens*) remember the relative time of caching as well as the location and content of their caches, *Journal of Comparative Psychology, 113,* 403–416.

Cook, R. G., Wright, A. A., & Sands, S. F. (1991). Interstimulus interval and viewing time effects in monkey list memory. *Animal Learning & Behavior, 19,* 153–163.

Crowder, R. G. (1976). *Principles of learning and memory* (pp. 229–241). Hillsdale, NJ: Erlbaum.

Crowder, R. G., & Neath, I. (1991). The microscope metaphor in human memory. In W. E. Hockley & S. Lewandowsky (Eds.), *Relating theory and data: Essays on human memory in honor of Bennet B. Murdock, Jr.* (pp. 111–125). Hillsdale, NJ: Erlbaum.

D'Amato, M. R. (1973). Delayed matching and short-term memory in monkeys. In G. H. Bower (Ed.), *The psychology of learning and motivation: Advances in research and theory,* Vol. 7 (pp. 227–269). New York: Academic Press.

Devine, J. B., & Jones, L. C. (1975). Matching-to-successive samples: A multiple-unit memory task with rhesus monkeys. *Behavior Research Methods and Instrumentation, 7,* 438–440.

Donaldson, W. (1996). The role of decision processes in remembering and knowing. *Memory & Cognition, 24, 523–533.*

Ebbinghaus, H. E. (1902) *Grundzuge der Psychologie* [Basic Psychology]. Leipzig: Von Veit.

Eddy, D. R. (1973). Memory processing in *Macaca speciosa*: Mental processes revealed by reaction time experiments. Unpublished doctoral dissertation, Carnegie Mellon University.

Etkin, M., & D'Amato, M. R. (1969). Delayed matching-to-sample and short-term memory in the capuchin monkey. *Journal of Comparative and Physiological Psychology, 69, 544–549.*

Foucault, M. (1928). Les inhibitions internes de fixation. *Annee Psychologique, 29,* 92–112.

Gaffan, D. (1977). Recognition memory after short retention intervals in fornix-transected monkeys. *The Quarterly Journal of Experimental Psychology, 29, 577–588.*

Gaffan, D., & Weiskrantz, L. (1980). Recency effects and lesion effects in delayed nonmatching to randomly baited samples by monkeys. *Brain Research, 196,* 373–386.

Gardiner, J. M., & Richardson-Klavehn, A. (2000). Remembering and knowing. In E. Tulving & F. I. M. Craik (Eds.), *The Oxford handbook of memory* (pp. 229–244). New York: Oxford University Press.

Gillund, G., & Shiffrin, R. M. (1984). A retrieval model for both recognition and recall. *Psychological Review, 91,* 1–67.

Glanzer, M., & Cunitz, A. R. (1966). Two storage mechanisms in free recall. *Journal of Verbal Learning and Verbal Behavior, 5,* 351–360.

Glenberg, A. M. (1987). Temporal context and memory. In D. S. Gorfein & R. R. Hoffman (Eds.), *Memory and learning: The Ebbinghaus centennial conference* (pp. 173–190). Hillsdale, NJ: Erlbaum.

Glenberg, A. M., Bradley, M. M., Kraus, T. A., & Renzaglia, G. J. (1983). Studies of the long-term recency effect: Support for a contextually guided retrieval hypothesis. *Journal of Experimental Psychology: Learning, Memory, and Cognition*, 9, 231–255.

Gorfein, D. S. (1987). Explaining context effects on short-term memory. In D. S. Gorfein & R. R. Hoffman (Eds.), *Memory and learning: the Ebbinghaus centennial conference* (pp. 153–172). Hillsdale, NJ: Erlbaum.

Graefe, T. M., & Watkins, M. J. (1980). Picture rehearsal: An effect of selectively attending to pictures no longer in view. *Journal of Experimental Psychology: Human Learning and Memory, 6,* 156–162.

Grant, D. S. (1975). Proactive interference in pigeon short-term memory. *Journal of Experimental Psychology: Animal Behavior Processes*, 1, 207–220.

Grant, D. S. (1976). Effect of sample presentation time on long-delay matching in the pigeon. *Learning and Motivation, 7,* 580–590.

Grant, D. S. (2000). Influence of intertrial interval duration on the intertrial agreement effect in delayed matching-to-sample with pigeons. *Animal Learning & Behavior, 28,* 288–297.

Grant, D. S., & Roberts, W. A. (1973). Trace interaction in pigeon short-term memory. *Journal of Experimental Psychology, 101,* 21–29.

Haarman, H., & Usher, M. (2001). Maintenance of semantic information in capacity-limited item short-term memory. *Psychonomic Bulletin & Review, 8,* 568–578.

Hampton, R. R. (2001). Rhesus monkeys know when they remember. *Proceeding of the National Academy of Sciences, 98,* 5359–5362.

Harper, D. N., McLean, A. P., & Dalrymple-Alford, J. C. (1993). List item memory in rats: Effects of delay and delay task. *Journal of Experimental Psychology: Animal Behavior Processes, 19,* 307–316.

Hogan, D. E., Edwards, C. E., & Zentall, T. R. (1981). Delayed matching in the pigeon: Interference produced by the prior delayed matching trial. *Animal Learning & Behavior, 9,* 395–400.

Hull, C. L. (1935). The conflicting psychologies of learning—A way out. *Psychological Review, 42,* 491–516.

Intraub, H. (1980). Presentation rate and the representation of briefly glimpsed pictures in memory. *Journal of Experimental Psychology: Human Learning and Memory, 6,* 1–12.

Jacoby, L. L. (1991). A process dissociation framework: Separating automatic from intentional uses of memory. *Journal of Memory and Language, 30,* 513–541.

Jacoby, L. L. (1998). Invariance in automatic influences of memory: Toward a user's guide for the process-dissociation procedure. *Journal of Experimental Psychology: Learning, Memory, and Cognition, 24,* 3–26.

Jacoby, L. L., Toth, J. P., & Yonelinas, A. P. (1993). Separating conscious and unconscious influence of memory: Measuring recollection. *Journal of Experimental Psychology: General, 122,* 139–154.

Keppel, G., & Underwood, B. J. (1962). Proactive inhibition in short-term retention of single items. *Journal of Verbal Learning and Verbal Behavior, 1,* 153–161.

Kesner, R. P., & Novak, J. M. (1982). Serial position curve in rats: role of the dorsal hippocampus. *Science, 218,* 173–175.

Knoedler, A. J., Hellwig, K. A., & Neath, I. (1999). The shift from recency to primacy with increasing delay. *Journal of Experimental Psychology: Learning, Memory, and Cognition, 25,* 474–487.

Koppenaal, R. J. (1963). Time changes in the strengths of A-B, A-C lists: Spontaneous recovery? *Journal of Verbal Learning and Verbal Behavior, 2,* 310–319.

Korsnes, M. S. (1995). Retention intervals and serial list memory. *Perceptual and Motor Skills, 80,* 723–731.

Korsnes, M. S., & Gilinsky, S. A. (1993). Aging and serial list picture memory. *Perceptual and Motor Skills, 76,* 1011–1014.

Mackintosh, N. J. (2000). Abstraction and discrimination. In C. Heyes & L. Huber (Eds.), *The evolution of cognition* (pp. 123–142). Cambridge, MA: MIT Press.

Macphail, E. M., & Reilly, S. (1989). Rapid acquisition of a novelty versus familiarity concept by pigeons (*Columba livia*). *Journal of Experimental Psychology: Animal Behavior Processes, 15,* 242–252.

Maki, W. S., Moe, J. C., & Bierley, C. M. (1977). Short-term memory for stimuli, responses, and reinforcers. *Journal of Experimental Psychology: Animal Behavior Processes*, 3, 156–177.

Mandler, G. (1980). Recognizing: The judgment of previous occurrence. *Psychological Review, 87,* 252–271.

Miles, R. C. (1971). Species differences in "transmitting" spatial location information. In L. E. Jarrard (Ed.), *Cognitive processes of nonhuman primates* (pp. 165–179). New York: Academic Press.

Mishkin, M., & Delacour, J. (1975). An analysis of short-term visual memory in the monkey. *Journal of Experimental Psychology: Animal Behavior Processes, 1,* 326–334.

Moise, S. L. (1976). Proactive effects of stimuli, delays and response position during delayed matching to sample. *Animal Learning & Behavior, 4,* 37–40.

Neath, I. (1993a). Distinctiveness and serial position effects in recognition. *Memory & Cognition, 21,* 689–698.

Neath, I. (1993b). Contextual and distinctive processes and the serial position function. *Journal of Memory and Language, 32,* 820–840.

Neath, I., & Knoedler, A. J. (1994). Distinctiveness and serial position effects in recognition and sentence processing. *Journal of Memory and Language, 33,* 776–795.

Neath, I., & Surprenant, A. M. (2003). *Human memory: An introduction to research, data, and theory.* Belmont, CA: Wadsworth/Thomson Learning.

Nipher, F. E. (1876). On the distribution of numbers written from memory. *Transactions of the Academy of St. Louis, 3,* 79–80.

Olton, D. S. (1978). Characteristics of spatial memory. In S. H. Hulse, H. Fowler, & W. K. Honig (Eds.), *Cognitive processes in animal behavior* (pp. 341–373). Hillsdale, NJ: Erlbaum.

Overman, W. H., & Doty, R. W. (1980). Prolonged visual memory in macaques and man. *Neuroscience, 5,* 1825–1831.

Peterson, L. R., & Peterson, M. J. (1959). Short-term retention of individual verbal items. *Journal of Experimental Psychology, 58,* 193–198.

Postman, L., & Phillips, L. (1965). Short-term temporal changes in free-recall. *The Quarterly Journal of Experimental Psychology, 17,* 132–138.

Postman, L., Stark, K., & Fraser, J. (1968). Temporal changes in interference. *Journal of Verbal Learning and Verbal Behavior, 7,* 672–694.

Premack, D. (1978). On the abstractness of human concepts: Why it would be difficult to talk to a pigeon. In S. H. Hulse, H. Fowler, & W. K. Honig (Eds.), *Cognitive processes in animal behavior* (pp. 423–451). Hillsdale, NJ: Erlbaum.

Premack, D. (1983). Animal cognition. *Annual Review of Psychology, 34,* 351–362.

Premack, D., & Premack, A. J. (1983). *The mind of an ape.* New York: W. W. Norton.

Proctor, R. W. (1983). Recognition memory for pictures as a function of poststimulus interval: An empirical clarification of existing literature. *Journal of Experimental Psychology: Learning, Memory, and Cognition, 9,* 256–262.

Reed, P., Croft, H., & Yeomans, M. (1996). Rats' memory for serially presented novel flavours: Evidence for non-spatial primacy effects. *The Quarterly Journal of Experimental Psychology, 49B,* 174–187.

Roberts, W. A. (1980). Distribution of trials and intertrial retention in delayed matching to sample with pigeons. *Journal of Experimental Psychology: Animal Behavior Processes, 6,* 217–237.

Roberts, W. A. (1998). *Principles of animal cognition.* New York: McGraw-Hill.

Roberts, W. A., & Grant, D. S. (1976). Studies of short-term memory in the pigeon using the delayed matching-to-sample procedure. In D. L. Medin, W. A. Roberts, & R. T. Davis (Eds.), *Processes of animal memory.* Hillsdale, NJ: Erlbaum.

Roberts, W. A., & Kraemer, P. J. (1981). Recognition memory for lists of visual stimuli in monkeys and humans. *Animal Learning & Behavior, 9,* 587–594.

Roitblat, H. L., & Scopatz, R. A. (1983). Sequential effects in pigeons delayed matching-to-sample performance. *Journal of Experimental Psychology: Animal Behavior Processes, 9,* 202–221.

Rundus, D. (1971). Analysis of rehearsal processes in free recall. *Journal of Experimental Psychology, 89,* 63–77.

Sands, S. F., & Wright, A. A. (1980). Primate memory: Retention of serial list items by a rhesus monkey. *Science, 209,* 938– 940.

Shapiro, K. L., Jacobs, W. J., & LoLordo, V. M. (1980). Stimulus-reinforcer interactions in Pavlovian conditioning of pigeons: Implications for selective associations. *Animal Learning & Behavior, 8,* 586–594.

Surprenant, A. M. (2001). Distinctiveness and serial position effects in tonal sequences. *Perception & Psychophysics, 63,* 737–745.

Thompson, R. K. R., & Herman, L. M. (1981). Auditory delayed discriminations by the dolphin: Nonequivalence with delayed matching performance. *Animal Learning & Behavior, 9,* 9–15.

Tulving, E. (1972). Episodic and semantic memory. In E. Tulving & W. Donaldson (Eds.), *Organization of memory* (pp. 381–403). New York: Academic Press.

Tulving, E. (1983). *Elements of episodic memory.* New York: Oxford University Press.

Tulving, E. (1985). Memory and consciousness. *Canadian Journal of Psychology, 26,* 1–12.

Tulving, E. (2002). Episodic memory and common sense: How far apart? In A. Baddeley, M. A. Conway, & J. P. Aggleton (Eds.), *Episodic memory* (269–287). New York: Oxford University Press.

Tulving, E., & Bower, G. H. (1974). The logic of memory representations. In G. H. Bower

(Ed.), *The psychology of learning and motivation: Advances in research and theory*. Vol. 8. New York: Academic Press.

Underwood, B. J. (1948a). Retroactive and proactive inhibition after five and forty-eight hours. *Journal of Experimental Psychology, 38,* 29–38.

Underwood, B. J. (1948b). "Spontaneous recovery" of verbal associations. *Journal of Experimental Psychology, 38,* 429–439.

Vander Wall, S. B. (1982). An experimental analysis of cache recovery in Clark's nutcracker. *Animal Behaviour, 30,* 84–94.

Watkins, M. J. (1989). Willful and nonwillful determinants of memory. In H. L. Roediger III & F. I. M. Craik (Eds.), *Varieties of memory and consciousness: Essays in honour of Endel Tulving* (pp. 59–71). Hillsdale, NJ: Erlbaum.

Watkins, M. J., & Graefe, T. M. (1981). Delayed rehearsal of pictures. *Journal of Verbal Learning and Verbal Behavior, 20,* 176–288.

Waugh, N. C., & Norman, D. A. (1965). Primacy memory. *Psychological Review, 72,* 89–104.

Wheeler, M. A. (1995). Improvement in recall over time without repeated testing: Spontaneous recovery revisited. *Journal of Experimental Psychology: Learning, Memory and Cognition, 21,* 173–184.

Wickens, D. D., Born, D. G., & Allen, C. K. (1963). Proactive inhibition and item similarity in short-term memory. *Journal of Verbal Learning and Verbal Behavior, 2,* 440–445.

Winograd, E. (1971). Some issues relating animal memory to human memory. In W. K. Honig & P. H. R. James (Eds.), *Animal memory.* New York: Academic Press.

Wixted, J. T., & Stretch, V. (2004). In defense of the signal-detection interpretation of remember/know judgments. *Psychological Bulletin & Review, 11,* 616–641.

Wright, A. A. (1997). Concept learning and learning strategies. *Psychological Science, 8,* 119–123.

Wright, A. A. (1998a). Auditory list memory in rhesus monkeys. *Psychological Science, 9,* 91–98.

Wright, A. A. (1998b). Auditory and visual serial position functions obey different laws. *Psychonomic Bulletin & Review, 5,* 564–584.

Wright, A. A. (1999a). Visual list memory in capuchin monkeys (*Cebus apella*). *Journal of Comparative Psychology, 113,* 74–80.

Wright, A. A. (1999b). Auditory list memory and interference in monkeys. *Journal of Experimental Psychology: Animal Behavior Processes, 25,* 284–296.

Wright, A. A. (2002). Monkey auditory list memory: Tests with mixed and blocked retention delays. *Animal Learning & Behavior, 30,* 158–164.

Wright, A. A., Cook, R. G., Rivera, J. J., Shyan, M. R., Neiworth, J. J., & Jitsumori, M. (1990). Naming, rehearsal, and interstimulus interval effects in memory processing. *Journal of Experimental Psychology: Learning, Memory, and Cognition, 16,* 1043–1059.

Wright, A. A., & Roediger H. L. III. (2003). Interference processes in monkey auditory list memory. *Psychonomic Bulletin & Review, 10,* 696–702.

Wright, A. A., Santiago, H. C., Sands, S. F., Kendrick, D. F., & Cook, R. G. (1985). Memory processing of serial lists by pigeons, monkeys, and people. *Science, 229,* 287–289.

Wright, A. A., Urcuioli, P. J., & Sands, S. F. (1986). Proactive interference in animal memory. In D. F. Kendrick, M. E. Rilling, & M. R. Denny (Eds.), *Theories of animal memory* (pp. 101–125). Hillsdale, NJ: Erlbaum.

Yonelinas, A. P. (2002). The nature of recollection and familiarity: A review of 30 years of research. *Journal of Memory and Language, 46,* 441–517.

IV

SPATIAL COGNITION

10

Arthropod Navigation: Ants, Bees, Crabs, Spiders Finding Their Way

KEN CHENG

Arthropods are a much-studied group of animals. They are characterized by a hard exoskeleton and no internal bones. They include insects, spiders, and hard-shelled invertebrates such as crabs. In this chapter, I review four broad topics on the navigational behavior of arthropods. The first is path integration, the ability to keep track of the straight-line distance and direction from one's starting point. The second is route behavior, in which landmarks figure in various ways. The third is image matching, the use of landmarks to pinpoint a target. The fourth is map-like navigational behavior.

My aim is to present an overview including some classic work and current trends and issues. Recent reviews on arthropod navigation are plentiful (Cheng, 2000a; T. S. Collett & M. Collett, 2002; T. S. Collett, Fauria, & Dale, 2003; T. S. Collett & Zeil, 1998; Wehner & Srinivasan, 2003). I see no point in simply re-presenting all the data. Rather, I aim for a selection tailored for an audience from the field of comparative cognition, laced with my concepts, which will, I hope, frame the data and aid in understanding.

PLACE-FINDING SERVOMECHANISMS

As before (Cheng, 1995, 2000a), I describe navigation in terms of place-finding servomechanisms (figure 10.1). A servomechanism, called control system in engineering terminology, has ongoing control by appropriate stimuli. The system can be characterized has having a standard, a specification of a target place, to which it "aims." The current state of affairs (input data) is compared with the standard, and the difference is an error. The system is designed to move so as to reduce the error.

Navigation typically requires a string of servomechanisms. Crucial to navigation is the switching on and off of servomechanisms. The right one needs to be used at the right time. A broad suite of stimulus conditions, often called context cues (for a review, see T. S. Collett et al., 2003), plays a role in the retrieval and operation of servomechanisms. To use learning-theoretic terminology, we can say that these cues set the occasion for the operation of a servomechanism. This theme will ring throughout the chapter.

PATH INTEGRATION

Across a featureless Tunisian salt pan wandered a desert ant circuitously in search of prey who have succumbed to the heat. After covering a path length of almost 600 m, the ant found a dead fly. It seized the prey and ran home in a nearly straight path of 141-m path length. The ratio of the homebound path length to the straight-line distance between the food and its nest was a mere 1.06 (Wehner & Wehner, 1990). This example features

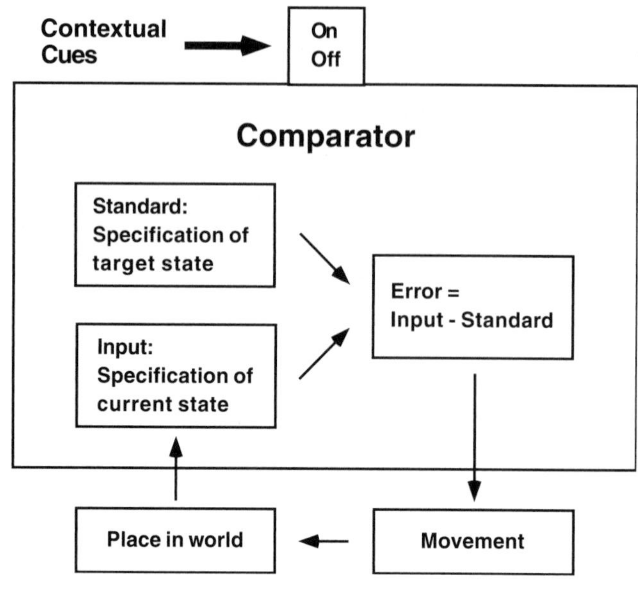

Figure 10.1. Place-finding servomechanism. Central to the operation of a servomechanism is a comparator. It compares a standard to "aim" for with input data, typically perceptual data broadly defined (including vision, proprioception, and efferent commands). Different servomechanisms specify the target differently. It might be the way landmarks should look, a compass direction, or a vector to be executed. The difference between the input and the standard constitutes error, and error drives action (movement). If the system is working correctly, this makes a negative feedback loop and reduces the error. Also illustrated are contextual cues, broadly construed. These can serve as occasion setters for the operation of servomechanisms. Contextual cues can switch on and off servomechanisms to coordinate navigation.

the navigational mechanism of path integration, for which the ant, of the genus *Cataglyphis*, is famous. This particular ant had kept track of its distance and direction from the starting point, its home, as it traveled. The march home was based upon the distance and directional information calculated en route. Path integration is found in a wide range of vertebrate animals (for a review, see Etienne & Jeffery, 2004) and invertebrate animals: ants (Wehner, Michel, & Antonsen, 1996; Wehner & Srinivasan, 1981, 2003; Wehner & Wehner, 1990); bees (von Frisch, 1967); spiders (Görner, 1958; Moller & Görner, 1994); and fiddler crabs (Zeil, 1998), among others.

Von Frisch (1967), famous for describing the dance "language" of the bees, also described examples of path integration in bees. The bee dance proved a handy measure because it was equivalent to a verbal indication of the direction and distance to a food source. In the experiments, an experimental hive was set up on one side of the spur of a mountain. Foragers were trained to go around the jutting spur, making two sides of a triangle to get to the food site and back. Their dances indicated neither the first leg nor the second leg of the journey to the food. Instead, it was the vector sum of the two legs, thus indicating that they had integrated the two legs of the journey.

Global Vector and Search Pattern

In a series of field experiments, Wehner and Srinivasan (1981) revealed two components in the desert ant's search for home. Experimentally, the ant typically comes to a reliable food source (feeder). The homing motivation is induced by giving the ant a small crumb of cookie to grasp with its mandibles; the ant then runs home. The straight run home is based on the calculated vector from the present location to the nest, known as the global vector. The global vector, however, is rarely accurate enough to lead the ant to its actual home. Errors that accumulate with travel mean that the tip of the global vector points to the neighborhood of the nest but typically not the nest itself. A search system is thus necessary to complement the global vector.

The search system for finding the nest also relies on path integration. The ant makes a sharp turn at the end of its global vector to initiate the search. In searching, it makes larger and larger loops, occasionally returning to the starting point of its search (Wehner & Srinivasan, 1981). The frequent returns to the start of search necessitate path integration. Experimentally, the use of path integration is demonstrated by displacing the ant. If the ant is displaced before it runs its global vector, the vector remains the same. That is, the ant heads off in a parallel course, in the direction and distance that would take it home had it not been displaced. Similarly, the ant can be displaced in the midst of its search pattern. Upon release, it behaves as if it had not been displaced; its search is now centered on a point that reflects the distance and direction from which it had been displaced.

The search behavior makes sense for a searcher who might miss the small nest entrance even at close range. In this case, a systematic outward spiral would mean a good chance of missing the nest and never finding it. Instead, the pattern of searching resembles what is theoretically predicted to be optimal for an animal whose navigation and nest detecting abilities are not perfect. Wehner and Srinivasan thus provide a functional explanation of search behavior. Although not recognized as such, this work contributes to the behavioral ecology of animal cognition.

In these servomechanisms, the execution of the global vector is triggered by the homing motivation brought about by the finding of food. The search pattern is initiated when the global vector has been run. The triggers or occasion setters for these servomechanisms are not external landmark cues. For these ants, the sky and ground typically look much the same wherever it forages. Many other servomechanisms, however, have landmarks as occasion setters (reviewed later).

Telling Direction: Sky-Compass

The sky-compass is the major mechanism for compass direction in insects (Rossel, 1987; Rossel & Wehner, 1986; Wehner, 1994). The term "sun-compass" is often used, but this term is misleading in that the direction of the sun is only a small part of the source for direction. Insects perceive the pattern of polarized light in the sky. Wehner (1994) provides a detailed summary; here are a few highlights.

Desert ants, honeybees, and crickets have been used to study the sky-compass because each offers its own advantages. The ants move on the ground and their movements can be readily tracked, something that is not true of flying bees. Honeybees, on the other hand, do a dance that indicates the direction and distance to a food source (von Frisch, 1967), so that their representation of a vector can be sampled by watching them dance at the hive. Crickets are sufficiently large insects and are the preferred species for neurophysiological recordings (Labhart, 1988, 1996).

Polarized light results from sunlight going through the Earth's atmosphere. The pattern of polarization depends on the direction of the sun and moves as the sun moves. Using the pattern of polarization in the entire skylight has functional advantages over using the sun alone. The sun may sometimes be covered, while parts of the sky may be seen under all but overcast conditions. Furthermore, the sun fills a small part of the sky, while polarized light fills the entire sky. Not surprisingly, the compass is more accurate when the entire sky can be used (Wehner, 1994).

The sky-compass in insects is characterized by a private channel (Wehner, 1994), a specialized module. It has its own receptors, in the eyes and in the brain, and its own computational principles (Rossel & Wehner, 1986). Specialized receptors at the dorsal (top) rim of the eye feed information to wide-field interneurons sensitive to the direction of polarized light. The interneurons work in three opponent-process systems (Labhart, 1988, 1996) analogous to the two opponent-process channels in color vision in bees (Backhaus, 1991). A polarization-sensitive interneuron is excited by polarized light from one direction but inhibited by light from an orthogonal direction. The opponent processes serve to neutralize overall level of illumination. A higher level of overall illumination would not increase a directional signal because it increases both the excitation and the inhibition of an interneuron. In this way, the system is most sensitive to the direction of polarized light and not to overall illumination.

Telling Direction: Landmarks

Cataglyphis travels typically (but not always) over barren ground devoid of Earth-based directional cues. Not so for honeybees, who may fly over landmark-rich terrain. Classic experiments showed that foraging bees use large-scale landmarks to tell direction. von Frisch and Lindauer (1954) set feeders out for bees along routes with prominent continuous landmarks, along a road, a shoreline, or a line of trees. Overnight, the hive was moved to a different location that had the same kind of prominent landmarks but running in a different direction from the hive. Thus, the feeder direction according to the sky-compass conflicted with the direction according to landmarks. Most bees relied on the landmarks to specify direction. The results were replicated more recently by Dyer and Gould (1981, 1983).

Thus, continuous Earth-based cues trump the sky-compass. The continuity and large directional discrepancy between sky-based and Earth-based cues are both important factors. von Frisch and Lindauer's bees did not follow a single salient landmark (a large tree or clump of trees) when it conflicted with sky-compass cues by a large amount; in this case, the sky-compass was followed. Similarly, desert ants (*C. bicolor*) follow the sky-compass rather the directional dictates of a single prominent landmark (a large, black board; Wehner, 1970). With smaller directional discrepancies between landmarks and sky-compass (7.5° to 15°), however, honeybees use both landmarks and sky-compass cues (Chittka & Geiger, 1995). In servomechanistic terms then, both sky-compass and landmarks can set the standard for the directional component of path integration.

Computing Distance Traveled: Odometry

Odometry, or the estimation of distance traveled, has been studied in honeybees and desert ants (*C. fortis*). The story differs for the two species and this probably reflects the different functional demands of flying versus walking. In honeybees, optic flow plays a major role in odometry. Optic flow is the systematic motion created on its eyes as the bee flies. An older hypothesis is that the bee estimates distance flown from energy expended (von Frisch, 1967). Esch and Burns (1995, 1996) recently put this hypothesis in doubt by having bees forage from a feeder on a hot-air balloon. The authors examined the reported distance from the foragers' dances as the balloon was lifted up in the air. In contradiction to the energy hypothesis, the higher the balloon, the *less* was the distance that foragers reported. Their interpretation is that flying to a higher goal results in less optic flow, which translates to less perceived distance traveled.

The bulk of work on odometry comes from Srinivasan, Zhang, and Bidwell (1997) and Srinivasan, Zhang, Lehrer, and T. S. Collett (1996) used long narrow tunnels covered by transparent Perspex. Bees were lured into the tunnel to reach a feeder offering sugar water. The feeder was set at a constant distance inside the tunnel. To offer optic flow, the sides or bottom (or both) of the tunnel was lined with visual texture (random black-and-white patterns or vertical black-and-white stripes). After suitable training, bees were tested individually in a new but identical looking tunnel with the feeder removed. The bees searched at about the correct distance from the entrance into the tunnel. Searching consisted of flying back and forth around the area where the feeder should have been.

Experimental manipulations indicated a major role for optic flow in odometry (Srinivasan et al., 1997). No systematic effects were found when head wind or tail wind was added or when the vertical stripes on the walls were widened or narrowed. Thus, bees were unlikely to be measuring energy expenditure, total time of flying, or number of stripes passed. Use of optic flow predicts that the width of the tunnel should be crucial. A wider tunnel than that used in training produces less optic flow as the walls are farther from the flying bee. Conversely, a narrower tunnel produces more optic flow. If the amount of optic flow is used in odometry, then changing the width of the test tunnel should change the distance into the tunnel at which the bees search most. This prediction was confirmed (Srinivasan et al., 1997). Furthermore, having some optic flow was necessary for odometry in the tunnel. If the bees were trained and tested in a tunnel with axial stripes (which run horizontally along the wall), then they did not estimate distance at all. Instead, these bees just flew back and forth from one end of the tunnel to the other.

What does the optic flow encountered in a short but narrow tunnel represent in terms of flying in a normal outdoor environment? This question can be addressed by watching the dance of the bees trained to forage in a tunnel. They communicate a distance that is much larger than the 6 or 8 m that they have flown in the tunnel (Esch, Zhang, Srinivasan, & Tautz, 2001). Waggle duration in the waggle dance indicates distance to the food source. After a 6-m flight in a 20-cm wide tunnel, bees dance to indicate a distance over 100 m. A calibration study shows that each millisecond of waggle corresponds to about 18 degrees of visual flow (Srinivasan, Zhang, Altwein, & Tautz, 2000).

Si, Srinivasan, and Zhang (2003) found that the dance behavior after a trip to a tunnel is robust to variations in the spatial frequency and contrast of the patterns. Although they found significant effects for contrast level, the similarities outweigh the differences. Even at 20% contrast, bees performed waggle dances of substantial duration. Chittka and Tautz (2003) found that dance behavior after a trip to a tunnel was driven by contrast in the stripes to the "green" receptors, but not by chromatic contrast or overall brightness contrast. About half of all visual receptors are "green" receptors with peak sensitivity at 540 nm (Bernard & Wehner, 1980; Horridge, 1999; Menzel & Blakers, 1976). Again, a low level of 20% contrast was sufficient to drive the waggle dancing and, by implication, the odometer. The reliance of the odometer on "green" receptors is consistent with other forms of motion perception in bees, which are similarly color blind and rely only on the "green" receptors (Lehrer, 1994, 1996).

Odometry is not perfect. The bees do not search at a precise spot but fly back and forth in a region. One measure of the spread of search can be obtained from the standard deviation of the location of the first four turns. The spread is proportional to the distance being estimated, thus fitting Weber's law (Cheng, Srinivasan, & Zhang, 1999). This scalar property is analogous to the Weber's law found in vertebrate interval timing (Gibbon, 1977).

In servomechanistic terms, a measure of amount of optic flow serves as both the standard and the input data (for comparing against the standard) in odometry. Stimulus conditions or contextual cues help to determine the odometric standard that is retrieved for the servomechanism. Honeybees can reduce scalar uncertainty by starting the odometer from some obvious landmark along the route, thus shortening the distance they have to estimate. Evidence for such "resetting" was found by Srinivasan et al. (1997) and M. Collett, Harland, & T. S. Collett (2002). Here, then, is another role for landmarks. They can set the occasion for using a shorter standard for odometry, thus increasing the accuracy of performance.

In desert ants, the means of odometry have yet to be fully determined. Optic flow on the surface plays some role. Ronacher and Wehner (1995) tested odometry in *C. fortis* by moving a textured strip underneath a transparent Perspex walkway across which the ants were trained to forage. Thus, while the visual texture moved, the ants were not moved. The ants' distance estimate was influenced by the optic flow to a small but statistically significant extent. Optic flow to the sides, on the other hand, seems to have no effect on distance estimation (Ronacher, Gallizzi, Wohlgemuth, & Wehner, 2000). A clever experiment tested whether step counting was used for distance estimation. Ants were trained to move up and down hills or on a flat surface, with both arrangements inside channels (Wohlgemuth, Ronacher, & Wehner, 2001). If step counting influences odometry, then ants going out on hills but returning on flat surface should overestimate the horizontal distance. No such effect was found. Instead, the hill-traveling ants returned the same horizontal distance as ants that traveled out and back on a flat surface. This study showed instead that ants can path integrate in the third dimension, somehow accounting for the inclination of the surface.

Path Integration in Fiddler Crabs

Fiddler crabs of the genus *Uca* live on intertidal mudflats, sandflats, and sometimes mangroves (Zeil & Layne, 2002). Males are well known for an enlarged claw, which they often wave. The animals live in burrows, which are important resources. Burrows are useful for molting, mating, and escaping from predators. The crabs come out of the burrow during low tide to forage. A crab needs to have the ability to return to the burrow quickly, in case a predator threatens, or a rival conspecific approaches its burrow. Path integration plays a large role in this navigation.

Because of foreshortening, the burrow is not visible when the crab is more than about 20 cm away (Zeil & Layne, 2002). A view of the burrow, however, is not necessary for homing. When the burrow is covered experimentally, crabs still home (Layne, Barnes, & Duncan, 2003a; Zeil, 1998). The homing crab searches frantically in the vicinity of its covered burrow. While away from its burrow, the crab usually aligns itself sideways to the line connecting its present position to the burrow. It does this even when a barrier is interposed between it and the burrow. The crab thus shows on-line computation of the direction to its burrow. The functions for this alignment may be twofold. Crabs move sideways. Keeping this orientation to the burrow thus speeds up the trip home by eliminating the need to turn. Also, by keeping a constant orientation, the same part of the eye views the scene around the burrow. This might facilitate visual processing, for instance, in spotting conspecifics that go near the burrow. Hemmi and Zeil

(2003a, 2003c) found that a key determinant of when (and if) a fiddler crab dashed home was the distance between a dummy "conspecific" pulled on a string and the subject crab's burrow. Judging the distance of a conspecific to one's burrow might be facilitated by viewing the burrow area with the same part of the eye. Hemmi and Zeil (2003b) proposed a model using multiple neural filters, by which the crabs might extract the distance between the intruder and the crab's own nest.

As in *Cataglyphis* ants, direct evidence for path integration comes from experiments in which crabs were displaced before the return trip. The manipulation is done when the subject walks onto a piece of sandpaper attached to a thin thread. The paper can be pulled, thus displacing the crab. The displaced crab then heads home in the same direction as undisplaced crabs, that is, in the direction that would take it home had it not been displaced (figure 10.2). It does this even when a prominent landmark is right at its burrow (Layne et al., 2003a; Zeil, 1998).

In a more detailed analysis of path integrational performance, Layne, Barnes, and Duncan (2003b) manipulated conditions under which the crabs performed. Basically, the crabs cope with or account for rotations but not translations. In estimating distance, the crabs are also fooled by a slippery patch over which they have to walk. That is, when they slip, they underestimate the distance home. This implicates some kind of step counting (proprioception or efferent command) in estimating distance.

In this brief space, I have not done justice to the richness of this work. The fiddler crab is a wonderful system for examining path integration (and other behaviors, too). Natural ecology, readily observable and recordable behavior, the possibility of experimental manipulations, and the potential for comparative research all make this system attractive. And the results so far have proved to be interesting.

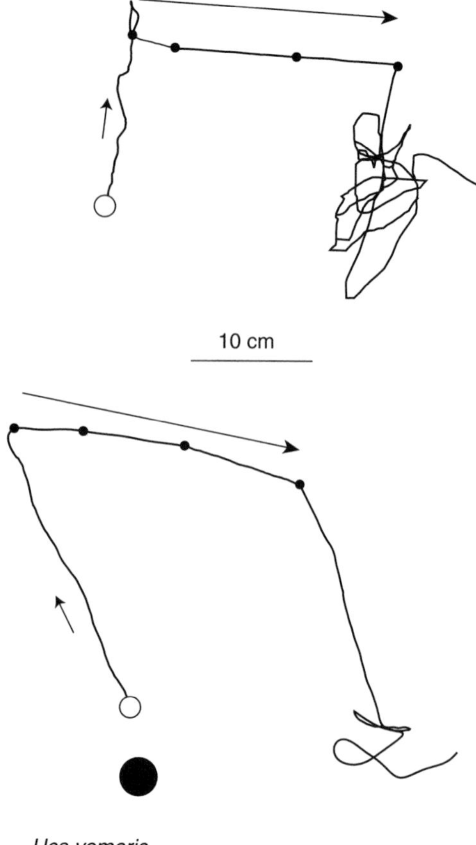

Figure 10.2. Path integration in fiddler crabs, *Uca lactea annulipes* and *Uca vomeris*. Shown is burrow entrance (*open circle*), landmark (*filled circle*), outward path (*line beside short arrow*), path of crabs as they sat on a piece of sandpaper and were pulled (dots every 200 ms) (*line joined by circles*), and homeward path (*unmarked line*). (Adapted from "Homing in Fiddler Crabs (*Uca lactea annulipes* and *Uca vomeris:* Ocypodidae)," by J. Zeil, 1998, *Journal of Comparative Physiology A, 183,* p. 373. Copyright 1998 by Springer-Verlag. Adapted with permission.)

Learning and Path Integration

By just about any definition of learning, path integration constitutes learning. The experience of the outbound journey must drive the march home. More specifically, metric information from the outbound journey is required. Furthermore, path integration has to be largely one-trial learning. A desert ant that has not learned enough from the current outbound trip will not get home, and thus will not have a second learning trial. The animal should be tuned primarily to the current outbound trip, and not previous trips. M. Collett, T. S. Collett, Chameron, and Wehner (2003) tested the primacy of the most recent outbound trip in *C. fortis*. For a minimum of 4 days, ants were trained to follow an L-shaped route to a feeder. The second leg of the route was lined with landmarks. On the crucial test, the outbound route was altered, for example, by shortening the first leg. The usual landmarks were there on the second leg. Thus, landmarks and all previous outbound journeys dictated one vector home, while the global vector computed from the current outbound trip dictated a different vector home. Ants overwhelmingly followed the global vector from the latest outbound trip.

But both the global vector and the search pattern can be modified by experience over a number of journeys, which is the reason the qualifiers "largely" and "primarily" were in the previous paragraph. The experimental manipulation to induce this learning is to displace the ant before letting it run home (Cheng & Wehner, 2002; M. Collett, T. S. Collett, & Wehner, 1999; Wehner, Gallizzi, Frei, & Vesely, 2002). M. Collett et al. (1999) trained ants to go to a feeder in a channel that constrained their movement along the channel. Ants were displaced to a different channel to go home in a direction that differed from the 180° reversal of the outbound direction. Trained ants were then tested after the outbound journey on open ground. Their direction home reflected a compromise between the direction home based on all their outbound journeys and the direction home based on all their homebound journeys. Wehner et al. (2002) trained ants without any constraining channels. The ants came to a feeder over open ground and went home over open ground. Before the return trip, however, they were displaced (figure 10.3). After the displacement experience, both the global vector and the search pattern were adjusted, and the adjustment was noticeable on the second or third trip (i.e., after one or two learning trials). The global vector was deflected to compensate for the displacement, although only a small compensation, about 10°, was made. The search pattern showed a systematic bias, again consistent with the displacement. Normally, a search pattern is centered at the starting point, with equal amounts of searching on either side of the global vector. After displacement experience, ants searched much more on the side where the nest was after displacement.

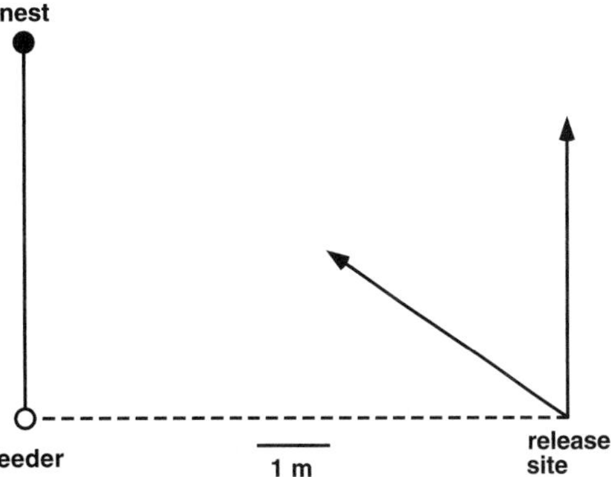

Figure 10.3. Illustration of one experimental paradigm from Wehner et al. (2002). Desert ants (*Cataglyphis fortis*) came from their nest to a feeder 5 m away. They were then displaced perpendicular to the nest-feeder direction (to release site) before being given a piece of cookie to take home. Ants were identified individually and given repeated training in this regimen. Arrows illustrate theoretical directions. If the ants rely only on the information from outbound trips, they should head in the feeder-nest direction, striking a parallel course (*vertical arrow*). If the ants rely only on past homebound vectors, they should take the diagonal arrow shown. The ants did neither but struck a compromise. The direction of their global vector was displaced some 10 degrees counterclockwise on average from the nest-feeder direction. Their search pattern was also asymmetrical, being about 80 degrees to the left of the vertical arrow shown. These patterns were evident by the third training trial.

Cheng and Wehner (2002) used the displacement manipulation in the distance dimension. Ants traveled in constraining channels. They traveled 6 m to a feeder in one channel and then returned in another identical looking channel. Control animals returned 6 m home, while experimental animals returned 12 m home. After five training trials, the ants were tested in a long channel. The first point at which the ants turned back in the channel provided an estimate of the length of the global vector. This did not differ between experimental and control animals, both averaging about 7 m. During subsequent searching in the channel, however, the experimental animals drifted farther and farther from the start (and toward the nest) as the test went on. The control animals showed no such bias. Thus, search behavior had adjusted in the experimental ants as a result of the experimental displacements. Altogether, these studies indicate malleability in both the global vector and the search pattern.

ROUTE FOLLOWING

The global vector of path integration, as already mentioned, is inaccurate. Error in the system accumulates with the length of travel. If the journey can be divided into shorter segments, one leading to another, accuracy can be much improved. This is what routes based on encountered landmarks do. Even if the route so constructed is not the most direct, it is likely to be the most successful and efficient. We can think of each piece of the route as an occasion for a particular servomechanism to come into play. The stimulus conditions set the occasion for a servomechanism, whose operation is typically based on different cues from the occasion setting cues. What follows are variations on this theme.

Early displacement experiments on *Cataglyphis bicolor* in Israel suggest that these ants use landmarks (Wehner, 1968). Foragers displaced a few meters from near their nest in a direction opposite to their usual foraging direction can nevertheless head in a homeward direction. Most nests of *C. fortis* are out on the open plain, where the nearest landmarks, bushes on the salt pan, are tens of meters away. Some nests, however, are found among the scrub, in which the bushes can serve as guides for plotting a route home. Examples of such stereotypical routes are shown in figure 10.4A. A highly thermophilic (heat-loving) Australian desert ant, the red honey ant *Melophorus bagoti*, lives in habitats with many bushes and even some trees, characteristic of good parts of arid central Australia. The behavior of *M. bagoti* has been little studied. Our preliminary studies indicate that *M. bagoti* also follows stereotypical routes (figure 10.4B). In the literature, the term "local vector" has been applied to the ants' performance, while the term "sensorimotor vector" has been applied to the bees' behavior. My view is that both these terms, along with beaconing (heading toward a recognized object), all reflect the concept of an occasion for the operation of a servomechanism.

Desert Ants' Local Vectors

Several examples of local vectors have been published (M. Collett, T. S. Collett, Bisch, & Wehner, 1998; T. S. Collett, M. Collett, & Wehner, 2001). I present just one example to illustrate the concept. In one set of experiments, the ants had to make an L-shaped journey to a feeder (M. Collett et al., 1998). The first leg was north over open ground, but the second leg was west in a channel in the ground (figure 10.5). The ants could see the sky from inside the channel, but they had to follow the route from the entrance of the channel to the end in order to reach the food. On the return journey, they had to make a similar L-shaped path in reverse, coming out of the channel first, and then turning south to head home over open ground.

After suitable training, ants were displaced far from the training grounds before their return trips under manipulated conditions. On these tests, the channel en route home might be shortened, or it might be turned so that the ants traveled northeast or southeast to get out of the channel instead of the usual east. Under all these conditions, the ants coming out of the channel tended to walk south for a short distance before heading in the true direction home, the direction according to their global vector. The authors called these short southward runs local vectors. They are local in the sense of being triggered by particular stimulus conditions, in this case coming out of a channel on the way home. What is triggered is a servomechanism, in this case using the sky-compass to head in a southerly direction.

If landmarks are dense enough, a sequence of such local vectors can guide the ant home. The behaviors shown in figure 10.4 probably consist of a sequence of local vectors. In executing local vectors, the global vector must be suppressed, at least temporarily. But the results of M. Collett et al. (1998) indicate that the global vector continues to be calculated as the ant follows a local vector. When needed, the global vector can guide behavior again.

Bees' and Wasps' Sensorimotor Vectors

In bees and wasps, the term *sensorimotor vector* was coined by T. S. Collett and colleagues (T. S. Collett & Baron, 1995; T. S. Collett, Baron, & Sellen, 1996; T. S. Collett & Rees, 1997). As with the local vector, a particular stimulus situation (the sensory part of the term) serves to trigger a vector (servomechanism).

A clear example comes from one of my experiments (Cheng, 1999a, Experiment 1). Free flying honeybees entered a lab and flew to a table in search of sugar water. On the table was a wall of

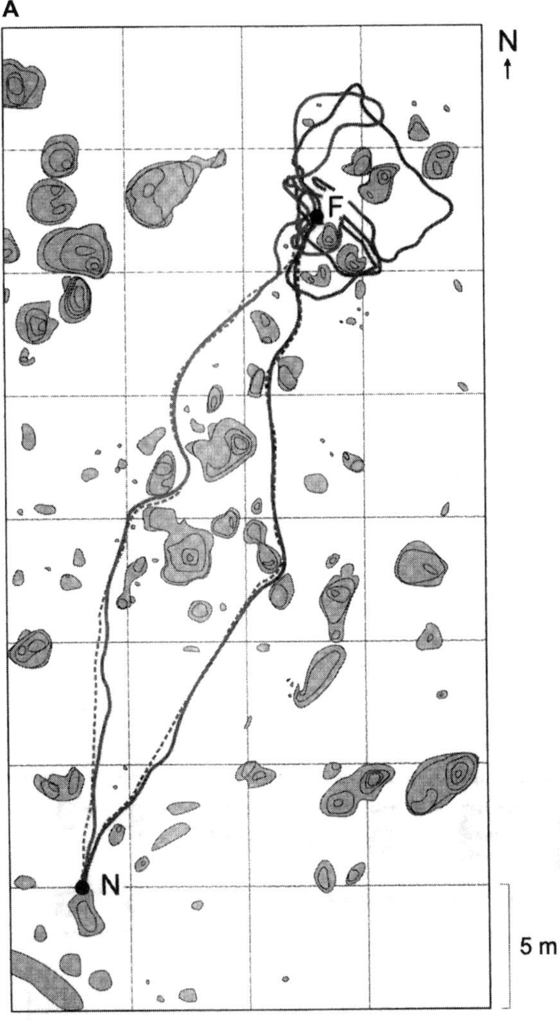

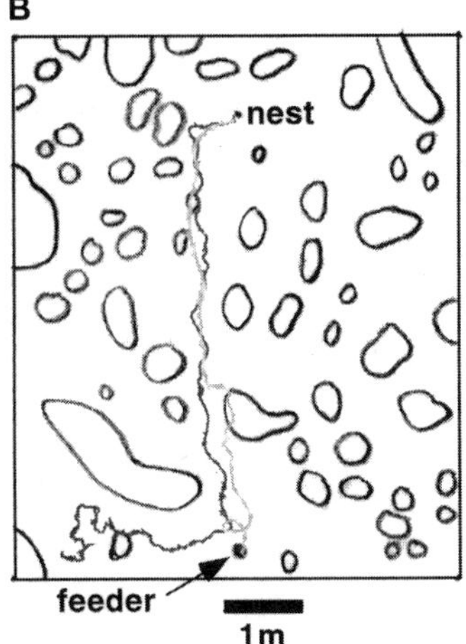

Figure 10.4. Route following in desert ants. (*A*) Homeward paths of two *Cataglyphis fortis* ants. *Dotted lines* show ants returning from the food site. *Solid lines* show ants displaced from near their nest to the food site. (*B*) Two paths of a red honey ant (*Melophorus bagoti*). In the lighter path, the animal was released at the feeder at which it was caught. In the darker path, the animal was displaced by 2.4 m to the left before release. In both panels, the irregular shapes represent plants. (Part *A* from "Visual Navigation in Insects: Coupling of Egocentric and Geocentric Information," by R. Wehner, B. Michel, and P. Antonsen, 1996, *Journal of Experimental Biology, 199,* p. 136. Copyright 1996 by the Company of Biologists. Reprinted with permission. Part *B* from K. Cheng, unpublished data.)

yellow blocks with a gap in it. The reward stood in front of the gap. On approach, the bees typically headed toward a part of the wall, and then flew parallel and close to the wall until they reached the gap. Flying along the wall is an example of a sensorimotor vector. The visual cues stemming from being near the wall set the occasion for the servomechanism of maintaining flight in a direction parallel to the wall.

T. S. Collett and Rees (1997) analyzed sensorimotor vectors in bees and wasps. The insects searched for an inconspicuous dish of sugar water near a single prominent landmark (cylinder). They first approached the landmark, and not the dish. When they were near the landmark, they then typically veered off on a sensorimotor vector toward the dish. In doing so, they tended to keep a view of the landmark on a particular part of the eye. Interestingly, in evolutionary simulations of this task on computer, such a two-part strategy (approach landmark followed by sensorimotor vector) evolved to solve this problem (Dale & T. S. Collett, 2001).

Another way to investigate sensorimotor vectors is to require the bees to execute them. T. S. Collett and Baron (1995) had bees enter an apparatus. The bees then had to fly one vector to enter a

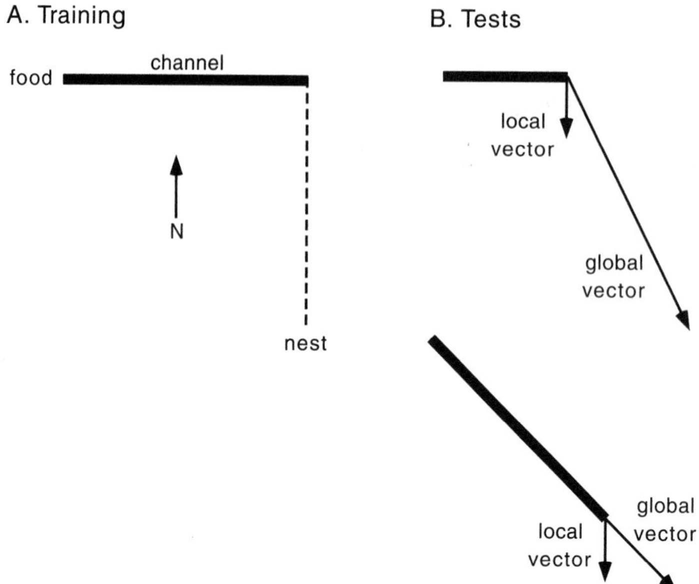

Figure 10.5. Illustration of an experimental paradigm from M. Collett et al. (1998). (*A*) Desert ants (*C. fortis*) were trained to go to a food source by heading north to the mouth of a constraining channel, and then heading west inside the channel to the food. (*B*) After sufficient training, the ant might be displaced far away to a modified channel for a (homebound) test. In the two examples, the channel was shortened (*top*) or rotated (*bottom*). The local vector refers to the usual heading direction upon coming out of the channel during training (south). The global vector is the calculated home direction according to continuing path integration. The ants usually took the local vector for 2 or 3 m before reverting back to using the global vector (which would now be different from what is shown because a local vector had been traveled).

second compartment. Another vector was required in the second compartment to reach a reward. For sensory context or cues, patterns were provided on the walls opposite to the entrance in the form of stripes at some orientation. For example, the first compartment might have 45° stripes, and the bees had to turn 45° right and fly 85 cm; the second compartment would have 135° stripes, and the bees had to turn 45° left and fly 85 cm. When presented with an ambiguous stimulus, for example, 90° stripes, bees averaged the learned vectors (T. S. Collett & Baron, 1995) using vector averaging (T. S. Collett et al., 1996). The entire vectors were averaged, distance and direction components together (figure 10.6). This stands in contrast to the averaging of vectors to landmarks, in which distance and direction components are separately averaged, in bees (Cheng, 1998) and pigeons (Cheng, 1994).

We might ask why bees would average sensorimotor vectors? Would it not be adaptive to adopt

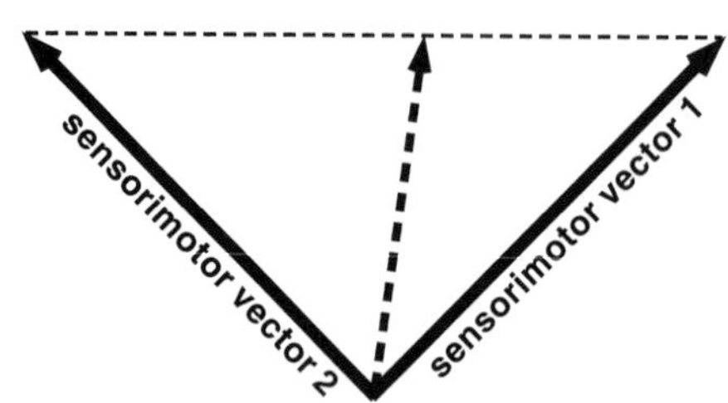

Figure 10.6. Vector averaging of sensorimotor vectors (T. S. Collett et al., 1996). The bee has learned to execute sensorimotor vector 1 to one stimulus pattern, and sensorimotor vector 2 to another stimulus pattern. If an intermediate stimulus pattern is presented, the bee executes a vector that is a weighted vector average of the two learned vectors. A vector average would be a vector to some point on the line segment connecting the tips of the two learned vectors, with the dashed vector being an example.

one of the learned vectors in an all-or-none fashion? Sometimes this strategy is adopted when contextual cues outside of the apparatus bias the bees to choose one sensorimotor vector over another (T. S. Collett, Fauria, Dale, & Baron, 1997). But averaging sensorimotor vectors may increase the versatility of such memories. This is explained in the section on map-like behavior.

The term "sensorimotor" might bring to mind the notion of a stimulus-response connection. I believe that this interpretation is a mistake. As I have been arguing, occasion setting is a far more apt description. If we look at the motor end, the behaviors are decidedly not single responses, such as a key peck or a button press. Rather, the behaviors require continuous servomechanistic control. Thus, an ant has to use its sky-compass to keep heading in a southerly direction, or a bee needs to maintain a flight parallel to a wall. The stimulus or context conditions pass the control on to a particular kind of servomechanism.

Beacons

Another form of route behavior is approaching a recognized, typically prominent object, called a beacon (Cheng, 2000a). Insects head to large beacons (e.g., tents, Chittka, Geiger, & Kunze, 1995) and small beacons (e.g., cylinders, T. S. Collett & Rees, 1997; Graham, Fauria, & T. S. Collett, 2003). We can again see beaconing as an occasion for a servomechanism. The stimulus conditions that set the occasion for beaconing involve sighting the beacon. The behavior called forth is the servomechanism of approaching the beacon. When honeybees are trained to a feeder at a tent, a substantial proportion would head to that beacon even if it is placed at a different distance from the usual training distance (thus, conflicting with odometric information; Chittka et al., 1995). Dale and Collett's (2001) evolutionary simulation of navigational strategies found that beacon strategies arose readily in artificial evolution. A combination of beaconing followed by a sensorimotor vector proved to be a successful strategy that most often evolved. These results suggest that breaking down the problem into two separate modules (servomechanisms of beacon and sensorimotor vector) is simpler by an "evolutionary metric"—simpler than computations to figure out from afar the correct direction to head directly to the target.

Beaconing behavior might be further subdivided into a series of segments, each controlled by a particular view of the beacon. Judd and T. S. Collett (1998) lured wood ants to a beacon on a flat surface. The beacon was either an upright or an inverted cone. The reward was at the bottom of the cone. As the ants approached an inverted cone, the bottom edge of the cone projected to a constant location on the eyes. As the ants approached the upright cone, however, the edges of the cone projected more and more laterally on the eyes. Judd and Collett measured the retinal position of the edge as the ant approached. Plotting the durations through which edge positions on the retina were maintained, a number of distinct peaks were found. This suggests that the ants were matching to a sequence of images, each specifying a particular retinal position for the edge of the cone. Hence, approaching a beacon really amounts to matching multiple images in series, a series of servomechanisms strung together.

Beacons might be natural attractions for navigating insects. Graham et al. (2003) placed food for wood ants at one end of an arena and a black cylinder as the sole salient object. The cylinder was not directly on the route to the food. The ants would first head toward the cylinder and then veer off toward the food. Thus, getting to a beacon, and then heading off from the beacon, was the preferred route. Interestingly, once this pattern of behavior was established, the ants followed a similar path even when the beacon was removed or displaced. That is, they headed first to where the beacon usually was and then veered off toward the food. This shows that some cues other than the beacon itself had been registered and were now used like a beacon. Clearly, some form of associative learning had taken place. Beaconing behavior coupled with associative learning might facilitate navigation by breaking down the task into easier subtasks, a strategy that characterizes all route learning. Having salient beacons on the route also helps to increase the chances of relocating the route after displacement.

Route Planning in Jumping Spiders

Bees and ants are central place foragers. They return home after foraging. They also show a good deal of foraging site fidelity, heading off time and again in a similar direction (Wehner, Harkness, & Schmid-Hempel, 1983). Stereotyped routes may often be used under these circumstances. Other arthropods hunt for a living. The circumstances surrounding each hunt differ from those of other hunts, and flexibility and route planning may be required. A spectacular example is found in jumping spiders of the genus *Portia*.

Jumping spiders typically do not catch prey in webs but hunt prey, including other spiders. *Portia* is characterized by a pair of high-resolution eyes, placed front and center (anterior medial eyes; Forster, 1982; Jackson & Pollard, 1996; Land, 1972). Other pairs of more laterally placed eyes function as motion detectors. The anterior medial eyes work like telescopes, but like a fovea, this telescopic vision has a narrow range of about 2° width. This means that building up a perceptual picture of the world requires scanning and integrating across multiple views.

Aside from navigational prowess, *Portia* exhibits a number of clever hunting behaviors (Jackson & Pollard, 1996; Wilcox & Jackson, 1998). For example, it can mimic the vibratory mating signals of the male spiders of other species, luring out unsuspecting prey. Sometimes, this aggressive mimicry is produced by trial and error. *Portia* broadcasts a wide array of signals until it finds one that lures the prey. When walking onto another spider's web, *Portia* may use an irregular gait, making the vibrations on the web seem like mere noise. Wilcox and Jackson call other methods smokescreen tactics. *Portia* may move on a web only when the wind is blowing, masking its footsteps with the wind-blown vibrations. It may even create its own smokescreen, such as by setting the web into vibration with a violent movement. During the reverberations, its footsteps are harder to detect.

Sometimes, *Portia* cannot catch a sensitive prey by walking across its web. Detours are then necessary. A detour might take the hunter out of view of the target web, to arrive above the web (Jackson & Pollard, 1996; Jackson & Wilcox, 1993; Wilcox & Jackson, 1998). The jumping spider then drops beside the web and, with a deft swing, attacks the prey on the web. In nature, detours may be over 1 m in length and take over an hour to execute.

Portia's ability to plan routes has been tested in laboratory tasks (Tarsitano & Andrew, 1999; Tarsitano & Jackson, 1997). Tarsitano and Jackson tested *P. fimbriata*, a jumping spider found in Queensland, Australia. Each spider was tested only once and hence faced a novel problem. The subject was placed on top of a cylinder serving as the start platform. From there, it could see a prey (a dead spider) in one of two dishes. Each dish was hanging on a "branch," and the branch was connected to a twisting route of branches that eventually ended in a trunk standing on the ground. To get to the prey, the jumping spider had to come down from the start platform, in the process losing sight of its prey, and pick the correct trunk to climb. The spiders chose the correct trunk at well above chance levels. They did this even if the path to the correct trunk went past the incorrect trunk.

Tarsitano and Andrew tested female *P. labiata*, a species found in Sri Lanka. The subject was again placed on a starting platform for a test where it saw one prey. To the left and right of the prey were branch-and-trunk routes. When both routes were complete, unbroken paths to the prey, the jumping spiders chose each route equally often. If, however, one of the routes had a gap in the middle, so that it provided no unbroken path to the prey, then the spiders avoided that path and preferentially chose the connected path. Examination of the scanning movements of the spiders revealed that they tended to travel the path that they had scanned the most. This was true whether both routes were connected or only one. With only one connected route, *Portia* initially scanned the gap a lot. But as scanning continued, it scanned the connected route more.

Portia's detour behaviors are clearly dependent on its visual abilities. Finding a suitable route requires looking across an expanse of space. *Portia*'s primary eyes have a narrow range, which means that an overview of the visual world must be integrated from temporally successive inputs. It is not clear how this is done. Tarsitano and Andrew suggest that scanning might produce secondary goals for *Portia*. Again, the problem might be divided into simpler subproblems. A secondary goal does not have to be immediately reachable. Getting to the secondary goal might require further subgoals to the secondary goal, and so on. Visual scanning might be the means of establishing such subgoals. Secondary goals might function as attractive beacons toward which jumping spiders head, much like prominent cylinders for Graham et al.'s (2003) wood ants.

Much about how *Portia* navigates needs to be investigated. Their abilities make them an interesting system for study. I have put them in this section on routes, but others might think that they exhibit map-like behavior as well. Future research might address this and other issues.

Discussion

Route-based behavior is ubiquitous in arthropods. If a route can be followed, arthropods seem to prefer it over long-range path integration (global vector) or map-like behavior (which I discuss next). Visual landmarks are typically incorporated into routes, both in triggering and in guiding servomechanisms. In commenting on this use of landmarks, T. S. Collett and M. Collett (2002) conclude that "the principal role of a landmark might be to instruct an insect to perform a particular action, rather than telling the insect where it is within a large-scale coordinate system" (p. 551). In this way, Collett and Collett liken landmarks to signposts.

To reemphasize, in all the examples, the behavior signposted is never a single, monophasic action. Rather, the behaviors signposted are servomechanisms. Action is to be continuously controlled by a set of cues, whether it is to keep heading south or to keep heading toward a recognized object. The action runs until the stimulus conditions arise for adopting the next servomechanism. The stimulus contexts serve as occasion setters for passing control from one servomechanism to another. Route following strings together servomechanisms to do the navigational job.

We should also not identify route learning with inflexible behavior. The jumping spider *Portia* can plan new routes to a prey. And in central place foragers, routes have salient points (e.g., beacons), which may be reached from different positions. Once on a route, the chances of successful navigation are high. This increases flexibility in route use. Having a number of routes can also increase flexibility (Shettleworth, 1998, chapter 7).

LANDMARK-BASED IMAGE MATCHING

If landmarks are available for pinpointing a location, arthropods will use them, as do birds and mammals (for a review, see Cheng & Spetch, 1998). Conceptually, this is another servomechanism or control process (Cheng, 1995, 2000a), one that comes into play in the last stage of the journey. The idea is to move so as to reduce the discrepancy between two "images": what the surrounding landmarks look like now and what is remembered about how the surrounding landmarks appear at the target (the memory or standard of the servomechanism). The use of experimentally provided landmarks was first demonstrated in desert ants (Wehner & Räber, 1979) and honeybees (Cartwright & T. S. Collett, 1982, 1983). It has now been extended to wood ants (Durier, Graham, & T. S. Collett, 2003; Graham, Durier, & T. S. Collett, 2004) and spread to robotics (Franz, Schölkopf, Mallot, & Bülthoff, 1998) and a theoretical analysis of outdoor scenes (Zeil, Hofmann, & Chahl, 2003).

In "image" matching, the idea is that the insect tries to recover the view that it has previously encountered at the target location, a view based on a retinal code (Cheng, 2000a; T. S. Collett & Zeil, 1998). "Image" is meant to be vague here because different models posit different aspects of the image for use in matching. Thus, Cartwright and T. S. Collett's (1983) models for bees use independent elemental pieces (corresponding to landmarks and gaps between them) for matching, while Möller's (2001) model for ants extracts a global parameter for matching. Image matching models have also been devised for rats (Benhamou, 1998; Gallistel, 1990, chapter 6). Both match on global characteristics. Gallistel was modeling the use of the geometry of surfaces, based on the findings of Cheng (1986) and Margules and Gallistel (1988).

Behaviorally, honeybees and wasps typically face a limited set of directions while image matching (Cheng, 1999a; T. S. Collett & Baron, 1994; Frier, Edwards, Smith, Neal, & T. S. Collett, 1996; Zeil, 1993a, 1993b). This strategy cuts out the need to rotate either the animal or, equivalently, the remembered image during search. It also serves to equate compass direction to a landmark with place of projection on the eye. How the stereotypical direction is chosen is not clear and might depend on circumstances. It may also depend on magnetic cues (T. S. Collett & Baron, 1994), stimulus set up (Cheng, 1999a), or directions adopted in orientation flights on leaving the nest (Zeil, 1993a, 1993b).

MAP-LIKE NAVIGATION

The use of landmarks in image matching fits conceptually with the route-based use of landmarks. It is another servomechanism, whose occasion is the last stage of the journey. It is landmark based but not map-like. A classic map-like behavior is the ability to chart a direct path to a known target from anywhere in the familiar terrain. This issue has been lively in the recent study of large-scale navigation in the honeybee. To address this issue, the chosen method is testing behavior after displacement.

Classic work shows that bees can home after displacement with only little experience in exploring their surround (Becker, 1958). More recent work has examined variables (e.g., vanishing bearing) other than percent of homing success. Gould (1986) trained bees to go in one direction (A) to a feeder from their hive. While marked bees were on their way to A, he displaced them to a different location B. The bees headed directly to A from B. Likewise, bees trained to head to B would head to B when displaced to A. Gould suggested that bees possess a cognitive map of their familiar territory that allowed them to go from anywhere in the territory to anywhere else.

Gould's results, however, have not stood the test of replication. A number of attempts to reproduce the experiment showed results consistent with compass-based route following (Dyer, 1991; Menzel et al., 1990; Wehner, Bleuler, Nievergelt, & Shah, 1990; Wehner & Menzel, 1990). Displaced bees in those studies headed in the compass direction in which they were originally flying before displacement. Dyer (1991) suggested that Gould's bees could see some of the landmarks at the target site and were engaging in beaconing behavior.

But in another twist to the story, Menzel, Brandt, Gumbert, Komischke, and Kunze (2000) suggested that bees do possess what they call general landscape knowledge. This knowledge allows bees to home from anywhere within their home range. The key experimental manipulation for revealing the general landscape knowledge was to not train bees to a specific feeder location, the typical practice in virtually all experiments on foraging bees. Rather, bees were trained to go to a feeder near their hive (5 to 10 m) that was moved occasionally. These "variable" bees, when released from locations at a distance of 350 m from their hive in various directions, homed in good time. The authors calculated that the time taken to home was much shorter than that required by a random or systematic search algorithm. Bees trained to a specific feeder location, however, showed a preponderant dependence on the specific route that they had learned. When displaced from the feeder to another location, they still headed in the feeder-to-home direction. Menzel et al. concluded that in this case and in earlier studies the general landscape knowledge had been masked by this dominant specialized route memory.

The data in support of general landscape knowledge are indirect. Exciting direct data were recently collected by Menzel's group (Menzel et al., 2005). The work relies on a new technological advance in tracking free flying bees (Capaldi et al., 2000). A small radio transponder is attached to a foraging bee, so that her flight can be radiotracked (see Capaldi et al., 2000, figure 1). From this technique, Capaldi et al. learned about the nature of the honeybee's orientation flights. These are flights that the bee takes, presumably to learn about the landscape, before setting out to forage. The orienting bee typically explores one narrow sector on each flight, flying farther and farther from her hive as she gains experience. Menzel and colleagues used this technique on foragers, thus obtaining full flights rather than only the initial direction. The bees were trained to go to a feeder repeatedly. On crucial tests, bees were displaced, either on their way from hive to feeder, or on their way from feeder to hive. Many of these bees found their way quite directly, either to the hive or to the feeder (figure 10.7). If the bee was displaced and immediately released, it would typically first fly the route vector it was executing before displacement. This is the behavior that Dyer (1991), Menzel et al., (1990), Wehner et al. (1990), and Wehner and Menzel (1990) had observed. After that route vector, however, Menzel et al.'s bees then searched around the area, which was not the goal to which they were headed. This searching behavior was usually followed by a direct flight to the target (hive or feeder). Menzel et al.'s conclusion was that the bees could head directly to a significant goal from anywhere in their known territory. They considered this behavior to constitute the equivalent of a cognitive map.

Map-Based or Route-Based?

The mechanistic bases of this general landscape knowledge after displacement are not currently known. The behavior may be guided by a representation resembling a metric sketch map, one that encodes the metric relations (distances and directions)

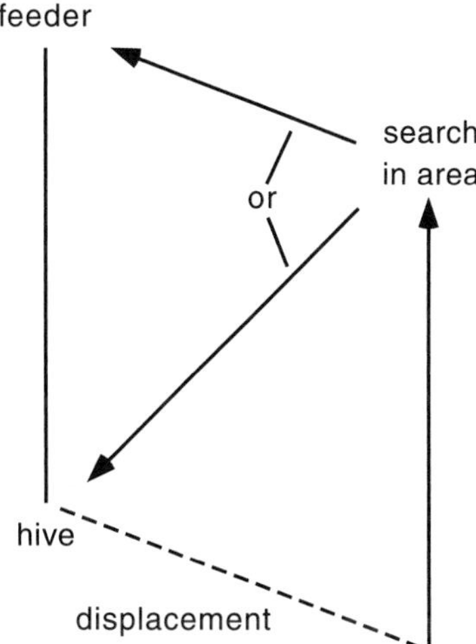

Figure 10.7. Schematic illustration of an experimental paradigm from Menzel et al. (2005). Individually marked honeybees were trained repeatedly to go from their hive to a feeder at a constant place. After some training, bees were captured on their way out and displaced to some arbitrary location. The subject bee carried a small transponder, which allowed its complete path to be tracked. Displaced bees typically first fly off their route vector, learned from their training. Then they search in the vicinity at which they had arrived. After some searching, they head directly to a target location, either the feeder or the hive.

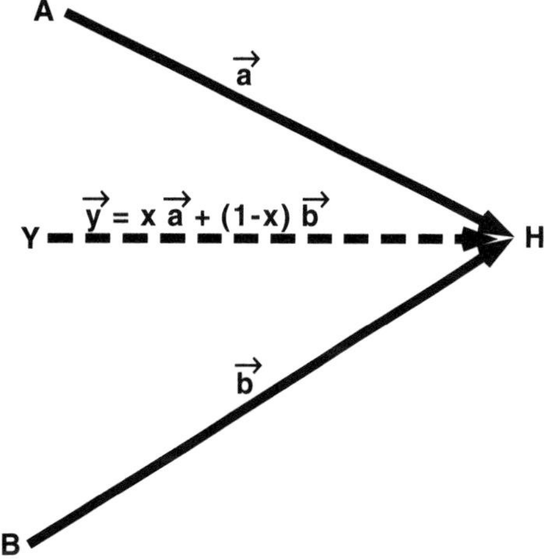

Figure 10.8. Vector averaging as a scheme for homing from an unfamiliar location. The bee has learned home vectors from A (vector **a**) and B (vector **b**). At the unfamiliar location Y, in between A and B, the scene resembles both A and B to some extent. The bee generalizes from both A and B and is hypothesized to travel a weighted average of vectors a and b. In the formula for vector **y**, x is a weighting factor that ranges between 0 and 1.

among the many salient landmarks in the area. Something along these lines has been proposed by Gould (1986) and Gallistel (1990). This would make the behavior truly map based. This map-like flexibility, however, also may be cobbled together by a combination of route-based mechanisms already demonstrated in bees.

Cartwright and T. S. Collett (1987) proposed that bees might use a network of vectors to obtain flexibility in navigation. View-based vectors to home from different locations might be learned on orientation flights. As already reviewed, sensorimotor vectors based on views have been well established in bees. In Cartwright and Collett's scheme, the bee chooses the remembered view that most resembles the current perceived scene and follows its dictates until the mismatch becomes high. Then it chooses another best-matching view, and so on. This is very much in the spirit of route behavior. The control is passed from one servomechanism (vector) to another, based on the occasion set by the stimulus context.

A generalization and averaging mechanism can add flexibility to this kind of navigation. The bee probably associates only a small number of views with vectors home. When it finds itself in a place without an associated vector, generalization and averaging take over. The current view presumably resembles learned views to either side of it. The bee generalizes from each of these views and averages the dictates of the two views (figure 10.8). This averaged vector would point approximately to the correct direction home. Generalization does two things. First, it lets a current view set the occasion for a vector even when the view does not match anything in memory very well. Second, it sets weights for the vectors to be averaged. I assume that the more similar a current view is to a remembered view, the more the vector associated with (occasioned by) that remembered view is weighted. Whatever metric of similarity the bee uses, similarity presumably decreases monotonically with distance from the place at which a view was committed to memory. The end result is a roughly sensible weighting of associated vectors based on the resemblance of the current view to various learned views. This system extends the utility of a limited number of view-based vectors. In bees studied in the laboratory, both spatial generalization (Cheng, 1999b, 2000b) and the averaging of sensorimotor vectors (T. S. Collett & Baron, 1995; T. S. Collett et al., 1996) have been demonstrated. It is reasonable to suppose that they play a role in large-scale navigation as well. Menzel, Geiger, Joerges, Müller, and Chittka (1998) found that under some circumstances, bees can home from a location intermediate between two feeding sites to which they had been trained to fly. Menzel et al. suggested that the averaging of two home vectors (associated with each of the feeding sites) might account for this behavior.

This scheme allows the bee to home from anywhere in its familiar terrain. An added component, literally, is needed to get to anywhere else, such as a feeder. To get to a feeder, the bee needs to add the home-to-feeder vector, which it presumably learns from flying repeatedly between home and the feeder. Vector from displaced location to home plus vector from home to feeder gives the bee the vector from the displaced location to the feeder. If we grant the bee vector averaging, then it is reasonable to grant it vector addition as well. Averaging is just the addition of weighted vectors.

This mechanism is map-like in having inference. Generalization and vector averaging and addition are proposed inference mechanisms. The inference uses "language" from the repertoire of routes, couched in terms of vectors. It is a more complex occasion setting of vectors. What is not explicitly present is an overall map plotting the geometrical relations of all significant locations. Whether this kind of mechanism constitutes a *cognitive map* depends on one's definition of the term. I suggest that it is more pertinent to test whether this or some other mechanism is being used.

GENERAL DISCUSSION

I describe here two themes suggested by the review. (1) Path integration requires metric encoding. This has clear implications for theories of learning and memory. Issues concerning learning in navigation need more study. (2) Many memories are used in navigation. This presents the arthropod with the problem of memory retrieval. How does the animal pick the right memory to do the task?

Metric Encoding

Path integration requires the encoding and use of metric information. The behavior to adopt in order to get home depends crucially on metrical properties (distances and directions) of the outbound trip. The information learned from the experience is decidedly quantitative (Cheng, in press). The computations that extract the requisite information (distance and direction from the starting point) must conform approximately to the geometrical properties of moving over a two-dimensional (or sometimes three-dimensional) Euclidean surface. Otherwise, the end result is useless for getting home. Gallistel (2000, 2002) views path integration as a specialized learning module, specifically devoted to calculating the metrical properties of the outbound trip.

What do these points imply for learning theory? They suggest that the learning mechanism for path integration is unlikely to be associative. By associative mechanism, I mean a theory in which learning is based on the strengthening (and weakening) of links between representations of entities (such as conditioned stimulus and unconditioned stimulus) that are nominal in nature (see Pearce & Bouton, 2000, for a review of such theories in classical conditioning). Problematic for associative theories are the metric characteristics of what is learned. How is it that the particular distance and direction home are learned, rather than any other distance and direction? Some mechanism must extract the distance and direction home as an ant or a bee travels. To date, only models with quantitative representations and computations can deliver the metric output necessary for the return journey (e.g., Maurer & Séguinot, 1995; Müller & Wehner, 1988).

Neurophysiologically, the emphasis is on the encoding of quantitative information, and not on the strength of connections, a point repeatedly raised by Gallistel (1990, 2000, 2002; Gallistel & Gibbon, 2002). Some entities in the brain correspond to or represent distances and directions in the world, and these represented entities, metrical in nature, are used to guide the march home. Hartmann and Wehner (1995) proposed a detailed neural architecture for path integration in desert ants. A key component of the model is the encoding of distance and direction. These are represented by the peak place of activity within chains of neurons. Thus, a circular chain, with a clever supporting cast, is used to compute and encode direction en route.

None of my arguments here apply to associative theories of conditioning. I am proposing that path integration seems to require a representational account. A representational theory of classic conditioning has also been proposed (Gallistel & Gibbon, 2000, 2002). But neither it nor an associative account can be readily adapted to explain path integration. Path integration requires its own brand of calculations and is an excellent example of specialized spatial learning.

The global vector, use of landmarks, and search biases all involve learning. Each is a behavioral mechanism requiring information input. In the case of the global vector and search bias, general strategies might also change over a number of trials of experience (Cheng & Wehner, 2002; M. Collett et al., 1999; Wehner et al., 2002). These longer-term learning effects have only been recently discovered. Their nature and the conditions under which they are found deserve more research.

Memory Retrieval

Arthropods use a range of strategies in navigation. This means that multiple memories are needed for one journey. Each memory must be retrieved at the right time to be useful. Memory retrieval thus becomes an interesting topic in navigation, one that deserves far more research. An emerging hypothesis is that context drives memory retrieval. By *context* is meant a host of physical and temporal characteristics of the circumstances in which the memory is needed. Surrounding scenery, time of day, and motivational state (out to get forage vs. back with forage) have all been proposed as contextual cues (for a comprehensive review, see T. S. Collett et al., 2003).

CONCLUSIONS

Path integration, route following, image matching, and map-like behavior in arthropods are described. Path integration is ubiquitous in the animal kingdom. In arthropods, a good deal of the underlying physiological and behavioral mechanisms are known, such as how polarized light is used to tell direction (see Wehner, 1994) and how optic flow is used by the honeybee to estimate distance (e.g., Srinivasan et al., 1997).

I have presented an overarching concept encompassing route behavior and much else in arthropod navigation. Stimulus conditions, sometimes called context cues (T. S. Collett et al., 2003), set the occasion for or call forth servomechanisms to be run. I have fit local vectors, sensorimotor vectors, beaconing, and image matching into this scheme. The global vector of path integration is also a servomechanism, computing in the background and ready to be run "on default" when occasion setters for other servomechanisms are not at hand. I have speculatively fit map-like behavior into this scheme as well.

It is important to keep separate the triggering or occasion setting stimuli from the stimuli that figure as standards for and inputs to servomechanisms. The two are usually distinct. Landmarks may play both roles. The surrounding landscape might set the occasion for retrieving a vector home. The animal might then use the sky-compass and optic flow for on-line guidance. A honeybee might also fly along a line of trees (von Frisch & Lindauer, 1954), thus using landmarks as the standard for servomechanistic control.

Finally, much of the data come from experiments in the natural habitat of the animals. The research combines experimental control with natural ecology and a realistic scale of navigation for the animals. The latter two characteristics are usually lacking in the confined spaces imposed on rats, pigeons, and humans in lab experiments. Field experiments might be used profitably to further investigate current issues surrounding learning and memory retrieval in arthropod navigation.

Acknowledgments This chapter was in part written while I was a Fellow at the Wissenschaftskolleg zu Berlin (Berlin Institute for Advanced Study), whose support is greatly appreciated. I thank Jochen Zeil and Rüdiger Wehner for supplying me with figures 10.2 and 10.4A, respectively, and Peter Carruthers, Sara Shettleworth, Mandyam Srinivasan, and Jochen Zeil for comments on earlier drafts.

References

Backhaus, W. (1991). Color opponent coding in the visual system of the honeybee. *Vision Research*, *31*, 1381–1397.

Becker, L. (1958). Untersuchungen über das Heimfindevermögen der Bienen [Studies on the homing abilities of bees]. *Zeitschrift für Vergleichende Physiologie*, *41*, 1–25.

Benhamou, S. (1998). Place navigation in mammals: A configuration-based model. *Animal Cognition, 1*, 55–63.

Bernard, G. D., & Wehner, R. (1980). Intracellular optical physiology of the bee's eye. I. Spectral sensitivity. *Journal of Comparative Physiology A, 137*, 193–203.

Capaldi, E. A., Smith, A. D., Osborne, J. L., Fahrbach, S. E., Farris, S. M., Reynolds, D. R., et al. (2000). Ontogeney of orientation flight in the honeybee revealed by harmonic radar. *Nature, 403*, 537–540.

Cartwright, B. A., & Collett, T. S. (1982). How honeybees use landmarks to guide their return to a food source. *Nature, 295*, 560–564.

Cartwright, B. A., & Collett, T. S. (1983). Landmark learning in bees. *Journal of Comparative Physiology A, 151*, 521–543.

Cartwright, B. A., & Collett, T. S. (1987). Landmark maps for honeybees. *Biological Cybernetics, 57*, 85–93.

Cheng, K. (1986). A purely geometric module in the rat's spatial representation. *Cognition, 23*, 149–178.

Cheng, K. (1994). The determination of direction in landmark-based spatial search in pigeons: A further test of the vector sum model. *Animal Learning & Behavior, 22*, 291–301.

Cheng, K. (1995). Landmark-based spatial memory in the pigeon. In D. L. Medin (Ed.), *The psychology of learning and motivation*, Vol. 33 (pp. 1–21). New York: Academic Press.

Cheng, K. (1998). Distances and directions are computed separately by honeybees in landmark-based search. *Animal Learning & Behavior, 26*, 455–468.

Cheng, K. (1999a). Landmark-based spatial search in honeybees: II. Using gaps and blocks. *Animal Cognition, 2*, 79–90.

Cheng, K. (1999b). Spatial generalization in honeybees confirms Shepard's law. *Behavioural Processes, 44*, 309–316.

Cheng, K. (2000a). How honeybees find a place: Lessons from a simple mind. *Animal Learning & Behavior, 28*, 1–15.

Cheng, K. (2000b). Shepard's universal law supported by honeybees in spatial generalization. *Psychological Science, 11*, 403–408.

Cheng, K. (in press). Common principles shared by spatial and other kinds of cognition. In F. Dolins & R. Mitchell (Eds.), *Spatial perception, spatial cognition: Mapping the self and space*. Cambridge: Cambridge University Press.

Cheng, K., & Spetch, M. L. (1998). Mechanisms of landmark use in mammals and birds. In S. Healy (Ed.), *Spatial representation in animals* (pp. 1–17). Oxford: Oxford University Press.

Cheng, K., Srinivasan, M. V., & Zhang, S. W. (1999). Error is proportional to distance measured by honeybees: Weber's law in the odometer. *Animal Cognition, 2*, 11–16.

Cheng, K., & Wehner, R. (2002). Navigating desert ants (*Cataglyphis fortis*) learn to alter their search patterns on their homebound journey. *Physiological Entomology, 27*, 285–290.

Chittka, L., & Geiger, K. (1995). Honeybee long-distance orientation in a controlled environment. *Ethology, 99*, 117–126.

Chittka, L., Geiger, K., & Kunze, J. (1995). The influence of landmarks on distance estimation of honey bees. *Animal Behaviour, 50*, 23–31.

Chittka, L., & Tautz, J. (2003). The spectral input to honeybee visual odometry. *Journal of Experimental Biology, 206*, 2393–2397.

Collett, M., Collett, T. S., Bisch, S., & Wehner, R. (1998). Local and global vectors in desert ant navigation. *Nature, 394*, 269–272.

Collett, M., Collett, T. S., Chameron, S., & Wehner, R. (2003). Do familiar landmarks reset the global path integration system of desert ants? *Journal of Experimental Biology, 206*, 877–882.

Collett, M., Collett, T. S., & Wehner, R. (1999). Calibration of vector navigation in desert ants. *Current Biology, 9*, 1031–1034.

Collett, M., Harland, D., & Collett, T. S. (2002). The use of landmarks and panoramic context in the performance of local vectors by navigating honeybees. *Journal of Experimental Biology, 205*, 807–814.

Collett, T. S., & Baron, J. (1994). Biological compasses and the coordinate frame of landmark memories in honeybees. *Nature, 368*, 137–140.

Collett, T. S., & Baron, J. (1995). Learnt sensori-motor mappings in honeybees: Interpolation and its possible relevance to navigation. *Journal of Comparative Physiology A, 177*, 287–298.

Collett, T. S., Baron, J., & Sellen, K. (1996). On the encoding of movement vectors by honeybees: Are distance and direction represented independently? *Journal of Comparative Physiology A, 179*, 395–406.

Collett, T. S., & Collett, M. (2002). Memory use in insect visual navigation. *Nature Reviews Neuroscience, 3*, 542–552.

Collett, T. S., Collett, M., & Wehner, R. (2001). The guidance of desert ants by extended landmarks. *Journal of Experimental Biology, 204*, 1635–1639.

Collett, T. S., Fauria, K., & Dale, K. (2003). Contextual cues and insect navigation. In K. J. Jeffery (Ed.), *The neurobiology of spatial behaviour* (pp. 31–47). Oxford: Oxford University Press.

Collett, T. S., Fauria, K., Dale, K., & Baron, J. (1997). Places and patterns—A study of context learning in honeybees. *Journal of Comparative Physiology A, 181*, 343–353.

Collett, T. S., & Rees, J. A. (1997). View-based navigation in Hymenoptera: Multiple strategies of landmark guidance in approach to a feeder. *Journal of Comparative Physiology A, 181*, 47–58.

Collett, T. S., & Zeil, J. (1998). Places and landmarks: An arthropod perspective. In S. Healy (Ed.), *Spatial representation in animals* (pp. 18–53). Oxford: Oxford University Press.

Dale, K., & Collett, T. S. (2001). Using artificial evolution and selection to model insect navigation. *Current Biology, 11*, 1305–1316.

Durier, V., Graham, P., & Collett, T. S. (2003). Snapshot memories and the use of landmarks in wood ants. *Current Biology, 13*, 1614–1618.

Dyer, F. C. (1991). Bees acquire route-based memories but not cognitive maps in a familiar landscape. *Animal Behaviour, 41*, 239–246.

Dyer, F. C., & Gould, J. L. (1981). Honey bee orientation: A backup system for cloudy days. *Science, 214*, 1041–1042.

Dyer, F. C., & Gould, J. L. (1983). Honey bee navigation. *American Scientist, 71*, 587–597.

Esch, H. E., & Burns, J. E. (1995). Honeybees use optic flow to measure the distance of a food source. *Naturwissenschaften, 82*, 38–40.

Esch, H. E., & Burns, J. E. (1996). Distance estimation by foraging honeybees. *Journal of Experimental Biology, 199*, 155–162.

Esch, H. E., Zhang, S. W., Srinivasan, M. V., & Tautz, J. (2001). Honeybee dances communicate distances measured by optic flow. *Nature, 411*, 581–583.

Etienne, A. S., & Jeffery, K. J. (2004). Path integration in mammals. *Hippocampus, 14*, 180–192.

Forster, L. (1982). Visual communication in jumping spiders (Salticidae). In P. N. Witt & J. S. Rovner (Eds.), *Spider communication: Mechanisms and ecological significance* (pp. 161–212). Princeton, NJ: Princeton University Press.

Franz, M. O., Schölkopf, B., Mallot, H. A., & Bülthoff, H. H. (1998). Learning view graphs for robot navigation. *Autonomous Robots, 5*, 111–125.

Frier, H. J., Edwards, E., Smith, C., Neal, S., & Collett, T. S. (1996). Magnetic compass cues and visual pattern learning in honeybees. *Journal of Experimental Biology, 199*, 1353–1361.

Gallistel, C. R. (1990). *The organization of learning*. Cambridge, MA: MIT Press.

Gallistel, C. R. (2000). The replacement of general-purpose learning models with adaptively specialized learning modules. In M. S. Gazzaniga (Ed.), *The new cognitive neurosciences* (pp. 1179–1191). Cambridge, MA: MIT Press.

Gallistel, C. R. (2002). The principle of adaptive specialization as it applies to learning and memory. In R. H. Kluwe, G. Lüer, & F. Rösler (Eds.), *Principles of human learning and memory* (pp. 250–280). Berlin: Birkhäuser Verlag.

Gallistel, C. R., & Gibbon, J. (2000). Time, rate and conditioning. *Psychological Review, 107*, 289–344.

Gallistel, C. R., & Gibbon, J. (2002). *The symbolic foundations of conditioned behavior*. Mahwah, NJ: Erlbaum.

Gibbon, J. (1977). Scalar expectancy theory and Weber's law in animal timing. *Psychological Review, 84*, 279–325.

Görner, P. (1958). Die optische und kinästhetishce Orientierung der Trichterspinne *Agelena labyrinthica* (Cl.) [The optical and kinesthetic orientation of the funnel-web spider *Agelena labyrinthica* (Cl.)]. *Zeitschrift für Vergleichende Physiologie, 41*, 111–153.

Gould, J. L. (1986). The locale map of honey bees: do insects have cognitive maps? *Science, 232*, 861–863.

Graham, P., Durier, V., & Collett, T. S. (2004). The binding and recall of snapshot memories in wood ants (*Formica rufa* L.). *Journal of Experimental Biology, 207*, 393–398.

Graham, P., Fauria, K., & Collett, T. S. (2003). The influence of beacon-aiming on the routes of wood ants. *Journal of Experimental Biology, 206*, 535–541.

Hartmann, G., & Wehner, R. (1995). The ant's path integration system: A neural architecture. *Biological Cybernetics, 73*, 483–497.

Hemmi, J. M., & Zeil, J. (2003a). Burrow surveillance in fiddler crabs. I. Description of behaviour. *Journal of Experimental Biology, 206*, 3935–3950.

Hemmi, J. M., & Zeil, J. (2003b). Burrow surveillance in fiddler crabs. II. The sensory cues. *Journal of Experimental Biology, 206*, 3951–3961.

Hemmi, J. M., & Zeil, J. (2003c). Robust judgement of inter-object distance by an arthropod. *Nature, 421*, 160–163.

Horridge, G. A. (1999). Pattern discrimination by the honeybee (*Apis mellifera*) is colour blind for radial/tangential cues. *Journal of Comparative Physiology A, 184*, 413–422.

Jackson, R. R., & Pollard, S. D. (1996). Predatory behaviour of jumping spiders. *Annual Review of Entomology, 41*, 287–308.

Jackson, R. R., & Wilcox, R. S. (1993). Observations in nature of detouring behaviour by *Portia fimbriata*, a web-invading aggressive mimic jumping spider from Queensland. *Journal of Zoology, London, 230*, 135–139.

Judd, S. P. D., & Collett, T. S. (1998). Multiple stored views and landmark guidance in ants. *Nature, 392*, 710–714.

Labhart, T. (1988). Polarization-opponent interneurons in the insect visual system. *Nature, 331*, 435–437.

Labhart, T. (1996). How polarization-sensitive interneurones of crickets perform at low degrees of polarization. *Journal of Experimental Biology, 199*, 1467–1475.

Land, M. F. (1972). Mechanisms of orientation and pattern recognition by jumping spiders (Salticidae). In R. Wehner (Ed.), *Information processing in the visual systems of arthropods* (pp. 231–247). New York: Springer-Verlag.

Layne, J. E., Barnes, W. J. P., & Duncan, L. M. J. (2003a). Mechanisms of homing in the fiddler crab *Uca rapax* 1. Spatial and temporal characteristics of a system of small-scale navigation. *Journal of Experimental Biology, 206*, 4413–4423.

Layne, J. E., Barnes, W. J. P., & Duncan, L. M. J. (2003b). Mechanisms of homing in the fiddler crab *Uca rapax* 2. Information sources and frame of reference for a path integration system. *Journal of Experimental Biology, 206*, 4425–4442.

Lehrer, M. (1994). Spatial vision in the honeybee: the use of different cues in different tasks. *Vision Research, 34*, 2363–2385.

Lehrer, M. (1996). Small-scale navigation in the honeybee: Active acquisition of visual information about the goal. *Journal of Experimental Biology, 199*, 253–261.

Margules, J., & Gallistel, C. R. (1988). Heading in the rat: Determination by environmental shape. *Animal Learning & Behavior, 16*, 404–410.

Maurer, R., & Séguinot, V. (1995). What is modelling for? A critical review of the models of path integration. *Journal of Theoretical Biology, 175*, 457–475.

Menzel, R., & Blakers, M. (1976). Colour receptors in the bee eye—Morphology and spectral sensitivity. *Journal of Comparative Physiology A, 108*, 11–33.

Menzel, R., Brandt, R., Gumbert, A., Komischke, B., & Kunze, J. (2000). Two spatial memories for honeybee navigation. *Proceedings of the Royal Society of London, Series B, Biological Sciences, 267*, 961–968.

Menzel, R., Chittka, L., Eichmüller, S., Geiger, K., Peitsche, D., & Knoll, P. (1990). Dominance of celestial cues over landmarks disproves map-like orienation in honey bees. *Zeitschrift für Naturforschung C, 45*, 723–726.

Menzel, R., Geiger, K., Joerges, J., Müller, U., & Chittka, L. (1998). Bees travel novel homeward routes by integrating separately acquired vector memories. *Animal Behaviour, 55*, 139–152.

Menzel, R., Greggers, U., Smith, A., Berger, S., Brandt, R., Brunke, S., et al. (2005). Honeybees navigate according to a map-like spatial memory. *Proceedings of the National Academy of Sciences, 102*, 3040–3045.

Moller, P., & Görner, P. (1994). Homing by path integration in the spider *Agelena labyrinthica* Clerck. *Journal of Comparative Physiology A, 174*, 221–229.

Möller, R. (2001). Do insects use templates or parameters for landmark navigation? *Journal of Theoretical Biology, 210*, 33–45.

Müller, M., & Wehner, R. (1988). Path integration in desert ants, *Cataglyphis fortis. Proceedings of the National Academy of Sciences, 85*, 5287–5290.

Pearce, J. M., & Bouton, M. E. (2000). Theories of associative learning in animals. *Annual Review of Psychology, 52*, 111–139.

Ronacher, B., Gallizzi, K., Wohlgemuth, S., & Wehner, R. (2000). Lateral optic flow does not influence distance estimation in the desert ant *Cataglyphis fortis. Journal of Experimental Biology, 203*, 1113–1121.

Ronacher, B., & Wehner, R. (1995). Desert ants *Cataglyphis fortis* use self-induced optic flow to measure distances travelled. *Journal of Comparative Physiology A, 177*, 21–27.

Rossel, S. (1987). Das Polarisationssehen der Biene [Polarization vision in bees]. *Naturwissenschaften, 74*, 53–62.

Rossel, S., & Wehner, R. (1986). Polarization vision in bees. *Nature, 323*, 128–131.

Shettleworth, S. J. (1998). *Cognition, evolution, and behavior*. New York: Oxford University Press.

Si, A., Srinivasan, M. V., & Zhang, S. (2003). Honeybee navigation: Properties of the visually driven "odometer." *Journal of Experimental Biology, 206*, 1265–1273.

Srinivasan, M. V., Zhang, S. W., Altwein, M., & Tautz, J. (2000). Honeybee navigation: Nature and calibration of the "odometer." *Science, 287*, 757–920.

Srinivasan, M. V., Zhang, S. W., & Bidwell, N. J. (1997). Visually mediated odometry in honeybees. *Journal of Experimental Biology, 200*, 2513–2522.

Srinivasan, M. V., Zhang, S. W., Lehrer, M., & Collett, T. S. (1996). Honeybee navigation en route to the goal: Visual flight control and odometry. *Journal of Experimental Biology, 199*, 155–162.

Tarsitano, M. S., & Andrew, R. (1999). Scanning and route selection in the jumping spider. *Portia labiata. Animal Behaviour, 58*, 255–265.

Tarsitano, M. S., & Jackson, R. R. (1997). Araneophagic jumping spiders discriminate between detour routes that do and do not lead to prey. *Animal Behaviour, 53*, 257–266.

von Frisch, K. (1967). *The dance language and orientation of bees.* Cambridge, MA: Belknap.

von Frisch, K., & Lindauer, M. (1954). Himmel und Erde in Konkurrenz bei der Orientierung der Bienen [Sky and Earth in competition in the orientation of bees]. *Naturwissenschaften, 41*, 245–253.

Wehner, R. (1968). Optische Orientierungsmechanismen im Heimkehr-Verhalten von *Cataglyphis bicolor* fab. (Formicidae, Hymenoptera) [Optical orientation mechanisms in homing behavior in *Cataglyphis bicolor* (Formicidae, Hymenoptera)]. *Revue Suisse de Zoologie, 75*, 1076–1085.

Wehner, R. (1970). Die Konkurrenz von Sonnenkompass- und Horizontmarken-Orientierung bei der Wüstenameisen *Cataglyphis bicolor* (Formicidae, Hymenoptera) [Competition in orientation according to the sun compass and landmark cues in the ant *Cataglyphis bicolor* (Formicidae, Hymenoptera)]. *Verhandlungen der Deutschen Zoologischen Gesellschaft, 64*, 238–242.

Wehner, R. (1994). The polarization-vision project: championing organismic biology. *Fortschritte der Zoologie, 39*, 103–143.

Wehner, R., Bleuler, S., Nievergelt, C., & Shah, D. (1990). Bees navigate by using vectors and routes rather than maps. *Naturwissenschaften, 77*, 479–482.

Wehner, R., Gallizzi, K., Frei, C., & Vesely, M. (2002). Calibration processes in desert ant navigation: Vector courses and systematic search. *Journal of Comparative Physiology A, 188*, 683–693.

Wehner, R., Harkness, R. D., & Schmid-Hempel, P. (1983). *Foraging strategies in individually searching ants* Cataglyphis bicolor *(Hymenoptera: Formicidae)*. Stuttgart/New York: Fischer.

Wehner, R., & Menzel, R. (1990). Do insects have cognitive maps? *Annual Review of Neurosciences, 13*, 403–414.

Wehner, R., Michel, B., & Antonsen, P. (1996). Visual navigation in insects: Coupling of egocentric and geocentric information. *Journal of Experimental Biology, 199*, 129–140.

Wehner, R., & Räber, F. (1979). Visual spatial memory in desert ants, genus *Cataglyphis* (Formicidae, Hymenoptera). *Experientia, 35*, 1569–1571.

Wehner, R., & Srinivasan, M. V. (1981). Search-ing behaviour of desert ants, genus *Cataglyphis* (Formicidae, Hymenoptera). *Journal of Comparative Physiology A, 142*, 315–338.

Wehner, R., & Srinivasan, M. V. (2003). Path integration in insects. In K. J. Jeffery (Ed.), *The neurobiology of spatial behaviour* (pp. 9–30). Oxford: Oxford University Press.

Wehner R., & Wehner, S. (1990). Insect navigation: Use of maps or Ariadne's thread? *Ethology, Ecology, and Evolution, 2*, 27–48.

Wilcox, R. S., & Jackson, R. R. (1998). Cognitive abilities of araneophagic jumping spiders. In I. Pepperberg, A. C. Kamil, & R. P. Balda (Eds.), *Animal cognition in nature* (pp. 411–434). New York: Academic Press.

Wohlgemuth, S., Ronacher, B., & Wehner, R. (2001). Ant odometry in the third dimension. *Nature, 411*, 795–798.

Zeil, J. (1993a). Orientation flights of solitary wasps (*Cerceris*; Sphecidae; Hymenoptera) I. Description of flight. *Journal of Comparative Physiology A, 172*, 189–205.

Zeil, J. (1993b). Orientation flights of solitary wasps (*Cerceris*; Sphecidae; Hymenoptera) II. Similarities between orientation and return flights and the use of motion parallax. *Journal of Comparative Physiology A, 172*, 207–222.

Zeil, J. (1998). Homing in fiddler crabs (*Uca lactea annulipes* and *Uca vomeris*: Ocypodidae). *Journal of Comparative Physiology A, 183*, 367–377.

Zeil, J., Hofmann, M. I., & Chahl, J. S. (2003). Catchment areas of panoramic snapshots in outdoor scenes. *Journal of the Optical Society of America A, 20*, 450–469.

Zeil, J., & Layne, J. (2002). Path integration in fiddler crabs and its relation to habitat and social life. In K. Wiese (Ed.), *Crustacean experimental systems in neurobiology* (pp. 227–246). Berlin/Heidelberg/New York: Springer-Verlag.

11

Comparative Spatial Cognition: Processes in Landmark- and Surface-Based Place Finding

MARCIA L. SPETCH AND DEBBIE M. KELLY

It is difficult to imagine how many animals could survive without an ability to remember and find places. Many everyday behaviors, such as returning home, remembering good places to find food and water, avoiding areas that are dangerous, selecting routes for efficient travel to desired locations, and keeping track of places visited during foraging, can depend on spatial memory processes. It is hardly surprising that various sophisticated cognitive mechanisms for spatial memory and navigation have been identified in animals ranging from invertebrates to humans.

One common way to remember the location of a goal is to encode its position relative to visual landmarks. If a landmark is located right at the goal or very near to it, then the animal can use the landmarks as a "beacon." In this case, heading directly toward the landmarks will get the animal to the vicinity of the goal. However, if the available landmarks are not right at the goal, but instead are some distance away from the goal, then the animal will need to encode not only something about the identity of the landmarks but also the distance and direction of the landmarks from the goal. When later searching for the goal, the landmarks can be used to find the goal using the process known as "piloting." The processes by which animals learn, remember, and use spatial information about landmarks for piloting to a goal have been the focus of numerous recent studies (for a review, see Cheng & Spetch, 1998).

Animals can also use the geometric shape of an environment to establish a directional frame of reference (i.e., to "get their bearings" or "determine heading"). Investigations of geometric orientation were pioneered in studies with rats by Cheng (1986) and have since been conducted on numerous organisms ranging from fish (Sovrano, Bisazza, & Vallortigara, 2002) to humans (e.g., Hermer & Spelke, 1994).

Research on both landmark-based and geometry-based spatial search has blossomed in the past couple of decades, and the variety of species investigated is increasing all the time, making it an exciting area of study in comparative cognition. In this chapter, we review a small selection of the extensive research concerning how animals, including humans, use discrete landmarks or the geometry of surfaces to locate a hidden goal.

METHODS USED TO STUDY LANDMARK- AND SURFACE-BASED SEARCH IN ANIMALS

Transformational Approach

As discussed by Cheng and Spetch (1998), most studies of landmark-based search use the transformational approach, as pioneered in the classic experiment by Tinbergen (1972) on landmark use by digger wasps. He placed pinecones in a circle around the entrance to a wasp's nest so that the pinecones would serve as conspicuous landmarks for the wasp to see when leaving the nest. Tinbergen then transformed the spatial information prior to the

Figure 11.1. Pigeon responding in an open-field (*left*) and in a touch-screen (*right*) landmark-based search task.

wasp's return to demonstrate that the pinecones were used as landmarks. Specifically, he displaced the pinecones a short distance away so that they surrounded a sham nest rather than the real nest. All of the 17 wasps that he tested landed on the sham nest rather than the real nest, indicating that the pinecones served as prominent landmarks for finding the nest.

Variations of this general transformational approach are used in contemporary laboratory studies of landmark-based search. In a typical study, an animal is trained to some criterion to find a goal that is hidden a certain distance and direction away from a landmark or landmark array. Sometimes the landmarks and corresponding goal location are translated within the search space across trials to make other cues uninformative about the goal location. After accurate search develops, the landmarks are manipulated in one of several ways. For example, the responses to the removal of a landmark can indicate the necessity of the landmark, whereas removal of all landmarks except one can indicate the sufficiency of that landmark for accurate search. Shifts of a landmark can indicate the weighting given to the landmark relative to nonshifted cues. Alterations in the distance between landmarks in an array or in the shape of the configuration of landmarks can indicate whether encoding is configural or elemental or whether encoding is relative or absolute. Finally, alterations in the properties of the landmark itself can indicate which features of the landmark are important (e.g., the color or shape) as well as whether the properties of the landmark itself are encoded as part of the spatial information (e.g., whether landmark size is used to gauge distance from the landmark as in Collett, Cartwright, & Smith, 1986, or whether an asymmetrical feature on a landmark is used to determine direction from the landmark as in Cheng, 1994).

The transformational approach is also used to study how animals use the geometry of surfaces to find a goal (Cheng, 1986). In this case, the subject searches for a goal within an enclosed environment. Subjects are disoriented so that directional information from outside of the enclosure is not available. On transformation tests, the orientation, shape, or size of the enclosure or the location of features within the enclosure is manipulated to assess the encoding of geometric or featural cues (e.g., Cheng, 1986; Hermer & Spelke, 1994; Kelly & Spetch, 2001; Kelly, Spetch, & Heth, 1998; Tommasi, Vallortigara, & Zanforlin, 1997).

Open-Field and Touch-Screen Tasks

Two general kinds of laboratory tasks have been developed for the study of landmark-based search in animals. The most commonly used task may be described as an open-field task, in which animals search for food in an open arena—often the floor of a laboratory room (see figure 11.1). Food is hidden (e.g., buried under bedding material) at a particular distance and direction from a landmark or landmark array (landmarks are typically simple objects such as a block of wood or a colored bottle) that is placed within the arena. The second general kind of task has been called a touch-screen task and is conducted within an operant-conditioning chamber, typically using birds or primates as the subjects (see figure 11.1). The vertical surface of a computer monitor serves as the spatial arena; pecks or touches at the monitor screen detected via a touch-frame serve as the search behavior, and graphic stimuli displayed on the screen serve as the landmarks. The goal is typically a small unmarked area; for nonhuman subjects, access to a feeder is provided as reinforcement when the animal responds in the goal area a set number of times.

It is worth noting some striking differences between these types of tasks. First, the scale of the search space differs by an order of magnitude of at least 10. Second, the behavior of searching is very different. In the open field task, the subject moves through the search space to find the goal; in the touch-screen task, the subject directs responses toward different areas of the screen as it searches for the goal. In the open field task, landmarks are three-dimensional objects that are viewed from a range of distances and directions as the subject moves through the search space; in the touch screen task, the landmarks are two-dimensional shapes or two-dimensional representations of three-dimensional objects. In either case, movement of the subject does not alter the direction by which the landmark is seen. Given these striking differences, any commonalities in results across these tasks are interesting and suggest the operation of central cognitive mechanisms governing landmark-based spatial search.

It should be noted, however, that similarity in principles of spatial search across touch-screen and real-world tasks cannot be taken as ironclad evidence that an animal recognizes the correspondence between pictures and real-world places. Instead, the animals may just apply the same processes to learning and remembering the spatial relationships between different kinds of stimuli. Determining whether two-dimensional stimuli seen on a touch-screen monitor are recognized as representing real three-dimensional objects is a separate question that must be addressed through other approaches, such as tests of transfer between environments (for a review, see Fagot, 2000).

LANDMARK-BASED SEARCH

Interactions Among Multiple Landmarks

In most natural settings in which an animal may search for a goal, myriad visual stimuli are present that could potentially serve as landmarks (e.g., a tree, the shape of a riverbank, a patch of yellow flowers, etc.). How much of the spatial information is encoded? If selection among the cues occurs, then what are the selection factors and processes? Is information from multiple landmarks used individually or jointly? Is the encoding absolute or relational? These and other questions have been the focus of numerous recent studies.

Hierarchical Use of Redundant Spatial Cues

Several studies have shown that animals will often encode multiple redundant spatial cues but use the information from these cues in a weighted or hierarchical fashion. For example, Spetch and Edwards (1988) trained pigeons to find food that was hidden inside the center carton of three identical cartons that were aligned along one wall of a test room. The location of the array of cartons was fixed during training, so that the correct carton could be found by attending to either the location in room (termed global cues) or the position in the array (termed local cues). Tests in which the array was shifted so that the global and local cues were placed in opposition revealed dominance by the local cues. However, when the local cues were removed, strong control by the global room cues was evident (see figure 11.2). This pattern of evidence indicates that both types of cues were encoded, but the local cues were weighted more heavily when both were available. It is not clear whether any overshadowing of the global cues occurred (i.e., whether stronger control by global cues would be seen in birds that were trained without local cues), because this possibility was not tested.

Brodbeck (1994) found a strong hierarchy when redundant cues were used by chickadees in both storing and food-finding tasks. The chickadees stored or found food in one of four spatially and visually distinct feeders. The baited feeder could be encoded in terms of its location in the room, its position in the array, or its visual features. The feeder array was transformed prior to the search test such that these three types of cues were specified by different feeders. The chickadees were required to inspect all four feeders to end the trial. The birds showed a strong hierarchy, choosing the correct absolute location first, the correct relative position next, and the correct feature third before choosing the feeder that was incorrect according to all cues. Thus, global room cues dominated, but choice of the featurally correct feeder over the incorrect

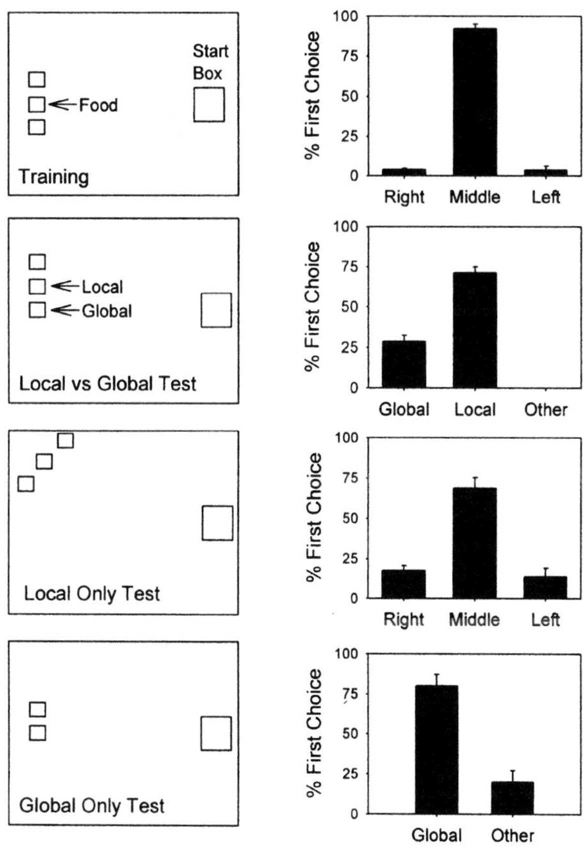

Figure 11.2. Example of spatial layout of choice sites in room (*left*) and average percentage of choices made to each site (*right*) during training and test trials. (From "Pigeons' (*Columba livia*) use of global and local cues for spatial memory," by M. L. Spetch and C. A. Edwards, 1988, *Animal Behaviour*, *36*, p. 294. Copyright 1998 by Association for the Study of Animal Behaviour. Adapted with permission.)

feeder indicated that even the less preferred featural cues were well encoded. Such hierarchical use of redundant cues presumably operates in nature, where the most informative cues are sometimes obscured or unavailable; hence, having a backup source of information is prudent.

Cue-Competition in Spatial Learning

Cue-competition effects are among the most well-studied and theoretically discussed findings in the field of associative learning. Kamin's (1969) classic blocking experiments demonstrated that the presence of an already conditioned stimulus can prevent a new one from being conditioned, thus highlighting the fact that simple pairing of a conditioned stimulus (CS) with an unconditioned stimulus (US) is not always sufficient for conditioning. Instead, the CS apparently needs to be informative about the occurrence of the US for good conditioning to occur, an assumption that forms the basis of the classic Rescorla-Wagner theory of associative learning (Rescorla & Wagner, 1972). Overshadowing, in which the presence of a salient CS can interfere with conditioning to a weak CS, is another common example of cue-competition. Although it remains unclear to what extent cue-competition reflects learning or performance factors (e.g., Denniston, Savastano, Blaisdell, & Miller, 2003), there is no doubt that such effects are pervasive and important in associative learning.

Recently, a growing number of investigators have asked whether cue-competition also occurs in the spatial domain. This seemingly simple question is interesting because of the dominant theoretical framework in which spatial learning has been viewed, namely as a cognitive mapping process (e.g., O'Keefe & Nadel, 1978; Tolman, 1948). Cognitive mapping has been viewed as curiosity driven and involves the accumulation of knowledge of the layout of the environment. As such, one might not expect to see cue-competition because additional cues would simply add more detail to the cognitive map. Evidence of overshadowing and blocking would seem to challenge such a view.

Evidence for Overshadowing Overshadowing has now been found in various spatial tasks, with rats

(Chamizo, Sterio, & Mackintosh, 1985; March, Chamizo, & Mackintosh, 1992; Sánchez-Moreno, Rodrigo, Chamizo, & Mackintosh, 1999), pigeons (Spetch, 1995), and humans (Chamizo, Aznar-Casnova, & Artugas, 2003; Spetch, 1995). For example, using a touch-screen task and a within-subject design, Spetch (1995) demonstrated overshadowing based on proximity to the goal in both pigeons and humans. Training included a mixture of two types of trials. Both trial types contained a target landmark as well as one or more competing landmarks. The absolute distance of the target landmark from the goal was the same on both types of trials, but the distance of the competing landmarks differed across the two types of trials. On overshadowing trials, a competing landmark was closer to the goal than the target landmark. On control trials, the competing landmark was farther from the goal than the target landmark. The features (color and shape) of the landmarks and their direction from the goal were counterbalanced across subjects. Following training, unreinforced test trials revealed that both pigeons and humans searched more accurately with the control landmark alone than they did with the overshadowed landmark alone (see figure 11.3).

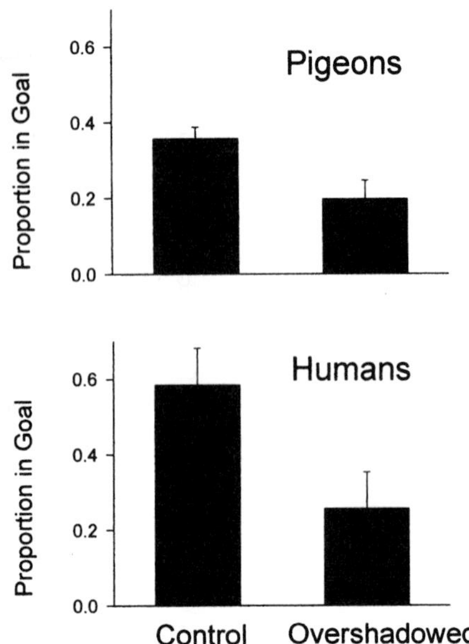

Figure 11.3. Proportion of responses in the goal area on tests with the control landmark alone and tests with the overshadowed landmark alone. (From "Overshadowing in Landmark Learning: Touch Screen Studies With Pigeons and Humans," by M. Spetch, 1995, *Journal of Experimental Psychology: Animal Behavior Processes, 21,* pp. 171, 174. Copyright 1995 by American Psychological Association. Adapted with permission.)

Evidence for Blocking Blocking has been demonstrated in spatial learning experiments with rats using radial arm mazes (Chamizo et al., 1985), open-field food searching tasks (Biegler & Morris, 1999), and water maze tasks (Roberts & Pearce, 1999; Rodrigo, Chamizo, McLaren, & Mackintosh, 1997). For an excellent review of these and other studies on blocking and overshadowing in spatial learning in rats, see Chamizo (2003). Recently, we (Cheng & Spetch, 2001) found blocking in spatial learning by honeybees. The task for the bees was to find sucrose that was located in a small dish on top of a table. Colored blocks served as landmarks. In the clearest demonstration of blocking (Experiment 2), two groups of bees were initially trained with a single landmark and the goal located to one side of the landmark. Phase 2 training then entailed presenting two landmarks with the goal in between. For the control group, the two landmarks were both novel, whereas for the blocking group, the phase 1 landmark was present in the same spatial relation to the goal and one novel landmark was added on the other side. Unreinforced tests with the novel landmark alone indicated that the control bees searched in the correct location more than the blocking group (see figure 11.4). Thus, the presence of the previously trained landmark appeared to block control by the novel landmark.

Absence of Cue-Competition Effects Despite the growing demonstrations of blocking and overshadowing in spatial learning, it is also the case that cue-competition is not always found. In particular, the presence of featural cues or beacons does not appear to overshadow or block learning about the geometric shape of an environment (Hayward, McGregor, Good, & Pearce, 2003; Kelly et al., 1998; Pearce, Ward-Robinson, Good, Fussell, & Aydin, 2001). We discuss these studies in the section on geometric shape.

ARRAYS OF IDENTICAL LANDMARKS

Absolute Versus Relative Relationships

Sometimes, the landmarks near a goal may be difficult to distinguish one from another, such as a row of similar-looking trees or a field of flowers. Rather

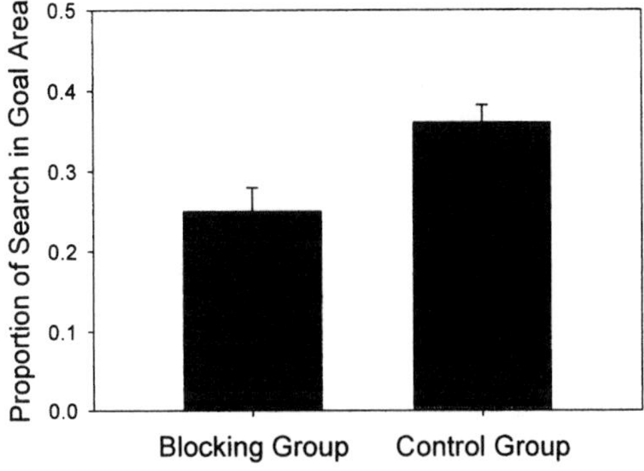

Figure 11.4. Proportion of time spent searching the goal area by honeybees in the blocking group and the control group of Experiment 2 of Cheng and Spetch (2001). (Based on data from "Blocking in Landmark-Based Search in Honeybees," by K. Cheng and M. Spetch, 2001, *Animal Learning & Behavior, 29*, pp. 1–9.)

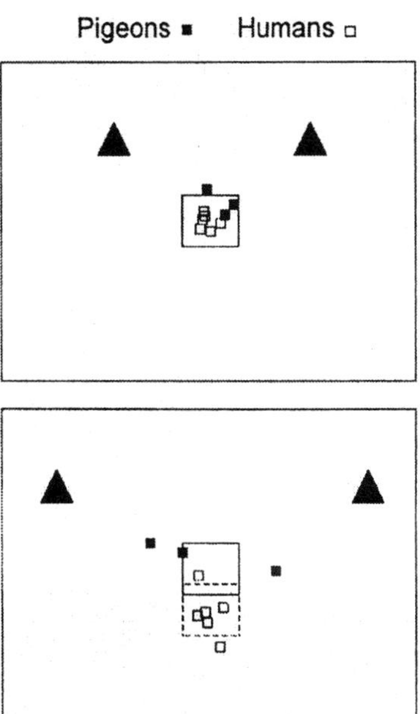

Figure 11.5. Peak place of searching by pigeons and humans on control trials (*top*), which were visually identical to training trials, and on expansion test trials (*bottom*) in which the landmarks were spread farther apart. *Top*, the *outlined square* indicates where the goal had been relative to the landmarks on training trials. *Bottom*, the *solid outlined square* indicates the goal location prior to the landmark shifts, and the *dotted outlined square* indicates that this location would be shifted downward if participants tried to maintain the same triangular shape formed by the landmarks and goal as in training. (From "Learning the Configuration of a Landmark Array, I: Touch-Screen Studies With Pigeons and Humans," by M. L. Spetch, K. Cheng, and S. E. MacDonald, 1996, *Journal of Comparative Psychology, 110*, p. 64. Copyright 1996 by American Psychological Association. Adapted with permission.)

than trying to encode the goal in terms of its relation to an individual landmark that might be confused with other similar-looking ones, an alternative strategy would be to encode the goal in relation to the array of landmarks. To investigate how animals search on the basis of landmark arrays, investigators have defined a goal location relative to a set of identical-looking landmarks. For example, Collett et al. (1986) trained gerbils to find a goal that was located midway between and at a fixed distance south of two identical landmarks. The array of landmarks and corresponding goal was translated in the search space across trials that forced the gerbils to attend to both landmarks. Tests in which one landmark was removed confirmed that both were needed to search accurately. However, interesting results emerged on tests in which the investigators spread the landmarks farther apart. On these tests, the gerbils searched at the two locations that maintained the correct vector from individual landmarks. Thus, although the array was used to determine which landmark was which, the gerbils did not appear to learn a rule based on the abstract relation between the landmarks and the goal, which would have led the gerbils to search midway between and farther south of the two landmarks.

Spetch, Cheng, and MacDonald (1996) used the touch-screen task to train both pigeons and humans on a two-landmark array like the one used by Collett et al. (1986). The goal was located below and between the landmarks. On expansion tests, humans remained centered between the landmarks and tended to shift their searching downward. Pigeons responded more like gerbils and showed no tendency to shift their searching downward or to respond in the middle of the landmarks (see figure 11.5).

Spetch et al. (1996) also tested pigeons and humans with a square array of four identical landmarks with the goal in the middle. Humans again appeared to use a relational rule and continued

Figure 11.6. Training set-up in the four-landmark task used for pigeons (*left*) and humans (*right*) in Spetch et al., 1997.

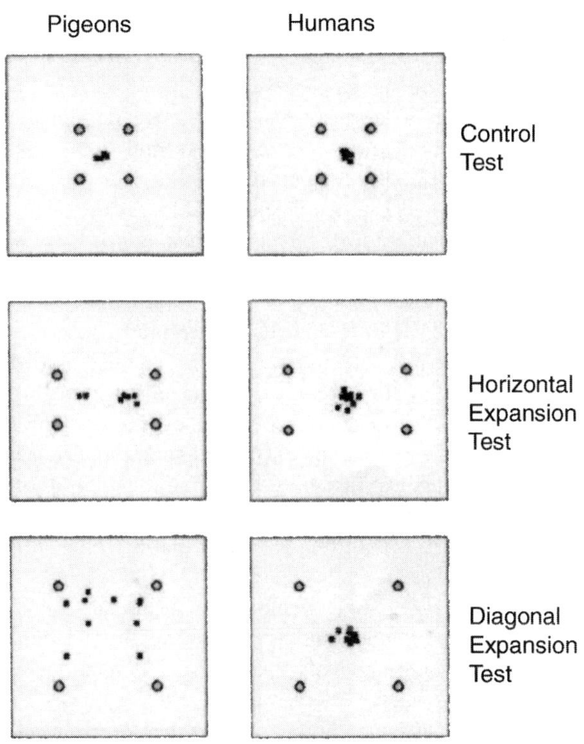

Figure 11.7. Peak places of search by pigeons (*left*) and location of search responses by humans (*right*) on control tests (*top*) and tests in which the landmark array was expanded in one dimension (*middle*) or in both dimensions (*bottom*). (From "Use of Landmark Configuration in Pigeons and Humans: II. Generality Across Search Tasks," by M. L. Spetch et al., 1997. *Journal of Comparative Psychology, 111*, pp. 18–19. Copyright 1997 by American Psychological Association. Adapted with permission.)

to search in the middle when the array was expanded. Pigeons, however, were more likely to search at location that maintained the same absolute vectors from individual landmarks as in training.

Spetch et al. (1997) conducted similar tests with both species using open field tasks. Humans were tested with the four-landmark array in an outdoor field, and pigeons were tested on the floor of a laboratory room (figure 11.6). Remarkably, the same distinct pattern of results shown by each species on the touch-screen task also emerged in the open field task: namely, humans used a middle rule whereas pigeons did not (figure 11.7). The similarity of results across tasks that differ so drastically in scale and dimensionality of space and in response requirements indicates that the results reflect central cognitive processes and are not an artifact of a particular spatial task.

It should be noted that, in the above studies, the array of landmarks and goal moved about in the search space across trials; so, to solve the training task, subjects needed to attend to the whole array of landmarks. To account for our results with pigeons, we (Spetch et al., 1997; Cheng & Spetch, 1998) suggested that landmark-based search may entail two processes: a landmark-matching process and a goal-matching process. In the former process, the animal matches the currently perceived landmarks to those stored in memory, and in the second step, the animal retrieves spatial information about the identified landmarks and goal. We suggested that pigeons may use configural information about the array of landmarks in the first step only, for example, to identify which is the top left landmark. The birds then appeared to use elemental information about the relationship between the identified landmarks and the goal.

Other species have since been trained with arrays of identical landmarks and tested with expansions of the array. Sutton, Olthof, and Roberts (2000) tested squirrel monkeys with a goal hidden in the middle of two-landmark and four-landmark arrays. On tests with expanded arrays, the monkeys searched primarily within the landmark array but did not search in the middle. Interestingly, in contrast to the pigeons and gerbils, the squirrel monkeys also showed little evidence of encoding vectors from individual landmarks and instead showed somewhat scattered search within the array. More recently, MacDonald, Spetch, Kelly, and Cheng (2004) tested marmoset monkeys with expansions of a four-landmark array. After being trained to find food in a cup that was centered among four landmarks, the monkeys did not search near the center on tests in which the landmarks were spread apart. Instead they searched in cups adjacent to the landmarks, but in contrast to the squirrel monkeys, the marmosets showed a significant tendency to search the cups that were at the training vector from the landmark to the goal.

Surprisingly, one species that appears to respond much like adult humans to expansions of a landmark array is the honeybee. Cartwright and Collett (1983) trained the bees to find food at a particular spot relative to a triangular array of three landmarks. When the distances between the landmarks was altered to expand or contract the array, the bees adjusted their distance of searching so that the compass bearings of the landmarks on the eye matched those seen from the food source during training. Although this tendency to search at the correct relative distance from the array of landmarks is similar to that shown by adult humans, it likely reflects the image-matching processes that are thought to characterize spatial search in bees. Adjusting the distance from the landmark array allows the bee to match the landmark locations on the eye with those stored in memory.

Learning Relative Relationships About Landmark Configurations

In the above studies, the training task could be solved on the basis of either absolute or relative spatial relationships. Moreover, the relative rule was represented by a single exemplar. Under these circumstances, humans and bees appear to spontaneously use a relative rule, whereas all other species tested appear to learn the absolute spatial relationship between the landmarks and the goal. A different question can be asked, however, namely, Can animals learn to use a relative rule if absolute metrics cannot be used? Kamil and Jones (1997, 2000) trained nutcrackers to find a goal that was located at a particular relative distance or direction from two landmarks. The distance between the landmarks varied across trials so that only the relative rule was informative. The nutcrackers learned the task and transferred to new interlandmark distances indicating use of the relative rule. Although less accurate than the nutcrackers, pigeons also solved the relative rule task (Jones, Anotoniadis, Shettleworth, & Kamil, 2002; Spetch, Rust, Kamil, & Jones, 2003). Thus, even though absolute learning appears to be the preferred strategy following single exemplar training, pigeons and nutcrackers can learn a relative relationship between an array of landmarks and goal when given multiple exemplar training.

Pigeons have also been found to use the configuration of landmark arrays to distinguish between identical sets of landmarks. In an interesting study, Sutton (2002) trained pigeons to search for food on the basis of four distinctly featured landmarks. Across trials, the landmarks were arranged according to one of two configurations, and the location of the goal differed depending on the configuration. The pigeons learned to distinguish between the configurations and to search in the appropriate location in each. Moreover, tests in which a single landmark was shifted indicated that multiple landmarks were used.

Clearly, spatial encoding processes are highly flexible in many animals. Transformation tests following training with a single spatial relationship suggest that an elemental use of landmarks for search-place matching is the dominant or preferred strategy. However, if training conditions discourage the use of an elemental/absolute approach, then relative encoding based on the configuration of landmarks is possible.

SEARCHING IN ENCLOSED SPACES: USE OF GEOMETRY OF SURFACES

Geometric Module

In his classic demonstration on use of geometry by rats, Cheng (1986) allowed rats to find food in one corner of a rectangular enclosure. The rat was permitted to eat half of the food, then was removed and disoriented, and then was placed into an identical-looking arena with the food hidden in the corresponding corner. Even with distinctive features on the surfaces of the enclosure, the rats confused the geometrically equivalent corners and made "rotational errors" of choosing the corner that was opposite to the correct one. If the food remained in the same corner trial after trial (a reference memory task), the rats eventually used the surface features to distinguish between the geometrically equivalent corners. However, on transformation tests in which the surface features were moved so that they were in conflict with geometry,

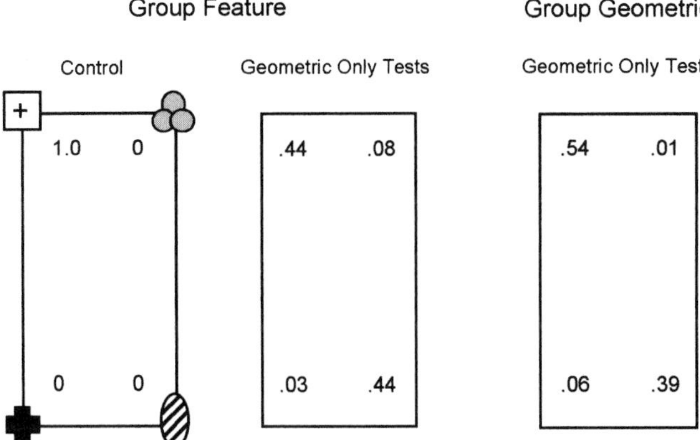

Figure 11.8. Proportion of choices to each corner during control and geometry tests for the feature group and the geometric group. Data are shown with the positive corner in the upper left; however, the actual positive corner was counterbalanced across birds. (From "Pigeons" (*Columbia livia*) encoding of geometric and featural properties of a spatial environment," by D. M. Kelly, M. L. Spetch, and C. D. Heth, 1998. *Journal of Comparative Psychology*, *112*, pp. 262, 264. Copyright 1998 by American Psychological Association. Adapted with permission.)

the rats frequently chose corners that were geometrically correct but featurally incorrect, suggesting that geometry was primary for rats.

Cheng's (1986) pioneering study on geometric orientation in rats triggered a number of comparative studies that have shown that other species also use the geometric shape of their environment for orientation (e.g., humans [adults and children]: Hermer & Spelke, 1994, 1996; chicks: Vallortigara, Zanforlin, & Pasti, 1990; pigeons: Kelly et al., 1998; and fish: Sovrano, Bisazza, & Vallortigara, 2002, 2003). Interestingly, evidence to date suggests that geometric encoding emerges early in development both in birds (Vallortigara et al., 1990) and in humans (Hermer & Spelke, 1994). Moreover, encoding of geometry appears to occur automatically: That is, geometry is encoded even when the goal's position can (and is) located on the basis of featural information (Kelly et al., 1998).

Features Do Not Appear to Overshadow Geometry

There is growing evidence that encoding of geometry is not overshadowed by the presence of salient features that signify the location of the goal during training. For example, Kelly et al. (1998) trained two groups of pigeons to find a goal in one corner of the rectangular enclosure. External visual and auditory cues were masked or blocked for both groups and internal orientation cues were disrupted by rotating the birds prior to each trial. For one group (geometric group), the enclosure was featureless, so geometry provided the only orientation cue. Birds in this group learned to search in the correct corner and in the geometrically equivalent corner, thus achieving a maximum accuracy of 50% overall. For the other group (feature group), distinct visual features were placed into each corner, so that both featural and geometric information was available. Birds in this group learned to search almost exclusively in the correct corner, indicating that the feature had been learned. Nevertheless, when all featural information was removed, the birds in the second group reverted to using geometry and chose the correct and the geometrically equivalent corner equally often. Moreover, there was no evidence of overshadowing, in that no significant differences emerged on these featureless tests between the birds trained with features and the birds trained with geometry only (figure 11.8). Thus, although the featural cues were salient and dominant for birds trained with both features and geometry, they did not seem to interfere with learning of geometry.

A similar failure of overshadowing of geometry by features was seen in humans on a two-dimensional spatial search task (Kelly & Spetch, 2004a). The participants viewed schematic displays of a rectangular environment shown in various orientations on a touch-screen monitor. The participants earned points for touching a correct corner of the rectangle. For one group of participants, initial training provided distinct features adjacent to each corner that could be used to identify the correct corner. For the other group, no distinct features were present, so the only information available was the geometry of the rectangle. Feature learning occurred much more readily than geometry learning in that almost all participants trained with features met criterion in learning to select the correct corner, whereas only some of the participants trained with geometry met our accuracy criterion in learning to select the two geometrically correct corners. Interestingly, however, when the distinctive features were removed from the display for the feature-trained participants, they showed a significant tendency to base choices on geometry and their geometry-based choices did not differ from those of the participants who learned to respond on the basis of geometry only. Thus, although learning about features seemed to be much easier than learning about geometry on the two-dimensional task, the features did not overshadow learning about geometry.

In a companion study to Kelly and Spetch (2004a), pigeons were trained and tested using a very similar procedure (Kelly & Spetch, 2004b). As in the study with humans, two groups of pigeons were trained to direct their responses to one corner of a schematic display of a rectangular environment. One group of pigeons was trained with distinctive features adjacent to each corner, whereas the second group of pigeons was trained with no distinctive features present. Overall, the birds trained with features took significantly fewer sessions to learn the task than did the birds trained with only geometric information. However, similar to the humans, the pigeons trained with features were also able to use a geometric strategy when tested in the absence of distinctive featural cues. Therefore, both humans and pigeons show facilitated learning with distinctive featural cues present. Furthermore, in both species, learning about the features did not overshadow learning about geometry.

Recent studies of rats in a swimming pool also found that encoding of geometry is not susceptible to overshadowing or blocking by featural cues. Pearce et al. (2001) successfully trained rats to find a hidden platform in a triangular swimming pool; however, the presence of a beacon (a rod attached to the platform) did not consistently overshadow or block learning based on the shape of the pool. Hayward et al. (2003) successfully trained rats to find a submerged platform in both rectangular and triangular pools. In their first two experiments, the researchers found that a landmark located near the platform in the pool did not overshadow or block learning based on geometric shape. In their third experiment, the researchers found that room cues external to the pool neither overshadowed nor were overshadowed by learning about the shape of the pool.

When these results are taken together and contrasted with the previously discussed results showing cue-competition between landmarks, beacons, and room cues, one is led to the conclusion that spatial learning based on the geometric shape of an environment is a robust encoding strategy. It appears to be rather impervious to interference by other types of spatial information.

Training Experience Matters

Although features do not seem to overshadow the encoding of geometric information, the presence of features during initial training in the environment can nevertheless affect the weighting given to features and geometry at the time of testing. As described, Kelly et al. (1998) trained two groups of disoriented pigeons in a fully enclosed rectangular environment. The feature group was trained from the outset with a distinct featural cue in each corner of the environment, so that both featural and geometric cues were available. The geometric group was initially trained without features, so that only the geometric information was available, but then was retrained with the features present. As previously mentioned, both groups showed strong control by geometry when no features were present. However, differences between the groups emerged on tests in which features and geometry provided conflicting information. For example, when tested with an affine transformation that essentially moved each feature one position clockwise, pigeons in the feature group showed strong control by the featural cues by choosing the corner with the correct feature, even though it was now in a geometrically incorrect position. On the other hand, pigeons in the geometric group divided their choices among the corner containing the correct feature and the two geometrically correct corners (figure 11.9). The difference between these groups on the conflict tests shows that the presence or absence of features during initial training in the rectangular enclosed environment played a key role in how the pigeons subsequently weighted featural and geometric cues.

Recent research using the touch-screen procedure with adult humans and pigeons has added an interesting twist to the experiential story (Kelly & Spetch, 2004a, b). In the first study (Kelly & Spetch, 2004a), two groups of adult humans were trained in a two-dimensional rectangular environment.

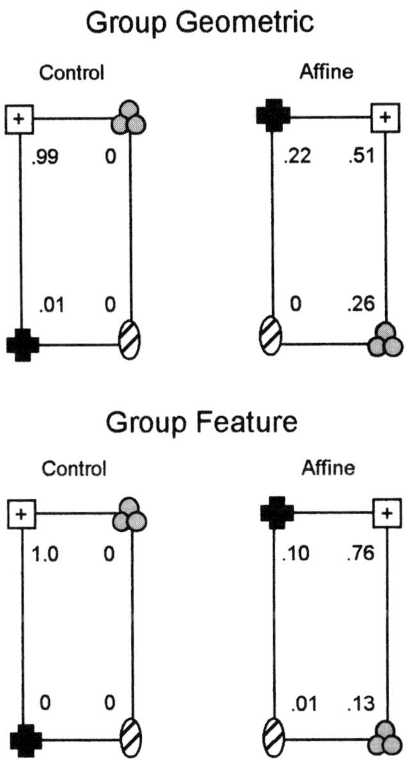

Figure 11.9. Proportion of choices during control tests and during the affine transformation test, averaged across the birds in the geometric group (*top row*) and the feature group. The corner containing the positive feature is represented by the square with a plus in the center (actual position was counterbalanced across birds). (Modified from Kelly, Spetch, & Heth, 1998.)

One group was trained with featural information from the outset and the other group was initially trained with geometry only and then was retrained with the features added. In this study, initial training experience had no significant effect on the weighting given to features and geometry on conflict tests. For example, when presented with an affine transformation, both groups of humans showed almost exclusive control by featural information. In the companion study (Kelly & Spetch, 2004b), two groups of pigeons were trained with the same two-dimensional rectangular environment as the humans. Again, initial training experience had no significant effect on the weighting of featural and geometric information on conflict tests. In this case, both groups of pigeons divided their choices among the two geometrically correct corners and the featurally correct corner

Thus, the humans in our two-dimensional schematic showed almost exclusive weighting of the featural information regardless of initial training (Kelly & Spetch, 2004a). For pigeons, initial training experience affected weighting of features and geometry in the enclosed environment (Kelly et al., 1998) but did not affect weighting in the two-dimensional task (Kelly & Spetch, 2004b). Although this result could reflect a difference between two-dimensional and three-dimensional environments, a difference in the training procedure provides a more likely reason for the conflicting results. In our study using the three-dimensional environment (Kelly et al., 1998), birds in the feature group were never specifically trained with geometry alone prior to the conflict tests. By contrast, in our study conducted with the two-dimensional environment (Kelly & Spetch, 2004b), the birds initially trained with features were subsequently retrained with geometry only, prior to the conflict tests. Thus, for pigeons at least, weighting of geometry and features may depend not on which training experience comes first but on whether any of the prior training requires an exclusive reliance on geometry.

Abstracting Geometry From Models and Two-Dimensional Schemata

Previous experiments investigating the conjoining of geometric and featural information in human and nonhuman animals have focused on the use of navigational tasks allowing the participant to freely locomote through an enclosed environment. However, recently Gouteux, Vauclair, and Thinus-Blanc (2001) and Kelly and Spetch (2004a, b) examined how geometric and featural information are used in nonnavigable space. Gouteux et al. used a small-scale three-dimensional model to represent an enclosed space, having the participants point to the location of the hidden goal. Remarkably, although this study showed some differences in the developmental aspects regarding the age at which geometric and featural information are conjoined, the overall results were very similar to a navigable environment. Indeed, even in a two-dimensional schematic of a room, we also found that adult humans showed conjoining of geometric and featural information (Kelly & Spetch, 2004a). We also examined whether encoding of geometric information in a two-dimensional environment was robust to translations and rotations. By presenting the schematic environment in a new position but maintaining the same rotation as in training, we found that the adults easily transferred to the translated environment. However, when we presented the environment at a novel rotation (one not seen during training), geometric responding fell to chance levels (a result also found with pigeons; Kelly & Spetch, 2004b). These results suggest that the geometric information was encoded using an orientation- and sense-specific code. Although previous research has shown that encoding of geometric properties may be robust to 180-degree rotations (Cheng, 1986; Kelly et al., 1998), few studies have examined the influence of intermediate rotations. Given that many studies use two-dimensional representations of space to examine navigation, understanding how geometry is encoded in such an environment is important (e.g., Albert, Rensink, & Beusmans, 1999; Sholl, 1999).

Nature of the Geometrical Representation

Geometric information can be encoded using either relative or absolute metrics. Consider, for instance, an animal orienting within a rectangular enclosure such as typical with many previously discussed tasks. If food is hidden in one corner of the environment such that a 200-cm wall is to the right of the corner and a 100-cm wall is to the left, then this information may be encoded using one or both of these absolute metrics. In particular, when facing the wall, the animal may encode that the wall on its right is 200 cm long, or that the wall on the left is 100 cm long, or it may encode the length of both walls. However, another way of encoding this information is to use a strategy of encoding relative metrics; that is, the animal might encode that the corner that contains the hidden food has a longer wall to the right and a shorter wall to the left. In this case, the geometric representation is abstracted away from the absolute metrics of the environment. Either of these two strategies would allow the animal to encode sufficient geometric information to limit its search to the two geometrically correct corners.

We examined whether pigeons encode absolute or relative metrics when reorienting within an enclosed rectangular space (Kelly & Spetch, 2001). We trained disoriented pigeons, on a reference memory task, to locate food in one of four identical containers within a fully enclosed rectangular room. Once the pigeons were accurately choosing between the containers in the two geometrically correct corners, we conducted transformation tests in which either the size or the shape of the environment was manipulated. We modified the size of the enclosure by reducing the long and short walls to two thirds of the original training size. Had the pigeons encoded the geometric shape of the environment using absolute metrics, none of the walls during testing would match the encoded information. Therefore, using an absolute encoding strategy would result in an unsolvable task and the pigeons should randomly choose between the corners. However, a representation based on relative metrics would not be affected by size transformation; hence, using a relative metrical encoding strategy would still allow the pigeons to choose between the geometrically correct corners. Indeed, we found that the pigeons chose the two geometrically correct corners more than expected by chance (50%) on the size transformation test, indicating that encoding was based at least in part on relative geometry. Furthermore, when we modified the shape of the environment, making it square, the pigeons' performance fell to chance (figure 11.10).

Tommasi and Polli (2004) assessed whether chicks' geometric representation included information about both the relative lengths of walls and the angles formed by the corners. They trained disoriented chicks to find food in one corner of a parallelogram-shaped enclosure. On test trials, they manipulated the shape of the environment in order to alter the angular information in the corners and/or the relative lengths of the walls. Specifically, they tested the chicks in a rectangular enclosure that preserved the ratio of wall lengths but removed the relevant angular information and in a rhombus-shaped enclosure that preserved the angles of the parallelogram but had walls of equal length. These tests revealed that the chicks could use either geometric cue when it was presented alone. On a third type of test, they tested the chicks in a mirror parallelogram that placed the corner angles in conflict with the wall–length ratios. The results of these conflict tests appeared to depend on the salience of the corners: chicks that were trained with 60 degrees as the positive corner showed control by the corner information, whereas chicks that were trained with 120-degree angles showed control

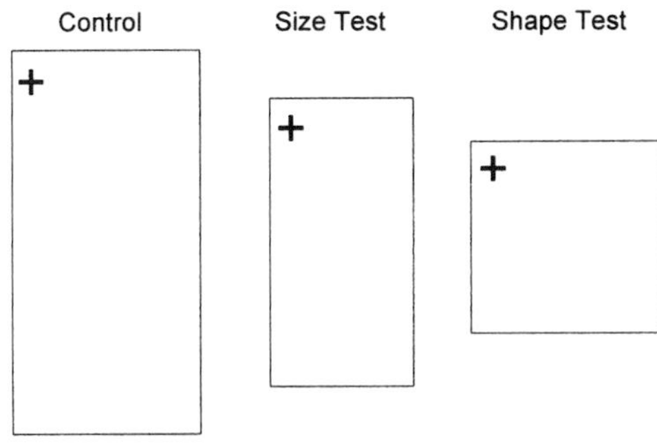

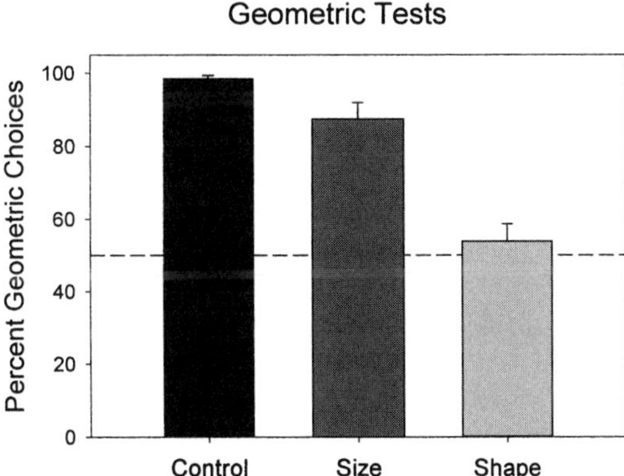

Figure 11.10. Diagram of spatial arenas (*top*) and search accuracy (*bottom*) for pigeons on control tests and on tests in which the size and/or shape of the arena was altered. (From Figures 1 and 2 of "Pigeons Encode Relative Geometry," by D. M. Kelly, and M. L. Spetch, 2001, *Journal of Experimental Psychology: Animal Behavior Processes, 27,* pp. 419, 420. Copyright 2001 by American Psychological Association. Reprinted with permission.)

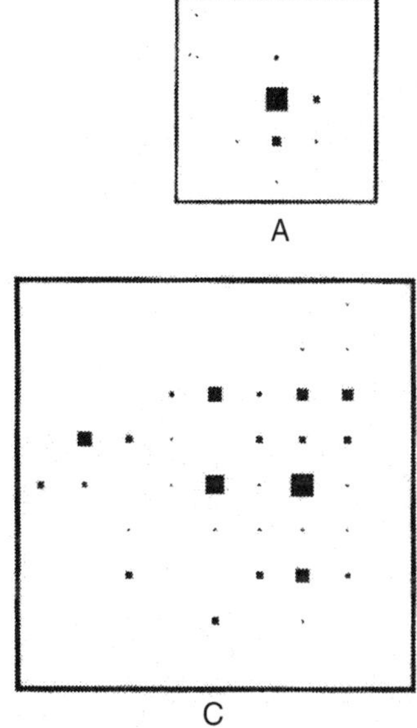

Figure 11.11. Search behavior of chicks in the training arena (*top*) and in the expanded arena (*bottom*). The size of the filled symbols is proportional to the density of searching in each location.(From Figure 1 [panels A and C] of "Searching for the Center: Spatial Cognition in the Domestic Chick (*Gallus gallus*)," by L. Tommasi and G. Vallortigara, 2000, *Journal of Experimental Psychology: Animal Behavior Processes, 26,* p. 479. Copyright 2000 by American Psychological Association. Adapted with permission.)

by wall–length information. Thus, the chicks in Tommasi and Polli's study showed a hierarchical use of redundant relevant geometric cues, much like the hierarchical use of redundant relevant local and global cues seen in pigeons by Spetch and Edwards (1988).

DIFFERENCES BETWEEN SURFACES AND DISCRETE LANDMARKS

Tommasi and colleagues (Tommasi & Vallortigara, 2000; Tommasi et al., 1997) conducted an interesting series of experiments with chicks that were procedurally similar to the aforementioned tests conducted by Spetch et al. (1997) with pigeons. The chicks were trained to search in the center of an arena and then were given expansion tests, in which the size of the arena was increased. The difference, however, was that the chicks searched in the center of an enclosed arena that blocked access to external orientation cues, whereas the pigeons searched in the center of an array of discrete landmarks that were placed within a search space that provided external cues for orientation. Interestingly, whereas pigeons showed no tendency to spontaneously encode a relative middle rule with the discrete landmarks, chicks showed both relative and absolute encoding of distance from the walls of the enclosure. Specifically, the chicks showed substantial searching both at the center of the expanded arena and at locations that maintained the absolute distance from walls (figure 11.11).

Do chicks encode spatial information differently from pigeons, or is there something different

Figure 11.12. Pigeon in square training arena. On training trials, food is hidden under the bedding in the center of the arena. The top is covered with mesh so that no external cues can be seen from inside the arena.

about encoding the location of a goal from surfaces of an enclosure than from discrete landmarks? To address this question, we (Gray, Spetch, Kelly, & Nguyen, 2004) tested pigeons in an enclosure like that used with chicks by Tommasi and Vallortigara (2000; see figure 11.12). Our training and testing procedures were similar to those used with chicks. Furthermore, we examined the pigeons' search behavior using both measures reported in the previous studies on chicks and measures used in our landmark-based search studies with pigeons. As shown in figure 11.13, both measures revealed considerable searching in the center region by the pigeons on the expansion tests. Thus, the pigeons' search behavior on expansion tests was clearly more like that seen with chicks than like that seen with pigeons on expansion tests with discrete landmarks. Apparently, birds are more likely to attend to relative distances when searching for a goal on the basis of continuous surfaces than when searching for a goal on the basis of discrete landmarks.

Research on hemispheric specialization in chicks (Tommasi & Vallortigara, 2001) further indicates a distinction between continuous surfaces and discrete landmarks. Here, chicks were trained binocularly to find food hidden under sawdust in the center of a square arena and then tested with size transformations under monocular conditions. Right-eyed chicks were more likely to search according to relative distances, whereas left-eyed chicks were more likely to search according to absolute distance from walls. In another condition, Tommasi and Vallortigara trained chicks binocularly with a discrete landmark placed near the food at the center of the arena and then tested them monocularly with shifts of the landmark, thus placing the landmark and wall cues in conflict. Right-eyed chicks followed the landmark, whereas left-eyed chicks did not. These results suggest that the left hemisphere (driven by the right eye) in birds may be specialized for encoding discrete landmarks and absolute distance spatial information, whereas the right hemisphere may encode

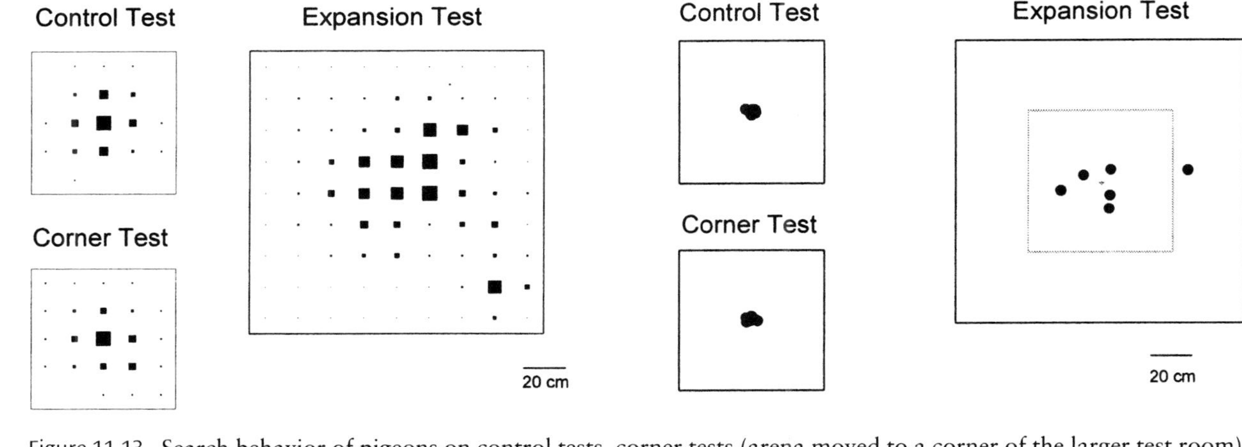

Figure 11.13. Search behavior of pigeons on control tests, corner tests (arena moved to a corner of the larger test room), and expansion tests in a larger arena. Left graphs show search behavior plotted in the same way as reported for chicks, in which the size of the square symbols is proportional to the density of searching. The right graph show peak places of searching as reported in previous studies on landmark-based search in pigeons. (From Figures 1 and 2 of "Searching in the Center: Pigeons (*Columba livia*) Encode Relative Distances from Walls of an Enclosure," by E. Gray, M. L. Spetch, D. M. Kelly, and A. Nguyen, 2004, *Journal of Comparative Psychology, 118,* pp. 115, 116. Copyright 2004 by American Psychological Association. Adapted with permission.)

global continuous surfaces and relative spatial information. These and subsequent studies (e.g., Tommasi & Vallortigara, 2004) provide an exciting approach to investigating how the avian brain processes spatial information.

CONCLUDING COMMENTS

The field of comparative spatial cognition has grown in the past few decades as researchers have expanded the range of species investigated, the environments and tasks used to study spatial behavior, and, most important, the questions and processes under investigation. Field and laboratory studies have revealed a rich array of cognitive mechanisms for finding places. In this chapter, we reviewed a small subset of recent work on spatial cognition, with a focus on how organisms use visual landmarks or the structure of surfaces to find a goal (other aspects of spatial cognition are reviewed in several other chapters in this volume). Some of the spatial processes identified are remarkably general across species and spatial environments. For example, the occurrence of cue-competition among discrete landmarks has been found in species ranging from honeybees to humans and with environments as different as swimming pools and computer screens. An ability to use the geometric shape formed by surfaces of an environment may also be universal—we are not aware of any reports of a species failing to display use of geometry for reorientation. Most interesting, the independence of geometric and landmark encoding may be general in that a lack of overshadowing between discrete landmarks and the geometric shape of an environment has now been seen in rodents, birds, and humans and in both three-dimensional arenas and two-dimensional environments.

However, comparative studies have also revealed some interesting differences between species in processes of landmark-based search. One such difference was disclosed by landmark array expansion tests. After being trained with an array of two or more landmarks that each have a fixed relation to each other and to the goal, the most frequently observed response to expansions of the array appears to be that of searching on the basis of individual landmarks. That is, most animals do not appear to spontaneously search according to the relational properties of the landmark array and goal (although they may be capable of learning such properties if training requires such learning). There are, however, two interesting exceptions. One is that honeybees appear to spontaneously respond to the relational properties of a landmark array; this appears to reflect some specialized aspects of their image-based navigational system (see chapter 10, this volume). Adult humans are the other exception. In tasks conducted on computer screens, table tops, and outdoors, humans almost uniformly respond to expansion tests according to relational properties of the landmark array and goal; this may reflect our extensive experience with scale transformations and representations of space in models and maps.

Many questions remain about the nature of the processes used, the conditions under which various strategies dominate, the role of development and experience, and the underlying brain mechanisms of spatial cognition. It seems likely that the next decade or two will bring exciting advances in the breadth and depth of our knowledge about place-finding mechanisms.

References

Albert, W. S., Rensink, R. A., & Beusmans, J. M. (1999). Learning relative directions between landmarks in a desktop virtual environment. *Spatial Cognition and Computation, 1,* 131–144.

Biegler, R. & Morris, R. G. M. (1999). Blocking in the spatial domain with arrays of discrete landmarks. *Journal of Experimental Psychology: Animal Behavior Processes, 25,* 334–351.

Brodbeck, D. R. (1994). Memory for spatial and local cues: A comparison of a storing and non-storing species. *Animal Learning & Behavior, 22,* 119–133.

Cartwright, B. A., & Collett, T. S. (1983). Landmark learning in bees. *Journal of Comparative Physiology, A, 151,* 521–543.

Chamizo, V. D. (2003). Acquisition of knowledge about spatial location: Assessing the generality of mechanisms of learning. *The Quarterly Journal of Experimental Psychology, 56B,* 102–113.

Chamizo, V. D., Aznar-Casnova, J. A., & Artugas, A. A. (2003). Human overshadowing in a virtual pool: Simple guidance is a good competitor against locale learning. *Learning and Motivation, 34,* 262–281.

Chamizo, V. D., Sterio, D., & Mackintosh, H. J. (1985). Blocking and overshadowing between intra-maze and extra-maze cues: A test of the independence of locale and guidance learning. *Quarterly Journal of Experimental Psychology, 37B*, 235–253.

Cheng, K. (1986). A purely geometric module in the rat's spatial representation. *Cognition, 23*, 149–178.

Cheng, K. (1994). The determination of direction in landmark-based spatial search in pigeons: A further test of the vector sum model. *Animal Learning & Behavior, 22*, 291–301.

Cheng, K., & Spetch, M. L. (1998). Mechanisms of landmark use in mammals and birds. In S. Healy (Ed.), *Spatial representation in animals* (pp. 1–17). Oxford: Oxford University Press.

Cheng, K., & Spetch, M. L. (2001). Blocking in landmark-based search in honeybees. *Animal Learning & Behavior, 29*, 1–9.

Collett, T. S., Cartwright, B. A., & Smith, B. A. (1986). Landmark learning and visuo-spatial memories in gerbils. *Journal of Comparative Physiology A, 158*,,835–851.

Denniston, J. C., Savastano, H. I., Blaisdell, A. P., & Miller, R. R. (2003). Cue competition as a retrieval deficit. *Learning & Motivation, 34*, 1–31.

Fagot, J. (2000). *Picture perception in animals.* East Sussex: Psychology Press.

Gouteux, S., Vauclair, J., & Thinus-Blanc, C. (2001). Reorientation in a small-scale environment by 3-, 4-, and 5-year-old children. *Cognitive Development, 16*, 853–869.

Gray, E., Spetch, M. L., Kelly, D. M., & Nguyen, A. (2004). Searching in the center: Pigeons (*Columba livia*) encode relative distances from walls of an enclosure. *Journal of Comparative Psychology, 118*, 113–117.

Hayward, A., McGregor, A., Good, M. A., & Pearce, J. M. (2003) Absence of overshadowing and blocking between landmarks and the geometric cues provided by the shape of a test arena. *Quarterly Journal of Experimental Psychology, 56B*, 114–126.

Hermer, L., & Spelke, E. S. (1994). A geometric process for spatial reorientation in young children. *Nature, 370*, 57–59.

Hermer, L., & Spelke, E. (1996). Modularity and development: The case of spatial reorientation. *Cognition, 61*, 195–232.

Jones, J. E., Anotoniadis, E., Shettleworth, S. J., & Kamil, A. C. (2002). A comparative study of geometric rule learning by nutcrackers, pigeons and jackdaws. *Journal of Comparative Psychology, 116*, 350–356.

Kamil, A. C., & Jones, J. E. (1997). The seed-storing corvid Clark's nutcracker learns geometric relationships among landmarks. *Nature, 390*, 276–279.

Kamil, A. C., & Jones, J. E. (2000). Geometric rule learning by Clark's nutcrackers (*Nucifraga columbiana*). *Journal of Experimental Psychology: Animal Behavior Processes, 26*, 439–453.

Kamin, L. J. (1969). Selective association and conditioning. In N. J. Mackintosh & W. K. Honig (Eds.), *Fundamental issues in associative learning* (pp. 46–64). Halifax, Nova Scotia: Dalhousie University Press.

Kelly, D. M., & Spetch, M. L. (2001). Pigeons encode relative geometry. *Journal of Experimental Psychology: Animal Behavior Processes, 27*, 417–422.

Kelly, D. M., & Spetch, M. L. (2004a). Reorientation in a two-dimensional environment. I: Do adults encode the featural and geometric properties of a two-dimensional schematic of a room? *Journal of Comparative Psychology, 118*, 82–94.

Kelly, D. M., & Spetch, M. L. (2004b). Reorientation in a two-dimensional environment II: Do pigeons encode the featural and geometric properties of a two-dimensional schematic of a room? *Journal of Comparative Psychology, 118*, 384–395.

Kelly, D. M., Spetch, M. L., & Heth, C. D. (1998). Pigeons' (*Columba livia*) encoding of geometric and featural properties of a spatial environment. *Journal of Comparative Psychology, 112*, 259–269.

MacDonald, S., Spetch. M. L., Kelly, D. M., & Cheng, K. (2004). Strategies in landmark use by children, adults and marmoset monkeys. *Learning and Motivation, 35*, 322–347.

March, J., Chamizo, V. D., & Mackintosh, N. J. (1992). Reciprocal overshadowing between intra-maze and extra-maze cues. *Quarterly Journal of Experimental Psychology 45B*, 49–63.

O'Keefe, J., & Nadel, L. (1978). *The hippocampus as a cognitive map.* Oxford: Oxford University Press.

Pearce, J. M., Ward-Robinson, J., Good, M., Fussell, C., & Aydin, A. (2001). Influence of a beacon on spatial learning based on the shape of the test environment. *Journal of Experimental Psychology: Animal Behavior Processes, 27*, 329–344.

Rescorla, R. A., & Wagner, A. R. (1972). A theory of Pavlovian conditioning: Variations in the effectiveness of reinforcement and nonreinforcement. In A. Black & W. F. Prokasy (Eds.), *Classical conditioning II* (pp. 64–99). New York: Appleton-Century-Crofts.

Roberts, A. D. L., & Pearce, J. (1999). Blocking in the Morris swimming pool. *Journal of Experimental Psychology: Animal Behavior Processes 25*, 225–235.

Rodrigo, T., Chamizo, V. D., McLaren, I. P. L., &. Mackintosh, N. J. (1997). Blocking in the spatial domain. *Journal of Experimental Psychology: Animal Behavior Processes 23*, 110–118.

Sánchez-Moreno, J., Rodrigo, T., Chamizo, V. D., & Mackintosh, N. J. (1999). Overshadowing in the spatial domain. *Animal Learning & Behavior 27,* 391–398.

Sholl, M. J. (1999). Egocentric frames of reference used for the retrieval of survey knowledge learned by map and navigation. *Spatial Cognition and Computation, 1,* 475-494.

Sovrano, V. A., Bisazza, A., & Vallortigara, G. (2002). Modularity and spatial orientation in a simple mind: encoding of geometric and non-geometric properties of a spatial environment by fish. *Cognition, 85,* B51–B59.

Sovrano, V. A., Bisazza, A., & Vallortigara, G. (2003). Modularity as a fish (*Xenotoca eiseni*) views it: Conjoining geometric and nongeometric information for spatial reorientation. *Journal of Experimental Psychology: Animal Behavior Processes, 29,* 199–210.

Spetch, M. L. (1995). Overshadowing in landmark learning: Touch-screen studies with pigeons and humans. *Journal of Experimental Psychology: Animal Behavior Processes, 21,* 166-181.

Spetch, M. L., Cheng, K., & MacDonald, S. E. (1996). Learning the configuration of a landmark array, I: Touch-screen studies with pigeons and humans. *Journal of Comparative Psychology, 110,* 55–68.

Spetch, M. L., Cheng, K., MacDonald, S. E., Linkenhoker, B. A., Kelly, D. M., & Doerkson, S. R. (1997). Use of landmark configuration in pigeons and humans: II. Generality across search tasks. *Journal of Comparative Psychology, 111,* 14–24.

Spetch, M. L., & Edwards, C. A. (1988). Pigeons' (*Columba livia*) use of global and local cues for spatial memory. *Animal Behaviour, 36,* 293–296.

Spetch, M. L., Rust, T. B., Kamil, A. C., & Jones, J. E. (2003). Searching by rules: Pigeons' landmark-based search according to constant bearing or constant distance. *Journal of Comparative Psychology, 117,* 125–132.

Sutton, J. E. (2002). Multiple-landmark piloting in pigeons (*Columba livia*): Landmark configuration as a discriminative cue. *Journal of Comparative Psychology. 116,* 391–403.

Sutton, J. E., Olthof, A., & Roberts, W. A. (2000). Landmark use by squirrel monkeys (*Saimiri sciureus*). *Animal Learning & Behavior, 28,* 28–42.

Tinbergen, N. (1972). *The animal in its world.* Cambridge, MA: Harvard University Press.

Tolman, E. C. (1948). Cognitive maps in rats and men. *The Psychological Review, 55,* 189–208.

Tommasi, L., & Polli, C. (2004). Representation of two geometric features of the environment by the domestic chick (*Gallus gallus*). *Animal Cognition, 7,* 53–59.

Tommasi, L., & Vallortigara, G. (2000). Searching for the center: Spatial cognition in the domestic chick (*Gallus gallus*). *Journal of Experimental Psychology: Animal Behavior Processes, 26,* 477–486.

Tommasi, L., & Vallortigara, G. (2001). Encoding of geometric and landmark information in the left and right hemispheres of the avian brain. *Behavioral Neuroscience, 115,* 602–613.

Tommasi, L., & Vallortigara, G. (2004). Hemispheric processing of landmark and geometric information in male and female domestic chicks (*Gallus gallus*). *Behavioural Brain Research, 155,* 85–96.

Tommasi, L., Vallortigara, G., & Zanforlin, M. (1997). Young chickens learn to localize the center of a spatial environment. *Journal of Comparative Physiology A: Sensory Neural and Behavioral Physiology, 180,* 248–254.

Vallortigara, G., Zanforlin, M., & Pasti, G. (1990). Geometric modules in animals' spatial representations: A test with chicks (*Gallus gallus domesticus*). *Journal of Comparative Psychology, 104,* 248–254

12

Properties of Time-Place Learning

CHRISTINA M. THORPE AND DONALD M. WILKIE

We live in a world that is always changing, sometimes predictably and sometimes not. The availability of food, mates, predators, and other biologically significant stimuli generally varies across both space and time. If these stimuli vary predictably, then it would be advantageous for animals to learn this spatiotemporal variability, so that they might maximally exploit these resources. The ability to learn spatiotemporal variability has become known as *time-place learning* (TPL).

In *The Organization of Learning*, Gallistel (1990) put forth a theory stating that whenever a biologically significant event occurs, a memory code is formed that includes the nature of the event, as well as the time and place in which it occurred. When the animal is later faced with a biological need, it can consult these time-place-event memory codes, determine when and where that need has been met in the past, and use that information to guide its current behavior.

In Gallistel's theory, animals' ability to tell time is of fundamental importance. The focus of this chapter is on this ability. Carr and Wilkie (1997a) distinguished among three timing systems: ordinal, phase, and interval. *Ordinal timing* allows an animal to predict the order in which events occur within a time period. For example, breakfast, dinner, and supper occur in the same order each day, but the time of the day at which they occur may not be constant. It has been shown that rats sometimes learn the order in which different levers provide food within a day without learning the actual time of day that they do so (Carr & Wilkie, 1997b, 1999). *Phase timing* allows an animal to predict events that are cyclic or occur with a fixed periodicity. This periodicity may be circadian, circalunar (tidal), or circannual. One of the first field studies of TPL observed seabirds called oystercatchers that learned the timing of the tides (Daan & Koene, 1981). These birds flew from inland roosts, over dykes, to mussel beds that were exposed at low tide. Because of coastal irregularities, mussels were exposed at different times at different spatial locations. The birds were able to learn the spatiotemporal variability of the mussels' availability as demonstrated by the ability to time their trips to the correct spatial locations, despite not being able to see the mussel beds from their roosts. *Interval timing* allows an animal to predict an event that reliably occurs at a fixed amount of time after some external event. For example, animals respond to a fixed-interval (FI) schedule with a typical "scalloped" pattern of responding. Interval timers are thought to measure durations in the range of seconds to minutes. Each of these three timers is specialized for durations of varying lengths. In addition, these timers have unique characteristics. Ordinal timers are resetable and focus on sequence information. Phase timers are self-sustaining and entrainable and run continuously. Interval timers have stopwatch properties of start, stop, reset, and restart (Carr & Wilkie, 1997a).

Why are there different types of timing systems? One speculation has been that multiple timing systems are thought to have evolved because the characteristics that make one timing system efficient are *functionally incompatible* with the efficient performance of other systems (see Sherry & Schacter, 1987, for a detailed discussion of this concept; see Wilkie, 1995, for a discussion of the different requirements of interval and phase timing).

In this chapter, we discuss recent research on interval and daily time-place (TP) tasks in both rats and pigeons. As will become apparent, rats and pigeons show both similarities and differences in how they respond to TP contingencies.

BACKGROUND INFORMATION ON INTERVAL TIME-PLACE LEARNING

Much of the knowledge about the timer involved in interval timing comes from research using the peak procedure. In this procedure, animals are first trained on an FI task in which there is a signal (tone or light) indicating the start of a trial. Once the animal has learned this task, peak probe trials are introduced, in which the signal remains on for approximately twice as long as the interval being timed and no reinforcement is given. When the response rate on these peak probe trials is plotted as a function of time elapsed since signal onset, a normal distribution is obtained with the peak response rate at the usual reinforcement time (e.g., Roberts, 1981). The width or spread of the response rate distribution is taken as a measure of error in the timing system. If the response rate distributions are acquired for many different FI durations, then it can be seen that as the duration of the FI timed increases, the error (spread) of the response distributions increases proportionally. Therefore, interval timing is said to obey Weber's law, a property also known as scalar timing (e.g., Cheng & Roberts, 1991; Gibbon, 1991). Scalar timing is also evidenced in interval TPL. Carr and Wilkie (1998) trained three groups on an interval TP task in which the levers provided reinforcement for 4, 6, or 8 min. As shown in figure 12.1, the greater the duration, the greater is the error.

Interval TP tasks differ from interval timing tasks in one fundamental way: Namely, there is an association between the time and a place. To ensure that animals are using an interval timer on the interval TP task rather than a circadian timer, animals are generally trained at variable times of day, so that the time of day information is irrelevant.

Wilkie and colleagues began the laboratory investigation of interval TPL using pigeons (Wilkie & Willson, 1992; Wilkie, Saksida, Samson, & Lee, 1994). The pigeons were tested in a square transparent box that contained a key and a hopper on each of the four walls. Illumination of the four keylights signaled the start of the session. Each key provided reinforcement on a variable interval schedule for 15 min. Only one key provided reinforcement at any given time, and the order in which the keys provided reinforcement remained constant from session to session. It was found that the pigeons restricted the majority of their responding to the key that was currently providing reinforcement. On this task, it is possible that the pigeons were not timing at all but rather were simply moving from a key when it stopped providing reinforcement (i.e., a win-stay/lose-shift strategy). Such a strategy did not seem to be the case, however, because the pigeons anticipated the next correct key before it started providing reinforcement and response rate on the key providing food started to decrease before the end of the reinforced period.

Also, data from probe trials, in which the keylights were turned out and no reinforcement was given, and from probe trials, in which the pigeons were temporally removed from the chamber and/or testing room partway through the session, suggested that movement from one key to the next was under temporal control. Data from these probe trials also helped to identify characteristics of the timer underlying the pigeon's TP behavior: namely, the interval timer used in this task has the properties of stop, restart, and reset (Wilkie et al., 1994), all properties of the internal clock model postulated by Church, Broadbent, and Gibbon (1992).

Can other animals learn TP contingencies? Do they do so in ways similar to pigeons? In the past few years, we have been investigating the properties of interval TPL in the rat. Some of this research is described in the following sections.

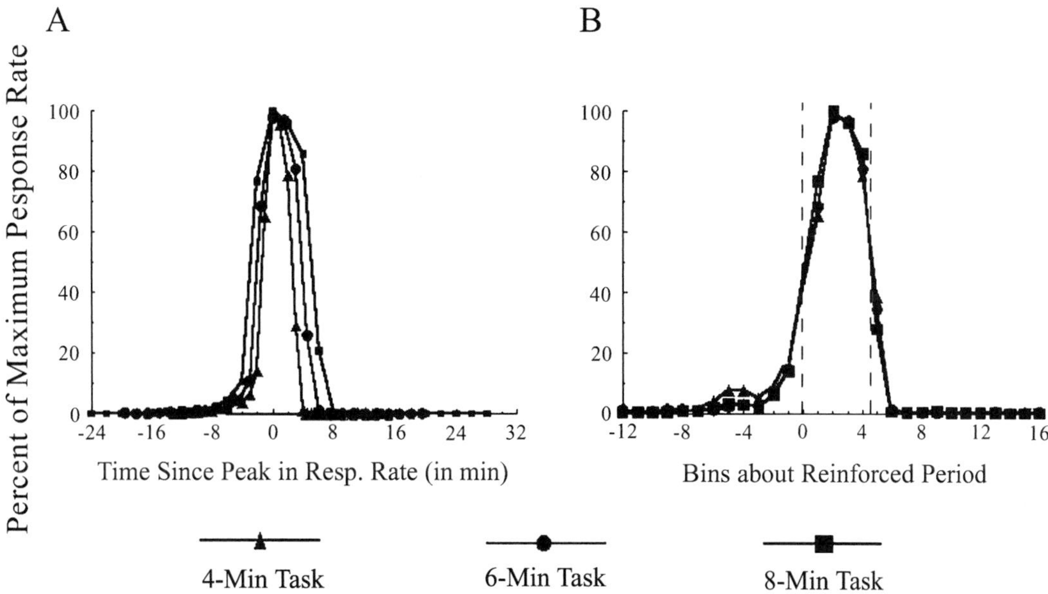

Figure 12.1. Three groups of rats were trained on an interval time-place task in which the levers provided reinforcement for 4, 6, or 8 min. The overall normalized response rate distributions for the 4-, 6-, and 8-min tasks (*A*) plotted about their peak overall normalized response rates and (*B*) plotted with time, in recording bins, on the abscissa. Responses were reinforced during the period bounded by the vertical dashed lines. As can be seen in *A*, the greater the duration, the greater is the spread (error). When the response rate distributions are plotted in relative time (*B*), the distributions superimpose. (From "Characterization of the Strategy Used by Rats in an Interval Time-Place Learning Task," by J. A. R. Carr and D. M. Wilkie, 1998, *Journal of Experimental Psychology: Animal Behavior Processes, 23,* 232–247. Copyright 1998 by the American Psychological Association. Redrawn with permission.)

ADVANCES IN INTERVAL TIME-PLACE LEARNING

Open Hopper Tests

Research has been conducted into the properties of interval TPL in rats using a similar paradigm as in pigeons. Similar to pigeons, rats restrict the majority of their responding to the correct lever and anticipate reinforcement on an upcoming correct (rewarded) lever (Carr & Wilkie, 1998). In addition, they anticipate depletion of reinforcement on a lever before it stops providing reinforcement; that is, response rate on a rewarded lever decreases as the time at which this lever ceases to produce food nears. Although anticipation indicates the use of a timing strategy, "open hopper" test (OHT) sessions confirm this property of TPL in a very convincing manner (Carr, Tan, Thorpe, & Wilkie, 2001). On OHT sessions, all levers provide reinforcement on a variable ratio schedule for the duration of the session; as can be seen in figure 12.2, under these conditions rats continue to move from lever to lever at approximately the correct times despite there being no contingencies in effect to necessitate their doing so.

This result rules out the possibility that the rats were using a nontemporal strategy, such as win-stay/lose-shift, in which case the rat would continue to press on a lever until it stopped providing reinforcement and then would shift to the next lever in the sequence. Such a strategy would be difficult (but not impossible) because the levers provide food on a variable ratio (VR)16 schedule. On a VR16 schedule, on average every 16th response is reinforced. Lack of reinforcement on a particular press could be due to either pressing an inactive lever or to the reinforcement schedule. It is worth noting, however, that there is more variability in OHT sessions than in baseline sessions. This finding suggests that there is a built-in error checker in baseline sessions similar to how known spatial

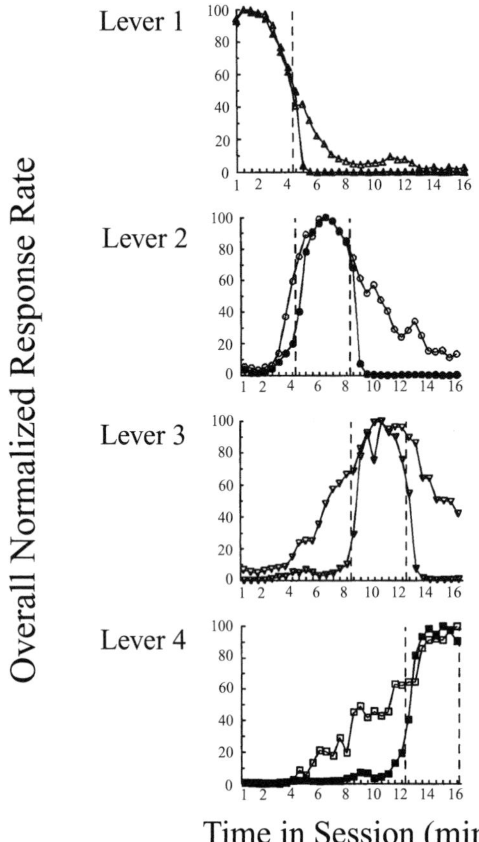

Figure 12.2. Overall normalized response rate on levers 1, 2, 3, and 4 throughout the baseline (*filled markers*) and open hopper (*open markers*) sessions. During baseline sessions, responses on each lever were reinforced during the period bounded by the vertical dashed lines. (From "Further Evidence of Joint Time-Place Control of Rats' Behavior: Results from an 'Open Hopper' Test," by J. A. R. Carr, A. O. Tan, C. M. Thorpe, and D. M. Wilkie, 2001, *Behavioural Processes, 53,* 147–153. Copyright 2001 by Elsevier Science. Redrawn with permission.)

landmarks are used to correct error in dead reckoning in the spatial domain. A likely candidate for the error checker in the TP domain is the food/no-food boundary.

There are two possible timing strategies that the rats could use in this task. First, they could time from the start of the session and move when the timer reaches three consecutive criterion values (i.e., a time session strategy). Second, they could time each lever separately (i.e., a time location strategy). If the rats were using a time session strategy, then we would expect the error (spread) to increase across levers, whereas if they were using a time location strategy, then we would not expect the error to increase. We found that the error did not increase across levers, suggesting that the rats timed each individual lever (Carr & Wilkie, 1998). It is not known, however, what starts the timer (although a likely candidate is the first reinforced response on a lever).

Effect of Distraction on Time-Place Behavior

From a foraging perspective, animals are sometimes distracted in the middle of a foraging bout. For example, an interesting field study of birds' foraging behavior was reported by Davies and Houston (1981). These authors studied the pied wagtail, a passerine bird that defends a feeding territory in the winter. These birds feed on dead insects that wash up onto river banks. The birds forage for 90% of daylight hours and must eat an insect every 4 s on average in order to achieve an energy balance. The defended territory averages about 600 m of river bank. Territory owners regularly circuit their territory, a strategy that avoids revisiting recently visited (and depleted) sites. Several circuits are made each day.

A remarkable phenomenon occurs when another bird intrudes into a defended territory. The territory owner breaks off feeding and chases the intruder from the territory, sometimes for distances of 500 m. Interestingly, after the intruder has been evicted, the owner returns to the place on the river bank at which it was feeding before chasing the intruder. There are two possible explanations for how this behavior occurs. First, the wagtails may continue to process spatiotemporal information about food availability during territory defense and return to the spatial location that is associated with the most recent temporally. The second possibility is that the wagtails do not keep track of the time that has passed while they were defending their territory, and simply remember their spatial location before the interruption and return to that location. It is impossible to determine from this field study which of these two strategies the wagtails are using.

Differences have been noted between rats and birds (pigeons) in their reactions to a disruption in an interval-timing task. This can be seen in interval timing when the signal is temporarily stopped partway through the peak procedure. Pigeons shifted their peak by approximately the length of the timeout period plus the elapsed time prior to the timeout, suggesting that pigeons reset their timers when the signal was turned off and restarted timing when it was turned back on (Roberts, Cheng, & Cohen, 1989). Rats, on the other hand, shifted their peak time by approximately the length of the timeout period, suggesting that the rats stopped and restarted their clocks when the signal came back on (Roberts & Church, 1978). Kaiser, Zentall, and Neiman (2002) propose that pigeons treat the gap as if it were an intertrial interval, whereas rats do not. Cabeza de Vaca, Brown, and Hemmes (1994) have suggested that, during breaks, the clock stops and the time accumulated before the break is gradually lost during the break. Therefore, the rightward shift would be somewhat less than would be expected if the clock had simply stopped and restarted.

In terms of interval TPL, we know that pigeons stop and restart their internal clocks when they are given a timeout (Wilkie, Carr, Galloway, Parker, & Yamamoto, 1994). However, in light of the differences between rats and pigeons on interval-timing tasks observed by Roberts et al., we could not be sure how the rats would respond to a distraction in the interval TP task.

After training on the interval TP task, the rats were given probe sessions in which a piece of highly preferred food—a piece of cheese—was dropped into the test chamber at selected times (Thorpe, Petrovic, & Wilkie, 2002). Several outcomes of the cheese distraction are theoretically possible: (1) the cheese could "disrupt" processing of the spatiotemporal sequence so that the rats will restart the sequence at a random location; (2) the cheese could "reset" processing of the spatiotemporal sequence so that the rats will start the TP sequence at the beginning (i.e., on lever 1); (3) the cheese could have no effect on processing of the spatiotemporal sequence so that the rats will continue the sequence at the "correct" TP location; or (4) the cheese could "stop" processing of the spatiotemporal sequence for the duration of the cheese consumption so that the rats will be "late" when restarting.

When rats were presented with a highly preferred food, they were able to keep an accurate record of the spatial location of the correct lever. That is, in most instances, they returned to the lever that had been providing food prior to the presentation of the cheese. This finding suggests that their spatial knowledge was intact. This retention was not the case for temporal knowledge. The rats' internal clock appeared to stop during cheese consumption. When rats began pressing after cheese consumption, their behavior was consequently "late." The usual anticipation effect was absent after the cheese presentation. A comparison of the response curves following cheese presentation and on baseline sessions shows a lack of anticipation following distraction (figure 12.3).

This lack of anticipation suggests that the rat was not timing during cheese consumption. One might argue that if the rats had in fact stopped their internal clock during cheese consumption and then restarted it upon completion of consumption, their response curves should be shifted to the right by an amount proportional to the time they were eating the cheese. This was not the case, however, because once the rats did not receive reinforcement on a lever for some criterion length of time, they shifted to the next lever. It is also possible that the rats stopped and reset their internal clock during cheese consumption as would be predicted by Matell and Meck (1999). This could occur only if there was a decoupling of spatial and temporal information and the rat simply returned to the spatial location where it was prior to distraction. If this was the case, we would also expect to see a rightward shift in the response curve. The magnitude of this shift would again be limited by the built-in error checker. Therefore, in the present study, although it is clear that the rats stopped timing when they were distracted, it is impossible to determine if the rats reset or restarted following distraction.

Overall, the pattern of results supports a timing process that resembles the common stopwatch, which has the properties of start, stop, restart, and reset. The results provide further evidence against an hourglass type of timing described by Daan and Koene (1981). Hourglass timers have only two properties: start and finish. These timers cannot stop and restart. Wilkie et al. (1994) argued similarly about pigeons' TP behavior.

This pattern of results has implications for the nature of memory representations formed on TP tasks. One possible representation is that both spatial and temporal information are integrated into a single entity. Another possibility is that temporal and spatial information are represented by two

Lever 3: Baseline and 6:00 Cheese Test

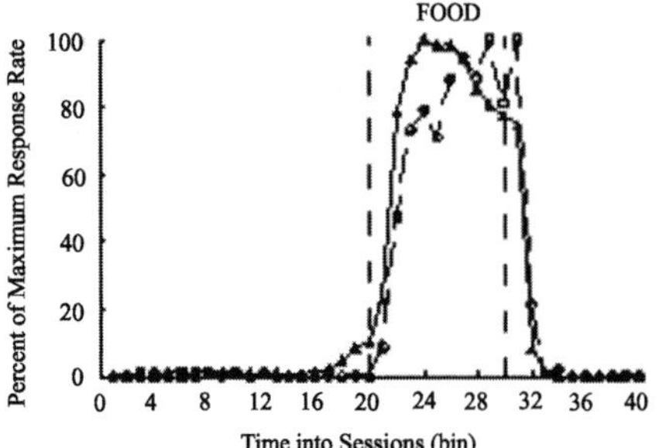

Lever 4: Baseline and 11:00 Cheese Test

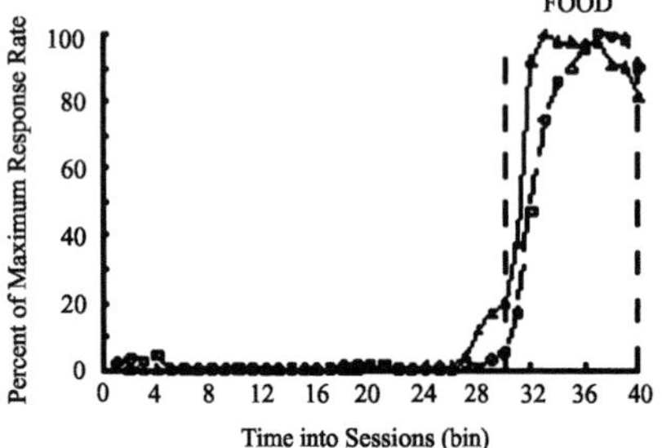

Lever 4: Baseline and 9:55 Cheese Test

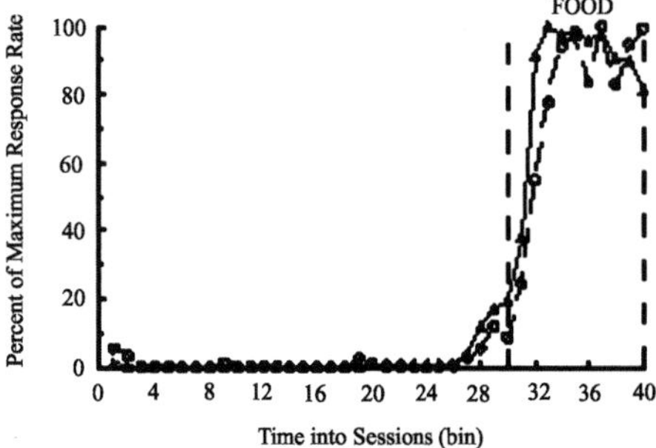

Figure 12.3. The overall response rate curves for the lever immediately following the presentation of cheese (*open circles*) and the overall response rate curves for the same lever on baseline sessions (*closed triangles*). *Top,* Probe and baseline response rate curves for lever 3 when cheese was presented at 06:00. *Middle and bottom panels,* Probe and baseline response rate curves for lever 4 on 11:00 and 09:55 cheese tests, respectively. (From "How Rats Process Spatiotemporal Information in the Face of Distraction," by C. M. Thorpe, V. Petrovic, and D. M. Wilkie, 2002, *Behavioural Processes, 58,* 79–90. Copyright 2002 by Elsevier Science. Redrawn with permission.)

entities that are processed in parallel. The fact that we observed a decoupling of spatial and temporal knowledge in the present experiment supports the latter possibility.

Unequal Interval Time-Place Task

In all of the TP learning experiments just discussed, the intervals of food availability for responding on a key or lever were equal (e.g., all levers produced food for 5 min). Such conditions probably do not hold in animals' natural environments. Thus, it is important to determine if animals can learn TP contingencies when the intervals of food availability are unequal.

Thorpe and Wilkie (2002) trained rats on an interval TP task in which lever 1 intermittently produced food for 6 min and then lever 2 produced food for 4 min. Levers 3 and 4 provided food for 2 and 8 min, respectively. The rats also received OHTs interspersed in baseline sessions to confirm that they were timing. The results of the baseline (figure 12.4) and OHT sessions confirmed that rats are able to learn an unequal interval TP task.

Although our results are clear in demonstrating that rats can perform the unequal interval task, our results do not indicate *how* rats performed the task. One possibility is that the rats used a single 20-min timer and switched from one lever to the next on the basis of different duration criteria stored in memory. Another possibility is that the rats engaged four separate timers, one for each of the four levers. For example, expiration of the first timer could serve as a cue for starting the second timer and so forth. Gallistel (1990) has suggested that this is the most likely scenario. A third possibility is that nonreinforcement could cause the first timer to stop and the second to start.

A second issue addressed by the unequal interval task was whether the data from this experiment conformed to scalar timing theory/Weber's law (Gibbon, 1991). Scalar timing theory states that the longer the duration being timed, the greater the error in that timing (Gibbon, 1991). Data from a previous experiment, in which different groups of rats received training on different intervals in an equal-interval TP task, showed that scalar expectancy theory/Weber's law did apply (Carr & Wilkie, 1998).

However, the rats' behavior on the unequal-interval task did not agree with scalar expectancy

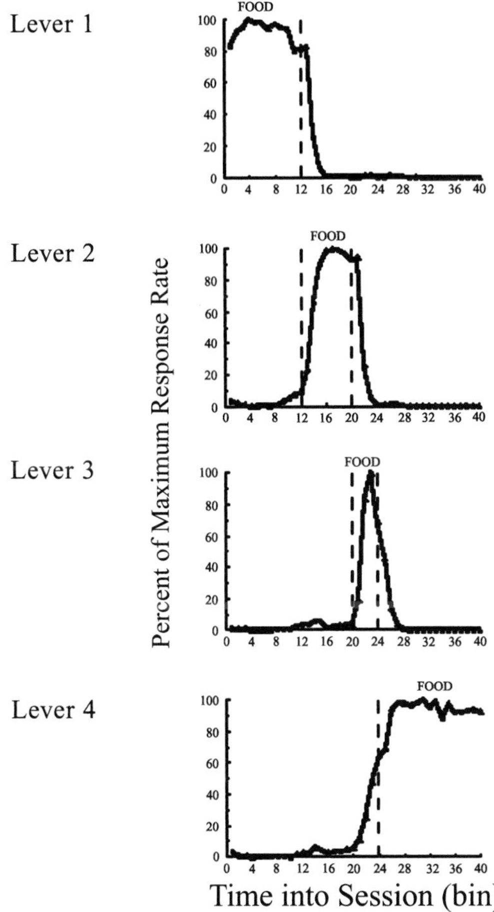

Figure 12.4. The normalized overall response rate distributions on the unequal interval time-place task. Responses on each lever were reinforced during the period bounded by the vertical dashed lines. (From "Unequal Interval Time-Place Learning," by C. M. Thorpe and D. M. Wilkie, 2002, *Behavioural Processes, 58*, 157–166. Copyright 2002 by Elsevier Science. Redrawn with permission.)

theory/Weber's law. The relative response rate curves for the different durations did not superimpose (figure 12.5), and the coefficient of variation (mean/standard deviation) was not constant for the different durations. This is not the only reported instance in which constant coefficients of variation were not found. Crystal and Miller (2002) also examined the properties of scalar timing using an interval TP task. Their rats were trained in a large, clear box with a lever centered on each of the four walls. Rats were trained so that each lever provided reinforcement in succession on an FI schedule (lever A = FI 60 s; lever B = 30 s; lever C = 30 s; lever D = 40 s). The sequence was repeated several times each session. The rats anticipated when a lever would provide food. Similar to the Thorpe and Wilkie (2002) findings, the response rate distributions did not superimpose. These authors suggested that simultaneously processing temporal and spatial information results in violations of Weber's law.

Similarly, Zeiler and Powell (1994) trained pigeons on FIs ranging in duration from 7.5 to 480 s. These authors found that the coefficients of variation of the pause durations increased as the FI durations increased, a finding inconsistent with Weber's law.

In a recent review of the timing literature, Grondin (2001) argued that Weber's law does not hold in situations where there is a sequence of intervals to be timed or in situations where there is extensive training. Both of these were the case in the Thorpe and Wilkie (2002) experiment, perhaps explaining why Weber's law did not apply here.

Crystal (2001) also argued that Weber's law does not hold in all cases. He trained rats to discriminate different durations of noise and calculated Weber fractions for the different durations. A Weber fraction is k in the formula

$$\Delta I = kI$$

where I is the intensity or magnitude of a stimulus, and ΔI is the change needed in I for a difference to be noticeable. According to Weber's law, k should be a constant for all durations. However, Crystal found that k varied for different durations.

Machado and colleagues (Machado & Guilhardi, 2000; Machado & Keen, 1999) have also reported instances in which scalar expectancy theory is unable to account for their data. These researchers argued that their Learning to Time model is better able to explain those instances in which scalar expectancy theory is violated. In summary, there is a growing body of evidence in the timing literature for which Weber's law does not hold.

Effect of Prefrontal Lesions on Time-Place Behavior

To date, there has been a paucity of information about the neural basis of rats' TP behavior.

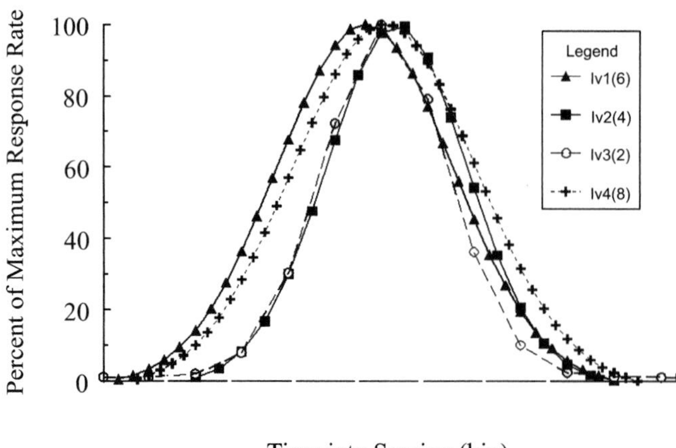

Figure 12.5. Gaussian curves fitted to the transposed distributions resulting from the open hopper tests in the unequal interval time-place experiment. The number in parentheses indicates the length of time in min that the lever provided food. (From "Unequal Interval Time-Place Learning," by C. M. Thorpe and D. M. Wilkie, 2002, *Behavioural Processes, 58,* 157–166. Copyright 2002 by Elsevier Science. Redrawn with permission.)

Although several brain areas are likely involved, we (Thorpe, Floresco, Carr, & Wilkie, 2002) chose to investigate the prefrontal cortex of the rat, because numerous studies have implicated this region as being involved in the organization of behavior across time (Fuster, 1980; Kolb, 1984).

Fuster (1980) posited that a primary function of the prefrontal cortex is to facilitate the temporal organization of behavior, allowing an organism to use information that was obtained at one time in order to guide behavior at a later point in time. Damage to the prefrontal cortex disrupts behaviors that require the execution of a planned sequence of events in both humans and rats. Damasio (1979, 1994) found that human neuropsychological patients with focal damage in the prefrontal cortex had difficulty planning their daily work schedule, despite otherwise largely preserved intellectual abilities. Similarly, in rats, damage to the medial prefrontal cortex disrupts behaviors such as food hoarding, which requires the animal to engage in a complex sequence of behaviors in order to store food efficiently (de Brabander, de Bruin, & van Eden, 1991).

We trained rats on a TP task in which each of four levers provided food intermittently for 3 min. Once the rats had mastered the interval TP task, half of the rats received electrolytic lesions restricted to the medial prefrontal cortex, whereas the other half received sham surgeries. Both lesioned and control rats were able to perform the task and switch from lever to lever; however, rats with lesions to the medial prefrontal cortex tended to perseverate, spending more time pressing a lever after a particular interval had expired. This difference was most pronounced in OHT probe sessions in which all levers provided reinforcement for the duration of the session. The behavior of the lesioned rats did not disclose a complete disruption of timing because rats were still able to shift from one lever to the other and they did not simply start responding on a lever and continue pressing on that lever until the session ended; instead, lesioned rats continued to move from one lever to the next but they were slower to shift from lever to lever relative to control rats. This finding suggests that an internal clock that lesioned rats consult to guide shifting behavior from lever to lever may have been running slow, thereby causing them to overestimate temporal intervals.

All rats were eventually trained on a new task in which the sequence of levers that provided reinforcement was switched, while the durations remained the same. Again, rats with lesions to the medial prefrontal cortex perseverated more than control rats (figure 12.6); however, there were no differences between the groups in acquisition of the new task.

In order to perform the TP task optimally, animals must learn two things. First, they must learn the sequence or order in which the different spatial

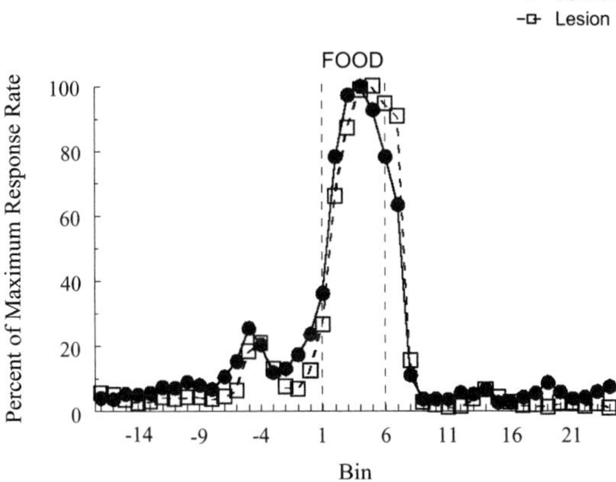

Figure 12.6. The normalized overall response rate distributions for the control (*closed circles*) and lesioned (*open squares*) rats collapsed over levers during baseline sessions. Results are shown for sessions after the sequence the levers provided reinforcement was changed. Responses on each lever were reinforced during the period bounded by the vertical dashed lines. (From "Alterations in Time-Tlace Learning Induced by Lesions to the Rat Medial Prefrontal Cortex," by C. M. Thorpe, S. B. Floresco, J.A.R. Carr, & D. M. Wilkie, 2002, *Behavioural Processes, 59,* 87–100. Copyright 2002 by Elsevier Science. Redrawn with permission.)

locations (levers) are to be visited. Second, they also have to learn how long to stay at each location. Contrary to our expectations, medial prefrontal lesions had no discernible effect on the rats' ability to visit the different levers in a previously learned sequence. In addition, these lesions did not have any discernible effect on the rats' ability to learn a new sequence, as lesioned rats learned a new lever sequence at the same rate as control rats. Thus, it appears that learning to switch from one location to another in order to receive food at preset intervals is a type of learning that does not require the integrity of the medial prefrontal cortex; instead, it was found that lesions to the medial prefrontal cortex resulted in a specific timing impairment. Similar peak shifts have been found by Olton (1989) in a peak procedure task using durations of 10 and 20 s.

DAILY TIME-PLACE LEARNING

The majority of research on TPL has been done using a daily TP task in which food is available at one spatial location at one time of day and at another spatially distinct location at another time of day. The theoretical question is whether this task is acquired using a circadian or ordinal timer.

Biebach, Gordijn, and Krebs (1989) provided the first laboratory demonstration of daily TPL. In their experiment, garden warblers were tested for 12 h each day in a chamber that was divided into a central living area and four compartments. Each compartment contained a grain dispenser that each day provided grain for a specific 3-h period. It was found that the birds entered the correct rooms at the correct times and in fact anticipated when the rooms would provide food as demonstrated by their tendency to enter a room before it started providing food. Furthermore, on test sessions in which no food was given, the birds continued to enter the rooms at the correct times. Anticipation and performance on test sessions suggest that the birds were using an endogenous timer to track the availability of food. To verify that the warblers were using a circadian timer (rather than an interval timer), tests were conducted in which the light-dark (LD) schedule was changed so that the lights remained on for 24 h a day (LL). This change did not disrupt the birds' performance on the first day of the test. Over continued days of testing, however, the periodicity dropped from 24 h to approximately 23 h (free running time). These results suggest that the timer being used was a circadian timer that was entrained to the LD cycle (Biebach, Falk, & Krebs, 1991).

There is also evidence to suggest that, in addition to using a circadian timer in this task, the birds use an ordinal timer (Carr & Wilkie, 1997b). Krebs and Biebach (1989) prevented warblers from entering any of the rooms for the first 3-h period. The warblers were then given free access to all of the rooms. If their behavior were driven solely by a circadian timer, then the birds should have gone to room 2; if, however, their behavior were driven by an ordinal timer, then they should have gone to room 1. In fact, five of the nine warblers preferred room 1, suggesting their behavior was at least partially controlled by an ordinal timer.

Daily TPL has also been demonstrated in pigeons (Saksida & Wilkie, 1994). Pigeons were trained in an operant chamber that contained a key on each of its four walls. The chamber was transparent to allow distal room cues to be available. Pigeons received two daily sessions: one in the morning and one in the afternoon. One key provided food in morning sessions, whereas another key provided food in afternoon sessions. The first few pecks never provided reinforcement and were recorded to see to which key the pigeons responded. Pigeons quickly learned to peck at the correct key. To verify that the pigeons were in fact timing, rather than using a nontemporal strategy such as alternation, skip session tests were conducted in which the morning or afternoon session on a probe day was omitted. If pigeons were alternating, then they should respond on the incorrect lever following all skip sessions. If they were using an ordinal timer, they should respond on the correct lever following skip afternoon sessions but not skip morning sessions. Following skipped sessions, the pigeons still responded on the correct lever, thus ruling out an alternation or ordinal timing strategy (figure 12.7). LD manipulations similar to those discussed above suggested that the pigeons were using a light-entrained circadian timer. Although not noticed by Saksida and Wilkie (1994), Carr and Wilkie's (1997a) reanalysis of these data found evidence that the pigeons, like the warblers, displayed some control by an ordinal timer.

In a similar study, Carr and Wilkie (1997b, 1999) observed TPL in rats. Rats were tested twice daily, once in the morning and once in the afternoon, in a chamber similar to that used for pigeons that had a lever mounted on each of its four walls. For each rat, one lever provided food during the morning sessions, whereas a different lever provided food during the afternoon sessions. Rats learned to press the appropriate lever depending on the time of day. Interestingly, skip-session probe tests conducted after the rats had successfully learned the discrimination revealed that the rats were not using a circadian timer, but rather an ordinal timer; that is, they learned the order in which the places provided food during the day. In the afternoon, after a skipped morning session, the rats responded on the morning lever; however, in the morning of a day following a skipped afternoon session, the rats responded on the correct morning lever (figure 12.8). The latter finding suggests that the ordinal timing system was reset by some (unknown) end of day or start of day cue. Another possibility is that the rats could not remember the afternoon omission; however, this

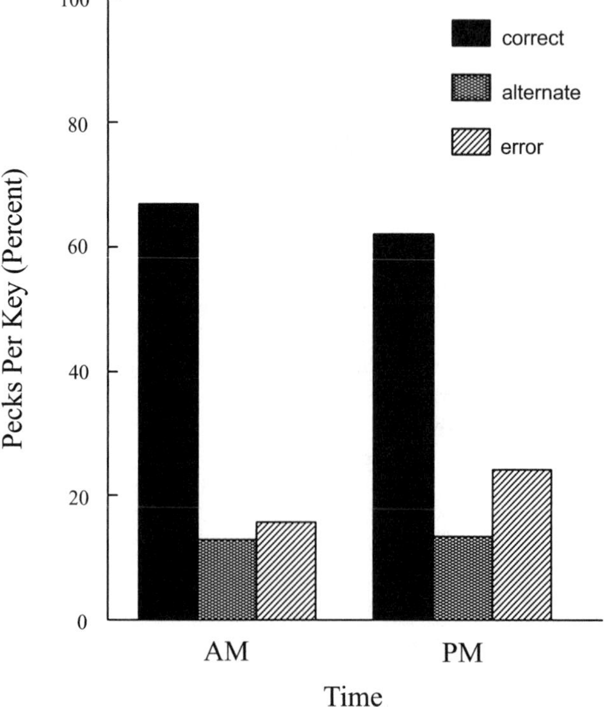

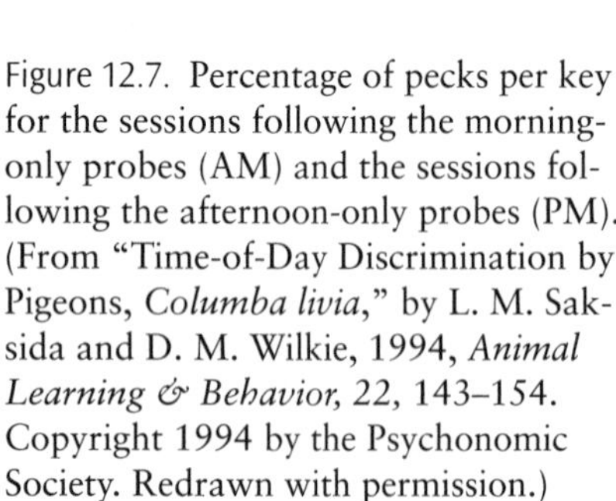
Figure 12.7. Percentage of pecks per key for the sessions following the morning-only probes (AM) and the sessions following the afternoon-only probes (PM). (From "Time-of-Day Discrimination by Pigeons, *Columba livia*," by L. M. Saksida and D. M. Wilkie, 1994, *Animal Learning & Behavior, 22,* 143–154. Copyright 1994 by the Psychonomic Society. Redrawn with permission.)

0930 SESSIONS

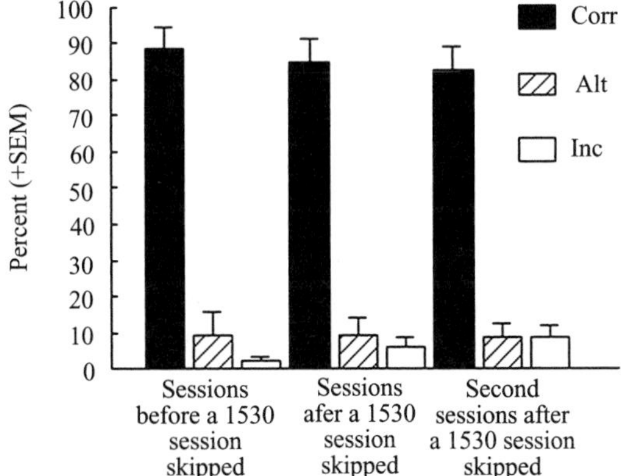

1530 SESSIONS

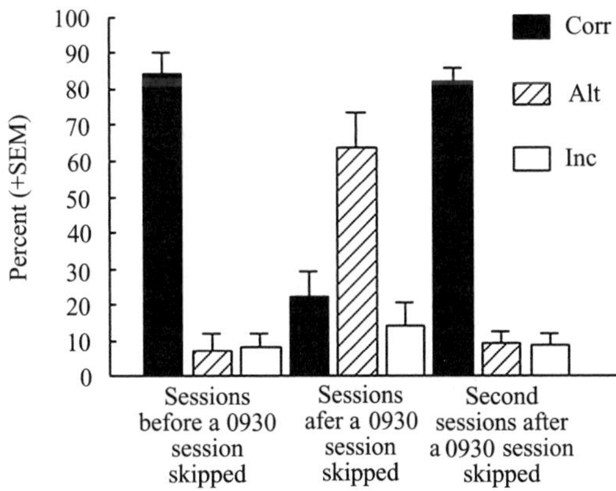

Figure 12.8. The rats' overall 09:30 (morning) and 15:30 (afternoon) Corr, Alt, and Inc scores (+SEM) during the sessions immediately before the skipped sessions, during the sessions immediately after skipped sessions, and during the second sessions after skipped sessions. Corr indicates the correct lever in that session; Alt, the correct lever in the alternate daily session; Inc, the two incorrect levers that never provided food. (From "Rats Use an Ordinal Timer in a Daily Time-Place Learning Task," by J. A. R. Carr and D. M. Wilkie, 1997, *Journal of Experimental Psychology: Animal Behavior Processes, 23,* 232–247. Copyright 1997 by the American Psychological Association. Redrawn with permission.)

possibility is unlikely given the rat's well-known spatial memory.

Other researchers have shown that rats sometimes use a circadian rather than an ordinal timer on a TPL task. Pizzo and Crystal (2002) successfully trained rats on a daily TPL task in which food was available at one of three locations depending on the time of day. There were two groups: group AB-C received two sessions in the morning and one in the afternoon, whereas group A-BC received one session in the morning and two in the afternoon. To determine whether a circadian or ordinal timer was in effect, the time of session B was shifted either very late or very early. It was found that by shifting the time of session B, performance dropped significantly contrary to what would be expected from ordinal timing. (Interval timing from light onset was ruled out by switching the rats to a continuous light schedule.)

Similarly, Mistlberger, de Groot, Bossert, and Marchant (1996) successfully trained rats to press a lever in one arm of a T-maze in morning sessions and a lever in the other arm in afternoon sessions. An alternation strategy was ruled out through skip sessions. Interestingly, rats with lesions of the suprachiasmatic nucleus were still able to learn this task, suggesting that the rats were not using a light-entrained circadian timer. The authors suggested that the circadian timer used was probably food entrained.

Laboratory studies also have shown daily TPL in honeybees (Wahl, 1932, as cited in Reebs, 1993), ants (Schatz, Beugnon, & Lachaud, 1994; Schatz, Lachaud, & Beugnon, 1999), and fish (inangas: Reebs, 1999), but these studies did not distinguish between circadian and ordinal timing.

Gallistel's (1990) theory leads us to believe that TPL is an almost automatic process that should be fairly easy to demonstrate in a variety of animals and circumstances. However, recent publications suggest that this may not be the case.

Reebs (1993) fed cichlid fish in different corners of their aquarium at different times of day. Although the fish learned the times at which food was given (as demonstrated by increased searching of the corners during the feeding times), they did not limit their searching to only the correct corner. Thus, they did not learn which corner was associated with which time of day. Reebs speculated that this failure to learn the TP association may have been due to the low response-cost ratio associated with not going to the correct place initially; that is, not much energy was expended and there was no punishment for going to the incorrect location. At the correct time of day, the fish could swim around the aquarium until they found the food. Alternatively, the failure to learn the TP association may have been due to interference among the locations.

Reebs (1996) was able to demonstrate TPL in another fish, the golden shiner. However, the fish were only able to learn the TP association when two places were involved. When the number of TP associations was increased to three, the fish no longer successfully anticipated the location of food. Similar findings were reported with another fish, the inanga; however, TPL was not shown with an aversive stimulus, namely simulated heron attacks (Reebs, 1999).

Boulos and Logothetis (1990) trained rats to press one lever during a 1- or 2-h time period and another lever located on the opposite side of the testing chamber during another 1- or 2-h time period. Only half of the rats showed pressing of the time appropriate lever on no food test sessions. The remaining rats showed a preference for one lever over another. White and Timberlake (1990, unpublished data cited in Widman, Gordon, & tImberlake, 2000) were unable to demonstrate TPL in rats using a paradigm similar to that of Boulos and Logothetis (1990). Furthermore, they could not demonstrate learning on a three-arm radial maze in which each arm provided food at a particular time of day.

Means, Ginn, Arolfo, and Pence (2000) were able to train rats to go to one arm of a T-maze for food in morning sessions and to the other arm for food in afternoon sessions. Only 63% of rats were able to learn this task after significant training. Furthermore, with continued training, rats' performance actually decreased. In addition, when external time-related cues such as noises and feeding were minimized, the trials to criterion increased. Skip session probes suggested that the rats were likely to have been using an ordinal timer.

In a later study, Means, Arolfo, Ginn, Pence, and Watson (2000) again showed that rats have difficulty learning a TP association in a T-maze. Neither making the two places more distinctive nor making the two times farther apart during the day significantly increased rats' success rate on the task. Rats were able to learn a time-of-day go–no-go discrimination, however. In this task, food was available on both arms of the T-maze in one session, but no food was available in the other session at a different time of day. Rats' latency to leave the start arm of the T-maze was significantly shorter on food sessions than on no food sessions.

Thorpe, Bates, and Wilkie (2003) were also unable to demonstrate daily TPL using a variety of tasks including a place preference task, a semiaversive water maze, a radial arm maze, and a T-maze. It was found that rats did learn the locations in which food was presented, as shown by their tendency to prefer those locations over others that had never been associated with food. If they know the locations, then why do they not connect them to the time of day? When the time part of the time-place-event code was removed by giving a discriminative cue informing them of the time of day, rats readily learned the task. When the place part of the code was removed by providing food at only one time (replication of Means, Ginn et al., 2000), rats also learned the task. (Interestingly, when skipped session probes were conducted, to rule out an alternation strategy, some rats used an ordinal timer, whereas other rats used a circadian timer; see figure 12.9.) Rats seem to face difficulty when they are required to use all three parts of the time-place-event code.

Widman et al. (2000) discovered that by increasing the response cost in TP tasks, they increased the probability that the rats would learn the task. In a simple radial arm maze similar to those described above (i.e., one arm baited in the morning sessions, another arm baited in the afternoon sessions), the rats did learn a general place preference (i.e., they learned which two arms were baited), but they did not learn when those places were baited. By switching to a vertical maze and increasing the height the rats had to climb for food (and thereby increasing

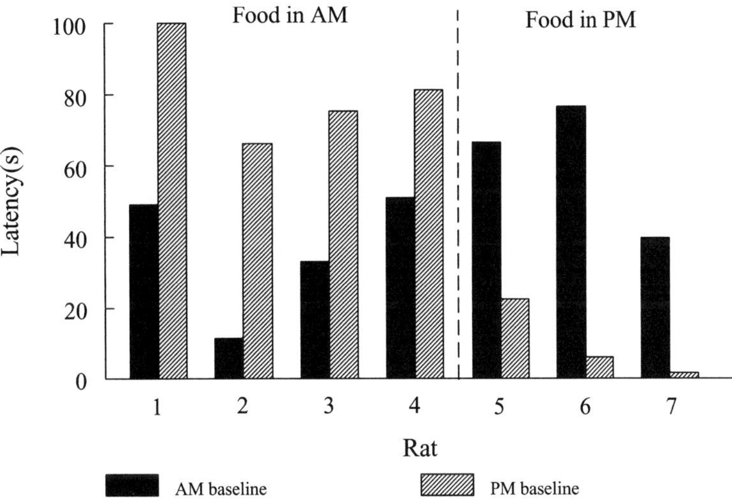

Figure 12.9. Results of the replication of the means, Ginn et al. (2000) go–no-go task conducted by Thorpe, Bates, and Wilkie (2003). Rats that received food in the morning (AM) had shorter latencies in the AM than in the afternoon (PM). Rats that received food in the PM had shorter latencies in the PM than in the AM. (From "Rats Have Trouble Associating All Three Parts of the Time-Place-Event Memory Code," by C. M. Thorpe, M. E. Bates, and D. M. Wilkie, 2003, *Behavioural Processes, 63,* 95–110. Copyright 2003 by Elsevier Science. Redrawn with permission.)

the response cost), they increased the success rate for TPL. Widman et al. also point out that this result seems to be contradict Gallistel's theory; that is, rats do not seem automatically to store and/or retrieve time-place-event information from their memory.

However, there are some obvious inconsistencies in the daily TPL literature. Some researchers have found daily TPL in operant response tasks (Carr & Wilkie, 1997, 1999; Mistlberger et al., 1996; Pizzo & Crystal, 2002), whereas others using very similar paradigms (and similar reinforcement schedules) have failed to find it (Boulous & Logothetis, 1990; Thorpe et al., 2003; White & Timberlake, 1990). Although Widman et al. (2000) believe that response-cost ratios (the relative cost of making an error) are the critical determinant of whether an animal learns a TP task, it is not clear why this should be the case. Nor does it account for the many inconsistencies in the research findings.

TIME-PLACE LEARNING AND THEORIES OF MEMORY

As noted earlier, Gallistel (1990) proposes that memory exists in the form of a time-place-event code. Furthermore, formation of a time-place-event memory representation is assumed to be an automatic low-level process. The memory code is stored effortlessly, immediately, with no executive control required. However, memory may operate in this manner only under certain conditions. Rats, like pigeons, readily learn interval TP contingencies, but they are reluctant to use circadian timing on daily TP tasks and they appear to do so only under limited circumstances.

One theory of memory failure is that the internal or external context in which memory was formed has been changed at the time of retrieval (e.g., Bouton, 1993). It has been suggested that the internal representation of time-of-day forms part of the context associated with learning and that retrieval is impaired when animals are tested at times other than training times (e.g., Holloway & Wansley, 1973). This notion has been recently questioned by McDonald, Hong, Ray, and Ralph (2002). These researchers trained rats on a battery of commonly used learning and memory tasks (water maze, shock avoidance, place learning, etc.). Training always occurred at the same time of day. On crucial test days, the rats were tested at a different time of day. McDonald et al. found no evidence of a performance decrement on test sessions. They concluded that circadian information does not contribute to the context in which learning and memory retrieval occur.

The evidence appears to show that rats, unlike birds such as warblers and pigeons, use little circadian information in discrimination procedures. Rats obviously display circadian rhythms and some rats seem to be able to consult the circadian clock under certain conditions; but, for the most part, time of day is not used by rats when they learn and remember. Why should rats and pigeons differ in this respect? Although clearly speculative, this difference might be related to the fact that pigeons are able to navigate over large spatial distances (e.g., Baker, 1984). In navigating (e.g., flying to the home loft), pigeons primarily use the sun as a compass (e.g., Bingmam & Jones, 1994) to direct their flight. Because the position of the sun varies over the course of the day, the sun's position can be used as a compass but only if the pigeon is able to determine the time of day. This requirement may permit pigeons to readily use circadian information in TPL.

One form of human memory, episodic memory or memory for personal experiences, also contains time-place-event information. For example, last night (time) one of us (D.W.) had pizza for supper (event) as he watched television in the den (place). Is the oystercatchers' time-place-event memory described earlier different from the author's episodic memory? These questions have recently generated much interest (see Clayton & Dickinson, 1998; Roberts, 2002; Tulving, 1972, 1984).

One obvious disparity is that the contents of D.W.'s episodic memory for today's events are likely to be very different from yesterday's memories, whereas the oystercatchers' memory may not change from day to day. In TP experiments, animals are trained to associate a time and place with a particular event. Although this procedure appears to be similar to the definition of episodic memory, we believe that there is a critical difference—the uniqueness/distinctiveness of the time-place-event code. In TP experiments, the time-place-event code consists of many trials of morning-Arm1-food and afternoon-Arm 2-food trials. If D.W. ate pizza at every supper and in the den, it is unlikely for him to have an episodic memory for any one particular instance. If something unique or unexpected happens, for example, the Toronto Maple Leafs winning the Stanley Cup, he would more likely remember that particular time-place-event.

But is it that simple? Oystercatchers can only eat mussels at low tide. The time of low tide changes from day to day as a function of the lunar cycle. Thus, the content of the oystercatchers' memory changes in some way from day to day over the 28-day lunar cycle. Are these changes in any way similar to the day-to-day variations in human episodic memory? The answer to this question is probably no. Whereas the oystercatchers' memory changes from day to day, the same sequence happens every month. This constraint does not occur in human episodic memory.

Further complexity can be seen in both field and laboratory data showing conditional TPL. Sibly and McCleery (1983) studied herring gulls that typically visited a grassy field at sunrise where they fed on earthworms. Later in the day, they visited a garbage dump and a beach. The gulls did not visit the grassy field during periods of drought, because of reduced earthworm availability. Thus, the presence of rainfall seemed to be a stimulus that modulated the gulls' TP behavior. Similarly, Wilkie et al. (1997) showed conditional TP behavior in laboratory pigeons. In one experiment, when three pecking keys were illuminated with red light, key 2 provided food for the first 10 min, followed by key 3, and then key 4. When the keys were lit with green light, key 1 provided food, followed by key 2, and then key 3. The pigeons learned these conditional TP contingencies. Both of these experiments show the flexibility that TPL can demonstrate under some conditions.

Similarly, the oystercatcher memory can be thought of as a conditional time-place-event memory in which the time of day information is modulated, or is conditional on, lunar cycle information. This suggestion that animals use the phase of a lunar oscillator fits nicely with Gallistel's (1990) notion that animals possess several oscillators having different periodicities.

CONCLUSION

In animals' environments, many biologically significant events occur with spatial and temporal regularity. This observation has prompted both field and laboratory study of TPL. An earlier paper (Wilkie, 1995) reviewed this research. The present chapter has provided an updated overview of the empirical understanding of TPL. The present chapter also comments on a prominent theory of how memory is organized. Gallistel (1990) has hypothesized that the brain automatically encodes time-place-event information as it occurs. When animals face a need for a particular resource, memory can then be scanned for information regarding the times and places relevant events (e.g., a meal) have happened in the past. An animal that uses such information to guide its behavior would have an advantage compared with animals that are incapable of such memory formation and use.

Despite the appealing power and simplicity of this view of memory, recent experiments have shown that this theory has constraints. In particular, there is empirical evidence questioning the automatic nature of time-place-event memory formation. As well, there seems to be species differences in TP behavior. Warblers and pigeons readily display TPL. Although rats can sometimes display TP behavior, for the most part they seem to be reluctant to do so. Demonstrating robust TP behavior in fish has also been somewhat difficult.

Acknowledgments This research was supported by grants and scholarships from the Natural Sciences and Engineering Research Council of Canada.

References

Baker, R. R. (1984). *Bird navigation: The solution of a mystery?* New York: Holmes and Meier.

Biebach, H., Falk, H., & Krebs, J. R. (1991). The effect of constant light and phase shifts on a learned time-place association in garden warblers (*Sylvia borin*): Hourglass or circadian clock? *Journal of Biological Rhythms, 6,* 353–365.

Biebach, H., Gordijn, M., & Krebs, J. (1989). Time-place learning by garden warblers, *Sylvia borin. Animal Behavior, 37,* 353–360.

Bingman, V. P., & Jones, T. J. (1994). Sun-compass-based spatial learning impaired in homing pigeons with hippocampal lesions. *Journal of Neuroscience, 14,* 6687–6694.

Boulos, Z., & Logothetis, D. E. (1990). Rats anticipate and discriminate between two daily feeding times. *Physiology & Behavior, 48,* 523–529.

Bouton, M., E. (1993). Context, time, and memory retrieval in the interference paradigms of Pavlovian learning. *Psychological Bulletin, 114,* 80–99.

Cabeza de Vaca, S., Brown, B. L., & Hemmes, N. S. (1994). Internal clock and memory processes in animal timing. *Journal of Experimental Psychology: Animal Behavior Processes, 20,* 184–198.

Carr, J. A. R., Tan, A. O., Thorpe, C. M., & Wilkie, D. M. (2001). Further evidence of joint time-place control of rats' behavior: Results from an "open hopper" test. *Behavioural Processes, 53,* 147–153.

Carr, J. A. R., & Wilkie, D. M. (1997a). Ordinal, phase, and interval timing. In C. M. Bradshaw, & E. Szabadi (Eds.), *Time and behavior: Psychological and neurobiological analyses* (pp. 265–327). Amsterdam: Elsevier.

Carr, J. A. R., & Wilkie, D. M. (1997b). Rats use an ordinal timer in a daily time-place learning task. *Journal of Experimental Psychology: Animal Behavior Processes, 23,* 232–247.

Carr, J. A. R., & Wilkie, D. M. (1998). Characterization of the strategy used by rats in an interval time-place learning task. *Journal of Experimental Psychology: Animal Behavior Processes, 24,* 151–162.

Carr, J. A. R., & Wilkie, D. M. (1999). Rats are reluctant to use circadian timing in a daily time-place task. *Behavioural Processes, 44,* 287–299.

Cheng, K., & Roberts, W. A. (1991). Three psychophysical properties of timing in pigeons. *Learning & Motivation, 22,* 112–128.

Church, R. M., Broadbent, H. A., & Gibbon, J. (1992). Biological and psychological description of an internal clock. In E. A. Wasserman & I. Gormezano (Eds.), *Learning and memory: The behavioral and biological substrates* (pp. 105–128). Hillsdale, NJ: Erlbaum.

Clayton, N. S., & Dickinson, A. (1998). Episodic-like memory during cache recovery by scrub jays. *Nature, 395,* 272–274.

Crystal, J. D. (2001). Nonlinear time perception. *Behavioural Processes, 55,* 35–49.

Crystal, J. D., & Miller, B. J. (2002). Simultaneous temporal and spatial processing. *Animal Learning & Behavior, 30,* 53–65.

Daan, S., & Koene, P. (1981). On the timing of foraging flights by oystercatchers, *Haematopus ostralegus*, on tidal mudflats. *Netherlands Journal of Sea Research, 15,* 1–22.

Damasio, A. R. (1979). The frontal lobes. In K. M. Heilman & E. Valenstein (Eds.), *Clinical neuropsychology* (pp. 360–412). New York: Oxford University Press.

Damasio, A. R. (1994). *Descartes' error: Emotion, reason, and the human brain.* New York: Grosset/Putnam.

Davies, N. B., & Houston, A. I. (1981). Owners and satellites: The economics of territory defense in the pied wagtail, *Motacilla alba. Journal of Animal Ecology, 50,* 157–180.

de Brabander, J. M., de Bruin, J. P., & van Eden, C. G. (1991). Comparison of the effects of neonatal and adult medial prefrontal cortex lesions on food hoarding and spatial delayed alternation. *Behavioral Brain Research, 42,* 67–75.

Fuster, J. M. (1980). *The prefrontal cortex: Anatomy, physiology, and neuropsychology of the frontal lobe.* New York: Raven Press.

Gallistel, C. R. (1990). *The organization of learning.* Cambridge, MA: MIT Press.

Gibbon, J. (1991). Origins of scalar timing. *Learning and Motivation, 22,* 3–38.

Grondin, S. (2001). From physical time to the first and second moments of psychological time. *Psychological Bulletin, 127,* 22–44.

Holloway, F. A., & Wansley, R. (1973). Multiphasiac retention deficits at periodic intervals after passive-avoidance learning. *Science, 180,* 208–210.

Kolb, B. (1984). Functions of the prefrontal cortex in the rat: A comparative review. *Brain Research Review, 8,* 65–98.

Krebs, J. R., & Biebach, H. (1989). Time-place learning by garden warblers (*Sylvia borin*): Route or map? *Ethology, 83,* 248–256.

Machado, A., & Guilhardi, P. (2000). Shifts in the psychometric function and their implications for models of timing. *Journal of the Experimental Analysis of Behavior, 74,* 25–54.

Machado, A., & Keen, R. (1999). Learning to time (LET) or scalar expectancy theory (SET)? A critical test of two models of timing. *Psychological Science, 10,* 285–290.

Matell, M. S., & Meck, W. H. (1999). Reinforcement-induced within-trial resetting of an internal clock. *Behavioural Processes, 45,* 159–171.

McDonald, R. J., Hong, N. S., Ray, C., & Ralph, M. R. (2002). No time of day modulation or time stamp on multiple memory tasks in rats. *Learning and Motivation, 33,* 230–252.

Means, L. W., Arolfo, M. P., Ginn, S. R., Pence, J. D., & Watson, N. P. (2000). Rats more readily acquire a time-of-day go no-go discrimination than a time-of-day choice discrimination. *Behavioural Processes, 52,* 11–20.

Means, L. W., Ginn, S. R., Arolfo, M. P., & Pence, J. D. (2000). Breakfast in the nook and dinner in the dining room: Time-of-day discrimination in rats. *Behavioural Processes, 49,* 21–33.

Mistlberger, R. E., de Groot, M. H. M., Bossert, J. M., & Marchant, E. G. (1996). Discrimination of circadian phase in intact and suprachiasmatic nuclei-ablated rats. *Brain Research, 739,* 12–18.

Olton, D. S. (1989). Frontal cortex, timing, and memory. *Neuropsychologia, 27,* 121–130.

Pizzo, M. J., & Crystal, J. D. (2002). Representation of time in time-place learning. *Animal Learning & Behavior, 30,* 387–393.

Reebs, S. G. (1993). A test of time-place learning in a cichlid fish. *Behavioural Processes, 30,* 273–282.

Reebs, S. G. (1996). Time-place learning in golden shiners (*Pisces: cyprinidae*). *Behavioural Processes, 36,* 253–262.

Reebs, S. G. (1999). Time-place learning based on food but not on predation risk in a fish, the inanga (*Galaxias maculates*). *Ethology, 105,* 361–371.

Roberts, S. (1981). Isolation of an internal clock. *Journal of Experimental Psychology: Animal Behavior Processes, 7,* 242–268.

Roberts, S., & Church, R. M. (1978). Control of an internal clock. *Journal of Experimental Psychology: Animal Behavior Processes, 4,* 318–337.

Roberts, W. A. (2002). Are animals stuck in time? *Psychological Bulletin, 128,* 473–489.

Roberts, W. A., Cheng, K., & Cohen, J. S. (1989). Timing light and tone signals in pigeons. *Journal of Experimental Psychology: Animal Behavior Processes, 15,* 23–35.

Saksida, L. M., & Wilkie, D. M. (1994). Time-of-day discrimination by pigeons, *Columba livia. Animal Learning & Behavior, 22,* 143–154.

Schatz, B., Beugnon, G., & Lachaud, J. P. (1994). Time-place learning by an invertebrate, the ant *Ectatomma ruidum* Roger. *Animal Behavior, 48,* 236–238.

Schatz, B., Lachaud, J. P., & Beugnon, G. (1999). Spatio-temporal learning by the ant *Ectatomma ruidum. The Journal of Experimental Biology, 202,* 1897–1907.

Sherry, D. F., & Schacter, D. L. (1987). The evolution of multiple memory systems. *Psychological Review, 94,* 439–454.

Sibly, R. M., & McCleery, R. H. (1983). The distribution between feeding sites of herring gulls breeding at Walney Island, U. K. *Journal of Animal Ecology, 52,* 51–68.

Thorpe, C. M., Bates, M. E., & Wilkie, D. M. (2003). Rats have trouble associating all three parts of the time-place-event memory code. *Behavioural Processes, 63,* 95–110.

Thorpe, C. M., Floresco, S. B., Carr, J. A. R., & Wilkie, D. M. (2002). Alterations in time-place learning induced by lesions to the rat medial prefrontal cortex. *Behavioural Processes, 59,* 87–100.

Thorpe, C. M., Petrovic, V., & Wilkie, D. M. (2002). How rats process spatiotemporal information in the face of distraction. *Behavioural Processes, 58,* 79–90.

Thorpe, C. M., & Wilkie, D. M. (2002). Unequal interval time-place learning. *Behavioural Processes, 58,* 157–166.

Tulving, E. (1972). Episodic and semantic memory. In E. Tulving & W. Donaldson (Eds.),

Organization of memory (pp. 381–403). San Diego: Academic Press.

Tulving, E. (1984). Precis of elements of episodic memory. *Behavioral & Brain Sciences, 7,* 223–268.

Wahl, O. (1932). Neue Untersuchungen uber das Zeitgedachtnis der Bienen. *Zeitschrift fur Vergleichende Physiologie, 9,* 259–338.

Widman, D. R., Gordon, D., & Timberlake, W. (2000). Response cost and time-place discrimination by rats in maze tasks. *Animal Learning & Behavior, 28,* 298–309.

Wilkie, D. M. (1995). Time-place learning. *Current Directions in Psychological Science, 4,* 85–89.

Wilkie, D. M., Carr, J. A. R., Galloway, J., Parker, K. J., & Yamamoto, A. (1997). Conditional time-place learning. *Behavioural Processes, 40,* 165–170.

Wilkie, D. M., Saksida, L. M., Samson, P., & Lee, A. (1994). Properties of time-place learning by pigeons, *Columbia livia. Behavioural Processes, 31,* 39–56.

Wilkie, D. M., & Willson, R. J. (1992). Time-place learning by pigeons, *Columba livia. Journal of the Experimental Analysis of Behavior, 57,* 145–158.

Zeiler, M. D., & Powell, D. G. (1994). Temporal control in fixed-interval schedules. *Journal of Experimental Analysis of Behavior, 61,* 1–9.

V

TIMING AND COUNTING

13

Behavioristic, Cognitive, Biological, and Quantitative Explanations of Timing

RUSSELL M. CHURCH

There are many types of explanations for the results of experimental studies of animal behavior, including behavioristic, cognitive, biological, and quantitative. In an overview of the field of animal cognition during the twentieth century, I expressed the opinion that all of these types of explanations were used in the nineteenth century and they continued to be used throughout the twentieth century (Church, 2001a). Of course, the extent of use of the different types of explanations is seldom the same in different decades.

This chapter is a review of the types of explanations of animal timing behavior that I have used in articles published between 1956 and 2003. Most of these articles were published with collaborators who were influential at all stages of the research. The substantive topics included: avoidance learning, conditioned suppression, competition, response contingency, temporal perception, temporal memory, timed performance, and temporal choice. In retrospect, it is clear that most of the research on this wide range of substantive topics has been about time perception and timed performance. *Time perception* refers to behavior that varies as a function of the temporal characteristics of a stimulus; *timed performance* refers to the temporal characteristics of behavior. The focus of this chapter is on the explanation of the results of 17 of the articles on timing. The types of explanations were behavioristic, cognitive, biological, and quantitative. They were used roughly in this chronological order, with the use of behavioristic general principles of behavior in the 1950s and 1960s, the concept of a cognitive internal clock in the 1970s, biological mechanisms in the 1980s, and quantitative models of timing behavior from the 1980s until the present. These are all legitimate types of explanations that provide bases for the prediction and understanding of behavioral observations.

EXPLANATIONS BY GENERAL PRINCIPLES (BEHAVIORISTIC)

In the 1950s, explanations of behavior in my articles were often deductions from a general law of behavior, an approach that was supported by philosophers of science at that time (Carnap, 1995; Hempel & Oppenheim, 1948). These explanations involved a statement of a general law or principle, a factual claim, and a deduction. The structure of an explanation by general principle is as follows:

General principle: If P then Q
Definitions: P
Deduction: Q

Inhibition of Delay: Avoidance Learning

Inhibition of delay is a general principle of classical conditioning that may be stated as "the latency of conditioned response (CR) increases as a function of the conditioned stimulus (CS)-unconditioned stimulus (US) interval." Given the definitions that a response A is a CR, a stimulus B is a CS, and a stimulus C is a US, it can be deduced that the latency of A increases as a function of the B-C interval. This deduction from the principle may be considered to be either an explanation of the result or a prediction of the result, and to test the explanation or prediction of the result, the deduction can be compared with the data.

In shuttlebox avoidance procedures, dogs readily learn to avoid shocks by crossing to the other side of the box after a warning stimulus. The primary goals of this research were to describe factors affecting acquisition and extinction of avoidance behavior and to examine the interrelationship between learning and emotion. In a trace conditioning experiment, after a mean of 3 min (uniformly selected from 2, 3, and 4 min), a warning stimulus (a buzzer) was sounded for 2 s (Kamin, 1954). A shock was scheduled to occur 5, 10, or 20 s after the onset of the stimulus (for different groups of animals). If the dog crossed to the other side of the shuttlebox before the shock was scheduled, then this was recorded as an "avoidance response," and the latency of the response was recorded; if the dog did not cross to the other side of the shuttlebox before the shock was scheduled, then the shock would go on and, when the dog crossed to the other side of the shuttlebox, this was recorded as an "escape response," and the latency of the response was recorded. The criterion of avoidance learning was five consecutive avoidance responses. The focus of this experiment was on the effects of the CS-US interval on the acquisition and extinction of the avoidance response and on the development of emotional responses, but one of the results of this procedure was that the mean latency of the five criterion avoidance responses was a linear function of the interval between the onset of the warning stimulus and the time at which a shock was scheduled (the CS-US interval) (figure 13.1).

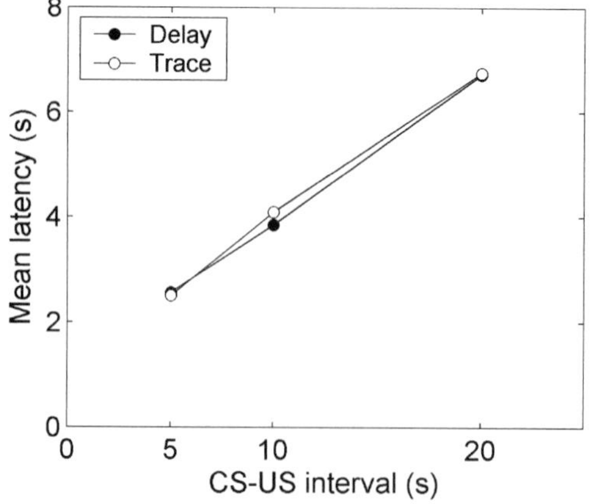

Figure 13.1. Signaled avoidance as a function of the CS-US interval. Mean latency of an avoidance response in trace and delay conditioning. (From "Traumatic Avoidance Learning: The Effects of CS-US Interval with a Delayed-Conditioning Procedure in a Free-Responding Situation," by R. M. Church, F. R. Brush, and R. L. Solomon, 1956, *Journal of Comparative and Physiological Psychology, 49,* 301–308. Copyright 1956 by American Psychological Association. Reprinted with permission.)

This procedure was called "trace conditioning" because there was an interval of time between the termination of the stimulus and the onset of a shock. A similar experiment with a "delay conditioning" procedure was conducted in which the warning stimulus continued until an avoidance response was made (Church, Brush, & Solomon, 1956). The focus of this experiment also was on the effects of the CS-US interval on the acquisition and extinction of the avoidance response, and on the development of emotional results, but one of the results of this experiment was that the mean latency of the five criterion avoidance responses was a linear function of the CS-US interval, and the same linear function characterized the results of the trace and delay procedures. A positive relationship between the mean avoidance latency and the CS-US interval was also observed in another delay conditioning procedure that had many other procedural differences from the other two experiments (Brush, Brush, & Solomon, 1955).

The explanation of the increasing avoidance latency with the increase in the CS-US interval was based on the Pavlovian inhibition of delay principle. The two-process theory of avoidance learning included a Pavlovian classical conditioning factor and a Thorndikian instrumental learning factor. The classical conditioning factor involved the relationship between the warning stimulus (CS) and the shock (US); the instrumental learning factor involved the relationship between the avoidance response and its consequences and the relationship between the escape response and its consequences. The latency of the avoidance response was assumed to reflect the classical conditioning factor. The argument was:

General principle: The latency of the CR increases as a function of the CS-US interval (inhibition of delay)
Definitions: The buzzer was a CS; the shock was a US; the emotional reaction was a CR; the avoidance response was a manifestation of the emotional reaction.
Deduction: Therefore, the latency of the avoidance response will increase as a function of the interval between the buzzer and the shock, as observed.

This analysis extended the generality of the principle of inhibition of delay to avoidance learning.

Law of Effect: Competition

The law of effect is a general principle of instrumental training that may be stated as "the strength of a response is increased by the delivery of a reinforcer following the response." Given the definition of a response that includes attributes of its time of occurrence (relative to previous responses and stimuli) as well as its topography, location, and force and given the definition of an increase of strength as an increase in response probability; it can be deduced that the delivery of a reinforcer following a short interresponse time will increase the probability of a short interresponse time.

In a competitive social situation, reinforcement is determined not solely by the performance of one individual but by the performance of one individual relative to another. The primary goals of this research were to determine conditions under which competition facilitates or interferes with performance and to determine whether the principles based on the behavior of individuals could be extended to social situations. In two experiments, rats were trained on a 30-s variable-interval schedule of reinforcement and then were put into a competitive situation (Church, 1961). In Experiment 1, the rat making the greater number of responses in each 15-s interval received food following its next response; in Experiment 2, the rat making the lesser number of responses in each 15-s interval received food following its next response. A control rat was paired with each experimental rat; when the experimental rat received food, the control rat would receive food following its next response.

The mean number of responses per minute as a function of sessions of competition based on high rates of response (Experiment 1) are shown in figure 13.2 (top); the results of competition based on low rates of response (Experiment 2) are shown in figure 13.2 (bottom). Competition based on high rates of response increased the response rate; competition based on low rates of response decreased the response rate. The interpretation was based on the law of effect:

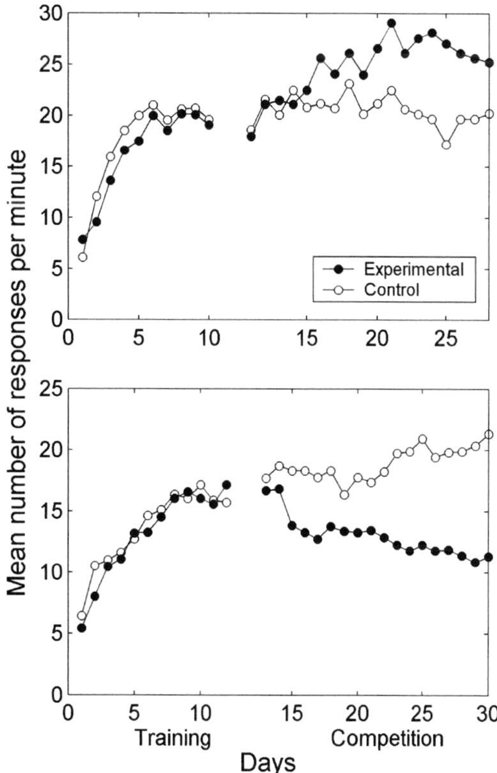

Figure 13.2. Competition with reinforcement of faster and slower response rates. Response rate as a function of days of training and competition. *Top*, Food was delivered to the rat in the experimental pair with the greater number of responses in each 15-s interval. *Bottom*, Food was delivered to the rat in the experimental pair with the fewer number of responses in each 5-s interval. (From "Effects of a Competitive Situation on the Speed of Response," by R. M. Church, 1961, *Journal of Comparative and Physiological Psychology, 54,* 162–166. Copyright 1961 by American Psychological Association. Reprinted with permission.)

Principle: Reinforcement of an attribute of a response will increase the probability of this attribute (law of effect).
Definitions: Response rate is an attribute of a response; food is a reinforcer. The competitive situation results in differential reinforcement of fast responses (in Experiment 1) and slow responses (in Experiment 2).
Deduction: Therefore, the response rate will increase in Experiment 1 and decrease in Experiment 2, as observed.

This analysis was intended to extend the generality of the law of effect to competitive social situations, although, shortly after this article was published, I appreciated there were alternative interpretations of results from the yoked control design (Church, 1964).

Stimulus Control: Differential Reinforcement of Short-Latency Responses

Of course, not all experiments support the wider application of a particular principle. In a reaction time experiment for rats, short-latency responses were reinforced (Church & Carnathan, 1963). According to the law of effect, this contingency should lead to an increase in the frequency of short-latency responses and to a corresponding decrease in the frequency of long-latency responses. But, there was reason to think that this pattern of conditioned responding might not occur. The evidence for selective reinforcement of low rates of response was much stronger than the evidence for selective reinforcement of high rates, particularly when rate was defined by single interresponse intervals. In fact, failures to selectively increase rapid responding by differential reinforcement of rapid responding had been reported (Anger, 1956; Logan, 1960).

For discrimination training, after 30 s of no responding on the lever, a white noise stimulus occurred. The first response after the onset of the noise turned off the noise and delivered a food pellet. For differential reinforcement of short-latency training, a criterion time was set at the median of a rat's reaction times on the previous session. Rats in the experimental condition received food only if a latency was less than the criterion; rats in the control condition received food following their first response in the stimulus if food had been received by the experimental rat with which it had been paired.

The results were that the differential reinforcement of short-latency responses did not significantly decrease the mean log latency—the mean log latency of the experimental group was actually greater than that of the control group. There was, however, a very large and significant increase in the standard deviation of the log latency in the experimental group. The basis for this result is shown in figure 13.3 (top) for one rat. Differential rein-

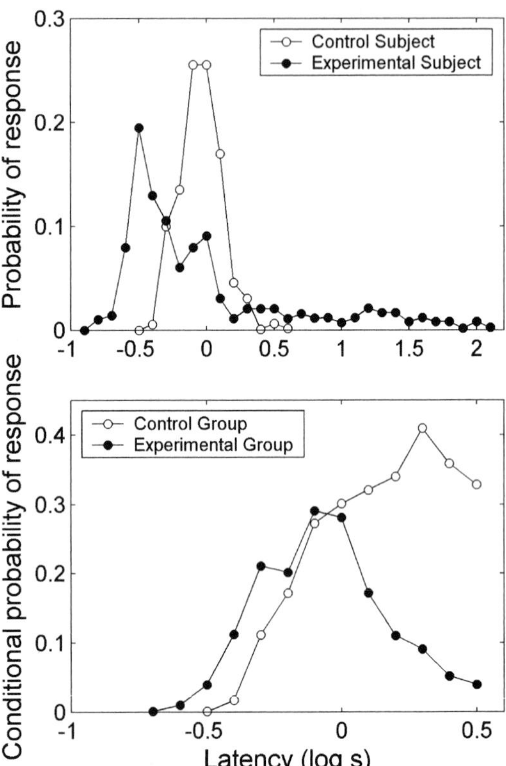

Figure 13.3. Selective reinforcement of short-latency responses. *Top*, Probability distribution of a response with different latencies from two individual rats matched with respect to reinforcement schedule. *Bottom*, Conditional probability of a response with different latencies for the experimental and control groups. (From "Differential Reinforcement of Short-Latency Responses in the White Rat," by R. M. Church and J. Carnathan, 1963, *Journal of Comparative and Physiological Psychology, 56,* 120–123. Copyright 1963 by American Psychological Association. Reprinted with permission.)

forcement of short-latency responses increased the probability of very short-latency responses, but it also increased the probability of long-latency responses. This same conclusion may be made on the basis of the conditional probability of a response as a function of log latency (figure 13.3, bottom, for all rats). In the control condition, the conditional probability of a response rises as a function of time because stimulus onset; in the experimental group, the conditional probability of a response less than about 0.8 s ($10^{-0.1}$ s) is greater for the experimental group; the conditional probability of a response greater than about 0.8 s is greater for the control group. How was this pattern of results to be explained?

According to the law of effect:

Principle: Reinforcement of an attribute of a response will increase the probability of this attribute (law of effect).

Definitions: Response latency is an attribute of a response; food is a reinforcer. The differential reinforcement of short-latency responses results in the probability of reinforcement of short-latency responses greater than that of long-latency responses.

Deduction: Therefore, the response latency will decrease. But this result did not occur. There are many ways to deal with the failure of a general principle to account for specific results. There may be questions about the data, such as the reliability of the data or the appropriateness of the data for the conditions under which the principle is supposed to be applicable. Alternatively, there may be questions about the principle, such as the generality of the principle (or any principle) and questions about the lack of specific information about the conditions under which the principle is supposed to be applicable. Or the principle may be reformulated to account for a wider range of results or even contradictory results, although this added flexibility destroys any value the theory may have had. Another alternative, and the one that was used by Church and Carnathan (1963), was to find another principle that did apply to the observed results.

The proposed solution was to describe a temporal interval, not as an attribute of a response, but as an attribute of a stimulus. According to the principle of stimulus control:

Principle: Reinforcement of a response in the presence of stimulus A will increase the probability of the response in the presence of stimulus A; nonreinforcement of a response in the presence of stimulus B will decrease the probability of the response in the presence of stimulus B.

Definitions: Time since onset of a noise is an attribute of a stimulus; stimulus A is a short time after onset of a noise; stimulus B is a long time after onset of a noise; food is a reinforcer.

Deduction: The differential reinforcement of a response after a short interval will increase the probability of short-latency responses; the nonreinforcement of a response after a long interval will decrease the probability of long-latency responses. Therefore, there will be an increase in the rate of short-latency responses and a decrease in the rate of long-latency responses.

This result did occur, as shown in the bottom panel of figure 13.3. The conditional probability of the short-latency responses was greater in the experimental than the control group, but the conditional probability of the long-latency responses was higher in the control than the experimental group.

In this case, the law of effect and the principle of stimulus control made different predictions. The availability of two or more principles that are applicable to a particular procedure but make different predictions is a serious problem for reliance on explanations based on principles. This can sometimes be solved by identifying a more general, but precise, principle.

EXPLANATIONS BY CHARACTERISTICS OF AN INTERNAL CLOCK (COGNITIVE)

In the 1970s, the explanations of animal timing behavior in my articles were based on the assumption that animals had an internal clock with properties that could be identified by experimental analysis. The properties of the internal clock were assumed to be revealed by the behavior of the rat based on the assumption that the response rate reflected the expected time to the food or shock. The first property was that the clock timed in proportional rather than absolute units. Subsequently, many other properties were identified; it appeared that the internal clock of a rat had all of the properties of a stopwatch.

Proportional Timing: Fixed and Random Times of Shock

The function relating response rate to the time since reinforcement provides evidence for control of behavior by the expected time to reinforcement. Evidence for timing in proportional units came from experiments that showed that a different relationship between responding and absolute time at different intervals became similar when time was measured in proportional units.

Three rats were trained on a 1-min random interval schedule of food reinforcement, in which food was primed according to an exponential waiting time distribution with a mean of 60 s (LaBarbera & Church, 1974). Then, in addition to the food reinforcement schedule, a mild shock was delivered at fixed times during the session. In successive phases of the experiment, the interval between shocks was a fixed 1-min, a fixed 2-min, or a random 1-min interval. The absolute response rate was maintained at approximately one half the rate at the end of training without shock by rules for the adjustment of the shock intensity between sessions and shock duration within a session.

The mean response rate for the rats during sessions with fixed times of 1 min and 2 min between shocks are shown as a function of the proportion of the fixed times in the left column of panels of figure 13.4 (LaBarbera & Church, 1974). The response rate gradients were approximately the same when shown as a function of the proportion of the interval; both decreased as a function of time since the last shock. The mean response rate for the rats during sessions with random times of 1 min between shocks is shown as a function of time after a shock in figure 13.4 (right column). The slope of the function relating the mean response rate to time after shock under the conditions of random shocks was not significantly different from 0; the rate was maintained with a lower intensity of shock in the 1-min random schedule of shock than in the 1-min fixed schedule of shock.

The conclusions were that the animals were estimating time in proportional units, that unpredictable shocks were more aversive than predictable shocks, and that a random schedule of shock is subjectively random. The basic explanation was that the response rate gradients were controlled by an internal clock that timed the expected time to shock in proportional units.

Proportional Timing: Sidman Avoidance Procedure

Another case of proportional timing comes from the Sidman avoidance procedure. In a Sidman avoidance schedule of reinforcement in a shuttlebox, any crossing from one compartment to the other results in a delay in the occurrence of a shock. In one experiment, the response-shock intervals under different conditions were 10, 20, or 40 s (Libby & Church, 1974). The conditional probability of a response (per s) is shown in figure 13.5 (top); this is a measure of response rate. The curves rose as a function of time since the last response, with the slopes progressively less steep for intervals of 10, 20, and 40 s. The response rate of its rat relative to its maximum response rate was calculated, and the mean across rats is shown in figure 13.5 (bottom) as a proportion of the interval. The proportion of the interval was calculated from an estimate of the time of response completion (5 s). The bottom panel shows an essential similarity of the three functions shown in the top panel: when the relative response rate was plotted as a function of the proportion of the interval, the three functions superposed.

The basic explanation for the response rate gradients was the same as the previous experiment: the response rate gradients were controlled by an internal clock that timed the expected time to shock in proportional units.

Expected Time to Reinforcement: The Conditional Emotional Response Procedure

Further evidence for the importance of the expected time to reinforcement comes from the conditioned emotional response procedure In this procedure, rats were trained to press a lever on a 1-min random interval schedule of reinforcement (Libby & Church, 1975). Then, there were cycles of a 1-min light stimulus followed by the light off for a minimum of 30 s and a random interval of 30 s. In one group of rats, shock occurred during the last 0.5 s of the 1-min stimulus (fixed); in the

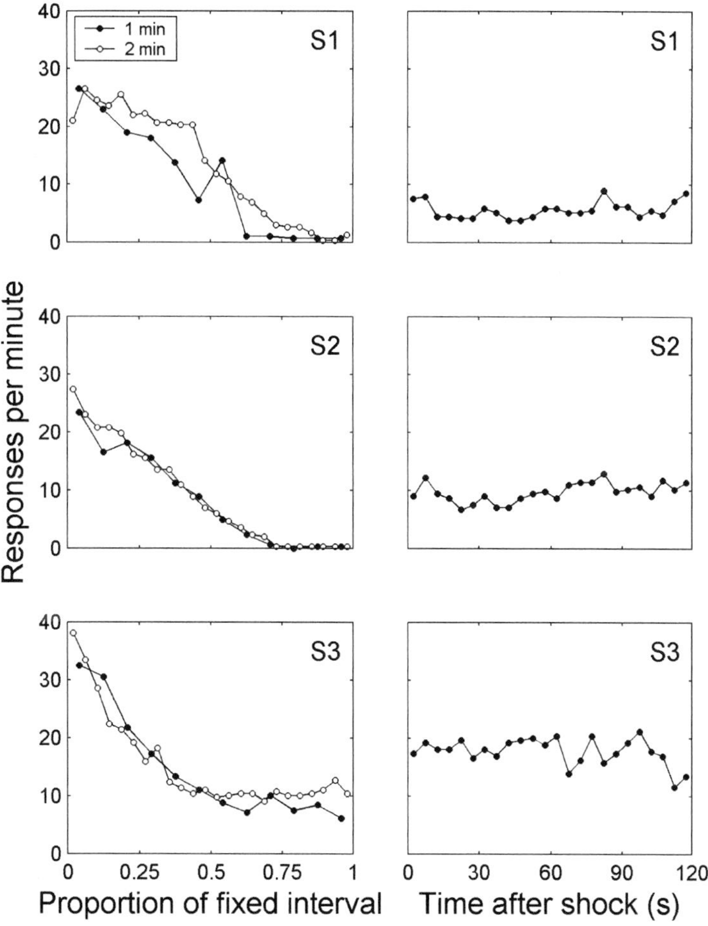

Figure 13.4. Fear gradients as a function of time of shock delivery. A single shock was delivered at 1-min intervals or 2-min intervals (*left*) or at random intervals with a mean of 1 min (*right*). Response rate is shown as a function of proportion of the 1- or 2-min fixed interval in the *left panels* and as a function of time since last shock in the *right panels*. (From "Magnitude of Fear as a Function of Expected Time to an Aversive Event," by J. LaBarbera and R. M. Church, 1974, *Animal Learning & Behavior, 2*, 199–202. Copyright 1974 by The Psychonomic Society. Reprinted with permission.)

other group, 0.5-s shocks occurred at random intervals during a stimulus at a mean rate of 1/min (random). With this random (exponentially distributed waiting time) distribution there could be no shocks, one shock, or more than one shock.

The fear ratio was defined as (A – B)/(A + B), where B was the response rate during the stimulus and A was the response rate during comparable periods without the stimulus. The mean fear ratio is shown as a function of time from stimulus onset in figure 13.6. After the first second, the fear ratio increases if shock is scheduled at the end of the stimulus; the fear ratio decreases if shock is scheduled at random during the interval.

The results were interpreted in terms of control of response rate by the expected time to the next shock. In the conventional conditioned emotional response procedure with shock at the end of a fixed-duration stimulus, the expected time to the next shock decreases linearly with time since stimulus onset; with shock at random times during a fixed-duration stimulus, the expected time to the next shock decreases as a function of time since stimulus onset. At the onset of the 1-min stimulus,

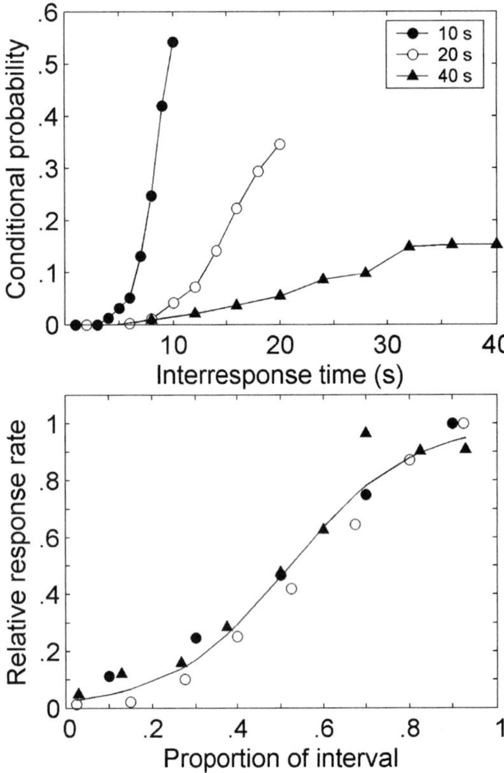

Figure 13.5. Unsignaled avoidance as a function of the response-shock interval. The conditional probability of a response (per second) as a function of the interresponse time in seconds for response-shock intervals of 10, 20, and 40 s (*top*). The relative response rate as a function of the proportion of the interval is shown for the three response intervals (*bottom*). (From "Timing of Avoidance Responses by Rats," by M. E. Libby and R. M. Church, 1974, *Journal of the Experimental Analysis of Behavior, 22,* 513–517. Copyright 1974 by American Psychological Association. Reprinted with permission.)

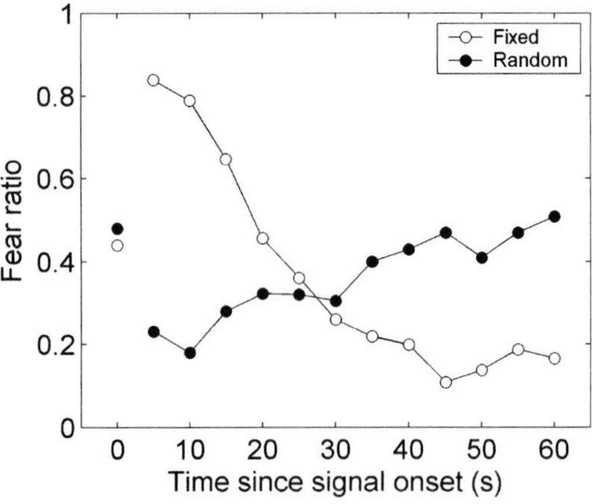

Figure 13.6. Conditioned suppression as a function of fixed and random shocks. The fear ratio during a 1-min stimulus as a function of time from stimulus onset for a condition in which shock occurred at the end of the stimulus (fixed) and a condition in which shock occurred at random times during the stimulus (random). (From "Fear Gradients as a Function of the Temporal Interval Between Signal and Aversive Event in the Rat," by M. E. Libby and R. M. Church, 1975, *Journal of Comparative and Physiological Psychology, 88,* 911–916. Copyright 1975 by American Psychological Association. Reprinted with permission.)

the expected time to the next shock is approximately 1 min, but near the end of the stimulus, with the interstimulus interval approaching, the expected time to the next shock is much longer. Consistent with this interpretation, the fear ratio decreased as a function of time since stimulus onset in the fixed condition and it increased as a function of time in the random condition.

This interpretation of the expected time to reinforcement was in contrast to the standard view that the instantaneous probability of a shock at any point during a stimulus (and in the absence of the stimulus) controlled the response rate (Rescorla, 1968).

Variability of the Internal Clock: A Titration Procedure

Psychophysics is the study of the relationship between psychological (behavioral) and physical variables. In the case of time perception, it is the study of the relationship between subjective time and physical time. One of the measures of psychological time is the difference limen (the just-noticeable-difference in durations) (DL) as a function of the base duration. In one experiment, an auditory stimulus was presented for a standard duration or for a longer comparison duration; the rat was reinforced if it pressed left lever after a standard duration or if it pressed the right lever after a comparison duration (Church, Getty, & Lerner, 1976). The standard durations were 0.5, 1, 2, 4, and 8 s. Based on the performance in blocks of eight trials, the duration of the comparison stimulus was decreased by a small amount if the proportion correct was greater or equal to 75%; the duration of the comparison stimulus was increased by a small amount if the proportion correct was less than 75%.

The results are shown in figure 13.7. The DL is the difference between the standard and comparison that was correctly identified 75% of the time. The top panels come from the experiment just described; the bottom panels come from an experiment with a procedure in which the DL was based on the interquartile range of the durations that rats held a lever down when reinforcement was contingent on exceeding a duration between 0.4 and 6.4 s (Platt, Kuch, & Bitgood, 1973).

In both cases of discrimination of time (top panels) and production of time (bottom panels), the relationship of the square of the DL was approximately linearly related to the square of the duration (T^2) rather than to the duration (T).

These experiments show that the variability of the judgment of a time interval, as well as its central tendency, increases with the duration to be judged. The linear relationship between the DL and the square of the duration provided support for Weber's law and, because of the small but reliable positive intercept, it supported a generalized Weber's law that involves an additive constant. An alternative conception of the clock as an emitter of pulses at random would have been led to linear psychophysical functions in the left panels rather than in the right panels. Psychophysical analysis may reveal specific properties of an internal clock.

Characteristics of the Internal Clock, Criterion, and Response Rule: A Bisection Procedure

In another psychophysical experiment, additional functional relationships were obtained between stimulus duration and response choice (Church & Deluty, 1977). The interpretation of this experiment included not only properties of an internal clock but also characteristics of a criterion and a response rule.

Eight rats were initially trained on a temporal discrimination procedure, in which a response on one lever was reinforced following a 2-s stimulus and a response on another lever was reinforced following an 8-s stimulus (Church & Deluty,

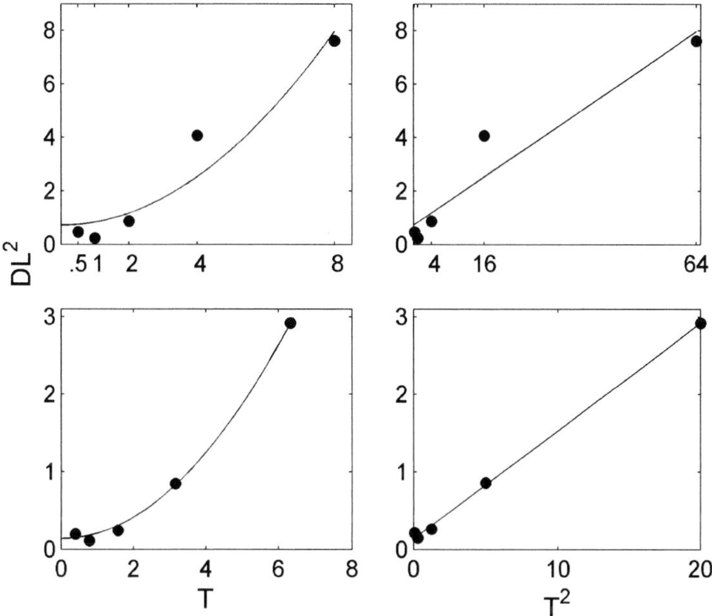

Figure 13.7. Variability of temporal discrimination as a function of stimulus duration. The squared difference limen is shown as a function of stimulus duration, and squared stimulus duration for data from Church, Getty, and Lerner, 1976 (*top*) and Platt, Kuch, and Bitgood, 1973 (*bottom*).

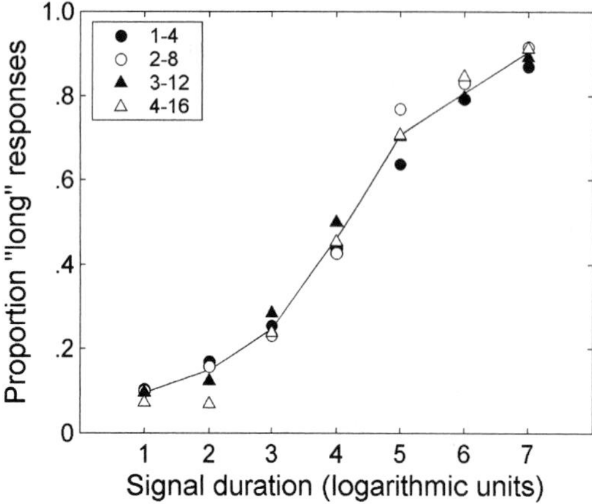

Figure 13.8. Bisection procedure. Proportion long responses as a function of stimulus duration in logarithmic units for four ranges of stimuli (1 vs. 4 s, 2 vs. 8 s, 3 vs. 12 s, and 4 vs. 16 s). (From "Bisection of Temporal Intervals," by R. M. Church and M. Z. Deluty, 1977, *Journal of Experimental Psychology: Animal Behavior Processes, 3,* 216–228. Copyright 1977 by American Psychological Association. Reprinted with permission.)

1977). In different phases of the experiment, rats were trained on different stimulus intervals that had the same 4:1 ratio of the long to the short stimulus. These ranges were 1 versus 4 s, 2 versus 8 s, 3 versus 12 s, and 4 versus 12 s. In these phases, in addition to the extreme durations, there were five additional stimulus durations between the shortest and longest in that series (logarithmically spaced), and responses to these intermediate stimuli were not reinforced. An important dependent variable was the proportion of "long" responses as a function of stimulus duration.

The major result is shown in figure 13.8. The proportion of long responses increased as a function of stimulus duration in an ogival manner. Most important, the functions for all of the ranges superposed when plotted in relative time units. The point of bisection (the time at which a rat was equally likely to respond on the left or right lever) was approximately at the geometrical mean between the short and long stimulus duration (rather than at the arithmetic or harmonic mean); the DL was also a linear function of the geometrical mean of the extreme durations.

The explanation of these results was in terms of an internal clock, a criterion, and a response rule. The onset of a stimulus started the clock, which continued to run until the stimulus terminated and the levers were inserted; the response rule was to respond on one lever if the clock value was below a criterion and to respond on the other lever if the clock value was above a criterion. One problem was to determine how subjective time (the value of the clock) varied as a function of physical time: linear, logarithmic, and reciprocal functions were considered. This experiment was interpreted as supporting Fechner's law that subjective time increases as a logarithm of the time. A comment was made that "there is no good a priori reason for expecting a biological process to be linear," although it was noted that this could fit the data with a different response rule.

Two sources of variability were also proposed: variability of the clock and of the criterion. Some variability of the clock was assumed to be necessary to fit the data and, with a logarithmic clock, a normal distribution with a constant standard deviation at all intervals might be sufficient. In this experiment, there was no attempt to assess the relative contribution of variability of the clock and criterion.

The interpretation of the results of this experiment were based on a relative, rather than an absolute, response rule. That is, the rat was assumed to respond relative to a criterion time, not at an absolute time. This assumption was supported by the greater difficulty of transfer from a 1- versus 4-s discrimination to a 4- versus 16-s discrimination if the correct response to the 4-s stimulus was maintained than if the correct response to the longer stimulus was maintained.

To account for the error rates on the extreme intervals, and the biases of some of the rats, the treatment of error described by Heinemann and Avin (1973) was used:

$$p_o(t) = \alpha p(t) + (1 - \alpha)p_b$$

where $p_o(t)$ is the observed behavior as a function of time, α is the probability of attending to time, $p(t)$ is the behavior as a function of time if the rat is attending to time, and p_b is the behavior as a function of time if the rat is not attending to time.

The explanation of the results of this experiment contained many ideas that would later be used for the development of a process model version of scalar timing theory, but it did not present a specific model that could be quantitatively fit to data.

Control of an Internal Clock: The Gap Procedure

If there is an internal clock, then perhaps it can be manipulated by experimental variables. One approach is to introduce a break in a previously continuous stimulus. In a temporal choice procedure, rats were trained to respond on one lever after a 5-s stimulus and on another lever after a 20-s stimulus (Roberts & Church, 1978). Then, the rats were trained on a range of stimuli and trained to respond to one lever if the interval was 4, 6, 8, or 10 s and to respond on the other lever if the interval was 12, 14, 18, or 22 s. In a later phase, a 4-s break began 2 s after the onset of some of the 8-, 10-, 12-, and 14-s stimuli. Figure 13.9 shows the probability of a "long" response following stimuli without a break (solid circles) and with a 4-s break (open circles). The "run" and "stop" groups refer to whether reinforcement on the break trials was based on the time since onset (run) or on the time since onset excluding the break interval (stop): The results were similar for the two reinforcement conditions. In both cases, a break produced an approximately 4-s rightward shift in the psychometric function relating the probability of a "long" response to time since stimulus onset, but the magnitude of the shift was reduced with training when reinforcement was based on time since stimulus onset (in the run group). In other conditions, the amount of shift depended on the duration of the break, but it did not depend on the location of the break during the stimulus; it appeared both in this choice procedure and in a fixed interval procedure.

The interpretation of the results of this experiment was that the internal clock of the rat began at stimulus onset, stopped during a break in the stimulus, and continued after the next stimulus onset. This operation of the internal clock led to a 4-s rightward shift in the stop group that was maintained and an initial 4-s rightward shift in the run group that adjusted to the reinforcement contingency. One of the strengths of this analysis is that a description of a qualitative hypothesis (the rat stops its clock during a break) provides a quantitative prediction of behavior (the rightward shift of the psychometric function will be equal to the duration of the break).

Temporal Memory: Effect of the Retention Interval in a Temporal Discrimination Procedure

In a typical temporal choice procedure, a stimulus of one of two durations is presented and then the animal has the opportunity to make a choice response immediately at the end of the stimulus. What is the effect of the introduction of a retention interval between the presentation of the stimulus and the opportunity to make a choice? Presumably, there is some loss of stimulus control with an increase in the retention interval. The question is whether this loss of stimulus control is due to subjective shortening of a remembered duration as a function of time.

In one experiment, rats were trained in a 2- versus 8-s temporal discrimination with retention

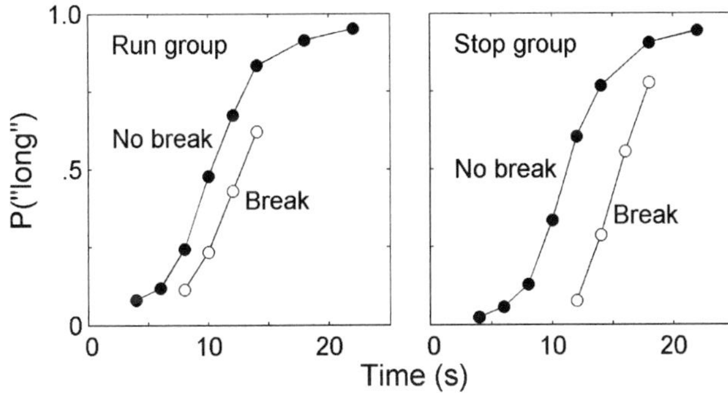

Figure 13.9. Stopping the internal clock. Probability of a long response as a function of duration since stimulus onset, with and without a 4-s break in the stimulus. (From "Control of an Internal Clock," by S. Roberts and R. M. Church, 1978, *Journal of Experimental Psychology: Animal Behavior Processes, 4,* 318–337. Copyright 1978 by American Psychological Association. Reprinted with permission.)

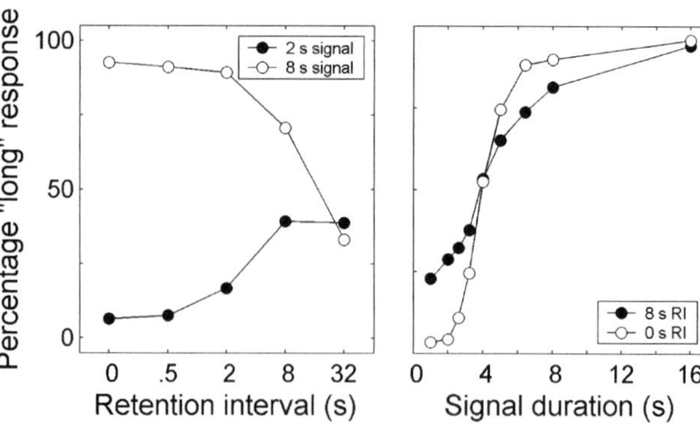

Figure 13.10. Memory of duration. Probability of long response as a function of stimulus duration at retention intervals of 0, 0.5, 2.0, and 8.0 s. *Right*, Percentage of long response as a function of signal duration for the 0-s and 8-s retention intervals. (From "Short-Term Memory for Time Intervals," by R. M. Church, 1980, *Learning and Motivation, 11*, 208–219. Copyright 1980 by Elsevier. Reprinted with permission.)

intervals of 0, 0.5, 2.0, 8.0, and 32.0 s (Church, 1980). The percentage of "long" responses is shown as a function of the retention interval in figure 13.10 (left). The temporal discrimination decreased as a function of the retention interval. The interpretation of this result is that there was no evidence in this experiment that forgetting occurred on the time dimension. If the reduction in the percentage of "long" responses following an 8-s stimulus was due to subjective shortening, then why did the percentage of "long" responses following the 2-s stimulus increase? The two functions were approximately at the same point after 32 s, which could represent the bias when choice is not based on the stimulus duration. This view was strengthened by the fact that the rats responded "long" less than half the occasions in which no stimulus was presented.

A more sensitive test for subjective shortening was also conducted. It involved the training of a 2- versus an 8-s temporal discrimination, and then with nine intervals between 1 and 16 s. A "short" response was reinforced following stimuli shorter than 4 s; a "long" response was reinforced following stimuli longer than 4 s; and neither response was reinforced following the 4-s stimulus. The results are shown in figure 13.10 (right). The open circles show the psychophysical function after a 0-s retention interval; the solid circles show the retention interval following an 8-s retention interval. Following the 8-s retention interval, the psychophysical function is much flatter, but the point of bisection remained near the geometrical mean of 4.0 s. The interpretation of the results of this experiment was that forgetting did not occur on the time dimension and that "the subjective duration of a signal did not appear to decrease during a retention interval" (Church, 1980, p. 218).

EXPLANATIONS BY NEURAL MECHANISMS (BIOLOGICAL)

One approach to the development of biological explanations of timing is to compare the behavior of animals with and without a particular brain lesion in timing tasks. The logic of these lesion studies is similar to the logic of studies of drug effects on behavior.

Rats were trained in a peak procedure following an electrolytic lesion of the fimbria fornix or a sham lesion (Meck, Church, & Olton, 1984). The peak procedure combines cycles with fixed-interval reinforcement with cycles without reinforcement (Roberts, 1981). During each cycle of the 20 sessions of training without gaps (breaks), after a random interval with a minimum of 5 s and a mean of 50 s, white noise was turned on during a cycle with a 20-s fixed interval or white noise was turned on for 50 s and then turned off. The three sessions of testing with gaps was the same, except that during a random half of the cycles without reinforcement there was a 5-s gap that began 10 s after stimulus onset. A dependent variable was the median time of the maximum response rate (peak) on cycles with and without a gap (figure 13.11).

Without a gap, the median peak time of the control rats was approximately 20 s, the time that food was sometimes available; the median peak

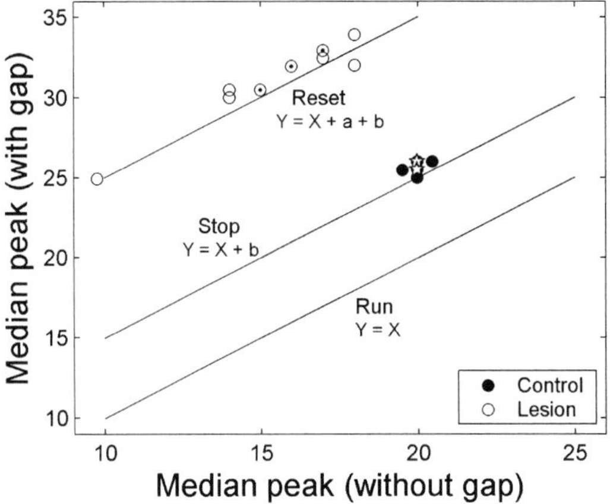

Figure 13.11. Effect of hippocampus on the internal clock. Median peak time with gap as a function of median peak time without gap for rats with hippocampal lesion and controls. (From "Hippocampus, Time, and Memory," by W. H. Meck, R. M. Church, and D. S. Olton, 1984, *Behavioral Neuroscience, 98,* 3–22. Copyright 1984 by American Psychological Association. Reprinted with permission.).

time of the rats with the fimbria fornix lesion was more variable and shorter. With a gap, the median peak time of the control rats was approximately 25 s; in the lesioned rats, the median peak time with a gap was about 15 s longer than that without a gap.

The interpretation was that the rats in the control group stopped their clocks during the 5-s gap and that the rats in the lesion group reset their clocks during the gap, thus adding 15 s to their peak times (the 10 s of stimulus and the 5 s of gap). The conclusion was that the fimbria fornix lesion did not interfere with the ability of rats to time intervals, but it did affect which intervals were timed or remembered.

EXPLANATIONS BY MATHEMATICAL MODELS (QUANTITATIVE)

In the 1980s, in collaboration with John Gibbon, the explanations of animal timing behavior in my articles were based on scalar timing theory. This theory originally was based on general principles, such as Weber's law for timing (Gibbon, 1977) and became a process theory of timing that was composed of modules for clock, memory, and decision (Gibbon, Church, & Meck, 1984).

Scalar Timing Theory: Time Left Procedure

In a concurrent chains procedure, a pigeon could choose between an elapsing time to food that began at 30 s and decreased to 0 s and a standard time to food that was 15 s. At a beginning of a trial the pigeon could choose to peck the left key that was illuminated with white light (for the elapsing time) or the right key that was illuminated with red light (for the standard time). At some time during after the beginning of the trial, the choice of the pigeon led to a terminal link. If it had most recently pecked on the left key, it received food after the time that was left; if it had most recently pecked on the right key, it received food after 15 s. Under such conditions, the pigeons usually responded initially on the standard key and then switched to respond on the elapsing key after about 7.5 s. In one experiment, the standard interval was either 15, 30, 60, or 90 s, and the elapsing interval began at twice the standard interval (Gibbon & Church, 1981).

The proportion of responses on the elapsing interval (L) is shown as a function since stimulus onset for the mean of three pigeons in figure 13.12. These curves were well fit by scalar timing theory with three free parameters for each of the four functions $\omega^2 \geq 0.995$: these were the probability of inattention, the coefficient of variation measure of sensitivity to time, and the threshold (b). The scalar timing model used a ratio decision rule:

$$(x_c - x_t)/x_s < b$$

where x_c is the initial duration of the elapsing standard, x_t is the time since stimulus onset, x_s is the duration of the standard, and b is the threshold (between 0 and 1).

The interpretation of the results of this experiment was that scalar timing theory provided a good fit to the data with plausible assumptions: these included the assumption that subjective time was linearly (rather than logarithmically) related to physical time.

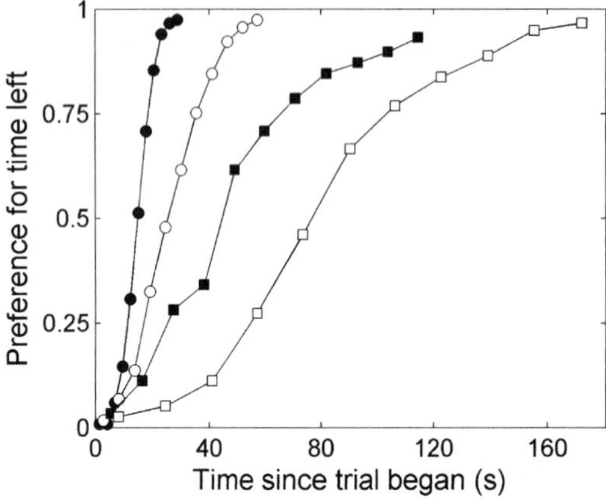

Figure 13.12. Time left. Probability of choosing the "time left" alternative as a function of time since a trial began. (From "Time Left: Linear Versus Logarithmic Subjective Time," by J. Gibbon and R. M. Church, 1981, *Journal of Experimental Psychology: Animal Behavior Processes, 7,* 87–108. Copyright 1981 by American Psychological Association. Reprinted with permission.)

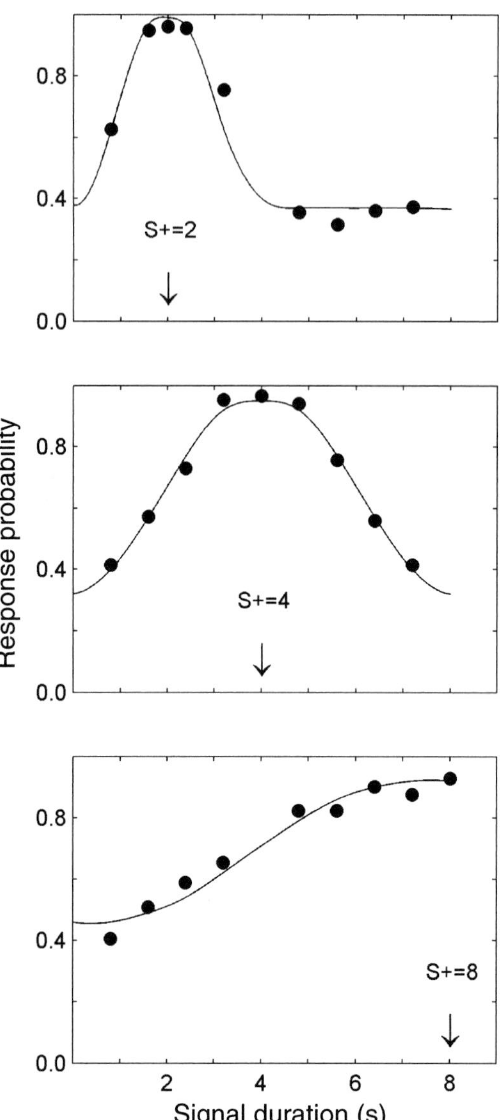

Figure 13.13. Temporal generalization. Probability of a response as a function of stimulus duration under conditions in which reinforcement of a response occurred after a stimulus duration of 2 s (*top*), 4 s (*middle*), and 8 s (*bottom*). (From "Temporal Generalization," by R. M. Church and J. Gibbon, 1982, *Journal of Experimental Psychology: Animal Behavior Processes, 8,* 165–186. Copyright 1982 by American Psychological Association. Reprinted with permission.)

Scalar Timing Theory: Temporal Generalization Procedure

A temporal generalization procedure provides a way to determine the ability of an animal to discriminate stimuli that differed in duration. In this procedure, stimuli of various durations are presented, but a response to only one of them is reinforced (Church & Gibbon, 1982). In different groups of rats, a response was reinforced for a response within 3 s following a 2-s stimulus, a 4-s stimulus, or an 8-s stimulus. The response probability as a function of stimulus duration is shown in figure 13.13. The maximum probability of responding was near the time of the reinforced stimulus duration; the variability of the response probability function increased as the reinforced interval increased. Quantitatively, for the estimated probability of a response given attention to time, the response probability as a function of relative time (duration of the stimulus divided by the reinforced interval) superposed for 12 different conditions in this experiment: log spacing, linear spacing, extended range, reinforcement at 2, 4, or 8 s, partial reinforcement, probability of presentation of the reinforced interval, and five quintiles of response probability.

The smooth functions near the data points are the quantitative predictions of scalar timing theory based on only two parameters that were fit to specific functions: the probability of attention to time and the probability of a response given inattention to time. The other parameters (sensitivity to time, mean of threshold, and standard deviation of threshold) were fixed at their median values. The median proportion of variance accounted for was 0.965. The interpretation of the results of the temporal generalization procedure was in terms of scalar timing theory.

Scalar Timing Theory: Simultaneous Temporal Processing Procedure

A simultaneous temporal processing procedure provided a way to assess the ability of animals to time more than one temporal interval at the same time. Ten rats were trained for 35 sessions on cycles of 130 s in the absence of a stimulus and then a houselight with a 50-s fixed interval of reinforcement (Meck & Church, 1984). Then there were 30 sessions in which half the trials were the same as during training, but the other half had 1-s presentations of a tone starting at 0, 10, 20, 30, and 40 s. The resulting response rate as a percentage of the maximum rate is shown as a function of time since stimulus onset in figure 13.14. The rats timed both of the intervals. There is an overall gradient of increasing response rate as a function of time since stimulus onset, plus local gradients of responding at the onset of each segment stimulus.

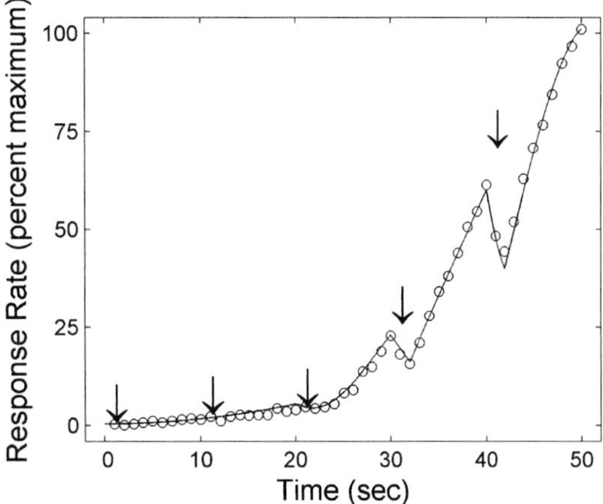

Figure 13.14. Simultaneous temporal processing. Response rate (percent maximum) as a function of time since onset of a stimulus (houselight). A 1-s stimulus (noise) was presented at the times indicated by the *arrows*. (From "Simultaneous Temporal Processing, by W. H. Meck and R. M. Church, 1984, *Journal of Experimental Psychology: Animal Behavior Processes, 10,* 1–29. Copyright 1984 by American Psychological Association. Reprinted with permission.)

The interpretation of the results of the simultaneous temporal processing procedure was in terms of the same version of scalar timing theory used for temporal generalization.

Scalar Timing Theory: The Peak Procedure

A peak procedure provides a way to assess the change in an animal's subjective time to reinforcement as a function of the objective time. Most studies of the performance of animals on the peak procedure have used the mean response gradients over many sessions. Although the information-processing version of scalar timing theory made assumptions about the performance of animals on individual cycles, their primary support had been that they led to adequate predictions of the mean response gradients. In an experiment with intervals in which food was delivered on half of the cycles following the first response after 15, 30, or 60 s, both the mean response gradients and the performance on individual cycles without food were analyzed (Church, Meck, & Gibbon, 1994). The purpose of the study was to determine the accuracy of the assumptions about the characteristics of the internal clock, temporal memory, and decision processes. The examination of performance on individual cycles also made it possible to assess the magnitude of the contributions of each of these sources of variability to performance on the peak procedure.

Some of the results are shown in figure 13.15. The three panels in the second column show the mean response gradients as a function of time since stimulus onset on nonfood trials. The thin line that is near the data points is based on scalar timing theory. Both the data and the model resulted in a maximum response rate near the time that food was sometimes available, a standard deviation of the gradients that was linearly related to the reinforced interval, a coefficient of variation (standard deviation divided by mean) that was relatively constant, and gradients that superposed when plotted in relative units.

The three panels in the first column show seven indices of performance on individual cycles. On individual cycles the response rate is typically low for some period of time, becomes high for some period of time that includes the time that food is sometimes

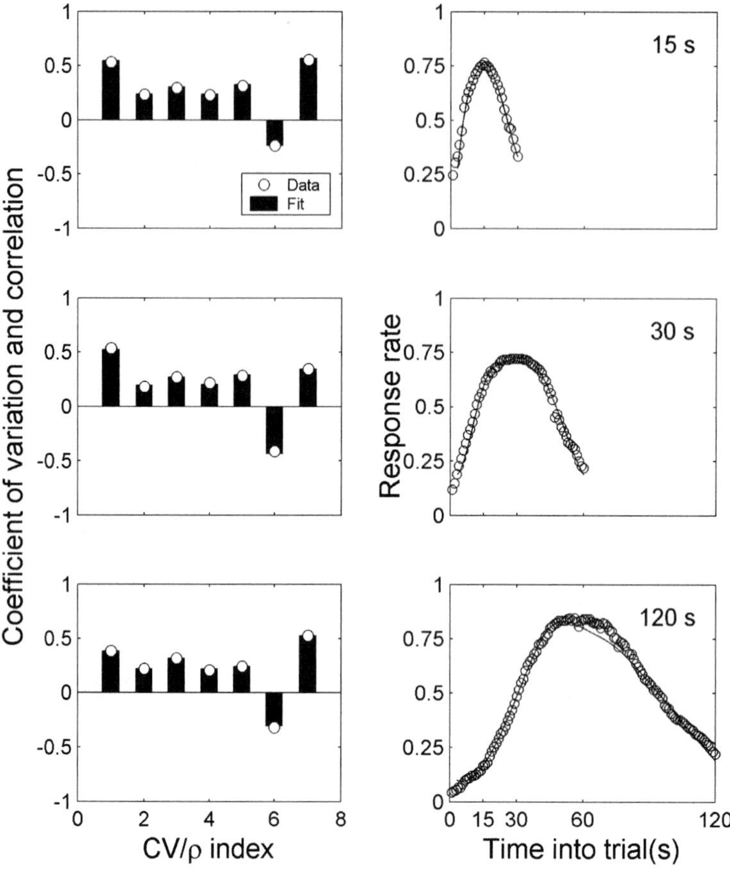

Figure 13.15. Single trial analysis. Fits of seven indices of performance on individual trials (*left*) and of the mean relative response rate as a function of time in a 15-s, 30-s, and 60-s peak procedure. The first four indices were the coefficient of variation of the start, end, duration, and middle (γ_{s1}, γ_{s2}, γ_d, and γ_m); the last three indices were the correlations between start and end, start and difference, and duration and mean ($\rho_{s1,s2}$, $\rho_{s1,d}$, and $\rho_{d,m}$). The white circles in the *left panels* and the thin line in the *right panels* are based on a fit of scalar timing theory. (From "Application of Scalar Timing Theory to Individual Trials," by R. M. Church, W. H. Meck, and J. Gibbon, 1994, *Journal of Experimental Psychology: Animal Behavior Processes, 20,* 135–155. Copyright 1994 by American Psychological Association. Reprinted with permission.)

delivered, and then becomes low again (the low-high-low pattern). An objective definition of the time of the start (s_1) and end (s_2) of the high state was used, and from these two times, the duration (d) and middle (m) of a high response rate could be calculated. Then, across cycles, it was possible to calculate the coefficient variation of the four indices (s_1, s_2, d, and m) and the correlations between pairs of indices. The observed values of these coefficients of variation and correlations are shown by the black bars in figure 13.15; the white circles near the top of the observed value are the values produced by scalar timing theory, with the same parameter values used for fitting the response rate gradients.

The covariance patterns between measures of start, end, duration, and middle individual trials, as well as the response rate gradients over many sessions, are accounted for by a two-threshold scalar timing theory with parameters for the mean and standard deviation of a start and an end threshold and a parameter for memory variance.

Multiple Oscillator Theory: The Ramped Interval Procedure

Although scalar timing theory has had many successes in providing a quantitative explanation of behavior in many timing procedures, its weaknesses are well known to both its critics and supporters. For example, it does not account for the learning of temporal discriminations or for extinction. Another concern is that it has a very large number of parameters that can be estimated from the data: these include the distribution form and the parameters of the clock, the latency to start and stop the clock, attention, memory storage, memory retrieval, and threshold or thresholds. These many parameters may give it too much flexibility. It is possible that a simpler model based on different assumptions could explain the data as well or better.

Many different quantitative models of timing have been proposed (Church & Kirkpatrick, 2001); one of them is a multiple oscillator model of timing (Church & Broadbent, 1990). A striking feature of this model is that many of its assumptions about the clock, temporal memory, and decision processes are quite different from the ones made by scalar timing theory. In multiple oscillator model, the clock consists of multiple oscillators (rather than a pacemaker-switch-accumulator system), temporal memory consists of a single autoassociation matrix rather than a store of exemplars, and the decision involves a correlation of the values in two vectors rather than a ratio comparison of two scalar values.

In a standard fixed interval procedure, food is made available after some interval of time (such as 60 s), and food is delivered at the next response. In a ramped interval procedure, the interval increases by some small amount after each reinforcement until it reaches some maximum, and then it decreases by some small amount until it reaches some minimum. In two experiments with a ramped interval procedure with 2-s steps between intervals, Crystal, Church, and Broadbent (1997) determined a start time for each cycle. This start time was an approximately linear function of the interval duration (figure 13.16, top left). The residual (the difference between the start time and the best-fitting straight line) was only a few seconds, but the deviations were clearly systematic (figure 13.16, bottom left).

The multiple oscillator model of timing was applied to these data, as shown in the right panels. The top right panel shows the approximately linear function of the start time, and the bottom right panel shows the systematic deviations which, although too large, occurred at approximately at the correct locations. For a description of other nonlinearities in animals' sensitivity to time and other quantitative models that produce them, see Crystal (2003).

Packet Theory: Fixed and Random Interval Schedules of Reinforcement

Many quantitative theories of timing have begun with what was regarded as plausible assumptions that could be applied to data; these assumptions could be adjusted as necessary if there were discrepancies between the predictions of the model and the data. Packet theory (Kirkpatrick, 2002; Kirkpatrick & Church, 2003) began with an examination of the time of occurrence of responses and was specifically designed to account for bouts of behavior, control of the pattern of responses by the expected time to reinforcement, and control of the overall response rate by the mean interreinforcement interval. The theory included quantitative assumptions regarding the characteristics of response bouts and the determinants of the pattern and rate of these bouts.

Perhaps the simplest timing experiment is one in which food is delivered at fixed or random times to a rat and the time of each head entry into the food cup is recorded. Eight groups of rats were trained with fixed times of 45, 90, 180, and 360 s or random times of 45, 90, 180, and 360 s (Kirkpatrick & Church, 2003).

The response rate as a function of time since food under each of the eight conditions is shown in figure 13.17 (left). After a bout of head-entry responses following the delivery of food, the response rate declined to a minimum. When food was delivered at fixed times, there was an increasing response rate with the slope and height inversely related to the interfood interval; when food was delivered at random times, the response rate gradient was nearly flat, but it was inversely related to the interfood interval. The right panels are based on a simulation of packet theory. A single set of two parameters was used for generating responses in a bout for all eight groups; a single parameter was estimated for responsiveness in all eight groups; and one learning rate parameter was used,

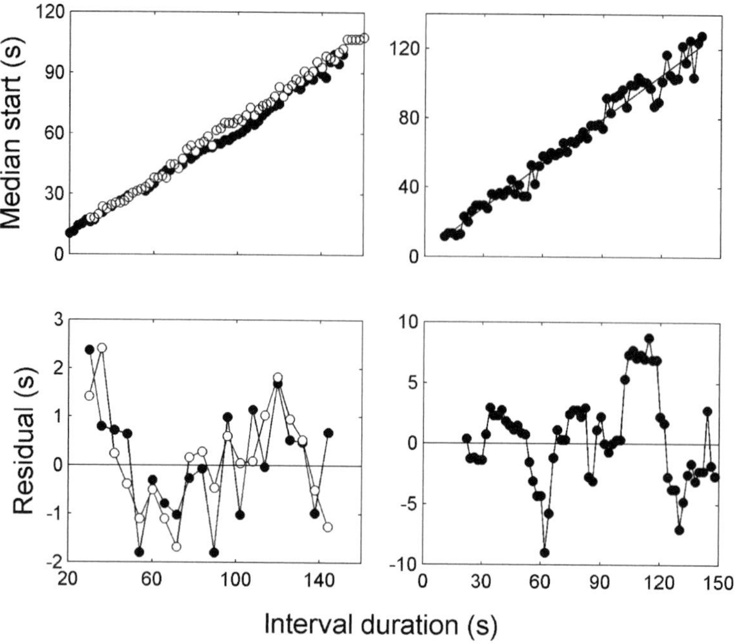

Figure 13.16. Ramped interval procedure. *Top left,* Median start time as a function of interval duration(s). *Bottom left,* Residual (difference between median start time and interval duration) as a function of interval duration(s). Rats tested on intervals between 20 and 150 s are shown by *closed circles;* those tested on intervals between 30 and 160 s are shown by *open circles. Top right,* Simulation of median start time. *Bottom right,* Simulation of residual. Both simulations based on the multiple oscillator model. (From "Systematic Nonlinearities in the Memory Representation of Time," by J. D. Crystal, R. M. Church, and H. A. Broadbent, 1997, *Journal of Experimental Psychology: Animal Behavior Processes, 23,* 267–282. Copyright 1997 by American Psychological Association. Reprinted with permission.)

but it had a negligible impact on the asymptotic behavior that is shown. The data (left panels) can be compared with the simulated results (right panels). Both showed an increase in response rate as a function of time since food for the fixed-time procedures and a relatively flat function relating response rate to the time since food; the mean response rate was inversely related to the interval in the data and simulations.

TYPES OF EXPLANATIONS

The four types of explanations (behavioristic, cognitive, biological, and quantitative) are not mutually exclusive or exhaustive. They do, however, focus on the enthusiasms of the times: the search for general principles of behavior, understanding of the animal mind, neural bases of behavior, and precise predictions of behavior.

Behavioristic

A conventional description of the history of research of animal cognition might include early conjectures about the nature of animal mental processes, the rise of behaviorism (Watson, 1913), and a successful cognitive revolution. A problem with this conventional history is that the decade in which behaviorism was overthrown has been reported to be sometime between 1926 and 1936 (Washburn, 1936), sometime between 1948 and 1959 (Gardner, 1985), and sometime late in the twentieth century (Griffin, 1992). (See Church, 2001a, for the bases of these reports.) With such uncertainty about date of the death of behaviorism, it is plausible to

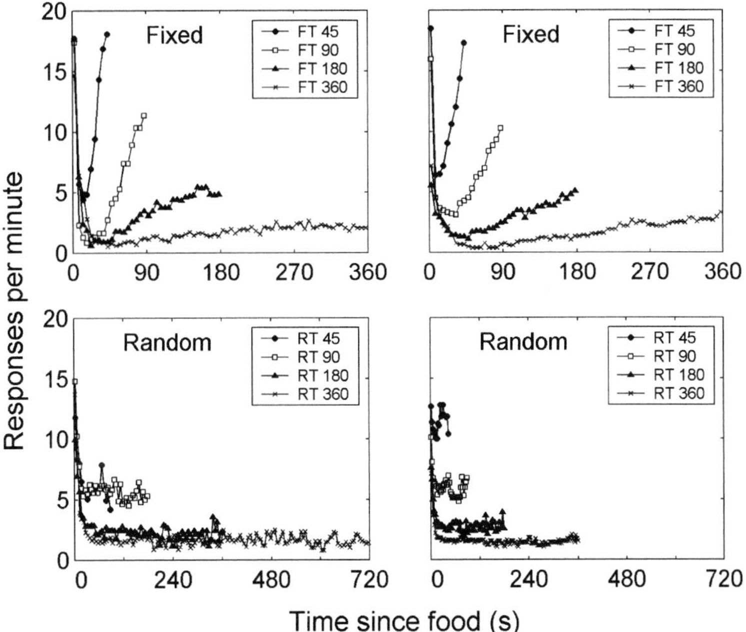

Figure 13.17. Tracking expected time to reinforcement. Response rate as a function of time since food in conditions in which food is delivered at fixed times (45, 90, 180, and 360 s) or at random times with means of 45, 90, 180, and 360 s. *Left panels* are data; *right panels* are simulations of packet theory. (From "Tracking of the Expected Time to Reinforcement in Temporal Conditioning Procedures," by K. Kirkpatrick and R. M. Church, 2003, *Learning & Behavior, 31,* 3–21. Copyright 2003 by American Psychological Association. Reprinted with permission.)

entertain the view that its essential ideas have been fully incorporated into research on animal behavior. These ideas include the use of well-defined behavioral dependent and intervening variables, well-controlled independent variables, and the experimental method.

Explanations based on general principles of behavior continue to be used extensively. They are very useful for identifying common features of apparently different phenomena. For example, the general principles of classical conditioning have unified such apparently different phenomena as salivary conditioning, eyelid conditioning, taste aversion, autoshaping, and the conditional emotional response.

One of the objections to the use of general principles is that there are no general principles of behavior. This may be because of individual differences, species differences, or the exceptions that may be found to any general principle of behavior. Such exceptions may readily be found if the boundary conditions are not precisely described and are obvious if a procedure produces inconsistent results. It is possible to focus either on similarities or on differences between results; the use of general principles for explanation clearly focuses on the similarities.

Another objection to the use of general principles is that no conclusions can be made if two or more principles apply to the same procedure. When this occurs, the variables are reported to be confounded, and efforts are made to find alternative procedures (and differences between the results of the procedures) that can be regarded as the consequence of a single factor.

Cognitive

The use of the clock metaphor provided a useful way to move from explanations based on principles to explanations based on processes. After a clock metaphor had been established, it was possible to consider other psychological processes (such as memory, attention, and decision) as other modules of a system. Then it was possible to develop hypotheses regarding the relationship of these intervening variables to each other and to the input (procedure) and the output (behavior). If a cognitive model is specified with sufficient precision to be a quantitative model, there is no rigorously defined distinction between cognitive models with and without a clock (or pacemaker).

Biological

One type of biological explanation is based on principles of evolution (genetic variation and selection) and ecology. This type of explanation has been used in timing interpretations of foraging behavior (Bateson, 2003), but it has not been represented in my research. Another type of biological explanation is based on brain mechanisms that can be described by the time, place, and nature of electrical and chemical activity. If a good biological explanation and a good cognitive explanation were available for the effects of timing procedures on timing behavior, then one could approach some understanding of the relationship of the mind to the body. At present, the biological variables are primarily alternative or additional dependent variables which can be correlated with behavioral dependent variables in timing experiments.

Quantitative

Quantitative models of timing can be modularized into parts that involve the procedures (independent variables), the theory (intervening variables), and the behavior (dependent variables). Many timing models have been developed. Each of them has particular strengths and weaknesses that are well known, but none of them would yet be able to pass a Turing test in which an investigator would be unable to determine whether data were being produced by an animal or by a quantitative model (Church, 2001b). However, the development of such a model no longer appears to be a particularly difficult task.

Acknowledgments Preparation of this chapter was supported by a grant from the National Institute of Mental Health (RO1-MH44234). Figures were prepared by Mika Macinnis, Paulo Guilhardi, and Elizabeth Kyonka.

References

Anger, D. (1956). The dependence of interresponse times upon the relative reinforcement of different interresponse times. *Journal of Experimental Psychology, 52,* 145–161.

Bateson, M. (2003). Interval timing and optimal foraging. In W. H. Meck (Ed.), *Functional and neural mechanisms of interval timing* (pp. 113–141). Boca Raton, FL: CRC Press.

Brush, F. R., Brush, E. L., & Solomon, R. L. (1955). Traumatic avoidance learning: The effects of CS-US interval with a delayed-conditioning procedure. *Journal of Comparative and Physiological Psychology, 48,* 285–293.

Carnap, R. (1995). *An introduction to the philosophy of science.* New York: Dover.

Church, R. M. (1961). Effects of a competitive situation on the speed of response. *Journal of Comparative and Physiological Psychology, 54,* 162–166.

Church, R. M. (1964). Systematic effect of random error in the yoked control design. *Psychological Bulletin, 62,* 122–131.

Church, R. M. (1980). Short-term memory for time intervals. *Learning and Motivation, 11,* 208–219.

Church, R. M. (2001a). Animal cognition: 1900–2000. *Behavioural Processes, 54,* 53–63.

Church, R. M. (2001b). A Turing test for computational and associative theories of learning. *Current Directions in Psychological Science, 10,* 132–136.

Church, R. M., & Broadbent, H. A. (1990). Alternative representations of time, number, and rate. *Cognition, 37,* 55–81.

Church, R. M., Brush, F. R., & Solomon, R. L. (1956). Traumatic avoidance learning: The effects of CS-US interval with a delayed-conditioning procedure in a free-responding situation. *Journal of Comparative and Physiological Psychology, 49,* 301–308.

Church, R. M., & Carnathan, J. (1963). Differential reinforcement of short-latency responses in the white rat. *Journal of Comparative and Physiological Psychology, 56,* 120–123.

Church, R. M., & Deluty, M. Z. (1977). Bisection of temporal intervals. *Journal of Experimental Psychology: Animal Behavior Processes, 3,* 216–228.

Church, R. M., Getty, D. J., & Lerner, N. D. (1976). Duration discrimination by rats. *Journal of Experimental Psychology: Animal Behavior Processes, 2,* 303–312.

Church, R. M., & Gibbon, J. (1982). Temporal generalization. *Journal of Experimental Psychology: Animal Behavior Processes, 8,* 165–186.

Church, R. M., & Kirkpatrick, K. (2001). Theories of conditioning and timing. In R. R. Mowrer & S. B. Klein (Eds.), *Handbook of contemporary learning theories.* Mahwah, NJ: Lawrence Erlbaum Associates.

Church, R. M., Meck, W. H., & Gibbon, J. (1994). Application of scalar timing theory to individual trials. *Journal of Experimental Psychology: Animal Behavior Processes, 20,* 135–155.

Crystal, J. D. (2003). Nonlinearities in sensitivity to time: Implications of oscillator-based representations of interval and circadian clocks. In W. H. Meck (Ed.), *Functional and neural mechanisms of interval timing.* Boca Raton, FL: CRC Press.

Crystal, J. D., Church, R. M., & Broadbent, H. A. (1997). Systematic nonlinearities in the memory representation of time. *Journal of Experimental Psychology: Animal Behavior Processes, 23,* 267–282.

Gardner, H. (1985). *The mind's new science: A history of the cognitive revolution.* New York: Basic books.

Gibbon, J. (1977). Scalar expectancy theory and Weber's law in animal timing. *Psychological Review, 84,* 279–325.

Gibbon, J., & Church, R. M. (1981). Time left: Linear versus logarithmic subjective time. *Journal of Experimental Psychology: Animal Behavior Processes, 7,* 87–108.

Gibbon, J., Church, R. M., & Meck, W. H. (1984). *Scalar timing in memory.* In J. Gibbon & L. G. Allan (Eds.), *Timing and time perception* (pp. 52–77). New York: New York Academy of Sciences.

Griffin, D. R. (1992). *Animal minds.* Chicago: University of Chicago Press.

Heinemann, E. G., & Avin, E. (1973). On the development of stimulus control. *Journal of the Experimental Analysis of Behavior, 20,* 183–195.

Hempel, C. G., & Oppenheim, P. (1948). *Philosophy of Science, 15,* 135–175.

Kamin, L. J. (1954). Traumatic avoidance learning: The effects of CS-US interval with a trace-conditioning procedure. *Journal of Comparative and Physiological Psychology, 47,* 1954, 65–72.

Kirkpatrick, K. (2002). Packet theory of conditioning and timing. *Behavioural Processes, 57,* 89–106.

Kirkpatrick, K., & Church, R. M. (2003). Tracking of the expected time to reinforcement in temporal conditioning procedures. *Learning & Behavior, 31,* 3–21.

LaBarbera, J. D., & Church, R. M. (1974). Magnitude of fear as a function of expected time to an aversive event. *Animal Learning & Behavior, 2,* 199–202.

Libby, M. E., & Church, R. M. (1974). Timing of avoidance responses by rats. *Journal of the Experimental Analysis of Behavior, 22,* 513–517.

Libby, M. E., & Church, R. M. (1975). Fear gradients as a function of the temporal interval between signal and aversive event in the rat. *Journal of Comparative and Physiological Psychology, 88,* 911–916.

Logan, F. A. (1960). *Incentive.* New Haven, CT: Yale University Press.

Meck, W. H., & Church, R. M. (1984). Simultaneous temporal processing. *Journal of Experimental Psychology: Animal Behavior Processes, 10,* 1–29.

Meck, W. H., Church, R. M., & Olton, D. S. (1984). Hippocampus, time, and memory. *Behavioral Neuroscience, 98,* 3–22.

Platt, J. R., Kuch, D. O., & Bitgood, S. C. (1973). Rats' lever-press duration as psychophysical judgments of time. *Journal of the Experimental Analysis of Behavior, 19,* 239–250.

Rescorla, R. (1968). Probability of shock in the presence and absence of CS in fear conditioning. *Journal of Comparative and Physiological Psychology, 66,* 1–5.

Roberts, S. (1981). Isolation of an internal clock. *Journal of Experimental Psychology: Animal Behavior Processes, 7,* 242–268.

Roberts, S., & Church, R. M. (1978). Control of an internal clock. *Journal of Experimental Psychology: Animal Behavior Processes, 4,* 318–337.

Washburn, M. F. (1936). *The animal mind.* New York: Macmillan.

Watson, J. B. (1913). Psychology as the behaviorist views it. *Psychological Review, 20,* 158–177.

14

Sensitivity to Time: Implications for the Representation of Time

JONATHON D. CRYSTAL

A central problem in the study of comparative cognition is to identify an animal's psychological representation of information in its environment (Roitblat, 1982). One of the critical features of the environment is the temporal relation between events (Gallistel, 1990). A powerful methodology for studying the representation of information is to identify its psychophysical properties. For example, a psychophysical approach to studying the representation of time seeks to identify the relation between psychological (i.e., subjective) estimates of time and physical estimates of time. The rationale for this approach is that identifying this relation will constrain the types of mechanisms that may be entertained to explain time estimation.

There is a long history of controversy over the psychophysical function for time (e.g., Nichols, 1891). Some of the earliest investigations in experimental psychology focused on identifying aspects of the psychophysical relation described above. Early psychophysical research suggested that the relationship between subjective and physical estimates of time is characterized by a power function with an exponent of less than 1 (Eisler, 1976; Stevens, 1957). Later research suggested that psychological time is linearly related to physical time (Allan, 1983; Gibbon & Church, 1981). The hypothesis that subjective estimates of time are linearly related to physical time is referred to as *linear timing*; linear timing is consistent with Weber's law (Gibbon, 1977, 1981). There is a growing body of recent evidence that suggests subjective estimates of time are nonlinearly related to physical time; this will be referred to as the *nonlinear timing* hypothesis. Small deviations from linearity have important theoretical implications (for details, see the section Implications for Theories of Time).

LINEAR TIMING

A major factor that contributes to the controversy over the psychophysical function for time is the selection of the number and spacing of interval conditions. For example, studies of timing often use two or three interval conditions, often with a doubling or a ten-fold relationship between successive intervals. The earliest example of linear timing by Dews (1970) appears in figure 14.1, documenting the similarity of 30, 300, and 3,000 s. Dews trained pigeons using a fixed interval procedure (i.e., the first response after a fixed interval has elapsed is rewarded). The key insight required to observe the similarity in Dews's data is that it is necessary to rescale the x-axis (i.e., time scale) with respect to the target interval and to rescale the y-axis (i.e., response rate) with respect to the maximum response rate. Three interval conditions is the minimum number that can be used to evaluate the linear timing hypothesis. This number, together with a sufficiently wide spacing of conditions, is adequate to compare a power function and a linear function

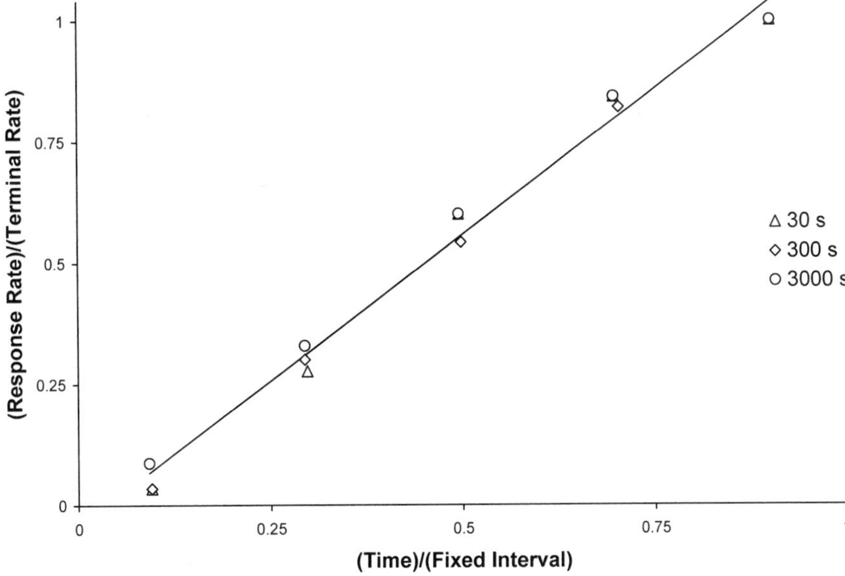

Figure 14.1. The response rate expressed as a proportion of the terminal rate is plotted as a function of elapsed time expressed as a proportion of the fixed interval (values of fixed intervals are given in the legend). Dews calculated response rate at successive fifths of the interval for three fixed intervals. The similarity across fixed intervals is consistent with the linear timing hypothesis. The solid line indicates the best fit by linear regression. (Adapted from Dews, 1970.)

(i.e., to identify the value of the exponent in a power function). However, it is inadequate to decide between linear and nonlinear timing hypotheses. Many studies of interval timing have been concerned with the generalized Weber function. For example, the relationship between standard deviation and time estimates is a plateau followed by a linear increase according to a generalized Weber function (e.g., Fetterman & Killeen, 1992). Therefore, a single bend in an otherwise linear function is anticipated for very short intervals (i.e., in the millisecond range) according to this proposal. For these studies, there are usually a few interval conditions, and the spacing between conditions increases as a function of interval duration. Increasing the spacing between conditions is particularly appropriate for evaluating a generalized Weber function because the single nonlinearity in the theoretical function occurs for the shortest intervals. However, this approach is less useful for evaluating nonlinearities that occur throughout the temporal range or that occur at intervals that are not known a priori.

The linear timing hypothesis predicts that measures of temporal performance are proportional (i.e., linear) to the target interval across a wide range of intervals. A more precise statement of the linear timing hypothesis is that timing estimates consist of a linear component plus random error. Consider fitting a theoretical function to a given data set. The *residuals* are the differences between the observed and expected values. A theoretical function provides an adequate description of the data when the residuals are randomly distributed with respect to the theoretical function (i.e., zero is an unbiased estimate of the residuals). By contrast, any systematic trend in the residuals would suggest that the theoretical function is not an adequate description of the data. This approach may be applied to timing by elaborating the linear timing hypothesis at two levels of detail. According to the most basic description, the linear timing hypothesis requires that psychological estimates of time increase as a constant proportion of physical estimates of time. According to a more detailed description, the linear timing hypothesis predicts that departures from the linear prediction are expected to be random.

A small number of interval conditions is adequate to evaluate the basic description of the linear

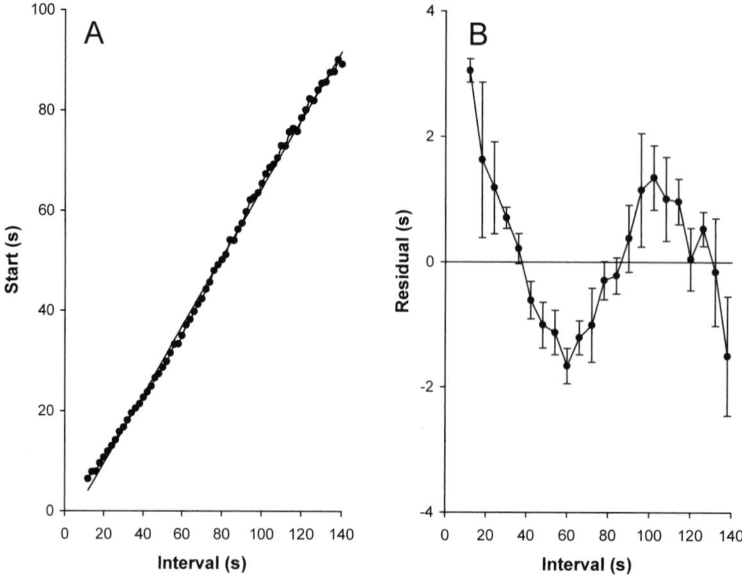

Figure 14.2. Start times are nonlinearly related to target intervals ($n = 20$). *A*, Start times increase as a function of intervals in an approximately linear fashion. The solid line is the best fitting linear regression function ($y = 0.685x - 4.15$, $r^2 = 0.998$). There is a systematic pattern of departures between the data and the linear function. *B*, Residuals (observed minus expected start times) from linear regression are not randomly distributed around zero [$r(19)_{\text{lag1}} = 0.834$, $p < .001$], departed from zero based on a binomial test ($p < .001$), and revealed a significant effect of interval duration [$F(21,399) = 7.94$, $p < .001$]. Mean *SEM* = 0.5. Error bars represent ± 1 *SEM*. (Adapted from Crystal, Church, & Broadbent, 1997.)

timing hypothesis. However, many closely space interval conditions are required to evaluate the detailed description of the linear timing hypothesis. It is well established that animals can track predictable changes in fixed-interval values across successive intervals (Church & Lacourse, 1998; Crystal, Church, & Broadbent, 1997; Higa, Wynne, & Staddon, 1991; Innis & Staddon, 1971; Wynne, Staddon, & Delius 1996); this approach provides an efficient means for testing many closely spaced target intervals. Figure 14.2 shows data from an experiment designed to test the detailed description of the linear timing hypothesis. In this *ramp procedure*, rats were trained to track a change in a fixed-interval value. The ramp procedure is similar to a fixed-interval procedure in that the first response after the fixed interval is rewarded, at which point the next fixed interval begins. However, in the ramp procedure, the fixed-interval value changes across successive intervals. For example, a rat might be trained with a ramp that ranges from 10 to 140 s with a 2-s step size. At the start of a daily session, the initial fixed interval and the direction (ascending or descending) are randomly selected for each rat. Next, the fixed interval changes on successive trials until an endpoint in the range is reached, at which point the direction changes, and the intervals continue to change in a predictable manner. To illustrate, suppose that the initial fixed interval was 136 s and the initial direction was ascending. The sequence of intervals in this case would be 136, 138, 140, 138, 136, 134, 132 s, and so on. The data in figure 14.2A show the start time plotted as a function of the interval; the start time is a measure of the time of transition from a low rate of responding to a high rate of responding on individual trials (Cheng & Westwood, 1993; Cheng, Westwood, & Crystal, 1993; Church, Meck, & Gibbon, 1994; Crystal et al., 1997; Gibbon & Church, 1990; Schneider, 1969). Start times increase as a function of intervals in an approximately linear fashion. These data are replotted as residuals in figure 14.2B; the data are the same across both panels of figure 14.2, with the only alteration being the removal of the linear trend. Note that this plot discloses a surprisingly systematic

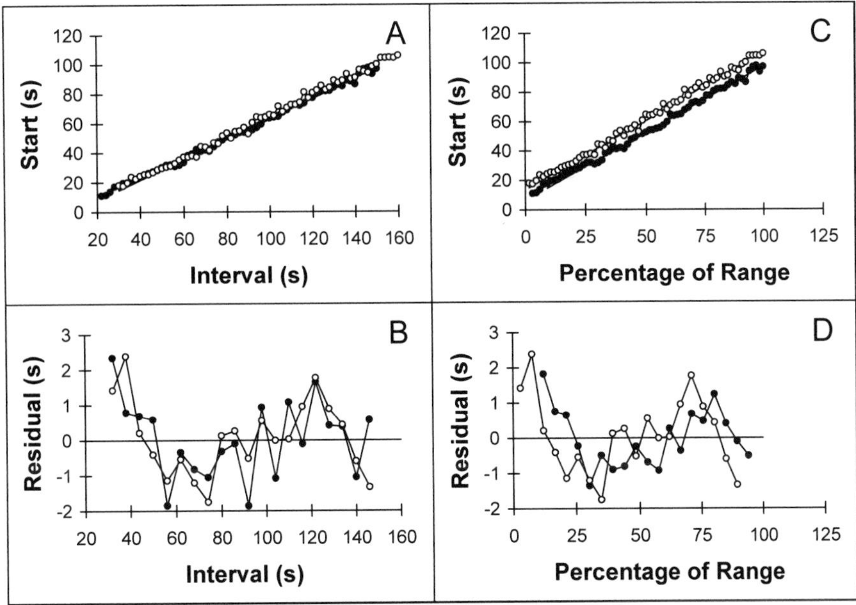

Figure 14.3. Start times (*top*) are plotted as a function of interval duration (*A*) and as a function of percentage into the range (*C*). *Filled circles* represent data from rats tested in the range of 20 to 150 s ($n = 10$). *Open circles* represent data from rats tested in the range of 30 to 160 s ($n = 10$). Residuals (observed minus expected start times) from linear regression (*bottom*) are plotted as a function of interval duration (*B*) and as a function of percentage into the range (*D*). Start times and residuals each superimpose when plotted as a function of interval duration and are displaced when plotted as a function of percentage into the range. Residuals for the two groups superimpose as a function of intervals [$r(18) = .659$, $p < .001$]. Residuals do not superimpose as a function of percentage of the range [$r(18) = .245$, $p > .05$]. The correlation with interval as the independent variable was higher than the correlation with percentage of range as the independent variable (Fisher's $z = 6.10$, $p < .001$), suggesting that the superposition was better as a function of absolute interval than as a function of percentage of the range. The residuals were nonrandom [$r(17)_{\text{lag1}} = .414$, $p < .05$], departed from zero based on a binomial test ($p < .001$), and exhibited a significant effect of interval duration [$F(19,361) = 1.99$, $p < .01$]. Mean $SEM = 0.7$. (Reproduced from "Systematic Nonlinearities in the Memory Representation of Time," by J. D. Crystal, R. M. Church, and H. A. Broadbent, 1997, *Journal of Experimental Psychology: Animal Behavior Processes, 23,* 267–282. Copyright © 1997 by the American Psychological Association. Reprinted with permission.)

trend in the residuals, given the original plot in figure 14.2A. This systematic trend suggests an empirical conflict with the linear timing hypothesis.

To establish that the nonlinear trend observed in the ramp procedure is characteristic of the intervals being timed (rather than, for example, regression to the mean or a range effect), it is necessary to compare two overlapping ranges of intervals. The data presented in figure 14.3 show start times as a function of intervals for two groups of rats; one group was trained with intervals between 20 and 150 s, whereas the other group was trained with intervals between 30 and 160 s; both groups were trained with a 2-s step size, and all other features of the experiment were the same as described above. Note that there is a substantial range in common between the groups (30–150 s). The purpose of this experiment was to identify the variable that controlled the nonlinear trend. There are two potential controlling variables: (a) the specific target interval or (b) the position of an interval within the range of intervals. The start times and residuals superimposed when they were plotted as a function of intervals (figure 14.3, left). When these same start times and residuals were plotted as a function of the percentage of the range, the data from the two groups were displaced from one another (i.e., the data did not superimpose;

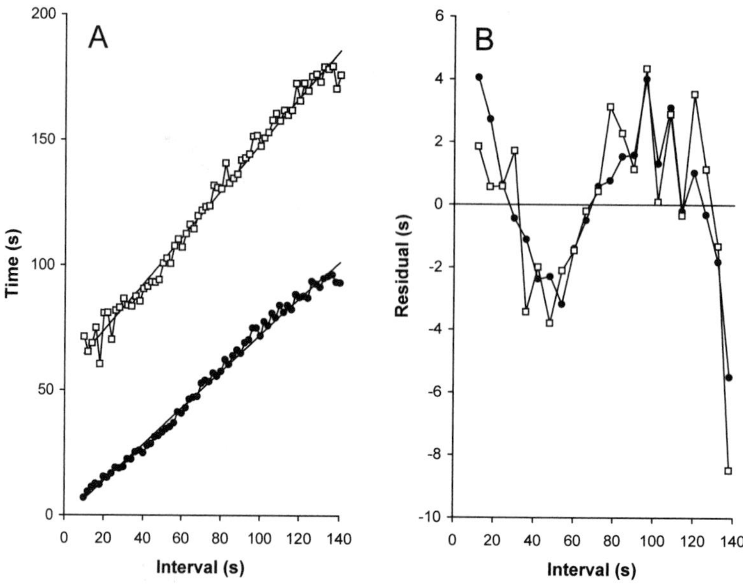

Figure 14.4. Start and end times (filled circles and open squares, respectively) are plotted as a function of intervals ($n = 20$). The solid lines are the best-fitting linear regression functions (start: $y = 0.730x - 0.980$, $r^2 = 0.992$; end: $y = 0.933x + 55.1$, $r^2 = 0.986$). Residuals (observed minus expected times) from linear regression are not randomly distributed around zero [start: $r(19)_{\text{lag1}} = 0.688$, $p < .001$; end: $r(19)_{\text{lag1}} = 0.403$, $p < .05$]. The correlation between start and end residuals was significant [$r(20) = 0.850$, $p < .001$]. (Adapted from Crystal, Church, & Broadbent, 1997.)

figure 14.3, right). These data support the conclusion that the nonlinearities are characteristics of timing specific intervals. Consequently, the nonlinearities represent an empirical conflict with the linear timing hypothesis.

The observation of nonlinearities in timing documented in figures 14.2 and 14.3 does not identify the mechanism of nonlinear timing. For example, the information-processing model of timing (Gibbon, Church, & Meck, 1984) proposes that timing involves clock, memory, and decision stages of processing temporal information. Nonlinearities may be introduced at any of these stages of information processing.

To identify the source of nonlinearities in timing, the ramp procedure was modified to permit an estimate of when the rat stops responding in the case that reward at the usual time is withheld (i.e., an *end* time in addition to the start time). In the ramp procedure (as in a standard fixed-interval procedure), the animal stops responding when it obtains food. By contrast, in the peak procedure (e.g., Roberts, 1981), food is withheld on a random subset of trials; the typical pattern of behavior on these trials is a low rate of responding followed by a high rate, followed by a low rate of responding, with the burst of responding centered on the target interval (e.g., Church et al., 1994). The end time is defined as the time of transition from the high to the low rate of responding. The ramp procedure was modified by randomly inserting 660-s fixed intervals into the sequence of ascending and descending intervals. Figure 14.4 shows start and end times plotted as a function of intervals. Note that the start and end residuals superimpose. This pattern of responding suggests that the source of the nonlinearities is not introduced at the decision stage of an information processing model of timing (Gibbon et al., 1984). Instead, the nonlinearity is introduced at the clock or memory stage (i.e., some intervals are remembered as relatively long and other intervals are remembered as relatively short). These findings suggest that the memory representation of time is nonlinear (Crystal et al., 1997).

The data from the ramp procedure suggest a different empirical description of the psychophysical properties of time, which leads to a basic question about the timing literature: Why was this pattern

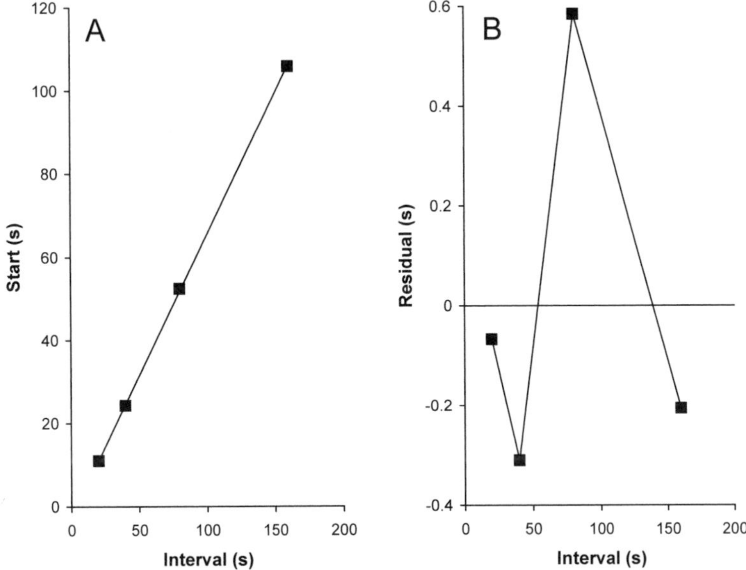

Figure 14.5. Start times are plotted as a function of intervals (n = 10–20). The interval conditions represent a subset of the conditions that appear in figure 14.3. The *solid line* is the best-fitting linear regression function ($y = 0.679x - 2.52$, $r^2 = 0.9999$). Note that with few, widely spaced interval conditions, it is not possible to detect the nonlinear pattern that appears in the complete data set with many, closely spaced interval conditions (cf. figure 14.3). (Adapted from Crystal, Church, & Broadbent, 1997.)

not observed previously? One explanation focuses on the number and spacing of interval conditions. To illustrate the problem, consider the situation in which a subset of the ramp-procedure data is selected using a number and spacing of conditions that is typical of the timing literature. Figure 14.5A plots start times as a function of four intervals. These data come from the larger data set that appears in figure 14.3A. With a few, widely spaced interval conditions (figure 14.5B), it is not possible to detect the nonlinear pattern that is apparent in the larger data set (figure 14.3B). The limitation of a data set with few, widely spaced interval conditions is that it is not possible to evaluate (or to detect) a nonlinear trend in the data, leading to a conclusion (linearity) that is at variance with the conclusion (nonlinearity) that emerges from a larger data set consisting of many, closely spaced interval conditions. Consequently, it can be argued that the timing literature has been interpreted as providing evidence for linear timing, in part because the literature does not provide many closely spaced interval conditions. Therefore, the observation of a systematic nonlinear pattern in figures 14.2, 14.3, and 14.4 does not reflect a data conflict with the published literature but rather the reliance on different procedural and quantitative methodologies.

NONLINEAR SENSITIVITY TO TIME

A critical feature of the linear timing hypothesis is the prediction that sensitivity to time is proportional to the interval being timed. Sensitivity to time has typically been evaluated by examining the coefficient of variation (CV), which is the standard deviation divided by the mean for a given distribution of data. The CV is constant across a wide range of interval conditions (e.g., Gibbon, 1977, 1991). Evaluating the constancy of the CV is a quantitative method to document the visual impression that timing distributions superimpose when the data are plotted in relative time (i.e., time divided by the target interval), a finding referred to as superposition (i.e., a version of Weber's law). However, exceptions to this rule have been noted for very short (in the millisecond range: Church, Getty, & Lerner, 1976; Crystal, 1999; Fetterman & Killeen, 1992; Gibbon, Malapani, Dale, & Gallistel, 1997) and very long (up to the range of hours: Brunner,

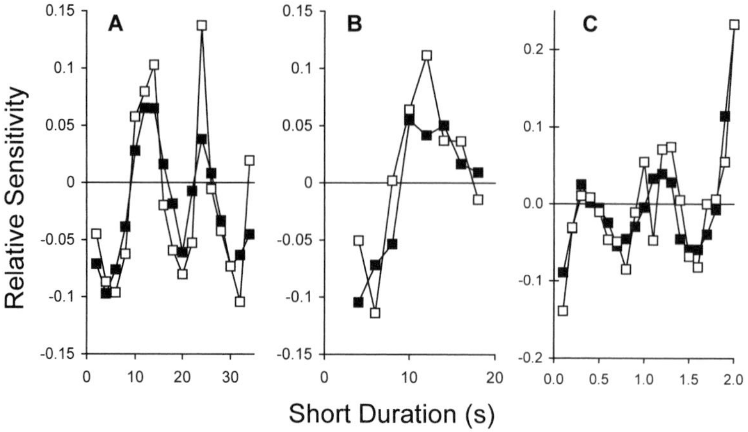

Figure 14.6. Sensitivity to time is characterized by local maxima at 12 and 24 s (*A*), 12 s (*B*), and 0.3 and 1.2 s (*C*). *Open symbols*, average across rats; *filled symbols*, a running median was performed on each rat's data and the smoothed data were averaged across rats to identify the most representative local maxima in sensitivity. *A*, Rats discriminated short and long noise durations with the duration adjusted to maintain accuracy at approximately 75% correct. Short durations were tested in ascending order with a step size of 1 s ($n = 5$) and 2 s ($n = 5$). Sensitivity was similar across step sizes [$r(15) = .701, p < .01$], departed from zero based on a binomial test ($p < .001$), and was nonrandom [$r(14)_{\text{lag1}} = 0.710, p < .01$]. Mean *SEM* = 0.03. *B*, Methods are the same as described in *A*, except short durations were tested in random order ($n = 7$) or with each rat receiving a single interval condition ($n = 13$); results from these conditions did not differ. Sensitivity departed from zero based on a binomial test ($p < .001$) and was nonrandom [$r(7)_{\text{lag1}} = 0.860, p < .01$]. Mean *SEM* = 0.02. *C*, Methods are the same as described in *A*, except intervals were defined by gaps between 50-ms noise pulses and short durations were tested in descending order with a step size of 0.1 s ($n = 6$). Sensitivity departed from zero based on a binomial test ($p < .001$) and was nonrandom ($r(18)_{\text{lag1}} = 0.736, p < .001$). Mean *SEM* = 0.04. Sensitivity was measured using d′ from signal detection theory. d′ = z[p(short response | short stimulus)] – z[p(short response | long stimulus)]. Relative sensitivity is d′ – mean d′. (Adapted from Crystal, 1999, 2001b.) (From "Nonlinearities in Sensitivity to Time: Implications for Oscillator-based Representations of Interval and Circadian Clocks," by J. D. Crystal, 2003. In W. H. Meck [Ed.], *Functional and Neural Mechanisms of Interval Timing*, pp. 61–75. Boca Raton, FL: CRC Press. Copyright CRC Press, Boca Raton, Florida. Reprinted with permission.)

Kacelnik, & Gibbon, 1992; Gibbon, Malipani, et al., 1997; Lejeune & Wearden, 1991; Zeiler, 1991; Zeiler & Powell, 1994) intervals. Nevertheless, the constancy of sensitivity to time across a wide range of target intervals has played a central role in the timing literature (Allan, 1998; Gibbon, 1991).

To evaluate the constancy of sensitivity to time, it is necessary to examine many closely spaced interval conditions. Figure 14.6 shows data from temporal discrimination procedures using many closely spaced target intervals. The data suggest that sensitivity to time is characterized by multiple local maxima. The data were obtained using a titration procedure (Crystal, 1999, 2001b). In particular, a "short" or a "long" noise was presented followed by the insertion of two levers. Left or right lever presses were required after short or long stimuli to obtain a reward. For each short duration, the duration of the long signal was adjusted (i.e., titrated) after blocks of discrimination trials to maintain discrimination accuracy at approximately 75% correct, which resulted in a long duration approximately 2 to 2.5 times the short duration. Sensitivity to time was measured using signal detection theory (Macmillan & Creelman, 1991). Sensitivity to time was approximately constant across short durations from 2 to 34 s. However, local peaks in sensitivity to time were observed at approximately 12 and 24 s (figures 14.6A and B). When short durations in the millisecond range were tested, local

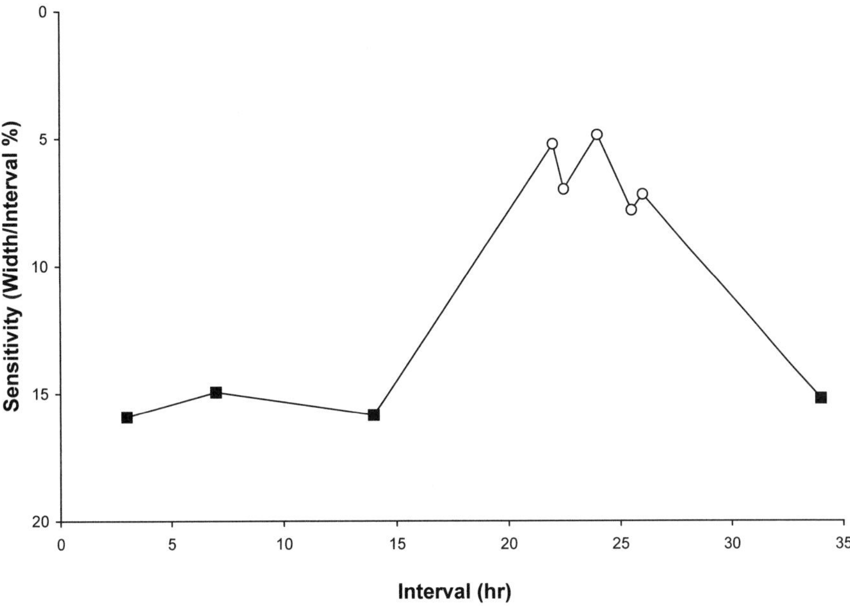

Figure 14.7. Intervals near the circadian range (*open circles*) are characterized by higher sensitivity than intervals outside this range (*filled squares*). Variability in anticipating a meal was measured as the width of the response distribution prior to the meal at 70% of the maximum rate, expressed as a percentage of the interval ($N = 29$). The interval is the time between light offset and meal onset in a 12-12 light-dark cycle (*leftmost two squares*) or the intermeal interval in constant darkness (all other data). The percentage width was smaller in the circadian range than outside this range [$F(1, 20) = 22.65$, $p < .001$]. The width/interval did not differ within the circadian [$F(4, 12) = 1$] or noncircadian [$F(3, 8) < 1$] ranges. The same conclusions were reached when the width was measured as 25, 50, and 75% of the maximum rate. The data are plotted on a reversed-order *y*-axis so that local maxima in the data correspond to high sensitivity, which facilitates comparison with other measures of sensitivity (e.g., figure 14.6). Mean *SEM* = 2.4. (Adapted from Crystal, 2001a.)

peaks in sensitivity were observed at 0.3 and 1.2 s (figure 14.6C). Multiple local maxima in sensitivity to time represent an empirical conflict with the linear timing hypothesis. The ability to directly compare nonlinearities in the ramp and titration procedures is limited by relatively little overlap in the interval conditions.

One interpretation of the data in figure 14.6 is that each local maximum in sensitivity to time identifies the period of an oscillator (for details, see the section Implications for Theories of Time). The hypothesis is that short-period oscillators mediate short-interval timing in ways that are similar to a circadian (i.e., approximately a day) oscillator mediating timing near 24 h. Consequently, if the local maxima in the milliseconds and seconds range identify short-interval oscillators, then we would predict that a local maximum in sensitivity to time will be identified near 24 h (i.e., near the well-established circadian oscillator). A series of experiments investigating meal anticipation was undertaken to test the hypothesis that the well-established feeding-entrainable circadian oscillator (for a review, see Mistlberger, 1994) is characterized by a local maximum in sensitivity to time (Crystal, 2001a). Figure 14.7 shows sensitivity data in the range of hours to a day. The data document a local maximum in sensitivity to time near 24 h (Crystal, 2001a). The data were obtained by restricting daily food availability to 3-h meals, which rats earned by breaking a photobeam in the food trough. The intermeal intervals were manipulated across groups of rats and ranged from 14 to 34 h, with several conditions using intermeal intervals near 24 h. The animals anticipated the arrival of the meal (i.e., response rate increased as a function of time prior to the meal). The dependent variable was the width of the anticipatory function (i.e., the width is a measure of the

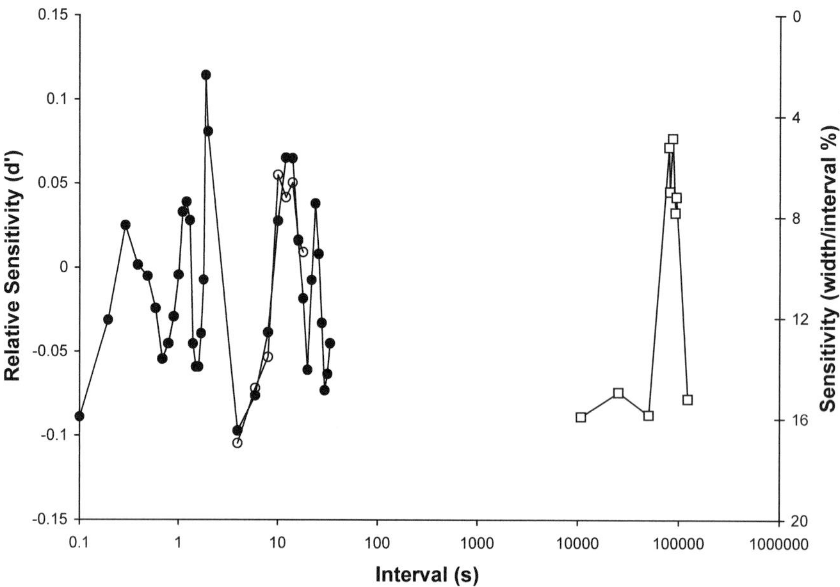

Figure 14.8. Multiple local maxima in sensitivity to time are observed in the discrimination of time across seven orders of magnitude. The existence of a local maximum near a circadian oscillator (peak on right side; *square symbols*) and other local maxima in the short-interval range (peaks on left side; *filled and open circles*) are consistent with the hypothesis that timing is mediated by multiple oscillators. Intervals in the blank region in the center of the figure have not been tested. *Left,* Rats discriminated short and long durations, with the long duration adjusted to maintain accuracy at 75% correct. Short durations were tested in sequential order (filled circles; $N = 26$) or independent order (open circles; $N = 20$). *Circles* represent relative sensitivity using d′ from signal detection theory and are plotted using the *y*-axis on the left side of the figure. *Right,* Rats received food in 3-h meals with fixed intermeal intervals by breaking a photobeam inside the food trough. The rate of photobeam interruption increased before the meal. *Squares* represent sensitivity, which was measured as the width of the anticipatory function at 70% of the maximum rate prior to the meal, expressed as a percentage of the interval ($N = 29$). The interval is the time between light offset and meal onset in a 12-12 light-dark cycle (*leftmost two squares*) or the intermeal interval in constant darkness (*all other squares*). Squares are plotted with respect to the reversed-order *y*-axis on the right side of the figure. The *y*-axes use different scales, and the *x*-axis uses a log scale. (Adapted from Crystal, 1999, 2001a, 2001b.) (From "Nonlinearities in Sensitivity to Time: Implications for Oscillator-based Representations of Interval and Circadian Clocks," by J. D. Crystal, 2003. In W. H. Meck [Ed.], *Functional and Neural Mechanisms of Interval Timing*, pp. 61–75. Boca Raton, FL: CRC Press. Copyright CRC Press, Boca Raton, Florida. Reprinted with permission.)

variability of timing functions). The observation of a local maximum in sensitivity to time near 24 h is consistent with the hypothesis that a property of an oscillator is improved sensitivity to time.

The conclusion that emerges from this series of experiments is that multiple local maxima in sensitivity to time are observed in the discrimination of time across several orders of magnitude (figure 14.8) (Crystal, 1999, 2001a, 2001b, 2003). The existence of a local maximum near a circadian oscillator (figure 14.8, peak on right side) and in the short-interval range (figure 14.8, peaks on left side) are consistent with timing based on multiple oscillators (Church & Broadbent, 1990; Crystal, 1999, 2001a, 2003; Gallistel, 1990).

We return to a basic question about the timing literature: Why have local maxima in sensitivity to time not been previously observed? As discussed, studies of timing generally test a few, widely spaced interval conditions. When large collections

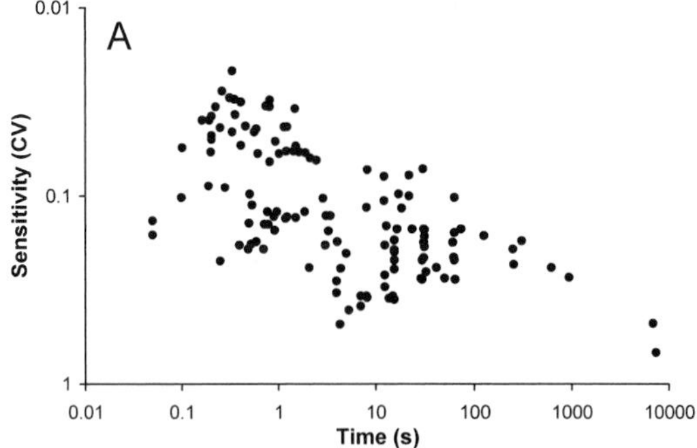

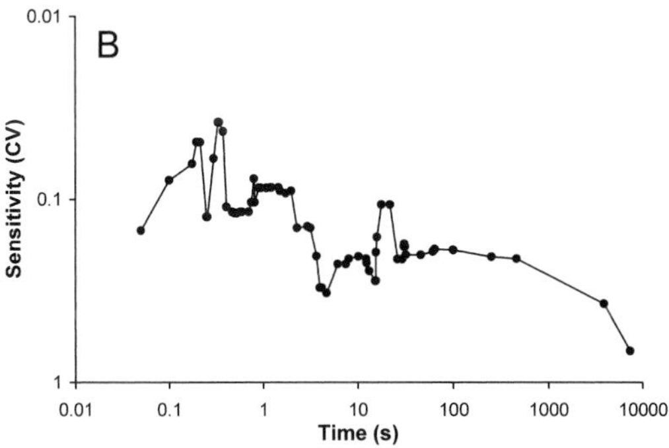

Figure 14.9. *A*, Sensitivity is plotted as a function of time across six orders of magnitude. The scatterplot reveals that sensitivity to time declines as a function of increasing intervals. The data are from figure 3 in Gibbon, Malapani, Dale, and Gallistel (1997). The published figure was enlarged by 375% and each datum was measured at 0.5-mm resolution. The residuals from linear regression (not shown) were not random [$r(128)_{\text{lag1}} = 0.454$, $p < .001$]. The data are plotted on a reversed-order *y*-axis to facilitate comparison with other measures of sensitivity. *B*, Sensitivity is plotted as a function of time across six orders of magnitude. The data from Gibbon, Malapani, et al. (1997) shown in *A* were averaged in two-point blocks and subjected to a three-point running median. Note that sensitivity to time is characterized by local maxima at approximately 0.2–0.3, 1.2, 10, and 20 s. Note that these values are similar to the local maxima that were observed by Crystal (1999, 2001b): 0.3, 1.2, 12, and 24 s (cf. figure 14.6). The residuals from linear regression (not shown) were not random [$r(63)_{\text{lag1}} = 0.869$, $p < .001$]. The data are plotted on a reversed-order *y*-axis to facilitate comparison with other measures of sensitivity. (Adapted from Gibbon, Malapani, Dale, & Gallistel, 1997.)

of interval conditions from many studies have been examined, the data have been presented as a scatterplot. Such scatterplots provide an opportunity to evaluate the published data for evidence of local maxima in sensitivity. To take a concrete example, Gibbon, Malapani, et al. (1997) plotted CV as a function of intervals using 43 data sets from the literature (figure 3 in their article). The scatterplot is replotted in figure 14.9A (the *y*-axis is plotted in reverse order so that high points in the figure correspond to high sensitivity to time). Gibbon and colleagues noted the overall increase in CV, with somewhat abrupt increases occurring at 1.5 and 500 s. They also noted that CV declined as a function of increasing intervals up to about 0.1 s. To examine the shape of the sensitivity function, the data from Gibbon and colleagues were averaged in two-point blocks and subjected to a three-point running median. These data appear in figure 14.9B (bottom). Note that sensitivity to time is characterized by multiple, local maxima. The middle of the local maxima in figure 14.9B occurs at approximately 0.2, 0.3, 1.2, 10, and 20 s. Clusters of relatively high points near these intervals can also be seen in figure 14.9A. Note that these values are strikingly similar to the local maxima that were observed in figure 14.6: 0.3, 1.2, 12, and 24 s (Crystal, 1999, 2001b, 2003). Although the shapes of the sensitivity functions in figures 14.6 and 14.9B differ, the similarity in the locations of local maxima is noteworthy given that the data in figure 14.9 come from 43 different data sets. Moreover, the data that appear in figure 14.9 were selected independently by Gibbon and colleagues; consequently, the selection of experiments for inclusion in the figure cannot be responsible for the observed local maxima. The quantitative similarity between the observed locations of local maxima in sensitivity provides an independent, converging line of evidence that suggests that sensitivity to time is nonlinear. In addition, a comparison of figures 14.9A and B reveals the importance of averaging the data to obtain a single function for evaluating nonlinearities.

IMPLICATIONS FOR THEORIES OF TIME

Sensitivity to time is characterized by multiple local maxima. This fact suggests that the representation of time is not linearly related to physical time. The violation of the linear timing hypothesis provides constraints for the development of timing theories. Four theories are reviewed here: scalar timing theory (Gibbon, 1977, 1991; Gibbon et al., 1984), multiple-oscillator theory (Church & Broadbent, 1990), broadcast theory (Rosenbaum, 1998, 2002), and stochastic counting cascades (Killeen, 2002; Killeen & Taylor, 2000).

Scalar Timing Theory

A central feature of scalar timing theory is a linear representation of time (i.e., sensitivity to time is predicted to be constant across a broad range of intervals). Scalar timing theory proposes that a pacemaker emits pulses that are gated across a switch into an accumulator. The number of pulses accumulated increases linearly as a function of time throughout a timing episode. The number of pulses at the time of reward is stored in reference memory (i.e., reference memory consists of a distribution of rewarded subjective intervals). The variability in reference memory is scalar, that is, proportional to the mean. The number of pulses accumulated during a timing episode is compared with a sample from memory of a previously stored rewarded duration, rendering a decision to respond or not to respond. Nonlinear sensitivity to time conflicts with current versions of scalar timing theory.

Multiple-Oscillator Theory of Timing

A central feature of the multiple-oscillator theory of timing is a nonlinear representation of time. The multiple-oscillator theory of timing proposes that elapsed time is represented by the phase of a set of oscillators, each with a unique period (e.g., 100, 200, 400, 800 ms, etc.). The representation of elapsed time increases nonlinearly as a function of time throughout a timing episode. The information about the phase of the oscillators at the time of reward is stored in reference memory (i.e., reference memory consists of a correlation matrix indicating the degree of association between the oscillators). The status of the oscillators during a timing episode is compared with the reference-memory representation of the rewarded duration, rendering a decision to respond or not to respond. Nonlinear sensitivity to time is predicted by the multiple-oscillator theory of timing.

The location of a local maximum can be used to identify an oscillator's period. This interpretation of local maxima suggests that the short-interval range (milliseconds to minutes) is characterized by several oscillators (e.g., 0.2–0.3, 1.2, 10–12, 20–24 s). The hypothesis that local peaks in sensitivity identify the period of an oscillator led to the prediction that a peak in sensitivity to time would be documented near 24 h, a prediction that was confirmed (figure 14.7; Crystal, 2001a). The long-interval range (hours, the region in the middle of figure 14.8 and the right side of figure 14.9) has not been systematically explored. Additional local maxima in sensitivity to time in the long-interval range may identify additional putative oscillators.

Broadcast Theory of Timing

The broadcast theory of timing proposes that timing of an interval is accomplished by subdividing the interval (i.e., time two short intervals instead of one relatively long interval). The theory proposes that timed performance is based on the time required for neural signals to travel different distances in the nervous system. Because the variance of travel delays is proportional to the square of the distance traveled, subdividing a delay will produce variances of timed performance that are characterized by multiple local peaks. This prediction is consistent with nonlinear sensitivity to time. However, there is no evidence to suggest that timing intervals near 24 h is based on neural signals that travel across a relatively long distance in the nervous system. Consequently, it is perhaps more parsimonious to explain local maxima in sensitivity to time in the short-interval and circadian ranges by applying a single mechanism (i.e., oscillators).

Stochastic Counting Cascades

A central feature of the stochastic-counting-cascades model is a nonlinear representation of time. The model proposes that counting events (e.g., pulses from a pacemaker) is characterized by failures to set the element in the next stage of a binary counter when a lower element is reset. Similarly, the model proposes that the resetting of a bit in a binary counter to its zero state may fail to occur. These set and reset failures result in underestimation and overestimation of the number of events, respectively. Fallible binary counters can produce nonlinearities in sensitivity to time. Moreover, the model may be considered a module that can be inserted into other theories of timing (i.e., a counting module; Church, 1997; Killeen, 2002; Killeen & Taylor, 2000). Indeed, the role played by oscillators in the multiple-oscillator theory of timing plays a similar role to Killeen's binary counters; the periods of the oscillators increase by powers of 2 in the multiple-oscillator theory of timing, and the behavior of elements in a binary counter oscillates with a period corresponding to each element in the counter.

Integration of Research from Short-Interval and Circadian Timing

Efforts to understand the discrimination of time have proceeded along two relatively independent paths: one focusing on timing short intervals and one focusing on timing intervals of approximately a day. These efforts involved study of different experimental manipulations and dependent variables, constructed different theoretical frameworks, and communicated findings to different research communities. These factors have led to the conclusion that the timing of short intervals and circadian rhythms is based on unrelated mechanisms. However, recent findings about the discrimination of short and circadian intervals suggest similarities in these two domains and raise the prospect of developing a theory of timing that encompasses the discrimination of temporal intervals across several orders of magnitude—from milliseconds to days.

The research program that emerges from this review involves integrating concepts and methods from short-interval and circadian domains. Can we test circadian concepts in the short-interval range? Can we test short-interval concepts in the circadian domain? An example of this integration is provided next.

A feature that distinguishes a pacemaker-accumulator from a circadian-oscillator is the reset characteristics of the mechanisms. The sensitivity to environmental stimuli is a defining feature that distinguishes the mechanisms. For example, an oscillator is only partially affected by the presentation of an environmental reset cue. A familiar example of this property of the circadian system is illustrated by jet lag. If you fly from the United States to Europe, then you will be exposed to environmental features of local time immediately upon arrival (unusual times at which the sun rises and sets, unusual times when alarm clocks ring in advance of early-morning appointments, unusual times for meals, etc.). The times are unusual because one's circadian system requires several days of environmental input before the system has been set to the new local time. In contrast, a hallmark of a short-interval clock is that it can be used to time arbitrary events signaled by the presentation of a stimulus. The analogy for short-interval timing is a stopwatch that can be reset at any time (Church, 1978).

The standard approach in the circadian literature for documenting gradual adjustment to environmental input is the phase-shift experiment. In a phase-shift experiment, the time of an event (e.g., a meal or light-cycle transitions) is shifted early or late and the amount of adjustment is measured until complete adjustment is achieved.

This circadian concept was applied in the short-interval domain as follows. Rats were trained with 100-s fixed intervals. A phase advance was introduced by providing an early, free food pellet (figure 14.10A). The phase shift produced partial adjustment on intervals immediately after the phase shift. Adjustment required four food cycles (figures 14.10A and B). An accumulator mechanism predicts 100% adjustment on the initial interval after the phase shift on the assumption of complete reset (Gibbon, Fairhurst, & Goldberg, 1997). An oscillator mechanism predicts initial incomplete adjustment. The experiment illustrates the application of circadian-oscillator concepts and methodology to investigate short-interval timing and the potential explanatory power of short-interval oscillators. Incomplete reset is consistent with an oscillator mechanism of short-interval timing (100 s).

CONCLUSIONS

The conclusion that emerges from this program of research is that the representation of time is nonlinear. The observation that time perception across many ranges is nonlinear may provide a basis for the development of a unified theory of timing that encompasses the discrimination of temporal intervals across several orders of magnitude—from milliseconds to days. The integration of concepts and methodologies from short-interval and circadian research may facilitate the development of such a unified theory.

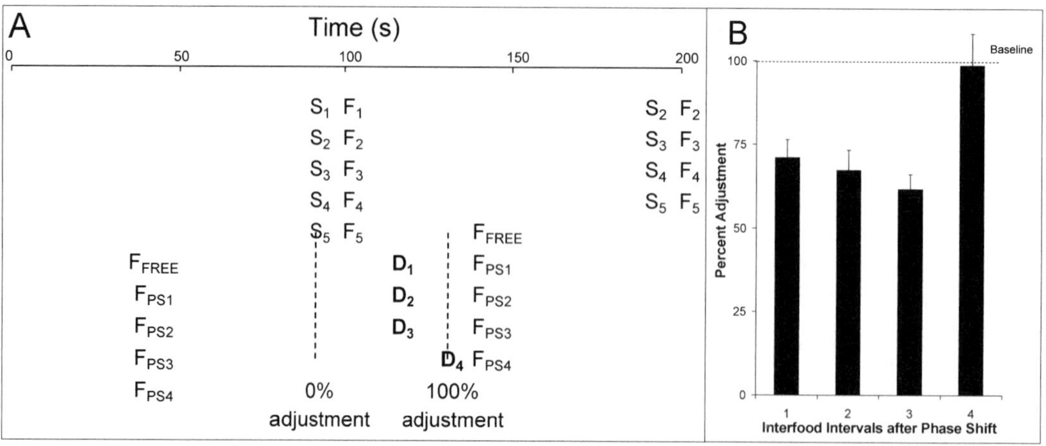

Figure 14.10. A phase shift produces partial reset in short-interval timing. *A*, Schematic representation of training, phase-shift manipulation, predictions, and data (double plotted to facilitate inspection of transitions across successive intervals; consecutive 100-s fixed intervals are plotted left to right and top to bottom). Rats ($n = 14$) timed 100-s intervals, and the last five intervals before the phase shift are shown (F = food pellet, S = start time of response burst). A 62-s phase advance (i.e., early pellet) on average was produced by the delivery of a response-independent food (F_{FREE}). All other food-to-food intervals were 100 s (F_{PS} = food post phase shift). Dashed lines indicate predictions if rats are insensitive (0% adjustment) or completely sensitive (100% adjustment) to the most recently delivered food pellet. A pacemaker-accumulator mechanism predicts 100% adjustment on the initial interval after the phase shift on the assumption of complete reset (Gibbon, Fairhurst, et al., 1997). An oscillator mechanism predicts initial incomplete adjustment. Data (D) indicate incomplete adjustment on the first three trials. *B*, Start times on the initial three trials were earlier than in preshift baseline [$t(13)$s > 2, *ps* < .05]. Resetting was achieved on the fourth trial ($t < 1$). Each 45-mg food pellet was contingent on a lever press after 100 s in 12-h sessions. The start of a response burst was identified on individual trials by selecting the response that maximized the goodness of fit of individual responses to a model with a low rate followed by a high rate (analysis as in Crystal et al., 1997). The same conclusions were reached by measuring the latency to the first response after food. Baseline was the average start time on the five trials before the phase shift. *B*, Zero on the *y*-axis corresponds to complete failure to adjust to the phase shift; 100% corresponds to complete resetting. Error bars represent 1 *SEM*.

Acknowledgments This work was supported by a grant from the National Institute of Mental Health (MH64799) to J.D.C. The author thanks Kenneth W. Maxwell for assistance with reanalyzing published data.

References

Allan, L. G. (1983). Magnitude estimation of temporal intervals. *Perception & Psychophysics, 33*, 29–42.

Allan, L. G. (1998). The influence of the scalar timing model on human timing research. *Behavioural Processes, 44*, 101–117.

Brunner, D., Kacelnik, A., & Gibbon, J. (1992). Optimal foraging and timing processes in the starling, *Sturnus vulgaris*: Effect of intercapture interval. *Animal Behaviour, 44*, 597–613.

Cheng, K., & Westwood, R. (1993). Analysis of single trials in pigeons' timing performance. *Journal of Experimental Psychology: Animal Behavior Processes, 19*, 56–67.

Cheng, K., Westwood, R., & Crystal, J. D. (1993). Memory variance in the peak procedure of timing in pigeons. *Journal of Experimental Psychology: Animal Behavior Processes, 19*, 68–76.

Church, R. M. (1978). The internal clock. In S. H. Hulse, H. Fowler, & W. K. Honig (Eds.), *Cognitive processes in animal behavior* (pp. 277–310). Hillsdale, NJ: Erlbaum.

Church, R. M. (1997). Quantitative models of animal learning and cognition. *Journal of*

Experimental Psychology: Animal Behavior Processes, 23, 379–389.
Church, R. M., & Broadbent, H. A. (1990). Alternative representations of time, number, and rate. *Cognition, 37,* 55–81.
Church, R. M., Getty, D. J., & Lerner, N. D. (1976). Duration discrimination by rats. *Journal of Experimental Psychology: Animal Behavior Processes, 2,* 303–312.
Church, R. M., & Lacourse, D. M. (1998). Serial pattern learning of temporal intervals. *Animal Learning & Behavior, 26,* 272–289.
Church, R. M., Meck, W. H., & Gibbon, J. (1994). Application of scalar timing theory to individual trials. *Journal of Experimental Psychology: Animal Behavior Processes, 20,* 135–155.
Crystal, J. D. (1999). Systematic nonlinearities in the perception of temporal intervals. *Journal of Experimental Psychology: Animal Behavior Processes, 25,* 3–17.
Crystal, J. D. (2001a). Circadian time perception. *Journal of Experimental Psychology: Animal Behavior Processes, 27,* 68–78.
Crystal, J. D. (2001b). Nonlinear time perception. *Behavioural Processes, 55,* 35–49.
Crystal, J. D. (2003). Nonlinearities in sensitivity to time: Implications for oscillator-based representations of interval and circadian clocks. In W. H. Meck (Ed.), *Functional and neural mechanisms of interval timing* (pp. 61–75). Boca Raton, FL: CRC Press.
Crystal, J. D., Church, R. M., & Broadbent, H. A. (1997). Systematic nonlinearities in the memory representation of time. *Journal of Experimental Psychology: Animal Behavior Processes, 23,* 267–282.
Dews, P. B. (1970). The theory of fixed-interval responding. In W. N. Schoenfeld (Ed.), *The theory of reinforcement schedules* (pp. 43–61). New York: Appleton-Century-Crofts.
Eisler, H. (1976). Experiments on subjective duration 1868-1975: A collection of power function exponents. *Psychological Bulletin, 83,* 1154–1171.
Fetterman, J. G., & Killeen, P. R. (1992). Time discrimination in *Columba livia* and *Homo sapiens. Journal of Experimental Psychology: Animal Behavior Processes, 18,* 80–94.
Gallistel, C. R. (1990). *The organization of learning.* Cambridge, MA: MIT Press.
Gibbon, J. (1977). Scalar expectancy theory and Weber's law in animal timing. *Psychological Review, 84,* 279–325.
Gibbon, J. (1981). On the form and location of the psychometric bisection function for time. *Journal of Mathematical Psychology, 24,* 58–87.
Gibbon, J. (1991). Origins of scalar timing. *Learning & Motivation, 22,* 3–38.
Gibbon, J., & Church, R. M. (1981). Time left: Linear versus logarithmic subjective time. *Journal of Experimental Psychology: Animal Behavior Processes, 7,* 87–107.
Gibbon, J., & Church, R. M. (1990). Representation of time. *Cognition, 37,* 23–54.
Gibbon, J., Church, R. M., & Meck, W. H. (1984). Scalar timing in memory. In J. Gibbon & L. Allan (Eds.), *Annals of the New York Academy of Sciences: Timing and time perception* (Vol. 423, pp. 52–77). New York: New York Academy of Sciences.
Gibbon, J., Fairhurst, S., & Goldberg, B. (1997). Cooperation, conflict and compromise between circadian and interval clocks in pigeons. In C. M. Bradshaw & E. Szabadi (Eds.), *Time and behaviour: Psychological and neurobehavioural analyses* (pp. 329–384). New York: Elsevier.
Gibbon, J., Malapani, C., Dale, C. L., & Gallistel, C. R. (1997). Toward a neurobiology of temporal cognition: Advances and challenges. *Current Opinion in Neurobiology, 7,* 170–184.
Higa, J. J., Wynne, C. D., & Staddon, J. E. R. (1991). Dynamics of time discrimination. *Journal of Experimental Psychology: Animal Behavior Processes, 17,* 281–291.
Innis, N. K., & Staddon, J. E. R. (1971). Temporal tracking on cyclic-interval reinforcement schedules. *Journal of the Experimental Analysis of Behavior, 16,* 411–423.
Killeen, P. R. (2002). Scalar counters. *Learning & Motivation, 33,* 63–87.
Killeen, P. R., & Taylor, T. J. (2000). How the propagation of error through stochastic counters affects time discrimination and other psychophysical judgments. *Psychological Review, 107,* 430–459.
Lejeune, H., & Wearden, J. H. (1991). The comparative psychology of fixed-interval responding: Some quantitative analyses. *Learning & Motivation, 22,* 84–111.
Macmillan, N. A., & Creelman, C. D. (1991). *Detection theory: A user's guide.* New York: Cambridge University Press.
Mistlberger, R. E. (1994). Circadian food-anticipatory activity: Formal models and physiological mechanisms. *Neuroscience and Biobehavioral Reviews, 18,* 171–195.
Nichols, H. (1891). The psychology of time. *American Journal of Psychology, 3,* 453–529.
Roberts, S. (1981). Isolation of an internal clock. *Journal of Experimental Psychology: Animal Behavior Processes, 7,* 242–268.
Roitblat, H. L. (1982). The meaning of representation in animal memory. *Behavioral & Brain Sciences, 5,* 353–406.
Rosenbaum, D. A. (1998). Broadcast theory of timing. In D. A. Rosenbaum & C. E. Collyer

(Eds.), *Timing of behavior: Neural, psychological, and computational perspectives* (pp. 215–235). Cambridge, MA: MIT Press.

Rosenbaum, D. A. (2002). Time, space, and short-term memory. *Brain and Cognition, 48*, 52–65.

Schneider, B. A. (1969). A two-state analysis of fixed-interval responding in the pigeon. *Journal of the Experimental Analysis of Behavior, 12*, 677–687.

Stevens, S. S. (1957). On the psychophysical law. *Psychological Review, 64*, 153–181.

Wynne, C. D. L., Staddon, J. E. R., & Delius, J. D. (1996). Dynamics of waiting in pigeons. *Journal of the Experimental Analysis of Behavior, 65*, 603–618.

Zeiler, M. D. (1991). Ecological influences on timing. *Journal of Experimental Psychology: Animal Behavior Processes, 17*, 13–25.

Zeiler, M. D., & Powell, D. G. (1994). Temporal control in fixed-interval schedules. *Journal of the Experimental Analysis of Behavior, 61*, 1–9.

15

Time and Number: Learning, Psychophysics, Stimulus Control, and Retention

J. GREGOR FETTERMAN

In a recent article (Fetterman, 1996b), I considered the issue of stimulus complexity in animal cognition research, pointing out that the resurgence of interest in animal cognition (e.g., Hulse, 1993; Wasserman, 1993) was accompanied by the use of increasingly complex stimulus arrangements—arrays of elements (e.g., Blough, 1992), textured patterns (e.g., Cook, 1992), color photographs (e.g., Herrnstein, Loveland, & Cable, 1976), musical selections (e.g., Porter & Neuringer, 1985), temporal events (e.g., Church & Deluty, 1977; Stubbs, 1968), numerosities (e.g., Meck & Church, 1983), and so forth. I made no claims about the direction of the causal relation because it seemed obvious that the renewed emphasis on cognitive constructs and theories in animal learning resulted from a dynamic interplay of a set of variables, including the "paradigm shift" in the study of human learning and memory that preceded changes in the approaches to learning in nonhumans by 20 years or more.

This chapter concerns research and theory on the ability of nonhuman animals to learn, remember, and discriminate between events that differ in duration (e.g., a 2-s light vs. a 4-s light) and between those that differ in number (e.g., two light flashes vs. four light flashes)—in each case, events with temporal extension, one of the dimensions of complexity considered by Fetterman (1996). This property of time-based and number-based discriminations raises interesting questions for research and theories of the underlying mechanisms, such as the role of memory and the weighting of events early in the sequence versus those that occur later (e.g., see Alsop & Honig, 1991). Events that involve temporal extension also raise questions about the nature of the stimulus that comprises such events (e.g., Gibson, 1966).

The chapter begins with a brief history of attempts to understand how nonhuman animals discriminate temporal intervals and moves to a brief presentation of how animals discriminate numerosities. The remainder of the chapter is devoted to comparisons of duration and numerosity discriminations and conclusions that may be drawn from the results of experiments on time and number discriminations. The main focus is on the role of stimulus information as opposed to underlying mechanisms (cf. Fetterman, 1996b).

The modern era of timing research in nonhuman animals began with two seminal publications that appeared in the late 1970s. Gibbon's article (1977) "Scalar expectancy theory and Weber's law in animal timing" summarized the regularities of timed behavior in nonhuman animals and provided a formal, mathematical model of the process. One year later, Church (1978) described the cognitive underpinnings of timing and the relationships among the various information-processing components of the timing system. The two approaches merged in the early 1980s when the mathematical model was used to specify the "behavior" of the cognitive components of the timing system (i.e., means and variances; Gibbon & Church, 1984). Since then, this theory has been further elaborated to encompass additional features of the timing process, including performance at the level of individual trials (e.g., Gibbon & Church, 1990).

Later, alternative timing systems were proposed, such as the behavioral theory of timing (BeT) described by Killeen and Fetterman (1988), the connectionist model of Church and Broadbent (1990), and the memory model of Staddon and Higa (1999). As a consequence of an extended interplay between data collection and theory development, research and theory on timing have achieved a level of theoretical sophistication that is probably unsurpassed compared with theoretical developments in most areas of animal learning, with the possible exceptions of models of Pavlovian conditioning and models of choice.

In terms of the theme of this chapter, an important elaboration of the timing model developed by Gibbon and Church appeared in 1984, when the model was extended to incorporate discriminations of numerosity, in which the numerical events (e.g., sequences of tones) were dispersed through time. Meck and Church (1983) proposed an extension of the model in which the timing mechanism could function in either one of two modes: a time mode or a count mode. In either mode, the "functional stimulus" consisted of pulses gated to an accumulator, such that both time and number were represented as pulse number values. This extension has subsequently been explored and further developed by researchers outside the Gibbon/Church camp (e.g., Roberts, 1995, 1997), who concluded that the dual-mode approach, having the virtue of economy of cognition, is a good approach.

It is not my goal to provide a detailed critique of extant theories of timing and numerosity discriminations. Instead, I offer a selective review of research on these topics, focusing on the content of time- and number-based events, common properties of these discriminations, and similarities and differences in empirical results. It will quickly become clear that the amount of research on numerosity discriminations, especially in the psychophysical domain, pales in comparison to the volume of research on timing.

LEARNING

Comparing the learning of different kinds of discriminations is difficult. If, say, a pigeon learns a hue discrimination faster than a line orientation discrimination, then we can conclude that the hue discrimination is "easier," but the reasons for the difference in learning are less transparent. A pair of hues may be more discriminable than a pair of line orientations if the proper values are selected, hue may be more salient than line orientation as a stimulus dimension, or both factors may contribute. Carter and Werner (1978) provided a comprehensive review of conditional discrimination learning in pigeons that addressed many aspects of variables that affect learning, demonstrating, among other things, that hue discriminations are acquired more rapidly than line discriminations. Their review also showed that symbolic and identity matching tasks are acquired at the same rate.

In this section, I consider how the learning of temporal and numerosity discriminations compares with discriminations of punctate visual stimuli, "all other things being equal." As noted, these comparisons are not without complications because it is difficult to say whether 2-s and 8-s temporal stimuli are as discriminable as are red and green lights. Nonetheless, research indicates that discriminations of both numerosity and duration take longer to learn than comparable visual discriminations, as illustrated later.

Fetterman and MacEwen (2003) trained pigeons on a symbolic matching-to-sample (SMTS) task with compound stimuli. The samples consisted of a fixed ratio (FR) requirement (FR5 or FR20) and a hue (red or green). For one group of pigeons (group H), the hue dimension was relevant to the correct comparison choice and the number of sample pecks was irrelevant. Thus, for example, a pigeon sometimes made 5 pecks to the red sample and sometimes made 20 pecks to the red sample. However, the correct comparison response was based on hue, not peck number. For another group (group N), the number of pecks to the sample key was the relevant dimension and the hue of the sample key was irrelevant. Thus, for instance, on FR5 trials, sometimes the sample key was red and other times it was green; the contingencies for comparison choice depended on peck number value, not sample key hue. Both groups received 96 trials per

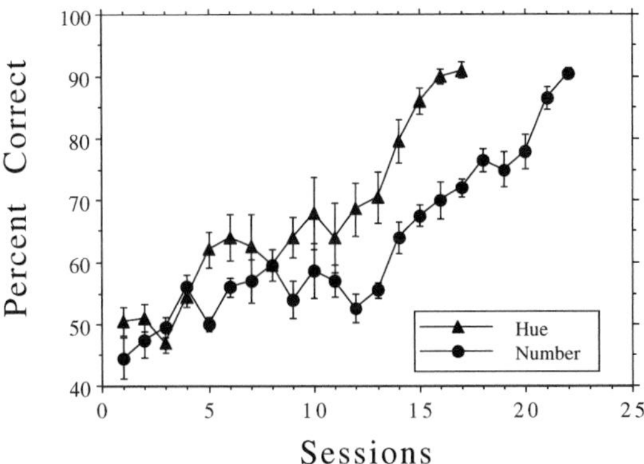

Figure 15.1. Percent correct choices as a function of number of training sessions. Data are the means of four pigeons for each group (represented by different symbols). The vertical bars show ±1 *SEM*. (From "Acquisition and Retention in Compound Matching with Hue and Peck Number Elements," by J. G. Fetterman and D. MacEwen, 2003, *Learning and Motivation*, *34*, 354–371. Copyright 2003 by Elsevier. Reprinted with permission.)

session with equal exposure to the pairs of hues and FR requirements.

Figure 15.1 displays the acquisition data for the two groups; the hue discrimination was learned considerably faster than the peck number discrimination. This result may or may not be surprising, depending on how one interprets the results of past research and what view is taken on the nature of stimuli. The review by Carter and Werner (1978) shows that hue discriminations are acquired rapidly, but other research (e.g., Cohen, Looney, Brady, & Aucella, 1976) demonstrates that such discriminations are acquired even faster when visual samples are correlated with differential sample behaviors, such as different FRs.

Urcuioli and Honig (1980) carried out an extensive series of experiments concerning the role of differential sample behaviors on the learning of conditional discriminations of visual stimuli. These authors concluded that behaviors directed toward the visual samples constituted a more potent source of stimulus control than the samples themselves, overshadowing the nominal visual stimulus. This conclusion is not entirely consistent with the finding that discriminations between different FR values take longer to learn than simple visual discriminations, except that it seems plausible that two cues for choice (sample and correlated behavior) are more effective than a single cue for choice.

Bowers and Richards (1990) used a task very similar to the one used by Fetterman and MacEwen, except that temporal samples, rather than FR samples, were combined with hue samples. These researchers presented pigeons with red or green sample hues that lasted for 5 or 30 s. One group was taught to choose between comparison stimuli based on hue, whereas another group was taught to choose between comparison stimuli based on sample duration. As in the case of Fetterman and MacEwen, the visual discrimination was learned faster than the (extended) temporal discrimination.

In the work of Fetterman and MacEwen and of Bowers and Richards, sample stimuli differed on two dimensions—hue and temporal extension. As noted, discriminations between stimuli differing in number or duration are more difficult to learn than hue discriminations. Fetterman and MacEwen (2003) conducted additional analyses of acquisition by separating trials according to number of pecks emitted to the samples (FR5 or FR20). Note that FR value was relevant for group N but not for group H. The results of this analysis are displayed in figure 15.2.

FR value made a difference in the rate of acquisition for group H. The hue discrimination was acquired faster for samples that required 20 pecks than for samples that required 5 pecks. Sacks, Kamil, and Mack (1972) reported a similar result, although they manipulated FR requirement between groups and we manipulated FR value within subjects. This finding implies better encoding of the hue sample on FR20 than FR5 trials. Group N displayed a different pattern with regard to acquiring the discrimination; there were no differences in learning the FRs when peck number value was the relevant dimension. I am not aware of published data comparing the rate of learning of short versus long temporal samples.

This brief summary of the time-course of acquisition of temporal and numerosity tasks reveals that these extended discriminations take longer to learn than discriminations of punctate stimuli, such as hue discriminations. Temporal and numerosity discriminations differ from these other discriminations in at least two ways. First, they involve extended events and the mechanisms involved in apprehending these events may be more cognitive than perceptual.

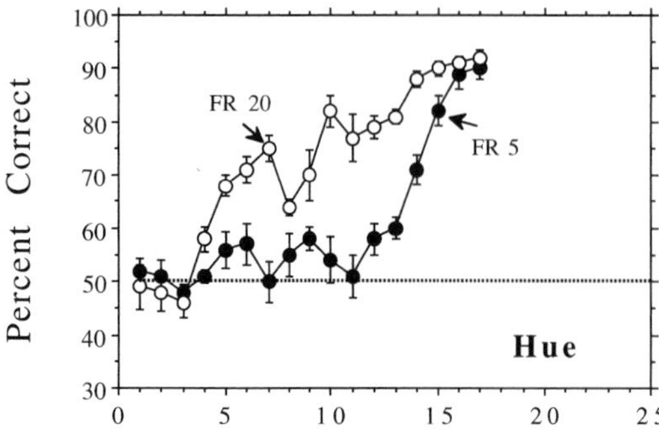

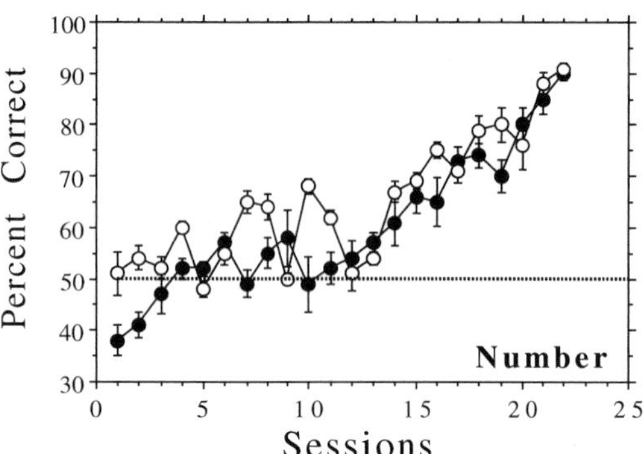

Figure 15.2. Percent correct choices as a function of number of training sessions. The data are shown separately for trials on which the sample pecking requirement was FR5 and for those on which it was FR20. Data are the means of four pigeons for each group. The vertical bars show ±1 *SEM*. (From "Acquisition and Retention in Compound Matching with Hue and Peck Number Elements," by J. G. Fetterman and D. MacEwen, 2003, *Learning and Motivation*, *34*, 354–371. Copyright 2003 by Elsevier. Reprinted with permission.)

Second, in the cases involving both temporal and numerical stimuli, the value of the sample cannot be determined until the sample period ends. Together, these features may result in slower learning compared with stimuli whose "identity" can be discerned immediately and do not require the integration of information over time.

PSYCHOPHYSICS

The development of theories of timing has benefited from a corpus of data that lend itself to quantification. These data have yielded what many regard as invariant principles of timing behavior that circumscribe the structure of timing theory (e.g., see Gibbon, 1991). Collectively, these principles are referred to as scalar timing (Gibbon, 1977) and they have different manifestations in different contexts. Under fixed-interval (FI) schedules, for example, response rate, expressed as a proportion of terminal rate, is a function of the relative temporal position (proportion of the FI value) of the subject in the FI (Dews, 1970). This invariance characterizes performance over a wide range of FI schedules.

Superposition

Under psychophysical discrimination tasks, the scalar property is manifest when psychometric functions involving different absolute values superpose when the abscissas are transformed from an absolute to a relative scale (e.g., by dividing the duration of a signal by the shortest test duration; see, for example, Church & Deluty, 1977; Gibbon, 1991; Stubbs, 1968). Fetterman and Killeen (1992) provided a demonstration of the range of generality of the superposition principle by training pigeons under a temporal discrimination task in which the stimuli varied over two orders of magnitude. The task was the method of single stimuli. Under a discrete trials procedure, pigeons were presented with a short or a long signal duration followed by a choice phase during which the pigeons chose between report keys. Responses to one of the two keys were reinforced after the short signal, whereas responses to the second key were reinforced after the long signal; each signal occurred often. In three conditions, the values of the short and long signals were 0.05 and 0.10 s, 0.5 and 1.0 s, and 5.0 and 10 s. Once the pigeons attained a learning criterion, they were given probe trials involving signal durations intermediate to the short and long signal training values; choices on these probe trials were not reinforced. This procedure allowed us to calculate psychometric functions relating signal duration to the probability of the pigeon choosing the key associated with the value of the "long" signal.

Figure 15.3 (top) displays the median data for three pigeons in a psychometric format. The abscissa identifies signal duration in relative terms by dividing test signal values by the value of the short-

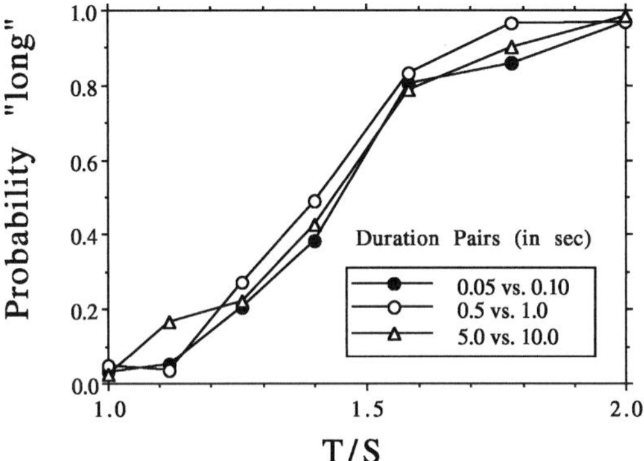

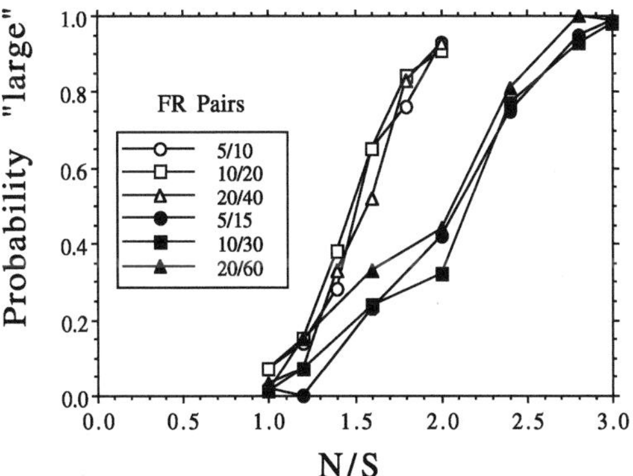

Figure 15.3. Probability of responding to the choice alternative associated with the longer of a pair of signal durations as a function of the relative duration (T/S) of the test signal (*top*). Probability of responding to the choice alternative associated with the larger sample FR as a function of the relative numerosity (N/S) of the FR sample (*bottom*). (Adapted from "Time Discrimination in *Columba livia* and *Homo sapiens*," by J. G. Fetterman and P. R. Killeen, 1992, *Journal of Experimental Psychology: Animal Behavior Processes*, *18*, 80–94.)

est signal. The dependent variable is the probability of responding to the key associated with the longest signal duration. An "eye" test indicates that the data in the figure demonstrate a close approximation to the superposition effect that characterizes timing behavior in many different contexts, consistent with the scalar timing principle. The impressive feature of the data in figure 15.3 is the range of intervals over which superposition may occur.

By comparison with the voluminous literature on the psychophysics of timing, there are very few studies concerned with the psychophysical principles of numerosity discriminations. Consequently, it is not clear whether there are ubiquitous principles of number-based discriminations, such as "scalar counting," comparable to those observed in the temporal domain. Accounts favoring a common mechanism approach to counting and timing (e.g., Meck, 1997; Roberts, 1997) imply that the same principles should apply to each kind of discrimination.

Fetterman (1993) conducted an extensive study of pigeons' discriminations of peck number using a psychophysical approach. In this study, pigeons were trained to discriminate between different numbers of pecks emitted to a sample key. One choice was reinforced after a small number of pecks had been emitted, whereas another choice was reinforced after a larger number of pecks had been emitted. Across conditions, various peck number pairs were used; the pairs differed in both the absolute and relative values of the pecking requirements. As in the experiment by Fetterman and Killeen (1992), the pigeons were given probe trials with intermediate stimulus values (number of key pecks) after the basic discrimination was acquired.

Figure 15.3 (bottom) shows the psychometric data as the mean of the four pigeons in Fetterman's (1993) study. The panel displays the probability of responding to the choice key associated with the larger pecking requirement as a function of relative numerosity, expressed as the value of the sample ratio (N) divided by the value of the smallest ratio (S) in a particular condition. The data in the figure represent six test conditions in which the relative and absolute values of the pecking requirements varied. Those values are identified in the figure legend. In its strongest form, superposition is observed across changes in the ratio of the reinforced endpoints (e.g., 2:1, 3:1); a somewhat weaker version predicts overlapping functions for a given stimulus ratio but not across conditions where the endpoints involve different stimulus ratios. The curves in figure 15.3, bottom, are orderly and ogival and, at the least, demonstrate the weaker version of the superposition property characteristic of temporal discrimination functions. This result suggests that numerosity discriminations, like temporal discriminations, obey the scalar principle as instantiated by the superposition property.

Bisection

A second point of psychophysical comparison between temporal and numerosity discriminations concerns the location of the subjective midpoint between reinforced values—the bisection point or point of subjective equality (PSE). The PSE typically is defined as the indifference point between reinforced values (e.g., a discrimination between a 2-s tone and an 8-s tone). It is measured by testing a subject with intermediate stimulus values and calculating the value of the stimulus at which the subject responds equally to choices associated with the shorter and longer values. The PSE can be taken as a measure of the underlying psychological scale (e.g., Gibbon, 1986) along a stimulus dimension. Its usefulness as an empirical constraint on theories of timing has been debated (e.g., Zeiler, 1985), but from a psychophysical perspective, many believe that this measure provides leverage on the machinery of timing.

Temporal bisection typically occurs at the geometrical mean of the reinforced stimuli (e.g., Allan & Gibbon, 1991; Church & Deluty, 1977; Fetterman & Killeen, 1992; Stubbs, 1976); this result appears robust across task and species differences (see Zeiler, 1985, for a different opinion). The bisection data appear less consistent for numerosity tasks, however. Fetterman, Dreyfus, and Stubbs (1985) used a free-operant scaling task and found that pigeons bisected pairs of fixed ratios at the harmonic mean of the ratio values. Fetterman, Stubbs, and Dreyfus (1986) used a similar task, except that the events comprised intermittent light flashes rather than pecking responses. Fetterman et al. (1986) found that pigeons bisected between the harmonic and geometrical mean of the reinforced values. Meck and Church (1983) trained rats to discriminate between different numbers of on-off noise cycles and obtained bisection at the geometrical mean of the noise quantities. A final point of comparison is provided by data reported by Martin-Iverson, Fibiger, and Wilkie (1988). They trained rats to discriminate between different numbers of tones or food pellets and found that bisection occurred near the harmonic mean for tone quantities but near the geometrical mean for food quantities, further complicating the comparison between time- and number-based bisection.

One problem with making comparisons of bisection data involving different tasks, species, carrier stimuli, and dimensions is that, often, predictions based on various candidate means (harmonic, geometrical, arithmetic) are very similar. Zeiler (1985) made this point and recommended a method called the power mean analysis that affords a clearer discrimination of bisection data. Other methods, such as regression analysis, also are useful as an assay of bisection data because they provide a greater degree of precision than less formal analyses.

Fetterman and Killeen (1992) used the power mean analysis recommended by Zeiler (1985) and found that the geometrical mean was the best predictor of bisection points for three pigeons tested across a wide range of temporal stimuli. These data are displayed in the upper panel of figure 15.4. Fetterman (1993) assessed bisection in a numerosity task by regressing the data against the harmonic, geometrical, and arithmetic means of the stimuli. The regression analysis based on the geometrical mean is shown in figure 15.4, bottom. The dashed line in the panel is an identity line, representing cases where bisection occurred exactly at the geometric mean; the solid line is the best-fitting regression line, produced by regressing the geometrical mean against the obtained PSEs pooled over subjects and conditions. The analysis was clear in demonstrating that the geometrical mean was the best predictor of bisection as the slope did not differ significantly from 1.0, whereas the slopes for the regressions based on the harmonic and arithmetic means were significantly different from 1.0.

Contextual Psychophysics

Students of timing recognize that scalar timing embodies a general principle of discrimination—Weber's law. Weber's law states that our ability to discriminate intensive stimuli is proportional to the magnitude of the stimuli discriminated. Weber's law is typically expressed in terms of a ratio of the variability of discriminative judgments (s) divided by the magnitude (M) of the discriminative stimulus; the resulting proportion is called a Weber fraction (k) that is presumed to reflect the acuity of discrimination ($s/M = k$). That proportion remains

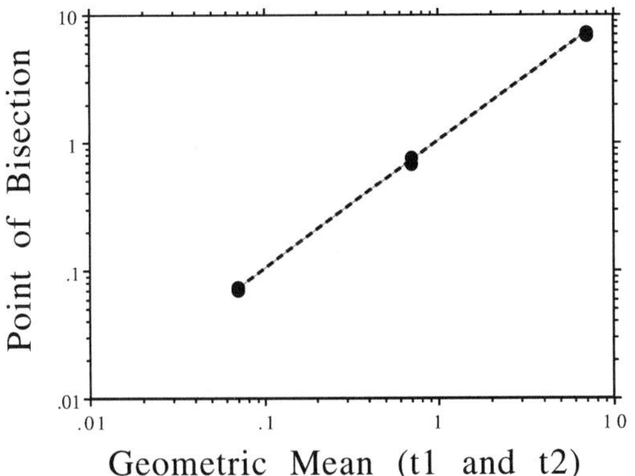

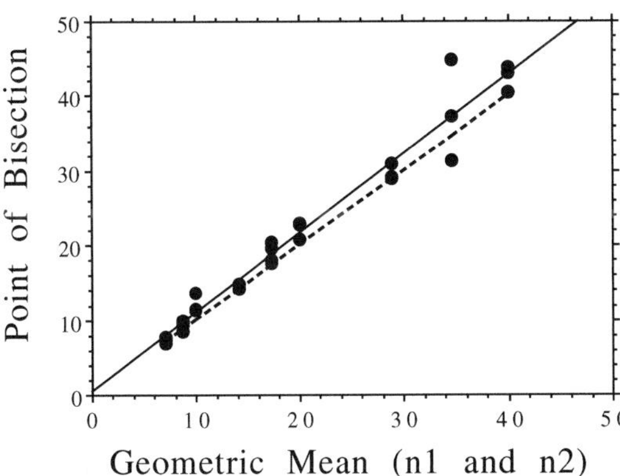

Figure 15.4. Point of bisection as a function of the geometric mean of a duration pair (*top*) or the geometric mean of a pair of fixed-ratio samples (*bottom*). The points represent data from individual pigeons. The *dashed lines* are identity lines that show the predicted bisection at the geometric mean of the training values. The *solid line* in the *bottom* is a best-fitting regression line. (*Top,* Adapted from "Time Discrimination in *Columba livia* and *Homo sapiens,*" by J. G. Fetterman and P. R. Killeen, 1992, *Journal of Experimental Psychology: Animal Behavior Processes, 18,* 80–94. *Bottom,* Adapted from "Numerosity Discrimination: Both Time and Number Matter, 1993, by J. G. Fetterman, *Journal of Experimental Psychology: Animal Behavior Processes, 19,* 149–164.)

constant over a fairly broad range of temporal stimuli (e.g., Stubbs, 1980).

The Weber fraction is a convenient way to depict the relative invariance of discrimination, but it is sometimes informative to rewrite the formula to emphasize changes in the variability of discriminative judgments in relation to stimulus magnitude: s = k * M. In this guise, Weber's law states that variability is proportional to stimulus magnitude. In other words, when the value of the stimulus is increased twofold (e.g., judging a 20-s interval as opposed to a 10-s interval), for example, the variability of the judgment should double. The psychophysical data for both temporal and numerical discriminations are consistent with either formulation. However, the story is more complicated because it turns out that the relation between variability and stimulus magnitude depends on context, defined as the collection of stimulus values experienced by the subject within and between conditions.

Relevant data are provided by a task called categorical scaling, first described by Fetterman and Killeen (1995). Fetterman and Killeen trained pigeons to time three intervals simultaneously by reinforcing responses to one key after a short time (e.g., 4 s), to a second key after an intermediate time (e.g., 8 s), or to a third key after a long time (e.g., 16 s). Food was primed for only one of the keys on each trial and reward opportunities were equally distributed among the key-interval pairs. Across conditions, the triplet of times comprised 4, 8, and 16 s (base 4), 8, 16, and 32 s (base 8), 16, 32, and 64 s (base 16), and 32, 64, and 128 s (base 32).

The pattern of behavior was similar in all conditions. Pigeons began a trial by responding on the "short" key, switched to the "intermediate" key if food was not obtained at the scheduled time on the short key, and switched to the "long" key at some point beyond the intermediate time if food was not delivered then. The birds became quite adept at procuring reinforcers, adjusting their switches so that very few reinforcers were missed (i.e., a pigeon rarely switched from the first to the second key or the second to the third key before the reinforced duration on that key had expired).

Switch times and their variability are the focus of the present discussion of contextual psychophysics. Figure 15.5 (top) shows the pairs of switch times (short → intermediate; intermediate → long) for each of the base conditions described above; switch times are displayed on the abscissa and their associated standard deviations on the ordinate. Mean switch times between key pairs occurred at the geometrical means of the times of reinforcement (see Fetterman & Killeen, 1995); the second switch time (intermediate → long) was approximately double the first (short → intermediate). The dashed lines in the figure indicate the predicted change in the standard deviation based on the scalar principle. Within a base, although the time of the second switch was roughly double that of the first, standard deviations increased by less than a factor of 2, being closer to a square root increase predicted by Poisson models of timing (i.e., the second switch points within each base fall below the dashed lines). Note, however, that the dashed line well predicts changes in standard deviations between the first switch point of one base and that of the next higher base, consistent with scalar timing. These results tell us that the timing of a particular interval is influenced by the temporal context in which the interval is presented. This finding may be interpreted in terms of classic adaptation level theory (Helson, 1964) or in terms of a theory of timing (Killeen & Fetterman, 1988). Fetterman and Killeen (1995) provide a detailed discussion of this contextual effect in relation to the BeT.

Fetterman (1996a) used a version of the categorical scaling procedure in which the number of pecks to different keys was the relevant dimension. Responses to one key were reinforced after a small number of pecks had been emitted (e.g., 4), to a second key after an intermediate number of pecks had been emitted (e.g., 8), and to a third key after a large pecking requirement had been met (e.g., 16). Pecks on all of the keys contributed to the response requirements. As in the procedure of Fetterman and Killeen (1995), reinforcement was arranged for only one of the keys on each trial; reinforcers were equally distributed among the keys. Performance was studied under three conditions with different bases: 4, 8, and 16 responses (base 4), 8, 16, and 32 responses (base 8), and 16, 32, and 64 responses (base 16). As above, the focus of the analysis was on switching between the keys, in this case the number of pecks emitted to the first key before a switch to the second key, and the number of pecks emitted to the second key before a switch to the third key. This measure was related to the variability in peck number values within and across base conditions.

Figure 15.5 (bottom) shows the results of the switching analysis with number of pecks as the relevant dimension. The results are very similar

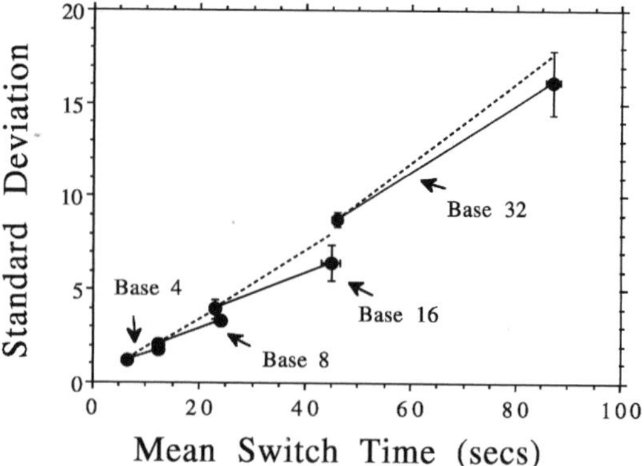

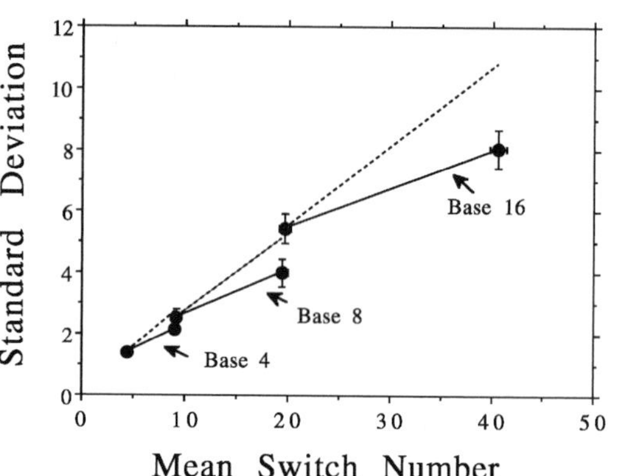

Figure 15.5. The standard deviations of switch times between the first and second keys and the second and third keys in a categorical scaling task (see text for details). The connected points show these values within a condition (base). *Top*, Results for an experiment in which responses to the keys were reinforced after different durations. *Bottom*, Data for an experiment in which the number of responses to the keys was the basis of reinforcement. The *dashed lines* indicate predictions based on a scalar process. (*Top*, From "Categorical Scaling of Time: Implications for Clock-Counter Models," by J. G. Fetterman and P. R. Killeen, 1995, *Journal of Experimental Psychology: Animal Behavior Processes*, *21*, 43–63. Copyright 1995 by American Psychological Association. Reprinted with permission. *Bottom*, From Fetterman, 1996a.)

to those displayed in the top panel. Within a base, the variability in the number of responses before a switch was less than predictions based on a scalar process (dashed lines). Between bases, however, the changes in variability relating number of responses to a switch and the variability of that number was almost perfectly scalar (the dashed lines connect the first switch points of each base).

The psychophysical properties of temporal and numerosity discriminations reviewed in this section support a conclusion that the psychophysics of these discriminations are very similar, if not identical. Superposition appears to hold for both dimensions, although there is a paucity of parametric data on numerosity discrimination. More could be done in this area. The bisection data, although complicated by differences in tasks, species, and carrier dimensions, indicate a fair, but not perfect, degree of correspondence across experiments—bisection at the geometrical mean, or a close approximation to it. Reviewing the bisection data, one could make a case for the contributions of multiple factors. All of the research agrees that bisection depends on relative stimulus differences. The differences in bisection have to do with the specific quantitative relation and the events that are used to construct event sequences (e.g., tones; lights; pecks; regular vs. irregular sequences). The influence of contextual factors on temporal psychophysical judgments (figure 5 first reported by Fetterman & Killeen, 1995) appears to hold for numerosity tasks, as well. The effects of stimulus context on temporal and numerical discriminations remain an area for further investigation.

CHANGING RATES OF REINFORCEMENT

Most theories of timing that rely on pacemaker countermechanisms (e.g., Church, 1984) assume that the mean rate of the pacemaker is relatively constant. In these theories, time is represented as an accumulation of pulse number values, and learning a discrimination between one duration and another requires long-term storage of the pulse number representations. As a consequence of the "fixed pacemaker" assumption, animals must adapt to different timing requirements by changing the criterial count number. If, for instance, the criterion is 10 counts and the temporal contingency is increased twofold, then a new criterion of 20 counts must be learned. Gibbon and Church (1984) showed how this property, in combination with other components of an internal clock and their associated variances, can produce the ubiquitous scalar property.

Killeen and Fetterman (1988) proposed an alternative pacemaker-counter framework for timing—the BeT. In BeT, temporal adaptation is accomplished by changes in the speed of the pacemaker rather than changes in the criterial count. Thus, with a twofold increase in a temporal criterion for reinforcement, Killeen and Fetterman posited that the speed of the pacemaker decreases by a factor of 0.5 while the criterial count remained the same. What could cause a change in the speed of the pacemaker? Killeen and Fetterman proposed that it was caused by changes in rate of reinforcement, with shifts to higher rates of reinforcement causing an increase in the rate of the pacemaker and shifts to lower rates of reinforcement causing a decrease in the speed of the pacemaker. In the original version of their theory, the relation between the rate of the pacemaker and the rate of reinforcement was held to be strictly proportional. This assertion led to a line of research focusing on how timing is impacted by changes in reinforcer frequency. In this section, some of this research is reviewed, and related work on numerosity discriminations that appears to be consistent with effects in the temporal domain is described.

In a typical timing experiment, reinforcement rate is highly correlated with the intervals to be timed (e.g., an FI schedule), leading to proportional changes in variability (i.e., scalar timing). It is possible, however, to dissociate these variables by manipulating reinforcement rate while holding the intervals to be timed constant. Under these conditions, if the rate of reinforcement is increased, then the mean judged duration of an interval should decrease because the criterion will be achieved sooner than the learned value (due to an increase in pacemaker speed). Correspondingly, if the rate of reinforcement is decreased, then the judged duration should increase because the criterion will be achieved later than the learned value (due to a decrease in pacemaker speed).

The prediction concerning changes in inferred pacemaker speed has now been confirmed in several experiments (e.g., Bizo & White, 1994a, 1994b; Fetterman & Killeen, 1991; Morgan, Killeen, & Fetterman, 1993). A particularly clear illustration of the effects of changes in reinforcer frequency on timing behavior is provided by Fetterman and Killeen (1995). Their categorical scaling procedure, described above, arranged reinforcers for three keys at different times (e.g., 4, 8, 16 s). Reinforcement was assigned to only one key on each trial, producing a pattern of behavior that could be described as temporal search. The birds moved from the first ("short") to the second ("intermediate") to the third ("long") in procuring the scheduled reinforcer; trials ended with reinforcer delivery. Responding on each of the keys was recorded as a function of time in a trial, yielding functions relating proportion of responses on each key (number of pecks to a key divided by total pecks to all keys) to trial time. Reinforcer frequency was manipulated by varying the probability of a trial ending with reinforcement in an ABA design: 1.0 (all trials end with food), 0.25 (one fourth of the trials end with food), and 1.0.

Figure 15.6 shows the results of the manipulation for a condition (base 8) in which the times of reinforcement were 8, 16, and 32 s. The data are averaged over four pigeons, but each bird showed the effects depicted in the figure. The curves are the proportion of responses on the intermediate (16-s) key. The unfilled symbols signify performance for the session before a decrease (top panel) or increase (bottom panel) in reinforcement probability. The filled symbols show performance for the session during which the change took place. The changes in both panels reflect clear shifts in temporal estimations consistent with a change in pacemaker speed. In the top panel, the response distribution shifted to the right, suggesting a decrease in the rate of a pacemaker. In the bottom panel, the response distribution shifted to the left, indicative of an increase in pacemaker speed. It is notable that the shifts occurred during the first sessions of the transitions in reinforcer probability, indicating a fast-acting process of temporal adjustment (e.g., Higa & Staddon, 1997).

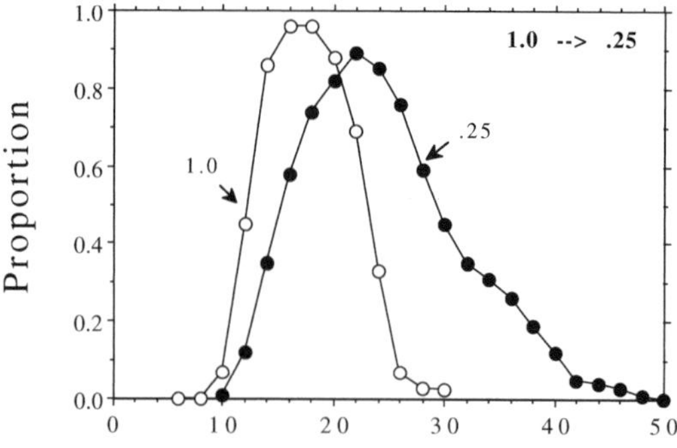

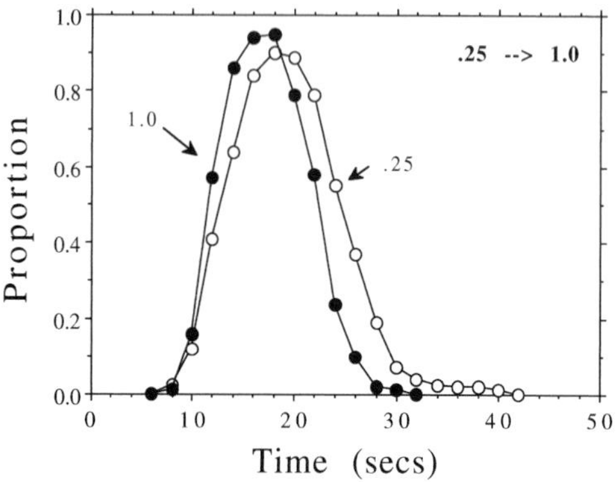

Figure 15.6. Proportion of responses on the intermediate key as a function of time for the session preceding (*open symbols*) a change in reinforcement probability and for the session in which the change occurred. The data are an average of four pigeons. (From "Categorical Scaling of Time: Implications for Clock-Counter Models," by J. G. Fetterman and P. R. Killeen, 1995, *Journal of Experimental Psychology: Animal Behavior Processes*, *21*, 43–63. Copyright 1995 by American Psychological Association. Reprinted with permission.)

Fetterman (1996a), using a response-based version of the categorical scaling procedure, manipulated reinforcement in the manner of Fetterman and Killeen (1995). The purpose was to determine whether the effects of changes in reinforcement on a numerosity discrimination were similar to those observed with temporal tasks. In this task, responses to three keys were reinforced after a small, intermediate, or large number of pecks had been emitted. In the conditions of interest, the pecking requirements were 8, 16, and 32 responses. During training, food was available on every trial (probability = 1.0); a reinforcer was primed for only one of the three keys on a trial, as in the task of Fetterman and Killeen. Once the basic task was learned, the probability that a trial ended with reinforcement was changed from 1.0 to 0.5. When food was not arranged, the trial ended after 32 responses had been emitted, followed by an intertrial interval. After lengthy exposure (about 25 sessions for each bird) to the partial reinforcement schedule, the original payoff structure was reinstated (probability = 1.0).

The results are shown in figure 15.7. The curves

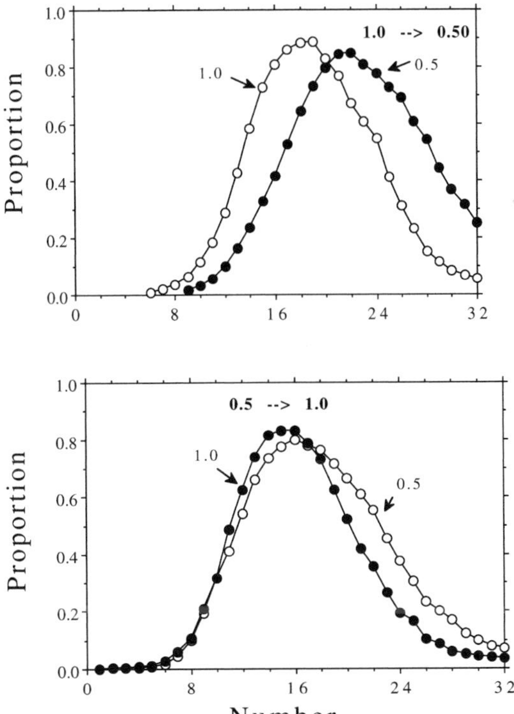

Figure 15.7. Proportion of responses on the intermediate key as a function of number of responses emitted for the session preceding (*open symbols*) a change in reinforcement probability and for the session in which the change occurred (*filled symbols*). The data are an average for four pigeons. (From Fetterman, 1996a.)

represent the proportion of total responses emitted to the intermediate (16 responses) key as a function of number of prior pecks emitted. The data represent an average of four pigeons. The top panel displays the effects of the change from a probability of 1.0 to 0.5, demonstrating that a reduction in reinforcement density produced a rightward shift in the choice function; that is, following the change from 1.0 to 0.5, pigeons emitted a larger number of responses before shifting into and away from the intermediate key than before the change in reinforcement. The bottom panel, representing the effects of an increase in reinforcement, show an opposite change (a leftward shift after the increase in reinforcement). The changes in figure 15.7 along the numerosity dimension are analogous to those shown in figure 15.6 along the temporal dimension.

There are sound theoretical reasons (Killeen & Fetterman, 1988) why temporal discriminations are affected by changes in the density of reinforcement, and there is converging evidence from a number of studies that these effects are robust. But, why should a numerosity discrimination be sensitive to changes in the frequency of reinforcement? A simple answer is that the birds were not counting their responses, but timing the duration of the pecking sequences. If the birds were timing rather than counting, then the effects of changing reinforcer density come as no surprise because they can be explained by a theory of timing. The answer is not so simple, however. First, multiple regression analyses of response number and response duration like those used by Fetterman (1993) show that the pigeons used both dimensions in performing the discrimination. Further, the analysis suggested that the number of responses was the more important dimension (larger beta weight). This point is developed further in the next section of the chapter. Second, in another variation of the categorical scaling procedure, the numerosities consisted of intermittent light flashes irregularly distributed in time (Fetterman, 1994). In this instance, the number of events was much more predictive of reinforcement than the duration of the event sequences. Under these circumstances, changes in reinforcer densities produced the same effects with light-flash numerosities as with response number. Thus, these results are not due simply to the fact that the birds always time sequences of events in which reinforcement is based on the number of events distributed through time.

Stimulus Control

Historically, approaches to duration and numerosity discrimination have focused on identifying a single stimulus dimension or underlying mechanism as the basis of the discrimination. In the case of duration discrimination, the emphasis has tended toward mechanism because duration is a dimension of a stimulus (the protensive dimension), not a stimulus itself. The method of presenting a duration to a pigeon or rat typically involves an unchanging light or tone, so (according to this view) there must be something that occurs during the stimulus or some internal temporal register that mediates the discrimination. As Gibson (1975) wrote, "events are perceivable, but time is not." In the case of numerosity discriminations, the potential controlling stimuli (if not the mechanism) are more obvious—pecks to a key, intermittent flashes of light, or periodic presentations of a tone. But, whether the focus concerns an underlying mechanism or external events, the emphasis has been on trying to identify a single entity that provides the causal basis of the discrimination.

Some of the early research on timing and counting illustrates this point. Rilling (1967) trained pigeons to discriminate between FI or FR schedules by reinforcing one choice after a small schedule value and another choice after a larger value. He correlated choices with the number of responses and the times taken to emit the responses. Rilling found that number of responses was the best predictor of choice for both time-based and number-based schedules, concluding that both discriminations were based on response number. Lydersen and Perkins (1974) varied the duration of a blackout between responses on a task involving a discrimination between two FR requirements. The effect of the changes in blackout duration was to alter the time taken to emit the response sequences while holding number constant. The results of the blackout manipulation led to the conclusion that the duration of the response sequence, not the number of responses, was the controlling dimension. Although Rilling and Lydersen and Perkins did not agree on the dimensions controlling duration and numerosity discriminations, each concluded that one dimension was primary.

More recently, researchers have sought to identify a single mechanism that underlies both temporal and numerosity discriminations. The primary candidate is the mode control version of the internal clock theory of timing, developed by Meck and Church (1983), and elaborated by W. A. Roberts (1995, 1997). This account specifies a flexible mechanism that may subserve discriminations of either the duration or the number of events by operating in different modes according to the demands of the task. This mechanism is also flexible in the sense that discriminations trained along one dimension may transfer to the other. However, not all students of timing and counting agree that a single mechanism suffices (Hobson & Newman, 1981).

The purpose of this section is to review temporal and numerosity discriminations from the perspective of a stimulus control analysis. I document instances when one or both discriminations are controlled by more than one stimulus variable. Normally, discriminative stimuli involving multiple features lend themselves to an analysis in terms of competition among the features, especially when the features are highly correlated and predict the same outcome (e.g., Kamin, 1969). But, this simple correlational approach does not capture the causal texture of complex environments, in which multiple sources of stimulus information are not completely redundant predictors of some target event. Under these circumstances, there is much to be gained by using more than one predictor (cf. Fetterman, 1993, 1996).

Consider an illustrative example from the foraging literature. Kamil, Yoerg, and Clements (1988) used a simulated foraging task and evaluated factors that influenced blue jays' decisions to give up on a depleting food source. They found that subjects based their decisions on multiple factors, including the number of prey received, the number of successive trials without a prey item (the "run of bad luck"), and a history of receiving a particular number of prey in the simulated patch. No single simple cue was involved.

Fetterman (1993) trained pigeons to discriminate different FR samples (e.g., FR10 vs. FR20) and recorded the times it took to complete the FR requirements. FR value and the associated duration of the pecking sequence were used as inputs of a multiple regression analysis, using the number of responses and the duration of response sequences as predictors of choice. The results showed that both time and number contributed to discrimination of the samples. The clearest statistical support for this conclusion was provided by squared semipartial correlations, which represent the increment in variance accounted for by one dimension (e.g., number) over and above that already accounted for by the other dimension (e.g., time). In the great majority of cases, the duration of the pecking sequences added significantly to the proportion of variance accounted for after FR value was taken into account. Similarly, the value of the FR contributed significantly to variance accounted for over and above the contribution of FR duration.

Figure 15.8 provides a visual representation of the joint contribution of number and time to the FR discrimination. The figure shows the times taken to emit different FRs (on the ordinate) against the values of the probe FRs (abscissa). The data are from a condition where the pigeons discriminated between FR10 and FR20 and were

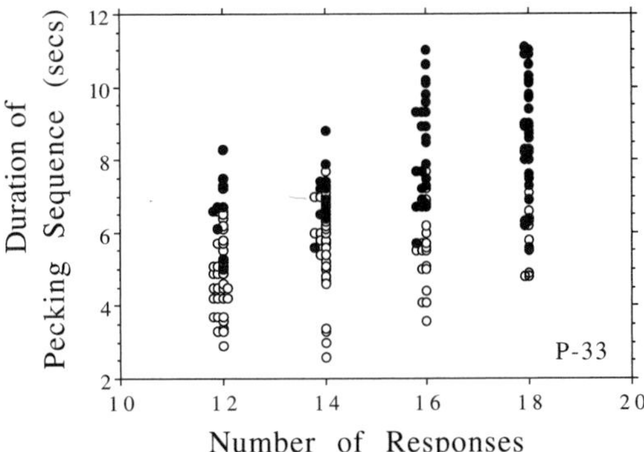

Figure 15.8. Scatterplots of the times taken by a pigeon to emit sample ratios as a function of the number of responses emitted. Each point represents the outcome of a single trial. *Open symbols* indicate a response to the small-choice alternative, and *filled symbols* indicate a response to the large-choice alternative. (From "Numerosity Discrimination: Both Time and Number Matter," by J. G. Fetterman, 1993, *Journal of Experimental Psychology: Animal Behavior Processes*, *19*, 149–164. Copyright 1993 by American Psychological Association. Reprinted with permission.)

tested with probe FRs of 12, 14, 16, and 18 responses. Data are shown for a single pigeon, but every subject displayed the pattern shown in the figure (i.e., the squared semipartial correlations were significant for all birds). Each point represents performance on a single trial. Unfilled symbols indicate a choice of the key associated with the smaller ratio and filled symbols indicate a choice of the "large" key. The visual representation is similar to the information provided by a semipartial correlation coefficient. The influence of response number, commingled with the duration of the pecking sequences, is represented by the increasing numbers of filled symbols ("large") for progressively larger probe ratios. The singular contribution of ratio time, over and above ratio value, is represented by the distribution of points in each column. Mostly, filled symbols lie above unfilled symbols, indicating that the pigeon was more likely to respond to the "large" choice when the time taken to emit a certain number of responses was longer than when it was shorter.

Although compelling, the data of Fetterman (1993) are correlational. Fetterman et al. (1986) provided a more direct assessment of the multiple control hypothesis by manipulating the timing of events in a numerosity discrimination. Pigeons were trained to produce intermittent flashes of a feeder light by pecking on a key that could be lit by red or green lights. Pecks on this key produced the light flashes according to a variable-interval (VI) 5-s schedule. Pecking on this key sometimes produced reinforcement after four light flashes, provided the key color was red. On other trials, pecking led to reinforcement after 16 light flashes, provided the key color was green. Reinforcement occurred equally after 4 flashes and 16 flashes. Trials began with the key lit red, but the pigeon could change the color to green by pecking a second (changeover) key; the only consequences of pecks to this key were to change the color of the main key and to darken and render inoperative the changeover key (i.e., only a single changeover response was allowed on a trial). The pigeons typically pecked on the red key, producing light flashes until food was delivered. When food was not scheduled for red key responses, the birds typically pecked on the red key until more than four flashes had occurred, and then pecked the changeover key, changing the color of the main key to green, and responded on the green key for the remainder of the trial.

Although reinforcement was based on the number of light flashes (4 or 16), temporal cues were also predictive. The flashes were presented aperiodically, but the fourth event occurred relatively soon after trial onset, whereas the 16th event occurred after an irregular, but longer time. The degree of control exerted by the duration of the flash sequences was assessed during probe sessions in which the timing of the light flashes was altered. In different sessions, flashes were presented more frequently (VI 3.75 s) or less frequently (VI 7.5 s) than the baseline rate (VI 5 s). If the number of events was the sole basis of discrimination, then the number of events produced before a switch from red (few) to green (many) should remain unchanged, even though the times taken to produce the events would be more (VI 7.5 s) or less (VI 3.75 s) than baseline. If, on the other hand, the birds based decisions to switch from red to green based on the duration of the event sequences, then the timing of the switches should remain the same, but the number of events before the switch would be fewer (VI 7.5 s) or greater (VI 3.75 s) than the baseline.

Figure 15.9 shows the results in terms of the mean number of events prior to a switch (top

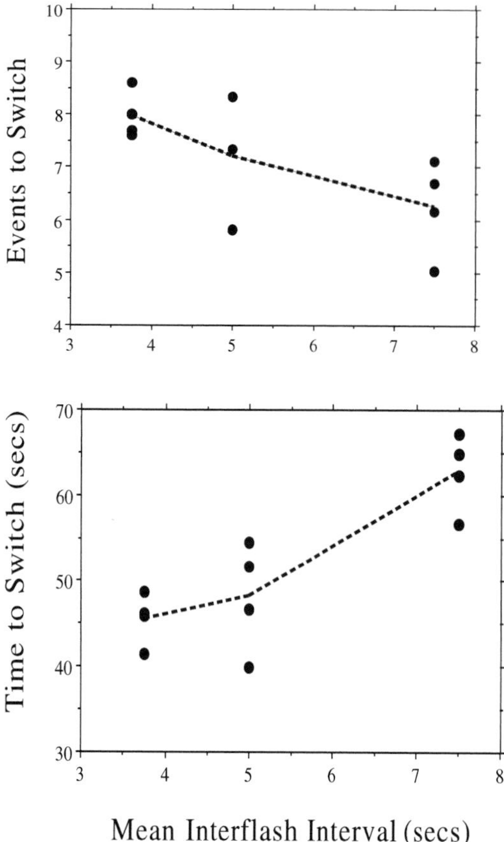

Figure 15.9. Mean number of events prior to a switch from a choice associated with "few" events to a choice associated with "many" events as a function of the average time between events (*top*). *Bottom,* Associated times before a switch from "few" to "many." Each column of points shows the data of individual pigeons. (Adapted from "Scaling of Events Spaced in Time," by J. G. Fetterman, D. A. Stubbs, and L. R. Dreyfus, 1986, *Behavioural Processes, 13,* 53–68.)

panel) and the mean time before a switch (bottom panel). Both measures are shown as a function of the mean interflash interval. Four pigeons were studied and each column of points represents the individual performances. The solid lines through the points represent the means of the four birds. When flash rate increased, the average number of events before a switch increased, and when flash rate decreased, the average number of events decreased (top panel). This pattern is consistent with a timing hypothesis. However, the bottom panel shows the opposite pattern for the time measure. When flash rate increased, the mean time to a switch decreased, and when flash rate decreased, the mean time to a switch increased. This pattern is consistent with a counting hypothesis. In combination, the patterns reflect a compromise between the hypotheses, demonstrating that the birds' choices were controlled by both the number of light flashes and the duration of the light flash sequences.

The review of numerosity discriminations supports the idea that both number and time contribute to perceived numerosity. But what of temporal discriminations, which typically are conveyed by presenting an unchanging light or tone for different durations? In the absence of stimulus information about the duration of events, explanations of timing in animals have quite naturally focused on cognitive mechanisms (Fetterman, 1996). Hence, little attention has been paid to the contribution of stimulus events to temporal discriminations. We do know that temporal discriminations are affected by the properties of the stimuli that are used to communicate a duration. For instance, filled durations (lights on) are discriminated more accurately than unfilled durations (lights off; Mantanus, 1981). Durations of access to food are discriminated more accurately than light durations (Spetch & Wilkie, 1981). And, pigeons discriminate light durations more accurately than they discriminate tone durations (Roberts, Cheng, & Cohen, 1989). However, we do not know much about the events during the various signals that contribute to the perception of stimulus duration (cf. Gibson, 1975).

Rilling's (1967) analysis of temporal discrimination suggested that pigeons' pecks to a key constituted the basis of the discrimination. But, more typically, there are varied and complex behavioral repertoires that occur during interreward intervals (e.g., Staddon & Simmelhag, 1971); these behavioral repertoires have been regarded as potential sources of stimulus control in timing tasks (e.g., see a review of the role of collateral behaviors in timing by Richelle & Lejeune, 1980). Killeen and Fetterman (1988) formally developed this idea and invoked it as a primary causal mechanism in their BeT, arguing that animals use their ongoing behaviors to judge their position in time with respect to a forthcoming reinforcement.

Fetterman, Killeen, and Hall (1998) assessed the behavioral mediation hypothesis by observing pigeons trained to discriminate between 6-s and 12-s presentations of a houselight. Some birds were trained on a spatial choice arrangement whereby left-key and right-key choices signified short and long durations. Other birds were trained under a nonspatial arrangement in which the position of the correct choice was identified by key color (red/green) rather than by key location. All birds were observed during daily sessions using the techniques pioneered by Staddon and Simmelhag (1971).

Figure 15.10 shows data from a representative pigeon trained under the spatial choice procedure. The figure shows the relative frequencies of different behaviors in 1-s bins. It is clear that a query about the duration of the signal could be answered accurately based on the ongoing behaviors. The figure shows that this pigeon engaged in different behaviors that occurred at different times and thus were predictive of the duration of the houselight stimulus. Pecking in front of the left ("short") key occurred early in the trial, whereas pecking in front of the right ("long") key occurred later in the trial.

Once the original discrimination (6 s vs. 12 s) had been learned, the task was made more difficult by reducing the value of the longer stimulus from 12 s to 9 s, with the goal of increasing error rates, affording a different method of analysis. Accuracy decreased from 95% correct responses to about 70% correct responses. The distributions of behavior did not change much in this new condition, such that the "short" behavior remained predictive, but both it and the "long" behavior predicted the time associated with the long choice alternative. If this pigeon used its behavior to discriminate signal duration, then choice accuracy should be higher on short than on long signal trials (because there would be more "behavioral confusion" on long trials). This prediction was borne out by the data (98% correct choices on short vs. 76% correct choices on long signal trials).

A more stringent test of the role of mediating behaviors in temporal discriminations is provided by a confusion analysis. Behaviors that immediately preceded choice on long signal trials were classified according to whether the choice response was correct or incorrect. If a "short" behavior preceded a choice when a long response was called for and that behavior provided the cue for choice, then the subject should incorrectly classify the signal duration. Conversely, when a "long" behavior preceded choice, the signal classification should be more accurate. The results support the behavioral mediation hypothesis. When a "short" behavior preceded choice, the accuracy of discrimination was 13% ($n = 44$). When a "long" behavior" preceded choice, the accuracy of discrimination was 98% ($n = 53$). These results provide compelling evidence of the role of mediating behaviors in temporal discriminations.

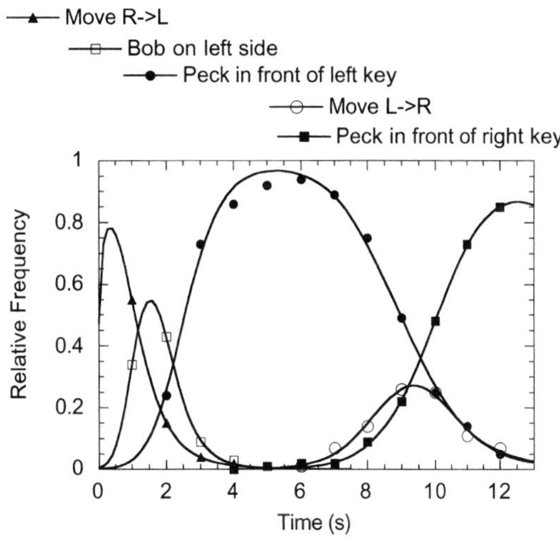

Figure 15.10. Relative frequency of different collateral behaviors in a temporal discrimination task. The figure legend identifies the behaviors. (From "Watching the Clock," by J. G. Fetterman, P. R. Killeen, and S. Hall, 1998, *Behavioural Processes, 44*, 211–224. Copyright 1998 by Elsevier. Reprinted with permission.)

DELAYED DISCRIMINATIONS

A final point of comparison between timing and numerosity tasks involves short-term retention of durations and numerosities as assessed by symbolic delayed-matching-to-sample (SDMTS) and related procedures. Normally, when the samples consist of simple, punctate stimuli (e.g., red vs. green), increases in a retention interval produce overlapping and parallel retention functions for the samples. A more precise statement is that the slopes and intercepts of individual sample retention functions are similar. When, however, samples consist of different durations or different numerosities, there is a divergence of the retention functions such that one sample is forgotten faster than the other (a difference in the slopes of the functions).

Spetch and Wilkie (1983) provided the prototype demonstration of this phenomenon in the temporal domain. After training pigeons to discriminate between short and long duration signals, the birds were given retention tests in which the presentation of the comparison stimuli was delayed from the offset of the signal. On these test trials, accuracy after short-signals remained roughly constant with increases in the retention interval (slope close to zero), whereas accuracy following long signals showed a sharp decline (negative slope) to levels below chance performance. The result, now well known and replicated many times (e.g., Fetterman, 1995; Spetch & Rusak, 1992), is referred to as the *choose-short* effect. Spetch and Wilkie (1983) advanced an account of this memory bias termed *subjective shortening*. According to this account, memory for each of the samples decays over time, with the decay process involving a shrinkage of the temporal representation stored in working memory. Accordingly, the representation of the "long" sample increasingly resembles that of the "short" sample, producing the bias to respond to the choice alternative associated with the short sample (see Roberts, 1997, for a detailed explication of this model and its relation to the mode control model of Meck & Church, 1983).

Fetterman and MacEwen (1989) were the first to provide evidence suggesting a biased forgetting effect along the numerosity dimension similar to the choose-short effect. Pigeons trained to discriminate between different FR samples (FR10 vs. FR40) were tested for retention of the samples using standard SDMTS procedures. The tests yielded divergent retention functions whereby retention of the small FR showed little or no decrease with increases in the retention interval and retention of the large FR showed a precipitous decline with increasing delays between the sample and choice—the *choose-small* effect.

Although the data of Fetterman and MacEwen (1989) appear to indicate a forgetting effect in the numerosity domain akin to temporal forgetting, Roberts, Macuda, and Brodbeck (1995) pointed out that the duration of the pecking sequences was confounded with peck number (i.e., FR10 samples took less time to emit than FR40 samples). In other words, the pigeons could have timed the FRs and the choose-small effect reported by Fetterman and MacEwen might, in fact, represent another instance of the choose-short effect.

Roberts et al. (1995) used a procedure in which the duration of different numerosities was the same—4 s for each numerosity sample. In their task, pigeons were presented with different numbers of light flashes and were trained to choose one key after two flashes and another key after eight flashes. When retention tests were given, the resulting forgetting functions for small and large numerosities revealed the choose-small effect. The function for the smaller numerosity was virtually flat, whereas the curve for the larger numerosity declined rapidly to accuracy levels well below chance. These findings appear to indicate that the biased forgetting of numerosities is not dependent on differences in the temporal extent of the numerosity samples and "that time and number are represented by a common mechanism" (Roberts, 1997).

A final point of comparison involves delayed discriminations of numerosity and discriminations of punctate events and is provided by data reported by Fetterman and MacEwen (2003). As noted (see figure 15.1), pigeons were trained to discriminate between samples composed of hue (red/green) and FR requirements (FR5/FR20). One group (H) of pigeons learned to discriminate based on hue; the pecking requirement was irrelevant to comparison choice. Another group (N) learned to discriminate based on FR value; hue was irrelevant. Retention tests were given following acquisition and the results of these tests for both groups are shown in figure 15.11.

The retention data in the figure are separated according to the pecking requirement and are displayed as a function of the delay between samples and choices. The retention functions for group N diverge with increasing delay embodying the choose-small effect, whereas the FR requirement did not affect retention for group H. The result for group H was somewhat surprising because, although FR was not a relevant feature of the sample, prior research with visual discriminations demonstrates that longer samples are retained better than shorter samples, perhaps due to better encoding (e.g., Grant, 1976). The lack of a difference in this case may be due to a ceiling effect.

Based on the similarity of biased forgetting results in numerosity and timing tasks described above, Roberts (e.g., Roberts, 1997; Roberts et al., 1995) has made a case for a common underlying mechanism based on the mode control model of timing and counting first described by Meck and Church (1983). The mechanism is an expanded version of the internal clock model of timing (e.g., Church, 1984) that is the most influential account of timing behavior in nonhuman animals. The important feature of the extension involves a "dual-mode" switch that can operate in a "count" or a

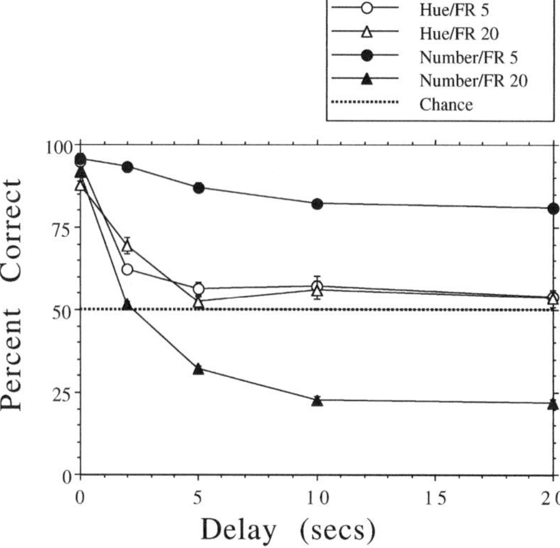

Figure 15.11. Percent correct responses as a function of delay between a sample stimulus and presentation of comparison choices. Data are the means of four pigeons, and the bars represent ±1 *SEM*. *Filled symbols* show performance for pigeons trained to discriminate hue samples, and *open samples* show performance for pigeons trained to discriminate samples based on FR value. Trials for both groups are separated according to whether a pigeon pecked 5 times (FR5) or 20 times (FR20) on the sample key. (From "Acquisition and Retention in Compound Matching with Hue and Peck Number Elements," by J. G. Fetterman and D. MacEwen, 2003, *Learning and Motivation, 34*, 354–371. Copyright 2003 by Elsevier. Reprinted with permission.)

"time" mode (see Roberts, 1997, for details). In either mode, the representation of the stimulus consists of pulses in an accumulator that, ultimately, reside in working memory. During retention intervals, pulses are lost from memory as a consequence of an unspecified decay process. The result is that the pulse number representation of the "bigger" stimulus increasingly resembles that of the "smaller" stimulus, producing the biased forgetting effect. This extended version of the internal clock model affords a complementarity of many of the principles of timing and counting discussed in this chapter. Hence, it has appeal as a parsimonious account of seemingly different discriminations.

Parsimony can be achieved in various ways, however, and a different account of biased forgetting in delayed discriminations of numerosity and temporal stimuli not only explains these effects but also provides an explanation for the forgetting of presence/absence discriminations. This different account does not rely on an internal clock mechanism. In a presence/absence discrimination, subjects (typically, pigeons) are taught to discriminate between the occurrence and nonoccurrence of an event, such as the presentation (or not) of food. When delays are inserted between the samples and choice alternatives, pigeons tend to select the choice alternative associated with the "absence" sample, regardless of the occurrence or nonoccurrence of the sample event (e.g., Grant, 1991). Wixted and Dougherty (1996) have made a case that the various instances of biased forgetting involve discriminations established on the basis of stimuli that differ in salience (e.g., short vs. long durations; few vs. many events; absence vs. presence of an event). Delayed tests of the samples have the effect of reducing the remembered salience of both samples, so that the memory of the more salient sample increasingly resembles that of the less salient sample. The result, akin to generalization along the dimension of event salience, is that subjects increasingly respond to the choice associated with the less salient sample, thereby producing biased forgetting.

It is not clear which account is correct. The dual-mode theory appeals to internal mechanisms, whereas the salience account focuses on properties of the stimulus events. These are different levels of analysis, with the latter approach being more consistent with the theme of this chapter. Yet another proposal (Zentall, 1997) suggests that these effects are due to instructional failure. It is a safe prediction that the retention of temporal and numerical stimuli will remain a topic of interest for the foreseeable future.

SUMMARY

Time and number are often interwoven, especially in ecologically valid contexts. For instance, an optimal forager might monitor the time spent foraging and the number of prey received, basing its decisions to leave a food patch on one or both of these sources of information. However, analyses of foraging have typically emphasized the role of temporal information (e.g., Kacelnik, Brunner, & Gibbon, 1990; Todd & Kacelnik, 1993) and have used timing theory as a proximal mechanism for explaining foraging behavior. This approach ignores the possibility that time and number together might serve as the heuristic guiding patch decisions. What might account for the failure to consider the contributions of both time and number to behavioral decision making?

One answer is that experimental research has typically focused on one dimension while controlling for correlated (confounding) features of the other. This analytical approach is most evident in recent investigations of numerosity discriminations in which the durations of sequences of different numerosities are equated. Although this approach is not without its virtues, it probably does not represent the causal structure of the real world (cf. Brunswik, 1956), in which time and number covary and where it is advantageous to rely on both sources of information. It is clear that such an approach begs the question of the role of stimuli, overlapping and otherwise, that contribute to the learning, perception, and retention of time- and number-based events.

References

Allan, L. G., & Gibbon, J. (1991). Human bisection at the geometric mean. *Learning and Motivation*, *22*, 39–58.

Alsop, B., & Honig, W. K. (1991). Sequential stimuli and relative numerosity discriminations in pigeons. *Journal of Experimental Psychology: Animal Behavior Processes*, *17*, 386–395.

Bizo, L. A., & White, K. G. (1994a). The behavioral theory of timing: Reinforcer rate determines pacemaker rate. *Journal of the Experimental Analysis of Behavior*, *61*, 19–33.

Bizo, L. A., & White, K. G. (1994b). Pacemaker rate in the behavioral theory of timing. *Journal of Experimental Psychology: Animal Behavior Processes*, *20*, 308–321.

Blough, D. S. (1992). Features of forms in pigeon perception. In W. K. Honig & J. G. Fetterman (Eds.), *Cognitive aspects of stimulus control* (pp. 263–278). Hillsdale, NJ: Erlbaum.

Bowers, R. L., & Richards, R. W. (1990). Pigeons' short-term memory for temporal and visual stimuli in delayed matching-to-sample. *Animal Learning and Behavior*, *18*, 23–28.

Brunswik, E. (1956). *Perception and the representative design of psychological experiments*. Berkeley: University of California Press.

Carter, D. E., & Werner, T. J. (1978). Complex learning and information processing by pigeons: A critical analysis. *Journal of the Experimental Analysis of Behavior*, *29*, 565–601.

Church, R. M. (1978). The internal clock. In S. H. Hulse, H. Fowler, & W. K. Honig (Eds.), *Cognitive processes in animal behavior* (pp. 227–310). Hillsdale, NJ: Erlbaum.

Church, R. M. (1984). Properties of the internal clock. In J. Gibbon & L. Allan (Eds.), *Timing and time perception* (pp. 566–582). New York: New York Academy of Sciences.

Church, R. M., & Broadbent, H. A. (1990). Alternative representations of time, number, and rate. *Cognition*, *37*, 55–81.

Church, R. M., & Deluty, M. Z. (1977). The bisection of temporal intervals. *Journal of Experimental Psychology: Animal Behavior Processes*, *3*, 216–228.

Cohen, L. R., Looney, R. A., Brady, J. H., & Aucella, A. F. (1976). Differential sample response schedules in the acquisition of conditional discriminations by pigeons. *Journal of the Experimental Analysis of Behavior*, *26*, 301–314.

Cook, R. G. (1992). The visual perception and processing of textures by pigeons. In W. K. Honig & J. G. Fetterman (Eds.), *Cognitive aspects of stimulus control*. Hillsdale, NJ: Erlbaum.

Dews, P. B. (1970). The theory of fixed-interval responding. In W. N. Schoenfeld (Eds.), *The theory of reinforcement schedules*. New York: Appleton-Century-Crofts.

Fetterman, J. G. (1993). Numerosity discrimination: Both time and number matter. *Journal of Experimental Psychology: Animal Behavior Processes*, *19*, 149–164.

Fetterman, J. G. (1994, May). *An experimental synthesis of timing and counting processes*. Paper presented at the meeting of the Society for Quantitative Analyses of Behavior, Atlanta, GA.

Fetterman, J. G. (1995). The psychophysics of remembered duration. *Animal Learning and Behavior*, *23*, 49–62.

Fetterman, J. G. (1996a, November). *Categorical scaling of number*. Paper presented at the meeting of the Psychonomic Society, Chicago.

Fetterman, J. G. (1996b). Dimensions of stimulus complexity. *Journal of Experimental Psychology: Animal Behavior Processes*, *22*, 3–18.

Fetterman, J. G., Dreyfus, L. R., & Stubbs, D. A. (1985). Scaling of response-based events. *Journal of Experimental Psychology: Animal Behavior Processes*, *11*, 388–404.

Fetterman, J. G., & Killeen, P. R. (1991). Adjusting the pacemaker. *Learning and Motivation*, *22*, 226–252.

Fetterman, J. G., & Killeen, P. R. (1992). Time discrimination in *Columba livia* and *Homo sapiens*. *Journal of Experimental Psychology: Animal Behavior Processes*, *18*, 80–94.

Fetterman, J. G., & Killeen, P. R. (1995). Categorical scaling of time: Implications for clock-counter models. *Journal of Experimental Psychology: Animal Behavior Processes, 21*, 43–63.

Fetterman, J. G., Killeen, P. R., & Hall, S. (1998). Watching the clock. *Behavioural Processes, 44*, 211–224.

Fetterman, J. G., & MacEwen, D. (1989). Short-term memory for responses: The "choose-small" effect. *Journal of the Experimental Analysis of Behavior, 52*, 311–324.

Fetterman, J. G., & MacEwen, D. (2003). Acquisition and retention in compound matching with hue and peck number elements. *Learning and Motivation, 34*, 354–371.

Fetterman, J. G., Stubbs, D. A., & Dreyfus, L. R. (1986). Scaling of events spaced in time. *Behavioural Processes, 13*, 53–68.

Gibbon, J. (1977). Scalar expectancy theory and Weber's Law in animal timing. *Psychological Review, 84*, 279–325.

Gibbon, J. (1986). The structure of subjective time: How time flies. In G. H. Bower (Ed.), *The psychology of learning and motivation* (pp. 105–135). San Diego, CA: Academic Press.

Gibbon, J. (1991). Origins of scalar timing. *Learning and Motivation, 22*, 3–38.

Gibbon, J., & Church, R. M. (1984). Sources of variability in an information processing theory of timing. In H. L. Roitblat, T. G. Bever, & H. S. Terrace (Eds.), *Animal cognition* (pp. 465–488). Hillsdale, NJ: Erlbaum.

Gibbon, J., & Church, R. M. (1990). Representation of time. *Cognition, 37*, 23–54.

Gibson, J. J. (1966). The problem of temporal order in stimulation and perception. *Journal of Psychology, 62*, 141–149.

Gibson, J. J. (1975). Events are perceivable but time is not. In J. T. Fraser & N. Lawrence (Eds.), *The study of time: II* (pp. 142–149). New York: Springer-Verlag.

Grant, D. S. (1976). Effect of sample presentation time on long-delay matching in the pigeon. *Learning and Motivation, 7*, 580–590.

Grant, D. S. (1991). Symmetrical and asymmetrical coding of food and no-food samples in delayed matching in pigeons. *Journal of Experimental Psychology: Animal Behavior Processes, 17*, 186–193.

Helson, H. (1964). *Adaptation-level theory: An experimental and systematic approach to behavior*. New York: Harper.

Herrnstein, R. J., Loveland, D. H., & Cable, C. (1976). Natural concepts in the pigeon. *Journal of Experimental Psychology: Animal Behavior Processes, 2*, 285–302.

Higa, J. J., & Staddon, J. E. R. (1997). Dynamic models of rapid temporal control in animals. In C. M. Bradshaw & E. Szabadi (Eds.), *Time and behaviour: Psychological and neurobehavioural analyses* (pp. 1–40). Amsterdam: Elsevier.

Hobson, S. L., & Newman, F. (1981). Fixed-ratio counting schedules: Response and time measures considered. In M. L. Commons & J. A. Nevin (Eds.), *Quantitative analyses of behavior: Discriminative properties of reinforcement schedules*. Cambridge, MA: Ballinger.

Hulse, S. H. (1993). The present status of animal cognition. *Psychological Science, 4*, 154–155.

Kacelnik, A., Brunner, D., & Gibbon, J. (1990). Timing mechanisms in optimal foraging: Some applications of scalar expectancy theory. In R. N. Hughes (Ed.), *Behavioural mechanisms of food selection* (pp. 61–82). Berlin: Springer-Verlag.

Kamil, A. C., Yoerg, S. I., & Clements, K. C. (1988). Rules to leave by: Patch departure in foraging blue jays. *Animal Behaviour, 36*, 843–853.

Kamin, L. J. (1969). Predictability, surprise, attention, and conditioning. In B. A. Campbell & R. M. Church (Eds.), *Punishment and aversive behavior* (pp. 279–296). New York: Appleton-Century-Crofts.

Killeen, P. R., & Fetterman, J. G. (1988). A behavioral theory of timing. *Psychological Review, 95*, 274–295.

Lydersen, T., & Perkins, D. (1974). Effects of response-produced stimuli upon conditional discrimination performance. *Journal of the Experimental Analysis of Behavior, 21*, 307–314.

Mantanus, H. (1981). Empty and filled interval discrimination by pigeons. *Behaviour Analysis Letters, 1*, 217–224.

Martin-Iverson, M. T., Fibiger, H. C., & Wilkie, D. M. (1988). Alteration in the perception of food quantity by rats induced by manipulations of hunger and food sweetness. *Learning and Motivation, 19*, 44–65.

Meck, W. H. (1997). Application of a mode-control model of temporal integration to counting and timing behavior. In C. M. Bradshaw & E. Szabadi (Eds.), *Time and behaviour: Psychological and neurobehavioural analyses*. Amsterdam: Elsevier.

Meck, W. H., & Church, R. M. (1983). A mode control model of counting and timing processes. *Journal of Experimental Psychology: Animal Behavior Processes, 9*, 320–334.

Morgan, L., Killeen, P. R., & Fetterman, J. G. (1993). Changing rates of reinforcement perturbs the flow of time. *Behavioural Processes, 30*, 259–272.

Porter, D., & Neuringer, A. (1985). Music discrimination by pigeons. *Journal of Experimental Psychology: Animal Behavior Processes, 10*, 138–148.

Richelle, M., & Lejeune, H. (1980). *Time in animal behavior*. Oxford: Pergamon Press.

Rilling, M. (1967). Number of responses as a stimulus in fixed interval and fixed ratio schedules. *Journal of Comparative and Physiological Psychology*, *63*, 60–65.

Roberts, W. A. (1995). Simultaneous numerical and temporal processing in the pigeon. *Current Directions in Psychological Science*, *4*, 47–51.

Roberts, W. A. (1997). Does a common mechanism account for timing and counting phenomena in the pigeon? In C. M. Bradshaw & E. Szabadi (Eds.), *Time and behaviour: Psychological and neurobehavioural analyses*. Amsterdam: Elsevier.

Roberts, W. A., Cheng, K., & Cohen, J. S. (1989). Timing light and tone signals in pigeons. *Journal of Experimental Psychology: Animal Behavior Processes*, *15*, 23–35.

Roberts, W. A., Macuda, T., & Brodbeck, D. R. (1995). Memory for number of light flashes in pigeons. *Animal Learning and Behavior*, *23*, 182–188.

Sacks, R. A., Kamil, A. C., & Mack, R. (1972). The effects of fixed-ratio sample requirements on matching-to-sample in the pigeon. *Psychonomic Science*, *26*, 291–293.

Spetch, M. L., & Rusak, B. (1992). Time present and time past. In W. K. Honig & J. G. Fetterman (Eds.), *Cognitive aspects of stimulus control* (pp. 47–67). Hillsdale, NJ: Erlbaum.

Spetch, M. L., & Wilkie, D. M. (1981). Duration discrimination is better with food access as the signal than with light as the signal. *Learning and Motivation*, *12*, 40–64.

Spetch, M. L., & Wilkie, D. M. (1983). Subjective shortening: A model of pigeons' memory for event duration. *Journal of Experimental Psychology: Animal Behavior Processes*, *9*, 14–30.

Staddon, J. E. R., & Higa, J. J. (1999). Time and memory: Towards a pacemaker-free theory of interval timing. *Journal of the Experimental Analysis of Behavior*, *71*, 215–252.

Staddon, J. E. R., & Simmelhag, V. L. (1971). The "superstition" experiment: A re-examination of its implications for the principles of adaptive behavior. *Psychological Review*, *78*, 3–43.

Stubbs, A. (1968). The discrimination of stimulus duration by pigeons. *Journal of the Experimental Analysis of Behavior*, *11*, 223–238.

Stubbs, D. A. (1976). Scaling of stimulus duration by pigeons. *Journal of the Experimental Analysis of Behavior*, *26*, 15–25.

Stubbs, D. A. (1980). Temporal discrimination and a free-operant psychophysical procedure. *Journal of the Experimental Analysis of Behavior*, *33*, 167–185.

Todd, I. A., & Kacelnik, A. (1993). Psychological mechanisms and the marginal value theorem: Dynamics of scalar memory for travel time. *Animal Behaviour*, *46*, 765–775.

Urcuioli, P. J., & Honig, W. K. (1980). Stimulus control of choice in conditional discriminations by sample-specific behaviors. *Journal of Experimental Psychology: Animal Behavior Processes*, *6*, 251–277.

Wasserman, E. A. (1993). Comparative cognition: Beginning the second century of the study of animal intelligence. *Psychological Bulletin*, *113*, 211–228.

Wixted, J. T., & Dougherty, D. H. (1996). Memory for asymmetric events. In D. L. Medin (Eds.), *The psychology of learning and motivation* (pp. 89–126). San Diego, CA: Academic Press.

Zeiler, M. D. (1985). Pure timing in temporal differentiation. *Journal of the Experimental Analysis of Behavior*, *43*, 183–193.

Zentall, T. R. (1997). Animal memory: The role of "instructions." *Learning and Motivation*, *28*, 248–267.

VI

CONCEPTUALIZATION AND CATEGORIZATION

16

Relational Discrimination Learning in Pigeons

ROBERT G. COOK AND EDWARD A. WASSERMAN

Stability and change—both of these fundamental features of the world must be discriminated and responded to in order for organisms to survive and reproduce. Being able to recognize and connect the continuity of the past and the present is key to unlocking the future. Thinking about the nature of complexity in general has suggested that the boundary between stability and change is a vital biological and psychological location that influences a wide variety of adaptive behaviors (Neuringer, 2004; Wasserman, Young, & Cook, 2004).

One important aspect of this border revolves around being able to detect the abstract relations among various kinds of stimuli. One such stimulus relation involves the complementary twin concepts of *sameness* and *difference*. William James suggested that the recognition and integration of the "sense of sameness is the very keel and backbone of consciousness" (James, 1910, p. 240). James also appreciated the crucial importance of its balance with the concept of difference: "We go through the world, carrying on the two functions abreast, discovering differences in the like, and likenesses in the different" (James, 1890, p. 529).

Recent research has shown that both humans and animals can perceive, discriminate, and produce constancy (sameness) and variability (difference) in a variety of settings (Delius, 1994; Nickerson, 2002; Wasserman et al., 2004). Although we have concentrated our independent empirical and analytical efforts on this issue within the stimulus domain, the recent work of Balsam (Balsam, Deich, Ohyama, & Stokes, 1998), Eisenberger (Eisenberger & Cameron, 1998), and Neuringer (Miller & Neuringer, 2000; Neuringer, 2004; Neuringer, Deiss, & Olson, 2000) has shed fresh light on when and how people and animals vary or repeat their behavior. Understanding how biological systems deal with the relational concepts of sameness and difference is essential to revealing the nature of an animal's adaptation to its environment and to the very origins of cognition.

Comparative psychologists have long sought to understand the types of intelligence that we share with other species (Cook, 2001; Darwin, 1897; Wasserman, 1993). Such knowledge elucidates the origins and nature of intelligent behavior, provides insight into the mechanisms of intelligence in both human and nonhuman animals, and suggests how this information is psychologically represented by the nervous system. Furthermore, such animal research greatly facilitates our understanding of the cognitive and neural substrates of behavior—without the involvement and complications of language. With this comparative agenda in mind, here we review and compare our recent research exploring how one avian species, the pigeon, processes the stimulus relations created by visual stimuli containing same and different items.

Being able to form and to use concepts is a key property of intelligence. Its great benefit is that it releases behavior from the direct control of the immediate stimulus and its history of reinforcement and permits flexible and adaptive solutions to novel problems and unfamiliar situations. As a result, we can engage in behaviors unshackled from our previous experience with specific stimuli. Such relational cognitive abilities allow us to make accurate inductions about new events and their interrelations, thus forming the basis for our use and appreciation of language, mathematics, abstract concepts, and even such fine arts as music.

Because of its importance to understanding animal cognition, our two laboratories, quite independently, started to investigate how pigeons learn one type of relational learning task—the same/different (S/D) discrimination. In a S/D discrimination task, the animal responds "same" when two or more stimuli are identical to one another and it responds "different" when one or more stimuli are different from one another. In 1995, we simultaneously published our first results examining this behavior (Cook, Cavoto, & Cavoto, 1995; Wasserman, Hugart, & Kirkpatrick-Steger, 1995). In both studies, the pigeons readily learned to perform our respective S/D discriminations and transferred this behavior to novel stimuli, suggesting that they had formed some type of generalized concept. At the time, we both proposed that the basis for this transfer might have been the formation of a relational S/D concept.

We now believe that these pigeons may have learned distinctly different things in our two tasks, despite the nominal procedural similarities they shared. As we develop later, this psychological divergence potentially reflects different, and perhaps flexible, cognitive mechanisms mediating how relational discriminations are acquired. If so, then our work documents an important case of a single animal species, besides humans, divergently processing and discriminating relational patterns of stimulation.

The purpose of the present chapter is to summarize our considerable, but previously separate, S/D discrimination findings in a single place in order to develop a more comprehensive picture of the cognitive mechanisms that may underlie relational conceptualization by pigeons. The next several sections outline our respective experimental procedures and convergent findings. The middle sections present and discuss our divergent and conflicting evidence. In the final sections, we sketch several theoretical perspectives regarding these data and potential routes to their reconciliation and integration.

BASIC SAME/DIFFERENT PROCEDURES AND RESULTS

To provide a firmer basis for understanding our results, we first review our basic S/D discrimination procedures. In both laboratories, testing is done using computer-driven, touchscreen-equipped, operant chambers. The pigeons are taught to respond differently depending on whether the items displayed on the computer screen are identical (a *same* trial) or contain one or more nonidentical elements (a *different* trial). The following describes a typical trial from each laboratory and the types of stimuli used to create these same and different displays, first with simultaneously presented elements and then with successively presented elements.

Cook: Simultaneous S/D Discrimination

Each S/D trial begins with a single peck at a small white ready signal on a black screen. This ready display is followed by the presentation of either a same or a different display. On different trials, the pigeons are required to locate the different item within a display and to peck it a fixed number of times. On same trials, a yoked number of pecks are required anywhere on the same display. After responding to the display is complete, two "choice" hoppers are illuminated, one on the left and one on the right side of the chamber. The pigeons indicate their reaction to the display by choosing between these hoppers (e.g., left = different, right = same). A correct hopper choice is reinforced with food, whereas an incorrect hopper choice results in a 15-s timeout.

Depending on the question being examined, up to five distinctively same and different classes of stimulus displays (texture, feature, geometric, object, and photograph; figure 16.1) varying heterogeneously in shape and color can be concurrently tested (Cook, Katz, & Cavoto, 1997; Cook, Katz, & Kelly, 1999). The top row of figure 16.1 shows the *texture* display type (Cook et al., 1995). These displays consist of 24 × 16 (18 × 12 cm) arrays of small colored shape elements. The individual elements of these displays are combined from as many as 54 shapes (4 to 7 mm in size) and 20 colors. *Color different* displays (not shown) have one or more elements within them differing in color but not shape, whereas *shape different* displays have elements that differ in shape but not color. *Same* displays consist of identically colored and shaped elements. The *feature* display type is similar (Cook, 1992), but these displays require the pigeon to detect the global S/D relations and to ignore the irrelevant local variations among the elements (again only a shape example is shown). The *geometric* display type is the same overall size, but these displays consist of a 3 × 2 array of geometric shapes defined by either a color (not shown) or shape difference presented as a single odd element, rather than a block of elements. The *object* display type is similar, but the elements of these displays consist of digitized depictions of natural objects (e.g., flowers, birds, fish, and humans). The *photograph* display type consists of digitized 200 × 200 pixel photographs of objects and landscapes. These latter two display types also require the pigeons to process the displays globally, because each element is composed of many local parts differing in shape and color. Both color and gray-scale versions of the object and photograph displays have been tested. Altogether, these different stimulus classes create an extremely wide variety of relational stimuli (over 10,000 trial-unique displays, given the numbers of colors, shapes, and pictures), with specific displays often not reappearing for months.

Wasserman: Simultaneous S/D Discrimination

Each S/D trial again begins with a single peck, but to a black ready signal on a white display screen. This ready display is followed by the presentation of a same or a different array of Macintosh

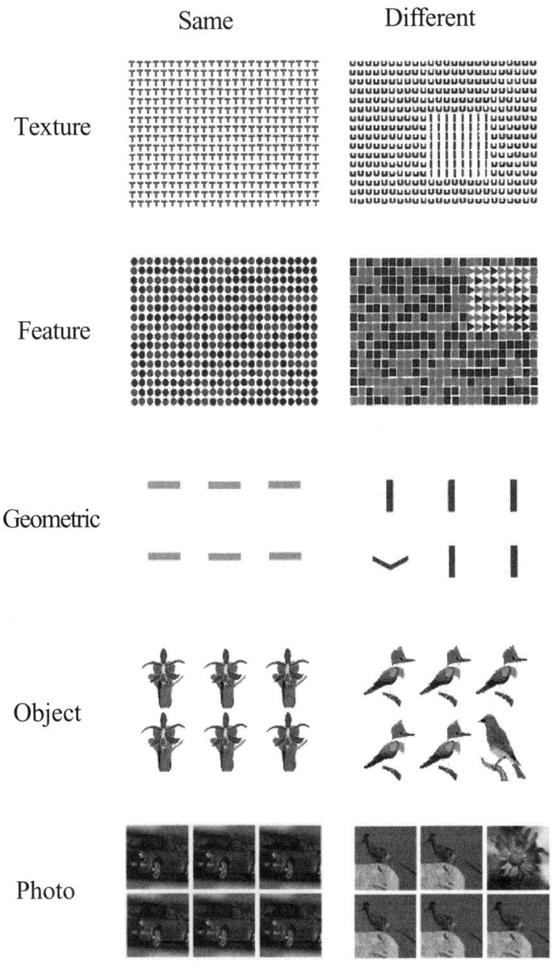

Figure 16.1. Examples of the five display types tested in Cook et al.'s (1997, 1999) experiments. *Left,* Examples of same displays for each display type (the example for the feature display type depicts a shape-same display). *Right,* Examples of different displays for each display type. The examples for the texture, feature, and geometrical display types depict shape-different displays, but comparable displays having color differences were also tested. (Modified from "Pigeon same/different concept learning with multiple stimulus classes," by R. G. Cook, J. S. Katz and B. R. Cavoto, 1997, *Journal of Experimental Psychology: Animal Behavior Processes, 23,* p. 417. Copyright 1997 by the American Psychology Association. Adapted with permission.)

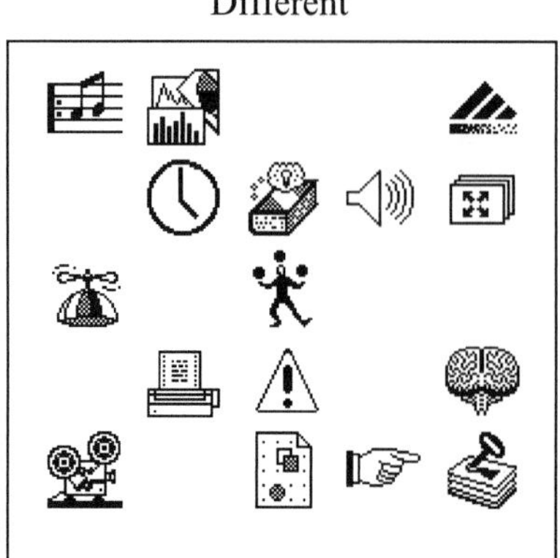

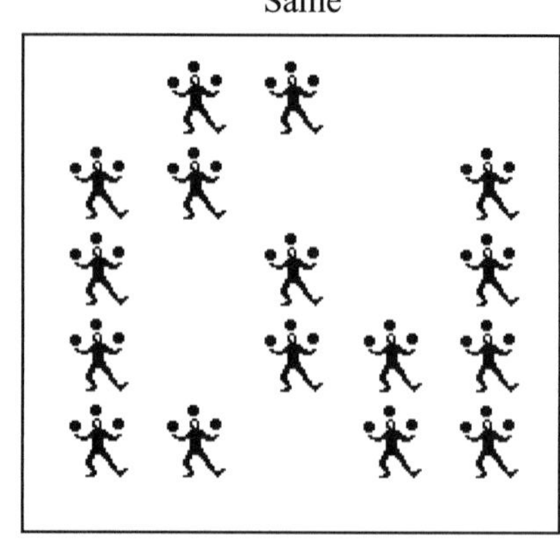

Figure 16.2. Examples of the simultaneous different (*left*) and same (*right*) icon-based same/different arrays tested by Young and Wasserman (1997).

computer icons (figure 16.2), which is then followed by illumination of green and red circular response buttons located to the left and right of the display area. The pigeons make their choice by pecking one of these two buttons (e.g., left = different, right = same). A correct choice delivers a food pellet reinforcer; an incorrect choice results in a 5-s timeout and a correction trial.

Depending on the experiment, a total of 16 black-on-white computer icons—typically chosen randomly from a set of 24 possible icons—are presented in the same and different displays. These icons are randomly placed into an invisible 5 × 5 grid. This spatial randomization minimizes the perceptual contribution of horizontal and vertical regularities to discriminative performance (Young & Wasserman, 1997). The same displays involve a single randomly selected icon repeated 16 times, whereas the different displays involve a randomly chosen 16 of the 24 icons in random spatial configurations.

We have found that both types of S/D discrimination procedure produce highly similar results as measured by acquisition and transfer. Acquisition with both procedures takes between 30 and 45 sessions, and both procedures support good discrimination transfer to novel displays formed within the classes of displays used during training (icons to icons, objects to objects, etc.: Cook et al., 1995, 1997; Wasserman et al., 1995; Young & Wasserman, 1997). Furthermore, Cook et al. (1999) found that most pigeons could transfer their discrimination behavior to a novel stimulus class never seen before (color and gray-scale photographs) and outside the range of the previous training displays.

This kind of transfer to novel stimuli supports the idea that the pigeons may have acquired a generalized concept based on relational S/D information in these displays, thus allowing the pigeons to generalize their past experience to new situations. Nevertheless, a skeptic could argue that these pigeons merely learned to detect simple perceptual features in these displays and did not have a deeper understanding of the conceptual relations of sameness and differentness. Although any single or simple feature fails to capture the opened-ended relations present within the many different types of display classes tested by Cook et al. (1997), a suitably revised perceptual account of these results might argue that the pigeons may have learned to detect the generalized presence or absence of large spatial discontinuities among the repeated mosaic of identical elements in these displays. This type of perceptual discontinuity account does not fare well, however, in accounting for Wasserman's results because of the more even distribution of spatial differences throughout in his icon-based displays. Nevertheless, the same skeptic could adjust the features attended to and suggest instead that Wasserman's pigeons were responding to differences in the spatial frequencies or patterns produced by multi-item icon displays.

Because the origins of most conceptual behavior begin with perception (Goldstone & Barsalou, 1998), we have been very sensitive from the beginning of our research programs to examine nonconceptual alternatives. In a variety of studies focused specifically on these issues, we have found little evidence to suggest that such perceptual accounts provide a unified or adequate explanation of our results (Cook et al., 1997, 1999; Cook, Kelly, & Katz, 2003; Wasserman, Frank, & Young, 2002; Wasserman, Young, & Nolan, 2000; Young & Wasserman, 2001b; Young, Wasserman, Hilfers, & Dalrymple, 1999).

To examine such perceptual accounts, for example, we independently developed S/D procedures using lists of successively presented same and different items. In these cases, items are presented one at a time, thereby eliminating perceptual features linked to the simultaneous presence of S/D relations within a display. Successful discrimination learning and transfer with lists of successively presented stimuli not only eliminates various nonconceptual interpretations of the simultaneous S/D discrimination results, but also demonstrates that any discrimination behavior must be founded on a memory-based comparison of past and present information.

Wasserman: Successive S/D Discrimination

Wasserman, Young, and Dalrymple (1997) first showed that pigeons can accurately discriminate lists or sequences of same and different items. The pigeons were trained to discriminate sequential lists of 16 same icons (AAAAAAA . . .) from lists of 16 different icons (ABCDEFG . . .) (figure 16.3). On each trial, the pigeon was shown a sequence of 16 items, each of which they pecked once, after which two choice keys (red and green) were illuminated, one on each side of the display, and the pigeon indicated its choice. A correct choice delivered a food pellet reinforcer; an incorrect choice resulted in a 5-s timeout and a correction trial. After learning this discrimination, the pigeons reliably generalized these "same" and "different" report responses to lists of novel items.

Cook: Successive S/D Discrimination

Cook has similarly conducted investigations using a successive S/D discrimination procedure but, unlike the above choice procedures, this test involved a go–no-go method (Cook et al., 2003). The pigeons were shown a sequence of temporally separated same stimuli (AAAAA . . .) or different stimuli, in which two color photographs alternated (ABABAB . . .) on the display for 20 s (figure 16.4). Pecks during same sequences were reinforced on a VI 10-s schedule (S+), whereas pecks during alternating different sequences (S–) produced no food and a dark time-out that depended on the number of pecks emitted. During each 20-s trial, each photograph was successively presented for 3 s with a 0.1- or 0.5-s blank interstimulus interval (ISI) separating each picture. Pigeons learned to discriminate these successive lists and transferred this behavior to both novel color and gray-scale photographs. Pigeons also showed considerable savings in learning a successive S/D discrimination based on brief video segments. In both of the above successive discriminations, the pigeons were sensitive to the temporal interval between successive items, being able to discriminate with as much as a 2- to 3-s gap between items (Cook et al., 2003; Young, Wasserman, & Garner, 1997).

The précis above of our simultaneous and successive acquisition and transfer results suggests that pigeons can readily learn S/D discriminations and transfer these discriminations across a wide variety of stimuli and settings (Cook, 2002; Cook et al., 1995, 1997, 1999, 2003; Cook & Wixted, 1997; Gibson & Wasserman, 2003; Wasserman et al., 1995, 1997, 2000, 2004; Young & Wasserman, 1997, 2002a, 2002b; Young et al., 1997, 1999). Table 16.1 provides a summary of the procedural differences among our tasks. It is rather compelling that, despite these many differences, the pigeons have consistently developed and shown S/D discrimination and transfer across all of these conditions. Although a different, nonconceptual alternative can be generated from each outcome, procedure, and display organization, the consistency and simplicity of interpreting these data within a single S/D framework have encouraged us to suggest that, like primates, relational information can come to control pigeons' discrimination behavior.

Part of our empirical success, in comparison to earlier studies of pigeon S/D discrimination behavior using pairwise combinations of stimuli, may be due to the increased number of items involved in our studies. This increased number is reflected both in the number of separate items used to train the pigeons, thus allowing more exemplars to be experienced during training, and by having more items appear within a specific display or list, which may lead to a heightened appreciation of the similarities and differences in the collections.

The critical point that we would next like to develop in this chapter, however, is that we are not

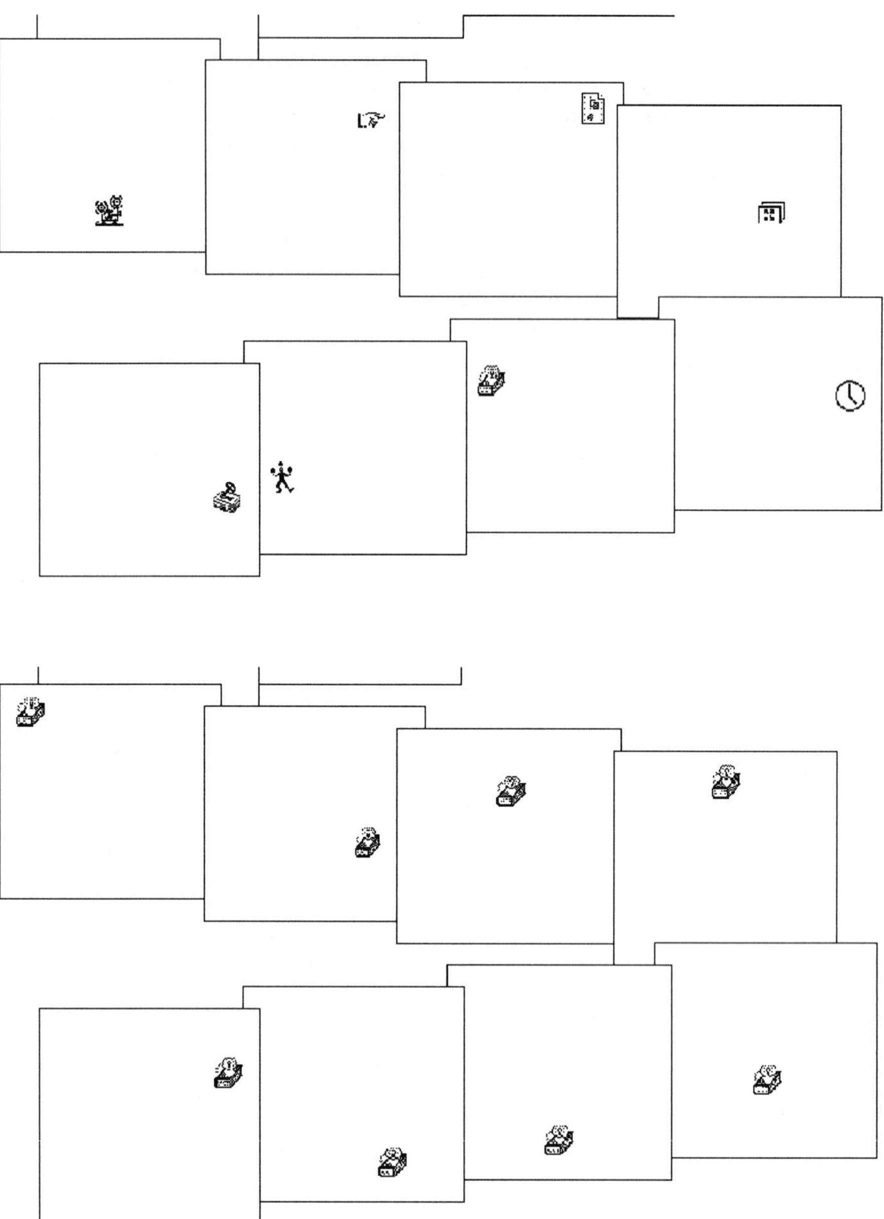

Figure 16.3. Examples of the successive different (*top*) and same (*bottom*) icon-based same/different arrays tested by Young and Wasserman (1997). Each item was displayed until the pigeon pecked it once. Time moves from front to back across the sequence of items.

sure whether the nature of stimulus control acquired in each of our S/D discriminations is the same. Despite the procedural and behavioral similarities evident in our acquisition, transfer, and temporal findings, we have also independently collected data suggesting that the controlling relations derived from our respective stimuli are *not* the same and may be related to how each of us chose to organize the increased number of items in our S/D displays. The next section describes the divergent results that point to this intriguing possibility.

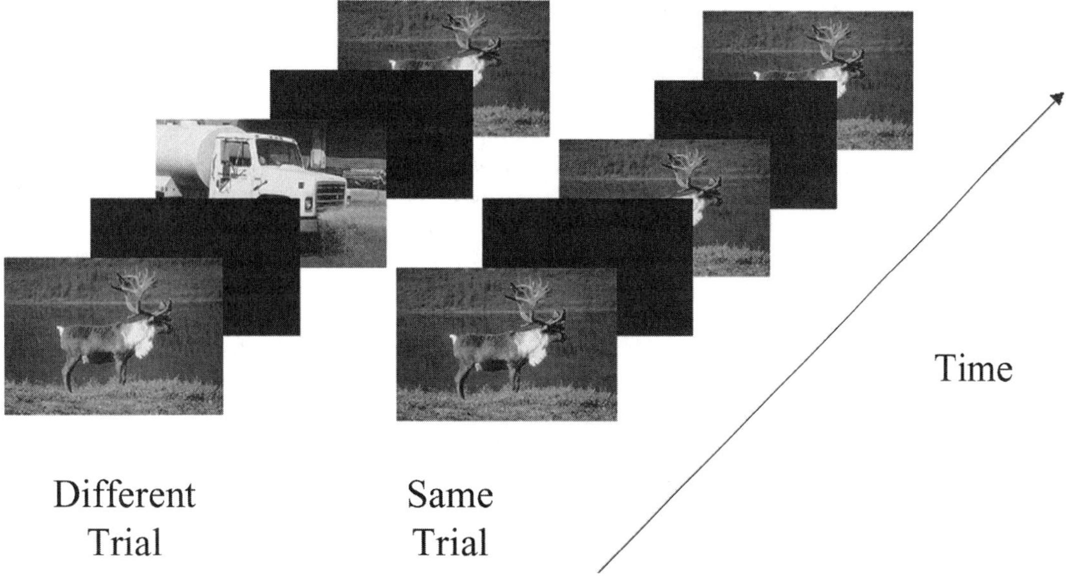

Figure 16.4. Examples of the successive different (*left*) and same (*right*) icon-based same/different arrays similar to those tested by Cook et al. (2003). Each picture was shown for 3000 ms and separated by one of two different dark interstimulus intervals (100 and 500 ms) across the trial.

Table 16.1. Summary of Procedural Differences Among Our Various S/D Discrimination Tasks

	Cook Simultaneous	Wasserman Simultaneous	Cook Successive	Wasserman Successive
Procedure type	Choice	Choice	Go–no-go	Choice
Stimulus types	Textures, objects, shapes, color and gray-scale photographs	Icons	Color and gray-scale photographs, videos	Icons
No. of display classes tested	5	1	2	1
Display organization	24×16, 3×2	5×5, 4×4	1×1	1×1
Odd item	Yes	No	No	No
Multiple differences in displays	No	Yes	No	No
Directed responses	Yes	No	No	Yes
No. and type of dimensions	2—Color and shape	1—Shape	2—Color and shape	1—Shape
Reinforcement	Mixed grain	Food pellets	Mixed grain	Food pellets
Timeouts	Yes	Yes	Yes	Yes
Correction procedure	No	Yes	No	Yes
Computer screen	Color on black	Black on white	Color on black	Black on white

WHAT'S THE DIFFERENCE?

We see strong merit in considering the general issue of stimulus control within the framework of signal detection theory (Cook & Wixted, 1997; Herbranson, Freemouw, & Shimp, 1999; Macmillan & Creelman, 1991; Swets, Tanner, & Birdsall, 1961). As pigeons learn to discriminate our same and different displays, they may set a decision criterion along a discriminative dimension based on their processing of the display's S/D organization. If the evidence from a display exceeds this criterion, then the pigeons make one response, and if not, then they make the other response. The same displays in our tasks represent one endpoint of this controlling dimension. The nature of the other endpoint of this controlling dimension—generated by the processing of the different displays—is the critical focus of the remainder of this chapter.

Several pieces of evidence suggest that a single dimension underlies our pigeons' S/D discrimination. For instance, Cook and Wixted (1997) conducted a series of experiments using same and different texture displays created by differences in either the color or shape dimension. Following manipulations of the relative number of same and different displays, Cook and Wixted tested the fit of various mathematical formulations of signal detection theory. In comparison to multidimensional models, they found that a unidimensional model yielded the best fit to the data—suggesting that a single common dimension controlled choice performance regardless of whether the different displays were created from color or shape disparities.

Cook et al. (1997) also found evidence consistent with a unidimensional model; they discovered that S/D acquisition proceeded at the same rate across the four display types (texture, feature, geometric, and object) tested in their task. The singular nature of this learning implicates a single generalized discrimination that encompassed all of the variations in the different training stimuli. Cook (2002) extended this finding using a pseudodiscrimination procedure. Using the same display types as Cook et al. (1997), Cook tested two groups of pigeons. In the consistent group, the same and different displays across the four display types were consistently assigned to the "same" and "different" response alternatives. This assignment allowed the identical relational codes to be shared across the display types. In the inconsistent group, however, the same and different displays of the four display types were inconsistently assigned to the response alternatives. For example, the same displays for the texture and geometrical displays and the different displays for the object and photographic display types might be assigned to one response alternative, whereas the complements of these display types were assigned to the other response alternative. Thus, in the inconsistent group, the categorical division of same and different ran orthogonal to their mapping to the two response alternatives. In two experiments, the consistent group learned its task much faster than the inconsistent group; what learning did occur in the latter group was isolated to a subset of displays. This difference in learning testifies to the importance of aligning the presented relations with the reported relations; failure to do so results in substantial interference in learning and prevents the formation of any relational concept. Collectively, these results provide substantial converging evidence that pigeons apply a single decision framework to multiple-stimulus class S/D discrimination (see figure 7 in Cook, 2002). The above results do not pinpoint the exact nature of this single dimension, but Cook has proposed that the controlling dimension is anchored by the relational values of "sameness" and "differentness."

Wasserman and his colleagues have also suggested that a single relational dimension controls discrimination in their icon-based task. However, the nature of this dimension is tied to the notion of item variability rather than "sameness" and "differentness." Because Wasserman and his colleagues used different displays that maximized the number of within-display differences, testing pigeons with displays containing various mixtures of identical and nonidentical icons was a natural outgrowth of their approach (Young & Wasserman, 1997). The typical result of these item mixture tests can be seen in the data summarized in figure 16.5. Across three different experiments, changes in S/D performance were a systematic function of different degrees of S/D mixture, strongly suggesting that the controlling dimension in this task is directly correlated with item variability. In fact, this variability dimension turns out to be well characterized by the information theoretic concept of *entropy*. Entropy measures the amount of variety or diversity in a categorical variable by a weighted average of the number of bits of information that are required to predict each of the categories of the variable. Rare or low-frequency categories convey a great deal of

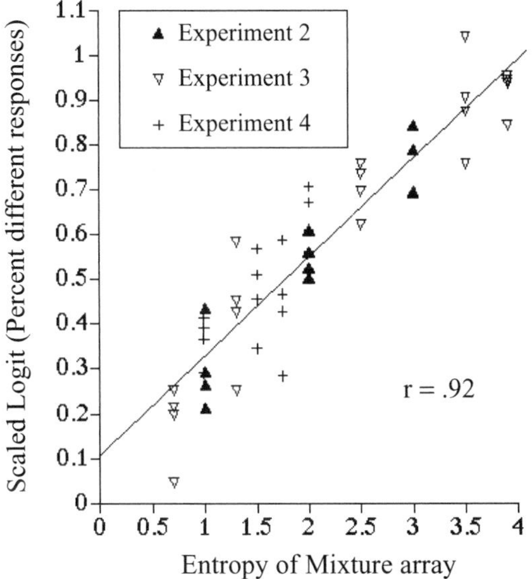

Figure 16.5. Summary of the results of three experiments conducted Young and Wasserman (1997), showing the mean amount of different responding as function of display entropy across different types of mixture displays. (From "Entropy detection by pigeons: response to mixed visual displays after same-different training," by M. E. Young and E. A. Wasserman, 1997, *Journal of Experimental Psychology: Animal Behavior Processes, 23,* p. 166. Copyright 1997 by the American Psychological Association. Adapted with permission.)

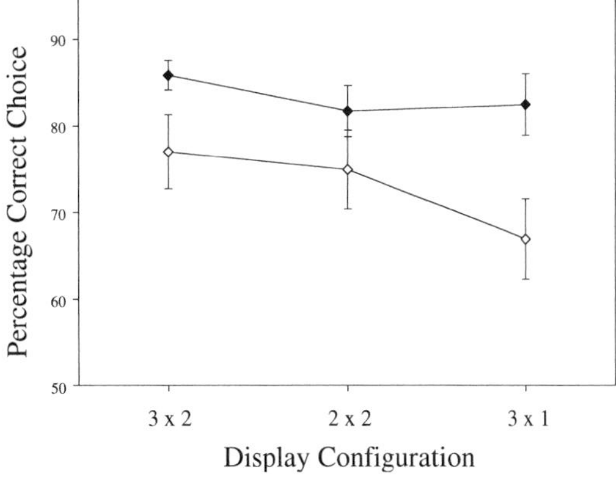

Figure 16.6. Results from Cook et al. (1997b) showing mean choice accuracy for same and different displays as a function of the three different display organizations tested. (From "Pigeon Same-Different Concept Learning with Multiple Stimulus Classes," by R. G. Cook, J. S. Katz, and B. R. Cavoto, 1997, *Journal of Experimental Psychology: Animal Behavior Processes, 23,* p. 431. Copyright 1997 by the American Psychological Association. Adapted with permission.)

information (they are very important), whereas common categories convey very little information (they are less important). Predicting the category of a variable that has only one value is easy and requires no information at all: entropy is zero. When all of the values of a categorical variable are equally likely, entropy is maximal for the given number of observed categories. So, same and different arrays represent endpoints of the entropy dimension: same arrays entail minimal entropy, whereas different arrays entail maximal entropy (see Young & Wasserman, 2001c, for more details about computing entropy and to access an online entropy calculator). A substantial body of additional results from Wasserman's laboratory strongly support the idea that entropy is the dimensional basis of the pigeons' performance following icon-based S/D training (Wasserman et al., 2000; Young & Wasserman, 1997, 2002a, 2002b; Young et al., 1997, 1999).

Given the above evidence, a key question to ask is whether Cook's S/D unidimensional results might also be accounted for by the single theoretical concept of entropy. If so, then we could offer a unified explanation of the entire set of S/D results from both laboratories. Interestingly, the answer appears to be "no" as determined by comparable experiments varying stimulus mixture conducted in Cook's laboratory.

Cook et al. (1997), for example, varied the number of common elements in a simultaneous display following training with one odd and five common elements in a 3 × 2 array made of either objects or geometric figures (see figure 16.1). As the number of common elements was reduced using 2 × 2 (one odd and three common elements) and 1 × 3 (one odd and two common elements) organizations, correct responses steadily fell on different trials with little effect on same trials. These data can be seen in figure 16.6. This decline on different trials is especially important because the entropy account predicts precisely the opposite result: namely, that accuracy should have increased. This prediction follows from the fact that decreasing the number of common elements should increase the entropy of the different displays and hence increase the number of correct responses on different trials.

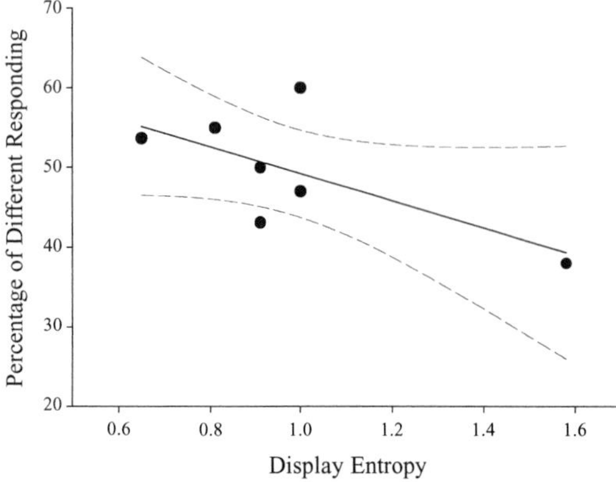

Figure 16.7. Mean percentage of "different" responding for different types of simultaneous mixtures as a function of display entropy. This experiment is a follow-up to those reported in Cook et al. (1997b) and tested the same animals but at a later point in training. The best fitting regression line (*solid line*) and its 95% confidence intervals (*dotted lines*) have been plotted through these data.

As well, in previously unpublished experiments, which tested the same birds at a later point in their training, we further manipulated the degree of mixture in the displays, testing a total of seven display organizations. These organizations included a row of three photographs, objects, or geometrical figures arranged with either one odd target (1 × 3/1; entropy = 1.58) or with all three items being different (1 × 3/3; entropy = 0.91), 2 × 2 arrays with either one odd item (2 × 2/1 entropy = 0.81) or two items being different (2 × 2/2; entropy = 1), and 3 × 2 arrays with either one odd target (3 × 2/1 entropy = 0.65), two contrasting items (3 × 2/2 entropy = 0.91) or three contrasting items (3 × 2/3; entropy = 1). Except for the 1 × 3 array, only two items (randomly selected each time) were used to make each different display, and these items were randomly distributed about the display dependent on the mixture condition within the display. One other important change from the earlier experiment was that the pigeons were not required to locate and peck at the odd item in this experiment; they simply pecked 40 times at each display prior to their choice.

The mean results from six sessions of testing are depicted in figure 16.7 as a function of display entropy. This portrayal provides the easiest contrast with the data summarized in figure 16.5. The solid line represents the best fitting regression function. As can be seen, the clear downward slope of this regression function ($r = -0.65$) contrasts with the strong upward slope observed in Young and Wasserman's stimulus mixture experiments. Further, for each display of the smaller display organizations (1 × 3; 2 × 2), the odd-item display supported numerically better discrimination than did similarly organized displays containing a greater number of differences. This result was true whether the displays were constructed from geometric, object, or photographic stimuli.

These contrasting data from our respective laboratories strongly suggest that the discriminative dimension for the pigeons in Cook's simultaneous task was not entropy. It thus appears that Cook's pigeons learned something very different from Wasserman's pigeons, despite receiving a superficially similar S/D task and training history.

Two interpretive possibilities can be entertained. The first is that that the pigeons in Cook's simultaneous task learned something related to the generalized "sameness" and "differentness" of the items in the display. A second possibility, suggested by the beneficial effects of increasing the number of common elements in both of Cook's experiments, is that display oddity is an important factor in controlling the "different" choice behavior of his pigeons (cf. Blough, 1989; Cook, 1992; Lombardi, Fachinelli, & Delius, 1984; Zentall, Hogan, Edwards, & Hearst, 1980).

We will have more to say about these different sources of stimulus control later, but we turn next to the divergent evidence in our successive S/D tasks. Here, again, we observed similar initial results with our respective successive discrimination tasks: rapid learning, reliable transfer to novel items, and common effects of ISI. But here, too, deeper empirical conflicts emerged upon further investigation.

Pursuing Young et al.'s (1997) observations regarding the effects of stimulus mixture, Young et al. (1999) found that their birds' icon-based successive S/D discrimination behavior was similarly controlled by item-to-item variability. The results can be seen in figure 16.8. After being trained to discriminate sequential lists of 16 same icons from lists of 16 different icons, the pigeons classified new mixture lists largely as a function of the number of different types of icons within the list. There was an increasing tendency for the pigeons to report "different" as

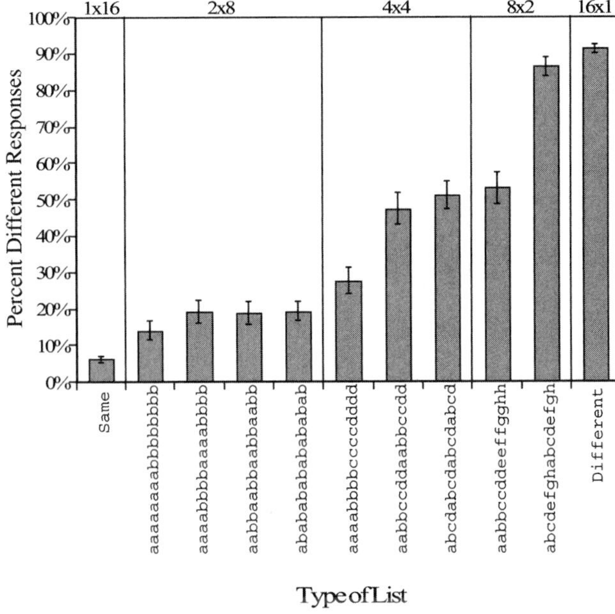

Figure 16.8. Mean percentage of "different" responses for different list mixtures in Experiment 1 of Young et al. (1999). (From "An examination of the pigeon's variability discrimination with lists of successively presented visual stimuli," by M. E. Young, E. A. Wasserman, M. A. Hilfers, and R. M. Dalrymple, 1999, *Journal of Experimental Psychology: Animal Behavior Processes, 25,* p. 478. Copyright 1999 by the American Psychological Association. Adapted with permission.)

the number of different types of icons increased from 1 (all identical) to 2 to 4 to 8 to 16 (all different). There was some suggestion of sensitivity to the number of transitions between icon types; this sensitivity increased when the number of icon types increased from 2 to 4 to 8. It is not clear, however, whether the effect of item transitions might have been mediated by memory processes; when the number of transitions did have a notable effect, there were fewer icon types at the end of the list (e.g., AABBCCDDAABBCCDD has four icon types among the last eight icons, whereas AAAABBBBCCCCDDDD has only two icon types among the last eight icons). It is possible that the pigeons are only sensitive to the number of icon types but that their memory of those types is limited to those that were encountered over the past few seconds.

These results again suggest that item variability or entropy is a powerful source of stimulus control when large numbers of different items are mixed together in either spatial or temporal proximity. One consequence of this type of dimensional control occurs when entropy-sensitized pigeons are tested with ABABAB sequences. In this case, the birds show a strong tendency to make "same" responses because of the minimal interitem variation in such lists. Does this weak "different" discrimination mean that pigeons cannot learn to make an S/D discrimination comprising only pairwise differences (Mackintosh, 2000)?

Consider for the moment the results of Cook's et al. (2003) successive S/D experiments. Recall that, in these experiments, the pigeons were trained with alternating sequences of different items (ABABA . . .) and same items (AAAA . . .) from the beginning. A notable advantage of the successive go–no-go discrimination procedure over choice tasks is it permits one to track on line the information contributed by each successive stimulus within a trial. Thus, we can examine at what point in the sequence the pigeons begin to discriminate between the same and different sequences. Figure 16.9 shows mean peck rates at each successive interval of baseline same (S+) and alternating (S–) trials for two different ISIs. For the present discussion, the most important thing to note is that only a single stimulus transition was needed for the pigeons to begin responding at different rates. That is, by the second image (the first one being ambiguous as to the type of sequence), the pigeons showed significant discrimination of the two trial types. This result indicates that pigeons can indeed learn to make S/D discriminations (and also show transfer) after experiencing only two items. The subsequent increases and decreases in peck rates for each trial type in figure 16.9 suggest that additional information accumulates over further stimulus presentations and transitions. Because of the use of only one (same) or two (different) items per trial, an entropy-based account does not easily capture

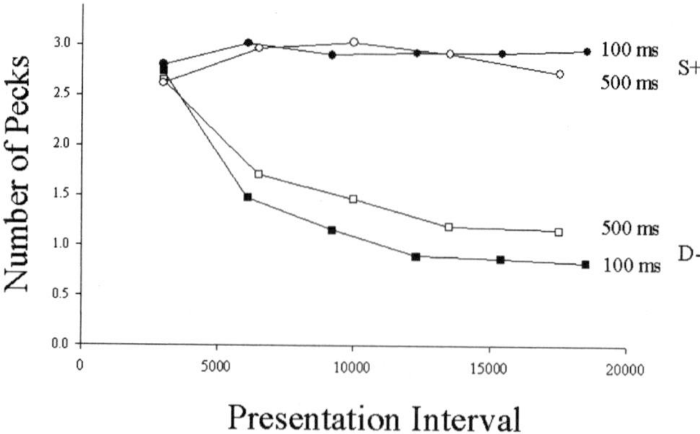

Figure 16.9. A subset of results from Experiment 1 of Cook et al. (2003). The figure shows mean number of pecks across successive intervals for same positive (S+) and alternating different negative (D–) sequences of pictures. Each picture was shown for 3,000 ms and separated by one of two different dark interstimulus intervals (ISI: 100 and 500 ms) across the trial. (Modified from "Successive two-item same-different discrimination and concept learning by pigeons," by R. G. Cook, D. M. Kelly, and J. S. Katz, 2003, *Behavioural Processes, 62,* 125–144.)

these monotonic changes in responding over item presentations. Under these conditions, entropy cannot grow beyond the second item on the different sequences and it remains constant at zero on the same sequences. These results suggest that pigeons can learn a two-item S/D concept when the potential contributions of the oddity or entropy dimensions are both minimized.

Thus, it appears here as well that Wasserman's pigeons learned something different in their AAAAAA versus ABCDEF successive discrimination than did Cook's pigeons in their AAAAAA versus ABABAB successive discrimination. This difference is most vividly seen in pigeons' response to alternating ABABAB . . . sequences. Cook's pigeons responded "different" when they were given such a sequence, whereas Wasserman's pigeons responded "same." Why does this notable disparity occur?

One possibility is that this disparity is due to the superficial differences between our tasks (icons vs. photographs, choice vs. go–no-go report responses, etc.). A second, and we think more likely, possibility is that this disparity is due to the nature of the stimulus sequences experienced during training, which caused the birds to attend to different attributes of the discriminative stimuli. We must therefore entertain the possibility that not all S/D discriminations are created equal.

DIALECTIC AND RECONCILIATION

Our individual lines of research have each pointed to unidimensional accounts of the S/D discrimination performance observed in our respective laboratories. At the start of this collaboration, we first attempted to reconcile our results by trying to fit a single-process account to our data: that is, could one dimension control both types of S/D discriminations? Entropy seemed the best initial candidate for such an account. According to this type of single-process account, the critical difference between our tasks involved the relative placement of the decision criterion. For example, in Cook's task, 6-item different displays with only a single odd item have a much smaller entropy value (0.65) than the 16-item different displays (entropy = 4.00) in Wasserman's task. This entropy disparity on different trials would have forced pigeons in Cook's S/D task to adopt a far stricter criterion relative to the common *same* displays than pigeons in Wasserman's task. This same type of analysis could be extended to the successive discrimination tasks, too. Nevertheless, such a single-process, criterion-shift account does not explain why Cook's pigeons responded so unexpectedly to displays with reduced numbers of items. Despite extended discussion, we could devise no single theoretical account that could reconcile these conflicting mixture results.

This situation leaves us with a second possibility: namely, that pigeons can flexibly process different features/dimensions from S/D stimulus organizations and use this disparate information to abstract different concepts. This multiprocess account explains the above contradictory effects by having the pigeons learn about the disparate relational properties of the different displays in our respective tasks. The same displays provide a common anchor for both tasks, but the disparate organizations of the different displays lead the birds to attend to orthogonal aspects of our S/D displays. Wasserman's results strongly suggested an entropy-based account of his pigeons' S/D behavior; Cook's results require an alternative account.

We see two possibilities to explain Cook's results. Cook has consistently suggested that stimulus "difference" is what is learned in these tasks and is a strong candidate for his successive discrimination results using alternating sequences. Another possibility that needs to be considered, however, is related to the role of stimulus "oddity," especially in the case of Cook's simultaneous displays. This "oddity" alternative contrasts with the discrete and categorical nature of a generalized S/D concept by being continuous in nature (here, we define oddity as the number of minority elements/number of items in the display, when the number of minority elements does not equal or exceed the number of majority elements).

One reason why we must consider continuous alternatives, such as entropy and oddity, is that the purely categorical property of difference would have all stimulus mixture displays being treated alike. Although the stimulus mixture results that we have independently collected go in opposite directions, the pigeons in both laboratories have consistently failed to exhibit exclusively categorical responding to various mixture differences. The birds instead show a clear sensitivity to continuous factors such as display entropy or oddity. Can human S/D behavior help to shed any light on the interaction of such categorical and continuous factors in these discriminations?

STIMULUS CONTROL OF HUMAN S/D BEHAVIOR

Adult humans readily exhibit S/D discrimination behavior. Because human performance provides an important comparison for the pigeon data, human behavior has also been examined in both laboratories. Our human results suggest that, similar to pigeons, people can also come to be controlled by different relational aspects of S/D displays. Consider first the recent research of Young and Wasserman (2001a). In these investigations, human participants were trained with a 16-item icon-based S/D task, virtually identical to what the pigeons had received. After learning this discrimination, the people were tested like the pigeons with varied mixtures of identical/nonidentical items and with different numbers of icons. The results revealed two dramatically different types or "clusters" of responding by the humans: One cluster behaved as if they were making a categorical S/D response to the mixed items and the other cluster showed a strong sensitivity to the entropy of the items in the display. These contrasting outcomes, labeled the categorical and continuous groups, are displayed in figure 16.10.

Participants in the smaller continuous cluster (n = 14) behaved as if display variability fell along a continuous dimension, exhibiting performance consistent with the use of entropy. These participants were more likely to choose "same" for the nonidentical arrays when the number of icons was reduced to two or four, but they consistently chose "same" for the identical arrays regardless of icon number. These results were expected by the entropy account because increasing the number of items increases entropy on nonidentical trials, but it has no effect on entropy on identical trials. The continuous participants also exhibited a strong sensitivity to the full range of display variability in the mixture arrays; as the mixture was changed from mostly identical to mostly nonidentical icons, responding changed from mostly "same" reports to mostly "different" reports.

Participants in the larger cluster (categorical, $n = 57$) behaved differently, treating the discrimination as a categorical one. These participants were largely unaffected by the number of icons in the identical and nonidentical displays, and they always preferred a "different" response for all of the mixtures, although there was some effect of the composition of the mixtures. When any of the icons were different, they tended to report "different"; only when all of the icons were identical did they consistently report "same," although a predominately same mixture (e.g., 2D/14S and 4D/12S) did prompt the occasional "same" report. The important implication of these two clusters is that humans can apparently attend to different aspects of these relational displays, much as it seems our pigeons did.

The difference in S/D display organization between our laboratories is a rather obvious candidate that might be responsible for the empirical disparities that we have identified in our pigeons. While we are only beginning to directly compare how pigeons respond to different display organizations (Gibson, Wasserman, & Cook, in press), recently collected data from human participants in Cook's laboratory support the idea that *same* versus *odd-item different* training (Cook's procedure) and *same* versus maximal *entropy* training (Wasserman's procedure) can lead to different patterns of responding. In this study (conducted with J. Holtzinger and I. Harnik), two groups of people were trained with

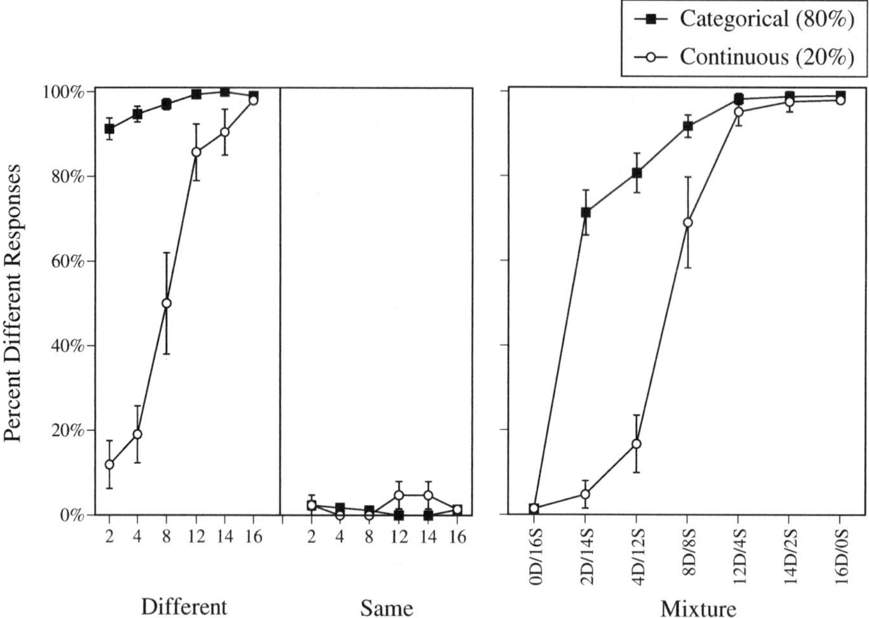

Figure 16.10. Mean percentage of "different responses" for the same, different, and mixture arrays of Experiment 1 of Young and Wasserman (2001). The response patterns are separately portrayed for the categorical and continuous participant clusters. (From Entropy and variability," by M. E. Young and E. A. Wasserman, 2001, *Journal of Experimental Psychology: Learning, Memory and Cognition, 27,* p. 281. Copyright 2001 by the American Psychological Association. Adapted with permission.)

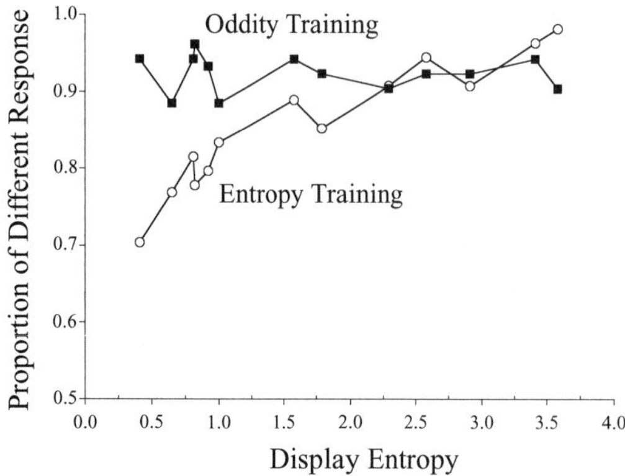

Figure 16.11. Mean proportion of "different responses" by two groups of humans exposed to different degrees of stimulus mixture during transfer testing. The entropy-trained group was initially trained with 3 × 4 different displays that were constructed from pictures that were all mixed and same displays that were all identical. The oddity-trained group was trained with 3 × 4 different displays that were constructed with only one odd picture and same displays that were all identical. For both groups, all 12 pictures were identical for the same displays.

3 × 4 arrays of 200 × 200 pixel photographs depicting natural objects and scenes. For the oddity group, the *different* trials were composed of one odd-item randomly located among 11 otherwise identical items. For the entropy group, the different trials were composed of 12 different randomly selected items. The same trials for both groups involved a single stimulus repeated 12 times. After learning to a set criterion, participants were then tested with displays containing different mixtures of identical and nonidentical elements.

The results of these mixture tests are depicted in figure 16.11 and show that the two groups responded differently to the test displays. The oddity group seemed to behave more categorically to all of the mixture tests by prominently responding "different." On the other hand, the entropy group showed a more continuous function in reaction to the mixed items, and they were significantly more likely to respond "same" to low entropy displays, although to a much weaker extent than pigeons or the people in Young and Wasserman (2001a). These data suggest that display organization on different trials is a critical factor in determining what is learned in an S/D task. It seems that both people and pigeons can be sensitive to the categorical and continuous features of S/D displays, depending on the circumstances. This fact raises the natural question of how these different relational representations come to control behavior and how they may interact with one another.

THE MULTIFACETED NATURE OF RELATIONAL REPRESENTATIONS

It appears that both pigeons and humans can use different representations of the various possible relations available in S/D problems. With identical same displays forming the common anchor, we have identified at least three approaches that are adopted by these species. The first approach is to use categorical S/D behavior much as traditionally defined, in which any difference among items is recognized as such. This behavior is clearly present in humans, as seen in the overall strong tendency to respond "different" to any set of nonidentical items in the above studies and the strong categorical response to mixtures by the majority of participants in our separate human studies. The strong human tendency to categorize S/D relations is reflected by the fact that even young children readily learn to make S/D reports when they are presented with only two items, as well as by the fact that they can label the source of any difference in similar pictures ("the balloons are different in that picture"). Although apparently not as robustly developed in pigeons, the transfer data from Cook's two-item successive S/D discrimination suggest that pigeons can make this type of categorical judgment as well.

The second and third approaches that we have identified suggest that the continuous factors of entropy and oddity can also play a role in S/D learning and transfer. Entropy or item variability as a dimension is apparently a highly salient one for pigeons, but we have documented that it can control human behavior, too (Young & Wasserman, 2001a). To compute entropy, subjects first have to use S/D information to differentiate among the contrasting classes of stimulus items within a display and then compute the extent of common representatives within each class. The other continuous factor that can play a role in S/D discrimination behavior is stimulus oddity. To compute oddity, subjects have to use S/D relations to differentiate the two classes of stimulus items within a display and then identify the relative oddity of one class of items compared with the other.

Thus far, we have found good evidence that each of these three approaches to S/D relations—categorical, entropy, and oddity—supports transfer to novel items, suggesting a conceptual basis for the discriminations. Furthermore, we seem to have reasonable evidence that experience with different types of S/D display organizations can have an important influence on the nature of the representation employed by both species. At the moment, however, beyond that statement, little is understood about what factors cause an animal to adopt one or more of these various relational approaches or their flexibility in detecting or switching among these different stimulus attributes.

Humans and pigeons are likely to be sensitive to all three of these relations to some degree. What factors promote one type of control over another? For pigeons, one preliminary answer seems to be display organization. Although this notion still needs to be directly studied in a uniform discriminative setting, in order to make sure that other factors (see table 16.1) are not responsible for our experimental differences, it seems clear that displays having strong oddity components encourage use of the oddity relation, whereas displays with large amounts of variability encourage use of the entropy relation. Thus, the stimulus context in which the S/D question is posed evidently makes an important difference to the pigeon's representation of the discrimination.

Context is certainly critical to understanding human S/D behavior. If asked which of the following words are the "same" (APPLE, BANANA, TRUCK), your answer would be very different depending on whether you are had recently been answering questions about basic objects or counting the number of letters in words. In fact, all questions about similarity and difference require a context to guide attention to any of the vast set of potential features available for such relational judgments (French, 1995). Thus, the highly contrasting reactions of our pigeons to different stimulus mixtures (see figures 16.5, 16.6, and 16.7) likely reflect the training context and organizations that they had experienced (high-variability vs. high-oddity displays).

Unlike pigeons, where continuous factors seem to dominate S/D judgments, humans generally tend to respond in a categorical manner. Although detectable, the contributions of continuous factors seem more easily overshadowed, perhaps because of the extended and explicit early childhood and educational experiences that bring categorical S/D relations more strongly to awareness (for more on the explicit/implicit distinction, see Stadler & Frensch, 1998). Children, who might be sensitive to continuous factors early, may soon learn to use a very strict criterion in responding to mixed displays to produce the desired categorical response. The dominance of categorical responding may also be further encouraged by our language and by its tendency to carve the world into categorical differences. In this vein, Premack (1978, 1983) previously suggested that language training may be critical to the emergence of S/D behavior in primates. As well, we seem to have a limited vocabulary for making distinctions among gradations of heterogeneity, perhaps forcing us to speak more categorically even when referring to continuous differences. Finally, our use of the terms "same" and "different" is decidedly asymmetrical; "sameness" suggests that each of the items in a group is identical to one another in at least one way, but "differentness" does not require that each item in a group to differ from every other item in at least one way.

Outside of the S/D discrimination, humans are often sensitive to the stimulus variability that is inherent in many circumstances (Wasserman, Young, & Cook, 2004). Humans have no problem responding appropriately to contextual and direct questions such as, "Which item is different?" "Which collection is the more variable?" "Which is the odd item?" Nevertheless, the cooperation and competition among these different stimulus relations may have important effects on human behavior. Although the roles of entropy and oddity have tended to be overlooked in the investigation of human S/D behavior, some intriguing hints do point to their interaction.

Young and Wasserman (2001a) attempted to increase the attention paid by humans to entropy. In one of their investigations, for example, they eliminated the same and different displays and instead trained people with displays that were either high or low in entropy. With this training, they found that humans who would generally be strong "categorical" responders were now far more sensitive to the dimension of variability, showing graded responding to new values of entropy tested from both inside and outside the range of training values. Such results suggest that humans can flexibly shift their attention between these different characteristics of "difference."

Mackay, Soraci, Carlin, Dennis, and Strawbridge (2002) also examined the interaction of these dimensions while looking at the acquisition of matching-to-sample behavior in mentally retarded youngsters. In particular, they were interested in identifying conditions that promoted the creation of this relational discrimination. The addition of visual oddity to the matching task was identified as one condition that promoted this behavior. During initial matching-to-sample training, the correct matching alternative in the test situation following the sample was further emphasized by making it the odd item among a larger set of eight repeated incorrect nonmatching items. Over successive training phases, the number of incorrect alternatives was gradually reduced until the children were finally able to perform the standard matching task—something they could not do before the supporting attentional oddity training. This outcome suggests that categorical and continuous stimulus relations do interact and that the right form of visual structuring in a task can promote the detection of relevant stimulus relations in humans.

Despite these suggestions that categorical and continuous factors interact, how they do so is still poorly understood in both pigeons and humans. Do these different stimulus relations compete for a limited pool of attention? If animals are attending to one feature, then does control by the other features decrease? Can animals divide their attention among these relations, or can they flexibly and simultaneously deploy all of these multiple strategies depending on the context? Does prior experience bias attention to these different S/D relations, and, if so, how long do these effects last? Are these relations hierarchical, with some being inherently more salient than others? How might control by S/D relations interact with the natural history of an animal? Clearly much research remains, to clarify how attention to these perceptual and conceptual factors influences behavior and its adaptive functions. The results of this work should provide important new insights into how animals process the many and complex stimulus relations present in the natural world.

References

Balsam, P., Deich, J., Ohyama, T., & Stokes, P. (1998). Origins of new behavior. In W. O'Donohue (Ed.), *Learning and behavior therapy* (pp. 403–420). Boston: Allyn & Bacon.

Blough, D. S. (1989). Odd-item search in pigeons: Display size and transfer effects. *Journal of Experimental Psychology: Animal Behavior Processes, 15,* 14–22.

Cook, R. G. (1992). Dimensional organization and texture discrimination in pigeons. *Journal of Experimental Psychology: Animal Behavior Processes, 18,* 354–363.

Cook, R. G. (Ed.). (2001). *Avian visual cognition.* Retrieved August 27, 2005, from http://www.pigeon.psy.tufts.edu/avc/.

Cook, R. G. (2002). The structure of pigeon multiple-class same-different learning. *Journal of the Experimental Analysis of Behavior, 78,* 345-364.

Cook, R. G., Cavoto, K. K., & Cavoto, B. R. (1995). Same/different texture discrimination and concept learning in pigeons. *Journal of Experimental Psychology: Animal Behavior Processes, 21,* 253–260.

Cook, R. G., Katz, J. S., & Cavoto, B. R. (1997). Pigeon same-different concept learning with multiple stimulus classes. *Journal of Experimental Psychology: Animal Behavior Processes, 23,* 417–433.

Cook, R. G., Katz, J. S., & Kelly, D. M. (1999). Pictorial same-different categorical learning and discrimination in pigeons. *Cahiers de Psychologie Cognitive, 18,* 805–844.

Cook, R. G., Kelly, D. M., & Katz, J. S. (2003). Successive two-item same-different discrimination and concept learning by pigeons. *Behavioural Processes, 62,* 125–144.

Cook, R. G., & Wixted, J. T. (1997). Same-different texture discrimination in pigeons: Testing competing models of discrimination and stimulus integration. *Journal of Experimental Psychology: Animal Behavior Processes, 23,* 401–416.

Darwin, C. (1897). *The descent of man: and selection in relation to sex* (new ed.). New York: Appleton.

Delius, J. D. (1994). Comparative cognition of identity. In P. E. P. Bertelson & G. d'Ydewalle (Ed.), *International perspectives on psychological science* (pp. 25–40). Hillsdale, NJ: Erlbaum.

Eisenberger, R., & Cameron, J. (1998). Rewards, intrinsic interest and creativity: New findings. *American Psychologist, 53,* 676–679.

French, R. M. (1995). *Subtlety of sameness.* Cambridge, MA: MIT Press.

Gibson, B. M., & Wasserman, E. A. (2003). Pigeons learn stimulus identity and stimulus relations when both serve as redundant, relevant cues during same-different discrimination training. *Journal of Experimental Psychology: Animal Behavior Processes, 29,* 84–91.

Gibson, B. M., Wasserman, E. A., & Cook, R. G. (in press). Not all same-different discriminations are created equal: Evidence against a unified account of same-different learning. *Learning & Motivation.*

Goldstone, R. L., & Barsalou, L. W. (1998). Reuniting perception and conception. *Cognition, 65,* 231–262.

Herbranson, W. T., Fremouw, T., & Shimp, C. P. (1999). The randomization procedure in the study of categorization of multidimensional stimuli by pigeons. *Journal of Experimental Psychology: Animal Behavior Processes, 25,* 113–135.

James, W. (1890). *The principles of psychology* (Vol. 1). New York: Henry Holt & Co.

James, W. (1910). *Psychology.* New York: Henry Holt & Co.

Lombardi, C. M., Fachinelli, C. C., & Delius, J. D. (1984). Oddity of visual patterns conceptualized by pigeons. *Animal Learning & Behavior, 12,* 2–6.

Mackay, H. A., Soraci, S. A., Carlin, M. T., Dennis, N. A., & Strawbridge, C. P. (2002). Guiding visual attention during acquisition of matching-to-sample. *American Journal of Mental Retardation, 107,* 445–454.

Mackintosh, N. J. (2000). Abstraction and discrimination. In C. Heyes & L. Huber (Eds.), *The evolution of cognition* (pp. 123–142). Cambridge, MA: MIT Press.

Macmillan, N. A., & Creelman, C. D. (1991). *Detection theory: A user's guide.* New York: Cambridge University Press.

Miller, N., & Neuringer, A. (2000). Reinforcing operant variability in adolescents with autism. *Journal of Applied Behavior Analysis, 33,* 151–165.

Neuringer, A. (2004). Reinforced variabililty in animals and people: Implications for adaptive action. *American Psychologist, 59,* 891–906.

Neuringer, A., Deiss, C., & Olson, G. (2000). Reinforced variability and operant learning. *Journal of Experimental Psychology: Animal Behavior Processes, 26,* 98–111.

Nickerson, R. S. (2002). The production and perception of randomness. *Psychological Review, 109,* 330–357.

Premack, D. (1978). On the abstractness of human concepts: Why it would be difficult to talk to a pigeon. In S. H. Hulse, H. Fowler, & W. K. Honig (Eds.), *Cognitive processes in animal behavior* (pp. 423–451). Hillsdale, NJ: Erlbaum.

Premack, D. (1983). The codes of beast and man. *Behavioral and Brain Sciences, 6,* 125–167.

Stadler, M. A., & Frensch, P. A. (1998). *Handbook of implicit learning.* Thousand Oaks, CA: Sage Publications.

Swets, J. A., Tanner, W. P., & Birdsall, T. G. (1961). Decision processes in perception. *Psychological Review, 68,* 301–340.

Wasserman, E. A. (1993). Comparative cognition: Beginning the second century of the study of animal intelligence. *Psychological Bulletin, 113,* 211–228.

Wasserman, E. A., Frank, A. J., & Young, M. E. (2002). Stimulus control by same-versus-different relations among multiple visual stimuli. *Journal of Experimental Psychology: Animal Behavior Processes, 28,* 347–357.

Wasserman, E. A., Hugart, J. A., & Kirkpatrick-Steger, K. (1995). Pigeons show same-different conceptualization after training with complex visual stimuli. *Journal of Experimental Psychology: Animal Behavior Processes, 21,* 248–252.

Wasserman, E. A., Young, M. E., & Cook, R. G. (2004). Variability discrimination in humans and animals: Implications for adaptive action. *American Psychologist, 59,* 879–890.

Wasserman, E. A., Young, M. E., & Dalrymple, R. M. (1997). Memory-based same-different conceptualization by pigeons. *Psychonomic Bulletin & Review, 4,* 552–558.

Wasserman, E. A., Young, M. E., & Nolan, B. C. (2000). Display variability and spatial organization as contributors to the pigeon's discrimination of complex visual stimuli. *Journal of Experimental Psychology: Animal Behavior Processes, 26,* 133–143.

Young, M. E., & Wasserman, E. A. (1997). Entropy detection by pigeons: Response to mixed visual displays after same-different discrimination training. *Journal of Experimental Psychology: Animal Behavior Processes, 23,* 157–170.

Young, M. E., & Wasserman, E. A. (2001a). Entropy and variability discrimination. *Journal of Experimental Psychology: Learning, Memory, and Cognition, 27,* 278–293.

Young, M. E., & Wasserman, E. A. (2001b). Evidence for a conceptual account of same-different discrimination learning in the pigeon. *Psychonomic Bulletin & Review, 8,* 677–684.

Young, M. E., & Wasserman, E. A. (2001c). Stimulus control in complex arrrays. In R. G. Cook (Ed.), *Avian visual cognition.* Retrieved August 27, 2005, from http://www.pigeon.psy.tufts.edu/avc/.

Young, M. E., & Wasserman, E. A. (2002a). Detecting variety: What's so special about uniformity? *Journal of Experimental Psychology: General, 131,* 131–143.

Young, M. E., & Wasserman, E. A. (2002b). The pigeon's discrimination of visual entropy: A logarithmic function. *Animal Learning & Behavior, 30,* 306–314.

Young, M. E., Wasserman, E. A., & Garner, K. L. (1997). Effects of number of items on the pigeon's discrimination of same from different visual displays. *Journal of Experimental Psychology: Animal Behavior Processes, 23,* 491–501.

Young, M. E., Wasserman, E. A., Hilfers, M. A., & Dalrymple, R. M. (1999). The pigeon's variability discrimination with lists of successively presented visual stimuli. *Journal of Experimental Psychology: Animal Behavior Processes, 25,* 475–490.

Zentall, T. R., Hogan, D. E., Edwards, C. A., & Hearst, E. (1980). Oddity learning in the pigeon as a function of the number of incorrect alternatives. *Journal of Experimental Psychology: Animal Behavior Processes, 6,* 278–299.

17

A Modified Feature Theory as an Account of Pigeon Visual Categorization

LUDWIG HUBER AND ULRIKE AUST

Categorization is one of the most enduring subjects in cognitive science. Considered as a process that permits us to understand, communicate, and make predictions about objects and events in our world, it is one of the most fundamental and pervasive cognitive activities. It is also basic for nonhuman animals, because it solves a central problem for brains. The sensory systems input more stimulus information into the nervous system than the motor system can possibly output as behavior patterns. This information bottleneck between the input layer and the output layer—to speak in computer language—demands a drastic information reduction (Delius, Jitumori, & Siemann, 2000). The pooling problem can be solved by detecting recurrences in the environment despite variations in local stimulus energies and by partitioning the wide variety of stimuli into smaller, more manageable, sets or classes, like friends and foes or food and nonfood (Herrnstein, 1990; Medin, 1989).

Although the benefit of categorization for animals is obvious, interest in the subject has for a long time been restricted to human cognition. Philosophers and psychologists believed that conceptual thought enables the subject to classify the world into categories, thereby forming the basis for the meaning of verbs, nouns, and adjectives. Only lately has categorization become a serious concern for comparative psychologists studying animals (Herrnstein & Loveland, 1964), and mounting evidence has been found for categorization at every level of the animal kingdom where it has competently been sought (Herrnstein, 1990). Focusing on the function of categorization as the propensity of an organism to respond differentially to a class of stimuli, animal discrimination learning paradigms have been used to illuminate how people might learn and represent new concepts.

Herrnstein and Loveland (1964) were the first to show that category discrimination in pigeons was not only possible but also was learned easily and generalized widely. These researchers trained pigeons to discriminate between sets of complex color photographs that were distinguished only by the presence of a human being in each member of one set. Extremely quick discrimination, complete transfer, and the failure to detect any trivial visual clues for discrimination performance such as wavelength, intensity, or frequency (Honig & Urcuioli, 1981; Lubow, 1974; Mostofsky, 1965) indicated that the pigeons readily came to respond to the "target" that we ourselves would call a person. Herrnstein and Loveland concluded that classification was based on a generalized concept rather than on the extraction of some simple features or on rote learning.

As a result, many experiments following the initial one adopted a more cognitive approach (e.g., Herrnstein, Loveland, & Cable, 1976; Lubow, 1974; Mallot & Siddall, 1972; Morgan, Fitch, Holman, & Lea, 1976; Poole & Lander, 1971). In particular, the notion of "concept" has been widely used in connection with complex discriminations since Herrnstein and Loveland published their famous study. The available evidence indeed seemed to suggest that pigeons possess an ability that transcends the discrimination of simple stimulus dimensions such as wavelength, intensity, or frequency.

Not surprisingly, the possibility that the pigeon may exploit texture, motion, color, and low-order statistics was seldom regarded as an alternative to higher-order concepts in categorization experiments (Huber, 1999). To some, even suggesting such a possibility seemed fatuous. Lea (1984), for example, called single features on which categorization may be based (e.g., properties of the frequency spectrum) "abstruse" (p. 266). In fact, some authors may dislike the possibility that animals function like the machines that became commercially available around 1976 for recognizing and counting different types of white blood cells; those machines actually take account of color and texture, as well as of shape. Color and texture are also often important in the automatic interpretation of satellite photography and other remotely sensed imagery (see Ullman, 1997).

The widespread view that pigeons' classification behavior is mediated by conceptual rules has, however, proved to be no less premature and misleading than its countercurrent, the view that nonhuman species are not able to categorize at all. The main trap for the unwary is that concept discrimination seems to imply concept formation. But, the mere fact that pigeons respond to visual classes according to some human language concept may tell us little or nothing about the underlying mechanism (Lea, 1984).

In fact, there are various ways in which a pigeon might solve a concept discrimination task. First, the ability to categorize may depend on remembering each trained instance and then generalizing responding to other members of the category to which the trained instances belong, as purported by early exemplar models (e.g., Astley & Wasserman, 1992). According to this view, categorization is exclusively based on item-specific information, with no category-specific properties being abstracted. Other versions of exemplar accounts also acknowledge the importance of single stimulus aspects that can be weighted differently (Kruschke, 1992; Pearce, 1988, 1991).

Second, as claimed by feature theory, categorization may be based on the abstraction of "common features" (i.e., a necessary set of defining features that characterize members of the same category). A category is thus represented as a list of the relative frequencies of those features (Cerella, 1982; D'Amato & Van Sant, 1988; Lea, 1984; Lubow, 1974; Morgan et al., 1976).

Finally, according to prototype theory, categorization may be accomplished by the abstraction of a summary representation of a category that corresponds to the average, or central tendency, of all of the exemplars that have been experienced. New exemplars can be classified on the basis of their similarities to this "best example" (Aydin & Pearce, 1994; Huber, 2001; Posner & Keele, 1968).

In this chapter, we propose a modified version of feature theory as an account of visual categorization in pigeons. Thus, our focus will be mainly on "natural" categories (e.g., "people"), which have become a matter of increasing interest as it appears that animals are not indifferent to where the dividing lines between classes are placed. For example, pigeons trained to sort color images according to four human language categories (cats, flowers, cars, and chairs) learned faster and more completely than did pigeons trained to sort the same pictures into arbitrary groupings (Bhatt, Wasserman, Reynolds, & Knauss, 1988; Wasserman, Kiedinger, & Bhatt, 1988). Nevertheless, the features that control pigeons' classification behavior have hitherto been successfully determined mostly in experiments using carefully constructed sets of artificial stimuli (e.g., Cerella, 1980; Huber & Lenz, 1993; Wasserman, 1991, 1993). This is because it is relatively straightforward to identify the controlling stimulus aspects of such patterns and to determine by which criteria the discrimination was made. By contrast, it is extremely difficult, if not impossible, to specify the defining features of natural classes and to analyze the specific properties or combinations thereof that the animals use for categorization (see Aust & Huber, 2001).

One reason that naturally occurring perceptual categories resist definition lies in the fact that they are polymorphous; this means that no single, isolated feature is necessary or sufficient but that each contributes to determining class membership. Of course, we can list features belonging to a certain category, but it is impossible to identify even a single property that reliably distinguishes that category from all others. Instead, each feature only weakly correlates with category membership and determines the latter only in combination with other features typical of the respective category. Thus, not all category features have to be present to allow for "correct" classification, but the more of them an instance contains, the more typical it is of the category that it is regarded to be (Aust & Huber, 2002; Jitsumori & Delius, 2001; Morgan et al., 1976).

Although natural categories are hard to describe, they appear to be easy to use. It has been shown that not only humans and nonhuman primates but also pigeons are able to discriminate polymorphous categories. In fact, experiments on pigeon categorization, which used an analytic approach involving natural patterns, have yielded great success (e.g., Herrnstein & Loveland, 1964; Malott & Siddall, 1972; Nakamura, Croft, & Westbrook, 2003; Poole & Lander, 1971; Watanabe, 1997, 2001).

In our pigeon laboratory, we also use natural stimuli such as color photographs in many experiments, because we believe that the composition and structure of such stimuli come closer to what pigeons encounter in their environment and what their visual system is prepared to process than do artificially created patterns. When stimuli are simplified, information is lost that may be crucial for comprehension (Cerella, 1982). Furthermore, naturalistic images engage perceptual processes that may not be deployed by line projections (Watanabe, 2001). For these reasons, the theory outlined in this chapter has primarily (although not exclusively) been developed from the results of experiments on natural categories. To what extent it may also apply to artificially constructed stimulus classes remains to be seen.

In the remainder of the chapter, we first provide a short outline of our modified feature theory as an account of the categorization of natural stimuli. Then, we discuss its characteristics in more detail and support its main assumptions by reporting evidence from experiments carried out in our pigeon laboratory.

A MODIFIED FEATURE THEORY OF CATEGORIZATION

A main characteristic of the present account of the categorization of natural, polymorphous, stimulus classes is that it is itself polymorphous. This means that we are going to list a set of features that, in combination, characterize classification according to modified feature theory (MFT), but none of them will be specific to our account alone nor will any of them be sufficient for distinguishing the present approach from any other model of visual categorization.

First, it is central to MFT that categorization is based on common features of the positive and/or the negative class (i.e., at least some kind of category-specific information is abstracted); this distinguishes the present account from prototype theory as well as from radical versions of the exemplar view. Whereas the former postulates the abstraction of a prototype containing information about the entire class, the latter claims that categorization is exclusively based on individual exemplars with no allowance for the possibility of abstraction of category-specific information. However, the assumption that categorization is based on the extraction of common features does not distinguish MFT from other versions of feature theory (e.g., Cerella, 1982; Lea, 1984; Morgan et al., 1976) or from other versions of the exemplar view (e.g., Medin & Schaffer, 1978; Pearce, 1988, 1991).

Second, MFT postulates flexibility in both feature creation and selection. As also put forward by other versions of feature theory, discriminative features are thought to be progressively extracted and continuously modified in the course of categorization (D'Amato & Van Sant, 1988; Huber, 2001; Lea, 1984; Schyns & Rodet, 1997; Smith & Medin, 1981). But, in addition, MFT acknowledges that pigeons can easily switch between features within a particular task, thereby frequently detecting surprising features that are not immediately obvious to a human observer. This latter aspect is often underrated or neglected by traditional theories of categorization, which presuppose that animals use exactly and exclusively the same criteria as we ourselves would use; consequently, animals' discrimination will have to fail as soon as those particular features are removed.

Finally, we show that pigeons are able to use various features from different dimensions and levels of complexity. Pigeons have proved to be able to abstract in parallel both item- and category-specific information about a stimulus. They can use global or local stimulus properties or both. They recognize isolated stimulus components but may at the same time comprehend the configuration of a stimulus. They may rely on "simple" physical dimensions (e.g., intensity or color) in one task but respond to a polymorphous class rule (some "higher" feature) in the next.

The pigeons' ability to extract such complex rules leads us to argue that pigeons are able to detect spatial relations among features, a fact about which traditional feature theories are usually silent. Most traditional feature theories are guided by the idea of "internal lists" consisting of independent features that incrementally contribute to class membership. According to MFT, by contrast, features are aligned and interconnected instead of simply being summed. In other words, individual features are not independent of but rather are related to one another.

ABSTRACTION OF CATEGORY-SPECIFIC FEATURES

In the continuing debate regarding the nature of the stored information used by pigeons during complex visual categorization, a distinction has been made between discriminable aspects of stimuli that are characteristic of individual instances of a class and cues that are common to many class instances and that are thus characteristic of the entire category. In short, category exemplars entail category-level information plus idiosyncratic, or item-specific, information (see Aust & Huber, 2001; Wasserman et al., 1988).

Accordingly, two different types of information may enter into the representation that is formed during a concept discrimination task; categorization can be accomplished by relying on either one or the other (Medin, Dewey, & Murphy, 1983; see Aust & Huber, 2001). On the one hand, animals may memorize item-specific features of the training stimuli and generalize to novel stimuli on the basis of psychophysical similarity to features of past exemplars of the reinforced and nonreinforced classes; this we may call an *item-specific* or *nonanalytic strategy.* On the other hand, animals may abstract the category-specific features and then react in the same way to novel stimuli possessing these features; this we may call a categorical or analytic solution. Item-specific information is needed to discriminate between instances of the same class, whereas category-specific information is needed to discriminate between instances of different classes.

Proponents of strict exemplar models assume that intact stimuli are stored in memory and that only item-specific information is thought to enter the representation (e.g., Reed, 1972). More tolerant versions assume that classification is based on retrieving only a subset of the stored exemplars, presumably the most similar ones. Furthermore, some exemplar models predict sensitivity to context, category size, exemplar variability, and correlated features (e.g., Medin & Schaffer, 1978; Pearce, 1988, 1991; see Smith & Medin, 1999). Nevertheless, the critical assumption of even those more liberal models is that exemplars play the dominant role in categorization.

Feature theory, by contrast, emphasizes the abstraction of common features that are characteristic of the entire category. Acquisition of item-specific knowledge in concept identification tasks is not denied, but item-specific knowledge is thought to be rendered nonfunctional and dominated by category-specific information during learning by an abstraction process (e.g., Restle, 1957).

In practice, it is extremely difficult to distinguish between exemplar and feature models. Although they are based on different premises, they frequently make quite similar predictions. Therefore, results obtained in visual categorization tasks have for the most part been deemed to be compatible with both explanatory accounts (see Huber, 2001).

There are two obvious ways in which this dilemma may be resolved. First, one can try to design a task for which the two competing models actually make different predictions (as done, for example, by Huber & Lenz, 1993). Second, one may investigate in more detail the actual role of item- versus category-specific information in visual categorization tasks (as done, for example, by Aust & Huber, 2001, and by Loidolt, Aust, Meran, & Huber, 2003). From the latter experiments, which were designed to allow a distinction between—and weighing of—item- and category-level information, we hoped to detect the nature of the underlying mechanism.

In Aust and Huber (2001), we replicated and extended the findings of Herrnstein and Loveland (1964), who successfully trained pigeons to discriminate pictures showing humans from pictures that did not. In particular, the study was aimed at determining which of the two types of information—item or category—was gathered and stored by the pigeons during training and which information was then used to classify novel instances. Pigeons of a local Austrian race (*Columba livia* "Strasser") were used as subjects. Each bird was assigned to one of two experimental groups.

For one group (group P), the stimuli containing at least one person (class P) were designated positive, whereas the stimuli that did not contain any persons (class NP) were designated negative. These contingencies were reversed for the other group (group NP). The birds were trained with a go–no-go procedure as described by Vaughan and Greene (1984). The stimuli were color photographs, presented on a computer monitor at a size of 128 × 128 pixels.

The pigeons readily acquired the initial discrimination and were also able to generalize discriminative responding to novel instances. The study included three experiments, the last of which directly addressed the role of item- versus category-specific information (Experiment 3). The key idea was to bring information about the presence or absence of people (category-relevant) into conflict with information about the background (category-irrelevant; figure 17.1, top. For instance, we showed images of familiar people on familiar backgrounds from nonpeople images (type Pf + Bf); those stimuli provided contradictory information about class membership with respect to what the pigeons had learned about the contingencies of the constituting elements (backgrounds and people) during training. Because item-specific information contained in the human figures could have been stored as well, we also presented familiar backgrounds from nonpeople images onto which novel persons had been inserted (type Pn + Bf); those stimuli provided a contradiction between the class rule (people-present) and experienced background contingency (NP). Conversely, other test stimuli consisted of familiar persons on novel backgrounds (type Pf + Bn); those stimuli did not contain any conflicting information and served mainly as a control.

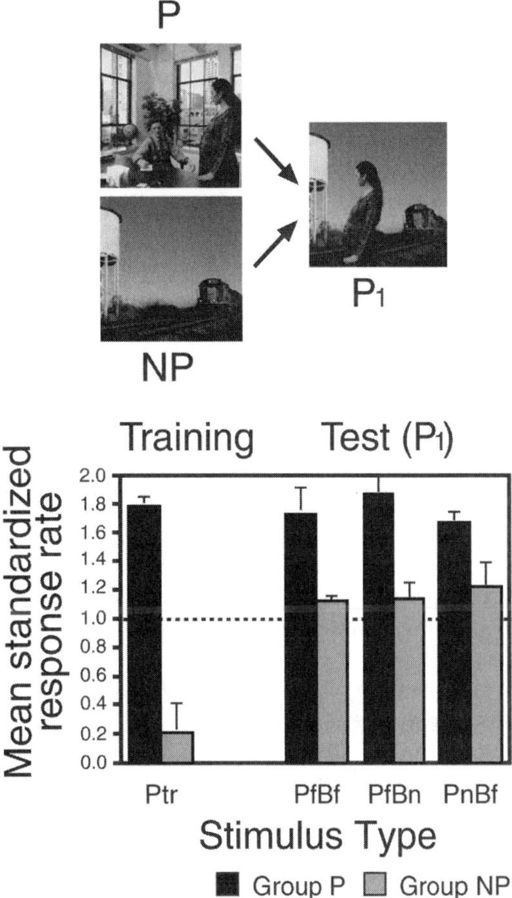

Figure 17.1. The results of the reversed contingency test in Aust and Huber (2001). *Top*, Example of a stimulus from class P1 and the original pictures from which it was derived. *Bottom*, Performance on the several types of test stimuli (P1: PfBf; PfBn; PnBf) shown in comparison with performance on the training stimuli of class P (Ptr). P, people; B, background; tr, training component; f, familiar; n, novel.

The most interesting finding to emerge from Experiment 3 was a significant difference between the groups (figure 17.1, bottom). In group P, performance was not at all disrupted by the modified contingency conditions. Even stimuli that contained conflicting information with respect to the previous contingencies (Pf + Bf) or in which the class rule was in conflict with the former background contingencies (Pn + Bf) were classified correctly; this result suggests that the birds made use of a category-based response rule, with classification being coupled to category-relevant features (i.e., features of the human figure). In group NP, performance was primarily controlled, neither by the category rule as in group P nor by irrelevant background information (as reported, for example, by Greene, 1983); instead, the pigeons responded to the test stimuli of all types at an intermediate level, which may have been due to a parallel use of both item- and category-specific information or, according to Greene's (1983) formulation, to the insufficient distinction between relevant and irrelevant features. If familiar stimuli are recognized by retrieving item-specific information and novel stimuli are classified by searching for a "target" (i.e., a person), then combinations of familiar and novel elements or of familiar elements belonging to different classes should lead to confusion and to decrements in performance.

We suspected that this between-group difference was rooted in the way in which the two sources of information—item-specific and category-specific—were weighed. The birds in group P appeared to favor category-specific over item-specific information, whereas the birds in group NP appeared to give these two kinds of information equal weight. Consequently, group P was able to deal more effectively than group NP with the present task. The fact that the target appeared on positive trials may have promoted the pigeons' ability to distinguish between relevant and irrelevant features in group P ("feature-positive effect") whereas the lack of reinforcement regarding the category-relevant features may have impeded correct weighing in group NP.

In summary, we found evidence that *both* types of information—item specific as well as category specific—were stored in parallel during category learning in both groups. This result is in keeping with the idea that identification and categorization need not occur to the exclusion of the other (Wasserman et al., 1988). However, as was shown in group P, novel items did not appear to be identified as belonging to class P because of the similarity between the new item and the exemplars of class P already stored in memory; had this been the case, then there should have been a drop in accuracy when novel people appeared in the pictures. Instead, the birds in group P appear to have used only category-level information to determine category membership of novel items; idiosyncratic information seems to have been irrelevant for that decision. Thus, different training conditions obviously encourage the use of different mixtures of these two types of information; more of one may imply less of the other (Medin et al., 1983; Wasserman et al., 1988).

In Loidolt et al. (2003), we trained pigeons to discriminate between pictures of human faces. Those images, developed at the Max Planck Institute for Biological Cybernetics in Tuebingen, Germany, to investigate human face processing, were used as stimuli in several pigeon studies in our laboratory (for details about the acquisition and the preprocessing of the images, see Troje & Bülthoff, 1996; Troje & Vetter, 1998; Vetter & Troje, 1995). The original picture collection was derived from a database of 200 three-dimensional head models obtained using a three-dimensional laser scanner. Those head models were sampled from humans between 20 and 40 years old, all of whom were free of make-up and any accessories such as glasses or earrings. Men were shaved and the hair on their head was digitally removed. The faces were shown from a frontal view, illuminated by ambient light and with a black background. Any variability in size and luminance was due to natural differences in head size and skin complexion.

The core experiment consisted of three experimental phases. In the first phase, which we called item-specific training, the subjects were exposed to a within-class discrimination problem. The pigeons had to discriminate among 20 faces of the same sex. In the second experimental phase, which we called category training, the same subjects were faced with a male–female classification problem using 100 stimuli not previously seen in item-specific training. In a subsequent test phase, the pigeons were presented with 100 test stimuli under nondifferential reinforcement test contingencies. The majority of the test stimuli ($n = 80$) were completely novel and tested the pigeons' transfer abilities: 50 were stimuli from the class that had not been used in item-specific training (type NN), 30 were stimuli from the class that had been used in item-specific training (type NI).

The test also included the presentation of the 20 stimuli shown during item-specific training (type II) to determine whether the pigeons would retain the previously formed associations (incorporating the item-specific aspects) despite subsequent category training. If that training resulted in the formation of class descriptions purely in terms of category-level invariants rather than in terms of complete exemplar descriptions, then all of the test faces should be classified according to that class description; previously formed associations with particular faces would thus be overruled by the category rule. If, however, category training were solved in the same way as item-specific training, namely by storing item-specific information together with the reinforcing consequence of each stimulus, then the faces of the first training phase should not change their associations (except to the extent that the stimuli from the two phases were similar; however, this possibility was controlled in a second experiment). In other words, the pigeons were retrained in the second training phase (category), but only at the abstract category level, not at the level of individual class instances, because the faces shown in the first training phase were not included in the second phase.

Thus, we were most interested in the responses to those 10 stimuli that entailed conflicting information: that is, different reinforcement contingencies during item-specific and category training. For example, if item-specific training required a discrimination between 10 positive (S+) and 10 negative (S–) male faces, and male was the positive class in subsequent category training, then would the S– stimuli shown in item-specific training continue to be signals for the absence of food in a subsequent test? The crucial question thus concerned the remaining associative strength of the idiosyncratic information in the test.

The test produced clear-cut results (figure 17.2). Not only were the completely novel test stimuli of type NI and of type NN classified according to their category information (sex) but so, too, were all 20 stimuli of type II. Thus, the 10 type II stimuli that bore conflicting information, that is, different reinforcement contingencies for item-specific and category-level stimulus aspects, had changed their associative value; this result strongly suggests that pecking was independent of the contingencies assigned to the stimuli in item-specific training but was completely dependent on category information. The associations between idiosyncratic memories and the reinforcement contingencies experienced during item-specific training (see also Heinemann & Chase, 1990) had no influence on the test performance of type II stimuli.

In two further experiments, we eliminated the possibilities that similarities between the training and test stimuli or the training sequence were responsible for the outcome of the main experiment. Finally, it might be argued that abstraction did not occur as a result of cue selection but because of forgetting, assuming that idiosyncratic information is more fragile than category-level information (Medin et al., 1983). However, given the enormous visual memory capacity demonstrated in pigeons (e.g., Vaughan & Greene, 1984; von Fersen & Delius, 1989), this possibility is unlikely.

In summary, the results indicated that (1) pigeons acquire tasks involving identification and categorization by attending to different sources of information provided by the training stimuli and (2) initially acquired item-specific information can be overruled by category-level information later acquired during categorization training. Together, the findings of these two studies (Aust & Huber, 2001; Loidolt et al., 2003) provide evidence of the pigeon's ability to abstract category-level information as a mechanism for true open-ended categorization. With the exception of group NP in Aust and Huber (2001), whose performance was probably contaminated by a feature-positive effect, our results are consistent with Restle's (1957) finding that idiosyncratic information can be rendered nonfunctional during classification learning.

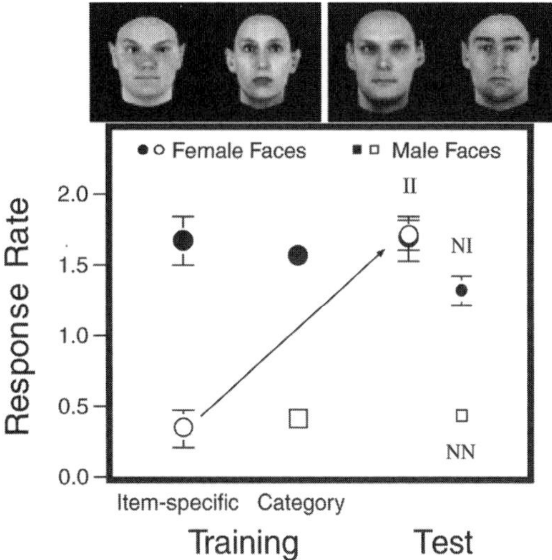

Figure 17.2. The test results of Experiment 1 of Loidolt et al. (2003) for one sample pigeon. We compared the mean pecking rates to test stimuli with the mean pecking rates to positive (*filled symbols*) and negative (*open symbols*) stimuli from item-specific and category training. The novel-novel type (NN) consisted of 50 novel stimuli from the class that had not been used in item-specific training. The novel-item type (NI) consisted of 30 novel stimuli from the class that had been used in item-specific training. The item-item type (II), finally, was represented by those 20 stimuli that had been learned individually in item-specific training. The most important results concern the differences in responding during the two presentations of the type II stimuli, shown first in item-specific training and then in test. The arrow indicates the radical shift of judgment by the pigeon.

FLEXIBILITY

A core assumption of MFT is that the pigeons are flexible in their use of strategies when acquiring a categorization task. This flexibility is two-fold. First, pigeons are extremely good at finding whatever attributes of a set of stimuli serve their purposes in relation to the contingencies of reinforcement (Greene, 1983; Herrnstein, 1990; Troje, Huber, Loidolt, Aust, & Fieder, 1999). Second, pigeons can flexibly shift their focus of attention between those features.

As already shown in the previous section, pigeons do not exclusively gather information about category-relevant features and neglect all other, category-irrelevant properties. Rather, they learn about any feature that occurs with some appreciable probability on trials and is followed by a specific reinforcing consequence such as food (D'Amato & Van Sant, 1988; Greene, 1983). Which features will actually be extracted depends on the demands of the specific task. This fact is acknowledged by recent versions of feature theory, including MFT, which assume that the features selected for classification depend on the nature of the category in question; the repertoire of features is continuously modified and adapted to the current demands of categorization ("feature learning").

Very often, pigeons have been found to use quite surprising attributes to help them distinguish between categories (Greene, 1983; Pearce, 1988, 1991). An example is provided by a study from our laboratory that examined the relative contributions of form (the morphology of a face) and visual texture information (the surface properties of a face) in the classification of human faces (Troje et al., 1999). The face images were chosen from the same stimulus pool as described earlier (Loidolt et al., 2003). However, due to a correspondence-based representation of the face models (for details, see Vetter & Troje, 1995), it was possible to separate form and texture information. The pigeons were assigned to one of three groups. Group O was presented with stimuli that contained both full texture and shape information. The stimuli presented to group T combined the average shape of all faces with individual texture information and thus could only be discriminated by making use of information about texture. The stimuli presented to group S combined the average texture of all faces with individual shape information and thus could only be discriminated by making use of information about shape.

The pigeons were trained in a go–no-go procedure to discriminate between 50 male and 50 female faces. The pigeons clearly preferred to extract texture rather than shape information, because only those birds that had texture information available (groups O and T) showed rapid acquisition and excellent transfer to 100 novel instances (figure 17.3). In fact, compared to training performance, the previously unseen 100 face images were spontaneously classified in the transfer test with no clear decrement in performance.

On closer inspection, it turned out that overall intensity in texture-only faces and overall size in shape-only faces provided strong cues for classification. On average, male faces were darker and larger than female faces. To investigate whether the successful birds had relied on those stimulus properties, the pigeons were presented with faces whose intensity (group T) or size (group S) corresponded to the average intensity or size, respectively, of the other class. Whereas pecking was reversed in group S, group T showed some evidence of positive transfer. These findings suggest that successful discrimination in group S, if any, was exclusively based on overall stimulus size, whereas in group T, average intensity was the main, but not the only, discriminative cue. In further experiments (Huber, Troje, Loidolt, Aust, & Grass, 2000), which were aimed at determining the residual information used by group T, we found evidence for the importance of color. In fact, male faces tended to be more reddish, whereas female faces tended to be more greenish and bluish.

The second aspect of flexibility concerns the fact that pigeons are able to cope with a particular classification task by shifting between various class-distinguishing features. For example, there is evidence that pigeons can flexibly shift their attention between global and local processing of hierarchical stimuli (see Cook, 2001, for a review). Cook concluded from several experiments that pigeons are quite flexible in how they process information from different spatial scales of a visual scene. Such shifts may be result from attentional factors or from stimulus factors, including variations in feature salience or stimulus organization. For example, removal of a particular class-distinguishing feature may make it necessary for a pigeon to compensate for its loss by shifting to other, reliable cues.

In a follow-up study by Troje et al. (1999), we found that the pigeons used cues related to color

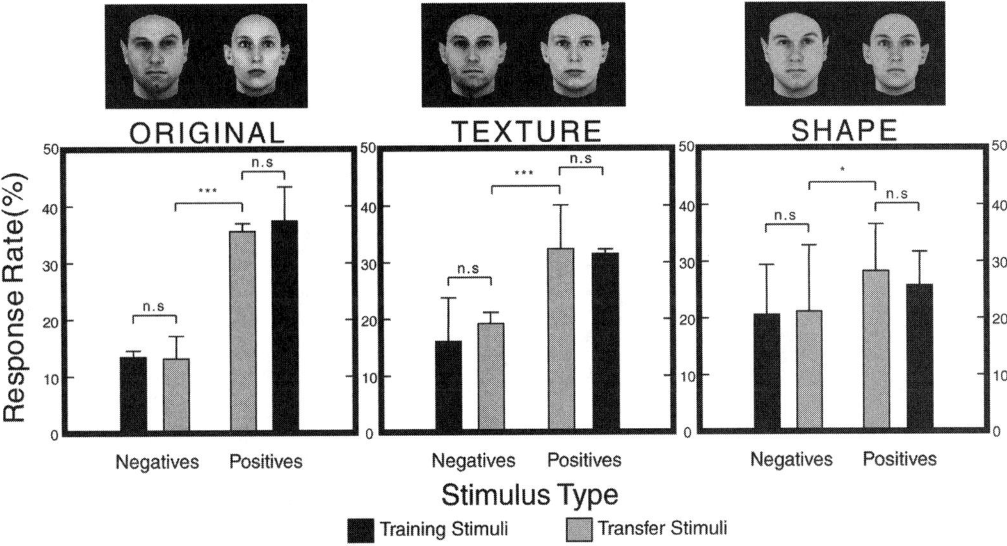

Figure 17.3. Training and transfer performance of three groups of pigeons presented with 100 training and 100 test stimuli in Troje et al. (1999). For each group, we computed the relative number of pecks emitted to positive and negative training stimuli as well as positive and negative test stimuli. Each bar represents the mean + *SEM* ($n = 8$).

and shading when intensity was ruled out as a category-distinguishing feature (Huber et al., 2000). Although the pigeons ($n = 11$) experienced considerable difficulty, they eventually solved that task. We investigated the pigeons' subjective separation of the feature space according to the experimenter-defined class rule using principal component analysis (PCA); PCA was applied to the stimuli in order to find those dimensions that account for most of the variance within the complete picture set. We found a significant correlation between pecking rate and the difference in relative luminance between the upper and lower halves of the face; this luminance difference was higher in men than in women, presumably because of the shadow created by the beard. We also found a significant correlation between pecking rate and face color. Male faces were more red than female faces, whereas female faces were more blue and green than male faces. Some correlation was found between pecking rate and patterns of shading. Presenting the birds "supernormal" faces (i.e., test stimuli that varied merely along one of those dimensions but exceeded the normal feature variation) revealed that their classification behavior was indeed controlled by these feature parameters (figure 17.4).

As final step in that study, we predicted that if a polymorphous combination of color, intensity, and shading information described the categorization code that was extracted by the pigeons in the task, then the subjects' classification behavior should be impaired in proportion to the degradation of that information. In contrast, degradation of the faces that retained the three components of the pigeons' class description should not influence the subjects' classification ability. We conducted only three such tests by presenting the pigeons with gray-scale versions, blurred versions, and block portraits of faces. Although the loss of color information produced substantial performance decrements in all subjects, neither blurring nor blocking led to a significant disruption of the pigeons' classification ability.

In sum, our systematic manipulation of the feature content revealed that the pigeons were able to track the complex categorization task by attending exactly to those feature dimensions that most accurately divided the stimulus classes into the experimenter-defined categories "male" and "female." Note, however, that we are not arguing in favor of traditional theories of similarity (e.g., Tversky, 1977), in which features are regarded as the building blocks of complex visual objects or scenes. In contrast to those static conceptions of similarity, we consider features to be *dynamic* (i.e., varying with the context and the task) and to be a

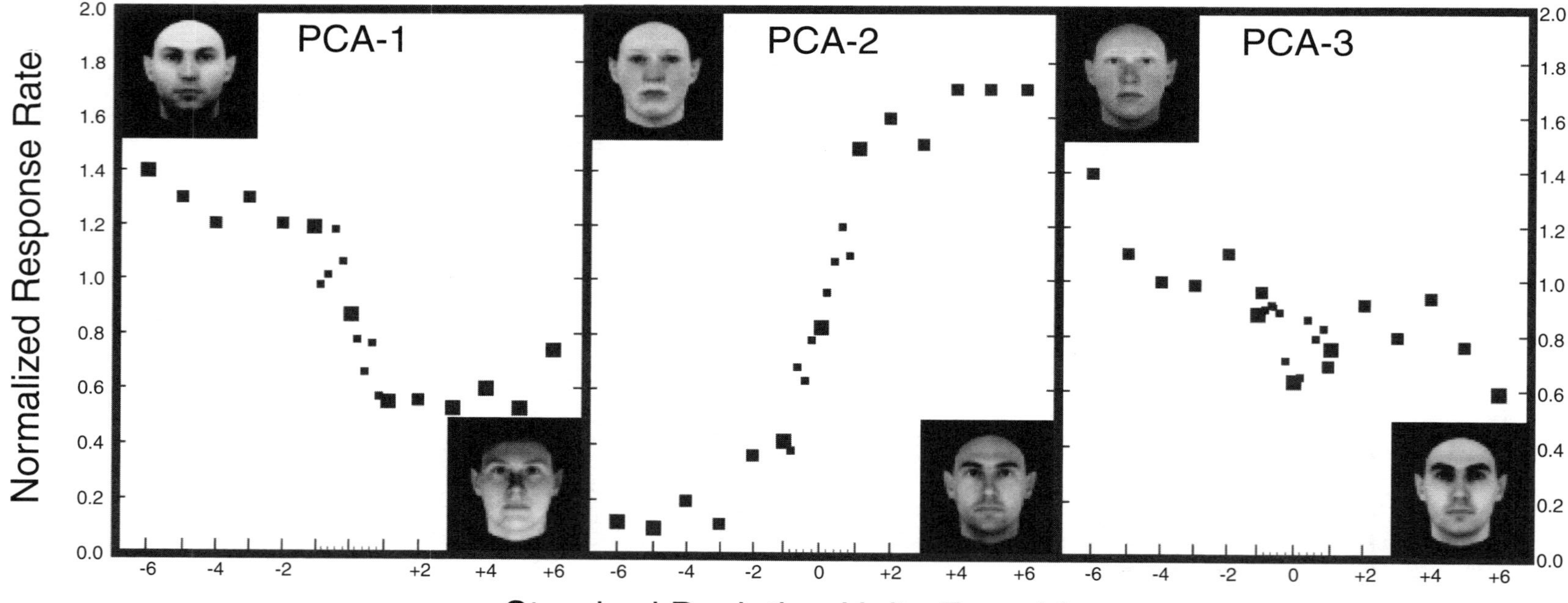

Figure 17.4. Results of the principal component test in Huber et al. (2000). Depicted are response rates as a function of distance from the average face (measured in standard deviations) along the first three principal components in both directions. In each graph, we included the response rates (mean of 11 subjects) to synthetic faces that varied within a naturally occurring range (from −1 to +1) as well as the "supernormal" faces that widely exceed that range.

product of the perceiver rather than of the objects themselves (Keane, Smyth, & O'Sullivan, 2001).

We may also use Herrnstein's (1984) carpentry metaphor to describe the categorization process as a kind of perceptual carpentry; from the available stimulus dimensions, differential reinforcement selects those that distinguish positive and negative instances. The resulting category features are then likely to be woven into a polymorphous rule for categorizing, even if item-specific information is also stored in picture memory. Ultimately, natural or "generic" visual categorization (Huber, 1999) should serve to abstract class-defining attributes from individual variations and to enact the correspondence between visual and natural categories (Cerella, 1979).

LEVELS OF ABSTRACTION

Animals may represent classes of stimuli in three rather distinct ways: (1) pictorially, as arrays or configurations of features or elements defined by their own absolute values (called "imaginal" representations by Premack, 1983); (2) abstractly, as relations between or among items; and (3) symbolically, as relations between relations. There is evidence to indicate that chimpanzees (Thompson & Oden, 1996) and baboons (Fagot, Wasserman, & Young, 2001) are capable of symbolic representations.

As to pigeons, there is clear evidence to suggest that they form pictorial representations but growing evidence that they form abstract representations (e.g., Wasserman, Hugart, & Kirkpatrick-Steger, 1995) and no evidence that they form symbolic representations (Mackintosh, 2000). Some birds, such as ravens and parrots, and most primates have been shown to be capable of abstract but not symbolic representation, whereas apes are probably able to form symbolic representations.

The difference between pictorial and abstract representation in pigeons is not always immediately obvious. This point is well illustrated by attempts to teach pigeons the relational concepts "same/different" and "symmetry." For example, Wasserman et al. (1995) claimed to have obtained strong evidence of *categorical* same/different conceptualization in pigeons because the birds in that study exhibited very good transfer to arrays of novel icons. However, Young and Wasserman (1997) later discovered that the pigeons' discriminative performance in that task may actually have been controlled by the degree of entropy inherent in the stimulus arrays. Furthermore, despite earlier claims that pigeons had formed symmetry concepts (Delius & Habers, 1978; Delius & Nowak, 1982), we have found this ability to be severely limited (Huber et al., 1999).

In many accounts of visual categorization in pigeons, researchers have taken extreme positions regarding the nature of the stimulus attributes that a pigeon might be able to exploit. For example, experiments were carried out in order to find evidence of perception being either dominated by global or by local stimulus properties. Objects were thought to be perceived as consisting either of independent elements or as coherent figures. Generally, pigeon categorization was interpreted as being mediated either by "concepts" or by simple physical dimensions. However, explanations in terms of such dichotomies are probably oversimplifications and insufficient to capture the diversity of pigeon classification behavior.

GLOBAL AND LOCAL PROPERTIES

As we use the term, *global features* are characteristics of the whole stimulus, such as size, orientation, and brightness. They roughly correspond to the types of features that are computed automatically and in parallel, at every location in the visual field at the same time (e.g., Treisman & Gelade, 1980). In contrast, distinct stimulus locations may be processed serially, one item and one location at a time, by driving an attentional focus through the visual field. In this sense, *local features* are restricted portions of an image that have semiautonomous, object-like status in visual perception (Palmer, 1999; see Aust & Huber, 2001). An image of a human body, for example, is perceived as being composed of a head, a torso, two arms, and two legs.

The extent to which pigeons exploit global stimulus aspects in comparison to local properties is still a matter of ongoing research. Some of the results obtained in our laboratory suggest a predominance of local features, whereas others point to the use of global properties.

In Aust and Huber (2001, Experiment 2), we investigated the relative importance of global compared with local features in the categorization of pictures according to the presence or absence of people by examining the effects of progressive stimulus fragmentation. Over the course of scrambling, many global properties of the images (e.g., overall brightness) remained intact, whereas local elements (e.g., human figures and objects or object-like parts) were gradually eliminated. If the pigeons mainly relied on local information, then fragmentation should result in a decrease in performance. If, however, classification was guided by global stimulus properties such as overall intensity, then performance should remain widely unaffected despite scrambling.

The pigeons were presented with scrambled versions of familiar as well as novel stimuli. There were six different degrees of scramble, defined by two interacting rules concerning size and distribution of the component square elements (for details, see Aust & Huber, 2001). In the extreme case (degree 6), the pictures were divided into 4,096 squares of 2 × 2 pixels, which were then distributed arbitrarily over the whole picture area (figure 17.5). We found that progressive scrambling resulted in a reduction of discrimination performance, which also depended on the familiarity of the test stimuli. Although the pigeons were able to discriminate even strongly scrambled versions of familiar stimuli, they generally failed on even low degrees of scrambling when the stimuli were novel.

We interpreted the decline in discrimination performance as evidence that the pigeons' classification of people-present/people-absent stimuli was not based on the computation of global features that remained intact across increased scrambling. Instead, we suggested that the birds relied on small identification elements of the previously learned exemplars that survived the fragmentation of the stimulus. Such information units are likely to be characterized by the specific appearance of individual pixels or small pixel blocks corresponding to distinct colors or brightness values.

A somewhat different result was obtained in our "male/female" discrimination experiment (Troje et al., 1999). As already outlined, global stimulus properties—namely, overall intensity and color in texture-only faces and overall size in shape-only faces—turned out to be strong classification cues. More local aspects, such as a brightness gradient or shading aspects, were less important and were used only after color and overall intensity had been removed.

Thus, on the one hand, we found that pigeons relied on local stimulus properties in a "people-present/people-absent" discrimination task (Aust & Huber, 2001); on the other hand, they attended to global information such as intensity and color in a "male/female" discrimination task (Huber et al., 2000; Troje et al., 1999). How can these conflicting results be reconciled? As noted by Cook

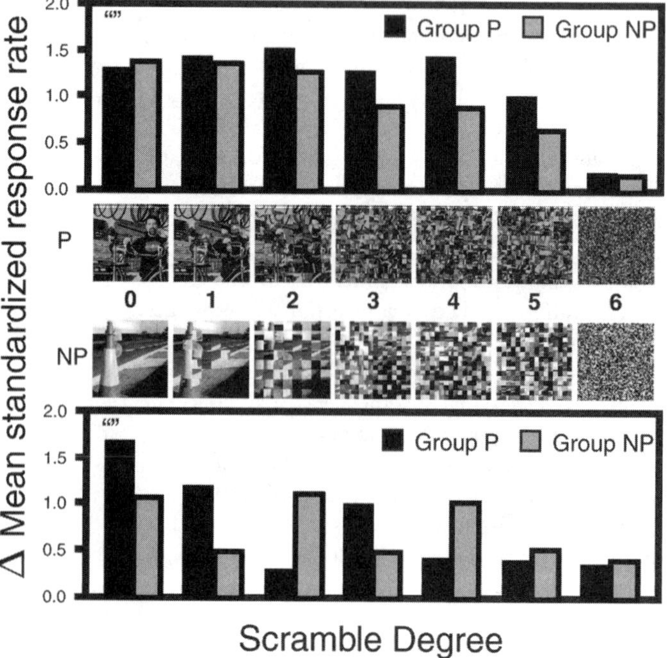

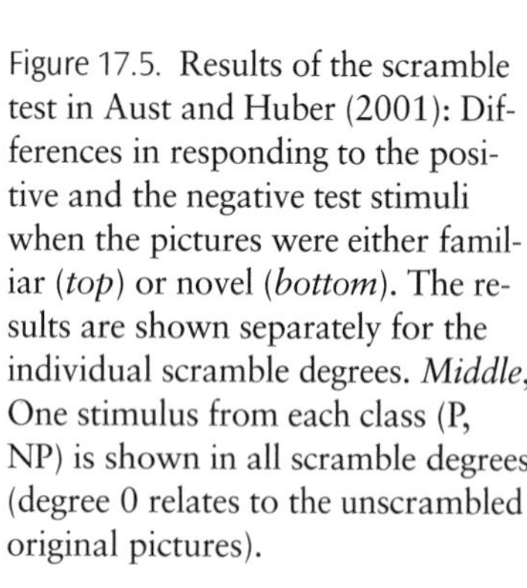
Figure 17.5. Results of the scramble test in Aust and Huber (2001): Differences in responding to the positive and the negative test stimuli when the pictures were either familiar (*top*) or novel (*bottom*). The results are shown separately for the individual scramble degrees. *Middle*, One stimulus from each class (P, NP) is shown in all scramble degrees (degree 0 relates to the unscrambled original pictures).

(2001), the answer must be more complex than simply saying that one level consistently dominates the other (see also Kirkpatrick-Steger & Wasserman, 1996; Kirkpatrick-Steger, Wasserman, & Biederman, 1996, 1998, 2000; Wasserman, Kirkpatrick-Steger, Van Hamme, & Biederman, 1993). Instead, the available evidence suggests that both levels are processed and that they interact with one another. Among other factors, the organization of the avian visual system, viewing distance, attention, stimulus organization, feature salience, and motion have been shown to be critical to determining which of these hierarchical levels will come to control behavior (see Cook, 2001).

ELEMENTAL AND CONFIGURAL PERCEPTION

The question of whether pigeons perceive objects as collections of independent elements or in the form of coherent entities has occasioned considerable controversy among researchers. In an early experiment by Cerella (1980), pigeons were trained to discriminate pictures of "Charlie Brown" from other characters of the "Peanuts gang"; later, the birds were found to generalize roughly equally to partial or obstructed views of Charlie Brown as well as to scrambled or inverted views. Cerella concluded that responding was guided by specific stimulus features and that spatial relations among features were not encoded. Recently, however, considerable evidence has emerged that pigeons are quite able to attend to organizational properties (e.g., Aust & Huber, 2003; Matsukawa, Inoue, & Jitsumori, 2004; Wasserman et al., 1993; Watanabe, 2001; also see Kirkpatrick, 2001, for a review).

In the third of our "people-present/people-absent" discrimination studies (Aust & Huber, 2003), we investigated whether the pigeons perceived the depicted human figures as compounds of unrelated, independent features associated with reinforcement or whether they recognized the spatial arrangement of the constituent target components. The birds were presented with "people-present" stimuli—both familiar and novel ones—that contained human figures that were distorted in various ways. Performance on these distorted stimuli decreased compared with the intact original pictures from which they had been derived. This result indicated that the birds must have recognized that parts of the depicted targets were not in their proper spatial order, reflecting the importance of relational information. At the same time, however, peck rates clearly exceeded the level of responding found for regular "people-absent" stimuli. This result indicated that the birds also recognized that the distorted versions contained the same elements as the intact originals. In summary, the pattern of results found was compatible with the notion that responding was controlled by both the constituting target components and their spatial relations (as earlier reported and discussed by Kirkpatrick-Steger et al., 1996, 1998; Van Hamme, Wasserman, & Biederman, 1992; Wasserman et al., 1993; Watanabe, 2001; Watanabe & Ito, 1991; see also Cook, 2001, and Kirkpatrick, 2001).

As a subsidiary result, we found that performance decrements were significant only when the test stimuli were derived from novel pictures. We concluded that with familiar, but not with novel, stimuli, the loss of configural integrity could be compensated for to some extent by item-specific information, acquired by experience with the training stimuli.

Obviously, pigeons can gather information about both the individual component parts of a stimulus and their spatial arrangement. This is, however, not to say that they always do, as shown in the Peanuts study by Cerella (1980). How and why these different types of stimulus perception develop is still poorly understood. But, as the elemental/configural problem is in many respects closely related to the question of global versus local processing, we suspect that discriminative stimulus control may depend on similar factors in both cases (see previous section).

"SIMPLE" VERSUS "HIGHER" FEATURES

For some time, Herrnstein and Loveland's (1964) pioneering experiment was taken as evidence that pigeons make category judgments on the basis of abstract or "conceptual" rules. In the late 1970s, a countercurrent to this view developed with the focus of pigeon classification studies shifting toward experimental designs that involved simpler sets of stimuli (Cerella, 1979; Lea & Harrison, 1978; Morgan et al., 1976; see Huber, 2001; Wasserman, 1991, 1993). A consensus grew that the results of most, if not all, of the previous data on pigeon

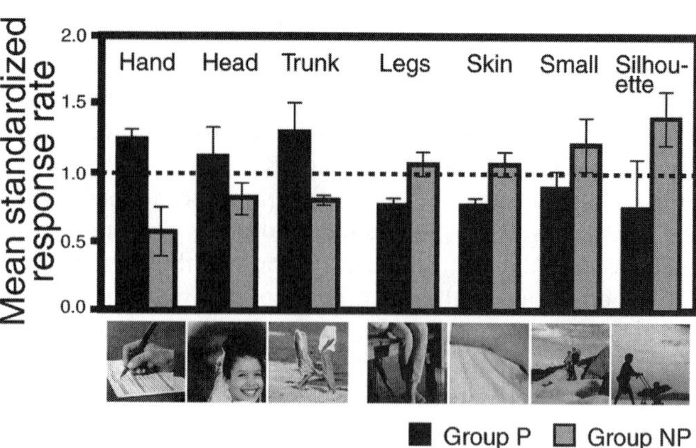

Figure 17.6. Performance to pictures showing impoverished versions of "people-present" stimuli in Aust and Huber (2002). *Left*, Stimulus types that were treated as members of class P (hands, heads, trunks). *Right*, Stimulus types that were treated as members of class NP (legs, patches of skin, particularly small human figures, silhouettes).

categorization could be explained by means of simple perceptual features.

Some researchers, such as Herrnstein (1985), tried to reconcile these contradictory positions by assuming that pigeons can categorize at high levels of abstraction, but they do not have to do so. He pointed out that pigeons "have surprisingly strong resources for learning specific exemplars," whereas "one form of discrimination at which pigeons . . . are deficient, is the relational" (p. 136).

MFT shares that view in assuming that pigeons are able to use various classification strategies involving different levels of complexity, depending on the specific task. Furthermore, categorization is claimed to have a purely perceptual basis. Although MFT does not explicitly rule out pigeons' ability to use abstract relations among stimuli (such as same/different, for example), it is assumed that pigeons are for the most part restricted to more concrete imaginal codes.

The spectrum of classification strategies taken into consideration by MFT ranges from the use of simple physical dimensions to the extraction of complex target figures. The former may, for example, include color or brightness cues, shading, or stimulus size, as found in our male/female classification experiment (Huber et al., 2000; Troje et al., 1999). The latter refers to the fact that pigeons frequently handle complex perceptual classes by combining various features in a manner that most closely corresponds to the given category (see Huber, 1999, 2001, for an extended discussion). Classification is then based on a collection of weighted category-relevant features, which are woven into a polymorphous class rule.

In our studies on "people-present/people-absent" discriminations (Aust & Huber, 2001, 2002), for example, we found that various target properties (e.g., target size, structural properties, presence of hands, heads, clothes, etc.) contributed to membership in class P (figure 17.6). Some features proved to be particularly central to class P and made good predictors of class P even when they were shown in isolation (e.g., hands and heads), whereas others turned out to be rather irrelevant (e.g., legs and skin color).

Furthermore, we found evidence that pigeons encoded the spatial relations among the individual parts of the target figures (Aust & Huber, 2003). Thus, MFT hypothesizes the use of relational features, not at an abstract and highly cognitive level but only in a strictly perceptual sense. In short, MFT accounts for the use of simple stimulus dimensions as well as for the use of feature compounds, including spatial relations among target components, but not for the extraction of abstract relations among stimuli.

CONCLUSION

In this chapter, we have presented a modified feature theory as an account of pigeon visual categorization. On the one hand, MFT combines important aspects of several other theories. For example, it rests on the premise that category-specific information is abstracted, as is also assumed by other versions of feature theory. But, additionally, it claims that item-specific features are learned, thereby finding itself in agreement with proponents of the exemplar view. Furthermore, MFT shares the assumption with other feature theories that features are flexible insofar as they are progressively extracted and developed in the course of category learning and are continuously adjusted to the demands of a particular task.

On the other hand, MFT clearly goes beyond traditional theories. First, in the domain of discrimination learning and categorization, traditional theories have for the most part assumed that animals exclusively learn relevant features and ignore irrelevant stimulus dimensions. MFT, by contrast, claims that any feature inherent to a stimulus may be learned, with a feature-weighing process rendering irrelevant and noninformative aspects nonfunctional. Furthermore—in contrast to other feature theories—MFT emphasizes that not only feature creation but also feature choice is characterized by considerable flexibility, meaning that a pigeon's focus may easily switch between features. For example, if a particular cue is made unavailable, then a pigeon may resort to other—perhaps formerly less important and even spurious—stimulus properties.

A cornerstone of MFT is the assumption that categorization may be based on various types of features and different ways of processing those features. The available evidence suggests that stimulus perception, feature selection, and processing mode strongly depend on the specifics of a particular task; different types of features may even coexist in a pigeon's internal representation of a category. Item- and category-specific learning, global and local processing, elemental and configural perception, or the extraction of simple, physical dimensions and "higher" features do not necessarily occur to the exclusion of the others in a particular task but may be stored in parallel. Which aspects will actually come to control categorization depends on a variety of parameters, including the size and structure of the category, stimulus design, training history, attentional factors, individual and species preferences, etc.

Finally, MFT differs from other feature theories with respect to the nature of the representation of a category. Traditionally, it has been assumed by proponents of feature models that the features used for categorization are independent and isolated from one another. This belief usually appears in the form of "internal feature lists," which makes one think of random accumulations of unrelated items at arbitrary positions that independently gain and lose predictive value (i.e., weight). By contrast, according to MFT, features are interconnected and frequently interact with each other. MFT can better be conceived as a three-dimensional network with interrelated nodes in various spatial dimensions representing the individual features. Representing features in the form of a net instead of a list emphasizes the fact that changes in the value of one feature affect the values of all other features. So, if some features gain predictive value, that is, they are—through feature learning—assigned more weight in the course of the categorization process, then they do so on the expense of other features represented as knots in the net. Conversely, if a feature loses weight or is even completely removed, then other features will gain predictive value instead.

For example, in Troje et al. (1999), the pigeons considered overall intensity and color information to be very effective discriminative cues. As a consequence, those stimulus aspects gained weight at the expense of other features, such as brightness gradients or shading cues; the latter were less important for discriminating between male and female faces in the first place. When, however, overall intensity and color were removed from the images, alternative cues such as brightness gradients and shading became important; that is, they gained relative weight.

To conclude, in this chapter, we have reported various experiments carried out in our laboratory to support the core assumptions of MFT. In testing the theory, we have only considered natural, polymorphous stimulus classes, mirrored by the polymorphous nature of MFT itself. We have described several key characteristics, none of which is singly necessary or sufficient to distinguish MFT from any other theory of categorization. Together, however, they provide a new and, we believe, more appropriate view of pigeon categorization than do previous accounts.

Acknowledgments The research reported in this chapter was supported by grants from the Austrian Science Foundation (P10975, P14175, T139). We acknowledge the collaboration of N. Troje.

References

Astley, S. L., & Wasserman, E. A. (1992). Categorical discrimination and generalization in pigeons: All negative stimuli are not created equal. *Journal of Experimental Psychology: Animal Behavior Processes, 18*, 193–207.

Aust, U., & Huber, L. (2001). The role of item- and category-specific information in the discrimination of people- vs. nonpeople images by pigeons. *Animal Learning and Behavior*, *29*, 107–119.

Aust, U., & Huber, L. (2002). Target-defining features in a "people-present/people-absent" discrimination task by pigeons. *Animal Learning and Behavior*, *30*, 165–176.

Aust, U., & Huber, L. (2003). Elemental versus configural perception in a "people-present/people-absent" discrimination task by pigeons. *Learning and Behavior*, *31*, 213–224.

Aydin, A., & Pearce, J. M. (1994). Prototype effects in categorization by pigeons. *Journal of Experimental Psychology: Animal Behavior Processes*, *20*, 264–277.

Bhatt, R. S., Wasserman, E. A., Reynolds, W. F., Jr., & Knauss, K. S. (1988). Conceptual behavior in pigeons: Categorization of both familiar and novel examples from four classes of natural and artificial stimuli. *Journal of Experimental Psychology: Animal Behavior Processes*, *14*, 219–234.

Cerella, J. (1979). Visual classes and natural categories in the pigeon. *Journal of Experimental Psychology: Human Perception and Performance*, *5*, 68–77.

Cerella, J. (1980). The pigeon's analysis of pictures. *Pattern Recognition*, *12*, 1–6.

Cerella, J. (1982). Mechanisms of concept formation in the pigeon. In D. J. Ingle, M. A. Goodale, & R. J. W. Mansfield (Eds.), *Analysis of visual behavior* (pp. 241–249). Cambridge, MA: MIT Press.

Cook, R. G. (2001). Hierarchical stimulus processing in pigeons. In R. G. Cook (Ed.), *Avian visual cognition*. Retrieved August 27, 2005, from http://www.pigeon.psy.tufts.edu/avc/.

D'Amato, M. R., & Van Sant, P. (1988). The person concept in monkeys (*Cebus apella*). *Journal of Experimental Psychology: Animal Behavior Processes*, *14*, 43–55.

Delius, J. D., & Habers, G. (1978). Symmetry: Can pigeons conceptualize it? *Behavioral Biology*, *22*, 336–342.

Delius, J. D., Jitsumori, M., & Siemann, M. (2000). Stimulus equivalences through discrimination reversals. In C. Heyes & L. Huber (Eds.), *The evolution of cognition* (pp. 103–122). Cambridge, MA: MIT Press.

Delius, J. D., & Nowak, B. (1982). Visual symmetry recognition by pigeons. *Psychological Research*, *44*, 199–212.

Fagot, J., Wasserman, E. A., & Young, M. E. (2001). Discriminating the relation between relations: The role of entropy in abstract conceptualization by baboons (*Papio papio*) and humans (*Homo sapiens*). *Journal of Experimental Psychology: Animal Behavior Processes*, *27*, 316–328.

Greene, S. (1983). Feature memorization in pigeon concept formation. In M. L. Commons, R. J. Herrnstein, & A. R. Wagner (Eds.), *Quantitative analysis of behavior* (Vol. 4, pp. 209–229). Cambridge, MA: Ballinger.

Heinemann, E. G., & Chase, S. (1990). A quantitative model for pattern recognition. In M. L. Commons, R. J. Herrnstein, S. Kosslyn, & D. Mumford (Eds.), *Quantitative analyses of behavior: Computational and clinical approaches to pattern recognition and concept formation* (Vol. 9, pp. 109–126). Hillsdale, NJ: Erlbaum.

Herrnstein, R. J. (1984). Objects, categories, and discriminative stimuli. In H. L. Roitblat, T. G. Bever, & H. S. Terrace (Eds.), *Animal cognition* (pp. 233–261). Hillsdale, NJ: Erlbaum.

Herrnstein, R. J. (1985). Riddles of natural categorization. In L. Weiskrantz (Ed.), *Animal intelligence* (Vol. 7, pp. 129–144). Oxford: Clarendon Press.

Herrnstein, R. J. (1990). Levels of stimulus control: A functional approach. *Cognition*, *37*, 133–166.

Herrnstein, R. J., & Loveland, D. H. (1964). Complex visual concept in the pigeon. *Science*, *146*, 549–551.

Herrnstein, R. J., Loveland, D. H., & Cable, C. (1976). Natural concepts in pigeons. *Journal of Experimental Psychology: Animal Behavior Processes*, *2*, 285–311.

Honig, W. K., & Urcuioli, P. J. (1981). The legacy of Guttman and Kalish (1956): 25 Years of research on stimulus generalization. *Journal of the Experimental Analysis of Behavior*, *26*, 405–445.

Huber, L. (1999). Generic perception: Open-ended categorization of natural classes. *Cahiers de Psychologie Cognitive/Current Psychology of Cognition*, *18*, 845–887.

Huber, L. (2001). Visual categorization in pigeons. In R. G. Cook (Ed.), *Avian visual cognition*. Retrieved August 27, 2005, from http://www.pigeon.psy.tufts.edu/avc/.

Huber, L., Aust, U., Michelbach, G., Ölzant, S., Loidolt, M., & Nowotny, R. (1999). Limits of symmetry conceptualization in pigeons. *Quarterly Journal of Experimental Psychology*, *52B*, 351–379.

Huber, L., & Lenz, R. (1993). A test of the linear feature model of polymorphous concept discrimination with pigeons. *Quarterly Journal of Experimental Psychology*, *46B*, 1–18.

Huber, L., Troje, N. F., Loidolt, M., Aust, U., & Grass, D. (2000). Natural categorization through multiple feature learning in pigeons. *Quarterly Journal of Experimental Psychology*, *53B*, 341–357.

Jitsumori, M., & Delius, J. D. (2001). Object recognition and object categorization in animals. In T. Matsuzawa (Ed.). *Primate origins of human cognition and behavior* (pp. 269–293). Tokyo: Springer.

Keane, M. T., Smyth, B., & O'Sullivan, J. (2001). Dynamic similarity: A processing perspective on similarity. In U. Hahn & M. Ramscar (Eds.), *Similarity and categorization* (pp. 179–192). Oxford: Oxford University Press.

Kirkpatrick, K. (2001). Object perception. In R. G. Cook (Ed.), *Avian visual cognition*. Retrieved August 27, 2005, from http://www.pigeon.psy.tufts.edu/avc/.

Kirkpatrick-Steger, K., & Wasserman, E. A. (1996). The what and the where of the pigeon's processing of complex visual stimuli. *Journal of Experimental Psychology: Animal Behavior Processes*, *22*, 60–67.

Kirkpatrick-Steger, K., Wasserman, E. A., & Biederman, I. (1996). Effects of spatial rearrangement of object components on picture recognition in pigeons. *Journal of the Experimental Analysis of Behavior*, *65*, 465–475.

Kirkpatrick-Steger, K., Wasserman, E. A., & Biederman, I. (1998). Effects of geon deletion, scrambling, and movement on picture recognition in pigeons. *Journal of Experimental Psychology: Animal Behavior Processes*, *24*, 34–46.

Kirkpatrick-Steger, K., Wasserman, E. A., & Biederman, I. (2000). The pigeon's discrimination of shape and location information. *Visual Cognition*, *7*, 417–436.

Kruschke, J. K. (1992). ALCOVE: An exemplar-based connectionist model of category learning. *Psychological Review*, *99*, 22–44.

Lea, S. E. G. (1984). In what sense do pigeons learn concepts? In H. L. Roitblat, T. G. Bever, & H. S. Terrace (Eds.), *Animal cognition* (pp. 263–276). Hillsdale, NJ: Erlbaum.

Lea, S. E. G., & Harrison, S. N. (1978). Discrimination of polymorphous stimulus sets by pigeons. *Quarterly Journal of Experimental Psychology*, *30*, 521–537.

Loidolt, M., Aust, U., Meran, I., & Huber, L. (2003). Pigeons use item-specific and category-specific information in the identification and categorization of human face stimuli. *Journal of Experimental Psychology: Animal Behavior Processes*, *29*, 261–276.

Lubow, R. E. (1974). Higher-order concept formation in the pigeon. *Journal of the Experimental Analysis of Behavior*, *21*, 475–483.

Mackintosh, N. J. (2000). Abstraction and discrimination. In C. Heyes & L. Huber (Eds.), *Evolution of cognition* (pp. 123–141). Cambridge, MA: MIT Press.

Malott, R. W., & Siddall, J. W. (1972). Acquisition of the people concept in pigeons. *Psychological Reports*, *31*, 3–13.

Matsukawa, A., Inoue, S., & Jitsumori, M. (2004). Pigeon's recognition of cartoons: Effects of fragmentation, scrambling, and deletion of elements. *Behavioural Processes*, *65*, 25–34.

Medin, D. L. (1989). Concepts and conceptual structure. *American Psychologist*, *44*, 1469–1481.

Medin, D. L., Dewey, G. I., & Murphy, T. D. (1983). Relationships between item and category learning: Evidence that abstraction is not automatic. *Journal of Experimental Psychology: Learning, Memory, and Cognition*, *9*, 607–625.

Medin, D. L., & Schaffer, M. M. (1978). A context theory of classification learning. *Psychological Review*, *85*, 217–238.

Morgan, M. J., Fitch, M. D., Holman, J. G., & Lea, S. E. G. (1976). Pigeons learn the concept of an "A". *Perception*, *5*, 57–66.

Mostofsky, D. (1965). *Stimulus generalization*. Stanford, CA: Stanford University Press.

Nakamura, T., Croft, D. B., & Westbrook, R. F. (2003). Domestic pigeons (*Columba livia*) discriminate between photographs of individual pigeons. *Learning & Behavior*, *31*, 307–317.

Palmer, S. E. (1999). *Vision science: Photons to phenomenology*. Cambridge, MA: MIT Press.

Pearce, J. M. (1988). Stimulus generalization and the acquisition of categories by pigeons. In L. Weiskrantz (Ed.), *Thought without language* (pp. 132–152). Oxford: Oxford University Press.

Pearce, J. M. (1991). The acquisition of abstract and concrete categories by pigeons. In L. Dachowski & C. Flaherty (Eds.), *Current topics in animal learning: Brain, emotion, and cognition* (pp. 141–164). Hillsdale, NJ: Erlbaum.

Poole, J., & Lander, D. G. (1971). The pigeon's concept of pigeon. *Psychonomic Science*, *25*, 157–158.

Posner, M. I., & Keele, S. W. (1968). On the genesis of abstract ideas. *Journal of Experimental Psychology*, *77*, 353–363.

Premack, D. (1983). Animal cognition. *Annual Review of Psychology*, *34*, 351–362.

Reed, S. K. (1972). Pattern recognition and categorization. *Cognitive Psychology*, *3*, 382–407.

Restle, F. (1957). Theory of selective learning, with probable reinforcement. *Psychological Review*, *64*, 182–191.

Schyns, P., & Rodet, L. (1997). Categorization creates functional features. *Journal of Experimental Psychology: Learning, Memory, and Cognition*, *23*, 681–696.

Smith, E., & Medin, D. (1981). *Categories and concepts*. Cambridge, MA: Harvard University Press.

Smith, E., & Medin, D. (1999). The exemplar view. In E. Margolis & S. Laurence (Eds.),

Concepts: Core readings (pp. 207–221). Cambridge, MA: MIT Press.

Thompson, R. K. R., & Oden, D. L. (1996). A profound disparity revisited: perception judgment of abstract identity relations by chimpanzees, human infants, and monkeys. *Behavioural Processes*, *35*, 149–161.

Treisman, A. M., & Gelade, G. (1980). A feature integration theory of attention. *Cognitive Psychology*, *12*, 97–136.

Troje, N. F., & Bülthoff, H. (1996). Face recognition under varying pose: The role of texture and shape. *Vision Research*, *36*, 1761–1771.

Troje, N. F., Huber, L., Loidolt, M., Aust, U., & Fieder, M. (1999). Categorical learning in pigeons: The role of texture and shape in complex static stimuli. *Vision Research*, *39*, 353–366.

Troje, N. F., & Vetter, T. (1998). Representations of human faces. In C. Taddei-Ferretti & C. Musio (Eds.), *Downward processing in the perception representation mechanism* (pp. 189–205). London: World Scientific.

Tversky, A. (1977). Features of similarity. *Psychological Review*, *84*, 327–352.

Ullman, J. R. (1997). Pattern recognition. In R. L. Gregory (Ed.), *The Oxford companion to the mind* (pp. 591–594). Oxford: Oxford University Press.

Van Hamme, L. J., Wasserman, E. A., & Biederman, I. (1992). Discrimination of contour-deleted images by pigeons. *Journal of Experimental Psychology: Animal Behavior Processes*, *18*, 387–399.

Vaughan, W. J., & Greene, S. L. (1984). Pigeon visual memory capacity. *Journal of Experimental Psychology: Animal Behavior Processes*, *10*, 256–271.

Vetter, T., & Troje, N. F. (1995). Separation of texture and two-dimensional shape in images of human faces. In S. Posch, F. Kummert, & G. Sagerer (Eds.), *Mustererkennung* 1995 (pp. 118–125). New York: Springer.

von Fersen, L., & Delius, J. D. (1989). Long-term retention of many visual patterns by pigeons. *Ethology*, *82*, 141–155.

Wasserman, E. A. (1991). The pecking pigeon: A model of complex visual processing. *Contemporary Psychology*, *36*, 605–606.

Wasserman, E. A. (1993). Picture perception: A bird's eye view. *Current Directions in Psychological Science*, *2*, 184–189.

Wasserman, E. A., Hugart, J. A., & Kirkpatrick-Steger, K. (1995). Pigeons show same-different conceptualization after training with complex visual stimuli. *Journal of Experimental Psychology: Animal Behavior Processes*, *21*, 248–252.

Wasserman, E. A., Kiedinger, R. E., & Bhatt, R. S. (1988). Conceptual behavior in pigeons: Categories, subcategories, and pseudocategories. *Journal of Experimental Psychology: Animal Behavior Processes*, *14*, 235–246.

Wasserman, E. A., Kirkpatrick-Steger, K., Van Hamme, L. J., & Biederman, I. (1993). Pigeons are sensitive to the spatial organization of complex visual stimuli. *Psychological Science*, *4*, 336–341.

Watanabe, S. (1997). Object-picture equivalence in the pigeon: An analysis with natural concept and pseudoconcept discriminations. *Behavioural Processes*, *53*, 3–9.

Watanabe, S. (2001). Discrimination of cartoons and photographs in pigeons: Effects of scrambling of elements. *Behavioural Processes*, *53*, 3–9.

Watanabe, S., & Ito, Y. (1991). Discrimination of individuals in pigeons. *Bird Behavior*, *9*, 20–29.

Young, M. E., & Wasserman, E. A. (1997). Entropy detection by pigeons: Response to mixed visual displays after same-different discrimination training. *Journal of Experimental Psychology: Animal Behavior Processes*, *23*, 157–170.

18

Category Structure and Typicality Effects

MASAKO JITSUMORI

The ability of organisms to categorize objects may enable them to learn about their environment economically, with a decrease in the amount of information that they would otherwise have to acquire. Smith and Medin (1981, p. 1) remarked that "without concepts, mental life would be chaotic." Concepts allow the large number of stimuli to be reduced to a small number of categories. Categorization allows human and nonhuman animals to cope with the stimulus variability that exists in the environment.

The classic approach to the problem of categorization was based on the assumption that categories are defined in terms of the conjunction of necessary and sufficient attributes, each of which is either present or absent at any given instant. A category, once established, divides stimuli into two sets with a clear boundary: those that are members of the category and those that are not. Thus, according to this approach, there are no instances that are better members of the category than others.

In contrast, empirical studies in the last several decades, specifically those pursued by Eleanor Rosch, revealed that some natural categories are internally structured into prototypical and nonprototypical members, with nonprototypical members tending toward an ordering from better to poorer exemplars (for more about the contrasting approaches, see Taylor, 1989). The basic assumptions of this view are as follows:

1. No single feature is likely to be a necessary or sufficient condition for determining category membership. The stimuli composed of such features are often referred to as *polymorphous* (Ryle, 1951).
2. Categorization of polymorphous stimuli is not an all-or-none process, thus forming an open-ended category identified by an ill-defined, fuzzy boundary (Herrnstein, 1985).
3. Category members are not equally representative of that category. Some exemplars are viewed as more prototypical than others (Mervis & Rosch, 1981).
4. Prototypical members of categories are those with the most attributes in common with other members of that category and with the least attributes in common with other categories (Rosch & Mervis, 1975).
5. Categories of highly variable members are structured by so-called *family resemblance* (Wittgenstein, 1953) or criss-crossing similarities. That is, each member has at least one, and probably several, attributes in common with one or more other members; but no, or few, attributes are common to all members (Rosch & Mervis, 1975).

Since the pioneering work of Herrnstein and Loveland (1964), it has been well documented that animals, particularly pigeons, can classify photographs that contain a particular type of natural object (for a recent review, see Huber, 2001).

However, little attention has been given to the relational structure of stimuli that enables animals to classify complex visual stimuli in accord with the human taxonomies of real-world objects. The purpose of this chapter is to review contemporary categorization studies in nonhuman animals, focusing on the structure of categories and on theoretical issues surrounding the learning of prototype categories.

LEVELS OF ABSTRACTION

Classic categories permit membership in an all-or-none fashion, so that all categories have equal status with respect to their inclusiveness. In contrast, most natural and artificial objects can be classified into several different categories that differ in inclusiveness. A chair can be categorized as *kitchen chair*, *chair*, *furniture*, *artifact*, and even *entity*, each of which is more inclusive than the preceding one. Across various levels of taxonomies, Rosch, Mervis, Gray, Johnson, and Boyes-Braem (1976) argued that there is a basic level of categorization (e.g., *chair*) at which perceptual as well as functional attributes are shared by all or most members of the category, but these attributes are different from those of contrasting categories (e.g., *table*, *bed*, and *closet*). At this basic level, objects in a category look very much like one another, whereas objects in different categories are perceptually distinct. Members of a category at the subordinate level (e.g., *kitchen chair*) also share a large number of attributes, but these attributes are also shared with members of contrasting categories at the same level (e.g., *dining-room chair*, *dentist's chair*), so that the category is not maximally distinct from other categories. At the superordinate level of categorization (*furniture*), members of a category share only a few attributes; members of superordinate categories are internally structured around prototypes of basic level categories (e.g., chair, lamp, and table). Rosch (1978) assumed that categorization in terms of prototypes provides maximal information with minimal cognitive effort for humans.

Animal Studies

From the perspective of comparative cognition, a question of interest is whether animals perceive the correlational feature structures existing in the real world. If basic level categories, as argued by Rosch, best mirror the correlational structures existing in the real world, then although perceived features and the salience of the features undoubtedly differ from species to species, basic concepts should also be learned easily by animals.

A comparative study by Roberts and Mazmanian (1988) examined categorization learning at different levels of abstraction in pigeons, squirrel monkeys, and humans. At the most concrete level, the positive items were pictures of a single species of bird, the common kingfisher, and negative items were pictures of other birds. At a more abstract level, subjects were trained to select pictures of birds from those of other animals. At the most abstract level, animal pictures in general were positive and pictures containing no animals were negative. Pigeons and monkeys learned the concrete categories more easily than the intermediate categories. Tests with novel pictures revealed that monkeys and pigeons can learn to identify novel exemplars at either the concrete or very abstract levels, but not at the intermediate level. At first glance, this finding appears to be the opposite of that predicted by Rosch. More recently, Vonk and MacDonald (2002) reported a similar finding with a gorilla given discrimination tasks at three levels of abstraction (animals vs. nonanimals, primates vs. nonprimate animals, orangutans vs. humans). The categories supposed to be at the most abstract level in these studies (animals vs. nonanimals) were mutually exclusive, whereas the intermediate categories shared features that could define the category at the next higher level. Note that superordination and subordination both existed for all the stimulus items used by Rosch, including those of the superordinate categories (see Rosch et al., 1976). There is a need to reconsider the levels of abstraction of the categories used in these studies.

Basic Objects in Natural Categories

In the biological kingdom, the domain of *plant* or *animal* is the highest level category that is often called as the "unique beginner" (Berlin, 1972). Naturally, the domains should be learned easily due to only a few, if any, overlapping perceptual features. The categories supposed to be at the most abstract level in the studies of Roberts and Mazmanian (1988) and Vonk and MacDonald (2002) are at this level. The remaining three levels, for example, *bird*, *cardinal*, *gray tailed cardinal*, are of interest with respect to the correlational structure of biological objects. Note that the categories that may depend on the development of mature adult naming or reasoning (e.g., *vertebrate* and its subordinate category *mammal*) are not in play here, because these categories are not relevant to the perceptual classifications of concrete objects.

Rosch assumed that, among the three levels of abstraction, the basic level is the most inclusive level at which the objects of a class begin to look very much alike. The categories *cardinal*, *robin*, *kingfisher*, and other various bird species are at the basic level and they are all included in the superordinate *bird* category. Easter cardinal and other different species of cardinal are subordinate members of the basic category *cardinal*. Category formation by animals is thus consistent with that predicted by Rosch, in the sense that animals showed better discrimination at the basic level (kingfisher vs. other birds) than at the superordinate level (bird vs. other animals). An earlier study by Cerella (1979) demonstrated that pictures of basic objects, oak leaves, are learned by pigeons with ease. These findings suggest that, for animal subjects, the basic level in biological taxonomies is the level at which categories are the most differentiated from one another.

Prototypicality in Superordinate Categories

With human subjects, Rosch et al. (1976) found that the basic level of biological objects, actually defined as numbers of shared attributes reported by the subjects, did not occur at the middle level but appeared at the level originally expected to be superordinate (e.g., *bird* rather than *cardinal*). Rosch et al. argued that biological taxonomies are probably of a type in which two basic level groupings are possible. A superordinate category, like *bird*, is structured around prototypes for humans. According to Rosch et al., although categories at this level are continuous rather than definitively bounded entities, the categories can be maintained as discrete by categorization in terms of prototypes. Rosch et al. pointed out that human subjects might be thinking of prototypical category members (for example, cardinals and robins) when making lists of attributes shared by members within a superordinate category (e.g., *bird*).

The findings reported by Roberts and Mazmanian (1988) and Vonk and MacDonald (2002) suggest that the placement of the basic level by animals is lower, or more concrete, than by humans. An important implication of the findings is that, for animal subjects, the hypothesized superordinate category, for example, *bird*, might not be internally structured into items that differ in their degree of prototypicality. However, categorization in terms of prototypes occurs only after the correlational structure of attributes has been learned. No one knows whether the restricted number of training stimuli used by Roberts and Mazmanian and Vonk and MacDonald are really enough for animals to perceive, if they can, the prototypicality of variable category members. Another possibility is that animals are insensitive to the correlational feature structure and merely learn to respond to the pictorial stimuli individually, by rote.

Several fundamental questions arise here: Do animals attend to multiple features and integrate information in the features to determine their responding? Do animals discriminate between different categories containing highly overlapping features? Do animals learn categories that have high within-category exemplar variability, with few features in common? Do animals' responses come under the control of degree of typicality? If so, then what are the determinants of the graded category membership? Empirical studies directed to these questions have progressed by using artificial stimuli rather than pictures of natural objects. An advantage of using artificial categories is that it is possible to analyze the way in which such well-defined features determine category membership.

M-OUT-OF-N POLYMORPHOUS CATEGORIES

Since the pioneering work by Lea and Harrison (1978), it has been well documented that pigeons are able to discriminate between artificial polymorphous categories. In the synthetic approach, artificial categories are constructed by mimicking the polymorphous feature structure of natural objects. One of the simplest of polymorphous categories, for example, is often referred to as the *two-out-of-three* polymorphous category. If one considers the logical values 1 and 0 as being binary-valued features on each dimension and category membership is defined by the possession of any two or all three relevant features, then the exemplars (110, 101, 011, and 111) would be in one category and the exemplars (001, 010, 100, and 000) would be in the other. Each of these features is independent of the others and overlaps the exemplars of the contrasting categories. Possession of one of these features does not determine the categories in an all-or-none fashion but merely raises the probability that an exemplar will be classified as a member of a given category. In contrast to a classic category, in which a perfect correlation of attributes permits only two degrees of membership (i.e., member and nonmember), some exemplars of a polymorphous category (e.g., 111) can be better members than are others depending on the number of independent features that they possess.

Gradient of Category Membership

Von Fersen and Lea (1990) trained pigeons to discriminate sets of color photographs of natural scenes, which differed along five two-valued dimensions (site, weather, camera distance, camera orientation, and camera height). One value of each dimension was designated as positive, and the pictures containing three or more positive features were defined as members of the positive category. In a go–no-go discrimination task, pigeons were trained to classify the pictures with the 32 feature-value combinations. The pigeons generally had difficulty in discriminating the stimuli, but they eventually used all five features to learn the discrimination. Asymptotic response rates revealed that the exemplars with more positive-valued features controlled higher response rates. Thus, the pigeons showed graded category membership, or a typicality effect, according to the number of positive features.

In another study, Huber and Lenz (1993) used schematic faces as stimuli, which differed along four facial feature dimensions (distance between the eyes, height of the forehead, length of the nose, and position of the mouth). Each of the four features took one of three values symbolized by –1, 0, or +1. The stimuli with feature sums of +1, +2, or +3 were defined as positives and those with feature sums of –1, –2, or –3 were defined as negatives. The faces in the positive category had, on average, smaller foreheads, more distantly separated eyes, longer noses, and higher chins than the faces in the negative category. Pigeons successfully learned the discrimination and variations in asymptotic peck rate were under control of the feature sum.

These studies consistently demonstrated that, for pigeons, category members are not equally valid with respect to their membership, but they are ordered according to the degree to which they belonged to the category. Thus, a typicality effect was demonstrated.

Prototype Effects

Von Fersen and Lea (1990) argued that the variations in response rate that were observed among stimuli within categories suggest that pigeons did not simply learn how to respond to each of the individual stimuli by rote. Rather, the pigeons may have learned the feature content of the stimuli, despite the ill-defined nature of the features involved. In other words, pigeons may learn the structure of between-category overlapping multiple features to cope with classification of variable exemplars. It is often assumed that the stimuli consisting of all positive or all negative features are the modal prototypes of the categories. In studies by von Fersen and Lea (1990) and Huber and Lenz (1993), prototypes were included in the acquisition sets and they were best discriminated by the pigeons. One way of testing the notion proposed by von Fersen and Lea is to search for a prototype effect (i.e., enhanced classification performance with novel prototypes) in generalization testing.

Jitsumori (1993, Experiment 1) explored a prototype effect, using *two-out-of-three* polymorphous categories consisting of three binary-valued features. In an attempt to facilitate categorization rather than "rote-learning," the full set of training stimuli was prepared to include a total of 60 different patterns consisting of 10 arrays of symbols for each of the six feature-value combinations (110, 101, and 011 in one category and 001, 010, and 100 in the other). Stimuli with all three positive (111) or all three negative (000) features were *not* used for training, but were reserved for a subsequent test. The relevant features of the stimuli were symbol color (black or white), symbol shape (circle or triangle), and background color (green or red). The alignment and the number of symbols were irrelevant, with each pattern containing three, four, or five identical symbols.

Pigeons learned to discriminate between the positive and negative stimulus sets with ease and

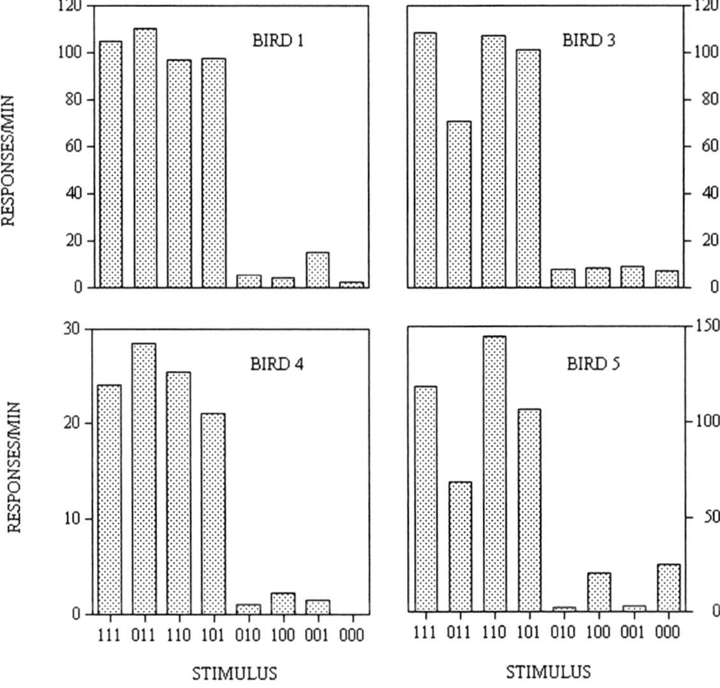

Figure 18.1. Response rates in responses per min for each of the eight feature–value combinations. The feature–value combinations are represented by binary-valued features on each of the three dimensions: symbol color, symbol shape, and background color. (Redrawn with permission from Jitsumori, 1993.)

they were then tested for transfer to novel array of symbols including the prototypes. Figure 18.1 shows response rates for each of the eight feature-value combinations during generalization testing. The pigeons showed a high level of transfer to the novel stimuli, but a prototype effect was not clearly obtained. Response rate to 111 was not always the highest nor was response rate to 000 always the lowest.

However, it was also found that the categories that the pigeons learned were flexible enough to permit membership even to stimuli that included a novel feature. Jitsumori (1993, Experiment 2) examined whether transfer would occur to the stimuli that had one of the three features replaced with a novel one; symbol color was gray, symbol shape was a star, or background color was blue. Transfer occurred to the stimuli including a novel feature. The mean relative rates of responding to the stimuli with two positive, one positive and one negative, and two negative features were 0.70, 0.27, and 0.03, respectively. The pigeons thus showed graded category membership with stimuli including a novel feature.

In contrast to the failure to obtain a prototype effect by Jitsumori (1993), Aydin and Pearce (1994) trained pigeons with a small number of visual patterns and successfully demonstrated a prototype effect. Pigeons were trained to discriminate between compound stimuli composed of three rectangles. Food was delivered after compounds ABF, AEC, and DBC but not after DEC, DBF, and AEF. Thus, A, B, and C tended to be associated with food, whereas D, E, and F tended to be associated with no-food. In a subsequent test, responding during the stimuli containing all three positive components (ABC) was faster and all three negative components (DEF) was slower than to any other stimulus used for training.

Classification Theories

Rosch (1978, p. 41) argued that "although prototypes must be learned, they do not constitute any particular theory of category learning." The typicality effects found with *m-out-of-n* polymorphous categories could be represented in terms of different types of classification theories, without the need to posit the abstraction of prototypes.

Independent Cue Models Independent cue models assume that the component attributes constituting a stimulus are processed independently and the category membership of a stimulus is determined by the weighted, additive integration of the information in its component attributes. A linear feature model offered by Lea and Ryan (1983) falls under this domain. The model assumes that subjects extract the features of visual stimuli that make it possible to discriminate between the experimenter-defined categories. All relevant features will eventually be detected, because all have imperfect correlations with reward and with each other. The information from the features is then combined in an additive manner to determine the response to any given stimulus. Due to perceptual salience or to a particular learning strategy, the feature dimensions may not be equally weighted. But, the weightings are adjusted through discrimination learning, as a result of reinforcement, until they correspond to a discrimination function that most nearly divides the stimuli into the experimenter-determined categories.

The linear feature model is consistent with the major findings in the above-mentioned studies. However, several difficulties arise in attempting to extend this model to the classification of complex visual stimuli. First, the features should be separable. Second, the categories to be discriminated should be linearly separable, so that the categories are "well structured" in the sense that they occupy different areas in a multidimensional feature space (e.g., Reed, 1972; Stanton, Nosofsky, & Zaki, 2002). Third, because the linear feature model is insensitive to correlational structure within categories, it may not be applicable to the classification of natural objects. Features of most natural objects are not independent but more or less correlated. Fourth, the ability of categorization is severely restricted by the number of features that can be processed simultaneously. Fifth, integration of the features in an additive manner does not economically deal with complex visual stimuli involving a large number of independent features.

Context Theory According to the context theory proposed by Medin and Schaffer (1978), people represent categories by storing individual exemplars as separate memory traces and classify stimuli based on their similarity to the stored exemplars. The ease of learning to classify a training stimulus into a given category and the likelihood of classifying a new stimulus into the category increases with the similarity of the stimulus to the stored exemplars in that category and decreases with its similarity to the alternative category exemplars. A basic idea of context theory is that a particular stimulus component serves a cue function and acts as context for other cues. The various feature dimensions that constitute the stimuli in a context are thus combined in a multiplicative manner to determine the overall similarity of two stimuli. Context theory was generalized by Nosofsky (1986) and later incorporated into a connectionist model by Kruschke (1992).

According to the Medin and Schaffer's (1978) context theory, the probability that a new stimulus containing all three positive features (111) will be classified into the positive category in the transfer test is

$$[(1 \cdot 1 \cdot c) + (1 \cdot b \cdot 1) + (a \cdot 1 \cdot 1)] \div [(1 \cdot 1 \cdot c) + (1 \cdot b \cdot 1) + (a \cdot 1 \cdot 1) + (a \cdot b \cdot 1) + (a \cdot 1 \cdot c) + (1 \cdot b \cdot c)]$$

where a, b, and c are the respective similarity parameters for the three binary-valued dimensions. The similarity parameter is set at 1 when the two values are identical. The probability that an old stimulus, for example 110, will be classified into the positive category is

$$[(1 \cdot 1 \cdot 1) + (1 \cdot b \cdot c) + (a \cdot 1 \cdot c)] \div [(1 \cdot 1 \cdot 1) + (1 \cdot b \cdot c) + (a \cdot 1 \cdot c) + (a \cdot b \cdot c) + (a \cdot 1 \cdot 1) + (1 \cdot b \cdot 1)].$$

When all three parameters are equal to the value 0.1, the probabilities of the positive prototype (111) and the old positives (110, 101, 011) being classified into the positive category are 0.91 and 0.84, respectively. Thus, a prototype effect will occur. Because each of the three old patterns of the same category are highly similar to two of the three members of the contrasting category (differing in only one dimension), very strong between-category confusion will occur and this confusion will interfere with performance on the training patterns more than the prototypes. If similarity is very low, then between-category confusion will decrease and training pattern performance will be as good as prototype performance (both are 95% correct when the similarity values are set to 0.05). Whether performance to a new prototype pattern is significantly better than performance to the old training patterns depends on the similarity parameters.

A similar prediction can be applied to performance when the prototypes are included in training, as in von Fersen and Lea (1990). When discriminative performance has reached asymptotic level, the probabilities of the best exemplars (prototypes), good exemplars, and poor exemplars being classified into the respective categories is 0.92, 0.81, and 0.63, with all five parameters being equal to 0.3.

The following predictions of the context model can explain the prevailing finding that animals are able to classify photographs of natural objects with ease and then show high levels of transfer to a variety of novel exemplars of the categories.

1. If differences on some feature dimensions are very salient, then variations in the similarity of less salient feature dimensions should not alter performance.
2. A new stimulus that is highly similar to one member, but that is dissimilar from another member of a category, should be assigned to that category more easily than a new stimulus that is moderately similar to both category members.
3. The categories involving a number of more or less correlated features will be discriminated with ease, even when these and other features overlap the categories.

Relational Frequency Models The attribute frequency model offered by Neumann (1974; 1977) assumes that the frequencies of attributes (dimension state) and their combinations (relational state) affect the recognition of familiar and novel instances. The prototype in a category receives the highest recognition rating because the dimension state and relational state frequencies are the highest for those states that are represented by the prototype.

In *two-out-of-three* polymorphous categories, the feature combinations that are unique to the positive training set (ABc, AbC, and aBC) are AB, AC, and BC, with the uppercase and lowercase letters representing positive and negative features on the three dimensions. Those of the negative training set (abC, aBc, and Abc) are ab, ac, and bc. Assuming that category membership of a new stimulus is determined by summing the relational state frequencies that are unique to the positive or negative training set, a prototype effect is readily predicted. Because the positive prototype ABC involves all three positive relational states (AB, AC, and BC) and the negative prototype abc involves all three negative relational states (ab, ac, and bc), the prototypes should be best discriminated. Note, however, that a simple sum of the dimension state frequencies also predicts the prototype effect. In this case, the feature frequency model is essentially equivalent to the linear feature model. A question of interest is whether animals use information about feature combinations to determine their responding to new stimuli.

A simple experiment (Jitsumori, 1993, Experiment 3) revealed that pigeons are capable of attending to individual features and their combinations simultaneously. In this experiment, the stimuli were arrays of symbols on colored backgrounds, as in the experiments described earlier, but only a single feature in each stimulus had a positive (P) or negative (N) value. The remaining two features were neutral (O) and were uncorrelated with the reinforcement contingencies. For example, the positive stimuli were black (P) stars (O) on a blue background (O), gray (O) circles (P) on a blue background (O), and gray (O) stars (O) on a red background (P). The negative stimuli were white (N) stars (O) on a blue background (O), gray (O) triangles (N) on a blue background (O), and gray (O) stars (O) on a green (N) background. There were 60 training stimuli, with 10 different arrays of symbols for each of the six feature–value combinations. Test stimuli were six new arrays of symbols for each of the 27 possible combinations of the features.

Figure 18.2 shows mean response rates as a function of the distribution of feature values. For example, PNO represents stimuli composed of one positive, one negative, and one neutral feature. Two pigeons (left panel) showed a peak at the feature–value distribution identical to that of the positive training stimuli (POO) and relatively high rates of responding to PNO and PPO, both of which include PO on two of the three feature dimensions. The remaining two pigeons (right panel) responded at low rates to the stimuli that included at least one negative feature. They showed a peak at OOO and a second peak at POO. Thus, the feature combinations OO and PO both controlled high rates of responding. With the stimuli that did not include neutral values, all of the pigeons consistently produced higher response rates to stimuli that included more positive features; the mean relative response rates to PPP, PPN, PNN, and NNN were 0.14, 0.07, 0.03, and 0.001, respectively. These findings revealed that pigeons are capable of using information about the between-feature relationships and also information about the individual features. It is

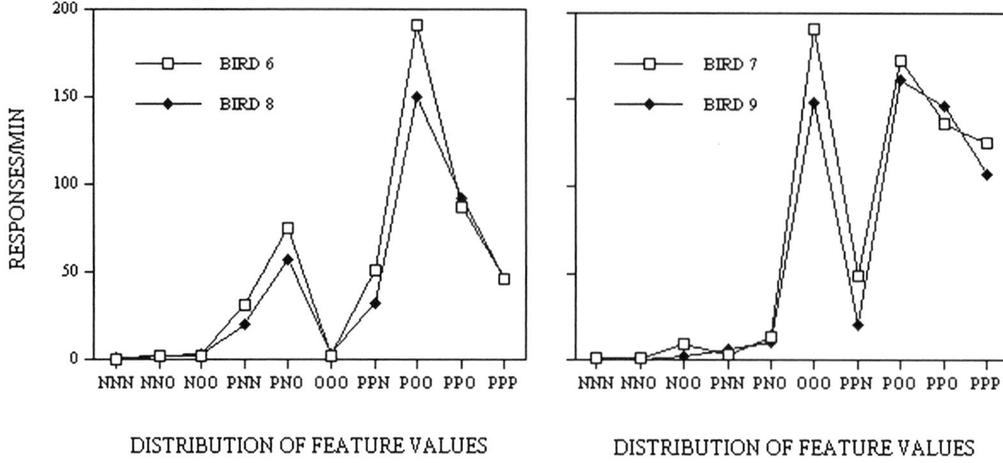

Figure 18.2. Response rates in responses per min as a function of feature–value distribution. (Redrawn with permission from Jitsumori, 1993.)

also worth noting that the results are not consistent with that predicted by context theory. According to context theory, classification of OOO as well as PNO should be at chance, regardless of the similarity parameters. Because these stimuli are equally similar to the positive and negative training exemplars, they should produce lower rates of responding than POO, PPO, and PPP. Clearly, this was not the case.

Peak-Shift Effects Based on the assumption that animals abstract a single "summary" dimension along which exemplars of contrasting categories are aligned in a linear fashion (Huber & Lenz, 1993), the peaks at the prototypes are often explained by Spence's (1937) interacting gradients of excitation and inhibition on this dimension. In the studies of Huber and Lenz (1993) and von Fersen and Lea (1990), more than half of the training stimuli were poor exemplars located near the category boundary. The sets of poor exemplars in the positive and negative categories were thus most frequently associated with reinforcement and nonreinforcement, respectively. Additive integration of gradients along the supposed "summary" dimension predicts that a positive peak will shift to the more positive side and a negative peak will shift to the more negative side.

One problem with this account is that it would have to find a special reason for assuming that the peak of the generalization gradient should occur at the positive prototype rather than at any other exemplars located away from the negative stimulus class. Another problem is that it assumes a "summary" dimension on which activation gradients are independent of one another. An unresolved theoretical issue is where the "summary" dimension originates. It is often said that a peak-shift account is the most parsimonious explanation of a prototype effect shown by animals, but this may not be correct.

An account of the distance-from-category-boundary peak-shift offered by Mackintosh (1995) provides a better account of the prototype effect. It assumes that the stimuli that have fewer elements in common with members of the opposite category (i.e., the exemplars located farther away from the category boundary) will be classified better than the exemplars located closer to the boundary. Under this hypothesis, the stimuli with all positive or all negative features of the *m-out-of-n* polymorphous categories should be best discriminated because they are located farthest away from the category boundary.

Mackintosh (1995) trained pigeons to classify wedge-shaped stimuli that varied along two physical dimensions (angle and length). The category boundary was a positive diagonal in a two-dimensional feature space, according to which the stimuli were to be classified into the "long and thin" and "short and fat" categories. The pigeons successfully learned the task, suggesting that they were attending to the two dimensions and integrating information from both. During generalization testing, the pigeons performed more accurately with the farther exemplars than with the closer ones; the generalization gradient peaked at the positive stimulus located farthest away from the boundary. Thus, a distance-from-category-boundary peak-shift effect was demonstrated.

Rosch (1978) stated that one way to achieve separateness and clarity of continuous, analog categories is by conceiving of each category in terms of its clear cases rather than its boundaries. In the categories used by Mackintosh, the length and angle of the closer exemplars are overlapping between the categories but those of the farther exemplars do not overlap. When the positive and negative stimuli were both presented at the beginning of classification training, the farther exemplars could be the clear cases. Generalization from the clear cases, instead of distance from the category boundary, may explain the peak of the generalization gradient at the farther exemplars, although these two effects are not separable with the categories used in this study.

The stimuli possessing all positive or all negative features are the clear cases of the *m-out-of-n* polymorphous categories and they are often referred to as the modal prototypes as noted earlier. Thus, it is impossible to distinguish a prototype effect and a distance-from-category-boundary peak-shift effect as an account of the generalization gradient peaked at the extreme positive stimulus. In contrast, the prototype of the category used by Mackintosh (1995) was defined as the central tendency of that category. Interestingly, when pigeons were first trained only with the positive stimuli and then received discrimination training with the positive and negative stimuli, they showed a generalization gradient peaked at the positive prototype rather than at the extreme positive stimulus. Thus, a prototype effect rather than a distance-from-category-boundary peak-shift effect was demonstrated by pigeons when they were first trained only with the positive category.

PROTOTYPE CATEGORIES

In *m-out-of-n* polymorphous categories, there is no correlation among the features. According to the view of classic categories, on the other hand, attributes are perfectly correlated with one another. Both kinds of categories are rare in the real world. Von Fersen and Lea (1990, p. 83) pointed out that "a concept would help organization the perceptual world in precisely those situations in which one feature value or one stimulus element is a good predictor of another." This notion agrees with the principles of categorization in terms of the prototypes proposed by Rosch (1978): that is, cognitive economy combined with the correlational structure of the real world.

Prototype Models

Reed (1972) showed students two categories each composed of five cartoon drawing of faces that differed along four feature dimensions. The faces in one category had, on average, smaller foreheads, eyes that were closer together, lower mouths, and shorter noses compared with those in the other category. The categories occupied different areas in a multidimensional feature space so that they were separable by a linear discriminant function. Linear separability is known as a necessary requirement for a prototype strategy to yield perfect classification performance (Reed, 1972; Stanton et al., 2002). The subjects were asked to classify novel faces into one of the two categories. Subjects' classification performance was best described by a distance-from-prototype model, with the prototype in each category defined as having the mean value on each of the four feature dimensions (but see Nosofsky, 1991). According to prototype models, people form a category prototype, which is usually assumed to be the central tendency of the training exemplars; people classify new items on the basis of how similar they are to the stored prototypes. More recently, Smith and Minda (2002) reported that human subjects refer to-be-categorized items to a representation near the category's center (prototype) rather than to the individual training exemplars.

However, because both prototype and exemplar models are powerful enough to explain many phenomena (Smith & Minda, 2002), the underlying mechanisms remain unresolved. Search for a better quantitatively fitting classification model may not be fruitful, not only because the predicted outcomes depend on parameters and parameter values determined by experimenters but also because of the theoretical problem of how to define prototypes.

Definition of Prototypes

Watanabe (1988) used dot patterns created by distortions from a prototype similar to those used by

Posner and Keele (1968). Pigeons were trained to respond to triangular patterns of dots distorted to a certain level and not to respond to random patterns of dots. After training, the pigeons were tested with the prototype and with dot patterns at different levels of distortion. The pigeons responded more often to the dot patterns at the original distortion levels than to the prototype. Watanabe (1988) concluded that pigeons failed to recognize the prototype as the best member of the stimulus set comprising the distorted triangles. This conclusion may have been premature. White, Alsop, and Williams (1993) correctly pointed out that because the visual pattern *triangle* has no prior relevance to pigeons, the pigeons must form the novel prototype on the basis of the distorted patterns alone, without the benefit of prior conceptual learning. Another possibility is that, for pigeons, distorted patterns rather than the triangle could be the prototypes of the distorted patterns used for training.

In another experiment, Pearce (1989) looked for a prototype effect with pigeons given artificial categories consisting of patterns of three colored bars, each of which varied in height from 1 to 7 units. Pigeons were trained to respond to patterns with a total height of 9 units (short category) and not to respond to patterns with a total height of 15 units (tall category), with some individual bars (bars 3, 4, or 5 units high) overlapping between the categories. All of the positive training patterns had either a 1-unit or a 2-unit bar and all the negative training patterns had either a 6-unit or a 7-unit bar, none of which appeared in the opposite category. Because the 3-unit and 5-unit bars, respectively, occurred most frequently in the short and tall categories, Pearce defined a pattern composed of three 3-unit bars as the short prototype and a pattern composed of three 5-unit bars as the long prototype. Testing with novel patterns revealed that the pigeons showed a better discrimination between the extra-short (a pattern composed of three 1-unit bars) and extra-tall (a pattern composed of three 7-unit bars) patterns than between the prototypes, a finding similar to the distance-from-category-boundary peak-shift reported by Mackintosh (1995).

The results of Pearce (1989) nicely revealed that cue validity is one of the most important factors that determine category membership. The validity of a given cue x as a predictor of a given category y increases as the frequency with which cue x is associated with category y increases and decreases as the frequency with which cue x is associated with categories other than y increases (Rosch, 1978). Cue validity is determined not only on the basis of the feature distribution in a given category but also on the basis of the feature distribution in the opposite category. The 3-unit or 5-unit bars overlap the two categories, so their cue validities should be much smaller than the cue validities of the diagnostic 1-unit and 7-unit bars. In this sense, the 3-3-3 and 5-5-5 patterns are ambiguous exemplars rather than the best exemplars (prototypes) of the categories.

PROTOTYPICALITY IN LINEARLY SEPARABLE CATEGORIES

Rosch (1978) claimed that "only in some artificial categories is there by definition a literal single prototype. For natural-language categories, to speak of a single entity that is the prototype is either a gross misunderstanding of the empirical data or a covert theory of mental representation" (p. 40). She characterized "prototypicality" merely as a relevant variable in terms of its effects on response rate, acquisition, priming effects, and other response measures in a variety of experiments. According to Rosch, the prototype is an abstraction of the central properties of an internally structured category and need not correspond to any example or schematic representation of the category. My concern is where prototypicality originates. Perhaps, the best way to investigate this issue in animals is to explore its determinants in the correlational structures of artificial categories.

Abstraction of Feature Distributions

Jitsumori (1996) used two categories containing drawings of a pseudo-butterfly that varied on three 6-valued feature dimensions. Exemplars of each category were generated by systematic transformations of the features from a single stimulus, a base pattern. The base pattern was 2-2-2 for one category and 5-5-5 for the other category, where the numbers refer, respectively, to the values of forewings, hind wings, and gray shade. The feature values 1, 2, and 3 were defined as positive and 4, 5, and 6 as negative for two pigeons, and vice versa for the remaining two pigeons. Either one, two, or

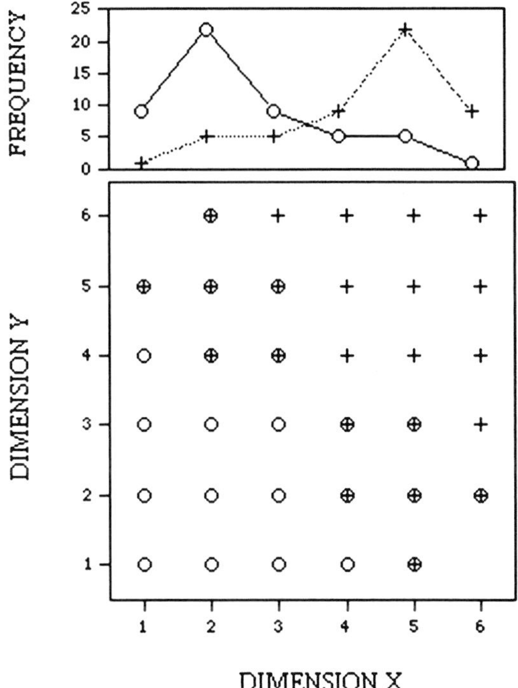

Figure 18.3. A two-dimensional projection of the three-dimensional stimulus space illustrating the distribution of the categories. (Redrawn with permission from Jitsumori, 1996.)

all three features received transformation under the restriction that the positive stimuli contained at least two positive features and the negative stimuli contained at least two negative features. The butterflies in the 555 category tended to have more complicated forewings and hind wings and darker shadings than the butterflies in the 222 category. A total of 51 patterns from each category were used as training stimuli, so that the positive and negative training stimuli were distinguished on the dimension of the sum of the feature values. Stimuli with a different feature sum from 4 to 10 belonged to the 222 category, whereas those with a different feature sum from 11 to 17 belonged to the 555 category. Thus, the training categories were linearly separable. The base patterns were not used in training but were reserved for a subsequent test.

Figure 18.3 shows the stimulus space represented by any two of the three feature dimensions. Open circles represent the training patterns in the 222 category, and crosses represent those in the 555 category. There is a highly overlapping region, as represented by superimposed circles and crosses. The feature-frequency distributions have a peak at the feature values 2 and 5. The base pattern thus contains the features that occur most frequently in its category. The central tendency of the base patterns was ensured because the total number of individual transformations required to produce the acquisition set was least when stimuli were generated from the base patterns.

The cue validity of each of the six feature values was calculated by subtracting the frequency with which the given feature occurred in the negative training set from the frequency with which it occurred in the positive training set. When the 222 category was positive and the 555 category was negative, the cue validities of the features valued 1, 2, 3, 4, 5, and 6 were 8, 17, 4, –4, –17, and –8, respectively. Thus, the features valued 2 and 5 had the highest cue validity.

All of the pigeons learned the task without difficulty. To examine whether cue validity actually controlled the pigeons' responding, I estimated the utility values of the features from the data in the last six training sessions, using a main-effects model. I found that the utilities were determined by, or linearly related to, cue validity and that the pigeons used all three feature dimensions to determine responding. A significant difference in dimensional salience was not found.

After training, the pigeons were tested with the base patterns and with other novel stimuli that were either closer to or farther from the category boundary than the prototypes. Figure 18.4 shows the results with the typical exemplars (111, 113, 222, 133, 333, 444, 446, 555, 466, and 666) with their features shared by many members within the categories. Note that the feature value combinations represented by three digit numbers involved different types of stimuli; for example, 113 was a stimulus set consisting of the 1-1-3, 1-3-1, and 3-1-1 patterns. The generalization gradient peaked at the positive base pattern (222 in the left panel, 555 in the right panel) rather than the extreme positive stimulus (111 in the left panel, 666 in the right panel). Thus, a prototype effect, rather than a peak-shift effect, was demonstrated. This finding indicated that an additive integration of utilities rather than the sum of feature values controlled the pigeons' responding to these stimuli.

A set of test stimuli located near the category boundary had a typical feature from its own category and one of the other two features transformed

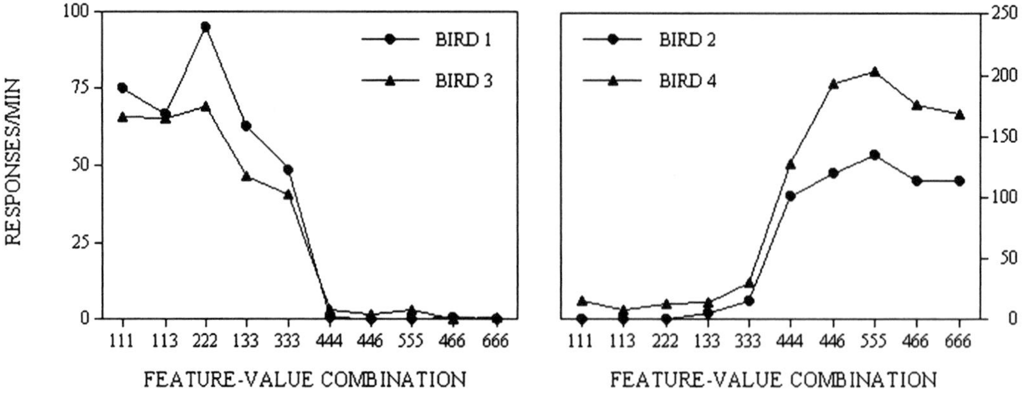

Figure 18.4. Response rates in responses per min as a function of the feature–value distributions of novel typical exemplars including the base patterns. (Redrawn with permission from Jitsumori, 1996.)

to an extreme value from the opposite category; they were 126(9) and 236(11) generated from 2-2-2 and 156(12) and 145(10) generated from 5-5-5 (numbers in parentheses represent the sum of feature values). An additive integration of utilities rather than the sum of feature values controlled pigeons' responding. That is, the pigeons discriminated the stimuli in accord with the categories defined by the base patterns from which they were generated. However, because these stimuli, as well as the prototypes, included the typical feature(s) of the category, there was a possibility that the pigeons used the typical feature as a cue to determine their responding. The remaining test stimuli received transformations on all three dimensions, some of which included a typical feature of the opposite category; 135(9), 334(10), 335(11), and 336(12) generated from 2-2-2 and 144(9), 244(10), 344(11), and 246(12) generated from 5-5-5. The pigeons did not respond to the poor exemplars by relying on the typical feature of the opposite category. But, the pigeons failed to discriminate the positive and negative stimuli with equal feature sum values. Because these stimuli were near the category border, the positive and negative stimuli might be inherently difficult for pigeons to discriminate.

Detailed analysis revealed that the pigeons' responding was best explained by an additive integration of utilities. Because utility was linearly related to the cue validity determined by the feature distributions of the two categories, we may conclude that the pigeons learned the feature structures represented by the training stimuli that were clustered around their prototypes. The key question then becomes whether there is a need to posit a prototype abstraction process to explain the prototype effect found in this study.

Notes on Prototype and Exemplar Models

Jitsumori (1996) suggested that the pigeons might have abstracted the prototypes from the feature combinations given during training, but this conclusion may have been premature. A prototype effect does not necessarily indicate that pigeons form the category prototypes, compare new stimuli with the prototypes, and then determine their responding to the new stimuli based on the similarity of the new stimuli to the prototypes. So far, the abstraction of prototypes is nothing more than a fiction that may explain the graded category membership that is actually shown by pigeons. On the other hand, a simple exemplar model failed to explain the steep generalization gradients shown by the pigeons to the stimuli surrounding the positive prototype (figure 18.4). According to context theory, responding to the prototypical stimuli (111, 113, 133, and 333 in the 222 category; 444, 446, 466, and 666 in the 555 category) should not differ, because the number of training exemplars that were very similar to each of these test stimuli was the same. It is thus unlikely that pigeons memorize the individual training exemplars and respond to new stimuli based on their similarity to old stored exemplars.

Taking ability to fly as an example of an attribute of bird, Taylor (1989) claimed that "prototypical instances of [the ability to fly] are exhibited by the prototypical members of the very category which the attribute is supposed to characterize. This state of affairs is not unusual. Other attributes of the BIRD prototype, such as the presence of feathers, wings, and a beak, the building of nests, and the laying of eggs, would appear prima facie to require, for their characterization, a prior understanding of what birds are" (p. 62). Here is a key that may integrate the learning of prototype categories at different levels: the exemplar, feature, and category levels, which are by no means exclusive to one another. The findings of Jitsumori (1996) suggest that pigeons are capable of learning prototypical features that maximize the information of the categories and enable the pigeons to economically classify variable exemplars.

NONLINEARLY SEPARABLE CATEGORIES

The categories used in the above-mentioned studies are linearly separable and thus well structured in the sense that they involve high within-category similarity and low between-category similarity. A question of interest is whether animals are able to cope with nonlinearly separable categories for which additive integration of features is not applicable.

Huber and Lenz (1996) used positive and negative sets of stimuli that were not linearly separable in terms of combinations of feature dimensions. The stimuli were cartoon drawings of faces consisting of four nine-valued features, thus providing up to 6,561 possible patterns. In a four-dimensional stimulus space, large numbers of positive and negative stimuli were located around a single standard stimulus (prototype). The positive and negative stimuli were on certain concentric spheres with different radii from the central prototype. The positive set was located closer to the central prototype than the negative set, but there were quite large numbers of positive and negative stimuli distributed similarly over the feature dimensions, thus impeding exemplar memorization. The positive and negative stimuli therefore consisted of highly overlapping features with a very weak correlation between the features and the stimulus set. Nevertheless, three of the five pigeons learned the discrimination. One of them showed a prototype effect that, according to the authors, could be explained in terms of similarity judgments to the central tendency of the category. However, because the prototype of the category was located a greater distance away from the negative set than the positive set, the authors argued that the prototype effect could be also explained in terms of Spencian generalization from learned exemplars (i.e., a peak-shift effect). A further interesting finding was the fact that the pigeons responded similarly to the exemplars that were distributed the same distance away from the central prototype, even though these stimuli were highly variable and might not be perceptually similar to each other.

SUPERORDINATE CATEGORIES STRUCTURED BY FAMILY RESEMBLANCE

Most of the prototype categories in the natural world consist of highly variable exemplars, but they are structured by so-called family resemblance (Wittgenstein, 1953) or a criss-crossing of similarities (Taylor, 1989). Ostriches and penguins do not have attributes shared by many other birds and they themselves are not very similar to each other, but we place them into the same category due to the existence of many other kinds of birds that differ in their degree of prototypicality. A simple category that bears such family resemblance comprises the exemplars AB, BC, CD, and DE. Although exemplars AB and CD do not have features in common, they can be associated with one another via the exemplar BC that contains one of the features of each of these exemplars. Similarly, BC and DE can be associated with one another via CD. The centrally located exemplars BC and CD are the most prototypical members of this category.

According to Rosch and Mervis (1975), the most prototypical members of categories bear the highest family resemblance to the other members of the category and they have the least resemblance to the members of other categories. Rosch and Mervis argued that in natural categories of concrete objects, these two aspects of family resemblance should coincide, so that categories tend to become organized in such a way that they reflect the correlational structure of the environment in a manner that renders them maximally discriminable from each other.

Makino and Jitsumori (2000) explored the effects of family resemblance on categorization by pigeons, using morphed images of human faces as stimuli. For example, AB was a 50%A–50%B

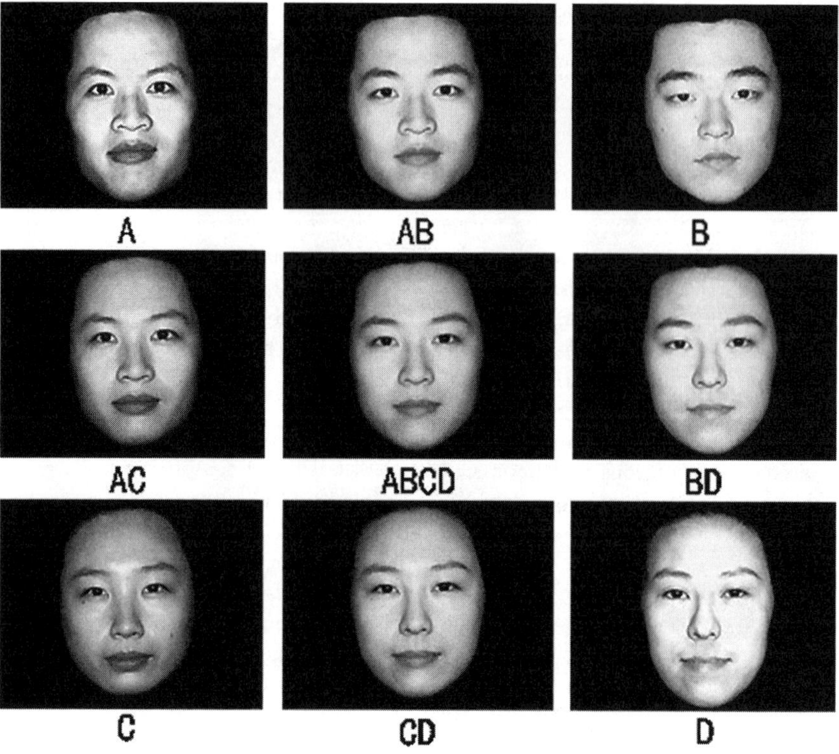

Figure 18.5. Black-and-white reproductions of the faces belonging to the same category structured by family resemblance. (Redrawn with permission from Makino & Jitsumori, 2000.)

morphed image created from A and B. Two stimulus sets were prepared, each of which consisted of four arbitrarily assigned faces (A, B, C, and D), six 50% averages of the possible pairs of these faces (AB, AC, AD, BC, BD, and CD), and an average face created by 25% morphing of the original faces (ABCD). Figure 18.5 shows black-and-white reproductions of the faces belonging to the same category (AD and BC are not shown). Note that AB and CD, AC and BD, or AD and BC are not particularly similar to one another, but they are structured by a network of criss-crossing similarities. Pigeons were trained to discriminate between the sets of 50% averages in a go–no-go discrimination procedure. They were then tested in extinction with the stimuli including the 50% morphed images used for training, the original faces, and the averages. The most pronounced discrimination occurred to the average faces (ABCD). The mean discrimination ratios for the average faces, the 50% morphs, and the original faces were 0.87, 0.84, and 0.76, respectively. Thus, a prototype effect was obtained, even though the prototypes contained novel features, none of which was exactly the same as those of the training stimuli.

Another important finding was that a high level of transfer occurred to the original faces (A, B, C, and D). Because these faces were arbitrarily assigned as members of the categories, there was no way to know which original face belonged to which category before categorization learning with the 50% morphed images (AB, AC, AD, BC, BD, and CD) had taken place. It is likely that similarity-based generalization from the training exemplars enabled the pigeons to classify the original faces into the same category. However, an important implication of this finding is that once a category is learned with its typical exemplars, poor exemplars that are not particularly similar to one another will be easily and correctly classified into the same category. This result represents the very nature of prototype categories structured by family resemblance, which may enable animals to categorize a wide variety of pictures of natural objects.

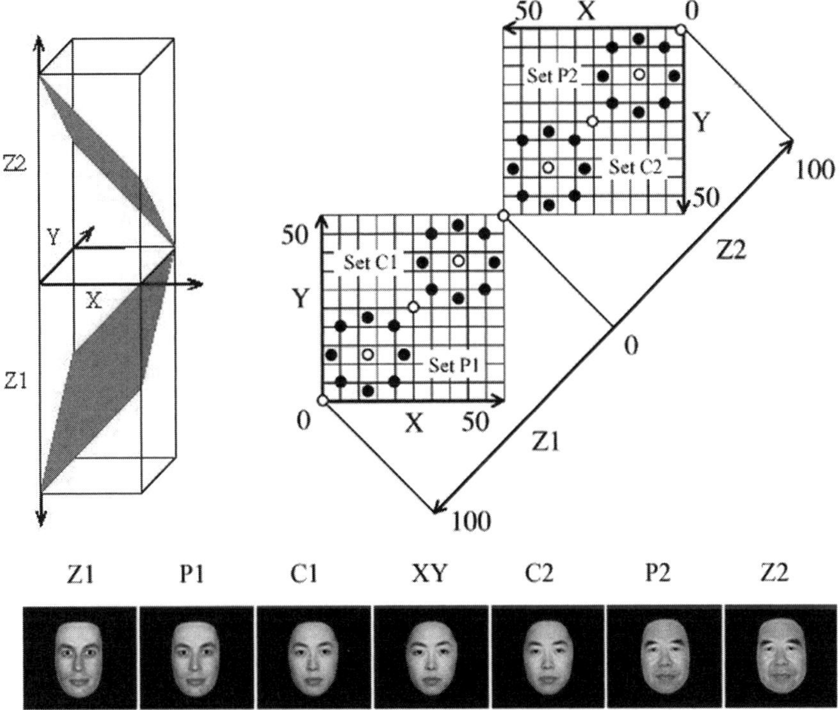

Figure 18.6. *Left,* A three-dimensional stimulus space represented by the three components of the morphed images of human faces. *Right,* A two-dimensional projection of the stimulus space. *Filled* and *open circles* represent the stimuli used for acquisition training and generalization testing, respectively. *Bottom,* Black-and-white reproductions of test stimuli. The test stimuli located between sets P1 and C1 and between sets C2 and P2 are not shown.

FUNCTIONAL EQUIVALENCE OF SUPERORDINATE CATEGORY MEMBERS

A question then arises as to whether animals treat highly variable poor exemplars as functionally equivalent when they are equally associated with a common event, for example, reinforcement or nonreinforcement (e.g., Vaughan, 1988). My students and I examined this issue in one of our recent studies, by training pigeons to discriminate between typical and atypical members of a category consisting of morphed images of human faces.

A 50%–50% average of two human faces denoted X and Y was defined as the center (a prototype) of the category. Exemplars surrounding around the prototype were created by means of morphing three faces: X, Y, and a third face, Z1 or Z2. The more typical an exemplar, the more it contains features provided by X and Y. Figure 18.6 (left) shows the stimulus space represented by three component dimensions (X, Y, and Z1 or Z2). Because the sum of the proportions of the components must be 100%, all of the morphed images are on the two-dimensional oblique planes. The X-Y-Z1 morphs are on one plane and the X-Y-Z2 morphs are on the other, with the two stimulus planes being connected at XY representing the 50%X–50%Y prototype. Figure 18.6 (right) shows a two-dimensional projection of the stimulus space. Filled circles represent the stimuli that were used for training. The centrally located sets C1 and C2 consisted of the exemplars containing large proportions of the features provided by X and Y. The peripherally located sets P1 and P2 are distantly away from the prototype in the opposite directions from Z1 and Z2. The centrally located sets C1 and C2 are highly similar to one another; one of these sets, set C1, is similar to set P1, and the other one, set C2, is similar

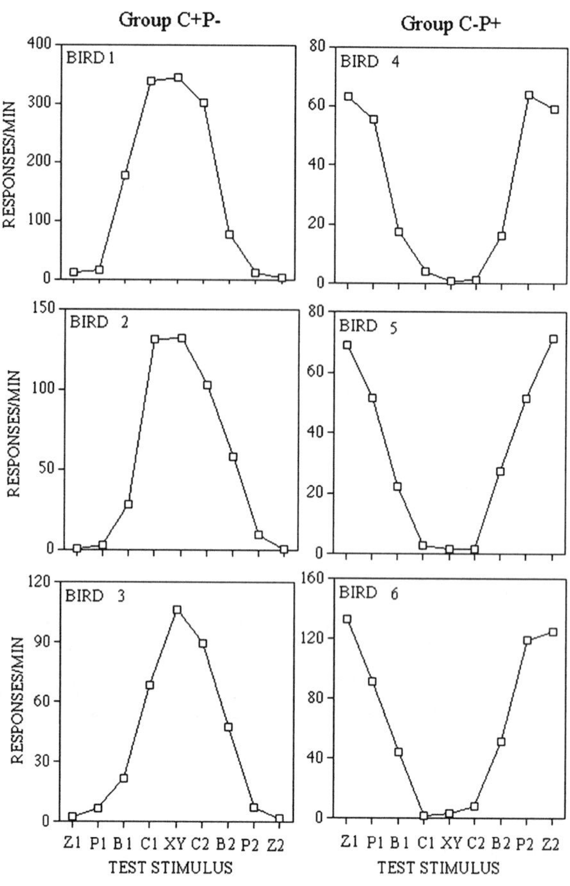

Figure 18.7. Generalization gradients for each subject in group C+P– (*left*) and group C–P+ (*right*).

to set P2. The highly dissimilar sets P1 and P2 can be related to one another by virtue of the existence of sets C1 and C2. The category is thus structured by family resemblance.

In a go–no-go discrimination procedure, two groups of pigeons were trained to discriminate between the good exemplar sets (sets C1 and C2) and the poor exemplar sets (sets P1 and P2). The stimuli drawn from sets C1 and C2 were positive and the stimuli drawn from sets P1 and P2 were negative for group C+P– (birds 1, 2, and 3), and vice versa for group C–P+ (birds 4, 5, and 6). The symbols C+ and P+ represent the positive stimuli in prereversal training sessions and those on training trials in testing sessions, respectively. After training, generalization testing was conducted to examine whether a pigeon's responding was under the control of the degree of typicality. The open circles in the right panel of figure 18.6 represent the stimuli used in generalization testing; they are XY, Z1, Z2, the average image of each of the four stimulus sets (C1, C2, P1, and P2), and the exemplars located on the boundary between sets C1 and P1 and between sets C2 and P2 (B1 and B2). The sequence of Z1, P1, C1, XY, C2, P2, Z2 is shown from left to right in figure 18.6 (B1 and B2 are not included).

In figure 18.7, response rates (responses/min) for each bird are plotted against the test stimuli. The sequence of test stimuli from left to right on the abscissa is Z1, P1, B1, C1, XY, C2, B2, P2, and ending with Z2. The birds in the group C+P– (left panels) showed gradients with a peak at XY, and the birds in the group C–P+ showed gradients with two peaks at Z1 and Z2 (one exception is that bird 4 showed a slightly higher rate of responding to P2 than Z2). Thus, the pigeons' responding was under the control of distance from the prototype. It may be worth noting that a simple exemplar model predicts peaks at C1 and C2 in the group C+P– and at P1 and P2 in the group C–P+. We may thus conclude that the pigeons did not merely learn to respond to the individual stimuli by rote.

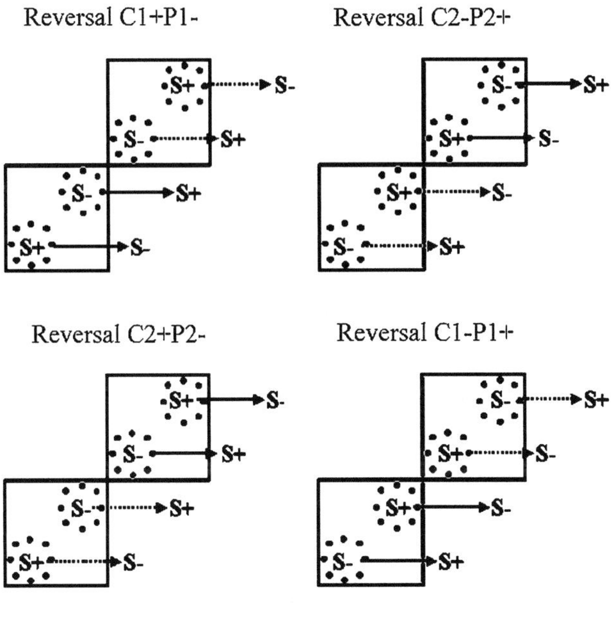

Reversal Training

Transfer

Figure 18.8. Sequences of prereversal training with the four sets of stimuli, selective reversal training, and reversal transfer testing.

A question of interest is whether the pigeons treated sets P1 and P2 as members of the same stimulus class or whether they separately learned to respond to each of these sets. Using a selective reversal design similar to that proposed by Lea (1984), we explored the formation of functional equivalence classes. More specifically, we trained the pigeons only with sets C1 and P1 or with sets C2 and P2, but the contingencies of reinforcement were reversed. Generalization of the reversal to the remaining stimulus sets that were not used for the reversal training would then indicate that the pigeons had formed functional equivalence classes. As in figure 18.8, a sequence of prereversal training with the four sets of stimuli, selective reversal training, and reversal transfer testing was repeated four times until each of the 32 stimuli was tested twice, once under C+P– condition and once under C–P+ condition. In testing sessions, reversal training contingencies were in effect on trials in which the birds were exposed to the reversal training stimuli, whereas responses had no consequences (no reinforcers and no penalties) on probe testing trials.

For the stimuli subjected to the test for reversal transfer, the rho values (Herrnstein, Loveland, & Cable, 1976) in the last prereversal training session ($n = 32$) and the testing sessions ($n = 32$) were calculated. Figure 18.9 shows the results for each bird in each of the training and testing sequences repeated four times (reversals 1, 2, 3, and 4). The positive set on training trials was P+ in the testing following reversal 1 and reversal 3 and C+ following reversal 2 and reversal 4 in group C+P– (left panels) and vice versa in group C–P+ (right panels). The region between the horizontal lines shows where the discrimination was not statistically significant ($p > .05$ on a two-tailed Mann-Whitney U test). The pigeons generally showed reversal transfers to the nonreversed stimulus sets, as indicated by rho values significantly lower than 0.5 in testing sessions. However, they showed less transfer of reversal effects in the C+P– testing sessions than in the C–P+ testing sessions. It is likely that after reversal training with poor negative exemplars, the pigeons had difficulty refraining from pecking the similarly poor but physically dissimilar exemplars that had been positive during prereversal training sessions. Nevertheless, the findings clearly indicated that the pigeons treated the various exemplars as functionally equivalent, in accord with degree of prototypicality.

One possible explanation of these findings is that sets P1 and P2 were learned to be equivalent because of "the absence (or the small proportion) of XY." If the pigeons responded solely on the basis of the

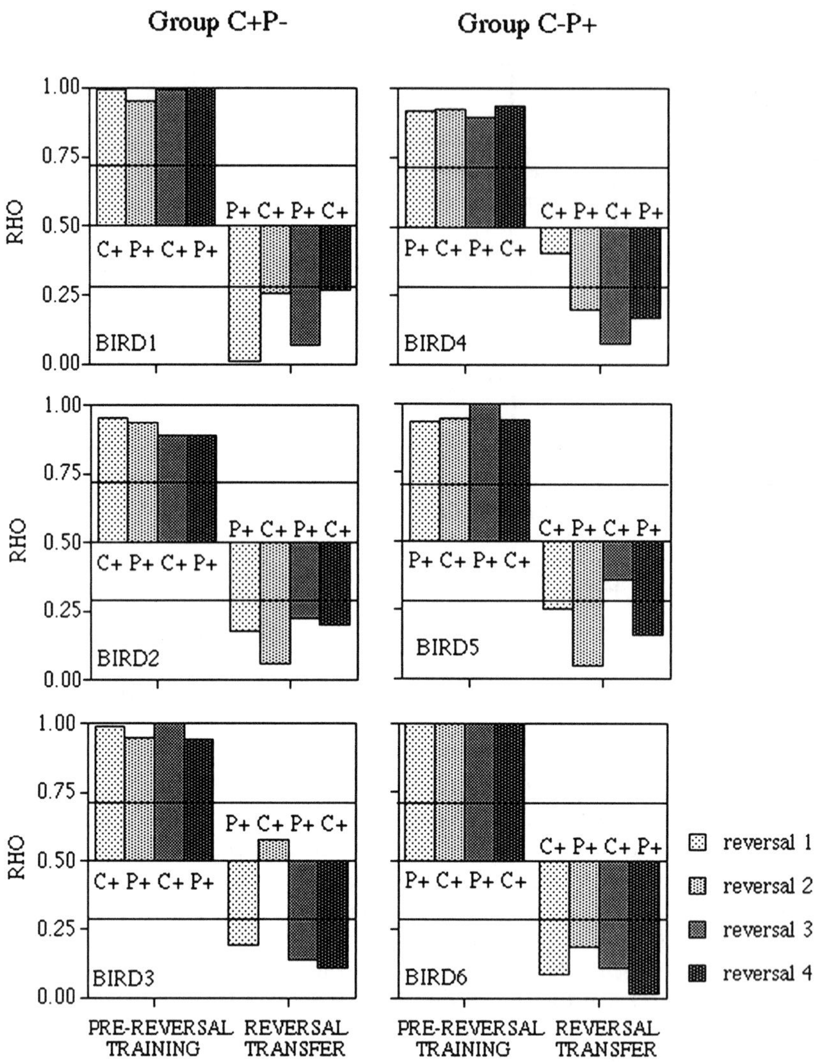

Figure 18.9. The rho discrimination statistic (Herrnstein et al., 1976) for the stimuli subjected to the test for reversal transfer. Rho expresses the proportion by which the rank for responding to a positive stimulus is above that to a negative stimulus under the contingencies of reinforcement in place before reversal.

presence and absence of the prototypical features provided by XY, then they should show substantial transfer to novel stimuli created by morphing X, Y, and a novel face. In subsequent generalization testing, the pigeons were tested for transfer to the novel positive and negative faces created from X, Y, and a new face Z3. The pigeons emitted more responses to the positive stimuli than to the negative ones (the discrimination ratios for birds 1, 2, 3, 4, 5, and 6 were 0.58, 0.55, 0.54, 0.70, 0.53, and 0.67, respectively), but the transfer was not significant. Facial components and surface properties are all changed by morphing. Therefore, structural features of the novel positive and negative faces might not be well specified prior to learning the features provided by Z3. This finding is consistent with the notion that analysis of natural stimuli into prototypical and nonprototypical features may occur only after learning of the category system. However, the finding that the pigeons still tended to discriminate between the novel positive and negative stimuli suggests that the categories are flexible and can be reconstructed to cope with novel circumstances.

CONCLUDING REMARKS

It has been well documented that pigeons are capable of learning artificial prototype categories. This learning may be accomplished by virtue of the structure of the artificial categories being carefully constructed by experimenters to mimic the supposed characteristics of natural categories existing in the real world. It may be reasonable to speculate that human and nonhuman animals have acquired basically similar perceptual and cognitive systems in accord with the existing structure of the real world. Although some of the findings that were reported in this chapter did not support a simple exemplar model, the prototype effects shown by pigeons can still be explained without the need to posit prototype-abstraction process.

Prototype effects should be understood as part of the general processes through which structures of prototype categories are learned. Eleanor Rosch initiated a line of research with human subjects primarily by using verbal stimuli. Comparative studies are needed to clarify similarities and differences in categorization between human and nonhuman animals. Such studies may very well advance our knowledge of object recognition and classification processes in ourselves.

Acknowledgments Preparation of this chapter and some of the research described in it were supported by a research grant from the Japan Society for the Promotion of Science (Grant-in-Aid 13610076) to Masako Jitsumori. The author thanks Yoko Tsukamoto, Mutsumi Daimon, Riye Ihou, Hiroshi Makino, Atsuko Matsukawa, Naoki Shimada, and Sana Inoue for their collaborations.

References

Aydin, A., & Pearce, J. M. (1994). Prototype effects in categorization by pigeons. *Journal of Experimental Psychology: Animal Behavior Processes, 20*, 264–277.

Berlin, B. (1972). Speculations on the growth of ethno botanical nomenclature. *Journal of Language and Society*, *1*, 63–98.

Cerella, J. (1979). Visual classes and natural categories in the pigeon. *Journal of Experimental Psychology: Human Perception and Performance*, *5*, 68–77.

Herrnstein, R. J. (1985). Riddles of natural categorization. In L. Weiskrantz (Ed.), *Animal intelligence* (Vol. 7, pp. 129–144). Oxford: Clarendon Press.

Herrnstein, R. J., & Loveland, D. H. (1964). Complex visual concept in the pigeon. *Science, 146*, 549–551.

Herrnstein, R. J., Loveland, D. H., & Cable, C. (1976). Natural concepts in pigeons. *Journal of Experimental Psychology: Animal Behavior Processes,* 2, 285–311.

Huber, L. (2001). Visual categorization in pigeons. In R. G. Cook (Ed.), *Avian visual cognition.* Retrieved August 27, 2005, from http://www.pigeon.psy.tufts.edu/avc/.

Huber, L., & Lenz, R. (1993). A test of the linear feature model of polymorphous concept discrimination with pigeons. *Quarterly Journal of Experimental Psychology, 46B*, 1–18.

Huber, L., & Lenz, R. (1996). Categorization of prototypical stimulus classes by pigeons. *Quarterly Journal of Experimental Psychology, 49B*, 111–133.

Jitsumori, M. (1993). Category discrimination of artificial polymorphous stimuli based on feature learning. *Journal of Experimental Psychology: Animal Behavior Processes, 19*, 244–254.

Jitsumori, M. (1996). A prototype effect and categorization of artificial polymorphous stimuli in pigeons. *Journal of Experimental Psychology: Animal Behavior Processes, 22*, 405–419.

Kruschke, J. K. (1992). ALCOVE: An exemplar-based connectionist model of category learning. *Psychological Review, 99*, 22–44.

Lea, S. E. G. (1984). In what sense do pigeons learn concepts? In H. L. Roitblat, T. G. Bever, & H. S. Terrace (Eds.), *Animal cognition* (pp. 263–276). Mahwah, NJ: Lawrence Erlbaum Associates.

Lea, S. E. G., & Harrison, S. N. (1978). Discrimination of polymorphous stimulus sets by pigeons. *Quarterly Journal of Experimental Psychology*, *30*, 521–537.

Lea, S. E. G., & Ryan, C. M. E. (1983). Feature analysis of pigeons' acquisition of concept discrimination. In M. L. Commons, R. J. Herrnstein, & A. R. Wagner (Eds.), *Quantitative analysis of behavior: Behavioral approaches to pattern recognition and concept formation* (Vol. 8, pp.165–185). Hillsdale, NJ: Lawrence Erlbaum Associates.

Makino, H., & Jitsumori, M. (2000). Category learning and prototype effect in pigeons: A study by using morphed images of human faces. *Japanese Journal of Psychology, 71*, 477–485.

Mackintosh, N. J. (1995). Categorization by people and pigeons: The twenty-second Bartlett Memorial Lecture. *Quarterly Journal of Experimental Psychology, 48B*, 193–214.

Medin, D. L., & Schaffer, M. M. (1978). Context theory of classification learning. *Psychological Review, 85*, 207–238.

Mervis, C. B., & Rosch, E. (1981). Categorization of natural objects. *Annual Review of Psychology, 32*, 89–115.

Neumann, P. G. (1977). Visual prototype information with discontinuous representation of dimension of variability. *Memory & Cognition, 5*, 187–197.

Nosofsky, R. M. (1986). Attention, similarity, and the identification-categorization relationship. *Journal of Experimental Psychology: General, 115*, 39–57.

Nosofsky, R. M. (1991). Tests of an exemplar model for relating perceptual classification and recognition memory. *Journal of Experimental Psychology: Human perception and Performance, 17*, 3–27.

Pearce, J. M. (1989). The acquisition of an artificial category by pigeons. *Quarterly Journal of Experimental Psychology, 41B*, 381–406.

Posner, M. I., & Keele, S. W. (1968). On the genesis of abstract ideas. *Journal of Experimental Psychology, 77*, 353–363.

Reed, S. K. (1972). Pattern recognition and categorization. *Cognitive Psychology, 3*, 382–407.

Roberts, W. A., & Mazmanian, D. S. (1988). Concept learning at different levels of abstraction by pigeons, monkeys, and people. *Journal of Experimental Psychology: Animal Behavior Processes, 14*, 247–260.

Rosch, E. (1978). Principles of categorization. In E. Rosch & B. B. Lloyd (Eds.), *Cognition and categorization* (pp. 27–48). Mahwah, NJ: Lawrence Erlbaum Associates.

Rosch, E., & Mervis, C. B. (1975). Family resemblances: Studies in the internal structure of categories. *Cognitive Psychology, 7*, 573–605.

Rosch, E., Mervis, C. B., Gray, W. D., Johnson, D. M., & Boyes-Braem, P. (1976). Basic objects in natural categories. *Cognitive Psychology, 8*, 382–439.

Ryle, G. (1951). Thinking and language. *Proceedings of the Aristotelian Society*, Suppl., *25*, 65–82.

Smith, E. E., & Medin, D. L. (1981). *Categories and concepts*. Cambridge, MA: Harvard University Press.

Smith, J. D., & Minda, J. P. (2002). Distinguishing prototype-based and exemplar-based processes in dot-pattern category learning. *Journal of Experimental Psychology: Learning, Memory, and Cognition, 28*, 800–811.

Spence, K. W. (1937). The differential response in animals to stimuli varying within a single dimension. *Psychological Review, 44*, 430–444.

Stanton, R., Nosofsky, R. M., & Zaki, S. R. (2002). Comparisons between exemplar similarity and mixed prototype models using a linearly separable category structure. *Memory & Cognition, 30*, 934–944.

Taylor, J. R. (1989). *Linguistic categorization: Prototypes in linguistic theory*. Oxford: Clarendon Press.

Vaughan, W. (1988). Formation of equivalence sets in pigeons. *Journal of Experimental Psychology: Animal Behavior Processes, 14*, 36–42.

von Fersen, L., & Lea, S. E. G. (1990). Category discrimination by pigeons using five polymorphous features. *Journal of Experimental Analysis of Behavior, 54*, 69–84.

Vonk, J., & MacDonald, S. E. (2002). Natural concepts in a juvenile gorilla (*Gorilla gorilla gorilla*) at three levels of abstraction. *Journal of the Experimental Analysis of Behavior, 78*, 315–332.

Watanabe, S. (1988). Failure of visual prototype learning in the pigeon. *Animal Learning & Behavior, 16*, 147–152.

White, K. G., Alsop, B., & Williams, L. (1993). Prototype identification and categorization of incomplete figures by pigeons. *Behavioural Processes, 30*, 253–258.

Wittgenstein, L. (1953). *Philosophical investigations*. New York: Macmillan.

19

Similarity and Difference in the Conceptual Systems of Primates: The Unobservability Hypothesis

JENNIFER VONK AND DANIEL J. POVINELLI

THE TWO FACES OF DIVERSITY

Biologists readily talk of genetic, physiological, morphological, behavioral, and organismal diversity. Indeed, every taxon is ultimately defined on the basis of some combination of variation at each of these levels of description, most of which are readily apparent and uncontested. Mammals are endothermic, whereas reptiles are exothermic. Birds can fly. Fish breathe underwater. Octopi emit ink jets; whales and dolphins emit sonar signals. Curiously, however, whereas biology was more or less founded on the tenets of diversity, psychology has exhibited a strong reluctance to embrace the idea of diversity among species—particularly among groups of closely related species, such as humans and other primates—focusing instead on trying to uncover universal laws of learning (for different perspectives on this problem, see Beach, 1950; Boakes, 1984; Hodos & Campbell, 1969; Macphail, 1987). As a consequence, the idea of psychological diversity—qualitative differences in the mental systems of different species—has not prominently entered the lexicon of comparative psychology, let alone become part of the general notion of biological diversity. Ironically, we believe at least part of this resistance stems from the operation of uniquely human systems that cause us to form strong empathic and intellectual identifications with other species (particularly with other primates).

From the opposite standpoint, however, humans have always possessed an unwavering interest in what makes us psychologically distinct from other species. Indeed, there is no shortage of time-honored proposals on this point. Just to list a few: Humans alone have evolved natural language (a communicative system that involves deep underlying semantic and syntactical structures); humans alone construct complex inventions and alter our environment in profound ways; humans alone have a meaningful culture; and the list goes on. Surely, then, when focused on this half of the question, it is easy to embrace the idea that we are very different from even our closest living relatives.

In the abstract, of course, this tension between similarity and difference does not present a real barrier to thinking about cognition from an evolutionary perspective (for recent attempts to explore cognitive evolution in a diverse array of taxa, see Gallistel, 2000; Gaulin, 1992; Kamil, 1984; Povinelli & Preuss, 1995; Tooby & Cosmides, 1995). After all, that is what evolution is all about—similarity *and* difference. The *similarities* among taxa at each nested level of the biological hierarchy are precisely what force us to the conclusion that life on this planet ultimately constitutes a single genealogy; traced back far enough, even elephants and fruitflies have a common ancestor. Conversely, the *differences* among taxa provide evidence that this unbroken genealogy of life is, and has been, sculpted by natural selection and other evolutionary processes, ultimately allowing us to represent the history of life on this planet as a branching tree or bush. And, finally, the combination of similarity and difference is what gives us such great confidence in the idea that the species we see today *evolved* on this planet, as opposed to having been specially created. In principle, then, the idea that the cognitive systems of humans and our closest living relatives are both profoundly similar *and* different should present little difficulty.

The general practice of comparative psychology has, however, largely been a deflationary one, attempting to explain away differences between species as unimportant, trivial, or simply a function of methodological artifacts. Psychologists have had a difficult time simultaneously embracing similarity and difference as equally important facets of cognitive evolution. More often than not, in the limited space that comparative psychology has given to seriously attempting to incorporate ideas about evolution, one or the other of these dimensions of evolution has been given the upper hand. Indeed, both possible mistakes have been made: (1) invoking the idea of evolution in an attempt to promote the idea of "unbridgeable" differences (usually in the case of attempting to set humans completely apart from other species) and (2) invoking evolution to support the idea of "unbreakable" similarities. These mistakes are exacerbated by the fact that, for much of its history, comparative psychology relied on the idea of the "phylogenetic scale" as opposed to the "phylogenetic tree" (Hodos & Campbell, 1969, 1991). The truth, of course, is that when it comes to entities whose ontological status is as nebulous as the "structures" or "systems" or "representations" investigated by cognitive scientists, and their connection to various behaviors, the fact of evolution creates little or no presumption about the phylogenetic distribution of such systems among closely related species. Indeed, because it largely sees the mind as a collection of innumerable systems and subsystems, cognitive science should herald an end to the sterile similarity/difference debate by allowing psychologists to recognize that each of these psychological systems may have its own evolutionary history, in the same manner as the various organs of the body. The distribution of these cognitive traits thus becomes an empirical question—just as the distribution of morphological, physiological, and behavioral traits was (and continues to be) an empirical question for those branches of biology that are interested in documenting diversity.

THE UNOBSERVABILITY HYPOTHESIS

What we have said about similarity and difference is true of cognitive evolution in general: The mental systems of closely related species can be both massively similar and massively different (depending on the degree of ecological divergence that occurred since their last common ancestor). But, the case of humans and our nearest living relatives—chimpanzees and the other great apes—would seem to constitute a vital "test case" for the project of incorporating "psychology" into the general list of dimensions along which species differ. After all, if we could not demonstrate that humans and chimpanzees differ from each other in fundamental ways, then the idea of psychological diversity might be harder for psychologists to take seriously—or at least harder to embrace as an important general fact about evolution, as opposed to a trivial fact about taxa that have not shared a common ancestor for many hundreds of millions of years. In other words, although many scholars might accept psychological differences between wasps and penguins, this idea is easily assimilated into the mistaken idea of evolution along a phylogenetic continuum (see Darwin, 1871). The case of humans and chimpanzees makes the point most clearly; if two such very closely related species that have evolved such radically different ways of life could not be shown to possess cognitive specializations, then psychologists (and biologists) might be convinced to politely agree with our general point about psychological diversity but fail to see how it has much to do with their day-to-day research activities.

In this chapter, we explore the possibility that one of the important ways in which humans differ from other species is that our minds form and reason about concepts that refer to unobservable entities or processes (see Povinelli, 2004). We use the term "unobservable" in its broadest sense to refer to entities or processes that cannot be directly perceived by the unaided senses. In short, we explore the possibility that whereas many species form concepts about observable things and use those concepts in flexible and productive ways, humans alone think about such things as God, ghosts, gravity, and other minds. Further, we speculate that although thinking about unobservables is by no means the only way in which the human mind differs from other species, it may serve as the foundation for many of the fundamental differences between our behavior and that of our closest living relatives. We note from the outset that this proposal does not conflict with other proposals that stress the importance of language in determining human uniqueness. Indeed, although we do not explore this idea at great length in this chapter, we suspect that the underlying "abstractive depth" that makes reasoning about unobservables possible co-evolved with natural language.

It is crucial to note that an ability to wield more concrete concepts may serve as the fundamental basis for much of what we deem "higher-order" cognition in humans. However, large swaths of these concepts are more than likely to be shared by other species; indeed, the more closely related the species, the more probable it is that their concepts of the observable world are similar. For example, although chimpanzees, humans, and fruitflies (*Drosophila melangaster*) all exploit bananas as an edible resource, the human and chimpanzee "banana" concept is undoubtedly highly similar and radically different from the banana concept found in the fruitfly (probably best described as a chemical gradient of some kind). Thus, although each species may represent only certain features of objects or events in the world and different species may overlap in the objects and events they represent, it would seem far fetched to imagine that even the same "objects" are conceptualized in the same manner across species.

However, it is our contention that the mental systems of most species, no matter how "abstract" the concepts they form, differ in one important respect from the human mind: They do not form concepts that refer to merely hypothetical things. Thus, we speculate that although many minds are adapted to represent events in terms of their observable properties and are able to extrapolate certain rules from these representations, these minds do not posit unobservable entities or processes as mediating variables to explain or to predict observable events or states. We are not the first to propose that the ability to reason about causal forces is a unique specialization of humans, an ability that leads to profound differences between the cognitive systems of humans and all other primates (e.g., see Kohler, 1925; Povinelli, 2000, 2004; Tomasello, 1998). However, we wish to focus the current discussion on the ability to represent concepts for unobservables, some of which represent causal forces and some of which do not. In addition, we wish to generalize this idea to emphasize the distinction between a mind that merely predicts events and a mind that strives to explain them (see Povinelli, 2004; Povinelli & Dunphy-Lelii, 2001). In what follows, we explore the unobservability hypothesis in the context of three areas of research—concept formation, theory of mind, and physical causality. In each of these research domains, we ask whether there is evidence to contradict the hypothesis that reasoning about strictly hypothetical constructs is a uniquely human specialization.

As we shall see, in each domain, the challenge lies in the tendency to conflate the outward manifestation of an unobservable construct with the construct itself. How does one determine when an organism is wielding concepts generalized from what he or she can directly perceive (the outward manifestation), as opposed to wielding those concepts plus additional, theoretical concepts that have no observable referent—concepts invoked both to explain *why* an observed event occurred and to assist in the prediction of future events (the underlying cause)? Viewed in this light, it should be readily apparent that teasing apart these two systems (one that reasons about unobservable causal forces and one that reasons about observables) will be far from a simple enterprise. Because of the close relationship between an event and its purported underlying cause, it is difficult to specify contrasting predictions of such systems. This point emphasizes another important fact that is often overlooked: A system that reasons about observables alone provides an organism with immense predictive abilities.

CONCEPT FORMATION

In asking whether reasoning about unobservable entities is a human specialization, a natural place to turn is to the literature on concept formation in animals. In this section, we address two main questions. First, do animals form the kinds of concepts that constitute theoretical class categories as well as concepts for tangible entities? For example, do they represent foods as a general category of items that encapsulates many different kinds of edible things or do they form only representations of individual food items, which may be associated to some degree by virtue of their obvious similarities but are not represented as belonging to a unitary conceptual class?

Second, is there any direct evidence to suggest that species other than humans form concepts about things that are so inherently abstract that they can be said to refer to unobservables? Our attempt here is not to review the literature on concept formation (see Jitsumori, 2001; Pearce, 1994); rather, in what follows, we examine some representative research in this area from the perspective of the unobservability hypothesis outlined earlier.

Exploring Animal Concepts

Studies that directly attempt to investigate the type and nature of concepts held by other species face great difficulty in determining whether subjects are responding on the basis of readily observable perceptual information or whether, in addition, they are able to reason about more abstract concepts which subsume those perceptual regularities. Typically, such studies involve the use of two-choice discrimination paradigms in which an animal responds in one way to a member of a (positive) class and in a different way to members of another (negative) class. Once a high level of performance is reached with a set of training stimuli, novel members of the "positive" and "negative" classes are presented as a test of transfer.

Another popular experimental design is the match-to-sample (MTS), or non–match-to-sample (NMTS) paradigm, in which an animal is shown a sample stimulus and either concurrently or successively (in delayed MTS or DMTS designs) is shown two or more comparison stimuli; the animal is then required to select the comparison stimulus that matches (or does not match) the sample. An animal may learn to make the correct response in such paradigms without using the experimenter-defined categories. The basis for correct categorization may depend more strongly on shared perceptual features and less on an overriding concept.

This distinction between categorizing on a conceptual versus a perceptual basis is a difficult one to make, particularly because conception is generally considered to be grounded in perception (e.g., Goldstone & Barsalou, 1988; Huber & Aust, chapter 17, this volume). Experiments testing for the presence of natural concepts, which consist of groupings of "infinite or open-ended classes of things that occur in nature" (Schrier, Angarella, & Povar, 1984, p. 564), make use of stimuli that must be discriminated perceptually. However, it is possible to construct categories whose members are visually dissimilar and yet are linked by virtue of an abstract construct that itself is not directly observable, as in the case of a category of items that are related by their function, not by the fact that they look, smell, feel, sound, or taste alike (e.g., categories such as "things that make good gifts" or "things that attract romantic partners"). In such cases, it would be difficult to understand the conceptual fabric binding the various category members together without a notion about constructs that cannot be directly perceived through the senses.

The extent to which other animals share the ability to form concepts in the more abstract sense just described has yet to be resolved. Indeed, it is difficult even to define what is meant by "abstract." The most commonly agreed on convention is to refer to abstract concepts as those that are not tied to directly perceivable features and to highlight the ability to create coherent conceptual categories across significant perceptual variance (Spalding & Ross, 2000). An "abstract concept" may then be a representation of constructs or theoretical entities as well as of material objects.

In practice, however, given the kinds of concepts that are typically explored with animals, common perceptual features between training and transfer stimuli must be present in order for subjects to make the discrimination in the first place. For instance, concepts such as "water" are typically exemplified by predominantly bluish-colored photographs, whereas stimuli exemplifying the concept "tree" typically consist of brown trunk and branch-like appendages with green leaves. Thus, it becomes difficult to distinguish between accounts whereby, for example, an animal learns to "choose blue" versus "choose water."

Of interest is the extent to which the amount of transfer is affected by the degree of perceptual overlap between the training and transfer stimuli (or between the sample and comparison stimuli in MTS designs). For instance, subjects may show less transfer to pictures of green or black water, or to pictures of trees without leaves. Thus, researchers have presented various animal subjects with categories that vary along a continuum of abstraction (with "abstraction" referring to the breadth of the category and the variance of physical features between the exemplars), testing the hypothesis that the most abstract categories will be more difficult to learn relative to more concrete level categories that share many perceptual features (e.g., Roberts & Mazmanian, 1988; Tanaka, 2001; Vonk & MacDonald, 2002, 2004).

For instance, Vonk and MacDonald presented a gorilla (2002) and six orangutans (2004) with a sequence of two-choice discrimination tasks in which the most concrete level category included members of only their own species and the most abstract category included diverse members of the animal kingdom, such as insects, birds, fish, mammals, and reptiles. Although the orangutans seemed to have the most difficulty learning the most abstract concepts, as expected, surprisingly, the gorilla, along with pigeons and squirrel monkeys that were presented with similar discriminations by Roberts and Mazmanian (1988), acquired the most abstract category discrimination more readily than an intermediate-level category discrimination. Vonk and MacDonald (2002) concluded that perhaps the degree of abstractness or breadth of the categories is not a reliable predictor of how readily nonhumans will form experimenter-defined categories; the degree of perceptual overlap both within and between categories in any given stimulus set may more strongly influence categorization.

Although some researchers have encountered difficulty determining the exact features used by their subjects to make the discriminations (Roberts & Mazmanian, 1988; Vonk & MacDonald, 2002; 2004), others have identified the use of features that are irrelevant to category membership, causing them to question the extent to which their subjects formed true concepts (D'Amato & Van Sant, 1988; Jitsumori & Matsuzawa, 1991; Schrier & Brady, 1987. Therefore, natural concept experiments may demonstrate little more than the fact that nonhuman primates are exceptionally skilled at tracking the presence or absence of various observable physical features of the stimuli presented to them. Indeed, such results suggest the possibility that nonhuman primates may operate on the basis of observing perceptual patterns rather than by forming overarching concepts, although the final assessment of this hypothesis awaits resolution.

Note that we are not suggesting that humans use concepts in the absence of, or to the exclusion of, relying on perceptual patterns; rather, both humans and nonhumans may rely on purely perceptual feature analyses to solve many discrimination problems. In fact, parallel studies with human infants and pigeons have revealed that these species sometimes make stimulus discriminations via parallel perceptual processes (Wasserman & Rovee-Collier, 2001). However, we speculate that humans may be uniquely capable of additionally reasoning about constructs that have no directly observable correlates.

Understanding First-Order Object Relations

Because of the difficulty in determining when natural classes of objects are discriminated on the basis of shared perceptual regularities between the objects, rather than by concepts defining the class itself, researchers have turned to studying the formation of relational concepts. It has been suggested that the concept of relatedness between items is independent of their physical properties and must be represented abstractly in the form of an analogy (Premack, 1983). For example, "darker" and "bigger" are relative concepts. Gray is darker than white, but black is darker than gray, so the idea of the "darker" color is relative and is not tied to a specific stimulus in a fixed manner.

However, the stimulus differences are still *perceived*, regardless of whether the difference is absolute or relative. In fact, in the discussion that follows, we shall see that there are perceptual processes that allow animals to make discriminations that humans perceive as conceptually "same" or "different." Thus, although the theoretical notions of "sameness" and "difference" cannot themselves be directly perceived, these relations can take the form of physical identity. An animal might perceive two objects that look similar as belonging together without representing the general concept of "sameness." In fact, some researchers have argued that, in order to demonstrate that an animal is classifying two stimuli as conceptually the same, one must first demonstrate that the stimuli are actually perceived as perceptually distinct (Vauclair & Fagot, 1996).

Conceptual categorization thus requires that stimuli are perceived as being distinct and yet are still classified as functionally or categorically equivalent. Without such evidence, one would not know whether the animal simply failed to discriminate between perceptually similar stimuli. Unfortunately, few researchers have incorporated such tests as an initial step in their categorization experiments.

Many researchers have repeatedly demonstrated that both pigeons and baboons can learn to discriminate large arrays in which all of the items are the same from those in which all or some of the items are unique (Cook, Cavoto, & Cavoto, 1995; Cook, Katz, & Cavoto, 1997; Cook & Wasserman, chapter 16, this volume; Wasserman, Hugart, & Kirkpatrick-Steger, 1995; Wasserman, Young, & Fagot, 2001; Young, Wasserman, & Garner, 1997). However, both species are unable to do so when the array contains fewer items, suggesting that the subjects rely on variability or entropy to perform the tasks (Wasserman, Fagot, & Young, 2001; Wasserman, Young, & Nolan, 2000; Young & Wasserman, 1997; Young, Wasserman, & Dalrymple, 1997). In other words, animals perceive the amount of perceptual variance to be greater in the "different" arrays than in the "same" arrays; this disparity in variance decreases as the number of items in the array decrease, causing deterioration in their ability to discriminate. These results suggest that the animals are in fact not relying on same/different concepts and instead are basing their responses on the perceived perceptual regularity of the stimulus.

Results from a slightly different procedure revealed that if pigeons were shown an entire list of items, composed of either identical or unique items, and executed their discriminative responses at the end of the lists, they were able to do so at above chance levels (Young et al., 1997; Young, Wasserman, Hilfers, & Dalrymple, 1999). At first glance, it might seem less likely that a perception of entropy could account for these results, because the individual components were presented successively in list form as opposed to being visible simultaneously as components of a single complex stimulus at the time of the response. However, if the pigeons are using a perceptual detector that is sensitive to variation among the stimuli, then ultimately it should not matter if the items are presented all at once or in succession. In fact, computational analyses done by Young et al. (1999) revealed that sensitivity to entropy remained a critical factor in accounting for the pigeons' performance with successively presented items. Still, in addition to entropy, memory was also revealed to be an important factor.

Young et al. (1997) suggested that their results constituted clear evidence of memory-based conceptualization in nonhuman animals. However, although the temporal organization of the list nominally required the animals to remember what had been presented, there is no clear evidence that what was held in memory was conceptual versus perceptual information. Furthermore, because viewing only the last two items provided all of the relevant information to make the same/different discrimination, given that none of the items were repeated in "different" lists and all of the items were repeated in "same" lists, and because the intertrial intervals were less than 10 s, the memory demand fell well within the range of short-term memory, in which the processing of perceptual information alone is sufficient to maintain a memory trace. It is possible for the pigeons to succeed at these tasks by relying on processing perceptual information, regardless of how the items are spatially or temporally configured. Although humans can be shown to rely on similar perceptual processing when performing the same or analogous tasks, it is not clear that these tasks possess the resolving power to disentangle the two accounts of performance—the representation of a concept of "sameness" versus a perceptual feature-matching process—because high levels of performance can be achieved using either mechanism.

The research discussed up to this point can be interpreted as showing that both pigeons and monkeys can perceive first-order relations—how two or more items are related to each other. However, "perceive" may be the key word. Success on such tasks can be achieved by attending solely to which items are perceptually more similar. In other words, animals may have a concept of "sameness" to the extent that one item is perceived as looking like another by virtue of shared physical features. However, there is a more abstract sense in which the concept of "same" may be represented: that is, whether both items belong to the same conceptual class of items, class being defined by potentially unobservable properties. That is, "same" can be represented perceptually as two or more things that visually match, lack variance, or present an impression of perceptual regularity, or "same" can be represented conceptually as a class of things bound by properties that may or may not be directly observed.

Understanding Second-Order Relations

In contrast to *first-order* relations, representing *second-order* relations—relations between relations—is thought to depend on an ability to understand that the relationship between two objects is the same as (or different from) the relationship between two other objects. Understanding second-order relations may thus require not only the detection of the perceptual relationships between objects, but also an understanding of the analogical relationship between pairs of objects that are perceptually dissimilar.

Early studies with chimpanzees suggested that only "language"-trained animals could process second-order relations (Gillan, Premack, & Woodruff, 1981; Premack, 1983). However, later experiments with adult chimpanzees who had not received formal language training, but who had learned abstract symbols representing the concepts "same" and "different," showed them to be capable of making explicit judgments about second-order relations (Thompson & Oden, 1996, 2000; Thompson, Oden, & Boysen, 1997). In addition, other researchers found that chimpanzees spontaneously sorted objects according to second-order classification schemes (Spinozzi, 1993; Tanaka, 1996).

Premack and Dasser (1991) suggested that requiring animals to make an instrumental response instantiating a categorical judgment satisfied the criteria for conceptually based behavior. One question we wish to pose is, Does an instrumental response, in the case of matching or sorting based on second-order relations, demand that the response be shaped by conceptual versus perceptual processes? Is it not possible that animals perceive variance discrepancies, or some other perceptual regularity or irregularity, between pairs of items without evoking a true concept for the perceived relations?

Interestingly, experiments involving spontaneous handling of object–object pairs suggested that infant chimpanzees who had not received any "language" or token training were capable of at least *perceiving* the relationships between objects, although they failed to make instrumental use of these observations (Oden, Thompson, & Premack, 1988, 1990). Clearly then, the capacity to perceive second-order relations can be dissociated from the ability to apply the concept operationally.

Thus, one hypothesis is that infant chimpanzees perceive the relations but have not yet formed an abstract representation of them, which they will ultimately develop. Another hypothesis is that although young chimpanzees cannot yet use their perceptions to guide their responses instrumentally, older chimpanzees can use these same perceptions to sculpt their instrumental responses, albeit still in the absence of having acquired a relational concept. If the infant chimpanzees can perceive the relations sufficiently to handle pairs of objects instantiating different relations for different lengths of time, then perhaps the adult chimpanzees use the same strictly perceptual information to succeed at the MTS tasks. Still, this leaves us with the question, What, other than a relational concept, would allow them to do so?

Although we are unable to resolve the issue as to whether sensitivity to second-order relations is based on more than perceptual processing, some evidence suggests that this sensitivity is greater in apes than in monkeys. Notably, Thompson and Oden (1996) reported that adult rhesus macaques tested in the same "preference for novelty tasks" failed to perceive these relations (although these data have not been published). Furthermore, the same authors suggest that human infants do not express tacit knowledge in relational MTS tasks, suggesting that the ability to make operational use of perceived second-order relations may be slow to develop in both chimpanzees and humans. Thus, there may be a gradient of relational understanding both ontogenetically and phylogenetically.

Fagot, Wasserman, and Young (2001) reported that baboons may also be sensitive to second-order relations. In an MTS task in which all of the items within a sample array were either the same or different, baboons chose at above-chance levels a matching array in which the different objects within that array were likewise either the same or different. Again, discriminative performance dissipated when only two items appeared in the stimulus array. It can be argued that the discrimination can be made on a purely perceptual basis. "All same" displays may appear more perceptually regular than "mixed" or "all different" displays, even when the components within the array are randomly arranged (Wasserman et al., 2000; Young & Wasserman, 1997). The fact that the performance of both baboons and pigeons falls apart when only two items appear in the array indicates that these animals are not representing "sameness" in the same sense that humans are capable of representing the concept "same." For humans, two identical items might represent the most salient case of "same." The fact that this is not the case for nonhumans suggests that different concepts are represented across species in these tasks.

A recent study by Vonk (2003) revealed that three orangutans and one gorilla were able to match stimuli containing only two components in an MTS task on the basis of a second-order relation: shared color or shape between items. Not only were the apes able to succeed at the task with only two items in the stimulus arrays, but they reached above-chance levels of responding much more quickly (i.e., within the first 24 trials) than did Fagot et al.'s (2001) baboons, who required hundreds of trials to match same and different arrays with multiple items within the array. The results of this study could be taken to suggest that both gorillas and orangutans, with no explicit "language" or token training, may be capable of representing second-order relations. One possible interpretation of these findings is that second-order relational information may be perceived only by the great apes, and not by the monkey species tested to date. This should be considered a testable hypothesis.

However, it is difficult to escape the problem discussed above in the context of first-order relations: The stimuli are almost always presented visually (slides or photographs) and the subjects can rely on only the perceptual features present in the stimuli in order to extrapolate the rule about which stimuli are "correct" or "reinforced" in a given experimental set. Thus, it becomes nearly impossible to surmise when the animals have gone beyond learning about perceptual regularities to form a more general concept. Transfer tests with discriminably different stimuli are important in this context because they provide a basis for surmising the generalization of learning from individual exemplars to novel examples of the same category.

However, transfer tests do not allow one to determine whether the subject is generalizing based on observable features or on the basis of constructs that may not be directly observable. For instance, an animal could generalize responding to photographs of particular humans to novel photos of different humans, but they may not be representing the concept "human"; instead they may be generalizing a more concrete list of features such as "two eyes, pale face, sparse hair etc." Even novel photographs must preserve the observable features that define the categories being discriminated, thus allowing transfer to be mediated by representations of physical features and not concepts per se.

For example, in another study, two orangutans and one gorilla matched stimuli that were created based on the experimenter's conception of social relationships between individual animals depicted in the stimuli (Vonk, 2002). For instance, they matched photos in a DMTS task based on whether the photographs depicted mother/offspring pairs, social groups of animals, mated pairs, or siblings. In this study, it is difficult to determine whether the high levels of performance were mediated by concepts for the relationships between the individuals depicted, such as "mother/offspring," versus nonrelational concepts, such as "young and old (or large and small) members of same species."

This problem is pervasive in studies of concept formation. Even when abstract symbols, such as lexigrams, are presented instead of the actual objects that they represent (as in Savage-Rumbaugh, Rumbaugh, Smith, & Lawson, 1980), the animal may base its response to those symbols on learned associations between the symbol and its referent, both of which must have been visually connected during training. Thus, it is only when the concept being wielded deals with properties that have no observable correlates that one can conclude that the concept is, in this strict sense, "theoretical."

Social Concepts

Researchers have also investigated whether nonhumans form social concepts about emotions and relationships, such as dominance, and have used evidence for such concepts to advance the idea that these primates are capable of representing concepts for unobservable constructs. However, even emotions have outward manifestations. Fear can be represented by the image of bristling hair, wide eyes, and shaking body. Anger can be represented in the form of bared teeth and scream vocalizations. Even love can be linked to the behaviors it evokes. When someone is in love, they presumably act differently from when they are not. Although humans might *describe* love in terms of its outward manifestations, they would *define* the concept as a subjective feeling that varies between individuals. Indeed, they would consider the concept somewhat nebulous and difficult to define. It is unclear how a nonhuman would define any emotion, given that they are incapable of communicating such thoughts to us. A limited number of studies have nonetheless sought to examine the nature of other primates' concept of emotions.

Parr (2001) reported that chimpanzees could correctly match photographs of chimpanzees expressing various emotions to the emotional valences of previously shown video. For instance, after being shown a video of chimpanzees being darted by veterinarians, the chimpanzees correctly selected the image of a chimpanzee presenting a bared teeth or scream expression over one presenting a neutral or positive expression. However, it is not possible to determine the nature of the subjects' underlying representations of the stimuli.

Surely, these chimpanzees had the necessary experience to form associations between various scenarios and the expressions present on the faces of their conspecifics during those episodes, without necessarily forming any representation of the underlying emotional experience of their counterparts. Furthermore, in order to comprehend the task, it is absolutely necessary that the chimpanzees had formed representations about the various behaviors depicted in the video, regardless of whether they had additionally mapped any concepts of "emotions," as internal states, onto those behaviors. Our point is that emotions could not be depicted in the video in the absence of the observable behaviors with which they are correlated. Behaviors, on the other hand, can clearly be represented in a manner that would allow the chimpanzees to match them to facial expressions, without necessarily also representing any underlying mental states.

The concept of dominance can likewise be represented as a series of behaviors that lead to similar outcomes—usually an unpleasant experience for the subordinate. A recent study by Bovet and Washburn (2003) exposed baboons to a series of short video clips depicting various scenes in which dominant unknown baboons interacted with other unknown group members. The monkeys were then rewarded for selecting the image of the dominant animal, based on the information available in the last still frame of the clip. Once criterion was reached with the initial category of video (e.g., "chasing"), the subjects were shown various clips exemplifying a different scenario (e.g., "avoidance" or "presentation"), up to a total of eight categories. The baboons were shown several different clips within each category. After the first two or three categories, two of the three subjects showed transfer on the very first opportunity with stimuli from a novel class of behavior, suggesting that they had extrapolated from the video clips a more general concept tying these clips together. At the very least, the baboons were able to accurately select those individuals whose attributes or behaviors resembled those of the "correct" individual from prior categories.

Bovet and Washburn's (2003) study experimentally corroborates observations of field researchers who have long noted the ability of group-living primates to assess the dominance relations of their peers (Cheney, Seyfarth, & Silk, 1995; Silk, 1999). Because these subjects were observing strangers, this experiment extends the conclusions based on field observations to more neutral scenarios by eliminating the opportunity for the baboons to rely on specific associations between the animals in the videos and representations of interactions directly witnessed in the past. The subjects' ability to select the image of the dominant animal in this case was independent of prior experience, in the sense that it was not a behavioral response with a long history of reinforcement through experiences with the particular conspecifics involved, such as displaying a submissive posture to a specific dominant.

Having said that, however, the concept of "dominance" revealed in this experiment could still be described by appealing solely to the various observable behaviors of the dominant (and perhaps the subordinate) animal and thus may constitute nothing more than a general category of behaviors that go together without a more abstract concept defining *why* this is so.[1] Thus, even in these cases, there is no unique evidence to suggest that the primates' understanding is tied to abstract social concepts about unobservables that underlie the observable behaviors, as opposed to concepts about strictly observable perceptual regularities apparent in the behaviors.

THEORY OF MIND

It is, in part, for the above reasons that researchers interested in the question of whether other species reason about unobservable entities have recently focused much of their energy on exploring concepts that, by their very nature, *require* inferences about unobservables. A central battleground for such questions is the current debate over whether the ability to reason about mental states is a uniquely human trait.

Premack and Woodruff (1978) coined the term "theory of mind" to describe this ability to make inferences about inherently unobservable mental states, such as desires, emotions, perceptions, and beliefs. Although inferences about mental states can lead to predictions about observable behavior (and hence presumably play some causal role in one's behavior), the mental states themselves cannot be directly observed. As in the case of our discussion of concept formation, the intimate connection between the directly observable aspects of behavior (avoiding a dominant whose hair is bristling) and an inferred unobservable mental state (the dominant is <*angry*>) makes it difficult to empirically disentangle whether a given animal is reasoning only about concepts abstracted from behavior (what we refer to as "behavioral abstractions") or whether, *in addition*, they are reasoning about the underlying mental states that (from the perspective of our folk psychology) give rise to those behaviors (see Povinelli & Vonk, 2003, 2004). We emphasize "in addition" because a trivial, but often overlooked, fact is that *a system for reasoning about mental states presupposes the presence and full operation of a system for reasoning about behaviors*—a fact that, when carefully considered, magnifies the challenge of disentangling the causal work that each kind of representation may perform (Povinelli & Vonk, 2004).

Do Nonhuman Primates Reason About Mental States?

Following Premack and Woodruff's (1978) initial report, early research explored the degree to which chimpanzees could make inferences about the knowledge states of others and, in particular, if they understood the connection between <*seeing*> and <*knowing*> (Call & Tomasello, 1999; Povinelli, Nelson, & Boysen, 1990; Povinelli, Rulf, & Bierschwale, 1994; Premack, 1988). The results of these empirical studies largely disconfirmed the hypothesis that other apes share the human ability to reason about epistemic states. Parallel attempts with several monkey species led to similar conclusions (e.g., Cheney & Seyfarth, 1990; Povinelli, Parks, & Novak, 1992). Since then, numerous methodologies have been deployed to explore whether various facets of theory of mind are present in nonhuman primates (see Cheney & Seyfarth, 1991, 1992; Heyes, 1998; Suddendorf & Whiten, 2001).

After initial attempts failed to clearly establish that chimpanzees or other nonhuman primates reason about knowledge states, we turned our attention to the possibility that humans and chimpanzees, for example, might share only certain aspects of theory of mind, with humans having elaborated on the system after the human lineage diverged from the chimpanzee lineage (Povinelli, 1996; Povinelli & Eddy, 1996c; for more recent views on this idea, see Tomasello, Call, & Hare, 2003a). In the context of our own research, we reasoned that our earlier studies investigating nonhuman primates' understanding that <*seeing*> something hidden leads to <*knowing*> its location, for example, had been constructed in such a way as to presuppose that they understood <*seeing*>. It followed then, that although chimpanzees had failed to demonstrate that they could make inferences about <*knowing*> in such contexts, they might nonetheless be capable of reasoning about <*seeing*> alone. In other words, chimpanzees might possess an ability to construe the movements and postures of the head and eyes in terms of the unobservable state of <*seeing*>, without having any idea about epistemic states (like <*knowing*>) that might be generated by such perceptual acts (for example, see John Flavell's Level 1/Level 2 visual perspective-taking distinction in Flavell, Everett, Croft, & Flavell, 1981).

To this end, in a lengthy series of cross-sectional and longitudinal studies, we systematically explored our chimpanzees' understanding of <*seeing*> (Povinelli, Dunphy-Lelii, Reaux, & Mazza, 2002; Povinelli & Eddy, 1996a, 1996b, 1996c, 1997; Povinelli, Bierschwale, & Cech, 1999; Reaux, Theall, & Povinelli, 1999; Theall & Povinelli, 1999). First, we were able to reliably document our chimpanzees' ability to follow the gaze of others (Povinelli & Eddy, 1996b, 1996c, 1997), a finding that has also been demonstrated and extended to other species in many other laboratories (e.g., Anderson & Mitchell, 1999; Emery & Clayton, 2001; Emery, Lorincz, Perrett, Oram, et al., 1997; Kaplan & Rogers, 2002; Tomasello, Call, & Hare, 1998; Tomasello, Hare, & Agnetta, 1999). Not only did our chimpanzees follow gaze in response to the movement of the head and eyes in concert, but they also did so in reaction to eye movements alone.

Furthermore, in certain contexts, our chimpanzees appeared to account for the opacity of the object at which the experimenter gazed (see Povinelli & Eddy, 1996a). For instance, they attempted to follow an experimenter's gaze to the other side of a solid partition as if they understood its obstructive properties, rather than looking past

Figure 19.1. A chimpanzee uses her species-typical begging gesture to request food from an experimenter.

the partition for an interesting object to which the experimenter was apparently orienting. In this context, we also demonstrated that chimpanzees could exploit gaze cues to locate hidden food (Povinelli et al., 1999, 2002; see also Barth, Reaux, & Povinelli, 2005). Thus, our results, taken in concert with those from other laboratories, provided strong evidence that chimpanzees (and other nonhuman primates) were very adept at monitoring and using the gaze of others.

At the same time, however, we discovered robust evidence that these same chimpanzees did not appreciate the psychological aspect of "seeing"; for example, the different visual experiences of someone with blindfolds over their eyes versus someone with blindfolds over their mouth. The chimpanzees were trained to use their species-typical begging gesture to request food from an experimenter (figure 19.1). Probe trials, in which the chimpanzees were required to choose between two experimenters, one of whom could see them and one of whom could not (figure 19.2), were interspersed with these single-experimenter trials. If the chimpanzees genuinely understood that, in each case, only one of the experimenters could see their gesture, then they should have preferentially gestured to that person.

Chimpanzees were presented with a variety of different conditions in which the experimenters were generally matched except for the critical variable ("able to see" versus "not able to see"). None of the chimpanzees spontaneously chose correctly from the first trial forward, except for the condition where one experimenter faced forward and the other had her back turned to the chimpanzee (Povinelli & Eddy, 1996c).

The results of a lengthy and carefully constructed series of more than a dozen follow-up studies consistently supported the conclusion that the chimpanzees were not making inferences about the experimenters' abilities to see them but were instead learning to predict who would respond to them on the basis of a prioritized set of observable features related to the experimenters' postures. For instance, chimpanzees first attended to the general frontal orientation of the experimenters' bodies, then to whether the experimenter's face was present, and then to whether the experimenter's eyes were visible. Over time, they learned to discriminate correctly across even the most initially difficult conditions. However, this learning did not seem to be retained when they were retested in a new series of tests several years later (Reaux et al., 1999).

In addition, the chimpanzees did not succeed at certain mixed conditions in which the previously "correct" experimenter posture from one condition was paired with the previously "incorrect" experimenter posture from a different condition (Reaux et al., 1999). Instead, the chimpanzees used their prioritized rule structure—even when it led them to choose the experimenter who could not see them! Thus, the chimpanzees started with some general rules about postural orientation, learned to

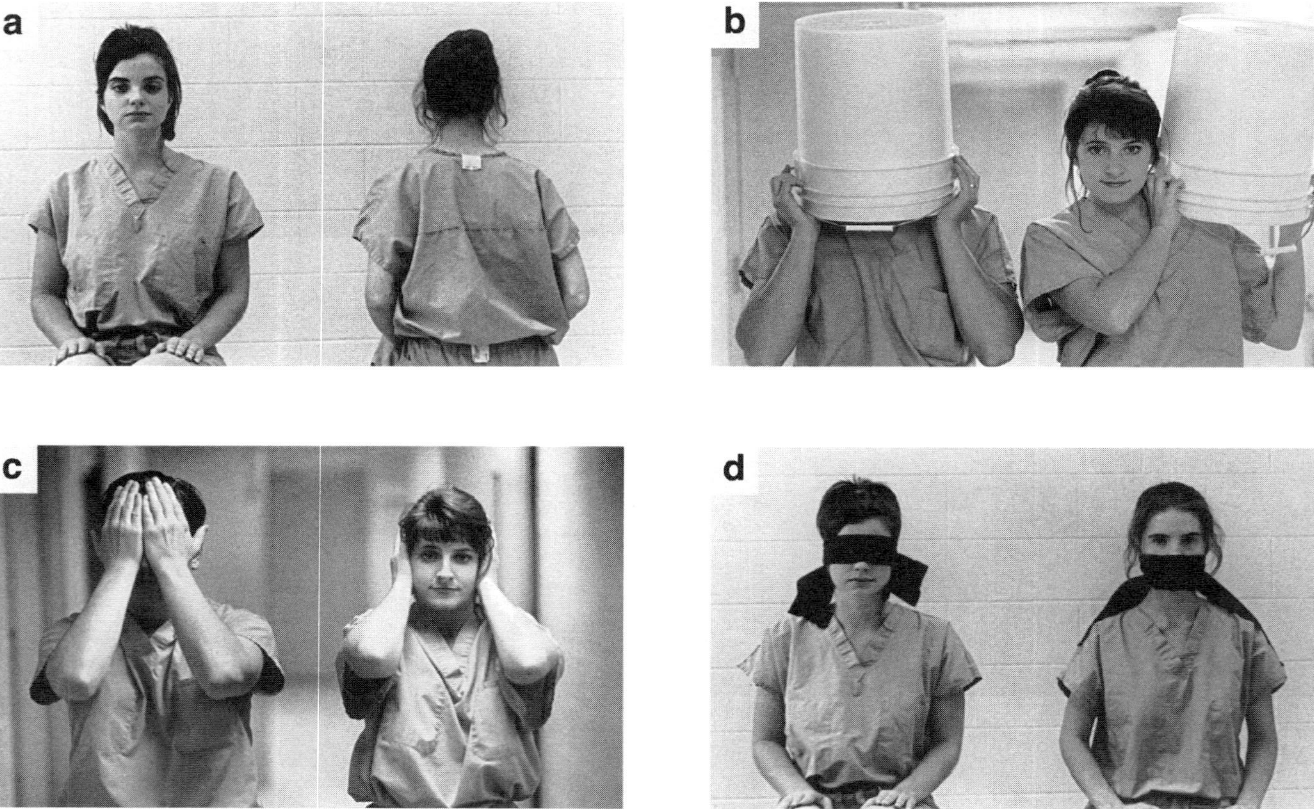

Figure 19.2. A subset of probe trial conditions presented to the chimpanzees in Povinelli and Eddy (1996c), in which one experimenter could see the chimpanzee and the other could not. *a*, Front/back, *b*, buckets, *c*, hands, *d*, blindfolds.

understand the importance of still others, but never appeared to understand them as indicators of unobservable visual attentional states. This pattern of results has been replicated in other species as well (Vick & Anderson, 2003), suggesting that a strategy of attending to prioritized rules about observable features is not an idiosyncratic adaptation of chimpanzees alone.

To be sure, our conclusion is controversial. Although initially concurring with these findings, Tomasello's research group has more recently argued that new studies warrant the conclusion that chimpanzees do, in fact, reason about perceptual states such as <*seeing*>. Hare, Call, and Tomasello (2000) reported the results of several studies using a competitive paradigm that they believe support the conclusion that chimpanzees do infer mental states such as <*seeing*> (see also Hare, 2001; Hare, Call, & Tomasello, 2001; Tomasello, Call, & Hare, 2003a, 2003b). However, foundational aspects of the results of those studies were not independently replicated (Karin-D'Arcy & Povinelli, 2002); more importantly, alternative interpretations of the results of such studies are possible (for a detailed discussion, see Povinelli & Vonk, 2003, 2004). Indeed, a logical analysis of these (and other studies) has shown that the observed outcomes can just as easily be produced by an organism that reasons solely about the observable behavioral features of the experiment—precisely because those are the observable features on which the chimpanzees are supposed to infer underlying states. In short, there may be no unique causal or predictive work to be performed by the inference of <*seeing*> in these studies (see Povinelli & Vonk, 2004).

Our purpose here is not to review the growing and controversial literature in detail (a good summary of the current controversy in this area can be found in the debate between Povinelli & Vonk, 2003, 2004, and Tomasello et al., 2003a, 2003b). However, by illustrating the general state of the controversy, we have sufficiently outlined our reasons for believing that, at present, there are no strong grounds for believing that nonhuman primates reason about unobservable mental states—consistent with our conclusion from the concept formation literature. At the same time, there is ample evidence to conclude what we already knew: chimpanzees are keen observers of readily perceivable features of the social world and make predictions about future states of that world on the basis of such features.

The Reinterpretation Hypothesis

If we are seriously to consider the possibility that chimpanzees and other species might not reason about mental states, then it is necessary to explain why, in our unstudied interactions with them, we readily attribute such abilities to them. Povinelli and colleagues have offered an evolutionary solution to this apparent tension and labeled it the *reinterpretation hypothesis*. They have proposed that theory of mind may be a *human* specialization that was grafted into existing cognitive systems for reasoning about social behavior that we inherited from our ancestor with the African apes (Povinelli, Bering, & Giambrone, 2001; Povinelli & Giambrone, 1999). Importantly, this new system for representing mental states did not replace the ancestral systems for representing behavioral abstractions but was integrated with such systems.

At a broader level, the model suggests that although evolution has sculpted the minds of virtually all social species to detect and reason about behavior, the ability to explain behaviors in terms of unobservable mental states is an innovation that is peculiar to humans. On this view, theory of mind can best be thought of as an additional social cognitive ability, unique to humans, that allows us to attribute mental states as the causes of overt behavioral acts—acts that all primates (and probably most vertebrates) have the ability to perceive.

Thus, the reinterpretation hypothesis clarifies an important confusion that pervades much of the writing about the evolution of theory of mind—the tendency to contrast the possibility that chimpanzees possess a theory of mind with a "behaviorist" strawman alternative account. On the "behaviorist" account, chimpanzees are seen as systems that form "simple" rules or learned associations (see Baldwin, 1988; Tomasello & Call, in press). And, after such an account is dismissed as being an intuitively unappealing explanation for their complex social behavior, the "alternative," that chimpanzees construe behavior in terms of mental states, is held up as more plausible.

For instance, in reference to the performance of Sarah, the chimpanzee who participated in the first attempts to investigate theory of mind in chimpanzees (see Premack & Woodruff, 1978), Tomasello writes, "This raises the possibility that what Sarah was doing was something cognitively much simpler than understanding the intentionality/mentality of other animate beings" (1999, p. 19).

Sarah had been required to choose a picture that depicted the logical next step in the completion of an intentional act performed by a human whom she had observed on video. Although Premack and Woodruff (1978) interpreted Sarah's ability to do so as evidence that she understood the intentions of the actor, it was later suggested that her choices may have been determined by knowledge of a logical sequence of events or pairing of objects, such as locks and keys, based on her prior experience in the world (Savage-Rumbaugh, Rumbaugh, & Boysen, 1978). The latter account of her behavior is generally deemed less cognitively interesting or sophisticated. The point often missed in such analyses is that the ability to reason about mental states *depends on* the ability to represent the behavioral associations. A human watching the same video clips would need to make use of the same behavioral information and form the same associations. The construction of such behavioral abstractions is exactly what the human theory of mind system "reads" in mentalistic terms. Thus, the human system for interpreting behaviors in mentalistic fashion is not independent of the behavior-reading system but instead depends on it.

The key insight of the reinterpretation hypothesis is that it *expects* humans and their nearest living relatives to behave in a highly similar manner, regardless of whether theory of mind is a human specialization. Furthermore, because the hypothesis posits that the theory of mind system was grafted into existing, highly "sophisticated" and "complex" systems for reasoning about behavior, it further expects that a large number of behaviors that become intimately connected with the theory of mind system in human development would be present in strictly hypothetical "theory-of-mindless" chimpanzees. On this view, it should be clear that the mere fact that we effortlessly attribute theory of mind to chimpanzees on the basis of the presence of such behaviors has no bearing whatsoever on whether they actually possess such a system.

And, finally, in anticipation of our conclusion, the generalized version of the reinterpretation hypothesis is that in each "domain" of knowledge, the human mind has evolved specializations for "reinterpreting" observables in terms of unobservables, with the foundation being ancient mechanisms for forming abstractions about the manifest features of the world (see also Povinelli, 2004).

PHYSICAL CAUSALITY

The distinction between concepts that refer to observable versus unobservable aspects of the world has also been investigated in the context of research exploring nonhuman primates' (especially chimpanzees') naïve or folk physics. Humans regularly invoke concepts about physical forces to explain events in the physical realm. At the most extreme level, humans have created theories about the observable world that rely on the causal power of unobservable entities or forces such as God, gravity, mass, quarks, and electricity.

The idea of gravity, for example, was posited as a theoretical construct to explain observable interactions of objects, not a description of an observable feature of those interactions. One can observe that an object falls when it is released above the ground and one can observe the relative effects of dropping objects of various sizes. However, in humans, at least, these representations of the observable features of the world are linked to systems that represent and reason about *unobserved* features of the world.

The distinction between the abstractions formed from the observable features of the world versus the theoretical notions that we map onto those abstractions is illustrated in table 19.1. Importantly, these theoretical notions are not present only in adults, but they appear to emerge at a very young age in human children (see review by Povinelli, 2000, chap. 3). In a series of exceptionally clever studies, for example, Shultz and colleagues have shown that by 2 or 3 years of age, children's causal explanations of simple events prioritize the unobserved features of the situation (e.g., "force" transfer) over the readily observed features (proximity, order of movement, etc.) (Shultz, Altmann, & Asselin, 1986).

Over the past decade or so, there has been a resurgence of interest in nonhuman primates' understanding of objects, both in the context of tool use and in the context of their systems for object representation in general (Boesch & Boesch, 1990; Cacchione & Krist, 2004; Fujita, Kuroshima, & Asai, 2003; Hauser, 1997; Hauser, Kralik, & Botto-Mahan, 1999; Hauser, Pearson, & Seelig, 2002; Hauser, Santos, Spaepan, & Pearson, 2002; Kohler, 1925; Matsuzawa, 1996, 2001; Munakata, Santos, Spelke, Hauser, & O'Reilly, 2001; Santos & Hauser, 2002, Santos, Ericson, & Hauser, 1999; Santos, Miller, & Hauser, 2003; Visalberghi &

Table 19.1. Observable Versus Unobservable Features Used to Describe a Small Subset of Physical Events

Observation	Observable Features	Unobservable Features
Collision	Proximity, order of movement, speed of movement, temporal succession	Transfer of force
Falling objects	Direction of movement, speed of movement	Gravity, force
Differential effects (kinesthetic sensations) caused by similarly sized objects	Deformation, noise, effects on contact with other objects, muscle tension	Weight/mass
Balanced objects	Surface area, slope, contact, shape, deformation	Strength/solidity, balance
Object–object correlated movement	Contact, movement patterns, containment	Physical connection
Unexplained occurrences	Noncontingent events, stypical object interactions	Supernatural forces

Tomasello, 1998). Much of this work has explored the generalization abilities of nonhuman primates and their understanding of means-ends relationships (e.g., Hauser, 1997; Hauser et al., 1999; Hauser, Santos, et al., 2002). A subset of this work, however, has specifically targeted the question of whether species other than humans are unique in their ability to reason about unobservable aspects of objects and their interactions (see Kralik & Hauser, 2002; Limongelli, Boysen, & Visalberghi, 1995; Povinelli, 2000; Santos & Hauser, 2002; Visalberghi, 1997, 2002; Visalberghi & Limongelli, 1994, 1996; Visalberghi & Tomasello, 1998; Visalberghi & Trinca, 1989).

For example, in the mid-1990s, we began confronting our chimpanzees with simple tool-using problems that were designed to explore their representation of the underlying causal structure of tool use—in particular, whether chimpanzees recruit folk concepts about things like gravity, weight, shape, and physical connection to predict the behavior of tools in novel situations. We introduced our chimpanzees to numerous problems through which we could probe their understanding of the role that various factors played in the behavior of the objects (Povinelli, 2000).

Although our apes were quite good at learning the problems with which we confronted them, they demonstrated little evidence that they understood the relevant but unobservable properties of gravity, transfer of force, physical connection, and so on; rather, consistent with their performance in the tasks designed to evaluate their understanding of abstract mental states such as <*seeing*>, they appeared to learn rules about the tasks based directly on observable features associated with success. For the chimpanzees, one of the most powerful of these heuristics that were derived from observable features of the world was the notion of "contact" (see also Cacchione & Krist, 2004; Kohler, 1925).

As one example of our chimpanzees' lack of use of a concept commonly used by humans to succeed at similar problems, consider their performance in the trap-tube problem, in which they had to insert, or to push an already inserted tool, through a tube in order to eject a food reward (see Limongelli et al., 1995; Visalberghi, 1993; Visalberghi & Limongelli, 1994, 1996; Visalberghi & Trinca, 1989). In this series of experiments, a number of our chimpanzees learned to insert the tool into the tube opening farthest from the reward (figure 19.3); but having learned this, in later variations of the task, they did not appear to give any consideration to the "up" versus "down" orientation of the trap (figure 19.4) (Povinelli, 2000, chap. 4). Even when we made it quite costly for them to use representations like "insert the stick into the end farthest from the reward" (figure 19.5), or when the representations were either irrelevant (the trap was in the "up" position) or led to losing the reward, the chimpanzees still relied on those heuristics. Thus, the subjects had apparently not learned something about the deep causal structure of the task.

Likewise, in an analogous procedure using a table with a trap (a large hole), although the chimpanzees learned to attend to specific relations

Figure 19.3. A chimpanzee inserts the tool into the tube opening farthest from the reward.

among the tool, reward, and substrate, their patterns of acquisition suggested that they did not appreciate the relevant factors within a framework of unobservable causal forces (Povinelli, 2000, chap. 5). In a related experiment, Hood, Hauser, Anderson, and Santos (1999) applied Hood's (1995) gravity-rules task to the behavior of cotton-top tamarins. In this task, objects were dropped down a chimney connected to various containers by an opaque tube. It was found that the tamarins continued to search in the container where the food was dropped on the first trial, regardless of whether the chimney was connected to that container, demonstrating a lack of understanding of the physical constraints operating in the task.

Hauser and colleagues have repeatedly shown that monkeys (cotton-top tamarins), after being trained how to use a tool, will readily transfer this learning to novel tools of different shapes and colors (Hauser, 1997; Hauser et al., 1999; Hauser,

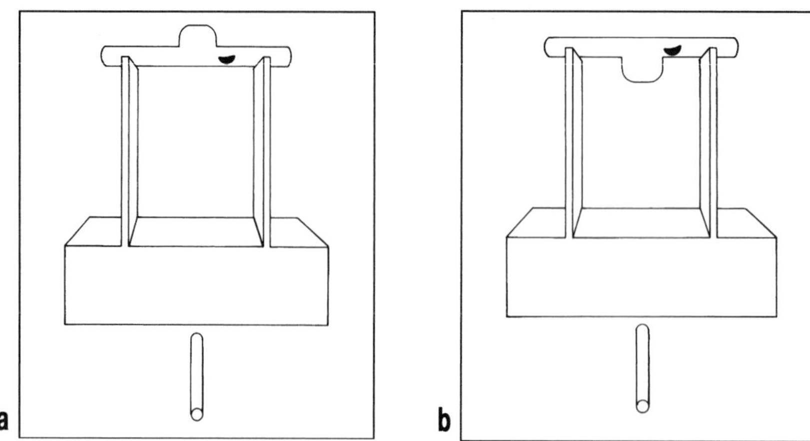

Figure 19.4. The trap is in the "up" orientation (*a*) versus the "down" orientation (*b*).

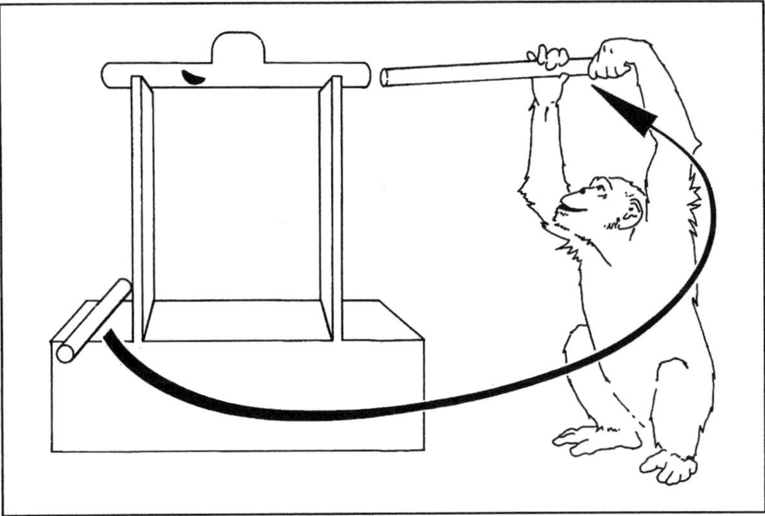

Figure 19.5. A cost to inserting the tool in the tube opening farthest from the reward is imposed by setting the tool closest to the tube opening closest to the reward.

Pearson, et al., 2002; Hauser, Santos, et al., 2002; for similar findings with chimpanzees, see Povinelli, 2000). A recent study with capuchin monkeys replicated this finding, but, in addition, showed that these animals, although not being distracted by those particular irrelevant features of the tools, still failed to attend to relevant task variables. For instance, like our chimpanzees, they did not learn to pull in the appropriate tool to procure a reward when obstacles or traps impeded performance (Fujita et al., 2003).

Although some authors have suggested that parallel representational abilities underwrite the tool-using abilities of capuchins and chimpanzees (Westergaard, Liv, Chavanne, & Suomi, 1998), others have implied that capuchins do not use tools with the same degree of cognitive complexity as chimpanzees (Westergaard, 1999). Some have hypothesized that the success of apes, but not capuchins, is based on the ability of apes to represent the causal relations between tool use and its consequence (Limongelli et al., 1995, Visalberghi, 1990; Visalberghi, Fragaszy, & Savage-Rumbaugh, 1995). However, our own studies have given strong reason to doubt such a construal on the part of even chimpanzees. For instance, in addition to the studies just described, in over two dozen studies, our chimpanzees (a) did not initially understand that the base of a tool used to procure reward would need to make contact with the reward, (b) failed to understand that they should select a rigid versus a malleable rake, (c) exhibited virtually no understanding of the distinction between "contact" and "physical connection," and (d), in simple tool-construction situations, failed to match the tool form to the problem type (Povinelli, 2000). Instead, although the chimpanzees appeared to form general concepts about observable features of the tests ("contact" versus "no contact"), they rarely, if ever, performed in a way consistent with the predictions of a model that posited that they were using unobservable causal concepts to predict how the objects would behave when they acted on them.

More recently, our laboratory has targeted a particular object property, weight, for analysis under the framework of the unobservability hypothesis in an extensive series of studies. Thus far, we are finding that chimpanzees' notions of weight and support are vastly different from our own. The chimpanzees' concept of weight appears to be tied directly to the kinesthetic sensations that are directly perceived by the lifting of objects of various weights; in direct contrast to human adults and children, chimpanzees do not appear to reason about weight as an independent and unobserved object property (e.g., Smith, Carey, & Wiser, 1985).

Finally, it is also worth noting that chimpanzees may not seek causal explanations for physical events at all. There is a great paucity of experimental research attempting to investigate this possibility. One relevant set of studies comparing the behavior of chimpanzees and children demonstrated that children, but not chimpanzees, attempted to seek an explanation for their failure to perform certain tasks (Povinelli & Dunphy-Lelii, 2001). For example, both species were trained to stand a wooden L-shaped block vertically upright. On occasion, probe trials were presented in which a visually identical block could not be stood upright by virtue of a hidden lead weight that made that block unbalanced. Children tended to turn the block over in an apparent attempt to investigate whether there was some property of the block that made it dysfunctional. Chimpanzees did not do so but did persist in attempting to stand the block upright for the full duration of the trial.

Thus, although chimpanzees and other nonhuman primates seem to be adept at attending to and learning about the observable features and propensities of objects, they do not appear to recruit unobservable forces or entities to explain *or* predict their behavior.

DIVERSITY WITHOUT HIERARCHY

We have limited the preceding review to three areas of research: concept formation, theory of mind, and physical causality. From this brief review, we conclude that there is little evidence that chimpanzees (or other primates) represent the world in ways that would suggest they posit "unobservable" entities or processes to explain or predict observable events. On the other hand, there is overwhelming evidence to suggest that closely related species share homologous mechanisms for forming abstract concepts about observable aspects of the world (in the case of humans and chimpanzees, for example, our respective species undoubtedly represent many macroscopic objects and events in similar ways). Likewise, in thinking about domains that we have not explored in this chapter (e.g., time, number, self), one could assert that humans and chimpanzees are extraordinarily similar in how they represent overt aspects of the world, but remain skeptical of the evidence that chimpanzees objectify these things as hypothetical entities in their own right. Finally, there are still other concepts that may be even farther removed from the observable features of the world (e.g., the concept of "memory"), such that at the present it is difficult to imagine how evidence that nonhumans reason about such things could ever be obtained. This observation should not be confused with the claim that no such evidence will ever be obtained or that it is impossible to obtain such evidence (for example, in the context of the current debate over theory of mind, although we have argued that there is no good evidence at the present that chimpanzees reason about mental states and that current techniques are not adequate to resolve such questions, we have positively highlighted techniques that could potentially provide such evidence; see Povinelli & Vonk, 2003, 2004).

If what we have just said is true, then the unobservability hypothesis becomes more complicated. It means that there are ontologically important distinctions in the ways in which humans reason about things that have no straightforward physical embodiments. We reason about God, ghosts, and other supernatural phenomena; as children, we engage in pretend relationships with imaginary objects; we create fantasy worlds populated by unicorns, Martians, and hobbits; in our folk ontologies, we treat "time," "memory," and "consciousness" as real entities or processes. The variety of such unobservables raises two questions: First, are all of these concepts equally theoretical under the framework of the unobservability hypothesis, and second, to what extent is our day-to-day behavior causally influenced by representations of unobservables like mental states and physical forces, as opposed to representations of their observable manifestations? We end this chapter by briefly reflecting on each of these questions.

ARE "UNOBSERVABLES" A HOMOGENEOUS CLASS?

To begin, we need to emphasize that the distinction we are drawing is between things that are in principle observable versus those that are in principle unobservable—not between things that are being or have been observed versus those that have not been. Building representations of novel situations or events (i.e., imagining, predicting), as long as they are composed from conceptual elements that are observable, would not seem to pose any special problem for nonhumans from the perspective we have adopted. We see no reason why chimpanzees, even if they do not think about mental states, could not imagine a novel consequence of some actions they have observed or some modification of a preexisting object. For example, Kohler's (1925) famous experiments with chimpanzees, if nothing else, showed that chimpanzees could imagine how a box could be moved into a novel position under a suspended banana, which would then allow them to reach it. We suspect such operations go on frequently in the mental workspace of chimpanzees (and an indefinitely large number of other species!). In any event, we do not see how such mental operations involving the manipulation of concepts that refer to potentially observable or tangible things has any bearing on the claim that they do not reason about unobservables (i.e., strictly theoretical entities that can have no perceptual embodiments).

Having said that, we can turn our attention to the important question, Are all nonreferring concepts equivalent? For example, unicorns and beliefs are both theoretical, nonreal entities, but there would seem to be an important difference between them: Whereas unicorns would seem to be a minor variant of an observable entity (i.e., a horse), "beliefs" or "forces" or "time" would seem to be constructs of a completely different kind, related to the entities with which they interact, to be sure, but of a qualitatively different nature. If so, then for chimpanzees that were to become familiar with both real horses and fictional portrayals of unicorns, there would be no particularly salient distinction between them. In fact, the only difference between humans and chimpanzees, in this regard, would be that although humans would represent the unobservable real versus unreal distinction between horses and unicorns, chimpanzees would not.

Does this distinction imply that certain kinds of unobservable things might be more likely to be represented by chimpanzees than would others? At present, we have no direct answer to this question. But, from the perspective of the unobservability hypothesis, we would insist on drawing a distinction between forming concepts about things that can be observed (a physical representation of a unicorn) versus forming concepts about the aspect of these things that cannot be observed (unicorns are not real).

THE CAUSAL ROLE OF UNOBSERVABLES IN BEHAVIOR

Humans can clearly reason about unobservables of the most abstract kind, the kind that in principle could never be directly observed. But, how much of our own behavior is causally influenced by such representations? Are we more likely to use representations of theoretical constructs rather than representations of observables in order to predict the behavior of other objects and entities in the world or to explain it? Or do we invoke such constructs equally in both contexts?

A recurring theme of this chapter has been the distinction between predicting events versus reasoning about and explaining the underlying causal forces involved in such events. As many scholars have noted, the world itself has an immense amount of information contained within it; systems that perceive and reason about these observable features have a large (and currently largely unspecified) power to predict future events (for examinations of how these systems might develop and operate in humans, see Baird & Baldwin, 2001; Zacks & Tversky, 2001). A critical question arises, then, as to when it is necessary to posit that a system is representing and using concepts that refer to underlying (unobservable) causes of an event or behavior. Note that we are not questioning whether humans do so or whether this ability can be demonstrated in experimental contexts; the answer to both of these questions is "yes." But, in what circumstances, exactly, are such concepts playing a causal role (see especially, Povinelli & Giambrone, 1999)? Humans undoubtedly use such concepts when attempting to generalize their understanding of the world to novel contexts and to transfer formal knowledge to others; there may be intimate causal connections between the human ability to reason about mental states and other aspects of human culture, such as pedagogy and ethics (see Povinelli & Godfrey, 1993; Russon, Mitchell, & Lefebvre 1998; Tomasello, 2000; Whiten, 1998).

Yet, important questions remain unanswered: What is the relative degree of the use of concepts about unobservables even in humans (e.g., Zacks & Tversky, 2001)? In what contexts are concepts about unobservables most activated? Can the causal work of such representations be fully understood and disambiguated from systems that do not possess such concepts? It is fully possible that although humans represent theoretical constructs, these constructs may not constitute the primary driving force in much of human behavior. Thus, although this additional representational capacity may lead to profound differences in the reasoning processes of humans and our closest relatives, in some contexts, the extent and specific role of such a capacity has not yet been fully specified.

TREATING SIMILARITY AND DIFFERENCE EQUALLY

Some may believe that the unobservability hypothesis is just another example of setting the bar too high, unnecessarily overlooking important abilities within various cognitive domains that different species have evolved or downplaying similarities between humans and other species in order to celebrate the superiority of the human mind. "Déjà vu!" the most extreme skeptic shouts. "Every time you psychologists try to define humans by one trait, you wind up embarrassing yourselves. Remember humans as the only tool using (then later, tool-making) species? Jane Goodall forever deflated that one!"

But, truly, these concerns are orthogonal to the central point of this essay—in fact, this outburst reveals the hegemony of the "phylogenetic scale" view that continues to grip comparative psychology. To make the point clearly: there is no bar to set. Identifying the abilities that one monophyletic group uniquely possesses is not a "test" for other species; it is only an attempt to fully characterize the psychology of each group.

In the case at hand, we seek to identify the uniquely derived features of human cognition so that, ultimately, we can develop a more complete picture of what is human about the human mind. Furthermore, thinking that broad categories, such as "tool-using," will capture meaningful differences between humans and chimpanzees, for example, misses the point that they exhibit massive differences in the number, method of construction, importance, and understanding of the tools they respectively make and use. Many of these differences may stem from tightly canalized differences between the species (see Johnson-Frey, 2004; Povinelli, 2000).

Thus, humans should not be misconstrued as some sort of cognitive benchmark by which all other species must be measured in order for us to be interested in what makes our minds unique. If, in the final analysis, it turns out that there are certain respects in which the chimpanzee's mind is massively different from our own, then this would in no way imply that their mind is any less efficient or any less interesting than our own. Chimpanzees need not be "inching closer to humanity" (de Waal, 1999, p. 635) in order to be of interest in their own right. We suggest that more insight will be gained by seeking and embracing the idea of psychological diversity—an idea that treats similarities and differences among species as equally important—than by treating other minds as watered-down, incomplete versions of our own.

Note

1. For instance, the subjects may have selected the animal whose image evoked more fear or anxiety within themselves without internally describing that animal as belonging to a general category of dominance. It would be interesting to know whether the subjects would have predicted dominance for individuals previously demonstrating dominant behaviors in novel scenarios rather than basing their responses on an immediately preceding event. This is not to suggest that correct categorization by nonhuman primates never reveals evidence for understanding "why" exemplars belong together in a category, but that the "why" may not rely on unobservable theoretical constructs.

References

Anderson, J. R., & Mitchell, R. W. (1999). Macaques but not lemurs co-orient visually with humans. *Folia Primatologica, 70*, 17–22.

Baird, J. A., & Baldwin, D. A. (2001). Making sense of human behavior: Action parsing and intentional inference. In B. F. Malle & L. Moses (Eds.), *Intentions and intentionality: Foundations of social cognition* (pp. 193–206). Cambridge, MA: The MIT Press.

Baldwin, J. D. (1988). Learning how to deceive. *Behavioral and Brain Sciences, 11*, 245.

Barth, J., Reaux, J. E., & Povinelli, D. J. (2005). Chimpanzees' (*Pan troglodytes*) use of gaze cues in object-choice tasks: Different methods yield different results. *Animal Cognition, 8*, 84–92.

Beach, F. A. (1950). The snark was a boojum. *American Psychologist, 5*, 115–124.

Boakes, R. A. (1984). *From Darwin to behaviorism: Psychology and the minds of animals.* Cambridge: Cambridge University Press.

Boesch, C., & Boesch, H. (1990). Tool use and tool making in wild chimpanzees. *Folia Primatologica*, *54*, 86–99.

Bovet, D., & Washburn, D. A. (2003). Rhesus macaques categorize unknown conspecifics according to their dominance relations. *Journal of Comparative Psychology*, *117*, 400–405.

Cacchione, T., & Krist, H. (2004). Understanding object relations: What chimpanzees know about support. *Journal of Comparative Psychology*, *118*, 140–148.

Call, J., & Tomasello, M. (1999). A nonverbal false belief task: The performance of children and great apes. *Child Development*, *70*, 381–395.

Cheney, D. L., & Seyfarth, R. M. (1990). Attending to behaviour versus attending to knowledge: Examining monkeys' attribution of mental states. *Animal Behaviour*, *40*, 742–753.

Cheney, D. L., & Seyfarth, R. M. (1991). Reading minds or reading behaviour? Tests for a theory of mind in monkeys. In A. Whiten (Ed.), *Natural theories of mind: Evolution, development and simulation of everyday mindreading*. Cambridge, MA: Blackwell.

Cheney, D. L., & Seyfarth, R. M. (1992). Precis of how monkeys see the world. *Behavioral & Brain Sciences*, *15*, 135–182.

Cheney, D. L., Seyfarth, R. M., & Silk, J. B. (1995). The responses of female baboons (*Papio cynocephalus ursinus*) to anomalous social interactions: Evidence for causal reasoning? *Journal of Comparative Psychology*, *109*, 134–141.

Cook, B. R., Cavoto, K. K., & Cavoto, B. R. (1995). Same-different texture discrimination and concept learning by pigeons. *Journal of Experimental Psychology: Animal Behavior Processes*, *21*, 253–260.

Cook, R. G., Katz, J. S., & Cavoto, B. R. (1997). Pigeon same-different concept learning with multiple stimulus classes. *Journal of Experimental Psychology: Animal Behavior Processes*, *23*, 417–433.

D'Amato, M. R., & Van Sant, P. (1988). The person concept in monkeys (*Cebus apella*). *Journal of Experimental Psychology: Animal Behaviour Processes*, *14*, 43–55.

Darwin, C. (1871). *The descent of man*. (Reprinted, Modern Library, New York, 1982.)

de Waal, F. (1999). Animal behaviour: Cultural primatology comes of age. *Nature*, *399*, 635.

Emery, N. J., & Clayton, N. S. (2001). Effects of experience and social context on prospective caching strategies by scrub jays. *Nature*, *414*, 443–446.

Emery, N. J., Lorincz, E. N., Perrett, D. I., Oram, M. W., et al. (1997). Gaze following and joint attention in rhesus monkeys (*Macaca mulatto*). *Journal of Comparative Psychology*, *111*, 286–293.

Fagot, J., Wasserman, E. A., & Young, M. E. (2001). Discriminating the relation between relations: The role of entropy in abstract conceptualization by baboons (*Papio papio*) and humans (*Homo sapiens*). *Journal of Experimental Psychology: Animal Behaviour Processes*, *27*, 316–328.

Flavell, J. H., Everett, B. A., Croft, K., & Flavell, E. R. (1981). Young children's knowledge about visual perception: Further evidence for the level 1–level 2 distinction. *Developmental Psychology*, *17*, 99–103.

Fujita, K., Kuroshima, H., & Asai, S. (2003). How do tufted capuchin monkeys (*Cebus apella*) understand causality involved in tool use? *Journal of Experimental Psychology: Animal Behavior Processes*, *19*, 233–242.

Gallistel, C. R. (2000). The replacement of general purpose learning models with adaptively specialized learning modules. In M. S. Gazzaniga (Ed.), The new cognitive neuroscience (2nd ed.) (pp. 1179–1191). Cambridge, MA: MIT Press.

Gaulin, S. J. C. (1992). Evolution of sex differences in spatial ability. *Yearbook of Physical Anthropology*, *35*, 125–151.

Gillan, D. J., Premack, D., & Woodruff, G. (1981). Reasoning in the chimpanzee: 1. Analogical reasoning. *Journal of Experimental Psychology: Animal Behaviour Processes*, *7*, 1–17.

Goldstone, R. L., & Barsalou, L. W. (1998). Reuniting perception and conception. *Cognition*, *65*, 231–262.

Hare, B. (2001). Can competitive paradigms increase the validity of experiments on primate social cognition? *Animal Cognition*, *4*, 269–280.

Hare, B., Call, J., & Tomasello, M. (2000). Chimpanzees know what conspecifics do and do not see. *Animal Behaviour*, *59*, 771–785.

Hare, B., Call, J., & Tomasello, M. (2001). Do chimpanzees know what conspecifics know? *Animal Behaviour*, *61*, 139–151.

Hauser, M. D. (1997). Artifactual kinds and functional design features: What a primate understands without language. *Cognition*, *64*, 285–308.

Hauser, M. D., Kralik, J., & Botto-Mahan, C. (1999). Problem solving and functional design features: Experiments on cotton-top tamarins (*Saguinus oedipus*). *Animal Behaviour*, *57*, 565–582.

Hauser, M. D., Pearson, H. M., & Seelig, D. (2002). Ontogeny of tool-use in cotton-top tamarins (*Saguinus oedipus*): Innate recognition of functionally relevant features. *Animal Behaviour*, *64*, 299–311.

Hauser, M. D., Santos, L. R., Spaepen, G. M., & Pearson, H. E. (2002). Problem solving, inhibition and domain-specific experience: Experiments on cottontop tamarins (*Saguinus oedipus*). *Animal Behaviour*, *64*, 387–396.

Heyes, C. M. (1998). Theory of mind in nonhuman primates. *Behavioural Brain Sciences*, *21*, 101–114.

Hodos, W., & Campbell, C. B. G. (1969). Scala naturae: Why is there no theory in comparative psychology? *Psychological Review*, *76*, 337–350.

Hodos, W., & Campbell, C. B. G. (1991). The Scala naturae revisited: Evolutionary scales and anagenesis in comparative psychology. *Journal of Comparative Psychology*, *105*, 211–221.

Hood, B. M. (1995). Gravity rules for 2–4-year-olds? *Cognitive Development*, *10*, 577–598.

Hood, B. M., Hauser, M. D., Anderson, L., & Santos, L. (1999). Gravity biases in a non-human primate? *Developmental Science*, *2*, 35–41.

Jitsumori, M. (2001). Object recognition and object categorization in animals. In T. Matsuzawa (Ed.), *Primate origins of human cognition and behavior* (pp. 269–292). New York: Springer-Verlag.

Jitsumori, M., & Matsuzawa, T. (1991). Picture perception in monkeys and pigeons: Transfer of rightside-up versus upside-down discrimination of photographic objects across conceptual categories. *Primates*, *32*, 473–482.

Johnson-Frey, S. (2004). The neural bases of complex tool use in humans. *Trends in Cognitive Sciences*, *8*, 71–78.

Kamil, A. C. (1984). Adaptation and cognition: Knowing what comes naturally. In H. L. Roitblat, T. G. Bever, & H. S. Terrace (Eds.), *Animal cognition.* Hillsdale, NJ: Erlbaum.

Kaplan, G., & Rogers, L. J. (2002). Patterns of gazing in orangutans (*Pongo pgymaeus*). *International Journal of Primatology*, *23*, 501–526.

Karin-D'Arcy, R., & Povinelli, D. J. (2002). Do chimpanzees know what each other see? A closer look. *International Journal of Comparative Psychology*, *15*, 21–54.

Kohler, W. (1925). *The mentality of apes.* New York: Liveright.

Kralik, J. D., & Hauser, M. D. (2002). A nonhuman primates' perception of object relations: Experiments on cottontop tamarins, *Saguinus oedipus*. *Animal Behaviour*, *63*, 419–435.

Limongelli, L., Boysen, S. T., & Visalberghi, E. (1995). Comprehension of cause-effect relations in a tool-using task by chimpanzees (*Pan troglodytes*). *Journal of Comparative Psychology*, *109*, 18–26.

Macphail, E. (1987). The comparative psychology of intelligence. *Behavioral and Brain Sciences*, *10*, 645–656.

Matsuzawa, T. (1996). Chimpanzee intelligence in nature and captivity: Isomorphism of symbol-use and tool-use. In W. C. McGrew, L. F. Marchant, & T. Nishida (Eds.), *Great ape societies* (pp. 196–212). New York: Cambridge University Press.

Matsuzawa, T. (2001). Primate foundations of human intelligence: A view of tool use in nonhuman primates and fossil hominids. In T. Matsuzawa (Ed.), *Primate origins of human cognition and behavior* (pp. 3–25). Tokyo: Springer-Verlag.

Munakata, Y., Santos, L. R., Spelke, E. S., Hauser, M. D., & O'Reilly, R. C. (2001). Visual representation in the wild: How rhesus monkeys parse objects. *Journal of Cognitive Neuroscience*, *13*, 44–58.

Oden, D. L., Thompson, R. K. R., & Premack, D. (1988). Spontaneous transfer of matching by infant chimpanzees. *Journal of Experimental Psychology: Animal Behaviour Processes*, *14*, 140–145.

Oden, D. L., Thompson, R. K. R., & Premack, D. (1990). Infant chimpanzees spontaneously perceive both concrete and abstract same/different relations. *Child Development*, *61*, 621–631.

Parr, L. A. (2001). Cognitive and physiological markers of emotional awareness in chimpanzees (*Pan troglodytes*). *Animal Cognition*, *4*, 223–229.

Pearce, J. M. (1994). Discrimination and categorization. In N. J. Mackintosh (Ed.), *Animal learning and cognition. Handbooks of perception and cognition series* (2nd ed.) (pp. 1009–1034). San Diego, CA: Academic Press.

Povinelli, D. J. (1996). Chimpanzee theory of mind? The long road to strong inference. In P. Carruthers & P. Smith (Eds.), *Theories of theories of mind* (pp. 293–329). Cambridge: Cambridge University Press.

Povinelli, D. J. (2000). *Folk physics for apes: The chimpanzee's theory of how the world works.* Oxford: Oxford University Press. [Reprinted with revisions, 2003]

Povinelli, D. J. (2004). Behind the ape's appearance: Escaping anthropocentrism in the study of other minds. *Daedalus*, *Winter*, 29–41.

Povinelli, D. J., Bering, J., & Giambrone, S. (2001). Toward a science of other minds: Escaping the argument by analogy. *Cognitive Science*, *24*, 509–541.

Povinelli, D. J., Bierschwale, D. T., & Cech, C. G. (1999). Comprehension of seeing as a referential act in young children, but not juvenile chimpanzees. *British Journal of Developmental Psychology*, *17*, 37–60.

Povinelli, D. J., & Dunphy-Lelii, S. (2001). Do chimpanzees seek explanations? Preliminary comparative investigations. *Canadian Journal of Experimental Psychology*, *55*, 93–101.

Povinelli, D. J., Dunphy-Lelii, S., Reaux, J. E., & Mazza, M. P. (2002). Psychological diversity in chimpanzees and humans: New longitudinal assessments of chimpanzees' understanding of attention. *Brain, Behavior, and Evolution*, *59*, 33–53.

Povinelli, D. J., & Eddy, T. J. (1996a). Chimpanzees: Joint visual attention. *Psychological Science*, *7*, 129–135.

Povinelli, D. J., & Eddy, T. J. (1996b). Factors influencing young chimpanzees' (*Pan troglodytes*) recognition of attention. *Journal of Comparative Psychology*, *110*, 336–345.

Povinelli, D. J., & Eddy, T. (1996c). What young chimpanzees know about seeing. *Monographs of the Society for Research in Child Development*, *61* (Serial No. 247).

Povinelli, D. J., & Eddy, T. J. (1997). Specificity of gaze-following in young chimpanzees. *British Journal of Developmental Psychology*, *15*, 213–222.

Povinelli, D. J., & Giambrone, S. (1999). Inferring other minds: Failure of the argument by analogy. *Philosophical Topics*, *27*, 167–201.

Povinelli, D. J., & Giambrone, S. (2001). Reasoning about beliefs: A human specialization? *Child Development*, *72*, 691–695.

Povinelli, D. J., & Godfrey, L. R. (1993). The chimpanzee's mind: How noble in reason? How absent of ethics? In M. D. Nílecki & D. V. Nílecki (Eds.), *Evolutionary ethics* (pp. 277–324). Albany: SUNY Press.

Povinelli, D. J., Nelson, K. E., & Boysen, S. T. (1990). Inferences about guessing and knowing by chimpanzees (*Pan troglodytes*). *Journal of Comparative Psychology, 104*, 203–210.

Povinelli, D. J., Parks, K. A., & Novak, M. A. (1992). Role reversal by rhesus monkeys, but no evidence of empathy. *Animal Behavior*, *44*, 269–282.

Povinelli, D. J., & Preuss, T. M. (1995). Theory of mind: Evolutionary history of a cognitive specialization. *Trends in Neuroscience*, *18*, 418–424.

Povinelli, D. J., Rulf, A. B., & Bierschwale, D. (1994). Absence of knowledge attribution and self-recognition in young chimpanzees (*Pan troglodytes*). *Journal of Comparative Psychology*, *108*, 74–80.

Povinelli, D. J., & Vonk, J. (2003). Chimpanzee minds: Suspiciously human? *Trends in Cognitive Science*, *7*, 157–160.

Povinelli, D. J., & Vonk, J. (2004). We don't need a microscope to explore the chimpanzee mind. *Mind and Language*, *19*, 1–28.

Premack, D. (1983). The codes of man and beasts. *The Behavioral and Brain Sciences*, *6*, 125–167.

Premack, D. (1988). "Does the chimpanzee have a theory of mind" revisited. In R. W. Byrne & A. Whiten (Eds.), *Machiavellian intelligence: Social expertise and the evolution of intellect in monkeys, apes and humans* (pp. 160–179). New York: Oxford University Press.

Premack, D., & Dasser, V. (1991). Perceptual origins and conceptual evidence for theory of mind in apes and children. In A. Whiten (Ed.), *Natural theories of mind*. Cambridge: Basil Blackwell.

Premack, D., & Woodruff, G. (1978). Does the chimpanzee have a theory of mind? *Behavioral and Brain Sciences*, *4*, 515–526.

Reaux, J. E., Theall, L. A., & Povinelli, D. J. (1999). A longitudinal investigation of chimpanzees' understanding of visual perception. *Child Development*, *70*, 275–290.

Roberts, W. A., & Mazmanian, D. S. (1988). Concept learning at different levels of abstraction by pigeons, monkeys, and people. *Journal of Experimental Psychology: Animal Behaviour Processes*, *14*, 247–260.

Russon, A. E., Mitchell, R. W., & Lefebvre, L. (1998). The comparative evolution of imitation. In J. Langer & M. Killen (Eds.), *Piaget, evolution, and development* (pp. 103–143). Mahwah, NJ: Lawrence Erlbaum Associates.

Santos, L. R., & Hauser, M. D. (2002). A nonhuman primate's understanding of solidity: Dissociations between seeing and acting. *Developmental Science*, *5*, F1–F7.

Santos, L. R., Ericson, B., & Hauser, M. D. (1999). Constraints on problem solving and inhibition: Object retrieval in cotton-top tamarins. *Journal of Comparative Psychology*, *113*, 1–8.

Santos, L. R., Miller, C. T., & Hauser, M. D. (2003). Representing tools: How two nonhuman primate species distinguish between the functionally relevant and irrelevant features of a tool. *Animal Cognition*, *6*, 269–281.

Savage-Rumbaugh, E. S., Rumbaugh, D. M., & Boysen, S. (1978). Linguistically mediated tool use and exchange by chimpanzees (*Pan troglodytes*). *Science*, *201*, 641–644.

Savage-Rumbaugh, E. S., Rumbaugh, D. M., Smith, S. T., & Lawson, J. (1980). The linguistic essential. *Science*, *210*, 922–925.

Schrier, A. M., Angarella, R., & Povar, M. L. (1984). Studies of concept formation by stump-tailed monkeys: Concepts, humans, and letter A. *Journal of Experimental Psychology: Animal Behaviour Processes*, *10*, 564–584.

Schrier, A. M., & Brady, P. M. (1987). Categorization of natural stimuli by monkeys (*Macaca mulatta*): Effects of stimulus set size and modification of exemplars. *Journal of Experimental Psychology: Animal Behaviour Processes*, *13*, 136–143.

Shultz, T. R., Altmann, E., & Asselin, J. (1986). Judging causal priority. *British Journal of Developmental Psychology*, *4*, 67–74.

Silk, J. B. (1999). Male bonnet macaques use information about third party rank relationships to recruit allies. *Animal Behaviour*, *58*, 45–51.

Smith, C., Carey, S., & Wiser, M. (1985). A case study of the development of the concepts of size, weight and density. *Cognition*, *21*, 177–237.

Spalding, T. L., & Ross, B. H. (2000). Concept learning and feature interpretation. *Memory and Cognition*, *28*, 439–451.

Spinozzi, G. (1993). Development of spontaneous classificatory behavior in chimpanzees (*Pan troglodytes*). *Journal of Comparative Psychology*, *107*, 193–200.

Suddendorf, T., & Whiten, A. (2001). Mental evolution and development: Evidence for secondary representation in children, great apes, and other animals. *Psychological Bulletin*, *127*, 629–650.

Tanaka, M. (1996). Information integration about object-object relationships by chimpanzees (*Pan troglodytes*). *Journal of Comparative Psychology*, *110*, 323–335.

Tanaka, M. (2001). Discrimination and categorization of photographs of natural objects by chimpanzees (*Pan troglodytes*). *Animal Cognition*, *4*, 201–211.

Theall, L. A., & Povinelli, D. J. (1999). Do chimpanzees tailor their attention-getting behaviors to fit the attentional states of others? *Animal Cognition*, *2*, 207–214.

Thompson, R. K. R., & Oden, D. L. (1996). A profound disparity revisited: Perception and judgement of abstract identity relations by chimpanzees, human infants and monkeys. *Behavioural Processes*, *35*, 149–161.

Thompson, R. K. R., & Oden, D. L. (2000). Categorical perception and conceptual judgments by nonhuman primates: The Paleological monkey and the analogical ape. *Cognitive Science*, *24*, 363–396.

Thompson, R. K. R., Oden, D. L., & Boysen, S. T. (1997). Language-naïve chimpanzees (*Pan troglodytes*) judge relations between relations in a conceptual matching-to-sample task. *Journal of Experimental Psychology: Animal Behaviour Processes*, *23*, 31–43.

Tomasello, M. (1998). Uniquely primate, uniquely human. *Developmental Science*, *1*, 1–16.

Tomasello, M. (1999). *The cultural origins of human cognition*. Cambridge: Harvard University Press.

Tomasello, M. (2000). Culture and cognitive development. *Current Directions in Psychological Science*, 37–40.

Tomasello, M., & Call, J. (in press). Do chimpanzees know what others see—or only what they are looking at? In. S. Hurley & M. Nudds (Eds.), *Rational animals*. New York: Oxford University Press.

Tomasello, M., Call, J., & Hare, B. (1998). Five primate species follow the visual gaze of conspecifics. *Animal Behaviour*, *58*, 769–777.

Tomasello, M., Call, J., & Hare, B. (2003a). Chimpanzees understand psychological states—the question is which ones and to what extent. *Trends in Cognitive Science*, *7*, 153–156.

Tomasello, M., Call, J., & Hare, B. (2003b). Chimpanzees versus humans: It's not that simple. *Trends in Cognitive Science*, *7*, 239–240.

Tomasello, M., Hare, B., & Agnetta, B. (1999). Chimpanzees, *Pan troglodytes*, follow gaze direction geometrically. *Animal Behaviour*, *58*, 769–777.

Tooby, J., & Cosmides, L. (1995). Mapping the evolved functional organization of mind and brain. In M. S. Gazzaniga (Ed.), *The cognitive neurosciences* (pp. 1185–1197). Cambridge, MA: MIT Press.

Vauclair, J., & Fagot, J. (1996). Categorization of alphanumeric characters by Guinea baboons: Within- and between-class stimulus discrimination. *CPC*, *15*, 449–462.

Vick, S., & Anderson, J. R. (2003). Use of human visual attention cues by olive baboons (*Papio anubis*) in a competitive task. *Journal of Comparative Psychology*, *117*, 209–216.

Visalberghi, E. (1990). Tool use in *Cebus*. *Folia Primatologica*, *54*, 146–154.

Visalberghi, E. (1993). Capuchin monkeys: A window into tool use in apes and humans. In K. R. Gibson & T. Ingold (Eds.), *Tools, language and cognition in human evolution*. New York: Cambridge University Press.

Visalberghi, E. (1997). Success and understanding in cognitive tasks: A comparison between *Cebus apella* and *Pan troglodytes*. *International Journal of Primatology*, *18*, 811–830.

Visalberghi, E. (2002). Insight from capuchin monkey studies: Ingredients of recipes for, and flaws in capuchins' success. In M. Bekoff & C. Allen (Eds.), *The cognitive animal: Empirical and theoretical perspectives on animal cognition* (pp. 405–411). Cambridge, MA: MIT Press.

Visalberghi, E., Fragaszy, D. M., & Savage-Rumbaugh, S. (1995). Performance in a tool-using task by common chimpanzees (*Pan troglodytes*), Bonobos (*Pan paniscus*), an Orangutan (*Pongo pygmaeus*), and capuchin monkeys (*Cebus apella*). *Journal of Comparative Psychology*, *109*, 52–60.

Visalberghi, E., & Limongelli, L. (1994). Lack of comprehension of cause-effect relations in tool-using capuchin monkeys (*Cebus apella*). *Journal of Comparative Psychology*, *108*, 15–22.

Visalberghi, E., & Limongelli, L. (1996). Acting and understanding: Tool use revisited through the minds of capuchin monkeys. In A. E. Russon & K. A. Bard (Eds.), *Reaching into thought: The minds of the great apes* (pp. 57–79). New York: Cambridge University Press.

Visalberghi, E., & Tomasello, M. (1998). Primate causal understanding in the physical and psychological domains. *Behavioral Processes*, *42*, 189–203.

Visalberghi, E., & Trinca, L. (1989). Tool use in capuchin monkeys: Distinguishing between performing and understanding. *Primates*, *30*, 511–521.

Vonk, J. (2002). Can orangutans (*Pongo abelii*) and gorillas (*Gorilla gorilla gorilla*) acquire relationships for social concepts? *International Journal of Comparative Psychology*, *15*, 257–277.

Vonk, J. (2003). Gorilla (*Gorilla gorilla gorilla*) and orangutan (*Pongo abelii*) understanding of first and second order relations. *Animal Cognition*, 6, 77–86.

Vonk, J., & MacDonald, S. E. (2002). Natural concept formation in a juvenile gorilla (*Gorilla gorilla gorilla*) at three levels of abstraction. *Journal of the Experimental Analysis of Behaviour*, *78*, 315–332.

Vonk, J., & MacDonald, S. E. (2004). Levels of abstraction in Orangutan (*Pongo abelii*), categorization. *Journal of Comparative Psychology*, *118*, 3–13.

Wasserman, E. A., Fagot, J., & Young, M. E. (2001). Same-different conceptualization by baboons (*Papio papio*): The role of entropy. *Journal of Comparative Psychology*, *115*, 42–52.

Wasserman, E. A., Hugart, J. A., & Kirkpatrick-Steger, K. (1995). Pigeons show same-different conceptualization after training with complex visual stimuli. *Journal of Experimental Psychology: Animal Behaviour Processes*, *21*, 248–252.

Wasserman, E. A., & Rovee-Collier, C. (2001). Pick the flowers and mind your As and 2s! Categorization by pigeons and infants. In M. E. Carroll & J. B. Overmier (Eds.), *Animal research and human health: Advancing human welfare through behavioral science* (pp. 263–279). Washington, DC: American Psychological Association.

Wasserman, E. A., Young, M. E., & Fagot, J. (2001). Effects of number of items on the baboon's discrimination of same from different visual displays. *Animal Cognition*, *4*, 163–170.

Wasserman, E. A., Young, M. E., & Nolan, B. C. (2000). Display variability and spatial organization as contributors to the pigeon's discrimination of complex visual stimuli. *Journal of Experimental Psychology: Animal Behaviour Processes*, *26*, 133–143.

Westergaard, G. C. (1999). Structural analysis of tool-use by tufted capuchins (*Cebus apella*) and chimpanzees (*Pan troglodytes*). *Animal Cognition*, 2, 141–145.

Westergaard, G. C., Liv, C., Chavanne, T. J., & Suomi, S. J. (1998). Token-mediated tool-use by a tufted capuchin monkey (*Cebus apella*). *Animal Cognition*, *1*, 101–106.

Whiten, A. (1998). Evolutionary and developmental origins of the mindreading system. In J. Lander & M. Killen (Eds.), *Piaget, evolution, and development* (pp. 73–99). Mahwah, NJ: Erlbaum.

Young, M. E., & Wasserman, E. A. (1997). Entropy detection by pigeons: Response to mixed visual displays after same-different discrimination training. *Journal of Experimental Psychology: Animal Behaviour Processes*, *23*, 157–170.

Young, M. E., Wasserman, E. A., & Dalrymple, R. (1997). Memory-based same-different conceptualization by pigeons. *Psychonomic Bulletin and Review*, *4*, 552–558.

Young, M. E., Wasserman, E. A., & Garner, K. L. (1997). Effects of number of items on the pigeon's discrimination of same from different visual displays. *Journal of Experimental Psychology: Animal Behaviour Processes*, *23*, 491–501.

Young, M. E., Wasserman, E. A., Hilfers, M. A., & Dalrymple, R. (1999). The pigeon's variability discrimination with lists of successively presented visual stimuli. *Journal of Experimental Psychology: Animal Behaviour Processes*, *25*, 475–490.

Zacks, J. M., & Tversky, B. (2001). Event structure in perception and conception. *Psychological Bulletin*, *127*, 3–21.

20

Rule Learning, Memorization Strategies, Switching Attention Between Local and Global Levels of Perception, and Optimality in Avian Visual Categorization

CHARLES P. SHIMP, WALTER T. HERBRANSON, THANE FREMOUW, AND ALYSON L. FROEHLICH

We begin with an uncontroversial statement: There is much diversity of opinion about the differences between human and nonhuman animal cognitive abilities. Diversity of opinion is found in the scientific community, where some researchers hold fast to associative learning accounts of animal performances and others welcome more cognitive accounts (Smith, Shields, & Washburn, 2003). Diversity of opinion is also found among the public. Some pet owners, on the one hand, seem to attribute to their pets cognitive abilities scarcely less complex than those of humans; on the other hand, others believe, perhaps for theological reasons deriving from Cartesian mind/body dualism, that a nonhuman animal cannot have a mental life, because to assume otherwise might jeopardize the exclusivity of the human soul. These differences of opinion obviously affect experimental research on animal cognition and issues related to the ethical treatment of animals and corresponding political issues (Plous, 1998; Shimp, Herbranson, & Fremouw, 2001).

In this chapter, we examine four specific beliefs about which we see major differences of opinion. First, only humans can deal with abstractions; nonhuman animals cannot. Second, only humans can flexibly adopt different memorization strategies depending on what momentarily is in their best interest; nonhuman animals cannot. Third, only humans can flexibly perceive complex stimuli differently depending on what is in their best interest; nonhuman animals cannot. Fourth, only humans can closely approximate optimal categorization performances in arbitrary tasks; nonhuman animals cannot.

Our first goal in this chapter is to describe recent research that shows how avian visual categorization transcends these specific cognitive limitations that are sometimes attributed to nonhuman animals. Our second goal is to view this research on avian categorization from the larger perspective of two philosophical positions that inform discussions of knowledge, language, concepts, perception, and other themes relevant to research on categorization. We suggest that each philosophy carries with it tangible implications for what is sensible research on cognition. A discussion of related issues is provided in Shimp (2004b), from which parts of the present chapter are drawn. First, we review some of our recent work on avian visual cognition.

EMPIRICAL RESEARCH ON AVIAN VISUAL CATEGORIZATION

Abstract Rule Learning in the Face of Ambiguity, the Flexibility of Attention, and Optimality in Categorizing Multidimensional Stimuli

A perceptual categorization procedure developed by Ashby, Maddox, their colleagues, and others is proving to be especially helpful in revealing the

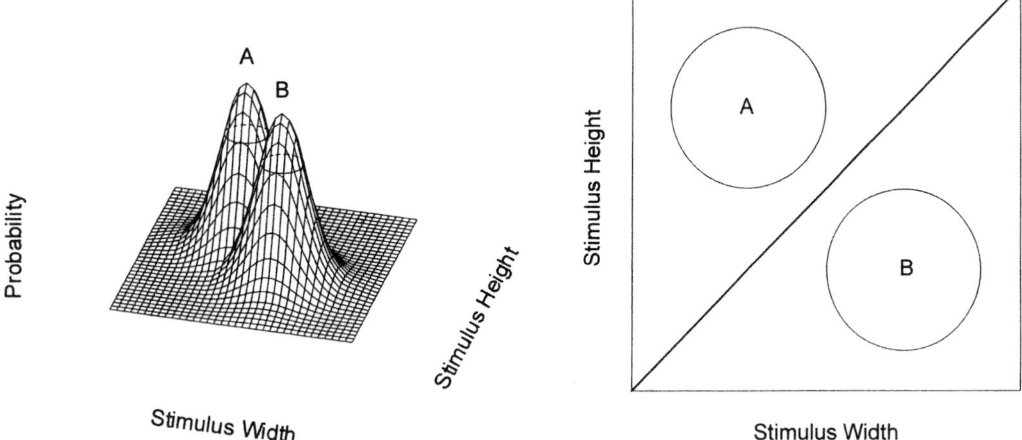

Figure 20.1. *Left*, Bivariate approximately-normal distributions represent likelihoods with which rectangles are sampled from either of two ill-defined (overlapping) categories: A and B. A rectangle is represented in the stimulus space as a point with coordinates equal to the corresponding width and height. A pigeon successively categorizes individual rectangles and is reinforced if a choice corresponds to the category, either A (left key) or B (right key), from which a rectangle was sampled. One arbitrary contour of equal likelihood is shown for each category. Each contour consists of all points corresponding to rectangles equally likely to be sampled from a category. *Right*, Arbitrary contours of equal likelihood for each category and the corresponding linear optimal decision bound, $x = y$, according to which a rectangle should be categorized as an A or as a B, depending on whether the rectangle is taller than wide or wider than tall, respectively. (From "The Randomization Procedure in the Study of Categorization of Multi-Dimensional Stimuli by Pigeons," by W. T. Herbranson, T. Fremouw, and C. P. Shimp, 1999, *Journal of Experimental Psychology: Animal Behavior Processes, 25,* 113–135. Copyright 1999 by the American Psychological Association. Reprinted with permission.)

cognitive and neurobiological mechanisms of categorization (Ashby & Ell, 2001; Ashby & Gott, 1988; Ashby & Maddox, 1998). The task more closely resembles the problems that organisms face in naturalistic settings than do many other categorization tasks, in the sense that it permits a category to have many exemplars and it permits exemplars to be ambiguous as to category membership (Herbranson, Fremouw, & Shimp, 1999, 2002). We have conducted several experiments using this procedure, two of which we review here. One involves static exemplars in the form of rectangles and another involves dynamic exemplars in the form of a moving object.

The general task requires participants to categorize stimuli that vary along two dimensions. For example, a specific task could require a participant to categorize rectangles varying in height and width or color patches varying in hue and brightness, and so on. All possible stimuli can be represented as points on a two-dimensional plane. A *category* is defined in terms of the corresponding sampling distribution that gives the likelihoods of all possible stimuli in that category.

Static Exemplars Figure 20.1 is a graphic representation of such a categorization task. Each of the two bell-shaped curves represents a category. A point on the surface of the mesh plot for a category shows the likelihood that a stimulus with a specific height and width will be sampled from that category. Note that both surfaces are approximately bivariate normal and that the likelihood of a stimulus from either category never quite reaches zero. Therefore, any possible stimulus in principle can be sampled from either category; that is, every stimulus has some degree of ambiguity as to its category membership. However, most stimuli are more likely to be sampled from one category than from the other. The exceptions are those stimuli that fall exactly on the line where the two categories intersect, as illustrated in figure 20.1. The diagonal line represents all stimuli that are equally likely to have been sampled from either category. This line also represents the optimal decision boundary. A participant who categorizes stimuli falling on one side as belonging to category A and stimuli falling on the other side as belonging to the category B will maximize the average number of correct responses.

Herbranson et al. (1999) arranged a task in which pigeons successively viewed on discrete trials a large number of different rectangles, one rectangle per trial. The reader is encouraged to consult the interactive, real-time, Web-based demonstration of this procedure that is available at Malloy et al. (2001). The pigeon's task was to categorize each rectangle: If the pigeon believed a rectangle was an exemplar of one category, then it was to peck the left key, whereas if the pigeon believed a rectangle was an exemplar of the second category, then it was to peck the right key. If the pigeon categorized a rectangle as an exemplar of the category from which it was sampled, then the pigeon received a small amount of grain; if the pigeon made an error, then it had to make a correction response to the correct key before the next trial could begin. The base rates of the two categories were equal; on average, the pigeon was reinforced equally often on the left and right.

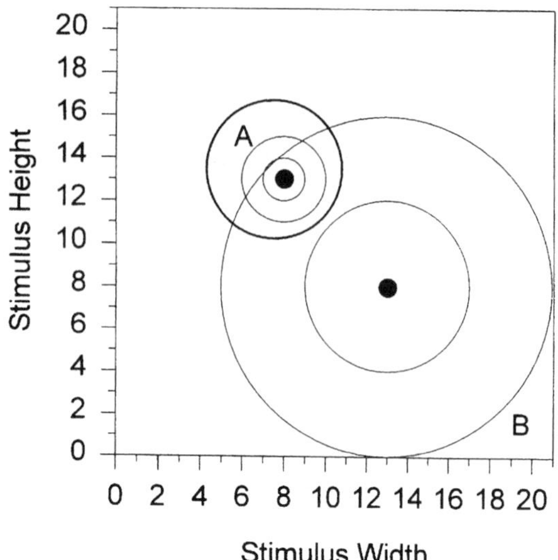

Figure 20.2. A task in which the optimal bound is nonlinear. An optimal response consisted of categorizing a rectangle as belonging to category A or B if its corresponding point in the stimulus space was or was not in the circular region indicated by the *bold circle*, respectively. Two contours of equal likelihood are shown for each category: A and B. For each category, the smaller and larger contours are 1 and 2 *SD*s from the mean (*filled circle*) of the corresponding normal bivariate distribution, respectively. The bold circular line represents the optimal decision bound. (From "The Randomization Procedure in the Study of Categorization of Multi-Dimensional Stimuli by Pigeons," by W. T. Herbranson, T. Fremouw, and C. P. Shimp, 1999, *Journal of Experimental Psychology: Animal Behavior Processes, 25,* 113–135. Copyright 1999 by the American Psychological Association. Reprinted with permission.)

We arranged tasks with two kinds of optimal decision bounds: linear and nonlinear. Among the tasks with linear optimal decision bounds, some required selective attention, whereas others required divided attention. That is, optimal categorization required the bird to attend either to both or to just one of the dimensions of a rectangle, respectively. (The actual psychological dimensions of a rectangle remain to be completely determined, and might be, for example, size and shape; however, for the present purposes it is adequate to write as though they are length and width.) In the selective attention conditions, only one element of a rectangle, either its length or its width, provided information about the category to which it belonged, whereas the other element continued to vary over trials without being diagnostic of the category from which the rectangle was sampled. In these linear conditions, optimal categorization was described by a linear decision rule in the two-dimensional stimulus space (for details, see Herbranson et al., 1999). Pigeons on the whole categorized stimuli more or less in accordance with this linear optimal decision rule. It is as though pigeons learned a simple abstract rule, such as, in one divided attention condition, "go left if width is greater than height, otherwise go right." In this linear task, the diagnosticity of a rectangle was an additive combination of the diagnosticities of the individual elements: length and width.

In the nonlinear task, optimal categorization could not be accomplished in terms of a rule according to which the separate diagnosticities of length and width combined additively: Figure 20.2 shows that in this task, the diagnosticities of the elements combined nonlinearly and that optimal decision rule was nonlinear, specifically, circular.

Pigeons nevertheless continued to do a respectable job in approximating the optimal solution. This outcome shows that, in at least this case, pigeons can combine the statistical diagnosticities of different elements of multidimensional stimuli in nonlinear ways, as presumably they must if they are to deal nearly optimally with many real-world categories that involve nonlinear combinations of their elements (Ashby & Maddox, 1998).

In summary, pigeons categorized rectangles in ways that were consistent with their having learned abstract decision rules when elements of complex stimuli combined either linearly or nonlinearly, depending on what a task required them to do. In passing, we note that pigeons therefore can categorize exemplars using either a strategy according to which a multidimensional stimulus is, in the linear case, an additive combination of its elements, corresponding to the case where "the whole is the sum of its parts" or, in the nonlinear case, a strategy according to which "the whole is different from the sum of its parts." The results are therefore compatible with the possibility that a pigeon can categorize complex stimuli either as a simple averaging machine, if that is the more adaptive behavior, or as a Gestalt processor, taking account of interactions among the elements of complex stimuli, if that is the more adaptive behavior. Pigeons also displayed considerable flexibility of attention, in that they could either selectively attend to an individual element of a complex stimulus or divide attention between elements, depending on which was adaptive given the task. Finally, in all cases, there was at least a crude approximation between categorization performance and the optimal decision rule.

Dynamic Exemplars The task described earlier can be used not only with rectangles but with nearly any kind of two-dimensional stimuli. A dimension of the natural world that is missing from stimuli in nearly all research on categorization, including research on what has come to be called "naturalistic visual concepts" (Herrnstein & Loveland, 1964) is time. Thus, to make our stimuli in this sense more naturalistically valid, we conducted an experiment in which the two dimensions were speed and direction of a moving object; the pigeon's task was to categorize the moving object into one or another category based not on the visual features of a static object, but on its dynamic features (Herbranson et al., 2002). We hasten to acknowledge that we do not believe that our stimuli were truly "naturalistic," even with the added dimension of time; the object that moved, for example, was merely a white circle, which had no particular ecological significance. We again encourage the reader to consult the interactive demonstration of this task for details (Malloy et al., 2001).

On each trial, a white circle appeared on a computer monitor in front of the pigeon, and after the circle moved for a brief period of time at a fixed speed in a fixed direction, the pigeon was asked to categorize the movement. If the stimulus (a speed/direction pair) had been sampled from one bivariate distribution, then a peck to one side location was reinforced; if it had been sampled from the second distribution, then a peck to the other side location was reinforced. As in the case of static stimuli described above, the two distributions overlapped, so that any stimulus could diagnose either category, but most stimuli were more likely to be sampled from one category than from the other, so that optimal performance was above the chance level of 50% correct but below 100% correct. As in the experiment with static stimuli, the task was changed over conditions so that in some conditions optimal performance could be achieved only if the pigeon divided attention between dimensions and integrated the information from each in a suitable manner. In other conditions, optimal performance required the pigeon to selectively attend to only speed or direction and to ignore the other, irrelevant dimension.

Results were similar to those when pigeons categorized static rectangles. Figure 20.3 summarizes how well the slopes and *y*-intercepts of the decision rules estimated from the birds' performances corresponded to the respective values in the linear optimal decision rule (for details of parameter estimation, see Herbranson et al., 2002). As can be seen, the correspondence was very close: In this sense, pigeons very closely approximated optimal performance. Thus, pigeons categorized moving objects as though they had learned an abstract rule approximating the optimal decision rule. Because the optimal decision rules varied across conditions in terms of whether attention was required to be allocated to either dimension alone or to both together, we can conclude that pigeons can display considerable flexibility in their attentional strategies; we may speculate that, to a considerable degree, pigeons use attention in ways that depend on

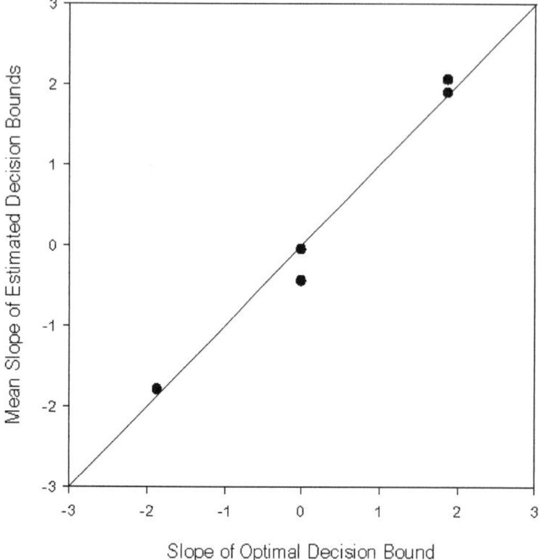

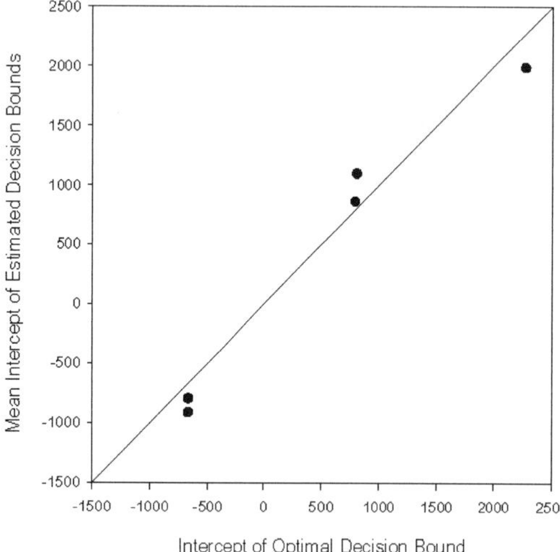

Figure 20.3. The average of the slopes of the individually estimated decision rules as a function of the optimal slope (*top*), and the average of the y intercepts of the individually estimated decision rules as a function of the optimal y intercept (*bottom*). (From "Categorizing a Moving Target in Terms of its Speed and Direction," by W. T. Herbranson, T. Fremouw, & C. P. Shimp, 2002, *Journal of the Experimental Analysis of Behavior (Special Issue on Categorization), 78,* 249–270. Copyright 2002 by the Society for the Experimental Analysis of Behavior. Reprinted with permission.)

what in any particular task is optimal—that is, on what produces higher reinforcement payoffs. This cognitive flexibility was displayed in the face of the statistical ambiguity produced by the overlap between the sampling distributions corresponding to the two categories.

Flexibility in the Use of Attention in the Local/Global Task

When we perceive the visual world, we can pay greater attention to either the forest or the trees. Stated in terms of contemporary cognitive vocabulary, recent history may momentarily prime us to be more inclined to pay attention to either local or global levels of perceptual analysis; what we have come to expect to see can facilitate our seeing a target at that expected level (Lamb & Robertson, 1988; Navon, 1977). The idea of mental continuity, combined with the Gestalt principle of figure-ground reversals, motivated us to determine if pigeons, like humans, could evidence shifts of attention between local and global levels of analysis. In order to do so, we presented pigeons with complex stimuli entailing both a global and a local level (Navon, 1977, 1981); we "primed" either the local or global level, and we rewarded the pigeons for responding to specific targets that could occur at either level. The reader is encouraged to consult an interactive, real-time, Web-based demonstration of this procedure (available at http://www.pigeon.psy.tufts.edu/avc/shimp/).

On each trial, pigeons were shown a compound stimulus composed of a large character created from a number of smaller characters (figure 20.4). Each stimulus contained a target character at either the global or local level and a distractor character at the other level. The task required the pigeon to indicate which target character was present by pecking a key to the left or to the right. For example, target letters H and S, regardless of the level at which they occurred, required a response to the left or right, respectively. A global target letter H, requiring a response to the left key, could be formed of local letters T or E; a global letter S, requiring a response to the right key, could also be formed of local letters T or E. A local target letter H, requiring a left response, could form either a global T or E; a local target letter S, requiring a right response, could similarly form either a global T or E. Thus, the complex stimuli were hierarchically organized; the pigeon had to search for a target that could be present at either the local or global level.

We used two different methods to train the pigeon to expect a target at a particular level, that is,

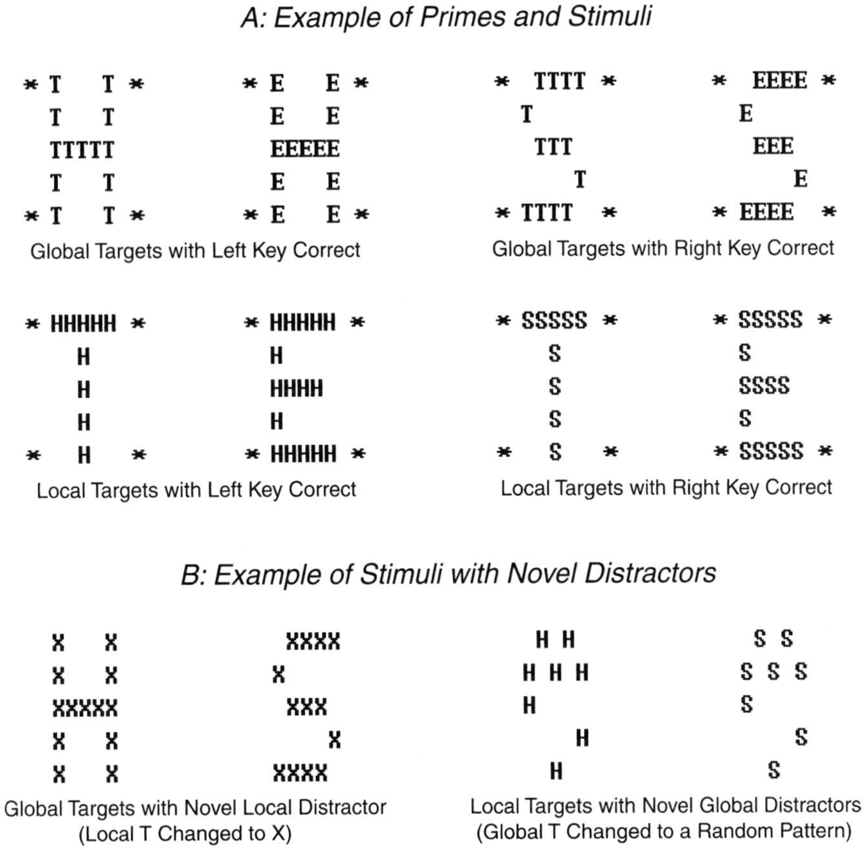

A: Example of Primes and Stimuli

```
* T   T *      * E   E *      *  TTTT *      *  EEEE *
  T   T          E   E         T               E
  TTTTT          EEEEE          TTT             EEE
  T   T          E   E             T               E
* T   T *      * E   E *      * TTTT  *      * EEEE  *
```

Global Targets with Left Key Correct

Global Targets with Right Key Correct

```
* HHHHH *      * HHHHH *      * SSSSS *      * SSSSS *
    H            H                S            S
    H            HHHH             S            SSSS
    H            H                S            S
*   H   *      * HHHHH *      *   S   *      * SSSSS *
```

Local Targets with Left Key Correct

Local Targets with Right Key Correct

B: Example of Stimuli with Novel Distractors

```
X   X          XXXX           H H            S S
X   X          X             H H H          S S S
XXXXX           XXX          H              S
X   X              X             H              S
X   X          XXXX            H              S
```

Global Targets with Novel Local Distractor (Local T Changed to X)

Local Targets with Novel Global Distractors (Global T Changed to a Random Pattern)

Figure 20.4. *A*, One set of stimuli used in Fremouw et al. (1998, 2002). Each hierarchical stimulus had a target stimulus (in this set either an H or an S) at either the local or global level, and an irrelevant distractor stimulus (in this set either a T or an E) at the other level. When the base-rate procedure was used to prime a level, the four stars at the corner of each stimulus did not appear: they were used only in the trial-by-trial priming cue procedure, where they served as the priming cue. The stars were presented about 1 s prior to the presentation of a hierarchical stimulus, and the first peck to the stars after 1 s elapsed presented the local/global stimulus. The local characters were white and the stars either red or green on a black/gray background. *B*, An example of stimuli with novel distractors used in Fremouw et al. (1998). In the two examples on the left, the original local distractor T has been replaced with the novel local distractor X. In the two examples on the right, the original global distractor T has been replaced with a novel random pattern global distractor.

to prime a level: a base-rate procedure and a trial-by-trial cuing procedure. In the base-rate procedure, we presented successive blocks of trials, within each of which, most targets occurred at one level: the primed level. Within a given block, targets at the primed level occurred a random 85% of the time, whereas targets at the nonprimed level occurred the other 15% of the time (Fremouw, Herbranson, & Shimp, 1998). We alternated blocks of trials with either global or local levels primed. In the trial-by-trial cuing procedure, on each trial, we presented a brief priming cue prior to the presentation of the hierarchical stimulus. The priming cue consisted of four stars, either all green or all red, that formed the corners of a box slightly larger that the stimuli (figure 20.4A). The color of the stars predicted, with 85% accuracy, the level at which the target would occur. Targets occurred at the global level a random 85% of the time and at the local level the other 15% of the time if the stars were red, and vice versa if the stars were green. Local and global targets occurred with equal

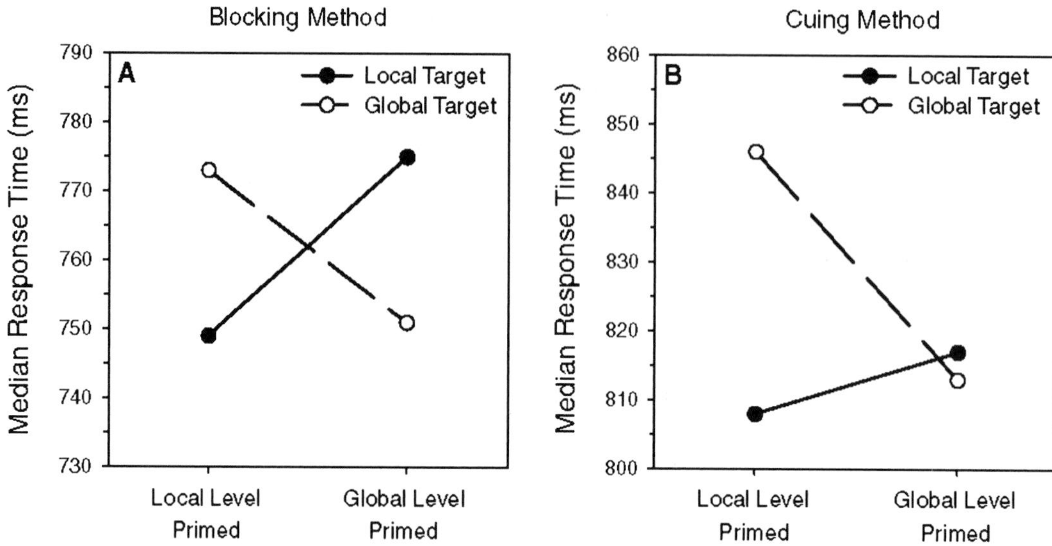

Figure 20.5. *A*, The overall mean median response time to global and local targets as a function of primed level when the blocking procedure was used to prime a level (Fremouw et al., 1998). Response time was significantly faster to local targets than to global targets during the blocks of trials in which targets appeared more frequently at the local level (local level primed). Response time was also significantly faster to global targets than to local targets when the global level was primed. In addition, response time to local targets was faster when the local level was primed than when the global level was primed, and response time to global targets was faster when the global level was primed than when the local level was primed (all ps < .05). *B*, The overall mean median response time to global and local targets as a function of primed level when the trial by trial priming cue procedure was used to prime a level (Fremouw et al., 2002). Response time was faster to global targets when the global level was primed than when the local level was primed. Response time was also faster to local targets than to global targets when the local level was primed (all ps < .05).

probabilities (Fremouw, Herbranson, & Shimp, 2002).

We asked if a pigeon saw a target at the primed level faster than at the nonprimed level. We therefore calculated the median response time to local and global targets when the targets occurred at the primed level and at the nonprimed level. Figure 20.5 summarizes the response time data from the two experiments; clearly, priming occurred with both the blocking method and the trial-by-trial cuing method. These results suggest that pigeons can flexibly switch attention between local and global levels of analysis.

We evaluated an alternative interpretation that each stimulus had some specific feature that could be used to distinguish it from the other stimuli that was independent of the local or global perceptual level. That is, perhaps birds can use some feature independent of local and global perceptual levels. To determine if this were so, we conducted transfer tests in which the original targets remained the same, but the original distractors were replaced. For example, the stimulus with a global target H composed of the local distractor T was changed so that it was composed of the local distractor X and the stimulus with a global distractor T composed of local target H was changed so that the global distractor was a random pattern composed of the local target H (figure 20.4B). If birds used some specific feature across perceptual levels, then a change to one of those levels should significantly reduce performance. There were no significant differences in median response time or percent correct responding between the original stimuli and the transfer stimuli, suggesting that the pigeons did not rely on a specific feature or set of features common to both perceptual levels (Fremouw et al., 1998). It appears that pigeons are indeed able to shift attention between local and global levels of perceptual analysis.

Both methods demonstrate shifts of attention between local and global levels of perceptual analysis in pigeons, but they do so over very different time frames. In the case of base-rate blocking, attention may build up slowly as the base rates are learned; once attention to a particular level has increased, it may simply remain "active" at that level until the base rate changes. That is, if the preponderance of targets is at the global level, then attention to the global level may slowly increase over the course of minutes or hours and then simply remain at the global level as long as the base rate remains the same. In the case of trial-by-trial cuing, the dynamics of attention must be much faster. The level at which the next target is likely to occur is not known until approximately 1 s before it occurs. Thus, attention must be dynamically readjusting on the scale of a second rather than on the scale of minutes or longer. That is not to say that attention cannot also operate on a similarly brief time scale in the base-rate blocking experiment; it simply does not have to do so.

The mechanisms responsible for local/global shifts of attention in humans and nonhuman animals are not yet fully understood and may depend on the specifics of the priming task. For example, Plaisted (1997) suggested that attention in experiments using the blocking procedure may depend on the fact that targets with higher base rates occur more frequently and thus may have more highly activated residual memories. The higher the activated state of the residual memory, the quicker it is that a target could activate the system to some threshold level that activates a response. It is unclear how such a purely time-based, decay-of-target-memory process could account for the attention switching that occurred in our cuing task. In that task, the base rates were the same for both local and global targets. A different kind of memory model might therefore be required to account for the attention switching in the cuing task.

For example, seeing the red stars might activate a memory of the red stars and that memory might be associated with the memories of the four stimuli that have targets at the global level. Activating the memory for red stars might therefore activate those associated global memories, and the higher level of activation for those four global memories might facilitate faster processing of a subsequent stimulus with a target at the global level. In addition, there are other models proposed in the contemporary human literature, including spatial frequency modulation (Lamb, Yund, & Pond, 1999; Shulman & Wilson, 1987) and activation of level-specific neural mechanisms (Lamb, London, Pond, & Whitt, 1998). We expect that the mechanisms underlying local/global attention will be found to involve the dynamic interaction of several processes, including basic memory processes, occurring along the full visual processing stream from the retina to associative cortex.

Recent neurophysiological findings from bats offer some intriguing possibilities for how feedback between cortex and lower sensory nuclei might play a role in attention phenomena on both slower time scales, such as in the blocking task, and on faster time scales, such as in the cuing task. Suga and his colleagues (Ma & Suga, 2003; Suga, Gao, Zhang, Ma, & Olsen, 2000; Yan & Suga, 1996; Zhang & Suga, 1997) showed that repetitive stimulation of auditory cortex can refine and strengthen neuronal firing in the inferior colliculus, a nucleus that is located earlier in the auditory processing stream than the auditory cortex. For example, stimulating an area of the cortex that responds best to a particular frequency range or to a particular delay between sounds seems to strengthen the response of neurons in the inferior colliculus that also respond to that particular frequency range or delay. Inactivating the cortex had the opposite effect: the response in the inferior colliculus was weakened. This neuronal modulation developed over time, from 2 to 30 min, and lasted from minutes to hours. Casseday, Fremouw, and Covey (2002) speculated that this process might help to select, enhance, and maintain processing of specific auditory features over the period of an evening's hunt in the case of a bat.

We wonder if a similar mechanism, perhaps working on spatial frequency, might play a role in local/global attention seen in the base-rate blocking experiments where the dynamics of attention may be relatively slow. Perhaps the high base rate of a particular target level leads to repetitive and prolonged activity of neurons tuned to the appropriate spatial frequency for the corresponding perceptual level. Perhaps once a target level is perceived on a trial, the neurons involved in encoding that level remain active longer and at a higher level than the neurons that encode the nontarget level. Such increased activity might then strengthen and fine-tune the response of neurons to that level in both visual cortex and earlier structures. This enhancement in neuronal response might in turn produce a faster or more accurate perception of subsequent targets at that perceptual level.

Activity in auditory cortex can also enhance specific auditory features in the inferior colliculus on a much faster, stimulus-by-stimulus time frame (Jen, Chen, & Sun, 1998; Zhou & Jen, 2000). Perhaps a similarly fast-acting mechanism plays a role in the visual system and at least partially mediates the local/global attention shifts seen in the priming cue task. We describe these highly speculative possibilities to illustrate how research on animal cognition and research on neurophysiology might mutually inform each other.

In summary, we showed that pigeons display flexibility in switching attention between local and global levels of perceptual analysis much as in the case of humans attending either to the forest or the trees. Thus, pigeons can flexibly display a kind of figure-ground reversal that forms part of the core metatheoretical perspective of Gestalt psychology.

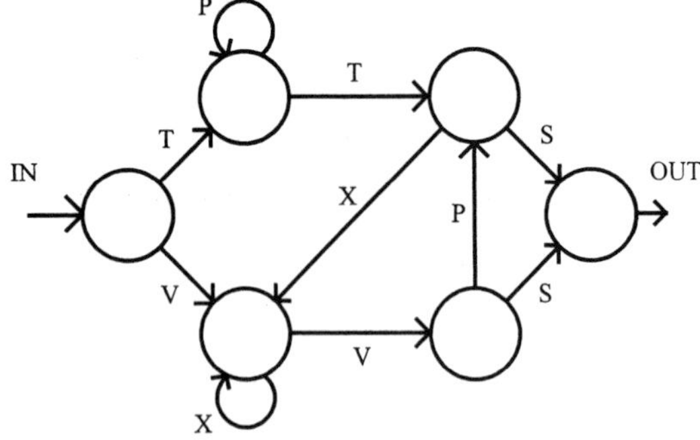

Figure 20.6. The artificial grammar that generated grammatical character strings of lengths 3 to 8. (Adapted from Chomsky and Miller, 1958, and Reber, 1967. From "Artificial Grammar Learning in Pigeons: A Preliminary Analysis," by W. T. Herbranson and C. P. Shimp, 2003, *Learning & Behavior, 31,* 98–106. Copyright 2003 by the Psychonomic Society. Reprinted with permission.)

Rule Learning and Memorization Strategies in Artificial Grammar Learning

Thus far, we have seen that pigeons can successfully attend either to one dimension or to both dimensions when they categorize two-dimensional rectangles, that they can attend to either or both of speed and direction of a moving object when they categorize the object in terms of its movement, and that they can be primed to see targets more quickly at one level of perceptual analysis than at another. In plain English, one might say in all these cases that pigeons used their attentional capacity in flexible ways. We next describe a very different task, in which the cognitive flexibility of pigeons is demonstrated in terms of the different memory strategies they use for different kinds of to-be-remembered material.

The idea of an "artificial grammar"[1] (Reber, 1967, 1989) has facilitated our understanding of the differences among various kinds of human memory systems. An artificial grammar is a set of rules for generating strings of characters. An example of one such grammar is depicted in figure 20.6. A character string is generated by entering the grammar at the left, with each transition from one state to another adding a character to the string, until exiting via the "out" arrow at the right. In this manner, each unique path through the grammar produces a different character string. Grammars containing loops like the one pictured here can generate an infinite number of character strings. Limiting the length of character strings naturally decreases this number, but it still results in many unique strings. The simple grammar depicted here, for instance, can generate 43 character strings between 3 and 8 characters in length.

In a prototypical artificial grammar experiment (e.g., Reber, 1967), undergraduates are shown grammatical character strings generated by a set of rules such as in figure 20.6 and are asked to memorize the strings. Later, they are presented with novel strings, told the earlier strings were generated by a grammar (but are not told the grammar), and asked whether the novel strings conform to the grammar. Despite the participants' inability to accurately describe the rules of the grammar, performance at diagnosing grammaticality is reliably above chance. This result is reminiscent not only of the performance of young children, who recognize grammatical sentences when they hear them without being able to describe grammatical rules, but also of the performance of both humans and pigeons on naturalistic categorization tasks. Naturalistic visual categories, such as "tree," are quickly learned, in the sense that a participant rapidly learns to discriminate visual scenes with or without a tree, even though the basis for the discrimination in the form of a simple rule-based criterion is unclear. From the perspective of the participants, artificial grammars have the virtue of preserving this "family resemblance" characteristic of naturalistic categories, where the basis for the discrimination seems complex and ambiguous. At the same time, from the perspective of the experimenter, artificial grammars have the virtue of simplicity: Unlike the case with naturalistic categories like "tree," the experimenter actually knows the rules, the true structure, of the category.

Recently, we showed that nonhuman animals, specifically pigeons, can learn an artificial grammar. We suspect that artificial grammar learning may be a nonlinguistic precursor of human language and, as such, deserves a comparative analysis (see Fitch & Hauser, 2004, and Seidenberg, MacDonald, & Saffran, 2002, for related discussion). We examined this possibility by attempting to train birds to discriminate between grammatical and nongrammatical character strings (Herbranson & Shimp, 2003). Birds were rewarded for pecking one key when a character string was displayed that conformed to the rules of the grammar in figure 20.6. They were rewarded for pecking a different key when the displayed character string violated the grammar. After extensive training (average of 179 days), birds reached a stable level of above chance performance (62.3% correct) on the training set of 62 character strings (31 grammatical and 31 nongrammatical), suggesting that they had learned something about the grammar.

In order to rule out the possibility that pigeons were simply memorizing specific training exemplars, at least some of which presumably seemed familiar to the pigeons by the end of training, we subsequently presented novel probe strings (12 novel grammatical and 12 novel nongrammatical strings) that the pigeons had not encountered during training. Performance on these novel strings was also reliably above chance (60.7%), supporting the notion that pigeons had acquired a flexible conception of the grammar that went beyond the specific stimuli presented during training. In addition to learning something abstract about the grammar, the pigeons also appeared to memorize some of the shorter strings. Thus, pigeons flexibly adopted different memorization strategies for different aspects of the same task.

Finally, we found that pigeons more accurately categorized grammatical than nongrammatical character strings. Although we initially found this difference to be puzzling, we now believe that this result nicely fits with the idea that artificial grammar learning is a form of learning abstract categories. Consider that grammatical strings shared a stronger family resemblance with each other than did nongrammatical strings with each other. Nongrammatical strings were random distortions of grammatical strings, and therefore necessarily violated the family resemblance shared by grammatical strings. We speculate this increased within-category variability might make the category of nongrammatical strings more difficult to learn.

In summary, pigeons learning an artificial grammar displayed cognitive flexibility in at least two ways familiar in human cognition, but less so in nonhuman animals. First, pigeons satisfied the traditional criterion for learning abstract concepts: they learned the training set of stimuli and generalized to novel stimuli. Although we do not know if the abstractions the pigeons learned corresponded exactly to the abstract rules of the grammar, the fact that learning generalized to new exemplars is part of the traditional definition of what it means to learn something abstract (although it has been shown that exemplar theory can generate what appears to be the learning of an abstract prototype, as in Medin & Schaffer, 1978). Second, pigeons demonstrated flexible memorization strategies, because it seems as though they used abstract concepts to categorize complex, more difficult-to-remember strings and simply memorized strings in some cases involving simple, easier-to-remember strings.

COMMENTS ON INTERRELATIONS WITH OTHER RESEARCH ON CATEGORIZATION

The following comments suggest how our research on avian visual categorization interrelates with the larger literature on animal and human cognition (also see Cook, 2001).

Rule Learning

The ability to learn abstract rules was formerly seen as a distinctly human ability, but two advances cast doubt on that simplistic view. First, philosophical and theoretical advances on the basic nature of an abstraction have clarified what it means to claim an organism has learned a rule (Ashby & Maddox, 1998; Ryle, 1949; Wittgenstein, 1953). Second, we have shown, at least by conventional standards, if not by entirely satisfactory theoretical standards, that pigeons behave as if they learn abstract rules both in the two-dimensional categorization task and in the artificial grammar learning task (see also Cook & Wasserman, chapter 16, Huber & Aust, chapter 17, and Jitsumori, chapter 18, this volume). We believe that further advances will depend greatly on whether corresponding theory is developed by which the various demonstrations of cognitive flexibility in nonhuman animals can be interpreted. We suggest that empirical progress will depend on theoretical and conceptual advances in our understanding of the rules that nonhuman animals can learn, on how these rules can be explained by evolutionary considerations, and on what it means to find the underlying neurobiological mechanisms.

Ambiguity and Gestalt Reversible Images

Ambiguity is rarely claimed to be a virtue of scientific theory. Ambiguity may look different, however, from the perspective of naturalistic categorization, from the perspective of family resemblance, and from the perspective of Gestalt psychology. We believe that ambiguity plays a necessary role in everyday categorization and, correspondingly, in empirical research and scientific theories of categorization. Ambiguity is not something that always needs to be replaced by logical clarity, given that one of our goals is to understand the messy complexity of everyday categorization. We note in passing that research on decision making in the face of uncertainty has recognized as much for many years.

Memorization Strategies

We believe that the ability of pigeons to switch memorization strategies merits further empirical investigation because it bears on the common, but we suspect incorrect assumption that few nonhuman animals can switch memorization strategies on a moment-to-moment basis, as a function of what is momentarily adaptive (Herbranson & Shimp, 2003; Wright, 2001; Wright, chapter 9, this volume).

Flexible Allocation of Attention

We believe that future progress in comparative cognition will hinge on the development of theories that can integrate demonstrations that pigeons can either selectively attend to individual elements or divide attention among them (e.g., Herbranson et al., 1999, 2002), can be primed either to see the forest or the trees in the local/global task, and can be primed in a multitude of other ways in visual search (Blough, 1991; Blough, chapter 5, this volume; Tinbergen, 1960). We tend to think that plain English is too often assigned the job of integrating these various phenomena; this job instead should be the task of well-articulated scientific theory.

Optimality

The question of whether humans and animals behave in optimal ways is so great in scope that a general treatment is far beyond the limits of this chapter (Gould & Lewontin, 1979; Kahneman, Slovic, & Tversky, 1982). We would like only to note that pigeons display a remarkable ability to behave not only in ways that appear rational but also in ways that are quantitatively close to optimal.

PERSPECTIVES ON CATEGORIZATION FROM WITTGENSTEIN'S TWO PHILOSOPHIES

Research on categorization, in general, and on rule learning and cognitive flexibility, in particular, raises difficult interpretative and evaluative issues because, by interrelating human and nonhuman animal cognition, it indirectly addresses the fundamental question of the nature of the human condition. Such a difficult question has many different kinds of answers; those who see the answer one way may disagree quite profoundly with those who see it some other way. Correspondingly, the same categorization literature may look either good or bad depending on the evaluative standards one adopts.

We believe that some of the important evaluative differences gain perspective when viewed in the light of Wittgenstein's two philosophies, both of which address some of the deepest issues in the nature of the human condition. Each of his philosophies carries with it its own evaluative standards. For our limited present purposes, there is no need to provide comprehensive descriptions, explanations, or criticisms of either of these philosophies. The following brief summary of those parts of the philosophies that are relevant to the present chapter is adapted from Shimp (2004a), which should be consulted for a somewhat more detailed treatment.

Relevant Features of the *Tractatus Logico-Philosophicus* (1922)

Wittgenstein's (1922) picture theory addressed the relation between language and reality; it assumed that a factual proposition in some sense has the same logical structure as the corresponding natural phenomenon. An examination of the visual appearance of the *Tractatus* reveals symbolically expressed logical propositions and truth tables but no pictures: the picture in the picture theory was abstract and static. (As an aside, we speculate that the development of the technology of motion pictures hastened the abandonment of this age-old tendency to think of mental representations in terms of static images.) In a manner not explained, a static factual proposition was supposed to capture what unfolds dynamically over time in actual behavior. Complex propositions were assumed to be built up from independent "atomic facts." The *Tractatus* assumes that logical clarity, logical rigor, unambiguity, and parsimony are vital virtues.

Relevant Features of the *Philosophical Investigations* (1953)

Wittgenstein is reputed to have rejected his first philosophy after having served briefly as an elementary school teacher, when he decided that his philosophy was of little practical use in dealing with how people really behave. He subsequently developed a system that was designed to show how to avoid making the kinds of conceptual and linguistic mistakes that led to the problems *Tractatus* was designed to solve.

Wittgenstein's *Philosophical Investigations* (1953) does not rely on logical rigor and abstract propositions; instead, it relies on careful analysis of how everyday language is used. An examination of the visual appearance of *Philosophical Investigations* reveals numerous drawings to illustrate Gestalt principles of visual perception, especially in the form of reversible images, figure/ground reversals (e.g., the duck/rabbit illustration), and the ambiguity inherent in the idea of family resemblance. It emphasizes how the same visual image can be an exemplar of either one or another category, as in the duck/rabbit illustration, and it examines in close detail actual, everyday, ordinary language use. It emphasizes how the meaning of elements depends on context: how the meaning of words in a sentence depends on grammatical context or how the meaning of a sentence depends on its larger context. Finally, through appeal to the Gestalt tradition, there is a sense of psychological dynamism in *Philosophical Investigations* that is lacking in *Tractatus*. Just as Gestalt psychology acknowledged a more dynamic approach to perceiving, remembering, and problem solving than did the more static and mechanical aspects of associative theories of learning and memory deriving from British empiricism, *Philosophical Investigations* acknowledged, or even welcomed, a more dynamic approach to perceiving, remembering, and problem solving than did *Tractatus*.

Wittgensteinian Evaluative Perspectives on Avian Visual Categorization

Wittgenstein's two philosophies offer different perspectives on what constitutes meaningful analyses of cognition, in general, and of categorization, in particular. These perspectives can even be seen as categories themselves; that is, we may try to categorize research on categorization into the two alternatives that Wittgenstein provided. When we look at the two alternatives in this way, we immediately see that they conform rather well to the idea of family resemblance in *Philosophical Investigations*, in the sense that exemplars of empirical research on categorization have no defining features that unambiguously assign them to one category or the other. It is still useful, we believe, to list ways in which the research that we have described fits one or the other of the perspectives, even if none of the research perfectly fits either.

First, *Tractatus* assumes that an understanding of complex cognition involves the use of simple logical rules and propositions. We made a similar assumption in three of our demonstrations of avian categorization, in our use of decision rules to interpret the results of both of our experiments on categorization of multidimensional stimuli (Herbranson et al., 1999, 2002), and in our use of abstract rules to interpret the results of our experiment on artificial grammar learning (Herbranson & Shimp, 2003). We believe that the contrasting perspectives of *Tractatus* and of *Philosophical Investigations* are illuminating in this case, because it was largely the "cognitive revolution" (Gardner, 1985; Shimp, 1989) that permitted rigorous experimental psychologists to feel comfortable attributing abstract rules, including grammatical rules, to humans. From the perspective of the cognitive revolution, rule learning looks modern; however, from the perspective of Wittgenstein's two philosophies, rule learning looks conceptually obsolete, because it was part of *Tractatus*, not *Philosophical Investigations*, from which perspective logical, abstract rules actually look old because they reflect a less-naturalistic, less-detailed, less-dynamic, more-idealized kind of mental representation.

Second, if we consider how *Philosophical Investigations* acknowledges some descriptive value in ambiguity and looks favorably on the dynamics of Gestalt reversible images, whereas *Tractatus* does not, then we get a different perspective on the statistical ambiguity in the multidimensional categorization task (Herbranson et al., 1999, 2002) and on the rapid, dynamic priming in the local/global task (Fremouw et al., 2002). In these ways, our research appears more constructive when viewed from *Philosophical Investigations* than from *Tractatus*.

Third, the two different memorization strategies that we hypothesized pigeons use to learn artificial grammars—the acquisition of abstract rules and the memorization of specific character strings—seem to us to reflect *Tractatus* and *Philosophical Investigations*, respectively. If one viewed it as a virtue to adopt a consistent position and to adhere to either *Tractatus* or *Philosophical Investigations*, but not both, then our attribution to pigeons of this kind of dual memorization strategy would seem inconsistent and undesirable. This dual strategy may also be viewed in terms of the distinction between explicit memory involving abstract rules and implicit memory involving memory for specific procedures or behaviors (Reber, 1967, 1989). Memory for the logical rules that form part of the definition of explicit memory seems more compatible with *Tractatus*, whereas memory for specific, detailed behaviors that form part of the definition of implicit memory seems more compatible with *Philosophical Investigations*. If we apply this distinction to our experiment on artificial grammar learning, we see that pigeons seem to have used two systems: a system for learning and remembering abstract, general, logical, clear, and unambiguous explicit grammatical rules, in a manner compatible with *Tractatus*, and a system for learning and remembering specific strings of characters, outside the context of a system of logical rules, in a manner more compatible with *Philosophical Investigations*.

Fourth, it is a prominent feature of *Philosophical Investigations*, but not of *Tractatus*, to address the flexibility of attention. Much of our work is therefore more consistent in this sense with *Philosophical Investigations* than with *Tractatus*, because we have interpreted much of our data in terms of attentional flexibility, a pigeon using either selective or divided attention (Herbranson et al., 1999, 2002) and using either local or global levels of perceptual analysis, whichever is primed. One might expect a researcher committed to *Philosophical Investigations* to strongly endorse this aspect of our work but a researcher committed to *Tractatus* to be much less favorably inclined toward it.

Fifth, the issue of optimality seems more closely to resemble *Tractatus* than *Philosophical Investigations* to the extent to which optimal behavior is viewed as related to the issue of whether behavior is efficient and parsimonious and displays logical, rule-driven solutions to environmental problems.

In summary, we believe that our work is characteristic, in important ways, of much contemporary research on categorization, and on cognition in general; contemporary research often displays a sort of methodological and theoretical incoherence if it is viewed from the perspectives of two of the most influential philosophies of the previous 100 years. If one wanted to adopt a consistent position, as Wittgenstein certainly did, then much contemporary research fails to meet his standard, because research methodology tends to be an uncomfortable hodgepodge of both positions. It has been our experience (Shimp, 2004a, 2004b) that some researchers are more comfortable with one of Wittgenstein's philosophies than with the other. As a result, it is likely that judgments of the scientific merit of a research program, as in peer review of publications and grants, are influenced by the extent to which a research program conforms to a preferred philosophical position (Shimp, 2004a, 2004b).

QUESTIONS FOR THE FUTURE

What are the important questions about categorization that need answering? Our review of Wittgenstein's two philosophies suggests that the answer to this question depends on what one thinks it means to categorize something. This, in turn, depends on how one prioritizes the important jobs for a philosophy of mind, language, and behavior.

If one were committed to *Tractatus*, for example, then one might believe that we need to discover simple, logical, and general rules in terms of which idealized laboratory categorization performance could be explained. If one were committed to *Philosophical Investigations*, on the other hand, then one might believe it was important to postpone or to abandon the search for such simple and general, or even universal, rules. Instead, one might concentrate on describing the complex details of specific, naturalistic, everyday categorizing.

It would therefore be presumptuous to try here to describe all facets of categorization that need theoretical description and explanation: The problem depends in too complex a manner on metatheoretical as well as conventional scientific choices. We can, nevertheless, try to imagine what kind of locally applicable theory might be able to handle the results that we have reviewed here, and we might try to look for ways in which such a theory might fit more closely with one philosophy than with the other.

It would appear that such a theory of categorization needs to deal with the learning of abstractions, including abstract rules that work in the face of ambiguity: how and why an animal, depending on task demands, learns abstractions or instead memorizes specific stimuli; how attention can be almost optimally selective or divided across tasks involving categorization of rectangles or moving objects; and, how attention can be primed, either through base rate manipulations or through trial by trial priming cues, to local or global levels of perceptual analysis. What kind of theory might be able to handle all of these results? In our judgment, there is at present no theory remotely capable of achieving all of these goals.

First, it seems to us that we can reject some entire categories of theory. For example, theories known as "molar" theories in behavior analysis seem unlikely candidates, because such theories typically reject the importance of fine-grain detail, deal with static aggregate summaries of behavior rather than with the reality of actual behavior streams, and emphasize instead logical rules and simple algebraic formulas. In short, their evaluative standards seem largely derived from *Tractatus* and it is not clear how they could be modified to satisfy the standards of *Philosophical Investigations*.

Second, where might one find sufficiently flexible theoretical methods that might handle our results? Consider the possible relevance of the field of robotics and of what has been called "behaving theory." A theory that generates real-time behavior streams, which then can be compared with behavior streams of actual participants, must deal with the fine-grain detail of behavior and automatically confront details of the local sequential patterning of behavior, as required by the complex evaluative standards of *Philosophical Investigations*. Such a theory, unlike a molar theory, which produces only aggregate averages of behavior, could control the movements of a robot. Such a "behaving theory" automatically generates the messy complexity of real behavior. We would like to offer computational processing models developed by Staddon and his colleagues (Staddon, 2001; Staddon & Higa, 1999), by Catania (2005), and by Shimp and his colleagues (Shimp, 1979, 1984a, 1984b, 1992, 1994; Shimp, Childers, & Hightower, 1990; Shimp & Friedrich, 1993) as preliminary examples of behaving theories that are somewhat more in the spirit of *Philosophical Investigations* than are most current quantitative theories.

Third, we can hear researchers committed to the methods of *Tractatus* objecting that a scientific theory need not deal with all the messy details of real-world, everyday behavior. In short, is a robotic behaving theory simple or complex, and which should it be? Consider that variability in laboratory behavior seems different from variability in naturalistic, everyday behavior. Indeed, that this is so is part of the justification for bringing real-world behaviors into the laboratory, where variability can be reduced. In short, one might say that laboratory behavior is relatively simple and that naturalistic behavior is relatively complex. As yet there is, however, no general theory, formula, or science to describe or to explain what is simplicity. In short, "fine-grain detail" is complex from the perspective of a theory that emphasizes logical rules or simple algebraic formulas, but it is simple from the perspective of a more naturalistic theory because it characterizes the very details without which one cannot describe or understand real-world, everyday behavior.

This same difference of perspective on simplicity is seen in research on categorization. Researchers examining naturalistic behavior, robotics, and the dynamics and sequential structure of behavior, appear, we believe, to be reducing the weight they give in evaluating research on categorization to a kind of parsimony based on "simple" laboratory behavior and increasing the weight they give to a newer kind of parsimony based on "complex" naturalistic behavior (Shimp, 2004a, 2004b). Accordingly, if research on nonhuman animal categorization continues to evolve in the direction of Wittgenstein's later views described in *Philosophical Investigations*, then the future may see a greater emphasis on how the fine-grain details of the local temporal structure of complex naturalistic behavior determine membership in a category. And, regardless of the accuracy of this prediction, researchers will probably continue for a long time to have their opinions about what constitutes good research on categorization determined in part by which of Wittgenstein's philosophies feels more compelling.

Fourth, we believe, however, that future advances in the real-time dynamics of the mechanisms of categorization may ultimately impact the necessity of choosing between philosophical positions. Consider that our research has shown that pigeons can apparently shift memorization strategies consistent with one philosophy or the other and that they can do so as a function of a particular trial's character string. Phenomena such as these encourage us to consider the possibility that different mechanisms compatible with either *Tractatus* or *Philosophical Investigations* may operate virtually simultaneously. That is, individual underlying mechanisms, such as rule-learning mechanisms or statistical-learning mechanisms, may resemble one philosophy more than the other (*Tractatus* or *Philosophical Investigations*, respectively). If we view the system as a whole, however, we may see performances that display features of both perspectives, so that an emerging literature on categorization, in particular, and on cognition, in general, may ultimately become more tolerant of what might appear, from the two philosophical perspectives, to be incoherence.

SUMMARY

Several psychological processes commonly associated more with human cognition than with nonhuman animal cognition have been identified in avian visual categorization. Pigeons learn abstract rules to categorize exemplars; pigeons demonstrate flexibility in how they memorize exemplars, that is, they demonstrate memorization strategies; pigeons switch attention between local and global levels of perceptual analysis; and in some cases, pigeons achieve levels of categorization performance that approach optimality.

We reviewed some of this evidence from our own experiments on how pigeons categorize rectangles varying in length and width or objects moving at varying speed and direction, how pigeons switch attention between local and global levels in hierarchically organized complex characters, and how they categorize character strings in artificial grammar learning tasks.

We gave perspective on these results by placing them in the context of Wittgenstein's two philosophies: those of *Tractatus* (1922) and *Philosophical Investigations* (1953). We suggested that certain traditional features of research consistent with *Tractatus*, especially unambiguous logic, parsimony, and highly simplified laboratory tasks, continue to describe some aspects of research, but there is a growing influence of features more consistent instead with *Philosophical Investigations*, especially influences from evolutionary biology and Gestalt psychology, in the form of naturalistic or everyday categorization and complex and ambiguous stimuli. We suggested that different research programs on categorization reveal different methodological commitments to one or another feature of Wittgenstein's two philosophies. A researcher's commitments may make some features of other research on categorization appear misguided, irrelevant, or simply wrong if the methodological commitments are different (Shimp, 2001, 2004a, 2004b). Finally, we suggested that some phenomena in avian categorization research imply that neither of Wittgenstein's philosophical perspectives provides a comprehensive account of categorization and that elements of both perspectives may be found to operate nearly simultaneously.

Acknowledgments The authors would like to thank Greg Ashby, Vince Filoteo, and Todd Maddox for their considerable assistance with our research on multidimensional categorization and Bryan Benham for his patient help with our views on Wittgenstein.

Note

1. While the term "grammar" carries linguistic connotations, artificial grammar learning appears to have relatively little to do with the notion of meaning as conveyed in natural language, but it has much to do with categorization and orthographic regularity (Herbranson & Shimp, 2003).

References

Ashby, F. G., & Ell, S. W. (2001). The neurobiological basis of category learning. *Trends in Cognitive Sciences, 5*, 204–210.

Ashby, F. G., & Gott, R. E. (1988). Decision rules in the perception and categorization of multidimensional stimuli. *Journal of Experimental Psychology: Learning, Memory, and Cognition, 14*, 33–53.

Ashby, F. G., & Maddox, W. T. (1998). Stimulus categorization. In M. H. Birnbaum (Ed.), *Measurement, judgment, and decision making: Handbook of perception and cognition* (pp. 251–301). San Diego, CA: Academic Press.

Blough, P. M. (1991). Selective attention and search images in pigeons. *Journal of Experimental Psychology: Animal Behavior Processes, 17*, 292–298.

Casseday, J. H., Fremouw, T., & Covey, E. (2002). The inferior colliculus: A hub for the central auditory system. In D. Oertel, R. R. Fay, & A. N. Popper (Eds.), *Integrative functions in the mammalian auditory pathway* (pp. 238–318). New York: Springer-Verlag.

Catania, A. C. (2005). The operant reserve: A computer simulation in (accelerated) real time. *Behavioural Processes, 69*, 257–278.

Chomsky, N., & Miller, G. A. (1958). Finite-state languages. *Information & Control, 1*, 91–112.

Cook, R. G. (Ed.). (2001). *Avian visual cognition.* Retrieved August 27, 2005, from http://www.pigeon.psy.tufts.edu/avc/.

Fitch, W. T., & Hauser, M. D. (2004). Computational constraints on syntactic processing in a nonhuman primate. *Science, 303*, 377–380.

Fremouw, T., Herbranson, W. T., & Shimp, C. P. (1998). Priming of attention to local or global levels of visual analysis. *Journal of Experimental Psychology: Animal Behavior Processes, 24*, 278–290.

Fremouw, T., Herbranson, W. T., & Shimp, C. P. (2002). Dynamic shifts of avian local/global attention. *Animal Cognition, 5*, 233–243.

Gardner, H. (1985). *The mind's new science: A history of the cognitive revolution.* New York: Basic Books.

Gould, S. J., & Lewontin, R. (1979). The spandrels of San Marco and the Panglossian paradigm: A critique of the adaptationist programme. *Proceedings of the Royal Society, B205*, 581–598.

Herbranson, W. T., Fremouw, T., & Shimp, C. P. (1999). The randomization procedure in the study of categorization of multi-dimensional stimuli by pigeons. *Journal of Experimental Psychology: Animal Behavior Processes, 25*, 113–135.

Herbranson, W. T., Fremouw, T., & Shimp, C. P. (2002). Categorizing a moving target in terms of its speed and direction. *Journal of the Experimental Analysis of Behavior (Special Issue on Categorization), 78*, 249–270.

Herbranson, W. T., & Shimp, C. P. (2003). Artificial grammar learning in pigeons: A preliminary analysis. *Learning & Behavior, 31*, 98–106.

Herrnstein, R. J., & Loveland, D. H. (1964). Complex visual concepts in the pigeon. *Science, 146*, 549–551.

Jen, P. H., Chen, Q. C., & Sun, X. D. (1998). Corticofugal regulation of auditory sensitivity in the bat inferior colliculus. *Journal of Comparative Physiology [A], 183*, 683–697.

Kahneman, D., Slovic, P., & Tversky, S. (1982). *Judgment under uncertainty: Heuristics and biases.* Cambridge: Cambridge University Press.

Lamb, M. R., London, B., Pond, H. M., & Whitt, K. A. (1998). Automatic and controlled processes in the analysis of hierarchical structure. *Psychological Science, 9*, 14–19.

Lamb, M. R., & Robertson, L. C. (1988). The processing of hierarchical stimuli: Effects of retinal locus, locational uncertainty, and stimulus identity. *Perception and Psychophysics, 21*, 226–232.

Lamb, M. R., Yund, E. W., & Pond, H. M. (1999). Is attentional selection to different levels of hierarchical structure based on spatial frequency? *Journal of Experimental Psychology: General, 128*, 88–94.

Ma, X., & Suga, N. (2003). Augmentation of plasticity of the central auditory system by the basal forebrain and/or somatosensory cortex. *Journal of Neurophysiology, 89*, 90–103.

Malloy, T. E., Jensen, G. C., Song, T., Herbranson, W. T., Fremouw, T., & Shimp, C. P. (2001). Interactive demonstration of avian categorization. Retrieved September 15, 2005, from http://www.psych.utah.edu/shimp/Avian_Categorization.htm.

Medin, D. L., & Schaffer, M. M. (1978). Context theory of classification learning. *Psychological Review, 85*, 207–238.

Navon, D. (1977). Forest before trees: The precedence of global features in visual perception. *Cognitive Psychology, 9*, 353–383.

Navon, D. (1981). The forest revisited: More on global precedence. *Psychological Research, 43*, 1–32.

Plaisted, K. (1997). The effect of interstimulus interval on the discrimination of cryptic targets. *Journal of Experimental Psychology: Animal Behavior Processes, 23,* 248–259.

Plous, S. (1998). Signs of change within the animal rights movement: Results from a follow-up survey of activists. *Journal of Comparative Psychology, 112,* 48–54.

Reber, A. S. (1967). Implicit learning of artificial grammars. *Journal of Verbal Learning & Verbal Behavior, 6,* 855–863.

Reber, A. S. (1989). Implicit learning and tacit knowledge. *Journal of Experimental Psychology: General, 118,* 219–235.

Ryle, G. (1949). *The concept of mind.* London: Hutchinson & Co.

Seidenberg, M. S., MacDonald, M. C., & Saffran, J. R. (2002). Does grammar start where statistics stop? *Science, 298,* 553–554.

Shimp, C. P. (1979). The local organization of behavior: Method and theory. In M. D. Zeiler & P. Harzem (Eds.), *Advances in analysis of behavior, Vol. 1: Reinforcement and the organization of behavior* (pp. 262–298). Chichester, UK: Wiley.

Shimp, C. P. (1984a). Relations between memory and operant behavior, according to an associative learner (AL). *Canadian Journal of Psychology (Special Issue on Animal Memory), 38,* 269–284.

Shimp, C. P. (1984b). Timing, learning and forgetting. In J. Gibbon & L. Allan (Eds.), *Timing and time perception,* Vol. 423 (pp. 346–360). New York: New York Academy of Sciences.

Shimp, C. P. (1989). Contemporary behaviorism versus the old behavioral straw man in Gardner's *The mind's new science: A history of the cognitive revolution. Journal of the Experimental Analysis of Behavior, 51,* 163–171.

Shimp, C. P. (1992). Computational behavior dynamics: An interpretation of Nevin (1969). *Journal of the Experimental Analysis of Behavior (Special Issue on Behavior Dynamics), 57,* 289–299.

Shimp, C. P. (1994). Computational behavior and behavior analysis: An interpretation of Catania and Reynolds (1968). In E. Ribes Inesta (Ed.), *B. F. Skinner, In memoriam.* Guadualajara, Mexico: University of Guadalajara Press. (In Spanish)

Shimp, C. P. (2001). Behavior as a social construction. *Behavioural Processes, 54,* 11–32.

Shimp, C. P. (2004a). Ambiguity, logic, simplicity, and dynamics: Wittgensteinian evaluative criteria in peer review of quantitative research on categorization. *Behavioural Processes, 66,* 333–348.

Shimp, C. P. (2004b). Scientific peer review: A case study from local and global analyses. *Journal of the Experimental Analysis of Behavior, 82,* 103–116.

Shimp, C. P., Childers, L. J., & Hightower, F. A. (1990). Local patterns in human operant behavior and a behaving model to interrelate animal and human performances. *Journal of Experimental Psychology: Animal Behavior Processes, 16,* 200–212.

Shimp, C. P., & Friedrich, F. J. (1993). Behavioral and computational models of spatial attention. *Journal of Experimental Psychology: Animal Behavior Processes, 19,* 26–37.

Shimp, C. P., Herbranson, W. T., & Fremouw, T. (2001). Avian visual attention in science and culture. In R. G. Cook (Ed.), *Avian visual cognition.* Retrieved August 27, 2005, from http://www.pigeon.psy.tufts.edu/avc/shimp/.

Shulman, G. L., & Wilson, J. (1987). Spatial frequency and selective attention to local and global information. *Perception, 16,* 89–101.

Smith, D. J., Shields, W. E., & Washburn, D. A. (2003). The comparative psychology of uncertainty monitoring and metacognition. *Behavioral and Brain Sciences, 26,* 317–373.

Staddon, J. E. R. (2001). *The new behaviorism: Mind, mechanism, and society.* Philadelphia, PA: Taylor & Francis.

Staddon, J. E. R., & Higa, J. J. (1999). Time and memory: Towards a pacemaker-free theory of interval timing. *Journal of the Experimental Analysis of Behavior, 71,* 215–251.

Suga, N., Gao, E., Zhang, Y., Ma, X., & Olsen, J. F. (2000). The corticofugal system for hearing: Recent progress. *Proceedings of the National Academy of Science U S A, 97,* 11807–11814.

Tinbergen, L. (1960). The natural control of insects in pinewoods. I. Factors influencing the intensity of predation by songbirds. *Archives Neerlandaises de Zoologie, 13,* 265–343.

Wittgenstein, L. (1922). *Tractatus logico-philosophicus.* London: Routledge & Kegan Paul.

Wittgenstein, L. (1953). *Philosophical investigations.* New York: Macmillan.

Wright, A. A. (2001). *Learning strategies in matching to sample.* In R. G. Cook (Ed.), *Avian visual cognition.* Retrieved August 27, 2005, from http://www.pigeon.psy.tufts.edu/avc/wright.

Yan, J., & Suga, N. (1996). Corticofugal modulation of time-domain processing of biosonar information in bats. *Science, 273,* 1100–1103.

Zhang, Y., & Suga, N. (1997). Corticofugal amplification of subcortical responses to single tone stimuli in the mustached bat. *Journal of Neurophysiology, 78,* 3489–3492.

Zhou, X., & Jen, P. H. S. (2000). Brief and short-term corticofugal modulation of subcortical auditory responses in the big brown bat, *Eptesicus fucus. Journal of Neurophysiology, 84,* 3083–3087.

21

Responses and Acquired Equivalence Classes

PETER J. URCUIOLI

The topic of this chapter is captured in the following remark by Dollard and Miller in their book *Personality and Psychotherapy*:

> Attaching the same cue-producing response to two distinctive stimulus objects gives them a certain *learned equivalence* increasing the extent to which instrumental and emotional responses will generalize from one to the other. (1950, p. 101)

What Dollard and Miller were saying was that humans (and, as we will see, other animals) will treat disparate things as belonging to the same class or category if they have learned to respond to them in the same manner. By definition, this type of equivalence is acquired through experience rather than being based on the inherent physical similarities between objects (Bhatt, Wasserman, Reynolds, & Knauss, 1988; Herrnstein & Loveland, 1964). More important, such learned or acquired equivalences produce behavioral effects that go beyond immediate training, as indicated by the mention of increased generalization. This increased generalization refers to the fact that other behavior directly conditioned or otherwise already occurring to some members of an equivalence class will, without explicit training, also occur to other class members (Goldiamond, 1962).

In their earlier book, *Social Learning and Imitation*, Miller and Dollard (1941) gave a hypothetical example of how a tribesman might show increased within-class generalization as a result of common-response training:

> The tribesman may learn at different times to respond to each of a number of different people with the same word, "enemy." . . . Once this response is learned, the cue which it produces may mediate the transfer of other responses . . . retreating, threatening, fighting, etc. . . . to any other person whom he calls an enemy. (p. 75)

Their example is also noteworthy because it suggests that even perceptually coherent groups of objects like "people" (Wasserman, Kiedinger, & Bhatt, 1988) can subdivide into discriminably different classes, like enemies and nonenemies (or friends), on the basis of the common responses occasioned by subsets of the group.

Learned or acquired equivalence classes, then, greatly expand the number and composition of categories that animals (including humans) can form. Like their perceptually based counterparts, learned or acquired equivalence classes provide considerable behavioral economy, in the sense that we need not learn through direct conditioning (Shipley, 1935) how to respond to each and every class member. Acquired equivalence also appears to be synonymous with the cognitive term "conceptualization" (Herrnstein, 1990; Lea, 1984) precisely because it does not require physical resemblance between class members (e.g., consider articles of clothing, toys, or modes of transportation). This type of experience-based categorization also permits more rapid adjustments to changing circumstances than do perceptually based categories, a point that can be appreciated by considering the change in reactions toward those who are no longer "enemies" but are "friends" (Miller & Dollard, 1941, p. 76; cf. Vaughan, 1988).

It can be tempting, especially in view of examples like those given, to regard human language as a necessary ingredient in the development of acquired equivalence. It is not. Although human language can facilitate class formation, given that many common responses to objects are the verbal labels we use to refer to them (e.g., Eikeseth & Smith, 1992; Lowe, Horne, Harris, & Randle, 2002), our names for things are just one *example* of common responding. There are many nonverbal, non–language-based responses that should, and indeed do, function in the manner described by Miller and Dollard.

This chapter describes research from my laboratory and those of colleagues and collaborators on the development and detection of acquired equivalence in pigeons and on the processes involved in it. Training pigeons to respond (peck) in a common fashion to distinctly different stimuli brings together those stimuli. This acquired equivalence is often revealed by showing that new behavior learned to just *some* of the originally trained stimuli transfers to *other* stimuli in the common-response class. This is an example of the within-class generalization mentioned by Dollard and Miller (1950, p. 101).

The first section of this chapter describes an acquired equivalence paradigm and some basic phenomena. Here, I illustrate the acquired equivalence litmus test, within-class generalization, show how it depends on common-response training, and draw parallels between the effects obtained in pigeons and those obtained in humans. The second section takes up the theoretical issue of what mechanism permits the generalization of new behavior across class members. The seminal idea about this generalization was proposed by Hull (1939) and is expressed in both of the opening citations: response-mediated (a.k.a. secondary) generalization. In short, the common responses conditioned to each class member have distinctive stimulus features that, even in their anticipatory form, can become "attached" to other behavior. As we shall see, however, there are data at odds with the mediated generalization explanation, thus raising the issue of how we should view the categorical properties of stimuli in an acquired equivalence class. The last section considers another type of relation between responding and equivalence classes—specifically, the possibility that different responses can themselves become class members.

Table 21.1. Two Equivalent Schematics of Common-Response/Many-to-One Training (Initial) and the Reassignment-Testing Procedure for Acquired Equivalence

Training		
Initial	Reassignment	*Testing*
S1 → R1+		
S2 → R2+	S1 → R3+	S3 → R3+
S3 → R1+	S2 → R4+	S4 → R4+
S4 → R2+		
A—B	A—D	C—D
C—B		

RESPONSES AS A SOURCE OF ACQUIRED EQUIVALENCE

To assist in the description of the experiments and data, table 21.1 presents two schematics of the common-response training and within-class generalization test procedures often used in studies of acquired equivalence. Individual stimuli and the responses required to them are depicted in the top portion of the table. The bottom portion of the table shows a condensed version of the top schematic using a notation commonly used in the human equivalence literature.

In initial training, subjects learn to make the same reinforced response (R1) to two different stimuli (S1 and S3) and an alternative reinforced response (R2) to two other stimuli (S2 and S4). Stimuli occasioning a common response are connected to each other by lines to emphasize this shared association and the potential for an acquired equivalence between them. With pigeons, S1-S4 are often the sample stimuli in two-choice matching-to-sample, and R1 and R2 are the choice responses made to the comparison alternatives that follow the sample on each matching trial. Only the correct/reinforced (+) choice response for each sample is shown in the schematic; the incorrect or nonreinforced choice is simply the response to the alternative comparison. This particular procedure is called many-to-one matching: multiple (many) samples occasion a single (common) choice response. Another way to represent the many-to-one relation is to use pairs of letters, the first of which represents the samples and the second of which represents the reinforced responses. Here, two sets of samples (A and C) are mapped onto a single or common set (B) of responses, as shown in the bottom half of the table.

Accurate many-to-one performance, by itself, does not mean that an acquired equivalence has developed between S1 and S3 or between S2 and S4. It is possible, for instance, that highly trained and highly accurate subjects have simply learned a set of independent stimulus-response relations (in this example, four of them). To establish an acquired equivalence, it is necessary to show that common-response training has increased within-class generalization between the ostensible class members.

Urcuioli, Zentall, Jackson-Smith, and Steirn (1989, Experiment 1) obtained some preliminary evidence for acquired equivalence by examining the effects of different types of trial-to-trial transitions in delayed many-to-one matching (i.e., with a retention interval separating the samples from the choice alternatives). An established finding in delayed matching with just two sample stimuli (e.g., red and green) is that accuracy on the retention (choice-response) test of a trial is lower if the sample on the preceding trial differs from the current one. Thus, if red = S1 and green = S2, subjects make more errors following S2 if the preceding trial required them to match S1 rather than S2. This effect is explained by postulating an antagonism between the physically based memory codes for the two different samples: The code operative on a previous trial proactively interferes with the current-trial code (Wright, Urcuioli, & Sands, 1986).

In many-to-one matching, there are (at least) three other samples that physically differ from the one occurring on a previous trial, and at least two often come from an entirely different stimulus dimension (e.g., S3 and S4 = white vertical and horizontal lines, respectively). Nonetheless, if common-response training produces an [S1, S3] acquired equivalence class and an [S2, S4] class, then accuracy involving an "across-dimension" sample should also be lower if the prior-trial sample came from the opposite class than if it came from the same class. Specifically, matching with S3 should be less accurate following an S2 trial than following an S1 trial; conversely, matching with S4 should be less accurate following S1 than S2.

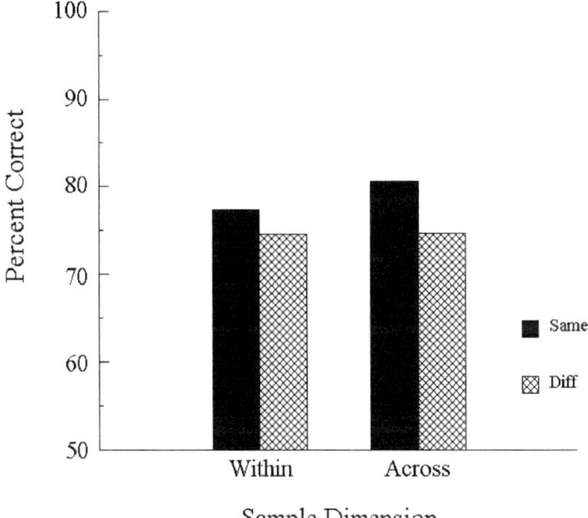

Figure 21.1. Pigeons' accuracy on delayed many-to-one matching as a function of whether the sample stimulus on Trial N occasioned the same or different choice response as the sample on Trial N-1 and whether the sample transition was within a stimulus dimension or across dimensions. (Adapted from "Evidence for Common Coding in Many-to-One Matching: Retention, Intertrial Interference, and Transfer, by P. J. Urcuioli, T. R. Zentall, P. Jackson-Smith, and J. N. Steirn, 1989, *Journal of Experimental Psychology: Animal Behavior Processes, 15*, 264–273, Experiment 1.)

Figure 21.1 shows that this pattern of results is exactly what occurs: Choice responding is less accurate on across-dimension, trial-to-trial transitions when the sample on the preceding trial is *associatively* different from the current-trial sample. (The typical within-dimension effect is also apparent.) Another way to think about these findings is that an acquired equivalence between S1 and S3, and between S2 and S4, increased within-class generalization of the choices responses they occasioned, such that performances were enhanced when trial-to-trial transitions involved samples from the same class.

Although consistent with acquired equivalence, these data provide, at best, only indirect evidence for class formation. A more conclusive test is one in which *new* responses learned to a subset of the putative class members are shown to generalize (emerge) to the other class members (Goldiamond, 1962). The full schematics in table 21.1 show how this sort of within-class generalization or transfer test is conducted. Following common-response (many-to-one) training, one member from each putative class (e.g., S1 and S2) is explicitly trained to occasion a new response (e.g., R3 and R4). Stated otherwise, one set of stimuli (A) now occasions a new set of responses (D). Following this so-called reassignment training (Wasserman, DeVolder, & Coppage, 1992), generalization of the new responses to the other (untrained or nonreassigned) class members (S3 and S4) is assessed. If the initial, common-response training had indeed produced two acquired equivalence classes, [S1, S3] and [S2, S4], then the new response learned to S1 should generalize more readily to S3 than to S4; likewise, the new response learned to S2 should generalize more readily to S4 than to S3.

Figure 21.2 shows first-session performances of pigeons given this sort of generalization test following many-to-one and reassignment training. The data in the left half of the figure show performances when the reinforced R3 and R4 choices following S3 and S4 (viz., C-D relations) were consistent with [S1, S3] and [S2, S4] classes: R3 was reinforced after S3, and R4 after S4 (cf. table 21.1). For these birds, accuracy was above chance, as an acquired equivalence/within-class generalization account would expect. The data in the right half of the figure show performances of other pigeons whose reinforced C-D relations during testing were *in*consistent with an [S1, S3] and an [S2, S4] acquired equivalence: R4 was reinforced after S3, and R3 after S4. Accuracy for these birds was below chance. In fact, for the "inconsistent" birds, too, there was greater generalization of R3 to S3 and R4 to S4, but these were the "wrong" (nonreinforced) choices in testing.

The large difference in accuracy between reinforcing class-consistent versus class-inconsistent responses in testing definitively shows that common-response (many-to-one) training does something more than produce learning of four independent sample-response relations. Specifically, pigeons treated S1 and S3, and S2 and S4, as belonging together (i.e., in the same class), creating an interchangeability between stimuli that transcended the explicitly reinforced responses that each stimulus occasioned in training. We (Urcuioli et al., 1989) originally called this effect "common coding," because pigeons had apparently coded the common *associative* features of the sample stimuli in addition to their physical features.

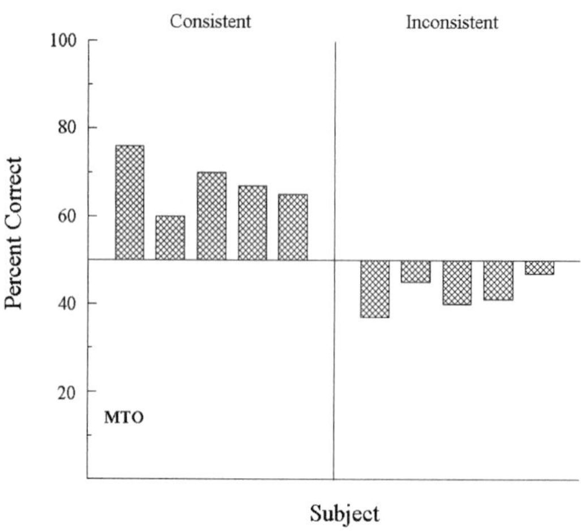

Figure 21.2. Matching accuracy by individual pigeons on novel sample-comparison relations that were either consistent or inconsistent with acquired sample equivalence following many-to-one training. (Adapted from "The Role of Common Responses in Acquired Sample Equivalence," by P. J. Urcuioli and K. M. Lionello-DeNolf, 2005, *Behavioural Processes, 69*, 207–222.)

A subsequent experiment (Zentall, Sherburne, & Urcuioli, 1993) showed how common coding could eliminate or reverse the normally disruptive effects of interpolating a stimulus during the retention interval of delayed matching-to-sample. Pigeons were initially trained on 0-delay many-to-one matching followed by reassignment training in which two samples, one from each common-response pair, were matched to new choice alternatives (cf. table 21.1). During reassignment training, 75% of the matching trials had a 2-s retention interval separating the sample to be matched and the choice alternatives. In testing, the reassignment task was split between baseline delayed matching trials and trials on which one of the remaining (nonreassigned) samples from many-to-one matching was inserted into the retention interval. On half of the latter trials, the interpolated stimulus was the sample that originally shared a common-response association with the sample to be matched; on the other half, the interpolated stimulus was from the other common-response set. This test amounts to a within-subject consistent versus inconsistent manipulation, in which the potentially interfering stimulus generated a "code" either associatively consistent or inconsistent with

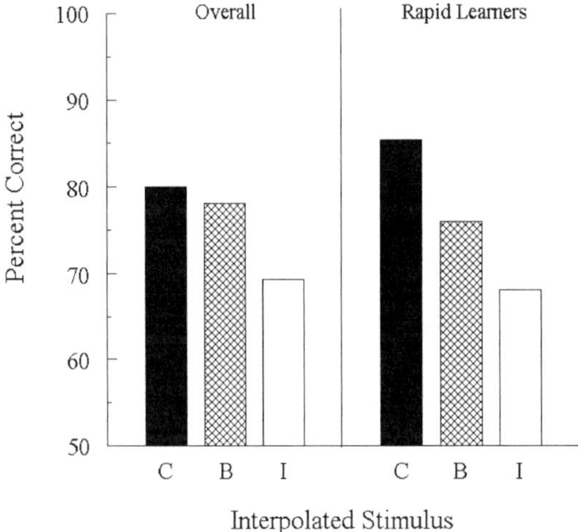

Figure 21.3. Delayed matching accuracy by pigeons as a function of whether a stimulus interpolated during the retention interval belonged to the same acquired equivalence class as the sample to be matched (class consistent) or to a different class (class inconsistent). B = baseline accuracy with no interpolated stimulus. (Adapted from "Common Coding by Pigeons in a Many-to-One Delayed Matching Task as Evidenced by Facilitation and Interference Effects," by T. R. Zentall, L. M. Sherburne, and P. J. Urcuioli, 1993, *Animal Learning & Behavior*, *21*, 233–237.)

the sample to be matched. Figure 21.3 shows the results.

Averaged across all eight subjects, an interpolated stimulus from the same common-response set as the sample to be matched (i.e., an associatively *c*onsistent stimulus) yielded the same level of choice accuracy on the retention test as that on baseline (no-interpolated-stimulus) trials. A stimulus from the other common-response set (i.e., an associatively *i*nconsistent stimulus), on the other hand, caused choice accuracy to drop substantially relative to baseline. For the four pigeons that acquired the baseline reassignment task most rapidly, the common-response or associatively consistent interpolated stimulus actually produced higher accuracy on the retention test than on baseline trials. The latter results in particular can be seen as another instance of within-class generalization: An interpolated stimulus from the same acquired equivalence class as the nominal sample preferentially cued the same, new choice response.

Do these within-class generalization effects truly depend on common-response training? Is it possible that similar results might be obtained even if the sample stimuli in original training did *not* occasion the same choice response? Although counterbalancing of reassignment relations in the three-stage many-to-one paradigm (cf. table 21.1) makes it very unlikely that the consistent versus inconsistent differences seen in testing arise from other uncontrolled factors, a definitive test of the importance of common-response associations in producing this pattern of results requires a separate (control) group in which each sample occasions a *unique* choice response. Its initial training can be designated A-B, C-X; otherwise, reassignment training and testing are exactly as shown in table 21.1. This "one-to-one" control group should not show preferential generalization of R3 (or R4) to either S3 or S4, except as would occur by chance; so, its first-session test accuracy should, on average, be close to chance. Urcuioli and Lionello-DeNolf (2005) recently confirmed this prediction, as seen in the top half of figure 21.4. Birds trained without common-response relations during initial training (Group OTO) matched R3 and R4 to S3 and S4 (the C-D relations) at chance levels. Also shown are the average performances of the consistent and inconsistent many-to-one (MTO) pigeons seen in figure 21.2. Thus, when each sample stimulus occasions a different response, that stimulus is in a class by itself.

The bottom half of figure 21.4 shows comparable results obtained from human subjects (Grover, Horton, & Cunningham, 1967), who were initially trained on a paired-associate task in which different stimulus terms either shared a common response (A-B, C-B) or did not (A-B, C-X). The stimuli were CVC syllables and the responses were past-tense verbs. Later, both groups learned new verb responses to the A stimuli (A-D), after which they were required to learn (and were thus tested on) C-D pairs. Half of the common-response (or many-to-one) subjects learned C-D pairs consistent with an acquired equivalence between the syllables originally paired with the same past-tense verb and the other half learned inconsistent C-D pairs. The performance measure, correct anticipation of the D response to the C stimuli, shows a pattern exactly like that exhibited by pigeons in two-choice matching.

There are many other studies showing these sorts of within-class generalization effects arising from common-response training or from procedures in which common responses develop to multiple stimuli as a result of training. For example, using a two-choice procedure and design almost

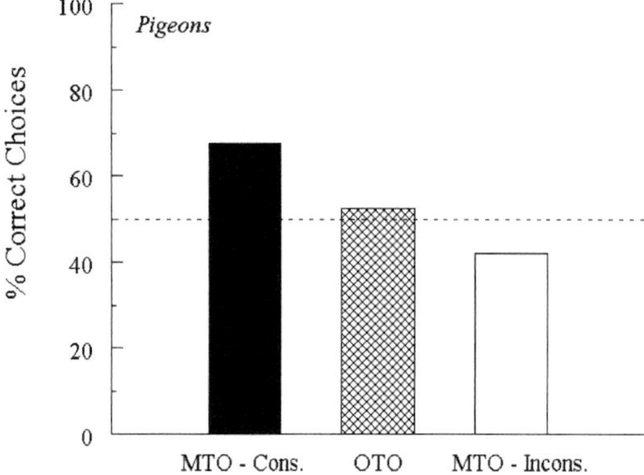

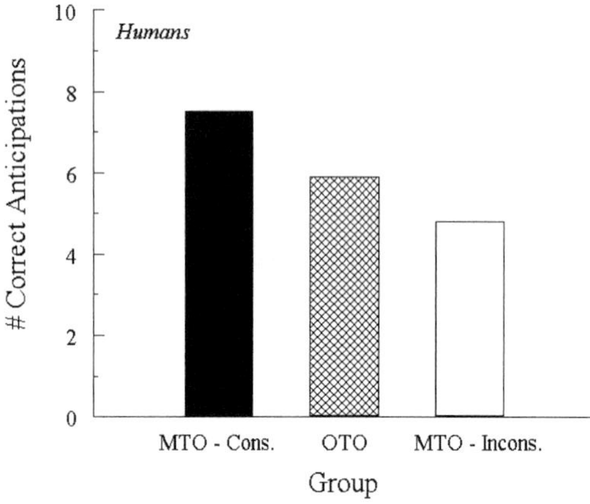

Figure 21.4. *Top*, First-session transfer performance by pigeons on novel sample-comparison relations following many-to-one (MTO) or one-to-one (OTO) matching and reassignment training. Transfer relations in the MTO conditions were either consistent or inconsistent with acquired sample equivalence. (Reprinted from "The Role of Common Responses in Acquired Sample Equivalence," by P. J. Urcuioli and K. M. Lionello-DeNolf, 2005, *Behavioural Processes, 69*, 207–222, with permission from Elsevier.) *Bottom*, Correct anticipation by humans of new responses to stimuli in a paired-associate task as a function of whether those stimuli were initially paired with the same responses (MTO) or unique responses (OTO) in training and whether there was a consistent or inconsistent mapping of the new responses to the MTO stimuli. (Adapted from Mediated Facilitation and Interference in a Four-Stage Paradigm," by D. E. Grover, D. L. Horton, and M. Cunningham, Jr., 1967, *Journal of Verbal Learning and Verbal Behavior, 4*, 42–46.)

identical to the one used with pigeons, Spradlin, Cotter, and Baxley (1973, Experiments 1 and 2) reported very strong C-D transfer in retarded adolescents initially trained on many-to-one matching. Wasserman and DeVolder (1993) showed within-class generalization effects *between* sets of photographs depicting different object categories (e.g., flowers and chairs) that previously occasioned the same response in preschool-aged children, a finding that replicated an earlier experiment with pigeons (Wasserman et al, 1992).

Bovet and Vauclair (1998, Experiment 1) initially gave baboons 41 different food objects and 41 different nonfood objects and found that, after training to pull one rope after seeing one food object (an apple) and to pull a different rope after seeing one nonfood object (a padlock), the rope-pulling response generalized to the remaining objects in the food and nonfood groups. Note that implicit in the initial exposure phase were common responses to food objects (eating) and to nonfood objects (manipulating). In differential Pavlovian eye blink conditioning with humans, Grice and Davis (1958; see also Grice, 1965b) reported greater generalization of the eye blink CR to a CS– to which subjects had to make the same lever-switching response as that required to the CS+ than to another CS– that required a different response. Foss and Jenkins (1966) manipulated the number of stimuli mapped onto the same response in paired associate learning and, like Grover et al. (1967), found that, with larger ratios, many-to-one training produced more or less accurate C-D performances relative to controls as a function of whether the stimulus-response mappings in testing were consistent or inconsistent, respectively, with the common-response classes (see also James & Hake, 1965). Finally, Lippa and Goldstone (2001) reported that spatially ambiguous or spatially neutral pictures acquire the left versus right response-biasing properties of arrows and fingers pointing in those directions if the spatially ambiguous/neutral stimuli occasioned the same categorical response ("up" versus "down") in humans as the spatially biased stimuli.

To this point, I've described the within-class generalization test results as indicating that *stimuli* will join the same acquired equivalence class if they occasion a common response. However, as Spradlin et al. (1973) noted, the initial and reassignment training phases in the many-to-one transfer design contain features conducive not only to the development of stimulus classes, but of response classes

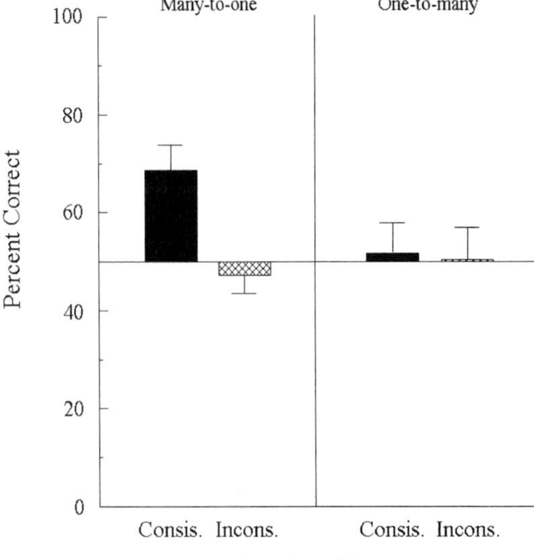

Figure 21.5. First-session transfer by pigeons to novel sample-comparison relations after training on the same set of baseline relations (A-B, C-B, and A-D) learned within the context of either many-to-one or one-to-many matching. Transfer (C-D) relations were either consistent or inconsistent with an acquired equivalence between the samples occasioning the same comparison response in training. (Adapted from "Transfer to Derived Sample-Comparison Relations by Pigeons Following Many-to-One Versus One-to-Many Matching with Identical Training Relations," by P. J. Urcuioli, T. R. Zentall, and T. DeMarse, 1995, *Quarterly Journal of Experimental Psychology*, *48B*, 158–178.)

too (Jenkins, 1963; Jenkins & Palermo, 1964). In other words, different responses (B and D) to the same stimulus (A)—note the A-B and A-D relations in Initial and Reassignment Training, respectively, in table 21.1—may become members of an equivalent class of *responses*. If so, then any other stimulus that exerts control over one of the responses (C-B) should control others in the same response class (C-D). Response equivalence, then, can generate accurate test performances if subjects match members of the same response class to the same antecedent stimulus.

The pigeon data, however, do not seem susceptible to this alternative interpretation. The reason is that if pigeons are explicitly trained from the outset to match one set of sample stimuli to two sets of comparison choice alternatives (i.e., A-B, A-D or "one-to-many" matching), they do *not* show the same pattern of transfer (C-D matching results) following reassignment training in which one set of responses is matched to new samples (C-B). In other words, the class-consistent versus class-inconsistent test differences seen after many-to-one matching are not apparent after one-to-many training, as figure 21.5 shows.

These data are especially noteworthy because pigeons in both groups, many-to-one and one-to-many, learned exactly the same set of baseline relations (A-B, C-B, and A-D) prior to testing. Despite this equilibration, the common-response associations in the many-to-one group generated an acquired equivalence between the occasioning samples, whereas common-stimulus associations in the one-to-many group did not produce an acquired equivalence between the different responses occasioned by each sample stimulus (Urcuioli & Lionello-DeNolf, 2001; Urcuioli, Zentall, & DeMarse, 1995).

MEDIATED GENERALIZATION: RESPONSES AS MEDIATORS OF C-D TRANSFER

Within-class generalization is a defining characteristic of acquired equivalence (Dollard & Miller, 1950; Goldiamond, 1962; Hull, 1939). It demonstrates an interchangeability or substitutability of stimuli for one another in their control over behavior that did not exist prior to common-response training or following training with other types of shared associations (e.g., Peterson, 1984; Urcuioli & Zentall, 1992; see also Zentall, Clement, & Weaver, 2003). The question addressed in this section is, By what *mechanism* is that interchangeability or substitutability realized? Does common-response training introduce new forms of stimulus control, such that explicit reassignment training with some class members automatically empowers the untrained class members to control new behavior?

Hull (1939) proposed that the mechanism underlying within-class generalization involves the common responses themselves—more specifically, the response-produced stimuli to which these responses give rise. His idea, known variously as secondary or mediated generalization (also response-mediated or anticipatory mediated generalization), is mentioned by Dollard and Miller (1950, p. 101) as "the same *cue-producing* response" (italics added). In short, the stimulus properties associated with the common responses acquire control over behavior.

For instance, when Grice and Davis (1958) required human subjects to make the same instrumental response to one CS– as to the CS+ in eye blink conditioning, their finding that eye blink CRs preferentially generalized more from the CS+ to that CS– is explicable if the cue-producing properties of that instrumental response had become associated with (a signal for) the UCS on CS+ trials. Generalization of the CRs was mediated, in other words, by that common response.

The purported mediator in the Grice and Davis paradigm was clearly observable, but applying this sort of analysis to pigeons' many-to-one matching requires postulating covert responses. Nonetheless, the logic and the mechanics of the mediated generalization account remain essentially the same (Urcuioli, 1996).

The top half of table 21.2 shows how this account could be applied to many-to-one matching. After many-to-one matching has been acquired to high levels of accuracy, the A and C samples not only directly control the same correct choice responses (B), but they presumably also give rise to the anticipation of those choices. ("Prospective coding" is another term for these anticipatory reactions [Honig & Thompson, 1982].) When one set of samples (A) is later matched to new choice responses (D), the anticipatory ("b") responses to A should also acquire control over the D choices, especially if continued, refresher training is provided on the original many-to-one task (cf. Urcuioli et al., 1989, 1995). These "b"-D associative links are shown under Reassignment (Phase 2) Training and represent this hypothesized stimulus control relation. Any other sample, then, that generates those same anticipatory responses—for example, the C samples in Testing—should cue the appropriate (i.e., class-consistent) D choices despite no direct training to do so. In short, within-class generalization of new (D) responses from the explicitly trained A samples in Reassignment to the "untrained" C samples in Testing occurs via their common, anticipatory-response mediators.

This theoretical account clearly predicts the consistent versus inconsistent transfer results following many-to-one training (cf. figure 21.2). In addition, it correctly predicts no transfer if the A and C samples occasion different choice responses during training (cf. figure 21.3) given that, under these conditions, the A and C samples cannot, by definition, give rise to a common mediator. Likewise, the absence of a consistent versus inconsistent difference in testing after initial one-to-many training is theoretically compatible on the assumption that subjects cannot reliably anticipate a particular choice response if each sample is followed unpredictably and equally often by two different reinforced choice alternatives (Urcuioli et al., 1995). The latter prediction is especially noteworthy because, after reassignment training in the one-to-many paradigm, the A and C samples do occasion common responses, albeit across separate training phases. Despite this fact, they do not exhibit the within-class generalization effect so routinely obtained following many-to-one training (Astley & Wasserman, 1998; Urcuioli et al., 1989, 1995; Wasserman et al., 1992; see also Ward-Robinson & Hall, 1999).

The mediated generalization account of acquired equivalence is also supported by studies in the human and animal literatures showing sizeable transfer effects when the (potentially) mediating common responses explicitly occur during reassignment and transfer (e.g., Birge, 1941; James & Hake, 1965; Jeffrey, 1953; Urcuioli & Honig, 1980; see also McIntire, Cleary, & Thompson, 1987). Nonetheless, the mediated generalization account cannot provide the sole explanation for within-class generalization effects.

For example, Grice (1965a) reported that the temporal dynamics of the instrumental response in his differential conditioning studies were at odds with their purported role as mediators of eye-blink generalization between the CS+ and the same-response CS–. For instance, the instrumental response very often occurred in conjunction with or after the CR. To reasonably explain generalization between CSs, this response (and its cue-producing properties) ought to consistently precede the CR.

More recently, we (Urcuioli & Lionello-DeNolf, 2001) conducted a direct test of anticipatory mediated generalization in many-to-one matching and also found results incompatible with this account. Our test involved measuring C-D transfer when many-to-one matching preceded reassignment training (the typical training sequence) versus when it followed such training. The experimental design of our study is shown in the bottom half of table 21.2. When many-to-one matching was the first task in the training sequence, response-mediation processes should be able operate in the fashion hypothesized by Hull (1939; cf. top half of table 21.2). However, when many-to-one training followed A-D matching (i.e., occurred second in the training sequence), any anticipatory "b" reactions developing

Table 21.2. Schematic Depiction of the Response-Mediated Generalization Account of Acquired Equivalence (*Top*) and a Procedure to Test It (*Bottom*)

Training		
Initial (Phase 1)	Reassignment (Phase 2)	*Testing*
A—B C—B	"b" A △ D	"b" C △ D

Group	*Training* Phase 1	*Training* Phase 2	*Testing*
First	A—B C—B	A—D	C—D
Second	A—D	A—B C—B	C—D

From Urcuioli and Lionello-DeNolf, 2001.

to the A and C samples should be unable to link to the D choices, because the latter have already been acquired during Phase 1 training. Consequently, Group Second should not show the typical consistent versus inconsistent differences in test (C-D) performances—that is, there should be no within-class generalization of the D choices from the A to the C samples.

To the contrary, however, transfer was clearly evident in this group (as well as in Group First). Figure 21.6 plots the accuracy of C-D matching over five successive transfer sessions for birds that learned many-to-one matching after reassignment training (Group Second) and those that learned that task initially (Group First). In both cases, higher accuracy in the consistent than in the consistent test condition is clearly apparent.

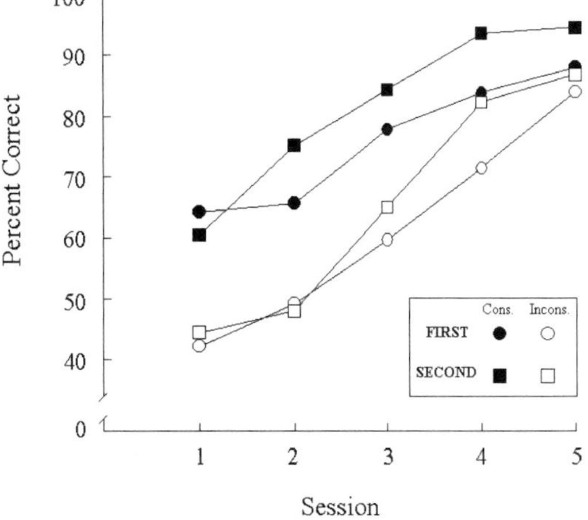

Figure 21.6. Matching accuracy by pigeons on novel sample-comparison relations following many-to-one and reassignment training in which many-to-one matching was either learned first (prior to reassignment) or second (after reassignment). Transfer relations were either consistent or inconsistent with acquired sample equivalence. (Adapted from Some Tests of the Anticipatory Mediated Generalization Model of Acquired Sample Equivalence in Pigeons' Many-to-One Matching," by P. J. Urcuioli and K. M. Lionello-DeNolf, 2001, *Animal Learning & Behavior*, *29*, 265–280.)

Jeffrey (1953) also used a reversed training order like our Group Second in his study of the effects of common-response training in preschool-aged children. Children named or manually responded to a gray stimulus card in the same way as they did to either a black or a white card. Most were required to make these potentially mediating responses during transfer and during immediately preceding refresher sessions on an initially learned "reassignment task." Children in two control groups, however, were not permitted to make the common response during refresher training nor during testing. Nonetheless, Jeffrey found a significant tendency by control subjects to make the same transfer-test response to gray as to the black (or white) stimulus with which it had shared a common-response association. Although nothing prohibited the control subjects from implicitly making the potentially mediating responses (especially when the cards were named), a mediated generalization explanation of their results would, at a minimum, seem to be stretched.

Likewise, the spatial biasing (transfer) effects reported by Lippa and Goldstone (2001) for otherwise ambiguous or neutral stimuli that occasioned the same "up" versus "down" response as left- versus right-pointing stimuli were evident even though the "reassignment" response, the response used to assess acquired equivalence (viz., left versus right reactions), had been learned and practiced well before common-response training.

Finally, Urcuioli et al. (1994, Experiment 1; see also Zentall et al., 1995) found retention asymmetries in pigeons' many-to-one delayed matching that also contradict the idea that anticipatory responses develop to the common-response samples. Table 21.3 shows the many-to-one contingencies used in Urcuioli et al. (1994). The task involved six different samples: two hues (red and green), two behaviors (20 pecks and 1 peck at a white triangle), and two hedonic events (presentation of food or "no food" = feeder light without food). One choice response (R1) was reinforced following the red hue, 20 pecks, and food, whereas the alternative choice response (R2) was reinforced following the green hue, 1 peck, and no food (see also Grant, 1982). After high levels of accuracy were achieved with no delay separating the samples from choice alternatives, retention intervals ranging from 1 to 6 s were added to the procedure.

Supposedly, anticipation (prospective coding) of the discrete choice responses (R1 and R2) should occur to each of the three samples in the two common-response sets. If so, then the form of the retention gradients for the various samples should be very similar (cf. Grant, 1991; Grant & Spetch, 1993), because coding and remembering "R1" should be no easier and no more difficult than coding and remembering "R2." Contrary to this prediction, however,

Table 21.3. Common-Response (Many-to-One) Matching Contingencies Used in Urcuioli, DeMarse, and Zentall (1994)

Red	→	R1+
Twenty pecks	→	R1+
Food	→	R1+
Green	→	R2+
One peck	→	R2+
No food	→	R2+

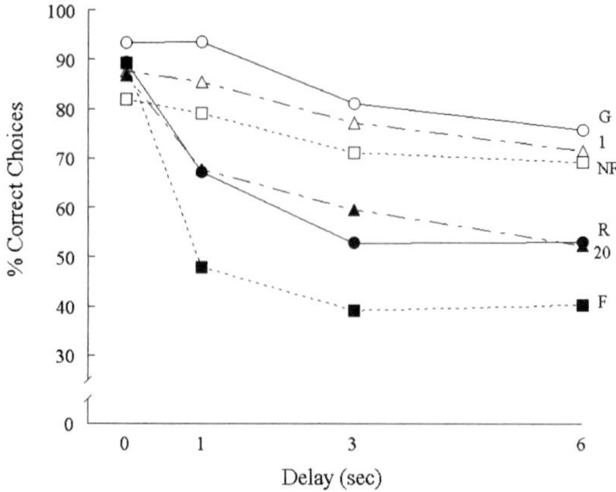

Figure 21.7. Delayed matching accuracy by pigeons in which two sets of three samples (Red, 20 Responses, and Food, and Green, 1 response, and No-Food) each occasioned the same comparison choice. (Reprinted from "Some Properties of Many-to-One Matching with Hue, Response and Food Samples: Retention and Mediated Transfer," by P. J. Urcuioli, T. DeMarse, and T. R. Zentall, 1994, *Learning and Motivation, 25*, 175–200, Experiment 1, with permission from Elsevier.)

matching accuracy fell much more rapidly over delays on food- than on no-food trials, on 20- than on 1-peck trials, and on red than on green trials, as can be seen in figure 21.7. The former two asymmetries have been well documented in the animal memory literature (see, e.g., Fetterman & MacEwen, 1989; Sherburne & Zentall, 1993) and are generally interpreted in terms of coding the sample stimuli (retrospective coding). Their presence here, along with the red versus green difference, contradicts the anticipatory response notion.

Together, then, these studies suggest that, although an acquired equivalence between stimuli can be response based (i.e., the result of their common response associations), within-class generalization may not be response mediated, at least in the sense originally envisioned by Hull (1939) and others (Dollard & Miller, 1950; Miller & Dollard, 1941). If this conclusion is correct, then how else might within-class generalization be explained?

Grice (1965a, 1965b) suggested the possibility of stimulus-based mediational links—a central, "common" code for each categorized stimulus (see also Hall, 1996). Similarly, Zentall (1998), Wasserman and DeVolder (1993), and Lippa and Goldstone (2001) proposed that stimuli in an acquired equivalence class act as retrieval cues for each other, a type of retrospective mediation (Honig & Thompson, 1982). These closely related ideas certainly fit with the observed interchangeability of stimuli following common-response training. But although these alternatives have intuitive appeal, it is unclear how to empirically evaluate them (i.e., to generate falsifiable predictions in the same way that is possible in tests of anticipatory mediation). Furthermore, some of their implicit assumptions (e.g., bidirectional associations between stimuli and responses) are questionable (e.g., Lionello-DeNolf & Urcuioli, 2002). Given these problems, there may be little to be gained by appealing to mediational accounts of acquired equivalence (Sidman, 1994). Perhaps it is sufficient to simply state that functional or acquired equivalence develops when stimuli occasion a common response or have other shared associations.

RESPONSES AS MEMBERS OF ACQUIRED EQUIVALENCE CLASSES

Sidman (1994, 2000) argues that equivalence is a basic stimulus function that is not derivable from other processes (such as mediated generalization). In other words, the ability of stimuli in an equivalence class to control behavior despite no reinforced history for doing so does not require that those stimuli give rise to other overt or covert processes that *do* have such a history. Sidman claims that equivalence relations (at least in humans) arise directly from the reinforcement contingency itself and consist of ordered pairs of all positive elements in that contingency: conditional and discriminative stimuli, responses, and reinforcers. His view is supported by results indicating that different reinforcers can join equivalence classes (e.g., Dube, McIlvane, Maguire, Mackay, & Stoddard, 1989; Kastak, Schusterman, & Kastak, 2001; Urcuioli & DeMarse, 1997, Experiment 2).

What about different responses or different patterns of responding? There are good reasons to suppose that, given proper training conditions, different response or response patterns should become functionally equivalent with other exteroceptive events. For instance, different patterns of responding have discriminative properties that serve very effectively as conditional cues in matching-to-sample (Urcuioli & Honig, 1980). Moreover, the retention results of Urcuioli et al. (1994, Experiment 1), in which number of responses served as one set of samples (cf. figure 21.7), suggest that responses had joined acquired equivalence classes with food versus no-food and red versus green samples. Urcuioli et al. (1994, Experiment 2) provided additional support for this notion by demonstrating that, under some reassignment conditions, it was possible to obtain within-class generalization of *new* comparison choices across samples, one of which was number of responses, that had participated in many-to-one training relations. Finally, in contemporary learning theory, responses are thought to participate in the same associative relations as stimuli (e.g., Colwill, 1994; Dinsmoor, 2001).

One recent finding in particular, however, has been cited as evidence for response membership in equivalence classes (e.g., Sidman, 1994, 2000). Manabe, Kawashima, and Staddon (1995) showed that budgerigars developed the same pattern of *sample responding* to samples that occasioned a common choice response. In their study, budgerigars were initially trained on two-sample, two-choice matching-to-sample, in which presentation of the choice alternatives was contingent on a high-pitched vocal call to one sample and a low-pitched vocal call to the other. After this task was acquired to high levels of accuracy, two new samples were introduced and mapped onto the same choice alternatives, thus creating many-to-one contingencies. On trials with the newly introduced samples, however, *any* vocal call (high or low) produced the comparisons.

Manabe et al. (1995) found that as the budgerigars learned to match accurately with the new samples, they began to call differentially to them despite no requirement to do so. Specifically, high-pitched calls emerged to the new sample that occasioned the same choice response as the original sample to which a high call was explicitly required, whereas low-pitched calls emerged to the new sample that occasioned the same choice response as the original sample to which a low call was required. In short, differential *sample behavior* emerged to samples associated with a common choice. One way this result could occur is if the explicitly required high versus low vocal calls had become members of an equivalence class that also contained the samples themselves (Sidman, 1994, 2000).

Using a procedure modeled after Manabe et al. (1995), Urcuioli, Pierce, Lionello-DeNolf, Friedrich, Fetterman, and Green (2002) replicated this emergent, differential sample behavior effect in

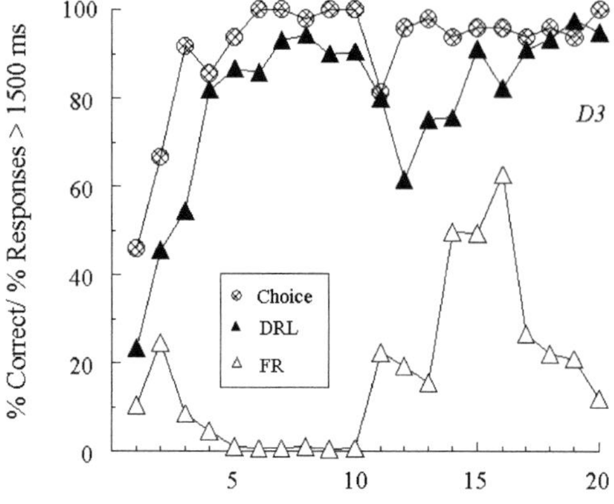

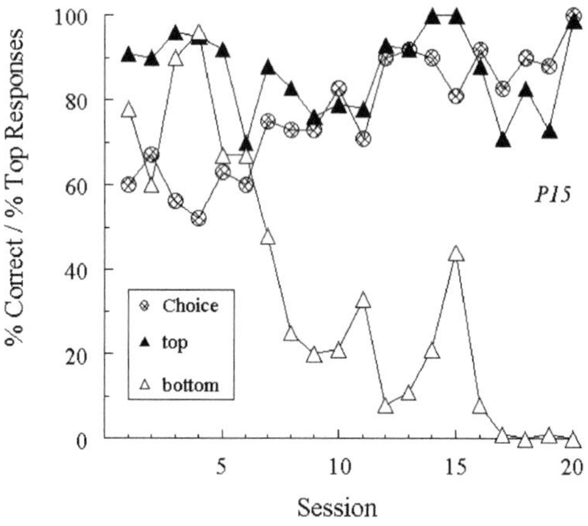

Figure 21.8. The emergence of differential responding (triangles) in two birds to new, target samples that occasioned the same comparison choice as samples to which differential responding was explicitly reinforced. Circles plot matching (choice) accuracy on target-sample trials. *Top,* The development of relatively long (>1500 ms) inter-response times (IRTs) to a target sample matched to the same comparison as a sample to which responding was reinforced on a differential-reinforcement-of-other-behavior (DRL) schedule, and relatively short IRTs to a sample matched to the same comparison as a sample to which responding was reinforced on a fixed-ratio (FR) schedule. *Bottom,* The development of top- versus bottom-key responding to samples matched to the same comparison as samples to which top- versus bottom-key responding was explicitly required. (Adapted from "The Development of Emergent Differential Sample Behavior in Pigeons," by P. J. Urcuioli, J. N. Pierce, K. M. Lionello-DeNolf, A. Friedrich, J. G. Fetterman, and C. Green, 2002, *Journal of the Experimental Analysis of Behavior*, *78*, 409–432.)

pigeons. The major difference between our study and theirs was the nature of the sample responses: we employed different patterns of sample responding and different response locations.

In one experiment, pigeons initially matched two samples to two choice alternatives that they obtained by completing a differential-reinforcement-of-low-rates-of-responding (DRL) 3-s schedule for one sample and a fixed-ratio (FR) 20 schedule for the other. In another experiment, the response requirements were to peck five times to the top versus bottom of two vertically aligned keys on which each sample was simultaneously displayed. After birds learned to respond appropriately to each sample and to accurately match them to the choice alternatives, two new samples were introduced. These samples were mapped onto the same comparison choices as the original samples, thus creating a many-to-one task. On trials with the new samples, however, the choice alternatives were obtained by completing *either* sample-response requirement. In other words, as in Manabe et al. (1995), there was a nondifferential requirement for responding to the newly introduced samples.

Despite this *nondifferential* requirement, many pigeons developed *differential* sample-response patterns as they learned to match accurately with the new samples. More important, the patterns that emerged coincided with the behavior explicitly required to the familiar samples that occasioned the same choice response. Figure 21.8 shows two examples of this effect: one from the experiment involving the DRL and FR schedules and the other from the experiment involving pecking the top and bottom keys.

Again, these results can be interpreted as evidence for response membership in equivalence classes under the assumption that samples will preferentially occasion the *behavior* that belongs to the same class as they do. However, these findings and those of Manabe et al. (1995) are amenable to another interpretation that does not appeal to equivalence. Saunders and Williams (1998) have convincingly argued that adventitious reinforcement can produce emergent differential sample behavior like that shown in figure 21.8. According to this analysis, two explicitly reinforced behavioral units are created during initial (two-sample) training: [sample behavior 1–choice response 1] and [sample behavior 2–choice response 2]. When later presented with new samples, birds are likely to emit either sample behavior 1 or sample behavior 2 and this, in turn, should cue choice response 1 or choice response 2, respectively (cf. Urcuioli & Honig, 1980). If that choice is reinforced, then the entire behavioral unit is strengthened to the sample that preceded it. Moreover, the common choice-response contingencies of many-to-one matching should enhance the likelihood that the [sample behavior 1–choice response 1] unit will develop preferentially to the new sample that occasions the same choice as the original sample to which sample behavior 1 was explicitly required, and likewise for the [sample behavior 2–choice response 2] unit.

Unfortunately, as we have noted elsewhere (Urcuioli et al. 2002, pp. 430–431), the predictions derived from the adventitious reinforcement account are identical to those derived from acquired equivalence. Consequently, this paradigm is poorly suited for establishing response membership in acquired equivalence classes. A different approach is needed.

A modified many-to-one matching procedure, depicted in table 21.4, is more promising in this regard. Initial common-response training will involve two exteroceptive samples (S3 and S4—e.g., red and green hues) and two behavioral patterns (DRL and FR). Unlike typical differential sample-response schedules, however, DRL and FR will *not* be occasioned by different stimuli. The omission of occasioning stimuli is done purposely to avoid the possibility that such stimuli, rather than the DRL and the FR themselves, will become members of acquired equivalence classes with S3 and S4 (Sidman, 1994).

Instead, the center key will always be lit white on DRL and FR "sample" trials, and a mixed DRL-FR schedule will be in effect. If the pigeon successfully completes the scheduled requirement to white, then the R1 and R2 choice alternatives will be presented. On the other hand, if the pigeon completes the *un*scheduled requirement (e.g., making 20 pecks on a DRL trial prior to meeting the DRL contingency or spacing two successive responses 3 s apart before completing the FR 20 contingency), then the white center-key stimulus will go off and, after a short interval, will reappear to permit the bird to "try again." Only when the scheduled response requirement is met will the choice alternatives appear. On trials with S3 and S4, a single peck will produce R1 and R2.

Table 21.4. Procedure to Evaluate Response Membership in Acquired Equivalence Classes

Training		
Initial	Reassignment	*Testing*
W-DRL 3 s → R1+		
W-FR20 → R2+	W-DRL 3 s → R3+	S3 → R3+
S3 → R1+	W-FR20 → R4+	S4 → R4+
S4 → R2+		

If the common choice-response contingencies of many-to-one training generate an acquired equivalence between any set of events that occasions a common choice, then this procedure should produce [DRL, S3] and [FR, S4] classes. Acquired equivalence between sample-response patterns and exteroceptive samples will then be assessed by reassigning one member from each presumed class (e.g., DRL and FR) to new choices (R3 and R4) and then testing the remaining samples for within-class generalization—that is, their ability to immediately occasion those new choices. If different responses join acquired equivalence classes, then the substitution of the remaining (S3 and S4) samples for them should produce transfer effects like those typically seen with a consistent versus inconsistent test manipulation (cf. figure 21.2).

The success of this experiment will depend, of course, on the ability of pigeons to learn to (1) immediately switch from one response pattern to another on the mixed DRL-FR schedule when initial responding to white is "unsuccessful" and (2) consistently make the reinforced choice response based on the sample-response pattern that produces the choice alternatives. In fact, pigeons possess both of these abilities. For example, Lionello-DeNolf and Urcuioli (2003) showed that pigeons can learn to switch to the "correct"/reinforced pattern when their initial pattern of responding to a mixed-schedule stimulus is "incorrect"/nonreinforced. With training, their rate of switching to the correct pattern on the first repeat attempt consistently exceeded 80% and often exceeded 90%. In addition, when required to match the correct patterns to two different comparison alternatives, pigeons were able to choose the reinforced alternative on 90% or more of all matching trials.

SUMMARY

In this chapter, I have discussed different "roles" that responses play in acquired equivalence. First, common responses that are occasioned by the same antecedent stimuli can bring those stimuli together into a class. Such responding, then, is one source of acquired equivalence, just as Dollard and Miller (1950) and Hull (1939) suggested long ago. Second, common responses can serve as "markers" for acquired equivalence; I described two ways in which this process has been observed. In one, new responses that are subsequently and explicitly trained to members of the class "emerge" or generalize without explicit training to the other members (e.g., Bovet & Vauclair, 1998, Experiment 1; Urcuioli et al., 1989; Zentall et al., 1993). In another, behavior *already* occasioned by certain stimuli begins to emerge to other stimuli that later become members of the same acquired equivalence class (Manabe et al., 1995; Urcuioli et al., 2002). Third, common responses in their actual or anticipatory form can potentially mediate within-class generalization of performance to the extent that their stimulus properties have had, at some point, the opportunity to gain control over that performance. Although I argued that anticipatory mediated generalization (Hull, 1939) is probably not necessary for transfer of performance across stimuli, it may certainly provide a means for such transfer when "available" (Urcuioli & Lionello-DeNolf, 2001; see also Hall, Mitchell, Graham, & Lavis, 2003, and Urcuioli & Honig, 1980). Fourth, I entertained the possibility that differential responding that shares a common association with other events could, like visual and auditory stimuli, join acquired equivalence classes. This possibility is entirely speculative at this point; but, unless a subject's behavior has special characteristics not shared by exteroceptive events, there is little reason to suspect otherwise.

One of the remaining challenges in this line of work is to see just how far the within-class generalization effect will go in nonhuman animals. For instance, humans will match stimuli that have previously occasioned a common reinforced response *to one another* (Spradlin & Saunders, 1986; see also Lowe et al., 2002). The matching of stimuli to one another has become a standard way in which human researchers assess *stimulus* equivalence, as defined by the concurrent properties of reflexivity, symmetry, and transitivity (Sidman & Tailby, 1982). Can other animals do the same after common-response training? The answer is currently unknown. Moreover, getting it will not be easy because such matching tests usually involve moving stimuli from previously trained locations to new ones. For pigeons and other animals, a change in location changes the functional stimulus (Iversen, 1997; Lionello & Urcuioli, 1998; Sidman, 1992). Nevertheless, once this stimulus-control problem is overcome or overridden, we may gain a clearer and more comprehensive picture of the categorization abilities of creatures other than ourselves.

References

Astley, S. L., & Wasserman, E. A. (1998). Novelty and functional equivalence in superordinate categorization by pigeons. *Animal Learning & Behavior*, *26*, 125–138.

Bhatt, R. S., Wasserman, E. A., Reynolds, W. F., Jr., & Knauss, K. S. (1988). Conceptual behavior in pigeons: Categorization of both familiar and novel examples from four classes of natural and artificial stimuli. *Journal of Experimental Psychology: Animal Behavior Processes*, *14*, 219–234.

Birge, J. S. (1941). The role of verbal responses in transfer. Unpublished doctoral dissertation, Yale University.

Bovet, D., & Vauclair, J. (1998). Functional categorization of objects and of their pictures in baboons (*Papio anubis*). *Learning and Motivation*, *29*, 309–322.

Colwill, R. M. (1994). Associative representations of instrumental contingencies. In D. Medin (Ed.), *The psychology of learning and motivation* (Vol. 31, pp. 1–72). New York: Academic Press.

Dinsmoor, J. A. (2001). Stimuli inevitably generated by behavior that avoids electric shock are inherently reinforcing. *Journal of the Experimental Analysis of Behavior*, *75*, 311–333.

Dollard, J., & Miller, N. E. (1950). *Personality and psychotherapy*. New York: McGraw-Hill.

Dube, W. V., McIlvane, W. J., Maguire, R. W., Mackay, H. A., & Stoddard, L. T. (1989). Stimulus class formation and stimulus-reinforcer relations. *Journal of the Experimental Analysis of Behavior*, *51*, 65–76.

Eikeseth, S., & Smith, T. (1992). The development of functional and equivalence classes in high functioning autistic children. *Journal of the Experimental Analysis of Behavior*, *58*, 123–133.

Fetterman, J. G., & MacEwen, D. (1989). Short-term memory for responses: The "choose-small" effect. *Journal of the Experimental Analysis of Behavior*, *52*, 311–324.

Foss, D. J., & Jenkins, J. J. (1966). Mediated stimulus equivalence as a function of the number of converging stimulus items. *Journal of Experimental Psychology*, *71*, 738–745.

Goldiamond, I. (1962). Perception. In A. J. Bachrach (Ed.), *Experimental foundations of clinical psychology* (pp. 280–340). New York: Basic Books.

Grant, D. S. (1982). Prospective and retrospective coding of samples of stimuli, responses, and reinforcers in delayed matching with pigeons. *Learning and Motivation, 13*, 265–280.

Grant, D. S. (1991). Symmetrical and asymmetrical coding of food and no-food samples in delayed matching in pigeons. *Journal of Experimental Psychology: Animal Behavior Processes, 17*, 186–193.

Grant, D. S., & Spetch, M. L. (1993). Analogical and nonanalogical coding of samples differing in duration in a choice-matching task in pigeons. *Journal of Experimental Psychology: Animal Behavior Processes, 19*, 15–25.

Grice, G. R. (1965a). Do responses evoke responses? *American Psychologist, 20*, 282–294.

Grice, G. R. (1965b). Investigations of response-mediated generalization. In D. I. Mostofsky (Ed.), *Stimulus generalization* (pp. 373–382). Stanford, CA: Stanford Univ. Press.

Grice, G. R., & Davis, J. D. (1958). Mediated stimulus equivalence and distinctiveness in human conditioning. *Journal of Experimental Psychology, 55*, 565–571.

Grover, D. E., Horton, D. L., & Cunningham, M., Jr. (1967). Mediated facilitation and interference in a four-stage paradigm. *Journal of Verbal Learning and Verbal Behavior, 4*, 42–46.

Hall, G. (1996). Learning about associatively activated stimulus representations: Implications for acquired equivalence and perceptual learning. *Animal Learning & Behavior, 24*, 233–255.

Hall, G., Mitchell, C., Graham, S., & Lavis, Y. (2003). Acquired equivalence and distinctiveness in human discrimination learning: Evidence for associative mediation. *Journal of Experimental Psychology: General, 132*, 266–276.

Herrnstein, R. J. (1990). Levels of stimulus control: A functional approach. *Cognition, 37*, 133–166.

Herrnstein, R. J., & Loveland, D. H. (1964). Complex visual concept in the pigeon. *Science, 146*, 549–551.

Honig, W. K., & Thompson, R. K. R. (1982). Retrospective and prospective processing in animal working memory. In G. H. Bower (Ed.), *The psychology of learning and motivation* (Vol. 16, pp. 239–284). New York: Academic Press.

Hull, C. L. (1939). The problem of stimulus equivalence in behavior theory. *Psychological Review, 46*, 9–30.

Iversen, I. (1997). Matching-to-sample performance in rats: A case of mistaken identity? *Journal of the Experimental Analysis of Behavior, 68*, 27–47.

James, C. T., & Hake, D. T. (1965). Mediated transfer in a four-stage stimulus-equivalence paradigm. *Journal of Verbal Learning and Verbal Behavior, 4*, 89–93.

Jeffrey, W. E. (1953). The effect of verbal and nonverbal responses in mediating an instrumental act. *Journal of Experimental Psychology, 45*, 327–333.

Jenkins, J. J. (1963). Mediated associations: Paradigms and situations. In C. N. Cofer & B. S. Musgrave (Eds.), *Verbal behavior and learning* (pp. 210–245). New York: McGraw-Hill.

Jenkins, J. J., & Palermo, D. S. (1964). Mediation processes and the acquisition of linguisitic structure. In U. Bellugi & R. Brown (Eds.), *The acquisition of language. Monographs of the Society for Research in Child Development, 29*, 141–169.

Kastak, C. R., Schusterman, R. J., & Kastak, D. (2001). Equivalence classification by California sea lions using class-specific reinforcers. *Journal of the Experimental Analysis of Behavior, 76*, 131–158.

Lea, S. E. G. (1984). In what sense do pigeons learn concepts? In H. L. Roitblat, T. G. Bever, & H. S. Terrace (Eds.), *Animal cognition* (pp. 263–276). Hillsdale, NJ: Erlbaum.

Lionello, K. M., & Urcuioli, P. J. (1998). Control by sample location in pigeons' matching to sample. *Journal of the Experimental Analysis of Behavior, 70*, 235–251.

Lionello-DeNolf, K. M., & Urcuioli, P. J. (2002). Stimulus control topographies and tests of symmetry in pigeons. *Journal of the Experimental Analysis of Behavior, 78*, 467–495.

Lionello-DeNolf, K. M., & Urcuioli, P. J. (2003). A procedure for generating differential "sample" responding without different exteroceptive stimuli. *Journal of the Experimental Analysis of Behavior, 79*, 21–35.

Lippa, Y., & Goldstone, R. L. (2001). The acquisition of automatic response biases through categorization. *Memory & Cognition, 29*, 1051–1060.

Lowe, C. F., Horne, P. J., Harris, F. D. A., & Randle, V. R. L. (2002). Naming and categorization in young children: Vocal tact training. *Journal of the Experimental Analysis of Behavior, 78*, 527–549.

McIntire, K. D., Cleary, J., & Thompson, T. (1987). Conditional relations by monkeys: Reflexivity, symmetry, and transitivity. *Journal of the Experimental Analysis of Behavior, 47*, 279–285.

Manabe, K., Kawashima, T., & Staddon, J. E. R. (1995). Differential vocalization in budgerigars: Towards an experimental analysis of naming. *Journal of the Experimental Analysis of Behavior, 63*, 111–126.

Miller, N. E., & Dollard, J. 1941. *Social learning and imitation*. New Haven, CT: Yale University Press.

Peterson, G. B. (1984). How expectancies guide behavior. In H. L. Roitblat, T. G. Bever, & H. S. Terrace (Eds.), *Animal cognition* (pp. 135–147). Hillsdale, NJ: Erlbaum.

Saunders, K. J., & Williams, D. C. (1998). Do parakeets exhibit derived stimulus control? Some thoughts on experimental control procedures. *Journal of the Experimental Analysis of Behavior*, *70*, 321–324.

Sherburne, L. M., & Zentall, T. R. (1993). Coding of feature and no-feature events by pigeons performing a delayed conditional discrimination. *Animal Learning & Behavior*, *21*, 92–100.

Shipley, W. C. (1935). Indirect conditioning. *Journal of General Psychology*, *12*, 337–357.

Sidman, M. (1992). Adventitious control by the location of comparison stimuli in conditional discriminations. *Journal of the Experimental Analysis of Behavior*, *58*, 173–182.

Sidman, M. (1994). *Equivalence relations and behavior: A research story*. Boston, MA: Authors Cooperative.

Sidman, M. (2000). Equivalence relations and the reinforcement contingency. *Journal of the Experimental Analysis of Behavior*, *74*, 127–146.

Sidman, M., & Tailby, W. (1982). Conditional discrimination vs. matching to sample: An expansion of the testing paradigm. *Journal of the Experimental Analysis of Behavior*, *37*, 5–22.

Spradlin, J. E., Cotter, V. W., & Baxley, N. (1973). Establishing a conditional discrimination without direct training: A study of transfer with retarded adolescents. *American Journal of Mental Deficiency, 77, 556–566.*

Spradlin, J. E., & Saunders, R. R. (1986). The development of stimulus classes using match-to-sample procedures: Sample classification vs. comparison classification. *Analysis and Intervention in Developmental Disabilities*, *6*, 41–58.

Urcuioli, P. J. (1996). Acquired equivalences and mediated generalization in pigeon's matching-to-sample. In T. R. Zentall & P. M. Smeets (Eds.), *Stimulus class formation in humans and animals* (pp. 55–70). Amsterdam: Elsevier.

Urcuioli, P. J., & DeMarse, T. (1997). Some further tests of response-outcome associations in differential outcome matching-to-sample. *Journal of Experimental Psychology: Animal Behavior Processes*, *23*, 171–182.

Urcuioli, P. J., DeMarse, T., & Zentall, T. R. (1994). Some properties of many-to-one matching with hue, response and food samples: Retention and mediated transfer. *Learning and Motivation*, *25*, 175–200.

Urcuioli, P. J., & Honig, W. K. (1980). Control of choice in conditional discriminations by sample-specific behaviors. *Journal of Experimental Psychology: Animal Behavior Processes*, 6, 251–277.

Urcuioli, P. J., & Lionello-DeNolf, K. M. (2001). Some tests of the anticipatory mediated generalization model of acquired sample equivalence in pigeons' many-to-one matching. *Animal Learning & Behavior*, *29*, 265–280.

Urcuioli, P. J., & Lionello-DeNolf, K. M. (2005). *The role of common responses in acquired sample equivalence. Behavioural Processes, 69*, 207–222.

Urcuioli, P. J., Pierce, J. N., Lionello-DeNolf, K. M., Friedrich, A., Fetterman, J. G., & Green, C. (2002). The development of emergent differential sample behavior in pigeons. *Journal of the Experimental Analysis of Behavior*, *78*, 409–432.

Urcuioli, P. J., & Zentall, T. R. (1992). Transfer across delayed discriminations: Evidence regarding the nature of prospective working memory. *Journal of Experimental Psychology: Animal Behavior Processes*, *18*, 154–173.

Urcuioli, P. J., Zentall, T. R., & DeMarse, T. (1995). Transfer to derived sample-comparison relations by pigeons following many-to-one versus one-to-many matching with identical training relations. *Quarterly Journal of Experimental Psychology*, *48B*, 158–178.

Urcuioli, P. J., Zentall, T. R., Jackson-Smith, P., & Steirn, J. N. (1989). Evidence for common coding in many-to-one matching: Retention, intertrial interference, and transfer. *Journal of Experimental Psychology: Animal Behavior Processes*, *15*, 264–273.

Vaughan, W., Jr. (1988). Formation of equivalence sets in pigeons. *Journal of Experimental Psychology: Animal Behavior Processes*, *14*, 36–42.

Ward-Robinson, J., & Hall, G. (1999). The role of mediated conditioning in acquired equivalence. *Quarterly Journal of Experimental Psychology*, *52B*, 335–350.

Wasserman, E. A., & DeVolder, C. L. (1993). Similarity- and non-similarity-based conceptualization in children and pigeons. *The Psychological Record*, *43*, 779–793.

Wasserman, E. A., DeVolder, C. L., & Coppage, D. J. (1992). Nonsimilarity-based conceptualization in pigeons. *Psychological Science*, *3*, 374–379.

Wasserman, E. A., Kiedinger, R. E., & Bhatt, R. S. (1988). Conceptual behavior in pigeons: Categories, subcategories, and pseudocategories. *Journal of Experimental Psychology: Animal Behavior Processes*, *14*, 235–246.

Wright, A. A., Urcuioli, P. J., & Sands, S. F. (1986). Proactive interference in animal memory. In D. F. Kendrick, M. E. Rilling, & M. R. Denny

(Eds.), *Theories of animal memory* (pp. 101–125). Hillsdale, NJ: Erlbaum.

Zentall, T. R. (1998). Symbolic representations in animals: Emergent stimulus relations in conditional discrimination learning. *Animal Learning & Behavior*, *26*, 363–377.

Zentall, T. R., Clement, T. S., & Weaver, J. E. (2003). Symmetry training in pigeons produces functional equivalences. *Psychonomic Bulletin & Review*, *10*, 387–391.

Zentall, T. R., Sherburne, L. M., & Urcuioli, P. J. (1993). Common coding by pigeons in a many-to-one delayed matching task as evidenced by facilitation and interference effects. *Animal Learning & Behavior*, *21*, 233–237.

Zentall, T. R., Sherburne, L. M., & Urcuioli, P. J. (1995). Coding of hedonic and nonhedonic samples by pigeons in many-to-one delayed matching. *Animal Learning & Behavior*, *23*, 189–196.

VII

PATTERN LEARNING

22

Spatial Patterns: Behavioral Control and Cognitive Representation

MICHAEL F. BROWN

LEARNING AS PATTERN DETECTION

It seems clear that objects and events in the world are related to each other in systematic ways. It seems very likely that the nervous system has evolved mechanisms that allow these relationships to be detected and used in adaptive ways. In this context, the study of learning can be understood as the study of these mechanisms that allow the systematicity in the world to affect behavior. The present chapter is concerned with systematic spatial relationships among the elements of a set of locations containing hidden goals. In the experimental paradigm that we use to study the effects of these systematic spatial relationships, the hidden goals form what would generally be considered to be a spatial form or spatial pattern. That is, the spatial relationships can be described (by the experimenter) and coded (by the subject) in a manner that is more efficient than coding each and every possible spatial relation among the locations. In the formal terms of information theory, there is informational redundancy in the set of spatial relations among the locations (Attneave, 1959). Our concern is with whether and, if so, how such spatial patterns are learned and how they affect the choices of locations made by the rat subjects as they search for the hidden goals.

Psychologists know a great deal about the detection and processing of perceptual patterns (e.g., Lockhead & Pomerantz, 1991; Uttal, 1988), but the processes involved in the perception of visual, auditory, and tactile patterns generally require that the elements of the pattern be simultaneously available as stimuli. Patterns considered to involve learning are often made up of elements that are experienced at different points in time, and so detection of such patterns requires the integration of information over time. A classic view of category learning, for example, is that systematic relations among particular stimuli are extracted as a result of exposure to those stimuli. This allows the formation of category prototypes that represent the systematic differences between elements of different categories and similarities among members of the same category (see Minda & Smith, 2001, for a discussion).

The study of associative learning can be described as the study of how systematic relations (patterns) among events in the world (in the case of classic conditioning) or between events in the world and behavior (in the case of instrumental conditioning) are detected and how those relations allow behavior and thought to become better adapted to the world (e.g., Dickinson, 1980). Although there is not complete agreement about the nature of the relationship(s) that underlie classical and instrumental conditioning, the dominant view is that the statistical correlations (contingencies) among events in the world (classical conditioning; e.g., Rescorla, 1988) or between events and behaviors (instrumental conditioning; e.g., Colwill &

Rescorla, 1986) are the conditions that determine associative learning, at least under natural conditions. Although traditionally explained in terms of binary associations that are produced by the systematicity among events, alternative views appeal to mechanisms that detect patterns using large databases of experienced events (e.g., Gallistel, Mark, King, & Latham, 2001).

There are, of course, systematic relations among events in the world other than the contingencies among them and some of these have also received experimental and theoretical attention. One category of such relations that corresponds to a well-developed area of study in comparative cognition involves the temporal relations among events (see Church, 2002, for a review). The study of interval timing can be seen as the study of how systematic temporal relations among events affect behavior.

Another domain in which learning can be understood as the detection of systematicity is control of behavior by serial patterns of magnitude. Behavior is controlled by systematic changes in the magnitude of reinforcement over trials (e.g., Capaldi, Blitzer, & Molina, 1979; Hulse & Dorsky, 1980). Two approaches have dominated attempts to explain this phenomenon. Hulse and his colleagues (e.g., Fountain, Evensen, & Hulse, 1984; Hulse, 1978) have proposed that animals learn rules that represent the molar properties of the pattern. Capaldi and his colleagues (e.g., Capaldi, Verry, & Davidson, 1981), on the other hand, have argued that control by serial patterns is best explained in terms of a set of associations between the reinforcement magnitude experienced on an earlier trial and an event (behavior or outcome) on a later trial in the series (see also Fountain, Benson, & Wallace, 2000; Self & Gaffan, 1983; Wallace & Fountain, 2002).

Behavior can also be controlled by serial patterns of interfood temporal intervals (Church & Lacourse, 1998; Staddon & Higa, 1999). Church and LaCourse showed that rats can be controlled by serial patterns of temporal intervals in an interval timing procedure. Their rats were exposed to a series of trials with fixed intervals ranging from approximately 2.5 s to approximately 210 s. In the critical conditions, the length of these intervals increased (or decreased) systematically over trials. There was clear evidence that behavior was controlled by this pattern of temporal intervals. Thus, serial pattern learning is not restricted to patterns of reward magnitude, but appears to be a more general phenomenon.

SPATIAL LEARNING AND SPATIAL PERFORMANCE

Spatial learning and performance in animals have been the targets of a large amount of recent empirical and theoretical work. Much of this was influenced by O'Keefe and Nadel's (1978) important work suggesting that the hippocampus is involved in a spatially organized representation of objects in space (termed the "cognitive map" following Tolman, 1948). Several distinct traditions have developed from this view, including a large body of work focused on the functions and mechanisms of the hippocampus and related brain structures (see Thinus-Blanc, 1996, for a review). In the behavioral and cognitive traditions, the focus has been on the content of the cognitive map and the ways in which it affects behavior (see Gallistel, 1990, for a review). A common theme is that stimuli with stable spatial locations serve as landmarks that allow animals to locate goal locations because the landmarks have consistent spatial relations with the goals. For example, honeybees find their way between sources of food and the hive using visual landmarks (Gould, 1986), food-storing birds locate their hidden caches of food using the spatial relations between the caches and visible landmarks (Kamil & Jones, 2000), and rats in the radial arm maze discriminate the location of maze arms using extra-maze visual stimuli (e.g., Suzuki, Augerinos, & Black, 1980). The use of visible landmarks to find hidden goals is well established and occurs in a wide variety of animals under a wide variety of circumstances.

A very different mechanism of spatial performance is enabled by cues inside rather than outside of the animal. Dead reckoning (also referred to as path integration) allows animals to determine the spatial relations among locations as they move among those locations using movement cues, such as vestibular or proprioceptive cues (e.g., Gallistel, 1990). In a classic demonstration of this ability, Wehner and Srinivasan (1981) showed that ants displaced during a foraging excursion would search for their nest in a location that was removed from the true location of the nest (in terms of distance and direction) in accordance with the displacement. Thus, the ants integrated their current distance and direction from the nest during the foraging excursion. Dead reckoning and landmark use can work together to allow a dead reckoned location to be calibrated based on learned visual cues (Collett, Collett, Bisch, & Wehner, 1998).

For present purposes, the critical feature of landmark use is that behavior is controlled by spatial relations among landmarks and goal locations. The critical feature of dead reckoning is that behavior is controlled by the spatial relations between one or more previously visited locations and the current location (as given by the animal's own movement).

Research in my laboratory has focused on a third type of spatial relation that also appears to control spatial performance. If goal locations have systematic spatial relations among themselves, that spatial pattern could allow rats to locate the goal locations more efficiently than would otherwise be possible. In particular, rats might learn about the spatial patterns among hidden goal locations and use the pattern in searching for the goals.

An early indication that the spatial relations among hidden goals can control spatial choices came from an experiment reported by Dallal and Meck (1990, Experiment 3). They trained rats in a 12-arm radial maze (Olton & Samuelson, 1976) in which eight of the arms were baited during each trial, and the remaining four arms were never baited. In the experimental condition, the locations of the baited and unbaited maze arms remained constant across training trials. Critically, the spatial relations among them also remained constant in a transfer phase of the experiment, in which the rats were tested with the maze moved to a second room with a very different set of extra-maze cues. The critical result was that choices during the transfer phase were more accurate under these conditions than they were among rats in control conditions, for which the spatial relations among the baited and unbaited arms were different in the transfer phase of the experiment than they had been during the training phase of the experiment. Dallal and Meck's results suggested that rats learned the spatial relations among the baited and unbaited arms of the maze in a manner that is independent of the extra-maze visual landmarks. That is, the spatial relations apparently were abstracted from the visual cues designating particular locations, and could then be used as cues to guide arm choices. However, Olthof, Sutton, Slumdkie, D'Addetta, and Roberts (1999) reported a careful series of attempts to replicate Dallal and Meck's basic result. They were unable to do so. So it is unclear whether spatial patterns of baited and unbaited arms in the radial maze can control choices.

LEARNING AND PERFORMANCE IN THE POLE BOX TASK

The work in my laboratory reviewed in this chapter has been concerned with further exploring the notion, first suggested by Dallal and Meck's results, that spatial navigation and spatial choices can be controlled by the spatial relations among hidden goals, which are abstracted from particular spatial locations and the landmarks that signify them. Most of our work on spatial pattern learning has involved an apparatus we refer to as the pole box. As illustrated in figure 22.1, the pole box is an arena with a matrix of vertical poles. Rats search for food (usually sucrose pellets) hidden in wells on top of the poles. On each trial, a subset of poles is baited. The identity of the baited poles is unpredictable prior to a trial and several lines of evidence make it clear that rats do not locate baited poles using odor or other perceptual cues. Odor cues are controlled in our recent experiments by the fact that all poles have a sham pellet, inaccessible to the rat, under a mesh false floor in the well of the pole (see figure 22.2). Locating the first pole in the baited subset occurs no more efficiently than would be expected by chance. However, because the baited poles form a spatial pattern, it is possible for additional poles in the baited set to be located more efficiently than would be expected by chance. If, in fact, baited poles are located more efficiently than would be expected by chance, that performance is taken as evidence that the spatial pattern has been learned and controls choice behavior.

We have studied three basic patterns that do, in fact, control choices. Brown and Terrinoni's (1996) initial report was of control by a square configuration of poles (a 2×2 arrangement of poles in a 5×5 matrix; see top panel of figure 22.3). The figure shows one exemplar of the square pattern among the 16 possibilities. In this and most of our experiments, the exemplar on any particular trial is chosen randomly. Thus, unlike in most spatial learning tasks, the problem is *not* to learn particular spatial locations. Only the spatial relations among the baited locations serve as valid cues that can increase search efficiency.

Isolating evidence relevant to such control is complicated by, among other factors, the strong effect of proximity (i.e., the tendency of rats to choose poles that are spatially proximal to the most recently chosen pole) and the ability of rats to

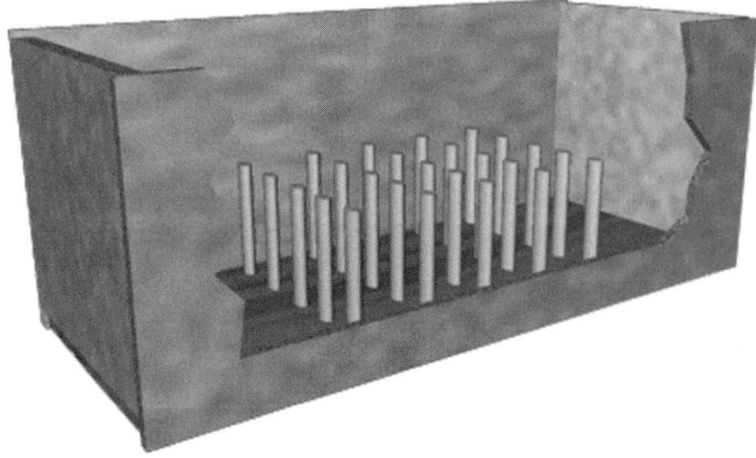

Figure 22.1. Cutaway view of a 5 × 5 pole box apparatus. Drawing by Morgan Terrinoni. (From "Sex Differences in Spatial Search and Pattern Learning in the Rat," by B. K. Lebowitz and M. F. Brown, 1999, *Psychobiology, 27*, 364–371. Copyright 1999 by The Psychonomic Society. Reprinted with permision.)

Figure 22.2. Inner core of pole with well for sham bait (*right*) and outer sleeve of pole with well for accessible bait (being held on left).

avoid revisits to poles that have already been chosen (just as they do in other spatial tasks, e.g., the radial arm maze [Olton et al., 1976]). Brown and Terrinoni developed a measure of control by the square pattern that involves a special subset of choices, thereby allowing both of these complicating variables to be controlled. This measure considers only choices of poles that are adjacent to the most recently visited pole and have not been visited earlier in the trial. Following discovery of the second baited pole in a square configuration (as illustrated in the top panel of figure 22.4), there are as many as three such poles. For each rat, the proportion of adjacent, previously unvisited poles that are consistent with the square pattern (marked with an S in the figure) among all such poles (S and X in the figure) is compared with the proportion of choices made to such poles. The fact that the latter proportion (of actual choices made) is greater than the former proportion (which represents the proportion of choices consistent with the pattern expected if rats are not controlled by the square pattern) provides evidence for control by the spatial pattern (top panel of figure 22.5). An analogous analysis of

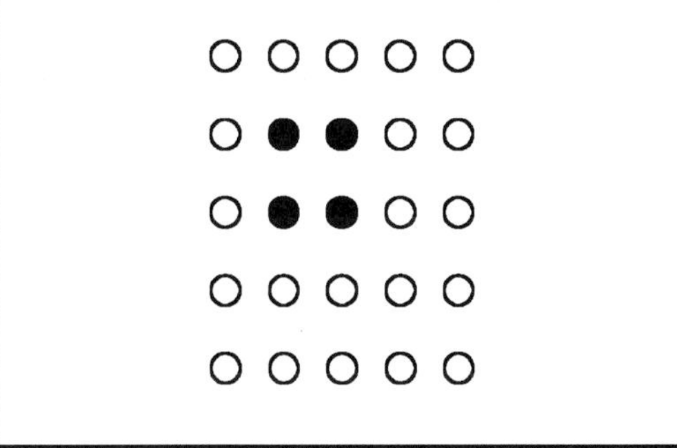

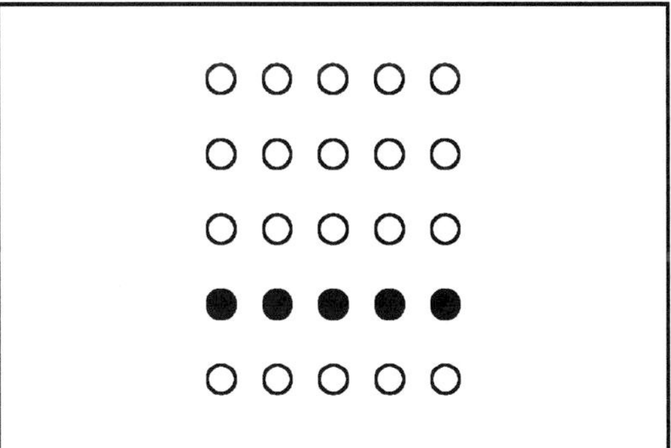

Figure 22.3. Exemplars of the square (*top*), line (*middle*), and checkerboard (*bottom*) spatial patterns. All three patterns have been shown the control choices in the pole box.

the actual and expected proportions of choices consistent with the square pattern following discovery of the third baited pole (bottom panel of figure 22.4) provided additional evidence for control by the square pattern of baited poles, in that the actual proportion of choices conforming to the pattern was substantially greater than the proportion

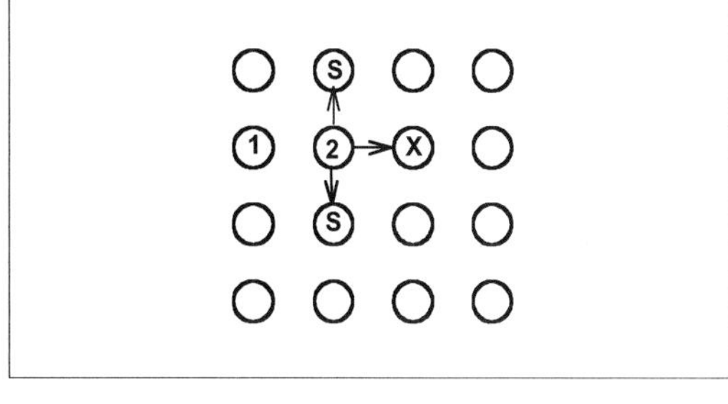

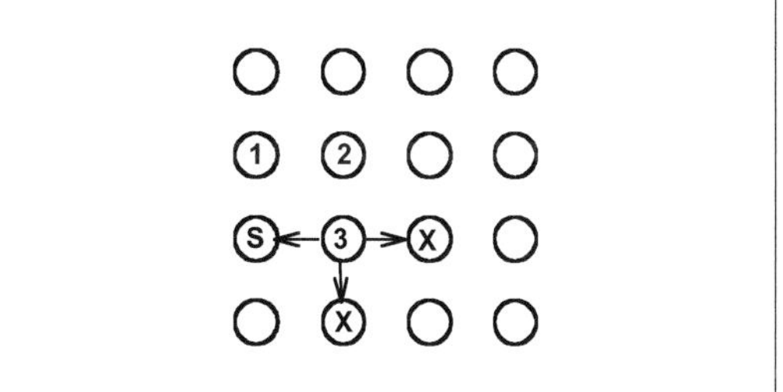

Figure 22.4. Logic of the Brown and Terrinoni analysis of control by a square spatial pattern. (From "Control of Choice by the Spatial Configuration of Goals," by M. F. Brown and M. Terrinoni, 1996, *Journal of Experimental Psychology: Animal Behavior Processes, 22*, 438–446. Adapted with permission of the American Psychological Association.)

expected on the basis of chance (bottom panel of figure 22.5).

Similar logic and an analogous set of behavioral measures have allowed us to show that, in addition to a square pattern, choices can be controlled by a linear arrangement of baited poles (an example of this pattern is shown in the middle panel of figure 22.3). Brown and Terrinoni (1996; Experiment 2) used a 4 × 5 pole box in which, for each trial, one of the four rows of poles or one of the five columns of poles was randomly selected as the set of baited poles. DiGello, Brown, and Affuso (2002) randomly selected one of the four rows of poles in a 4 × 4 pole box. In both cases (and based on somewhat different measures in the two cases) rats were more likely to choose a pole consistent with the linear spatial pattern than would be expected on the basis of chance.

The finding that choices can be controlled by a line pattern as well as a square pattern is particularly important because it rules out a potential alternative explanation for control by the square

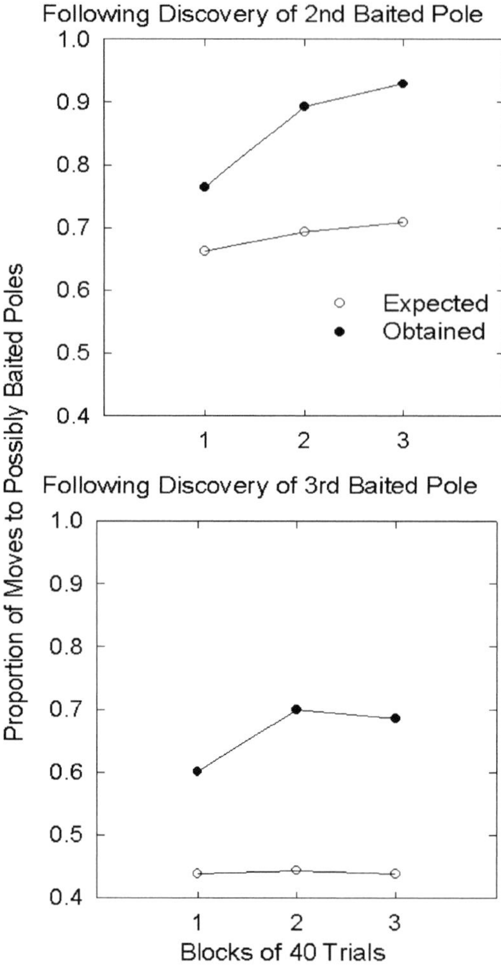

Figure 22.5. Results from Brown and Terrinoni, 1996, Experiment 1. (From "Control of Choice by the Spatial Configuration of Goals," by M. F. Brown and M. Terrinoni, 1996, *Journal of Experimental Psychology: Animal Behavior Processes, 22,* 438–446. Experiment 1. Copyright 1996 by American Psychological Association. Reprinted with permission.)

pattern. Choice of poles consistent with the square pattern could be explained as the effect of intersecting spatial generalization gradients of stimulus control from the two (or three) previously discovered poles. However, such an effect predicts a very different pattern of results than the one predicted by spatial pattern learning (and found) in the case of the linear pattern. In particular, if choice of poles consistent with a square pattern is produced by the combination of spatial generalization gradients centered on the two (or three) previously discovered poles, then rats should choose poles consistent with a square pattern even when they are trained with poles baited according to the square pattern (see Brown & Terrinoni, 1996, for details). Rats trained with a line pattern of baited poles, however, learn to choose poles consistent with the line pattern rather than those consistent with hypothetical generalization gradients.

Control by a very different sort of spatial pattern was demonstrated by Brown, Zeiler, and John (2001). In a 4×4 pole box (Experiment 1) or a 5×5 pole box (Experiment 2), half of the poles were baited on each trial, and the baited poles formed a checkerboard pattern (as illustrated in the bottom panel of figure 22.3). Unlike the square pattern, which has a large number of exemplars (16 in a 4×4 matrix, 25 in a 5×5 matrix), the checkerboard pattern has only two exemplars. In theory, then, it is possible for a subject to choose perfectly in the checkerboard pattern task following the first pole choice. In fact, however, accurate performance in the pole box requires overcoming a strong preexperimental tendency to choose poles that are spatially adjacent to the most recently chosen pole. The measure of control by the checkerboard pattern developed by Brown et al. takes advantage of this by examining spatial relations among poles serving as the target of consecutive choices. The majority of choices made in the pole box are to poles either adjacent to the previously chosen pole, poles separated by one pole in a row or one pole in a column from the most recently chosen pole, or poles removed by one row and one column from the most recently chosen pole. Such choices are referred to as *adjacent moves, skip moves,* and *diagonal moves*, respectively (figure 22.6). Following choice of an unbaited pole, an adjacent move leads to a baited pole, whereas following choice of a baited pole, a skip move, or a diagonal move leads to a baited pole. Figure 22.7 shows an example of the critical finding, which we have now found several times under a variety of experimental conditions. Over the course of the experiment, the tendency to make adjacent moves following choice of an unbaited pole increases, as does the tendency to make skip and diagonal moves following choice of a baited pole.

How does the existence of a pattern among hidden food locations come to control spatial choices and increase spatial choice accuracy? Our approach reflects our belief that there are two general sets of processes to be investigated. The first is the

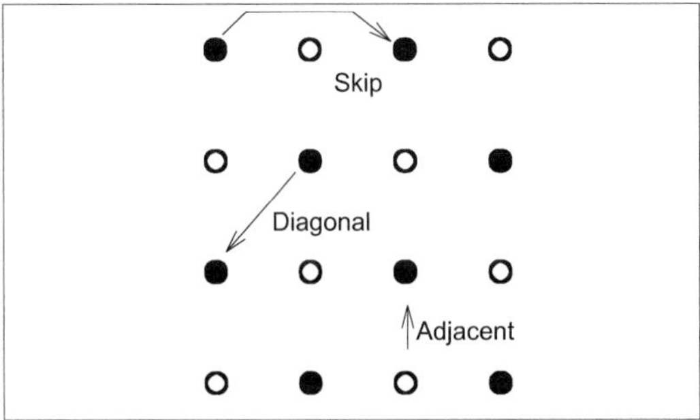

Figure 22.6. Move types used in the analysis of control by a checkerboard pattern. If filled symbols represent baited poles, then all three samples shown are moves consistent with the pattern. (From "Spatial Pattern Learning in Rats: Control by an Iterative Pattern," by M F. Brown, C. Zeiler, and A. John, 2001, *Journal of Experimental Psychology: Animal Behavior Processes, 27,* 407–416. Copyright 2001 by American Psychological Association. Reprinted with permission.)

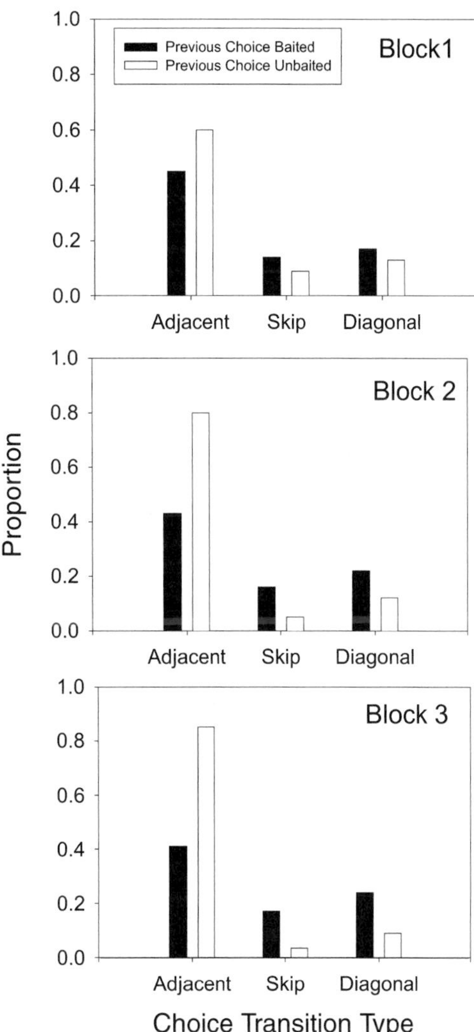

Figure 22.7. Control by the checkerboard pattern is shown by the increasing tendency for adjacent moves to follow choice of an unbaited pole and skip and diagonal moves to follow choice of a baited pole. (From "Spatial Pattern Learning in Rats: Control by an Iterative Pattern," by M F. Brown, C. Zeiler, and A. John, 2001, *Journal of Experimental Psychology: Animal Behavior Processes, 27,* 407–416. Copyright 2001 by American Psychological Association. Reprinted with permission.)

mechanism and content of pattern learning. Over the course of trials, rats must detect the spatial relations among the baited poles and code those relations in some behavioral or cognitive format. The second concerns the means by which the learned pattern influences spatial performance. That is, there must be dynamic processes that are engaged during each trial that allow the baited poles to be more efficiently located using the learned pattern.

WHAT IS LEARNED ABOUT THE PATTERN?

Pattern Representation or Response Learning?

One possible interpretation of control by a spatial pattern of hidden goals is that a motor response (or set of responses) comes to be occasioned by finding a baited pole (Olthof, Sutton, Slumskie, D'Addetta, & Roberts, 1999). In the case of the checkerboard pattern, for example, the move types used in our analysis used to detect control by the checkerboard pattern may also reflect the mechanism of that control. Rats may learn to make skip and/or diagonal moves in response to the stimulus of a baited pole. They might also (or alternatively) learn to make adjacent moves in response to an unbaited pole. Acquisition of either or both of these response tendencies could explain the development of choices consistent with the checkerboard spatial pattern without appealing to a representation of the pattern.

In the cases of square and line patterns, an explanation in terms of response learning is necessarily more complex, because the correct response is not

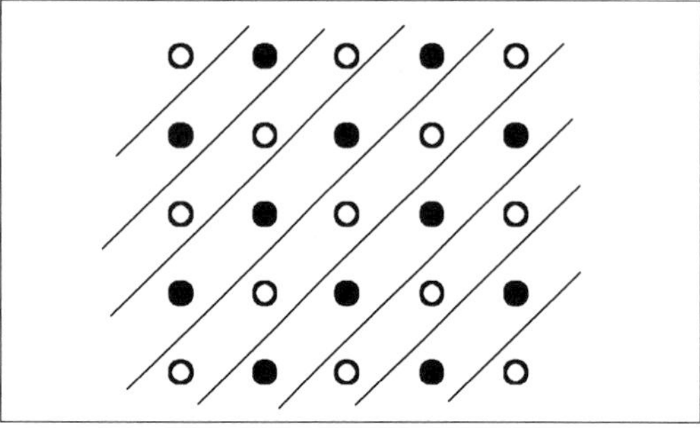

Figure 22.8. Barriers used to prevent adjacent and skip moves. (From "Spatial Pattern Learning in Rats: Control by an Iterative Pattern," by M F. Brown, C. Zeiler, and A. John, 2001, *Journal of Experimental Psychology: Animal Behavior Processes, 27*, 407–416. Copyright 2001 by American Psychological Association. Reprinted with permission.)

determined by the status (baited vs. unbaited) of the most recently chosen pole. Rather, a response that conforms to a line pattern or a square pattern depends on the location of at least two previously located baited poles. However, it is possible to explain our evidence for control by square and line patterns in terms of a learned response occasioned by locating the first two (or more) baited poles. So, for example, a rat might come to be controlled by the line pattern by learning to continue moving in the same direction after finding two adjacent baited poles. A rat controlled by the square pattern, on the other hand, might have learned to turn right or left after finding two adjacent baited poles.

Brown et al. (2001) tested the motor learning interpretation of control by a checkerboard pattern by training rats with barriers preventing the rats from making skip or adjacent moves (see figure 22.8). During this training, rats did learn to choose baited poles more efficiently than would be expected by chance, and they did so by learning to locate the baited "diagonal alleys" defined by the barriers, choosing poles in baited alleys in succession but tending to move on to another alley if the first pole in the alley was not baited. The critical result was that when the barriers were removed following training, rats showed the signature tendencies indicating control by the checkerboard pattern: There was a stronger tendency to make adjacent moves following choices of unbaited poles and to make skip moves following choices of a baited pole. Because only diagonal moves could be made during training, this control by the checkerboard pattern must have been produced by something other than response learning.

It therefore appears that rats develop a representation of the spatial relations among the baited poles that is independent of the particular responses that correspond to those relations (and serve as our measure of their behavioral control). Our evidence for this conclusion is analogous to the evidence that led to Tolman's classic conclusions regarding cognitive maps. But, as indicated earlier, the cognitive maps that were described by (Tolman, 1948), conceptually rejuvenated by O'Keefe and Nadel (1978), and continue to be widely studied differ in a fundamental way from the representations of spatial relations among the poles in our pole box task. Whereas the cognitive maps that have typically been proposed and investigated include representations of landmarks that are anchored in allocentric space, the spatial locations of baited poles in the box pole are represented only in relation to each other. They are not, and cannot be, represented in relation to allocentric space. Rather, the spatial relations among the baited locations are abstracted from particular locations in the pole box.

At least in the case of the checkerboard pattern, there is another possible mechanism of control by the pattern that should be considered. There are only two exemplars of the checkerboard pattern. It is possible that rats learn two sets of pole locations that function as equivalence sets (Vaughan, 1988). Just as in Vaughan's classic experiment, there are two sets of stimuli (poles) and the values of stimuli within each set (i.e., whether a pole is baited or nonbaited) change together over the course of trials. However, because the value of stimuli in the same set changes in the same way, subjects learn to respond to stimuli based on the value of other stimuli in the same set. In the pole box, it is possible that control by the checkerboard pattern is not a function of the consistent spatial relations among the baited poles but rather is due to the development of two equivalence sets of poles. The idea that rats might learn a small number of independent sets of spatial locations is not without precedence. Wathen and Roberts (1994) studied rats in a radial arm maze paradigm in which a subset of maze arms was baited on each trial. Trials were structured in daily sessions of eight trials each. In the critical condition, the set of baited arms varied systematically over the trials of each session. Wathen and Roberts argued that rats solved this problem by learning which set of arms was baited as a function of trial number (see also Neath & Capaldi, 1996). If rats are capable of coding several sets of locations chosen from among the same set of eight maze arms in Wathen and Roberts's paradigm, it seems plausible that they may solve the checkerboard pattern problem in the pole box by learning two sets of baited pole locations, and then determining which of the two sets is active on the current trial based on the first choice or first several choices.

We do not yet have data that directly address this alternative to representation of the spatial relations that constitute a checkerboard. However, even if it is a viable alternative explanation for control by the checkerboard pattern, equivalence sets of pole locations is not a feasible explanation of control by the square or line patterns, given the large number of pattern exemplars (and therefore equivalence sets) involved (16 different exemplars of the square pattern in a 5×5 pole box; nine exemplars in a 4×4 pole box).

Is Pattern Learning a Module Separate From Other Spatial Control Mechanisms?

It has been argued that processes involved in spatial learning and performance function in relative isolation from other learning and memory processes (Cheng, 1986; Gallistel, 1990) and function according to principles that are at least somewhat different from those governing learning in other domains. One of these differences is the apparent absence of cue competition effects under at least some conditions of spatial learning (Biegler & Morris, 1999; Pearce, Ward-Robinson, Good, Fussell, & Aydin, 2001). In a water escape task with a hidden platform goal, for example, Pearce et al. found control of spatial navigation by both the shape of the pool and a visual beacon that specified the goal location but no evidence that either of these cues overshadowed the other. They argued that the lack of cue competition between shape and a visual beacon supports the idea of a separate learning system responsible for control by the overall shape of the arena (the "geometric module" described by Cheng, 1986).

Similarly, Brown, Yang, and DiGian (2002) trained rats in a pole box task using either a square (Experiment 1) or checkerboard (Experiment 2) pattern. For rats in the critical experimental condition, the baited poles were also identified by distinct visual cues (Experiment 1: baited poles had white, horizontal stripes and the unbaited poles were black; Experiment 2: baited and unbaited poles differed by being either black or white). It was very clear that rats were controlled by these visual cues. However, when the cues were removed during the test phase of the experiment, these rats exhibited control by the spatial pattern and, critically, the extent to which they were controlled by the pattern was no different than rats in a control condition that had never experienced the visual cues. Thus, there was no evidence that very distinct visual cues (which did in fact control behavior during training) competed for behavioral control with the spatial pattern. This suggests that learning about spatial patterns occurs independently of learning about other kinds of cues. The isolation of spatial pattern learning from other forms of spatial cue learning would be adaptive in that allocentric landmarks are irrelevant to learning the pattern. Learning to locate goals in terms of their spatial relations with other goal locations would, in fact, require ignoring the landmarks that are otherwise often involved in spatial navigation and spatial choice.

Is Spatial Pattern Learning Part of a More General Pattern Learning Process?

As argued here, the spatial pattern learning process appears to be at least somewhat isolated from the processes involved in cue-based spatial learning and spatial navigation. However, it might be expected that the control of behavior by patterns in two-dimensional space would have processes in common with control of behavior by other kinds of patterns, such as the serial patterns of reward magnitude or temporal intervals mentioned above. To the extent that the learning of rules is involved in serial pattern learning, the attributes of those rules may be common to both serial and spatial patterns. For example, among the attributes of particular serial and spatial patterns are repetition and symmetry.

Brown, DiGian, Fabian, and Smith (2003) report two experiments in which rats are exposed to both a spatial pattern and a serial pattern. Five poles were baited during each trial in a 5×5 pole box, and the baited poles were always in a linear pattern (one of the five rows of the matrix, as in the middle panel of figure 22.3). There were three trials in each daily session. As illustrated in figure 22.9, one experimental group (Group Ordered)

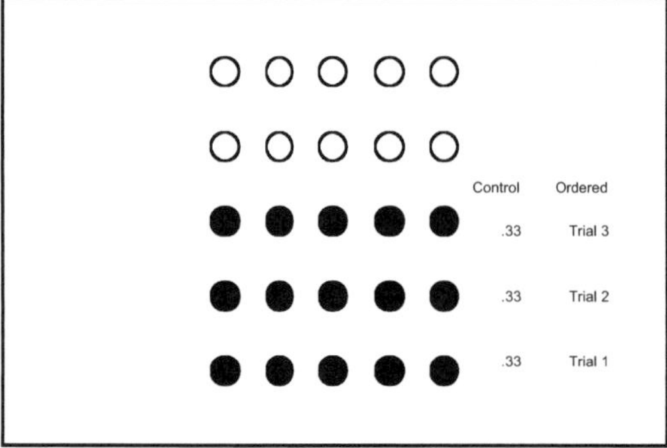

Figure 22.9. Experimental design in which one row was baited on each of three daily trials. The baited row varied systemically over the three trials of each session (ordered group) or was chosen randomly (control group). (From *Spatial and Serial Pattern Learning*, by M. F. Brown, K. A. DiGian, S. A. Fabian, and W. Smith, 2003. Unpublished data.)

was exposed to a serial pattern of spatial pattern exemplars during each daily session. In particular the identity of the baited row varied predictably in moving from an "outside row" on the first trial of each session to the adjacent row on the second trial to the next adjacent (middle) row on the third trial. Thus, in this condition (unlike in any of our other experiments with spatial patterns), the location of the baited poles was predictable prior to each trial on the basis of this serial pattern of baited rows. Performance in this condition was compared to a control group of rats in which the baited row varied unpredictably among the three possibilities.

The critical finding in this experiment was that the existence of the serial pattern of baited rows facilitated behavioral control by the rows. Rats in the group for which the identity of the baited row varied according to a serial pattern (over the three trials of each daily session) were controlled by the row to a greater extent than rats in the group for which the identity of the baited row was unpredictable (over trials). That is, the effect of serial patterns and the effect of spatial patterns interact. This interaction is evidence that some part of the processes involved in serial pattern learning and spatial pattern learning is common. This finding encourages the possibility that elements of systematicity that are common to serial and spatial patterns (such as repetition and symmetry) are detected by a common psychological process. In this particular case, there is repetition in the spatial pattern (a repeated adjacent relationship between the poles forming the pattern). There is also repetition in the serial pattern (the bait row is adjacent to the row baited on the previous trial, repeatedly over trials). This common attribute of the spatial and serial pattern may be detected by the same mechanism, thereby producing the interaction between the behavioral effects of the two patterns.

HOW DOES THE LEARNED PATTERN INFLUENCE SPATIAL SEARCH?

Whatever the particulars of the pattern learning process turn out to be, acquisition of pattern learning is only the first half of the story. Knowledge of the spatial pattern must be applied on each trial to locate baited poles on the basis of choices made during that trial. As pointed out earlier, at the time the rat makes its first choice, there is no information available regarding the location of the baited poles, and that is the case even for a rat with perfect information about the properties of the spatial pattern.

Empirical support for a distinction between the behavioral processes involved in searching for the first baited pole and searching for baited poles once information related to the pattern is available comes from an experimental dissociation reported by Lebowitz and Brown (1999). They compared the ability of male and female rats to locate baited poles arranged in a square pattern in a 5×5 pole box (subjects in all of our other experiments have been male rats). Based on our primary measure of control by a square pattern (as illustrated in figure 22.4), male rats were clearly controlled by the square pattern to a greater extent than were female rats. This is consistent with a number of lines of research indicating more control by spatial relations for male rats than for female rats (see Beatty, 1992, for a review). However, female rats were able to locate the first baited pole slightly more efficiently than male rats. This difference in the efficiency of spatial search could be explained in terms of preexperimental tendencies that have an impact on the spatial diversity of poles chosen during the early part of each trial. Choosing poles over a wider range of the matrix during the initial part of the trial decreases the number of choices made before locating the first baited pole (because a pole adjacent to the pole just chose cannot be part of the square that includes the just-chosen, unbaited pole). Lebowitz and Brown found that female rats did, in fact, have a weaker preexperimental tendency to choose adjacent poles than male rats. Whatever search tendencies are brought to the pole box paradigm, they must be modified to accommodate the properties of the pattern experienced by the rats. The sex difference found in this experiment indicates that these modifications are applied only after the rat locates one or two baited poles, thereby allowing it to use those locations in combination with the pattern to better locate the remaining poles. This in turn provides empirical support for the idea that the processes in force during the search for the first baited pole differ from those involved once a pattern element (the first baited pole) has been located and the pattern can thereby be used to guide subsequent choices.

Conditional Control by Two Spatial Patterns

Multiple spatial patterns can control behavior, conditional on a cue that indicates which pattern is in force. Brown, DiGello, Milewski, Wilson, and Kozak (2000) trained rats in a 4 × 4 pole box with one of two patterns in force. When the poles were baited with one of two food types (either sucrose pellets or halves of sunflower seeds), the baited poles formed a line (either a row or column of the matrix). When the poles were baited with the other food type, the baited poles formed a square pattern. After finding two adjacent baited poles, rats were more likely to choose the pole consistent with a line pattern if the food in those poles was the one signaling the line pattern but were more likely to choose a pole consistent with the square pattern if the food in the poles was the one signaling the square pattern. It is important to note that the choices measured by Brown et al. indicating control by the square or linear pattern were not only different but actually mutually incompatible with each other. After finding two adjacent baited poles, control by a square pattern was indicated by choice of a pole perpendicular to the line formed by those poles whereas control by a line pattern was indicated by choice of a pole along the same line formed by those poles. The existence of this conditional control by two spatial patterns shows that learned spatial patterns can be used in a flexible manner. Certainly in nature different resources can be distributed according to different spatial patterns, and the behavioral systems that use spatial pattern learning are able to accommodate that.

Use of Both Positive and Negative Information About the Location of the Pattern Exemplar

In searching for baited poles under the influence of a learned spatial pattern, the rat clearly could use the location of discovered baited poles in combination with the pattern to locate additional baited poles. The idea that discovery of a baited pole is critical in allowing the rat to locate the pattern exemplar within the matrix of poles is implied in the measures we use of control by the square pattern. In the case of a square pattern, for example, when the rat has discovered two adjacent baited poles, the location of those poles in combination with the learned pattern allows it to locate a third baited pole (as indicated, for example, in the top panel of figure 22.4). However, not only can the location of a baited pole provide information about the location of the pattern exemplar on a particular trial but also the location of an unbaited pole potentially provides such information. Consider, for example, the case of the square pattern shown in the top panel of figure 22.4. After locating the two indicated baited poles, the location of the two remaining baited poles is ambiguous: they are either the pair above the baited poles already located or they are the two below. If the rat chose one of those four poles and the pole is not baited, then the location of the two remaining baited poles is determined.

In the case of a checkerboard pattern, the potential value of such "negative information" (i.e., information available from choice of an unbaited ["incorrect"] choice) is even greater. Given the checkerboard pattern, the location of all baited (and unbaited) poles is determined following the first pole choice, regardless of whether that choice is of a baited pole or an unbaited pole. DiGello, Brown, and Affuso (2002) showed that rats do, in fact, use such negative information when searching for poles baited according to a row pattern. In a 4 × 4 pole box, one of the four rows of poles was baited on each trial. Control by this pattern would be indicated if rats acquired a tendency to choose poles in the same row after finding a baited pole (they did). In addition, control by the linear pattern would also be indicated if rats acquired a tendency to choose poles in a *different* row after choosing a pole that is *not* baited. The rats also acquired this tendency. Thus, both "positive" information (provided by finding a baited pole) and "negative" information (provided by finding that a pole is not baited) can allow a learned pattern to guide choices to baited poles.

This suggests that spatial patterns are represented in terms of both figure and ground. That is, the representation guiding choices to baited locations includes information not only about where yet-to-be-visited baited locations (goals) are relative to baited locations but also about where goals are relative to unbaited locations. Depending on the pattern, the ability to narrow down the location of goals based on where they have *not* been found is often possible, and this clearly occurs in the case of the checkerboard pattern.

Working Memory for the Location of Visited Poles: Separate Systems for Avoiding Revisits and Coding Pole Contents?

In the pole box task, memory for the location of poles already visited during the present trial is important for two reasons. First, as described here, the location of previously visited poles, together with their status as either baited or unbaited, is necessary to use knowledge of the pattern to locate additional baited poles. Second, performance in the pole box task would be enhanced by minimizing pole revisits. The ability of rats to avoid revisits of locations in spatial tasks has been well studied in the radial arm maze and related tasks (e.g., Olton et al., 1976). In the pole box, rats revisit locations much more than they do in a typical radial-arm maze experiment. We have assumed that this difference is due, at least in part, to the close proximity of the poles and the correspondingly small amount of time and effort required for a pole visit. It has been shown in the radial arm maze that reduced distance to the end of the maze arms increases the tendency to revisit arms (Brown & Huggins, 1993) and that this effect is due, at least in part, to a more lax choice criterion when the amount of effort required to make a choice is relatively low (Brown & Lesniak-Karpiak, 1993).

Are the memories used to keep track of pole visits for purposes of avoiding revisits the same memories that are used to keep track of where baited and unbaited poles are located? We assumed that the same memories would be used for both purposes, but recent data indicate that this in not the case (Brown & Wintersteen, 2004). The data are from an experiment using a special 5 × 5 pole box in which the base of each pole was constructed of an upside-down translucent funnel and could be illuminated from below. Rats were trained with a checkerboard pattern and were provided with a cue that signified whether a pole had been previously visited during the trial (for half of the rats, the pole was illuminated during the first visit; for the other half of the rats, all poles were illuminated at the beginning of each trial and the illumination was removed from a pole during the first choice of that pole). There was clear evidence of control by the checkerboard pattern, in terms of the same pattern of adjacent, skip, and diagonal moves described above for other experiments involving the checkerboard pattern. The extent to which, and manner in which, the illumination cue controlled choices was measured in a test phase in which half of the trials included the illumination cues but the remaining (probe) trials did not include them. Comparison of performance in the cue and no cue test trials showed clearly that the visual cues enhanced the ability of rats to avoid revisits to poles chosen earlier in the trial.

We expected that these cues, which allowed the rats to avoid revisits, would also allow them to discriminate the location of previous poles more generally and, in particular, would allow them to better determine which of the two pattern exemplars was in force on a particular trial. However, there was no indication whatsoever that choices were controlled by the pattern to a greater extent when the cues were present than when they were absent. Like any null result, these data must be interpreted with caution. However, they suggest the interesting possibility that the memory system that allows rats to avoid revisits and the memory system that allows them to determine the location of baited and unbaited poles are independent. Perhaps the baited status of locations (baited vs. unbaited at the beginning of each trial) and the visit status of locations (visited vs. unvisited) cannot be stored in the same memories without conflict. This might be because, for purposes of determining the pattern exemplar in force on each trial, the bait status does not change within a trial. The same pole, however, does change status in terms of whether it has been visited (and therefore whether it should be avoided). Thus, the cues provided to our rats in the Brown and Wintersteen experiment were valid only for purposes of avoiding revisits and were isolated from the memory module involved in representing whether a pole was part of the pattern "figure" or pattern "ground."

CONCLUSIONS

The spatial pattern learning phenomenon revealed by our experiments suggests a mechanism for the formation of representations of systematic spatial relations among hidden goals. Such a system would be of value when hidden resources have some systematic spatial distribution. The system may, however, be one expression of more general pattern recognition mechanisms that detect patterns over a variety of dimensions, including serial and temporal patterns. Regardless of its relationship to other forms of pattern learning, spatial pattern learning appears to be somewhat isolated from the spatial learning processes that rely on visual or other sensory cues to specify the location of goals. The representations of spatial patterns formed are flexible enough to allow more than one spatial pattern to control behavior at the same time and include spatial relations that allow choice of unbaited poles to guide subsequent choices to baited poles. Thus, we have begun to understand many of the properties of this form of spatial learning. The details of its mechanism and relation to other forms of spatial and nonspatial learning remain to be understood. However, we are guided by the idea that patterns of various varieties are likely to elicit learning and performance mechanisms that are, to at least some extent, common across the domains in which patterns occur.

Acknowledgments Much of the work described in this chapter was supported by National Science Foundation (NSF) Grant BNS-9982244. I am grateful to the many undergraduate and graduate students who participated in this project.

References

Attneave, F. (1959). *Applications of information theory to psychology*. New York: Henry Holt & Company.

Beatty, W. W. (1992). Gonadal hormones and sex differences in non-reproductive behaviors. In A. A. Gerall, H. Moltz, & I. L. Ward (Eds.), *Sexual differentiation* (pp. 85–128). New York: Plenum.

Biegler, R., & Morris, R. G. (1999). Blocking in the spatial domain with arrays of discrete landmarks. *Journal of Experimental Psychology-Animal Behavior Processes, 25*, 334–351.

Brown, M. F., DiGello, E., Milewski, M., Wilson, M., & Kozak, M. (2000). Spatial pattern learning in rats: Conditional control by two patterns. *Animal Learning & Behavior, 28*, 278–287.

Brown, M. F., DiGian, K. A., Fabian, S. A., & Smith, W. (2003). *Spatial and serial pattern learning*. Unpublished data.

Brown, M. F., & Huggins, C. K. (1993). Maze-arm length affects a choice criterion in the radial-arm maze. *Animal Learning & Behavior, 21*, 68–72.

Brown, M. F., & Lesniak-Karpiak, K. B. (1993). Choice criterion effects in the radial-arm maze: Maze-arm incline and brightness. *Learning and Motivation, 24*, 23–39.

Brown, M. F., & Terrinoni, M. (1996). Control of choice by the spatial configuration of goals. *Journal of Experimental Psychology: Animal Behavior Processes, 22*, 438–446.

Brown, M. F., & Wintersteen, J. (2004). Spatial patterns and memory for locations. *Learning and Behavior, 34*, 391–400.

Brown, M. F., Yang, S. Y., & DiGian, K. A. (2002). No evidence for overshadowing or facilitation of spatial pattern learning by visual cues. *Animal Learning & Behavior, 30*, 363–375.

Brown, M. F., Zeiler, C., & John, A. (2001). Spatial pattern learning in rats: Control by an iterative pattern. *Journal of Experimental Psychology: Animal Behavior Processes, 27*, 407–416.

Capaldi, E. J., Blitzer, R. D., & Molina, P. (1979). Serial anticipation pattern learning in two-element and three-element series. *Bulletin of the Psychonomic Society, 14*, 22–24.

Capaldi, E. J., Verry, D. R., & Davidson, T. L. (1981). Memory, serial anticipation pattern learning, and transfer in rats. *Animal Learning & Behavior, 8*, 575–585.

Cheng, K. (1986). A purely geometric module in the rat's spatial representation. *Cognition, 23*, 149–178.

Church, R. M. (2002). Temporal learning. In R. Gallistel (Ed.), *Stevens' handbook of experimental psychology. Volume 3: Learning, motivation, and emotion* (pp. 365–393). New York: Wiley.

Church, R. M., & Lacourse, D. M. (1998). Serial pattern learning of temporal intervals. *Animal Learning & Behavior, 26*, 272–289.

Collett, M., Collett, T. S., Bisch, S., & Wehner, R. (1998). Local and global vectors in desert ant navigation. *Nature, 394*, 269–272.

Colwill, R. M., & Rescorla, R. A. (1986). Associative structures in instrumental learning. In G. H. Bower (Ed.), *The psychology of learning and motivation* (Vol. 20). New York: Academic Press.

Dallal, N. L., & Meck, W. H. (1990). Hierarchical structures: Chunking by food type facilitates spatial memory. *Journal of Experimental Psychology: Animal Behavior Processes, 16*, 69–84.

Dickinson, A. (1980). *Contemporary animal learning theory*. Cambridge: Cambridge University Press.

DiGello, E., Brown, M. F., & Affuso, J. (2002). Negative information: Both presence and absence of spatial pattern elements guide rats' spatial choices. *Psychonomic Bulletin & Review, 9*, 706–713.

Fountain, S. B., Benson, A. M., & Wallace, D. G. (2000). Number, but not rhythmicity, of temporal cues determines phrasing effects in rat serial-pattern learning. *Learning and Motivation, 31*, 301–322.

Fountain, S. B., Evensen, J. C., & Hulse, S. H. (1984). Formal structure and pattern length in serial pattern learning by rats. *Animal Learning & Behavior, 11*, 186–192.

Gallistel, C. R. (1990). *The organization of learning*. Cambridge, MA: MIT Press.

Gallistel, C. R., Mark, T. A., King, A. P., & Latham, P. E. (2001). The rat approximates an ideal detector of changes in rates of reward: Implications for the law of effect. *Journal of Experimental Psychology: Animal Behavior Processes, 27*, 354–372.

Gould, J. L. (1986). The locale map of honey bees: Do insects have cognitive maps? *Science, 232*, 861–863.

Hulse, S. H. (1978). Cognitive structure and serial pattern learning by animals. In S. H. Hulse, H. Fowler, & W. K. Honig (Eds.), *Cognitive processes in animal behavior* (pp. 311–340). Hillsdale, NJ: Erlbaum.

Hulse, S. H., & Dorsky, N. P. (1980). Serial pattern learning by rats: Transfer of a formally defined stimulus relationship and the significance of nonreinforcement. *Animal Learning & Behavior, 7*, 211–220.

Kamil, A. C., & Jones, J. E. (2000). Geometric rule learning by Clark's nutcrackers (*Nucifraga columbiana*). *Journal of Experimental Psychology: Animal Behavior Processes, 26*, 439–453.

Lebowitz, B. K., & Brown, M. F. (1999). Sex differences in spatial search and pattern learning in the rat. *Psychobiology, 27*, 364–371.

Lockhead, G. R., & Pomerantz, J. R. (1991). *The perception of structure*. Washington, DC: American Psychological Association.

Minda, J. P., & Smith, J. D. (2001). Prototypes in category learning: The effects of category size, category structure, and stimulus complexity. *Journal of Experimental Psychology: Learning Memory and Cognition, 27*, 775–799.

Neath, I., & Capaldi, E. J. (1996). A "random-walk" simulation model of multiple-pattern learning in a radial-arm maze. *Animal Learning & Behavior, 24*, 206–210.

O'Keefe, J., & Nadel, L. (1978). *The hippocampus as a cognitive map*. Oxford: Oxford University Press.

Olthof, A., Sutton, J. E., Slumskie, S. V., D'Addetta, J., & Roberts, W. A. (1999). In search of the cognitive map: Can rats learn an abstract pattern of rewarded arms on the radial maze? *Journal of Experimental Psychology: Animal Behavior Processes, 25*, 352–362.

Olton, D. S., & Samuelson, R. J. (1976). *Journal of Experimental Psychology: Animal Behavior Processes, 2*, 97–116.

Pearce, J. M., Ward-Robinson, J., Good, M., Fussell, C., & Aydin, A. (2001). Influence of a beacon on spatial learning based on the shape of the test environment. *Journal of Experimental Psychology: Animal Behavior Processes, 27*, 329–344.

Rescorla, R. A. (1988). Pavlovian conditioning. It's not what you think it is. *American Psychologist, 43*, 151–160.

Self, R., & Gaffan, E. A. (1983). An analysis of serial pattern learning by rats. *Animal Learning & Behavior, 11*, 10–18.

Staddon, J. E. R., & Higa, J. J. (1999). Time and memory: Toward a pacemaker-free theory of interval timing. *Journal of the Experimental Analysis of Behavior, 71*, 215–251.

Suzuki, S., Augerinos, G., & Black, A. H. (1980). Stimulus control of spatial behavior on the eight-arm radial maze. *Learning and Motivation, 11*, 1–18.

Thinus-Blanc, C. (1996). *Animal spatial cogntion: Behavioral and neural approaches*. Singapore: World Scientific.

Tolman, E. C. (1948). Cognitive maps in rats and men. *Psychological Review, 55*, 189–208.

Uttal, W. R. (1988). *On seeing forms*. Hillsdale, NJ: Erlbaum.

Vaughan, W. J. (1988). Formation of equivalence sets in pigeons. *Journal of Experimental Psychology: Animal Behavior Processes, 14*, 36–42.

Wallace, D. G., & Fountain, S. B. (2002). What is learned in sequential learning? An associative model of reward magnitude serial-pattern learning. *Journal of Experimental Psychology: Animal Behavior Processes, 28*, 43–63.

Wathen, C. N., & Roberts, W. A. (1994). Multiple-pattern learning by rats on an eight-arm radial maze. *Animal Learning & Behavior, 22*, 155–164.

Wehner, R., & Srinivasan, M. V. (1981). Searching behavior of desert ants, genus Cataglyphis (Formicidae, Hymenoptera). *Journal of Comparative Physiology, 142*, 315–338.

23

The Structure of Sequential Behavior

STEPHEN B. FOUNTAIN

A fundamental feature of behavior is that it occurs sequentially in time. Likewise, events are often arranged so that an organism must learn ordered relationships among them if meaningful predictions are to be made about the occurrence of future events. Thus, a classic problem has been the nature of the mechanisms mediating sequential learning and behavior. In recent years, it has become clear that humans and other animals have much in common in terms of sequential behavior and the processes that seem to be responsible for sequential learning and behavior (Kesner, 2002; McGonigle & Chalmers, 2002; Sands & Wright, 1980, 1982; Terrace & McGonigle, 1994). However, rather than a consensus emerging regarding the nature of the mechanisms responsible for sequential behavior, competing hypotheses and theories to describe sequential behavior have multiplied. No general process theory is currently adequate to describe all sequential learning phenomena. We propose that, in sufficiently complex paradigms, sequential learning involves multiple, concurrently active behavioral and brain processes.

CURRENT MODELS OF SEQUENTIAL BEHAVIOR

For decades, beginning with Lashley's (1951) celebrated paper or even earlier with the work of Ebbinghaus and others (Hunter, 1920; Skinner, 1934), sequential learning and memory research has repeatedly aroused debate over the fundamental nature of sequential learning, memory, and representation in humans and animals. In recent years, debate has centered on whether nonhuman animals can use nonassociative symbolic processes such as rule-induction to learn about the structure of patterned sequences ("serial patterns") of events. The work by Hulse and colleagues on rats' serial-pattern learning of food reward magnitude in runways, in particular, supported a rule-learning theory (e.g., Fountain, Evensen, & Hulse, 1983; Fountain & Hulse, 1981; Hulse, 1978; Hulse & Campbell, 1975; Hulse & Dorsky, 1977, 1979). Rule-learning theory proposed that rats learned some representation of the abstract rules that described organized sequences (Fountain, 1986; Roitblat, Pologe, & Scopatz, 1983; Wathen & Roberts, 1994). The implication was that rats did not have to rely on chaining or remote associations alone to master sequences. Later work in our laboratory involved a somewhat different serial-pattern learning paradigm using patterns of stimuli drawn from another stimulus dimension (viz., a spatial dimension rather than food reward magnitude). This work also supported the rule-learning view of serial-pattern learning in both rats and mice (e.g., Fountain, 1990; Fountain, Krauchunas, & Rowan, 1999; Fountain & Rowan, 1995a, 1995b).

Very early on, Capaldi and colleagues contested the rule-learning view, proposing as a competing view that serial-pattern learning in rats could be accounted for by associative mechanisms alone (e.g., Capaldi, 1986; Capaldi & Molina, 1979; Capaldi, Nawrocki, Miller, & Verry, 1985; Capaldi, Nawrocki, & Verry, 1982; Capaldi, Verry, & Davidson, 1980a, 1980b). Capaldi likened sequential learning to other discrimination learning problems. However, as Capaldi himself admitted at the time (Capaldi et al., 1980a), his "sequential memory" model lacked sufficient parametric power to make strong predictions regarding the outcome of sequential learning tasks involving long patterns like those used by Hulse and colleagues. Adding to the complexity of the issue, the rule-learning view has frequently failed to predict outcomes for shorter patterns; even Hulse (1980) conceded that Capaldi's sequential memory theory was a better account in that domain because, according to Hulse, short patterns approximate the paradigm of paired-associate learning rather than that of rule learning.

Roitblat, Pologe, and Scopatz (1983) proposed yet another view: namely, that serial position (SP) played an important role in rat serial-pattern learning. SP models assume that sequence elements become associated with their position in the sequence, not with other sequence items (Burns & Gordon, 1988; Burns, Hulbert, & Cribb, 1990; Chen, Swartz, & Terrace, 1997; Roitblat et al., 1983). Although serial position models may have much in common with Capaldi's sequential memory view, the critical difference is that sensitivity to SP, the central construct here, seems to imply the additional cognitive ability of counting or timing the serial pattern events.

Clearly, the most fundamental question that is not yet fully answered is, "What is learned in sequential learning?" In the area of animal sequential learning research, claims that animals chunk information and form hierarchical representations to facilitate sequential learning and memory (Dallal & Meck, 1990; Fountain, Henne, & Hulse, 1984; Macuda & Roberts, 1995; Roberts, 1979; Terrace, 1987) have inspired research designed to determine what processes mediate chunking and related phenomena. For example, serial learning research has investigated a number of factors thought to affect how animals encode sequences of events (Capaldi, 2002; Capaldi, Verry, Nawrocki, & Miller, 1984; Fountain, 1990; Fountain et al., 1984; Fountain & Rowan, 1995a; Fountain, Wallace, & Rowan, 2002; Swartz, Chen, & Terrace, 1991; Terrace, 1987, 1991, 2002; Terrace & Chen, 1991a, 1991b). As indicated in the earlier discussion, evidence has accumulated that performance in sequential learning tasks can be mediated by discrimination learning processes (e.g., Capaldi, 1985, 1994; Capaldi & Miller, 1988), by a representation of the SP of items (e.g., Chen et al., 1997; Roitblat et al., 1983), or by a representation of pattern organization through some form of rule learning (Fountain et al., 1984; Fountain & Rowan, 1995a, 1995b). Although the foregoing models were originally proposed by some as mutually exclusive accounts of sequential learning and memory, recent behavioral and psychobiological work has produced evidence to support each of these positions, sometimes suggesting that rats may use more than one strategy or type of information to encode and reproduce a single complex behavioral sequence (Fountain, 1990; Fountain & Rowan, 1995a, 2000). Recent work in our laboratory involving behavioral, computational, and psychobiological approaches to understanding serial pattern learning support this view. Some of that evidence will be reviewed later. Our conclusion, for now, is that no general process theory is currently adequate to describe all serial-pattern learning phenomena; in all likelihood, serial-pattern learning involves multiple, concurrent behavioral and brain processes.

Similarly, research from behavioral neuroscience and related fields has found evidence for more than one process and more than one brain area mediating sequential learning. Nissen and Bullemer's (1987) paper on sequence learning has been particularly influential. Nissen's work on brain correlates of her human serial reaction time task (Knopman & Nissen, 1987; Nissen, Knopman, & Schacter, 1987) has supported the idea that serial learning is subserved by both declarative and nondeclarative memory systems. Nissen and co-workers showed that human Alzheimer's patients and scopolamine-treated experimental participants could improve their reaction times for a repeating 10-element pseudo-random response sequence (Knopman & Nissen, 1987; Nissen et al., 1987). Both groups showed no recognition that they were learning a repeating sequence, thus suggesting that learning could occur implicitly (or "procedurally"). Huntington disease patients, however, exhibited no improvement; that is, they showed a deficit in serial learning described as a procedural memory deficit (Knopman & Nissen, 1991). Given that basal ganglia are severely affected by

Huntington's disease, the results contribute to the growing evidence implicating the basal ganglia in sequence learning. For example, Huntington's disease and Parkinson's disease patients who have basal ganglia dysfunction have motor learning deficits that are characterized as deficits in sequencing and sequence learning independent of general motor performance deficits (Heindel, Butters, & Salmon, 1988; Willingham, 1998).

In animal studies, injections of the dopaminergic antagonist haloperidol into the caudate nucleus of cats produces disruptions of "nonexteroceptively directed" motor sequences that were not cued by exteroceptive stimuli but did not affect cued "exteroceptively directed" sequences of behavior (Jaspers, Schwarz, Sontag, & Cools, 1984). Lesions of hippocampus and medial caudoputamen produce a double dissociation of processes relevant to serial-pattern learning (DeCoteau & Kesner, 2000), and hippocampal lesions have also been shown to cause deficits in rats' ability to disambiguate sequences (Agster, Fortin, & Eichenbaum, 2002). In Fountain and Rowan (2000), we showed that MK-801, an *N*-methyl-D-aspartate (NMDA) receptor antagonist, caused severe deficits in serial-pattern learning in rats but only for elements of serial patterns that interrupted or violated pattern structure. More recent work in our laboratory has indicated that these effects of MK-801 were not likely the results of impairment of hippocampus or medial frontal cortex, thus perhaps implicating subcortical structures. Heindel, Butters, and Salmon (1988) stated that "knowledge of the anatomical substrate underlying the acquisition of motor skills and other memory capacities preserved in amnesia is extremely limited." It is possible that identifying the "critical" brain circuits involved in sequential learning and behavior has been difficult because, as the foregoing suggests, sequential behavior may be mediated by multiple brain systems and multiple concurrently active behavioral processes.

THE IDENTIFICATION AND STUDY OF CONCURRENTLY ACTIVE BEHAVIORAL PROCESSES IN SEQUENTIAL LEARNING

If we are to determine whether multiple behavioral processes act concurrently to produce sequential behavior, then we have to study forms of sequential behavior that are sufficiently complex that they would likely recruit multiple processes concurrently. Our serial-pattern learning task for rats seems to be well suited for this purpose. The method we use is a functional analog of nonverbal human pattern learning tasks that require participants to anticipate a series of positions in a spatial array. In our task, rats learn to press levers in a circular array of eight levers in the proper sequential order to obtain reinforcement. Rats must learn to produce long and elaborate sequences of responses. With this method, we can create serial patterns with many items that could be associated, with spatial and temporal cues that could be relevant, with particular pacing or rhythmic structures, and with patterns of movements that could potentially be coded internally as motor patterns or as rule-based structures. Typically, many of these cues and features are concurrently available to the rat as the sequence training takes place, and, as we shall show, it appears that rats concurrently make use of multiple sources of cues and behavioral processes to learn to navigate these serial patterns. Evidence to support this latter assertion comes from behavioral studies, from our work with the drug MK-801, and with specific brain lesions.

SERIAL-PATTERN LEARNING METHOD FOR RATS

Our method for studying serial-pattern learning in rats is a functional analogue of human pattern learning tasks that require subjects to learn to choose items from an array in the proper sequential order (Hartman, Knopman, & Nissen, 1989; Knopman & Nissen, 1991; Reber, 1989; Restle, 1970, 1973; Restle & Brown, 1970a, 1970b; Willingham, Nissen, & Bullemer, 1989; Willingham, 1998). Rats learn to press levers in an array in the proper sequential order. Our current procedure involves training rats in an octagonal Plexiglas box equipped with a retractable lever mounted on each wall (Fountain & Rowan, 1995a, 1995b; Rowan, Fountain, Kundey, & Miner, 2001). The levers are designated levers 1 through 8 in clockwise order with lever 8 adjacent to lever 1. All of the levers are presented at the beginning of each trial and the rat may press any of the eight levers. If the correct lever is pressed, then the rats receive hypothalamic brain-stimulation reward. If an incorrect lever is pressed, then all of the levers except the correct lever are removed from the box and the animal is not reinforced until the correct response is emitted. This method is easily learned by the rat without pretraining procedures other than leverpress shaping. It provides the rat with a continuous (circular) stimulus array and allows us to record response latency (in addition to accuracy measures) on a trial-by-trial basis while the rat performs the task at its own pace. Rats have been trained with up to fifty 24-element patterns per daily session (Fountain & Rowan, 2000). Our method is an improvement over earlier methods used with rats because it allows us to study how rats learn long, elaborate serial patterns and because it provides measures of correct-response rates, error rates, and "intrusion" rates (i.e., the number of specific kinds of errors produced at particular locations in the pattern) on a trial-by-trial basis throughout the serial pattern.

BASIC SEQUENTIAL LEARNING PHENOMENA: RATS APPEAR TO BE SENSITIVE TO STRUCTURE AND VIOLATIONS OF STRUCTURE IN HIERARCHICALLY ORGANIZED AND INTERLEAVED SERIAL PATTERNS

Hierarchically Organized Serial Patterns

One prediction from the rule-learning view is that a highly organized, hierarchically structured sequence should be easier to learn than a sequence having little or no higher-order structure. We have already reported several studies that explored whether pattern structure would determine the ease or difficulty of learning long and elaborate patterns.

In one experiment (Fountain & Rowan, 1995b), we tested whether pattern structure described as "runs" (e.g., 1-2-3-4-5- . . .) or "trills" (e.g., 1-2-1-2-1- . . .) would determine the ease or difficulty of rats' anticipating a final sequence item that either conformed to the implied structure of the sequence or violated pattern structure. Rats received patterns having either perfect structure or one sequence element (the last in the series) that violated an otherwise perfect structure:

"Perfect Runs"	123 234 345 456 567 678 781 812 . . .
"Violation Runs"	123 234 345 456 567 678 781 818 . . . (violation element indicated)
"Perfect Trills"	121 232 343 454 565 676 787 818 . . .
"Violation Trills"	121 232 343 454 565 676 787 812 . . . (violation element indicated)

A 1-s intertrial interval (ITI) was used except where spaces indicate 3-s phrasing cues. [Note: given that lever 1 is adjacent to lever 8, a 6-7-8-1-2 sequence would be a quite natural "run" series.] We observed high error rates in acquisition on the violation trial (the last trial of the pattern) for both Violation Runs and Violation Trills patterns (Fountain & Rowan, 1995b), despite the fact that one view might predict that the generalization of associations from other parts of the pattern should have predisposed the animals to learn the violation patterns easily. For example, in the violation trills pattern, a correct response on lever 1 should always predict that the next response should be to lever 2, yet rats had great difficulty learning to respond on lever 2 on the last trial of the pattern but not on the second trial of the pattern. No comparable errors were observed for the perfect runs or perfect trills patterns. An alternative view is that rats learned about the highly repetitive structure of the sequence that resulted in highly repetitive patterns of response to learn the sequence, even when doing so produced errors at the violation element, and even though these errors might have been avoided by adopting another strategy. CF1 mice show the same pattern of results as rats when learning the perfect and violation runs patterns described here (Fountain et al., 1999).

As we have indicated, violation elements (elements that violate pattern structure) are particularly difficult for rats to learn, although eventually they can be learned to a high level of accuracy. In a recent series of studies conducted with graduate student, Melissa Muller, we investigated what cues contribute to proper tracking of violation elements in serial patterns. Groups of rats learned two-level hierarchical sequences containing a violation. For some groups, sequences started on different levers of the chamber on a pattern-by-pattern basis, and patterns were separated by a long (9-s) interpattern interval to mark the beginning of patterns. The violation always appeared at the end of a chunk. Which chunk contained the violation for a given sequence was determined for the SP group by position in the sequence; the violation was always the last (24th) element of the pattern (Group SP24). In the item-associative/place (IA/P) group, the violation always occurred at the end of a chunk starting with a unique pair of items (which of necessity was confounded with a given place in the chamber). Performance for these groups was compared with that of a group where both SP and item associative/place cues were relevant (SP24 + IA/P) and with that of a group where neither SP and IA/P cues were relevant (NC).

Group SP24 + IA/P. Violation (underlined) consistently in the same spatial location and SP:

Constant pattern: 123 234 345 456 567 678 781 818

Group SP24. Randomized presentation; violation (underlined) located in constant SP:

Starting lever 1: 123 234 345 456 567 678 781 818
Starting lever 2: 234 345 456 567 678 781 818 121
Starting lever 3: 345 456 567 678 781 818 123 232 etc.

Group IA/P. Randomized presentation; violation (underlined) located relative to item associative/place cues:

Starting lever 1: 123 234 345 456 567 678 781 818
Starting lever 2: 234 345 456 567 678 781 818 123
Starting lever 3: 345 456 567 678 781 818 123 234 etc.

Group NC. Violation with no relevant cues: a control condition in which a violation was randomly positioned at the end of a different chunk of the group SP pattern.

Rats experienced 24 pattern repetitions a day (3 each from each possible starting location in groups SP24 and IA/P). Patterns were presented with 1-s ITIs for elements within chunks and 3-s ITIs (phrasing cues) at chunk boundaries (indicated by spaces in the above patterns) in the manner described by Fountain and Rowan (1995b). For groups that met a criterion of fewer than 10% errors on the violation, a series of 1-day transfers were conducted to determine what controlled responding to the violation element.

Acquisition results under the foregoing condition manipulations were very clear. Rats in the two conditions with relevant item/place cues (viz., SP24 + IA/P and IA/P) learned the sequence equally quickly, with all rats reaching criterion for the violation element in 14 to 22 days. Rats with SP cues alone (viz., group SP) never reached criterion; rats in SP, like those with no cues in NC, mastered other elements of their pattern, but they continued to make approximately 100% errors on the violation element throughout 40 days of acquisition. We found no evidence that rats used SP cues, either when presented alone or in combination with other cues, to anticipate the violation element when it was located in SP24.

In subsequent transfer phases, rats in SP24 + IA/P and IA/P experienced transfer conditions presented on separate days; transfer days were separated by retraining to criterion on the original pattern. On one day, rats in both conditions received SP cues only (i.e., 1 day of training under Group SP24 conditions). Under these conditions, all rats failed to anticipate the violation element (making nearly 100% errors), indicating that training with SP cues in SP24 + IA/P did not give them an advantage in transfer over the group that never experienced consistent SP cues for the violation element. On another transfer day, rats were trained in their usual chamber that had been rotated 180°. Under these conditions, rats' performance on the violation did not change, indicating that anticipation of the violation element was controlled in large measure by intrachamber cues (perhaps cues from the floor, walls, levers, or associated apparatus) rather than by extrachamber spatial cues. On another transfer day, rats were transferred to a new chamber in a different testing room. With both extrachamber and intrachamber cues removed, rats made nearly 100% errors on the violation element, but their performance was unchanged on all other elements of the pattern. Thus, intramaze cues were important for anticipating the violation element, but they otherwise played little role in rats' performing the sequential behavior. Finally, rats in Group IA/P were transferred for 1 day to IA/P only conditions (i.e., SP cues were removed). No effects were observed, providing additional evidence that SP cues were not important for anticipating the violation element.

It should be noted that having identified the relevant cues for the violation element as involving intrachamber cues, we have still not identified the specific cue or set of cues that control the behavior. A close examination of the serial pattern that rats learned reveals that no single exteroceptive or interoceptive cue, except the cues that define SP24, reliably predict the violation element. Rats encounter all of the intrachamber and interoceptive cues surrounding the violation element more than once in the course of producing each serial pattern. More will be said about this problem later.

In a separate study, other groups of rats were trained with the violation element in serial position 6 or 12 (SP6 and SP12, respectively, where the violation element appears as the third element of chunks 2 and 4, respectively, of the eight-chunk pattern). The results indicated that rats in SP6 learned to anticipate the violation, but only with great difficulty, requiring approximately 50 days to reach asymptote at approximately 25% errors. SP6 rats were further tested until day 70, but they never improved. Rats in SP12 never diverged from 100% errors in 70 days of training (24 patterns per day). Clearly, rats have great difficulty using SP as a cue for anticipating important sequential events such as violation elements, even when SP is the only reliable cue for the event. Indeed, rats may not be able to do so at all for serial positions 12 or beyond.

In another set of studies, we tested whether pattern structure would determine the ease or difficulty of pattern learning by developing patterns with hierarchical structure, then reordering chunks of the pattern to produce "linear" structure, that is, incompletely nested hierarchical structure (Fountain & Rowan, 1995a). The hierarchical (H) and linear (L) patterns were:

H pattern: 123 234 345 456 567 876 765 654 543 432 . . .
L pattern: 123 234 <u>543</u> 456 567 876 765 654 <u>345</u> 432 . . .

For both groups, the digits indicate the clockwise position of the correct response on successive trials and the spaces indicate brief pauses.

The completely nested H pattern is described by a simple hierarchical rule structure: elements within three-element chunks are related by first-order rules, chunks within the first and second halves of the pattern, respectively, are related to each other by second-order rules, and the first half of the pattern is related to the second half of the pattern by a third-order rule.

The incompletely nested L pattern was generated by exchanging the two underlined three-element chunks in the H pattern. In so doing, however, it should be noted that all pairwise associations were maintained; rats were always required to press a lever immediately to the left or right of the last correct response in both patterns, and the number of transitions from a given lever to any other was conserved across patterns. In this structure, elements within any chunk are related by a rule, but chunks are not related to each other in any systematic way.

The results showed that, for rats, pattern complexity predicted pattern learning difficulty (Fountain & Rowan, 1995a). The formally simpler H pattern was easier to learn than the formally more complex L pattern. In addition, rats in H were sensitive to the hierarchical structure of their pattern. For rats, as in humans, in the H pattern groups, the difficulty of learning to respond appropriately on any trial was a function of the hierarchical level of the rule required to predict the item. Rats produced significantly more errors on the first trial of chunks 1 and 6 than on all other trials. These trials corresponded to the highest-order rule transitions in the pattern structure (i.e., third-order rule transitions). Fewer errors were observed on the first trial of other chunks; these trials corresponded to second-order rule transitions. The fewest errors occurred within chunks, where trials corresponded to first-order rule transitions. Thus, in the completely hierarchical pattern, the difficulty of learning to respond appropriately on any trial was a function of the hierarchical level of the rule required to predict the item. Rats in L did not show the three-level hierarchical pattern of errors observed for H rats.

In the hierarchical versus linear structure experiment just described, rats demonstrated sensitivity to multilevel hierarchically organized pattern structure. Rats found learning completely nested hierarchical patterns easier than learning less organized patterns, even when pairwise associations and pattern length were conserved across patterns. In another study from the same series (Fountain & Rowan, 1995a), a three-level hierarchy was easier to learn than a four-level hierarchy when pattern length was conserved across patterns. As a rule, then, pattern complexity was a better predictor of acquisition difficulty in these studies than was pattern length. These acquisition results alone are strong evidence that pattern organization, that is, pattern complexity, was the primary determinant of pattern difficulty, as argued by a rule-learning view of sequential learning.

Interleaved Serial Patterns

One question of significance for animal sequential learning research is whether animals are constrained to learn sequences on the basis of pairwise associations between successive elements, for example, as in chaining (Skinner, 1934). A significant body of evidence suggests that animals are able to be more flexible in representing sequential events, conceivably by coding hierarchical representations characterized by relations for nonadjacent events (Roitblat, Bever, Helweg, & Harley, 1991; Roitblat, Scopatz, & Bever, 1987). The mechanisms of learning involving nonadjacent events are not well understood. Terrace (1987), for example, indicated that little evidence existed that animals are able to spontaneously reorganize sequentially presented items into chunks not presented by the experimenter. As Terrace noted, such processes are readily observed in human free-recall (Tulving, 1962). Additionally, it should be noted that chunking of nonadjacent items in human serial-pattern learning has been studied extensively using patterns of letters and digits (Hersh, 1974). We have previously shown that rats, when presented a sequence of reward quantities, can spontaneously sort quantities from nonadjacent SPs into chunks to facilitate learning (Fountain & Annau, 1984). A comparable strategy in humans would be to learn the pattern 2555455565558 by sorting pattern elements into 555 chunks and a 2468 chunk. Other work also supports the view that rats have this capacity. For example, Capaldi and Miller (1988) have shown that rats can keep count of different kinds of rewards by chunking nonadjacent items in series into different food categories. In two recent studies in our laboratory (Fountain, Rowan, & Benson, 1999), rats learned either a structured (ST) or unstructured (UNST) sequence interleaved with elements of a repeating (R) sequence in one experiment or an alternation (A) sequence in another experiment. The question was whether rats would learn the interleaved subpatterns at different rates as a function of subpattern complexity.

The first experiment sought to determine whether rats would show signs of being sensitive to the organization of nonadjacent items from interleaved subpatterns when one subpattern was a composed of simple, repeating element and the second subpattern was either highly structured or not. For rats in the structured (ST) subpattern condition, a 123 234 345 456 567 subpattern was interleaved with a repeating (R) subpattern, 888 888 888 888 888, resulting in the ST-R pattern that rats were required to learn:

182838 283848 384858 485868 586878.

For rats in the unstructured (UNST) subpattern condition, a 153 236 345 426 547 subpattern was interleaved with the same R subpattern to create the UNST-R pattern in the same manner. For both patterns, integers represent the clockwise position of correct levers in the octagonal chamber on successive trials and spaces represent pauses that served as phrasing cues.

Acquisition of the interleaved structured pattern (i.e., ST-R) was significantly faster than for the interleaved unstructured pattern (i.e., UNST-R). The unstructured pattern was generated by exchanging only two pairs of elements in the structured pattern, as described above. In so doing, however, all pair-wise associations in the interleaved patterns were maintained because all of the relocated items were preceded by "8" trials. Nevertheless, the effects of disrupting pattern structure were apparent throughout the pattern. UNST-R rats' performance was poorer even in the third (middle) chunk that was not altered in producing the unstructured pattern; rats found this chunk, 384858, harder to learn in the context of the UNST-R pattern than in the ST-R pattern. In the second experiment, rats learned two interleaved sequences, where both were created from sets composed of more than one element. As before, longer patterns were composed of two interleaved subpatterns; either a structured or unstructured subpattern was interleaved with a subpattern of two alternating elements. For one group of rats, the structured (ST) subpattern, 1 2 3 4 5 6, was interleaved with the alternating (A) subpattern, 7 8 7 8 7 8 to create the ST-A pattern. For another group of rats, the unstructured (UNST) subpattern, 1 5 3 4 2 6, was likewise interleaved with the same alternating subpattern to produce the UNST-A pattern. Note that the unstructured subpattern was generated by exchanging two items of the structured subpattern. Rats learned the subpatterns of their interleaved patterns at different rates both within and between pattern groups. As predicted based on subpattern structure, in the case of the UNST-A pattern, the A subpattern was acquired faster than the UNST subpattern. The A subpattern would be expected to be acquired faster because it is formally simple, whereas the UNST subpattern has little structure (Hulse, 1978; Hulse & Dorsky, 1977; Jones, 1974). Based on similar reasoning, it was expected that the ST subpattern should be easier to learn than the UNST subpattern; this result was obtained. In the case of the ST-A pattern, because both subpatterns were structured, it might be difficult to predict in advance based on subpattern structure alone whether rats should find either the ST or A subpattern easier to learn than the other. However, if structural complexity is equated (i.e., if the same number of rules are needed to describe subpattern structure), then rats might show the same predisposition that humans do (Kotovsky & Simon, 1973) to detect repeating items before other structural features of patterns. In fact, evidence for the latter assertion was obtained in this experiment. Rats in the ST-A pattern group showed better acquisition for A with its repeating "7" and "8" elements than ST subpatterns of their interleaved pattern despite the fact that both ST and A subpatterns have simple structure that can be described by a single rule (viz., a "+1" rule for the 123456 ST subpattern versus an "alternate" rule for the 787878 A subpattern). The results of differential acquisition of ST and UNST subpatterns support the notion that accurate performance on these interleaved subpatterns was dependent on a mnemonic representation characterized by relations for nonadjacent events (Roitblat et al., 1991, 1987). The results indicate that rats are sensitive to the organization of nonadjacent elements in serial patterns and that they can detect and sort structural relationships in interleaved patterns. Pattern and subpattern structures appear to drive how animals sort, chunk, and represent nonadjacent pattern elements that are related by common rules or features.

PHRASING CUES AS DISCRIMINATIVE STIMULI THAT CHUNK PATTERNS BY OVERSHADOWING

Fountain et al. (1984) argued that phrasing cues speed learning by facilitating chunking vis-à-vis pattern structure. Rats were trained to anticipate food quantities presented in a series of trials in a runway, such as in the five-element pattern, 14-7-3-1-0. Structurally, this pattern is highly organized; that is, it is formally simple, because successive elements can be described by a single "less than" rule (Hulse, 1978). A longer pattern was produced by presenting a 14-7-3-1-0 subpattern of food quantities five times in succession. Fountain et al. reported that, when spatial or temporal cues were placed congruent with boundaries between subpatterns, the cues facilitated pattern learning. This result tended to support the notion that phrasing facilitated learning by highlighting salient features of pattern structure rather than by cueing specific responses. However, one distinction between spatial and temporal cues was noted. When phrasing cues were removed, rats trained with spatial cues alone showed savings relative to controls that had never experienced cues. In contrast, rats trained with temporal cues alone or in combination with spatial cues showed no savings after cue removal, suggesting that spatial and temporal cues may have facilitated learning via different mechanisms (Fountain et al., 1984). Capaldi, Verry, Nawrocki, and Miller (1984) replicated the effects of spatial cues reported by Fountain et al. but argued that phrasing effects, like other aspects of serial-pattern learning, should be explained by appealing to traditional associative processes rather than rule-learning processes.

Echoing these earlier ideas, in Stempowski, Carman, and Fountain (1999), we argued that discriminative cues might serve at least two functions in serial learning. One possibility is that temporal intervals signal or guide responses as traditional discrimination learning theory suggests (Capaldi et al., 1984). In the case of temporal intervals inserted into patterns at chunk boundaries, the intervals presumably would overshadow the naturally occurring interitem associations and would become the principal signal of the correct response or the next item in the trial following the temporal pause (Capaldi et al., 1984). If this were the effect of inserting temporal cues into sequences, then rats should become dependent on these cues for producing the cued responses and should fail to respond correctly if the cues are removed. A second hypothesis is that temporal cues bias the perception of pattern organization (Fountain et al., 1984, 2002). According to this view, temporal cues identify salient features of pattern structure, for example, by indicating transitions between chunks. According to the hypothesis that intervals serve as cues for structure, the differential intervals located at chunk boundaries simply facilitate encoding pattern structure and should thus result in savings in pattern tracking even after phrasing cues are removed (for a similar argument, see Fountain et al., 1984).

Consistent with the views of Capaldi and associates, two recent experiments in our laboratory on the effects of temporal phrasing in rat pattern learning showed that temporal intervals positioned at chunk boundaries facilitated pattern learning by serving as discriminative cues that overshadowed associations between sequence items (Stempowski et al., 1999). One experiment showed that rat serial-pattern learning could be facilitated when distinct temporal intervals preceded chunk boundaries, regardless of whether the intervals were longer or shorter than the intervals within chunks. A second experiment replicated the acquisition results of the first with a different, more difficult serial pattern. In addition, after both 14 and 35 days of acquisition with phrasing cues, cue removal produced severe deficits in tracking the first element of chunks, the element directly after the phrasing cues during acquisition (Stempowski et al., 1999). The results indicated that rats used both short and long temporal phrasing intervals as discriminative cues, and that facilitated learning due to phrasing is not the result of additional processing time provided by longer intertrial intervals at chunk boundaries (Terrace, 1991). Furthermore, many of the finer details of the results could be accounted for by the additional assumption that phrasing cues overshadowed interitem associations.

DECONSTRUCTING SEQUENTIAL BEHAVIOR: PROBE METHODS

Our recent work has shown that transfer procedures and probe patterns can be very efficient and informative procedures for determining what behavioral processes determine rats' behavior in sequential learning tasks. Rats can easily be trained to perform 20 to 50 patterns per day during acquisition, and then continue with 20 to 50 patterns per day plus up to 10 interspersed probe patterns per day thereafter with the order of presentation of probe patterns randomized.

In a recent study conducted with graduate students Denise Smith and Melissa Muller, rats were initially trained on a two-level hierarchical pattern with a violation element as the last pattern element. Because the foregoing studies suggested that rats were sensitive to a chunk length equal to three elements, we wondered whether this sensitivity to chunks of three elements represented a bias caused by training with a pattern composed of three-element chunks or a limitation (or bias) in cognitive capacity (cf. Terrace, 2002). We also wished to identify the factors that control rats' behavior in sequential tasks on an element-by-element basis. To begin to answer these questions, rats were trained with a 16-element pattern composed of four four-element chunks, 1234 3456 5678 781<u>8</u>, where the violation element is indicated. The results were somewhat surprising in that rats took considerably longer to learn this pattern than the 24-element, eight-chunk pattern described in several studies above, despite the fact that the pattern's two-level structural organization is very similar. Additionally, rats found chunk boundaries (the first element of new chunks) at least as difficult to learn as the violation element. This outcome deserves further scrutiny because it appears to challenge a rule-learning interpretation of hierarchical pattern learning, which predicts that patterns with similar structure should also be similar in difficulty.

Once rats learned this pattern to a high level of accuracy (no more than 10 percent errors on any element type within a day), they experienced a series of 10-day probe phases, wherein they were trained with 20 patterns of the training pattern each day with three probe patterns presented in random order after the fifth, tenth, and fifteenth pattern of each day. We thus obtained data for 10 probe trials for each of three probe patterns for each 10-day probe phase. Between probe phases, rats were returned to normal training for a minimum of 3 days to ensure that they still met criterion performance before going to the next probe phase. The following sections describe some of the probe results we obtained.

RATS USE DIFFERENT CUES TO ANTICIPATE DIFFERENT PATTERN ELEMENTS, INCLUDING COMPOUND CUES TO ANTICIPATE CHUNK BOUNDARIES

After rats were trained to a high level of accuracy, they experienced three patterns that varied in length from 12 elements to 20 elements. These probe patterns also contained chunks with as few as 1 element and as many as 6 elements between phrasing cues. However, in each case, the violation element was the last element of the pattern and remained in the same spatial location in the chamber

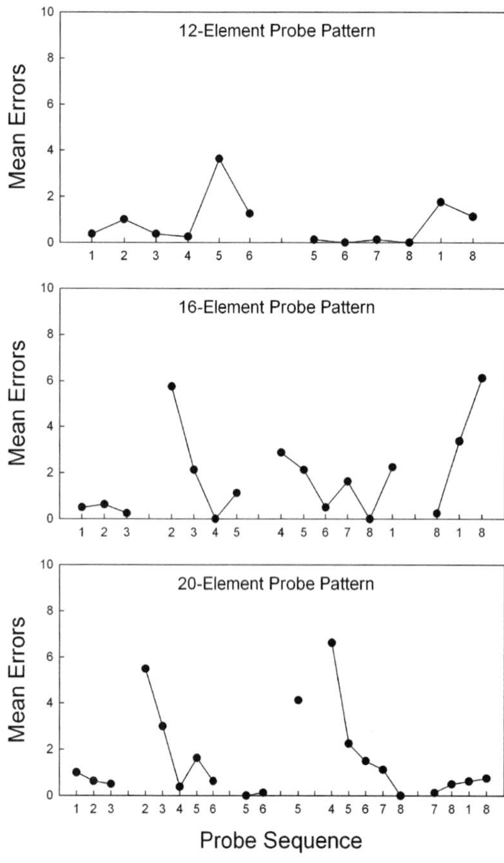

Figure 23.1. Rats' group mean number of pattern tracking errors for the successive elements of the 12-, 16-, and 20-element probe patterns.

(i.e., on lever 8). Response requirements after phrasing cues and within chunks were conserved; phrasing cues continued to signal left turns in the probes, and within-chunk responses were always right turns, as in training. The probe patterns were:

12-Element probe pattern: 123456 567818
16-Element probe pattern: 123 2345 456781 818
20-Element probe pattern: 123 23456 56 5 45678 7818

Rats received one of each transfer pattern as probe patterns interspersed with normal training for 10 days.

Figure 23.1 shows rats' performance on each of the three probe patterns. The results reveal that rats use different cues to anticipate different elements of the pattern and that they use compound cues to anticipate chunk boundaries. First, one should note that rats' performance on the violation element (the last element of each pattern) was excellent in the 12- and 20-element probe patterns, despite large changes in SP and in the pattern leading up to the violation. Ironically, performance on the violation element suffered in the 16-element probe only, even though the violation occurred in the same SP as in training patterns. This profile of results is consistent with the idea that rats were using spatial cues to anticipate the violation element and that SP in the pattern and chunk played little role in anticipation of the violation element.

Second, it should be noted that performance on the first element of chunks in probe patterns—elements that followed phrasing cues indicated by breaks in the curves in figure 23.1—varied from excellent to quite poor. A close perusal of the data indicates that phrasing cues were effective as a cue for the next response whenever the preceding chunk was composed of four elements or more. When phrasing cues followed chunks that were one, two, or three elements long, performance on the trial after the phrasing cue was poor. Thus, in the probes, rats were using phrasing cues to anticipate chunk boundary elements, but only when chunks were as long as or longer than they were in training patterns. Although it is clear that the phrasing cue should have been sufficient to inform the animals what to do at chunk boundaries ("always turn left"), the rats learned about chunk length even when phrasing cues should have been perfectly adequate for anticipating the next event of the sequence.

The foregoing results parallel and extend the results from an earlier study with a similar design (Fountain et al., 2002). In that study, rats were trained to a high level of accuracy on a 24-element pattern composed of eight three-element chunks, 123 234 345 456 567 678 781 818, where the violation element is indicated. In transfer patterns, rats experienced three patterns that varied in length from 18 elements to 30 elements. As in the current study, chunk length was manipulated in transfer testing, so that transfer patterns contained chunks with as few as one element and as many as five elements between phrasing cues. However, in each case, the violation element was the last element of the pattern and remained in the same spatial location in the chamber; the response requirements after phrasing cues and within chunks were conserved. Results paralleled those obtained here; evidence indicated that rats used spatial cues rather than SP to

Table 23.1. Manipulation of Three Factors Potentially Responsible for Poor Performance on the Violation Element in the 16-Element Probe Pattern of Figure 23.1 (2 × 2 × 2 Design)

"7" or "1" Response on Element 1 of Training Chunk 4	Phrasing Cue or No Phrasing Cue Before Training Chunk 4	Extra Phrasing Cue after Element 1 in Training Chunk 4	Resulting Probe Pattern
7	P	No Extra Cue	1234 3456 5678 7818*
1	P	No Extra Cue	1234 3456 5678 1818
7	NoP	No Extra Cue	1234 3456 56787818
1	NoP	No Extra Cue	1234 3456 56781818
7	P	Extra Cue	1234 3456 5678 7 818
1	P	Extra Cue	1234 3456 5678 1 818
7	NoP	Extra Cue	1234 3456 56787 818
1	NoP	Extra Cue	1234 3456 56781 818

*Training pattern.

anticipate the violation element and that rats used compound cues composed of phrasing and SP cues to anticipate chunk boundaries after chunks composed of three elements (Fountain et al., 2002).

Taken together, the results of the foregoing studies indicate that rats can be explicitly trained to anticipate chunk boundaries after either three- or four-chunk elements. This outcome indicates that the results of the foregoing studies suggesting that rats were sensitive to a chunk length equal to three elements were not due to a limitation (or bias) in cognitive capacity (cf. Terrace, 2002), but were the result of a bias caused by training with a pattern composed of three-element chunks. When rats were trained with phrasing and pattern structure implying an interpretation of the pattern composed of four-element chunks, rats internalized that interpretation of the pattern. Although rats may indeed have some native cognitive limitations or biases that could affect how they chunk patterns, these results show that rats can be flexible in how they chunk serial patterns and that they respond to some of the same kinds of pattern features that humans do in parsing sequential information.

RATS USE COMPOUND CUES TO ANTICIPATE A VIOLATION ELEMENT

It should be noted that the 16-element sequence under study, 1234 3456 5678 781<u>8</u> (where the violation element is underlined), has severe associative "branching": that is, many elements of the sequence, here indicated as digits but representing spatial locations in a circular array, predict multiple future outcomes. For example, "1" is followed by "2" early in the sequence but is followed by "8" at the end of the sequence. If one imagines recoding the sequential behavior as right and left turns, then right turns are followed by right and left turns approximately equally often. Using individual cues for responses, the problem is insoluble, yet rats have little difficulty learning this sequence and sequences like it to high levels of accuracy. Some authors have argued that rule learning is the solution that rats adopt, but even a rule-learning strategy fails when the target is the violation element. The violation element by definition cannot be predicted by pattern rules, is not anticipated based on pattern SP, and cannot be anticipated based on any single cue, spatial or proprioceptive, that directly precedes it. What cues do rats use to anticipate the violation element?

A clue comes from the results depicted in figure 23.1. Rats do quite well in terms of anticipating the violation element in the 12-element probe (top panel) and in the 20-element probe (bottom), but they do poorly in the 16-element probe (middle panel). The 16-element probe differed from training in three ways: the "7" response required as element 1 of training chunk 4 was changed to a "1" response, the training chunk 4 phrasing cue was removed, and an extra phrasing cue was added before the final "818" sequence. As shown in table 23.1, we used a 2 × 2 × 2 factor design to ascertain which of these changes or combinations of changes to the training pattern was responsible for poor performance in the 16-element probe. Figure 23.2 shows rats' group mean errors on the violation element of each probe in table 23.1. The results show that rats' performance on the violation element did not differ

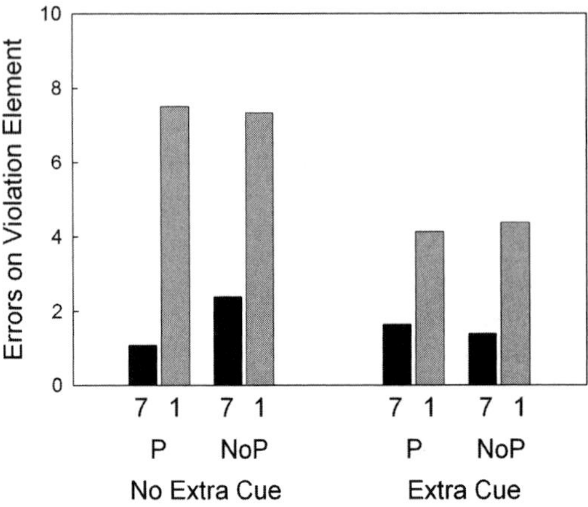

Figure 23.2. Rats' group mean number of errors on the violation element when element 1 of chunk 4 remained "7" or was changed to "1," when the probe had training phrasing (P) or the phrasing cue removed (NoP), and when no extratemporal cue was inserted into chunk 4 of the probe (No Extra Cue) or had an extra cue added (Extra Cue). Of these changes to the pattern presented as probes, only changing element 1 of chunk 4 from "7" to "1" significantly increased errors on the violation element.

Table 23.2. Probe Patterns Created by Changing the Required Response to a "3" Response for Individual Elements of Chunks 3 and 4 Leading Up to the Violation Element

Location of Element Change (Number of Trials before Violation Element)	Resulting Probe Pattern
1	1234 3456 5678 7838
2	1234 3456 5678 7318
3	1234 3456 5678 3818
4	1234 3456 5673 7818
5	1234 3456 5638 7818
6	1234 3456 5378 7818
7	1234 3456 3678 7818

from training as long as the "7" element was not replaced by a requirement to respond on lever 1. Removing the phrasing cue at the beginning of training chunk 4 had little effect generally. This result is consistent with the results of figure 23.1, where phrasing cue removal in the 12-element probe had little effect on anticipation of the violation element. Adding an extra cue within what had been chunk 4 of training actually improved performance for rats that had "7" changed to "1."

One question of interest is why rats used "7" as a cue for the violation element. Close perusal of the pattern shows that, logically, only the "81" elements of the last chunk are necessary to anticipate the violation element because the "81" event sequence is unique in the pattern. This question led us to investigate the factors influencing which cues come to control behavior in this situation.

CHUNK FORMATION INDEPENDENT OF ASSOCIATIVE DEMANDS

To ascertain which elements of the pattern actually served as cues for the violation element, rats were presented seven probes as before with one pattern element changed in each probe. Instead of the response learned in training, rats were required to make a "3" response. Different probes required rats to make a "3" response rather than the response learned in training for each element of chunks 3 and 4 leading up to the violation element, as shown in table 23.2.

Figure 23.3 shows rats' group mean errors on the violation element as a function of the location of an element change in the sequence. The results demonstrated a discontinuity between chunks 3 and 4; element changes in chunk 3 had no effect on anticipation of the final violation element of the sequence, whereas any change in chunk 4 produced serious disruption of anticipation. The results indicate that rats used the sequence of elements "781" as a compound cue to anticipate the violation element. Changing any element of this three-element sequence produced a profound disruption of anticipation of the violation element. Given that, logically, only the "81" elements of the last chunk are necessary to anticipate the violation element, the fact that rats uniformly also included the "7" element in the stimulus compound "781" used to anticipate the terminal violation element indicates that a chunking mechanism contributed to the organization of rats' behavior. Chunk formation was not determined by the minimum number of cues necessary for accurate anticipation of the violation element. This phenomenon deserves further scrutiny because it implies that concurrent and potentially independent item associative and cognitive chunking processes were involved in sequence learning.

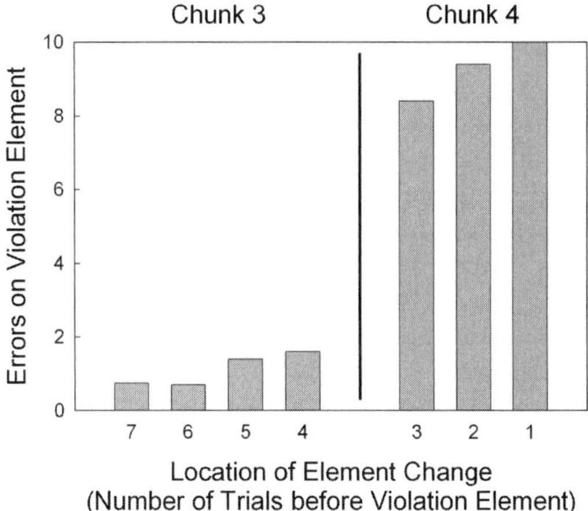

Figure 23.3. Violation element errors as a function of the location of earlier element changes. Element changes in chunk 3 had little effect on anticipation of the violation element, whereas changes in chunk 4 caused profound deficits in anticipation of the violation element.

CHUNKING INDEPENDENT OF ASSOCIATIVE DEMANDS IN INTERLEAVED SEQUENCES

Here, we digress to describe additional evidence for the notion of chunking apparently independent of associative demands. In a separate study conducted with graduate student Don Benson, rats learned interleaved patterns (Fountain et al., 1999) based on two simple subpatterns, but for different groups of rats, pattern structure was manipulated by introducing no, two, or four violations into the first subpattern of the interleaved pattern. Rats were randomly assigned to three pattern conditions. One group learned an interleaved pattern based on the two formally simple (S) subpatterns, 1-2-3-4-5-6-7-8 and 5-6-7-8-1-2-3-4. Thus, the interleaved S-S serial pattern was 1-5-2-6-3-7-4-8-5-1-6-2-7-3-8-4. Both subpatterns are considered formally simple because they can be described by a single rule, namely, a "+1" rule that indicates that, on successive trials, the rat must choose the lever to the right of the last correct lever. In fact, the subpatterns are structurally the same, differing only in terms of where the pattern begins in the octagonal box (lever 1 vs. lever 5 as starting lever). This interleaved pattern was called "S-S", to signify that it was composed of two subpatterns of simple structure. A second group learned an interleaved 2V-S serial pattern composed of two subpatterns, one with two violation (2V) elements and the other with simple structure: 1-2-4-3-5-6-7-8 and 56781234. Thus, for the second group, the interleaved 2V-S pattern was: 1-5-2-6-4-7-3-8-5-1-6-2-7-3-8-4. Note that the 2V subpattern contains two "violation" elements that break the +1 rule that describes the elements constituting the rest of this subpattern. The 2V subpattern was created by exchanging the "4" and "3" elements of the first subpattern of the S-S pattern. The second subpattern of 2V-S is identical to the second subpattern of the S-S pattern. A third group learned an interleaved 4V-S pattern was composed of two subpatterns, one with 4 violation (4V) elements and the other with simple structure: 1-2-4-3-6-5-7-8 and 5-6-7-8-1-2-3-4. Thus, the interleaved 4V-S serial pattern was 1-5-2-6-4-7-3-8-6-1-5-2-7-3-8-4. The 4V subpattern was created by exchanging the "3" and "4" elements and the "5" and "6" elements of the first subpattern of the S-S pattern. The second subpattern of 4V-S is identical to the second subpattern of the S-S and 2V-S patterns.

Figure 23.4 shows the acquisition curves for the component subpatterns of S-S, 2V-S, and 4V-S (top to bottom panels, respectively). As we predicted based on rule-learning theory, the interleaved serial pattern, S-S, composed of two subpatterns of simple structure, was learned faster than interleaved serial patterns containing violation elements. Further, in each interleaved pattern, subpatterns were acquired at different rates. Even though the two S subpatterns in the interleaved serial pattern S-S were essentially identical, rats were still able to chunk items with respect to constituent subpattern; most rats learned the first S subpattern faster than the second S subpattern. With reference to the 2V-S and 4V-S interleaved patterns, the subpattern containing the violation elements was acquired first. Generally, then, rats learned the first subpattern of the interleaved patterns before the second subpattern, even in the case where the subpatterns were essentially identical (i.e., in the S-S pattern). These results are not easily explained by rule learning, which predicts that simple subpatterns should be learned before more complex subpatterns. Just the opposite occurred in 2V-S and 4V-S. The results are also not easily explained from an associative perspective, which, if any predictions can be made, predicts that the S-S subpatterns should be learned at the same pace. The results fit best with the idea that rats cognitively chunked the sequences, but the phenomenon deserves further study given that our other studies with interleaved serial patterns

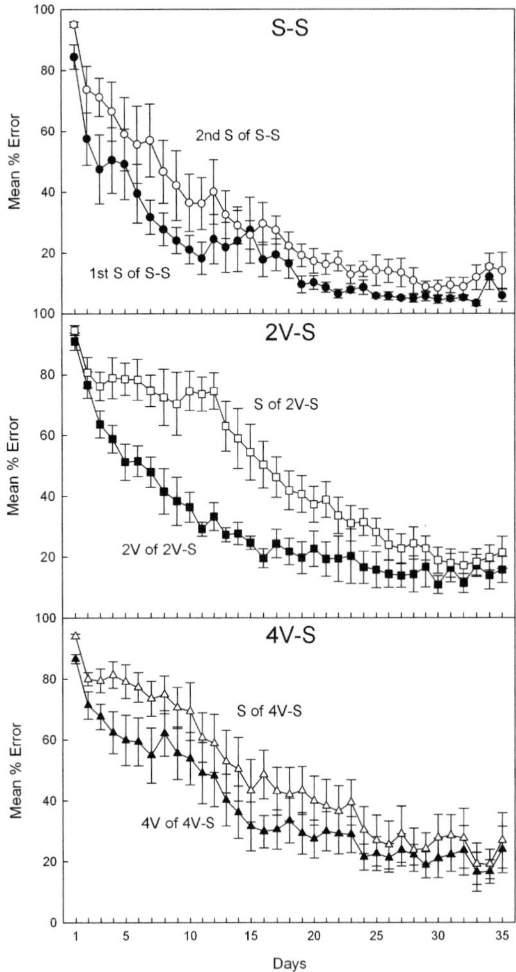

Figure 23.4. Acquisition curves comparing the component first and second subpatterns of S-S, 2V-S, and 4V-S (*top* to *bottom*, respectively) over the 35 days of the experiment. Percentages of daily mean errors were averaged across all elements of the patterns. Error bars indicate ±SEM.

showed that rats do not always learn the first subpattern of an interleaved pattern faster than a later subpattern (Fountain et al., 1999).

THE ROLE OF PATTERN ELEMENTS AS CUES IN SEQUENTIAL PATTERNS

Returning to our study of the 16-element sequence, 1234 3456 5678 7818, we recall from figure 23.3 that rats used the sequence of elements "781" as a compound cue to anticipate the violation element; the chunk 4 phrasing cue played little role in anticipation of the violation element. To examine the role of pattern elements as cues throughout the pattern, we presented rats with three probes where the pattern was shifted around the array of levers. That is, the pattern was structured the same, with four chunks with phrasing cues and a violation element at the last element of the sequence, but the pattern began on three different levers with the probe patterns starting on levers 2, 4, and 8. The resulting probe patterns were:

Lever 2 start: 2345 4567 6781 8121
Lever 4 start: 4567 6781 8123 2343
Lever 8 start: 8123 2345 4567 6787

Figure 23.5 shows rats' group mean trial-by-trial performance on these three probe patterns. First, it should be noted that rats failed to anticipate the violation elements located at the end of each probe pattern. Error rates were high on this element for all of the probes. It is also interesting to note that, with regard to anticipating the violation element, there was little evidence of generalization from the training pattern. Two similar probes were started one lever to the left and right of the training pattern on lever 2 or 8, so the final chunk and violation element of these probes were shifted only one lever to the left or right of those experienced in training. The other different probe was started on the opposite side of the chamber, on lever 4, so that the final chunk and violation were three levers away from their location in training. Under these conditions, rats were no better at anticipating the violation element in the two similar conditions than they were in the different condition, indicating that rats acquired a very precise discrimination of the "781" sequence that cued the violation element in training and that resulted in little generalization to similar probes.

Second, rats were also not able to anticipate the first element of each probe pattern, producing very high error rates on element 1, as expected because the probes appeared in random order and thus could not be anticipated. Rats made the response expected from training; they chose lever 1 uniformly, indicating that spatial cues controlled element 1 responses.

Third, what is remarkable, given the magnitude of the two foregoing effects, is that rats were uniformly good at anticipating almost all of the other elements of the three probe patterns. Rats anticipated both within-chunk elements and chunk-boundary elements with a high degree of accuracy.

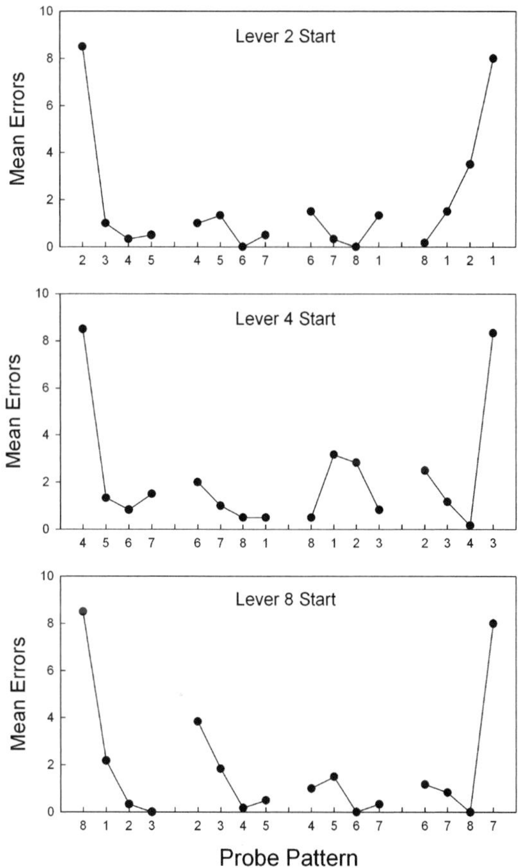

Figure 23.5. Rats' group mean number of pattern tracking errors for the successive elements of the probe patterns shifted to start on lever 2, 4, or 8 (*top* to *bottom*, respectively).

These results indicate that the compound of cues controlling responding at chunk boundaries—which included temporal cues and cues correlated with SP, as indicated above—did not include spatial cues. Likewise, responses to within-chunk elements also were not controlled by pattern element cues. Clearly, rats used spatial pattern element cues on element 1 and to anticipate the violation element, but not elsewhere in the pattern. The factors that influence or determine which cues come to control rats' behavior on a trial-by-trial basis are not yet clear.

THE RESILIENCE OF WITHIN-CHUNK RESPONSE SEQUENCES

Through a number of different studies involving cue removal or cue manipulation, probe trials, or transfer phases, we have been struck by the resilience of within-chunk response sequences once they are learned. In the case of our 16-element sequence, 1234 3456 5678 7818, we apply the term, within-chunk elements, to elements beyond chunk boundaries that are not violation elements, such as "234" of chunk 1 and "456" of chunk 2. Universally, we have found that responses to chunk boundary elements and to violation elements are significantly more difficult to acquire than responses to within-chunk elements. Rats learn to anticipate within-chunk elements quickly, and these responses resist disruption by temporal cues, spatial cues, and even structural manipulations such as changing chunk length. In rule-learning terms, within-chunk responses are described by the lowest-order (first order) rules of the pattern structure, such as "+1" or "move-one-to-the-right" rule, in this case, that are typically applied repeatedly to generate individual multi-element chunks. From a proprioceptive cue-learning perspective, within-chunk elements in our paradigm can be described as repetitions of the same movement. From the rule-learning perspective, these rules are abstract in the sense that they have meaning when applied to any element in the stimulus array; a "+1" rule can be applied to any starting position with the same meaning, namely, increment within the array. From the proprioceptive cue learning perspective, these left and right turns have a similar "abstract" quality since they are self-referential; the rat can conceivably make the same "right turn" from any position in the array. From both perspectives, the prediction would be that within-chunk response sequences should be disrupted only minimally by changes in exteroceptive or other interoceptive cues such as spatial cues or temporal cues. This is the result we have typically observed. For example, shifting the starting lever of patterns within the octagonal chamber or transfer to a different operant chamber causes disruption of anticipation of violation elements (see figure 23.5), but has no measurable effect on within-chunk performance. Similarly, probes with phrasing cue removal disrupt performance on the element cued by the phrasing cue in training, but have little effect on within-chunk performance, as we showed in earlier studies with different patterns (Stempowski et al., 1999). The results show that within-chunk response sequences are indeed "abstract" in the sense that they are not directly tied to exteroceptive cues. Instead, these responses appear to be related to interoceptive cues, such as proprioceptive feedback from left and right turns, or interoceptive information from cognitive systems, such as rule-based representations of chunks or the sequence as a whole.

NEUROBEHAVIORAL STUDIES OF SEQUENTIAL BEHAVIOR IN RATS

Recently, we began to explore the neural basis of sequential learning and behavior in a systematic manner. Our first approach was to investigate the effects of drugs thought to have effects on learning by their impact on specific receptor systems. This approach had the advantage that we could choose drugs that could be injected systemically and thus avoid the problem of producing lesions in animals to be implanted with bipolar electrodes. Thus, in these studies rats learned leverpress response patterns for brain-stimulation reward (BSR). In one series of experiments (Fountain & Rowan, 2000), rats were trained on two patterns: one that was structurally "perfect" and a second virtually identical to the first, but containing a single element that violated the otherwise simple structure. The perfect (P) and violation (V) patterns were:

P pattern: 123 234 345 456 567 678 781 812
V pattern: 123 234 345 456 567 678 781 818

As before, the digits indicate the reinforced lever for successive trials and spaces indicate the location of phrasing cues. The last "8" item of the V pattern (underlined) was the violation element. Rats from one group for each pattern condition were injected with 0.0625 mg/kg MK-801 daily before training. MK-801 is a systemically administered NMDA receptor antagonist that blocks neuronal plasticity in the hippocampus and other areas of the brain, including amygdala and basal ganglia. We observed that MK-801 had little effect on learning to respond to rule-governed elements within chunks. However, it did impair responding for the violation element and for cued responses at chunk boundaries. Another recent study conducted in collaboration with James Rowan and Michael Wollan for his dissertation examined the effects of cholinergic blockade on performance of a well-learned serial pattern with phrasing cues and a violation element (the violation pattern described above). Rats received 50 mg/kg atropine sulfate injections prior to testing. Cholinergic blockade by atropine produced greatly elevated response rates on chunk boundaries and the violation element but almost no effect on within-chunk elements.

In a more recent study conducted by Denise Smith for her master's thesis, rats were trained to make nose poke responses for water reinforcement in the octagonal chamber to produce the pattern just described. The results replicated our earlier results (Fountain & Rowan, 2000) by showing little effect of MK-801 on acquisition of within-chunk, rule-governed elements—although a reduction in accuracy at asymptote was observed. We also observed that MK-801 produced profound deficits for learning to perform cued responses at chunk boundaries and for the violation element over the 49 days of the experiment. Thus, parallel results were obtained in the two types of octagonal chambers under different response and reward conditions. This study also examined the role of hippocampus in sequential learning. One group of rats received radiofrequency lesions of the dorsal hippocampus at least one week prior to training on the aforementioned serial pattern with phrasing cues and a violation element: 123 234 345 456 567 678 781 818. Rats were trained for 49 days in the octagonal chamber with nose poke for water reward. The results indicated that dorsal hippocampus plays no significant role in rats' ability to learn to perform rule-governed within-chunk responses or, somewhat surprisingly, to anticipate the difficult violation element. Dorsal hippocampal lesions did produce a significant retardation of learning about cued responses at chunk boundaries, but lesioned rats eventually achieved the same level of performance as controls. To ensure ourselves that our lesions were good (and our histology later confirmed large lesions in dorsal hippocampus), these rats were later tested on a radial maze task and showed spatial memory deficits. Clearly, this relatively simple pattern recruits hippocampal function for only a small role in learning about chunk boundaries, and it will be interesting to determine what function it plays and whether hippocampus is more important for more demanding tasks, such as disambiguating interleaved patterns (cf. Agster et al., 2002).

From both a learning theory perspective and a neural systems perspective, it is important to (a) determine whether multiple neural systems are recruited in sequential learning, as evidence seems strongly to indicate, (b) identify the neural systems involved, and (c) determine whether multiple neural systems are recruited concurrently, as we have proposed above for the concomitant behavioral processes. As for the behavioral processes, it is also important to identify factors that determine when these neural systems come into play, whether or not they are recruited concurrently. This information is critical for developing a coherent general model of behavioral and neural function in sequential learning.

ANIMALS AS MULTIMODALITY SEQUENTIAL PROCESSORS

The general goal of the foregoing studies was to begin to identify which behavioral processes contribute to control of rats' responses in serial patterns of behavior on an element-by-element basis, in order to develop a more complete picture of how sequential behavior is acquired, represented, and produced. The approach was to determine the extent to which rats' sequential behavior is controlled by extrasequence stimuli through associative processes, such as temporal or spatial cues acting as discriminative cues, by some other mechanisms, such as internal motor patterns or cognitive structures, or by multiple processes acting concurrently. The behavioral evidence that we have accumulated strongly supports the view that rats can be described as multimodality sequential processors. Evidence supports the view that rats concurrently track multiple interoceptive, exteroceptive, and cognitive sources of information to organize their behavior through time.

The outcomes of these studies are relevant to current research problems in several domains. First, the results are important for building a better understanding of the mechanisms of serial-pattern learning, because they begin the process of cataloging the conditions under which item associations, extrasequence cues, and pattern structure, individually or collectively, control sequential behavior. This information will be critical in developing an integrative model of serial-pattern learning. Second, if rats are concurrently using multiple cues to anticipate upcoming pattern elements, as suggested by several studies reported here, then this research is also potentially relevant to more generally understanding how animals use cues concurrently either in stimulus compounds that remain "elemental" or that become "configural" (Pearce, 1987; Pearce & Bouton, 2001). The results could help clarify whether cues in complex serial-pattern learning tasks are treated the same or differently by the organism compared with when they are encountered in simpler instrumental or classical conditioning settings. Third, the results of these studies will be very useful in informing behavioral neuroscience research that is attempting to understand the cortical and subcortical circuits responsible for sequential behavior. For example, if sequential behavior routinely includes temporal coding for SP of pattern elements even when other processes are also coding item associations (as indicated in the foregoing studies), then neural models will benefit from that information. This type of information could be particularly useful to those attempting to understand the sequential processes mediated by the hippocampal system, the medial prefrontal cortex, the caudate-frontal cortical loop, and the putamen–supplementary motor area (SMA) cortical loop, especially as these relate to processes in Alzheimer's, Parkinson's, and Huntington's diseases. Finally, this line of work can be potentially relevant to understanding how multiple behavioral processes are selected and controlled to produce efficient and accurate behavior through time, a problem central to both serial-pattern learning and to the concept of "executive function."

Acknowledgments This work was supported in part by National Institute of Mental Health Grant MH48402.

References

Agster, K. L., Fortin, N. J., & Eichenbaum, H. (2002). The hippocampus and disambiguation of overlapping sequences. *Journal of Neuroscience, 22,* 5760–5768.

Burns, R. A., & Gordon, W. U. (1988). Some further observations on serial enumeration and categorical flexibility. *Animal Learning & Behavior, 16,* 425–428.

Burns, R. A., Hulbert, L. G., & Cribb, D. (1990). A test for order relevance in a three-element serial learning task. *Journal of General Psychology, 117,* 91–98.

Capaldi, E. J. (1985). Anticipation and remote associations: A configural approach. *Journal of Experimental Psychology: Learning, Memory, and Cognition, 11,* 444–449.

Capaldi, E. J. (1986). Serial learning and trimethyltin: An unfortunate case of ad hoc conclusions. *Physiological Psychology, 14,* 71–72.

Capaldi, E. J. (1994). The sequential view: From rapidly fading stimulus traces to the organization of memory and the abstract concept of number. *Psychonomic Bulletin & Review, 2,* 156–181.

Capaldi, E. J. (2002). The discriminative stimulus and response enhancing properties of reward produced memories. In S. B. Fountain, M. Bunsey, J. H. Danks, & M. K. McBeath (Eds.), *Animal cognition and sequential behavior: Behavioral, biological, and computational perspectives* (pp. 91–113). Boston: Kluwer Academic.

Capaldi, E. J., & Miller, D. J. (1988). The rat's simultaneous anticipation of remote events and current events can be sustained by event memories alone. *Animal Learning & Behavior, 16,* 1–7.

Capaldi, E. J., & Molina, P. (1979). Element discriminability as a determinant of serial-pattern learning. *Animal Learning & Behavior, 7,* 318–322.

Capaldi, E. J., Nawrocki, T. M., Miller, D. J., & Verry, D. R. (1985). An examination into some variables said to affect serial learning. *Animal Learning & Behavior, 13,* 129–136.

Capaldi, E. J., Nawrocki, T. M., & Verry, D. R. (1982). Difficult serial anticipation learning in rats: Rule-encoding vs. memory. *Animal Learning & Behavior, 10,* 167–170.

Capaldi, E. J., Verry, D. R., & Davidson, T. (1980a). Memory, serial anticipation pattern learning, and transfer in rats. *Animal Learning & Behavior, 8,* 575–585.

Capaldi, E. J., Verry, D. R., & Davidson, T. (1980b). Why rule encoding by animals in serial learning remains to be established. *Animal Learning & Behavior, 8,* 691–692.

Capaldi, E. J., Verry, D. R., Nawrocki, T. M., & Miller, D. J. (1984). Serial learning, interitem associations, phrasing cues, interference, overshadowing, chunking, memory, and extinction. *Animal Learning & Behavior, 12,* 7–20.

Chen, S., Swartz, K. B., & Terrace, H. S. (1997). Knowledge of the ordinal position of list items in rhesus monkeys. *Psychological Science, 8,* 80–86.

Dallal, N. L., & Meck, W. H. (1990). Hierarchical structures: Chunking by food type facilitates spatial memory. *Journal of Experimental Psychology: Animal Behavior Processes, 16,* 69–84.

DeCoteau, W. E., & Kesner, R. P. (2000). A double dissociation between the rat hippocampus and medial caudoputamen in processing two forms of knowledge. *Behavioral Neuroscience, 114,* 1096–1108.

Fountain, S. B. (1986). Serial-pattern learning: A unitary process? *Physiological Psychology, 14,* 67–70.

Fountain, S. B. (1990). Rule abstraction, item memory, and chunking in rat serial-pattern tracking. *Journal of Experimental Psychology: Animal Behavior Processes, 16,* 96–105.

Fountain, S. B., & Annau, Z. (1984). Chunking, sorting, and rule-learning from serial patterns of brain-stimulation reward by rats. *Animal Learning & Behavior, 12,* 265–274.

Fountain, S. B., Evensen, J. C., & Hulse, S. H. (1983). Formal structure and pattern length in serial pattern learning by rats. *Animal Learning & Behavior, 11,* 186–192.

Fountain, S. B., Henne, D. R., & Hulse, S. H. (1984). Phrasing cues and hierarchical organization in serial pattern learning by rats. *Journal of Experimental Psychology: Animal Behavior Processes, 10,* 30–45.

Fountain, S. B., & Hulse, S. H. (1981). Extrapolation of serial stimulus patterns by rats. *Animal Learning & Behavior, 9,* 381–384.

Fountain, S. B., Krauchunas, S. M., & Rowan, J. D. (1999). Serial-pattern learning in mice: Pattern structure and phrasing. *Psychological Record, 49,* 173–192.

Fountain, S. B., & Rowan, J. D. (1995a). Coding of hierarchical versus linear pattern structure in rats and humans. *Journal of Experimental Psychology: Animal Behavior Processes, 21,* 187–202.

Fountain, S. B., & Rowan, J. D. (1995b). Sensitivity to violations of "run" and "trill" structures in rat serial-pattern learning. *Journal of Experimental Psychology: Animal Behavior Processes, 21,* 78–81.

Fountain, S. B., & Rowan, J. D. (2000). Differential impairments of rat serial-pattern learning and retention induced by MK-801, an NMDA receptor antagonist. *Psychobiology, 28,* 32–44.

Fountain, S. B., Rowan, J. D., & Benson, D. M., Jr. (1999). Rule learning in rats: Serial tracking in interleaved patterns. *Animal Cognition, 2,* 41–54.

Fountain, S. B., Wallace, D. G., & Rowan, J. D. (2002). The organization of sequential behavior. In S. B. Fountain, M. Bunsey, J. H. Danks, & M. K. McBeath (Eds.), *Animal cognition and sequential behavior: Behavioral, biological, and computational perspectives* (pp. 115–150). Boston: Kluwer Academic.

Hartman, M., Knopman, D. S., & Nissen, M. J. (1989). Implicit learning of new verbal associations. *Journal of Experimental Psychology: Learning, Memory, and Cognition, 15,* 1070–1082.

Heindel, W. C., Butters, N., & Salmon, D. P. (1988). Impaired learning of a motor skill in patients with Huntington's disease. *Behavioral Neuroscience, 102,* 141–147.

Hersh, H. M. (1974). The effects of irrelevant relations on the processing of sequential patterns. *Memory and Cognition, 2,* 771–774.

Hulse, S. H. (1978). Cognitive structure and serial pattern learning by animals. In S. H. Hulse, H. Fowler, & W. K. Honig (Eds.), *Cognitive processes in animal behavior* (pp. 311–340). Hillsdale, NJ: Erlbaum.

Hulse, S. H. (1980). The case of the missing rule: Memory for reward vs. formal structure in serial-pattern learning by rats. *Animal Learning & Behavior, 8,* 689–690.

Hulse, S. H., & Campbell, C. E. (1975). "Thinking ahead" in rat discrimination learning. *Animal Learning & Behavior, 3,* 305–311.

Hulse, S. H., & Dorsky, N. P. (1977). Structural complexity as a determinant of serial pattern learning. *Learning and Motivation, 8,* 488–506.

Hulse, S. H., & Dorsky, N. P. (1979). Serial pattern learning by rats: Transfer of a formally defined stimulus relationship and the significance of nonreinforcement. *Animal Learning & Behavior, 7,* 211–220.

Hunter, W. S. (1920). The temporal maze and kinaesthetic sensory processes in the white rat. *Psychobiology, 2,* 1–17.

Jaspers, R., Schwarz, M., Sontag, K. H., & Cools, A. R. (1984). Caudate nucleus and programming behaviour in cats: Role of dopamine in switching motor patterns. *Behavioural Brain Research, 14,* 17–28.

Jones, M. R. (1974). Cognitive representations of serial patterns. In B. Kantowitz (Ed.), *Human information processing: Tutorials in performance and cognition.* Hillsdale, NJ: Erlbaum.

Kesner, R. P. (2002). Neural mediation of memory for time: Role of the hippocampus and medial prefrontal cortex. In S. B. Fountain, M. Bunsey, J. H. Danks, & M. K. McBeath (Eds.), *Animal cognition and sequential behavior: Behavioral, biological, and computational perspectives* (pp. 201–226). Boston: Kluwer Academic.

Knopman, D., & Nissen, M. J. (1991). Procedural learning is impaired in Huntington's disease: Evidence from the serial reaction time task. *Neuropsychologia, 29,* 245–254.

Knopman, D. S., & Nissen, M. J. (1987). Implicit learning in patients with probable Alzheimer's disease. *Neurology, 37,* 784–788.

Kotovsky, K., & Simon, H. A. (1973). Empirical tests of a theory of human acquisition of concepts for sequential patterns. *Cognitive Psychology, 4,* 399–424.

Lashley, K. S. (1951). The problem of serial order in behavior. In L. A. Jeffress (Ed.), *Cerebral mechanisms in behavior* (pp. 112–146). New York: Wiley.

Macuda, T., & Roberts, W. A. (1995). Further evidence for hierarchical chunking in rat spatial memory. *Journal of Experimental Psychology: Animal Behavior Processes, 21,* 20–32.

McGonigle, B., & Chalmers, M. (2002). The growth of cognitive structure in monkeys and men. In S. B. Fountain, M. Bunsey, J. H. Danks, & M. K. McBeath (Eds.), *Animal cognition and sequential behavior: Behavioral, biological, and computational perspectives* (pp. 269–314). Boston: Kluwer Academic.

Nissen, M. J., & Bullemer, P. (1987). Attentional requirements of learning: Evidence from performance measures. *Cognitive Psychology, 19,* 1–32.

Nissen, M. J., Knopman, D. S., & Schacter, D. L. (1987). Neurochemical dissociation of memory systems. *Neurology, 37,* 789–794.

Pearce, J. M. (1987). A model for stimulus generalization in Pavlovian conditioning. *Psychological Review, 94,* 61–73.

Pearce, J. M., & Bouton, M. E. (2001). Theories of associative learning in animals. *Annual Review of Psychology, 52,* 111–139.

Reber, A. S. (1989). Implicit learning and tacit knowledge. *Journal of Experimental Psychology: General, 118,* 219–235.

Restle, F. (1970). Theory of serial pattern learning: Structural trees. *Psychological Review, 77,* 481–495.

Restle, F. (1973). Serial pattern learning: Higher order transitions. *Journal of Experimental Psychology, 99,* 61–69.

Restle, F., & Brown, E. R. (1970a). Serial pattern learning. *Journal of Experimental Psychology, 83,* 120–125.

Restle, F., & Brown, E. R. (1970b). Serial pattern learning: Pretraining of runs and trills. *Psychonomic Science, 19,* 321–322.

Roberts, W. A. (1979). Spatial memory in the rat on a hierarchical maze. *Learning and Motivation, 10,* 117–140.

Roitblat, H. L., Bever, T. G., Helweg, D. A., & Harley, H. E. (1991). On-line choice and the representation of serially structured stimuli. *Journal of Experimental Psychology: Animal Behavior Processes, 17,* 55–67.

Roitblat, H. L., Pologe, B., & Scopatz, R. A. (1983). The representation of items in serial position. *Animal Learning & Behavior, 11,* 489–498.

Roitblat, H. L., Scopatz, R., & Bever, T. (1987). The hierarchical representation of three-item sequences. *Animal Learning & Behavior, 15,* 179–192.

Rowan, J. D., Fountain, S. B., Kundey, S. M. A., & Miner, C. L. (2001). A multiple species approach to sequential learning: Are you a man or a mouse? *Behavior Research Methods and Instrumentation, 31,* 435–439.

Sands, S. F., & Wright, A. A. (1980). Serial probe recognition performance by a rhesus monkey and a human with 10- and 20-item lists. *Journal of Experimental Psychology: Animal Behavior Processes, 6,* 386–396.

Sands, S. F., & Wright, A. A. (1982). Monkey and human pictorial memory scanning. *Science, 216,* 1333–1334.

Skinner, B. F. (1934). The extinction of chained reflexes. *Proceedings of the National Academy of Sciences U S A, 20,* 234–237.

Stempowski, N. K., Carman, H. M., & Fountain, S. B. (1999). Temporal phrasing and overshadowing in rat serial-pattern learning. *Learning and Motivation, 30,* 74–100.

Swartz, K. B., Chen, S., & Terrace, H. S. (1991). Serial learning by rhesus monkeys: I. Acquisition and retention of multiple four-item lists. *Journal of Experimental Psychology: Animal Behavior Processes, 17,* 396–410.

Terrace, H. S. (1987). Chunking by a pigeon in a serial learning task. *Nature, 325,* 149–151.

Terrace, H. S. (1991). Chunking during serial learning by a pigeon: I. Basic evidence. *Journal of Experimental Psychology: Animal Behavior Processes, 17,* 81–93.

Terrace, H. S. (2002). The comparative psychology of chunking. In S. B. Fountain, M. Bunsey, J. H. Danks, & M. K. McBeath (Eds.), *Animal cognition and sequential behavior: Behavioral, biological, and computational perspectives* (pp. 24–55). Boston: Kluwer Academic.

Terrace, H. S., & Chen, S. (1991a). Chunking during serial learning by a pigeon: II. Integrity of a chunk on a new list. *Journal of Experimental Psychology: Animal Behavior Processes, 17,* 94–106.

Terrace, H. S., & Chen, S. (1991b). Chunking during serial learning by a pigeon: III. What are the necessary conditions for establishing a chunk? *Journal of Experimental Psychology: Animal Behavior Processes, 17,* 107–118.

Terrace, H. S., & McGonigle, B. (1994). Memory and representation of serial order by children, monkeys, and pigeons. *Current Directions in Psychological Science, 3,* 180–185.

Tulving, E. (1962). Subjective organization in free recall of "unrelated" words. *Psychological Review, 69,* 344–354.

Wathen, C. N., & Roberts, W. A. (1994). Multiple-pattern learning by rats on an eight-arm radial maze. *Animal Learning & Behavior, 22,* 155–164.

Willingham, D. B. (1998). A neuropsychological theory of motor skill learning. *Psychological Review, 105,* 558–584.

Willingham, D. B., Nissen, M. J., & Bullemer, P. (1989). On the development of procedural knowledge. *Journal of Experimental Psychology: Learning, Memory, and Cognition, 15,* 1047–1060.

24

Truly Random Operant Responding: Results and Reasons

GREG JENSEN, CLAIRE MILLER, AND ALLEN NEURINGER

In his influential book on evolutionary game theory, John Maynard Smith wrote, "I cannot see . . . (why) . . . animals do not have roulette wheels in their heads. . . . If it were selectively advantageous, a randomising device could surely evolve. . . ." (1982, p. 76).

We submit that such a device has evolved. In support, this chapter discusses evidence for three related claims: Response variability can be reinforced (i.e., it is an operant); reinforcers exert precise control over what, where, when, and how much to vary; and the resulting responses are at least sometimes stochastic (or random) in nature (i.e., they are emitted probabilistically and therefore unpredictably).

These are controversial claims, but their roots go back to the early history of Western thought. Epicurus suggested that random swerves of atoms help to explain novelty, creativity, and the initiation of action. He was objecting to Democritus's deterministic philosophy. Many philosophers and psychologists since that time, including Gustav Fechner and William James, have posited random-like behaviors (see Neuringer, 2003, 2004). But an operant "randomizing device in the head" flies in the face of an assumption dear to most psychologists: namely, that psychological phenomena are determined by prior events—and therefore ultimately predictable. Until recently, there has been little direct evidence concerning the existence, characteristics, and functions of an operant variability-generating process. We describe current evidence, including three previously unreported experiments, but first provide some definitions.

DEFINITIONS

Variability Variability has many meanings. Sometimes, it implies ignorance of causal factors. Other times it is used in a statistical sense to indicate the spread of values, as in standard deviation and confidence intervals. Sometimes the term implies random-like outputs or a high degree of uncertainty. The term also refers to a dimension or continuum, ranging from repetition (and therefore high predictability) to random (and therefore maximal uncertainty). Context provides the appropriate meaning.

Random In lay terms, *random* often connotes "do anything" or "without reason." That is not what we intend. Rather, we use *random* and *stochastic* interchangeably in their technical senses, to indicate that members of a specified set occur independently of prior events, and therefore that although a knowledgeable observer can predict relative frequencies (or probabilities, these terms also used interchangeably), particular instances cannot be predicted or explained at a more precise level than that of the probability statements.

Because stochasticity is often misunderstood, an example might help. Imagine a large, revolving barrel filled with 1,000 blue (B) and 1,000 green (G) balls. A blindfolded individual picks balls one at a time and an observer notes the color before the ball is replaced in the barrel. The resulting sequence of Bs and Gs is stochastic, meaning that knowledge of past selections enables an observer to predict future relative frequencies—approximately equal numbers of Bs and Gs—but not the next color (or sequence of colors). The barrel could contain unequal numbers, e.g., 900 Bs and 100 Gs, and, under those conditions, B would be much more likely than G, but the resulting sequence would nevertheless be stochastic (probabilities of 0.9 and 0.1, respectively). This same analysis holds no matter how many different colors were in the barrel—two, four, eight, and so on—because blind selection would in each case result in stochastic outcomes.

Operant A rat pressing a lever for food pellets provides an example of the relationship between operant response and reinforcer. The lever press produces food and the food influences the action of pressing, both being necessary for the response to be defined as an operant and for the consequence to be defined as a reinforcer. Reinforcement shapes and maintains operant responses. Reinforcement also affects individual dimensions of responses, such as response force and speed. For example, if food depends on rapid responding, then high response rates may result.

EVIDENCE FOR THE OPERANT NATURE OF VARIABILITY

Reinforcement

Variability is influenced by reinforcers contingent on it. For example, when porpoises were reinforced for novel responses, they came eventually to emit behaviors not previously observed in any porpoise (Pryor, Haag, & O'Reilly, 1969). When pigeons were reinforced if their interresponse times—the intervals between consecutive pecks to a response key—were distributed in random-like fashion, pecks came to resemble the random emission of atomic particles (Blough, 1966). In another experiment, when pigeons were reinforced for infrequently occurring sequences of pecks across two response keys, the distribution of sequences came to match that expected from a random source (Machado, 1989). In yet another example, when high-school students were reinforced for random-like generation of sets of 100 responses across two computer keys, the students' performances came to approximate the random model (Neuringer, 1986). In many other experiments as well, animals and people have successfully been reinforced for generating highly variable behaviors (Barba & Hunziker, 2002; Machado, 1997; Neuringer, Deiss, & Olson, 2000; Neuringer & Huntley, 1992; Page & Neuringer, 1985).

There are many possible sources of variability, of course, including noise in the environment and withholding or decreasing reinforcement, and control procedures are required before we can conclude that variability is an operant. As one example, pigeons in an experimental condition were reinforced whenever a sequence of eight responses across left (L) and right (R) keys differed from each of the preceding 50 sequences, a contingency referred to as lag 50 (Page & Neuringer, 1985). In a "yoked" control condition, the same frequency and distribution of reinforcers were presented but now contingent only on the pigeon responding eight times per trial. Thus, in the experimental condition, trials terminated with food only if sequences varied, but under the yoked condition, the food did not depend on variability—the pigeons could vary or not without penalty. The important finding was that response variability was significantly higher when explicitly reinforced than not. This type of comparison provides strong evidence for the operant nature of response variability (see also Blough, 1966; Machado, 1989; Neuringer, 1986).

Discriminative Cues

Another characteristic of an operant is influence by discriminative cues. For example, if response-contingent food is available only when a 1,000-Hz tone sounds, rats learn to respond when the tone is on and not in its absence. The same is true for response variability: For example, when rats were reinforced for varying in the presence of one stimulus and reinforced independently of variability in a different stimulus (the yoked control), levels of variability were significantly higher in the experimental period than in the yoked period (Denney & Neuringer, 1998). Other studies showed stimulus control over varying versus response repetitions (Cohen, Neuringer, & Rhodes, 1990; Page &

Neuringer, 1985). In summary, variability—of response topography, speed, and sequencing—is controlled in ways that are characteristic of operant responses.

Response Dimensions

As suggested earlier, reinforcers also control individual dimensions of response, a phenomenon that applies to variability as well. For example, human participants were reinforced for drawing rectangles on a computer screen, and three attributes of the response were monitored—the area of the rectangle, its location on the screen, and its shape (Ross & Neuringer, 2002). Participants were reinforced for varying along two of the dimensions (e.g., shape and size), while simultaneously keeping the third constant (e.g., repeating the location of the rectangle). Participants learned quickly to satisfy the contingencies.

Response Sets

Reinforcement also establishes the set of responses from which variations emerge. This fact is shown indirectly by all experiments on operant variability: Animals and people tend to limit their responses to the potentially reinforced ones, although others are certainly possible (see, for example, Neuringer, Kornell, & Olufs, 2001). A more direct demonstration was provided by Mook, Jeffrey, and Neuringer (1993): Rats were reinforced for varying sets of four responses across L and R levers, but, to be reinforced, sequences had to start with two L responses. The rats learned to limit their sequences while, at the same time, their responses varied among the potentially reinforced options. Another example: when variations among four-response sequences across L and R levers were reinforced in rats, except that one particular sequence, LLLL, was never reinforced, the rats learned to vary among all of the sequence other than LLLL (Neuringer, 1993). Thus, reinforcement not only engenders variations, but it helps to define the operative set.

Levels of Variability

Just as particular response rates can be reinforced, or response forces, so, too, different minimum levels of variability can be required for reinforcement. For example, Page and Neuringer (1985) used a lag schedule in which, across phases of the experiment, the current sequence of eight responses by pigeons had to differ from at least 1, 5, 10, 20, or 50 previous sequences (lag 1, 5, 10, 20, or 50); variability generally increased with the demands. Similar results were observed by Blough (1966), Machado (1989), and Grunow and Neuringer (2002). These studies leave unanswered, however, whether responding is sensitive to requirements for specific levels of variability (rather than the more permissive minimum levels required in previous experiments), and if so, whether variability can change rapidly in response to reinforcement demands. As described later, important theories of behavior, including matching theory and game theory, require such rapid sensitivity.

EXPERIMENT 1: REINFORCEMENT OF STOCHASTIC DISTRIBUTIONS

Experiment 1 may best be introduced by returning to the balls-in-barrel example used above. Our question is whether behavioral allocations can change rapidly in a way analogous to what happens when the proportions of Gs and Bs change, such as from equal numbers of Bs and Gs to 3 Bs for 1 G. That is, does reinforcement exert precise and rapid control over distributions of stochastic responses?

A positive finding would be consistent with two influential theories of choice. Matching theory predicts that ratios of choices (analogous to Gs and Bs) will be an orderly function—a power function—of the ratios of reinforcements for those choices (Herrnstein, 1997). Matching theory is supported by much evidence (Davison & McCarthy, 1988), but the theory is silent with respect to how responses are allocated—stochastically or systematically. For example, if the rate of reinforcement for left responses were three times higher than for right, an animal would "match" responses to reinforcers by responding systematically with a 3:1 ratio (e.g., LLLRLLLRLLLR . . .) or, alternatively, by responding stochastically with the same 3:1 ratio (e.g., LRLLLLRLRLLL . . .). Stochastic generation is predicted by a second theory, however, namely game theory, developed to explain choices when individuals compete with one another for resources. In such situations, it would be ineffective for one animal to permit an opponent to predict its choices—the opponent could take countermeasures—whereas stochastic responding is functional. The Nash equilibrium combines matching and game theories in its prediction that, in many competitive situations, reinforcement will be optimized when relative frequencies of stochastic responses match relative frequencies of obtained reinforcers. The Nash equilibrium therefore predicts both matching and stochastic allocation. Glimcher (2003) found evidence for such stochastic matching: monkey and human subjects allocated choices in a way that was consistent with both matching and game theory (i.e., stochastic choices matched reinforcement proportions). This is an important result because it provides experimental support for applying the Nash formulation to operant choices. Experiment 1 used a different procedure to test whether reinforcement directly controls stochastic allocation of choice responses and, if so, to ascertain how rapidly that control is achieved.

Procedure

College students were divided into Experimental ($n = 116$) and Yoke control ($n = 30$) groups, both gaining points for responding on two keys of a computer keyboard, to be referred to as L and R. The experiment consisted of five phases, each terminating after at least 150 responses and at least 25 points, with the different phases not cued and seamlessly joined in a single session lasting approximately 20 min. In most cases, 150 responses sufficed to gain the required 25 points per phase.

Experimental Condition

Each of the five phases reinforced a different distribution of stochastic responses across the L and R keys: 0.25–0.75, 0.33–0.67, 0.40–0.60, 0.50–0.50, and back to 0.25–0.75, respectively. Thus, in the first phase, approximately 0.25 of responses were required on one key and 0.75 on the other. In the second phase, the required distribution was approximately 0.33 and 0.67, and so on, with Phase 5 repeating Phase 1. We say that responses had to "approximate" a given distribution because there was a delta window for each distribution such that if the response frequency fell within that window, the participant would be rewarded. Delta windows were created by assessing the performance of a stochastic model and using boundaries that resulted in the model being "reinforced," according to the contingencies to be described later, on 80% of its trials.

Responses had to satisfy stochastic contingencies simultaneously at three levels of analysis, as described, based on separate response counters at each level. Level 1 analysis was based on overall percentages of L and R responses, their frequencies maintained in two associated counters. The particular keys were not specified; some participants responded more on the left key than the right and others did the opposite, but the response percentages had to be within required delta windows. Thus, in the first phase, for example, the relative frequencies of L and R responses were required to be approximately 0.25 and 0.75 on L and R keys or vice versa.

Level 2 analysis was based on the percentages of pairs of responses, with pair frequencies recorded in four counters: LL, LR, RL, and RR. If LRRLRLLLR had just been emitted, then (in order of occurrence) one count would be added to the LR counter, one to the RR counter, one to the RL counter, and so on, with the most recent pair being indicated by the rightmost LR in the example. For a response to be reinforced, relative frequencies of the current "possible pairs" were required to fall within the defined delta windows. Referring back to the example, the most recent responses were L followed by R. Therefore, given the L response, LR and LL were the current "possible pairs," because (again, given that an L response had occurred previously) only those two pairs were possible. Level 2 proportions were calculated by dividing the sum in one of the possible-pair counters (the pair that had actually been emitted) by the sum of the two possible-pair counters—in the example given by dividing the LR counter by the sum of LR + LL counters—and in all other ways treating the data as described for level 1.

Similarly, level 3 consisted of eight counters, LLL, LLR, . . . RRR, with, in the just given example, the terminal triplet being LLR. Level 3 analyses similarly required concordance with the stochastic model for response triplets and, in the example given, the number of LLR sequences was divided by the sum of LLR + LLL sequences—these being the only possible triplets given that LL had been emitted prior to the terminal response. In brief, in Phase 1 (where a 0.25–0.75 distribution was required), the last response in our example was reinforced if Ls and Rs had occurred with approximately the required 0.25–0.75 distribution; if LR and LL had occurred with the same approximate percentages; and similarly if approximately 0.25–0.75 distributions were obtained for LLR and LLL. Of course, the particular "possible" pairs and triplets changed with each response. Thus, for example, if following emission of LLR, another R were to be emitted, then the current (i.e., prior to the last response) possible pairs would be RL and RR, and the current possible triplets, LRL and LRR. The beauty of the procedure lies in the fact that although increasingly demanding conditional probabilities are assessed, the required relative frequencies—0.25 and 0.75 in our example—remain constant.

One additional detail: In order to differentially weight current responses more heavily than those emitted earlier in a phase, each of the "possible" counters was multiplied by an amnesia coefficient of 0.95 following every response. Returning to our example, following the last R response, the level 1 L and R counters were each multiplied by 0.95 (because both L or R were possible), as well as the level 2 LR and LL counters and the level 3 LLR and LLL counters. Each phase began with all counters preset with a value of 1, and the data and calculations in each phase were independent of all others (see Miller, 2003, for additional procedural details).

Participants, naive to the nature of the task, received feedback that indicated how closely response percentages approximated the stochastic model at each of the three levels of analysis. This feedback consisted of a horizontal line across the center of the computer screen and three pairs of colored dots—red, green, and blue—moving symmetrically around the line. Response percentages at the three levels were normalized so that they could be represented by the single horizontal line and the distance of the dots from the line represented the difference between the participant's relative frequencies and the stochastic model at each of the three levels. A point was awarded when all dots were sufficiently close to the line, that is, within the delta windows, with cumulative points shown by a counter. The participant's task was to keep the balls as close to the horizontal line as possible. Rapid responding was discouraged by a "slow down" message appearing in the middle of the screen whenever response rates exceeded 4/s. In brief, human participants were rewarded for distributing responses in a way that matched (within delta windows) a stochastic model, with the model's response probabilities differing across the five phases.

Yoked Condition

All aspects of the procedure were the same as for the Experimental participants, except that response distributions and variability had no influence on the displayed dots or the presentation of points. Rather, for each Yoked participant individually, these depended on an arbitrarily paired Experimental player's responses and rewards; that is, feedback to each Yoked participant was identical to that received by the paired Experimental participant. Thus, when Yoked participants responded, they were reinforced at exactly the same rate and intermittency as the Experimentals. Experimental and Yoked participants were given minimal instructions and told only to try to keep the colored dots close to the horizontal line in order to maximize points.

Measures

A common measure used to assess the stochasticity of responses is *U value*, which evaluates the distribution of relative frequencies of responses (Evans & Graham, 1980; Machado, 1989; Page & Neuringer, 1985; Stokes, 1995). If eight unique responses are possible, $i = 1$ to 8, then the U value is given by:

$$U_{i=1 \text{ to } 8} = -[RF_i * \log_2(RF_i)]/\log_2(8)$$

where RF_i = relative frequencies (or percentages) of each of the eight responses. U values approach 1.0 when relative frequencies approximate one another, as would be expected over the long run from stochastic generation of equiprobable instances, and 0 when a single instance is repeated. U values can be applied as well to sequences of responses. Given a series of Ls and Rs, U values can be based on sets of three responses, (e.g., LLR, LLL), constructed from a moving window across the entire series. For example, if the emitted sequence had been LLRLRRRLLRL . . . , then the sets of three would be LLR, LRL, RLR, LRR, and so on. Note that there are eight possible patterns of L and R taken three at a time, and thus, as in the just-described example, the U value would be based on eight possibilities. The U value thus is an index of the overall equality of members of a set of possible outcomes. Of course, when contingencies reinforce unequal distributions of responses (e.g., 0.25–0.75), U values are expected to be lower than when equality is reinforced (0.50–0.50). In the present study, participant-generated U values were compared to those from a stochastic model in each of the five phases.

Stochasticity can be evaluated in another way, namely by comparing proportions of participant-generated responses—L and R instances, pairs of instances, triplets, and so forth—to that expected from the stochastic model. In the balls-in-barrel example, assuming equal numbers of blue and green balls, a stochastic process would yield not only equal relative frequencies of Bs and Gs, but also equal pairs, i.e., blue followed by blue (BB) would approach 0.25, as would green followed by green (GG), blue followed by green (BG), and green followed by blue (GB). Similarly relative frequencies of BBB, BBG, BGB, etc., would each approach 0.125. More precisely, a stochastic process is indicated if the relative frequencies of pairs of instances is the multiplicative value of the first-order proportions (e.g., if B = 0.50 and G = 0.50, then BB = 0.50 * 0.50 = 0.25), and the same is true for GG, BG, and GB. Similarly, BBB = 0.50 * 0.50 * 0.50 = 0.125, and so on. When baseline proportions are unequal (e.g., if three Gs were selected for each B), then if the process were stochastic, the probability of BB would be 0.25 * 0.25 = 0.0625, of GG, 0.75 * 0.75 = 0.5625, and BG and GB = 0.25 * 0.75 = 0.1875. The same holds for triplets. Thus, when first-order relative frequencies are unequal, a test for stochasticity involves predicting second order, third order, etc., proportions from the observed first-order values. The main questions asked in the present experiment were whether human participants would distribute their responses across two keys in a way predicted from a stochastic model, and whether they could learn to do so rapidly.

Results

We first tested consistency with matching theory. Figure 24.1 plots, on log-log coordinates, the ratio of left to right responses (total Ls in a phase divided by total Rs in the phase) as a function of the ratio of left to right reinforcers, as commonly done in testing for matching. Each data point represents one participant under one phase, with all participants and all phases represented. Consistent with matching theory, response ratios were related to reinforcement ratios by a power function, with the least-squares best fitting line accounting for 68.6% of the variance. As is often the case in choice experiments, "under-matching" was observed (i.e., response distributions tended to be closer to 0.50–0.50 than the proportions of reinforcements), this indicated by the 0.583 value of the exponent. In the present case, undermatching may partly be explained by the fact that relatively few responses were collected in each phase (approximately 150), that all of these responses were included in the analyses, and that participants could, within a given phase, switch preferences from one key to the other. To a first order of approximation, however, the distributions of choices were consistent with predictions from matching theory.

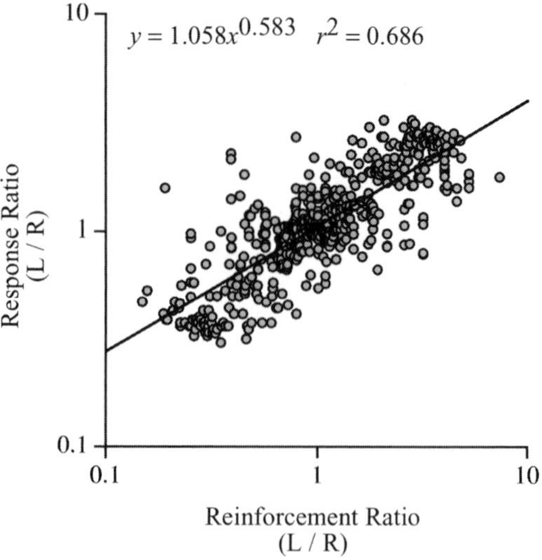

Figure 24.1. Log ratios of left to right responses (L/R) as a function of log ratios of obtained numbers of reinforcements (L/R) for all Experimental participants ($n = 116$) in each of the five phases of Experiment 1. The least-squares best-fitting power function accounts for 68.6 percent of the variance.

Levels of variability were also influenced by the contingencies, this shown by the U values in figure 24.2. U values were calculated for each subject in each of the five phases based on proportions of response triplets, with group averages represented in figure 24.2. Experimental (filled circles) and Yoked participants (open circles) differed significantly, $F(1, 144) = 96.119$, and phase and interaction effects were also significant, $F(4, 576) = 5.747$ and $F(4, 576) = 37.278$, respectively. Reinforcement contingencies therefore clearly influenced levels of response variability.

For comparison, figure 24.2 also shows performance of the stochastic model (Xs), programmed to generate L and R responses with the target probabilities and for the same number of responses as the human participants. Experimental participants' U values approximated those of the stochastic model, although the participants' U values were higher than the model's in Phases 1 and 5 (i.e., human participants distributed their responses more equally) and slightly lower in Phase 4.

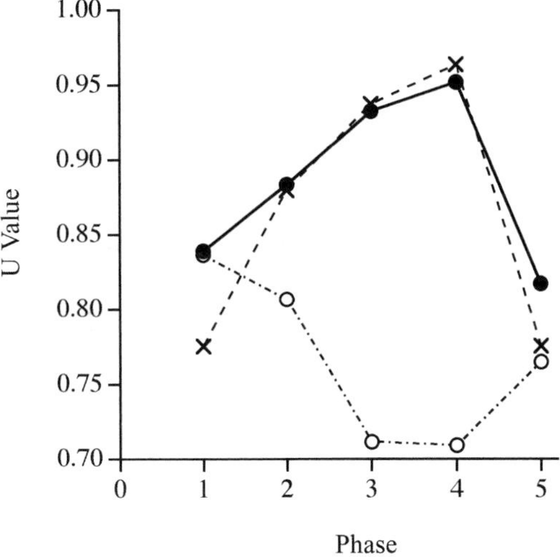

Figure 24.2. Filled circles show average U values for the Experimental participants, reinforced for responding with differing levels of stochastic allocations in the 5 phases of Experiment 1. Phase 1 required 0.75–0.25 distributions; Phase 2, 0.67–0.33; Phase 3, 0.60–0.40; Phase 4, 0.50–0.50; and Phase 5 was a replication of Phase 1. Xs represent a random model, programmed to respond with the five appropriate levels of stochastic allocation, and open circles represent Yoked control participants, whose reinforcement was presented independently of levels of variability.

Finer-grained analyses of pairs and triplets were also consistent with stochastic generation. Because we did not specify which key, L or R, had to be responded to more frequently and to facilitate the comparison between people and stochastic model, these analyses are based on Stays (Ss) and Changes (Cs)—the predictions for these being independent of whether L was preferred or R. A *Stay* was defined as two consecutive responses on the same key, LL or RR; a *Change* was defined as an alternation, LR or RL. Stochasticity was tested by ascertaining if S and C pairs (an S followed by another S, an S followed by a C, and so on) and triplets (SSS, SSC, and so on) could be predicted from the level 1 proportions of Ss and Cs, this being done for each participant individually and in exactly the same manner as described above in the B and G colored balls example. As described there, when response frequencies (or, in this case, Stay and Change frequencies) are unequal, stochasticity can be tested by calculating expected percentages of pairs and triplets based on level 1 frequencies. For example, if a participant emits relative frequencies of 0.90 Cs and 0.10 Ss, then if Cs and Ss were generated by a stochastic process, CC would equal 0.81, CCC, 0.729, and so on. We therefore used each participant's level 1 relative frequencies to predict that subject's pair (level 2) and triplet (level 3) proportions.

The results, shown in table 24.1, are based on the average of all Experimental participants across

Table 24.1 Relative frequencies of Stays (S) and Changes (C) given in five phases of Experiment 1

	Phase 1		*Phase 2*		*Phase 3*		*Phase 4*		*Phase 5*	
Type	Observed	Predicted	Observed	Predicted	Observed	Predicted	Observed	Predicted	Observed	Predicted
S	.671	.750	.641	.670	.577	.600	.553	.500	.660	.750
C	.329	.250	.358	.330	.424	.400	.447	.500	.340	.250
SS	.485	.451	.424	.412	.336	.333	.320	.306	.464	.436
SC	.186	.221	.218	.230	.241	.244	.233	.247	.196	.224
CS	.189	.221	.216	.230	.239	.244	.233	.247	.196	.224
CC	.141	.108	.142	.128	.184	.179	.214	.200	.144	.116
SSS	.372	.302	.294	.264	.204	.192	.191	.170	.346	.288
SSC	.112	.148	.130	.148	.131	.141	.130	.137	.118	.148
SCS	.115	.148	.150	.148	.169	.141	.154	.137	.122	.148
SCC	.072	.073	.067	.082	.072	.103	.079	.110	.074	.076
CSS	.113	.148	.128	.148	.129	.141	.130	.137	.117	.148
CSC	.075	.073	.089	.082	.111	.103	.103	.110	.079	.076
CCS	.072	.073	.067	.082	.072	.103	.078	.110	.075	.076
CCC	.069	.036	.075	.046	.113	.076	.136	.089	.069	.039

Note: The observed level-1 values (S and C) were used to generate the predicted level-2 (S, SC . . .) and level-3 (SSS, SSC . . .) values. The reinforced response distributions in the five phases were .75–.25, .67–.33, .60–.40, .50–.50, and .75–.25, respectively.

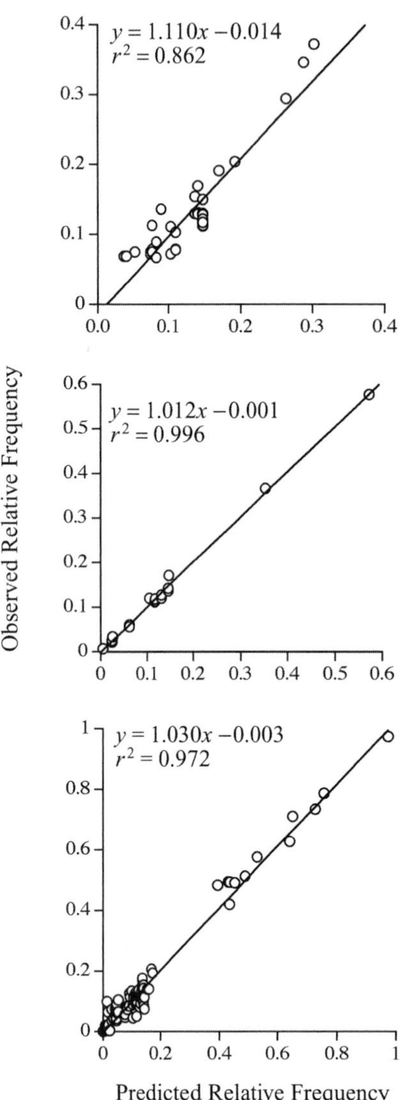

Figure 24.3. Percentages of Stays (S) and Change (C) triplets (SSS, SSC, SCS . . .) as a function of the predicted percentages based on a stochastic model. *Top*, Experiment 1 performances in which different distributions of stochastic responses were required for human participants responding across two keys. *Middle,* Data from Experiment 2a in which pigeons were reinforced for stochastic responding across different number of response operanda. *Bottom*, Human participants responding under the same conditions as Experiment 2a. To the extent that the least squares best fitting function has a slope of 1.0 and intercept of 0.0, the performances were predicted by a stochastic model.

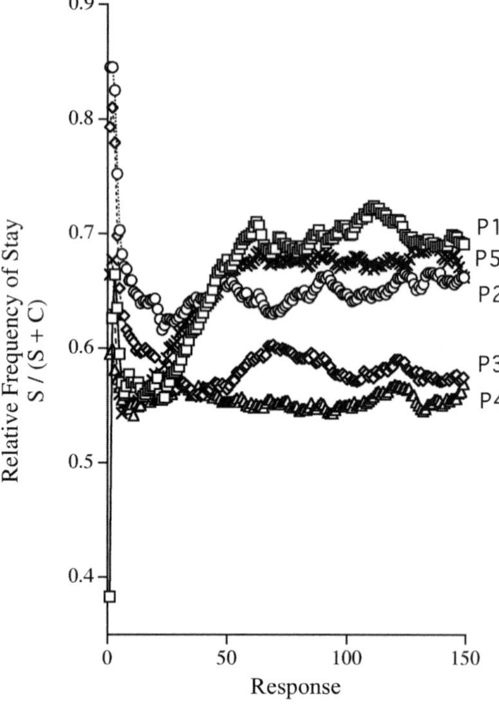

Figure 24.4. Relative frequencies of Stays (S/S + C) across each of the 150 responses in each of five phases, when Phase 1 (P1) required 0.75–0.25 distributions, P2 required 0.67–0.33, P3 required 0.60–0.40, P4 required 0.50–0.50, and P5 was a replication of P1. Each data point is an average across a moving window of 20 responses and across all Experimental participants.

the five phases, but these well represent individual performances. The participants' pairs and triplets values closely approximate those predicted from a stochastic model. A graphic representation of the goodness of the triplets' predictions is shown in figure 24.3, top: Observed percentages of triplets is plotted as a function of the values predicted by the stochastic model. The slope of the least-squares best-fitting line is close to 1, the intercept is close to 0, and the function accounts for 86% of the variance. Thus, the participants' responses—and levels of variability—were consistent with those generated by a stochastic model (table 24.1 and figure 24.3).

Furthermore, variability changed rapidly when the reinforcement contingencies were changed. Figure 24.4 shows probabilities of Stays (S/S + C) over a moving window of 20 responses in each of the five phases. The leftmost points in each phase

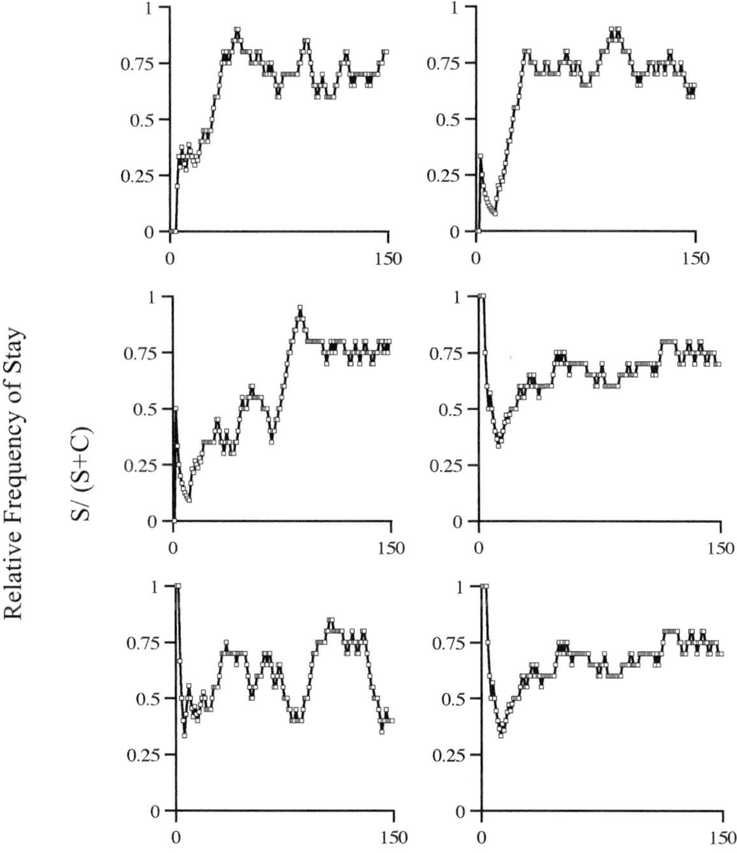

Figure 24.5. Relative frequencies of Stays (S/S + C) in Component 1 when the required distribution was 0.75–0.25, for six Experimental subjects. Each data point is an average of a moving window of 20 responses.

indicate the average number of Ss and Cs when the second response in a phase had been emitted—two responses being the minimum necessary to define an S or C—the next point, the average over the first three responses, the next, first four, and so on until the 20th response, whereupon a constant 20-response moving window was represented. The distributions approximated asymptotic values generally within 75 responses. Again, these averages well represent individual performances, as seen in figure 24.5, which shows performances for six arbitrarily selected Experimental participants under Phase 1 conditions. These results are all consistent with stochastic allocation of responses and high sensitivity to reinforcement contingencies.

However, the "stochastic-generator hypothesis" can be challenged on at least two grounds. First, many studies have reported that people are unable to respond randomly when requested to do so, for example, to call out heads or tails randomly (Brugger, 1997; Nickerson, 2002). Later we attempt to explain why our results are consistent with the stochastic hypothesis, whereas this large body of literature is not. But, first we consider a second objection: Namely, that an alternative hypothesis, one consistent with deterministic assumptions, can account for our results, as well as those from other experiments purporting to show stochastic-like responding (Blough, 1966; Machado, 1989; Neuringer, 1986). This alternative is that memory-based or deterministic computational processes can generate variable responses, including those that appear to match a stochastic model. We consider memory-based theories as an introduction to our second experiment.

MEMORY-BASED OPERANT VARIABILITY

Memorial processes can produce highly variable responses in a number of different ways. For example, a person can memorize a long list of "random" numbers and use these to generate responses.

Alternatively, an algorithm (e.g., an equation) that yields random-like sequences can be learned. Chaotic algorithms are one such class and these will be described below. Or one might attempt to remember previous responses or sequences and not repeat these, or remember frequencies of responses or sequences and attempt to equalize these. Each of these strategies relies on memory (explicit or implicit) for past responses or sequences to generate highly variable and, indeed, sometimes random-like outputs.

We first show that animals and people sometimes do manifest an "avoid repetition" or other memorial strategy when satisfying operant variability contingencies; and then we will turn to the question of how memory and stochastic hypotheses might be compared. Our claim is that there are multiple ways in which functionally variable responses can be generated, including memory based, and that responding stochastically is one such strategy.

As described, Pryor et al. (1969) reinforced porpoises for emitting "novel" responses, ones that had not previously been emitted in the same situation. Similar contingencies with human children resulted in novel drawings and block constructions (Holman, Goetz, & Baer, 1977). Other examples of memory-based "do not repeat" strategies include rats learning to avoid previously entered arms of a radial maze (Cook, Brown, & Riley, 1985); and pigeons, rats, or monkeys learning to choose a novel stimulus under a non–matching-to-sample paradigm.

Also, as indicated earlier, iterations of nonlinear dynamical or chaotic equations—one example is the logistic-difference equation—yield random-like outputs under some parameters. One important characteristic of such chaotic algorithms is that each instance is determined by prior instances and that the overall sequence may be "noisy." In one experimental demonstration, human participants received feedback showing how closely their responses matched that expected from iterations of the logistic-difference function. The logistic-difference function can be represented as:

$$y_n = 4 * y_{n-1} * (1 - y_{n-1})$$

where y_n represents the value of the current response and y_{n-1} represents the value of the just-preceding response. The "4" in the equation is a parameter value, namely the value that generates the most chaotic, or "noisy" outcome, and the process is initiated with some arbitrary value for y that is less than 1. The interested reader can reiterate the equation, always using the just-obtained value to seed the next iteration, and see that a highly variable series of outputs results. Neuringer and Voss (1993) showed that human participants could learn to generate responses that were increasingly like iterations of the chaotic model.

Memory insufficiencies have been posited to explain why people often fail to respond randomly, e.g., as found in the human random-generation literature (Brugger, 1997; Wagenaar, 1972). It is suggested that participants are unable to recall the number of responses in each category or the numbers of individual sequences and subsequences that, according to these memory-based theories, are necessary to satisfy randomness criteria (Wagenaar, 1972; Weiss, 1964, 1965). One particularly influential theory suggests that an executive monitor assesses the output of an internal response generator and, depending on prior responses and the individual's criterion of random, inhibits those potential responses that fail to meet the criterion (Baddeley, 1966). As cognitive or memory loads increase, the executive monitor is hypothesized increasingly to fail.

Direct tests of the stochastic nature of operant variability. It is difficult to assess whether a memory-based or stochastic-based processes is involved, because both can generate identical sequences of responses. The iteration of pi is a case in point (the sequence of digits in pi being indistinguishable from random according to most tests), the iterated algorithms used by computer-based random-number generators is another, and chaotic algorithms a third. Each of these algorithms is memory based, in the sense that each instance is determined completely by the prior instance(s) while yielding sequences that cannot easily be distinguished from that of a stochastic source. There are, however, cases for which memory and stochastic theories make different predictions and these provide a way to test underlying processes. For example, memory-based theories predict that response interference—produced, for example, by interposing long pauses—should degrade approximations to a random model (because they degrade memory for prior responses), whereas a stochastic-generator hypothesis predicts no such effect.

As an example, if one were using memory to approximate a random sequence of B and G colored balls, then long pauses between each response, or any other type of interference, would be expected to degrade performance. But, random selection of Bs and Gs from a large barrel would not be influenced by increasing the time between selections. Thus, if interresponse interference adversely affects the generation of variable responses, then memorial processes are likely to be involved. An absence of such effects would be consistent with an underlying stochastic process.

To test these opposing predictions, Neuringer (1991) reinforced two groups of rats: one for repeating a fixed, LLRR sequence of responses across two levers and the other for varying (under a lag contingency). The underlying assumption was that successful repetitions of LLRR depended in part on memorial processes, implicit or explicit, whereas the variability contingencies could be met by stochastic selection of Ls and Rs. Testing this possibility was the goal of the experiment. Following acquisition of the two types of behaviors to approximately equal levels of proficiency, pauses were interposed between consecutive responses, with pause lengths systematically increased across phases. The results were that LLRR performance was severely degraded as pause lengths increased, but performance under the variability contingencies was not, results consistent with stochastic generation of the variable responses.

In a related study, McElroy and Neuringer (1990) showed that administering alcohol caused performance decrements for a group of rats that was reinforced for repeating an LLRR sequence but had no effect on a variability-reinforced group. In another test, human participants were trained to alternate between chaotic-like sequences—thought to be memory based, as described earlier—and stochastic-like sequences—those that met a number of tests of randomness. When pauses or other interfering events were interposed between responses, only the chaotic-like sequences showed decrements (Neuringer, 2002). The evidence therefore supports a stochastic process being involved in at least some cases of operant variability.

However, there is conflicting evidence. Under human random-number-generation procedures (as described earlier), increasing the "memory load" is found to interfere with ability to vary. Memory load has been manipulated by increasing the number of possible responses in the to-be-varied set. For example, Rath (1966) compared random generation in human participants when the set of responses included the digits 0 through 9 versus another case in which the responses were the letters A through Z. Greater deviations from a stochastic model were found with the latter task than the former, results interpreted as indicating that, as memory load increases (from 10 to 26), ability to vary decreases. In a more direct test, Wagenaar (1972) found that, as number of response alternatives increased from two to eight, approximations to an equiprobable model decreased (however, see also Towse, 1998). Consistent with these findings, when a competing task was concurrently presented with a random-generation task, decrements in ability to vary were again observed (Towse & Valentine, 1997). Also consistent with a memory hypothesis, Towse (1998) showed that when available responses were presented visually (e.g., the digits 1 through 10), better approximation to a stochastic model was observed than when the participants had to keep these options in memory.

Might these opposing results—memory interference leaves variability generation unaffected in some cases (e.g., Neuringer, 1991, 2002), whereas it adversely affects it in others (e.g., Rath, 1966; Wagenaar, 1972)—indicate that stochastic processes are involved in the one and memorial processes in the other? Almost all of the human random-generation experiments (with the exception of Neuringer, 1986) required relatively few responses (generally 100 total) and feedback was not provided: participants were simply asked to respond randomly. In most operant cases, including the Neuringer (1986) human random generation experiment, tens of thousands of responses were practiced with reinforcement contingent on high variability. A reasonable interpretation is that memorial strategies are invoked given few responses without feedback, whereas a stochastic-based strategy is employed given the long-term demands of reinforcement-of-variation contingencies.

To test the effects of memory load in an operant situation, Page and Neuringer (1985) studied pigeons responding under a lag 3 contingency, in which the current sequence had to differ from each of those in the preceding three trials. Memory load was varied by changing the required number of responses per trial: four, six, or eight responses per trial across different phases of the experiment. It was reasoned that if memory load had an effect, performance would be degraded when the number of responses increased (i.e., eight responses per trial requires subjects to remember more than four responses). The stochastic hypothesis predicts the opposite result, as demonstrated by the following example. If responses were directed by the toss of a coin, then if trials consisted of only two responses (a small number used for the sake of this example), the probability of one trial repeating the previous trial is 0.25. (There are four possible sequences in the first trial—RR, RL, LR, and LL; thus, the second trial has a 1 in 4 chance of matching the first.) If a trial consisted of four responses, again directed by coin tosses, then the probability of a repetition by chance is 0.0625, or 1 in 16, and with eight responses per trial, the probability of repetition is .0039, or 1 in 256. So, if subjects used a stochastic process to generate Ls and Rs, performances should be more likely to satisfy a lag 3 contingency as responses per trial increased, but if subjects were trying to remember each of their sequences, then the opposite result might emerge. Results were precisely those predicted by the stochastic hypothesis and inconsistent with a memory strategy: increasing numbers of responses per trial, and therefore memory-load, resulted in an increased probability of meeting the contingencies. Stated differently, eight-response trials resulted in more frequent reinforcement than four-response trials, as would be expected if L and R responses were stochastically generated. These findings are all the more important because presumably the memory and cognitive capacities of pigeons are smaller than those of humans.

Two objections can be raised to the Page and Neuringer interpretation, however. First, because the number of possible sequences increased across the phases—given four responses per trial, there are a total of 16 unique sequences, but with eight responses per trial, there are 256—any "noise" in the generating system would more likely result in reinforcement under the eight than under the four phase (Peter Balsam & Pat Stokes, personal communication). Second, responses were distributed across two keys rather than the many distinct operanda or verbal responses used in the human random generation literature.

Thus, there is disagreement. Memory-based theories predict that as numbers of alternative responses increase, it should be more and more difficult to approximate random outputs, and data from the human random literature support that prediction. A stochastic-generator hypothesis predicts that approximations to random should be at least as readily obtained with many alternatives as with few (i.e., stochastic sequences are as likely when there are eight different colors in the barrel as two), and one study, involving different numbers of responses per trial, reported data consistent with the stochastic prediction (Page & Neuringer, 1985).

In an attempt to disambiguate these different results, Experiment 2a varied the number of different response operanda (two, four, and eight), as is characteristically done in the human random-generation literature, but within an operant-conditioning context in which pigeons were given long-term practice and were provided with feedback to indicate successful variations. Because the data supported the stochastic hypothesis, a similar experiment was performed with human participants in Experiment 2b.

EXPERIMENT 2A: PROCEDURE

Five mature male Racing Homer pigeons were maintained at 85% of their normal body weights and reinforced for pecking small response squares (1 cm) projected on the monitor (33-cm Apple color monitor) of a touchscreen (Carroll Touch Smart-frames) located in a Gerbrands operant conditioning chamber. At a right angle to the touchscreen, a food hopper provided access to food pellet reinforcement. Additional details concerning this apparatus can be found in Vickrey and Neuringer (2000).

The procedure is diagramed at the top of figure 24.6. Each "trial" began with a 1-cm black square projected at the center of the screen—it will be referred to as the trial-initiating square—a response to which resulted in projection of two, four, or eight squares (depending on the condition), each of these 1 cm in size—to be referred to as the choice squares. Figure 24.6, bottom, shows how these choice squares were oriented—in the two-, four-, and eight-choice cases, respectively. (The numbers next to the squares were not shown during the experiment and are provided to facilitate description of the procedure.) A single peck to one of the choice squares resulted in a cue for reinforcement, if the variability contingency had been satisfied; otherwise, the trial-initiating square reappeared to indicate a new trial. The reinforcement cue was a green star, projected at the center of the screen, a single peck to which resulted—with a 0.25 probability—in access to food for 1.2 s, after which the trial-initiating square reappeared. Those pecks to the star that did not produce food (because of the 0.25 probability) led immediately to the reappearance of the trial-initiating square.

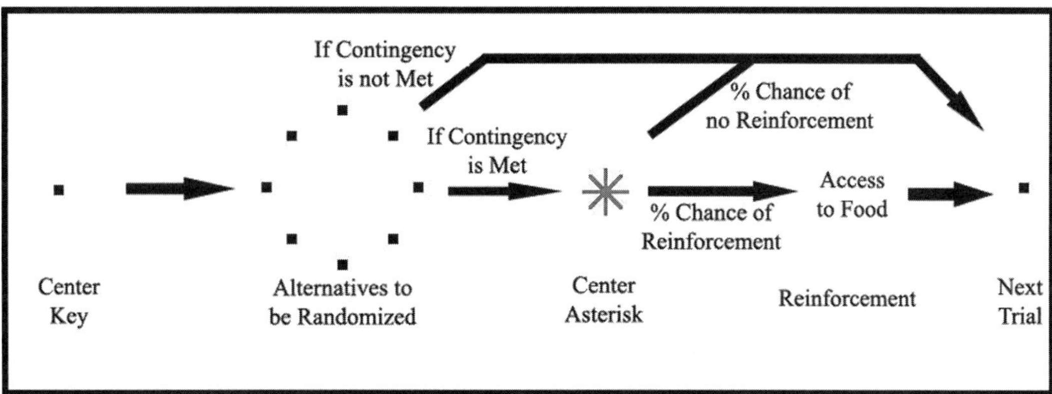

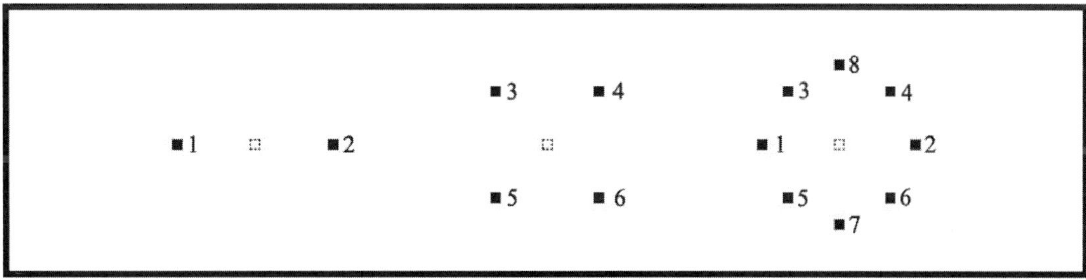

Figure 24.6. *Top,* Outline of the procedure in Experiment 2a. *Bottom,* Orientation of the response squares during the 2-choice condition *(left),* 4-choice condition *(middle)* and 8-choice condition *(right).* The squares are numbered for reference purposes.

Thus, a trial consisted of an initiating response to a center square followed by a response to one of the two-, four-, or eight-choice squares (depending on the condition in effect), and (if the contingency had been satisfied) a peck to a star that led to food 25% of the time and other times to initiation of the next trial. Response variability was reinforced according to the contingencies described later, and the main question was whether levels of variability would differ under the two-, four-, and eight-choice conditions.

Sessions cycled through the two, four, and eight conditions in that order, one session per condition, repeated over and over (two, four, eight, two, four, eight, etc.), with each session terminating after 2,000 responses. Approximately 75 sessions were provided (25 per condition), during the early portion of which parameters were modified to ensure stable responding (e.g., variations were made in the number of trials per session, amount of reinforcement, and probability of food access when the variability contingency was met).

Variability Contingency

To be reinforced, a response had to complete a sequence—to be defined shortly—that had occurred infrequently, according to a variability contingency related to those used by Blough (1966) and by Denney and Neuringer (1998). For the contingency to be equivalently demanding across the two-, four-, and eight-choice conditions (and therefore avoid the objection to Page and Neuringer's interpretation), the number of possible sequences was kept constant at 64 in the following way. In the two-choice condition, each sequence was defined by 6 consecutive responses, with $2^6 = 64$ possible sequences. (It is important to note that sequence length was a variable internal to the computer and that no external stimulus indicated length of trial.) As an example, assume that the responses were 1 and 0, and that the pigeon pecked 1010000101101, with the rightmost digit indicating the most recent response. The current sequence was defined by the last six responses, or 101101, which (translating from binary to decimal) was sequence number 45. The just-prior sequence was defined by moving to the left by one, or 010110 = 22, and the same procedure was used throughout the two-choice condition, with each sequence defined by a moving window consisting of 6 responses. In the four-choice case, $4^3 = 64$ (with instances designated as zero, one, two, and three) and therefore three responses were used to define a "sequence." The eight-choice case involved sets of two responses, $8^2 = 64$ (with instances designated as zero through seven). The response windows were therefore of different lengths (i.e., lengths of six in the two-choice condition, three in the four-choice condition, and two in eight-choice), in order to keep the amount of information constant (64, or 6 bits). Page and Neuringer held the window size constant (lag 3), while permitting information (number of possible sequences) to vary. It is not possible to hold both constant simultaneously. As will be seen, the consistency of results across these two procedures supports the conclusion that responses were generated stochastically.

Additional details are as follows. Each possible sequence was associated with a counter, for a total of 64 counters per condition. At the beginning of the experiment, all counters were initialized with a value of 20 units. Each response increased the value of its associated counter by 1 unit. In order for all responses to contribute equally, whether emitted early in a condition or later, a constant sum was maintained across all counters by subtracting $\frac{1}{63}$ from each of the other 63 counters. To meet the variability contingency, the value of a sequence's counter had to be less than 21.6. These values, together with other parameters, were chosen so that a stochastic model would be reinforced on approximately 70% of trials. Each counter was multiplied by an amnesia coefficient (.984) following reinforcement for the same reasons as in Experiment 1. Counter values were maintained across sessions of a given condition (i.e., the values at the beginning of one session were the same as at the end of the previous session under the same condition) but were independent of the other conditions. Additional procedural details are given in Jensen (2003).

The final 18 sessions were used for all analyses, with 6 sessions per condition, 2,000 responses per session, and therefore 12,000 responses per condition. U values were computed for each pigeon, based on the 64 possible sequences in each condition.

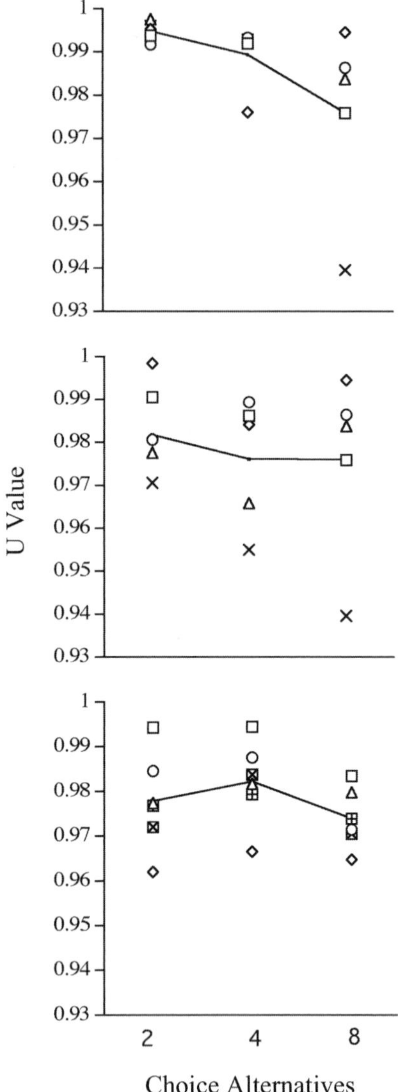

Figure 24.7. U values as a function of number of choice alternatives in Experiment 2a (*top* and *middle*), where pigeons served as subjects, and Experiment 2b (*bottom*), where human participants were studied. Each subject is represented with the solid line showing the average of all subjects.

Results

Figure 24.7, top, shows U values for each of the pigeons as a function of number of choice alternatives. The line connects the group mean. Although U values decreased somewhat across conditions, the y-axis is highly magnified (beginning at .93) and a repeated measures analysis of

Table 24.2 Relative frequencies of Stays (S) and Changes (C) given two, four, or eight choice alternatives with pigeons

Type	Observed (2)	Predicted (2)	Observed (4)	Predicted (4)	Observed (8)	Predicted (8)
S	.529	.500	.293	.250	.170	.125
C	.477	.500	.707	.750	.830	.875
SS	.291	.280	.095	.086	.033	.029
SC	.238	.252	.198	.207	.137	.141
CS	.238	.252	.198	.207	.137	.141
CC	.233	.228	.509	.500	.693	.689
SSS	.171	.148	.034	.025	.007	.005
SSC	.128	.132	.061	.061	.026	.024
SCS	.120	.132	.056	.061	.022	.024
SCC	.118	.120	.140	.147	.116	.117
CSS	.128	.132	.061	.061	.026	.024
CSC	.114	.120	.136	.147	.112	.117
CCS	.118	.120	.142	.147	.112	.117
CCC	.120	.109	.366	.353	.577	.572

Note: The observed level-1 values (S and C) were used to generate the predicted level-2 (SS, SC . . .) and level-3 (SSS, SSC . . .) values.

variance (ANOVA) showed that effects were not statistically significant, $F(2, 5) = 2.30$.

The stochastic nature of these responses is indicated in table 24.2, which presents percentages of Stays and Changes, as in Experiment 1, together with the percentages of pairs and triplets, for each of the three conditions. As in Experiment 1, Stay was defined as two consecutive responses to the same square (e.g., in the eight-choice case, a response on square 4 followed by another response to 4 was a Stay, whereas a 4 response followed by one to any other square was a Change). In the two-choice condition, a stochastic generator is expected to repeat with a probability of .5, and the same for changes. For the four-choice case, a stochastic generator's expected Stay equals 0.25; and for the eight-choice case, expected Stays equal .125. As shown by the level 1 percentages in the top two lines of the table, the pigeons tended to repeat more than predicted. However, when, as in Experiment 1, percentages of pairs and triplets (SS, SC . . . ; SSS, SSC . . .) were calculated from the subjects' own level 1 percentages, they closely matched the predictions from a stochastic model. Figure 24.3, middle, plots the pigeons' percentages of triplets on the y-axis as a function of the predicted values on the x-axis. The fit is almost perfect: Triplet percentages were precisely those predicted by a stochastic model.

In addition to the slight tendency to repeat, indicated by the level 1 percentages in table 24.2, some of the birds showed a bias for or against particular response locations. This bias was especially noticeable in the eight-choice case where, for example, one subject responded to square 1, the top square, with a relative frequency less than 0.01, whereas the relative frequency of responses to square 6, on the bottom left was 0.22. The expected proportion (given an unbiased distribution) was 0.125 for each case. Other subjects showed similar, although less extreme, biases. We noticed that the smallest birds had the most difficulty responding to the top square (1), and when we measured birds' heights, a significant inverse correlation was found between height and percentage of responses to the top choice location ($r^2 = 0.909$, Fisher's r to z test ($p < .04$).

Only the eight-choice condition contained the top choice location and that might have contributed to the marginally lower U values in the eight-choice case. To evaluate this possibility, we replicated the two- and four-choice conditions, but with different square locations from those in the initial phase of the study. In particular, we compared levels of variability in the two-choice condition when the locations were one and two; three and six; four and five; and seven and eight, respectively (shown in figure 24.6, bottom). We compared the four-choice conditions when the locations were three, four, five, and six versus when they were one, eight, two, and seven. Figure 24.8 indicates that locations in fact influenced levels of variability. Indeed, location exerted a much larger effect on U value than did number of choice alternatives. Figure 24.7, middle, shows the U values averaged across these repeated conditions together

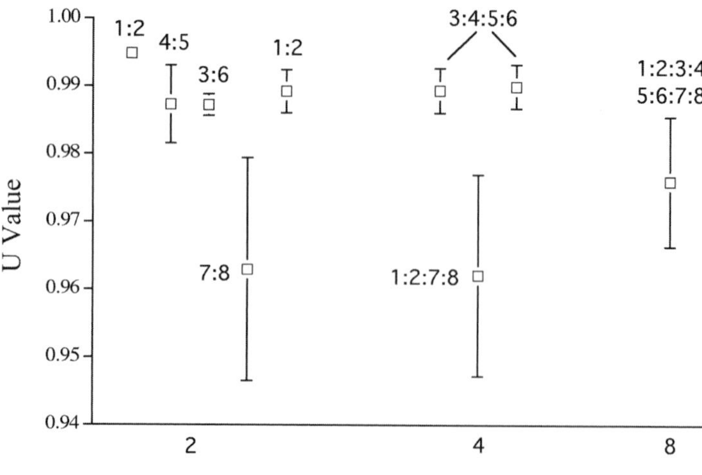

Figure 24.8. U values as a function of number of choice alternatives (two, four, or eight), when the particular response-square locations differed, these indicated by the numbers (e.g., 1:2; 4:5) above or to the left of the individual points. Bars show standard errors.

with the eight choices for comparison and clearly indicates that number of response alternatives had no significant impact on levels of variability. To the extent that number of choice alternatives appeared to affect response variability, biases for and against particular locations were responsible.

Figure 24.9, top, shows the one statistically significant effect of number of alternatives: namely the time between pecks to the trial-initiating center key and the response to one of the available choice alternatives, $F(2, 8) = 14.26$, $p < .003$. More time was required to choose among eight alternatives than for four, and likewise for four than for two. This result is consistent with that reported by Baddeley (1966) for human participants.

The main finding was that number of operanda did not significantly influence response variability. These results differ from human random-generation experiments and support a stochastic-generator theory of operant variability, as did Page and Neuringer's earlier findings. However, both Page and Neuringer's study and the experiment just described studied pigeons, whereas the random generation literature is based exclusively on human participants. To test for species differences, we repeated Experiment 2a with human participants.

EXPERIMENT 2B: PROCEDURE

Unless otherwise specified, the procedure was identical to that in Experiment 2a. Each of six college students was paid $8 per hour for 5 hours of participation plus the possibility of two additional incentives. If the participant's lowest U value (in the two, four, or eight condition) was higher than the lowest U value of the pigeons in Eperiment 2a, then an additional $25 was awarded; and the participant whose lowest U value was higher than all other human participants' lowest values received an additional $50.

Participants responded on the numeric keypad of an e-Mac computer. Keys 4 and 6 were used in the two-choice case; keys 1, 3, 7, and 9 in the four-choice condition; and keys 1 through 9, except 5, in the eight-choice condition. A visual representation of the active keys was shown on the screen, with the key's image illuminated after each response. The procedure differed from Experiment 2a in that center-key presses and responses to a star were not required, and participants were rewarded with points rather than food. Each session was divided into "blocks" consisting of 150 responses in two-, four-, or eight-choice conditions, with order of conditions randomized such that every set of three blocks contained each of the conditions. Additional feedback was provided at the end of each block in the form of percentage of reinforced responses, with a graph on the computer's screen showing all blocks of the condition just completed.

Results

Each participant's final 3,600 responses (a number chosen because all participants emitted at least that number of responses per condition) provided the data for the analyses. Figure 24.7, bottom, shows U values as a function of number of choice alterna-

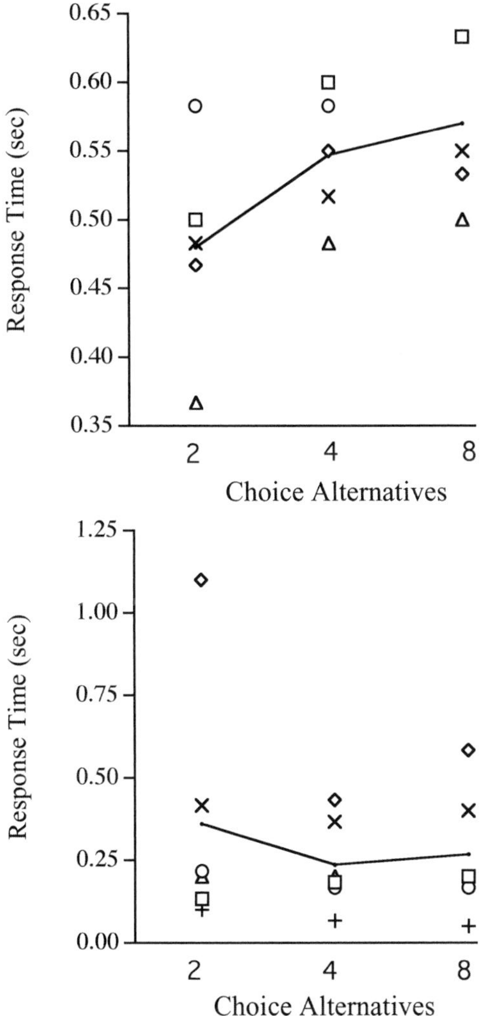

Figure 24.9. Average interresponse time under the 2-, 4- and 8-choice conditions of Experiments 2a (*top*) and 2b (*bottom*).

tives. A repeated-measures ANOVA indicated a significant effect of conditions, $F(2, 6) = 6.26$, $p < .02$, with the four-choice condition differing from the eight-choice (Fisher's PLSD). The two-alternative condition did not differ significantly from either of the other two conditions. Participants succeeded at achieving high levels of variability, and three of the six participants had higher lowest scores than the pigeons in Experiment 2a. Thus, although a significant difference emerged, the difference was small and a consistent decrease in variability across two-, four-, and eight-choice conditions was not observed.

Table 24.3 shows relative frequencies of Stays and Changes, as in Experiment 2a. The human results were comparable to the pigeons' with percentages close to those predicted from a stochastic model. Figure 24.3, bottom, shows the high correlation between stochastic-based predictions and observed triplet values.

Figure 24.9, bottom, shows the mean of all participants' median response times. Apart from a higher mean in the two-choice condition (largely due to one participant responding especially slowly in that condition), no pattern emerged across conditions, and a repeated-measures ANOVA showed no significant effects. The difference between these findings and those from pigeons, where response latencies increased with number of choice alternatives, may partly be due to the location biases demonstrated by the pigeons, which were not seen with the human participants. Also, the procedures differed somewhat. In the pigeon case, latencies were measured from a trial initiating peck; in the human case, responding to the choice alternatives was continuous—there was no trial initiator in order to minimize the tedium of the experiment—and the datum therefore was average interresponse time rather than latency. That the response time data differ also from those previously reported in the human randomness literature (e.g., Baddeley, 1966) may be due to the fact that, in the present case, many thousands of responses were emitted, under control of reinforcing feedback, whereas, as noted above, few responses and the absence of feedback characterize the previous human random-generation research.

The main finding was that, for both pigeons and people, levels of variability were not consistently affected by number of choice alternatives, a result predicted by stochastic theory. We conclude that there are multiple sources of operant variability. We know that people can memorize random sequences (Ericsson & Chase, 1982) and can respond in chaotic-like ways (Neuringer & Voss, 1993). Furthermore, when people are asked to respond randomly, but few responses are required and feedback is not provided, memory for instances and subsequences may well be involved. However, when reinforcement is contingent on approximations to a stochastic model and extended practice is provided, the evidence supports a stochastic-generating process (Experiments 2a and 2b), one that is highly sensitive to changing contingencies (Experiment 1).

We turn now to the general question of why ability to respond unpredictably, whether based on memorial or stochastic processes, might be adaptive.

Table 24.3 Relative frequencies of Stays (S) and Changes (C) given two, four, or eight choice alternatives with people

Type	Observed (2)	Predicted (2)	Observed (4)	Predicted (4)	Observed (8)	Predicted (8)
S	.409	.500	.240	.250	.110	.125
C	.501	.500	.760	.750	.890	.875
SS	.257	.167	.060	.058	.018	.012
SC	.233	.205	.177	.182	.093	.098
CS	.233	.205	.177	.182	.093	.098
CC	.277	.251	.585	.577	.797	.792
SSS	.117	.068	.010	.014	.001	.001
SSC	.141	.085	.051	.044	.016	.011
SCS	.116	.085	.074	.044	.030	.011
SCC	.116	.103	.103	.139	.062	.087
CSS	.141	.085	.051	.044	.016	.011
CSC	.092	.103	.128	.139	.076	.087
CCS	.116	.103	.103	.139	.062	.087
CCC	.161	.126	.482	.439	.727	.705

Note: The observed level-1 values (S and C) were used to generate the predicted level-2 (SS, SC . . .) and Level-3 (SSS, SSC . . .) values.

REASONS TO RESPOND UNPREDICTABLY

Protection

Driver and Humphries (1988) describe "protean behavior . . . (that) is sufficiently unsystematic in appearance to prevent a reactor predicting in detail the position or actions of the actor" (p. 36). Stochastic-like protean responses have evolved in many species as a means of protection from attack or predation. Examples include the unsystematic zigzag flights of butterflies and similar movements by other species—mosquitoes, stickleback fish, ptarmigan, squirrels, rabbits, antelopes—in response to the threat of attack by a predator. Mobbing behaviors are similarly protean in nature, such as unpredictable attacks by gulls against a potential predator or the aerial mobbing by hawks of starlings. Driver and Humphries note that, besides providing immediate protection, protean behaviors interfere with the ability of an opponent to learn to anticipate antipredation responses. They also note that protean behavior is "not so random as to be formless; it is a structured system within which predictability is reduced to a minimum" (p. 157). This point parallels one made above: Selection pressures, whether phylogenetic or ontogenetic, help to establish the set of possibly functional responses from which instances emerge stochastically.

Attraction

Habituation is basic: Repeated stimuli tend to be ignored and unexpected variations attract attention. "Variations attract" describes mating preferences in some species, such as songbirds (Catchpole & Slater, 1995). Female mockingbirds, for example, prefer males who sing complex songs; female sparrows display sexually more to song variety than stereotypy; and great tits demonstrate sexual interest in males with the largest song repertoires. Implied by these studies is that females can discriminate levels of stochasticity (or entropy); evidence supporting this conjecture comes from a series of studies showing that pigeons and people can discriminate among levels of entropy in visual displays (Young & Wasserman, 2001). That males respond to female preferences for variability was shown by Searcy and Yasukawa (1990), who observed that when male red-winged blackbirds were presented with a female dummy, song variability increased. Evidence of direct sensitivity of song complexity to reinforcement contingencies was shown by Manabe, Staddon, and Cleaveland (1997): The variability of budgerigar songs was directly reinforced with food under a lag schedule and song complexity was sensitive to the value of the lag. Thus, attention and attraction by conspecifics may reinforce variations.

Competition

When animals compete for such resources as food, shelter, and mates, predictable responding may be disadvantageous, as a competitor might thereby take countermeasures. As indicated above, game theory shows that, in such competitive situations, optimization of reinforcement may depend on stochastic allocation of choices; in particular, the Nash equilibrium predicts that animals should match relative allocations of stochastic responses to relative frequencies of reward.

Exploration

We use exploration in its generic sense to imply the exploration of a problem space—geographic, artistic, scientific, or personal. The goal may be to discover new resources, as in exploration of spatial locations or new lands (Peterson, 1996; Viswanathan et al, 1996), or the discovery of solutions to some problem, as in scientific exploration or solving mechanical problems (Beveridge, 1950; Maier, 1933), or exploration with an aesthetic goal, as in artistic and literary creativity (Campbell, 1960). Stochastic responding within circumscribed limits may be functional in these cases, because it avoids overreliance on previous patterns of response that may no longer be effective. As with all of the other cases described in this chapter, it is important for a functional set to be circumscribed or defined, a point emphasized by Stokes with respect to creativity (Stokes, 2001; Stokes & Harrison, 2002).

Knowledge and Skill Acquisition

Choosing varied over repetitive stimulation (Fiske & Maddi, 1961) enables acquisition of knowledge. Variations in behaviors and strategies also facilitate the acquisition of cognitive and motor skills. For example, Siegler (1996) has shown that children who vary their strategies are most successful in acquiring mathematical skills. Varying practice routines facilitates acquisition of motor skills (Manoel & Connolly, 1997; Mechner, 1992; Schmidt & Lee, 1999). And, acquisition of difficult-to-learn operant sequences is facilitated by reinforcement of response variations (Neuringer et al., 2000; Seymour, 2003).

Volition

The operant may be conceptualized as a class of responses, with instances emerging stochastically (Skinner, 1974). In an example of rat's lever-pressing given above, the class may comprise pressing with left paw, right paw, or mouth; with high or low force; and so on. Discriminative cues may increase the likelihood of an operant class, but the particular instances cannot be predicted, either in terms of time of occurrence or topography; the individual responses emerge stochastically. This view of the operant provides a model of voluntary action because voluntary actions are both functional—they are goal-directed actions that can be explained, at least in part, by reinforcement—and potentially unpredictable or stochastic (see Neuringer, 2002). Operant variability manifests both of these characteristics—functionality and stochasticity—and therefore may play an important role any explanation of voluntary action.

In each of these cases—protection, attraction, competition, exploration, acquisition, and volition—controlled variability appears to be functional. In some instances, variability is a species-typical, evolved response to a stimulating situation (e.g., varied bird songs). In other cases, variability is not selected by evolutionary pressures but rather by reinforcing consequences experienced by the individual organism. Thus, many normal, ongoing activities involve controlled, stochastic-like emission of functional responses—for both phylogenic and ontogenic reasons. Absence of such controlled variability may characterize some psychopathologies. For example, levels of variability in those diagnosed with depression tend to be lower than in nondepressed individuals (Channon & Baker, 1996; Hopkinson & Neuringer, 2003), and the same is true for individuals with autism (Baron-Cohen, 1992; Lee, McComas, & Jawor, 2002; Miller & Neuringer, 2000). Individuals with attention deficit-hyperactivity disorder may manifest the opposite, that is, abnormally high (and uncontrolled) levels of variability.

We again emphasize the importance of controlled variability, because "doing anything" may have low probability of success or be deleterious. By "controlled," we mean that operant reinforcement and phylogenic survival shape the set from which possible responses emerge, establish when and where variations are adaptive, establish within-class probability distributions, and, no doubt, determine when it is adaptive to use memorial processes to behave variably and when to use stochastic ones. Operant stochasticity therefore combines two views: one in which behavior is determined by genes and experiences and the other in which some behaviors are unpredictable or indeterminate, even assuming high-quality knowledge of prior experiences and genetic contributions. There is determination of response classes and potential indetermination of within-class instances. Stated differently, operant variability is a process of stochastic-like emissions from a defined set of possible instances.

Why Stochastic?

But why is the emission process stochastic, at least under some circumstances? At present, we can only speculate. Stochastic variability may be adaptive in protection, attraction, and competition for reasons indicated by game theory: namely, to counter prediction by another animal or person. Stochastic variability maximizes unpredictability. Stochastic variability may be generated in nonsocial cases as a way to avoid behavioral traps and to produce reinforcing effects. For example, in human creativity, stochastic behaviors may result in effects that are surprising to the creator himself or herself, and therefore are autoreinforcing. Additionally, randomizing heuristics may have evolved because memory for instances and sequences, as well as iterative computations based on chaotic-like functions, require more "computational power" than stochastic emission.

Acknowledgments The research and preparation of this manuscript were in part supported by National Institutes of Health Grant MH068259. Parts of the research were submitted as senior theses to Reed College by G. J and C. M.

References

Baddeley, A. D. (1966). The capacity for generating information by randomization. *Quarterly Journal of Experimental Psychology, 18,* 119–129.

Barba, L. S., & Hunziker, M. H. (2002). Variabilidade comportamental produzida por dois esquemas de reforçamento (Behavioral variability produced by two reinforcement schedules). *Acta Comportamentalia, 10,* 5–22.

Baron-Cohen, S. (1992). Out of sight or out of mind? Another look at deception in autism. *Journal of Child Psychology and Psychiatry, 33,* 1141–1155.

Beveridge, W. I. B. (1950). *The art of scientific investigation.* New York: Vintage Books.

Blough, D. S. (1966). The reinforcement of least frequent interresponse times. *Journal of the Experimental Analysis of Behavior, 9,* 581–591.

Brugger, P. (1997). Variables that influence the generation of random sequences: An update. *Perceptual and Motor Skills, 84,* 627–661.

Campbell, D. T. (1960). Blind variation and selective retention in creative thought as in other knowledge processes. *Psychological Review,* 67, 380–400.

Catchpole, C. K., & Slater, P. J. (1995). *Bird song: Biological themes and variations.* Cambridge: Cambridge University Press.

Channon, S., & Baker, J. E. (1996). Depression and problem-solving performance on a fault-diagnosis task. *Applied Cognitive Psychology, 10,* 327–336.

Cohen, L., Neuringer, A., & Rhodes, D. (1990). Effects of ethanol on reinforced variations and repetitions by rats under a multiple schedule. *Journal of the Experimental Analysis of Behavior, 54,* 1–12.

Cook, R. G., Brown, M. F., & Riley, D. A. (1985). Flexible memory processing by rats: use of prospective and retrospective information in the radial maze. *Journal of Experimental Psychology: Animal Behavior Processes, 11,* 453–469.

Davison, M., & McCarthy, D. (1988). *The matching law.* Hillsdale, NJ: Lawrence Erlbaum Associates.

Denney, J., & Neuringer, A. (1998). Behavioral variability is controlled by discriminative stimuli. *Animal Learning and Behavior, 26,* 154–162.

Driver, P. M., & Humphries, D. A. (1988). *Protean behavior: The biology of unpredictability.* Oxford: Oxford University Press.

Ericsson, K. A., & Chase, W. G. (1982). Exceptional memory. *American Scientist, 70,* 607–615.

Evans, F. J., & Graham, C. (1980). Subjective random number generation and attention deployment during acquisition and overlearning of a motor skill. *Bulletin of the Psychonomic Society, 15,* 391–394.

Fiske, D. W., & Maddi, S. R. (1961). *Functions of varied experience.* Homewood, IL: Dorsey Press.

Glimcher, P. W. (2003). *Decisions, uncertainty and the brain.* Cambridge, MA: MIT Press.

Grunow, A., & Neuringer, A. (2002). Learning to vary and varying to learn. *Psychonomic Bulletin & Review, 9*, 250–258.

Herrnstein, R. J. (1997). *The matching law*. Cambridge, MA: Harvard University Press.

Holman, J., Goetz, E. M., & Baer, D. M. (1977). The training of creativity as an operant and an examination of its generalization characteristics. In B. Etzel, J. LeBland, & D. Baer (Eds.), *New development in behavior research: Theory, method and application* (pp. 441–471). Hillsdale, NJ: Erlbaum.

Hopkinson, J., & Neuringer, A. (2003). Modifying behavioral variability in moderately depressed students. *Behavior Modification, 27*, 251–264.

Jensen, G. (2003). *Mechanisms and variables involved in aptitude for random generation*. Unpublished undergraduate thesis, Reed College.

Lee, R., McComas, J. J., & Jawor, J. (2002). The effects of differential and lag reinforcement schedules on varied verbal responding by individuals with autism. *Journal of Applied Behavior Analysis, 35*, 391–402.

Machado, A. (1989). Operant conditioning of behavioral variability using a percentile reinforcement schedule. *Journal of the Experimental Analysis of Behavior*, *52*, 155–166.

Machado, A. (1997). Increasing the variability of response sequences in pigeons by adjusting the frequency of switching between two keys. *Journal of the Experimental Analysis of Behavior, 68*, 1–25.

Maier, N. R. F. (1933). An aspect of human reasoning. *British Journal of Psychology, 24*, 144–155.

Manabe, K., Staddon, J. E. R., & Cleaveland, J. M. (1997). Control of vocal repertoire by reward in Budgerigars (*Melopsittacus undulatus*). *Journal of Comparative Psychology, 111*, 50–62.

Manoel, E. J., & Connolly, K. J. (1997). Variability and stability in the development of skilled actions (pp. 286–318). In K. J. Connolly & H. Forssberg (Eds.), *Neurophysiology and neuropsychology of motor development*. London: MacKeith Press.

McElroy, E., & Neuringer, A. (1990). Effects of alcohol on reinforced repetitions and reinforced variations in rats. *Psychopharmacology, 102*, 49–55.

Mechner, F. (1992). *Learning and practicing skilled performance*. New York: Behavior Science Applications.

Miller, C. (2003). *Metavariability: Interrelations with creativity, depression, and SAT/GPA*. Unpublished undergraduate thesis, Reed College.

Miller, N., & Neuringer, A. (2000). Reinforcing variability in adolescents with autism. *Journal of Applied Behavior Analysis, 33*, 151–165.

Mook, D. M., Jeffrey, J., & Neuringer, A. (1993). Spontaneously hypertensive rats (SHR) readily learn to vary but not to repeat instrumental responses. *Behavioral and Neural Biology, 59*, 126–135.

Neuringer, A. (1986). Can people behave "randomly?": The role of feedback. *Journal of Experimental Psychology: General, 115*, 62–75.

Neuringer, A. (1991). Operant variability and repetition as functions of interresponse time. *Journal of Experimental Psychology: Animal Behavior Processes, 17*, 3–12.

Neuringer, A. (1993). Reinforced variation and selection. *Animal Learning & Behavior, 21*, 83–91.

Neuringer, A. (2002). Operant variability: evidence, functions, and theory. *Psychonomic Bulletin & Review, 9*, 672–705.

Neuringer, A. (2003). Creativity and reinforced variability. In K. A. Lattal & P. N. Chase (Eds.), *Behavior theory and philosophy* (pp. 323–338). New York: Kluwer Academic/Plenum.

Neuringer, A. (2004). Reinforced variability in animals and people. *American Psychologist, 59*, 891–906.

Neuringer, A., Deiss, C., & Olson, G. (2000). Reinforced variability and operant learning. *Journal of Experimental Psychology: Animal Behavior Processes, 26*, 98–111.

Neuringer, A., & Huntley, R. (1992). Reinforced variability in rats: Effects of gender, age and contingency. *Physiology & Behavior, 51*, 145–149.

Neuringer, A., Kornell, N., & Olufs, M. (2001). Stability and variability in extinction. *Journal of Experimental Psychology: Animal Behavior processes, 27*, 79–94.

Neuringer, A., & Voss, C. (1993). Approximating chaotic behavior. *Psychological Science, 4*, 113–119.

Nickerson, R. A. (2002). The production and perception of randomness. *Psychological Review, 109*, 330–357.

Page, S., & Neuringer, A. (1985). Variability is an operant. *Journal of Experimental Psychology: Animal Behavior Processes, 11*, 429–452.

Peterson, I. (1996). Trails of the wandering albatross. *Science News, 150*, 104–105.

Pryor, K. W., Haag, R., & O'Reilly, J. (1969). The creative porpoise: Training for novel behavior. *Journal of the Experimental Analysis of Behavior, 12*, 653–661.

Rath, G. J. (1966). Randomization by humans. *American Journal of Psychology, 79*, 97– 103.

Ross, C., & Neuringer, A. (2002). Reinforcement of variations and repetitions along three independent response dimensions. *Behavioural Processes, 57*, 199–209.

Schmidt, R. A., & Lee, T. D. (1999). *Motor control and learning: A behavioral emphasis.* Champaign, IL: Human Kinetics.

Searcy, W. A., & Yasukawa, K. (1990). Use of song repertoire in intersexual and intrasexual contexts by male red-winged blackbirds. *Behavioral & Ecological Sociobiology, 27,* 123–128.

Seymour, K. H. (2003, May). The effects of reinforcing operant variability on task acquisition. Presented at the Association for Behavior Analysis, San Francisco.

Siegler, R. S. (1996). *Emerging minds: The process of change in children's thinking.* New York: Oxford University Press.

Skinner, B. F. (1974). *About behaviorism.* New York: Knopf.

Smith, J. M. (1982). *Evolution and the theory of games.* Cambridge: Cambridge University Press.

Stokes, P. D. (1995). Learned variability. *Animal Learning & Behavior, 23,* 164–176.

Stokes, P. D. (2001). Variability, constraints, and creativity: Shedding light on Claude Monet. *American Psychologist, 36,* 355–359.

Stokes, P. D., & Harrison, H. M. (2002). Constraints have different concurrent effects and aftereffects on variability. *Journal of Experimental Psychology: General, 131,* 552–566.

Towse, J. N. (1998). On random generation and the central executive of working memory. *British Journal of Psychology, 89,* 77–101.

Towse, J. N., & Valentine, J. D. (1997). Random generation of numbers: A search for underlying processes. *European Journal of Cognitive Psychology, 9,* 381–400.

Vickrey, C., & Neuringer, A. (2000). Pigeon reaction time, Hick's law, and intelligence. *Psychonomic Bulletin & Review, 7,* 284–291.

Viswanathan, G. M., Afanasyev, V., Buldyrev, S. V., Murphy, E. J., Prince, P. A., & Stanley, H. E. (1996). Levy flight search patterns of wandering albatrosses. *Nature, 381,* 413–415.

Wagenaar, W. A. (1972). Generation of random sequences by human subjects: A critical survey of literature. *Psychological Bulletin, 77,* 65–72.

Weiss, R. L. (1964). On producing random responses. *Psychological Reports, 14,* 931–941.

Weiss, R. L. (1965). "Variables that influence random-generation": An alternative hypothesis. *Perceptual and Motor Skills, 20,* 307–310.

Young, M. E., & Wasserman, E. A. (2001). Entropy and variability discrimination. *Journal of Experimental Psychology: Learning, Memory, & Cognition, 27,* 278–293.

25

The Simultaneous Chain: A New Look at Serially Organized Behavior

HERBERT TERRACE

Serial learning is one of the oldest and most widely studied phenomena of experimental psychology, as well it should be. Compared with discrete responses, the focus of most experiments in psychology, serially organized action is the norm in everyday behavior. It is also fundamental for the mastery of skills at all levels of complexity: skills as simple as knowing how to get from point A to point B and as complex as knowing how to speak and comprehend language.

Until the middle of the twentieth century, it was assumed that chaining theory could explain all serially organized behavior, both human and nonhuman. The basic premise was that any learned sequence could be reduced to a series of successive stimulus-response associations (Hull, 1935; Skinner, 1934). In 1951, Karl Lashley (1951) challenged that assumption in one of the most influential papers in modern psychology.

Lashley argued that chaining theory could not account for knowledge of relationships between nonadjacent items in serially organized behavior and presented two important examples to support his argument. First, he noted that all human languages assume knowledge of relationships between words from different parts of a sentence. For example, if someone told you that the girl wearing the blue uniform won the race, you would understand that it was the girl, and not the uniform, that won the race. Lashley also cited various human skills that could not be characterized as sequences of chained S-R units because the interresponse times between successive responses are often shorter than the time it would take for feedback from one response to trigger the next (e.g., typing or playing a musical instrument).

Lashley's critique of chaining theory, and his proposal that the organization of language and skilled sequences was hierarchical, is often regarded as a herald of the human "cognitive revolution." Hierarchical organization, a level of complexity that cannot be derived from chaining theory, is central to the concept of chunking (Miller, 1956) and contemporary theories of language (Jackendoff, 2002).

Because Lashley did not use examples of animal behavior in his critique of chaining theory, its implication for animal cognition is less clear than it is for human cognition. Indeed, it has been argued that Lashley's arguments do not apply to animals because there is no evidence that they engage in learned behavior that approaches the complexity of typing or playing a musical instrument and because animal communication is simpler and less arbitrary than human language (Lewandowsky & Murdock, 1989). However, recent advances in our understanding of serially organized behavior in animals have confirmed that Lashley's critique of chaining theory applies with the same force to sequence learning by animals as it does to sequence learning by humans.

INFLUENCE OF "APE LANGUAGE" STUDIES

Ironically, the main impetus for recent interest in serially organized behavior in animals was the failure of various projects that attempted to show that apes (mainly chimpanzees) have grammatical competence (Premack, 1976; Rumbaugh, 1977; Terrace, Petitto, Sanders, & Bever, 1979) and by the success of the *simultaneous chaining paradigm* in training nonhuman primates to produce complex sequences without the benefit of any "linguistic" training (Straub & Terrace, 1981). Strange as it may seem, the failure of ape language projects had an important silver lining. It motivated a new line of research on serially organized behavior that provides a glimpse of how animals think without language!

Analysis of Lana's "Linguistic" Sequences

Thompson and Church's (1980) analysis of a corpus of purported sentences produced by Lana provides a good example of the shift of attention from training a nonhuman ape to learn a language to new paradigms for investigating an animal's ability to learn arbitrary, but meaningless sequences. Lana was trained to arrange symbols called *lexigrams* in a particular sequence (Rumbaugh, Gill, & von Glasersfeld, 1973). Each symbol was composed of a particular geometric configuration on a particular colored background.

Lana's training was modeled after the training used in an earlier study by Premack (1976) in which the chimpanzee Sarah learned to use an artificial visual language, composed of plastic chips of different colors and shapes, to obtain different incentives. Premack's study was criticized because it did not provide adequate controls for cues that Sarah's trainers could have provided when they asked her to chose a lexigram to obtain an incentive (Terrace, 1979). Rumbaugh et al. (1973) controlled for cueing by using a computer to present lexigrams to Lana and to record her responses. Initially, Lana learned to obtain various rewards by pressing the appropriate lexigram on the console. Lana subsequently learned to produce sequences composed of lexigrams (e.g., *Please → machine → give → M and M*).

After analyzing more than 14,000 of Lana's combinations, Thompson and Church (1980) concluded that most of them were paired-associates and conditional discriminations. First, Lana learned that particular lexigrams were associated with particular incentives (e.g., $lexigram_{apple}$ → apple). She then learned to use six stock sequences in particular contexts. For example, if the incentive was in view, then the required stock sequence was, *Please machine give piece of X*. (*X* refers to the symbolic member of the paired associate, e.g., apple, music, banana, and chocolate.) Similarly, if there was no incentive in view, then the required stock sequence was, *Please put into machine X*. The symbol for the incentive was typically inserted in the last position of the stock sentence.

Lana's ability to use particular lexigrams to obtain different rewards provides clear evidence that she understood the meanings of those lexigrams. There is, however, no evidence that she understood the meanings of the other lexigrams she used to assemble stock sentences (e.g., *Please, machine, give, put*, and *piece of*). Similar arguments have been made about the plastic symbols that Sarah used to produce sequences such as *Mary give Sarah apple* (Terrace, 1979).

Obtaining food and other incentives appears to have been the only function of the sequences reported by Sarah, Lana, and other "linguistic chimps." For example, the sequence glossed as *Please machine give food* could just as well have been described as a sequence composed of four arbitrarily selected letters, say, X → N → F → G. That a nonhuman primate could be taught to touch symbols in a particular sequence, one that its trainer glossed as *please → machine → give → food,* is of interest not because of the purported meanings of those symbols but because it raises important questions about the actual nature of those sequences. They are not linguistic and they cannot be reduced to S-R chains.

SIMULTANEOUS CHAINS

Maze learning is the classic example of sequential learning by animals. According to chaining theory, learning a maze entails nothing more than learning a sequence of S-R associations. At a particular choice point, make a particular turn. While running through a maze, an animal encounters each choice point one at a time. Having made a correct turn at one choice point, the subject proceeds to the next one. That action removes the subject from the cues associated with the prior choice point. As a result, the cues from one choice point do not compete for the subject's attention with those from other choice points.

The last point about the isolation of one choice point from another is critical. The sequences Lana was trained to produce on her keyboard differ from those trained in a maze because all of the lexigrams to which Lana had to respond were presented simultaneously and because they remained in view until she completed the required sequence. Given the simultaneous presentation of all of the relevant lexigrams, it is not clear how Lana's sequences could be explained by chaining theory.[1] That feature of Lana's protocol struck me as a basis for defining a new paradigm for training arbitrary sequences. To emphasize that feature, I referred to the new method as the *simultaneous* chaining paradigm and to the traditional method as the *successive* chaining paradigm (Terrace, 1984).

The simultaneous chaining paradigm provides an opportunity for investigating a wide range of cognitive phenomena in humans that do not "scale up" from traditional chaining theory, for example, serial expertise (Terrace, Son, & Brannon, 2003), distance and magnitude effects (Brannon & Terrace, 2000), the production of numerical sequences (Brannon & Terrace, 1998), meta-cognition (Son & Kornell, 2005), and cognitive imitation (Subiaul, Cantlon, Holloway, & Terrace, 2004). It also appears that the ability to use simultaneous chains may be a relatively recent evolutionary development. As we see in the next section, certain characteristics of performance on simultaneous chains have not been observed in species that are phylogenetically older than primates (Terrace & McGonigle, 1994). For example, even after extensive training, pigeons can barely master short simultaneous chains, and what they do learn about those sequences is basically different from what a nonhuman primate learns.

S-R Chains Versus Cognitive Maps

The experience of mastering a maze is familiar to anyone trying to find their way through a strange town (e.g., turn left at the library, right at the bank, right at the gas station). Notice that the driver in this example needs to learn only the correct response at each choice point, not its relationship to any of the other choice points. For example, a four-item maze is a successive chain composed of four S-R associations: $[S_1{:}R_1]$, $[S_2{:}R_2]$, $[S_3{:}R_3]$, and $[S_4{:}R_4]$. Responding correctly to S_1 ensures that the subject will encounter S_2, and only S_2. Thus, learning a maze can be characterized as follows (Skinner, 1938):

$$S_1{:}R_1 \rightarrow S_2{:}R_2 \rightarrow S_3{:}R_3 \rightarrow S_4{:}R_4 \rightarrow S^R \quad (1)$$

Tolman and his students performed a series of experiments in which they prevented rats from reaching particular choice points in a maze by blocking their normal route (Tolman, 1948; Tolman, Ritchie, & Kalish, 1946). The rat's ability to immediately find alternative paths led Tolman to question the adequacy of the successive chaining model of learning sequences. Instead of a chain of S-R units, Tolman concluded that the rat had formed a cognitive map of the maze and that the cognitive map functioned as a spatial representation of the relationships among the choice points. Tolman's insight did not bear fruit until 1969, when his hypothesis about cognitive maps was confirmed in experiments on a rat's ability to navigate a radial maze (Olton & Samuelson, 1976). As we shall see, the representation needed to execute a simultaneous chain shares many features of a cognitive map.

Simultaneous Versus Successive Chains

The most important difference between a simultaneous and a successive chain is the manner in which a subject encounters successive choice points within a sequence. In contrast to a successive chain, all of the choice points that comprise a simultaneous chain are displayed for the entire duration of the trial. For example, at the start of a trial in which a subject is required to produce a four-item simultaneous chain, the stimuli S_1 S_2 S_3 S_4 are presented simultaneously and they continue to appear, either until the subject makes an error or until it earns a reward by responding to the four stimuli in the sequence $S_1 \rightarrow S_2 \rightarrow S_3 \rightarrow S_4$. Thus, in contrast to a successive chain (1), a simultaneous chain would be characterized as (Terrace, 1984):

$$S_1\ S_2\ S_3\ S_4{:}R_1 \rightarrow R_2 \rightarrow R_3 \rightarrow R_4 \rightarrow S^R \quad (2)$$

Another important difference between successive and simultaneous chains is the location of the choice

A. Required Sequence

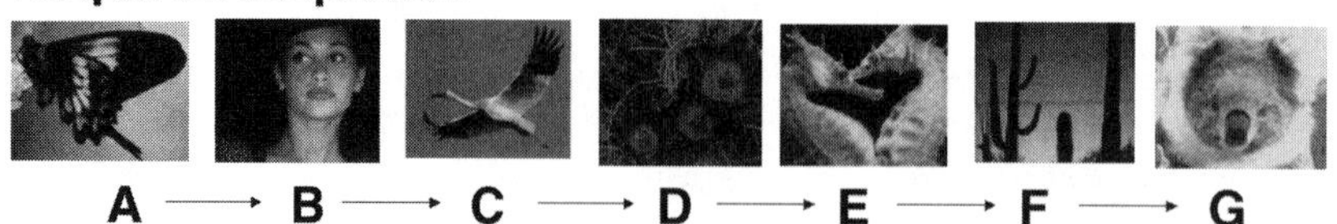

B. Examples of Changes in Item Configuration

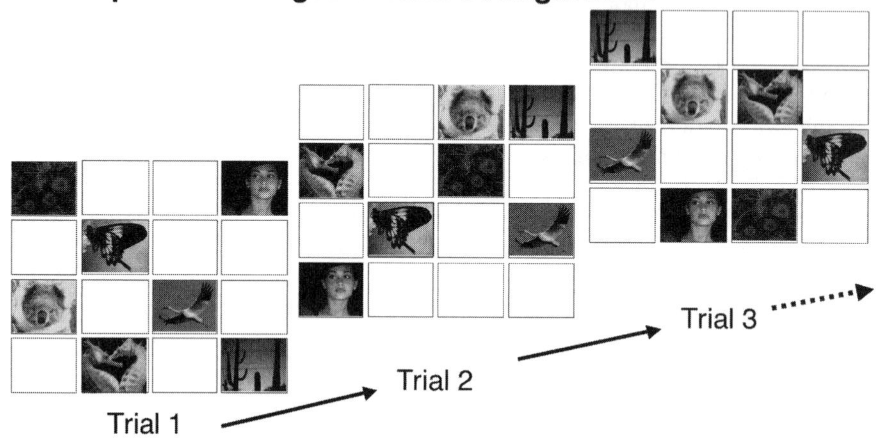

C. Types of Responses

	1st Response	2nd Response	3rd Response	4th Response	5th Response	6th Response	7th Response
Backward Errors							$R_A \rightarrow$ TO
						$R_A \rightarrow$ TO	$R_B \rightarrow$ TO
					$R_A \rightarrow$ TO	$R_B \rightarrow$ TO	$R_C \rightarrow$ TO
				$R_A \rightarrow$ TO	$R_B \rightarrow$ TO	$R_C \rightarrow$ TO	$R_D \rightarrow$ TO
			$R_A \rightarrow$ TO	$R_B \rightarrow$ TO	$R_C \rightarrow$ TO	$R_D \rightarrow$ TO	$R_E \rightarrow$ TO
Correct Responses	**$R_A \rightarrow$ Trial Continues**	**$R_B \rightarrow$ Trial Continues**	**$R_C \rightarrow$ Trial Continues**	**$R_D \rightarrow$ Trial Continues**	**$R_E \rightarrow$ Trial Continues**	**$R_F \rightarrow$ Trial Continues**	**$R_G \rightarrow$ FOOD PELLET**
Forward Errors	$R_B \rightarrow$ TO	$R_C \rightarrow$ TO	$R_D \rightarrow$ TO	$R_E \rightarrow$ TO	$R_F \rightarrow$ TO	$R_G \rightarrow$ TO	
	$R_C \rightarrow$ TO	$R_D \rightarrow$ TO	$R_E \rightarrow$ TO	$R_F \rightarrow$ TO	$R_G \rightarrow$ TO		
	$R_D \rightarrow$ TO	$R_E \rightarrow$ TO	$R_F \rightarrow$ TO	$R_G \rightarrow$ TO			
	$R_E \rightarrow$ TO	$R_F \rightarrow$ TO	$R_G \rightarrow$ TO				
	$R_F \rightarrow$ TO	$R_G \rightarrow$ TO					
	$R_G \rightarrow$ TO						

D. Possible Paths for Guessing A

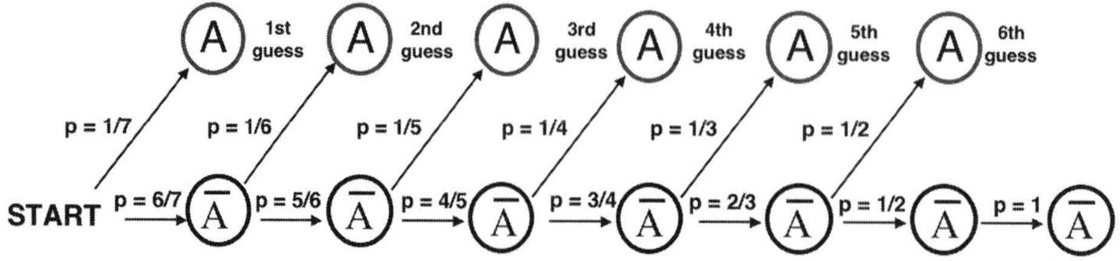

points on each trial. On a successive chain, the locations of the choice points remain fixed throughout training. That allows a subject to learn the maze as a sequence of specific motor responses. That is not possible on a simultaneous chain because the configuration of the choice points is changed randomly from trial to trial. A third difference follows from the first two. On a simultaneous chain, no information is provided following a correct or an incorrect response as to the identity of the next correct item. On a successive chain, S_3 appears automatically and S_2 disappears after the subject responds to S_2. On a simultaneous chain, however, there is nothing in the subject's external environment that can function as a cue for responding to S_3, as opposed to S_1 or S_4. Taken together, these features of a simultaneous chain require a subject to form a representation of the required sequence and to update its position in that sequence before making each response. The following thought experiment illustrates the cognitive processes that are needed to execute a simultaneous chain.

Imagine trying to enter your personal identification number (PIN) at a cash machine, say 9-2-1-5-8-4-7, on which the positions of the numbers were changed each time you tried to obtain cash. You could not enter your PIN by executing a sequence of distinctive motor movements (i.e., first pressing the button in the lower right corner of the number pad to enter 9, then the button in the upper middle position to enter 2, and so on). Instead, you would have to search for each number and mentally keep track of your position in the sequence as you pressed different buttons. Another problem is the absence of any information after a correct response to one item as to the identity the next item. For example, after responding to "1," the subject is not given any information that the next response should be directed to "5" (as opposed to "9," "2," "8," "4," or "7").

As difficult as this task may seem, it would be far more difficult if you did not know your PIN and you had to discover it by trial and error. Any error ends that trial and results in a new trial on which the digits were displayed in a different configuration. Thus, to determine your PIN, you would have to recall the consequences of the many types of logical error you could make while attempting to produce the required sequence. Further, you would have to determine the first six digits without getting as much as a penny from the cash machine.

The above example is virtually identical to the type of problem that an animal would have to solve when learning a seven-item simultaneous chain. As described later, subjects were trained to respond to photographs instead of numerals, and they were given food reward instead of cash. An example of a seven-item list of photographs is shown in figure 25.1A. Figure 25.1B illustrates how the configuration of list items is changed from trial to trial. The 21 types of logical error that can occur while learning a seven-item list are shown in figure 25.1C.

Differences in List Learning by Pigeons and Monkeys

For reasons that are not relevant to this chapter, the first experiments that used the simultaneous chaining paradigm were conducted with pigeons. A replication of those experiments with *Cebus* monkeys revealed some important differences in the manner in which each species learned a simultaneous chain (Swartz, Himmanen, & Terrace, 1993). It was not very surprising that *Cebus* monkeys learned lists much more rapidly than pigeons. What was surprising was the difference in the manner in which each species represented list items.

Figure 25.1. Simultaneous chaining paradigm. (*A*) An example of a 7-item list. Subjects are required to respond to each photograph in a prescribed order (A → B → C → D → E → F → G). (*B*) Variation of the configuration of list items. List items were presented on a touch-sensitive video monitor in randomly configured displays. Prior to each trial, a new configuration is selected at random from the more than 5.8 million configurations that could be generated by presenting 7 items in any of 16 positions. (*C*) Types of forward and backward errors. The row in boldface type shows the types of logical errors a subject can make before discovering the correct sequence. See text for additional details. (*D*) Determining the ordinal position of a list item. The probability of guessing A while making logical errors to eliminate B, C, D, E, F, and G.

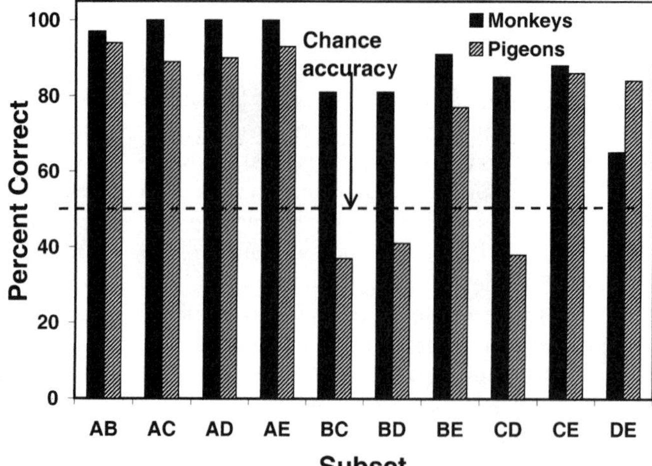

Figure 25.2. Average percentage of correct responses to each of the ten 2-item subsets that can be derived from a 5-item list by monkeys (D'Amato & Colombo, 1988) and pigeons (Terrace, 1987).

Lashley and others have argued that chaining represents the simplest form of serial learning. On that view, a subject that executes a list solely on the basis of associations between adjacent items should be unable to respond to two-item subsets of the list that contain nonadjacent items (e.g., items B and E from the five-item list A → B → C → D → E). Pigeons did respond accurately to some pairs of nonadjacent items from a well-learned list, but only if the subset contained a start and/or an end item. For example, after a pigeon learned a five-item list, it responded at uniformly high levels of accuracy to the subsets, AB, AC, AD, AE, BE, CE, and DE, but at chance levels of accuracy to the subsets BC, BD, and CD. This result suggests that a pigeon's performance on a subset test is not based on associations between items of the sequence, either adjacent or remote. The relevant data are shown in figure 25.2.

Straub and Terrace (1981) have shown that a pigeon's performance on the subset test can be accounted for by the following rules: (1) respond to item A first, (2) respond to item E last, and (3) respond to any other item by default. The validity of these rules is demonstrated by the reaction time (RT) data shown in figure 25.3. RTs of initial pecks to subsets that begin with A (1.0 s) were significantly faster than those that begin with B, C, and D (1.4 s). These aspects of a pigeon's performance indicate that a pigeon's cognitive resources for executing a two-item subset are limited and that they do not rise to the level of a simple chain. By contrast, *Cebus* monkeys performed at high levels of accuracy to all 10 subsets (D'Amato & Colombo, 1988).

Unlike pigeons, monkeys form a linear representation of a list. In order to decide which member of a pair to respond to first, a monkey starts at the beginning of its representation of the list and moves through the list until it locates one of the items displayed on the subset test. The more items it has to check, the longer is the RT. Having responded to the first item, the subject begins a similar search for the second item. Assuming a fixed increment in search time for each item, the RT of the monkey's response to the first item of each subset should increase linearly as a function of that item's ordinal position on the original list. Similarly, the latency of responding to the second item should increase linearly as a function of the number of items from the original list that intervene between the first and the second items of the subset pair. Precisely such functions were obtained from *Cebus* monkeys, which were trained by D'Amato and Colombo (1988) to produce a five-item list (cf. figure 25.3); from rhesus monkeys that were trained to produce four- and six-item lists (Terrace, 2001b); and from 4-year-old children who were trained to produce five-item lists (Chalmers & McGonigle, 1993). As can be seen in figure 25.3, analogous RT functions obtained from pigeons were flat.

Serial Expertise

During our initial experiments on simultaneous chaining with monkeys, list items were added one at a time to avoid the risk of extinction at the start

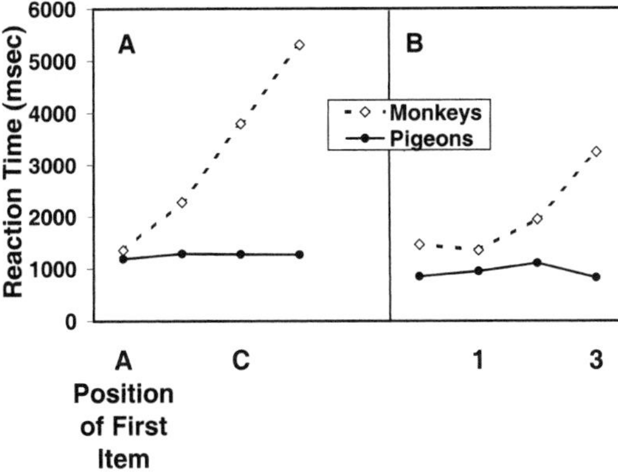

Figure 25.3. Reaction times of responses to first and second items of two-item subsets by monkeys (D'Amato & Colombo, 1988) and pigeons (Terrace, 1987). (*A*) Mean reaction time of responding to the first item as a function of that item's position on the original list 5-item list. (*B*) Mean reaction time of responding to the second item as a function of the number of items that intervened between those items on the original list.

of training on a new list (Swartz, Chen, & Terrace, 1991). For example, the four-item list A → B → C → D would be trained in the following phases: A, A → B, A → B → C, and A → B → C → D. Advancement from one phase to the next was contingent on satisfying an accuracy criterion for the current phase. The subjects of the Swartz et al. experiment, which were trained to master four lists by the successive phase method, showed a modest but steady increase in the efficiency with which they acquired new lists. That increase suggested that it might be possible to dispense with the cumbersome successive phase method entirely and train lists on which all items were present from the start of training. To see if that were possible, we performed an experiment that was based on Harlow's classic paradigm for training learning sets (Harlow, 1949).

Harlow showed that it was easier for a subject to induce a general strategy for learning a particular type of cognitive task ("win-stay," "lose-shift" problems) by working on many exemplars of a problem than by waiting for a subject to achieve a high level of accuracy on a particular exemplar. Accordingly, we trained monkeys on multiple three- and four-item lists on which all items were presented from the start of training (Terrace et al., 2003).[2] None of the subjects had any prior training on a serial task. With the exception of the first list, each new list was presented for a maximum of three sessions.[3] The idea was to see if a monkey could induce a strategy for identifying the ordinal position of items on new lists.

The strategy of training multiple exemplars of three- and four-item lists produced an unexpected dividend. Not only were subjects able to learn lists without the benefit of the successive phase method, but also they became progressively more efficient at mastering new and longer lists. After training on only seven three-item lists and 11 four-item lists, monkeys were able to learn seven-item lists in which all of the items were present from the start of training.

Difficulty of a Simultaneous Chain as a Function of List Length

To place the difficulty of learning a seven-item list into perspective, I digress briefly to compare the difficulty of learning successive chains with n choice points and a simultaneous chain composed of n items. Both types of sequence have to be learned by trial and error. However, the consequences of correct responses and errors differ radically in each paradigm. During training on a successive chain, a subject receives a reward no matter how many errors it makes on a particular trial. The only requirement is that the subject finds its way to the goal box. On a simultaneous chain, an error at *any* point in the sequence terminates the trial and produces a brief time out. Food reward occurs if, and only if, the subject responds to all of the items in the correct order. To learn the first $n - 1$ items of an n-item list, a subject has to rely exclusively on secondary reinforcement. The only consequence of a correct response to each of the first $n - 1$ items is brief auditory and visual feedback when the response is detected, and the continuation of the trial.

The difficulty of acquiring a simultaneous chain increases nonlinearly as its length increases. Because all list items are displayed for the duration of each trial, it is possible to make both forward and backward errors while attempting to execute a correct sequence. As the length of a list increases, the number of potential forward and backward errors increases exponentially and the probability of guessing the correct sequence decreases exponentially. Figure 25.4 shows how these variables change as a function of list length.

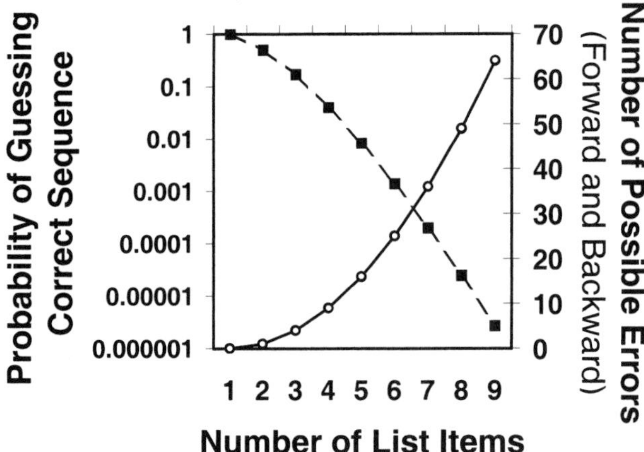

Figure 25.4. The number of possible forward and backward errors (*open circles*) during the acquisition of simultaneous chain grows exponentially as list length increases. *Filled squares* show chance accuracy.

Logical Errors

At the start of training on a new list, a subject has a 1/n! chance of responding to each item in the correct order—that is, without making any errors (cf. figure 25.4). Unless the subject guesses the correct sequence by chance, it must make some errors; these will be referred to as *logical errors*. A logical error, which actually functions as an hypothesis about the position of a particular item, is the first incorrect guess a subject makes to any of the list items at a particular position of the sequence. If, for example, a subject responds to G at the second position of a seven-item list, then that error disproves the hypothesis that G is the second item. If the subject responds to G as the second item on a later trial, that response would be called a *perseverative error* because it provides no new information about the identity of the second item. A perseverative error simply indicates that the subject has forgotten the consequences of the logical error it made to G on an earlier trial.

Ideal List Learner

It is possible to make 21 different types of logical errors at the start of training on a new seven-item list (cf. figure 25.1C). By definition, each type of logical error can occur only once. An *ideal list learner* remembers the consequences of each logical error and does not repeat that error while learning a new list. If an ideal list learner does not guess an item's ordinal position correctly with its first response to that item (see figure 25.1D), then its best strategy would be to make logical errors until it encounters the correct item. The extent to which the number of logical errors approximates that of an ideal list learner is therefore a measure of the subject's expertise at learning new lists.

The average number of logical errors an ideal list learner would make while learning a new seven-item list is the product of the maximum number of logical errors that can be made at a given position and the probability of guessing the correct item at that position. For example, the maximum number of logical errors needed to determine A on a seven-item list is 21 (6 + 5 + 4 + 3 + 2 + 1), and the probability of a correct logical guess of A is 1/7. Thus, the expected number of logical errors needed to determine A is 21/7 (or 3). Similarly, the maximum number of logical errors needed to determine B is 15/6 (or 2.5); the maximum number to determine C is 10/5 (or 2), and so on. The value of the expected number of logical errors at each position decreases linearly, by 0.5 guess at each position, until it reaches a value of 0 at item F. It is not possible to make logical error at F, the seventh position, because F can be identified by default. Figure 25.5 shows the average number of errors an ideal list learner would make while learning the identity of each item on a seven-item list.

The Development of Serial Expertise

Panels A and B of figure 25.6 show the mean accuracy of responding on successive three- and four-item lists during the first and last sessions of training on each list. As expected, none of the

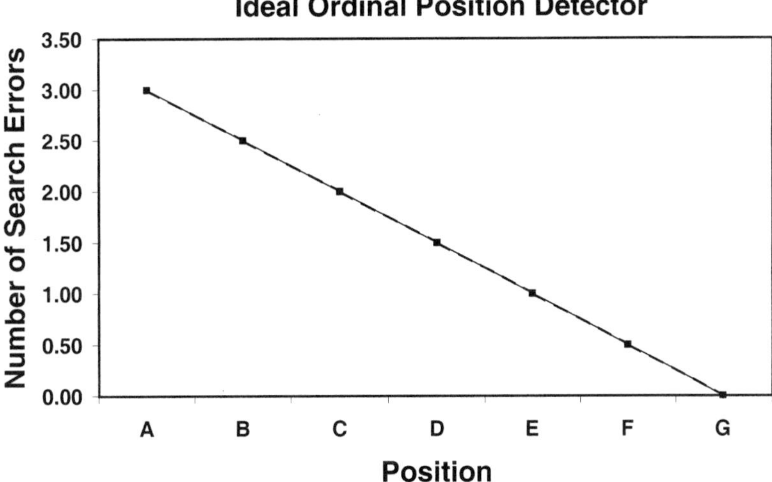

Figure 25.5. Average number of errors an ideal list learner would make at each position of a 7-item simultaneous chain.

subjects exceeded the chance level of accuracy (.17) during the first session of training on their first three-item list. However, all subjects exceeded that level during the first session of training on at least five of the seven remaining lists. Benedict and Oberon exceeded the chance level of accuracy (.04) during the first session of training on all four-item lists; Rosencrantz and Macduff, on approximately two thirds of those lists. The mean accuracy level during the last session of training on three-item lists was approximately 57%; on four-item lists, it was approximately 61%.[4]

After four-item training, subjects were trained on four seven-item lists, each to a criterion of completing correctly at least 65% of the trials in a single session. Subjects learned each of those lists and required progressively fewer sessions to satisfy the accuracy criterion on each new list. As can be seen in panel C, subjects needed an average of 31.5, 17.5, 13, and 12.25 sessions, respectively, to satisfy the accuracy criterion on their first, second, third, and fourth seven-item lists (ranges: 21 to 55, 11 to 25, 11 to 19, and 7 to 17, respectively).

The seven-item lists trained in this experiment were only the nineteenth, twentieth, twenty-first, and twenty-second lists (of any length) that the subjects had learned. Similar reductions in the amount of training needed to satisfy an accuracy criterion have been observed in experiments in which adult human subjects were trained to memorize successive lists of arbitrarily selected words (Keppel, Postman, & Zavortink, 1968). However, compared with the monkeys trained in this experiment, human subjects had the benefit of learning thousands of lists prior to their experimental training.

Accuracy on Partially Completed Trials

The functions shown in figure 25.6 underestimate subjects' serial knowledge because they are based entirely on correctly completed trials. The conditional probability of responding correctly to each item is a more sensitive measure of serial knowledge because it provides credit for partially correct trials. In contrast to an overall measure of accuracy, which assigns a single value to the outcome of each trial (correct or incorrect), conditional probabilities assign an equal weight to each correct response on a given trial.

Figure 25.7 shows three conditional probability functions that provide additional evidence of subjects' serial expertise. Each function depicts subjects' performance during the first session of training on three new lists: their last four-item list, their first seven-item list, and their last seven-item list.

The probability of responding to all of the items correctly on a particular trial is the product of the

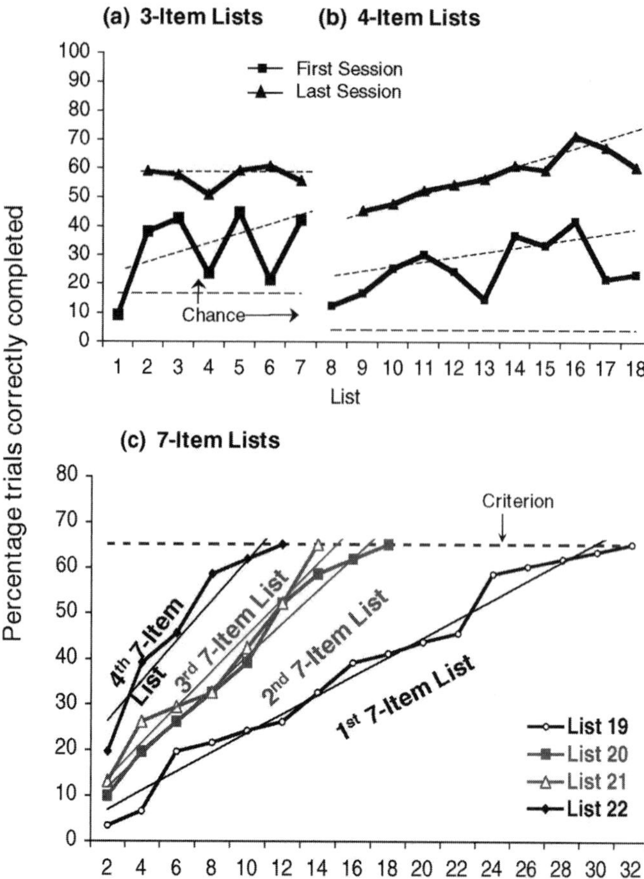

Figure 25.6. Learning curves for 3-, 4-, and 7-item lists in the Terrace, Son, and Brannon (2003) experiment. (*a*, *b*) Each panel shows the percentage of correctly completed trials during the first and the last sessions of training on 3- and 4-item lists (lower and upper functions, respectively). (*c*) Each function shows the mean accuracy of responding on each 7-item list during even-numbered sessions. The probability of executing a new 7-item list correctly by chance is 1/7! = 1/5,040 (assuming no backward errors). Note that the abscissa of *c* represents session (not list).

conditional probabilities of responding correctly to each item. For example, the conditional probabilities of a correct response to A, B, C, D, E, F, and G during the first session of training on the last seven-item list were, respectively, .79, .62, .49, .46, .32, .27, and .29. However, the probability of completing a trial correctly was only .003 (the product of the seven conditional probabilities).

Also shown in figure 25.7 is the performance of an ideal list learner.[5] On a seven-item list, an ideal list learner would need, on average, 3 logical errors to identify A; 2.5 logical errors to identify B; 2 logical errors to identify C, and so on. A comparison of the performance of an ideal list learner, with that of our subjects at the start of training on their fourth seven-item list, provides powerful evidence of our subjects' serial expertise. In particular, our subjects identified positions A and B almost as rapidly as does an ideal list learner. On average, subjects made only four errors at position A (accuracy = 0.92) and five errors at position B (accuracy = 0.88) during the first session of training on that list. Thus, at the start of training on their fourth seven-item list, subjects were able to induce the position of the first two items with almost perfect efficiency.

Knowledge of Ordinal Position

The availability of list-sophisticated monkeys makes it possible to ask questions about the serial organization of memory that, previously, could only be addressed in experiments on human subjects. We exploited that opportunity in two experiments (Chen, Swartz, & Terrace, 1997; Terrace et al., 2003). The first was a replication of a classic experiment on knowledge of the ordinal position of

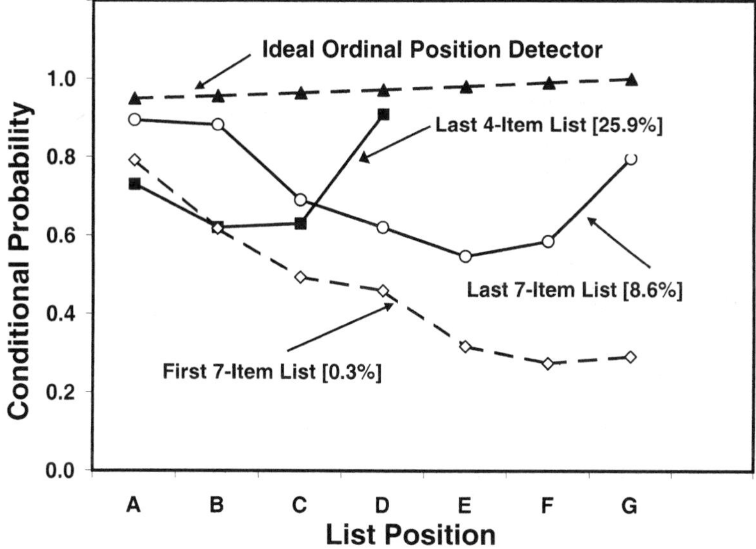

Figure 25.7. Serial position functions from Brannon and Terrace (2003) experiment. Each function shows the average conditional probability of a correct response at each position during initial training on the last 4-item list (overall list 18) and each of the 7-item lists (overall lists 19 through 22). The numbers in brackets to the right of each function show the probability of correctly responding to all of the items on a particular trial. That is the product of the conditional probabilities of responding correctly to each item.

list items in human subjects (Ebenholtz, 1963) that is based on the Ebbinghaus method of derived lists (Ebbinghaus, 1964). The second experiment used two-item subset tests to probe knowledge of ordinal position of list items in subjects trained on seven-item lists (see section below on distance and magnitude effects with arbitrary list items).

Derived Lists

The subjects in the Chen et al. (1997) experiment were two male monkeys that had been trained previously to produce four four-item lists at a high level of accuracy (Swartz et al., 1991). Those lists will be referred to as A1 → B1 → C1 → D1, A2 → B2 → C2 → D2, A3 → B3 → C3 → D3, and A4 → B4 → C4 → D4. Four new lists were also trained in the Chen et al. experiment that were constructed by the method of derived lists (Ebbinghaus, 1964). Each derived list was constructed from the items used in the four lists trained in the Swartz et al. (1991) experiment, with the constraint that no two items came from the same original list. Thus, each derived list contained only one item from each of the first four lists that these subjects learned. The ordinal position of each item was maintained on two of the derived lists (maintained lists 1 and 2: A2 → B4 → C1 → D3 and A3 → B1 → C4 → D2, respectively). On the other two derived lists (changed lists 1 and 2), the original ordinal position of each item was changed (B3 → A1 → D4 → C2 and D1 → C2 → B3 → A4). The original and the derived lists used in this experiment are shown in figure 25.8.

Subjects were trained on the four derived lists in an ABBA order, with A being maintained list 1 or 2 and B being changed list 1 or 2. To counterbalance possible differences in list difficulty, the order of the derived lists used for Franklin was the reverse of that followed for Rutherford. Training on the four derived lists began with all items present from the start of training. When a subject satisfied the accuracy criterion on one derived list, it was advanced to the next one.

If a monkey's knowledge of the four original lists was limited to item-item associations, each derived list should be equally difficult to acquire. If, however, a monkey learned each item's ordinal position in the original lists, then the two maintained

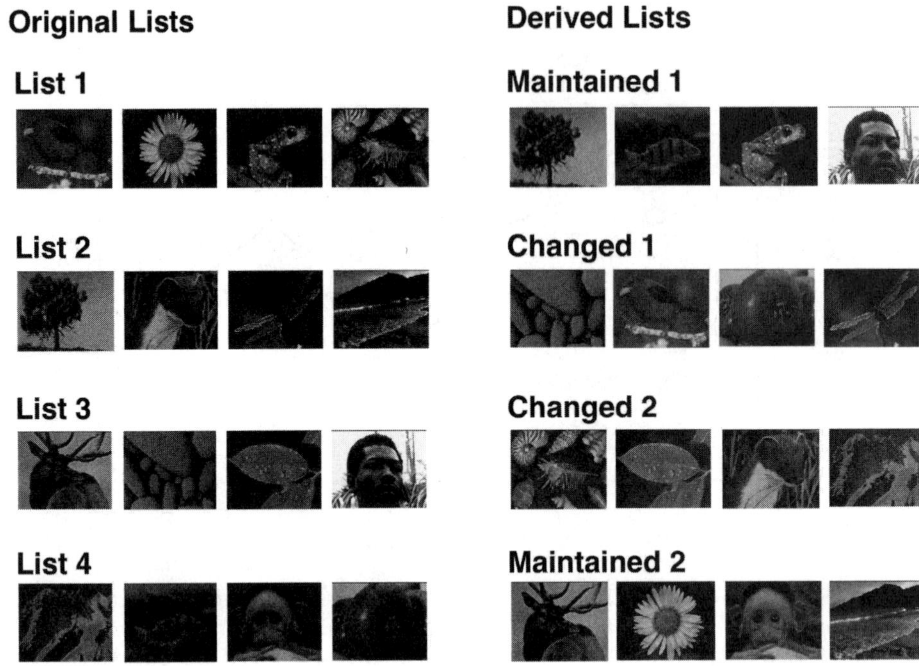

Figure 25.8. Composition of original and derived lists used in experiment by Chen, Swartz, and Terrace (1997).

lists should be easier to learn than the two changed lists. The performance of both subjects confirmed the latter prediction. The relevant data are shown in figure 25.9. Both monkeys rapidly acquired maintained list 1 in the minimum number of trials needed to satisfy the accuracy criterion (120). On maintained list 2, Franklin satisfied the accuracy criterion in 120 trials, while Rutherford required 180 trials.[6]

By contrast, both subjects had difficulty learning changed list 1 and changed list 2, in particular changed list 2, the derived list on which the ordinal positions of the two end items were switched. Rutherford and Franklin needed 599 and 358 trials, respectively, to satisfy the accuracy criterion for changed list 1, and 1655 and 1938 trials, respectively, for changed list 2.[7]

NUMERICAL SEQUENCES

It is convenient to refer to items of an arbitrary list by using letters of the alphabet. Given the arbitrary nature of an alphabet, there is no logical difference between a list composed of photographs and lists composed of letters of the alphabet. Indeed, if monkeys could discriminate letters as well as photographs, then they should be able to learn alphabetic sequences, for example, ABCDEFG, DGAECFB, CFBEGD, and so on. We could even use letters that form words, for example, SUBJECT, PROVIDE, ORDINAL, and so on, in their familiar (to us) arrangements or in arbitrary arrangements, for example, TSBEJCU, OVPIRDE, RLNOADI, and so on. In principle, all of these lists should be equally difficult, and equally meaningless, because changing the order of the items should have no effect on the rate of acquisition of a new list.

Given that the choice of an item in a simultaneous chain is arbitrary, we could have also used other symbols, for example, Arabic numbers. Just as a telephone number has no meaning for us, a sequence of Arabic numbers would have no meaning for a monkey. You may object that telephone numbers may be arbitrary but the sequence 1-2-3-4-5-6-7 is not. The symbol 5 comes after the symbol 4 because it represents a numerosity that is exactly 1 more than the numerosity represented by the symbol 4. The same is true for all of the other adjacent

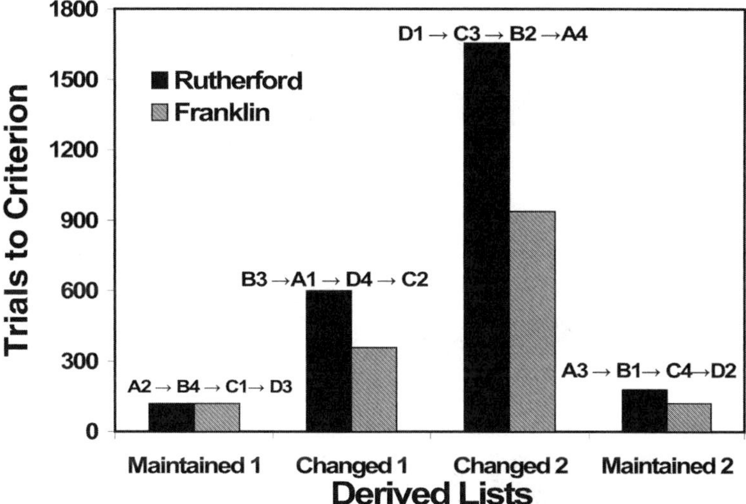

Figure 25.9. Number of trials needed to satisfy the accuracy criterion on four derived lists in the Chen, Swartz, and Terrace (1997) experiment. The order in which the derived lists were trained is shown in figure 25.8.

numbers. Also, the symbol 4 can be used to describe all sets of composed of four objects, the symbol 5, all sets composed of five objects, etc. Just the same, the sequence 1-2-3-4-5-6-7 would be meaningful only to a subject that had learned the ordinal relationships between each pair of numbers.

These examples should make it clear that learning to produce the sequence 1-2-3-4-5-6-7 by rote is a far cry from learning to count. It is generally agreed that learning to count entails, among other abilities, the ability to discriminate sets of objects on the basis of their numerosity and to understand the ordinal and cardinal properties of numbers (Gelman & Gallistel, 1978). For practical reasons, and also because all normal children readily acquire numerical skills, the necessary conditions for learning to count have not been studied systematically.

Investigators of the numerical abilities of animals face a fundamentally different problem. Animals do not normally count. Hence, claims about their knowledge of the ordinal and cardinal properties of numerical symbols have been met with considerable skepticism. Experiments on the numerical ability of animals have had to bear the burden of proof when attributing to animals any of the components of numerical ability that seem natural in children.

That burden notwithstanding, investigators of animal behavior have shown that many species possess some numerical ability (a for review, see Davis & Perusse, 1988). Those observations have led some psychologists to hypothesize that human mathematical ability evolved from numerical abilities that can be observed in animals (Dehaene, 1997; Gallistel & Gelman, 1992). In our research program, we have collected considerable evidence on the ordinal abilities of rhesus monkeys that support the continuity hypothesis (Brannon & Terrace, 1998, 2000, 2002).

A basic premise of our research was that a monkey must be trained to discriminate the numerosity of different sets of objects before it can learn the ordinal or the cardinal properties of numbers. We began by training monkeys to acquire simultaneous chains composed of numerically defined stimuli. Those stimuli, which were composed of geometric shapes that varied in color, number, and size, could be perceived as arbitrary shapes or as exemplars of a particular numerosity. Some examples of numerical lists are shown in figure 25.10.

Our first goal was to show that a monkey could learn a sequence of numerically defined stimuli by following a numerical rather than an arbitrary rule (Brannon & Terrace, 1998). We trained two monkeys (Rosencrantz and Macduff) on 35 four-item lists composed of exemplars of the numerosities 1, 2, 3, and 4 in an ascending order.[8] Subjects were then tested on novel lists to see if they abstracted a

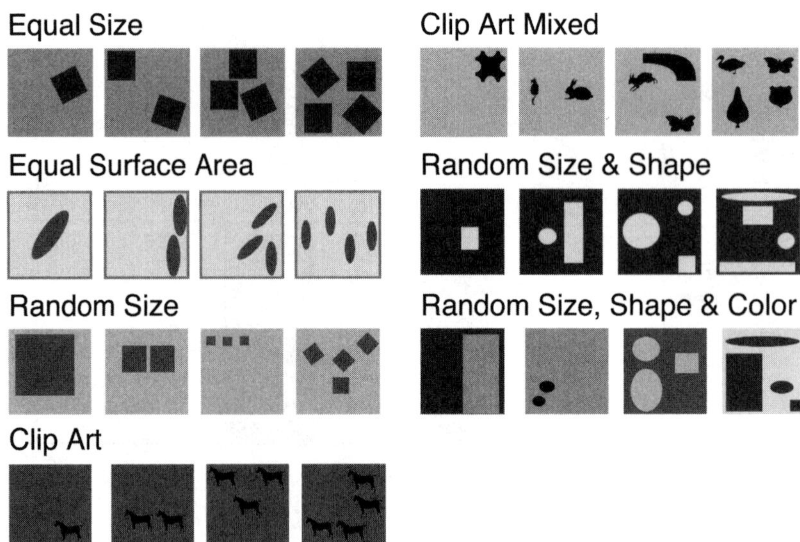

Figure 25.10. Exemplars of the seven different types of stimulus sets used in the Brannon and Terrace (1998) experiment. Equal size: elements were of same size and shape. Equal area: cumulative area of elements was equal. Random size: element size varied randomly across stimuli. Clip art: identical nongeometrical elements selected from clip art software. Clip art mixed: clip art elements of variable shape. Random size and shape: elements within a stimulus were varied randomly in size and shape. Random size, shape, and color: same as previous with background and foreground colors varied between stimuli.

numerical rule during their initial training. Exemplars of the numerosities 1, 2, 3, and 4 were selected from a large library of stimuli in which surface area, shape, size, and color were varied systematically to ensure that those dimensions could not serve as cues for discriminating numerosities.

The same stimuli were used on each trial for each of the 35 lists used during training, albeit in randomly selected configurations (chance level of accuracy ~4%). Subjects were trained for a maximum of three sessions on any of the 35 lists before being moved to a new list. If the subject responded to 30 percent or more of the trials correctly during sessions 1 or 2 of training on a particular training list, then a new list would be introduced at the start of the following session. As can be seen in figure 25.11a, subjects responded in the correct order on at least 45% of the trials on each of the last 10 lists.

Memory of Particular Stimuli or of Numerical Categories?

To rule out the possibility that subjects memorized each of the 35 lists on which they were trained, we tested their ability to respond in the correct order on 150 *novel* lists, all composed of exemplars of the numerosities 1 through 4. Each novel list was presented only once, that is, they were trial unique. Subjects continued to respond at approximately the same level of accuracy (40%) as they did at the end of training on the 35 original lists. Because they had no opportunity to memorize any of the novel lists, the absence of a performance decrement provides clear evidence that subjects used the numerosity of each stimulus (as opposed to some physical feature) to determine the order in which to respond on the novel lists. The relevant data are shown in figure 25.11b.

Representation of Numerical Sequences

Less clear is how a monkey represents the numerosities 1 through 4. One possibility is that the monkeys assigned each numerosity to one of four distinct nominal categories. Under this scenario, the monkeys would have learned an arbitrary ordering of the four categories, just as if we had

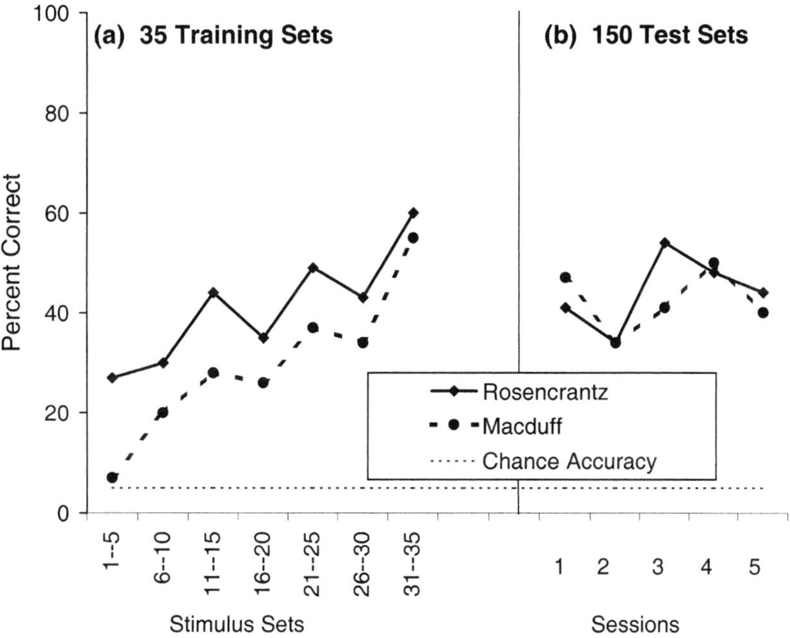

Figure 25.11. (*a*) Percentage of correctly completed trials during the first session for each of 35 training stimulus sets (blocks of five sessions). (*b*) Percentage of correctly completed trials on the 150 test sets. (Data from Brannon & Terrace, 1998, experiment.)

taught them to respond to different exemplars of, say, birds, flowers, trees, and rocks.

On this view, it should be just as easy for monkeys to learn a list composed of numerical stimuli in the order 3-1-4-2 as it would be to learn a list in which the subject had to respond in an ascending order, 1-2-3-4. Contrary to that hypothesis, the one subject (Macduff) trained on a 3-1-4-2 sequence showed no signs of improvement during training on 13 stimulus sets. However, as can be seen in figure 25.12, Macduff's performance improved rapidly once he was required to respond to list items in an ascending numerical order. The ease of learning a monotonic rule, as compared with a nonmonotonic rule, provides strong evidence that monkeys perceive the ordinal relations between the numerosities on which they were trained.

Given that evidence, we used the same subjects to evaluate a monkey's ability to perceive ordinal relations between novel numerosities. Specifically, we asked whether a monkey could apply the ascending rule it had learned with respect to the numerosities 1 through 4 to the novel numerosities 5 through 9. To answer that question, subjects were tested on exemplars of all possible pairs of the numerosities 1 through 9. As shown in figure 25.13, each pair can be classified as familiar-familiar, familiar-novel, and novel-novel. Reinforcement for responding to pairs in an ascending order was available only on trials on which one of the six familiar-familiar pairs were presented (1-2, 1-3, 1-4, 2-3, 2-4, 3-4). There was, therefore, no basis for learning the ordinal relationship of a novel numerosity with any other numerosity, novel or familiar.

Subjects responded correctly on between 70% and 75% of the trials on which novel-novel pairs were presented. The relevant data are shown in figure 25.14. On these tests, both subjects were just as accurate in their responses to pairs in which the larger numerosity covered a smaller area than to pairs in which the larger numerosity covered a larger area (not shown). That result ruled out nonnumerical features of the test stimuli as an explanation of subjects' accuracy. As neither subject had any previous training with the numerosities 5 through 9, their ability to respond to those numerosities in an ascending order provides clear evidence that a monkey can extrapolate an ascending rule to novel numerosities.

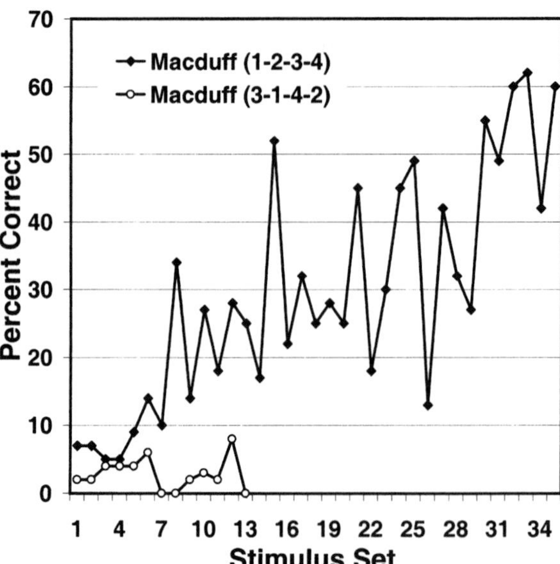

Figure 25.12. Comparison of Macduff's performance on a nonmonotonic ($3 \rightarrow 1 \rightarrow 4 \rightarrow 2$) and a monotonic ($1 \rightarrow 2 \rightarrow 3 \rightarrow 4$) sequence of numerical stimuli. (Data from Brannon & Terrace, 2002.)

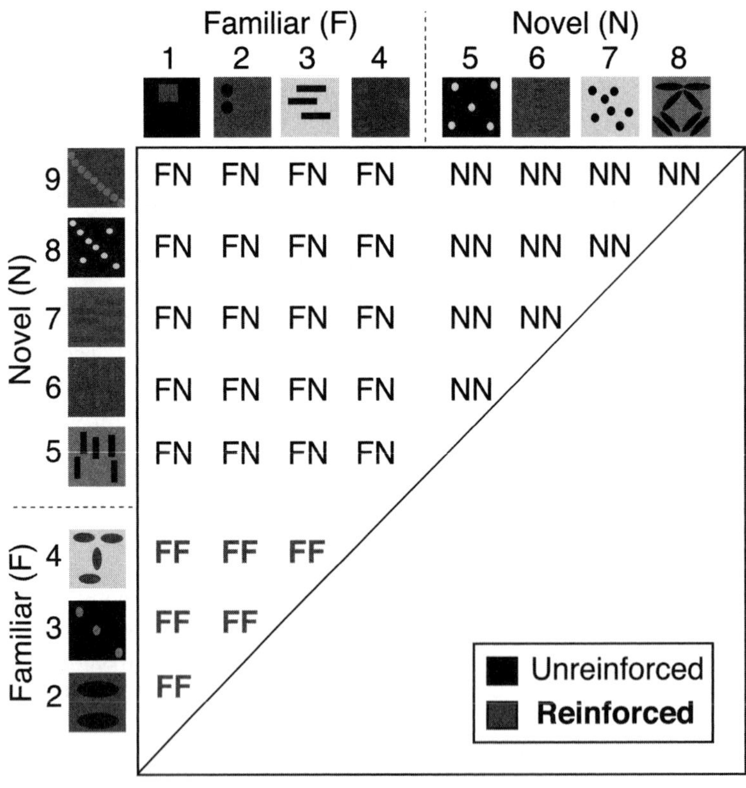

Figure 25.13. The 36 pairs of the numerosities 1 through 9 used in subset test in Brannon and Terrace's (1998) experiment. These were defined with respect to the subjects' prior experience with the constituent numerosities: familiar-familiar (FF), familiar-novel (FN), novel-novel (NN). Only FF subsets were reinforced.

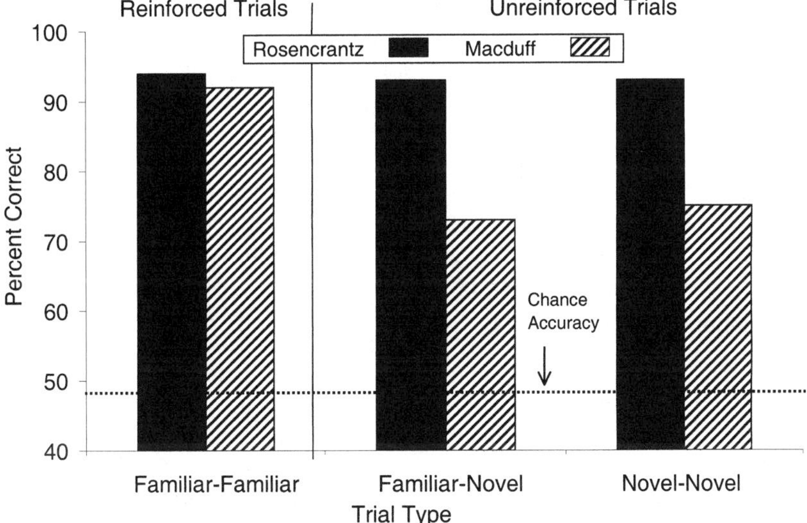

Figure 25.14. Accuracy of responding on familiar-familiar, familiar-novel, and novel-novel subsets in Brannon and Terrace (1998) experiment.

Distance and Magnitude Effects

In what is arguably the oldest and most reliable experiment in psychology, subjects are asked to judge the relative magnitude of two stimuli from some physical continuum, such as line length, light intensity, sound energy, and so on (Herrnstein & Boring, 1965). The same paradigm has also been used to obtain judgments of the relative magnitude of stimuli defined by their psychological characteristics (e.g., judgments of the relative numerical magnitude of Arabic numerals). In a classic experiment, Moyer and Landauer (1967) showed that RT decreased as the numerical distance between two numerals increased. For example, when asked to select the larger number from pairs 2-4 and 2-7, subjects respond more rapidly to the latter. Moyer and Landauer referred to the inverse relationship between distance and RT as a *distance effect*. Figure 25.15 shows a distance function that is based on their data.

Distance effects have also been obtained on arbitrary continua (e.g., the alphabet). For example, Hamilton and Sanford (1978) showed that RTs of judgments about the alphabetical order of pairs of letters decreases as the distance between the letters increase (e.g., a more rapid response to the letters G and S than to the letters G and M). Data from the Hamilton and Sanford experiment are shown in figure 25.16.

Judgments of the relative magnitude of two stimuli are affected by the magnitude of the smaller item as well as by the distance between the items. At a constant distance between the smaller and the larger item, RTs of judgments of relative magnitude increase with the magnitude of the smaller item. That relationship, which is analogous to Weber's

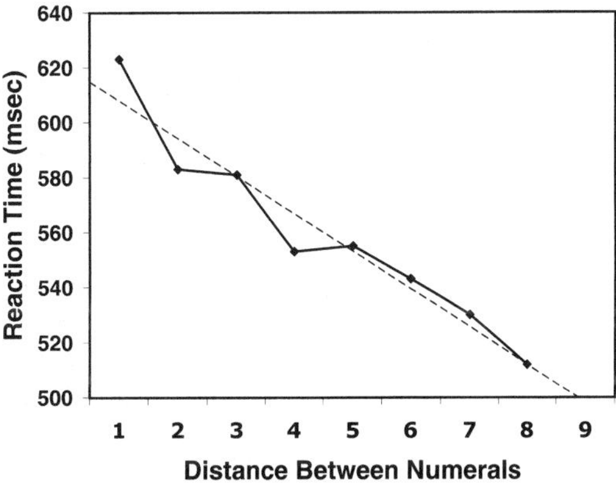

Figure 25.15. Reaction times of human subjects asked to select the larger of two simultaneously presented Arabic numerals. (Data from Moyer & Landauer, 1967.)

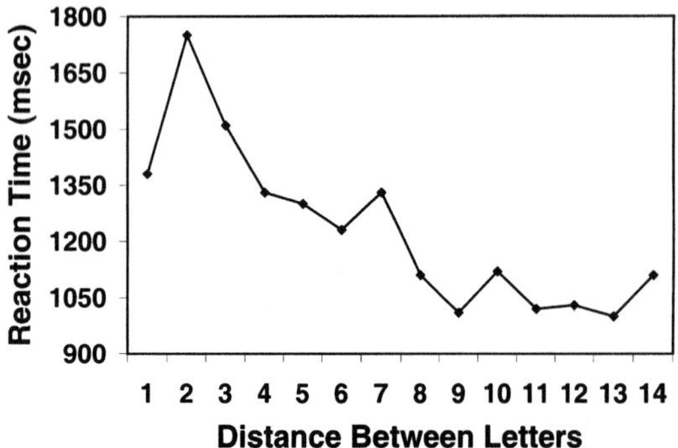

Figure 25.16. Reaction times of human subjects asked to select which of two simultaneously presented letters comes first in the English alphabet. (Data from Hamilton & Sanford, 1978.)

law in the case of natural continua, has been referred to as a *magnitude effect*. Thus, when subjects are asked, which number is larger, 7 or 8, RT is longer than when the same question is asked about the numbers 3 and 4. Similarly, in the case of alphabetical stimuli, RTs to the pair J and K are longer than RTs to the pair C and D.

Distance and Magnitude Effects in Rhesus Macaques

The ability of our monkeys to learn arbitrary and numerical sequences provides an unprecedented opportunity to assess distance and magnitude effects in a nonhuman primate. Positive results would factor out language as a necessary condition for distance and magnitude effects. It would also provide an animal model of ordinal representation that could guide investigations of the neural substrates of distance and magnitude effects. For example, a recent study by Nieder, Freedman, and Miller (2002) shows how psychological distance and magnitude effects can be used in analyses of the activities of single cells in the brain that are tuned to specific numerosities.

Experiments on magnitude and distance effects in human subjects are based mainly on variations in the RTs of subjects' judgments of relative magnitude. In principle, subjects' accuracy of responding to particular pairs of stimuli could also serve as a dependent variable. For example, one would predict that accuracy should increase as the distance between the members of a pair increases and that it should decrease as the magnitude of the smaller item increases. Accuracy has not been used as dependent variable because subjects' error rates were virtually nil, hardly a surprise in experiments in which college students were tested with stimuli they learned to use as children: letters of the alphabet and numbers. Although our subjects had considerable expertise in ordering arbitrary and numerical stimuli, they still made errors. We were therefore able to use accuracy, as well as RT, to measure of distance and magnitude effects in monkeys.

Distance and Magnitude Effects Obtained With Numerical Stimuli

To assess distance and magnitude effects in monkeys trained to order numerical stimuli, we analyzed the accuracy and the RT of subjects' responses to the 36 numerical pairs on which subjects were tested in the Brannon and Terrace (1998) experiment. As

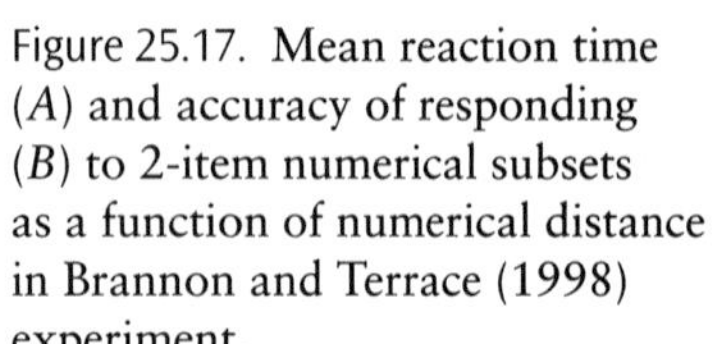

Figure 25.17. Mean reaction time (*A*) and accuracy of responding (*B*) to 2-item numerical subsets as a function of numerical distance in Brannon and Terrace (1998) experiment.

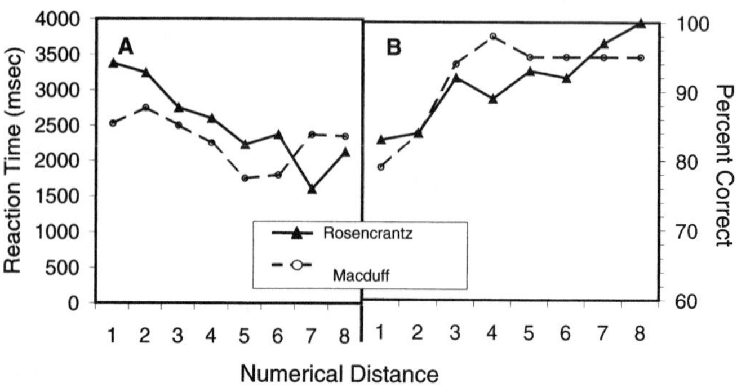

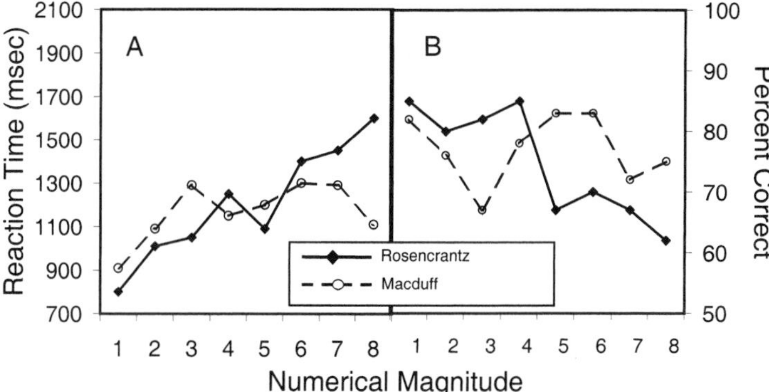

Figure 25.18. Mean reaction time (*A*) and accuracy of responding (*B*) to 2-item numerical subsets as a function of numerical magnitude in Brannon and Terrace (1998) experiment.

described earlier, those pairs were derived from stimuli whose numerical value ranged from 1 to 9. We found clear evidence of both distance and magnitude effects. As can be seen in figure 25.17, RT decreased and accuracy increased as the numerical distance between the members of a pair increased. Analogously, as shown in figure 25.18, RT increased and accuracy decreased as the magnitude of the first item of each pair increased.

The value of each point shown in figure 25.17 is the average of all pairs separated by a distance of 1 (1-2, 2-3, 3-4, 4-5, 5-6, 6-7, 7-8, and 8-9) a distance of 2 (1-3, 2-4, 3-5, 4-6, 5-7, 6-8, and 7-9), a distance of 3 (1-4, 2-5, 3-6, 4-7, 5-8, and 6-9), and so on. In figure 25.18, the value of each point is the average of all pairs in which the first item had a magnitude of 1 (1-2, 1-3, 1-4 . . .), a magnitude of 2 (2-3, 2-4 . . .), and so on. Those averages do not provide information about the uniformity of the effect of distance across all pairs. It is conceivable, for example, that distance might only influence pairs in which the magnitude of the first item exceeded 3.

To evaluate the uniformity of the effects of distance and magnitude on accuracy and RT, the data shown in figures 25.17 and 25.18 were analyzed with distance or magnitude held constant. The result of that analysis is shown in figures 25.19 and 25.20. In general, distance and magnitude exerted uniform effects on accuracy and RT. The one exception was the effect of magnitude on accuracy. Were it not for a ceiling effect of 100% accuracy, it is likely that the influence of magnitude on accuracy would have been more pronounced. Figure 25.19 also shows that the lowest accuracy for any pair of numerosities was significantly greater than that predicted by chance. The effect of distance and magnitude on RT was unambiguous. As can be seen in figure 25.20, that effect was most striking for distances 1 and 2. On average, each increment in magnitude resulted in an increase in RT of sapproximately 250 ms.

Distance and Magnitude Effects With Arbitrary List Items

To assess distance and magnitude effects on arbitrary continua, we administered a two-item subset test to the subjects that mastered seven-item lists of photographs in the Terrace et al. (2003) experiment. All 28 of the items used to construct the four seven-item lists those subjects learned were used to construct the subset test. From those items, we derived 84 within-list subsets and 252 between-list subsets. Within-list subsets were composed of items from a particular list (e.g., from list 3, the subsets A_3B_3, A_3C_3 . . . A_3G_3; B_3C_3, B_3D_3 . . . F_3G_3). Between-list subsets were composed of items drawn from different lists (e.g., the subsets A_2B_4 from lists 2 and 4, C_3F_5 from lists 3 and 5, E_1G_3 from lists 1 and 3, etc.).

For the purpose of analysis, these subsets were assigned to one of six categories on the basis of the distance between their ordinal positions on the original lists (e.g., pairs of items separated by a distance of 1: the subsets A_1B_1, B_2C_2 . . . A_1B_2; B_2C_3, C_3D_4 . . . F_3G_4; a distance of 2: A_1C_1, B_2D_2 . . . A_1C_2; B_2D_3, C_3E_4 . . . E_3G_4; a distance of 6: A_1G_1,

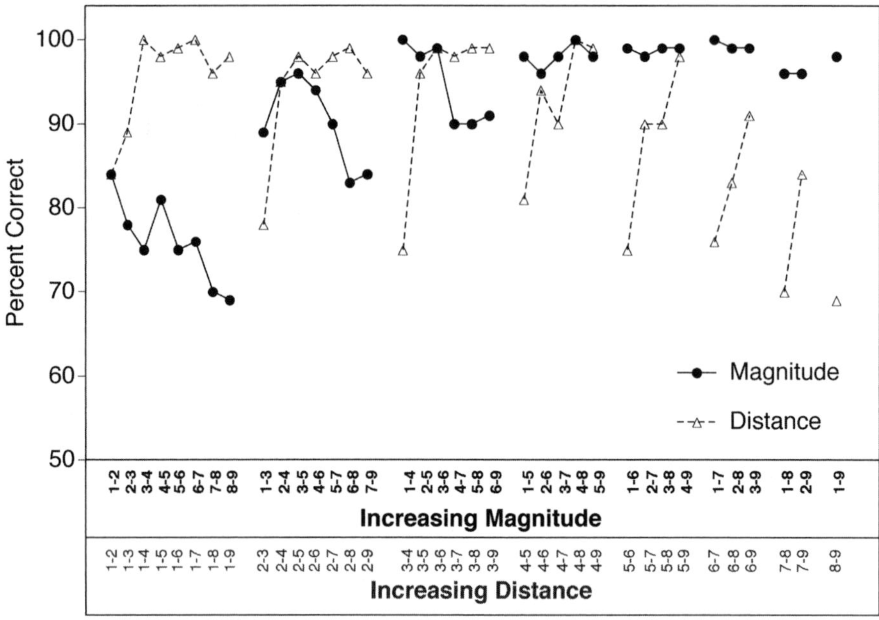

Figure 25.19. Mean accuracy of responding to each of the 36 numerical pairs presented in the Brannon and Terrace (2000) experiment when distance (gray functions) and magnitude (black functions) were held constant.

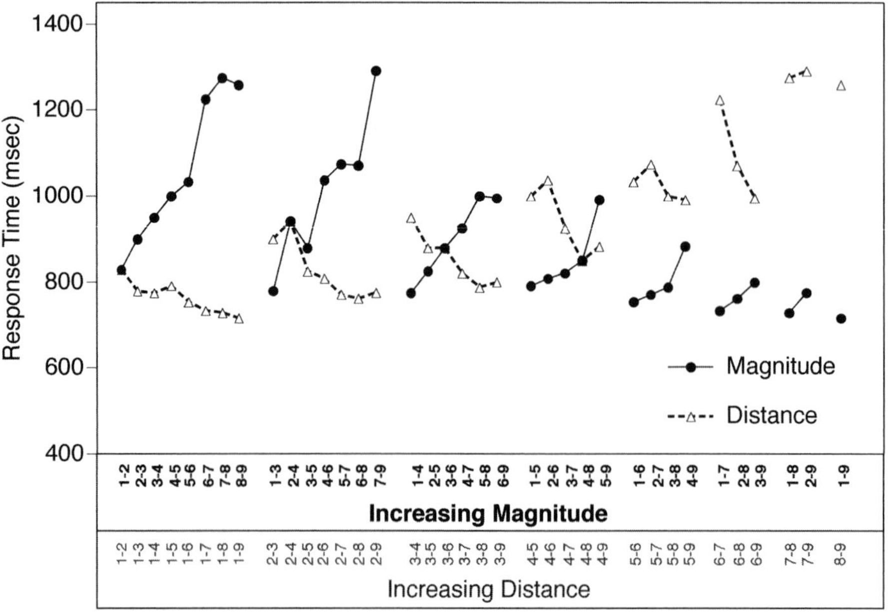

Figure 25.20. Mean reaction times to each of the 36 numerical pairs presented in the Brannon and Terrace (2000) experiment when distance (gray functions) and magnitude (black functions) were held constant.

(A)

Cyrillic

Д Ж Я Ю Б Э Ч

Greek

Σ Δ Ψ Ω Θ Λ Π

Hebrew

ע פ ת ד ט מ ב

Thai

น บ ซ ต ฮ ฝ ษ

(B)

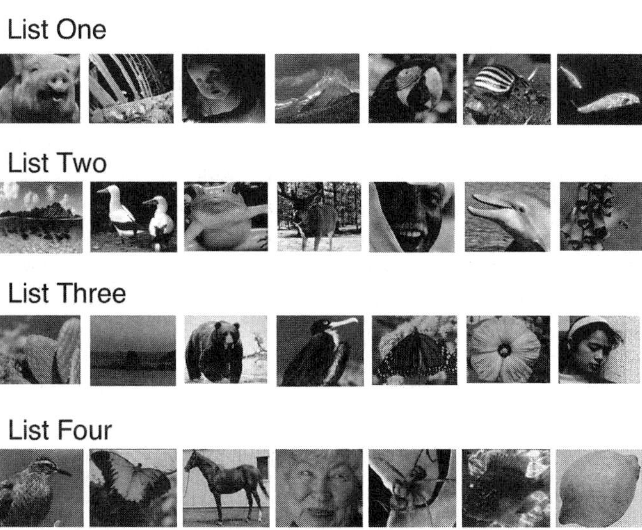

Figure 25.21. (*A*) Examples of letters from the Cyrillic, Greek, Hebrew, and Thai alphabets. (*B*) Photographs used to compose four 7-item lists on which monkeys were trained in the Terrace, Son, and Brannon (2003) experiment.

$A_2G_1 \ldots A_2G_1$, A_2G_2, $A_2G_3 \ldots A_4G_4$). Excluded from the subset test were the 21 pairs that could be composed of items occupying the same ordinal positions on the four seven-item lists (e.g., the subsets A_1A_2, $A_1A_3 \ldots G_3G_4$). Within- and between-list pairs were interspersed randomly throughout the subset test. Subjects were rewarded if they responded in the order specified by their ordinal positions on the original list. For example, subjects were rewarded for responding to items C and F, in that order, whether or not they came from the same or different lists (e.g., C_3F_3 or C_2F_6).

Here again, a human analogy is helpful to explain the monkey's task. Suppose that you took a course in which you learned four new languages: Greek, Finnish, Russian, and Hebrew. Seven letters of those alphabets are shown in figure 25.21A. One day, you are given a surprise quiz on which you are shown pairs of letters that were drawn at random from each of the four alphabets you learned. Any of the 28 letters could be chosen as the first letter. The choice of the second letter was restricted to 24 of the remaining letters. Excluded were the three letters that occupy the same ordinal position as the first letter. For each subset, your task is to say which letter comes first in the alphabet from which it was selected, a difficult task by any standard.

Now, imagine monkeys taking a similar quiz based on the 28 photographs that were used to compose the four seven-item lists trained in the Terrace et al. (2003) experiment. Those photographs are shown in figure 25.21B. From the monkey's point of view, the order of the photographs on each of the four lists is just as arbitrary as the order of the letters in any of the four alphabets. Consider, for example, the English alphabet. There is no inherent reason why *d* has to come after *c*. A child would find either order equally difficult to master. However, a child has an important advantage over a monkey because the child could use *numerical* symbols as a mnemonic for remembering a letter's position in the alphabet from which it was drawn. There is no reason to assume that a monkey could use that strategy.

Before we examine the results of the subset test based on photographs, we should consider what chaining theory would predict. Because associative strength between items decreases with distance, chaining theory would predict that accuracy of responding to subset pairs would *decrease* and that RT would *increase* as the distance between the items increased. By contrast, theories of serial learning based on cognitive maps or spatial representations of lists (e.g., Holyoak & Patterson, 1981) would make the opposite prediction. Because larger distances are more discriminable than smaller distances, a spatial theory would predict that accuracy *increases* and that RTs *decrease* as the distance between the items increases.

Both predictions of spatial theory were confirmed. Even though accuracy of responding was nearly perfect on many subset types, there was clear evidence of a distance effect. As shown in figure 25.22, accuracy on both within- and between-list subsets increased as the distance between the subset items increased. For both types of subset, accuracy was well above the chance level of accuracy, with accuracy on within-group subsets was slightly greater than accuracy on between-group subsets (by ~250 ms). Analogously, figure 25.23 shows that the RT of the response to the first item of each subset decreased with distance between the subset items.

To evaluate the uniformity of the effects of distance and magnitude on accuracy and RT, we analyzed the data from the subset test using arbitrary list items holding distance and magnitude constant. The results of that analysis are shown in figure 25.24. In each instance, the functions we obtained using arbitrary stimuli were strikingly similar to those obtained from subset tests based on numerical stimuli (cf. figures 25.19 and 25.20). As was the case with numerical pairs, the functions based on accuracy were compressed because of a ceiling effect. Consider, for example, the upper set of functions in

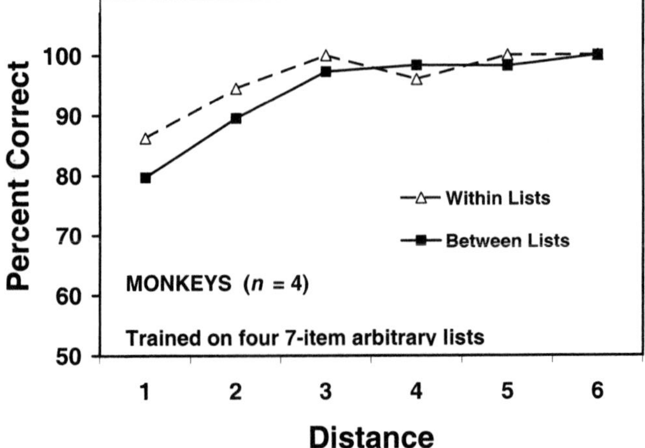

Figure 25.22. Mean accuracy to between- and within-list subsets as a function of distance between items on original lists in Terrace, Son, and Brannon (2003) experiment.

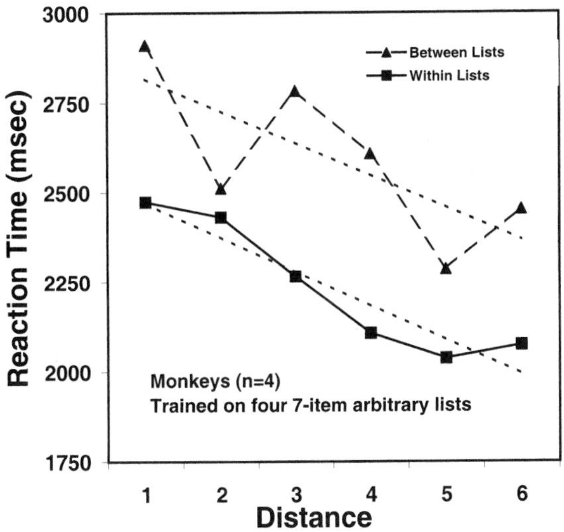

Figure 25.23. Mean reaction times of the first response on between- and within-list subsets as a function of distance between items on original lists in Terrace, Son, and Brannon (2003) experiment.

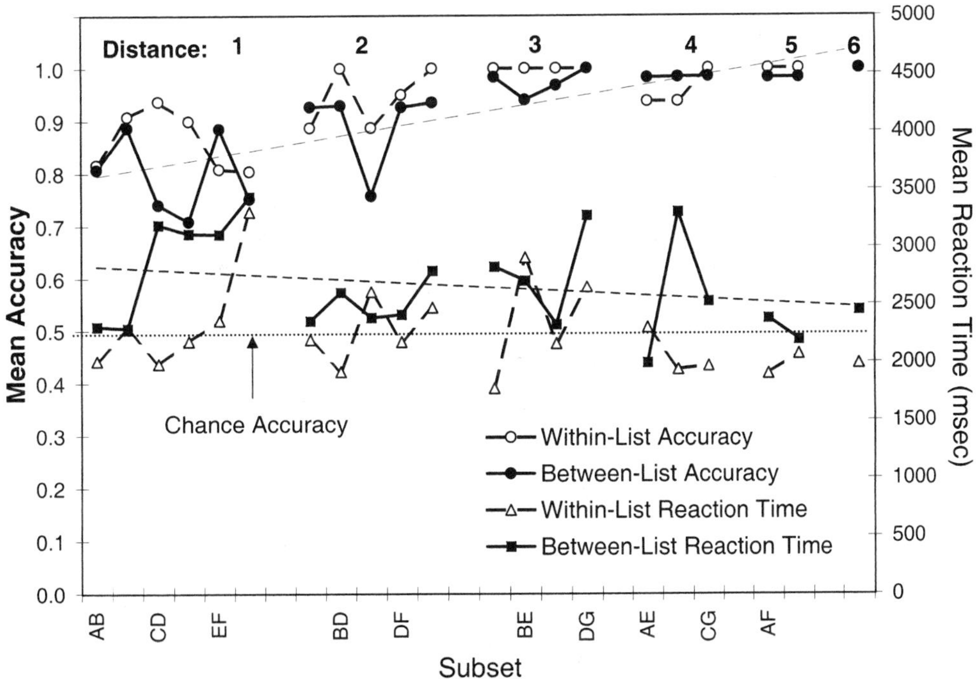

Figure 25.24. Mean reaction times and accuracy of responding to within- and between-list subsets in the Terrace, Son, and Brannon (2003) experiment with distance and magnitude were held constant.

figure 25.24 (shown in gray). At a distance of 1, the mean level of accuracy was 83%; at a distance of 2, accuracy was 92%. For distances greater than 2, the average level of accuracy was 99% for all subsets.

The RT functions in the lower portion of figure 25.24 (shown in black) were obtained with distance held constant and are quite similar to the analogous RT functions shown in figure 25.20. For example, at distance 1, RTs increased approximately 470 ms for each increment in ordinal position. The median RT to the first item on AB trials was 2,180 ms. On FG trials, it was 3,374 ms. Similar RT functions have been obtained from human subjects in experiments on the discriminability of adjacent pairs of letters of the alphabet when the alphabetical position of the first item is varied from trial to trial (Hamilton & Sanford, 1978; Lovelace & Snodgrass, 1971).

Comparison of Distance and Magnitude Effects in Humans and Monkeys

We have seen that the distance and magnitude effects that were obtained from monkeys are strikingly similar to those obtained from human subjects, in the case of both arbitrary and numerical sequences. In each instance, RT decreased and accuracy increased with increasing distance between the items used in two-item subset tests. Conversely, RT increased and accuracy decreased as the magnitude of the first item increased. To be sure, human subjects were tested on such overlearned sequences as the alphabet and Arabic numbers, whereas our monkeys were trained on lists of arbitrarily selected photographs and numerical stimuli composed of geometrical shapes. How could we be sure that the similarities we observed were not artifacts of the stimuli on which each species was trained?

To rule out that possibility, we performed experiments on college students using stimuli that were identical or comparable to those we used with our monkeys. In one experiment, we used the same numerical stimuli we used with our monkeys and gave them the same pairwise comparison task. Subjects were instructed to respond to the stimulus with the smaller number of elements as quickly as possible by pressing the appropriate key on a computer keyboard. As shown in figure 25.25, the numerical distance and magnitude effects obtained from college students were indistinguishable from those obtained from monkeys (Brannon & Terrace, 2002). These data provide compelling evidence that animals and humans use the same numerical comparison process.

In another experiment (Terrace, 2001), college students were trained on arbitrary lists composed of complex black and white geometrical shapes of the type shown in figure 25.26 (Attneave, 1955). We chose geometrical stimuli rather than photographs because pilot data showed that human subjects were likely to verbally encode photographic, but not

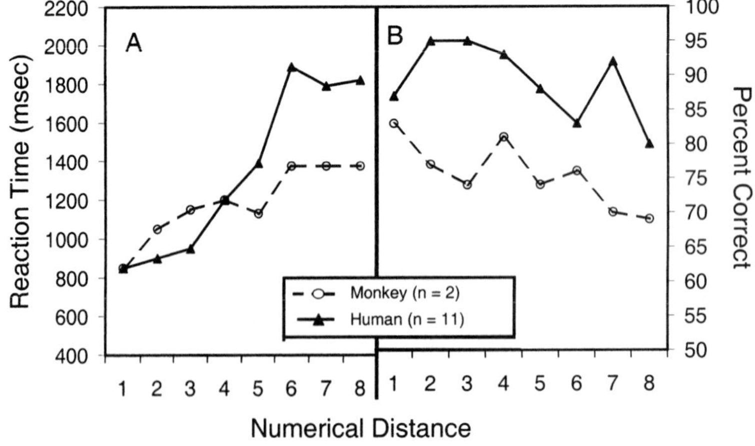

Figure 25.25. Comparison of performance on 2-item numerical subsets by human subjects and monkeys. (*A*) Mean reaction time. (*B*) Mean accuracy of the first response as a function of numerical distance. (Data are from Brannon & Terrace, 2002.)

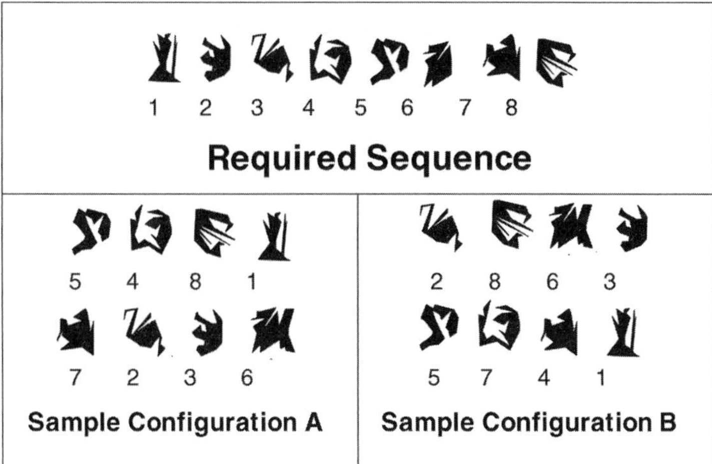

Figure 25.26. Stimuli used to construct 8-item lists for human subjects trained by the simultaneous chaining paradigm in the experiment by Terrace (2003).

geometric, stimuli. After subjects were familiarized with the task on a three-item simultaneous chain, they were instructed to apply the same logic to four eight-item lists. Subjects were trained to a criterion of completing at least 65% of the trials correctly in a single session on each list. After mastering each list, subjects were given a two-item subset test. As can be seen in figure 25.27A and B, subjects' RTs resembled those obtained from monkeys (cf. figure 25.20); they decreased with increasing distance between the subset items and increased as the position of the first item increased (Brannon & Terrace, 2000).

Differences in the absolute value of RTs to arbitrary and numerical stimuli are evident both within and between species and indeed, in some cases, within individual subjects. Consider, for example, the magnitude functions for numerical and arbitrary stimuli obtained from Rosencrantz and Macduff shown in figure 25.28. RT increased from 600 to 1,500 ms as the magnitude of the first item of a numerical pair increased from 1 to 9. By contrast, on the subset test with photographic stimuli, RT increased from 2,250 to 3,000 ms as the position of the first item advanced in the seven-item list on which the subject was trained.

Why should it take two to three times as long to make a judgment about arbitrary stimuli than it does about numerical stimuli? Assuming that comparisons of both types of stimuli are made in working memory, it appears that the longer RTs for arbitrary stimuli include the time needed to retrieve information about the ordinal position of such stimuli from long-term memory. That does not seem to be the case for numerical stimuli whose ordinal position can be determined algorithmically in working memory (Carey, 2004).

The data shown in figure 25.28 raise another interesting question about differences between distance functions obtained with arbitrary stimuli that is absent from those obtained with numerical

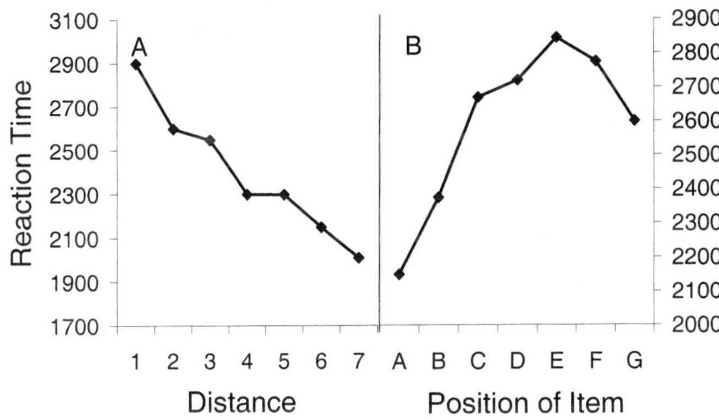

Figure 25.27. Mean reaction time of responding of human subjects as a function of distance (*A*) and position of first item (*B*) to 2-item subsets derived from 8-item lists in the experiment by Terrace (2001).

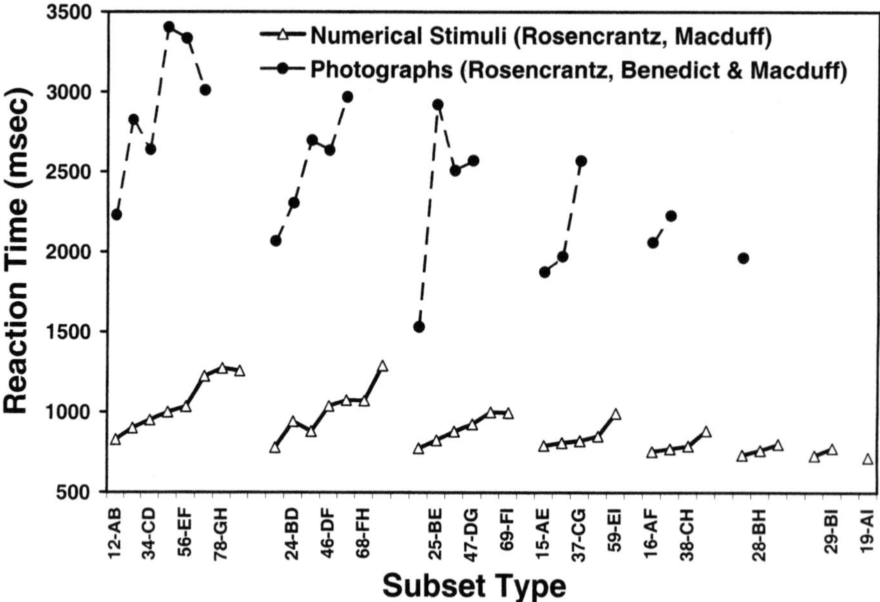

Figure 25.28. Reaction times of monkeys to 2-item subsets composed of numerical (Brannon & Terrace, 1998) and arbitrary (Terrace, Son, & Brannon, 2003) stimuli.

stimuli. In the case of arbitrary stimuli, RTs often assume their maximal values to items from the middle of the list. Returning to the data shown in figure 25.28, we see that, at a distance of 1, RT for the monkeys trained on seven-item arbitrary lists increases from 2,200 ms at the first position to 3,450 ms at position E and then drop to 2,900 ms at position H. By contrast, the absolute values of RT functions that were obtained from the same monkeys on numerical subsets increase monotonically as the numerical value of the first item of the subset increases. Similar patterns of unimodal magnitude functions for arbitrary stimuli and monotonic magnitude functions for numerical stimuli can be seen in figure 25.29, which depicts RT functions from both human and nonhuman primates.

The drop in RT for judgments about items from the end of an arbitrary list suggests that subjects scan a representation of those lists from both ends. The asymmetry of those distance functions suggests that the rate of forward scanning for items from the beginning of an arbitrary list to the end of an arbitrary list is faster than the rate of backward scanning of items from the end of the list. This pattern is hardly surprising given the huge disparity in subjects' experience in executing a list in a forward and a backward manner.

A dual scanning process should be expected with overtrained lists of arbitrary stimuli but not with overtrained lists of numerical stimuli. On arbitrary lists, the last item becomes more salient during overtraining.[9] As a result, subjects tend to scan a list forward, starting from the first item, and backward, starting from the last item. On a numerical list, the last item is not salient because subjects rely on an ordinal rule to execute such sequences and because the physical appearance of the last item varies from trial to trial. Thus, there is no reason to expect a backward scanning process in the case of numerical lists.

The distance and magnitude functions we obtained from human and nonhuman primates, for both arbitrary and numerical stimuli, are remarkably similar to those reported by other investigators. Indeed, when the functions shown in figure 25.29 are combined with those reported in the literature, they coalesce into two neatly segregated and nonoverlapping categories that can be defined by the absolute value of RTs: one for arbitrary stimuli, the other for numerical stimuli. A summary of these functions is shown in figure 25.30.

These functions have important implications for theories of animal cognition. They show that the ordering of arbitrary and numerical stimuli

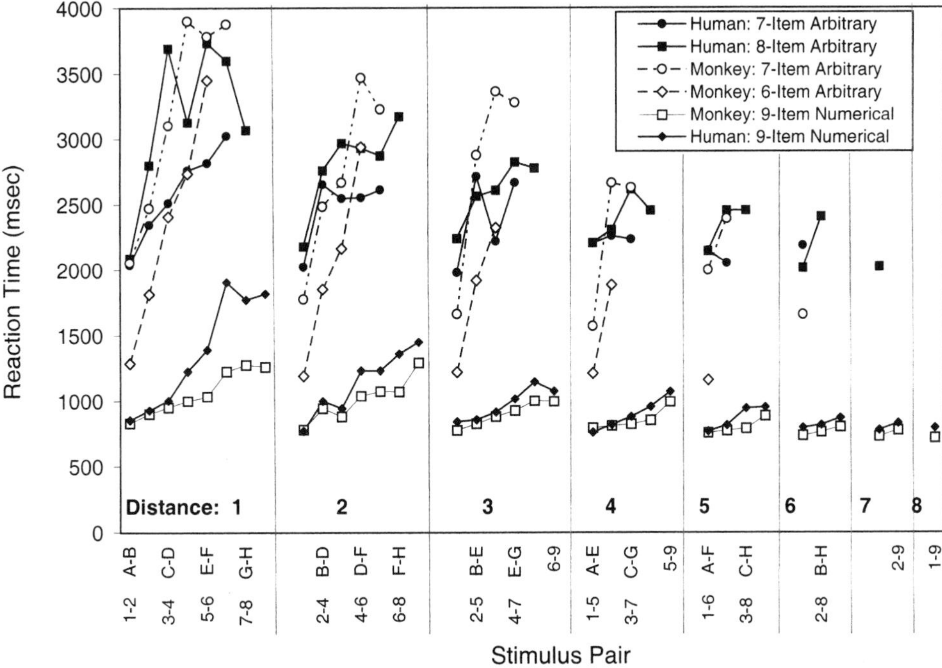

Figure 25.29. Reaction times of monkeys and humans to 2-item subsets composed of numerical and arbitrary stimuli containing 6 to 9 items. (Data are from experiments by Brannon & Terrace, 1998, 2002; Terrace, 2001; and Terrace, Son, & Brannon, 2003.)

does not require language and that there is a considerable overlap in the processes that human and nonhuman primates use to make ordinal judgments of the relative magnitude of arbitrary and numerical stimuli. They also provide a basis for performing experiments on mental chronometry, a paradigm that has helped to shape theories of human cognition (Posner, 1989; Sternberg, 1969, 1975).

In addition, distance effects obtained with arbitrary stimuli have two important theoretical implications. As noted previously, chaining theory predicts an *increase* in RT with increasing distance between arbitrary stimuli because associative strength decreases as the ordinal distance between items increases. As can be seen in figure 25.25, the slopes of the distance function are the exact opposite of what chaining theory would predict. Of broader interest are the implications of the data shown in figure 25.25 for theories of representation. Many computational theories claim that cognitive representations are propositional, that is, they are based upon rules of syntax and semantics (Fodor & Pylyshyn, 1988; Pylyshyn, 1981). In experiments with human subjects, it is difficult to tease apart the influence of propositional thinking, which requires language, from the influence of perceptual-analogical processing, which may not (Kosslyn, 1994). A monkey's knowledge of the ordinal position of arbitrary items cannot, of course, be based on nonlinguistic representations. A more plausible candidate is analog coding of ordinal position, which can account for knowledge of ordinal position and distance effects based on arbitrary stimuli (Kosslyn, 1994). Analog coding can also account for RTs of judgments of the numerical magnitude of stimuli. Interestingly, recent experiments on the neural basis of numerical judgments by monkeys suggest a continuum of analog processes that are shared by human and nonhuman primates (Nieder et al., 2002).

CONCLUSION

The simultaneous chaining paradigm provides an important bridge for comparing animal and human cognition. Its success in training animals to order arbitrary and numerical stimuli stems from the

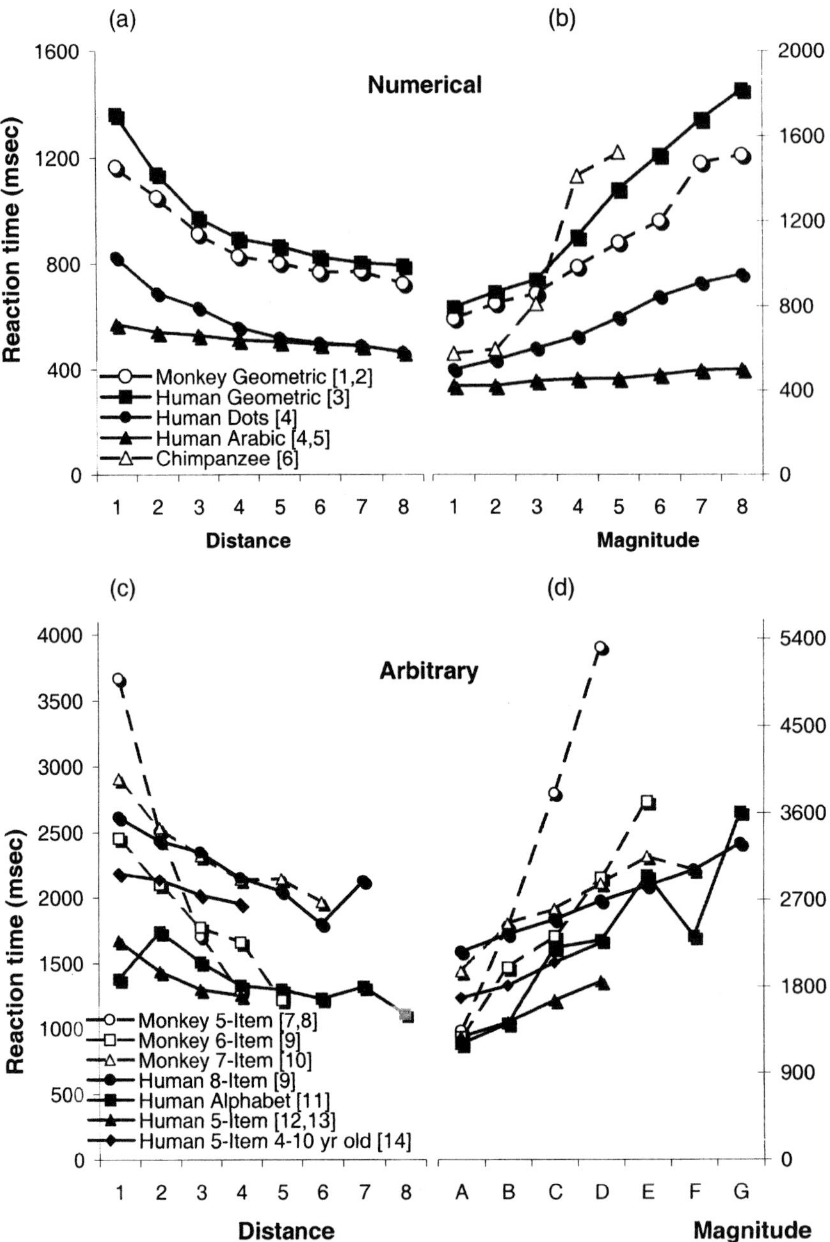

Figure 25.30. Distance and magnitude functions obtained from human subjects and monkeys. These functions were obtained on subtest tests composed of numerical and arbitrary items. All of the nonhuman primates were first trained by the simultaneous chaining paradigm to learn lists of arbitrary or numerical stimuli. They were then tested with 2-item subsets composed of items from a given list. The data shown in this figure are the median reaction times of correct responses to the first item of each subset. Also shown in this figure are distance and magnitude functions obtained from human subjects that were tested on their ordinal knowledge of Arabic numbers and letters of the alphabet. These are similar to functions obtained from nonhuman primates in experiments that used arbitrary and numerical stimuli. The sources of the functions shown here are as follows. [1] Brannon and Terrace, 1998; [2] Brannon and Terrace, 2002; [3] Murofushi, 1997; [4] D'Amato and Colombo, 1988; [5] Terrace, 2001b; [6] Terrace et al., 2003; [7] Terrace, 2001a; [8] Hamilton and Sanford, 1978; Brannon and Terrace, 2002; [9] Colombo and Frost, 2001; Guyla and Colombo, 2004; [10] Guyla and Colombo, 2004; [11] Brannon and Terrace, 2002; [12] Buckley and Gillman, 1974; [13] Moyer and Landauer, 1967; Buckley and Gillman, 1974; [14] Chalmers and McGonigle, 1984.

absence of any requirement for subjects to learn new motor responses while learning a new sequence. In addition to the experiments described in this article, the simultaneous chaining paradigm has provided a basis for performing experiments on cognitive imitation (Subiaul et al., 2004), on meta-cognition (Son & Kornell, 2005), and on neural mechanisms that mediate serially organized behavior (Carpenter, Georgopolous, & Pellizzer, 1999; Grafton et al., 1995; Marshuetz, Smith, Jonides, DeGutis, & Chenevert, 2000; Nieder et al., 2002; Ninokura, Mushiake, & Tanji, 2004). Given that many of the discoveries about simultaneous chaining have been serendipitous, I anticipate that the future of research on this topic will contain various surprises that will help to fill many gaps in our understanding of how the verbal human mind evolved from the poorly understood nonverbal animal mind.

Notes

1. Because of the fixed position of the lexigrams on each trial, Lana could have learned sequences as a series of rote responses. That possibility was eliminated in the experiment by Terrace, Son, & Brannon (2003) described here.

2. We started with three-item lists because a meaningful list cannot be constructed with fewer than three items. A two-item list does not have to be learned as a sequence because a subject simply has to identify A and then respond to the second item by default. That default strategy cannot be used on a three-item list. After the subject learns A, it has to chose one of the two remaining items.

3. The first list was trained to a criterion of correct completion of 65% of the trials in a single session to be sure that subjects learned to execute at least one three-item list and one four-item list at a high level of accuracy.

4. The reader should keep in mind that accuracy level refers to correctly completed trials and not responses to individual items. Thus, an accuracy level of 61% means that on 61% of the trials, the subject made four correct responses, one to A, one to B, one to C, and one to D.

5. Given 60 trials per session and an average of three logical errors at A, the conditional probability of a correct response by an ideal ordinal position detector at position A would be 57/60 = .95; given an average of 2.5 logical errors at position B, 54.5/57 = .96.

6. Rutherford needed an extra session to satisfy the accuracy criterion for maintained list 2 most likely because he followed the "changed" rule that was relevant on changed list 2. On changed list 2, the original ordinal positions of the end items were reversed. Virtually all of Rutherford's errors on maintained list 2 reflected the reversal of the original ordinal positions of items A and D.

7. Additional evidence of a monkey's knowledge of the ordinal position of list items has been presented in an experiment by Orlov, Yakovlev, Hochstein, and Zohary (2000).

8. Rosencrantz and Macduff served as subjects in the experiment described earlier on serial expertise. Brannon and Terrace (2002) have also successfully trained monkeys to learn numerical list in which the rule was to respond in a descending order (4-3-2-1). Certain aspects of subjects' performance on descending lists differed from those observed in an ascending series. Because those differences are more relevant to theories of numerical representation in nonhuman primates than our understanding of simultaneous chains, they will not be pursued in this chapter.

9. Nonmonotonic magnitude effects have also been found with lists of verbal stimuli that refer to objects of different sizes (Clark, 1973). Although these effects have been attributed to backward scanning, it would make for to long a digression to describe them in this chapter.

References

Attneave, F. (1955). Symmetry information and memory for patterns. *American Journal of Psychology, 68*, 209–222.

Brannon, E. M., & Terrace, H. S. (1998). Ordering of the numerosities 1-9 by monkeys. *Science, 282*, 746–749.

Brannon, E. M., & Terrace, H. S. (2000). Representation of the numerosities 1-9 by rhesus monkeys. *Journal of Experimental Psychology: Animal Behavioral Processes, 25*, 31–49.

Brannon, E., & Terrace, H. (2002). The evolution and ontogeny of ordinal behavior. In M. Bekoff, C. Allen, & G. M. Burghardt (Eds.), *The cognitive animal* (pp. 197–204). New York: Oxford University Press.

Buckley, P. B., & Gillman, C. B. (1974). Comparisons of digit and dot patterns. *Journal of Experimental Psychology, 103*, 1131–1136.

Carey, S. (2004). Bootstrapping and the origin of concepts. *Daedalus,* Winter, 59–68.

Carpenter, A. F., Georgopolous, A. P., & Pellizzer, G. (1999). Motor control encoding of serial position in a context-recall task. *Science, 283*, 1752–1757.

Chalmers, M., & McGonigle, B. (1984). Are children any more logical than monkeys on the five term series problem? *Journal of Experimental Child Psychology, 37*, 355–377.

Chalmers, M., & McGonigle, B. (1993). An experimental analysis of size seriation skill in children. *Quarterly Journal of Experimental Psychology*.

Chen, S., Swartz, K., & Terrace, H. S. (1997). Knowledge of the ordinal position of list items in rhesus monkeys. *Psychological Science, 8*, 80–86.

Clark, E. (1973). Nonlinguistic strategies and the acquisition of word meanings. *Cognition, 12*, 161–182.

Colombo, M., & Frost, N. (2001). Representation of serial order in humans: A comparison to the findings with monkeys (*Cebus appela*). *Psychonomic Bulletin & Review, 8*, 262–269.

D'Amato, M. R., & Colombo, M. (1988). Representation of serial order in monkeys (*Cebus apella*). *Journal of Experimental Psychology: Animal Behavior Processes, 14*, 131–139.

Davis, H., & Perusse, R. (1988). Numerical competence in animals: Definitional issues current evidence and a new research agenda. *Behavioral and Brain Sciences, 11*, 561–591.

Dehaene, S. (1997). *The number sense: How the mind creates mathematics*. New York: Oxford University Press.

Ebbinghaus, H. (1964). *Memory: A contribution to experimental psychology* (originally published 1885; translated 1913 ed.). New York: Dover.

Ebenholtz, S. M. (1963). Serial learning: Position learning and sequential associations. *Journal of Experimental Psychology, 66*, 353–362.

Fodor, J. A., & Pylyshyn, Z. W. (1988). Connectionism and cognitive architecture: A critical analysis. In S. Pinker & J. Mehler (Eds.), *Connections and symbols* (pp. 3–72). Cambridge, MA: MIT Press.

Gallistel, C. R., & Gelman, R. (1992). Preverbal and verbal counting and computation. *Cognition, 44*, 43–74.

Gelman, R., & Gallistel, C. R. (1978). *The child's understanding of number*. Cambridge, MA: Harvard University Press.

Grafton, S. T., Hazeltine, E., & Ivry, R. (1995). Functional mapping of sequence learning in normal humans. *Journal of Cognitive Neuroscience, 7*, 497–510.

Guyla, M., & Colombo, M. (2004). The ontogeny of serial-order behavior in human (*Homo sapiens*) representation of a list. *Journal of Comparative Psychology, 118*, 71–81.

Hamilton, J. M. E., & Sanford, A. J. (1978). The symbolic distance effect for alphabetic order judgements: A subjective report and reaction time analysis. *Quarterly Journal of Experimental Psychology, 30*, 33–43.

Harlow, H. F. (1949). The formation of learning sets. *Psychological Review, 56*, 51–65.

Herrnstein, R. J., & Boring, E. G. (1965). *A sourcebook in the history of psychology*. Cambridge, MA: Harvard University Press.

Holyoak, K. J., & Patterson, K. K. (1981). A positional discriminability model of linear-order judgments. *Journal of Experimental Psychology, 7*, 1283–1302.

Hull, C. L. (1935). The mechanism of the assembly of behavior segments in novel combinations suitable for problem solution. *Psychological Review, 42*, 219–245.

Jackendoff, R. (2002). *Foundations of language: Brain, meaning, grammar, evolution*. Oxford: Oxford University Press.

Keppel, G., Postman, L., & Zavortink, B. (1968). Studies of learning to learn: VIII. The influence of massive amounts of training upon the learning and retention of paired-associate lists. *Journal of Verbal Learning and Verbal Behavior, 7*, 790–796.

Kosslyn, S. M. (1994). *Image and brain: The resolution of the imagery debate*. Cambridge, MA: MIT Press.

Lashley, K. S. (1951). The problem of serial order in behavior. In L. A. Jeffries (Ed.), *Cerebral mechanisms in behavior* (pp. 112–136). New York: Wiley.

Lewandowsky, S., & Murdock, B. B. (1989). Memory for serial order. *Psychological Review, 96*, 25–57.

Lovelace, E. A., & Snodgrass, R. D. (1971). Decision times for alphabetic order of letter pairs. *Journal of Experimental Psychology, 88*, 258–264.

Marshuetz, C., Smith, E. E., Jonides, J., DeGutis, J., & Chenevert, T. (2000). Order information in working memory: fMRI evidence for parietal and prefrontal mechanisms. *Journal of Cognitive Neuroscience, 12*, 130–144.

Miller, G. A. (1956). The magical number seven plus or minus two: Some limits on our capacity for processing information. *Psychological Review, 63*, 81–96.

Moyer, R. S., & Landauer, T. K. (1967). Time required for judgments of numerical Inequality. *Nature, 215*, 1519–1520. Murofushi, K. (1997). Numerical matching behavior by a chimpanzee (*Pan troglodytes*): Subitizing and analog magnitude estimation. *Japanese Psychological Research, 39*, 140–153.

Nieder, A., Freedman, D. J., & Miller, E. K. (2002). Representation of the quantity of visual items in the primate prefrontal cortex. *Science, 297*, 1708–1711.

Ninokura, Y., Mushiake, H., & Tanji, J. (2004). Integration of temporal order and object information in the monkey lateral prefrontal cortex. *Journal of Neurophysiology, 91*, 555–560.

Olton, D. S., & Samuelson, R. J. (1976). Remembrance of places passed: Spatial memory in rats. *Journal of Experimental Psychology: Animal Behavior Processes, 2*, 97–116.

Orlov, T., Yakovlev, B., Hochstein, S., & Zohary, E. (2000). Macaque monkeys categorize images by their ordinal number. *Nature, 404*, 77–80.

Posner, M. I. (Ed.). (1989). *Foundations of cognitive science*. Cambridge, MA: MIT Press.

Premack, D. (1976). *Intelligence in ape and man*. Hillsdale, NJ: Lawrence Erlbaum.

Pylyshyn, Z. (1981). The imagery debate: Analogue versus tacit knowledge. *Psychological Review, 88*, 16–45.

Rumbaugh, D. M. (1977). *Language learning by a chimpanzee: The Lana Project*. New York: Academic Press.

Rumbaugh, D. M., Gill, T. V., & von Glasersfeld, E. C. (1973). Reading and sentence completion by a chimpanzee. *Science, 182*, 731–733.

Skinner, B. F. (1934). The extinction of chained reflexes. *Proceedings of the National Academy of Science U S A, 20*, 234–237.

Skinner, B. F. (1938). *The behavior of organisms*. New York: Appleton-Century-Crofts.

Son, L., & Kornell, N. (2005). Metaconfidence judgments in rhesus macaques: Explicit versus implicit mechanisms. In H. S. Terrace & J. Metcalfe (Eds.), *The missing link in cognition: Origins of self-reflective consciousness*. New York: Oxford University Press.

Sternberg, S. (1969). Memory-scanning: Mental processes revealed by reaction-time experiments. *American Scientist, 57*, 421–457.

Sternberg, S. (1975). Memory scanning: New findings and current controversies. *Quarterly Journal of Experimental Psychology, 27*, 1–32.

Straub, R. O., & Terrace, H. S. (1981). Generalization of serial learning in the pigeon. *Animal Learning and Behavior, 9*, 454–468.

Subiaul, F., Cantlon, J., Holloway, R., & Terrace, H. (2004). Cognitive imitation in rhesus macaques. *Science, 305*, 407–410.

Swartz, K., Himmanen, S., & Terrace, H. S. (1993). Strategies for list execution by list-sophisticated monkeys. *Bulletin of the Psychonomic Society, 31*, 362.

Swartz, K. B., Chen, S., & Terrace, H. S. (1991). Serial learning by rhesus monkeys. I: Acquisition and retention of multiple four-item lists. *Journal of Experimental Psychology: Animal Behavior Processes, 17*, 396–410.

Terrace, H. S. (1979). Is problem solving language? A review of Premack's *Intelligence in Apes and Man*. *Journal of the Experimental Analysis of Behavior, 31*, 161–175.

Terrace, H. S. (1984). Simultaneous chaining: The problem it poses for traditional chaining theory. In M. L. Commons, R. J. Herrnstein, & A. R. Wagner (Eds.), *Quantitative analyses of behavior: Discrimination processes* (pp. 115–138). Cambridge, MA: Ballinger Publishing.

Terrace, H. S. (1987). Chunking by a pigeon in a serial learning task. *Nature, 325*, 149–151.

Terrace, H. S. (2001a). Chunking and serially organized behavior in pigeons, monkeys and humans. In R. G. Cook, (Ed.), *Avian visual cognition*. Retrieved August 27, 2005, from http://www.pigeon.psy.tufts.edu/avc/.

Terrace, H. S. (2001b). Comparative psychology of chunking. In S. Fountain, M. Bunsey, H. Danks, & K. McBeath (Eds.), *Animal cognition and sequential behavior* (pp. 23–56). Dordrecht, the Netherlands: Kluwer Academic Publishing.

Terrace, H. S., & McGonigle, B. (1994). Memory and representation of serial order by children, monkeys, and pigeons. *Current Directions in Psychological Science, 3*(6), 180–185.

Terrace, H. S., Petitto, L. A., Sanders, R. J., & Bever, T. G. (1979). Can an ape create a sentence? *Science, 206*, 891–902.

Terrace, H. S., Son, L., & Brannon, E. (2003). Serial expertise of rhesus macaques. *Psychological Sciences, 14*, 66–73.

Thompson, C. R., & Church, R. M. (1980). An explanation of the language of a chimpanzee. *Science, 208*, 313–314.

Tolman, E. C. (1948). Cognitive maps in rats and men. *Psychological Review, 55*, 189–208.

Tolman, E. C., Ritchie, B. F., & Kalish, D. (1946). Studies in spatial learning. I. Orientation and the short-cut. *Journal of Experimental Psychology, 36*, 13–24.

VIII

TOOL FABRICATION AND USE

26

Cognitive Adaptations for Tool-Related Behavior in New Caledonian Crows

ALEX KACELNIK, JACKIE CHAPPELL, BEN KENWARD, AND ALEX A. S. WEIR

In the semitropical rain forest of the Pacific islands of New Caledonia, a crow detects the presence of a succulent grub (a beetle larva) deep in an inaccessible burrow in a tree. The crow flies to a nearby tree, breaks off a small branch, and removes leaves and minor twiglets, until a stick is left. The crow returns and, holding the twig in its beak, probes into the burrow until the grub has grasped the tip with its mouth parts. The crow then slowly withdraws the stick to expose and eat the grub. We know from laboratory studies that these crows can prepare twigs of different lengths or diameters, depending on their needs, and that they can also make tools of many different shapes for other purposes.

Elsewhere in the tree, a spider moves between the branches and the ground, releasing various mixtures of liquid proteins with different proportions to form different kinds of silk on its trail. The spider's movements are such that the trail of silk forms a perfectly designed web with a sticky spiral held by strong, nonsticky lines supporting the structure. This web building is achieved for an almost infinite variety of geometric configurations of the branches that provide potential support, thus creating a new solution to each problem. When the web is finished, the spider waits at its hub until an insect is trapped, when its own reward materializes.

Meanwhile, at a laboratory of artificial intelligence, a robot has been trained to select among a hammer, a spanner, and a screwdriver when presented with tasks involving nails, bolts, or screws, respectively. Using its experience, the robot recognizes tools by decomposing images into segments of component shapes, somewhat like a cubist depiction of a natural object. On one occasion, the robot is presented with a nail and a piece of wood. The robot faces these materials and turns toward the tool panel; but, on this day, the experimenters have forgotten to hang the hammer in place. The robot "hesitates" in front of the panel and finally picks the screwdriver, turns to the wood and nail and, holding the screwdriver by its blade, proceeds to hammer the nail into the wood by hitting it with the screwdriver's handle. The robot had never before done such a thing.[1]

New Caledonian crows, spiders, and robots use and can construct objects outside their own body ("tools") to act on the outside world toward some goal. In all cases, each instance of tool making or use is different from previous ones, so that variability in the tasks' needs leads to variations in behavior. Tool use is considered by many to be one of the defining features of advanced intelligence and to have played an important role in, or at least to have been correlated with, the specific features of human evolution. Quotes like the following are not rare:

> The first indications that our ancestors were in any respect unusual among animals were our extremely crude stone tools that began to appear in Africa by around two-and-a-half million

> years ago. The quantities of tools suggest that they were beginning to play a regular, significant role in our livelihood. Among our closest relatives, in contrast, the pygmy chimpanzee and gorilla do not use tools, while the common chimpanzee occasionally makes some rudimentary ones but hardly depends on them for its existence. . . . Clear evidence of a Great Leap Forward in our behaviour appears suddenly in Europe around 40,000 years ago, coincident with the arrival of anatomically modern *Homo sapiens* from Africa via the Near East. At that point, we began displaying art, technology based on specialized tools, cultural differences from place to place, and cultural innovation with time. (Diamond, 1992, p. 328)

To understand why tool making and use elicits such respect, and to form a judgment on whether this respect is justified, we need to examine nonhuman examples in some detail. We chose the spider and robot examples arbitrarily, to highlight the breadth of tool-related behaviors that may need to be considered and the reactions they generate in us as observers, but, as will become clear, our focus is on the crows.

TOOLS AND COGNITION

Few people attribute high cognitive abilities to spiders despite their extremely sophisticated engineering achievements and the flexibility with which they tackle different geometric configurations of the support available. Few, again, would attribute complex cognition to the robot, despite its evident "creativity" in generating a new solution to a problem never faced before (for devotees of artificial intelligence, it is worth stating that we are not judging the correctness of these intuitions but simply exposing them for analysis). The reasons for these presumed denials of cognitive respectability are varied, but they include arguments of the following kind.

Spiders have a complex, but rigid, built-in set of rules, shaped by evolution over many generations, and they respond to the spatial configuration of potential web supports with precisely preprogrammed behaviors. Spiders even have rules for how to behave if they happen to lose one or more legs. The fact that the list of such rules is large does not require the attribution of intelligence.

In the case of the robot, its behavior can be explained by generalization from its previous training, following a program devised by its human creators. Hammers are identified by an elongated "business end" shape attached perpendicularly by its middle to an elongated holding part (the "handle"). When in search of a hammer, the robot picks the shape that most closely resembles the compounds that have been successful before and uses it by assigning to each subcomponent the role their model played in the training tool (the "handle" is the thinnest and most elongated shape in the compound). In this case, we can make explicit the robot's internal mechanisms leading to innovative behavior, even when the emergent behavior itself was not preprogrammed and surprises its creators. For some people, this putative complete understanding of the mechanisms removes the need to invoke cognition and, for others, leads to redefining the concept of cognition to make it equivalent to information processing.

Explanations such as the above are tempting, but problematic because, when faced with a human being performing any of the above tasks, our intuition leads us to assume that a process of planning, judgment, and decision-making involving emotions, unconscious and conscious representations, abstract thinking, and even language has taken place.

We do not believe that these double standards are necessarily wrong, because our intuition—deceptive as it may often be—is informed by much more than the sketches of behavior we presented above. We rather believe that both intuition and explicit understanding may be improved by analysis of the formal and informal criteria that lead human observers to make such attributions. Here, we focus on one example, that of New Caledonian crows (*Corvus moneduloides*), and air some views on what constitutes advanced tool-related cognition by relating and comparing our species' behavior with that of other animals that make and/or use tools. We have no illusions of solving the problem of formulating a universally acceptable definition of cognition and then assigning each candidate to a well-defined category; we believe this is not possible. It should be possible, however, to inform the discussion and to identify which behavioral data can influence our judgment and which questions are more likely to offer some guide for future research.

THE NEW CALEDONIAN CROW IN THE WILD

Natural History

The New Caledonian crow is endemic to the Grande Terre island of New Caledonia, but it has also been introduced to the smaller island of Maré. It is common throughout the range of forest types found on Grande Terre (Hunt, 2000a; our personal observations) and it is also found in the Niaouli savanna (Hannécart & Létocart, 1980). The crow's diet is only partially composed of food obtained with tools, and includes insects and their larvae, snails, nuts, fruit, seeds, flowers, and other birds' eggs (Layard & Layard, 1882). It lives in social groups and there is a high level of parental care, with juvenile birds being fed by adults for at least 6 months after fledging and (if the behavior of captive birds reflects life in the wild) probably much longer (Kenward, Rutz, Weir, Chappell, & Kacelnik, 2004). The size of social groups varies, with some flocks reaching around 30 individuals. However, groups are usually of around three or four birds (Kenward et al., in press), consistent with a breeding pair plus the clutch size of one or two eggs (Hannécart & Létocart, 1980); the larger groups are probably temporary conglomerations (Hunt, 2000b). Because field studies with marked individuals have not yet been carried out, it is not known how stable or closely related these groups are.

In addition to using tools, the New Caledonian crows display behaviors found in other corvids that are often thought to be associated with high cognitive abilities, such as breaking nuts by dropping them from branches (Hunt, Sakuma, & Shibata, 2002; Layard & Layard, 1882) and food-caching (Hunt, 2000b; our personal observations in the laboratory).

Tool Use

Almost everything known about crows' tool use in the wild is from the work of Gavin Hunt and his colleagues. Tool use of several kinds is widespread throughout the crows' range. One sort of tool, cut from Pandanus leaves, has been found at 20 sites throughout Grande Terre and also on Maré (Hunt & Gray, 2003). Other kinds of hooked and straight tools have been found in at least 11 sites in the south of Grande Terre (Hunt & Gray, 2002). These tools are used and manufactured in different ways. Stick-type tools are made from a variety of different materials, including tree twigs, fern stolons, bamboo stems, tree leaf midribs, and thorny vines (Hunt & Gray, 2002). In our laboratory, crows readily make similar straight tools by removing the barbs from long feathers and then using the stem formed by the quill and shaft (see figure 26.1a, c, and d).

Two issues are of particular interest: the method of manufacturing hooks and the way that Pandanus leaf cutouts are made. The hooks sometimes occur naturally on the raw material, such as on lengths of thorny vines cut by the crows (Hunt & Gray, 2002). In other cases, however, the crows detach a secondary twig from the primary one by nipping at the joint with their beaks, leaving a piece of the primary twig to form a hook. After a twig is detached, crows typically remove leaves and bark, and have even been observed sculpting the shape of the hook with their beak (Hunt, 1996; Hunt & Gray, 2004a).

The Pandanus leaf tool manufacture is interesting because it appears to require the use of a rule system that dictates a complex sequence of actions resulting in the finished tool (Hunt, 2000a; Hunt & Gray, 2004b). The edge of the stiff, barbed leaf is cut and torn in a sequence which results in the cutting-out from the leaf of a flat tool that may have various shapes, from long and rectangular to a tapering shape achieved by stepped cuts (see figure 26.1b). The steps give the tool strength, because it is broad at the proximal end (where it is held), and also precision, because it is thin at the distal, probing end. Unlike, for example, the removal of twigs and bark from a stick, each action does not result in a progressively more effective tool: the final step is the removal of the tool from the leaf, so that until this point the tool is nonfunctional.

The design of the Pandanus leaf tools varies in complexity from area to area: In some areas, only unstepped tools are found, whereas across most of the island the more complex multistep tools are made. There is no identified variation in availability of raw materials or in ecological correlates that could indicate different needs, so these design differences are suggestive of cultural transmission of tool design. If the more complex stepped tools are derived from the simpler rectangular tools, then social transmission may operate as a ratchet to preserve and accumulate design improvements (Hunt

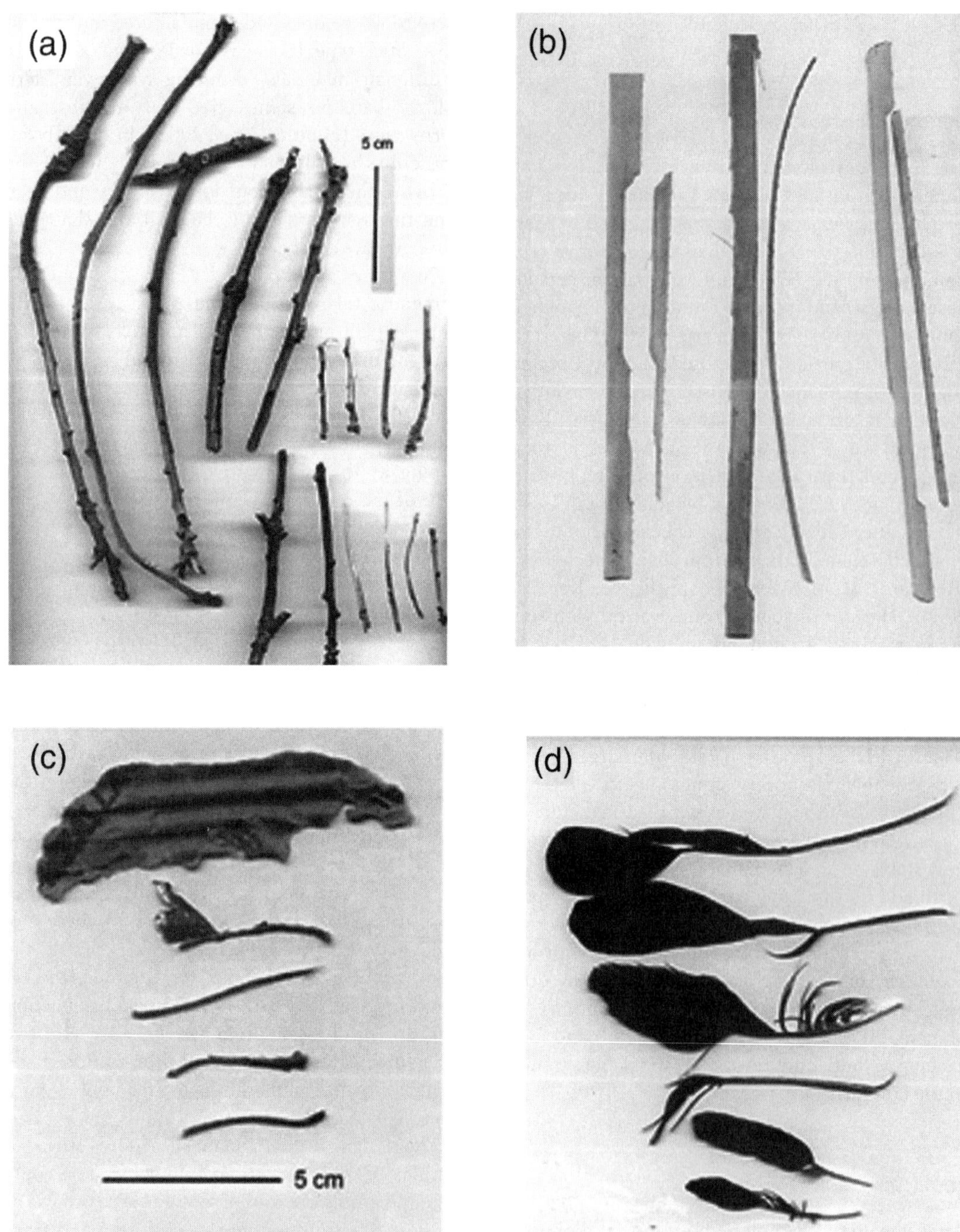

Figure 26.1. Tools made by New Caledonian crows in the wild and captivity. (*a*) Twig tools (captivity). (*b*) Pandanus tools (wild). (*c*) Leaf petiole and cardboard tools (captivity). (*d*) Feather tools (captivity).

& Gray, 2003). This historical sequence is likely, as it seems improbable that the most complex tool design would have emerged at once.

At least two main techniques of tool use have been described. One method involves the use of tools (with or without hooks) to extract small invertebrates hiding under tree bark and crevices in the base of palm leaves (Hunt, 1996; Hunt & Gray, 2002). With Pandanus tools, a wild crow has been observed using the barbs on the leaf margin (which always point away from the tip of the tool) as hooks to facilitate the extraction of food from a hole (Hunt & Gray, 2004b). The other main technique is the beetle larvae fishing described in the opening paragraph. In this case, the tools are not hooked but end in a straight tip (Hunt & Gray, 2002).

There remain many important gaps in our knowledge of these crows' behavior in the wild. We know very little about:

- Their sociobiology
- Their dependency on the food provided by tools
- The development of individual skills
- The mechanism of cultural transmission
- The putative specialization of individuals or family groups in tool variety
- The role of individual creativity
- The role of tool and food caching

It is crucial to know the answers to these questions if we are to make inferences about the cognitive processes that accompany this species' extraordinary behavior. Equally crucial, however, is to compare what is known about these crows with the tool-related behavior of other species.

COMPARISONS WITH OTHER ANIMALS

We have seen in the preceding section that New Caledonian crow tool behavior may be characterized by four striking features: it is very common, possibly universal, in that (as far as we know) all populations of this species hitherto studied show high levels of tool use; it involves a wide diversity of types of tool; it involves highly complex manufacture, most strikingly for the Pandanus tools; and (although this feature is still not fully demonstrated) the design of Pandanus tools may have been cumulatively improved through cultural transmission.

These characteristics all intuitively seem to be related to cognitive sophistication—so to what extent are they found in other animals? We are currently developing a framework for formal analysis of animal tool use within these and other categories; in this chapter, we restrict ourselves to briefly discussing the extent to which other animals demonstrate similar behavior.

Frequency

To our knowledge, New Caledonian crows and chimpanzees (*Pan troglodytes*) (McGrew & Marchant, 1997; Whiten et al., 1999) are the only nonhuman vertebrates where all populations show routine tool use. Woodpecker finches (*Cactospiza pallida*) (Grant, 1999; Tebbich, Taborsky, Fessl, & Dvorak, 2002) and orangutans (*Pongo pygmaeus*) (van Schaik et al., 2003) show high frequencies of tool use in some populations, but there are other populations that never use tools. In all other animal tool users, either there are insufficient data to assess tool use frequency or tool use is known to be absent from many populations.

Diversity

The diversity of tool types shown by New Caledonian crows is also rare. No other bird is known to routinely make more than one type of tool (tools are considered as being different "types" if they are used for different functions or are acquired or made in substantially different ways), and the only mammals, other than humans, that are known to use a diversity of tools are the great apes (chimpanzees and orangutans) (e.g., van Schaik et al., 2003; Whiten et al., 1999) and capuchin monkeys (*Cebus* spp.) (Fragaszy, Izar, Visalberghi, Ottoni, & de Oliveira, 2004; Moura & Lee, 2004).

Complexity

Defining *complexity* unambiguously is a philosophical challenge that goes beyond the scope of this chapter. However, a factor that seems closely allied to complexity is the degree of transformation necessary to produce a functional tool from the raw material. Using this as a working definition allows us to describe four levels of complexity in tool manufacture (levels 1 and 2 are modified from Beck, 1980).

0. *None:* Unmodified objects are used.
1. *Detach/subtract:* Severing a fixed attachment between environmental objects (or the substrate) or removing object(s) from another unattached object, so the latter is a more useful tool.
2. *Add/combine/reshape*: Connecting two or more objects to produce a tool; fundamentally restructuring material to produce a functional tool.
3. *Multistep manufacture/fine crafting:* Involves either several (more than two) manufacturing steps to produce a functional tool or fine, three-dimensional sculpting of the raw material (see Hunt & Gray, 2004a).

If wild tool behavior only is taken into account, then no nonhuman vertebrates apart from New Caledonian crows have ever been reported to manufacture tools in a multistep fashion or by fine crafting (Hunt & Gray, 2004a). Chimpanzees and orangutans have been reported to use crumpled leaves as sponges (Beck, 1980; van Schaik et al., 2003), which could be regarded as "reshaping"; all other animal tool manufacture involves nothing more complex than detaching or subtracting objects from each other.

Cumulative Cultural Evolution

Human technology is entirely dependent on the transmission of techniques between generations and the resulting cumulative improvement in tool design. Although there is now reliable evidence for tool "traditions" in chimpanzee and orangutan populations (van Schaik et al., 2003; Whiten et al., 1999), there is no evidence that their technology has improved cumulatively (Boyd & Richerson, 1996; Tomasello, 1999). This evidence contrasts with the observations that New Caledonian crows make Pandanus tools of differing complexity in different areas of New Caledonia in the absence of detectable habitat differences. The present geographical distribution of complexity and the fact that complex tools are likely to be modifications from simpler patterns are consistent with cumulative cultural transmission of improvements in design (Hunt & Gray, 2003). Experiments involving cross-fostering or hand-raising (e.g., Tebbich, Taborsky, Fessl, & Blomqvist, 2001) are ultimately necessary to demonstrate that social learning is responsible for these differences, but the current evidence makes it plausible.

As the previous analysis illustrates, we can compare animals' tool using proclivities based on behavior in the wild alone. However, many questions about the cognitive processes that underlie such behavior are only answerable in the laboratory. The following section therefore outlines our program of experimental work with New Caledonian crows.

THE NEW CALEDONIAN CROW IN THE LABORATORY

We started our research using two subjects, Abel (a male) and Betty (a female), but we have since formed a colony of several groups totaling 21 subjects. All of the experiments described below were conducted with the original two subjects. Betty was captured from the wild in March 2000 in Yaté, New Caledonia. We infer from her behavior that she was probably a nutritionally independent juvenile at the time of capture. Abel came from the Parc Forestier, a zoo in Noumea, New Caledonia, where he had been captive for at least 17 years (his age at capture was unknown). The pair lived together in a large room, with free access to an outdoor flight cage. They were fed ad libitum on a varied diet, but, for the experiments, we used their preferred food (pig or lamb heart), which was not included in their daily ration.

The main issues we have tackled so far are the extent to which tool-related behavior showed anticipation ("planning") and the level of apparent "understanding" of the physical relations involved in the birds' actions. We have examined the degree of anticipation by testing whether, when facing a task that requires a tool, the crows pick a random available object within the range of shapes that can be used as tools or instead choose (or make) an object that is suited for the task being faced.

The question of understanding is more debatable—indeed, the very term is not easy to define and we will not attempt to do so other than operationally. What we are addressing here is the level of abstraction of the rules that the crows use in performing their actions. Most tasks can be solved either by learning task-specific responses or by applying wider principles; this difference may be informative as to how sophisticated the cognitive mechanisms involved may be. For instance, Wilson, Mackintosh, and Boakes (1985) showed that, in a delayed matching- (or nonmatching-) to-sample task, pigeons formed specific associations involving precise sequences of stimuli, whereas corvids (jackdaws, rooks, and jays) seemed to use concepts of sameness and oddity. In another example, Povinelli (2000) has recently called attention to the fact that humans and chimps appear to solve similar problems using different concepts about physical interactions between objects. We replicated some experiments previously conducted with primates to examine whether the crows used the principles of gravity and rigidity or instead solved the problems by learning specific rules. Finally, we describe an experiment triggered by a serendipitous observation that gives an indication of the level of individual creativity these animals possess.

Selectivity

Tool Length Making or using a tool that is unsuitable to extract a given food item because of its size (too short to reach, too long to handle accurately) incurs costs in terms of time and associated potential loss of the prey to another predator. It seems reasonable to expect that, having judged the geometry of a burrow, the crows may be able to show anticipation by selecting a tool that is well suited for each case.

We tested the ability of our two original crows to select a tool of an appropriate length to obtain a piece of food in a horizontal tube (Chappell & Kacelnik, 2002). The birds were presented with food that, in 20 different trials, could be at 10 different distances from the open end of the tube (each distance occurred twice). The birds were also provided, in all 20 trials, with 10 sticks, each of a length matching the distances at which food was placed in the different trials.

Our goal was to see if tool choice was determined by the food distance in each trial; figure 26.2 shows the results. Both crows significantly avoided selecting tools shorter than the distance to food (and hence unsuitable). Furthermore, they selected tools that precisely matched this distance significantly more often than chance, thus reducing the frequency of use of tools that were longer than

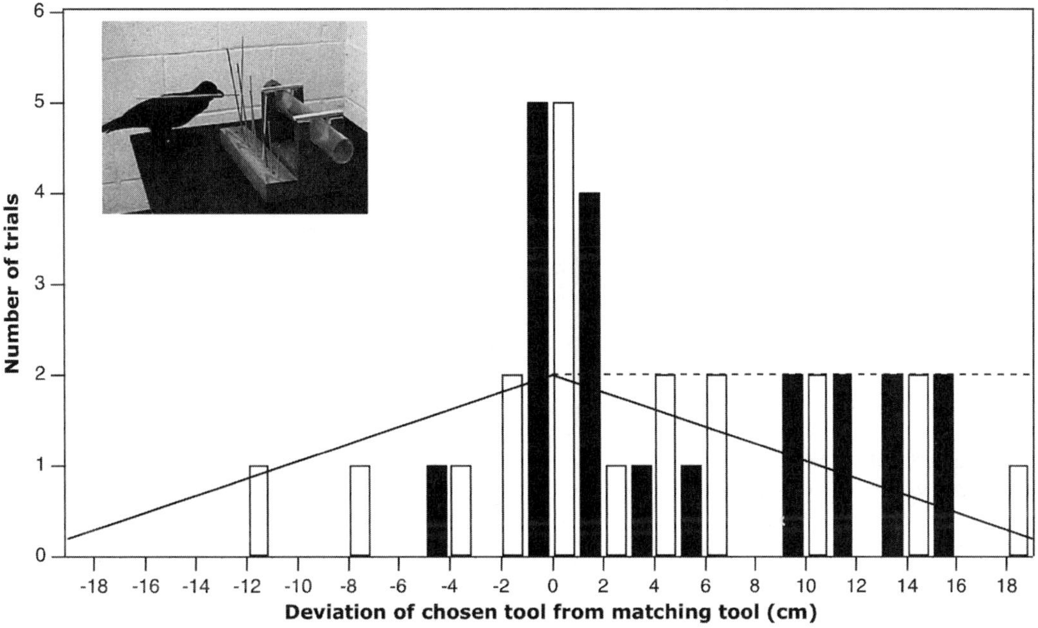

Figure 26.2. Choice of tools in a length selection experiment. Distribution of sticks chosen by Abel (*filled bars*) and Betty (*open bars*) relative to the matching tool (at 0). *Solid line* shows the expected distribution if the crows chose at random, and *dotted line* shows the expectation if they always chose the longest tool. The *inset* photograph shows Betty choosing a tool from the "tool box." (Reprinted with permission from Fig. 3 in Chappell & Kacelnik [2002]. © Springer-Verlag 2002.)

required. When, in a different experiment, the sticks were placed behind a screen so that the birds could not see both the tools and the food tube simultaneously, Abel still chose suitable tools more frequently than expected by chance, whereas Betty (who was still a juvenile at the time) seemed to lose motivation and did not perform the task.

Tool Diameter The diameter of tools is another dimension of size that affects suitability. In further experiments with the original two crows, we tested their ability to select and make tools with an appropriate diameter (Chappell & Kacelnik, 2004). For testing both selectivity and tool making, the task was to insert a tool through the end cap of an upside-down L-shaped tube and to push a small cup containing food along the horizontal leg, so that it would fall down the vertical leg of the tube (see apparatus in figure 26.3). The diameter of the hole in the end cap was varied between trials.

In the first part of this study, we tested selectivity alone, using Betty. She was provided with three sticks of different diameters. The thinnest could be inserted through all of the holes, the medium diameter stick could only be inserted into the two widest holes, and the widest would only fit the widest hole. Even though she was capable of using all three diameters, Betty showed a strong preference for the narrowest tool, regardless of the diameter of the hole. When given a choice between two tools in a bundle and one loose one, she only dismantled the bundle when it contained the thinnest tool, thus paying the cost of disassembling the bundle only when required.

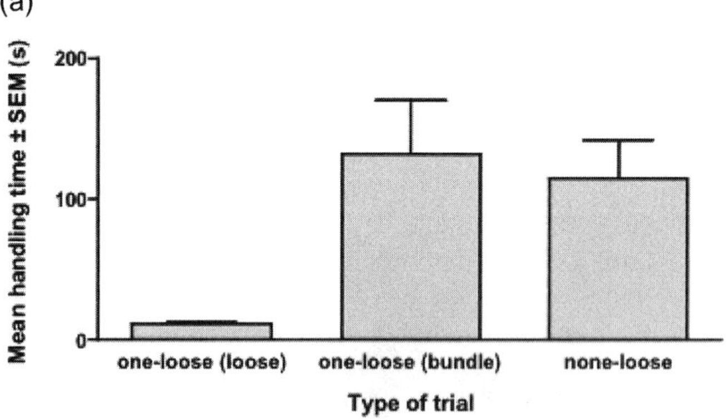

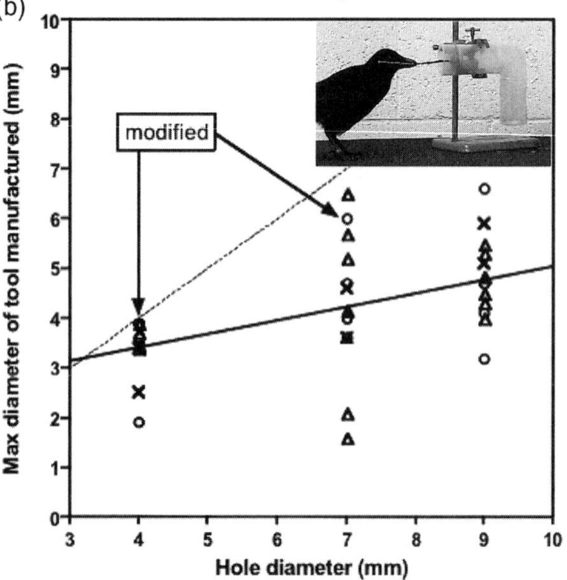

Figure 26.3. Choice and making of tools in relation to diameter. (*a*) Cost of dismantling the tool bundle. The *left* and *central columns* show mean time to obtain food in trials when one tool was loose and the other two were in a bundle. The *left column* shows trials in which the tool used was the loose one and the *central* one trials in which the tool used was in the bundle. The *right column* shows trials in which all three tools were in the bundle and hence the bundle had to be dismantled. Dismantling the bundle took substantially longer than using the loose tool. (Reprinted with permission from Fig. 2 in Chappell & Kacelnik [2004]. © Springer-Verlag 2003.) (*b*) Diameter of manufactured tools. Maximum diameter of tool manufactured as a function of the diameter of the hole. *Open circles* are tools made by Betty, *open triangles* are tools made by Abel, and *crosses* are tools that were made and then discarded. Significantly wider tools were made when the hole was wider. The photograph shows Betty inserting a tool into the apparatus. (Modified with permission from Fig. 4 in Chappell & Kacelnik [2004]. © Springer-Verlag 2003.)

In the second part of the experiment, both crows were exposed to the same apparatus, but they were not provided with tools. Instead, we placed tree branches into the aviary from which tools could be made. Both birds readily made tools by cutting segments of the branches and removing leaves and minor twiglets. The diameter of the tools that were made increased significantly with the diameter of the hole (see figure 26.3b). The birds made tools that were too thick to fit into the hole on only 2 (of 29) trials; in both cases, they modified the tools by sculpting the thickenings that blocked their use immediately after first trying them, until they were suitable. Thus, in all but two cases, the birds made tools of appropriate final dimensions before actually trying to use them, correctly anticipating the hole size in that trial.

Specific Associations Versus General Principles

Rigidity This experiment was inspired by similar experiments with chimpanzees by Daniel Povinelli (2000, Experiments 9 and 10). In it, we preexposed Betty to two rakelike objects with different levels of rigidity in a nonfunctional context and then tested her in a situation where only one of the tools would serve (Chappell & Kacelnik, 2005). The idea was to examine whether, when she needed to pick a tool among a set of objects that were familiar to her but had not been used before as tools, she would choose according to the suitability afforded by the objects' properties.

The rakes differed in their business ends. One had a solid head made of wood, whereas the other had a flexible head made of thin plastic. Betty was allowed to freely manipulate the tools without the apparatus for several days prior to the start of the experiment. The rakes were then placed into a box with a transparent lid that was internally divided into two compartments (see figure 26.4a). The two compartments each contained a food-filled cup placed in front of the head of each rake. The cup could be retrieved from the box by pulling the rake with the rigid, but not the flexible, head. If Betty had learned the properties of the rakes and used this knowledge, then she should choose the rigid tool; otherwise, she might be expected not to pull at all or to pull both rakes with equal probability. Betty was 100% accurate on the first trial on each day, but she seemed to lose motivation quickly, and her accuracy decreased sharply over the course of each session (see figure 26.4b). This drop in performance may be because if she made an error, then she could choose again without penalty; or she may have been inclined to explore the consequences of the alternative action. Betty's success on the first trial of each session contrasts with the results from Povinelli's chimpanzees, where six of seven subjects performed at chance throughout the experiment (Experiment 9), and the only successful subject reverted to chance when a different experimental design was used (Experiment 10).

Gravity Here, we used another experimental design originally used with primates (Limongelli, Boysen, & Visalberghi, 1995; Povinelli, 2000; Visalberghi & Limongelli, 1994) to test whether the crows responded directly to the action of gravity or gave priority to local stimulus relations (Chappell & Kacelnik, 2005). The essence of the task was to expose the subject to a problem where to obtain the reward it was necessary to avoid a gravity trap (a blind-ending trap in a horizontal tube) and, once the subject had learned this, to transform the task so that gravity was no longer a problem. If the subject was driven by local features of the trap, then the subject may continue to avoid it; however, if the subject was using the concept of gravity, then it may ignore the now inconsequential stimuli associated with it.

After about 100 trials with the apparatus, Betty reached criterion (trap avoided on 8 of 10 trials or more on three consecutive blocks of 10 trials). This performance is comparable to that shown by chimpanzees and capuchin monkeys (*Cebus apella*) (Limongelli et al., 1995; Povinelli, 2000; Visalberghi & Limongelli, 1994).

When the trap was inverted during the testing phase, responding did not return to random; instead, Betty continued to avoid the now irrelevant trap—a result that had previously been observed in chimps and capuchin monkeys, although one woodpecker finch did return to random responding on an inversion test (Tebbich & Bshary, 2004). Human infants have not been tested with an inverted trap to our knowledge, but when children aged between 27 and 66 months were tested with the simple trap tube task, those under 3 years responded essentially at random, whereas those over 3 years learned to solve the task within a few trials (Limongelli, 1995; cited in Visalberghi, 2000).

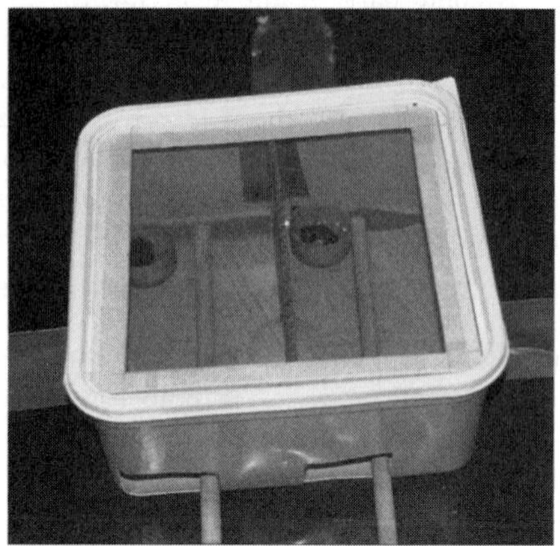

(b)

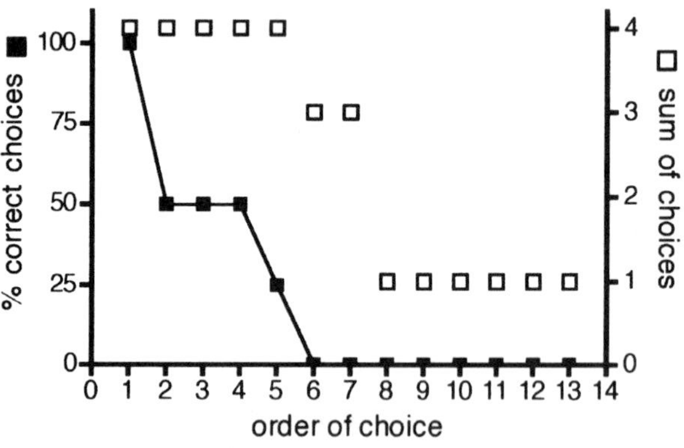

Figure 26.4. Choice in a "rigidity" concept experiment. (*a*) The "rake box." The rigid tool is on the *left*, and the nonrigid tool on the *right*. (*b*) Tools chosen in the rake experiment. The percentage of correct choices analyzed by the within-session order of choice. In all sessions, Betty chose the correct tool on the first trial.

This task is, however, difficult to interpret for all species, whatever the outcome. Even if subjects do return to random performance after inversion, then it may not be due to the use of gravity as a concept; subjects could be following local cues so narrowly that avoidance may not generalize to the inverted trap because it just looks different. The continued avoidance of the trap excludes the interpretation of a direct use of gravity, but it does not prove that Betty and the other nonhuman subjects tested in this task cannot use this concept. Nonhumans may use local cues rather than general principles when the former are effective. After all, subjects experience 100% success after the trap is inverted whatever they do, so there is no incentive to change the technique.

Innovation We had an insight into the level of individual creativity of New Caledonian crows through a serendipitous observation that was made during the course of an experiment on selectivity. In the planned experiment, we were testing whether the crows would choose a hooked piece of wire over a straight piece, where the task was to lift a bucket containing food (using the handle) from a vertical tube. On one trial, Abel took the (suitable) hooked wire away, leaving Betty with an unsuitable straight wire. After attempting unsuccessfully to extract the bucket with the unsuitable straight wire, Betty spontaneously secured the distal end in a crevice and made a hook by pulling perpendicularly on the proximal end. With the hook thus made, she proceeded to retrieve the food.

To explore the phenomenon further, we repeated the task but offered only the straight wire. Now, Betty bent the piece of wire and used it successfully on virtually every opportunity (occasionally she or Abel dropped the tool into the pipe, where it was out of reach) (Weir, Chappell, & Kacelnik, 2002). She used at least two techniques and three locations to bend the wire (and has subsequently used a third technique), and she often corrected the shape of the tool several times before attempting to use it.

As far as we know, Betty did not have any experience with flexible wire or similarly pliant material prior to this episode nor were the techniques she used possible with natural materials. It is therefore clear that at least one member of this crow species is able to innovatively shape tools in anticipation of specific needs.

DISCUSSION

The behavior of New Caledonian crows both in the wild and in captivity conveys the impression that these animals' cognitive capacities are out of the ordinary. Indeed, they fashion and select tools according to apparently preconceived projects to an extent not reported so far in any other bird and hardly in any other animal. They show inventiveness in solving new problems with flexibility. And they seem, in the case of the Pandanus stepped-cut leaves, to make tools to a design that is socially transmitted, so that regional differences are explained by cultural history. But, this impression of cognitive exceptionality glosses over a deep uncertainty as to whether these birds are indeed genetically special and, if so, why they have evolved these unusual traits. We turn now to discuss several angles of this problem. These comments are not aimed at providing mutually exclusive alternatives but to indicate what issues lie ahead of us.

Ecological Explanations

It remains possible that nothing is intrinsically special about New Caledonian crows' cognition, even if the behavior is. This could be the case if the ecological circumstances in New Caledonia are so uniquely favorable for tool use (for instance, the absence of competitors exploiting beetle larvae hidden in tree holes) that any population of corvids or indeed other birds would develop similar behavior under the circumstances. It is possible that not even the ecology is special. A fortunate accident could have led to an individual discovery that became culturally fixed in the population because of the nature of island life.

These hypotheses (unlikely in our view) can only be answered by developmental studies, including rearing individuals of this and other species under controlled conditions, including cross-fostering. Observation of experienced individuals from wild populations, even if transported to the laboratory, cannot disprove these "killjoy" hypotheses, but they seem improbable to us. It is likely instead that special ecological circumstances led to unusual selective pressures, and this in turn led to the evolution of a heritable specialization underlying the behavior we see today.[2]

If the species does possess genetic peculiarities, then they could be at many different levels. The birds could, for instance, have particularly fine motor control of their beaks. An early manifestation of such a genetic specialization could lead to reinforcing experiences with object manipulation and a further cascade of acquired skills through practice. Alternatively, the birds could simply be particularly confident and neophilic (as many island living birds are as a consequence of the scarcity of predatory mammals), so that they experience greater exposure to random manipulation of objects and consequent learning by reinforcement. Under this option, any genetic adaptations responsible for tool behavior need not necessarily be associated with an unusual degree of cognitive sophistication.

Social Learning

It is worth distinguishing the factors influencing the original emergence of the behavior (and any subsequent "re-invention" by other individuals) from those influencing the spread of the behavior through the population. Both are likely to play a role in the complexity and frequency of tool behavior, but the latter is likely to be particularly important in determining both the proportion of tool users in the population and the frequency with which tool behavior occurs. Thus, if New Caledonian crows are particularly and heritably adept at social learning, then tool behavior could be maintained in the population from an initial fortuitous invention, without the need for any heritable cognitive adaptations (other than possessing a tendency to learn socially).

It is well established that the behavior of a single individual can spread and become established in a population. For example, a new song type spread and became established among a population of saddlebacks (*Philesturnus carunculatus*) in New Zealand as a consequence of one individual having an unusual vocalization—probably due to a mistake in song learning (Jenkins, 1977). If juveniles live an exceptionally long period next to their parents and other relatives and forage close to them, then the transmission of such skills would be facilitated. New Caledonian crows do indeed live in groups that seem to be familial, so their social structure could provide opportunities for the social transmission of tool behavior.

Rearing experiments may help to determine to what extent social learning is involved. Tebbich and colleagues (Tebbich et al., 2001) found that young woodpecker finches developed proficient tool-using skills even when raised with non–tool-using adults. The young finches showed a strong spontaneous tendency to use sticks, and they refined and consolidated the habit by their own experience. These observations suggest that social learning is not essential for the development and transmission of tool use in woodpecker finches.

However, in New Caledonian crows, the presence of geographic diversity in tool shape (Hunt & Gray, 2003) in the absence of detectable habitat differences strongly argues in favor of a cultural component, because geographic diversity can hardly result from purely individual acquisition in similar environments. In the context of the questions addressed in this chapter, the presence of a strong cultural component adds further uncertainty, because it opens the possibility that New Caledonian crows may simply be better at advanced forms of social learning than other corvids, rather than being particularly advanced in their cognitive abilities.

However, we know from our observations of hook making (Weir et al., 2002) that New Caledonian crows do excel in creative problem solving. So, it seems unlikely that advanced social learning skills are a complete answer to the question, "What is special about this species?"

Cognitive Adaptations: Generalized or Specialized?

Perhaps at the other extreme of the possibilities just discussed, New Caledonian crows might have an enhanced cognitive ability (compared, for example, with other Corvidae) that is not specifically related to tool behavior. They might have better general problem-solving abilities, be better able to deal with abstract or conditional rules, or have more accurate memories than other species. These abilities may explain tool behavior, but they extend well beyond it. We have not yet had the opportunity to test these aspects of their cognition. An obvious route, that we are following now, is to compare behavior of this and other species in tasks requiring problem solving but not involving tools.

Alternatively, the crows may have cognitive adaptations strictly within the domain of tool behavior. Even then, we can ask about the nature of the adaptation: Do they learn specific solutions for each task they encounter, or can they abstract more general principles? These abstractions could be very specific—for example, the individual might simply understand that pushing *that* object with *this* stick will cause it to move away from self; or fairly general—an object has an effect on another if and only if there is a direct, physical connection between them, regardless of the exact circumstances and objects involved. The latter allows for greater behavioral flexibility and improvisation in the face of variable availability of materials and differing tasks requiring tools.

For example, if a human finds herself in need of a screwdriver to remove a screw but does not have one readily available, then she can attempt to use a blunt knife tip or a thin coin to serve the same purpose. She is able to do so because she "understands" the required physical forces involved and is able to generalize that knowledge to different objects. We all do something similar every time we try to use a new piece of computer software—with varying levels of success. The laboratory experiments described earlier suggest that New Caledonian crows have an impressive ability to generalize their tool expertise and to create new solutions. Making a hook out of an unfamiliar material and using a variety of different techniques that would not result in a working tool with natural materials seems even more impressive than loosening a screw with a blunt knife.

If New Caledonian crows do have a generalized cognitive adaptation, then it is most likely to be founded on knowledge about physical causality and object relations. But, is it conceivable that an organism without language would be able to deal with these rather abstract concepts? Neonatal human infants of 3 months of age have been shown to possess knowledge about physical causality (Spelke, Breinlinger, Macomber, & Jacobson,

1992). They expect objects to move only on connected paths, rather than jumping discontinuously from one location to another (*continuity*), and they expect objects to move only on unobstructed paths, so that no parts of two distinct objects can occupy the same space and time (*solidity*). Other knowledge about the physical world (such as *gravity* and *inertia*) appears to develop at a much later stage. If such young infants possess this kind of knowledge—long before the acquisition of language, and before extensive motor exploration of the environment—then it does not seem impossible that nonhuman species might also be able to form some of these concepts. Time (and much more work) will tell.

Acknowledgments This work was funded by the Leverhulme Trust and the Wellcome Trust.

Note

1. We are grateful to Prof. M. Brady for this example.

2. We have recently provided evidence supporting this hypothesis, by demonstrating that New Caledonian crows develop tool use even if reared in isolation without ever witnessing another individual using tools (Kenward, Weir, Rutz, & Kacelnik, 2005), and that successful tool use is preceded by nonfunctional, stereotyped "precursor" behaviors (Kenward, Rutz, Weir, & Kacelnik, in press).

References

Beck, B. B. (1980). *Animal tool behavior*. New York: Garland.

Boyd, R., & Richerson, P. J. (1996). Why culture is common, but cultural evolution is rare. In W. G. Runciman, J. Maynard Smith, & R. I. M. Dunbar (Eds.), *Evolution of social behaviour patterns in primates and man: A joint discussion meeting of the Royal Society and the British Academy* (pp. 77–93). Oxford: Oxford University Press.

Chappell, J., & Kacelnik, A. (2002). Tool selectivity in a non-mammal, the New Caledonian crow (*Corvus moneduloides*). *Animal Cognition, 5*, 71–78.

Chappell, J., & Kacelnik, A. (2004). Selection of tool diameter by New Caledonian crows *Corvus moneduloides. Animal Cognition, 7*, 121–127.

Chappell, J., & Kacelnik, A. (2005). *Folk physics in New Caledonian crows: Do crows understand gravity?* Unpublished manuscript.

Diamond, J. M. (1992). *The rise and fall of the third chimpanzee*. London: Vintage.

Fragaszy, D., Izar, P., Visalberghi, E., Ottoni, E. B., & de Oliveira, M. G. (2004). Wild capuchin monkeys (*Cebus libidinosus*) use anvils and stone pounding tools. *American Journal of Primatology, 64*, 359–366.

Grant, P. R. (1999). *Ecology and evolution of Darwin's finches*. Princeton, NJ: Princeton University Press.

Hannécart, F., & Létocart, Y. (1980). *Oiseaux de Nouvelle Calédonie et des Loyautés*. Noumea, Nouvelle Calédonie: Les Editions Cardinalis.

Hunt, G. R. (1996). Manufacture and use of hook-tools by New Caledonian crows. *Nature, 379*, 249–251.

Hunt, G. R. (2000a). Human-like, population-level specialization in the manufacture of Pandanus tools by New Caledonian crows *Corvus moneduloides. Proceedings of the Royal Society of London B, 267*, 403–413.

Hunt, G. R. (2000b). Tool use by the New Caledonian crow *Corvus moneduloides* to obtain Cerambycidae from dead wood. *Emu, 100*, 109–114.

Hunt, G. R., & Gray, R. D. (2002). Species-wide manufacture of stick-type tools by New Caledonian Crows. *Emu, 102*, 349–353.

Hunt, G. R., & Gray, R. D. (2003). Diversification and cumulative evolution in New Caledonian crow tool manufacture. *Proceedings of the Royal Society of London B, 270*, 867–874.

Hunt, G. R., & Gray, R. D. (2004a). The crafting of hook tools by wild New Caledonian crows. *Proceedings of the Royal Society of London B, 271(suppl)*, S88–S90.

Hunt, G. R., & Gray, R. D. (2004b). Direct observations of Pandanus-tool manufacture and use by a New Caledonian crow (*Corvus moneduloides*). *Animal Cognition, 7*, 114–120.

Hunt, G. R., Sakuma, F., & Shibata, Y. (2002). New Caledonian crows drop candle-nuts onto rock from communally-used forks on branches. *Emu, 102*, 283–290.

Jenkins, P. F. (1977). Cultural transmission of song patterns and dialect development in a free-living bird population. *Animal Behaviour, 25*, 50–78.

Kenward, B., Rutz, C., Weir, A. A. S., Chappell, J., & Kacelnik, A. (2004). Morphology and sexual dimorphism of the New Caledonian Crow *Corvus moneduloides*, with notes on its behaviour and ecology. *Ibis, 146*, 652–660.

Kenward, B., Rutz, C., Weir, A. A. S., & Kacelnik, A. (in press). Development of tool use in New Caledonian crows (*Corvus moneduloides*): Stereotyped action patterns and social influence. *Animal Behaviour*.

Kenward, B., Weir, A. A. S., Rutz, C., & Kacelnik, A. (2005). Tool manufacture by naive juvenile crows. *Nature, 433,* 121.

Layard, E. L., & Layard, E. L. C. (1882). Notes on the avifauna of New Caledonia. *Ibis, 6,* 520–522.

Limongelli, L. (1995). *Comprehensione delle realzioni di causa-effetto nei Primati: uno studio sperimentale.* Unpublished doctoral dissertation, University of Rome, Rome, Italy.

Limongelli, L., Boysen, S. T., & Visalberghi, E. (1995). Comprehension of cause-effect relations in a tool-using task by chimpanzees (*Pan troglodytes*). *Journal of Comparative Psychology, 109,* 18–26.

McGrew, W. C., & Marchant, L. F. (1997). Using the tools at hand: Manual laterality and elementary technology in *Cebus* spp. and *Pan* spp. *International Journal of Primatology, 18,* 787–810.

Moura, A. C. de A., & Lee, P. C. (2004). Capuchin stone tool use in Caatinga dry forest. *Science, 306,* 1909.

Povinelli, D. J. (2000). *Folk physics for apes.* Oxford: Oxford University Press.

Spelke, E. S., Breinlinger, K., Macomber, J., & Jacobson, K. (1992). Origins of knowledge. *Psychological Review, 99,* 605–632.

Tebbich, S., & Bshary, R. (2004). Cognitive abilities related to tool use in the woodpecker finch, *Cactospiza pallida. Animal Behaviour, 67,* 689–697.

Tebbich, S., Taborsky, M., Fessl, B., & Blomqvist, D. (2001). Do woodpecker finches acquire tool-use by social learning? *Proceedings of the Royal Society of London B, 268,* 2189–2193.

Tebbich, S., Taborsky, M., Fessl, B., & Dvorak, M. (2002). The ecology of tool-use in the woodpecker finch (*Cactospiza pallida*). *Ecology Letters, 5,* 656–664.

Tomasello, M. (1999). The human adaptation for culture. *Annual Review of Anthropology, 28,* 509–529.

van Schaik, C. P., Ancrenaz, M., Borgen, G., Galdikas, B., Knott, C. D., Singleton, I., et al. (2003). Orangutan cultures and the evolution of material culture. *Science, 299,* 102–105.

Visalberghi, E. (2000). *Tool use behavior and the understanding of causality in primates.* In E. Thommen & H. Kilcher (Eds.), *Comparer ou prédire: Exemples de recherches comparatives en psyhologie aujourd'hui* (pp. 17–35). Fribourg, Suisse: Les Editions Universitaires.

Visalberghi, E., & Limongelli, L. (1994). Lack of comprehension of cause-effect relations in tool-using capuchin monkeys (*Cebus apella*). *Journal of Comparative Psychology, 108,* 15–22.

Weir, A. A. S., Chappell, J., & Kacelnik, A. (2002). Shaping of hooks in New Caledonian crows. *Science, 297,* 981.

Whiten, A., Goodall, J., McGrew, W. C., Nishida, T., Reynolds, V., Sugiyama, Y., et al. (1999). Cultures in chimpanzees. *Nature, 399,* 682–685.

Wilson, B., Mackintosh, N. J., & Boakes, R. A. (1985). Transfer of relational rules in matching and oddity learning by pigeons and corvids. *Quarterly Journal of Experimental Psychology, 37B,* 313–332.

27

What Is Challenging About Tool Use? The Capuchin's Perspective

ELISABETTA VISALBERGHI AND DOROTHY FRAGASZY

Our fascination with the use of tools by nonhuman animals reflects a profound appreciation of the importance of tools to our own species. There is no doubt that the use of tools has empowered humans to diversify their way of life and to exploit resources not available to other primates. The paleontological and archaeological records show that changes in tools throughout human history reflect an accumulating mastery of physical relations and knowledge of natural processes. The tools themselves provide a record of human workmanship, and, from the earliest periods of human history, one of the best records from which to infer the behavior of our ancestors. Moreover, using tools is linked in our minds to intelligence; the emergence of tools in human history is thought to reflect the evolution of human intelligence.

Apart from the issue of intelligence, animals using tools interest biologists because tool use is a means by which an individual can expand available resources. For example, chimpanzees (*Pan troglodytes*) can open certain kinds of nuts only by cracking them with a stone. These nuts are a rich food source for the animals. Similarly, using a cactus needle, the woodpecker finch (*Cactospiza pallida*) can obtain prey not otherwise accessible. Although it is often an assumption, using a tool to solve an ecologically important problem (such as obtaining food or constructing shelter) is generally thought to confer an advantage over solving the same problem by some other means without using a tool, usually because the tool confers some mechanical advantage or some protection to the user.

We all understand what we mean by the word "tool" and by the phrase "using a tool." However, as is often the case for words and phrases used in everyday speech, these terms are actually too vague for scientific purposes. To determine whether and under what circumstances other species use tools, we need a more precise definition. Beck (1980) offered a widely accepted functional definition of tool use in his book *Animal Tool Behavior*, which is still the most complete catalog of tool use in animals. Beck states that "tool use is the external employment of an unattached environmental object to alter more efficiently the form, position, or condition of another object, another organism, or the user itself when the user holds or carries the tool during or just prior to use and is responsible for the proper orientation of the tool" (p. 10). To distinguish exploratory behaviors from tool use, we need to make a further distinction that must be inferred from the animal's behavior. Tool use requires that the agent pursue a goal. Exploration can lead to fortuitous discovery of how to use an object as a tool, but it is the purposeful repetition of that sequence of actions to reach a goal that is recognized as tool use.

As Beck (1980) shows convincingly, tool use is widely distributed across the animal kingdom; it is clearly not restricted to primates. However, it is thought that tool use is more flexible in format and more varied in function in primates than in other orders (Tomasello & Call, 1997). In the wild, tool use is widespread among chimpanzees, observed less often in orangutans (*Pongo pygmaeus*), and even less often in the other great apes (gorillas, *Gorilla gorilla*, and *bonobos Pan paniscus*), and capuchins (genus *Cebus*). Only wild chimpanzees use tools habitually, in varied formats, and for diverse purposes. However, all of these species use tools spontaneously and readily in captivity in flexible and diverse ways. Many other species of nonhuman primates occasionally use objects as tools (e.g., *Macaca tonkeana*: Ueno & Fujita, 1998; *Macaca fascicularis*: Zuberbühler, Gygax, Harley, & Kummer, 1996; *Macaca silenus*: Westergaard, 1988; *Papio papio*: Beck, 1973; see Beck, 1980, for review). But none are habitual users of tools, although they can easily be trained to use tools (*Macaca fuscata:* Hihara, Obayashi, Tanaka, & Iriki, 2003). Clearly, use of an object as a tool is challenging for all primates and an unusual accomplishment for most.

For many years, we have studied tool use and other features of manipulative behavior and problem solving in tufted capuchin monkeys (*Cebus apella*), the most adept and frequent users of tools among monkeys. In this chapter, we use capuchins as a vehicle to discuss tool use in nonhuman primates. After providing some background on capuchins and an overview of the forms and contexts of tool use commonly observed in this genus, we review experimental studies focusing on the number and kind of relations among object, substrate, and actions required to use an object to achieve a goal. This section is framed in terms of a particular view of tool use that we believe holds promise for a broad understanding of the phenomenon as a particular kind of perceptual-motor challenge.

To the best of our knowledge, capuchins learn to use tools in much the same way that other species do. Understanding how they learn to use tools, and the aspects of using tools that challenge them, gives us a new understanding of tool use in our own species as well as other species of nonhuman animals. Finally, to better understand why captive capuchins readily use tools, but capuchins in the wild rarely do so, we discuss the behavioral and environmental factors that promote and constrain the occurrence of tool use in these monkeys.

CAPUCHIN MONKEYS

Capuchin monkeys have been popular subjects for research in the laboratory as well as in the field (see Fragaszy, Visalberghi, & Fedigan, 2004, for a review). They are robustly built monkeys weighing between 2.5 and 5 kg. Capuchins are named for the distinctive caps on their crowns that appear in various colors and shapes in different species. They have an unusual life history: capuchins live an anomalously long time (up to 55 years in captivity), and they have a long period of maternal care and immaturity. A large ratio of brain size to body size also distinguishes capuchins from other monkey species. Capuchins live in groups ranging from around 10 to more than 40 individuals that contain one or more adult males, several adult females, and immatures. In general, each group contains a clearly dominant male and female. Although group members can be assigned to different dominance classes, social relations are characterized by a high degree of tolerance among individuals.

Capuchins are very widely distributed in Central and South America, ranging from Honduras to the north of Argentina and from Peru to the Atlantic coast of Brazil. Such a wide distribution is possible because they can thrive in a variety of habitats. They spend most of their time in trees. However, in response to local conditions, they may also spend time feeding on the ground (including raiding crops), drinking, playing, or moving across open ground between patches of forest.

Capuchins are omnivores. They eat mostly fruits but include varying portions of other vegetable items (leaves and shoots, flowers, buds, etc.), invertebrates (mollusks, insects, worms, etc.), and vertebrates (birds and their eggs, small mammals, lizards, etc.) in their diet. Many other South American monkeys eat the same items as capuchins, but what distinguishes the latter is their destructive manner of foraging. Capuchins are renowned as extractive foragers, meaning that they exploit hidden and encased foods. Their foraging behavior is distinctive for its inclusion of a large variety of strenuous actions (e.g., dig, rip, bite, bang, grab, break; see figure 27.1) as well as dexterous and precise ones (e.g., pull or pick with precision grip, scoop, open by peeling).

One particular form of strenuous foraging activity typifies wild capuchins: breaking open hard-shelled fruits, nuts, and invertebrates. *C. apella* repeatedly bang the shelled item against a tree

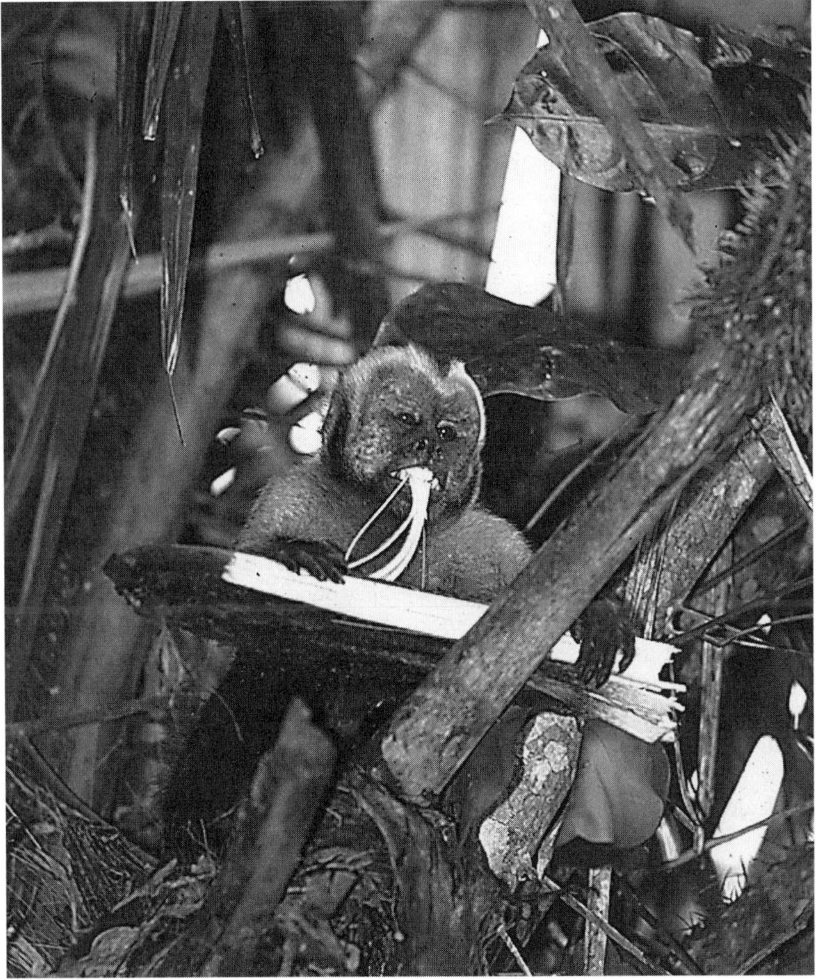

Figure 27.1. Manu National Park, Peru. An adult male *C. apella* strips pieces from a branch using strong arms and teeth. (Photograph courtesy of Charles Janson.)

trunk or other hard surface until cracks appear in the shell. Then, they peel or remove the cracked rind with the teeth and hands or bang the nut or shell again until the husk breaks and the flesh or kernels can be extracted.

Capuchins are comparable to other species of monkeys in their achievements in tasks commonly used to assess memorial, attentional, and conceptual abilities (e.g., Piagetian sensorimotor tasks, various discrimination, matching, and conceptual learning tasks, as well as social cognition tasks; Adams-Curtis, 1990; Anderson, 1996; Antinucci, 1989; D'Amato & Salmon, 1984; De Lillo & Visalberghi, 1994; see Tomasello & Call, 1997, and Fragaszy, Fedigan, & Visalberghi, 2004, for a comparative review). However, their engagement with objects is unique. Captive capuchins of all ages devote considerable attention, time, and energy to manipulating objects; moreover, they frequently combine objects and surfaces in actions (e.g., bang objects on surfaces and poke objects into surfaces), leading to fortuitous spontaneous discoveries and innovations.

HISTORICAL OVERVIEW OF TOOL USE REPORTS

The Complete Capuchin (Fragaszy, Fedigan, et al., 2004, chap. 10) contains the most updated and exhaustive information on the tool using skills of capuchins. The use of tools has been observed mainly in captive capuchins; the first report dates back about 500 years. The Spanish naturalist Gonzalo Fernández de Oviedo y Valdés (de Oviedo, 1526/1996, cited by Urbani, 1998) was the first to describe a capuchin monkey cracking open a nut with a tool. Hundreds of years later, Erasmus Darwin, the grandfather of the more famous Charles Darwin, observed this same behavior in a park in London (Darwin, 1794). A century later, naturalists and psychologists began to report serendipitous observations as well as systematic studies of captive capuchins using tools (e.g., Klüver, 1933, 1937; Nolte, 1958; Romanes, 1883/1977; Watson, 1908; for further details, see Beck, 1980; Fragaszy, Fedigan, et al., 2004; Visalberghi, 1990). At this point, it became clear that these South American monkeys were capable of using many different tools to reach many different goals (sticks to rake/push/insert, hard objects to crack open nuts, etc.).

According to Hill (1960), Buffon writes that Dampier (1697) provided the first report of tool use by wild capuchins (living on the island of Gorgona off the coast of Colombia) cracking open mollusks by banging them on the rocks or using a stone as a tool to smash the shells. Note that according to Beck's definition (1980), only the latter case can be considered tool use. However, Dampier merely wrote that the monkeys ate mollusks by digging them out of the shells. Unless different editions of the book contain different information, the earlier references to Dampier reporting tool use were apparently in error. In other words, Dampier did not report that he saw wild capuchins using tools. Although there are second-hand reports of capuchins using pounding tools (e.g., Hernández-Camacho & Cooper, 1976), Fernandes (1991) published the first report of direct observation of tool use by wild capuchins. Fernandes described, 300 years later, what Buffon and Hill erroneously attributed to Dampier: a wild capuchin using a broken oyster shell to strike oysters still attached to the substrate, successfully breaking them open. Another instance of tool use by wild *C. capucinus* was carefully documented by Boinski (1988); she observed a male killing a snake by hitting it with a branch obtained from nearby vegetation.

In a photograph report that appeared in the popular press, Oxford (2003) documented a group of wild *C. apella* in the "cerrado" habitat of Brazil that feed routinely on the nuts of the Attalea palm. He photographed these monkeys opening the hard nuts by first placing them on a large stone and then pounding them with stones that often weighed more than a kilogram. Prompted by his astonishing photos, we conducted an exploratory investigation in this same area (Fragaszy, Izar, Visalberghi, Ottoni, & Gomes de Oliveira, 2004). Direct observation of several instances of tool use by wild capuchin monkeys (male and female) convinced us that the phenomenon was indeed a legitimate discovery. In surveying the surrounding area, we found indirect physical evidence that monkeys cracked nuts on numerous rock outcrops, boulders, logs, and even the tops of mesas. The abundance of shell remains and depressions in the anvil surface at numerous anvil sites indicate that nut-cracking activity is common and long enduring. The presence of abundant anvil sites, limited alternative food resources, the abundance of palms, and the fact that the palms in this region produce fruit at ground level all likely contribute to the monkeys' routine exploitation of palm nuts via cracking them with stones. In our opinion, ecologically and behaviorally, capuchins' nut-cracking appears to parallel nut-cracking observed in wild chimpanzees. Further systematic long-term studies are needed.

In the last two decades of the last century, a surge of interest in capuchins' tool use developed that continues to the present. This increased interest was partly inspired by Parker and Gibson's (1977, 1979) argument that higher forms of intelligence evolved as an adaptation for extracting embedded food resources. Pursuing this idea, some researchers investigated the development of tool-using behaviors in young individuals as well as the achievements of adults within a Piagetian framework (Chevalier-Skolnikoff, 1989, 1990; K. R. Gibson, 1990; Natale, 1989; Parker & Potì, 1990). Others (e.g., Anderson, Fragaszy, Visalberghi, & Westergaard—see table 27.1 for references) undertook studies to clarify (1) how behavior, morphology, and cognition contribute to the emergence of tool use, (2) the range of capuchins' tool use, (3) the extent to which social influences affect individuals learning to use objects as tools, (4) the flexibility of tool use with varying objects and surfaces, and (5) what this flexibility means about underlying comprehension of the task. Recently, reports of tool use by wild or semifree capuchins carried out in the capuchins' natural habitats have appeared (e.g., Jalles-Filho, da Cunha, & Salm, 2001; Ottoni & Mannu, 2001; Rocha, dos Reis, & Sekiama,

Table 27.1 Recent Studies on Tool Use in Capuchins, Chronologically Ordered

Task	Relational Category[a]	Specific Aim(s) of the Study	No. of Tool Users/No. Total[b]	Species	Source
Studies in Captivity[c]					
Nut cracking	First dynamic	Selection among differently effective tools	1/6	*C. apella*	Antinucci & Visalberghi, 1986
Nut cracking	First dynamic	Acquisition of the behavior and social learning	2/42	*C. apella*	Visalberghi, 1987
Dipping	First static	Acquisition of the behavior and social learning	6/9	*C. apella*	Westergaard & Fragaszy, 1987a
Sponging	First static		9/9		
Stick directed to a wound	First static	Serendipitious observation	n.a.	*C. apella*	Westergaard & Fragaszy, 1987b
Stick directed to a wound	First static	Serendipitious observation	n.a.	*C. apella*	Ritchie & Fragaszy, 1988
Raking/digging/probing	Ambiguous description	Observational study	n.a./12	*C. apella* *C. albifrons*	Chevalier-Skolnikoff, 1989
Nut cracking	First static	Social influences on tool use acquisition	5/20	*C. apella*	Fragaszy & Visalberghi, 1989
Stick to push	First static		5/20		
Stick to rake	First dynamic	Sensorimotor intelligence	3	*C. apella*	Natale, 1989
Stick to push a reward out of a tube	First dynamic	Appreciation of how the tool should be modified	3/4	*C. apella*	Visalberghi & Trinca, 1989
Nut cracking	First dynamic	Benefits in terms of time and success due to the use of tools	5/6	*C. apella*	Anderson, 1990
Stick to rake	First dynamic	Sensorimotor intelligence	3/5	*C. apella*	Parker & Potì, 1998
		Developmental	1		
Sticks to push a reward out of a tube	First dynamic	Selection of the appropriate tool	4	*C. apella*	Visalberghi, 1993
Nut cracking and probing	First static	Sequential use of tools (tool-set)	3/9	*C. apella*	Westergaard & Suomi, 1993
	First static				
Probing	First static	Selection of the appropriate tool	2	*C. apella*	Anderson & Henneman, 1994
Dipping	First static	Tool acquisition in juveniles and influence of the context	3juv/9juv	*C. apella*	Fragaszy, Fedigan, et al., 1994
Nut cracking	First static		3juv/9juv		
Stick to push a reward out of a tube	Second simult.	Understanding of cause-effect relations	4	*C. apella*	Visalberghi & Limongelli, 1994
Aimed throwing	First static	Modeling early hominid technology	4	*C. apella*	Westergaard & Suomi, 1994a
Stone flaking	First dynamic	Production of flakes	6/11	*C. apella*	Westergaard & Suomi, 1994b
Stones as cutting tools	First static	Stones as cutting tools	3/15		
Bone modification due to the use of tools	First static	Modeling early hominid technology	5/10	*C. apella*	Westergaard & Suomi, 1994c

(continued)

Table 27.1 (*Continued*)

Task	Relational Category[a]	Specific Aim(s) of the Study	No. of Tool Users/No. Total[b]	Species	Source
Nut cracking	First static	Use and modification of bone tools	3/9	*C. apella*	Westergaard & Suomi, 1994d
Bone fragments as cutting tools	First static		3/9		
Stick to displace a reward out of a tube	First dynamic	Comparison with apes	6	*C. apella*	Visalberghi et al., 1995
Dipping	First static	Modeling East Asian hominid bamboo technology	5/18	*C. apella*	Westergaard & Suomi, 1995a
Cutting	First static		6/18		
Digging tools	First static	Modeling hominid subsistence technology	4/10	*C. apella*	Westergaard & Suomi, 1995b
Stone throwing	First static	Modeling hominid throwing capabilities	4	*C. apella*	Westergaard & Suomi, 1995c
Pestle use	First static	Use of different objects as pestle	10/18	*C. apella*	Westergaard et al., 1995
Nut cracking	First static	Modeling hominid metal-tool technology	5/14	*C. apella*	Westergaard et al., 1996
Cutting	First static		5/14		
Stones as cutting tools	First static	Transfer of tools and food	3/11	*C. apella*	Westergaard & Suomi, 1997
Ant gathering	First static	Use of sticks to extract ants	7/14	*C. apella*	Westergaard et al., 1997
Stones as cutting tools	First static	Use of a tool-set	3/14		
Nut cracking	First static	Use of color chips to request tools	1	*C .apella*	Westergaard, Chavanne, et al., 1998
Dipping	First static				
Dipping	First static	Role of sex and age on tool use acquisition	21/36	*C. apella*	Westergaard, Lundquist, et al., 1998
		Factors associated with tool use and modification	31/61		
Container for water	First static	Serendipitious observation	1/11	*C. olivaceus*	Urbani, 1999
Sponging	Zero		1/11		
Stick as cane	NA		1/11		
Bait for fishing	First static	Observational study	4/6	*C. apella*	Mendes et al., 2000
Cracking open a baited box	First static	Modeling hominids' behavioral evolution and the transport of tools	8/13	*C. apella*	Jalles-Filho et al., 2001
Transport tools to the box			1/13		
Transport tools to the nuts and nut cracking	First dynamic		7/8		
Dipping	First static	Influence of task location of tool use	2/4	*C. olivaceus*	Dubois et al., 2001
Tool choice, obstacles, and traps	First dynamic and second simult.	Selection of the appropriate tool and understanding of cause-effect relations	4	*C. apella*	Fujita et al., 2003

Table 27.1 (*Continued*)

Task	Relational Category[a]	Specific Aim(s) of the Study	Condition	No. of Tool Users/No. Total[b]	Species	Source
Studies in Semifree and Wild Conditions[d]						
Throwing, probing	NA[e]	Observational study	W	NA/21	*C. capucinus*	Chevalier-Skolnikoff, 1990
Pounding to open oysters	First static	Serendipitious observation	W	NA	*C. apella*	Fernandes, 1991
Exploratory probing	First static	Serendipitious observation	W	NA	*C. capucinus*	Garber & Paciulli, 1997
Nut cracking	? Second sequential	Serendipitious	W	NA	*C. apella*	Langguth & Alonso, 1997
Nut cracking for inside larvae	Second sequential	Use of suitable pounding tools and anvils	S-F	no data/44	*C. apella*	Rocha et al., 1998
Dipping	First static	Selection and modification of tools	S-F	3/11	*C. apella*	Lavallee, 1999
Nut cracking	Second sequential	Search of suitable anvil and pounding tools	S-F	15/18	*C. apella*	Ottoni & Mannu, 2001
Leaves to absorb liquid	Zero	Serendipitious observation	W	NA	*C. albifrons*	Phillips, 1998
Branches to kill a snake	First static	Serendipitious observation	W	NA	*C. capucinus*	Boinski, 1988
Nut cracking[f]	? Second sequential	Observational study	W	NA	*C. apella*	Boinski et al., 2001
Stick to push	First dynamic	Acquisition of tool use by providing a tool task	W	0/15	*C. capucinus*	Garber & Brown, 2004
Nut cracking	Second sequential	Use of pounding tools and anvils	W	Several	*C. apella*	Oxford, 2003; Fragaszy, Izar, et al., 2004

[a]Relational categories are defined in table 27.2 according to the number (zero, first, or second order) and type of relations (static and dynamic) embodied in the task. We include a few cases reported in the literature as tool use involving a zero order relation that do not fit our criterion of tool use.

[b]Number of individuals using tools and total number of individuals tested. When there is only one value, it means that the study focussed only on those subjects. NA = not applicable, meaning that the information is not provided by the author(s).

[c]Captivity includes cages, outdoor enclosures, and small islands.

[d]In semifree ranging (S-F) conditions, the animals have access to large areas from which they obtain a substantial part of their food. W = wild.

[e]In our view, the instances described are not cases of tool use. Most of them refer to explorative behaviors and to dropping branches.

[f]Boinski et al., 2001, did not actually see the capsule of the *Couratari oblongifolia* open or the capuchin bring its content to the mouth.

Note: From *The Complete Capuchin,* by D. Fragaszy, L. Fedigan, and E. Visalberghi, 2004, Cambridge: Cambridge University Press. Updated with permission of the publisher.

1998), and, as mentioned, we have observed wild capuchin monkeys cracking open palm nuts using stones and anvils (Fragaszy, Izar, et al., 2004). Table 27.1 provides a list of published reports on tool use in capuchins from 1980, the vast majority of which (about two-thirds) refer to studies carried out in captivity. Instead of reviewing the above studies (for this, we direct interested readers to Fragaszy, Fedigan, et al., 2004), we describe only a few of them to illustrate the types of tool-using problems that capuchins master readily and the types that are more challenging for them.

A PERCEPTION-ACTION VIEW OF TOOL USE

Before we review research reports, we need to present and explain our particular treatment of tool use. The definition of tool use from Beck (1980) that we quoted at the opening of the chapter is sufficient to identify tool use across a broad spectrum of species and contexts, as it was intended to do. However, this definition still leaves ambiguous the status of some actions. Consider the case where an individual rubs a substance on the body (called "anointing" in monkeys; e.g., Baker, 1996), presumably because the astringent substance feels good on the skin (and also because it likely provides insecticidal or antibacterial protection; Valderrama, Robinson, Attygalle, & Eisner, 2000). In this case, the actor, to paraphrase Beck's definition, uses a material (an unattached environmental object) to alter the condition of its skin while the user holds or carries the material during use and the user is responsible for the proper orientation of the material. However, several elements are not clear: for example, whether rubbing something on the body counts as orienting a material. Given this ambiguity, we do not classify anointing as tool use.

Beck's functional definition presents a further problem for us: Namely, it is meant only to distinguish tool use from other categories of action. But, identifying an action as tool use does not help to evaluate the relative complexity of the action; thus, it does not help to establish whether or why some forms of tool use are more challenging than others. For this purpose, we need a principled psychological framework of tool use.

We can think about tool use in terms of the relations among objects, surfaces, effectors, and movements that must be recognized or produced to achieve a goal.[1] This framework was first explicated by Lockman (2000) in a discussion of the origins of tool use in human infancy through exploratory action with objects and surfaces. In this framework, the actor, through common exploratory actions in the species-typical behavioral repertoire (Lockman refers to these as "perception-action routines"), (a) discovers the properties of objects and surfaces, and the consequences of combining them in various ways, (b) learns to recognize and manage the mobile spatial frames of reference that govern the relation of body, objects, and surfaces to each other, and (c) practices modulating actions to achieve particular consequences. Thus, combinatorial exploration leads to tool use.

An important element in this framework is that the actor produces information through action that guides subsequent activity, and action and perception occur in inextricably linked cycles. This insight applies to all action, as explicated by J. J. Gibson (1966, 1979; see E. J. Gibson & Pick, 2000). In this view, the actor must produce at least one needed relation between one object and another object or a surface in order for the action to qualify as tool use. Merely recognizing the appropriate relation, but not producing it, is not tool use.

To make this point clearer, consider the following example. A dog attending closely to a bicycle or to a stone is using neither the bicycle nor the stone as a tool. These objects become tools only when they are used for reaching a goal (traveling efficiently or cracking open a nut) and only when the actor is responsible for producing the relevant relation. Even if the dog has gone on runs with its owner riding the bicycle or received nuts after its owner cracked them, so that it anticipates a fast run or bits of nuts when these objects are present, the dog is not yet a tool user. Similarly, preferential attention toward one of two (or more) objects or choice of an object (Fujita, Kuroshima, & Asai, 2003; Hauser, 1997; Povinelli, 2000; Santos, Miller, & Hauser, 2003) may inform us about the actor's recognition of spatial relations that are relevant for tool use, but attention and choice are not tool use.

TOOL USE IN CAPUCHINS

To be conservative, we focus on cases in which capuchins use objects to achieve a tangible goal (thus ruling out banging to make noise and anointing the body with material with no clear immediate goal, among other actions). Moreover, we add to the definition of tool use given here (using an object as a functional extension of the body to act on another object or surface) the requirement that the actor itself produce a relation between the tool and another object or surface, and not simply use a preexisting relation (labeled as zero-order relations in table 27.2). This definition excludes some situations that others commonly include as examples of tool use, such as pulling in a cane where the curve of the cane already surrounds a piece of food when the actor arrives on the scene. In our scheme, the monkey itself has to place the cane in relation to the food (producing a first-order relation) for the action to be classified as tool use.

An animal may not use a tool consistently in all contexts; it may use a tool to solve one task but be unable to use it to solve another. What determines the difficulty of a tool-using task? According to the perception-action framework, the number and kind of relations among objects, surfaces, and movements that must be recognized or produced to achieve a goal determine the complexity of a tool-using task (see table 27.2).

Table 27.2 Relations Produced Through Action With an Object That Are Evident in Capuchins' Use of Tools

Relational Category	Definition	Examples
Zero Order		
	Act on one object; action on second object occurs by default.	Pull in a cane positioned with food inside the hook and the straight part of the cane within reach. Pull in cloth with food on the cloth.
First Order		
Static first-order relations	Acting with an object on a fixed surface (or on a fixed object) to reach the goal.	Probe into an opening with a stick ("dip"). Pound a stone on a nut fixed on a surface.
Dynamic first-order relations	Acting with an object A in relation to an object B that moves. Because action with A alters the state of B, B must be monitored as action progresses.	Push food out of a tube with a stick. Pull in an object with a stick when they are not already positioned so that pulling is effective. Pound a loose nut with a stone.
Second Order		
Sequential second-order relations	Acting with an object A in relation to object B following placement of object B in relation to a third object C (surface or object). In this case, one static relation between B and C and then one dynamic relation between A and B are produced.	Pound a stone against a nut placed on a second stone.
Simultaneous second-order relations	Acting with an object A in relation to object B while maintaining B in relation to C (surface or object). In this case two dynamic relations (between A and B, and between B and C) are coordinated simultaneously.	Push food through tube with a stick while avoiding a hole. Pull food with a rake across a surface with a hole. Pound a stone against a nut on an anvil surface while holding the nut (to prevent the nut from falling off the anvil).

Note: In our view, an action involving a zero-order relation is not tool use; tool use requires producing a first-order relation. Order refers to the number of relations between objects and surfaces that are required to reach the goal, and not to the number of actions in a sequence.

We recognize two types of spatial relations here: static and dynamic. Static relations are produced once, such as placing a nut on a specific surface. Dynamic relations must be maintained through time, such as holding a nut on an inclined surface or keeping an object behind the blade of a hoe while sweeping it laterally. Other thing being equal, a dynamic relation is more difficult to achieve than a static relation, because it requires continuous monitoring. The boundary between static and dynamic relations may not always be clear (for example, the case of a nut placed on an inclined stone), but it is still useful, we think, to keep this dimension of action in mind when thinking about a particular tool problem.

First-Order Problems (Single Relations)

Captive capuchins are often successful in tasks where they must produce a single static spatial relation. Probing into an opening with a stick or pounding a nut or other object fixed to a surface (see figure 27.2, top left and right) are examples of actions embodying static first-order relations. Dipping and banging are very common actions performed frequently by all capuchins. Actions producing dynamic single relations are also fairly common, such as pushing or pulling an object with a stick (figure 27.2, bottom left). Pounding a loose nut with a stone can involve a static relation if the nut remains where it is placed without support (see figure 27.2, bottom right) or a dynamic relation if the object slips unless supported.

A dipping/probing task is a good example of a tool-using task involving a single static relation that has been used many times with captive capuchins (see figure 27.2, top left). In this task, a container is filled with a viscous food (e.g., syrup, applesauce, yogurt) or ants (Westergaard, Lundquist, Kuhn, & Suomi, 1997) that can be retrieved through an opening that is too small for a capuchin's hand. The container is fixed to a rigid surface and suitable objects (stick, straw, dowels, and branches from which smaller pieces can be used) are presented. Capuchins master this task before their first birthday (Westergaard & Fragaszy, 1987a; Westergaard, Lundquist, Haynie, Kuhn, & Suomi, 1998) or shortly thereafter (Fragaszy, Vitale, & Ritchie, 1994).

In a variation of this task, capuchins struck an acetate film with sharp-edged stones and cut an opening into a closed food container (Westergaard & Suomi, 1994b). When sticks to probe with are not readily available near the apparatus, capuchins collect them from somewhere out of view and bring them to the work site (Fragaszy & Visalberghi, 1989; Lavallee, 1999; Visalberghi, 1987). Planning is implied by the collection of tools distant from the work site (see also Jalles-Filho et al., 2001).

Once capuchins have learned to dip for food, they do not forget how to do this, even after several years. For example, two capuchins that learned to dip for syrup, dipped years later when given similar opportunities, although the setting was completely different (from indoor to semifree conditions) (Lavallee, 1999). However, applying a strategy successfully adopted in the past is not necessarily efficient for the task at hand. Figure 27.3 shows a female tufted capuchin that years before had used sticks to dip for syrup. Now, she has an opportunity to work for a new food item, a walnut. She is holding a straw and touching the shell of the walnut with it. Clearly, dipping will not work in this context. In this case, the monkey will have to abandon the remembered action—object combination and learn new ones. It is evident from this example that capuchins do not always appreciate the appropriate elements of a task in the same way as an adult human observer.

SECOND-ORDER PROBLEMS (TWO RELATIONS)

Inserting a stick into an opening is a fairly probable action for capuchins, as their success in dipping tasks suggests (see earlier). Capuchin monkeys also readily discover that after they insert a stick into a horizontal tube, they can push food out of the tube using a stick (figure 27.4). Pushing food through a tube requires producing one static relation (inserting the stick into the tube) and then one dynamic relation (a sustained push on the food with the stick).

Visalberghi and Trinca (1989) used a transparent tube, which allowed the experimenter and subject alike to view the food inside and to see the tool entering the tube, to study the tool-using behavior of four tufted capuchin monkeys. The monkeys mastered this problem within 101 min without any training or demonstrations. This general finding has been replicated with other capuchins and other primate species (for a review, see Visalberghi, 2000).

Figure 27.2. *Top left*, Adult female tufted capuchin dips for applesauce while holding her newborn infant in one arm. She holds the stick with a power grip. (Photograph courtesy of Elisabetta Visalberghi.) This is an example of producing a static first-order relation; see table 27.2. *Bottom left*, Tufted capuchins use a C-shaped tool to retrieve a reward. Once the monkey has placed the hook around the food, the task becomes easy, but the monkey must still monitor that the food remains within the hook of the tool as it slides across the surface. This task involves producing a dynamic first-order relation. (Photograph courtesy of S. Cummins-Sebree.) *Top right*, Juvenile uses a metal object to crack open a walnut glued in the wooden board. (Photograph courtesy of Elisabetta Visalberghi.) This is an example of producing a static first-order relation. *Bottom right*, Adult male effectively cracks open a nut by striking it with a log, demonstrating skillful use of a tool (from video by Elisabetta Visalberghi). This involves a static first-order relation if the nut remains stationary during the cracking process. If the nut must be supported to prevent it from moving (not shown), this is an additional, dynamic relation that the actor must produce.

The four monkeys tested by Visalberghi and Trinca (1989) subsequently encountered the same tube apparatus in three new conditions in which the tools had to be modified before use or used in succession (see figure 27.4). In one condition, the object (a bundle of thin canes held together by tape) was too large in diameter to fit into the tube. In another condition, the stick had thin pieces of dowel, inserted transversely at each end, so that the ends of the stick could not enter the tube. To insert the stick into the tube, the dowel had to be pulled out or broken off. In the third condition, the sticks were so short that two of them had to be inserted one behind the other inside the tube in order to move the food far enough for the monkey to reach it. The capuchins succeeded under all conditions within a few minutes. Despite their success, they made many attempts to use the original object without modifying it and to use parts of the object (e.g., the tape, a splinter; see figure 27.4) that did not have the necessary properties (e.g., rigidity, length) to displace the food from the tube. Over the 10 trials in each

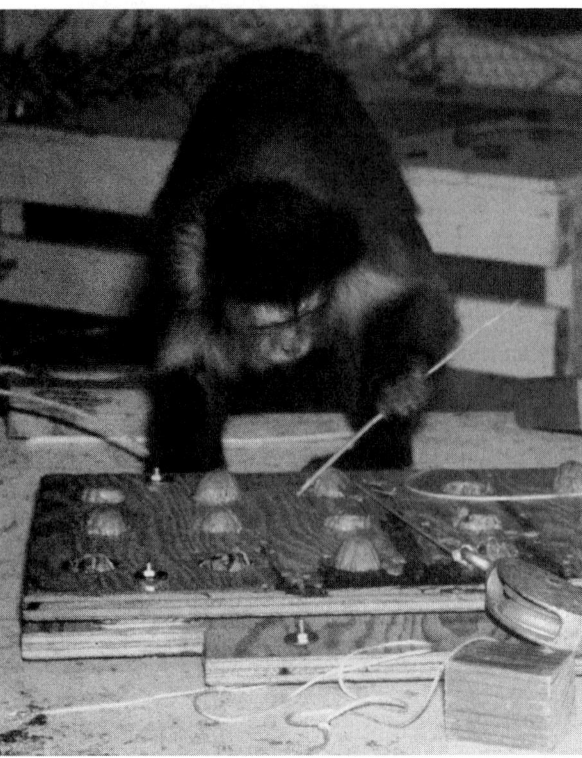

Figure 27.3. An adult female tufted capuchin, proficient in using straw for dipping syrup, touches a nut glued on a wooden board with a straw, using the same action that she used previously to retrieve syrup from a closed container. She ignores the adjacent hard objects (one shown in the foreground) that could be used effectively to crack open nuts. Striking a nut glued in place would be producing a first-order static relation. (Photograph courtesy of Elisabetta Visalberghi.)

condition, the number of errors produced by each monkey and the nature of their errors decreased only slightly. After an interval of 5 years, when these same capuchins encountered these objects and the tube again for a filming session, they made the same kinds of errors (Visalberghi & Limongelli, 1992). These findings indicate that the monkeys did not quickly learn what properties of the objects, surfaces, and actions were most important for success, and they were willing to produce multiple actions in sequences in attempts to solve the problem.

In another experiment, the same four capuchins were given a choice among four different objects to use to push food out of the tube (Visalberghi, 1993). Three of the objects could not be inserted or would not reach the food (one was too thick, one was too short, and one had a transverse block at one end that prevented its insertion), whereas the fourth was the appropriate diameter and length. Although they made a few wrong choices throughout the 16 test trials, all the capuchins selected the correct tool far more often than would be expected by chance. Similarly, Anderson and Henneman (1994) found that capuchins selected an appropriate object for dipping from among an array of appropriate and inappropriate objects. It appears that recognizing an appropriate object to insert is easier for monkeys than modifying an object appropriately beforehand.

Cracking open a nut sometimes requires managing two spatial relations in succession. For example, if the nut is loose and most of the ground surface is relatively soft but hard objects are present, the monkey can use one hard object as an anvil and another to pound. Positioning the nut on a specific hard surface (an anvil) is the first spatial relation; pounding the nut with a hard object is the second. The monkey must often hold the nut in place to make sure that it stays on the anvil as it is struck, adding a dynamic element to the first of the two relations.

Capuchins, in semifree conditions, crack nuts placed on an anvil from about 2 years of age (Ottoni & Mannu, 2001; Resende & Ottoni, 2002; Rocha et al., 1998). And, as noted, in Piauí (Brazil), wild *C. apella libidinosus* (or *Cebus libidinosus* according to the more recent classification of the genus by Groves, 2001; Rylands, Schneider, Mittermeier, Groves, & Rodriguez-Luna, 2000;

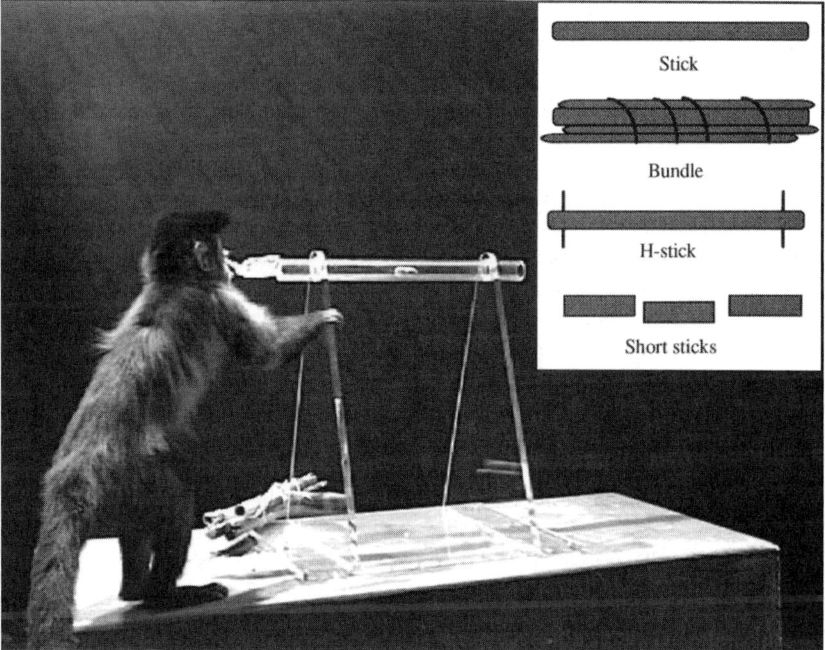

Figure 27.4. The tube task consists of a transparent horizontal tube baited in the center with a food treat. Pushing food through a tube requires producing one static relation (inserting the stick into the tube) and then one dynamic relation (a sustained push on the food with the stick). The objects provided to the subject that can be used as tools are shown in the *top right* of the figure. (From *top* to *bottom*) A stick that can be used to push the treat out of the tube. A bundle consisting of several reeds firmly held together by tape; the diameter of the intact bundle is too large to fit into the tube. The H-stick consisting of a dowel with two smaller sticks placed transversally near the end; the transverse sticks block the insertion of the dowel into the tube. Short sticks at least two of which must be inserted into the tube one behind the other to displace the reward. (Drawing by S. Marta.) The capuchin in the figure has dismantled the bundle of reeds (visible at her feet) and is inserting the tape, not a reed, into the tube. Errors of this type (selecting inappropriate objects as tools) are common in capuchin monkeys. (Photograph courtesy of Elisabetta Visalberghi.)

see also Fragaszy, Fedigan, et al., 2004) routinely open hard nuts with tools (Fragaszy, Izar, et al., 2004). This appears to be a very promising setting in which to study tool use in wild capuchins, as Matsuzawa and colleagues have done with wild chimpanzees (Inoue-Nakamura & Matsuzawa, 1997; Matsuzawa, 1994; Matsuzawa et al., 2001).

It is clear that capuchins are capable of solving a variety of different tasks requiring first- and second-order relations, more so than monkeys of other genera tested so far. However, in most studies with captive capuchins, not all individuals were successful at any particular task (e.g., Westergaard et al., 1998). Some individuals ignored the task, whereas others, although they explored the context, did not solve the task, even if they had many opportunities to watch others using an object and obtaining food. In contrast, many of the wild tufted capuchin monkeys observed by Fragaszy, Izar, et al. (2004) cracked open nuts (Marino Gomes de Oliveira, personal communication), and all individuals except infants cracked nuts in Ottoni and Mannu's (2001) study.

Several factors may account for more consistent use of tools to obtain food by individuals in seminatural or natural groups than in captive groups. More frequent exposure to the task over a longer period of time, exposure to the task from an early age, richer social context, and greater motivation in obtaining food are some of the more obvious ones (see Fragaszy & Visalberghi, 2004, for discussion of variables that affect learning in social settings). In most of the laboratory studies, the tool task is presented for a limited duration and a limited number of times, sometimes with few or no companions present, and the monkeys are typically well nourished and fully adult when they first encounter the task. In a natural setting, the task (embedded food to open) is present daily for weeks or months, for year after year. All individuals have repeated opportunity and a strong interest in obtaining the food, and materials are distributed in space and cannot be monopolized by any single individual. In other words, whereas the experimental data reflect cross-sectional testing, field observations reflect longitudinal exposure.

Moving Objects Across Irregular Surfaces: An Extreme Challenge for Capuchins

Visalberghi and Limongelli (1994) presented a variation of the tube task, the trap-tube task, to four capuchin monkeys already proficient in pushing food out of a tube. The apparatus consists of a transparent tube with a hole in the center and a "trap" underneath the hole (figure 27.5). The experimenter placed the reward on one side of the hole. To get the food, the capuchin had to insert the stick into the tube (first relation) and push the food (second relation) away from the trap (third relation). The monkey could avoid the trap while retrieving the reward by taking into account the outcome of its action with the stick on the movement of the food (toward or away from the trap). Once the stick is inserted into the tube, avoiding moving the food over the trap embodies two dynamic relations: one that the monkey must produce (between the stick and the food) and one that it must recognize beforehand (between the movement of the food over the trap and the food falling into the trap).

The four capuchins were tested for 140 trials. Three of them succeeded at only chance levels, whereas the fourth (3 years old) succeeded on 86% of trials in the second half of the experiment. Careful observation of this monkey's performance revealed that she adopted a distance-based rule: She looked inside the tube from either end and only then did she insert the stick into the opening farthest from the reward (Visalberghi & Limongelli, 1994). However, when the tube was modified so that one "arm" was longer than the other, as shown in figure 27.6, the distance rule became counterproductive. When the trap was not centered, inserting the stick into the side of the tube from which the reward was farther away led to failure. As expected from the use of a distance rule, when the trap was not centered, the monkey's rate of success fell significantly below chance level (Limongelli, Boysen, & Visalberghi, 1995).

A distance-based strategy seems odd to us. As adult humans, we anticipate or we imagine the effect of pushing the food with the stick and (simultaneously) the fate of the food when it moves above a hole. Thus, the position of the food with respect to the trap is integral to how we decide to push the food. The four capuchins probably anticipated that pushing with the stick causes the food to move, but they did not simultaneously recognize that the food will fall into the hole when they push it toward the hole. The behavior of the three monkeys that never scored better than chance with the trap tube supports this view. This view is also supported the thorough analysis of the behavior of the fourth monkey who discovered an effective strategy based on a spatial relation instead of one based on the recognition beforehand of the relation between the movement of the food over the trap and the food falling into the trap.

When the trap tube was presented to five chimpanzees, two solved it at above-chance level (Limongelli et al., 1995), but their strategy was not based on the same distance rule as was used by the successful capuchin, Roberta (see Experiment 2, in Limongelli et al., 1995). It is possible that these two apes might have understood the relevant relation between the food and the hole, as do children above 3 years of age (Visalberghi & Limongelli, 1996; Want & Harris, 2001). However, Reaux and Povinelli (2000) found that several chimpanzees behaved like Roberta; they solved the task by inserting the stick into the end of the tube farthest from the food. When they encountered the tube with the trap rotated 180 degrees vertically (so that the reward cannot fall into it and be lost), they continued to use the same distance rule. Therefore, identifying the second spatial relation in the trap problem is not easy for either apes or capuchins, even though they can see the hole and the food and see that, when they push the food into the hole, it falls into the trap.

To better understand what makes the trap tube difficult for capuchins and chimpanzees, we should consider whether they perceive the hole in the tube and whether they anticipate the path of motion of the food when it enters the hole. Would

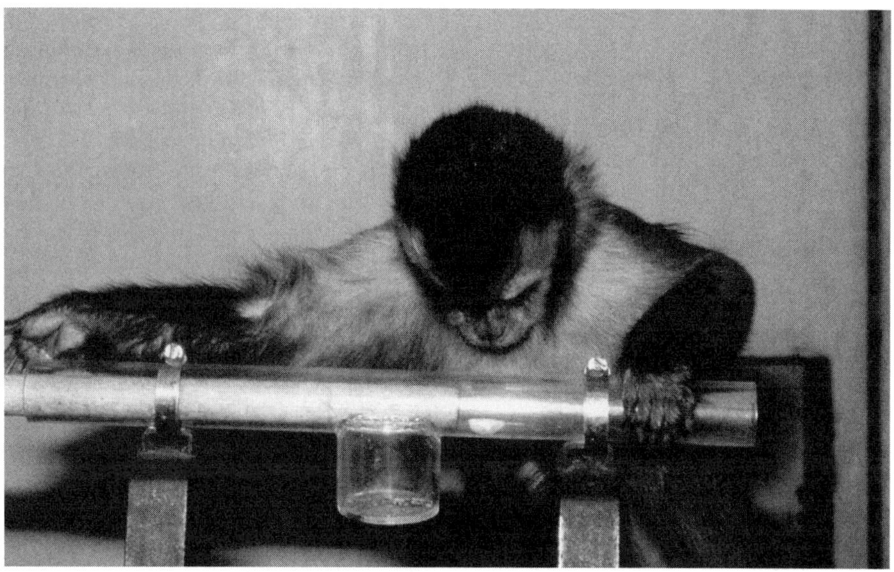

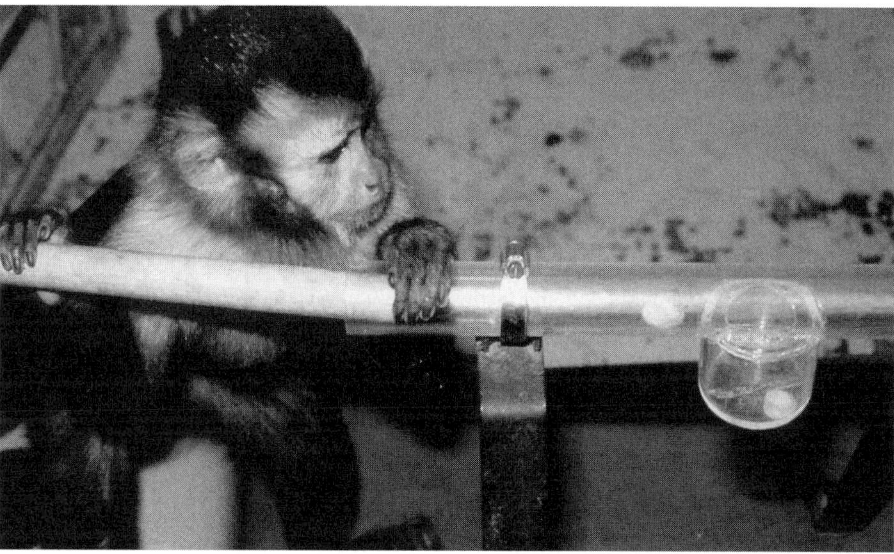

Figure 27.5. Trap-tube is a transparent tube with a hole in the center and a trap underneath it. The *upper panel* shows an example of correct insertion of the stick; the reward is on the right side of the trap. Note how delicately the monkey (Roberta) moves the stick with the fingertips of her right hand while at the same time monitoring the slow movement of the reward. The *lower panel* shows an example of insertion of the stick in the wrong side of the tube. Note that the reward, lost on a previous trial by Roberta, is already inside the trap. (Photographs courtesy of Elisabetta Visalberghi.)

they eventually learn to solve this problem effectively if they generated more or different kinds of feedback from their own actions concerning objects moving across surfaces? Experiments to test these hypotheses have begun.

Cummins (1999) investigated the ability of four capuchin monkeys to deal with two kinds of aberrations of a surface (a barrier and a hole) while using a hoe to retrieve a piece of food (figure 27.7). When the hoe struck the hole, the monkey could

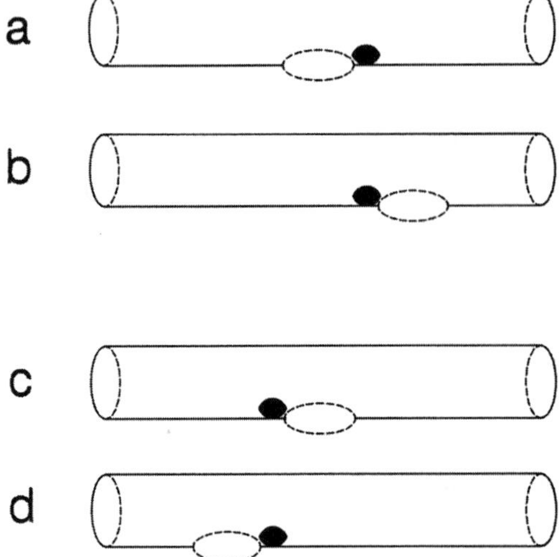

Figure 27.6. Control tests presented to Roberta, the only capuchin that solved the trap-tube task above chance level. These tubes were used to test whether Roberta was using a distance strategy to solve the trap-tube task. When the reward falls into the hole, it is lost to the monkey. The figure shows the possible locations of the reward at the beginning of each trial. In *a* and *c*, the hole is centered; in *b* and *d* the food is in the same position as in *a* and *c* but the hole is displaced from the middle part of the tube. Note that in *a* and *b* the reward is closer to the opening on the right and farther from the opening to the left and that in *c* and *d* the reward is closer to the opening on the left and farther from the opening to the right. Roberta did not solve the problem when it was presented as in *b* and *d*. (Redrawn by S. Marta from Limongelli et al., 1995.)

see and feel the blade of the hoe falling into it. When the hoe struck the barrier, the monkey could see that the hoe was partly occluded and could feel the impediment to movement. In this task, capuchins detected barriers on surfaces more readily than holes and they moved an object past a barrier more successfully than past a hole. In subsequent testing, the monkeys avoided moving a reward toward a hole placed anywhere on a surface. They also readily moved the reward across a location where, on a previous trial, the hole had been (Cummins-Sebree & Fragaszy, 2005). In other words, their successful performance was not based on the spatial rule of avoiding the area where a hole sometimes appears. These results suggest that feedback from action is very important for learning; when capuchin monkeys had enough of the right kinds of experience, they learned to use one object to move another object past a hole, just as they learned to move an object past a barrier.

The four capuchins tested by Fujita et al. (2003) used cane tools effectively to pull in food across a smooth surface but failed when they encountered new situations involving obstacles and traps. The fact that these same subjects were proficient in tasks requiring a choice between cane tools of varying shape, size, color, or material led Fujita et al. to argue that capuchins are able to appreciate relationships between items (namely, tool and reward), but they have difficulty mastering relationships among items (namely, tool, food, and a constraining environmental feature, such as a trap).

Visalberghi and Néel (2003) provide an example where experience acting on objects resulted in excellent discrimination by capuchin monkeys in a different kind of task. In terms of time and energy, opening an embedded food is a costly activity. Therefore, it is important for the monkey to determine, before opening it, whether a particular shell is empty or full. Visalberghi and Néel permitted the monkeys to choose one of two visually identical nuts to open. The nuts were hung on the side of the cage with string; the monkey could take one and the other was immediately removed. One of the nuts was empty (worthless); the other was full (valuable). Before making their choice, the capuchins lifted the nuts (presumably to judge their weight) and tapped the shells (presumably to listen). The monkeys could discriminate between nuts differing by as little as 2 to 3 gm, a 21 to 30% difference in weight. Either tapping or lifting was sufficient for accurate discrimination between the full and empty nuts. By their action, the monkeys produced information about the nuts that permitted them to make informed choices.

We suggest that the same processes apply to behavior in tool-using situations. Tool users act to produce information about objects and surfaces that guide further action. To the extent that the context permits effective production of salient information from their own action, capuchins are likely to master the problem.

The notion that individuals act to produce relevant perceptual information, and that this information guides further action and further learning, opens a new avenue for investigating how and when monkeys will master using objects as tools.

Figure 27.7. A capuchin monkey faces the choice of retrieving one of the two pieces of food with a hoe. Success depends on the type of surface the food must traverse. In the *lower panel*, the monkey is moving the hoe to collect a piece of food by sliding it across a solid, smooth surface (the surface on the monkey's left; on the right side of the picture) instead of trying to collect the piece of food placed behind a hole (the dark rectangle on the surface to the monkey's right; on the left side of the picture); in the *upper panel*, the monkey moves the food around the barrier (the raised block on the right) rather than toward the hole on the left. Coping with moving food past the hole posed a greater challenge to the monkeys than coping with moving food around the barrier. (Photographs courtesy of S. Cummins-Sebree.)

We anticipate an active program of research to investigate these ideas.

Behavioral and Environmental Factors Promoting and Constraining Tool Use

Captive capuchins' impressive achievements in using tools contrast sharply with the scarcity of reports of tool use by wild capuchins. What aspects of capuchins' behavior and ecology might result in the discovery of how to use an object as a tool? And conversely, what can constrain or prevent capuchins from using tools, or prevent the scientist from noticing it? Considering these questions may help us understand why captive and wild monkeys differ in tool use and may suggest new ways to look for tool use in wild capuchins.

Like other monkeys, capuchins possess sensory, anatomical, and behavioral characteristics that enable them to use objects as tools (e.g., they have grasping hands and stereoscopic vision, they coordinate vision and prehension, and they manipulate objects dexterously). In addition to these characteristics, as mentioned earlier in this chapter, capuchins possess behavioral characteristics that are less widely shared with other primates and that are particularly relevant to using objects as tools. Both wild and captive capuchins reliably and spontaneously combine objects with substrates and with other objects by pounding and rubbing; they also insert their hands and objects in holes and crevices (Boinski, Quatrone, & Swartz 2001; Fragaszy, 1986; Fragaszy & Adams-Curtis, 1991; Janson & Boinski, 1992; Panger, 1998). These actions are sufficient to support the discovery of tool use by captive capuchins (Visalberghi, 1987). When captive capuchins encounter objects they consider benign, whether novel or familiar, they quickly approach, explore, and manipulate them enthusiastically. Interest in objects, even familiar ones, persists over time (Visalberghi, 1988; Westergaard & Fragaszy, 1985). On encountering an interesting set of objects or an interesting substrate with loose objects available, and with the time and security to investigate, a capuchin monkey will reliably produce actions with objects on surfaces. This form of activity is more likely when the monkey is on the ground, so that the object does not fall out of reach when the monkey drops it (as would occur if the monkey is in a tree), when a substrate to bang the object against is easily within reach, and when the monkey itself is at no risk of falling.

These optimal conditions are less likely to be present for wild capuchins (Visalberghi, 1993), which do not respond as enthusiastically to novel objects as do captive monkeys (Visalberghi, Janson, & Agostini, 2003). Capuchins' arboreal lifestyle limits their opportunities to manipulate objects and makes the use of objects as tools more challenging. When in the trees, capuchins' hands are more often needed for support, loose objects that could be used as tools are less available and are less easily set aside and retrieved, and stable, strong, and appropriately shaped supporting substrates are less available than on the ground. Although arboreality may limit opportunities, it does not preclude tool use as both chimpanzees and orangutans do sometimes use tools in trees (Boesch & Boesch-Achermann, 2000; van Schaik, 2003; van Schaik, Fox, & Sitompul, 1996). Finally, capuchins have not yet been studied extensively in the wild and activities carried out high in the forest canopy are more difficult for terrestrial humans to view than activities occurring on the ground (but see later). All of these points may account for the rarity of observations of tool use in wild capuchins.

Let us now consider the circumstances under which wild capuchins should be expected to use tools. Tool using would provide an alternative feeding strategy when other important resources are scarce. For example, the exploitation of nuts and the pith of oil palms (*Elais guineensis*) by wild chimpanzees in Bossou (Guinea, West Africa) is strongly negatively correlated with the availability of fruit (Yamakoshi, 1998). Visalberghi (1997) argued that the general disposition to act with objects that leads capuchins to use tools for exploiting embedded food resources is more likely when readily available foods are scarce or undesirable. In addition, using a tool is more likely when direct pounding or biting does not suffice (Visalberghi & Vitale, 1990). Thus, we should expect to find capuchins using tools when seasonal reductions in fruit availability are particularly harsh and an embedded food that is difficult to open is abundant or highly desirable due to its nutritional value, or when the diversity of foods is consistently low and an embedded food is an important staple item in the diet.

Evidence supporting this view is slowly accumulating. The few reports of wild capuchins using tools are all cases in which easily obtained food was scarce or abundant food was very difficult to obtain. Fernandes (1991, p. 530) argues that the ability to open oysters by using a tool allowed capuchins to be "the only permanent primate resident" in the mangrove swamp he surveyed. There is strong, but indirect evidence (remains of Syagrus nuts on and near stones on the ground in areas where tufted capuchin monkeys ranged) that, during a period of severe drought, wild *C. apella* used stones to pound open nuts (Langguth & Alonso, 1997). We expect that, as we look more widely at wild capuchins in areas where they search for encased foods on the ground, we may find additional populations of monkeys using stones as tools to pound open hard foods.

In short, the strong motivation imposed by harsh ecological conditions, a certain degree of terrestriality, and the ready availability of stones and hard surfaces on which to place the embedded food to be pounded all favor the emergence of using tools to open hard foods. Tool use, in turn, may give capuchins a chance to inhabit otherwise inhospitable areas and to deal with seasonal changes in food availability.

CONCLUDING REMARKS

Tool use among nonhuman animals will certainly remain of interest to behavioral scientists for many reasons for years to come. Nevertheless, in part because it is of interest to so many communities for diverse reasons, there is more discussion about tool use than research on the topic; indeed, we find the literature on tool use, as a whole, to be theory poor.

For most of the twentieth century, studies of tool use in animals were descriptive or documentary. Documentary studies will remain important (i.e., reports of new discoveries from the field that individuals of a particular species use an object as a tool, such as van Schaik & Knott, 2001, for orangutans; Hunt, 1996, and Weir, Chappell, & Kacelnik, 2002, for New Caledonian crows). However, we have entered a new millenium and it is time to face a new challenge. The challenge for the field of comparative cognition that we are now in a position to address is understanding the origins and mechanisms that support the use of tools in diverse species. This task requires theoretically driven empirica, and particularly experimental investigations. There is no comprehensive "theory of tool use" to guide us. Instead, theoretical treatments of tool use, particularly by nonhuman primates, have included adaptations of Piagetian theory by Parker and colleagues (Parker & Gibson, 1977; Parker, Langer, & McKinney, 2000; Parker & Potì, 1990) and Antinucci (1989), innate knowledge and causal comprehension theory by Visalberghi and Tomasello (1998) and Povinelli (2000), and hierarchical ordering theories by Greenfield (1991) and Matsuzawa (2001).

We have proposed using perception-action theory, offered some examples of research with capuchin monkeys based on this theory, and applied it post-hoc to previous studies with capuchins (see table 27.1). This theory seems to us to offer promising new directions for comparative research. We suggest that theoretical diversity is a healthy state for the field at this time; we look forward to continuing experimental work guided by several theoretical orientations.

Where should research on tool use in capuchins go in the near future? Three directions seem to us to be very promising. First, descriptive studies of tool use and other forms of combinatorial behavior by wild capuchins (e.g., Boinski et al., 2001; Panger, 1998) will continue to be enormously important to our understanding of developmental processes and functional consequences of these activities.

Second, we look forward to the start of experimental studies on tool use at field sites where this is permissible. Ottoni and colleagues (Ottoni & Mannu, 2001; Resende & Ottoni, 2002) have begun such a line of work. A site where capuchins are provisioned and provided with opportunities to use tools could create a natural laboratory of the kind that Matsuzawa and colleagues have done at Bossou (Inoue-Nakumura & Matsuzawa, 1997; Matsuzawa et al., 2001). Natural laboratories provide opportunities for many kinds of longitudinal, developmental, and experimental studies, such as investigating how animals cope with altered conditions (new kinds of nuts or tools, altered abundance or distribution, etc.). Moreover, naturally occurring phenomena, such as immigration of skillful individuals into groups whose members do not use tools in the same manner, can tell us about the contribution of social context to skill development in a natural setting. Overall, the more comparable data we have obtained on wild capuchins and wild chimpanzees, the more powerful will be our comparisons of these two tool-using genera. We are now beginning to collect such data.

Third, we look forward to experimental studies in the laboratory using perception-action theory to examine how capuchins detect, produce, and modulate spatial relations among objects. In general, this theory directs our attention to the physical and perceptual challenges of using objects as tools. One can ask, for example, how monkeys progress from banging a hard object erratically on a nut and the surface surrounding the nut, to carefully modulated, accurate strikes that break the nut efficiently. Or, one can ask what features of the repertoire contribute to initial discoveries of useful relational properties, how easily the monkeys learn to detect and produce appropriate spatial relations, and so forth. We know virtually nothing about these topics at present for any nonhuman species. We are particularly interested in the possibility that producing and sustaining dynamic and static relations pose differential challenges to the monkeys. One of the advantages of this line of investigation is that it leads naturally to links with neuroscience, biomechanics, morphology, and related fields in the life sciences.

A final thought: Seeking compatible explanations for behavioral phenomena at multiple levels (mechanism, function, development, and evolution) invigorates the field of animal behavior (Kamil, 1998). Comparative cognition would do well to follow the model of the larger field of animal behavior and work to maintain multiple levels of explanation and multiple links with other fields. Researchers interested in tool use in nonhuman species should keep this in mind.

Acknowledgments This work was supported by grants from the Italian Ministry of Education, University and Research (MIUR/FIRB) to Elisabetta Visalberghi and from the National Science Foundation to Dorothy Fragaszy. The authors thank J. Lockman, H. Takeshita, and S. Itakura for discussions about the model of tool use presented in table 27.1.

Notes

1. This view of tool use is similar in many respects to those presented by Greenfield (1991).

2. Hauser (1997) tested cotton-top tamarins (*Saguinus oedipus*) in a choice paradigm (previously adopted by Brown, 1990, to test human infants), and Povinelli (2000) used the same paradigm with chimpanzees. In these studies, the subject had to choose between objects to retrieve a reward. The choice, not the actual use of the object as tool, was the dependent variable used to evaluate the monkeys' representation of the functionally relevant features of a tool. Santos and co-workers (in press) used looking time to test whether tamarins and rhesus (*Macaca mulatta*) distinguished between relevant and irrelevant features of a tool. In Hauser and Santos's studies, macaques and tamarins reliably distinguished relevant and irrelevant features of objects that could be used to pull in food. As mentioned earlier, we consider the two variables of choice and looking time to indicate something about the subjects' interest in objects or events but not about tool use per se.

References

Adams-Curtis, L. (1990). Conceptual learning in capuchin monkeys. *Folia primatologica, 54*, 129–137.

Anderson, J. (1996). Chimpanzees and capuchin monkeys: Comparative cognition. In A. Russon, K. Bard, & S. Parker (Eds.), *Reaching into thought. The minds of the great apes* (pp. 23–55). Cambridge: Cambridge University Press.

Anderson, J. R. (1990). Use of objects as hammers to open nuts by capuchin monkeys (*Cebus apella*). *Folia Primatologica, 54*, 138–145.

Anderson, J. R., & Henneman, M. C. (1994). Solutions to a tool-use problem in a pair of *Cebus apella*. *Mammalia, 58*, 351–361.

Antinucci, F. (1989). *Cognitive structure and development in nonhuman primates*. Hillsdale, NJ: Erlbaum.

Antinucci, F., & Visalberghi, E. (1986). Tool use in *Cebus apella*: A case study. *International Journal of Primatology*, *7*, 351–363.

Baker, M. (1996). Fur rubbing: Use of medicinal plants by capuchin monkeys (*Cebus capucinus*). *American Journal of Primatology, 38*, 263–270.

Beck, B. B. (1973). Observation learning of tool use by captive Guinea baboons (Papio papio). *American Journal of Physical Anthropology, 38*, 579–582.

Beck, B. B. (1980). *Animal tool behavior*. New York: Garland Press.

Boesch, C., & Boesch-Achermann, H. (2000). *The chimpanzees of the Taï Forest*. Oxford: Oxford University Press.

Boinski, S. (1988). Use of a club by wild white-faced capuchin (*Cebus capucinus*) to attack a venomous snake (*Bothrops asper*). *American Journal of Primatology, 14*, 177–179.

Boinski, S., Quatrone, R. P., & Swartz, H. (2001). Substrate and tool use by brown capuchins in Suriname: Ecological contexts and cognitive bases. *American Anthropologist, 102*, 741–761.

Brown, A. (1990). Domain-specific principles affect learning and transfer in children. *Cognitive Science, 14*, 107–133.

Chevalier-Skolnikoff, S. (1989). Spontaneous tool use and sensorimotor intelligence in *Cebus* compared with other monkeys and apes. *Behavioral and Brain Sciences, 12*, 561–627.

Chevalier-Skolnikoff, S. (1990). Tool use by wild Cebus monkeys at Santa Rosa National Park, Costa Rica. *Primates, 31*, 375–383.

Cummins, S. E. (1999). *Detection of environmental constraints in a tool-use task by tufted capuchins monkeys* (Cebus apella). Unpublished master's thesis, University of Georgia, Athens, GA.

Cummins-Sebree, S. E., & Fragaszy, D. M. (2005). Detecting environmental constraints during toll-use by capuchin monkeys (*Cebus apella*). Manuscript in preparation.

D'Amato, M. R., & Salmon, D. P. (1984). Cognitive processes in Cebus monkeys. In H. L. Roitblat, T. G. Bever, & H. S. Terrace (Eds.), *Animal Cognition* (pp. 149–168). Hillsdale, NJ: Erlbaum.

Dampier, W. (1697). A new voyage round the world. London: J. Knapton, at the Crown in St. Paul's Church-yard.

Darwin, C. (1794). *Zoonomia or laws of organic life*. London: J. Johnson.

De Lillo, C., & Visalberghi, E. (1994). Transfer index and mediational learning in tufted capuchins (*Cebus apella*). *International Journal of Primatology, 15*, 275–286.

de Oviedo, F. G. (1526/1996). *Sumario de la natural historia de las Indias*. Biblioteca Americana. Fondo de Cultura Económica (279 pp; first edition, Toledo, Spain, 1526).

Dubois, M., Gerard, J. F., Sampaio, E., Galvão, O., & Guilhem, C. (2001). Spatial facilitation in a probing task in *Cebus olivaceus*. *International Journal of Primatology, 22*, 991–1006.

Fernandes, E. B. M. (1991). Tool use and predation of oysters (*Crassostrea rhizophorae*) by the tufted capuchin, *Cebus apella apella*, in brackish water mangrove swamp. *Primates, 32*, 529–531.

Fragaszy, D. (1986). Time budgets and foraging behavior in wedge-capped capuchins (*Cebus olivaceus*): age and sex differences. In D. Taub & F. King (Eds.), *Current perspectives in primate social dynamics* (pp. 159–174). New York: Van Nostrand.

Fragaszy, D., Fedigan, L., & Visalberghi, E. (2004). *The complete capuchin: The biology of the genus* Cebus. Cambridge: Cambridge University Press.

Fragaszy, D., Izar P., Visalberghi, E., Ottoni, E., & Gomes de Oliveira, M. (2004). Wild capuchin monkeys (*Cebus libidinosus*) use anvils and stone pounding tools. *American Journal of Primatology, 64*, 359–366.

Fragaszy, D., & Visalberghi, E. (1989). Social influences on the acquisition and use of tools in tufted capuchin monkeys (*Cebus apella*). *Journal of Comparative Psychology, 103*, 159–170.

Fragaszy, D., & Visalberghi, E. (2004). Socially biased learning in monkeys. *Learning & Behavior, 32*, 24–35.

Fragaszy, D. M., & Adams-Curtis, L. E. (1991). Generative aspects of manipulation in tufted capuchin monkeys (*Cebus apella*). *Journal of Comparative Psychology, 105*, 387–397.

Fragaszy, D. M., Vitale, A. F., & Ritchie, B. (1994). Variation among juvenile capuchins in social influences on exploration. *American Journal of Primatology, 32*, 249–260.

Fujita, K., Kuroshima, H., & Asai, S. (2003) How do tufted capuchin monkeys (*Cebus apella*) understand causality involved in tool use? *Journal of Experimental Psychology, 29*, 233–242.

Garber, P. A., & Brown, E. (2004). Wild capuchins (*Cebus capucinus*) fail to use tools in an experimental field study. *American Journal of Primatology, 62*, 165–170.

Garber, P. A., & Paciulli, L. (1997). Experimental field study of spatial memory and learning in wild capuchin monkeys (*Cebus capucinus*). *Folia Primatologica, 68*, 236–253.

Gibson, E. J., & Pick, A. D. (2000). *An ecological approach to perceptual learning and development*. New York: Oxford University Press.

Gibson, J. J. (1966). *The senses considered as perceptual systems*. Boston: Houghton-Mifflin.

Gibson, J. J. (1979). *The ecological approach to visual perception*. Boston: Houghton-Mifflin.

Gibson, K. R. (1990). Tool use, imitation, and deception in a captive Cebus monkey. In S. Parker & K. Gibson (Eds.), *"Language" and intelligence in monkeys and apes* (pp. 205–218). Cambridge: Cambridge University Press.

Greenfield, P. M. (1991). Language, tools, and the brain: The ontogeny and phylogeny of hierarchically organized sequential behavior. *Behavioral and Brain Sciences, 14*, 531–595.

Groves, C. P. (2001). *Primate taxonomy*. Washington, DC: Smithsonian Institution Press.

Hauser, M. (1997). Artifactual kinds and functional design features: What a primate understands without language. *Cognition, 64*, 285–308.

Hernández-Camacho, J., & Cooper, R. W. (1976). The nonhuman primates of Colombia. In R. W. Thorington & P. G. Heltne (Eds.),

Neotropical primates: Field studies and conservation (pp. 35–69). Washington, DC: National Academy of Sciences.

Hihara, S., Obayashi, S., Tanaka, M., & Iriki, A. (2003). Rapid learning of sequential tool use by macaque monkeys. *Physiology and Behavior, 78*, 427–434.

Hill, W. C. O. (1960). *Primates. Vol. 4: Cebidae, part A*. Edinburgh: Edinburgh University Press.

Hunt, G. R. (1996). Manufacture and use of hook-tools by Caledonian crows. *Nature, 379*, 249–251.

Inoue-Nakamura, N., & Matsuzawa, T. (1997). Development of stone tool use by wild chimpanzees (*Pan troglodytes*). *Journal of Comparative Psychology, 111*, 159–173.

Jalles-Filho, E., da Cunha R. G. T., & Salm, R. A. (2001). Transport of tools and mental representation: Is capuchin monkey tool behavior a useful model for Plio-Pleistocene hominid technology? *Journal of Human Evolution, 40*, 365–377.

Janson, C. H., & Boinski, S. (1992). Morphological and behavioral adaptations for foraging in generalist primates: The case of the Cebines. *American Journal of Physical Anthropology, 88*, 483–498.

Kamil, A. C. (1998). On the proper definition of cognitive ethology. In R. P. Balda, I. M. Pepperberg, & A. C. Kamil (Eds.), *Animal cognition in nature* (pp. 1–28). London: Academic Press.

Klüver, H. (1933). *Behavior mechanisms in monkeys*. Chicago: Chicago University Press.

Klüver, H. (1937). Re-examination of implement-using behavior in a Cebus monkey after an interval of three years. *Acta Psychologica, 2*, 347–397.

Langguth, A., & Alonso, C. (1997). Capuchin monkeys in the Caatinga: Tool use and food habits during drought. *Neotropical Primates, 5*, 77–78.

Lavallee, A. C. (1999). Capuchin (*Cebus apella*) tool use in a captive naturalistic environment. *International Journal of Primatology, 20*, 399–414.

Limongelli, L., Boysen, S., & Visalberghi, E. (1995). Comprehension of cause and effect relationships in a tool-using task by common chimpanzees (*Pan troglodytes*). *Journal of Comparative Psychology, 109*, 18–26.

Lockman, J. J. (2000). A perception-action perspective on tool use development. *Child Development, 71*, 137–144.

Matsuzawa, T. (1994). Field experiments on use of stone tools by chimpanzees in the wild. In R. W. Wrangham, W. C. McGrew, F. B. M. de Waal, & P. G. Heltne (Eds.), *Chimpanzee cultures* (pp. 351–370). Cambridge, MA: Harvard University Press.

Matsuzawa, T. (2001). Primate foundations of human intelligence: A view of tool use in nonhuman primates and fossil hominids. In T. Matsuzawa (Ed.), *Primate origins of human cognition and behavior* (pp. 3–25). Tokyo: Springer-Verlag.

Matsuzawa, T., Biro, D., Humle, T., Inoue-Nakamura, N., Tonooka, R., & Yamakoshi, G. (2001). Emergence of culture in wild chimpanzees: Education by master-apprenticeship. In T. Matsuzawa (Ed.), *Primate origin of cognition and behavior* (pp. 557–574). Tokyo: Springer.

Mendes, F. D. C., Martins, L. B. R., Pereira, J. A., & Marquezan, R. F. (2000). Fishing with a bait: A note on behavioral flexibility in *Cebus apella*. *Folia Primatologica, 71*, 350–352.

Natale, F. (1989). Causality. II: The stick problem. In F. Antinucci (Ed.), *Cognitive structure and development in nonhuman primates* (pp. 121–133). Hillsdale, NJ: Erlbaum.

Nolte, A. (1958). Beobachtungen über das Instinktverhalten von Kapuzzineraffen (*Cebus apella* L.) in der Gefangenschaft. *Behaviour, 12*, 183–207.

Ottoni, E. B., & Mannu, M. (2001). Semi-free ranging tufted capuchin monkeys (*Cebus apella*) spontaneously use tools to crack open nuts. *International Journal of Primatology, 22*, 347–358.

Oxford, P. (2003). Cracking monkeys. *BBC Wildlife, 21*, 26–29.

Panger, M. A. (1998). Object-use in free-ranging white-faced capuchins (*Cebus capucinus*) in Costa Rica. *American Journal of Physical Anthropology, 106*, 311–321.

Parker, S. T., & Gibson, K. R. (1977). Object manipulation, tool use and sensorimotor intelligence as feeding adaptations in Cebus monkeys and great apes. *Journal of Human Evolution, 6*, 623–641.

Parker, S. T., & Gibson, K. R. (1979). A developmental model for the evolution of language and intelligence in early hominids. *Behavioral and Brain Sciences, 2*, 367–408.

Parker, S. T., Langer, J., & McKinney, M. L. (Eds.). (2000). *Biology, brains, and behavior: The evolution of human development*. Santa Fe, NM: SAR Press.

Parker, S. T., & Potì, P. (1990). The role of innate motor patterns in ontogenetic and experiential development of intelligent use of sticks in Cebus monkeys. In S. T. Parker & K. R. Gibson (Eds.), *"Language" and intelligence in monkeys and apes: Comparative developmental perspectives* (pp. 219–243). New York: Cambridge University Press.

Phillips, K. A. (1998). Tool use in wild capuchin monkeys (*Cebus albifrons trinitatis*). *American Journal of Primatology, 46*, 259–261.

Povinelli, D. J. (2000). *Folk physics for apes: The chimpanzee's theory of how the world works.* Oxford: Oxford University Press.

Reaux, J. E., & Povinelli, D. J. (2000). The trap-tube problem. In D. J. Povinelli (Ed.), *Folk physics for apes: The chimpanzee's theory of how the world works* (pp. 108–131). Oxford: Oxford University Press.

Resende, B. D., & Ottoni, E. B. (2002). *Ontogeny of nutcracking behavior in a semifree-ranging group of tufted capuchin monkeys.* Poster presented at the XIX International Primatological Society Meeting, Beijing, China, August 4–9.

Ritchie, B. G., & Fragaszy, D. M. (1988). Capuchin monkey (*Cebus apella*) grooms her infant's wound with tools. *American Journal of Primatolology, 16*, 345–348.

Rocha, J. V., dos Reis, N. R., & Sekiama, M. L. (1998). Uso de ferramentas por *Cebus apella* (Linnaeus) (Primates, Cebidae) para obtenção de larvas de Coleoptera que parasitam sementes de *Syagrus romanzoffianum* (Cham.) Glassm. (Arecaceae). *Revista Brasileira de Zoologia, 15*, 945–950.

Romanes, G. J. (1883/1977). *Significant contributions to the history of psychology 1750-1920.* Washington: University Publications of America (first edition 1883).

Rylands, A. B., Schneider, H., Mittermeier, R. A., Groves, C. P., & Rodriguez-Luna, E. (2000). An assessment of the diversity of new world primates. *Neotropical Primates 8*, 61–93.

Santos, L. R., Miller C. T., & Hauser, M. D. (2003). Representing tools: how two nonhuman primate species distinguish between the functionally relevant and irrelevant features of a tool. *Animal Cognition, 6*, 269–281.

Tomasello, M., & Call, J. (1997). *Primate cognition.* Oxford: Oxford University Press.

Ueno, Y., & Fujita, K. (1998). Spontaneous tool use by a Tonkean macaque (*Macaca tonkeana*). *Folia Primatologica, 69*, 318–324.

Urbani, B. (1998). An early report on tool use by neotropical primates. *Neotropical Primates, 6*, 123–124.

Urbani, B. (1999). Spontaneous use of tools by wedge-capped capuchin monkeys (*Cebus olivaceus*). *Folia Primatologica, 70*, 172–174.

Valderrama, X., Robinson, J. G., Attygalle, A. B., & Eisner, T. (2000). Seasonal anointment with millipedes in a wild primate: A chemical defense against insect? *Journal of Chemical Ecology, 26*, 2781–2790.

van Schaik, C. P. (2003). Local traditions in orangutans and chimpanzees: Social learning and social tolerance. In D. Fragaszy & S. Perry (Eds.), *Traditions in nonhuman animals: models and evidence* (pp. 297–328). Cambridge: Cambridge University Press.

van Schaik, C. P., Fox, E. A., & Sitompul, A. F. (1996). Manufacture and use of tools in wild Sumatran orangutans. *Naturwissenschaften, 83*, 186–188.

van Schaik, C. P., & Knott, C. D. (2001). Geographic variation in tool use on *Neesia* fruits in orangutans. *American Journal of Physical Anthropology, 114*, 331–342.

Visalberghi, E. (1987). Acquisition of nut-cracking behavior by 2 capuchin monkeys (*Cebus apella*). *Folia Primatologica, 49*, 168–181.

Visalberghi, E. (1988). Responsiveness to objects in two social groups of tufted capuchin monkeys (*Cebus apella*). *American Journal of Primatology, 15*, 349–360.

Visalberghi, E. (1990). Tool use in *Cebus*. *Folia Primatologica, 54*, 146–154.

Visalberghi, E. (1993). Tool use in a South American monkey species: An overview of the characteristics and limits of tool use in *Cebus apella*. In A. Berthelet & J. Chavaillon (Eds.), *The use of tools by human and non-human primates* (pp. 118–131). Oxford: Clarendon Press.

Visalberghi, E. (1997). Success and understanding in cognitive tasks: A comparison between *Cebus apella* and *Pan troglodytes*. *International Journal of Primatology, 18*, 811–830.

Visalberghi, E. (2000). Tool use behaviour and the understanding of causality in primates. In E. Thommen & H. Kilcher (Eds.), *Comparer ou prédire: Exemples de recherches en psychologie comparative aujourd'hui* (pp. 17–35). Fribourg, Switzerland: Les Editions Universitaires.

Visalberghi, E., Fragaszy, D. M., & Savage-Rumbaugh, S. (1995). Performance in a tool-using task by common chimpanzees (*Pan troglodytes*), bonobos (*Pan paniscus*), and orangutan (*Pongo pygmaeus*), and capuchin monkeys (*Cebus apella*). *Journal of Comparative Psychology, 109*, 52–60.

Visalberghi, E., Janson, C. H., & Agostini, I. (2003). Response towards novel foods and novel objects in wild tufted capuchins (*Cebus apella*). *International Journal of Primatology, 24*, 653–675.

Visalberghi, E., & Limongelli, L. (1992). *Experiments on the comprehension of a tool-use task in tufted capuchin monkeys* (Cebus apella). Video presented at XIV Congress of the International Primatological Society, August 16–21, 1992, Strasbourg, France.

Visalberghi, E., & Limongelli, L. (1994). Lack of comprehension of cause-effect relations in tool-using capuchin monkeys (*Cebus apella*). *Journal of Comparative Psychology, 108*, 15–22.

Visalberghi E., & Limongelli L. (1996). Action and understanding: Tool use revisited through the mind of capuchin monkeys. In A. Russon, K. Bard, & S. Parker (Eds.), *Reaching into thought: The minds of the great apes* (pp. 57–79). Cambridge: Cambridge University Press.

Visalberghi, E., & Néel C. (2003). Tufted capuchins (*Cebus apella*) use of sound and weight to optimise their choice between full and empty nuts. *Ecological Psychology, 15*, 215–228.

Visalberghi, E., & Tomasello, M. (1998). Primate causal understanding in the physical and in the social domains. *Behavioural Processes, 42*, 189–203.

Visalberghi, E., & Trinca, L. (1989). Tool use in capuchin monkeys: Distinguishing between performing and understanding. *Primates, 30*, 511–521.

Visalberghi, E., & Vitale, A. F. (1990). Coated nuts as an enrichment device to elicit tool use in tufted capuchins (*Cebus apella*). *Zoo Biology, 9*, 65–71.

Want, S., & Harris, P. L. (2001). Learning from other people's mistakes. *Child Development, 72*, 431–443.

Watson, J. (1908). Imitation in monkeys. *Psychological Bulletin, 5*, 169–178.

Weir, A. S., Chappell, J., & Kacelnik, A. (2002). Shaping of hooks in New Caledonian crows. *Science, 297*, 981–981.

Westergaard, G. C. (1988). Lion-tailed macaques (*Macaca silenus*) manufacture and use tools. *Journal of Comparative Psychology, 102*, 152.

Westergaard, G. C., Chavanne, T. J., & Suomi, S. J. (1998). Token-mediated tool-use by tufted capuchin monkey (*Cebus apella*). *Animal Cognition, 1*, 101–106.

Westergaard, G. C., & Fragaszy, D. M. (1985). Effects of manipulatable objects on the activity of captive capuchin monkeys (*Cebus apella*). *Zoo Biology, 4*, 317–327.

Westergaard, G. C., & Fragaszy, D. M. (1987a). The manufacture and use of tools by capuchin monkeys (*Cebus apella*). *Journal of Comparative Psychology, 101*, 159–168.

Westergaard, G. C., & Fragaszy, D. M. (1987b). Self-treatment of wounds by a capuchin monkey (*Cebus apella*). *Human Evolution, 1*, 557–562.

Westergaard, G. C., Greene, J. A., Babitz, M. A., & Suomi, S. J. (1995). Pestle use and modification by tufted capuchins (*Cebus apella*). *International Journal of Primatology, 16*, 643–651.

Westergaard, G. C., Greene, J. A., Menuhin-Hauser, C., & Suomi, S. J. (1996). The emergence of naturally-occurring copper and iron tools by monkeys: Possible implications for the emergence of metal-tool technology in hominids. *Human Evolution, 11*, 17–25.

Westergaard, G. C., Lundquist, A. L., Haynie, M. K., Kuhn, H. E., & Suomi, S. J. (1998). Why some capuchin monkeys (*Cebus apella*) use probing tools (and others do not). *Journal of Comparative Psychology, 112*, 207–211.

Westergaard, G. C., Lundquist, A. L., Kuhn, H. E., & Suomi, S. J. (1997). Ant-gathering with tools by captive tufted capuchins (*Cebus apella*). *International Journal of Primatology, 18*, 95–104.

Westergaard, G. C., & Suomi, S. J. (1993). Use of a tool-set by capuchin monkeys (*Cebus apella*). *Primates, 34*, 459–462.

Westergaard, G. C., & Suomi, S. J. (1994a). Aimed throwing of stones by tufted capuchin monkeys (*Cebus apella*). *Human Evolution, 9*, 323–329.

Westergaard, G. C., & Suomi, S. J. (1994b). A simple stone-tool technology in monkeys. *Journal of Human Evolution, 27*, 399–404.

Westergaard, G. C., & Suomi, S. J. (1994c). Stone-tool bone-surface modification by monkeys. *Current Anthropology, 35*, 468–470.

Westergaard, G. C., & Suomi, S. J. (1994d). The use and modification of bone tools by capuchin monkeys. *Current Anthropology, 35*, 75–77.

Westergaard, G. C., & Suomi, S. J. (1995a). The manufacture and use of bamboo tools by monkeys: Possible implications for the development of material culture among east Asian hominids. *Journal of Archeological Science, 22*, 677–681.

Westergaard, G. C., & Suomi, S. J. (1995b). The production and use of digging tools by monkeys: A nonhuman primate model of a hominid subsistence activity. *Journal of Anthropological Research, 51*, 1–8.

Westergaard, G. C., & Suomi, S. J. (1995c). Stone-throwing by capuchins (*Cebus apella*): A model of throwing capabilities in *Homo habilis*. *Folia Primatologica, 65*, 234–238.

Westergaard, G. C., & Suomi, S. J. (1997). Transfer of tools and food between groups of tufted capuchins (*Cebus apella*). *American Journal of Primatology, 43*, 33–41.

Yamakoshi, G. (1998). Dietary responses to fruit scarcity of wild chimpanzees at Bossou, Guinea: Possible implications for ecological importance of tool use. *American Journal of Physical Anthropology, 106*, 283–295.

Zuberbühler, K., Gygax, L., Harley, N., & Kummer, H. (1996). Stimulus enhancement and spread of a spontaneous tool use in a colony of long-tailed macaques. *Primates, 37*, 1–12.

IX

PROBLEM SOLVING AND BEHAVIORAL FLEXIBILITY

28

Intelligences and Brains: An Evolutionary Bird's Eye View

JUAN D. DELIUS AND JULIA A. M. DELIUS

Whenever reporting on the cognitive abilities of animals to lay audiences, one is regularly confronted with the question of whether one is suggesting that animals are, in fact, intelligent. The senior author has often found himself sidestepping this question. But, having taken over a seminar on intelligence in animals, humans, and machines, he could no longer evade it. Moreover, the participants complained that the seminar's readings conveyed a mere mass of disconnected knowledge. They wanted a succinct text that would organize the material. This chapter is an updated version of that text, which presents what the authors consider to be an interdisciplinary consensual overview of intelligence as a behavioral disposition displayed by some animals, humans included.

There has never been any doubt about the fact that the human species is the cleverest on Earth. However, there has been much preoccupation with the circumstance that not all human individuals are equally bright. In nearly all areas of human endeavor, it is appreciated that the degree of cleverness or stupidity of an individual is a factor that defines the efficiency with which (s)he can execute all but the most routine tasks. This efficiency is mostly judged by the accuracy, the speed, and the effortlessness with which a person can solve everyday problems. These problems might involve finding the way in unknown terrain with a map, baking a cake when ingredients and implements are lacking, assembling kit furniture without the instructions, or setting straight a muddled scientific text. Although there is no undisputed definition of intelligence, there is some consensus that it has to do with varying abilities to successfully adapt behavior to novel situations, or more abstractly, with varying capacities for a goal-conducive processing of cognitive information (Hunt, 1980).

A test that measured intelligence was first devised by Alfred Binet (1857–1911). Intelligence tests were steadily improved so that now several of them provide a consistent, replicable, and predictive measure of individual intellectual ability (Kaufman, 2000). Early tests tended to yield scores that were much influenced by the cultural background and the formal education that the subjects had experienced. Modern intelligence tests are designed to be largely insensitive to these factors. An extreme in this respect are the so-called Raven scales which are thought to give nearly ideal measures of the general intelligence of individuals independently of their particular expertises and also independently of their more special cognitive abilities (Snow, Kyllonen, & Marshalek, 1984). Figure 28.1 shows both an easy and a difficult example of Raven scale items. They must be solved quickly, as the full test consists of many such items and has to be completed in a limited time. These items have been designed so that their solution is unlikely to be influenced by previous knowledge that individuals might or might not have. The scales are constructed so that even extended experience with one

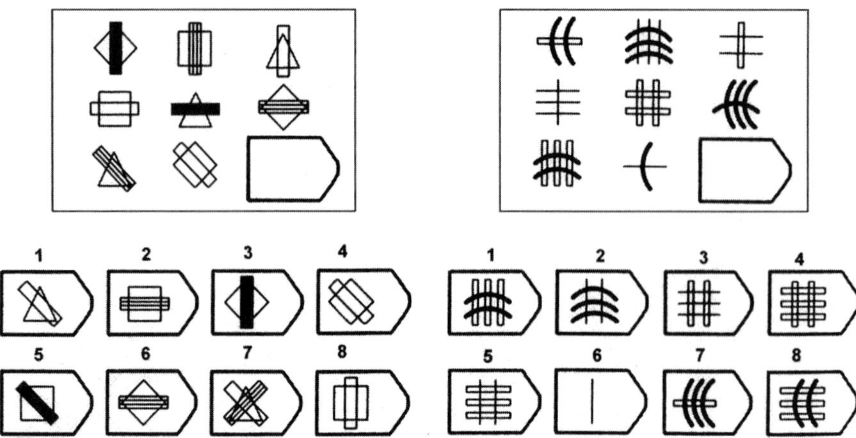

Figure 28.1. An easy item and a difficult item from the Raven intelligence scales. The gaps must be filled with one of the panels offered. (Based on Carpenter, Just, & Shell, 1990.)

version of them has only a negligible influence on how well one performs with the next version of them. The fact that the intelligence gauged by such tests is an ability that cannot be easily taught and learned is undoubtedly the source of widespread uneasiness. What the test measures is often felt not to correspond with the everyday connotations—whatever they precisely are—of the term *intelligence* (Lenz, 2000). Many textbooks of cognitive psychology avoid the subject of individual differences in cognitive competencies perhaps because of political correctness (e.g., Matlin, 2002; Medin, Ross, & Markman, 2001; but see Sternberg, 1996). The notion of innate individual differences seems to go against the fact that experience can improve one's performance with tasks such as improving texts or assembling furniture. On the other hand, some of us seem inherently good at drawing (or mathematics), but inherently poor at writing (or singing). We will return to these issues later.

ANIMAL INTELLIGENCES

Even before Darwin (1809–1882) proposed that one must look for the roots of human intellect in animals, their intelligence was of much practical interest. Shepherds and cowboys were aware of the differences in working intelligence among individual collies or horses. Older members of the senior author's laboratory still remember one extraordinary pigeon that could solve complex behavioral tasks within hours or days, problems that other pigeons would not solve within weeks or months. Because they are after universals rather than particulars, animal behavioral scientists have largely ignored the interindividual variations in cognitive capacities of their subjects (but see B. Anderson, 2000; Matzel et al., 2003). But also, anybody watching mountain sheep and macaque monkeys at the zoo is likely to be sure that the latter are more intelligent than the former. The same applies to more gross phyletic groups, such as birds being rated more clever than fishes (Nakajima, Arimatsu, & Lattal, 2002). Using more scientific methods, scholars have been interested in such interspecific differences as, for example, are dolphins more cognitively capable than monkeys? But the design of a universal test of animal intelligence has turned out to be difficult.

Learning Sets

Harry Harlow (1905–1981) and colleagues attempted to assess the intelligence of various species by judging how well they would acquire learning sets. The learning-to-learn procedure they used involved challenging individual animals with a series of discrimination learning problems, all of which were procedurally identical, but each involved new stimuli. For example, macaques first had to learn in repeated trials that lifting a toy car rather than a simultaneously presented toy airplane would reveal a hidden peanut reward. Next, they had to learn that a cup, but not a can, signaled reward, and so on with a number of "junk–object" pairs. The animals initially took a considerable number of trials with each pair of new objects before consistently picking the rewarded one, but, by about the 100th pair, the macaques had learned to choose correctly by the second trial with each novel pair (Warren, 1973). It was found that some species, foremost chimpanzees, showed near-perfect discrimination on the second pair after experience with only about a dozen stimulus pairs (Schusterman, 1964). Other species, such as the rat, only show minor improvements in this learning-to-learn task. The latter species were accordingly considered to be less intelligent than the former. Most 6- to 7-year-old schoolchildren are quicker than chimpanzees at acquiring this optimal strategy, needing only pre-experience with two or three pairs of stimuli, but apparently, whether the individual performance of children on this kind of task correlates with their test intelligence has not been examined (S. Buschio, personal communication). Learning-set tasks can be viewed as the learning of a special expertise that helps to solve a particular kind of problem but it is not quite what human intelligence tests attempt to measure (see later). Some work has been done on the learning-set task with nonmammalian species, and some bird species have done quite well (Kamil, Lougee, & Schulman, 1973; Plotnik & Tallarico, 1966).

There are data on a somewhat wider range of species for another task of a similar, but simpler nature: serial reversal learning (Warren, 1973). Subjects learn to discriminate a pair of stimuli as before, but once they have acquired the discrimination, instead of being confronted with a new pair, they continue with the same pair, now with the contingencies of reinforcement reversed. That is, if choices of A were rewarded and choices of B were not rewarded previously, choices of B are now rewarded and choices of A are not. When the subjects have learned to respond adequately to this reversal, the reinforcement allocation is reversed again, and so on. A cognitively gifted species can be expected to learn to behave according to the rule, "if a stimulus ceases to yield reward, switch to the other stimulus on the next trial." Indeed, most macaques manage to adopt such a strategy within a few reversals. Pigeons show improvements in learning the successive reversals, but never achieve such an immediate switching strategy (Delius, Ameling, Lea, & Staddon, 1995; Diekamp, Prior, & Güntürkün, 1999; Staddon & Frank, 1974). Some other bird species performed better on this task, achieving levels comparable to those of monkeys (Gossette & Gossette, 1967; Kamil, Jones, Pitrewicz, & Mauldin, 1977). Of a sample of 20 university students, many achieved nearly rule-like behavior after five reversals on a task involving the concurrent discrimination of two pairs of irregular polygons. However, a few students did not exhibit any significant performance improvements. Remarkably, among the successful students, several could not verbally explain at all what rule they had finally used (Siemann, von Selzam, & Borchert, 2004; see later).

According to an early study, rats show comparatively little learning-to-learn ability (Warren, 1973). The rats had been trained to jump toward a pair of doors bearing different visual patterns such as a triangle and a circle. The door displaying the triangle would, for example, be designated correct and open to give access to a food reward. The other displaying the circle would be the incorrect one and would be locked, the rats falling onto a net as a penalty. However, rats are night-active animals and are not well adapted for the recognition of visual patterns in daylight. When Slotnik and Katz (1974; see also Slotnick, Hanford, & Hodos, 2000) used different odors as stimuli and arranged a more suitable procedure, they found that rats were considerably more capable than originally judged. Unsurprisingly, rats were better with stimuli that they are better equipped to recognize. One can expect that humans, being relatively microsmatic, would conversely do worse on an olfactory test than on a visual test, even if the odors were chosen to be discriminable for them (cf. Danthiir, Roberts, Pallier, & Stankow, 2001). The point is that it is hard to design a testing situation that is sufficiently uniform to yield comparable measures while being equally appropriate to the perceptual, motivational, and motoric dispositions of species that are adapted to quite diverse environments. The difficulties are not unlike those arising when human psychologists attempt to design intelligence tests, which are also fair to motorically disabled or blind persons. The upshot of this conundrum is that behaviorists have largely given up trying to design a universal animal intelligence test. They have rather turned to examining the performance of animals on a wider range of cognitive tasks (Wasserman, 1993; Zentall, 2000).

Concept Formation

Being able to group different perceptual items under one cognitive category is undoubtedly a basic prerequisite for intelligent information processing. Humans' singular ability to form multifarious concepts is considered an essential element of our intellectual superiority. Interestingly, though, as research on humans has progressed, it has become ever less certain how concept formation should be operationally defined (Murphy, 2002). A capacity of categorizing items of somewhat diverse appearances as belonging (or not belonging) to a class is certainly a precursor to concept formation. Thus, we can recognize animals such as canaries, hummingbirds, penguins, and owls as belonging to the class of avians because they are all feathered and have a beak, two legs, and a pair of wings. It is well established that monkeys and pigeons are capable of similar classificatory feats, but it is less well established whether, for example, rats can do so, perhaps because human experimenters find it difficult to design corresponding tasks within the olfactory realm (Herrnstein, 1990).

A more abstract classification applies when humans, for example, group very different looking animals such as snails, aphids, geese, manatees, and giraffes as belonging to the class of herbivores on the basis of what they eat. This kind of item grouping is viewed as an instance of true concept formation (Sloman & Rips, 1998). Anagenetically advanced animals can associate different stimuli according to analogous functional criteria (Astley & Wasserman, 1999; Zentall, 1998). We ourselves have investigated the issue by training pigeons to discriminate two pairs of differently looking stimuli A+C– and B+D–, where + and – signify that the choice of the corresponding stimuli out of serially randomly presented pairs was rewarded and not rewarded, respectively. When the birds had learned to choose the positive stimuli, the reinforcement allocations were reversed: A–C+ and B–D+. As soon as the pigeons had switched their stimulus preferences, the reinforcement allocations were again reversed, and so on several times, until the birds had learned to quickly alter their stimulus choices. The birds were then tested to determine whether they had formed two functional classes involving the stimuli such that, if A was rewarded in a given session, B would be rewarded too, and if C was rewarded in another session, D would also be rewarded. For this test, a reinforcement reversal would begin with only one of the pairs being shown until the birds switched their choice behavior to it (the leading pair); only then would the other stimulus pair be presented (the trailing pair) to assess transfer of the choice reversal.

Figure 28.2 shows how well pigeons performed on the first three presentations of the leading pair after the reversal and how well they did on the first three trailing pair presentations after they had mastered the current reinforcement allocation on the leading pair. It is apparent that they did far better, though by no means perfectly, with the second pair than with the first pair (Delius, Jitsumori, & Siemann, 2000). This finding demonstrates that, because of the stimulus equivalencies learned, the pigeons could transfer short-term information acquired with the first pair to solve the task posed by the second pair. Using a more sophisticated version of the reversing reinforcement allocation and eight different stimuli, we could demonstrate that pigeons were able to conceptualize them as belonging to two different equivalence classes. We then added further stimuli to build up a network of equivalencies. The more capable pigeons—individual variations proved to be important here—were able to associate stimuli by their conjoint property of switching from yielding reward to yielding nonreward and back again (Jitsumori, Siemann, Lehr, & Delius, 2002).

Von Fersen and Delius (2001) taught two bottlenosed dolphins the basic serial-reversal task with two stimulus pairs. The dolphins easily succeeded in discriminating the visual stimuli, but they never showed any reversal transfer from one pair of stimuli to the other as the pigeons had done. However, when four auditory stimuli were used, the dolphins easily acquired the equivalence relations among them. With the auditory stimuli, their performance was better than that of the pigeons with visual stimuli. It is very unlikely that pigeons would perform better with auditory stimuli than with visual stimuli, as they are more adept at cognitively processing visual stimuli than auditory stimuli (Delius & Emmerton, 1978). It seems likely that much as rats were earlier suspected to be more cognitively capable with olfactory than with visual stimuli, dolphins may be more intelligent when

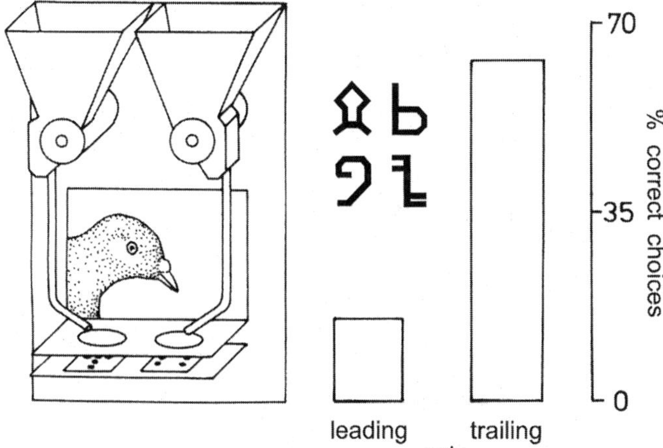

Figure 28.2. Concept formation according to functional equivalencies in pigeons. (Modified from Siemann, von Fersen, & Delius, 1998.)

dealing with auditory than with visual stimuli (Roitblat & von Fersen, 1992).

Siemann et al. (2004) found that, although university students were naturally more efficient than pigeons or dolphins at learning the basic discriminations constituting the serial reversal task, they still varied individually in their ability with tests involving equivalence class transfer. The students also differed considerably in their awareness of the task's logical structure, but the relation between the students' transfer performance and their test intelligence was not examined. Experiments using a different methodology have shown that mentally handicapped schoolchildren have considerably more difficulty forming equivalences than same-age controls (Sidman, 1992). In any case, these studies suggest that some behavioral tasks with which at least some birds and mammals can cope also challenge the cognitive competencies of younger or lesser gifted humans, even if it is not clear whether these competencies are those measured by intelligence tests.

What is obvious, however, is that the uniform assessment of the intelligence of animal species is made difficult by the different specializations that the various species have evolved. It is reasonable to speculate that the olfactory intelligence of rats is linked to their nocturnal way of life and that the auditory intelligence of dolphins is related to their sonar mode of orientation (Shettleworth, 1998). Similar ecological arguments have been proposed in connection with the presence of an enhanced memory competency in bird species that cache surplus food in many different locations for later, leaner times (Krebs, 1990; but see Macphail & Bolhuis, 2001). Indeed, this faculty appears to be associated with a relative enlargement of the hippocampus, a brain area that appropriately, among other things, is known to be involved in encoding the spatial layout of the environment. However, it is not altogether certain whether the latter enlargement is not a secondary ontogenetic adaptation (cf. Ekstrom et al., 2003; Maguire et al., 2000).

Transitive Responding

It is not immediately obvious that if $x<d$, $m>d$, and $f<x$, then it must follow that $f<m$. The more terms that are involved and the less well ordered the premises that are presented, the harder it is to draw the correct conclusions. Transitive inference problems of a similar nature have been designed so that they can be given to very young children or, indeed, to animals. In the simplest case, they learn over many trials to discriminate concurrently four overlapping pairs of five stimuli, A+B–, B+C–, C+D–, and D+E–, randomly ordered, until they achieve a criterion level of choice accuracy. Then, animals and children are presented with a test pair of stimuli not previously presented together, BoDo, without reinforcement (o) for their choice. If the subjects interpret the task in terms of a transitive inference problem ($A>B$, $B>C$, $C>D$, $D>E$), then they should prefer B to D. In fact, that is what subjects actually do (children, squirrel monkeys: Chalmers & McGonigle, 1984; pigeons: von Fersen, Wynne, Delius, & Staddon, 1991; cf. figure 28.3). Note that all three species did about equally well with test pair BoDo. However, the pigeons

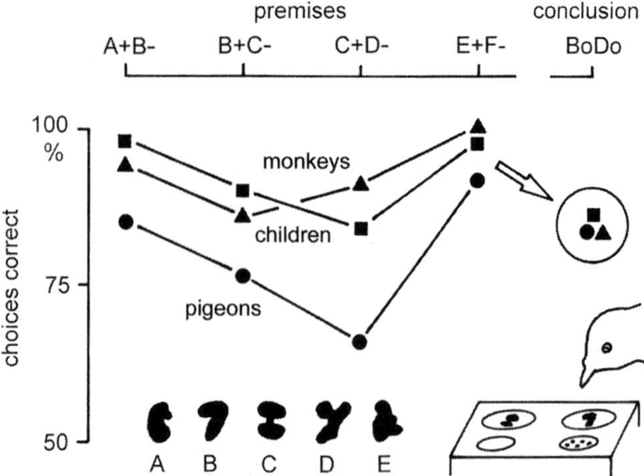

Figure 28.3. Transitive responding in pigeons, squirrel monkeys, and humans. (Based on Siemann, von Fersen, & Delius, 1998.)

took longer to learn the premise pairs than the monkeys, who took longer than the children.

Siemann and Delius (1998; see also Delius & Siemann, 1998) conducted analogous experiments with students. As reinforcements for correct and incorrect stimulus choices, students gained or lost symbolic coins. The students learned the premises far faster than pigeons or indeed children, but they were not much better on the conclusion pairs. When faced with the test pairs, two thirds of the students did quite well, but about one third of the students chose randomly. Interestingly, these failures were not linked with lower test intelligence. Rather, it appeared that these individuals had learned to correctly respond to the various stimulus pairs (AB, BC, etc.) as compound patterns without attending to the fact that the component elements (B for example) recurred in different pairs. When later faced with BoDo conclusion pairs, these students did not have any ready response to these new compound stimuli. It is likely that an enhanced capacity for configural perception is a part of human intelligence (Matsumoto Ohigashi, Fujimori, & Mori, 2000), but here it was counterproductive because it could not provide the information needed to solve the problem.

Questionnaires after the experiment revealed that about half of the students who solved the test pairs were aware of the logical structure of the inference task but that the other half were not. Nevertheless, the students with an explicit understanding did not perform better than did the ones without. We assume that the former—despite knowing about the principle on which the task was based—could not bring this explicit knowledge to bear because of the requirement to choose as fast as possible (cf. Greene, Spellman, Dusek, Eichenbaum, & Levy, 2001). The deliberative reasoning that would be needed is [illegible]vely slow process that could not be applie[illegible] the short reaction times recorded (about [illegible] Leighton & Sternberg, 2003). Indeed it [illegible] that the transitive inference problem pr[illegible] here mainly challenges the efficiency of [illegible]rm learning mechanisms rather than t[illegible]ty of the working memory system with [illegible] intelligence tests are mainly concerned (se[illegible] Nevertheless, it is remarkable that pigeon[illegible] outperform humans on this task.

Just as primates stand out intellectually among mammals, parrots and corvids tend to stand out among birds. The productive language feats by African grey parrots (Pepperberg, 1999) and the insightful problem solution by American ravens (Heinrich, 2000; cf. Emery & Clayton, 2004; Weir, Chappell, & Kacelnik, 2002) can only be usefully compared with performances by apes. Not even monkeys do as well. One can find antecedents of particular competencies in pigeons (e.g., Nakajima & Sato, 1993; Xia, Emmerton, Siemann, & Delius, 2001), but the ease with which parrots and corvids cope with many tasks that are difficult for pigeons must be stressed (Mackintosh, Wilson, & Boakes, 1985). More generally stated, birds often turn out to be on par with mammals regarding specific intellectual competencies. Birds certainly stand above reptiles, amphibians, and fish, for which competencies like learning sets, concept learning, or transitive responding are borderline or absent (but see Bshary, Wickler, & Fricke, 2002). This picture appears to be true despite the fact that Macphail (1987) has proposed that all vertebrates except humans are of about equal intelligence.

Rotation Invariance

A kind of item that appears in several human intelligence and ability tests involves a spatial skill known as mental rotation (Eysenck, 1990). An example is shown in the lower inset of figure 28.4. Subjects have to identify which one of the various patterns shown deviates by being a mirror image of the others. The accuracy and speed with which individual humans solve such items correlate highly with their test intelligence (Kail & Pellegrino, 1985). A related procedure has been used to assess the mental rotation abilities of both animal and human subjects. For pigeons, three stimuli were presented side by side and one or the other of the lateral stimuli was odd with respect to the middle stimulus (see upper inset in figure 28.4). Pigeons first learned that pecking the odd lateral stimuli yielded food reward. This was always the mirror image of the sample stimulus. Choices of the sample-identical lateral stimulus were penalized with a period of darkness. It was important that the birds learned to perform this task with several different visual shapes to ensure that they had acquired a general preference for the mirror stimuli. Pigeons were earlier thought to be unable to learn such an "always choose odd stimulus" rule, but it is now clear that they can do so under propitious conditions (Cook, 2002; Delius, 1994; Young & Wasserman, 2001).

The test stage involved presenting both comparison stimuli rotated by the same angle relative to the sample stimulus. Apart from the 0° training disparity, the pigeons were tested with 45°, 90°, 135°, and 180° sample-comparison disparity triplets. The tests showed that the pigeons made about the same number of errors, about 10%, and took about the same amount of time (just under a second) to choose, regardless of the varying orientation disparities (figure 28.4; Hollard & Delius, 1982; Lombardi, 1987). It needs to be stressed that this result does not mean that pigeons are invariably insensitive to the orientation of visual patterns, as some critics seem to have assumed (e.g., Hamm & Matheson, 1997). In differently designed experiments, we ourselves showed that, under different

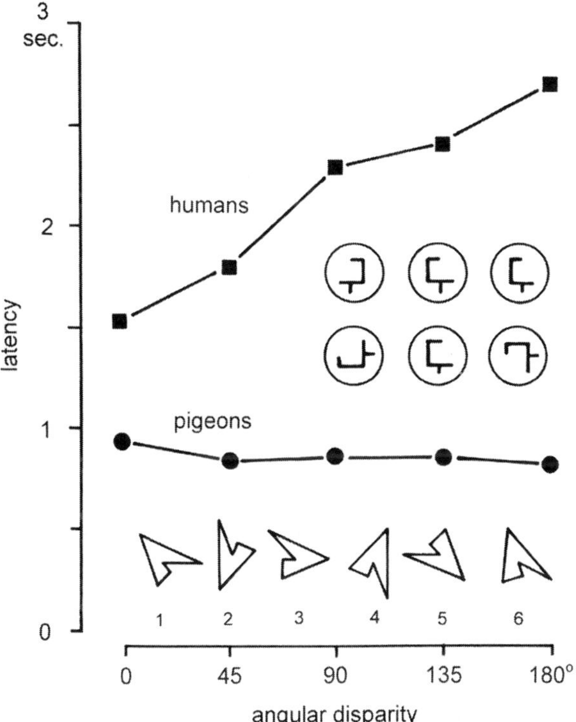

Figure 28.4. Mental rotation in humans and pigeons. *Lower inset*, Item out of a human intelligence test; subjects have to identify which one of the various patterns shown deviates by being a mirror image of the others. *Upper inset*, Present experiment with humans and pigeons; three stimuli were presented side by side; subjects had to identify which of two lateral stimuli was odd with respect to the middle stimulus. (Based on Eysenck, 1990, and Hollard & Delius, 1982.)

circumstances, pigeons are quite sensitive to orientation differences (Lohmann, Delius, Hollard, & Friesel, 1988). A related alternative responsiveness or nonresponsiveness to pattern orientation disparities can, by the way, also be demonstrated in humans (Förster, Gebhard, Lindlar, Siemann, & Delius, 1996).

Much the same rotation invariance experiment was carried out with students. They received money instead of food for correct choices. With the help of verbal instructions, the students only needed a few training trials with the 0° disparity trials. In terms of errors, they did slightly better than pigeons in test trials. But, they were generally slower in choosing and took longer as the orientation disparity between sample and comparison stimuli was greater. This finding replicates the typical results of many mental rotation experiments with humans (Delius & Hollard, 1995). Some people can mentally rotate quickly and produce shallow reaction functions, while others can only mentally rotate slowly and produce steep functions. This rotation speed correlates appreciably with their test intelligence. However, no human seems to be able to mentally rotate as fast as pigeons can. In this very narrow respect, pigeons are more test-intelligent than humans.

Why are pigeons so good at mental rotation problems while humans are not? The likely distal explanation is that there is considerable selection pressure on pigeons to recognize objects regardless of their orientation with reference to the observer, whereas there is far less such pressure on humans. This selection pressure has to do with the fact that pigeons, from their pronate stance, predominantly look down on the horizontal ground plane, where objects have no standard alignments vis-à-vis observers. In contrast, humans, from their upright stance, look predominantly at frontal, vertical planes, where objects and observers tend to have fixed orientations due to gravity. As to a proximal explanation, computational analyses of the information processing required for such invariant recognition show that both a serial and a parallel processing strategy are viable. The former is economical in terms of processing units but slow and error-prone when large orientation disparities have to be bridged (human performance), whereas the second is insensitive to increasing degrees of disparity but expensive in terms of processing units (pigeon performance; Delius, Siemann, Emmerton, & Xia, 2001). Furthermore, the parallel processing circuitry must be tuned to the particular task, but the serially processing circuitry—more amenable to reprogramming—can probably be used in other cognitive tasks. This difference is perhaps what underlies the distinction between special abilities and general intelligence treated later.

INTELLIGENCE ORIGINS

Evolving Intelligence

How did intelligence evolve as the property of a few organisms and not of many others? The key protagonists of biological evolution are ribonucleic acid molecules. As soon as they arose from precursor organic molecules about 4.5 billion years ago, they began to play the evolutionary game (Dawkins, 1989). They did this because of their unique capacity of nearly perfect replication. From the very beginning, the persistence and multiplication of these molecules, that is, their Darwinian fitness, would have been threatened by inimical environmental conditions. Their replication rates were dependent on their capacity to requisition material and energetic resources from the environment. Different variants of these gene molecules turned out to be more efficacious than others in different environmental niches. The gene variants arose because of a not altogether perfect replication (i.e., their capacity for mutation). Over billions of generations, this process led to the appearance of millions of different species of organisms, only some of which still populate the Earth. Genes of organisms that could synthesize a protective envelope, a soma, for themselves at some point of this biological history were at an advantage over those that could not. Their cellular membrane and the cytoplasm it enclosed interposed a *milieu interieur* that buffered the genes from the harshness of the environment (Futuyma, 1998).

Pluricellular organisms would evolve because of an improved encapsulation of the inner environment. Later in evolutionary history, genes that could instruct the synthesis of structures that ensured a physicochemical reactivity would be selected in some species because they allowed individual adaptation to unstable environments. The adaptability of individuals among species inhabiting spatially varying environments would be enhanced by the emergence of mutants phenotypically capable of sensing promising niches and growing into them. Mutants capable of instructing mechanisms that ensured motility would perfect the competence to seek fitness-promoting environments.

In the beginning, all behavioral responses to sensed events would have been genetically, innately determined. Some pluricellular organisms underwent mutations that would lead to cellular networks exclusively dedicated to a signaling mechanism to mediate between sensory receptors and motor actuators (Bonner, 1988). A genome capable of instructing intercalated neurons that would enable these organisms to convert differing arrays of sensory inputs into varying patterns of motor outputs would have been beneficial. Proper nervous systems began to evolve. A set of mutant genes that allowed neural structures to adjust according to individual experiences would again have been advantageous to some organisms, given the right circumstances. The capability for learning and memory had emerged. Any genes that instructed mechanisms enabling a more rapid information processing, detection of ever more complex interrelationships between stimuli, allowing the storage of these associative complexities, and ever more differentiated manners of responding to them might again provide a selective advantage in some socioecological niches. A property that one might be inclined to call intelligence would have arisen (Bullock, 1993; Heschl, 1998).

Note that, at every stage of this sketch of the progressive, anagenetic evolution of intelligence, there is always the qualifier that the right circumstances had to apply for the selection of improved cognitive abilities to occur. Of the million or so species that exist on earth, only a very small proportion is capable of showing any behavior, an even smaller proportion capable of any learning, and only exceedingly few qualify as possibly intelligent. The influenza and HIV viruses do very well with no behavior at all, liver flukes and sea urchins thrive despite the fact that they are virtually incapable of any learning, and the common toad and the stickleback fish manage fine without much intelligence. There is hardly any doubt that occasional mutants have arisen in these organisms that might have provided them with some behavior, with improved learning and expanded intelligence, but probably the costs of such capabilities exceeded the benefits in terms of fitness. The price of intelligent behavior is grossly that of having more neurons and therefore larger nervous systems.

Of course, it is not only sheer brain enlargement that can bring overall information processing improvements but also increased conduction speed, improved synaptic efficacy, augmented neural connectivity, more synaptic variety, an extra neuron miniaturization, tighter neural packing, superior metabolic efficiency, pronounced hemispheric asymmetries, and so forth (Arbas, Meinertzhagen, & Shaw, 1991; Güntürkün et al., 2000; Matzel, Gandhi, & Muzzio, 2000; Roth, Blanke, & Wake, 1994; Volman, 1990). The best example of the fact that cognitive cleverness is not a mere matter of absolute brain size are honeybees, whose abilities often approach and occasionally may even exceed those of avians and mammals (Giurfa & Menzel, 2003). Still, much of the cleverness of social insects is more the product of the cooperative functioning of their colonies than of the cognitive capacities of individuals (Franks, 1989). By and large, however, significantly increased information-processing capacities can only arise from a large and complex brain. But of course, these capacities have to develop meaningfully during individual growth, have to be metabolically maintained in adulthood, and, not the least, have to be carried around. In many of the varied environmental contexts in which the members of most species find themselves, the fancier brains afforded by advanced intelligence would simply not result in an overall, net fitness advantage (Delius et al., 2001; cf. Köhler & Moyà-Solà, 2004; Scott, Jones, & Wilkinson, in press).

Intelligent Brains

It is important to realize that it is the selection pressure for more varied behavior, improved learning, and expanded intelligence that bring about the evolution of more voluminous and more sophisticated brains. It is not, as some have suggested, due to some intrinsic drive that makes brains ever larger and more intricate and then allows them to produce increasingly complex and refined behavior. The first requirement is the chance appearance of gene mutations that enable the ontogenetic development of a brain with improved cognitive capabilities. The probability of any odd mutation leading to such improvement is low. For it to be effective, the mutation must first fit in with the preexisting genome. For it to spread through the population, it is a requisite that the socioecological circumstances be such that the enabled intelligent behavior brings about a fitness advantage to the individuals displaying it. This advantage entails that, in the course of evolutionary time, the genome of some species—but definitely not that of others—ended up instructing the development and maintaining the functioning of large and complex brains. Note though that, in terms of sheer numbers, the microcephalic and unintelligent tuna fish, for example, are still doing considerably better than the nearly same body-sized but macrocephalic and intelligent chimpanzees.

Figure 28.5 summarizes the relationship between body and brain weights of vertebrates. Generally speaking, small animals have small brains and large animals have large brains, mainly because a larger body mass necessarily incorporates more sensory, secretory, and motor elements that need to be interconnected (Jerison, 2001). However, the oblique polygons that enclose the brain weights of birds and the brain weights of mammals in figure 28.5 lie above those that enclose the brain weights of reptiles. Within the mammalian polygon, open circles represent the brain weight of a selection of nonhuman primates, which obviously lie somewhat above the remainder of the mammals. The filled circle represents the human species. Within the avian polygon, the open squares, representing a few species of corvids and parrots, similarly lie in its upper half. The polygons corresponding to amphibian and fish species (not shown) overlap closely with that of the reptiles. Thus, the relative brain weights correspond to the assumed intelligence rankings informally assigned to the various vertebrate groups (Van Dongen, 1998). Even within the human species, the brain sizes of individuals correlate weakly, but significantly, with their test intelligences (Deary, 2000). That the size and structuring of brains can be shaped by the bioevolutionary process relies on the fact that both characteristics are under considerable genetic control (Cheverud et al., 1990; Kaschube et al., 2001).

The large size of the human brain is principally due to our relatively oversized forebrain. The highly convoluted folding of the human telencephalic cortex is its salient feature. The convolution has to do with an increased number of cortical columns, thought to be the elementary neural networks that implement cortical processing (Fuster, 2002). The folding is apparent in several mammalian groups, but in primates and particularly in humans, it is particularly pronounced (Rehkämper, Frahm, & Mann, 2001). Still, cortex volume and folding are not invariably indexes of intelligence. Dolphins are endowed with a remarkably large and folded cortex, but its neuron and neuropil densities are remarkably low. Indeed, the behavioral intelligence of dolphins, thought a few years ago to be on par with that of apes, has lately been judged

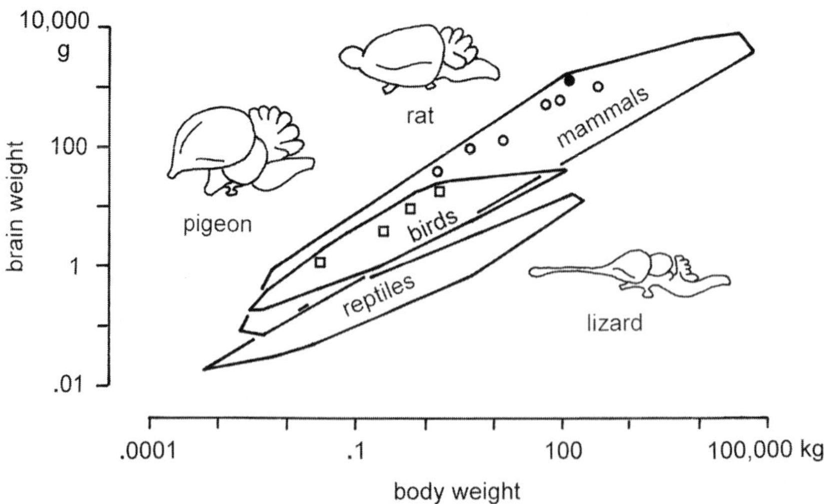

Figure 28.5. Brain weights as a function of body weights in reptilian, avian, and mammalian species. The inserts illustrate the brains of a rat, a pigeon, and a lizard, all three species having about the same body weight. (Based on Van Dongen, 1998.)

as not so particularly outstanding (Güntürkün & von Fersen, 1998; cf. Kingsbury, Rehen, Contos, Higgins, & Chun, 2003).

It is now accepted that birds possess an overgrown dorsal pallium that is analogous to the mammalian neocortex and makes up a considerable portion of the avian telencephalon (Butler & Hodos, 1996; Jarvis et al., 2005; Veenman, 1997). The small dorsal pallium of reptiles is assumed to be the structural predecessor of both the avian and the mammalian cortex. However, the avian cortex does not possess the tidily layered and columnar organization typical of the mammalian neocortex. But, as well known to electronics technicians, a superficially not so tidy circuit can function just as well as one that is tidier. Indeed, if very fast signal processing is at a premium, then an apparently disorderly circuit can have an edge over an obviously better ordered one. Birds even appear to have a cortical area that is equivalent to the prefrontal cortex of mammals, a structure that, as discussed later, is central to human intelligence (Aldavert-Vera, Costa-Miserachs, Divac, & Delius, 1999; Güntürkün & Durstewitz, 1998; see also Wild & Williams, 2000).

Birds also posses a voluminous cerebellum that is as complexly structured histologically as that of mammals (Dubbledam, 1998). The cerebellar cortex, at least in humans, is not, as classically assumed, solely dedicated to the coordination of movements but is also involved in cognitive functions that contribute to intelligence (Paradiso, Andreasen, O'Leary, Arndt, & Robinson, 1997; Schmahmann, 1997). Birds, moreover, possess the most tidily layered and neatly columnar neural structure found anywhere. Santiago Ramón y Cajal (1852–1934) listed some 14 neuronal layers in the optic tectum of birds, whereas he only recognized about six in the cerebral cortex of mammals. But it must be conceded that there is only meager evidence that the optic tectum participates in intelligent information processing (Hardy, Audinat, & Jassik Gerschenfeld, 1987; Hellmann, Manns, & Güntürkün, 2001; Wiltschko & Wiltschko, 2002). Nevertheless, in principle, birds are neurally very well equipped for complex information-processing operations.

Inasmuch as intelligence is a characteristic that transcends the elementary capacity for efficient learning and is best captured by the range of cognitive operations of which a given species is capable, birds and mammals are a league above that of all other animals. On a geological scale, the origins of intelligent behavior would therefore go back to the early Permian period, about 300 million years ago, when the ancestors of birds, the theropodans, branched off. The small arms of some of these dinosaurs evolved into feathered, although still clawed, appendages. These feathered arms probably assisted in the fanning-in of volatile prey while jumping upward and forward. By the time proper birds had evolved in the early Cretaceous era (about 150 million years ago), true wings enabled flight (Alonso, Milner, Ketcham, Cookson, & Rowe, 2004; Feduccia, 1996; Zhou, Barrett, & Hilton, 2003). This energy-demanding motor activity was dependent on a level of metabolic turnover that only a regulated body temperature could ensure. Homeothermy would arise, and this in turn would open the way to an efficient utilization of the nervous system. The therapsids, the saurian ancestors of mammals, branched off soon after the theropodans, about 280 million years ago. The mammals that derived from them about 180 million years ago went on to occupy a nighttime niche where they did not have to compete with the reptiles but where homeothermy was an imperative requirement. The renewed emergence of homeothermy entailed another flourishing of behavior potentialities among mammals (Gisolfi & Mora, 2000; Ruben, 1995).

The intellectual backwardness of fishes, amphibians, and reptiles is largely ascribable to the fact that they remained poikilothermic. Even if simpler neural functions, such as action potential conduction, are not impeded by this condition, other functions such as synaptic transmission and synaptic plasticity may be (Janssen, 1992). Lethargy at lower temperatures certainly restricts the possibility that intelligent behavior might have an impact on evolutionary fitness. In mammals and birds, however, warm-bloodedness ensured that intelligent behavior would acquire crucial importance. The large and intricate brains that resulted gave rise to the evolution of extended and involved styles of parental care; these in turn demanded more sophisticated behaviors and brains. A run-away evolutionary process began to operate that, however, could never quite escape the surplus costs of having larger brains.

Social Intelligence

The course of evolution is importantly shaped by chance events. Not only is the emergence of mutations a stochastic process, but also their selection is often determined by haphazard events. The evolution of mammals and birds was in all probability critically influenced by the sudden extinction of the dinosaurs and other large reptiles due to the impact of a very large meteorite about 65 million years ago. The growth of tropical forests caused by climate changes in the aftermath might have promoted the evolution of primates about 50 million years ago. This environment offered spatially and seasonally patchy food supplies: trees bearing fruit here and there, now and then. That uncertainty favored the emergence of socially organized groups. Competition within the groups would become the prime selective agency affecting the behavior of ancestral primates. This is what the Machiavellian theory of primate intelligence basically proposes (Byrne, 1995; Whiten & Byrne, 1997; cf. Bond, Kamil, & Balda, 2003, about corvid birds).

What advanced the evolution of primate intelligence was less the harshness of the environment or the presence of predators than the intricate demands of social life. The fact that body-size—compensated whole brain volumes—and more specially, cortical volumes—of mammals, and more so primates, are correlated with the size of the social groups they typically form accords with this hypothetical evolutionary scenario (Clark, Mitra, & Wang, 2001; Dunbar, 1998). It may also be symptomatic that several cognitive reasoning problems are better solved by human subjects when they are posed within the context of a social interaction than when presented in a nonsocial format (Cosmides, 1989; Gigerenzer, 1997).

The complexities of ape society have been aptly captured by the catch phrase "chimpanzee politics" (de Waal, 1988). The strategies that these apes use involve more sophisticated mental processes than those that they implement when coping with the physical environment (Povinelli, Reaux, Theall, & Giambrone, 2000). Shifting alliances and active deception are used, among other things, to further social status or to evade the consequences of low status (reduced access to quality feeding and mating opportunities, for example). In such contexts, apes appear to operate with some understanding of causality, some representation of the self, and some appreciation of the beliefs of others, competencies that are certainly less developed in monkeys (Tomasello & Call, 1997). Humans are, of course, well known to use many different strategies to alter the behavior of social partners to their own advantage. Even small children, some more successfully than others, can use a variety of social bargaining techniques, such as alternatively endearing themselves, asking for more than they expect to get, or throwing a tantrum in public (cf. Klimes-Dougan & Kopp, 1999). The issue is complicated because strategies that might yield small gains in the short term may produce large losses in the long term. Aggressive behavior can yield immediate access to resources, but it can also prevent a lasting and more profitable friendly cooperation. In any case, the ability to manipulate the behavior of others to one's own or one's group's advantage clearly involves special social skills (cf. Vignal, Mathevon, & Mottin, 2004).

Tests that attempt to assess individual differences in this social ability have been developed, but no really satisfactory measurement instrument has emerged. More important, the relevant tests do not reliably measure anything sufficiently different from what is assessed by cognitive intelligence tests (Riggio, Messamer, & Throckmorton, 1991; but see Ramnani & Miall, 2004). The main difficulty is that problems requiring social operations cannot be as easily translated into formalized paper-and-pencil tasks as problems involving academic reasoning processes (see later). Nevertheless, it is notable that individual bargaining skills measured in game situations vary considerably and are correlated with personality characteristics when the interaction involved is simple but with test intelligence when the interaction involved is complex (Barry & Friedman, 1998; Brandstätter & Königstein, 2001).

It is fashionable to hypothesize a separate and ancestral emotional intelligence (Goleman, 1995). When animals, including humans, behave emotionally, it functions predominantly to communicate to others their motivational state (Evans, 2001). An adequate externalization of emotional states is a necessity for successful social functioning. Howler monkeys with a pathological facial paralysis, characteristically, had great difficulty being accepted into their troop and were subjected to bouts of both excessive neglect and exaggerated antagonism (J. D. Delius, personal observations). Among humans, a body-shove is interpreted as friendly if the perpetrator has a playful facial expression but as aggressive if she or he has a threatening facial expression. Additionally, emotional states can modulate the efficiency of cognitive functioning. Both fear and rage, for example, tend to paralyze rational reasoning (Salovey, Bedell, Detweiler, & Mayer, 2000). Our innate emotional constitution may be better adapted to life in earth-caves than to life in skyscrapers. It is conceivable that some individuals are neurally better equipped than others to neocortically control their limbic emotional states in socially or academically conducive ways (cf. Ledoux, 1998).

The difficulty with emotional intelligence is that, like social intelligence, there are no reliable instruments to measure it. Existing tests are only indirect questionnaires. A typical test item reads: "Assuming that the driver of the car in which you are traveling is angered by a supposed infraction of another driver, what would you do: (a) tell him to pipe down as the incident was of no consequence, (b) start playing his preferred music-cassette, (c) join him in cursing at the other driver, or (d) tell him that something similar happened to you and that on that occasion you found out that the guilty party was on his way to an emergency ward?" It is doubtful that any answer adequately gauges the subject's actual capability for emotional self-control. It is not even clear that what is being assessed is not just social intelligence and, indeed, whether the emotional intelligence trait is sufficiently distinct from that of general intelligence (Ciarrochi, Chan, & Caputi, 2000; Newsome, Day, & Catano, 2000; but see Mayer, Caruso, & Salovey, 2000).

HUMAN INTELLIGENCE

Why are humans such particularly intelligent primates? A probable evolutionary scenario is that a lineage we have in common with chimpanzees and that occupied an arboreal niche had to cope with a freak climate change resulting in the savannization of east Africa about 5 million years ago. This change meant a forced shift away from a vegetarian diet to a carnivorous one. Note that chimpanzees, although still predominantly vegetarian, do occasionally also engage in communal hunts and eat meat (Goodall, 1986). Not being equipped with claws or fangs like longstanding carnivores, these prehominids had to employ tools such as spears and clubs. Some tool use in connection with feeding, although not with hunting, also occurs in chimpanzees. Initially, hunting could only be successful if it was carried out by social intelligence–demanding cooperative gangs. Hunting-pack organization generated selective pressure for enhanced communication (Delius, 1990; Wilson, 1975). The labeling property of language in turn improved intellectual functioning through an enhanced structuring of the mental representations of the world and the self. Language-trained chimpanzees and parrots outdo linguistically naive peers in the performance of demanding cognitive tasks (Pepperberg, 1999; Premack, 1988). But, also by involving symbolic sequential operations, language required a serial mode of information processing that is not particularly natural for neuronal networks, which are more suited for parallel information processing (Nowak, Komarova, & Niyogi, 2003). The language faculty undoubtedly facilitated the evolution of a propositional form of information processing considered essential for the deliberative, rational reasoning needed to solve problems like those shown in figure 28.1 (Carruthers, 2002; but see also Goldin-Meadow, 2003; Hespos & Spelke, 2004; see later). It is certainly no accident that a propositional mode of processing is frequently used in artificial intelligence programming (Russel & Norvig, 1995).

Practical Intelligence

Until advanced cultures began to emerge about 10,000 years ago, the cognitive problems that humans had to solve were of a practical, applied sort, not of an abstract, academic kind. Indeed, some of the dissatisfaction with intelligence tests arises because they seem divorced from everyday problem solving. The criticism is akin to that often raised regarding the nonecological nature of laboratory experiments on animal learning (Timberlake & Lucas, 1989; see also Gigerenzer, 1998).

As tests of practical intelligence, computerized games were introduced by Dörner and Reither (1978) to assess the managerial abilities of individuals. They involve subjects having to run a virtual factory. Several variables are related to each other through a varied set of equations. The input variables represent outlays (buying prime materials, investing in machines, paying personnel, borrowing money, etc.) and the output variables represent income (production volume, price level, etc.). The subjects had to try to adjust the input variables so as to maximize the factory's profitability within an hour. The success of subjects in reaching this goal varied considerably and was found not to correlate with their test intelligence. Later studies, however, showed that this lack of correlation arose because the original factory games were not really rationally soluble within the time that the subjects had to play them. The performance differences arose because some subjects hit on good settings by chance and other subjects were not so lucky. When the games were modified to be more cognitively penetrable, a substantial correlation was observed between individuals' test intelligence and their purported management ability (Putz-Osterloh & Lüer, 1981; but see Berry & Broadbent, 1987).

Individual differences in managerial ability may exist, but they cannot be adequately measured with these factory games and they are unlikely to be totally divorced from test intelligence. Nor are they likely to be commensurate with individual differences in horserace betting ability that were unearthed by another remarkable study of practical intelligence (Ceci & Liker, 1986). The wide range of practical abilities that have been looked into are not easy to subsume within one practical intelligence disposition, nor are they easy to separate from special abilities or, indeed, acquired expertise (Sternberg et al., 2000; Sternberg & Grigorenko, 2002).

It is nevertheless widely accepted that there are a number of special intellectual abilities, such as verbal, spatial, or mathematical, that are at least partially independent of general intelligence. Indeed, many intelligence tests, as, for example, the Binet and Wechsler tests, include a proportion of items that tap some of these special abilities (Lohman, 2000). But, the assessment of these abilities often requires special instruments: Musical ability, for example, because it is not properly measurable with a paper-and-pencil test alone, requires an additional tape recorder. Further on this theme, although developers of intelligence tests recognized early the desirability of including an assessment of the creative abilities of individuals, a reliable measure of this competence, beyond a fraction that is already represented in the general intelligence score, has proved elusive (Glover, Ronning, & Reynolds, 1989).

The term *abilities* that is habitually used, reflects a persisting doubt as to whether all these competencies refer to true separate intelligences or are merely special skills that are in addition to a core intelligence gift. The possession of absolute auditory pitch perception, for example, may be considered significant for musical ability but would be hardly considered an element of general intelligence (Rae & McAnulty, 1995; Zatorre, 2005). The fact that brain imaging studies reveal different areas being activated by tasks associated with various cognitive abilities suggests that there may be different intelligences. Nevertheless, all of them may be modulated by variations in elementary neuronal functions that have to do with general intelligence (Houdé & Tzourio-Mazoyer, 2003; Murphy, 2003). Although the existence of several separate, modular intelligences instead of a single, molar intelligence has often been promoted (M. Anderson, 1998; Ceci, Nightingale, & Baker, 1993), this notion has just as often been denied (Gerrans, 2002; Neubauer & Bucik, 1996; Petrill, 2002).

General Intelligence

Regardless of how one views it, there appears to be a general quality, conventionally called *g*, that is at the base of all human intellectual abilities (Detterman, 2000; Jensen, 2000). What is more, there are batteries of psychometric tests that measure it quite well. Note, however, that the tests are necessarily limited to tapping cognitive processes that can be demonstrated within a relatively short time span, that is, within the time frame of the tests. For example, it is typical to perceive a person's poor capacities in retaining episodic events over periods of a few days to several months as reflecting low intelligence. But it should be noted that the correlation between measures of earlier occurring episodic events and standard intelligence test scores is rather weak (Alexander & Smales, 1997). Tests that would measure cognitive competencies over longer periods of time are plainly unwieldy.

Standard intelligence tests are specially designed to avoid the influence of special expertise, such as can be provided by relevant episodic or indeed procedural memories. Of course, there are also separate tests designed to measure the expertise that people like aircraft pilots or computer programmers may or may not have. A more interesting kind of test would be one that would measure the individual potential for the acquisition of any cognitive expertise rather than the actual possession of a particular expertise. This test would come close to the comparative assessment of the learning-to-learn capabilities of species described in the earlier section on animal intelligence. Note, however, that the capacity for higher-level learning in humans, if it were possible to reliably measure such a thing, would be unlikely to be totally divorced from short-term cognitive processing ability, the capacity that standard intelligence tests tend to assess.

Research into how people solve intelligence-test items, such as those shown in figure 28.1, has revealed that they mainly challenge the working memory system (Baddeley, 1986; Logie & Della Sala, 2001). This mechanism apparently consists of two kinds of short-term memory: one dedicated to storing auditory-verbal (phonological) information and another dedicated to storing visuospatial information over time spans lasting several seconds to several minutes. Both of these stores have quite a limited capacity as captured by the statement that they can hold no more than about 7 ± 2 chunks of information at a given time. The access to these buffers and the processing of their contents is controlled by a central executive mechanism. This agency is conceived as a serially operating device that is in some ways similar to the central processor of a computer. There is evidence that this working memory device plans and guides the course of our ongoing conscious behavior, but probably not the execution of more automated activities, the details of which we are largely unaware.

The neural networks that constitute working memory seem to be mainly located in the prefrontal cortex. In monkeys, lesions in this area impair the performance of tasks that require short-term information retention (Fuster, 1989). Moreover, electrophysiological recordings reveal neurons with response characteristics that are congruent with working memory functions (Funahashi & Kubota, 1994; Wallis, Anderson, & Miller, 2001). In humans, brain imaging procedures consistently reveal that the prefrontal cortex is activated by mental tasks that resemble intelligence tests items (D'Esposito et al., 1995; see also Koechlin, Basso, Pietrini, Panzer, & Grafman, 1999) and that it is more strongly activated by such items in lower-intelligence than in high-intelligence persons (Duncan, Burgess, & Emslie, 1995; but see Haier, Jung, Yeo, Head, & Alkire, 2004).

Intelligence tests can thus be thought to assess the information-processing capacity of working memory. Part of this quality seems to reside in the number of items that the audioverbal and visuospatial buffers can hold. Indeed, the so-called digit span—the average number of digits that an individual can reliably recall shortly after hearing or reading randomized lists of them—is a simple index known to appreciably correlate with the intelligence quotient (Schofield & Ashman, 1986). But undoubtedly, the relevant quality is also a function of the storage durability, the processing speed, the operational precision, and the computational complexity that the neuronal networks constituting the working memory system are capable of sustaining. At the species level, the fact that animals, pigeons more so than monkeys, have less capacious and less lasting short-term memories than humans might indeed be a reason why they are comparatively less intelligent (Wright, 1990; see also Higashijima, 2003). How fast signals can be transmitted along axons and across synapses in the nervous system can be assessed at the individual level in humans by measuring the conduction velocity of polysynaptic pathways, for example, by recording the latency of cortical potentials evoked by peripheral stimuli (Reed & Jensen, 1993). Much like reaction times in multiple-choice tasks, where subjects must select a target stimulus among several distracter stimuli, these conduction velocities have been shown to partially correlate with their test intelligence. These two measures of neural performance have been found to be quite stable, lifelong traits of individuals, as long as no pathological events intervene (Neubauer, Spinath, Riemann, Borkenau, & Angleitner, 2000; Vernon, 1987).

Given the assumption that working memory for verbal and spatial information processing are somewhat independent, it may be that the effectiveness of the prefrontal cortex also depends on the processing capability of the several neural structures that provide it with inputs and outputs. Some of these accessory structures are undoubtedly functionally specialized networks supporting auditory, visual, verbal, manual, and other such functions, whose processing qualities may well surface behaviorally as one of the individually varying special abilities discussed earlier.

Is it possible that a high level of development of a particular modular ability could inhibit the expression of general intelligence? Excessive allocation of neuronal processing capacities to one sort of cognitive operation might restrict the capacities available for other kinds of cognitive functioning. The occurrence of so-called idiots savant suggests that there may be a competitive partitioning of computational resources (Heaton, Pring, & Hermelin, 1999; Hermelin, 2001; but see Snyder & Mitchell, 1999).

Developing Intelligence

Most of the studies that have examined concordances in intelligence quotients within pairs of monozygotic and dizogotic twins and between the intelligence quotients of adoptive children and that of their biological and adoptive parents have concluded that the ontogeny of intelligence is importantly, but not exclusively, determined by the individual's genome (Bouchard, 1993; Plomin, De Fries, McClearn, & Rutter, 1997). This general conclusion is warranted despite the fact that the heritability of intelligence is an intricately complex issue (Grigorenko, 2000; Turkheimer, Haley, Waldron, D'Onofrio, & Gottesman, 2003). The undoubted role of the environment is still difficult to detail, largely because it is such a complex factor and because the effective environment is partly created by individuals themselves (Dickens & Flynn, 2001; Scarr & McCartney, 1983). For instance, the availability of books at home is probably an intelligence-promoting factor, but of course, it can only become effective if the child is disposed to reading them.

The influence of the developmental environment on intelligence is possibly reflected in the fact that, over the decades since standardized intelligence tests have come into widespread use, average intelligence of the population has been slowly, but steadily rising, at least in developed countries (Neisser, 1998). This rise has occurred despite the fact that, in the same countries, there is a tendency for less intelligent couples to produce more offspring than more intelligent couples, a trend that should genetically depress the population's overall intelligence (Kirk et al., 2001; Lynn, 1999). The rise in average test intelligence seems to reflect improving standards of nutrition, health, and education. But, the rise might alternatively reflect increased outbreeding due to augmented mobility, which may counter the decline in intelligence that occurs in less mobile, inbred populations (Agrawal, Sinha, & Jensen, 1984).

Individual intelligence is also affected by birth order within the family, earlier born siblings being at a slight statistical advantage over later born siblings. This trend probably arises because intellectual nurturing diminishes in growing families—for example, baby babble increases and adult discussion decreases (Zajonc, 2001). But, the effect might also come about through a deleterious genetic aging of parental oocytes (and, less so, spermatocytes). Recall that Down syndrome (chromosome 21 trisomy) is more frequent in later born children because of this aging (Carr, 1995).

Dire environmental events such as rubella infection during early pregnancy, protracted protein deprivation during childhood, or chronic lead poisoning during adulthood (Barth et al., 2002; Brown & Pollit, 1996; Zgorniaknowosielska, Zawilinska, & Szostek, 1996) can have a sizeable impact on the development and maintenance of test intelligence: More mundane environmental variants like bottle- or breast-feeding, maternal smoking or nonsmoking, and parental education levels have comparatively small impacts, but these and other similar factors may interact and result in appreciable effects (Johnson, Swank, Baldwin, & McCormick, 1999; Neiss & Rowe, 2000; Rogan & Gladen, 1993).

One must keep in mind that the tens of thousands of structural and enzymatic proteins that make up the neurons of an individual are essentially products of the individual's genome present in each of these cells. Inasmuch as intelligence is importantly determined by the sophistication of neuronal network operations and these depend pivotally on the proteins that the genes can instruct, it has to be the case that the degree of intelligence that different species and different individuals exhibit must depend heavily on the genetic endowments that the species have come to possess and that the individuals have chanced to inherit. The decisive influence of genes on intelligence is illustrated, among other mutational defects, by the havoc that the fragile X chromosome mutant frequently wreaks in the intelligence of male and, more rarely, female persons (Dykens, Hodapp, & Leckman, 1994; see also Plomin, 2001).

Why it is that humans are so much more intelligent than chimpanzees when both species have about 99% of their almost 20,000 genes in common? The probable answer is that the several hundred genes that they do not share are crucially involved in regulating the expression of several thousand genes that determine brain development (Kaessmann & Pääbo, 2002; Levine & Tjian, 2003; Weissenbach, 2004). Both the proteinic composition and the anatomical structure of human brains are demonstrably more complex than those of chimpanzee brains (Enard et al., 2002; Holloway, 2001).

EPILOGUE

Even though, nowadays, test intelligence in many countries is no longer correlated with individual Darwinian fitness, as measured by the number of reproductively mature offspring produced, it still needs to be primarily understood as one of the many historical products of biological evolution. The cognitive competencies of some present-day animals unquestionably reflect some of the phylogenetic antecedents of human intelligent behavior. Tests that measure human intelligence yield scores that are characterized by a remarkable lifelong stability and a high genetic heritability. They assess the quality of neurobiological factors that determine the computational power of components of the brain that underlie problem-solving through short-term reasoning. Longer-term learning and memory capacities, and the flexibilities that are part of more vernacular concepts of human intelligence (cf. Booth, 2002), and that also frequently play an important role in animal intelligence assessments, are not really measured by these tests.

Egalitarian oriented people are frequently uncomfortable with the notion that intelligence is effectively, as suggested by E. G. Boring (1886–1968), defined by whatever the trait is that intelligence tests measures, and that what they measure is an individual disposition that is not easily improvable by a simple amelioration of the economic, educational, and social environment. They point out that test intelligence correlates only moderately with outward success in life (Mackintosh, 1998). It is indeed obvious that other traits, such as an intellectuality disposition (wanting to know) and an achievement motivation (wanting to succeed) also contribute to determining how well one does in life (Lloyd & Barenbatt, 1984). The assessment of their exact effects is hindered by the fact that these dispositions cannot be measured as precisely as can general intelligence. Furthermore, it seems that these partly heritable dispositions are somewhat correlated with general intelligence (Gagne & St Père, 2002). The upshot is that test intelligence is still by far the best predictor of scholastic achievement and life-long income that is available (Amelang, 1994; Schmidt & Hunter, 1998). But, one must note, it is clearly not at all a serviceable index of satisfaction with life (Pastuovic, Kolesaric, & Krizmanic, 1995).

The role of deliberative reasoning in intelligent behavior remains to be briefly considered. It is a process much involved in the solution of problems such as those presented in figure 28.1. Humans can mostly state verbally, or pictorially, which analytical steps they undertook and what logical rules they applied when solving them (Carpenter et al., 1990). However, when examining the performance of humans on some tasks used to assess animal intelligence, one finds that many subjects cannot provide explicit after-the-event accounts (Siemann et al., 2004; Siemann & Delius, 1998). Moreover, those individuals who can provide explicit accounts do not as a rule exhibit any performance advantage. The solution of these tasks seems to rely on automatic processes that appear not to be fully consciously accessible. Phenomenologically, explicitly declarable, but usually covert, deliberative reasoning appears to correspond to a simulative neural operation that has similarities with overt trial-and-error learning. The learning takes place within an elaborate memorial representation (mental model) of the world and the self (cf. Damasio, 2003; Ehrsson, Spence, & Passingham, 2004; Smith Churchland, 2002). This simulatory activity seems to rely heavily on a chess-playing-program–like mode of information processing: "Suppose I try this particular action, . . . no, it is not likely to lead to success, ... let's try this alternative action instead, . . . yes, this seems likely to work, . . . now I'll try this next step, . . ." and so on. Such deliberative reasoning may, in fact, often largely devolve in terms of corresponding sequences of visually imagined scenes (Knauff, Mulack, Kassubek, Salih, & Greenlee, 2002; Wohlschläger & Wohlschläger, 1998). Pictorial in-brain simulations of this kind are conceivably within the capabilities of clever animals such as corvids and might well underlie their "insightful" problem-solving feats (Heinrich, 2000). The evolution of language competence in humans, besides advancing a more clearly propositional style of covert deliberation (Fitch & Hauser, 2004; Premack, 2004), might have also favored an increase in the informational definition and persistence of the mental representation. These modifications would have better allowed them to be semantically and syntactically explainable to others. Still, the continuing salience of the modeling imagery may possibly be what makes us feel that we, and perhaps others, our dogs included, are consciously aware of at least some of our thought processes (Griffin & Speck, 2004).

Acknowledgments The present chapter is a much modified version of an earlier Spanish text (Delius, 2002). We thank I. Morgado-Bernal (Barcelona), M. J. Cleaveland (Poughkeepsie), S.-C. Li (Berlin), and J. M. Lee (Konstanz) for helpful comments and suggestions. J. D. D. is grateful to the Deutsche Forschungsgemeinschaft, Bonn, for steady research support.

References

Agrawal, N., Sinha, S. N., & Jensen, A. R. (1984). Effects of inbreeding on Raven matrices. *Behavior Genetics, 14,* 579–585.

Aldavert-Vera, L., Costa-Miserachs, D., Divac, I., & Delius, J. D. (1999). Presumed "prefrontal cortex" lesions in pigeons: Effects on visual discrimination performance. *Behavioural Brain Research, 102,* 165–170.

Alexander, J. R. M., & Smales, S. (1997). Intelligence, learning and long-term memory. *Personality & Individual Differences, 23,* 815–825.

Alonso, P. D., Milner, A. C., Ketcham, R. A., Cookson, M. J., & Rowe, T. B. (2004). The avian nature of the brain and inner ear of Archaeopteryx. *Nature, 430,* 666–669.

Amelang, M. (1994). Intelligenz [Intelligence]. In M. Amelang (Ed.), *Verhaltens- und Leistungsunterschiede: Enzyklopädie der Psychologie* (pp. 245–328). Göttingen: Hogrefe.

Anderson, B. (2000). The g factor in non human animals. In G. R. Bock, J. A. Goode, & K. Webb (Eds.), *The nature of intelligence* (pp. 79–104). Chichester, UK: Wiley.

Anderson, M. (1998). Mental retardation, general intelligence, and modularity. *Learning & Individual Differences, 10,* 159–178.

Arbas, E. A., Meinertzhagen, I. A., & Shaw, S. R. (1991). Evolution in nervous systems. *Annual Review of Neuroscience, 14,* 9–38.

Astley, S. L., & Wasserman, E. A. (1999). Superordinate category formation in pigeons: Association with a common delay or probability of food reinforcement makes perceptually dissimilar stimuli functionally equivalent. *Journal of Experimental Psychology: Animal Behavior Processes, 25,* 415–432.

Baddeley, A. (1986). *Working memory.* Oxford: Oxford University Press.

Barry, B., & Friedman, R. A. (1998). Bargainer characteristics in distributive and integrative negotiation. *Journal of Personality & Social Psychology, 74,* 345–359.

Barth, A., Schaffer, A. W., Osterode, W., Winker, R., Konnaris, C., Valic, E., et al. (2002). Reduced cognitive abilities in lead-exposed men. *International Archives of Occupational & Environmental Health, 75,* 394–398.

Berry, D. C., & Broadbent, D. E. (1987). The combination of explicit and implicit learning in task control. *Psychological Research, 49,* 7–15.

Bond, A. B., Kamil, A. C., & Balda, R. P. (2003). Social complexity and transitive inference in corvids. *Animal Behaviour, 65,* 479–487.

Bonner, J. T. (1988). *The evolution of complexity.* Princeton, NJ: Princeton University Press.

Booth, M. Z. (2002). Swazi concepts of intelligence: The universal versus the local. *Ethos, 30,* 376–400.

Bouchard, T. J. (1993). The genetic architecture of human intelligence. In Vernon, P. A. (Ed.), *Biological approaches to the study of human intelligence* (pp. 33–93). Norwood, NJ: Ablex.

Brandstätter, H., & Königstein, M. (2001). Personality influences on ultimatum bargaining decisions. *European Journal of Personality, 15,* S53–S70.

Brown, L., & Pollitt, E. (1996). Malnutrition, poverty and intellectual development. *Scientific American, 274,* 26–31.

Bshary, R., Wickler, W., & Fricke, H. (2002). Fish cognition: A primate's eye view. *Animal Cognition, 5,* 1–13.

Bullock, T. H. (1993). How are more complex brains different? *Brain, Behavior & Evolution, 41,* 88–96.

Butler, A. B., & Hodos, W. (1996). *Comparative vertebrate neuroanatomy: Evolution and adaptation.* New York: Wiley.

Byrne, R. W. (1995). The ape legacy: The evolution of Machiavellian intelligence and anticipatory interactive planning. In E. N. Goody (Ed.), *Social intelligence and interaction* (pp. 37–52). Cambridge, UK: Cambridge University Press.

Carpenter, P. A., Just, M. A., & Shell, P. (1990). What one intelligence test measures: A theoretical account of the processing in the Raven progressive matrices test. *Psychological Review, 97,* 404–431.

Carr, J. H. (1995). *Down's syndrome: Children growing up.* Cambridge: Cambridge University Press.

Carruthers, P. (2002). The cognitive functions of language. *Behavioral & Brain Sciences, 25,* 657–674.

Ceci, S. J., & Liker, J. K. (1986). Academic and nonacademic intelligence: An experimental separation. In R. J. Sternberg & R. K. Wagner (Eds.), *Practical intelligence* (pp. 119–142). Cambridge: Cambridge University Press.

Ceci, S. J., Nightingale, N. N., & Baker, J. G. (1993). The ecologies of intelligence: Challenges to traditional views. In D. K. Detterman (Ed.), *Is the mind modular or unitary? Current topics of human intelligence* (pp. 61–82). Norwood, NJ: Ablex.

Chalmers, M., & McGonigle, B. (1984). Are children any more logical than monkeys on the five term series problem? *Journal of Experimental Child Psychology, 37,* 355–377.

Cheverud, J. M., Falk, D., Vannier, M., Konigsberg, L., Helmkamp, R. C., & Hidebolt, C. (1990). Heritability of brain size and surface features in rhesus macaques (*Macaca mulatta*). *Journal of Heredity, 81,* 51–57.

Ciarrochi, J. V., Chan, A. Y. C., & Caputi, P. (2000). A critical evaluation of the emotional intelligence construct. *Personality & Individual Differences, 28,* 539–561.

Clark, D. A., Mitra, P. P., & Wang, S. S.-H. (2001). Scalable architecture in mammalian brains. *Nature, 411,* 189–193.

Cook, R. G. (2002). Same–different concept formation in pigeons. In M. Bekoff, C. Allen, & G. M. Burghardt (Eds.), *The cognitive animal* (pp. 229–237). Cambridge, MA: MIT Press.

Cosmides, L. (1989). The logic of social exchange: Has natural selection shaped how humans reason? Studies on the Wason selection task. *Cognition, 31,* 187–276.

Damasio, A. (2003). The person within. *Nature, 423,* 227.

Danthiir, V., Roberts, R. D., Pallier, G., & Stankow, L. (2001). What the nose knows: Olfaction and cognitive abilities. *Intelligence, 29,* 337–361.

Dawkins, R. (1989). *The selfish gene* (2nd ed.). Oxford: Oxford University Press.

Deary, I. J. (2000). *Looking down on human intelligence: From psychometrics to the brain.* Oxford: Oxford University Press.

Delius, J. D. (1990). Sapient sauropsids and hollering hominids. In W. A. Koch (Ed.), *Geneses of language* (pp. 1–29). Bochum: Brockmeyer.

Delius, J. D. (1994). Comparative cognition of identity. In P. Bertelson, P. Eelen, & G. d'Ydewalle (Eds.), *International perspectives on psychological science: Leading themes* (pp. 25–40). Howe, UK: Erlbaum.

Delius, J. D. (2002). Inteligencias y cerebros: Un enfoque comparativo y evolucionario [Intelligences and brains: A comparative and evolutionary view]. In I. Morgado Bernal (Ed.), *Cerebro, inteligencia y emoción* (pp. 17–65). Barcelona: Tuskets.

Delius, J. D., Ameling, M., Lea, S. E. G., & Staddon, J. E. R. (1995). Reinforcement concordance induces and maintains stimulus associations in pigeons. *Psychological Record, 45,* 283–297.

Delius, J. D., & Emmerton, J. (1978). Stimulus dependent asymmetry in classical and instrumental discrimination learning by pigeons. *Psychological Record, 28,* 425–434.

Delius, J. D., & Hollard, V. D. (1995). Orientation invariance in pattern recognition by pigeons (*Columba livia*) and humans (*Homo sapiens*). *Journal of Comparative Psychology, 109,* 278–290.

Delius, J. D., Jitsumori, M., & Siemann, M. (2000). Stimulus equivalencies through discrimination reversals. In C. Heyes & L. Huber (Eds.), *Evolution of cognition* (pp. 103–122). Cambridge, MA: MIT Press.

Delius, J. D., & Siemann, M. (1998). Transitive inferences in animals and humans: Adaptation or exaptation? *Behavioural Processes, 42,* 107–137.

Delius, J. D., Siemann, M., Emmerton, J., & Xia, L. (2001). Cognitions of birds as products of evolved brains. In G. Roth & M. F. Wulliman (Eds.), *Brain evolution and cognition* (pp. 451–490). New York: Wiley.

D'Esposito, M., Detre, J. A., Alsop, D. C., Shin, R. K., Atlas, S., & Grossman, M. (1995). The neural basis of the central executive system of working memory. *Nature, 378,* 279–281.

Detterman, D. K. (2000). General intelligence and the definition of phenotypes. In G. R. Bock, J. A. Goode, & K. Webb (Eds.), *The nature of intelligence* (pp. 136–144). Chichester: Wiley.

de Waal, F. (1988). Chimpanzee politics. In R. Byrne & A. Whiten (Eds.), *Machiavellian intelligence: Evaluations and extensions* (pp. 122– 131). Oxford: Clarendon.

Dickens, W. T., & Flynn, J. R. (2001). Heritability estimates versus large environmental effects: The IQ paradox resolved. *Psychological Review, 108,* 346–369.

Diekamp, B., Prior, H., & Güntürkün, O. (1999). Functional lateralization, interhemispheric transfer and position bias in serial reversal learning in pigeons (*Columba livia*). *Animal Cognition, 214,* 187–196.

Dörner, D., & Reither, F. (1978). Über das Problemlösen in sehr komplexen Realitätsbereichen [On problem-solving in very complex realities]. *Zeitschrift für experimentelle und angewandte Psychologie, 25,* 52–55.

Dubbeldam, J. J. (1998) Birds. In R. Nieuwenhuys, H. J. ten Donkelaar, & C. Nicholson (Eds.), *The central nervous system of vertebrates* (pp. 1525–1636). New York: Springer.

Dunbar, R. I. M. (1998). The social brain hypothesis. *Evolutionary Anthropology, 6,* 178–190.

Duncan, J., Burgess, P., & Emslie, H. (1995). Fluid intelligence after frontal lobe lesions. *Neuropsychololology, 33,* 261–268.

Dykens, E. M., Hodapp, R. M., & Leckman, J. F. (1994). *Behavior and development in fragile X syndrome.* Thousand Oaks, CA: Sage.

Ehrsson, H. H., Spence, C., & Passingham, R. E. (2004). That is my hand! Activity in the premotor cortex reflects feeling of ownership of a limb. *Science, 305,* 875–879.

Ekstrom, A. D., Kahana, M. J., Caplan, J. R., Fields, T. A., Isham, E. A., Newman, E. L., et al. (2003). Celullar networks underlying human spatial navigation. *Nature, 425,* 184–187.

Emery, N. J., & Clayton N. S. (2004). The mentality of crows: Convergent evolution of intelligence in corvids and apes. *Science, 306,* 1903–1907.

Enard, W., Khaitovich, P., Klose, J., Zollner, S., Heissig, F., Giavalisco, P., et al. (2002). Intra- and interspecific variations in primate gene expression patterns. *Science, 296,* 233–235

Evans, D. (2001). *Emotion: The science of sentiment.* Oxford: Oxford University Press.

Eysenck, H. J. (1990). *Check your own IQ.* London: Penguin Books.

Feduccia, A. (1996). *The origin and evolution of birds.* New Haven, CT: Yale University Press.

Fitch, T. W., & Hauser, M. D. (2004). Computational constraints on syntactic processing in a nonhuman primate. *Science, 303,* 377–380.

Förster, B., Gebhardt, R.-P., Lindlar, K., Siemann, M., & Delius, J. D. (1996). Mental rotation: A function of elementary stimulus discriminability. *Perception, 25,* 1301–1316.

Franks, N. R. (1989). Army ants: A collective intelligence. *Scientific American, 77,* 139–145.

Funahashi, S., & Kubota, K. (1994). Working memory and prefrontal cortex. *Neuroscience Research, 21,* 1–11.

Fuster, J. M. (1989). *The prefrontal cortex: Anatomy, physiology and neuropsychology of the frontal lobe* (2nd ed.). New York: Raven.

Fuster, J. M. (2002). *Cortex and mind: Unifying cognition.* London: Oxford University Press.

Futuyma, D. J. (1998). *Evolutionary biology* (3rd ed.). Sunderland, MA: Sinauer.

Gagne, F., & St. Père, F. (2002). When IQ is controlled, does motivation still predict achievement? *Intelligence, 30,* 71–100.

Gerrans, P. (2002). Modularity reconsidered. *Language & Communication, 22,* 259–268.

Gigerenzer, G. (1997). The modularity of social intelligence. In A. Whiten & R. W. Byrne (Eds.), *Machiavallian intelligence: Evaluations and extensions* (pp. 264–288). Cambridge: Cambridge University Press.

Gigerenzer, G. (1998). Ecological intelligence: An adaptation for frequencies. In D. Cummins & C. Allen (Eds.), *The evolution of mind* (pp. 9–29). New York: Oxford University Press.

Gisolfi, C. V., & Mora, F. (2000). *The hot brain: Survival, temperature and the human body.* Cambridge, MA: MIT Press.

Giurfa, M., & Menzel, R. (2003). Cognitive architecture of a mini-brain. In R. Kühn, R. Menzel, U. Ratsch, M. M. Richter, & I. O. Stamatescu (Eds.), *Adaptivity and learning: An interdisciplinary debate.* Berlin: Springer.

Glover, J. A., Ronning, R. R., & Reynolds, C. R. (Eds.). (1989). *Handbook of creativity.* New York: Plenum.

Goleman, D. (1995). *Emotional intelligence: Why it can matter more than IQ.* New York: Bantam.

Goldin-Meadow, S. (2003). *Hearing gesture: How our hands help us think.* Cambridge, MA: Belknap.

Goodall, J. (1986). *The chimpanzees of Gombe: Patterns of behavior.* Cambridge, MA: Belknap.

Gossette, R. L., & Gossette, M. F. (1967). Examination of the reversal index across fifteen different mammalian and avian species. *Perceptual & Motor Skills, 24,* 987–990.

Greene, A. J., Spellman, B. A., Dusek, J. A., Eichenbaum, H. B., & Levy, W. B. (2001). Relational learning with and without awareness: Transitive inference using nonverbal stimuli in humans. *Memory & Cognition, 29,* 893–902.

Griffin, D. R., & Speck, G. B. (2004). New evidence of animal conciousness. *Animal Cognition, 7,* 5–18.

Grigorenko, E. L. (2000). Heritability and intelligence. In R. J. Sternberg (Ed.), *Handbook of intelligence* (pp. 53–91). New York: Cambridge University Press.

Güntürkün, O., Diekamp, B., Manns, M., Nottelmann, F., Prior, H. Schwarz, A., et al. (2000). Asymmetry pays: Visual lateralization improves discrimination in pigeons. *Current Biology, 10,* 1079–1081.

Güntürkün, O., & Durstewitz, D. (2000). Multimodal areas in the avian forebrain: Blueprints for cognition? In G. Roth & M. F. Wullimann (Eds.), *Brain evolution and cognition* (pp. 431–450). New York: Wiley.

Güntürkün, O., & von Fersen, L. (1998). So wenig graue Zellen; ein Mythos wird angetastet [So few grey cells, a myth is challenged]. *Rubin, 1,* 6–13.

Haier, R. J., Jung, R. E., Yeo, R. A., Head, K., & Alkire, M. T. (2004). Structural brain variation and general intelligence. *Neuroimage, 23,* 425–433.

Hamm, J., & Matheson, W. R. (1997). Mental rotation in pigeons (*Columba livia*). *Journal of Comparative Psychology, 111,* 76–81.

Hardy, O., Audinat, E., & Jassik Gerschenfeld, D. (1987). Intracellular recordings from slices of the pigeon optic tectum. *Neuroscience, 23,* 305–318.

Heaton, P., Pring, L., & Hermelin, B. (1999). A pseudo-savant, a case of exceptional musical splinter skills. *Neurocase, 5,* 503–509.

Heinrich, B. (2000). Testing insight in ravens. In C. Heyes & L. Huber (Eds.), *Evolution of cognition* (pp. 289–306). Cambridge, MA: MIT Press.

Hellmann, B., Manns, M., & Güntürkün, O. (2001). Nucleus isthmi, pars semilunaris as a key component to the tectofugal visual system in pigeons. *Journal of Comparative Neurology, 436,* 153–166.

Hermelin, B. (2001). *Bright splinters of the mind.* London: Kingsley.

Herrnstein, R. J. (1990). Levels of stimulus control: A functional approach. *Cognition, 37,* 133–166.

Heschl, A. (1998). *Das intelligente Genom* [The intelligent genome]. Berlin: Springer.

Hespos, S. J., & Spelke, E. S. (2004). Conceptual precursors to language. *Nature, 430,* 453–456.

Higashijima, J. (2003). Spatial working memory in pigeons. In S. Watanabe (Ed.), *Comparative analysis of mind* (pp. 31–47). Tokyo: Keio University.

Hollard, V. D., & Delius, J. D. (1982). Rotational invariance in visual pattern recognition by pigeons and humans. *Science, 218,* 804–806.

Holloway, R. (2001). Brain, evolution of. In N. J. Smelser & P. B. Baltes (Eds.), *International encyclopedia of the social and behavioral sciences* (pp. 1338–1345). Oxford: Elsevier Science.

Houdé, O., & Tzourio-Mazoyer, N. (2003). Neural foundations of logical and mathematical cognition. *Nature Reviews Neuroscience, 4,* 507–514

Hunt, E. (1980). Intelligence as an information-processing concept. *British Journal of Psychology, 71,* 449–474.

Janssen, R. (1992). Thermal influences on nervous system function. *Neuroscience & Biobehavioral Reviews, 16,* 399–413.

Jarvis, E., Güntürkün, O., Bruce, L., Csillag, A., Karten, H., and 24 further authors. (2005). Avian brains and a new understanding of vertebrate brain evolution. *Nature Reviews Neuroscience, 6,* 151–159.

Jensen, A. R. (2000). The g factor, psychometrics and biology. In G. R. Bock, J. A. Goode, & K. Webb (Eds.), *The nature of intelligence* (pp. 37–57). Chichester: Wiley.

Jerison, H. J. (2001). The evolution of neural and behavioral complexity. In G. Roth & M. F. Wulliman (Eds.), *Brain evolution and cognition* (pp. 524–553). New York: Wiley.

Jitsumori, M., Siemann, M., Lehr, M., & Delius, J. D. (2002). A novel approach to the formation of equivalence classes in pigeons. *Journal of the Experimental Analysis of Behavior, 78,* 397–408.

Johnson, D. L., Swank, P. R., Baldwin, C. D., & McCormick, D. D. (1999). Adult smoking in the home environment and children's IQ. *Psychological Reports, 84,* 149–154.

Kaessmann, H., & Pääbo, S. (2002). The genetical history of humans and the great apes. *Journal of Internal Medicine, 250,* 1–18.

Kail, R., & Pellegrino, J. W. (1985). *Human intelligence: Perspective and prospects.* New York: Freeman.

Kamil, A. C., Jones, T. B. Pitrewicz, A. M., & Mauldin, J. E. (1977). Positive transfer from successive reversal training to learning set in blue jays. *Journal of Comparative & Physiological Psychology, 91,* 79–86.

Kamil, A. C., Lougee, M., & Schulman, R. J. (1973). Learning-set behaviour in the learning-set experienced blue-jay. *Journal of Comparative & Physiological Psychology, 82,* 394–405.

Kaschube, M., Wolf, F., & Geisel, T. (2002). Genetic influence on quantitative features of neocortical architecture. *Journal of Neuroscience, 22,* 7206–7217.

Kaufman, A. S. (2000). Tests of intelligence. In R. J. Sternberg (Ed.), *Handbook of intelligence* (pp. 445–476). Cambridge: Cambridge University Press.

Kingsbury, M. A., Rehen, S. K., Contos, J. J. A., Higgins, C. M., & Chun, J. (2003). Nonproliferative effects of lysophosphatic acid enhance cortical growth and folding. *Nature Neuroscience, 6,* 1292–1299.

Kirk, K. M., Blomberg, S. P., Duffy, D. L., Heath, A. C., Owens, I. P. F., & Martin, N. G. (2001). Natural selection and quantitative genetics of life-history traits in western women: A twin study. *Evolution, 55,* 423–435.

Klimes-Dougan, B., & Kopp, C. B. (1999). Childrens conflict tactics with mothers: A longitudinal investigation on the toddler and preschool years. *Merrill-Palmer Quarterly Journal of Developmental Psychology, 45,* 226–241.

Knauff, M., Mulack, T., Kassubek, J., Salih, H. R., & Greenlee, M. W. (2002). Spatial imagery in deductive reasoning: A functional MRI study. *Cognitive Brain Research, 13,* 203–212.

Koechlin, E., Basso, G., Pietrini, P., Panzer, S., & Grafman, J. (1999). The role of the anterior prefrontal cortex in human cognition. *Nature, 399,* 148–151.

Köhler, M., & Moyà-Solà, S. (2004). Reduction of brain and sense organs in the fossil insular bovid *Myotragus. Brain, Behavior & Evolution, 63,* 125–140.

Krebs, J. R. (1990). Food storing birds: Adaptive specialization in brain and behaviour. *Philosophical Transactions of the Royal Society of London, Series B, 329,* 153–160.

Ledoux, J. (1998). *The emotional brain: The mysterious underpinnings of emotional life.* New York: Simon & Schuster.

Leighton, J. P., & Sternberg, R. J. (Eds.). (2003). *The nature of reasoning.* Cambridge: Cambridge University Press.

Lenz, P. (2000). The concept of intelligence in psychology and philosophy. In H. Kruse, J. Dean, & H. Ritter (Eds.), *Prerational intelligence: Interdisciplinary perspectives on the behaviour of natural and artificial systems* (pp. 19–30). Dordrecht: Kluwer.

Levine, M., & Tjian, R. (2003). Transcription regulation and animal diversity. *Nature, 424,* 147–151.

Lloyd, J., & Barenbatt, L. (1984). Intrinsic intellectuality: Its relations to social class, intelligence and achievement. *Journal of Personality & Social Psychology, 46,* 664–654.

Logie, R. H., & Della Sala, S. (2001). Working memory, psychology of. In N. J. Smelser & P. B. Baltes (Eds.), *International encyclopedia of the social and behavioral sciences* (pp. 16587–16593). Oxford: Elsevier Science.

Lohman, D. F. (2000). Complex information processing and intelligence. In R. J. Sternberg (Ed.), *Handbook of intelligence* (pp. 285–340). New York: Cambridge University Press.

Lohmann, A., Delius, J. D., Hollard, V., & Friesel, M. (1988). Discrimination of shape reflections and shape orientations by *Columba livia. Journal of Comparative Psychology, 102,* 3–13.

Lombardi, C. M. (1987). Shape oddity recognition by pigeons is independent of shape orientation. *Revista Mexicana del Análisis de la Conducta, 13,* 265–272.

Lynn, R. (1999). New evidence for dysgenic fertility for intelligence in the United States. *Social Biology, 46,* 146–153.

Mackintosh, N. J. (1998). *IQ and human intelligence.* Oxford: Oxford University Press

Mackintosh, N. J., Wilson, B., & Boakes, R. A. (1985). Difference in mechanisms of intelligence among vertebrates. In L. Weiskrantz (Ed.), *Animal intelligence* (pp. 53–65). Oxford: Clarendon.

Macphail, E. M. (1987). The comparative psychology of intelligence. *Behavioral & Brain Sciences, 10,* 645–656.

Macphail, E. M., & Bolhuis, J. J. (2001). The evolution of intelligence: Adaptive specialization versus general processes. *Biological Reviews, 76,* 341–364.

Maguire, E. A., Gadian, D. G., Johnsrude, I. S., Good, C. D., Ashburner, J., Frackowiak, R. S. J., et al.. (2000). Navigation-related structural change in the hippocampi of taxi drivers. *Proceedings of the National Academy of Sciences USA, 97,* 4398–4403.

Matlin, M. W. (2002). *Cognition* (5th ed). Fort Worth, TX: Harcourt.

Matsumoto, E., Ohigashi, Y., Fujimori, M., & Mori, E. (2000). The processing of global and local visual information in Alzheimer's disease. *Behavioral Neurology, 12,* 119–125.

Matzel, L. D., Gandhi, C. C., & Muzzio, I. A. (2000). Synaptic efficacy is commonly regulated within a nervous system and predicts individual differences in learning. *Neuroreport, 11,* 1253–1257.

Matzel, L. D., Han, Y. R., Grossman, H., Karnik, M. S., Patel, D., Scott, N., et al. (2003). Individual differences in the expression of a "general" learning ability in mice. *Journal of Neuroscience, 23,* 6423–6433.

Mayer, J. D., Caruso, D. R., & Salovey, P. (2000). Emotional intelligence meets traditional standards for an intelligence. *Intelligence, 27,* 267–298.

Medin, D. L., Ross, B. H., & Markman, A. B. (2001). *Cognitive psychology* (3rd ed.). Fort Worth, TX: Harcourt.

Murphy, G. (2003). Lost for words. *Nature, 425,* 340–342.

Murphy, G. L. (2002). *The big book of concepts.* Cambridge, MA: MIT Press.

Nakajima, S., Arimatsu, K., & Lattal, K. M. (2002). Estimation of animal intelligence by university students in Japan and the United States. *Anthrozoös, 15,* 194–204.

Nakajima, S., & Sato, M. (1993). Removal of an obstacle: Problem solving behavior in pigeons. *Journal of the Experimental Analysis of Behavior, 59,* 131–145.

Neiss, M., & Rowe, D. C. (2000). Parental education and child's verbal IQ in adoptive and biological families. *Behavioral Genetics, 30,* 487–495.

Neisser, U. (1998). *The rising curve: Long term gains in IQ and related measures.* Washington, DC: American Psychological Association.

Neubauer, A. C., & Bucik, V. (1996). The mental speed–IQ relationship: Unitary or modular? *Intelligence, 22,* 23–46.

Neubauer, A. C., Spinath, F. M., Riemann, R., Borkenau, P., & Angleitner, A. (2000). Genetic and environmental influences on two measures of speed of information processing and their relation to psychometric intelligence. *Intelligence, 28,* 267–289.

Newsome, S., Day, A., & Catano, V. M. (2000). Assessing the predictive validity of emotional intelligence. *Personality & Individual Differences, 29,* 1005–1016.

Nowak, M. A., Komarova, N. L., & Niyogi, P. (2003). Computational and evolutionary aspects of language. *Nature, 417,* 611–617.

Paradiso, S., Andreasen, N. C., O'Leary, D. S., Arndt, S., & Robinson, R. G. (1997). Cerebellar size and cognition, correlations with IQ, verbal memory and motor dexterity. *Neuropsychiatry, Neuropsychology, & Behavioral Neurology, 10,* 1–8.

Pastuovic, N., Kolesaric, V., & Krizmanic, M. (1995). Psychological variables as predictors of quality of life. *Review of Psychology, 2,* 49–61.

Pepperberg, I. M. (1999). *The Alex studies: Cognitive and communicative abilities of grey parrots.* Cambridge, MA: Harvard University Press.

Petrill, S. A. (2002). The case for general intelligence: A behavioural perspective. In R. J. Sternberg & E. L. Grigorenko (Eds.), *The general factor of intelligence: How general is it?* (pp. 281–298). Mahwah, NJ: Erlbaum.

Plomin, R. (2001). Genetics of intelligence. In N. J. Smelser & P. B. Baltes (Eds.), *International encyclopedia of the social and behavioral sciences* (pp. 7645–7651). Oxford: Elsevier Science.

Plomin, R., De Fries, J. C., McClearn, G. E., & Rutter, M. (1997). *Behavioral genetics.* New York: Freeman.

Plotnik, R. J., & Tallarico, R. B. (1966). Object-quality learning-set formation in the young chicken. *Psychonomic Science, 5,* 195–196.

Povinelli, D. J., Reaux, J. E., Theall, L. A., & Giambrone, S. (2000). *Folk physics for apes.* Oxford: Oxford University Press.

Premack, D. (1988). Minds with and without language. In L. Weiskrantz (Ed.), *Thought without language* (pp. 46–65). Oxford: Clarendon.

Premack, D. (2004). Is language the key to human intelligence? *Science, 303,* 318–320.

Putz-Osterloh, W., & Lüer, G. (1981). Über die Vorhersagbarkeit komplexer Problemlöseleistungen durch Ergebnisse in einem Intelligenztest [About the predictability of problem-solving competencies by intelligence test results]. *Zeitschrift für experimentelle und angewandte Psychologie, 28,* 309–334.

Rae, G., & McAnulty, H. (1995). Relationship between musical ability and intelligence after correction for attenuation. *Perceptual & Motor Skills, 81,* 746.

Ramnani, N., & Miall, R. C. (2004). A system in the human brain for predicting the actions of others. *Nature Neuroscience, 7,* 85–90.

Reed, T. E., & Jensen, A. R. (1993). Conduction velocity in a brain nerve pathway of normal adults correlates with intelligence level. *Intelligence, 16,* 259–272.

Rehkämper, G., Frahm, H. D., & Mann, M. D. (2001). Evolutionary constraints of large telencephala. In G. Roth & M. F. Wulliman (Eds.), *Brain evolution and cognition* (pp. 49–76). New York: Wiley.

Riggio, R. E., Messamer, J., & Throckmorton, B. (1991). Social and academic intelligence: Conceptually distinct but overlapping constructs. *Personality & Individual Differences, 12,* 695–702.

Rogan, W. J., & Gladen, B. C. (1993). Breastfeeding and cognitive development. *Early Human Development, 31,* 181–193.

Roitblat, H. L., & von Fersen, L. (1992). Comparative cognition: Representations and processes in learning and memory. *Annual Review of Psychology, 43,* 671–710.

Roth, G., Blanke, J., & Wake, D. B. (1994). Cell size predicts morphological complexity in the brains of frogs and salamanders. *Proceedings of the National Academy of Sciences USA, 91,* 4796–4800.

Ruben, J. (1995). The evolution of endothermy in mammals and birds: From physiology to fossils. *Annual Review of Physiology, 57,* 69–95.

Russel, S. J., & Norvig, P. (1995). *Artificial intelligence: A modern approach.* Englewood Cliffs, NJ: Prentice Hall.

Salovey, P., Bedell, B. T., Detweiler, J. B., & Mayer, J. D. (2000). Current directions in emotional research. In M. Lewis & J. M. Haviland-Jones (Eds.), *Handbook of emotions* (pp. 504–520). New York: Guilford.

Scarr, S., & McCartney, K. (1983). How people make their environments: A theory of genotype-environment effects. *Child Development, 54,* 424–435.

Schmahmann, J. D. (Ed.). (1997). *The cerebellum and cognition.* San Diego: Academic Press.

Schmidt, F. L., & Hunter, J. E. (1998). The validity and utility of selection methods in personnel psychology: Practical and theoretical implications of 85 years of research findings. *Psychological Bulletin, 124,* 262–274.

Schofield, N. J. & Ashman, A. F. (1986). The relationship between digit span and cognitive processing across ability groups. *Intelligence, 10,* 59–73.

Schusterman, R. J. (1964). Successive discrimination-reversal training and multiple discrimination training in one trial learning by chimpanzees. *Journal of Comparative & Physiological Psychology, 58,* 153–156.

Scott, P., Jones, K. E., & Wilkinson, G. S. (in press). Mating system and brain size in bats. *Proceedings of the Royal Society B: Biological Sciences.*

Shettleworth, S. J. (1998). *Cognition, evolution and behavior.* Oxford: Oxford University Press.

Sidman, M. (1992). *Equivalence relations and behavior: A research story.* Boston: Authors' Cooperative.

Siemann, M., & Delius, J. D. (1998). Algebraic learning and neural network models for transitive and nontransitive responding in humans and animals. *European Journal of Cognitive Psychology, 10,* 307–334.

Siemann, M., von Fersen, L., & Delius, J. D. (1998). Kognition bei Tieren [Cognition in animals]. In E. Irle & H. J. Markowitsch (Eds.), *Enzyklopädie der Psychologie: Vergleichende Psychobiologie* (pp. 695–738). Göttingen: Hogrefe.

Siemann, M., von Selzam, A., & Borchert, K. (2004). *Functional equivalence extraction in students.* Unpublished manuscript, Universität Konstanz.

Sloman, S. A., & Rips, L. J. (Eds.). (1998). *Similarity and symbols in human thinking.* Cambridge, MA: MIT Press.

Slotnick, B. M., Hanford, L., & Hodos, W. (2000). Can rats acquire an olfactory learning set? *Journal of Experimental Psychology: Animal Behavior Processes, 26,* 399–415.

Slotnik, B. M., & Katz, H. M. (1974). Olfactory learning-set formation in rats. *Science, 185,* 796–798.

Smith Churchland, P. (2002). Brain-wise: Studies in neurophilosophy. Cambridge, MA: MIT Press.

Snow, R. E., Kyllonen, P. C., & Marshalek, B. (1984). The topography of ability and learning correlations. In R. J. Sternberg (Ed.), *Advances in the psychology of human intelligence* (Vol. 2, pp. 47–103). Hillsdale, NJ: Erlbaum.

Snyder, A. W., & Mitchell, D. J. (1999). Is integer arithmetic fundamental to mental processing? The mind's secret arithmetic. *Proceedings of the Royal Society of London, Series B, 266,* 587–592.

Staddon, J. E. R., & Frank, J. (1974). Mechanisms of reversal learning. *Animal Behaviour, 22,* 806–828.

Sternberg, R. J. (1996). *Cognitive psychology.* Fort Worth, TX: Harcourt Brace.

Sternberg, R. J., Forsythe, G. B., Hedlund, J., Horvath, J. A., Wagner, R. K., Williams, W. M., et al. (2000). *Practical intelligence in everyday life.* Cambridge: Cambridge University Press.

Sternberg, R. J., & Grigorenko, E. L. (2001). Unified psychology. *American Psychologist, 56,* 1069–1079.

Sternberg, R. J., & Grigorenko, E. L. (Eds.). (2002). *The psychology of abilities, competencies, and expertise.* Cambridge: Cambridge University Press.

Thompson, P. M., Cannon, T. D., Narr, K. L., van Erp, T., Poutanen, V. P., Huttunen, M., et al. (2001). Genetic influences on brain structure. *Nature Neuroscience, 4,* 1253–1258.

Timberlake, W., & Lucas, G. A. (1989). Behaviour systems and learning: From misbehavior to general principles. In S. B. Klein & R. R. Mowrer (Eds.), *Contemporary learning theories: Instrumental conditioning and the impact of biological constraints on learning* (pp. 237–275). Hillsdale, NJ: Erlbaum.

Tomasello, M., & Call, J. (1997). *Primate cognition.* Oxford: Oxford University Press.

Turkheimer, E., Haley, A., Waldron, M., D'Onofrio, B., & Gottesman, I. I. (2003). Socoeconomic status modifies heritability of IQ in young children. *Psychological Science, 14,* 623–628.

Van Dongen, P. A. M. (1998). Brain size in vertebrates. In R. Nieuwenhuys, H. J. ten Donkelaar, & C. Nicholson (Eds.), *The central nervous system of vertebrates* (pp. 2099–2134). Berlin: Springer.

Veenman, C. L. (1997). Pigeon basal ganglia: Insights into the neuroanatomy underlying telencephalic sensorimotor processes in birds. *European Journal of Morphology, 35,* 220–233.

Vernon, P. A. (Ed.). (1987). *Speed of information-processing and intelligence.* Norwood, NJ: Ablex.

Vignal, C., Mathevon, N., & Mottin, S. (2004). Audience drives male songbird responses to partner's voice. *Nature, 430,* 448–450.

Volman, S. F. (1990). Neuroethological approaches to the evolution of neural systems. *Brain, Behavior & Evolution, 36,* 154–165.

von Fersen, L., & Delius, J. D. (2001). Acquired equivalences between auditory stimuli in dolphins (*Tursiops truncatus*). *Animal Cognition, 3,* 79–83.

von Fersen, L., Wynne, C. D. L., Delius, J. D., & Staddon, J. E. R. (1991). Transitive inference formation in pigeons. *Journal of Experimental Psychology: Animal Behavior Processes, 17,* 334–341.

Wallis, J. D., Anderson, K. C., & Miller, E. K. (2001). Single neurons in prefrontal cortex encode abstract rules. *Nature, 411,* 953–962.

Warren, J. M. (1973). Learning in vertebrates. In D. A. Dewsbury & D. A. Rethlingshafer (Eds.), *Comparative psychology: A modern survey* (pp. 471–509). New York: McGraw-Hill.

Wasserman, E. A. (1993). Comparative cognition: Beginning the second century of the study of animal intelligence. *Psychological Bulletin, 113,* 211–228.

Weir, A., Chappell, A. S., & Kacelnik, A. (2002). Shaping of hooks in New Caledonian crows. *Nature, 297,* 981.

Weissenbach, J. (2004). Differences with relatives. *Nature, 429,* 353–355.

Whiten, A., & Byrne, R. W. (Eds.). (1997). *Machiavallian intelligence: Evaluations and extensions.* Cambridge: Cambridge University Press.

Wild, J. M., & Williams, M. N. (2000). Rostral wulst in passerine birds: Origin, course, and terminations of an avian pyramidal tract. *Journal of Comparative Neurology, 416,* 429–450.

Wilson, E. O. (1975). *Sociobiology: The new synthesis.* Cambridge, MA: Harvard University Press.

Wiltschko, W., & Wiltschko, R. (2002). Magnetic compass orientation in birds and its physiological basis. *Naturwissenschaften, 89,* 445–452.

Wohlschläger, A., & Wohlschläger, A. (1998). Mental and manual rotation. *Journal of Experimental Psychology: Human Perception and Performance, 24,* 397–412

Wright, A. A. (1990). Memory processing by pigeons, monkeys and people. In Bower, G. H.

(Ed.), *The psychology of learning and motivation* (Vol. 24, pp. 25–70). New York: Academic Press.

Xia, L., Emmerton, J., Siemann, M., & Delius, J. D. (2001). Pigeons learn to link numerosities with symbols. *Journal of Comparative Psychology, 115,* 83–91.

Young, M. E., & Wasserman, E. A. (2001). Evidence for a conceptual account of same-different discrimination learning in the pigeon. *Psychonomic Bulletin & Review, 8,* 677–684.

Zajonc, R. B. (2001). The family dynamics of intellectual development. *American Psychologist, 56,* 490–496.

Zatorre, R. J. (2005). Music the food of neuroscience? *Nature, 434,* 312–316.

Zentall, T. R. (1998). Symbolic representation in animals: Emergent stimulus relations in conditional discrimination learning. *Animal Learning & Behavior, 26,* 363–377.

Zentall, T. R. (2000). Animal intelligence. In R. J. Sternberg (Ed.), *Handbook of intelligence* (pp. 197–215). New York: Cambridge University Press.

Zgorniaknowosielska, I., Zawilinska, B., & Szostek, S. (1996). Rubella infection during pregnancy in the 1985–86 epidemic: Follow-up after seven years. *European Journal of Epidemiology, 12,* 303–308.

Zhou, Z., Barrett, P. M., & Hilton, J. (2003). An exceptionally preserved lower cretaceous ecosystem. *Nature, 421,* 807–814.

29

How Do Dolphins Solve Problems?

STAN A. KUCZAJ II AND RACHEL THAMES WALKER

Much of an animal's life consists of problems that it must overcome if it is to survive. The solutions to some problems have been provided by an animal's evolutionary history, and so require little thought. For example, an animal that accidentally touches a hot surface will automatically and immediately retract the body part that is in contact with the surface and thereby avoid more serious damage to that body part. Although not initially reflexive, solutions to other problems may become automatic as the result of experience. For example, rats learn to avoid novel tastes that are associated with illness (Garcia & Koelling, 1966) and decrease their chances of ingesting potentially poisonous substances if they survive the first encounter with the substance. Reflexively removing a body part from a painful situation or avoiding tastes that have been associated with illness does not require awareness of the problem or a conscious decision to implement behaviors to solve the problem, demonstrating that problem solving need not involve insight or conscious effort.

Of course, not all problem solving is automatic. Problems that involve the presence of a desired state of affairs and the absence of an immediately apparent way to achieve this state may be said to require conscious effort if a solution is to be found (Holyoak, 1995). In such cases, problem solving may be purposeful. Some animals appear to engage in purposeful problem solving. An orangutan that mimics the clothes-washing behaviors of a human (Russon, 1996) and a raven that uses its feet and beak to obtain a piece of meat dangling from its perch on a piece of string (Heinrich, 1999) each appears to be doing something more than simply reacting to external stimuli. Nonetheless, it is not clear exactly what sorts of cognitive processes, if any, are necessary to explain the orangutan's clothes-washing behavior or the raven's apprehension of the need to step on the string after having lifted it with its beak. Did the orangutan intend to mimic the clothes-washing behaviors it had witnessed? Or were the clothes and soap simply made more salient by its observations of others interacting with these objects? Did the raven learn via trial and error to use both beak and feet? Or did it arrive at this behavior by reflectively considering the problem and determining the best solution?

Trial-and-error learning and conscious reflection appear to lie at opposite ends of the problem-solving spectrum. Trial-and-error learning is one of the least sophisticated forms of problem solving; it requires only that the organism keep trying new behaviors until the desired goal is achieved (Baron, 1988). In contrast, consciously considering possible outcomes before determining the correct solution involves the ability to mentally represent aspects of the world and the ability to manipulate these representations (Piaget, 1955).

The distinction between trial-and-error learning and the sorts of reflection involved in planning and insight is important in the history of the comparative study of problem solving. Romanes (1883) suggested that some animals are capable of relating ends to means and that this capacity is the hallmark of intelligence:

> Reason or intelligence is the faculty which is concerned with the intentional adaptation of means to ends. It therefore implies the conscious knowledge of the relation between means employed and ends attained, and may be exercised in adaptation to circumstances novel alike to the experience of the individual and to that of the species. (p. 17)

Romanes's assertions have not gone unchallenged. Thorndike (1911) argued that animals solved problems via trial-and-error learning rather than insight. Watson (1914), Hull (1943), and Skinner (1938) believed that explanations of behavior need rely only on analyses of the relationships between stimuli and responses. Morgan (1894) cautioned against interpreting behaviors in terms of more complex cognitive abilities when explanations involving simpler abilities would suffice, but he acknowledged the possibility that animals might possess higher-order cognitive abilities. Washburn (1936) argued that animals were able to mentally represent absent stimuli and that such abilities must be included in explanations of animal behavior (see also Yerkes, 1934). Tolman (1932) proposed that animals are active processors of information and can anticipate stimuli rather than simply react to them. According to Tolman, some animals are capable of inventive ideation, the end result of an attempt to solve a problem. When an animal encounters a novel problem, Tolman believed that they first attempt to solve the problem via trial and error. If this fails, then some animals cease overt responses and "reflect" on the problem. Tolman suggested that visual inspection and scratching one's head might be overt indications of such reflection. However, the best evidence for inventive ideation is the subsequent sudden appearance of the correct response. Although Tolman recognized the importance of cognitive abilities for explanations of animal behavior, he hedged his bets insofar as abstract thought was concerned.

> Perhaps in all cases of true problem-solving, the growth in means-end-readiness . . . is an outgrowth of *fooling around with* either actual or hypothetical particulars [author's italics]. The thinker would . . . perceive or mnemonize himself into the presence of a particular and be led to "infer" new responses which he might make to this particular. Perhaps . . . there is fundamentally no such thing as "abstract" thought. There are abstractions behind one's thought, and these abstractions grow, but one's thought itself is perhaps always a running-over of presented or imagined particulars or groups of particulars. (p. 231)

The debate over the roles of trial-and-error learning and insight/planning in animal problem solving has not abated. Many species are capable of trial-and-error learning. For example, certain spiders improve their predatory success via trial and error (Jackson & Wilcox, 1998), but they seem to be unlikely candidates for conscious planning or insight. Other species (including our own) engage in behavior that might seem to involve some sort of planning, but actually involves less cognitive sophistication.

For instance, it is not clear exactly what processes are involved in animal imitation (or even which animals are capable of true imitation; see Heyes, 1996; Kuczaj, Paulos, & Ramos, 2005; Tomasello, 1996; Zentall, 1996). If we consider imitation as a problem in which the animal must determine both the behavior to be imitated and how to reproduce the performance of the model, then imitation takes on a cognitive flavor reminiscent of that suggested by Romanes and Tolman. In such a case, the orangutan that learned to mimic clothes washing might have done so by observing the human activity, storing the representation of this behavior in memory, mentally rehearsing the washing behaviors, and then producing the behaviors. Alternatively, its attention may have been drawn to the soap and clothes by the witnessed activity; the subsequent mimicry may merely be the result of trial-and-error learning with salient objects. The latter scenario requires less representational sophistication than does the intentional imitation possibility. Clearly, the interpretation of observed behaviors determines the types of cognitive abilities that investigators grant to animals (see Berthelet & Chavaillon, 1993; Bradshaw & Rogers, 1993; Gibson & Ingold, 1993, for discussions of the relative roles of trial-and-error learning and planning in tool use).

In this chapter, we explore the problem-solving capabilities of bottlenose dolphins. Dolphins possess relatively large brains (Marino, 1998; Ridgway & Brownson, 1979), and have demonstrated a variety of cognitive abilities (e.g., Harley, Roitblat, & Nachtigall, 1996; Herman, Matus, Herman, Ivancic, & Pack, 2001; Kellogg & Rice, 1966; Mercado, Murray, Uyeyama, Pack, & Herman, 1998; Richards, Wolz, & Herman, 1984; von Fersen & Delius, 2000). However, relatively little is known about the manner in which dolphins solve problems. We first consider two cases (dolphin "syntax" and dolphin "pointing") in which dolphins derived strategies in response to problems posed to them by humans. Although neither of these studies was designed to directly study problem solving, the dolphins' solutions to the problems they encountered revealed the types of strategies that they spontaneously used. We next summarize a series of studies designed to assess the ability of dolphins to plan their behavior when confronted with novel problems. We then present recent findings on dolphin play and consider the role of play in the emergence of problem-solving skills.

DOLPHIN PROCESSING OF GESTURAL SEQUENCES: EVIDENCE OF SYNTACTIC ABILITIES OR INFORMATION-PROCESSING STRATEGIES?

Little is known about the structure and function of dolphin communication systems (Tyack, 2000). The meaningful units of dolphin communication have yet to be determined, making it impossible to ascertain the referential functions of dolphin communication or to investigate whether dolphins spontaneously combine such units in some meaningful way (see Hauser, 1996; Kuczaj & Kirkpatrick, 1993, for discussions of the significance of specifying the units of communication systems). Nonetheless, there are claims in the literature that dolphins are capable of learning syntax (e.g., Griffin, 2001; Herman, Richards, & Wolz, 1984). These claims are based in large part on the accomplishments of one female dolphin, Akeakamai (Ake). She was taught an artificial comprehension-based communication system consisting of individual gestures that could be combined into short sequences. Although we occasionally use terms like language, verb, and grammar as convenient labels in our discussion of Ake's performance with this gestural communication system, we do not mean to imply that the system Ake learned is in fact like a human language or that she conceptually represents notions like "verb" or "grammar." The artificial communication system that Ake acquired is vastly different from any human language, and it is unlikely that she learned the system in terms of grammatical rules or categories such as verb.

Two types of sequences formed the core of the language that Ake learned to comprehend. Action sequences contained two gestures: (1) a gesture that designated an object and (2) a gesture that referred to an action to be performed with the object. Thus, action sequences instructed Ake to perform a single action on a single object. For example, the sequence PIPE UNDER instructed Ake to swim under the pipe that was floating in the tank. Relational sequences contained two object gestures and one "relational action" gesture. Relational sequences required Ake to first obtain a particular object and then either take it to or put it into (or on) another object. For example, the sequence HOOP BALL IN instructed Ake to first get the ball and then put it inside the hoop. Although modifiers were also occasionally included in action and relational sequences, our main concern is the difference between action sequences and relational sequences, specifically the number of object gestures that preceded the (relational) action term. Action sequences contained one object gesture and relational sequences contained two object gestures. In a relational sequence, the object gesture that occurred closest to the relational action term was always the direct object (the one that Ake was supposed to act on first) and the object gesture farthest from the relational action term was the indirect object. In both types of sequences, the action to be performed was the last gesture to be produced.

As noted above, the language Ake was taught was strictly unidirectional. Humans could use the system to ask Ake to perform specific actions, but Ake could not use the system to communicate with humans. Thus, Ake was required to learn to comprehend the gestural system but not to produce it. Despite this limitation, her performance with novel sequences suggested a facile command of this artificial language and perhaps even an appreciation for the grammatical rules that governed it (Herman et al., 1984).

However, not everyone agreed that Ake had actually learned something that approximated syntax (see Herman, 1987; Herman & Uyeyama, 1999;

Kako, 1999; Schusterman & Gisiner, 1988, 1989, for discussions of this issue, and Hauser, Chomsky, & Fitch, 2002, for a broader consideration of the comparative study of language faculties). For example, Schusterman and Gisiner (1989) argued that Ake's performance had been overinterpreted by Herman and his colleagues and that there was insufficient evidence to conclude that Ake used grammatical rules and symbolic representations in her responses to the gestural sequences of her language. Instead, Schusterman and Gisiner proposed that both Ake and the sea lion they studied had learned to form connections between gestures and their referents, to classify gestures into various types, and to make conditional discriminations about the relationships between sequences of gestures.

Ake's correct responses to grammatical sequences (i.e., those that did not violate the rules of the system she was taught) do not clarify the nature of the information she used to process the sequences. The same problem exists for those who study human children's language acquisition: correct use has multiple possible explanations (Brown, 1973; Kuczaj, 1977). Asking children to respond to anomalous sentences has helped determine their understanding of the language they are learning (Carr, 1979; Kuczaj & Brannick, 1979; Kuczaj & Maratsos, 1975; Tyler & Marslen-Wilson, 1981). Such sentences violate either semantic or syntactic rules and are processed by young children in terms of their existing grammatical and semantic knowledge. As a result, children's responses to anomalous sentences can sometimes be particularly revealing of their developing grammatical and semantic knowledge. Anomalous sequences were thus given to Ake in the hope that her responses would reveal the information she used to interpret the grammatical sequences to which she was normally exposed (Herman, Kuczaj, & Holder, 1993; Holder, Herman, & Kuczaj, 1993).

At the time of testing, Ake knew 14 object gestures, 17 action gestures, and 2 relational action gestures. She also understood a small number of other gestures, such as the modifiers RIGHT and LEFT. Over an 8-month period, Ake received 31 different types of anomalous sequences and 201 distinct anomalous sequences. Anomalies were embedded in sessions of grammatical sequences, the ratio usually being one or two anomalies in a session of 20 or so sequences (see Herman et al., 1993, and Holder et al., 1993, for more detailed discussions of the procedure).

Ake's performance on anomalies that contained an uninterrupted grammatical sequence provided the most useful information about her processing of grammatical sequences. These anomalies were grouped into three broad categories. (1) Initial embedded grammatical sequences: These anomalies had uninterrupted grammatical strings embedded at the beginning of each sequence. For example, PIPE UNDER TOSS contained the grammatical sequence PIPE UNDER at the beginning of the sequence and was made anomalous by adding one more action gesture (TOSS) to the end of the sequence. (2) Middle embedded grammatical sequences: These anomalies contained uninterrupted grammatical strings in the middle of each sequence. For example, in WATER PIPE BASKET IN FETCH, the grammatical relational sequence PIPE BASKET IN is preceded by an object term (WATER) and followed by an additional relational action term (FETCH). (3) Final embedded grammatical sequences: These anomalies ended with an uninterrupted grammatical string. For example, SPIT PHOENIX BALL IN concluded with the grammatical relational sequence PHOENIX BALL IN.

There were various ways in which Ake could have responded to each of these anomalies. She could have simply not responded at all, suggesting that she was unable to interpret the strange sequence. Failures to respond occurred for all three types of anomalies but more so for middle embedded anomalies. Ake failed to respond to both initial embedded and final embedded anomalies on approximately 25% of the occasions in which she received such anomalies, but she did not respond to middle embedded anomalies approximately 43% of the time.

When Ake did respond to an anomaly, one possibility was that she would respond to the first uninterrupted grammatical sequence to occur. She did so for 54% of the initial embedded anomalies (excluding those to which she failed to respond). For example, having received the sequence BASKET TOSS BALL, Ake went to the basket and tossed it. She also produced responses consistent with the first uninterrupted grammatical sequence for 36% of the final embedded grammatical sequences (again excluding those to which she failed to respond). Thus, WATER FRISBEE BALL FETCH resulted in Ake taking the ball to the Frisbee. However, Ake rarely responded to a middle embedded grammatical sequence by producing behaviors that corresponded to the sequence, doing so only on 14% of the occasions in which she produced a response to such anomalies. An example of such a response involved Ake taking the pipe to a person after being given WATER PERSON PIPE FETCH PECTOUCH.

We have considered two of the ways in which Ake responded to anomalous sequences: failing to respond at all or acting out the first uninterrupted grammatical sequence. Before turning to Ake's other response types, we should note that there were many reasonable interpretations that Ake could have made. For example, after seeing the PIPE UNDER TOSS sequence, Ake could have swum under the pipe if she was responding to the first uninterrupted grammatical sequence (PIPE UNDER), tossed the pipe if she organized her response around the last action gesture (the normal state of affairs in her language), or swum under the pipe and then tossed it if she wished to respond to every gesture in the sequence. SPEAKER PIPE OVER FETCH could have resulted in Ake jumping over the pipe or the speaker (or both) or taking the pipe to the speaker. Despite the range of possible interpretations, Ake provided consistent responses to the anomalies. Her consistent interpretations of anomalies helped to determine the manner in which she processed the grammatical sequences she had been taught.

Ake's responses suggested that her performance could be explained in terms of the following strategies, each of which is consistent with the rules of the language she was taught.

STRATEGY 1: If a gestural sequence contains more than one object gesture, then anticipate a relational action gesture.

STRATEGY 2: If a gestural sequence contains more than one object gesture, but no relational action gesture, then respond to the last action gesture.

The first strategy directly reflects Ake's experience with her language. Normal sequences that contained two object terms were always followed by one of two relational action gestures; Ake seems to have developed a processing strategy that was strongly biased by this regularity. The second strategy reflects Ake's attempts to make sense of sequences that violated what she has learned—two (or more) object gestures followed by an action gesture rather than a relational action gesture. When she responded to such sequences, Ake's performance suggested that she had been waiting for a relational action term. When none appeared, she used the default option described in strategy 2 and incorporated the last action gesture into her response.

The evidence for these two strategies comes from Ake's responses to anomalies that contained two or more object gestures and some combination of two action/relational action gestures. When an anomaly contained two action gestures and Ake produced a response that involved one of the signed actions, she produced the action specified by the last action gesture 96% of the time (e.g., she jumped over the ball after seeing BASKET BALL MOUTH OVER and touched the basket with her tail after seeing BASKET OVER TAILTOUCH). However, when an anomaly contained multiple object gestures and a relational action gesture, Ake always responded to the first relational gesture to appear. This tendency was true regardless of whether an action gesture preceded the relational action gesture (e.g., PHOENIX FRISBEE SPIT FETCH resulted in Ake taking the Frisbee to Phoenix), an action gesture followed the relational action gesture (e.g., Ake took the ball to the person after seeing PERSON PIPE BALL FETCH TOSS), or there were two relational action gestures (e.g., PHOENIX BALL PIPE IN FETCH resulted in Ake taking the pipe and putting it/on Phoenix).

Clearly, Ake had learned that the presence of two objects in a sequence meant that a relational action term should follow. Once a relational term was given in such a context, Ake organized her response around it. Moreover, her incorporation of the objects indicated by the object gestures in a testing anomaly depended on both their sequential location and the type of "verb." Anomalies with multiple object gestures, but no relational action gesture confused Ake. When she responded to the action term in such contexts, she substituted objects that were not signed in 71% of her responses. For example, PIPE SURFBOARD MOUTH SPIT resulted in Ake spitting at the person and BALL WATER TAILTOUCH resulted in Ake touching the surfboard with her tail. In contrast, object substitutions occurred in only 26% of Ake's responses to anomalies that contained a relational action term; instead, Ake typically incorporated two of the signed objects into her response if the anomaly contained a relational action gesture. She was most likely to incorporate the first object gesture and the object gesture closest to the relational action gesture into her response. Thus, PERSON PIPE FRISBEE IN FETCH resulted in Ake taking the Frisbee and putting it on the person. This pattern demonstrates that adjacency of gestures was not a requisite for Ake to organize a subset of the gestures into a coherent response. Instead, there was an effect of primacy (the first object gesture was frequently incorporated into her response) and an effect of adjacency to the relational action gesture (objects that were indicated by gestures closest to the relational action gesture were also likely to be used in Ake's responses).

Object substitutions in relational anomalies were most likely to occur when an action term interrupted the normal flow of a relational sequence. For example, when the action gesture PECTOUCH intruded in SPEAKER HOOP PECTOUCH IN, Ake took the hoop and put it into a basket. Similarly, inserting the action term MOUTH in WATER MOUTH SURFBOARD FETCH resulted in Ake taking a hoop to the water. If an action term happened to precede the entire sequence, as in OVER PHOENIX PIPE FETCH, then Ake might substitute both objects and take the Frisbee to the water.

These results demonstrate that Ake organized her responses to the gestural sequences of her language in two ways. First, she used the number of object gestures to anticipate the type of verb that should follow. Single-object signs indicated that an action gesture should follow; multiple-object gestures indicated that a relational action gesture should follow. These biases were so ingrained that Ake's use of signed objects was impaired when one of her expectations was violated. Specifically, when multiple-object signs were not followed by a relational action sign, Ake's use of the actual signed objects was less likely. This result is consistent with the notion that Ake had interpreted multiple-object gestures in terms of a relational response, and so consequently found it difficult to use either object in an action response when a relational action gesture did not occur in the sequence.

Second, despite her use of object gestures to anticipate verb type, Ake organized her responses around the action to be performed. When she responded to an anomalous sequence, Ake almost always used a verb that had occurred in the sequence (there were only two instances in which Ake used a verb that had not been used in the anomaly). So, even if her expectations about verb type were violated, Ake incorporated the signed verb into her response, sometimes at the expense of the signed objects. Additional evidence for this strategy comes from Ake's performance on semantically anomalous sequences such as WINDOW TOSS or SURFBOARD TWIRL (see Holder et al., 1993). These anomalies asked Ake to perform impossible actions. She rarely failed to respond to such anomalies; instead, she was more likely to substitute a nonsigned object with which to perform the requested action.

The relative significance of actions over objects for dolphins was also demonstrated by Mercado, Uyeyama, Pack, and Herman (1999). They asked a dolphin that had been trained with the same language as Ake to repeat actions that it had just performed on an object. For example, the dolphin may have been initially asked to swim under a basket. If it did so, then it might then be asked to repeat what it had just done. The dolphin was most likely to err by producing the correct action with the wrong object, suggesting that memory for actions was better than memory for objects. These results are consistent with the notion that actions are more salient than objects for dolphins, but it is also possible that the characteristics of the artificial language produced this bias. Verbs always occurred at the end of a sequence; the dolphins may have learned to organize their responses around such terminal terms. Replicating the Mercado et al. study with dolphins that had not been taught a similar system would help to tease apart these two possibilities.

It seems, then, that Ake's comprehension of the sequences in the language she had been taught was governed by both serial order information and by strategies she used to more readily interpret such information. She developed a set of processing strategies consistent with the rules of the language she was taught. If the language had been less predictable, then perhaps Ake would have developed strategies that went beyond the ones reported here.

The strategies that Ake used seem to reflect both rule learning and associative learning, as is the case in humans' and pigeons' acquisition of artificial grammars (Herbranson & Shimp, 2003; Knowlton & Squire, 1996). The nature of the rules to be learned in such situations depends in part on the complexity of the artificial grammar and in part on processing biases brought to the task by the learner. Determining processing biases will require fine-grained analyses of performance on anomalous sequences and the generalization of acquired rules. For example, the extent to which human children who have been exposed to artificial grammars overgeneralize regular rules to irregular instances depends on the specific instances of regular rules to which they have been exposed (Kuczaj & Borys, 1989).

Although Ake's performance suggests that she attempted to make sense of the anomalies, her flexibility was limited. She responded in ways that made sense given the language she had been taught, but she produced few creative responses. For example, she did not leap over two objects when the anomalous sequence leant itself to that interpretation. Nor did she conjoin two actions, such as swimming under the pipe and then tossing it after seeing PIPE UNDER TOSS. This finding contrasts sharply with the performance of human children, whose novel solutions to anomalies are often the most revealing of their linguistic prowess (Kuczaj & Brannick, 1979; Kuczaj & Maratsos, 1975). Ake's failure to produce such spontaneous innovations did not reflect an inability to perform such actions. She was later taught to act on two objects by teaching her the conjunctive AND (Prince, 1993; also reported in Herman & Uyeyama, 1999). Although Herman and Uyeyama reported that learning this new term "required effort," Ake did learn to interpret sequences such as HOOP AND BALL OVER and so jump over both the hoop and the ball. However, she had to be taught to do so.

We thus agree with Schusterman and Gisiner (1989) that it is not necessary to think of Ake's abilities in linguistic terms. As James (1890) cautioned in his discussion of the psychologist's fallacy, it is important that psychologists distinguish their own perspective from that of the subject they are studying. Failure to do so opens the door to overly rich interpretation of behavior (Morgan, 1894). In this case, Ake's performance can be interpreted in terms of human language processing (see Herman et al., 1993; Herman et al., 1994; Holder et al., 1993), but such an interpretation imposes a human linguistic perspective on her performance. We believe that Ake's performance can be explained without recourse to analogies to human grammatical capabilities. Instead, Ake's performance reflects reasonable strategies that she adopted when faced with the problem of most efficiently interpreting the communication system she was being taught. The extent to which these strategies reflect the inherent sequential processing biases that dolphins may have and the particular elements of the system Ake was taught (verbs always at the end of a sequence; only one object gesture before an action gesture; only one verb per sentence, etc.) requires additional research.

DOLPHIN POINTING: A SPONTANEOUS COMMUNICATION STRATEGY?

Gory, Xitco, and Kuczaj (1992, 1993) designed a two-way communication system for dolphins and humans that involved an underwater keyboard, the large structure shown in figure 29.1. Two adult male dolphins (Bob and Toby), housed at Epcot's Living Seas Pavilion, participated in this project. In this project, humans used the symbols on the keyboard as if they were words and so indirectly modeled keyboard use for the dolphins. Specifically, humans used the keyboard to describe the dolphins' environment, ask the dolphins simple questions, and announce impending activities. The most common activities involved searching for food and for toys and tools that might be of interest to the dolphins and that had been placed in various locations in the large aquarium.

During the course of this project, dolphins and humans often foraged together for desirable objects. Although Gory et al. had hoped that dolphins would use the keyboard to communicate with humans (which they did do, albeit in a limited manner), the dolphins also solved the problem of indicating objects of interest by adopting a novel behavior. Each dolphin began to spontaneously point at desired objects that required human assistance to obtain (Xitco, Gory, & Kuczaj, 2001). Dolphins lack arms, hands, and fingers and so engaged in "full-body" pointing by stopping and aligning the anterior/posterior axis of their body with the designated object.

Humans used pointing, with an extended arm and index finger, while interacting with the dolphins. It is possible, then, that the dolphins could have learned when to point, if not the exact form of the pointing gesture, by observing humans. However, this possibility does not seem to have been the case. Humans tended to point mostly to tools, toys, and other individuals. Although dolphins did occasionally point to such things, they were most likely to point at food or at containers that might have food inside.

Figure 29.1. A dolphin and a human at the underwater keyboard.

Other differences between dolphin and human pointing involved proximity to the indicated object and the receiver. The dolphins typically got very close to the object before pointing. In contrast, humans were more likely to point to more distant objects. In addition, humans almost always pointed to objects when the dolphin receiver was near. Dolphins were more likely to point when the human receiver was farther away. We suspect that these differences reflected both the relative swimming speeds of dolphins and humans and the relative distinctiveness of pointing behavior in the two species. Humans are much slower swimmers than are dolphins, resulting in humans in the company of a dolphin being more likely to point to distant objects toward which they were beginning to swim. The faster swimming dolphins were more likely to discover interesting objects while exploring away from their human partner, and so were more likely to begin to point while the human was farther away. It is also possible that dolphins must be near an object in order for humans to apprehend their points. Dolphin pointing is less distinctive than is human pointing (at least to humans); the dolphins may have learned that humans did not respond to their points unless the indicated object was near.

These spontaneous pointing behaviors were the first evidence of wild or captive dolphins pointing at objects. If the dolphins had pointed at the objects regardless of the location of their human partner, then the points could simply have been some form of superstitious behavior the dolphins learned to produce when they saw something they wanted but could not obtain without a human's aid. However, the dolphins often combined their pointing behavior with alternating orientation between the human and the object, suggesting that the dolphins were attempting to communicate something to their human counterpart. For example, figure 29.2 shows a sequence of pointing and monitoring behaviors. In the first photograph, the dolphin is pointing to a transparent jar of food that rests on the bottom (the jar of food is not visible in the photograph). After pointing for approximately 1 s, he then turns his head to look back at an approaching human diver, while maintaining the alignment of his body with the jar of food (photograph 2). The dolphin next pointed a second time at the food (photograph 3) and followed this point with another look at the human (photograph 4). The dolphin again pointed at the jar as the human arrived on the scene (photograph 5) and received a fish once the trainer opened the jar (photograph 6).

Were the dolphins actually trying to communicate with their human partners? Although this is a difficult question to answer, there are a number of behaviors that suggest some sort of communicative

Figure 29.2. Sequence of a dolphin's pointing and monitoring behavior.

intent. These include (1) monitoring the behavior of companions while pointing, (2) refraining from pointing if others are out of sight or cannot see the point, and (3) modifying pointing behavior in response to the receiver's behavior.

This sort of pointing behavior has proven to be difficult to document for animals in the wild, leading some to suggest that referential pointing is uniquely human (Butterworth, 1998; Werner & Kaplan, 1963). Apes do use gestures to mediate social interactions (de Waal, 1988; Goodall, 1986; Plooij, 1978), and pointing has been reported for captive apes, particularly those engaged in intense interaction with humans in the course of research on symbolic communication and problem solving (Hopkins & Leavens, 1998; Krause & Fouts, 1997; Leavens, Hopkins, & Bard, 1996; Mitchell & Anderson, 1997; Savage-Rumbaugh, 1986; Woodruff & Premack, 1979). There is some controversy about the meaning of such behaviors in captive apes (e.g., Povinelli, Nelson, & Boysen, 1990; Tomasello, Call, & Hare, 1998), particularly the extent to which the apes monitor the behavior of their audience to facilitate communication.

Analyses of the development of the dolphins' pointing and monitoring behaviors suggest that the dolphins were using their points to indicate objects of concern to humans. The first pointing event for each dolphin was a point followed by a look at the receiver. Thus, monitoring behavior (or at least something that resembled monitoring behavior) was present in the dolphins from the time they began to point at objects. Nonetheless, most of their early points did not involve a look toward the human diver. As the dolphins gained experience with the consequences of their pointing behaviors, most points were followed by looks. However, this pattern changed as the project continued. Toward the end of the project, the percentage of points preceded by looks declined and most dolphin pointing events involved a single point without a look or a single point followed by a single look back toward the trainer. Perhaps because humans moved so slowly through the water, the dolphins may have learned that a held single point was sufficient to produce the results they wanted.

Xitco, Gory, and Kuczaj (2004) tested the two dolphins' ability to take into account the perspective of the human for whom they were pointing. The procedure was similar to that used by Call and Tomasello (1994) to test orangutans. Xitco et al. placed a human and a dolphin on opposite sides of a fence that allowed the dolphin and human to observe one another but prevented the dolphin from touching the food jar. In the initial phase of the study, the human placed food into one of two clear plastic jars, and then placed one jar to the left and one jar to the right. When the dolphin pointed to the jar that contained food, the human opened the jar and fed the dolphin through the fence. After the dolphins became proficient at this task, three test conditions were introduced. In the face-forward condition, the trainer looked directly at the dolphin for 30 s after the food had been placed into a jar but did not respond to any dolphin behavior during this time. The human did respond to the dolphin's first point after the 30-s delay had ended. In the back-turned condition, the human turned his back to the dolphin after placing the food into a jar. After 30 s, the human turned around to face the dolphin and responded to the dolphin's first point. In the swim-away condition, the human placed food into a jar and then turned and swam away to hide behind a nearby reef. The human returned to his normal post in 30 s and responded to the dolphin's first point.

The results are summarized in figure 29.3. The dolphins pointed most often in the face-forward condition, less often in the back-turned condition, and least often in the swim-away condition. Dolphin pointing in the swim-away condition often started as the experimenter was placing the food jar and before he began to swim away. If these initial points were eliminated, then approximately half of the swim-away trials contained no points whatsoever. Moreover, dolphins rarely continued to point after the human had turned or begun to swim away.

These results, in conjunction with the data for spontaneous pointing during keyboard sessions, suggest that the dolphins' pointing behavior was dependent on the attentional behavior of a receiver. However, it is not clear if the dolphins understood that the divers could not see the dolphins pointing when the divers had their backs turned or were swimming away or if the dolphins had learned a set of stimulus-based strategies for pointing. In other words, it is not clear if the dolphins had a "theory of mind" concerning the visual perspective of the humans or if they had simply learned the most suitable conditions under which to point to a desired object. This issue is significant in terms of what it tells us about an animal's awareness of others. For example, chimpanzees are more likely to produce manual gestures when a human is facing them rather than looking away and they are also more likely to produce vocalizations when the human cannot see them, but can nonetheless hear their sounds (Hostetter, Cantero, & Hopkins, 2001), suggesting that chimpanzees may have some sort of theory of mind that incorporates human perspective. However, Povinelli and his colleagues have reported that chimpanzees do not appear to truly understand what humans can see (Povinelli & Eddy, 1996; Reaux, Theall, & Povinelli, 1999). Reaux et al. suggested that the chimpanzees in their studies had learned to attend to the various characteristics of human receivers, including frontal orientation, the face, and eyes, but had not learned to understand what all this meant in relation to "seeing" or "not seeing."

To sum up, the dolphins in the two studies that we have described in this section had clearly learned an adaptive communication strategy to help them obtain aid from humans when they were faced with the problem of obtaining something they could not otherwise have. However, it is not clear if the dolphins understood the perspective of the humans or if they had simply learned when it was most effective to point. We also do not know if the dolphins were capable of comprehending the points of others (including other dolphins). Dolphins can learn to comprehend human points when they are rewarded for doing so (Herman et al., 1999; Tschudin, Call, Dunbar, Harris, & van der Elst, 2001), but nothing is known about a dolphin's willingness to point for another dolphin and the receiving dolphin's ability to interpret such points. In addition, the two dolphins studied by Xitco and his colleagues may have pointed only to

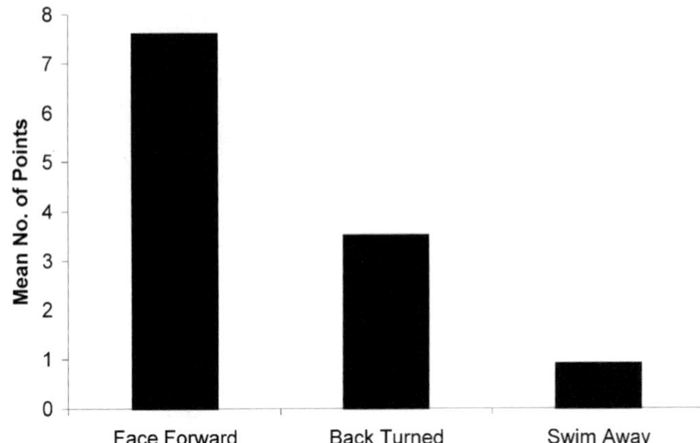

Figure 29.3. Dolphin pointing as a function of the receiver's attentional behavior.

induce humans to give them desirable things like food. One of the hallmarks of pointing in human infants is the use of pointing to direct the attention of others to interesting things, including the moon, fire trucks, and Big Bird (Butterworth, 1998), but such referential pointing has not been shown in chimpanzees (Povinelli, Reaux, Bierschwale, Allain, & Simon, 1997). It is not clear if dolphins can use pointing referentially or only point instrumentally (to obtain something they want).

CAN DOLPHINS PLAN THEIR BEHAVIOR?

The above considerations of Ake's processing of gestural sequences and Bob's and Toby's pointing behavior illustrate types of problem-solving behavior that are spontaneously used by dolphins. However, it is not clear exactly how the dolphins learned the strategies that they used. The dolphins could have acquired the strategies gradually as a consequence of their experiences, or they may have gained some sudden insight into the nature and solution of the specific problems they encountered. It is one thing to solve a problem via trial and error, and another to do so by planning a solution before one acts. The use of planning to solve problems requires that an individual represent the nature of a problem and at least some of the possible future states and behaviors that might achieve a solution, including ones that the individual has never seen or done previously (Hauser, Kralik, & Botto-Mahan, 1999; Procyk & Joseph, 1996; Tolman, 1932; Washburn, 1936). Thus, planning is creative and involves some understanding of the causal relationships between behavior and its consequences (Holyoak, 1995). Such understanding permits the creation of novel solutions that allow one to achieve a goal without trial-and-error learning, and thus allows the planner to avoid the consequences of unnecessary errors.

Observations of behavior suggest that dolphins and whales may plan at least some of their behaviors. For example, Mercado et al. (1998) asked two dolphins to repeat actions they had just produced. During the training phase of this project, the two dolphins typically abandoned an object after they had performed the requested behavior. However, during the experimental phase, the dolphins were more likely to keep the object with them when they returned to the trainer, suggesting that they had learned to anticipate the request to repeat the action they had just performed and had learned to plan ahead by keeping the object. Connor, Smolker, and Richards (1992) reported that male dolphins cooperate with one another to herd female dolphins away from female groups in order to make it easier for the males to mate with the females. In addition, dolphins and whales use air bubbles to confuse, encircle, and trap prey (Fertl & Wilson, 1997), and killer whales and dolphins herd fish into balls and take turns feeding (Similä & Ugarte, 1993). Killer whales cooperate to force large schools of herring from their deep-water habitat to the surface so that the whales may more easily feast on the herring (Nottestad, Ferno, & Axelsen, 2002), and dolphins in South America cooperate with human fisherman to catch fish (Pryor, Lindbergh, Lindbergh, & Milano, 1990). Some dolphins carry large sponges on the tips of their rostrums (noses), which they may use to prevent injury from stingrays and other sharp hazards as they scour the bottom for small fish (Smolker, Richards, Connor, Mann, & Berggren, 1997). Killer whales use bits of fish to lure gulls close enough to catch, after which the gulls are used as play objects (Kuczaj, Lacinak, Garver, & Scarpuzzi, 1997). Each of these examples could be viewed as planned actions. But, how can we be sure that planning actually occurred?

To begin to answer this question, it is necessary to define *planning* (Gory & Kuczaj, 1998, 2001). Many animals engage in behaviors that might appear to be intelligent planned actions but are instead instinctive (Tinbergen, 1951). Likewise, animals may accidentally discover useful behaviors for obtaining goals through trial-and-error learning. In the cases of instincts and serendipitously learned behaviors, the animal need not mentally create a novel solution to a problem prior to executing the solution. For Gory and Kuczaj, this creative mental act is the essence of planning. Given the difficulty of ascertaining a mental act, how can we ever know if an animal can plan its behavior?

In the absence of detailed knowledge of the individual developmental history of naturally occurring behaviors, it is difficult to determine if such behaviors are instinctual, serendipitously learned, or planned. However, in an experimental setting, it is possible to expose animals to novel problems and to document the complete history of any behaviors that emerge during the animals' attempts to solve the problems (e.g., Hauser, Santos, Spaepen, & Pearson, 2002). Gory and Kuczaj (1998, 2001) used this approach to more directly assess the ability of dolphins to plan their behavior. The two dolphins described in the above section on dolphin pointing participated in the planning studies. The tests were designed so that the dolphins could more efficiently obtain a goal if they planned their behavior.

In the multiple-weight task, the dolphins are required to drop four weights into a container in order to release a food fish that is visible inside the cube. The dolphins first learned to use the weights by observing human divers. During the learning phase, one dolphin was released from a separate holding area. When the dolphin approached the diver, the diver first looked at the cube until the dolphin noticed the fish. The diver then picked up one of the weights and dropped it into the cube. The diver then looked to see if the food was released. When it was not, the diver got one more weight and dropped it into the cube, again looking at the food compartment. This process continued until the fourth weight was deposited, which released the food for the dolphin to consume.

The dolphins quickly learned to take part by dropping weights into the cube, and the divers were gradually faded out of the setting. It is important to emphasize that the divers always gathered and deposited a single weight tool at a time. Gory and Kuczaj were curious to see if the dolphins would continue to use one weight at a time or realize that it was more efficient to gather and to deposit multiple weight tools on each trip to the tool site. Of course, the most efficient strategy would be to gather and deposit all four weight tools in one trip. At the time testing began, the dolphins had neither seen multiple weights used nor ever done so themselves.

The results from the first set of tests failed to demonstrate planning on the dolphins' part. Over 50 trials, the dolphins continued to use one weight at a time to obtain the fish. During these trials, the eight weights were placed within 6 meters of the cube. Perhaps they were too close to motivate the dolphins to do more than they had witnessed the human diver do—use one weight at a time. To test this possibility, the weight tools were placed 45 meters from the cube during the second set of trials, thereby making it much more costly to use one weight at a time. In this condition, the dolphins quickly began gathering multiple weight tools when the weights were far away. Figure 29.4 shows the average number of weights each dolphin carried per trip to the cube within five successive 10 trial blocks in this far condition. Toby quickly began to pick up an average of two weights per trip. His average increased to almost three weights per trip, but he returned to a two-weights-per-trip strategy (perhaps because it still took two trips to obtain a sufficient number of weights to release the fish). Bob steadily increased the number of weights he carried per trip until he was carrying four or five weights per trip to the cube and so had to make only one trip (see figure 29.5). The dolphins' behavior in this task suggested that they were capable of simple planning: namely, carrying more than one weight when the distance to be traveled made this a more efficient strategy.

In the retaining weight site test, the dolphins needed to drop a single weight into a cube in order to obtain a fish. One weight and three cubes were present for each trial. Two of the cubes had open

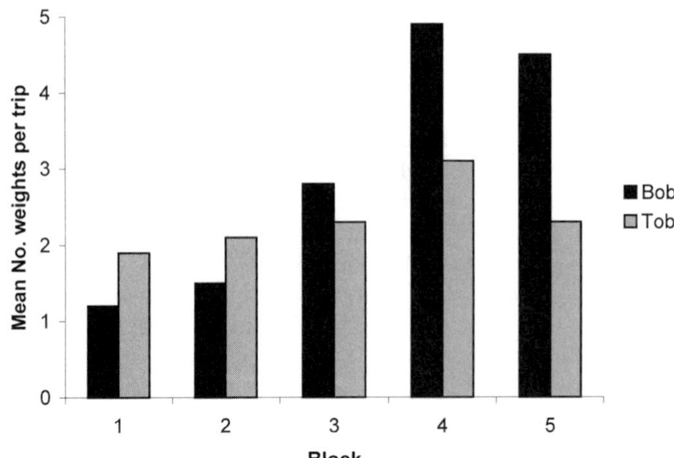

Figure 29.4. Average number of weights carried per trip in each block of trials in the far condition of the multiple-weight test.

bottoms. When a dolphin dropped a weight into the top of one of these cubes, the weight fell through the open bottom after deflecting a hinged surface and releasing the fish. This mechanism allowed the dolphin to retrieve the weight and to use it on one of the other tool sites. The remaining cube had a vertical tube that extended down to the floor of the aquarium. When the weight was dropped into this cube, the weight was contained inside the extension, so the dolphin could not retrieve it for further use. This retaining cube was visually distinct from the other two cubes. The location of the retaining cube varied randomly across trials at each of the three possible positions in the array. If the dolphin used the retaining cube last, then it would obtain all of the available food. If not, then the dolphin would receive only one or two loads of food, depending on whether it used the retaining cube on the first or second attempt.

If a dolphin is incapable of planning the order in which it used the cubes, then it should use the retaining cube equally often as the first, second,

Figure 29.5. The dolphin Bob carrying multiple weights.

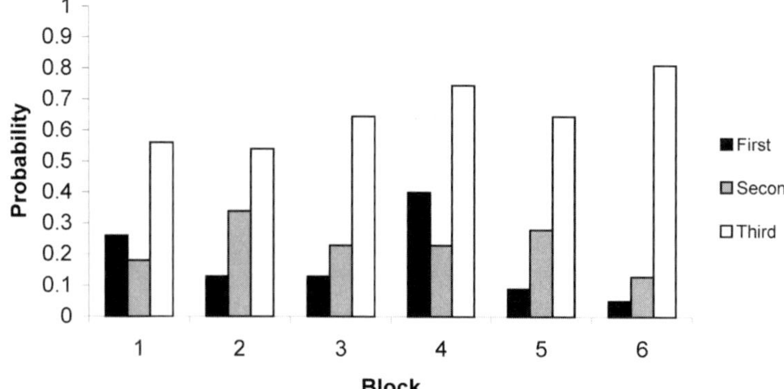

Figure 29.6. Relative probability with which dolphins used retaining weight site as the first, second, or third choice.

and third choice. However, if a dolphin can plan the order in which it used the cubes, then it should use the retaining cube more often as the third choice. Figure 29.6 shows the relative frequency with which the dolphins used the retaining cube as the first, second, or third site across six 30-trial blocks. The dolphins quickly learned to use the retaining cube last. These results are consistent with the notion that the dolphins were able to learn that the retaining cube prevented immediate future use of the weight and to plan their use of the weight to optimize their foraging.

The final task that we discuss was more challenging. This two-step time-limited test involved the use of two tools: (1) a weight such as that used in the other two tasks and (2) a stick (which the dolphins grasped with their mouth). The dolphin first had to deposit a weight into the top of the apparatus. This caused a bin of air to be rotated and dumped into a second inverted bin that was attached to a sliding door. The buoyancy of the air caused the sliding door to rise, which exposed an opening. The dolphin could then insert the stick tool to push the food capsule to the rear of the apparatus, which resulted in the food fish being released. In order to obtain the fish, the dolphins had to use both tools in the proper order.

In addition, the dolphins had to use the stick within a certain amount of time. The second bin of air leaked at a controlled rate. When enough air leaked out, the sliding door closed and the dolphin could not insert the stick tool. Thus, after the dolphin had deposited the weight tool, he had approximately 15 s to retrieve and use the stick. This was ample time if both tools were near the tool site, as they were when the dolphins first learned how to operate the tool site by observing humans. Once the dolphins were proficient at obtaining the fish by using the weight and stick in the correct order, the locations of the tools were changed.

On the first set of test trials, the weight remained near the apparatus, but the stick was placed 25 meters away. At this distance, the sliding door closed if the dolphin deposited the weight tool and then swam to get the stick tool. Once the door closed, the dolphins were unable to obtain the fish. Gory and Kuczaj were interested in the dolphins' reaction to such failures; they predicted that if the dolphins were able to understand the nature of the problem (i.e., that there is a time limit), then the dolphins would first swim faster to try to compensate for the time limit.

This is just what the dolphins did. Both dolphins swam faster in apparent attempts to beat the time limit but abandoned this behavior when it was not successful. However, the failure of this strategy did not result in the dolphins adopting the more successful plan of moving the stick closer to the apparatus prior to using the weight; instead, the dolphins lost interest in trying to solve the problem when the stick was far away.

Subsequent trials with Bob varied the distance of both the stick and the weight. Although this manipulation seemed to increase Bob's interest in the stick when it was far away, it did not result in him moving the stick closer to the apparatus. Instead, when the stick was too far away for it to be used in time, Bob rarely tried to obtain the fish in the apparatus. However, when Bob was allowed to observe a human model solve the problem by moving the stick closer before using the weight, he quickly began to do so himself when the stick was too far away to otherwise use successfully.

In summary, the dolphins' behavior in these tasks suggested a limited ability to plan their behavior. The multiple-weight test showed that the dolphins could plan their behavior to be more efficient at obtaining a goal. They created a behavior (carrying more than one weight at a time) that they had neither seen nor done previously. In the retaining weight site test, the dolphins were able to create and follow a simple plan to use the retaining site last in order to optimize their reward. Although the dolphins were unable to generate the ideal solution to the more complex two-step time-limited task, one dolphin was able to recognize the solution quickly when observing it. The two-step problem required the dolphins to reorganize their behavior in opposition to their initial learning. The ability to analyze, reflect, and reorganize action sequences into novel behaviors that are appropriate to obtain a goal in a novel problem is one of the abilities that characterize good human problem-solvers (Baron, 1988; Holyoak, 1995). Perhaps dolphins are limited in the extent to which they can restructure their behavior to solve problems, or they may simply need more experience to solve more difficult problems. Problem-solving success in human children is positively correlated with the level of problem-solving experience (Case, 1985; DiLisi, 1987; Siegler, 1986); the same may be true of dolphins.

DOLPHIN PLAY AND THE ONTOGENY OF PROBLEM SOLVING

Observations of the spontaneous play behaviors of captive bottlenose dolphin calves have revealed that they play both with one another and with a wide array of objects (Kuczaj & Highfill, 2005; Kuczaj, Makecha, Trone, Paulos, & Ramos, in press; Kuczaj & Trone, 2001; McBride & Hebb, 1948; McCowan, Marino, Vance, Walke, & Reiss, 2000; Pace, 2000; Tavolga, 1966). These objects include those they are given by humans (e.g., a ball), objects they find in their tanks (e.g., a leaf), objects they catch (e.g., a seagull), and objects they create (e.g., a bubble ring that is produced by forcing air out of their blow hole). For all types of objects, the ontogeny of play is characterized by increasingly complex behaviors (Kuczaj & Trone, 2001; Kuczaj et al., in press). For example, one dolphin calf first bit the air bubbles produced by his mother (which had modeled the bubble-biting behavior of self-produced bubbles on earlier occasions). The calf next attempted to bite bubbles that he himself produced. Once he had perfected this technique, the calf began to produce more bubbles to bite at a time, which made it more difficult for the calf to bite all of the bubbles before they reached the water's surface. After the calf became adept at biting large numbers of bubbles, he began to produce bubbles of variable sizes at different depths and from a variety of body positions prior to biting them. The calf's manipulations invariably resulted in failure to bite as many bubbles when a new technique was first initiated. We believe that the calf changed his behavior to make bubble biting more difficult because the challenge of the activity was more important than the actual biting of the bubbles. In this case, and in many other forms of object play, the dolphins seem to have made their task more difficult, perhaps to keep the activity interesting.

The tendency of dolphin calves to make their play activities more complex suggests that the play process is more important than the play product and that dolphins use play to create moderately discrepant events as they actively seek stimulation (Kuczaj & Trone, 2001). The motivation to seek stimulation during play may reflect a genetic predisposition that evolved, because it facilitates skill acquisition and therefore the survival of the individual and the continuation of the species.

Moderately discrepant events are both somewhat familiar and somewhat novel and so provide optimal contexts for learning cognitive skills (Piaget, 1952). Markus and Croft (1995) reported that infant and juvenile chimpanzees preferred to play with other chimpanzees that were slightly older or slightly younger than themselves, a finding that fits well with the notion that play that results in moderately discrepant events is the most rewarding. In addition to fueling cognitive development, the stimulating environments provided by moderately discrepant events may help to maintain cognitive functioning throughout the life span. We believe that dolphins' interest in moderately discrepant events helps them to create their own stimulating environments, which facilitates the development and maintenance of flexible problem-solving skills. If this hypothesis is correct, then dolphin play may have evolved to enhance adaptations to novel situations, particularly those that require flexible problem solving (see Spinka, Newberry, & Bekoff, 2001, for similar arguments regarding the function of play in a variety of species).

Peers play important roles in the acquisition of novel behaviors by bottlenose dolphin calves.

Kuczaj et al. (in press) found that the ontogeny of play behaviors was accelerated by the presence of other calves. Calves tended to learn to produce particular forms of play behavior more quickly if there were other calves already producing these behaviors. For example, a comparison of the play of five calves that had been reared together in a community tank revealed a number of cases in which younger calves produced a play behavior at an earlier age than had their older counterparts. For example, the second oldest calf (Katelyn) first tossed a ball while swimming at the age of 124 days. Eli, the youngest calf, first tossed a ball while swimming at the age of 56 days. Katelyn first held a ball between her pectoral fins while swimming at the age of 442 days. Eli did so at 147 days of age. The difference between Katelyn and Eli was not due to the simple presence or absence of models. Katelyn was exposed to many adult dolphins and one older calf that frequently played with balls (including adults that tossed balls and carried balls between their pectoral fins). However, Eli was exposed to more calf models (four compared with the one calf model available to Katelyn). It seems that some models may have been more salient than others. Simply put, the presence of older calves may have facilitated dolphin calf play behavior. As shown in figure 29.7, the more older calves that were part of a calf's environment, the more types of play behaviors were produced by a calf early in life.

Some of the behaviors shown in figure 29.7 are behaviors that the calf introduced to the group. Calves with slightly older peers were most likely to experiment with and to introduce novel play behaviors into the group. Although some mother dolphins led the way in the development of some play behaviors, innovations were more likely to occur during or immediately following interactions among calves. For example, for three of our calves, the mother first produced bubbles and bit them in the calf's presence. Each mother later produced bubbles that the calf was allowed to bite. Later still, calves produced and bit their own bubbles. Thus, the mothers seemed to play an important role in the ontogeny of bubble play for these calves (as suggested by McCowan et. al., 2000). Nonetheless, subsequent innovations involving bubble play occurred only when the calves were alone or were interacting with one another. Similar findings were reported by Pace (2000). Her description of the development of fluke-made bubble rings by two male dolphin calves emphasized the calves' imitation of each another's fluke-slapping technique and is consistent with our belief that peers both provide important models for behavioral development and facilitate the emergence of flexible problem-solving skills.

Although dolphins have been reported to mimic the behavior of their mothers (McCowan et al., 2000), adult tank mates (Brown, Caldwell, & Caldwell, 1966; Pryor, Haag, & O'Reilly, 1969), and other species (Taylor & Saayman, 1973), our own observations lead us to speculate that peers are particularly important in two ways: (1) they provide models of behaviors that can be reproduced (albeit rarely exactly) and (2) they open the door to the realm of possible behaviors. Peers thus facilitate the emergence of behaviors that are already in the repertoire of other animals in the group as well as the creation of novel behaviors. For the animals studied by Kuczaj et al. (in press), calves were more likely to introduce a new behavior into the group than were adults and they were also more likely than adults to be the second animal to produce the new behavior (see figure 29.8).

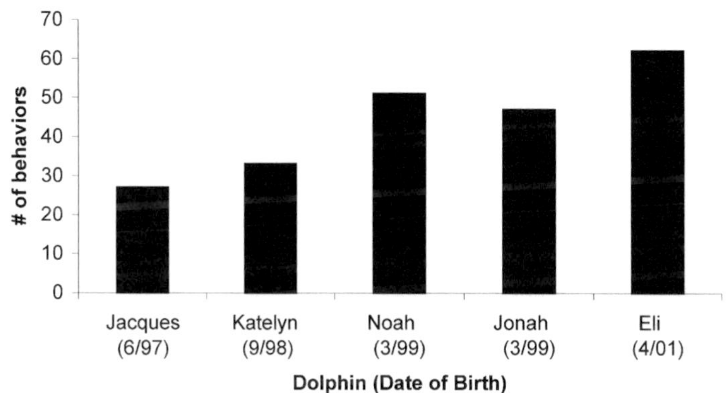

Figure 29.7. Number of different types of play behaviors exhibited by dolphins during the first 6 months of life.

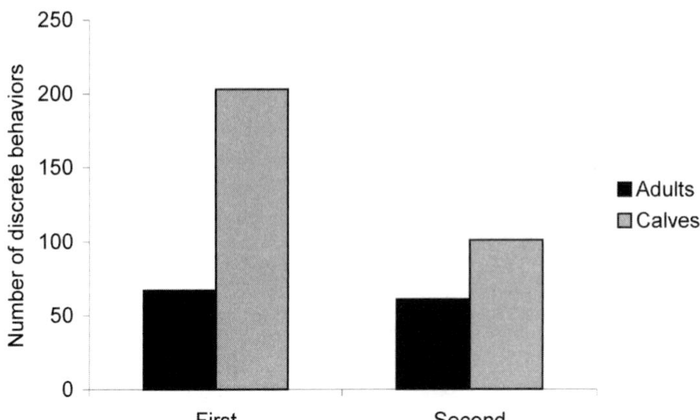

Figure 29.8. Number of behaviors that were produced first or second by adults and calves.

CONCLUSIONS

How do dolphins solve problems? Like many species, they attempt to solve some problems via trial and error. We suspect that trial-and-error learning resulted in the information-processing strategies that Ake used to process and respond to the gestural sequences in the language she was taught. Nonetheless, Ake's strategies were appropriate for the circumstances in which she found herself; it is unlikely that anything in her previous experience or the evolutionary history of her species would have prepared her to respond to gestural commands or requests in the absence of trial-and-error learning.

Not all dolphin problem solving depends entirely on trial-and-error learning. Dolphins' use of multiple weights in the multiple weight task and their use of the retaining site last in the retaining site task both suggest rudimentary forms of planning, as does their attempt to swim faster to beat the time limit in the two-step time-limited task. Of course, the dolphins had to learn from their experiences that their success on a task could be enhanced by changing their behaviors. When the weights were far enough away to make it more efficient for the dolphins to carry more than one weight at a time, they quickly came to do so. Once the dolphins learned that the retaining site prevented future use of the weight, they were more likely to use the retaining site last. Similarly, they swam more quickly in the two-step task in an apparent attempt to beat the time constraints in that task. The dolphins' performance in these tasks is consistent with Tolman's (1932) suggestion that animals typically first try to solve a problem via trial and error but then engage in some form of "inventive ideation" if trial and error is unsuccessful. But what sort of "inventive ideation" might dolphins use?

A number of comparative psychologists in the 1920s and 1930s suggested that animals' "ideational behavior" was best revealed by sudden solutions to problems (Bingham, 1929; Köhler, 1925; Maier 1929; Tolman, 1932; Yerkes, 1934). The dolphins in the multiple weight task and in the retaining site task learned the correct solutions quickly, which suggests some sort of "insight." However, the spontaneous pointing behavior described by Xitco et al. (2001) is the most likely candidate for the type of inventive ideation described by Tolman. This behavior emerged suddenly and appeared to be fully functional from its onset. The dolphins in this study appear to have apprehended a novel (and to them, unnatural) behavior that they could use to direct human's attention to objects that the dolphins desired.

DiLisi (1987) described the development of children's problem-solving skills in terms that closely parallel Piaget's (1952; Piaget & Inhelder, 1969) description of children's cognitive development. The earliest form of problem solving involves planning in action. This need not involve representations of behavior or of the relationship between behavior and the desired result. Instead, the infant produces behaviors that result in some goal (such as getting the thumb into the mouth to suck). This seems to involve trial-and-error learning more than planning, but DiLisi suggested that these primitive plans (or proto-plans, as suggested by Parker & Milbrath, 1993) set the stage for the infant to purposely modify his behavior, to determine the consequence of such modifications, and eventually to anticipate the consequences of his behavior (see also Piaget, 1952). The next type of problem solving to emerge is planning of action, in which children are able to mentally represent simple behavioral plans. However, children's representational capacity is limited during this phase; they cannot reflect on their plans, and so require external feedback to evaluate the consequences of their behavior. The third type of planning emerges when children become aware of the significance of planning and know how to formulate and execute plans; they are able to consider multiple possibilities and mentally anticipate the consequence of each possible course of action without actually producing the imagined behaviors. The most mature form of planning occurs when adolescents can produce and evaluate purely representational acts. As a result, the adolescent can consider hypothetical problems and their solutions as well as actual problems.

Although most animals appear to behave in a purposeful manner (as Tolman, 1932, and others recognized long ago), the nature of the planning in which nonhuman animals engage is far from clear. Parker and Milbrath (1993) suggested that most animal planning is limited to planning in action, and that more advanced planning is largely limited to the great apes (see Boesch & Boesch, 1984; Heinrich, 1999; Rumbaugh & Washburn, 2003, for discussions relevant to this issue). We believe that the dolphins, in the studies we have discussed, engaged in both planning in action and planning of action but that there is little evidence of more advanced planning skills. We suspect that planning of action skills is perfected in dolphin play and that the play context is an ideal one in which to evaluate the consequences of one's actions. Moreover, if dolphins prove capable of more advanced forms of planning, then we believe that the requisite abilities will be facilitated by opportunities for increasingly challenging play.

These views are consistent with the notion that organisms learn by doing (Piaget, 1952; Wilson, 2002) and so learn about problem solving by trying to solve problems (Baron, 1988; Holland, Holyoak, Nisbett, & Thagard, 1986). There is an obvious need for additional research to assess the factors that affect the acquisition of problem-solving and planning skills in dolphins, the flexibility and complexity of such abilities, and the manner in which these skills are limited. This research should compare dolphin planning and problem solving with that of other species, but we must also compare dolphins with one another. Tolman (1932) recognized that both species and individuals differ in terms of their capacity for inventive ideation; an understanding of both sorts of differences is necessary for the comparative psychology of problem solving.

References

Baron, J. (1988). *Thinking and deciding.* New York: Cambridge University Press.

Berthelet, A., & Chavaillon, J. (1993). *The use of tools by human and non-human primates.* New York: Oxford University Press.

Bingham, H. C. (1929). Chimpanzee translocation by means of boxes. *Comparative Psychology Monographs, 5,* 1–91.

Boesch, C., & Boesch, H. (1984). Mental maps in wild chimpanzees: An analysis of hammer transports for nut cracking. *Primates, 25,* 160–170.

Bradshaw, J. L., & Rogers, L. J. (1993). *The evolution of lateral asymmetries, language, tool use, and intellect.* New York: Academic Press.

Brown, B. B. (1973). Language disorders in children. *Public Health, 87,* 115–118.

Brown, D. H., Caldwell, D. K., & Caldwell, M. C. (1966). Observations on the behavior of wild and captive false killer whales, with notes on associated behavior of other genera of captive delphinids. *Natural History Museum of Los Angeles County Contributions in Science, 95,* 1–32.

Butterworth, G. (1998). What is special about pointing? In F. Simion & G. Butterworth (Eds.), *The development of sensory, motor, and cognitive abilities in early infancy* (pp. 169–188). London: Psychology Press.

Call, J., & Tomasello, M. (1994). Production and comprehension of referential pointing by orangutans (*Pongo pygmaeus*). *Journal of Comparative Psychology, 108,* 307–317.

Carr, D. B. (1979). The development of young children's capacity to judge anomalous sentences. *Journal of Child Language, 6,* 227–241.

Case, R. (1985). *Intellectual development.* New York: Academic Press.

Connor, R., Smolker, R., & Richards, A. (1992). Two levels of alliance formation among male bottlenose dolphins (*Tursiops* sp.). *Proceedings of the National Academy of Sciences U S A, 89,* 987–990.

de Waal, F. (1998). *Chimpanzee politics: Power and sex among apes.* Baltimore: The Johns Hopkins University Press.

DiLisi, R. (1987). A cognitive-development model of planning. In S. Friedman, E. Scholnick, &

R. Cocking (Eds.), *Blueprints for thinking* (pp. 79–109). New York: Cambridge University Press.

Fertl, D., & Wilson, B. (1997). Bubble use during prey capture by a lone bottlenose dolphin (*Tursiops truncatus*). *Aquatic Mammals, 23,* 113–114.

Garcia, J., & Koelling, R. A. (1966). The relation of cue to consequence in avoidance learning. *Psychonomic Science, 5,* 123–124.

Gibson, K. R., & Ingold, T. (1993). *Tools, language and cognition in human evolution.* New York: Cambridge University Press.

Goodall, J. (1986). *The chimpanzees of Gombe: Patterns of behavior.* Cambridge, MA: Harvard University Press.

Gory, J. D., & Kuczaj, S. A. I. (1998, November). *Planning and problem solving in bottlenose dolphins.* Paper presented at the annual meeting of the Psychonomic Society, Dallas, TX.

Gory, J. D., & Kuczaj, S. A. I. (2001, March). *More planning by bottlenose dolphins.* Paper presented at the International Conference on Comparative Cognition, Melbourne Beach, FL.

Gory, J. D., Xitco, M. J., & Kuczaj, S. A. I. (1992, November). *Dolphin cognitive research at the Living Seas.* Paper presented at the 20th annual meeting of the International Marine Animal Trainers Association, Freeport, Grand Bahamas.

Gory, J. D., Xitco, M. J., & Kuczaj, S. A. I. (1993, November). *Cognitive studies of symbolic communication, tool use, and echolocation at the Living Seas, Epcot Center.* Paper presented at the 10th annual biennial conference on The Biology of Marine Mammals, Galveston, TX.

Griffin, D. R. (2001). *Animal minds.* Chicago: University of Chicago Press.

Harley, H. E., Roitblat, H. L., & Nachtigall, P. E. (1996). Object representation in the bottlenose dolphin (*Tursiops truncatus*): Integration of visual and echoic information. *Journal of Experimental Psychology: Animal Behavior Processes, 22,* 164–174.

Hauser, M. D. (1996). *The evolution of communication.* Cambridge, MA: MIT Press.

Hauser, M. D., Chomsky, N., & Fitch, W. T. (2002). The faculty of language: What is it, who has it, and how did it evolve? *Science, 298,* 1569–1579.

Hauser, M. D., Kralik, J., & Botto-Mahan, C. (1999). Problem solving and functional design features: Experiments on cotton-top tamarins, *Saguinus oedipus. Animal Behavior, 57,* 565–582.

Hauser, M. D., Santos, L. R., Spaepen, G. M., & Pearson, H. E. (2002). Problem solving, inhibition, and domain-specific experience: Experiments on cottontop tamarins, *Saguinus oedipus. Animal Behavior, 64,* 387–396.

Heinrich, B. (1999). *Mind of the raven.* New York: Harper Collins.

Herbranson, W. T., & Shimp, C. P. (2003). "Artificial grammar learning" in pigeons: A preliminary analysis. *Learning & Behavior, 31,* 98–106.

Herman, L. M. (1987). Receptive competencies of language trained animals. In J. S. Rosenblatt, C. Beer, M. C. Busnel, & P. B. J. Slater (Eds.), *Advances in the study of behavior* (Vol. 17, pp. 1–60). New York: Academic Press.

Herman, L. M., Abichandani, S. L., Elhajj, A. N., Herman, E. Y. K., Sanchez, J. L., & Pack, A. A. (1999). Dolphins (*Tursiops truncatus*) comprehend the referential character of the human pointing gesture. *Journal of Comparative Psychology, 113,* 347–364.

Herman, L. M., Kuczaj, S. A., & Holder, M. D. (1993). Responses to anomalous gestural sequences by a language-trained dolphin: Evidence for processing of semantic relations and syntactic information. *Journal of Experimental Psychology: General, 122,* 184–194.

Herman, L. M., Matus, D. S., Herman, E. Y. K., Ivancic, M., & Pack, A. A. (2001). The bottlenosed dolphin's (*Tursiops truncatus*) understanding of gestures as symbolic representations of its body parts. *Animal Learning & Behavior, 29,* 250–264.

Herman, L. M., Richards, D. G., & Wolz, J. P. (1984). Comprehension of sentences by bottlenosed dolphins. *Cognition, 16,* 129–219.

Herman, L. M., & Uyeyama, R. K. (1999). The dolphin's grammatical competency: Comments on Kako (1999). *Animal Learning & Behavior, 27,* 18–23.

Heyes, C. M. (1996). Imagination and imitation: Input, acid test, or alchemy? *Behavioral and Brain Sciences, 19,* 131.

Holder, M. D., Herman, L. M., & Kuczaj, S. A. (1993). A bottlenosed dolphin's responses to anomalous sequences expressed within an artificial gestural language. In H. L. Roitblat, L. M. Herman, & P. E. Nachtigall (Eds.), *Language and communication: Comparative perspectives* (pp. 443–456). Hillsdale, NJ: Lawrence Erlbaum Associates.

Holland, J. H., Holyoak, K. J., Nisbett, R. E., & Thagard, P. R. (1986). *Induction: processes of inference, learning, and discovery.* Cambridge, MA: MIT Press.

Holyoak, K. J. (1995). Problem solving. In E. E. Smith & D. O. Osherson (Eds.), *Thinking* (Vol. 3, pp. 267–296). Cambridge, MA: MIT Press.

Hopkins, W. D., & Leavens, D. A. (1998). Hand use and gestural communication in chimpanzees (*Pan troglodytes*). *Journal of Comparative Psychology, 112,* 95–99.

Hostetter, A. B., Cantero, M., & Hopkins, W. D. (2001). Differential use of vocal and gestural communication by chimpanzees (*Pan troglodytes*) in response to the attentional status of a human (*Homo sapiens*). *Journal of Comparative Psychology, 115,* 337–343.

Hull, C. L. (1943). *Principles of behavior.* New York: Appleton.

Jackson, R. R., & Wilcox, R. S. (1998). Spider-eating spiders. *American Scientist, 86,* 350–357.

James, W. (1890). *The principles of psychology.* New York: Holt.

Kako, E. (1999). Elements of syntax in the systems of three language-trained animals. *Animal Learning and Behavior, 27,* 1–14.

Kellogg, W. N., & Rice, C. E. (1966). Visual discrimination and problem solving in a bottlenose dolphin. In K. S. Norris (Ed.), *Whales, dolphins, and porpoises* (pp. 731–754). Berkeley: University of California Press.

Knowlton, B. J., & Squire, L. R. (1996). Artificial grammar learning depends on implicit acquisition of both abstract and exemplar-specific information. *Journal of Experimental Psychology-Learning Memory and Cognition, 22,* 169–181.

Kohler, W. (1925). *The mentality of apes.* New York: Harcourt, Brace & Co.

Krause, M. A., & Fouts, R. S. (1997). Chimpanzee (*Pan troglodytes*) pointing: Hand shapes, accuracy, and the role of eye gaze. *Journal of Comparative Psychology, 111,* 330–336.

Kuczaj, S. A., II. (1977). The acquisition of regular and irregular part tense forms. *Journal of Verbal Learning and Verbal Behavior, 16,* 589–600.

Kuczaj, S. A., II, & Borys, R. H. (1989). The overgeneralization of morphological forms as a function of experience. *Language Sciences, 10,* 111–122.

Kuczaj, S. A., II, & Brannick, N. (1979). Children's use of the wh question modal auxiliary placement rule. *Journal of Experimental Child Psychology, 28,* 43–67.

Kuczaj, S. A., II, & Highfill, L. E. (2005). Dolphin play: Evidence for cooperation and culture? *Behavioral and Brain Sciences, 28,* 31–32.

Kuczaj, S. A., II, & Kirkpatrick, V. M. (1993). Similarities and differences in human and animal language research: Toward a comparative psychology of language. In H. L. Roitblat, L. M. Herman, & P. E. Nachtigall (Eds.), *Language and communication: Comparative perspectives* (pp. 45–63). Hillsdale, NJ: Lawrence Erlbaum Associates.

Kuczaj, S. A., II, Lacinak, C. T., Garver, A., & Scarpuzzi, M. (1997, October). *Can animals enrich their own environment?* Paper presented at the Third International Conference on Environmental Enrichment, Orlando, FL.

Kuczaj, S. A., II, Makecha, R. N., Trone, M., Paulos, R. D., & Ramos, J. A. (in press). The role of peers in cultural transmission and cultural innovation: Evidence from dolphin calves. *International Journal of Comparative Psychology.*

Kuczaj, S. A., II, & Maratsos, M. P. (1975). What children can say before they will. *Merrill-Palmer Quarterly, 21,* 89–112.

Kuczaj, S. A., II, Paulos, R. D., & Ramos, J. A. (2005). Imitation in apes, children and dolphins: Implications for the ontogeny and phylogeny of symbolic representation. In L. Namy (Ed.), *Symbol use and symbolic development* (pp. 221–243). Cambridge, MA: MIT Press.

Kuczaj, S. A., II, & Trone, M. (2001). Why do dolphins and whales make their play more difficult? *Genetic Epistemologist, 29,* 57.

Leavens, D. A., Hopkins, W. D., & Bard, K. A. (1996). Indexical and referential pointing in chimpanzees (*Pan troglodytes*). *Journal of Comparative Psychology, 110,* 346–353.

Maier, N. R. (1929). Reasoning in white rats. *Comparative Psychology Monographs, 6.*

Marino, L. (1998). A comparison of encephalization levels between odontocete cetaceans and anthropoid primates. *Brain, Behavior and Evolution, 51,* 230–238.

Markus, N., & Croft, D. B. (1995). Play behavior and its effects on social-development of common chimpanzees (*Pan troglodytes*). *Primates, 36,* 213–225.

McBride, A. F., & Hebb, D. O. (1948). Behavior of the captive bottle-nose dolphin, *Tursiops truncatus. Journal of Comparative and Physiological Psychology, 41,* 111–123.

McCowan, B., Marino, L., Vance, E., Walke, L., & Reiss, D. (2000). Bubble ring play of bottlenose dolphins (*Tursiops truncatus*): Implications for cognition. *Journal of Comparative Psychology, 114,* 98–106.

Mercado, E., Murray, S. O., Uyeyama, R. K., Pack, A. A., & Herman, L. M. (1998). Memory for recent actions in the bottlenosed dolphin (*Tursiops truncatus*): Repetition of arbitrary behaviors using an abstract rule. *Animal Learning & Behavior, 26,* 210–218.

Mercado, E. I., Uyeyama, R. K., Pack, A. A., & Herman, L. M. (1999). Memory for action events in the bottlenose dolphin. *Animal Cognition, 2,* 17–25.

Mitchell, R. W., & Anderson, J. R. (1997). Pointing, withholding information, and deception in capuchin monkeys (*Cebus apella*). *Journal of Comparative Psychology, 111,* 351–361.

Morgan, C. L. (1894). *An introduction to comparative psychology.* London: Walter Scott.

Nottestad, L., Ferno, A., & Axelsen, B. E. (2002). Digging in the deep: killer whales' advanced hunting tactic. *Polar Biology, 25,* 939–941.

Pace, D. S. (2000). Fluke-made bubble rings as toys in bottlenose dolphin calves (*Tursiops truncatus*). *Aquatic Mammals, 26,* 57–64.

Parker, S. T., & Milbrath, C. (1993). Higher intelligence, propositional language, and culture as adaptations for planning. In K. R. Gibson & T. Ingold (Eds.), *Tools, language and cognition in human evolution* (pp. 314–333). New York: Cambridge University Press.

Piaget, J. (1952). *The origins of intelligence in children.* New York: W.W. Norton.

Piaget, J. (1955). *The language and thought of a child.* New York: World Publishing.

Piaget, J., & Inhelder, B. (1969). *The psychology of the child.* New York: Basic Books.

Plooij, F. X. (1978). *Tool use during chimpanzees bushpig hunt. Carnivore, 1,* 103–106.

Povinelli, D. J., & Eddy, T. J. (1996). Reconstructing the evolution of psychological development. *Monographs of the Society for Research in Child Development, 61,* 1.

Povinelli, D. J., Nelson, K. E., & Boysen, S. T. (1990). Inferences about guessing and knowing by chimpanzees (*Pan troglodytes*). *Journal of Comparative Psychology, 104,* 203–210.

Povinelli, D. J., Nelson, K. E., & Boysen, S. T. (1992). Comprehension of role reversal in chimpanzees: Evidence of empathy. *Animal Behavior, 43,* 633–640.

Povinelli, D. J., Reaux, J. E., Bierschwale, D. T., Allain, A. D., & Simon, B. B. (1997). Exploitation of pointing as a referential gesture in young children, but not adolescent chimpanzees. *Cognitive Development, 12,* 327–365.

Prince, C. G. (1993). *Conjunctive rule comprehension in an bottlenosed dolphin.* Unpublished master's thesis, University of Hawaii, Honolulu.

Procyk, E., & Joseph, J. P. (1996). Problem solving and logical reasoning in the macaque monkey. *Behavioural Brain Research, 82,* 67–78.

Pryor, K., Haag, R., & O'Reilly, J. (1969). The creative porpoise: Training for novel behavior. *Journal of the Experimental Analysis of Behavior, 12,* 653–661.

Pryor, K., Lindbergh, J., Lindbergh, S., & Milano, R. (1990). A dolphin-human fishing cooperative in Brazil. *Marine Mammal Science, 6,* 77–82.

Reaux, J. E., Theall, L. A., & Povinelli, D. J. (1999). A longitudinal investigation of chimpanzees' understanding of visual perception. *Child Development, 70,* 275–290.

Richards, D. G., Wolz, J. P., & Herman, L. M. (1984). Vocal mimicry of computer-generated sounds and vocal labeling of objects by a bottlenosed dolphin, *Tursiops truncatus. Journal of Comparative Psychology, 87,* 10–28.

Ridgway, S. H., & Brownson, R. H. (1979). Brain size and symmetry in 3 dolphin genera. *Anatomical Record, 193,* 664–664.

Romanes, G. J. (1883). *Animal intelligence.* New York: Appleton.

Rumbaugh, D. M., & Washburn, D. A. (2003). *Intelligence of apes and other rational beings.* New Haven, CT: Yale University Press.

Russon, A. E. (1996). Imitation in everyday use: Matching and rehearsal in the spontaneous imitation of rehabilitant orangutans (*Pongo pygmaeus*). In A. Russon, K. A. Bard, & T. Parker (Eds.), *Reaching into thought.* Cambridge: Cambridge University Press.

Savage-Rumbaugh, E. S. (1986). *Ape language: From conditioned response to symbol.* New York: Columbia University Press.

Schusterman, R. J., & Gisiner, R. (1988). Artificial language comprehension in dolphins and sea lions: The essential cognitive skills. *Psychological Record, 38,* 311–348.

Schusterman, R. J., & Gisiner, R. C. (1989). Please parse the sentence: Animal cognition in the procrustean bed of linguistics. *Psychological Record, 39,* 3–18.

Siegler, R. (1986). *Children's thinking.* New York: Prentice Hall.

Similä, T., & Ugarte, F. (1993). Surface and underwater observations of cooperatively feeding killer whales in Northern Norway. *Canadian Journal of Zoology, 71,* 1494–1499.

Skinner, B. F. (1938). *The behavior of organisms. An experimental analysis.* New York: Appleton-Century-Crofts.

Smolker, R., Richards, A., Connor, R., Mann, J., & Berggren, P. (1997). Sponge carrying by dolphins (*Delphinidae, Tursiops* sp.): A foraging specialization involving tool use? *Ethology, 103,* 454–465.

Spinka, M., Newberry, R. C., & Bekoff, M. (2001). Mammalian play: Training for the unexpected. *Quarterly Review of Biology, 76,* 141–168.

Tavolga, M. C. (1966). Behavior of bottlenose dolphins (*Tursiops truncatus*): Social interaction in a captive colony. In K. S. Norris (Ed.), *Whales, dolphins, and porpoises* (pp. 718–730). Berkeley: University of California Press.

Taylor, C. K., & Saayman, G. (1973). Imitative behavior by Indian Ocean bottlenose dolphins (*Tursiops aduncus*) in captivity. *Behavior, 44,* 286–298.

Thorndike, E. L. (1911). *Animal intelligence: Experimental studies.* New York: Macmillan.

Tinbergen, N. (1951). *The study of instinct.* New York: Oxford University Press.

Tolman, E. C. (1932). *Purposive behavior in animals and men.* Berkeley: University of California Press.

Tomasello, M. (1996). Do apes ape? In B. G. J. Galef & C. M. Heyes (Eds.), *Social learning in animals: The roots of culture* (pp. 319–346). New York: Academic press.

Tomasello, M., Call, J., & Hare, B. (1998). Five primate species follow the visual gaze of conspecifics. *Animal Behavior, 55,* 1063–1069.

Tschudin, A., Call, J., Dunbar, R. I. M., Harris, G., & van der Elst, C. (2001). Comprehension of signs by dolphins (*Tursiops truncatus*). *Journal of Comparative Psychology, 115,* 100–105.

Tyack, P. L. (2000). Dolphins whistle a signature tune. *Science, 289,* 1310.

Tyler, L. K., & Marslen-Wilson, W. D. (1981). Children's processing of spoken language. *Journal of Verbal Learning and Verbal Behavior, 20,* 400–416.

von Fersen, L., & Delius, J. D. (2000). Acquired equivalences between auditory stimuli in dolphins (*Tursiops truncatus*). *Animal Cognition, 3,* 79–83.

Washburn, M. F. (1936). *The animal mind.* New York: Macmillan.

Watson, J. B. (1914). *Behavior: An introduction to comparative psychology.* New York: Holt.

Werner, H., & Kaplan, B. (1963). *Symbol formation.* New York: Wiley.

Wilson, M. (2002). Six views of embodied cognition. *Psychonomic Bulletin & Review, 9,* 625–636.

Woodruff, G., & Premack, D. (1979). Intentional communication in the chimpanzee: Development of deception. *Cognition, 7,* 333–362.

Xitco, M. J., Gory, J. D., & Kuczaj, S. (2001). Spontaneous pointing by bottlenose dolphins (*Tursiops truncatus*). *Animal Cognition, 4,* 115–123.

Xitco, M. J., Gory, J. D., & Kuczaj, S. A. I. (2004). Dolphin pointing is linked to the attentional behavior of a receiver. *Animal Cognition, 7,* 231–238.

Yerkes, R. M. (1934). Modes of behavioral adaptation in chimpanzee to multiple-choice problems. *Comparative Psychology Monographs, 10,* 1–108.

Zentall, T. R. (1996). An analysis of imitative learning in animals. In C. M. Heyes & B. G. J. Galef (Eds.), *Social learning in animals: The roots of culture.* New York: Academic.

30

The Comparative Cognition of Caching

S. R. DE KORT, S. TEBBICH, J. M. DALLY, N. J. EMERY, AND N. S. CLAYTON

The avian food-caching paradigm has greatly contributed to our understanding of a number of cognitive capacities. Although the early work focused on spatial memory, contemporary studies of the cognitive abilities of food-caching birds have a much broader scope, ranging from episodic-like memory and mental time travel to aspects of social cognition such as observational spatial memory of other birds' caches and elements of mental attribution. A major strength of using the food-caching paradigm to test for cognitive abilities lies in the combination of ethological validity coupled with rigorous experimental control. Thus, food-caching is a naturally occurring behavior, but one that birds will readily perform in the laboratory. And, unlike many of the standard psychological tests of animal memory, the birds do not need to be trained to cache or to recover food.

Yet, the very fact that memory for food caches can be tested in captive birds allows a level of control that would be difficult, if not impossible, in the field. For example, we can control for the time elapsed between caching and the first opportunity to recover that cache, as well as whether the animal can use cues emanating directly from the caches at the time of recovery. And, we can test hand-raised birds that have spent their life in captivity, ones whose reinforcement histories are well documented and whose previous experiences can be experimentally manipulated.

Our current approach to the comparative cognition of caching capitalizes on an integrative knowledge of behavioral ecology and comparative psychology. An understanding of behavioral ecology allows one to pose questions about the selective pressures that drive the evolution of cognitive abilities in food-caching birds and how a bird's decisions concerning both caching and cache-recovery are shaped by ecological factors.

For example, reliance on cached food may be greater for those individuals that live in harsher environments, where access to food supplies is limited and unpredictable, because failure to recover food caches in the winter may lead to death from starvation (Pravosudov & Grubb, 1997). The prediction, therefore, is that an individual living in harsh conditions should cache more food and/or show more efficient recovery of caches (e.g., fewer searches to find its cached seeds) than one that lives in a more temperate environment. Support for this claim comes from population differences in the caching behavior of black-capped chickadees (*Poecile atricapillus*). Alaskan chickadees that have to endure severely cold winters cache considerably more seeds and are much more efficient at cache recovery than are chickadees from low-elevation Colorado, even when the two populations are housed for 2 months in identical laboratory conditions (Pravosudov & Clayton, 2002).

In comparative psychology, the emphasis is on understanding the general processes of learning, memory, and cognition, and the questions are often inspired by the logical structure of the task. Adopting a psychological approach allows us to ask questions about whether, and to what extent, food-caching birds rely on various cognitive abilities such as whether a potential pilferer uses observational spatial memory to steal another bird's caches or whether it simply relies on olfactory cues to detect the hidden cache at a later date. In the case of the Alaskan and Colorado chickadees, the psychological approach inspired the comparison of these birds' performance on other tasks that rely on spatial and nonspatial memory (Pravosudov & Clayton, 2002).

By combining the two approaches, we can use natural variations in food-caching behavior across different species, and even different populations of the same species, to investigate the cognitive mechanisms that might underlie caching and recovery decisions. Indeed, studies comparing the caching abilities and spatial memory capabilities of different species in relation to their ecological demands have been particularly productive for assessing species differences in cognition, especially the studies of Balda and Kamil on different species of North American corvids, notably the Clark's nutcracker (*Nucifraga columbiana*), the pinyon jay (*Gymnorhinus cyanocephalus*), and the Western scrub-jay (*Aphelocoma californica*), which differ in their reliance on caches of pine nuts and in their performance on a battery of spatial and nonspatial memory tasks (e.g., Balda & Kamil, 1989).

Most of the comparative work on food-caching birds has been conducted on two families of birds: the *Paridae* (tits and chickadees) and the *Corvidae* (the crow family, which includes ravens, jays, magpies, and nutcrackers). So, we shall begin this chapter with a brief overview of the variations among species in caching in relation to ecological and cognitive demands. The main body of this chapter is focused on the role of cognition for caching and cache-recovery decisions in members of the *Corvidae*, because this family of food-caching birds is well known for its relatively large brain-to-body size ratio and its complex cognition (see Emery & Clayton, 2004, for a review).

Our approach to comparative cognition is also informed by an evolutionary perspective, because a knowledge of the evolutionary history of the species is of critical importance when interpreting species differences in cognitive ability, particularly for teasing apart the role of current ecological factors and the role of previous pressures imposed on their ancestors; to do so, one needs to know the evolutionary relatedness among those species (phylogeny). We therefore conclude this chapter with a discussion of why an understanding of evolution in general, and of the phylogeny of the studied species in particular, is essential for how we interpret species differences in cognition.

TO CACHE OR NOT TO CACHE

Many bird species hide food for later consumption and rely on memory to recover their caches, often several days, if not months, later, when food supplies are less abundant (Vander Wall, 1990). Within the Corvids and the Parids, the amount of caching varies considerably, from species that do not cache at all to species that cache thousands of items per year. Food-caching and recovery behavior is thought to have evolved in response to temporal food scarcity (R. C. Roberts, 1979). For example, the Clark's nutcracker can winter at higher latitudes and breed earlier in the spring than other corvids by relying on caches of pinyon seeds that it has deposited during the previous fall (Vander Wall & Balda, 1981).

Species differences in cache propensity are thought to correlate with differences in fluctuating food availability in the environments in which birds live; the common assumption is that caching intensity is linearly related to the dependence on caches for survival. Those species that depend on their caches for survival tend to live in extreme environments where food availability follows a discrete seasonal pattern, such as at high altitudes in mountainous areas or in high latitudes. Species living in more temperate areas, with a year-round availability of food, are usually less dependent on their caches for survival and they tend to cache less (see Andersson & Krebs, 1978; McNamara, Houston, & Krebs, 1990).

The Siberian jay (*Perisoreus infaustus*) is largely dependent on cached food for survival during the hostile winters of Siberia, and it is likely to be a prolific cacher that can store thousands of items a season (Ekman, Brodin, Bylin, & Sklepkovych, 1996). The same is true of willow tits (*Parus montanus*) and Siberian tits (*P. cinctus*) that occupy a similarly harsh climate (Pravosudov, 1986). In contrast, the more southerly distributed Eurasian jackdaw (*Corvus monedula*) and magpie jay (*Calocitta formosa*) cache little, if at all. Similarly, within the

Parids, species such as the blue tit (*P. caeruleus*) and the great tit (*P. major*) are also classified as nonstorers.

Species differ not only in the amount of food they cache but also in the average time elapsed between caching and recovery. Some species of corvids, such as Clark's nutcrackers, are relatively long-term hoarders that recover their caches mainly in periods of food scarcity; they may have to remember the locations of their caches for months. Other species, such as the Northwestern crow (*C. caurinus*), only hoard for short intervals; they recover their caches within a day (James & Verbeek, 1983). Similarly, marsh tits (*P. palustris*) are thought to recover the majority of their caches within the first few days after caching (Stevens & Krebs, 1986).

THE ROLE OF COGNITION IN CACHING

What, When, and Where to Cache

At the initiation of every caching event, food-caching birds need to make complex decisions about the type and amount of food to cache, where to cache it, and when to cache it. These decisions may be directed by the animals' anatomy, physiology, and motivational state, as well as by ecological factors. In order to make these decisions, animals also have to process complex information; cognitive abilities may constrain these decision processes.

The adaptive specialization hypothesis suggests that different environmental conditions may select for different cognitive abilities among species. By contrast, the general process view assumes that all food-caching species possess general learning and memory abilities that allow them to make these decisions; thus, one should not expect any variation in cognitive abilities to be directly related to caching. Figure 30.1 outlines some of the decisions a food-storer needs to make, the information required to make those decisions, and the potential cognitive abilities that might be used. In the following sections, we discuss these caching and recovery decisions in turn.

The decision about what to cache is determined by a number of factors, such as the type of food available to the bird, anatomical adaptations for eating specific foods or caching in different substrates, and whether the species in question is a specialized or a generalized feeder. However, what is cached also determines what needs to be remembered. For instance, the Clark's nutcracker is a specialized cacher that eats and caches predominantly pine seeds (Vander Wall, 1990). Because seeds do not perish, there is no need to encode the time of caching. It therefore seems likely that the main information a nutcracker needs to remember is the location of the cache, although it does retain information about the cache size (Möller, Pavlick, Hile, & Balda, 2001). By contrast, Western scrub-jays cache perishable items such as beetle larvae as well as nonperishable seeds (Clayton & Dickinson, 1999c; Clayton, Yu, & Dickinson, 2001). The rate at which a perishable item degrades depends on a number of ecological factors, including the temperature and humidity of the environment, the type of substrate in which the food is cached, and the depth and location of a cache within a particular substrate. Caches that consist of invertebrates degrade rapidly in the heat and more slowly in the cold. The problem for the food-storer is not only to learn how quickly a particular food type degrades but also to update this information in a flexible manner, based on the ecological conditions that occur in the interim between caching the food and recovering it. Elsewhere, we have argued that such flexible deployment of information relies on a declarative memory system (Clayton, Yu, & Dickinson, 2003).

The type and amount of food items that are cached, rather than eaten, are not randomly selected; the decision to cache rather than eat is based on the size and quality of the item, its composition, and its perishability, as well as the cacher's motivational state at the time of caching. Scrub-jays have been shown to select the highest quality peanuts based on visual assessment and handling (Langen, 1999). In captivity, magpies (*Pica pica*) and jackdaws (*Corvus monedula*) will eat small pieces of bread but will cache large ones (Henty, 1975), although the jackdaw is deemed a noncaching species under natural conditions. Eurasian jays (*Garrulus glandarius*) preferentially cache large acorns, which are undamaged and without a cavity between the kernel and the shell (Bossema, 1979).

Motivational state at the time of caching can have important effects on the decision to cache or not to cache as well as on the decision of what to cache. In one experiment, Western scrub-jays were

Select cache site

Quality & suitability of substrate
Topography of cache site
Privacy of cache site

Store information on spatial location including large scale topography
Visual perspective-taking

Assess social context

Presence or absence of observer
Identity & status of observer
Visual access of observer

Store information on social context
Individual recognition
Deception & Theory of Mind

Select food item to cache

Quality & size of food item
Nutritional value
Perishability

Store information about the content of cache & time of caching

Figure 30.1. Some of the decisions a corvid has to make while caching (gray), the information it needs to process these decisions (white), and the potential cognitive abilities that might be used (black). (Artwork by N. J. Emery.)

prefed either powdered peanuts or dog-food kibble, which could be eaten but not cached; the birds were later given the opportunity to cache whole peanuts or dog-food kibble. Prefeeding on powdered peanuts selectively reduced caching levels of peanuts, but not of dog-food kibble, and vice versa (Clayton & Dickinson, 1999b). Clayton and Dickinson therefore argued that caching behavior is controlled by two independent systems: one for feeding and one for caching. The control exerted by the different systems appears to be mediated by the incentive value of specific items rather than by a general motivational state.

Many corvids demonstrate marked seasonal patterns in caching intensity. For example, Eurasian jays cache significantly more acorns in the autumn than in the spring and summer (Bossema, 1979; Clayton, Mellor, & Jackson, 1996). Clark's nutcrackers and pinyon jays commence caching in late August when pinyon seeds are mature and begin to recover them in early winter (Vander Wall, 1990). In some species at least, the preference for what to cache also changes seasonally. Thus, independent of food availability, laboratory-housed Eurasian jays prefer to cache worms in the spring and nuts in the autumn and winter (Clayton et al., 1996).

One of the key decisions that a caching bird has to make is where to cache. Corvids may reduce their memory load by caching next to landmarks or in locations that increase the likelihood of successful recovery. For example, pinyon jays tend to cache on the south side of trees, which receive half the snow cover of other locations and which are the first to melt in the spring (Balda & Bateman, 1971). Eurasian jays prefer to cache along the edges of substrates, next to conspicious landmarks (Bossema, 1979). And, Clark's nutcrackers make most of their caches within 5 meters of large objects

(Vander Wall, 1982). A featureless landscape is not likely to be selected as a suitable caching environment and, indeed, most corvids cache in areas that contain multiple landmarks. Large vertical landmarks may also serve to constrain the view of the cache site from other birds and thus act as barriers protecting the cache site from potential pilferers.

The number of food items that can be carried away and cached depends on morphological adaptations such as pouches. Species that are capable of carrying large amounts of food items at once tend to cache at larger distances from their feeding grounds than do species that are more limited in their transport capacities. Clark's nutcrackers can transport around 100 seeds up to 22 km away, held in their large, sublingual pouch (Vander Wall & Balda, 1977), whereas pinyon jays can transport only about 40 seeds, 8 to 10 km away (and usually only 1 km) in their Oesophagus. As scrub-jays have no specialized food-carrying structures, they are limited in the amount of food items they can carry (about three seeds); most of their caches are made within 1 km of the food source (Vander Wall, 1990). It therefore seems that the decision where to cache is partly determined by morphological constraints rather than cognitive decisions.

However, in the Eurasian jay, the amount of food transported correlates with the distance it is carried. A larger number of acorns (three to five) is carried over 100 m, but one acorn is only carried 20 m (Bossema, 1979). So, for Eurasian jays, the decision of how far to cache from the food source varies between caching episodes and it is not solely dependent on a morphological limitation.

Social Aspects of Caching: For My Eyes Only

Another factor that affects caching decisions is the potential for pilfering by other birds (Emery & Clayton, 2001; Vander Wall & Jenkins, 2003). When a bird is observed during a caching episode, the observer may return later to pilfer the cache. In response, food-storers will develop strategies to prevent their caches from being pilfered; these strategies may or may not involve complex cognitive processes (Emery, Dally, & Clayton, 2004).

There is substantial variation in social structure among different caching species and consequently in the social cognitive demands related to caching. For instance, solitary species like the Eurasian jay and the Clark's nutcracker are less likely to be observed while caching than are birds that live in social groups. Group structure can vary from colonies consisting of many, often unrelated individuals (e.g., the rook [*Corvus frugilegus*]) to smaller family units, such as cooperative breeders (e.g., the Florida scrub-jays [*Aphelocoma coerulescens*]). Cooperative breeding is a complex, strongly hierarchical social system in which several, usually related, birds help raising the offspring of one dominant breeding pair. Pilfering of caches within such groups is not necessarily detrimental to a particular food-storer because the recovered food may be used to feed the communal young, provided the pilferer is not an intruder. The caching behavior of these birds may thus require the ability to recognize certain individuals, and surely to distinguish intruders from group members.

Food-storers that live in large groups have to balance the benefits of being in a social group with the costs of pilfering by conspecifics (Andersson & Krebs, 1978). Any member of a social group may either be a storer or a stealer; each role may require a number of different cognitive abilities. For example, if pilferers are unable to obtain another's caches aggressively (e.g., if they are subordinate to the cacher), then they may use cognitive strategies that are independent of aggression. An example may be remembering the location of a storer's caches, so that they can be recovered when the storer has departed the scene. Pilferers may also use "deceptive" strategies, such as concealing themselves when observing another caching or observing at a distance, to increase the opportunity of recovering more caches and to reduce retaliatory aggression. Similarly, individuals storing food may use cognitive counterstrategies to outwit potential pilferers, such as caching out of sight (i.e., behind obstacles), caching at a distance, caching when pilferers are distracted, or re-caching in new places at the time of recovery.

There is a considerable amount of support from field observations that caching corvids do indeed use these cognitive strategies. In common ravens, it has been shown that storers will delay caching if other ravens are in the vicinity and wait until potential pilferers are distracted or have disappeared (Bugnyar & Kotrschal, 2002; Heinrich & Pepper, 1998). Ravens and Northwestern crows (Heinrich, 1999; James & Verbeek, 1983) make "false" caches; these birds either cache nonedible objects or they probe the bill into the ground without burying an item of food. Ravens preferentially store food behind obstacles such that other ravens cannot see where the caches are being made (Bugnyar & Kortschal, 2002). Clarkson, Eden, Sutherland, & Houston (1986) found that magpies adjusted the density of their caches by spacing them farther apart and placing them farther away from the central food source if the risk of pilfering was high. Individuals of several corvid species return alone to caches they had hidden in the presence of conspecifics and re-cache them in new places (Bugnyar & Kotrschal, 2002; DeGange, Fitzpatrick, Layne, & Woolfenden, 1989; Emery & Clayton, 2001; Goodwin, 1956; Heinrich, 1999).

In a recent set of experiments, Dally, Emery, and Clayton (2005) examined which strategies Western scrub-jays use to protect their caches from being pilfered. In the first experiment, the jays were provided with two caching trays: one located close to an observer and the other located as far as possible from the observer. The jays cached preferentially in the tray farthest from the observer, but only when they were observed; the jays did not discriminate between the trays when they were allowed to cache in private. Interestingly, the jays only re-cached food from the near tray, suggesting that they treated the food items in that tray as the most likely to be pilfered.

In a second experiment, jays were provided with two trays at equal distance from the observer: one tray was located in the open and the other was located behind an opaque screen (i.e., hidden from the observer's view). In test trials, the jays preferentially cached behind the opaque screen. To determine whether the jays feared the open (and so failed to cache there), control trials were run in which powdered (noncacheable) food was provided. The jays did not spend any longer eating behind the barrier than in the open. Therefore, during caching, scrub-jays appear to process the presence of conspecifics, their distance from the cache sites, and whether the cache sites are in view.

Bugnyar and Kotrschal (2002) have suggested that caching and raiding ravens may present an example of tactical deception through their attempts to manipulate another individual's attention. This deception is either manifest as the storer's attempts to prevent opponents from gaining opportunities to steal or the raider's attempts to gain opportunities to learn the location of the storer's caches.

The investigators examined two forms in which another's attention can be manipulated: withholding information and directing another's attention away from the caches. During caching, storers tended to withdraw from conspecifics and were located at a greater distance from conspecifics during caching than during other activities, such as feeding and resting. Cachers moved their caches if an observer moved toward them and also protected their cache sites. Cache raiders also used a number of strategies, seemingly to increase the potential for learning about cache sites and for stealing caches. If a storer was close to a cache site, then the observers delayed pilfering until the cacher moved away from the caches. These behaviors suggest that caching and raiding ravens appreciate the visual perspective of one another and may produce strategies and counterstrategies to influence the behavior of the other.

COGNITION IN CACHE RECOVERY

Remembering the "What-Where-and-When" of Caching Events: Episodic-like Memory

During the interval between caching and recovery, a bird needs to make several decisions that may or may not require complex cognitive processes. To successfully recover caches, food-storing animals need to form representations of the location of the cache site, the type and perishability of the cached item, and the social context during caching. Figure 30.2 outlines some of these recovery decisions, along with the information required and the potential cognitive abilities that might be used. Note that these representations may be based on purely spatial memories in animals that cache large numbers of a *single* food type over a wide area or more complex declarative memories of which foods have been cached where and when in species that cache a *variety* of food items that differ in their levels of perishability.

Vander Wall (1990) discussed several hypotheses for how animals may find their food-caches. First, animals may find hidden food through use of olfactory cues produced by the cache. Observations suggest that this method is unlikely to be used by corvids; strong-smelling food items are not located with greater accuracy than nonsmelling objects (Bunch & Tomback, 1986; James & Verbeek, 1983). Second, animals may find their caches by

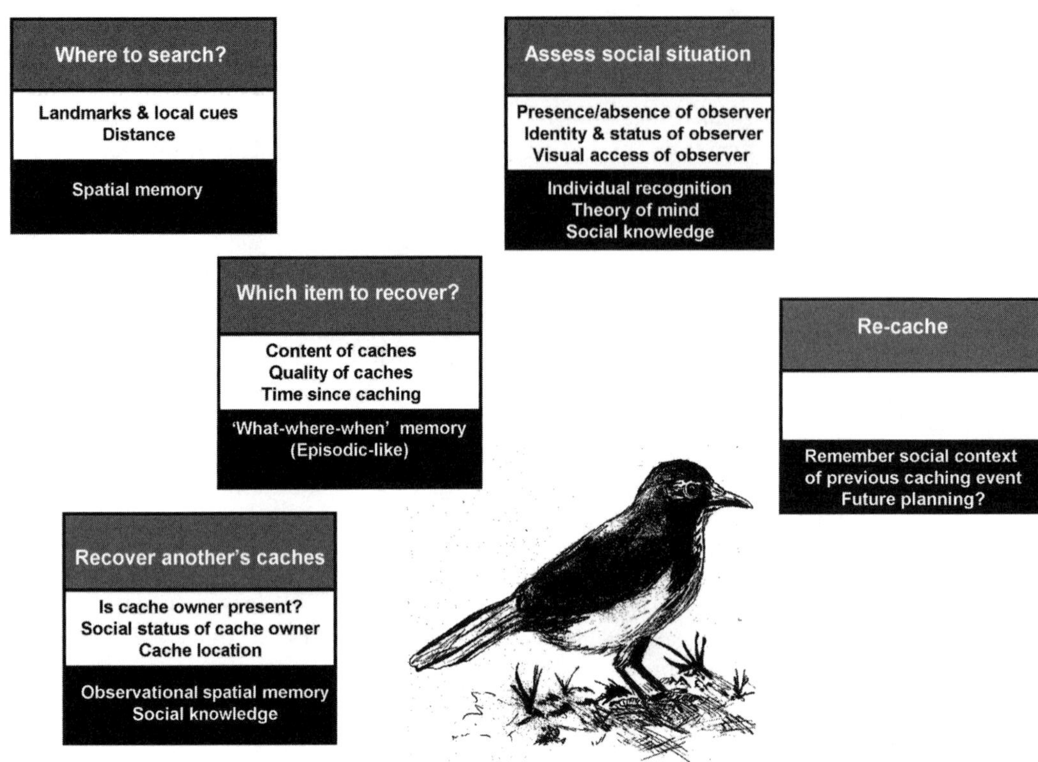

Figure 30.2. Some of the decisions a corvid has to make while recovering caches (gray), the information it needs to make these decisions (white), and the potential cognitive abilities it might use (black). Note that the recovering individual does not need to be the same as the caching individual. Thus, some of these recovery decisions could also be made by a pilferer, even an individual from a nonstoring species (e.g., a jackdaw). (Artwork by N. J. Emery.)

following visual cues created during the act of caching, such as disturbance to the substrate or protuberance of the food itself. Balda (1980) smoothed over the soil in which Eurasian nutcrackers had previously made a cache, but the birds nevertheless searched in the correct sites, suggesting that the birds did not use direct visual cues. Third, the birds may locate their caches through random foraging instead of aimed searching. However, such random foraging cannot explain the exceptionally high success rates (50 to 99%) in recovering caches by several corvids (Balda, 1980; Bossema, 1979; James & Verbeek, 1983, 1984; Vander Wall, 1982). Finally, animals may remember the precise location of each cache site using spatial memory. Indeed, there is ample evidence that birds find their caches using predominantly spatial memory (Shettleworth, 1995; Vander Wall, 1990).

What exactly is remembered about a cache location has been examined in several studies, and there is now consensus that landmarks form a major contribution to spatial memory. Nevertheless, there seems to be variation among species in the types of cues used (such as local feature cues around the cache site [e.g., color and the shape of leaves]) and more global position cues (such as the location of various trees and rocks). In memory tests in the laboratory, Eurasian jays tended to rely on global position cues, whereas nonstoring jackdaws made more use of local cues in the same test (the same difference between storers and nonstorers was also found for species of tits; Clayton & Krebs, 1994). Clark's nutcrackers appear to use either local or global spatial cues, depending on which are available to them (Gould-Beierle & Kamil, 1998). Large landmarks provide more information to a caching animal than just the general location of a cache site.

For example, Vander Wall (1982) allowed Clark's nutcrackers to cache in an arena containing multiple objects. Between caching and recovery, the arena was extended by 20 cm to the right, and all objects in the right half were also moved by 20 cm. A large landmark in the left of the arena (rock) remained in place. The nutcrackers displayed errors in recovery accuracy for the caches the birds had made in the right-hand side of the arena, whereas the caches made in the left-hand side of the arena were recovered accurately. This pattern of results suggests that the nutcrackers assess the actual distance between the cache site and a landmark. However, there are multiple landmarks present in most caching environments, so cachers should possess the ability to calculate the relative distance between cache sites and two or more landmarks. Clark's nutcrackers can learn to find the half-way point between landmarks, and they transfer this "rule" to changes in the distance between the landmarks (Kamil & Jones, 1997).

Corvids also appear to remember the specific content of their caches. When approaching cache sites containing large seeds, Clark's nutcrackers use a wide bill gape, but they use a small bill gape for caches containing small seeds (Möller et al., 2001). As noted earlier, when Western scrub-jays were prefed powdered peanuts, they ceased recovering peanuts, but not dog-food kibble, and vice versa (Clayton & Dickinson, 1999b). This pattern of results suggests that the jays had remembered the content as well as the locations of their caches. Further evidence that scrub-jays remember not only the content of their caches but also the relative perishability of different foods has been provided by a series of experiments on episodic-like memory in Western scrub-jays (see Clayton, Bussey, & Dickinson, 2003, for a review). One important factor in accurate recovery of caches is the ability to differentiate caching actions from recovery actions. Western scrub-jays appear to search selectively in those cache sites that still contain food rather than in cache sites from which food items had earlier been recovered (Clayton & Dickinson, 1999c).

Scrub-jays form integrated memories of "what" item was cached "where" and "when." When caching perishable food, it would appear to be prudent to have learned something about the decay properties of the cached food and, if two or more perishable foods are cached, then to learn their relative decay rates, so as to increase recovery efficiency. Clayton and Dickinson (1999a) trained one group of scrub-jays (degrade group) that wax worms were still fresh after a 4-h retention interval between caching and recovery but that the worms had degraded after a 124-h retention interval. A second group of jays (replenish group) always received fresh wax worms at recovery no matter what the retention interval had been. Less-preferred peanuts were also available for caching that never degraded. The degrade group birds rapidly learned to avoid searching for wax worms at the 124-h retention interval when they had perished. On probe testing trials (in which the food and any food odor cues had been removed) after caching both worms and peanuts in different parts of a trial-unique caching tray, the birds in the degrade group searched in wax worm sites at the 4-h retention interval, but they switched to searching in peanut sites at the 124-h retention interval, suggesting that they had learned "when" and "where" wax worm and peanut caches had been made (Clayton & Dickinson, 1998, 1999a).

In natural situations, scrub-jays may need to remember about several caches that contain food items with varying perishability rates. Using a similar paradigm, but this time with three different retention intervals and three different food types, Clayton et al. (2001) showed that scrub-jays can indeed learn about the relative perishability rates of two degradable foods. These studies provide convincing evidence that, during cache recovery, Western scrub-jays remembered not only the location of their caches but also the different food types located within individual cache sites and the relative time since they were cached. This representation of the time since caching is essential for the efficient recovery of perishable food items; Clayton and colleagues have argued that Western scrub jays deploy a flexible, declarative memory system in their food-caching and recovery behaviors (Clayton, Bussey, et al., 2003; Clayton et al., 2001).

Social Aspects of Cache Recovery

Western scrub-jays have been shown to use cognitive social strategies during cache recovery. Emery and Clayton (2001) allowed hand-raised scrub-jays to cache either in private or while a conspecific was watching. Individuals that had prior experience (outside of the experiment) pilfering another bird's caches subsequently re-cached food in new cache sites but only when they had been observed during caching. By contrast, those birds without pilfering experience did not move their caches to new sites, even though they had observed the caching behavior of others. The inference is that these birds engage in experience projection (i.e., the jays relate information about their previous experience as a pilferer to the possibility of future stealing by another individual and modify their recovery strategy accordingly). By focusing on the counterstrategies of the storer when previously observed by a potential stealer, this experiment raises the intriguing possibility that recaching behavior is based on mental attribution.

A second experiment focused on the counter strategies of the storer when previously observed by a potential stealer. Scrub-jays that had previously observed some of their caches being stolen by a conspecific subsequently switched recovery strategies from checking that their caches were still available to eating them. The birds also continued to re-cache, but they were more selective in their choice of re-cache location, moving caches to places inside their home cage that could not be accessed by other birds (Emery et al., 2004).

Cache raiding may be interpreted as another form of recovery (of another's caches). For pilferers, their ability to locate caches made by others quickly and efficiently may be an important difference between successful pilfering and potential aggression from the storer. Therefore, pilferers may require a sophisticated observational spatial memory for learning about the precise location of another individual's caches.

Note that, although parids have an excellent spatial memory for their own caches and they readily pilfer conspecific's food caches, the mechanisms they use do not appear to be based on observational spatial memory (Baker et al., 1988; Brodin, 1994; Bunch & Tomback, 1986; Hitchcock & Sherry, 1995). By contrast, corvids have been demonstrated to use observational spatial memory to locate and subsequently pilfer other's caches.

Bednekoff and Balda (1996a, b) tested the ability of pinyon jays, Clark's nutcrackers, and Mexican jays (*Aphelocoma ultramarina*) to remember where another bird had cached food, by examining their cache pilfering efficiency. The birds were allowed to observe another bird caching and were given the opportunity to recover those caches either 1 day or 2 days later. All three species were accurate at recovering both self-made and observed caches after a 1-day interval. The asocial Clark's nutcracker was not able to recover caches made by another individual after a 2-day interval, but the other two species were (Bednekoff & Balda, 1996b). By contrast, ravens can only locate another's caches accurately when the duration between observing and pilfering is short (Bugnyar & Kortschall, 2002). Because the cached food is often perishable in ravens, they may not require an elaborate observational spatial memory over an interval of similar duration as seed-caching corvids.

The flexibility required in this complex network of decisions that a caching corvid needs to make suggests that all of this information is processed using a declarative memory system (e.g., one that can be updated if new information comes available). Evidently, the cognitive processes involved in caching behavior are affected by a plethora of factors that may vary within individuals in different seasons, between individuals in different populations, and between species. These factors include temperature, food availability, food type, social structure, and habitat type. This variation in cognitive requirements is not likely to show a simple linear relationship with the amount of caching a species performs or with the amount of time elapsing between caching and recovery. Nonetheless, such variation in caching and recovery behavior allows for comparative tests of different cognitive abilities in relation to prevailing ecological demands.

We must stress that it is crucial for the study species to be carefully selected in order to allow the correct comparisons to be drawn. For instance, within the Old World corvids, the jackdaw has a relatively small hippocampus; it is also one of the few species that caches little or no food (Healy & Krebs, 1992). The jackdaw is often presented as the typical example of a nonstoring species, and it is used as a baseline to test for a relationship between spatial memory and relative hippocampus size in other species of corvids. However, if all of its close relatives cache, then it may be more parsimonious to assume that the common ancestor of the corvids also cached, in which case caching behavior in jackdaws has been secondarily lost. So, within these corvids, *loss* of caching in jackdaws might be seen to be the adaptive specialization. What needs to be explained then is not why most species cache but rather why the nonstoring species lost this trait (for loss of behavioral traits, see, e.g., de Kort & ten Cate, 2004; Wiens, 2001) and whether this loss had consequences for related cognitive abilities such as spatial memory and episodic-like memory. Indeed, the evolutionary history of a group of related species is a factor that has often been neglected in comparative cognition, yet it may have far-reaching consequences, as we shall explain.

WHY EVOLUTION MATTERS

The adaptive specialization hypothesis assumes that brain and behavior, just like any other aspect of an organism, are shaped through natural selection. In much the same way as different demands of foraging have selected for different beak shapes in the Darwin's finches, different cognitive demands have selected for different brains and behaviors.

The capacity and longevity of cache location memories have led a number of authors to hypothesize that the increased visuospatial demands of remembering the locations of so many scatter-hoarded food caches are associated with an enlargement of the hippocampus (e.g., Krebs, 1990). According to the adaptive specialization hypothesis, food-caching animals should not only have larger hippocampal volumes (relative to overall brain and body size) than their noncaching counterparts but also outperform noncaching species on tests of spatial memory. By contrast, there should be no difference on nonspatial memory tasks. Indeed, a number of studies have suggested that species that are dependent on stored food are more accurate at retrieving caches than are nonstoring species (Kamil, Balda, & Olson, 1994; Olson, Kamil, Balda, & Nims, 1995) and that the hippocampus is larger in birds that cache large amounts than in those that cache little or none at all (Basil, Kamil, Balda, & Fite, 1996; Healy & Krebs, 1996). These results were interpreted as supporting the adaptive specialization hypothesis (Healy & Braithwaite, 2000; Shettleworth, 2003).

Recently, the adaptive specialization hypothesis has been criticized on the grounds that there is no conclusive evidence that there are adaptive specializations in the brain that are related to ecological demands (Bolhuis & Macphail, 2001; Macphail & Bolhuis, 2001; Papini, 2002). These critics maintain the general process view: namely, that the mechanisms of learning and memory are fundamentally the same across species. Their critique has prompted a lively debate (Bolhuis & Macphail, 2002; Dwyer & Clayton, 2002; Hampton, Healy, Shettleworth, & Kamil, 2002; Healy, de Kort, & Clayton, 2005; Shettleworth, 2003).

A crucial point raised by Papini (2002), but which has largely been ignored in the field of comparative cognition, is the concept of homology/homoplasy. Homology refers to a similarity in certain traits between species based on common ancestry, while homoplasy refers to similarities that evolved independently as a result of common selection pressures. Homology and homoplasy are relative concepts, and therefore their categorization depends on the taxonomic level of the comparison and the definition of the trait under study. Consider the wings of birds, bats, and bees as an example. As forelimbs, wings are homologous between birds and bats because they derived from those of their common reptilian ancestor. As wings (i.e., forelimbs to fly with), they are homoplasous because these structures evolved independently in birds and bats, even though they have the same function. The wings of bees are homoplasous at any level of comparison to those of both birds and bats.

The distinction between homology and homoplasy is important because it allows for an assessment of whether a comparison between species is meaningful with respect to a given hypothesis. Food caching probably developed independently in the parids and corvids (Papini, 2002). Therefore, enhanced spatial memory in these two groups is a case of homoplasy and not of homology. Thus, although the current behavior pattern (caching) appears similar, the underlying ways to solve the problem may differ. Consequently, one does not necessarily expect to find a similar relationship between caching propensity and size of the hippocampus when these two groups are compared (Brodin & Lundborg, 2003).

Spatial memory is a trait that is present in all vertebrates and in the vast majority of invertebrates, having most likely arisen as early as when organisms began to engage in active locomotion. Spatial memory is thus not confined to food caching animals and it is certainly a homologous trait across all families of birds that cache food. At this level, there is no reason to compare species for differences in spatial memory, just as one would not compare them for the presence or absence of having feathers.

The adaptive specialization hypothesis tests for specific enhanced spatial memory capacities in food-storing species in relation to their natural history (caching), whereas the general process hypothesis looks for similarities among species. The adaptive specialization hypothesis thus focuses on homoplasies, whereas the general process hypothesis focuses on homologies. At this point, it is important to emphasize once more that homoplasy/homology are relative concepts. For instance, when the adaptive specialization hypothesis is tested using the relationship among caching, enhanced spatial memory, and enlarged hippocampus, it is implicitly assumed that caching is a homoplasous trait. However, one must consider what traits were likely to be possessed by the common ancestor of the species being compared. As stated at the end of the previous section, within the Corvidae, it is likely that the common ancestor already possessed spatial memory as an adaptive specialization. Consequently, all species within that group are derived from a species that already had the adaptive specialization, and it is therefore a homologous trait.

Below, we outline five historical scenarios about the ancestor of corvids, based on a hypothetical phylogeny of the five species illustrated in figure 30.3. We contrast two different starting points: one in which the ancestor was a cacher and one in which the ancestor was a noncacher. Note that, in the absence of a detailed phylogenetic analysis, it is not clear which of these scenarios is the most plausible. For each scenario, we make predictions about whether the presence or absence of caching behavior is correlated with two aspects of cache recovery: namely, accuracy of spatial memory and hippocampal size. Although it need not be the case, for simplicity, we assume that hippocampal size and performance on spatial memory tasks (referred to here simply as "spatial memory") go hand in hand; they are thus treated as one trait.

Five Evolutionary Scenarios for Caching by Corvids

Scenarios A, B, and C assume that the common ancestor was a cacher; therefore, caching is a homology in corvids. Thus, the noncaching species lost the ability or motivation to cache.

Scenario A: Retain Noncaching species did not lose the associated traits for caching such as a preference to use large landmarks when remembering food locations and other features that allow for enhanced performance on spatial memory tasks (including hippocampal volume changes), because there was no counterselection against such traits. According to this scenario, no relationship between hippocampus size and performance on spatial memory tasks is expected.

Scenario B: Co-opt Rather than necessarily retaining the trait for spatial memory, a second scenario is that the trait was co-opted for other cognitive tasks in some of the descendants (e.g. Western scrub-jays may have co-opted spatial memory to also encode timing of caching, i.e., episodic-like memory). This scenario also makes no prediction about the relationship between caching, performance on spatial memory tasks, and hippocampus size.

Scenario C: Too Costly According to this scenario, the adaptations underlying spatial memory and hippocampal size are too costly to maintain in those species that do not cache. Selection pressure will therefore result in noncachers having reduced hippocampal volumes and less accurate performance on spatial memory tests. This scenario might be named the adaptive despecialization of noncachers.

Scenarios D and E assume that the common ancestor was not a cacher; therefore, caching is a homoplasy in corvids. According to this hypothesis, not all species of corvids develop the ability to cache.

Scenario D: Spinoff The enhanced performance on spatial memory tests and the enlarged hippocampal size is a consequence of a general increase in cognitive capacities, as opposed to one that is specifically related to caching behavior. Thus, no clear relationship between size of hippocampus, spatial memory, and caching is predicted. Note that the prediction is the same as in Scenario A, but the evolutionary trajectory differs.

Scenario E: Adaptive Specialization According to this scenario, only those species that developed caching behavior evolved an enhanced spatial memory and increased hippocampal size. This scenario has the same prediction as Scenario C, but the evolutionary trajectory differs fundamentally in suggesting that the difference between cachers and noncachers results from an adaptive specialization of cachers as opposed to an adaptive despecialization of noncachers.

According to Scenario E, the extant caching species would have independently developed the caching behavior and the associated enhanced spatial memory and hippocampal enlargement, as

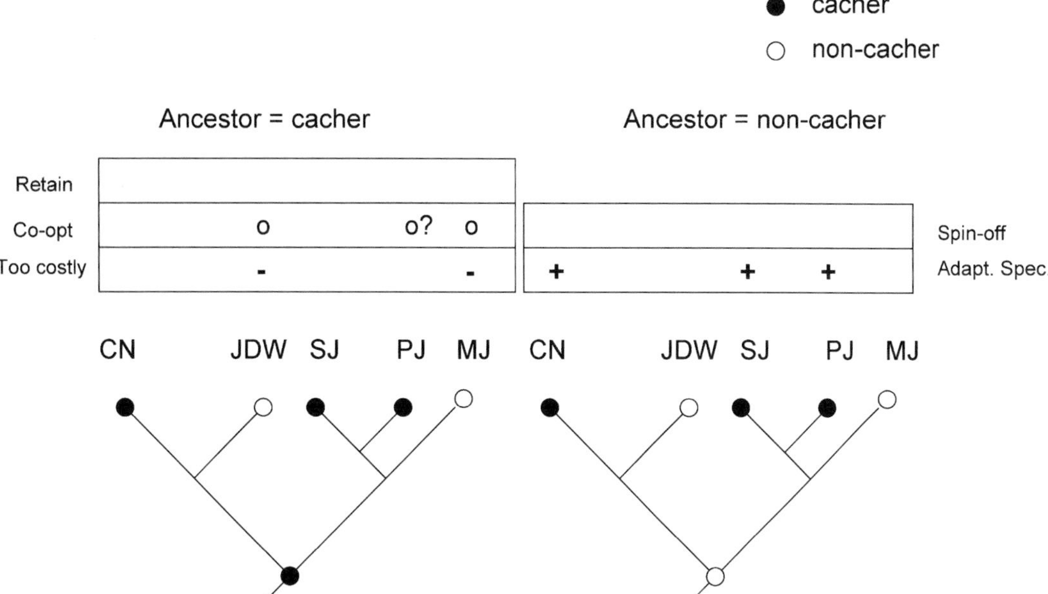

Figure 30.3. A hypothetical phylogeny of five species of corvids (two Old World and three New World species): namely, the food-caching Clark's nutcracker (CN), the noncaching jackdaw (JDW), the food-caching Western scrub-jay (SJ) and pinyon jay (PJ), and the noncaching magpie jay (MJ). Note that the evolutionary trajectories are not based on any known data but serve simply to illustrate five possible historical scenarios. Two of these scenarios are based on the assumption that the ancestor of these species was a noncacher, whereas the other three scenarios are based on the assumption that the ancestor was a cacher. The five scenarios make different predictions about the relationship between (a) food-caching and (b) performance on spatial memory tasks and hippocampal size. Blank spaces indicate that there is no clear relationship between caching and memory and the hippocampus, whereas + indicates that a particular species has gained the trait (i.e., enhanced spatial memory performance and increased hippocampal size) and – indicates that a particular species has lost the trait. O refers to the case where a species may have co-opted the trait for a different function. For example, it is hypothesized that the Western scrub-jay may have co-opted its spatial memory capabilities for use in episodic-like recall. See text for further details.

shown in figure 30.3. Thus, pinyon jays and Clark's nutcrackers might show differences in some aspects of the hippocampal enlargement and enhanced spatial memory. One might argue that the better performance of the Clark's nutcracker at accurate cache recovery over long retention intervals (e.g., Balda & Kamil, 1992) and the better spatial performance of the pinyon jay (and the scrub-jay for that matter) on the radial arm maze (Gould-Beierle, 2000) constitute support for this claim.

The take-home message from this analysis is that an assumption based purely on the caching behavior of current-day corvids may lead one to predict that a noncaching species has an inferior spatial memory and reduced hippocampal volume compared with a caching species, but this assumption may be incorrect. Distinguishing among the five scenarios is not possible without using phylogenetic techniques to establish the evolutionary history of the corvids, and thus whether the ancestor was a cacher. Below, we discuss two other examples that may gain relevance if these evolutionary processes are considered.

Comparison of Corvid Species for Spatial Capacities

The consensus from a series of comparative studies of memory in food-caching corvids is that species with the highest dependence on cached food generally perform the best on tests for spatial memory (e.g., Balda & Kamil, 1989; Kamil et al., 1994). However, there were some notable exceptions that have been notoriously difficult to interpret (Bolhuis & Macphail, 2001).

In one study, four corvid species were compared for their spatial memory in an analogue of the radial maze (Gould-Beierle, 2000). In light of the adaptive specialization hypothesis, the results were surprising; a less dependent species (the Western scrub-jay) performed better at the task than a species highly dependent on caching (the Clark's nutcracker), whose performance was about equal with that of the nonstoring jackdaw. And, the Western scrub-jay performed equally to the pinyon jay, which, like the nutcracker, is also highly dependent on caching. As pointed out by the author, the four species are not equally related. The New World jays (the pinyon jay and the Western scrub-jay) are more closely related to each other than they are to the other two species (Cibois & Pasquet, 1999; Hope, 1989). Although the Western scrub-jay does not cache large quantities of food, the common ancestor that it shares with the pinyon jay may have done so. The scrub-jay may still have the capacity to perform well in this particular memory test, because its ancestor evolved the capacity to do so in relation to efficient recovery of large numbers of cached seeds, and the capacity was maintained even though the selection for intensive caching may have been reduced. In other words, the scrub-jay shares this trait (as shown by the capacity to perform well on the radial-arm memory task) with the pinyon jay through homology. The ancestor of the jackdaw and the nutcracker may never have evolved this specific trait; consequently, these species do not perform as well as the two jay species. Although the caching behavior of the nutcracker is similar to that of the pinyon jay, efficient cache recovery may be homoplasous in these two species, which means that they both need enhanced spatial memory for accurate cache recovery, but the specific way in which they solve the problem may differ.

Comparison Between the Parids and Corvids

A well-established technique used in comparative research addressing adaptive specializations is to test for a correlation between traits. The technique relies on the assumption that there is a positive relationship between the species best adapted to a certain selection pressure and a measure of the selected-for trait (Pagel, 1997). Several studies show that there is a positive relationship between relative hippocampal volume and dependency on caching in both parids and corvids (Basil et al., 1996; Healy & Krebs, 1992, 1996). However, Brodin and Lundborg (2003) presented a meta-analysis of these studies, combining the previously published data on parids and corvids, which they complemented with additional data from both parids and corvids. Based on this larger sample, the authors found no significant effect of food storing on relative hippocampal volume. However, as we argued earlier, the common ancestor of the corvids, and possibly also the parids, was a food-storer. Therefore, the adaptive specialization tested for in these sorts of analyses has developed only twice, once for the corvids and once for the parids, which makes the effective sample size two, not the total number of species for which the hippocampal volume is known in each family.

Furthermore, as Felsenstein (1985) has argued, species are not independent data points in such a between-species comparison. All species are interrelated to some extent, and one has to correct for this lack of independence in the data. Several statistical techniques have been developed to deal with this problem of nonindependent data points (Harvey & Pagel, 1991). It is beyond the scope of this chapter to review them all, but suffice it to say that there is now wide agreement that phylogenetic correction is required. There is extensive literature that deals with the subject, and an important next step will be to integrate such methods into the study of comparative cognition. An obvious reason for the paucity of these types of analyses in the study of corvids and parids is that the required tools are missing. Unfortunately, there are no comprehensive modern phylogenies available for the food-storing birds. However, the fact that such information is missing is not a justification for ignoring the necessity to use it.

The discussion between the adaptive specialization hypothesis and the general process hypothesis is currently difficult to resolve. It is not possible to provide a convincing case that certain cognitive abilities are due to adaptation to specific ecological needs without looking at the evolutionary history of the species involved. The only way to resolve these problems is to reconstruct the evolutionary pathways of each species and to analyze the transitions that took place along the phylogeny of the species concerned. Evolutionary history cannot be reconstructed without reference to the phylogeny of the species in question. To resolve this question, a modern comprehensive phylogeny for both corvids and parids is required. An alternative solution, and one that circumvents the lack of a phylogeny, is to test several pairs of sister species (species that share a common ancestor) in which one of the pair does possess the trait and the other member of the pair does not. A problem with this approach is that it is difficult, if not impossible, to find a sufficient number of such sister-species pairs to allow meaningful statistical analyses.

CONCLUDING REMARKS

The food-caching paradigm has been a productive combination of two traditionally separated fields of research: namely, behavioral ecology and comparative psychology. Current work has moved beyond just spatial memory to encompass other aspects of cognition. For instance, mental time travel has been considered a uniquely human trait (Suddendorf & Corballis, 1997), but several aspects of retrospective cognition have been investigated in food-caching corvids (Clayton, Bussey, & Dickinson, 2003; Clayton & Dickinson 1998, Clayton et al., 2001; Clayton, Yu, et al., 2003), although the debate is still continuing (Clayton, Bussey, Emery, & Dickinson, 2003; W. A. Roberts, 2002; Suddendorf & Busby, 2003). Similarly, the work on the social context of caching has opened new directions for testing various aspects of social cognition in non-primate animals (Emery & Clayton, 2001; Emery et al., 2004). Tests of the strategies used by food-storers to protect their caches from theft by others provides insight into various aspects of complex social cognition, including experience projection, tactical deception, and other aspects of theory of mind.

The time is now ripe to place more emphasis on an evolutionary perspective to comparative cognition. So far, evolutionary thinking has been considered in the field of comparative cognition only from a theoretical perspective (Hauser & McDermott, 2003; Papini, 2002; Wasserman, 1993). Comparative psychology was warned in the 1950s that it should not be founded on laboratory studies of the white rat alone (Beach, 1950). By analogy, Ryan (1996) pointed out that comparative biology cannot be done without taking evolutionary history into consideration. For the same reason, we suggest that the study of comparative cognition should not be conducted without due consideration to evolutionary history.

Acknowledgments This work was supported by grants NS35465-05 and MH2602 to N. S. C. from the National Institutes of Health, BBSRC grant S16565, and the University of Cambridge. S. de K. was funded by the Biotechnology and Biological Sciences Research Council and Schlumberger Interdisciplinary Research Fellowship at Darwin College, Cambridge, UK. S. T. was funded by a Marie-Curie postdoctoral fellowship. J. M. D. received financial support from Clare College, the University of Cambridge, the Sir Richard Stapeley Educational Trust, and the Sefton Educational Trust, and N. J. E. was funded by a Royal Society University Research Fellowship. We thank Anders Brodin for his comments on the manuscript.

References

Andersson, M., & Krebs, J. R. (1978). On the evolution of hoarding behavior. *Animal Behaviour*, *26*, 707–711.

Baker, M. C., Stone, E., Baker, A. E. M., Shelden, R. J., Skillicorn, P., & Mantych, M. D. (1988). Evidence against observational learning in storage and recovery of seeds by black-capped chickadees. *The Auk*, *105*, 492–497.

Balda, R. P. (1980). Recovery of cached seeds by a captive *Nucifraga caryocatactes*. *Zietschrift fur Tierpsychologie*, *52*, 331–346.

Balda, R. P., & Bateman, G. C. (1971). Flocking and annual cycle of the pinyon jay, *Gymnorhinus cyanocephalus*. *Condor*, *73*, 287–302.

Balda, R. P., & Kamil, A. C. (1989). A comparative study of cache recovery by three corvid species. *Animal Behaviour*, *38*, 486–495.

Balda, R. P., & Kamil, A. C. (1992). Long-term spatial memory in Clark's nutcrackers, *Nucifraga columbiana*. *Animal Behaviour*, *44*, 761–769.

Basil, J. A., Kamil, A. C., Balda, R. P., & Fite, K. V. (1996). Differences in hippocampal volume among food storing corvids. *Brain Behavior and Evolution*, *47*, 156–164.

Beach, F. (1950). The snark was a boojum. *American Psychologist*, *5*, 115–124.

Bednekoff, P. A., & Balda, R. P. (1996a). Observational spatial memory in Clark's nutcrackers and Mexican jays. *Animal Behaviour*, *52*, 833–839.

Bednekoff, P. A., & Balda, R. A. (1996b). Social caching and observational spatial memory in Pinyon jays. *Behaviour 133*, 807–826.

Bolhuis, J. J., & Macphail, E. M. (2001). A critique of the neuroecology of learning and memory. *Trends in Cognitive Sciences, 4*, 426–433.

Bolhuis, J. J., & Macphail, E. M. (2002). Everything in neuroecology makes sense in the light of evolution: Response from Bolhuis and Macphail. *Trends in Cognitive Sciences, 6*, 7–8.

Bossema, I. (1979). Jays and oaks: An eco-ethological study of a symbiosis. *Behaviour, 70*, 1–117.

Brodin, A. (1994). Separation of caches between individual willow tits hoarding under natural conditions. *Animal Behaviour, 47*, 1031–1035.

Brodin, A., & Lundborg, K. (2003). Is hippocampal volume affected by specialization for food hoarding in birds? *Proceedings of the Royal Society of London Series B–Biological Sciences, 270*, 1555–1563.

Bugnyar, T., & Kotrschal, K. (2002). Observational learning and the raiding of food caches in ravens, *Corus corvax*: Is it "tactical" deception? *Animal Behaviour, 64*, 185–195.

Bunch, K. G., & Tomback, D. F. (1986). Bolus recovery by grey jays: an experimental analysis. *Animal Behaviour, 34*, 754–762.

Cibois, A., & Pasquet, E. (1999). Molecular analysis of the phylogeny of 11 genera of corvidae. *Ibis, 141*, 297–306.

Clarkson, K., Eden, S. F., Sutherland, W. J., & Houston, A. I. (1986). Density dependence and magpie food hoarding. *Journal of Animal Ecology, 55* 111–121.

Clayton, N. S., Bussey, T. J., & Dickinson, A. (2003). Can animals recall the past and plan for the future? *Nature Reviews Neuroscience, 4*, 685–691.

Clayton, N. S., Bussey, T. J., Emery, N. J., & Dickinson, A. (2003). Prometheus to Proust: The case for behavioural criteria for "mental time travel." *Trends in Cognitive Sciences, 7*, 436–437.

Clayton, N. S., & Dickinson, A. (1998). Episodic-like memory during cache recovery by scrub jays. *Nature, 395*, 272–278.

Clayton, N. S., & Dickinson, A. (1999a). Memory for the contents of caches by scrub jays (*Aphelocoma coeruleus*). *Journal of Experimental Psychology: Animal Behavior Processes, 25*, 82–91.

Clayton, N. S., & Dickinson, A. (1999b). Motivational control of caching behaviour in the scrub jay, *Aphelocoma coerulescens. Animal Behaviour, 57*, 435–444.

Clayton, N. S., & Dickinson, A. (1999c). Scrub jays (*Aphelocoma coerulescens*) remember the relative time of caching as well as the location and content of their caches. *Journal of Comparative Psychology, 113*, 403–416.

Clayton, N. S., & Krebs, J. R. (1994). Memory for spatial and object-specific cues in food storing and non-storing birds. *Journal of Comparative Physiology A, 174*, 371–379.

Clayton N. S., Mellor, R., & Jackson, A. (1996). Seasonal patterns of food storing in the European jay (*Garrulus glandarius*). *Ibis, 138*, 250–255.

Clayton, N. S., Yu, K. S., & Dickinson, A. (2001). Scrub jays (*Aphelocoma coerulescens*) form integrated memories of the multiple features of caching episodes. *Journal of Experimental Psychology: Animal Behavior Processes, 27*, 17–29.

Clayton, N. S., Yu, K. S. & Dickinson, A. (2003). Interacting cache memories: Evidence of flexible memory use by scrub jays. *Journal of Experimental Psychology: Animal Behavior Processes, 29*, 14–22.

Dally, J. M., Emery, N. J., & Clayton, N. S. (2005). Cache protection strategies by western scrub-jays (*Aphelocoma californica*): Implications for social cognition. *Animal Behaviour, 70*, 1251–1263.

DeGange, A. R., Fitzpatrick, J. W., Layne, J. N., & Woolfenden, G. E. (1989). Acorn harvesting by Florida scrub-jays. *Ecology, 70*, 348–56.

de Kort, S. R., & ten Cate, C. (2004). Repeated decrease in vocal repertoire size in Streptopelia doves. *Animal Behaviour, 67*, 549–557.

Dwyer, D. M., & Clayton, N. S. (2002). A reply to the defenders of the faith. *Trends in Cognitive Sciences, 6*, 109–111.

Ekman, J., Brodin, A., Bylin, A., & Sklepkovych, B. (1996). Selfish long-term benefits of hoarding in the Siberian jay. *Behavioral Ecology, 7*, 140–144.

Emery, N. J., & Clayton, N. S. (2001). Effects of experience and social context on prospective caching strategies by scrub jays. *Nature, 414*, 443–446.

Emery, N. J., & Clayton, N. S. (2004). Comparing the complex cognition of birds and primates. In Rogers, L. J. & Kaplan, G. S. (Eds.), *Comparative vertebrate cognition: Are primates superior to non-primates* (pp. 3–55). The Hague: Kluwer Academic Press.

Emery, N. J., Dally, J. M., & Clayton, N. S. (2004). Western scrub-jays (*Aphelocoma californica*) use cognitive strategies to protect their caches from thieving conspecifics. *Animal Cognition, 7*, 37–43.

Felsenstein, J. (1985). Phylogenies and the comparative method. *The American Naturalist, 125*, 1–15.

Goodwin, D. (1956). Further observations on the behaviour of the jay. *Ibis, 98*, 186–219.

Gould-Beierle, K. (2000). A comparison of four corvid species in a working and reference memory task using a radial maze. *Journal of Comparative Psychology*, *114*, 347–356.

Gould-Beierle, K. L., & Kamil, A. C. (1998). The use of local and global cues by Clark's nutcrackers, *Nucifraga columbiana*. *Animal Behaviour*, *52*, 519–528.

Hampton, R. R., Healy, S. D., Shettleworth, S. J., & Kamil, A. C. (2002). "Neuroecologists" are not made of straw. *Trends in Cognitive Sciences*, *6*, 6–7.

Harvey, P. H., & Pagel, M. (1991). *The comparative method in evolutionary biology*. Oxford: Oxford University Press.

Hauser, M. D., & McDermott, J. (2003). The evolution of the music faculty: a comparative perspective. *Nature Neuroscience*, *6*, 663–668.

Healy, S., & Braithwaite, V. (2000). Cognitive ecology: A field of substance? *Trends in Ecology & Evolution*, *15*, 22–26.

Healy, S., de Kort, S. R., & Clayton, N. S. (2005). The hippocampus, spatial memory and food hoarding: A puzzle revisited. *Trends in Ecology and Evolution*, *20*, 17–22.

Healy, S. D., & Krebs, J. R. (1992). Food storing and the hippocampus in corvids: Amount and volume are correlated. *Proceedings of the Royal Society London Series B*, *248*, 241–245.

Healy, S. D., & Krebs, J. R. (1996). Food storing and the hippocampus in Paridae. *Brain Behavior and Evolution*, *47*, 195–199.

Heinrich, B. (1999). *Mind of the raven*. New York: Harper Collins.

Heinrich, B., & Pepper, J. W. (1998). Influence of competitors on caching behavior in the common raven. *Animal Behaviour*, *56*, 1083–1090.

Henty, C. J. (1975). Feeding and food-hiding responses of jackdaws and magpies. *British Birds*, *68*, 463–466.

Hitchcock, C. L., & Sherry, D. F. (1995). Cache pilfering and its prevention in pairs of black-capped chickadees. *Journal of Avian Biology*, *26*, 181–192.

Hope, S. (1989). *Phylogeny of the avian family Corvidae* (p. 280). New York: City University of New York.

James, P. C., & Verbeek, N. A. M. (1983). The food storage behavior of the Northwestern crow. *Behaviour*, *85*, 276–291.

James, P. C., & Verbeek, N. A. M. (1984). Temporal and energetic aspects of food storage in northwestern crows. *Ardea*, *72*, 207–216.

Jones, J. E., & Kamil, A. C. (2001). The use of relative and absolute bearings by Clark's nutcrackers, *Nucifraga columbiana*. *Animal Learning & Behavior*, *29*, 120–132.

Kamil, A. C., Balda, R. P., & Olson, D. J. (1994). Performance of four seed-caching corvid species in the radial-arm maze analog. *Journal of Comparative Psychology*, *108*, 385–393.

Kamil, A. C., & Jones, J. E. (1997). The seed-storing corvid Clark's nutcracker learns geometric relationships among landmarks. *Nature*, *390*, 276–279.

Krebs, J. R. (1990). Food-storing birds: Adaptive specialization in brain and behavior? *Philosophical Transactions of the Royal Society London B*, *329*, 55–62.

Langen, T. A. (1999). How western scrub-jays (*Aphelocoma californica*) select a nut: Effects of the number of options, variation in nut size, and social competition among foragers. *Animal Cognition*, *2*, 223–233.

Macphail, E. M., & Bolhuis, J. J. (2001). The evolution of intelligence: Adaptive specializations versus general process. *Biological Reviews*, *76*, 341–364.

McNamara, J. M., Houston, A. I., & Krebs, J. R. (1990). Why hoard? The economics of food storing in tits, *Parus* spp. *Behavioural Ecology*, *1*, 12–23.

Möller, A., Pavlick, B., Hile, A. G., & Balda, R. P. (2001). Clark's nutcrackers *Nucifraga columbiana* remember the size of their cached seeds. *Ethology*, *107*, 451–461.

Olson, D. J., Kamil, A. C., Balda, R. P., & Nims, P. J. (1995). Performance of four seed-caching corvid species in operant tests of nonspatial and spatial memory. *Journal of Comparative Psychology*, *109*, 173–181.

Pagel, M. (1997). Inferring evolutionary processes from phylogenies. *Zoologica Scripta*, *26*, 331–348.

Papini, M. R. (2002). Pattern and process in the evolution of learning. *Psychological Review*, *109*, 186–201.

Pravosudov, V. V. (1986) Individual differences in the behavior of the Siberian tit (*Parus cinctus*) and the willow tit (*Parus montanus*) in foraging and storing food. *Soviet Journal of Ecology*, *17*, 237–241.

Pravosudov, V. V., & Clayton, N. S. (2002). A test of the adaptive specialization hypothesis: Population differences in caching, memory, and the hippocampus in black-capped chickadees (*Poecile atricapilla*). *Behavioral Neuroscience*, *116*, 515–522.

Pravosudov, V. V., & Grubb, T. C., Jr. (1997). Energy management in passerine birds during the non-breeding season: A review. *Current Ornithology*, *14*, 189–234.

Roberts, R. C. (1979). The evolution of avian food storing behavior. *American Naturalist*, *114*, 418–438.

Roberts, W. A. (2002). Are animals stuck in time? *Psychological Bulletin*, *128*, 473–489.

Ryan, M. J. (1996). Phylogenetics and behavior: Some cautions and expectations. In: E. Martins

(Ed.), *Phylogenies and the comparative method in animal behavior* (pp. 1–21). New York: Oxford University Press.

Shettleworth, S. J. (1995). Comparative studies of memory in food storing birds: from the field to the Skinner box. In: E. Alleva, A. Fasolo, H.-P. Lipp, L. Nadel, & L. Ricceri (Eds.), *Behavioral brain research in naturalistic and semi-naturalistic settings* (pp. 159–194). Dordrecht: Kluwer Academic Press.

Shettleworth, S. J. (2003). Memory and hippocampal specialization in food-storing birds: Challenges for research on comparative cognition. *Brain Behavior and Evolution, 62,* 108–116.

Stevens, T. A., & Krebs, J. R. (1986) Retrieval of stored seeds by marsh tits (*Parus palustris*) in the field. *Ibis, 128,* 513–515.

Suddendorf, T., & Busby, J. (2003). Mental time travel in animals? *Trends in Cognitive Sciences, 7,* 391–396.

Suddendorf, T., & Corballis, M. C. (1997). Mental time travel and the evolution of the human mind. *Genetic Social and General Psychology Monographs, 123,* 133–167.

Vander Wall, S. B. (1982). An experimental analysis of cache recovery in Clark's nutcracker. *Animal Behaviour, 30,* 84–94.

Vander Wall, S. B. (1990). *Food hoarding in animals.* Chicago and London: The University of Chicago Press.

Vander Wall, S. B., & Balda, R. P. (1977). Coadaptations of the Clark's nutcracker and the pinyon pine for efficient seed harvest and dispersal. *Ecology Monographs, 47,* 89–111.

Vander Wall, S. B., & Balda, R. P. (1981). Ecology and evolution of food-storage behavior in conifer-seed-caching corvids. *Zeitschrift für Tierpsychologie, 56,* 217–242.

Vander Wall, S. B., & Jenkins, S. H. (2003). Reciprocal pilferage and the evolution of food-hoarding behavior. *Behavioral Ecology, 14,* 656–667.

Wasserman, E. A. (1993). Comparative cognition: Beginning the second century of the study of animal intelligence. *Psychological Bulletin, 113,* 211–228.

Wiens, J. J. (2001). Widespread loss of sexually selected traits: How the peacock lost its spots. *Trends in Ecology & Evolution, 16,* 517–523.

31

The Neural Basis of Cognitive Flexibility in Birds

SHIGERU WATANABE

Cognitive flexibility has a number of different aspects. Here, I examine three of them. First, cognitive flexibility means expansion of knowledge, so I discuss concept discrimination as one example. Second, I analyze reversal learning and repeated acquisition as a modification of already acquired knowledge. Finally, innovation, or the emergence of novel knowledge, is discussed.

NEURAL BASIS OF VISUAL CONCEPTS

Generalization and Concept Discrimination

After discriminative training, animals respond not only to all of the trained stimuli but also to new stimuli, depending on the similarity of the new stimuli to the trained ones. This phenomenon is known as *stimulus generalization*. Although generalization depends on perceptual similarity, it differs from mere confusion between the trained stimuli and testing stimuli because it can be shown that the subjects can be trained to discriminate between the training and the testing stimuli (Wasserman, Kiedinger, & Bhatt, 1988). Usually, responses to the testing stimuli decrease as sensory distance from the originally trained stimulus increases. We thereby obtain a stimulus generalization gradient.

Unlike generalization, in concept discrimination, the animal responds equally to testing stimuli within a class. Concept discrimination refers to generalization of stimuli *within* a class and discrimination *between* classes. Thus, instead of a generalization gradient, a rectangular pattern of responding is obtained. Since Herrnstein and Loveland (1964) first found evidence for a complex visual concept in pigeons, there have been many studies demonstrating higher visual functioning in pigeons (e.g., Herrnstein, Vaughan, Mumford, & Kosslyn, 1989; Wasserman et al., 1988; Watanabe, 1988; Watanabe, Wakita, & Sakamoto, 1995).

Concepts With and Without Explicit Rules

In concept discrimination, subjects are usually exposed to multiple exemplars. Figure 31.1 presents responses to different types of triangles after discriminative training with either a single exemplar or with multiple exemplars (reanalyzed data from Watanabe, 1991). After discriminating between a single triangle and three randomly placed lines (top panel), the birds responded to different types of triangle, thereby showing a kind of generalization gradient. However, they responded more often to a trapezoidal pattern than to novel triangles. Interestingly, an inverted V-shape induced more responding than did an ordinary V-shape. Three lines

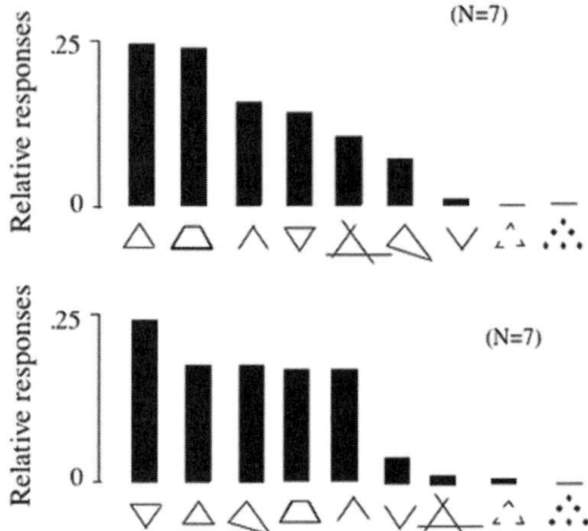

Figure 31.1. The concept of a triangle in pigeons. Results of a generalization test after discriminative training with single (*top*) and multiple (*bottom*) exemplars. (Reanalyzed data from Watanabe, 1991.)

whose inside area formed a triangle also engendered considerable responding (the fifth stimulus from the left in the upper graph of figure 31.1). Thus, what the pigeons had learned through the discrimination with the single triangle differs from our concept of "triangle."

On the other hand, the pattern of response to test stimuli after discrimination training with *multiple* exemplars produced a more rectangular response pattern (the lower graph of figure 31.1). There was no differential response among the five test stimuli from the left in the figure. These pigeons seem to have learned our concept of "triangle." Nevertheless, the pigeons responded to trapezoidal and inverted V-shapes as if they were triangles. These two patterns had never been observed during discriminative training. Interestingly, the three vertices of a triangle or a triangle formed by six dots did not induce responding. Therefore, the pigeon and human concepts of triangle do differ, even though pigeons' discriminative behavior is largely categorical rather than exhibiting a generalization gradient of responding.

Of course, humans' geometrical definition of a triangle is a rule that can be described verbally. Pigeons have to establish nonverbal definition-like rules through behavioral experience alone. Comparing the pigeons' patterns of responding after training with multiple exemplars and after training with a single exemplar suggests that exposure to multiple exemplars may be essential to the formation of an artificial geometrical concept based on a definition-like rule.

Some other concepts have no single rule or feature, even for humans. The discrimination of pictures may entail such a concept. We can easily identify artists, such as Picasso or Van Gogh, when we see their pictures, even though we have never before seen these particular paintings. I have demonstrated successful discrimination of paintings by pigeons (Watanabe, 2001b; Watanabe et al., 1995). Pigeons that had been trained to discriminate paintings by a particular artist from those by another artist could discriminate other paintings that they had never seen before. Furthermore, the birds maintained their discrimination for black-and-white paintings and for partially occluded paintings. Pigeons could also discriminate unfocused paintings or monochromatic paintings. It is hard to single out particular cues for these complex discriminations, but on a perceptual level, there is clearly some similarity between the training and testing stimuli. We may be able to explain this cognitive behavior in terms of polymorphous concepts based on perceptual cues (Lea & Harrison, 1978) in which several different cues, but none in particular, are integrated to define the concept.

Do Negative Concepts Go Beyond Polymorphous Concepts?

In the case of human concepts, we can easily make a list of concepts whose members differ perceptually from each other: for example, the concepts "vehicle," "furniture," and "cooking tool" comprise highly varied members. However, until relatively recently, it had been difficult to detect such concepts in animals (Bovet & Vauclair, 1998; Wasserman, DeVolder, & Coppage, 1992).

Using real objects as discriminative stimuli, I trained pigeons to discriminate food and nonfood objects (Watanabe, 1991). Figure 31.2 shows birds' responses to the test stimuli after training. Corn, peas, buckwheat, and wheat were used as exemplars of food; responding to these stimuli was reinforced. Stones, twigs, yellow paper clips, and nuts were used as exemplars of nonfood; responding to these stimuli was not reinforced. After the birds learned the discrimination, they were tested with kaoliang, safflower seed, hemp seed, coins, electric resistors, and bolts, in addition to two of the already trained

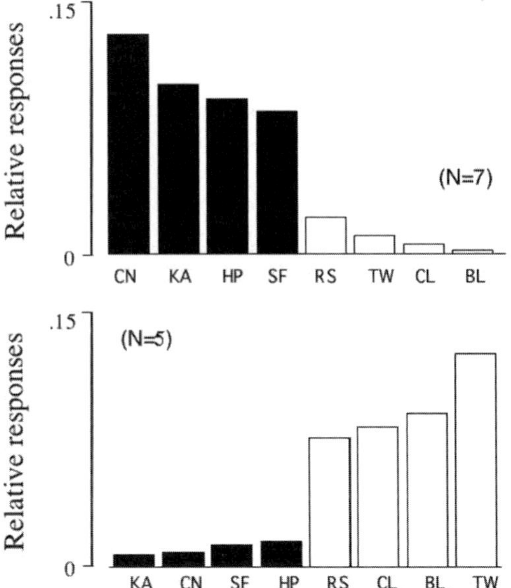

Figure 31.2. The concepts of food (*top,* food+/nonfood– discrimination) and nonfood (*bottom,* nonfood+/food– discrimination). Dark and open bars represent food and nonfood items. BL, bolt; CN, corn; CL, coin; HP, hemp seed; KA, kaoliang; RS, electric resistor; SF, safflower; TW, twig. (Reanalyzed data from Watanabe, 1991.)

stimuli (corn and twigs). The birds responded to the test stimuli according to the categorical discriminative training they had received. Thus, they showed evidence of concept discrimination.

In the case of the "positive" food concept, the pigeons showed a somewhat rectangular response pattern. This pattern might be explained in terms of a polymorphous concept (Lea & Harrison, 1978): There may be no single visual feature of "edible objects," but there surely are several features of the edible objects. In the case of food for pigeons, size (most of the food is not so big), color (objects with metallic color are usually not edible), or shape (most food is round) may be such features. Therefore, pigeons could recognize an object as edible if the object has some of such features (*n-out-of-m* rule).

In the case of "the negative" nonfood concept, the pigeons cannot use the polymorphous concept discrimination strategy, because nonfood stimuli have greater variability in appearance compared with food stimuli. In fact, the concept of nonfood is entirely open-ended; it is impossible to list perceptual features that define "not food," "not vehicle," or "not cooking tools." Thus, negative concepts may go beyond polymorphous concepts. Still the pigeons responded in testing after nonfood training in much the same way as they did after food training (figure 31.2).

I can provide another example of a negative concept. Detecting "abnormal" behavior has special importance, because an abnormal conspecific may be dangerous or may be a signal of a dangerous environment. For example, an animal can avoid a toxic food by observing illness behavior in other animals that have consumed the food. In fact, social transmission of taste aversion has been observed in red-winged black birds (Mason & Reidinger, 1982), although social transmission of taste aversion has not been confirmed in rats (Galef, McQuoid, & Whiskin, 1990; Galef, Wigmore, & Kennett, 1983). Abnormal behavior is varied in appearance. Hyperactive behavior or a manic state is abnormal, as is hypoactive behavior or a depressive state. Thus, the concept of abnormal behavior consists of perceptually different members.

We used movie images to examine the classification of abnormal behavior in quail (Yamazaki, Shinohara, & Watanabe, 2004). The quail were trained to discriminate between moving video images of quail injected with psychoactive drugs and those in a normal (nondrugged) condition. Methamphetamine (stimulant) or ketamine (anesthetic) was used to produce drug-induced behaviors; the former induced hyperactive behavior, and the latter, hypoactive behavior. Thus, the degree of activity could be perceived as hyperactive, normal, or hypoactive in this order. Human observers could easily discriminate these three kinds of behavior by the quail.

One group of quail was trained to peck images of a hyperactive quail but not those of a normal quail. The other group was trained to peck images of a hypoactive quail but not those of a normal quail. After discriminative training, the subjects received a generalization test with images of hyperactive, normal, and hypoactive quail. The quail did learn the discrimination and showed generalization to novel images of the drug-induced behaviors. They did not, however, show discriminative behavior according to the kind or dosage of the drugs. In other words, the quail did not classify different behaviors of conspecifics along the "activity" dimension but classified different drug-induced behaviors into a single category ("abnormal") representing behavior that differed from normal behavior.

The nonfood concept and the concept of abnormal behavior support the idea of an open-ended concept. However, members belonging to the complementary S– concept ("food" or "normal behavior") are probably similar to one another, so discriminative behavior in these "negative" concept tasks might be based on one or more properties of the S– stimuli. If the birds use the strategy of not responding to particular stimuli (food or normal behavior) but of responding to any other stimuli, then they can learn "negative" concepts via a simple sensory discrimination. Therefore, we cannot exclude the possibility that discrimination is based on sensory similarity in the case of "negative" concepts.

The Neural Basis of Conceptual Cognition—Visual Agnosia or Learning Deficit?

Both mammals and birds have two visual pathways: the lemnothalamic and the collothalamic pathways. In birds, the telencephalic terminal of the former pathway is the visual Wulst that consists of the hyperstriatum accessorium, the hyperstriatum intercalatus superior, and the hyperstriatum dorsale. The Wulst or hyperpallium may be homologous to the neopallium, but it does not have a laminated structure like the mammalian cortex. The ectostriatum or entopallium is the telencephalic terminal of the collothalamic pathway and a part of the dorsal ventricular ridge. In primates, the lateral geniculate-visual cortex pathway (lemnothalamic pathway) is the main visual pathway, whereas the collothalamic pathway is the main visual pathway in pigeons. Thus, the ectostriatum is the main visual processing structure in the telencephalon.

Simple Pattern Discrimination An earlier study by Hodos and Karten (1970) demonstrated deficits in pattern discrimination after ectostriatal lesions. In contrast, I did not find deficits in the discrimination of two stimuli—namely, a triangle and lines—after ectostriatal lesions (Watanabe, 1991). However, Hodos and Karten used a simultaneous discrimination, whereas I used a successive discrimination. Powers, Halasz, and Williams (1982) trained pigeons in a line discrimination (vertical line vs. blank key) with multiple schedules that were similar to those I used and found no deficits in discrimination after ectostriatal lesions. However, a more important procedural difference is that the pigeons in Hodos and Karten's experiment were trained on five visual discriminations concurrently, whereas my birds (and also those of Powers) were trained on only one task. Thus, the deficits observed by Hodos and Karten might represent difficulties in mastering concurrent discriminations.

Artificial Concept I trained pigeons on a triangle concept task using multiple exemplars (described above) and found that ectostriatal lesions caused severe deficits (Watanabe, 1991). The birds could not relearn the task after the lesions, but they still could learn a one-pair task. These results suggest deficits in concept discrimination, but not in simple pattern discrimination.

Natural Concept A visual image of a conspecific must be a familiar natural concept for pigeons. I trained pigeons on a pigeon-versus-quail discrimination with a color monitor using still images (Watanabe, 1992). After discriminative training, the birds responded to images of other pigeons (one white pigeon and one with a green patch on white feathers), but they responded less often to other species (ring dove, diamond dove, and Indian quail). Interestingly, the pigeons did not respond to images of squab. Neither ectostriatal nor Wulst lesions disturbed the conspecific discrimination. On the other hand, discrimination between two individual pigeons was impaired after the ectostriatal lesions. Thus, there may be a dissociation between discrimination of conspecifics and individuals. Wulst lesions did not cause deficits in discrimination of individuals. Sensory differences between species might be larger than those within a species. In another experiment, I trained pigeons to discriminate between avian species (Java sparrow and grey starling) and I made lesions after the training (Watanabe, 1996). The pigeons showed deficits after ectostriatal lesions. Thus, there appears to be a functional dissociation between the discrimination of conspecifics and between the discrimination of different species. In the case of food, another natural concept, pigeons did not show deficits after ectostriatal lesions (Watanabe, 1991). These results concur with those for the conspecific discrimination. I also trained pigeons to discriminate using pseudo-concepts. The birds had to learn to classify eight items (four food items and four nonfood items) into two arbitrary (pseudo) groups. They were the same items as those used for the food-versus-nonfood concept discrimination, but there was no rule for classification, so the animals had to memorize each item. The birds with ectostriatal damage showed deficits. Because the same items were used in both concept and pseudo-concept discriminations, the dissociation depends on the rules of classification rather than the kinds of training stimuli.

Two- and Three-Dimensional Discrimination The relationship between a two-dimensional (2D) stimulus and a three-dimensional (3D) stimulus is interesting because there are many 2D stimuli representing 3D stimuli in the human environment. Newspapers, books, and television are such 2D stimuli. On the other hand, pure 2D stimuli are quite rare in the environment of most animals. Thus, 2D stimuli are artificial. To investigate this issue, pigeons were trained on a discrimination task with real objects and their photographs (Watanabe, 1997). The training stimuli were real food (grains), photographs of food, various inedible objects, and photographs of them. One task was to discriminate between real objects and their photographs. The other task was to discriminate between food (real items and their photographs) and nonfood (real objects and their photographs). The birds could discriminate real objects from their pictures and also food from nonfood, suggesting that pigeons can integrate real stimuli and their photographs into one category. Unlike the previous food concept experiment, however, bilateral ectostriatal lesions caused deficits in this food-versus-nonfood discrimination. The birds responded less often to novel stimuli in the generalization test. Photographs of buckwheat (an untrained food item) were classified as nonfood after training to respond to nonfood objects but not to food objects. The birds seemed unable to learn the concept discrimination because they did not show clear generalization based on the concept, nevertheless learning the discrimination task by discriminating each stimulus. Pigeons could learn the arbitrary classification of objects (pseudo-concept discrimination) by such item-by-item discrimination. The birds should have employed an item-by-item learning strategy for the discrimination of composition of real objects and their photographs, as in the learning of pseudo-concepts. In other word, the birds learned real objects and their photographs not as one group of stimuli but individually. The birds learned real corn and its photograph as different two items; they did not use concept discrimination for this task. The object-versus-picture discrimination, in which both real objects and their pictures appeared, was not affected by ectostriatal lesions. Again, the stimuli were the same as those used in the food concept. This dissociation suggests that different brain mechanisms are involved in the two visual discriminations that use the same stimuli.

Table 31.1 Effects of the ectostriatal lesions on visual cognition in pigeons

No Deficits	Deficits
Simple pattern discrimination	Concept of triangle
Food/no-food concept	Pseudoconcept
Object/picture discrimination	Integration of objects and pictures
Conspecific discrimination	Individual discrimination
	Species discrimination

Table 31.1 summarizes the deficits and the absence of deficits after ectostriatal lesions. The tasks showing deficits seem not to be category specific. The birds showed deficits not only in artificial concepts but also in individual or species concepts. Common to the tasks that show deficits is the acquisition of knowledge through discriminative training. Pseudo-concepts and the concept of triangle, as well as of individual and unknown species, have to be learned by training. On the other hand, the concepts of food and conspecific should already involve acquired knowledge for the pigeons in our experiments. The discrimination of 2D (photographs) and 3D stimuli (real objects) may also involve knowledge that is already present.

We do have to consider task difficulty as a factor responsible for the observed deficits. It may be easier to discriminate natural concepts than pseudo-concepts. However, the number of sessions needed to reach the criterion for learning the object/picture discrimination did not differ from that needed for the discrimination of objects and the integration of pictures. The correlation between the number of sessions before the ectostriatal lesions and individual deficits was not significant (Watanabe, 1996, 1997).

CHANGING LEARNED BEHAVIOR

Category learning involves an expansion of knowledge. Another type of cognitive flexibility involves a change or replacement of learned behavior.

Learning Set

Animals not only can expand their knowledge but also can modify it according to environmental changes. Such cognitive flexibility has traditionally been examined by two methods: reversal learning and learning set. Learning set has been considered a form of species IQ test. Researchers rank different mammals according to their performance on the second trial of a problem, because the animal should know the correct stimulus on the second trial in a two-choice discrimination. Comparisons indicate that rhesus monkeys perform better than squirrel monkeys, squirrel monkeys better than cats, and cats better than rats. Interestingly, the performance of blue jays is similar to that of monkeys. The mean percentage correct on trial 2 was 72% over the last 100 of 700 problems for these species (Hunter & Kamil, 1971). Critics of learning set as an intelligence test note its dependence on sensory modality. For example, rats behave more accurately in an olfactory learning set task than in a visual learning set task (Eichenbaum, Fagan, & Cohen, 1986). However, there also appear to be qualitative differences in cognitive strategy. Comparison of pigeons with corvids shows an improvement in the percentage correct on trial 2 in corvids, but not in pigeons (Mackintosh, 1988). Mackintosh suggested that the corvids employed rule learning, whereas pigeons used rote learning. Yamazaki (2001) compared pigeons and crows in their performance of matching symbolic samples. The crows performed well with 10 concurrent matching pairs, but the pigeons could not complete the task, even though they could learn each pair independently. Despite these differences, we still do not have a reliable quantitative method of comparing the cognitive abilities of different species, but there is also much debate about the measurement of human intellectual ability.

Reversal Learning

Reversal learning and reversal learning set are further methods for examining cognitive ability. These methods have often been used in brain lesion studies (Rajalakshmi & Jeeves, 1965). The role of the area prefrontalis in reversal learning has been well documented in monkeys (e.g., Harlow & Dagnon, 1943). Relative to controls, lesions of the medial prefrontal cortex impair reversal in rats (Ferry, Lu, Xi-Chun, & Price, 2000). Damage to the nucleus basalis also impairs reversal learning in the marmoset (DeBrulin, Sanchez-Santed, Heinsbroek, Donker, & Postmes, 1992). Pigeons with Wulst lesions exhibit impaired reversal of position discriminations (Macphail, 1971, 1975; Macphail & Reilly, 1985), orientation discriminations (Powers et al., 1982; Macphail & Reilly, 1983), and color discriminations (Macphail, 1976a; Shimizu & Hodos, 1989). Most of these experiments employed simultaneous discrimination, but reversal with a go–no go procedure is also impaired by Wulst lesions (Shimizu & Hodos, 1989). Single reversal (Macphail, 1971), reversals within 3 days (Macphail, 1976a), and repeated reversals (Macphail, 1976b) are all sensitive to Wulst lesions. Wulst lesions in chicks (Benowitz & Lee-Teng, 1973) and quail (Stettner & Schultz, 1967) also impair reversal learning. Although there has been some variability in the extent of the lesions in these studies, deficits in reversal learning are consistently observed after Wulst lesions. Because OPT (thalamic nucleus of the lemnothalamic pathway) lesions did not result in deficits in reversal learning (Chaves, Hodos, & Gunturkun, 1993), the brain area that is likely to be responsible for reversal deficits is the Wulst itself. Lesions in the nucleus rotundus, which transmits visual information from the tectum to the ectostriatum, also causes deficits in reversal learning (Chaves & Hodos, 1998). Thus, visual information from the collothalamic pathway seems to be processed for reversal learning through the hyperstriatum ventrale and neostriatum intermedials pars laterale (NIL). Although deficits in reversal learning have been well documented after Wulst lesions, deficits in the acquisition of horizontal-vertical discrimination have also been reported. Reilly (1987) suggested the possibility that the deficits in reversal learning are due to deficits in acquisition because Wulst lesions also disturb autoshaping. Macphail (1975) also found both acquisition and reversal deficits in a simultaneous position discrimination; he suggested that there were deficits in the ability to shift responses to an alternative stimulus, although the same author later reported that there were deficits in response inhibition (Macphail, 1976b). In reversal learning using go–no go procedures, the animal has to learn to respond to the previously negative stimulus. Wulst lesions impaired such responding in reversals of a go–no go color discrimination (Powers, 1989). Thus, the ability to acquire a new response to the previously negative stimulus was retarded. These observations suggest difficulty in the acquisition of a new behavior, rather than perseverance of responding. Deficits in reversal learning may be caused by increased difficulty in shifting the response or by new learning. Another telencephalic structure, which when damaged impairs reversal learning, is the neostriatum caudolateralis (NCL) (Hartmann & Gunturkun, 1998). The NCL has dense dopaminergic innervations and can be assumed to be homologous to the mammalian prefrontalis. Lesions in this area cause deficits in reversal learning, but lesions in the nucleus dorsolateralis posterior thalami, which projects into the NCL, have no effect. Therefore, two structures in the telencephalon, the Wulst and NCL, are involved in reversal learning. Recently, Husband and Shimizu (2003) reported impairment of reversal learning after lesions in the medial lobus parolfactorius (LPO) (medial striatum) that were assumed to be the nucleus accumbens. Thus, two dorsal structures (Wulst and NCL) and one ventral structure (LPO) appear to be involved in reversal learning.

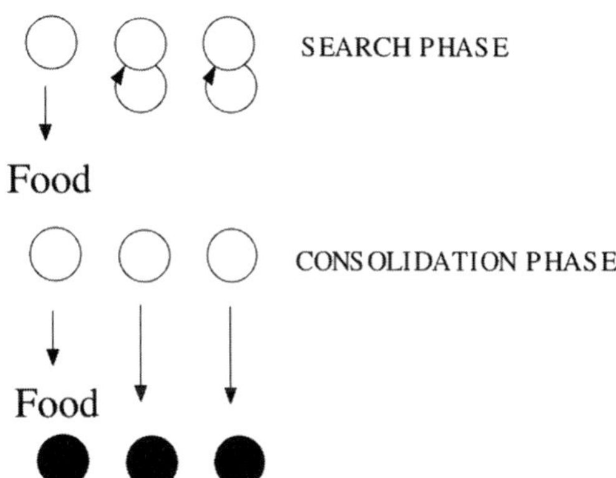

Figure 31.3. The repeated acquisition procedure. Bird can search for the correct key in the first trial (SEARCH PHASE). An incorrect peck causes nothing. In the following trials (CONSOLIDATION PHASE), a peck to the correct key causes food presentation but a peck on the incorrect keys terminates the key lights without food. The Consolidation Phase continues until 10 successive correct pecks are achieved.

The Repeated Acquisition Procedure

The repeated acquisition procedure is another method of examining cognitive flexibility. The procedure of repeated acquisition was originally developed for pharmacological study and used the learning of a sequential response. The animal has to learn the order of pecking three (or more) keys. I modified the repeated acquisition procedure to examine cognitive flexibility in pigeons. In serial reversal learning, animals are repeatedly trained on two contradictory discriminations. In repeated acquisition, animals have to learn a new discrimination each time they accomplish one discrimination. Novel stimuli are presented for each discrimination in a learning set task, whereas the same stimulus set is repeatedly used in the repeated acquisition procedure. Thus, the difficulty of each discrimination task is identical in the repeated acquisition procedure.

A within-subject design is a powerful way to assess the effects of a lesion, because damage to brains may differ between subjects. However, it is difficult to use this method to examine the effects of lesions on acquisition processes, because it is impossible to repeat acquisition before and after the lesions. The repeated acquisition procedure makes it possible to obtain a baseline of acquisition, so comparison of the steady state of learning before and after lesions is possible. I used a position discrimination with three pecking keys, so the correct response was to peck one particular key. Another modification that I made to this procedure was to separate the search and consolidation phases. Figure 31.3 demonstrates the sequence of the procedure. On the first trial, a peck on the incorrect key produces no reward, but a peck on the correct key is followed by reinforcement. All keys are lit until the subject pecks the correct key. This part of the task is defined as the search phase, because the subject has to search for the correct key. If the subject continues to respond according to previous learning—in other words, the subject lacks cognitive flexibility—then it produces many error pecks on incorrect keys before finding the correct key. On the second and subsequent trials, a peck on the incorrect keys causes immediate blackout, whereas a peck on the correct key causes reinforcement. The intertrial interval is a 10-s blackout. Training continues until the subject produces 10 successive correct choices. If the subject reached the criterion, then one of the previous two incorrect keys is assigned as the correct key in the next session. Therefore, the subject has to learn a new spatial discrimination problem every time it masters an old one. The subjects received more than 15 problems.

The repeated acquisition procedure shares some features with reversal learning, because three contradictory discriminations are repeatedly trained. The procedure shares some features with the card sorting task described later, because the subject has

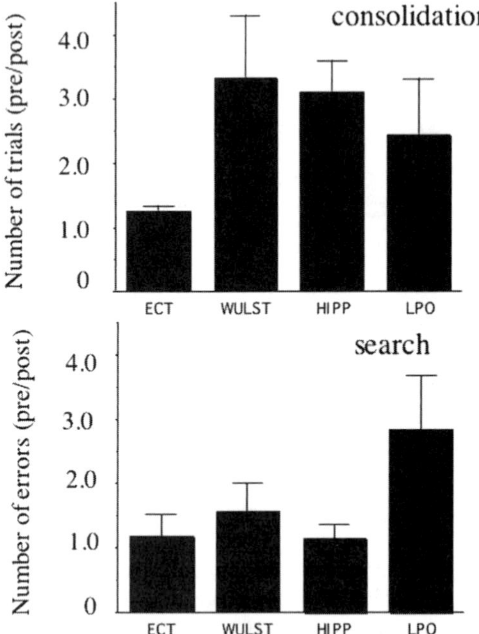

Figure 31.4. Effects of lesions on repeated acquisition. *Top* and *bottom*, Number of trials to reach the discrimination criterion (consolidation) and the number of errors on the first trial (search), respectively. The *vertical axis* indicates the ratio of postlesion to prelesion scores. (From "Effects of Wulst and Ectostriatum Lesions on Repeated Acquisition of Spatial Learning in Pigeons," by S. Watanabe, 2003, *Cognitive Brain Research, 17,* 286–292. Copyright 2003 by *Behavioural Brain Research.* Reprinted with permission.)

to change its discrimination. I trained pigeons on this repeated acquisition procedure to obtain a baseline of acquisition and then made lesions. If lesions impair cognitive flexibility, then the main effect should be an increase in the number of errors in the search phase. If lesions impair the consolidation of memory, then the main effect should be an increase in the number of trials to reach criterion. Figure 31.4 presents the results of the experiment.

Ectostriatum (Entopallium) As described earlier, the ectostriatum is an area that processes complex visual information. The repeated acquisition procedure is a kind of visual discrimination, but figure 31.4 shows that ectostriatal lesions did not affect performance (Watanabe, 2003). Identification of the position of the three keys does not seem to need higher-level processing via the ectostriatum. As described earlier, the ectostriatum is not involved in simple discriminations (e.g., a triangle versus three lines) of the kind required for repeated acquisition.

Hippocampus The dorsomedial telencephalon in birds has been considered the avian counterpart of the mammalian hippocampus. Anatomical studies of neural connections suggest similarities between the avian and mammalian hippocampus (Benowitz & Karten, 1976; Bingman, Casini, Nocjar, & Jones, 1994; Casini, Bingman, & Bagnoli, 1986; Erichsen, Bingman, & Krebs, 1991; Kahn, Hough, Ten Eyck, & Bingman, 2003; Krebs, Erichsen, & Bingman, 1991). Visual discrimination in pigeons is not impaired by hippocampal lesions. Hippocampal lesions does not affect visual acuity (Bingman & Hodos, 1992), color discrimination (Reilly & Good, 1987), color delayed matching to a sample (Colombo, Cawley, & Broadbent, 1997), or the concurrent acquisition of six different visual discriminations (Colombo et al., 1997). A trial unique object recognition task is not disrupted by hippocampal damage (Good & Macphail, 1994). It has been suggested that the hippocampus of rats plays a role in integrating information (Murray & Ridley, 1999), but the avian hippocampus seems not to play a role in complex discriminations. Negative patterning, in which elements are associated with reinforcement individually but not in combination, can be learned after hippocampal lesions in pigeons (Papadimitriou & Wynne, 1999). Broadbent, Gallagher, and Colombo (1999) used auditory and visual stimuli as elements, and pigeons with hippocampal damage learned negative patterning as well as control animals. I trained pigeons before and after hippocampal lesions on a conditional discrimination, in which a conditional color stimulus determined the position of the correct key (Watanabe, 2002a). The position of the correct key was on the left side when all keys were red, in the center when all keys were green, and on the right side when all keys were white. Pigeons with hippocampal damage learned the task as well as intact birds. These results suggest that the pigeon hippocampus does not play a role in conditional spatial discrimination. The results are interesting, because hippocampal lesions in rats caused deficits in conditional spatial discriminations (Raffaele & Olton, 1988) and conditional brightness discriminations (Sutherland, McDonald, Hill, & Rudy, 1989). On the other hand, there have been several reports demonstrating that the avian hippocampus has a spatial function. A correlation between the size of the hippocampus and food-storing behavior has been reported (Krebs, Sherry, Healy, Perry, & Vaccarino, 1989), although more recent work has not found a significant correlation (Brodin & Lundborg, 2003). On the other hand, deficits in homing (Bingman, Ioale, Casini, & Bagnoli, 1990) and in spatial discrimination (Fremouw, Jackson-Smith, & Kesner, 1997) after lesions suggest that there is in fact a spatial function of the hippocampus. I trained pigeons on a spatial autodiscrimination, in which the presentation of one of two keys was followed by food but the presentation of the other key was not (Watanabe, 1999). Intact birds easily learned to peck one key, but not the other; however, birds with hippocampal damage did not. When hippocampal lesions were made after the pigeons had been trained on the autodiscrimination task, the subjects with hippocampal damage did not show deficits. Furthermore, hippocampal damage did not impair a color autodiscrimination, in which presentation of one of the two colors was followed by food. These results strongly suggest that one function of the avian hippocampus is specific to spatial learning. I also examined effects of hippocampal lesions on a repeated acquisition procedure (figure 31.3). In the first trial of this task, three keys remain lit until the subject finds the correct key. A peck on the correct key results in reinforcement. This is a search phase and the number of pecks on the incorrect keys is counted as an index of searching. In the second and following trials, any incorrect response terminates trials. The training continues until the subject emits 10 successive correct choices. This is the consolidation phase. The number of errors in the first trial represents searching. The number of trials to reach the criterion represents consolidation. Once the subject reaches the criterion, it is trained on a new task in which one of the two previously incorrect keys becomes the new correct key. This procedure is repeated to obtain a baseline of acquisition. Then, a brain lesion is made. The acquisition after the lesion is compared with that before the lesion by dividing performance before the lesion by that after the lesion. A ratio of 1.0 means that there was no effect of the lesion. Figure 31.4, top, depicts pre/post ratios for the number of trials to reach the criterion (consolidation), and the bottom depicts pre/post ratios for the number of errors (search). We can thus separately compare deficits in consolidation and search. Hippocampal lesions did increase the number of trials to learn, suggesting deficits in consolidation in the repeated acquisition procedure (Watanabe, 2001a). The deficits shown in figure 31.4 concur with previous reports, because the procedure involved acquisition of a spatial discrimination. Interestingly, when color cues were added to the keys, such deficits in repeated acquisition disappeared (Watanabe, 2001). This finding fits well with the results from the color autodiscrimination. If the animal has difficulty in changing a previously learned behavior, then it should commit many errors in the search phase, because a previously correct key just became an incorrect one. Figure 31.4 shows that subjects with a damaged hippocampus did not commit many errors in the search phase, suggesting no deficits in their flexibility of learning. This observation agrees with intact reversal learning after hippocampal lesions (Good, 1987; Good & Honey, 1991). On the other hand, the pigeons required many trials to reach the criterion, suggesting difficulty in learning. Thus, the function of the hippocampus in the repeated acquisition of spatial discrimination may be the consolidation of spatial memory.

Basal Ganglion (LPO) or Medial Striatum The avian paleostriatal complex can be divided into three parts: the paleostriatum augmentatum (PA) or lateral striatum, the paleostriatum primitivum or globus pallidus, and the LPO. One structure involved in repeated acquisition is the LPO. Figure 31.4 clearly shows that LPO damage disturbed consolidation of a spatial discrimination and caused severe deficits in searching, with the latter effect a bit stronger than the former (Watanabe, 2002b). The deficits concur with deficits in reversal learning observed after LPO lesions (Husband & Shimizu, 2003). Unlike hippocampal lesions, adding color cues did not improve learning after the LPO lesions. Thus, although the hippocampus plays a crucial role in consolidation specific to spatial learning, LPO has more general effects on learning. The role of the LPO in learning has been studied mostly with one-trial passive avoidance in 1-day-old chicks. Bilateral LPO lesions after, but not before, training cause learning deficits (Gilbert, Patterson, & Rose, 1991), suggesting that the LPO has a memory storage function. Contrary to these results, when Izawa, Yanagihara, Atsumi, and Matsushima (2001) examined a go–no go discrimination with water reward in chicks after LPO lesions, they reported acquisition deficits rather than retention deficits. Although the lesions were made after baseline training in the repeated acquisition experiment, the results in figure 31.4 demonstrate deficits in acquisition rather than retention. Several procedural differences between the chick experiments and the present experiment can be pointed out, such as the type of reward, the developmental stage of the subjects, and the difficulty of the tasks; therefore, it is hard to identify which factor(s) produced the different results. One possible mechanism responsible for the many errors produced in the search phase concerns the difficulty of response inhibition. The birds may have pecked an incorrect key because they might be not have been able to inhibit such behavior. Unfortunately, paleostriatal lesions have been shown to cause either facilitation or suppression of responding (Mitchell, 1983; Mitchell & Hall, 1984; Wesp & Goodman, 1978). These results are interesting, but the damage was restricted to the lateral part of the paleostriatum (PA) rather than the LPO. I did not find any facilitative effects of LPO damage, which suggests that the LPO and PA may have different functions. Deficits in locomotion have been observed after paleostriatal lesions in pigeons (Ruskin & Goodman, 1971), which suggests that the avian paleostriatum and mammalian basal ganglion have a similar function. However, I did not observe any severe motor deficits. Because the damage in the present experiment was mostly restricted to the LPO, this area did not have an important role in motor coordination. One interesting function of the LPO is its role in birdsong production. Area X, which is a part of the LPO of songbirds, has catecholaminergic projections from the area ventralis. It was suggested that area X-LPO may be equivalent to the mammalian nucleus accumbens (Lewis, Ryan, Arnold, & Butcher, 1981). Lesions in area X result in the repetition of fixed notes in the song of Bengalese finches (Kobayashi, Uno, & Okanoya, 2001), suggesting rigidity or perseverance of behavior patterns. These observations are compatible with the present results.

Clinical research shows both motor and cognitive stereotypy in basal ganglia dysfunction in humans (Ridley, 1994). Patients with Huntington's disease show impaired reversal of a probabilistic discrimination due to perseverant responses (Lawrence, Sahakian, Rogers, Hodges, & Robbins, 1999). The basal ganglion is involved in the motor circuit and in the "cognitive circuit." The orbitofrontalis and medial prefrontalis project into the ventromedial striatum, including the nucleus accumbens, and into the ventral palladium. The ventral pallidum sends projections to the mediodorsal thalamus and the thalamus sends projections back to the frontalis. Lesions in this pathway impair reversal leaning in rats (Ferry et al., 2000). Reiner, Medina, and Veenman (1998) suggested an evolutionary homology between the avian LPO–PA and the mammalian striatum. The ventromedial LPO can be considered to be equivalent to the nucleus accumbens, and the lateral part of the LPO, part of the caudate-putamen. These anatomical studies suggest that birds also have a palliostriatal system similar to that of mammals; behavioral deficits after the LPO lesions support the idea that the system has a cognitive flexibility function.

Wulst As described earlier, the Wulst is a telencephalic visual structure of the lemnothalamic pathway, but damage to it does not impair visual conceptual behavior. On the other hand, damage to it results in deficits in reversal learning. In figure 31.4, we see deficits in both search (mild) and consolidation (severe) phases (Watanabe, 2003). Birds with damage to the Wulst had difficulty changing their discriminative behavior, whereas those with ectostriatal lesions did not. The present results concur with data from reversal learning after Wulst lesions. Deficits in reversal learning after Wulst lesions can be explained in terms of perseverance of learned behavior or deficits in acquisition. In the repeated acquisition procedure, perseverative errors on the previous correct key can be separated from errors committed on the other key. Wulst lesions in the present experiment only slightly increased the number of errors on the first trial (search), whereas such lesions had a more pronounced negative effect on the acquisition of new behavior (consolidation). The deficits caused by pallial lesions can be considered a form of cognitive rigidity. In other words, it is suggested that the LPO and pallium form a system for cognitive flexibility similar to a frontal cortex–basal ganglion system in mammals. In mammals, abnormal function of the interconnection between the frontal cortex and the basal ganglia is thought to be critical in such cognitive rigidity (Graybiel, 1997). The relationship between the avian pallio-LPO system and the mammalian corticostriatal system are also considered in the following section.

The Card Sorting Task

In human patients, the Wisconsin Card Sorting Test (WCST) is a standard test for examining cognitive flexibility. Originally, it was developed for the study of normal persons (Berg, 1948). The site of lesions that cause deficits in this test is the frontal lobe (Cronin-Golomb, 1990). Both event-related potentials and near-infrared spectroscopy suggest a role of the prefrontalis in the card sorting test (Barcelo, 1999; Fallgatter & Strik, 1998). Lesions in the dorsolateral part of the prefrontalis result in difficulty in changing card sorting strategy (Verin et al., 1993), whereas lesions in the inferomedial part have no effect (Stuss et al., 2000). Patients with damage to the basal ganglia show deficits in the WCST (Milner, 1963). Parkinson's disease also results in deficits in the card sorting test (Dimitrov, Grafman, Soares, & Clark, 1999). Thus, the prefrontal-striatal system seems to play a crucial role in the cognitive flexibility of humans. Recently, O'Reilly, Noelle, Braver, and Cohen (2002) developed a WSCT-like test for monkeys and found that damage to the dorsolateral prefrontalis causes deficits in dimensional shift, whereas damage to the orbitofrontal part results in errors involving specific features of the stimuli. Although poor WCST performance has been commonly observed in patients with frontal lobe dysfunction, the hippocampus is another region that may play a role in this test. Hermann, Wyler, and Richey (1988) suggested that a kind of neural noise caused by temporal epilepsy propagated to the frontalis, thereby disturbing WCST performance. Corcoran and Upton (1993) observed poor card sorting performance in patients with hippocampal sclerosis, supporting the notion of the hippocampus as a comparator. More recently, Giovagnoli (2001) examined 112 patients with temporal epilepsy and observed severe deficits in patients with left hippocampal lesions. She explained the deficits in terms of the learning or associative function of the hippocampus. Thus, there are cases of deficits in WCST due to hippocampal dysfunction, but different researchers have proposed different explanations for the deficits. Repeated acquisition has aspects in common with the card sorting test, because subjects are requested to repeatedly find a new correct response. However, the repeated acquisition task always involves a position discrimination, even though the correct position is changed. In other words, there is an intradimensional shift, but not an extradimensional shift. Recently, I developed an analog card sorting test for pigeons (Watanabe, 2005). The test consists of four discriminations: two position discriminations and two color discriminations. Two keys are illuminated by either green or red lamps. In the color discriminations, the position of the keys is irrelevant, so the pigeons have to ignore position. In the position discriminations, the color of the keys is irrelevant, so the pigeons have to ignore the color. On each trial, two keys are illuminated until the subject pecks the correct key. Pecking on the incorrect key indicates cognitive rigidity. These four discriminations were trained in a random sequence. Each time the subjects reached the discrimination criterion, the task was changed. We can thus compare an intradimensional shift (from the red S+ to the green S+ and from the left S+ to the right S+) with an extradimensional shift (from a spatial discrimination to a color discrimination and vice versa). After subjects were trained on this WCST analog, I made hippocampal or LPO lesions (Watanabe, submitted). The main effect of the hippocampal lesions was an increase in the number of trials to reach criterion, whereas the main effect of the LPO lesions was an increase in the number of errors. The number of errors indicates cognitive flexibility, because the animal that was trapped in the previous learning had many initial errors. On the other hand, the number of trials to the criterion indicates the role of consolidation, because the animal that did not firmly learn the task had difficulty in making successive correct responses even though it might know the correct response. The deficits were more severe after the LPO lesions than after the hippocampal lesions. These results confirm my previous results with repeated acquisition and support the idea that the LPO is involved in searching, whereas the hippocampus supports memory. This position also agrees with the poor performance observed in patients with hippocampal lesions. I expected selective deficits in the spatial discrimination, but not in the color discrimination, after the hippocampal lesions; however, such selective deficits were not observed. Perhaps an interaction between the intradimensional and extradimensional shifts masked dimension-specific deficits. Differences between the intradimensional and the extradimensional shift were not clear following lesions in either area.

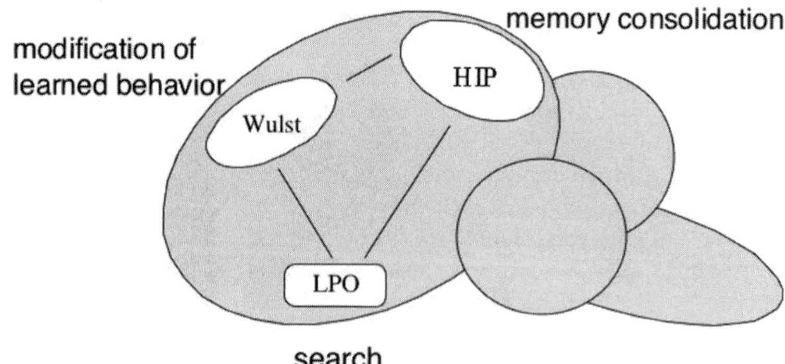

Figure 31.5. The hypothesized function of the avian telencephalon in cognitive flexibility.

The Neural Structure of Changing Learned Behavior

The discrimination tasks that I discussed in this section have several common features: (1) the subject must be free from the previous learning, (2) the subject has to find a new correct response by searching, and (3) the subject has to memorize the new learning. Figure 31.5 presents a model of telencephalon involvement in modifying learned behavior.

The LPO plays a crucial role in finding the correct behavior, whereas the hippocampus plays a crucial role in the consolidation of that learning. The functions of the Wulst and other pallial structures are not well understood. Impairment in reversal learning suggests a preservation of, or adherence to, previous learning without the Wulst. However, analysis of error preservation in repeated acquisition does not support such a conclusion. The LPO-Wulst system probably plays a role in new learning as a linking system, similar to the mammalian prefrontalis-striatum system, whereas the LPO-hippocampal system may be a search and memory system.

INNOVATION

The previous two aspects of cognitive flexibility, conceptualization and modifying acquired behavior, do not involve the creation of new knowledge. Innovation is a kind of creation of new knowledge. The most popular examples of innovation in animals are sweet potato washing by monkeys and bottletop opening by robins. These are novel behaviors never observed before that innovation. There are several definitions of *innovation* (see Reader & Laland, 2003). Here, I define innovation as the creation or productive synthesis of knowledge.

Tool Using and Tool Making

Tool use is one kind of innovation, because a tool is used for a new purpose or in a new situation. Tool using has been observed to occur over a wide range of species. Powell and Kelly (1977) examined tool use in crows. After training through successive approximation, the crows could operate a pecking key using a wooden stick, but they were unable to perform this act spontaneously. Subsequently, the crows could use different materials as a tool. In this case, the crows did not make or modify their tool, but in other cases, they could shape the tool (Weir, Chappell, & Kacelnik, 2002); indeed, New Caledonian crows make hook-like sticks. A female captive crow was shown a bucket that contained meat in a transparent vertical pipe. Using a piece of straight wire that was available, the bird made a hook by bending the wire and then it retrieved the bucket. Pigeons also used a tool in a situation that was similar to that of Kohler's chimpanzee. The situation is not real tool making as described below but the creation of a new combination of different behaviors. Pigeons, which had a history of training to move a box toward a particular position and to climb onto a fixed box and peck a suspended plastic banana, showed problem-solving behavior similar to that of the chimpanzee (Epstein, Kirshnit, Lanza, & Rubin, 1984). The history of training in Kohler's chimpanzees was not clear, but pigeons that had no history of training to move a box to a particular position could not solve the problem. Thus, pigeons could interconnect different repertoires of behavior forming a new sequence to solve the problem if they had a repertoire of each component skill. Several field studies have demonstrated more skillful tool-using and tool-making behavior by corvids. A crow pulled a fishing line from a hole in the ice to get a fish (Homberg, 1957). Recently, Hunt reported two types of tools made by New Caledonian crows (Hunt, 1996, 2000): one is a tool made from leaf edges and the other is a hook made from twigs. According to Hunt, there are three aspects of tool making: (1) imposition of form on raw materials in the sculpted sense, (2) skilled tool-making techniques, and (3) morphological standardization of finished tools. Hunt gathered many samples of the tools made by crows and found a kind of standardization of manufacturing. Crows from different areas produced different tools, some of which were of simpler construction than others. Apparently, there had been an evolution of tool making. The hook was used to extract larvae from holes in dead wood. Making a hook is an advanced technique in the history of tool making in humans. Hunt concluded that the tools made by the crows are similar to human tools of the Lower Paleolithic era. Observational learning also occurred in juvenile crows; they observed the tool use of adults and sometimes picked up dropped tools and made holes. Occasionally, juveniles tried to make their tool from inappropriate materials. These observations suggest learning through tool manufacturing.

Innovation and the Brain

Some species, such as the panda, depend on special food, whereas others, such as rats and humans, enjoy many different food items. Opportunists have to explore new kinds of food. Some of the items may be toxic, but others are edible. The opportunists have to decide to eat food at their own risk. Natural study of birds has showed that successful invaders in new regions have a higher innovation rate in foraging than do unsuccessful species (Sol, Timmermans, & Lefebvre, 2002). In laboratory study, the innovation rate appears to be negatively correlated with the number of errors during reversal learning in eight species of birds (Timmermans, Lefebvre, Boire, & Basu, 2000). Thus, cognitive flexibility appears to be involved in both innovation in a natural environment and learning in the laboratory. There is positive correlation between innovation rate and learning speed, tool use, or reversal learning, whereas negative or zero correlation between the innovation and food storing (Lefebvre & Bolhuis, 2003). These observations suggest that spatial learning and innovation constitute separate "modules." According to Fodor (1983), modules are domain specific, innately specified, and hard-wired; this does not necessarily mean localization of modules within the brain, but the localization of brain function supports the modularity of function. Lefebvre, Whittle, Lascaris, and Finlestein (1997) examined the foraging behavior of 40 species as reported in nine ornithological journals. These workers tabulated the ingestion of new foods and new foraging techniques as innovation and found a correlation between innovation rate and forebrain size (forebrain/brain stem) ($r = 0.93$). Using a different index of forebrain size (residual) in birds from New Zealand and Australia, these researchers confirmed their previous results (Lefebvre et al., 1998). Timmermans et al. (2000) also found a positive correlation between innovation rate and the size of four structures of the telencephalon from 17 taxa ($r = 0.554$ for Wulst, 0.598 for neostriatum, 0.599 for striopallidal, and 0.637 for hyperstriatum ventrale). Based on a multivariate analysis, the size and complexity of the neostriatum and the hyperstriatum ventrale appear to predict the innovation rate. Therefore, several different behavioral indices of flexibility, obtained from either natural or laboratory environments, are correlated with the size of the forebrain. We do not have a good IQ test for animals, but behavioral or cognitive flexibility is probably one factor in their general intelligence, because cognitive flexibility in birds not only can function in specific contexts but also can generalize to other contexts. On the other hand, as described earlier, innovation does not correlate with spatial learning; lesion studies in pigeons showed a dissociation between LPO and hippocampal functions. The former functions to find correct behavior, whereas the latter functions to consolidate memory, particularly spatial memory. These findings suggest both general and specific intelligence in birds. I do want to point out a problem with the allometric study of brains. Brain volume may not be a good measure of the number of neurons in the brain. Further, neuronal number may not represent the complexity of the nervous system. The density of synapses and the number of axons or the shape of the cell body may influence the complexity of the system. Although allometric comparisons may be problematic, when applied to the hippocampus in food-storing birds, it has yielded a positive correlation between hippocampal volume and spatial memory. Such a correlation between hippocampal size and spatial cognition is observed not only in birds but also in mammals, including humans. In the case of innovation in birds, however, the function of the hyperstriatum ventrale is not well understood. Although different regions in the forebrain have dif[illegible] these regions work as a whole t[illegible] A combination of all [illegible] studies is needed to clarify relation between behavioral function and particular brain structures.

The Origin of Cognitive Flexibility

At first glance, more flexible behavior suggests more adaptive behavior; however, from the viewpoint of technology, a flexible system costs more than a fixed system. For example, a computer is more expensive than a simple calculator without programming functions. Adaptation is the cost/benefit balance of the system. In fact, many species enjoy adaptive success without large brains. The nervous system is one of the distinctive features of animals when compared with plants, but not all animals develop large brains. Mammals and birds are animals that have a large brain and a particularly large telencephalon. Among mammals, primates have larger brains. Among birds, parrots and crows have the largest brains (see Emery, 2003). Even among fish, some species have a developed brain. Therefore, enlargement of the brain emerged independently in different lines of evolution. If the environment is constant, then animals do not need to change their behavior. Animals have to change their behavior only if the environment changes. Seasonal changes in the environment may necessitate a change in foraging behavior. Difficulty in obtaining food also requires flexibility in foraging. For example, the Kea, a New Zealand parrot, is one such type of animal. They are well known for their curiosity and how skillfully they manipulate objects (Huber, Rechberger, & Taborsky, 2001). Environmental intelligence is one indication of cognitive flexibility. Another well-documented origin of cognitive flexibility is social intelligence. Many primate researchers have advocated the idea that our intelligence may have such an origin. Unfortunately, the social behavior of birds has not been well examined; interestingly, the gray parrot, which exhibits cognitive flexibility such as the acquisition of vocal communication, has a complex social life (Pepperberg, 1999). However, Emery (2003) examined the development of the forebrain and social complexity in birds (solitary, pairs, family group, small flocks, medium flocks, and large flocks) and did not find a significant enlargement of the forebrain depending on social complexity. Thus, we do not have direct evidence documenting a correlation between brain size and social intelligence in birds. Differences between environmental intelligence and social intelligence have not been well studied; in particular, the brain mechanisms underlying the two types of intelligence are not known. The development both types of intelligence may result in a common cognitive ability, such as the g-factor, or may result in the evolution of different cognitive modules. Both types of intelligence may involve enlargement of the same structure in the brains or may involve the enlargement of different structures. Both behavioral and neural analysis of birds with large brains (parrots and corvids) should contribute to our understanding of the evolution of higher cognitive functions, including our own.

Acknowledgments This research was supported by the 21st Century Center of Excellence Program (D-1). The author expresses his gratitude to T. Shimizu for his comments on this chapter.

References

Barcelo, F. (1999). Electrophysiological evidence of two different types of errors in the Wisconsin Card Sorting Test. *Neuroreport, 10,* 1299–1303.

Benowitz, L., & Lee-Teng, E. (1973). Contrasting effects of three forebrain ablations on discrimination learning and reversal in chicks. *Journal of Comparative & Physiological Psychology, 84,* 391–397.

Benowitz, L. I., & Karten, H. J. (1976). The tractus infundibulli and other afferents to the parahippocampal region of the pigeon. *Brain Research, 102,* 174–180.

Berg, M. (1948). A simple objective test for measuring flexibility of thinking. *Journal of Generic Psychology, 39,* 15–22.

Bingman, V. P., Casini, G., Nocjar, C., & Jones, T.-J. (1994). Connections of the piriform cortex in homing pigeons (*Columba livia*) studies with fast blue and WGA-HRP. *Brain Behavior & Evolution, 43,* 206–218.

Bingman, V. P., & Hodos, W. (1992). Visual performance of pigeons following hippocampal lesions. *Behavioural Brain Research, 51,* 203–209.

Bingman, V. P., Ioale, P., Casini, G., & Bagnoli, P. (1990). The avian hippocampus: Evidence for a role in the development of the homing pigeon navigation map. *Behavioral Neuroscience, 104,* 906–911.

Bovet, D., & Vauclair, J. (1998). Functional categorization of objects and of their pictures in baboons (*Papio anubis*). *Learning and Motivation, 29,* 309–322.

Broadbent, N., Gallagher, S., & Colombo, M. (1999). Hippocampal lesions and negative patterning in pigeons. *Psychobiology, 27,* 51–56.

Brodin, A., & Lundborg, K. (2003). Is hippocampal volume affected by specialization for food hoarding in birds? *Proceedings of Royal Society of London B, 270,* 1555–1563.

Casini, G., Bingman, V. P., & Bagnoli, P. (1986). Connections of the pigeon dorsomedial forebrain studies with WGA-HRP and 3H-proline. *Journal of Comparative Neurology, 245,* 454–470.

Chaves, L. M., & Hodos, W. (1998). Color reversal-learning deficits after tectofugal pathway lesions in the pigeon telencephalon. *Behavioural Brain Research, 90,* 1–12.

Chaves, L. M., Hodos, W., & Gunturkun, O. (1993). Color-reversal learning: Effects after lesions of thalamic visual structures in pigeons. *Visual Neuroscience, 10,* 1099–1107.

Colombo, M., Cawley, S., & Broadbent, N. (1997). The effects of hippocampal and area parahippocampalis lesions in pigeons: II. Concurrent discrimination and spatial memory. *Quarterly Journal of Experimental Psychology, 50B,* 172–189.

Colombo, M., Swain, N., Harper, D., & Alsop, B. (1997). The effects of hippocampal and area parahippocampalis lesions in pigeons: I. Delayed matching to sample. *Quarterly Journal of Experimental Psychology, 50,* 149–171.

Corcoran, R., & Upton, D. (1993). A role for the hippocampus in card sorting? *Cortex, 29,* 293–304.

Cronin-Golomb, A. (1990). Abstract thought in aging and age-related disease. In F. Boller & J. Grafman (Eds.), *Handbook of neuropsychology* (Vol. 4, pp. 279–310). Amsterdam: Elsevier.

de Bruin, J. P., Sanchez-Santed, F., Heinsbroek, R. P., Donker, A., & Postmes, P. (1994). A behavioural analysis of rats with damages to the medial prefrontal cortex using the Morris water maze: Evidence for behavioural flexibility, but not for impaired spatial navigation. *Brain Research, 652,* 323–333.

Dimitrov, M., Grafman, J., Soares, A. H., & Clark, K. (1999). Concept formation and concept shifting in frontal lesions and Parkinson's disease patients assessed with the Californian Card Sorting Test. *Neuropsychology, 13,* 135–143.

Eichenbaum, H., Fagan, A., & Cohen, N. J. (1986). Normal olfactory discrimination learning set and facilitation of reversal learning set after medial-temporal damages in rats: Implications for an account of preserved learning abilities in amnesia. *Journal of Neuroscience, 6,* 1876–1884.

Emery, N. J. (2003). Are corvids "feathered apes"?—Cognitive evolution in crows, jays, rooks and jackdaws. In S. Watanabe (Ed.), *Comparative analysis of mind* (pp. 181–214). Tokyo: Keio University Press.

Epstein, R., Kirshnit, C. E., Lanza, R. P., & Rubin, L. C. (1984) "Insight" in the pigeon: Antecedents and determinants of an intelligent performance. *Nature, 308,* 61–62.

Erichsen, J. T., Bingman, B. P., & Krebs, J. R. (1991). The distribution of neuropeptides in the dorsomedial telencephalon of the pigeon (*Columba livia*): A basis for regional subdivisions. *Journal of Comparative Neurology, 314,* 478–492.

Fallgatter, A. J., & Strik, W. K. (1998). Frontal brain activation during the Wisconsin Card Sorting Test assessed with two-channel near-infrared spectroscopy. *European Archives of Psychiatry and Clinical Neuroscience, 248,* 245–249.

Ferry, A., Lu, T., Xi-Chun, M., & Price, J. L. (2000). Effects of excitotoxic lesions in the ventral striatopallidal-thalamocortical pathway an odor reversal learning: Inability to extinguish incorrect response. *Brain Research, 131,* 320–335.

Fodor, J. A. (1983). *The modularity of mind: An essay on faculty psychology.* Cambridge, MA: MIT Press.

Fremouw, T., Jackson-Smith, P., & Kesner, R. P. (1997). Impaired place learning and unimpaired cue learning in hippocampal-lesioned pigeons. *Behavioral Neuroscience, 111,* 963–975.

Galef, B. G., Jr., McQuoid, L. M., & Whiskin, E. E. (1990). Further evidence that Norway rats do not socially transmit learned aversions to toxic baits. *Animal Learning & Behavior, 18,* 199–205.

Galef, B. G., Jr., Wigmore, S. W., & Kennett, D. J. (1983). A failure to find socially mediated taste aversion learning in Norway rats (*R. norvegicus*). *Journal of Comparative Psychology, 97,* 358–363.

Gilbert, D. B., Patterson, T. A., & Rose, S. P. (1991). Dissociation of brain sites necessary for registration and storage of memory for a one-trial passive avoidance task in the chick. *Behavioral Neuroscience, 105,* 553–561.

Giovagnoli, A. R. (2001). Relation of sorting impairment to hippocampal damages in temporal lobe epilepsy. *Neuropsychologia, 39,* 140–150.

Good, M. (1987). The effects of hippocampal-area parahippocampalis lesion on discrimination learning in the pigeon. *Behavioural Brain Research, 26,* 171–184.

Good, M., & Honey, R. C. (1991). Conditioning and contextual retrieval in hippocampal rats. *Behavioral Neuroscience, 105,* 499–509.

Good, M., & Macphail, E. M. (1994). The avian hippocampus and short-term memory for spatial and non-spatial information. *Quarterly Journal of Psychology, 47B,* 293–317.

Graybiel, A. M. (1977). The basal ganglia and cognitive pattern generators. *Schizophrenic Bulletin, 23,* 459–469.

Harlow, H. F., & Dagnon, J. (1943). Problem solving by monkeys following bilateral removal of the prefrontal areas: 1. The discrimination and discrimination reversal problems. *Journal of Experimental Psychology, 32,* 351–356.

Hartmann, B., & Gunturkun, O. (1998). Selective deficits in reversal learning after neostriatum caudolaterale lesions in pigeons: possible behavioral equivalencies to the mammalian prefrontal system. *Behavioural Brain Research, 96,* 125–133.

Hermann, B. P., Wyler, A. R., & Richey, E. T. (1988). Wisconsin Card Sorting Test performance in patients with complex partial seizures of temporal-lobe origin. *Journal of Clinical and Experimental Neuropsychology, 10,* 467–476.

Herrnstein, R. J., & Loveland, D. H. (1964). Complex visual concept in the pigeon. *Science, 146,* 549–551.

Herrnstein, R. J., Vaughan, W. Jr., Mumford, D. B., & Kosslyn, S. M. (1989). Teaching pigeons on abstract rule: Insideness. *Perception & Psychophysics, 46,* 56–64.

Hodos, W., & Karten, H. (1970). Visual intensity and pattern discrimination deficits after lesions of ectostriatum in pigeons. *Journal of Comparative Neurology, 140,* 53–68.

Homborg, L. (1957). Fiskande Krator. *Fauna och Flora, 5,* 182–185 (cited in Powell & Kelly, 1977).

Huber, L., Rechberger, S., & Taborsky, M. (2001). Social learning affects object exploration and manipulation in Keas, *Nestor notabilis. Animal Behavior, 62,* 945–954.

Hunt, G. R. (1996). Manufacture and use of hook-tools by New Caledonian crows. *Nature, 379,* 249–251.

Hunt, G. R. (2000). Tool use by the New Caledonian crow *Corvus moneduloides* to obtain Cerambycidae from dead wood. *Emu, 100,* 109–114.

Hunter, M. W., & Kamil, A. C. (1971). Object-discrimination learning set and hypothesis behavior in the northern bluejay (*Cynaocitta cristata*). *Psychonomic Science, 22,* 271–273.

Husband, S., & Shimizu, T. (2003). Reversal learning after lesions in the presumptive nucleus accumbens in pigeons. *Proceedings of the International Conference in Comparative Cognition, 10,* 25.

Izawa, E., Yanagihara, S., Atsumi, T., & Matsushima, T. (2001). The role of basal ganglia in reinforcement learning and imprinting. *NeuroReport, 12,* 1743–1747.

Kahn, M. C., Hough, G. E., Ten Eyck, G. R., & Bingman, V. P. (2003). Internal connectivity of the homing pigeon (*Columba livia*) hippocampal formation: An anterograde and retrograde tracer study. *Journal of Comparataive Neurology, 459,* 127–141.

Kobayashi, K., Uno, H. & Okanoya, K. (2001). Partial lesions in the anterior forebrain pathway affect song production in adult Bengalese finches. *NeuroReport, 12,* 353–358.

Krebs, J. R., Erichsen, J. T., & Bingman, V. P. (1991). The distribution of neurotransmitters and neurotransmitter-related enzymes in the dorsomedial telencephalon of the pigeon (*Columba livia*). *Journal of Comparative Neurology, 314,* 467–477.

Krebs, J. R., Sherry, D. F., Healy, S. D., Perry, V. H., & Vaccarino, A. L. (1989). Hippocampal specialization of food storing birds. *Proceedings of the National Academy of Science U S A, 86,* 1388–1392.

Lawrence, A. D., Sahakian, B. J., Rogers, R. D., Hodges, J. R. & Robbins, T. W. (1999). Discrimination, reversal, and shift learning in Huntington's disease: Mechanisms of impaired response selection. *Neuropsychologia, 37,* 1359–1374.

Lea, S. E. G., & Harrison, S. N. (1978). Discrimination of polymorphous stimulus sets by pigeons. *Quarterly Journal of Experimental Psychology, 30,* 521–537.

Lefebvre, L., & Bolhuis, J. J. (2003). Positive and negative correlations of feeding innovations in birds: Evidence for limited modularity. In S. M. Reader & K. N. Laland (Eds.), *Animal innovation* (pp. 40–61). Oxford: Oxford University Press.

Lefebvre, L., Gaxiola, A., Dawson, S., Timmermans, S., Rosza, L. & Kabai, P. (1998). Feeding innovations and forebrain size in Australasian birds. *Behaviour, 135,* 1077–1097.

Lefebvre. L., Whittle, P., Lascaris, E., & Finlestein, A. (1997). Feeding innovations and forebrain size in birds. *Animal Behavior, 53,* 549–560.

Lewis, J. W., Ryan, S. M., Arnold, A. P., & Butcher, L. L. (1981). Evidence for a catecholaminergic projection to area X in the zebra finch. *Journal of Comparative Neurology, 196,* 347–354.

Mackintosh, N. J. (1988). Approaches to the study of animal intelligence. *British Journal of Psychology, 79,* 509–525.

Macphail, E. M. (1971). Hyperstriatal lesions in pigeons: Effects on response inhibition, behavioral contrast and reversal learning. *Journal of Comparative and Physiological Psychology, 75,* 500–507.

Macphail, E. M. (1975). Hyperstriatal function in the pigeon: Response inhibition or response shift? *Journal of Comparative and Physiological Psychology, 89,* 607–618.

Macphail, E. M. (1976a). Effects of hyperstriatal lesions on within-day serial reversal performance in pigeons. *Physiology & Behavior, 16,* 529–536.

Macphail, E. M. (1976b). Evidence against the response-shift account of hyperstriatal function in the pigeon (*Columba livia*). *Journal of Comparative and Physiological Psychology, 90,* 547–559.

Macphail, E. M., & Reilly, S. (1983). Probability learning in pigeons (*Columba livia*) is not impaired by hyperstriatal lesions. *Physiology & Behavior, 31,* 279–284.

Macphail, E. M., & Reilly, S. (1985). Hyperstriatal lesions and short-term retention of nonvisual information in pigeons. *Quarterly Journal of Experimental Psychology, 37B,* 121–153.

Mason, J. R., & Reidinger, R. F. (1982). Observational learning of food aversions in red-winged blackbirds (*Agelaius phoeniceus*). *Auk, 99,* 548–554.

Milner, B. (1963). Effect of different brain lesions on card sorting. *Archives of Neurology, 90,* 90–100.

Mitchell, J. A. (1983). Paleostriatal lesions in the pigeons (*Columba livia*) potentiate classical conditioning: Evidence from fixed-interval responding, free operant go–no-go discrimination, and alternation. *Behavioral Neuroscience, 97,* 171–194.

Mitchell, J. A., & Hall, G. (1984). Paleostriatal lesions and instrumental learning in the pigeon. *Quarterly Journal of Experimental Psychology, 36B,* 93–117.

Murray, T. K., & Ridley, R. M. (1999). The effect of excitotoxic hippocampal lesions on simple and conditional discrimination learning in the rat. *Behavioural Brain Research, 99,* 103–113.

O'Reilly, R. C., Noelle, D. C., Braver, T. S., & Cohen, J. D. (2002). Prefrontal cortex and dynamic categorization tasks: Representational organization and neuromodulatory control. *Cerebral Cortex, 12,* 246–257.

Papadimitriou, A., & Wynne, C. D. L. (1999). Preserved negative patterning and impaired spatial learning in pigeons (*Columba livia*) with lesions of the hippocampus. *Behavioral Neuroscience, 113,* 683–690.

Pepperberg, I. M. (1999). *The Alex studies: Cognitive and communicative abilities of Grey parrots.* Cambridge, MA: Harvard University Press.

Powell, R. W., & Kelly, W. (1977). Tool use in captive crows. *Bulletin of the Psychonomic Society, 10,* 481–483.

Powers, A. (1989). Wulst lesions in pigeons disrupt go/no-go reversal. *Physiology & Behavior, 46,* 337–339.

Powers, A. S., Halasz, F., & Williams, S. (1982). The effects of lesions in telencephalic visual areas of pigeons on dimensional shifting. *Physiology & Behavior, 29,* 1099–1104.

Raffaele, K. C., & Olton, D. S. (1988). Hippocampal and amygdaloid involvement in working memory for nonspatial stimuli. *Behavioral Neuroscience, 102,* 349–355.

Rajalakshmi, R., & Jeeves, M. A. (1965). The relative difficulty of reversal learning (reversal index) as a basis of behavioral comparisons. *Animal Behaviour, 13,* 203–211.

Reader, S. M., & Laland, K. N. (2003). Animal innovation. In S. M. Reader & K. N. Laland (Eds.), *Animal innovation* (pp. 3–38). New York: Oxford University Press.

Reilly, S. (1987). Hyperstriatal lesions and attention in the pigeon. *Behavioral Neuroscience, 101,* 74–86.

Reilly, S., & Good, M. (1987). Enhanced DRL and impaired forced-choice alternation performance following hippocampal lesions in the pigeon. *Behavioural Brain Research, 26,* 185–197

Reiner, A., Medina, L., & Veenman, C. L. (1998). Structural and functional evolution of the basal ganglia in vertebrates. *Brain Research Review, 28,* 235–285.

Ridley, R. M. (1994). The psychology of perserverative and stereotyped behavior. *Progress in Neurobiology, 44,* 221–231.

Ruskin, R. S., & Goodman, I. J. (1971). Changes in locomotor activity following basal forebrain lesions in the pigeon. *Psychonomic Science, 22,* 181–188.

Shimizu, T., & Hodos, W. (1989). Reversal learning in pigeons: Effects of selective lesions of the Wulst. *Behavioral Neuroscience, 103,* 262–272.

Sol, D., Timmermans, S., & Lefebvre, L. (2002). Behavioural flexibility and invasion success in birds. *Animal Behaviour, 63,* 495–502.

Stettner, L. J., & Schultz, W. J. (1967). Brain lesions in birds: Effects on discrimination acquisition and reversal. *Science, 155,* 1689–1692.

Stuss, D. T., Levine, B., Alexander, M. P., Hong, J., Palumbo, C., Hamer, L., et al. (2000). Wisconsin Card Sorting Test performance in patients with focal frontal and posterior brain damage: Effects of lesion location and test structure on separable cognitive processes. *Neuropsychologia, 38,* 388–402.

Sutherland, R. J., McDonald, R. J., Hill, C. R., & Rudy, J. W. (1989). Damage to the hippocampal formation in rats selectively impairs the ability to learn cue relationships. *Behavioral & Neural Biology, 52,* 331–356.

Timmermans, S., Lefebvre, L., Boire, D., & Basu, P. (2000). Relative size of hyperstriatum ventrale in the best predictor of feeding innovation rate in birds. *Brain, Behavior & Evolution, 56,* 196–203.

Verin, M., Partiot, A., Pillon, B., Malapani, C., Aqid, Y., & Duboias, B. (1993). Delayed response tasks and prefrontal lesions in man: Evidence for self generated patterns of behaviour with poor environmental modulation. *Neuropsychologia, 31,* 1379–1396.

Wasserman, E. A., DeVolder, C. L., & Coppage, D. J. (1992). Nonsimilarity-based conceptualization in pigeons via secondary or mediated generalization. *Psychological Science, 3,* 374–379.

Wasserman, E. A., Kiedinger, R. E., & Bhatt, R. S. (1988). Conceptual behavior in pigeons: Categories, subcategories, and pseudocategories. *Journal of Experimental Psychology: Animal Behavior Processes, 14,* 235–246.

Watanabe, S. (1988). Failure of visual prototype learning in the pigeon. *Animal Learning & Behavior, 16,* 147–152.

Watanabe, S. (1991). Effects of ectostriatal lesions on natural concept, pseudo concept and artificial pattern discrimination in pigeons. *Visual Neuroscience, 6,* 497–506.

Watanabe, S. (1992). Effects of ectostriatum and Wulst on species and individual and species discrimination in pigeons. *Behavioural Brain Research, 49,* 197–203.

Watanabe, S. (1996). Effects of ectostriatal lesions on discriminations of conspecific, species and familiar object discrimination in pigeons. *Behavioural Brain Research, 81,* 183–188.

Watanabe, S. (1997). Visual discrimination of real objects and pictures in pigeons. *Animal Learning and Behavior, 25,* 185–192.

Watanabe, S. (1999). Effects of hippocampal lesions on spatial operant discrimination in pigeons. *Behavioural Brain Research, 103,* 77–84.

Watanabe, S. (2001a). Effects of hippocampal lesions on repeated acquisition of spatial discrimination in pigeons. *Behavioural Brain Research, 120,* 59–66.

Watanabe, S. (2001b). Van Gogh, Chagall and pigeons. *Animal Cognition, 4,* 147–151.

Watanabe, S. (2002a). Effects of hippocampal lesions on conditional spatial discrimination in pigeons. *Physiology & Behavior, 77,* 183–187.

Watanabe, S. (2002b). Effects of lobus parolfactorius lesions on repeated acquisition of spatial discrimination in pigeons. *Brain Behavior & Evolution, 58,* 333–342.

Watanabe, S. (2003). Effects of Wulst and ectostriatum lesions on repeated acquisition of spatial learning in pigeons. *Cognitive Brain Research, 17,* 286–292.

Watanabe, S. (2005). Lesions in the basal ganglion and hippocampus on performance in a Wisconsin Card Sorting–like task in pigeons. *Physiology & Behavior, 85,* 324–332.

Watanabe, S., Wakita, M., & Sakamoto, J. (1995). Discrimination of Monet and Picasso in pigeons. *Journal of the Experimental Analysis of Behavior, 63,* 165–174.

Weir, A. S., Chappell, J., & Kacelnik, A. (2002). Shaping of hooks in New Caledonian crows. *Science, 297,* 981.

Wesp, R., & Goodman, I. (1978). Fixed interval responding by pigeons following damages to corpus striatal and limbic brain structures (paleostriatal complex and parolfactory lobe). *Physiology & Behavior, 20,* 571–577.

Yamazaki, Y. (2001). *Effects of reinforcement history on establishment of equivalence relations.* Unpublished doctoral dissertation, Keio University, Tokyo.

Yamazaki, Y., Shinohara, T., Watanabe, S. (2004). Visual discrimination of normal and drug induced behavior in quails (*Coturnix coturnix japonica*). *Animal Cognition, 7,* 128–132.

X

SOCIAL COGNITION PROCESSES

32

Chimpanzee Social Cognition in Early Life: Comparative–Developmental Perspective

MASAKI TOMONAGA, MASAKO MYOWA-YAMAKOSHI, YUU MIZUNO, SANAE OKAMOTO, MASAMI K. YAMAGUCHI, DAISUKE KOSUGI, KIM A. BARD, MASAYUKI TANAKA, AND TETSURO MATSUZAWA

In this chapter, we summarize parts of our ongoing research project on the cognitive development of chimpanzee infants. Among various research topics, here we focus on their social cognition (Tomonaga et al., 2004).

Since Premack and Woodruff's (1978) article on "theory of mind" in the chimpanzee, studies on social cognition in nonhuman primates from comparative and developmental perspectives have attracted considerable attention. The idea of *theory of mind*, the ability to infer the mental state of a conspecific, has been elaborated by developmental psychologists, and many experimental studies have been conducted with human children using "false belief" tasks (e.g., Wimmer & Perner, 1983). In humans, theory of mind is not believed to be present at 3 years of age but emerges at 4 or 5 years. Researchers have tried to find evidence for the prerequisites of theory of mind in younger children (Baron-Cohen, 1995; Wellman, 1992). Such research on the development of human social cognition has been linked to the hypothesis proposed by several primatologists in the mid-1980s that human intelligence evolved to deal with the complexities in social living (Byrne & Whiten, 1988; Whiten & Byrne, 1997). This hypothesis is called the *social intelligence* or Machiavellian-intelligence hypothesis. Since then, comparative (evolutionary) and developmental approaches to social cognition have been recognized as important to the understanding of human social cognition. During the 1990s, findings on various aspects of social cognition in nonhuman primates (especially great apes) have accumulated: tactical deception, imitation, observational learning in cultural behavior including tool use, gaze following, understanding of the relationship between seeing and knowing, empathy, social referencing, and false belief (e.g., Call, 2001; Tomasello & Call, 1997; Whiten & Byrne, 1997).

Many of these studies, however, tested only adult subjects. These studies have clarified the social cognitive abilities of great apes, but the developmental course of these abilities is not still well understood. Although there have been many studies on the development of human-raised chimpanzees since the 1930s (e.g., Gardner & Gardner, 1969; Hayes, 1951; Kellogg & Kellogg, 1933; Okano, 1978), the problem of "enculturation," that is, the effects of physical, social, and cultural aspects of human environments on the development of human-raised (enculturated) chimpanzees, is still controversial (Tomasello & Call, 1997). It is reasonable to expect that interactions between the human caregiver and the infant ape would affect the emergence of social cognitive abilities (cf. Russell, Bard, & Adamson, 1997). To understand the comparative development of social cognition in chimpanzees, the natural emergence of these abilities should be investigated during the course of development. To this end, the Primate Research Institute of Kyoto University (PRI) began a longitudinal study

Figure 32.1. (*A*) Outdoor compound for the chimpanzees at the Primate Research Institute, Kyoto University. (*B*) Mother-infant pairs in the outdoor compound. (Photographs courtesy of The Mainichi Shimbun.)

of chimpanzee development in 2000 (Matsuzawa, 2002, 2003; Tanaka, Tomonaga, & Matsuzawa, 2002; Tomonaga, Tanaka, & Matsuzawa, 2003). To the best of our ability, we set up the necessary conditions for the natural development of captive chimpanzees: enriched environment, community, and mother-infant bonds (figure 32.1). In 2000, three infants were born to chimpanzees at the PRI. Each mother living in a community successfully held her baby and demonstrated good maternal competence (e.g., Bard, 2002). Based on this criterion, we investigated the development of various social cognitive abilities in mother-raised chimpanzees. With regard to the development of social cognition, we also focused on the social transmission of knowledge from mother to infant (Hirata & Celli, 2003; Sousa, Okamoto, & Matsuzawa, 2003).

In this chapter, we focus on the interrelated abilities of early social cognition with special reference to gaze: recognition of the mother's face, mutual gaze, gaze following, and triadic interactions. Recently, these topics were extensively discussed, and they are the center of controversy concerning the evolutionary origin of primate cognition (Tomasello, 1999; Tomasello & Call, 1997). In the last section of this chapter, we discuss the relationship between early social cognition in chimpanzees and the social transmission of cultural behaviors in the wild.

RECOGNITION OF THE MOTHER'S FACE

The most familiar individual for the infant is its mother. Human infants recognize their mother's face at around 1 month of age (Bushnell, Sai, & Mullin, 1989). We investigated developmental changes in chimpanzee infants' recognition of their mother's face from the first week of life (Tomonaga, Yamaguchi, Myowa-Yamakoshi, Mizuno, & Kanazawa, 2003). We prepared two types of stimulus sets: the mother's face and a prototypic averaged chimpanzee face developed by computer software based on the mother's face and those of the other members in the PRI community (cf. Yamaguchi, Myowa, Kanazawa, & Tomonaga, 2000). We presented a photograph in front of the infant and repeatedly moved the photograph slowly to the left and right five times (the preferential tracking procedure; Bard, Platzman, Lester, & Suomi,

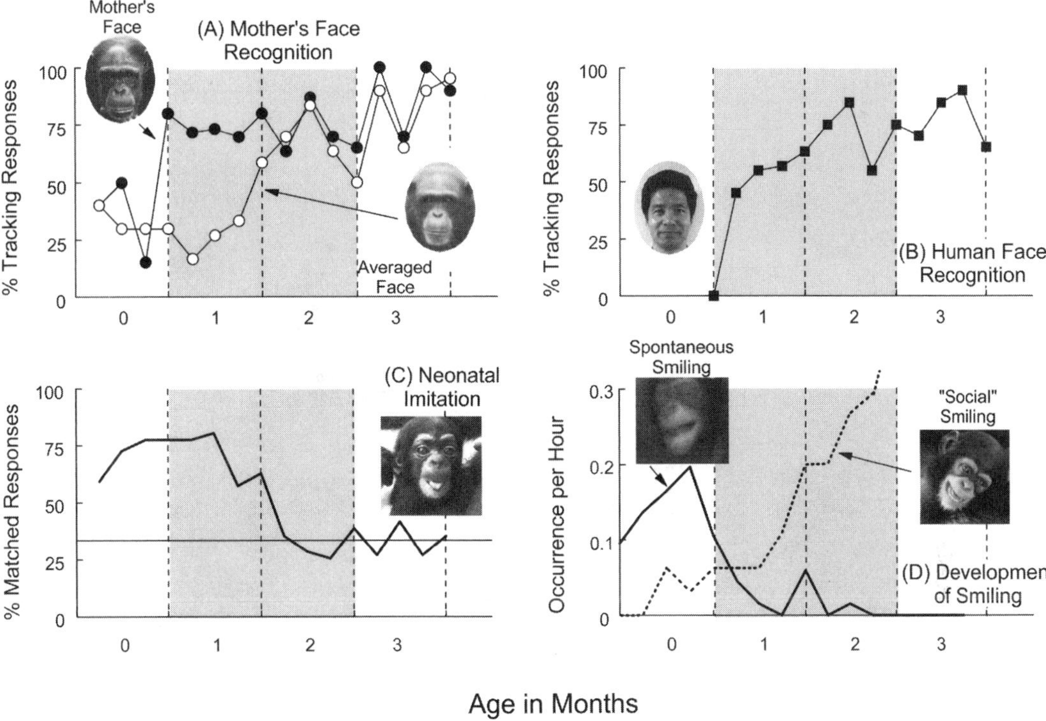

Figure 32.2. Developmental changes in the recognition of mother's face and their relationship to other developmental changes. (*A*) Recognition of the mother's face. The data are averaged across the three infants. (Adapted from Tomonaga, Yamaguchi, et al., 2003.) (*B*) Recognition of a human face. The data are averaged over the infants. (Adapted from Tomonaga, Yamaguchi, et al., 2003.) (C) Neonatal imitation. The data are averaged over two infants and over three types of model gestures. The horizontal line at 33.3% shows chance performance. (Adapted from Myowa-Yamakoshi et al., 2004.) (*D*) Developmental changes in smiling responses. Vertical axis indicates the mean number of occurrences per hour. (Adapted from Mizuno, 2004.)

1992; Johnson & Morton, 1991). The number of tracking responses (eye movements or head turning) to each of the photographs was compared.

The results are summarized in figure 32.2A. As shown in this figure, we found three phases in the development of mother's face recognition in chimpanzees. At less than 1 month old, infants showed very few tracking responses and no difference between the faces. At 1 month of age, however, all of the infants exhibited more orienting responses to their mother's face than to the averaged face. These results suggest that the infant chimpanzees recognized their mother's face, at least at 1 month of age, an age that generally corresponds to results for human infants (Bushnell et al., 1989). At 2 months old, however, the infants increasingly looked at both faces. This pattern of looking at faces was also found in an experiment with human faces (figure 32.2B) and schematic faces (Kuwahata et al., 2003).

From 1 to 2 months of age, other important changes related to those found with face recognition were also observed. Myowa-Yamakoshi, Tomonaga, Tanaka, and Matsuzawa (2004) examined the neonatal imitation of facial expressions in chimpanzees and found that matched facial-expression responses to the facial expressions made by the human experimenter decreased to chance level during this period (figure 32.2C). Furthermore, Mizuno and Takeshita (2002; Mizuno, 2004) found that spontaneous smiling responses, during rapid-eye-movement sleep, decreased at 1 month of age, whereas extraneous (or "social") smiling responses caused by explicit stimulation such as presenting objects and face-to-face interactions increased from 1 to 2 months of age (figure 32.2D).

Figure 32.3. Mutual gaze between Ai (mother) and Ayumu (infant, at 1 month). (Photograph courtesy of The Yomiuri Shimbun.)

Although it is still controversial whether neonatal imitation in chimpanzees is reflexive, these results, taken together with face-recognition experiments, suggest that developmental changes occurred in chimpanzees, from reflex-like (nonsocial) responses to social responses between the first and second months of age. The social cognitive abilities of chimpanzees emerge during this period.

MUTUAL GAZE AND GAZE RECOGNITION

As infants develop recognition and preference for their mother's face, there is also an increase in mutual gaze between mother and infant. Mutual gaze is defined by looking at the each other's face (figure 32.3). Okamoto, Kawai, et al. (2002) reported that while a mother chimpanzee was working on an experimental computer-controlled task, she looked at her infant's face 6.3% of the experimental time when the infant was in the first month of life, whereas she looked at its face 23.5% of the time when the infant was 4 months old. The infant also increased the time spent looking at the mother's face in this situation from 3.4% to 11.8% of the experimental time. Mizuno (2004) measured the duration of "mutual" gaze, in which the mother and infant simultaneously looked at each other's face, and found that it increased from 0 to 50 s/h from the age of 1 week to 12 weeks.

We also conducted more detailed observations of the development of mutual gaze in a natural setting (Bard et al., 2005). We videorecorded the behavior of mother and infant in the indoor living area from 2 to 12 weeks of the infant's life, classifying both eye gaze and interactive behaviors. The three mother-infant pairs increased the occurrence of mutual gaze from 11 times/h when the infants were 2 to 4 weeks old, to 28 times/h when the infants were 10 to 12 weeks of age. This increase in mutual gaze corresponded to a decrease in cradling behavior by the mother: The frequency of mutual gaze was negatively correlated with that of physical contact between mother and infant. A similar tendency has been reported in human mother-infant pairs (LaVelli & Fogel, 2002).

Presumably, the mother's responses were reinforced by the infant's behavioral change that occurred during the second month of age and vice versa. In addition to these changes, it is quite possible that sensitivity to the other's gaze also changes

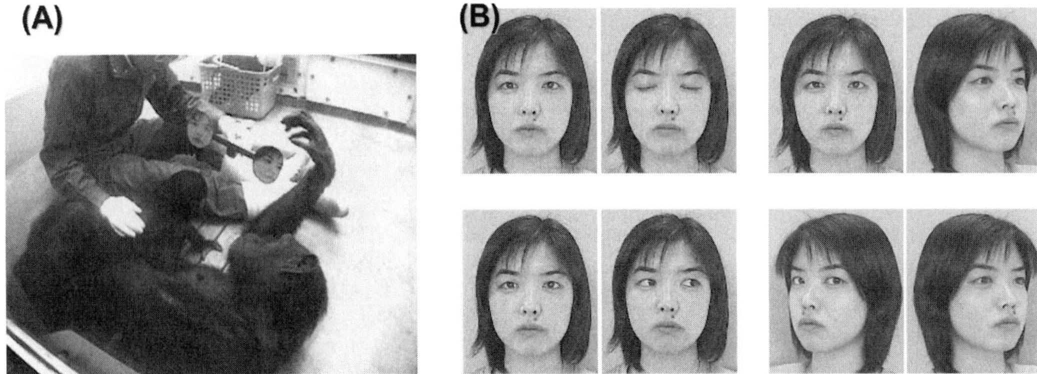

Figure 32.4. (*A*) Setting for the gaze recognition experiment. The human experimenter presented a pair of photographs of directed- and averted-gaze faces to the infant. Looking behavior of the infant was recorded by the small CCD (charge coupled device) camera mounted at the center of photographs. (Photograph courtesy of Masako Myowa-Yamakoshi.) (*B*) Selected stimulus sets used in the experiment.

during this period. To investigate this possibility, we tested infant chimpanzees for their ability to discriminate gaze direction of the other's face (Myowa-Yamakoshi, Tomonaga, Tanaka, & Matsuzawa, 2003) (figure 32.4A). In humans, neonates younger than 2 days old looked longer at a photograph of a face with the eyes open than at the same face with the eyes closed (Batki, Baron-Cohen, Wheelwright, Connellan, & Ahluwalia, 2000). Furthermore, several studies reveal that human infants discriminate eye gaze direction when they are 3 to 4 months old (Farroni, Johnson, Brockbank, & Simon, 2000; Samuels, 1985; Vecera & Johnson, 1995). In nonhuman primates, there are very few reports on the development of discrimination of eye gaze direction. Myowa-Yamakoshi and Tomonaga (2001) reported that a nursery-raised agile gibbon infant preferred a schematic directed-gaze face over an averted-gaze face when it was younger than 1 month.

We tested the infant chimpanzees from 10 to 32 weeks of age using a forced-choice preferential looking procedure. We prepared various sets of photographs of human faces with directed and averted eye gaze as shown in figure 32.4B. We presented these faces to the infants for 15 sec and measured looking time for each of the photographs (figure 32.4A). All three infants looked longer at the directed-gaze faces than at the averted-gaze faces. These results indicate that the chimpanzee infants, at least those who were around 2 months of age or older, clearly discriminate eye gaze direction and, further, prefer directed-gaze faces to averted-gaze faces. Mutual gaze in mother-infant chimpanzees appears to be based on the infant's preference for the directed-gaze face and is maintained by the mother's reaction to the infant.

Bidirectional mother-infant interactions on the basis of mutual gaze may facilitate *primary intersubjectivity* (Trevarthen & Aitken, 2001), defined as a dyadic social relationship maintained by mutual gaze between mother and infant chimpanzees. In humans, the social functions of eye gaze develop beyond the dyad, to those involving a triad of the infant, social partner, and object (i.e., shared attention; Emery, 2000). This developmental change in chimpanzees is discussed in a later section.

FOLLOWING THE OTHER'S GAZE

Chimpanzee infants, as young as 1 month, initially discriminate their mother's face from others and their social-cognitive abilities emerge between 1 to 2 months of age as evidenced by a decrease in reflex-like responsiveness. In parallel with these changes, they come to recognize the other's eye gaze direction, pay attention to directed-gaze face, and engage in dyadic social interactions with the mother via mutual gaze. The next developmental step for the infants is to follow the other's gaze. *Gaze following* refers to when an individual detects that another's gaze is not directed toward him and follows the line of sight of the other onto a point or an object in space (cf. Emery, 2000).

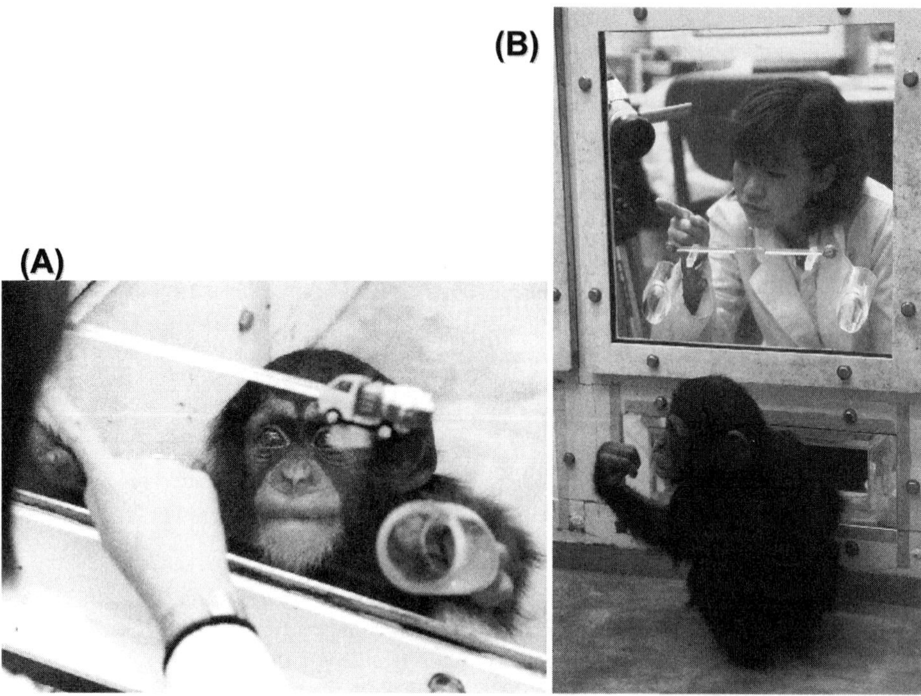

Figure 32.5. (*A*) Ayumu at 1.5 years followed the experimenter's pointing. (*B*) Ayumu at 2 years looked back by following the experimenter's pointing. (Photographs courtesy of The Mainichi Shimbun.)

Human infants, who are around 6 months old, begin to follow gaze direction of others, and this ability is refined during the course of development (Butterworth & Jarrett, 1991; Moore & Dunham, 1995). The ability to follow another's gaze has been intensively examined in various nonhuman primates from prosimians to great apes (see Emery, 2000, for review). However, there are few studies on gaze following from a comparative-developmental perspective (e.g., Tomasello, Hare, & Fogleman, 2001).

We tested a chimpanzee infant longitudinally from age 7 months to 2 years for its ability to follow a human experimenter's social cues, including gaze (Okamoto, Tanaka, & Tomonaga, 2004; Okamoto, Tomonaga, et al., 2002). In these experiments, the human experimenter outside the experimental booth gives various cues to the infant in the booth (figure 32.5A). The cues are directed to one of two identical objects. They consist of tapping it, pointing to it, head turning toward it, and eyes directed toward it. Three seconds after presentation of the social cue, the experimenter delivered food reward to that side, irrespective of the infant's responses. The infant reliably followed the pointing cue before the age of 9 months and the head-turn cue by the age of 10 months. Furthermore, the infant began to follow the eye gaze cue (without head movements) by 13 months (Okamoto, Tomonaga, et al., 2002).

These experiments clearly show that an infant chimpanzee followed social cues, including gaze, at around 9 months. Although our experimental design provided nondifferential reinforcement to avoid learning by differential reinforcement, in fact, the infant may have "learned" to follow human gaze because of the outcomes provided by the experimenter. Nevertheless, the infant's performance was constrained by the social cues, especially in the latter phase of the experiment. Okamoto et al., (2004) reported that the infant at 13 to 20 months old did not "look back" by following the human pointing to an object behind the subject. This looking-back response became evident after 21 months (figure 32.5B). To some degree, such constraints in gaze following may be due to the nature of the social cues, such as their saliency, but the possibility of developmental constraints cannot be ruled out. Taken together with these results, the gaze following ability of chimpanzee infants seems to develop in a step-by-step manner as has also been found in human infants.

SHARED ATTENTION AND TRIADIC INTERACTIONS

A large qualitative change in social communication occurs in humans at around 9 months (Carpenter, Nagell, & Tomasello, 1998; Ohgami, 2002). Human infants, at 6 months, interact dyadically with objects or with a person in a turn-taking (or reciprocal exchange) sequence. However, they do not interact with a person who is manipulating objects (Tomasello, 1999). At this age, the dyadic format of social interaction is prototypical; however, this format soon changes in a marked way. From around 9 months on (probably to 12 months), infants start to engage in triadic exchanges with others. Their interactions involve both objects and persons, resulting in the formation of a referential triangle involving the infant, an adult, and an object to which they share attention (Rochat, 2001; Tomasello, 1999). Shared attention is different from gaze following and emphasizes the role of communicative interactions via gaze (cf. Emery, 2000). This is a decisive, critical development occurring at around 9 months. Some researchers call this change "the 9-month revolution" (e.g., Tomasello, 1999). The 9-month revolution appears to be based on the ability to follow gaze and to understand the intention or goal-directedness of others; this ability then becomes the basis for understanding others' mental states (Baron-Cohen, 1995; Tomasello, 1999).

Chimpanzees, on the other hand, begin to interact with objects in a very simple manner at 3 to 5 months and show more complex, combinatorial manipulations at 8 to 9 months (Hayashi & Matsuzawa, 2003). They also begin to move away from their mother and to search for things in the environment at around 4 months and start to interact with the other individuals, including human experimenters, at around 6 to 8 months (Nakashima, 2003; Okamoto, Kawai, et al., 2002). Furthermore, chimpanzees' interactions with others are all emotionally based (e.g., with facial expressions) as occurs with human infants (figure 32.6).

Although a decisive conclusion cannot be made at this time, the 9-months revolution does not appear to occur in chimpanzees (Tomasello & Call, 1997). In an opportunistic observation, we tried to engage in triadic exchange with the chimpanzee infants using various kinds of objects, but they did not interact with humans in a reciprocating manner. When the human experimenter played with the infant chimpanzee at the age of 1 to 2 years by using a towel, the infant showed both social and solitary play, but it did not engage in reciprocal exchange with us. In another case, when we tried to reciprocate with the infant using a ball, she "stole" the ball away and started solitary play with it: only when the ball was exchanged for food did she give it back to the experimenter (cf. Tomonaga & Hayashi, 2003). The chimpanzee infants never engaged in "showing object" and "giving object, " which are indicative of referential communication in a triadic relationship in human infants, behavior that was found in an 18-month-old nursery-raised chimpanzee by Russell et al. (1997). Okamoto et al. (2004) also reported that after looking back by following the human pointing, the infant did not look at the experimenter's face again. This represents one of the common shared attention behaviors shown by human infants (e.g., Carpenter et al., 1998).

Figure 32.6. Ayumu at 10 months dyadically interacts with the human experimenter with a playful facial expression. (Photograph courtesy of The Mainichi Shimbun.)

In addition to these observations, we conducted more controlled investigations (Kosugi et al., 2003). We presented a novel remotely controlled toy to the mother-infant pairs when the infants were 1 and 2 years old and observed the mother—infant interactions. Initially, the infants showed some fearful responses toward this novel object, such as withdrawing from the object and hiding behind their mothers. When the infants manipulated the object, they always kept in contact with the mother's body with their unoccupied hand. However, the infants often watched the mother manipulating the object and tried to touch it, and the mother never refused this kind of approach behavior. Such triadic interactions or "shared (joint) engagement" was frequently observed both when the infants were 1 and 2 years old (figure 32.7). However, when the infant manipulated the object, she seldom looked back to her mother, showing the object to her or giving it to her. Similarly, the mothers did not engage in showing and giving behaviors. These results suggest that mother—infant interactions with an object were not based on shared attention between them. This observation may imply that chimpanzee mother-infant pairs interact without referential triadic relationships. However, there might be precursors for triadic interactions in chimpanzees. As described above, the infant chimpanzees showed fearful responses toward a novel object at first, and they did not manipulate it by themselves. After they saw the mother's manipulation of the object or participated in shared engagement, however, they actively tried to manipulate it by themselves. This behavior can be interpreted as one type of "social referencing" (e.g., Feinman, 1982; Sorce, Emde, Campos, & Klinnert, 1985); that is, the infant obtained some information concerning the ambiguous object through watching and joining in the manipulation of it by the mother.

At the present, we have not observed complex triadic exchanges among mother-infant chimpanzees and an object that are based on "shared attention" or "reciprocity." It is still unclear whether this is a cognitive constraint on chimpanzees or this ability will emerge at a later age. To address this question, we need to continue the longitudinal observations and experiments.

LACK OF TRIADIC INTERACTIONS AND "EDUCATION BY MASTER-APPRENTICESHIP"

We can conclude, at least, that chimpanzees appear to lack complex triadic interactions that are commonly observed in humans. This species-specific property of social interactions presumably affects the processes involved in the acquisition of a cultural or community-specific repertoire of behaviors in wild chimpanzees. In the community of wild chimpanzees, it is well known that they use tools and that there exist "cultural differences" in repertoires of tool-using behaviors among communities (Whiten et al., 1999). Many researchers agree that the chimpanzee learns tool-using behavior through the observation of another's behavior, although the exact processes involved are still controversial. Matsuzawa et al., (2001) summarized the social learning process of chimpanzees using the term "education by master-apprenticeship" (cf. de Waal, 2001). For long periods of time, the infants observe the adult's tool-using behaviors (especially that of their mothers) closely and intensively and try those behaviors themselves (cf. Hirata & Morimura,

Figure 32.7. Joint engagement in a triadic context. Cleo (infant, 1 year) manipulated the novel object (model car) held and manipulated by the mother. (Photograph courtesy of Daisuke Kosugi.)

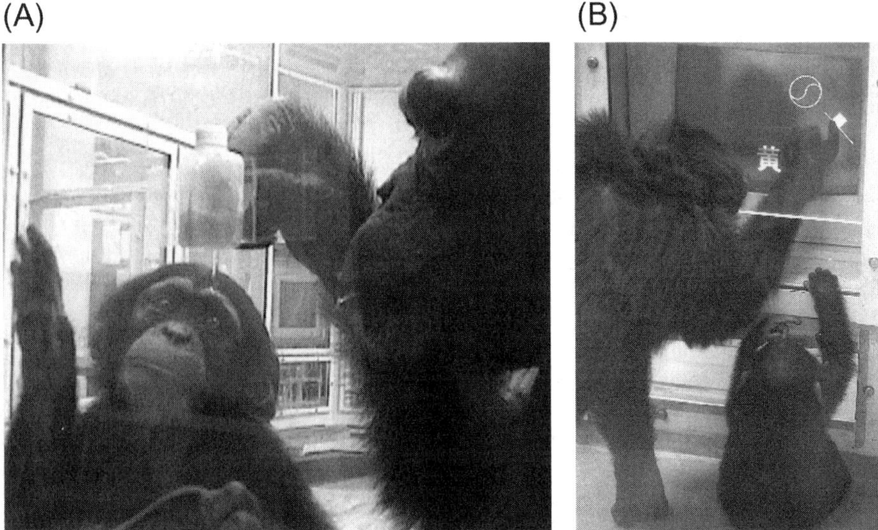

Figure 32.8. Social transmission of cognitive skills from the mother to the infant. (*A*) Ayumu (1½ years) watching his mother's tool-using (honey-dipping) behavior. (Photograph courtesy of Satoshi Hirata.) (*B*) Ayumu (1½ years) watching his mother performing a computer-controlled task. (Photograph courtesy of The Mainichi Shimbun.)

2000; Tonooka, Tomonaga, & Matsuzawa, 1997). Adults are relatively tolerant of being observed or even of being interrupted by the infants, but they do not actively teach infants. Apparently, it is very rare for mothers and infants to interact triadically in the context of tool use.

This was also the case in our research project. To simulate the tool-using behaviors found in the wild, longitudinal studies were conducted with chimpanzees on the acquisition of various cognitive skills such as tool-using behavior (Hirata & Celli, 2003) and computer-controlled tasks (Sousa et al., 2003). Both experiments reported that the infants watched the adults' behaviors very intensively and tried these target behaviors for themselves (figure 32.8). These responses by infants were in part based on local stimulus enhancement processes (Inoue-Nakamura, Myowa-Yamakoshi, Hayashi, & Matsuzawa, 2003). However, the most important point is that the chimpanzee mother did not actively interact with the infant under these contexts (i.e., there was lack of active teaching). There were very rare triadic interactions between the mother and infant. The mothers did not model, guide, mold, punish, or praise the infant's behavior. The infants paid attention to the mother's behavior, but the attention was not shared. Social (observational) learning in chimpanzees has been hypothesized because of their ability to imitate the actions of another. But differences in social learning processes between humans and chimpanzees appear to result from the absence of social-communicative abilities other than the absence of imitative abilities by chimpanzees.

CONCLUDING REMARKS

In this chapter, we summarized some of the ongoing research on cognitive development in infant chimpanzees with special reference to their social cognitive abilities. Mother-raised chimpanzee infants seemingly lack the human-like ability for triadic social interactions. Early social cognitive development, including face and gaze recognition, however, is similar to that of humans. These abilities are the basis for dyadic social interactions. In the latter part of development in infancy, mother-raised chimpanzees diverge from the path taken by Western humans. As some researchers note, triadic interactions may be required for more advanced cognitive abilities, such as self-recognition, understanding other's mental states, and so on (Tomasello, 1999; Tomasello & Call, 1997). Based on Baron-Cohen's (1995) "mind-reading system" model, the detection of intentionality and eye gaze following are prerequisites for shared attention, which is the basis of theory of mind. The apparent inability of chimpanzees to understand the mental state of another (Call & Tomasello, 1999; cf. Hirata & Matsuzawa, 2001) therefore may be due to the lack of shared attention. Our research project will continue to focus on these topics to attempt to understand the development of the human mind from a comparative-cognitive-developmental perspective.

Acknowledgments This chapter is based on a paper by the same authors (Tomonaga et al., 2004). The research reported here and the preparation of the manuscript were financially supported by Grants-in-Aid for Scientific Research 07102010, 09207105, 10CE2005, 11710035, 12002009, 13610086, 14000773, 16300084, and 16002001 from the Japan Society for the Promotion of Science (JSPS), and the Ministry of Education, Culture, Sports, Science and Technology (MEXT); an MEXT Grant-in-Aid for the 21st Century COE Programs (A2 and D2 to Kyoto University); a research fellowship to M.M.-Y. and D.K. from JSPS for Young Scientists and to K.A.B. from The British Council; the Cooperative Research Program of the Primate Research Institute; Kyoto University; and Basic Research 21 for Breakthroughs in Info-communications from the Support Center for Advanced Telecommunications Technology Research (SCAT). The authors thank O. Takenaka, G. Hatano, K. Fujita, S. Itakura, N. Kawai, S. Hirata, M. Celli, C. Sousa, C. Douke, Y. Mizuno, M. Hayashi, T. Matsuno, T. Imura, C. Murai, N. Nakashima, T. Ochiai, R. Oeda, A. Ueno, M. Uozumi, Y. Fukiura, T. Takashima, K. Kumazaki, N. Maeda, A. Kato, S. Yamauchi, and K. Matsubayashi for their help throughout this research project.

References

Bard, K. A. (2002). Primate parenting. In M. Bornstein (Ed.), *Handbook of parenting: Vol. 2. Biology and ecology of parenting* (2nd ed., pp. 99–140). Mahwah, NJ: Lawrence Erlbaum Associates.

Bard K. A., Myowa-Yamokoshi, M., Tomonaga, M., Tanaka, M., Quinn, J., Costal, A., & Matsuzawa, T. (2005). Cultural variation in the mutual gaze of chimpanzees (*Pan troglodytes*). *Developmental Psychology, 41*, 616–624.

Bard, K. A., Platzman, K. A., Lester, B. M., & Suomi, S. J. (1992). Orientation to social and nonsocial stimuli in neonatal chimpanzees and humans. *Infant Behavior and Development, 15*, 43–56.

Baron-Cohen, S. (1995). *Mindblindness*. Cambridge, MA: MIT Press.

Batki, A., Baron-Cohen, S., Wheelwright, S., Connellan, J., & Ahluwalia, J. (2000). Is there an innate module? Evidence from human neonates. *Infant Behavior and Development, 23*, 223–229.

Bushnell, I. W., Sai, F., & Mullin, J. T., (1989). Neonatal recognition of the mother's face. *British Journal of Developmental Psychology, 7*, 3–15.

Butterworth, G. E., & Jarrett, N. L. M. (1991). What minds have in common is space: Spatial mechanism serving joint visual attention in infancy. *British Journal of Developmental Psychology, 9*, 55–72.

Byrne, R. W., & Whiten, A. (Eds.). (1988). *Machiavellian intelligence: Social expertise and the evolution of intellect in monkeys, apes, and humans*. New York: Oxford University Press.

Call, J. (2001). Chimpanzee social cognition. *Trends in Cognitive Sciences, 5*, 388–393.

Call, J., & Tomasello, M. (1999). A nonverbal false belief task: The performance of chimpanzees and human children. *Child Development, 70*, 381–395.

Carpenter, M., Nagell, K., & Tomasello, M. (1998). Social cognition, joint attention, and communicative competence from 9 to 15 months of age. *Monographs of the Society for Research in Child Development, 63*, 1–143.

de Waal, F. (2001). *The ape and the sushi master: Cultural reflections of a primatologist*. New York: Basic Books.

Emery, N. J. (2000). The eyes have it: The neuroethology, function and evolution of social gaze. *Neuroscience and Biobehavioral Reviews, 24*, 581–604.

Farroni, T., Johnson, M. H., Brockbank, M., & Simon, F. (2000). Infants' use of gaze direction to cue attention: The importance of perceived motion. *Visual Cognition, 7*, 705–718.

Feinman, S. (1982). Social referencing in infancy. *Merrill Palmer Quarterly, 28*, 445–470.

Gardner, R. A., & Gardner, B. T. (1969). Teaching sign language to a chimpanzee. *Science, 165*, 664–672.

Hayashi, M., & Matsuzawa, T. (2003). Cognitive development in object manipulation by infant chimpanzees. *Animal Cognition, 6*, 225–233.

Hayes, C. (1951). *The ape in our house*. New York: Harper.

Hirata, S., & Celli, M. L. (2003). Role of mothers in the acquisition of tool use behaviour by captive infant chimpanzees. *Animal Cognition, 6*, 235–244.

Hirata, S., & Matsuzawa, T. (2001). Tactics to obtain a hidden food item in chimpanzee pairs (*Pan troglodytes*). *Animal Cognition, 4,* 285–295.

Hirata, S., & Morimura, N. (2000). Naive chimpanzees' (*Pan troglodytes*) observation of experienced conspecifics in a tool-using task. *Journal of Comparative Psychology, 114,* 291–296.

Inoue-Nakamura, N., Myowa-Yamakoshi, M., Hayashi, M., & Matsuzawa, T. (2003). Effect of stimulus enhancement on preference to objects in mother and infant chimpanzees. In M. Tomonaga, M. Tanaka, & T. Matsuzawa (Eds.), *Cognitive and behavioral development in chimpanzees: A comparative approach* (pp. 254–257). Kyoto, Japan: Kyoto University Press. [In Japanese]

Johnson, M. H., & Morton, J. (1991). *Biology and cognitive development: The case of face recognition.* Oxford: Blackwell.

Kellogg, W. N., & Kellogg, L. A. (1933). *The ape and the child.* New York: McGraw-Hill.

Kosugi, D., Murai, C., Tomonaga, M., Tanaka, M., Ishida, H., & Itakura, S. (2003). Relationship between the understanding of causality in object motion and social referencing in chimpanzee mother-infant pairs: Comparisons with humans. In M. Tomonaga, M. Tanaka, & T. Matsuzawa (Eds.), *Cognitive and behavioral development in chimpanzees: A comparative approach* (pp. 232–242). Kyoto, Japan: Kyoto University Press. [In Japanese]

Kuwahata, H., Fujita, K., Ishikawa, S., Myowa-Yamakoshi, M., Tomonaga, M., Tanaka, M., et al. (2003). Recognition of schematic face in infant chimpanzees. In M. Tomonaga, M. Tanaka, & T. Matsuzawa (Eds.), *Cognitive and behavioral development in chimpanzees: A comparative approach* (pp. 89–93). Kyoto, Japan: Kyoto University Press. [In Japanese]

LaVelli, M., & Fogel, A. (2002). Developmental changes in mother-infant face-to-face communication. *Developmental Psychology, 38,* 288–305.

Matsuzawa, T. (2002). Chimpanzee Ai and her son Ayumu: An episode of education by master-apprenticeship. In M. Bekoff, C. Allen, & G. M. Gordon (Eds.), *The cognitive animal.* (pp.190–195). Cambridge, MA: MIT Press.

Matsuzawa, T. (2003). The Ai project: Historical and ecological contexts. *Animal Cognition, 6,* 199–211.

Matsuzawa, T., Biro, D., Humle, T., Inoue-Nakamura, N., Tonooka, R., & Yamakoshi, G. (2001). Emergence of culture in wild chimpanzees: Education by master-apprenticeship. In T. Matsuzawa (Ed.), *Primate origins of human cognition and behavior* (pp. 557–574). Tokyo: Springer.

Mizuno, Y. (2004). *Communications between mother and infant chimpanzees: Developmental changes in the first 4 months of life.* Unpublished doctoral thesis, University of Shiga Prefecture, Shiga, Japan. [In Japanese]

Mizuno, Y., & Takeshita, H. (2002). Behavioral development of chimpanzees in the first month of life: Observation of mother-infant pairs at night. *Japanese Psychological Review, 45,* 352–364.[In Japanese with English abstract]

Moore, C., & Dunham, P. J. (Eds.). (1995). *Joint attention: Its origins and role in development.* Hillsdale, NJ: Lawrence Erlbaum Associates.

Myowa-Yamakoshi, M., & Tomonaga, M. (2001). Perceiving eye gaze in an infant gibbon (*Hylobates agilis*). *Psychologia, 44,* 24–30.

Myowa-Yamakoshi, M., Tomonaga, M., Tanaka, M., & Matsuzawa, T. (2003). Preference for human direct gaze in infant chimpanzees (*Pan troglodytes*). *Cognition*, 89, B53–B64.

Myowa-Yamakoshi, M., Tomonaga, M., Tanaka, M., & Matsuzawa, T. (2004). Imitation in neonatal chimpanzees (*Pan troglodytes*). *Developmental Science*, *7*, 437–442.

Nakashima, N. (2003). *Developmental changes of the responses to the vocalizations in infant chimpanzees.* Unpublished masters thesis, Primate Research Institute, Kyoto University, Aichi, Japan. [In Japanese]

Ohgami, H. (2002). The developmental origins of early joint attention behaviors. *Kyushu University Psychological Research, 3,* 29–39. [In Japanese]

Okamoto, S., Kawai, N., Sousa, C., Tanaka, T., Tomonaga, M., Ishii, K., et al. (2002). Interaction between of mother and infant chimpanzees in the experimental setting. *Primate Research, 18,* 394. [Japanese abstract only]

Okamoto, S., Tanaka, M., & Tomonaga, M. (2004). Looking back: The "representational mechanism" of joint attention in an infant chimpanzee (*Pan troglodytes*). *Japanese Psychological Research*, *46*, 236–245.

Okamoto, S., Tomonaga, M., Ishii K., Kawai N., Tanaka, M., & Matsuzawa, T. (2002). An infant chimpanzee (*Pan troglodytes*) follows human gaze. *Animal Cognition, 5,* 107–114.

Okano, T. (1978). *Chimpanzee intelligence.* Tokyo, Japan: Brain Shuppan. [In Japanese]

Premack, D., & Woodruff, G. (1978). Does the chimpanzee have a theory of mind? *Behavioral and Brain Sciences*, 1, 515–526.

Rochat, P. (2001). *The infant's world.* Cambridge, MA: Harvard University Press.

Russell, C. L., Bard, K. A., & Adamson, L. B. (1997). Social referencing by young chimpanzees (*Pan troglodytes*). *Journal of Comparative Psychology, 111*, 185–193.

Samuels, C. A. (1985). Attention to eye contact opportunity and facial motion by three-month-old infants. *Journal of Experimental Child Psychology, 40,* 105–114.

Sorce, J. F., Emde, R. N., Campos, J. J., & Klinnert, M. D. (1985). Maternal emotional signaling: Its effect on the visual cliff behavior of 1-year-olds. *Developmental Psychology, 21,* 195–200.

Sousa, C., Okamoto, S., & Matsuzawa, T. (2003). Behavioral development in a matching-to-sample task and token use by an infant chimpanzee reared by his mother. *Animal Cognition*, 6, 259–267.

Tanaka, M., Tomonaga, M., & Matsuzawa, T. (2002). A developmental research project with three mother-infant chimpanzee pairs: A new approach to comparative developmental science. *Japanese Psychological Review, 45,* 296–308. [In Japanese with English abstract]

Tomasello, M. (1999). *The cultural origins of human cognition.* London: Harvard University Press.

Tomasello, M., & Call, J. (1997). *Primate cognition.* New York: Oxford University Press.

Tomasello, M., Hare, B., & Fogleman, T. (2001). The ontogeny of gaze following in chimpanzees, *Pan troglodytes*, and rhesus macaques, *Macaca mulatta. Animal Behavior, 61,* 335–343.

Tomonaga, M., & Hayashi, M. (2003). Object exchange between infant chimpanzees and humans. In M. Tomonaga, M. Tanaka, & T. Matsuzawa (Eds.), *Cognitive and behavioral development in chimpanzees: A comparative approach* (pp.153–157). Kyoto, Japan: Kyoto University Press. [In Japanese]

Tomonaga, M., Myowa-Yamakoshi, M., Mizuno, Y., Yamaguchi, M. K., Kosugi, D., Bard, K. A., et al. (2004). Development of social cognition in infant chimpanzees (*Pan troglodytes*): Face recognition, smiling, gaze and the lack of triadic interactions. *Japanese Psychological Research, 46,* 227–235.

Tomonaga, M., Tanaka, M., & Matsuzawa, T. (Eds.). (2003). *Cognitive and behavioral development in chimpanzees: A comparative approach.* Kyoto, Japan: Kyoto University Press. [In Japanese]

Tomonaga, M., Yamaguchi, M. K., Myowa-Yamakoshi, M., Mizuno, Y., & Kanazawa, S. (2003). Recognition of mother's face in infant chimpanzees. In M. Tomonaga, M. Tanaka, & T. Matsuzawa (Eds.), *Cognitive and behavioral development in chimpanzees: A comparative approach* (pp. 94–99). Kyoto, Japan: Kyoto University Press. [In Japanese]

Tonooka, R., Tomonaga, M., & Matsuzawa, T. (1997). Acquisition and transmission of tool use and making for drinking juice in a group of captive chimpanzees (*Pan troglodytes*). *Japanese Psychological Research*, 39, 253–265.

Trevarthen, C., & Aitken, K. J. (2001). Infant intersubjectivity: Research, theory, and clinical applications. *Journal of Child Psychology and Psychiatry, 42,* 3–48.

Vecera, S. P., & Johnson, M. H. (1995). Gaze detection and the cortical processing of faces: Evidence from infants and adults. *Visual Cognition, 2, 59–87.*

Wellman, H. M. (1992). *The child's theory of mind.* Cambridge, MA: MIT Press.

Whiten, A., & Byrne, R. W. (Eds.). (1997). *Machiavellian intelligence. II: Extensions and evaluations.* New York: Cambridge University Press.

Whiten, A., Goodall, J., McGrew, W. C., Nishida, T., Reynolds, V., Sugiyama, Y., et al. (1999). Cultures in chimpanzees. *Nature, 399,* 682–685.

Wimmer, H., & Perner, J. (1983). Beliefs about beliefs: Representation and constraining function of wrong beliefs in young children's understanding of deception. *Cognition, 13,* 103–128.

Yamaguchi, M. K., Myowa, M., Kanazawa, S., & Tomonaga, M. (2000). Early development in the recognition of familiar faces: Comparative-developmental studies with humans, Japanese macaques, and chimpanzees. *The Technical Report of the Proceeding of the Institute of Electronics, Information and Communication Engineers, HCS2000-41,* 21–28. [In Japanese]

33

Stimuli Signaling Rewards That Follow a Less-Preferred Event Are Themselves Preferred: Implications for Cognitive Dissonance

THOMAS R. ZENTALL, TRICIA S. CLEMENT, ANDREA M. FRIEDRICH, AND KELLY A. DIGIAN

Comparative research, once at the center of American behaviorism, has recently broadened its base to focus more on cognitive processes and social learning. That shift has come about through influences from cognitive and developmental psychology as well as from behavioral ecology. But, these various influences have also resulted in some ambiguity about the goals of our research.

Behavioral ecologists, who study ecological systems, are interested in the adaptive value of behavior to the animal; for this reason, they typically start by observing naturally occurring behavior. When they bring that behavior into the laboratory to get better control of the conditions under which it occurs, to the degree possible, they attempt to maintain the natural conditions under which it was found. From their perspective, if the laboratory conditions do not mimic those of the natural environment, then the behavior under study may be distorted or may not even occur. For this reason, behavioral ecologists often do not grasp the relevance of exposing animals to conditions that differ from what they would encounter in their natural environment.

Psychologists, on the other hand, study all kinds of behavior—both natural and unnatural. Memorizing numbers, reading text, playing a cello, and piloting an airplane are not natural behaviors, certainly not in an evolutionary sense; but psychologists are interested in how humans accomplish these challenging tasks. Comparative psychologists who study analogous tasks in other animals are also interested in the mechanisms responsible for such performance.

On the one hand, comparative psychologists may be interested in the generality of processes that some theorists believe are unique to humans. Given that animal species share some general requirements for the survival of their genes—such as obtaining food, water, shelter, and a mate—it may be helpful for them to possess certain cognitive abilities that are characteristic of humans, like the ability to categorize, to learn relationships, and to imitate. This is not to say that all animals should show similar abilities, but rather that a capacity that is useful for one species may also have evolved in others.

This hypothesis is based on an important assumption that may not be recognized by either psychologists or behavioral ethologists. The ability of humans to successfully perform unnatural tasks such as those already mentioned must have some genetic basis, even if it is just the general flexibility to adapt to new environments. But, if the need for such flexibility is rare in nature (see Boice, 1973), then what is it that maintains those genes in the gene pool? One possibility is that we are only able to take a "snapshot" of an animal's behavior (in evolutionary time) and that snapshot does not represent enough time to see important, but rare, events. Alternatively, these abilities may be maintained in a "reservoir" of capacity, for occasional use by attaching themselves to genes that are more highly selected for. Whatever the mechanism that maintains them, moving an animal into an unnatural environment involving challenging tasks may not be a good model of the animal's natural behavior, but it may be a reasonable model of what we humans have done to ourselves in the past few thousand years, as we moved from a hunter-gatherer environment to this artificial modern environment in which we now live.

On the other hand, there may be a more subtle reason to study cognitive behavior in animals. In studying human behavior, psychologists often take a logical rather than a psychological approach to the identification of responsible mechanisms. An example of this approach is Piaget's (1962) theory of imitation in children. To account for a child's ability to copy the body position of an adult without being able to see that change in its own body position (e.g., placing its hand on top of its head), Piaget proposed, not unreasonably, that the child must be able to take the perspective of a third party and reason, "What do I have to do, such that a third party would say that my body position matches that of the adult." The problem with this hypothesis is that imitation of this kind can be found is children much younger than the age at which perspective taking is supposed to occur (Meltzoff, 1988). Even more convincing is the finding that several bird species, including pigeons (Zentall, Sutton, & Sherburne, 1996) and Japanese quail (Akins & Zentall, 1996, 1998), show imitative behavior of this kind. Thus, if nonhuman species can be shown to have an ability (e.g., imitation) that is thought to be mediated by a particularly advanced cognitive process (i.e., perspective taking), then one is more likely to consider the possibility that the underlying mechanism may be simpler (Gallese, Fadiga, Fogassi, & Rizzolatti, 1996; Mitchell, 2002). The present chapter takes this approach with regard to a well-studied phenomenon in human social psychology—cognitive dissonance (Festinger, 1957).

COGNITIVE DISSONANCE IN HUMANS

Cognitive dissonance is a conflict that arises when one's behavior (e.g., one treats a friend badly) is discrepant from one's beliefs (e.g., one should be nice to one's friends). According to cognitive dissonance theory, one should work to resolve this discrepancy. As one's behavior is difficult to take back, one tends to alter one's beliefs. In this case, one might justify the inappropriate behavior by proposing that our friend had done something to deserve the bad treatment.

In Festinger's classic experiment (Festinger & Carlsmith, 1959), after completing a tedious task, participants were paid either \$1 or \$20 to lie to another participant about how interesting the task was. When then asked to evaluate the task, those who were paid only \$1 rated the task more interesting than those who were paid \$20. Festinger explained these results as follows: Participants who were paid \$20 could justify lying in terms of the large value of the payment. However, those who were paid only \$1 could not justify lying; for them, the only way to explain their behavior was to alter their belief that it was an uninteresting task.

The complexity of Festinger's experimental design, as well as its important language component, makes it difficult to translate this task for use with animals. Fortunately, later research has used procedures that are more tractable.

JUSTIFICATION OF EFFORT IN HUMANS

In a variant of the cognitive dissonance experiment called justification of effort, Aronson and Mills (1959) had participants read aloud as a test before being permitted to listen to a group discussion. Participants who had to read aloud embarrassing sexually explicit material (severe test) judged the later group discussion as more interesting than those who read material that was not sexually explicit (mild test). Aronson and Mills explained their results in terms of cognitive dissonance. To justify their behavior (reading embarrassing material aloud), participants had to increase the value of group discussion that followed. Was this effect really produced by the discrepancy between behavior and beliefs, or was there a simpler explanation? Our approach to this question was to see if animals would show an analogous effect when they were asked to evaluate (comparatively) outcomes that were preceded by a mildly aversive event. If they did so, this result would suggest that a simpler mechanism was responsible for their behavior.

Festinger, himself, believed that his theory also applied to the behavior of nonhuman animals

(Lawrence & Festinger, 1962), but the examples that he provided were only remotely related to the cognitive dissonance research that had been conducted with humans and the results that were obtained were easily accounted for with simpler behavioral mechanisms (e.g., the partial reinforcement extinction effect, which was attributed by others to a generalization decrement [Capaldi, 1967] or to an acquired response in the presence of frustration [Amsel, 1958]). Thus, the purpose of the research presented here was to develop an analog design that could be used with nonhuman animals to determine if they too would show a similar justification of effort effect.

JUSTIFICATION OF EFFORT IN PIGEONS

The paradigm used by Aronson and Mills (1959) can be adapted for use with animals by training them to make many pecks to a response key for food on some trials and to make few pecks to the same response key for the same food on other trials, and then asking them which of the two outcomes they prefer. As this design, with minor variations, was used in a number of experiments, some details of the procedure are presented.

The research was conducted in a typical three-response-key operant chamber. All trials began with the illumination of the center response key with a circle. In the preliminary experiment, on some trials, one peck was required to turn off the circle key and replace it with a red hue; five pecks to the red hue resulted in reinforcement (2-s access to mixed grain). On the remaining trials, 20 pecks to the circle were required to turn off the key and it was then replaced with a green hue, and 5 pecks to the green key resulted in reinforcement (the colors associated with the different response requirements were counterbalanced and the 1-peck and 20-peck trials were randomly alternated). After several sessions of training, test trials were introduced. On test trials, we asked the pigeons which colored key they preferred by giving them a choice between red and green response keys. On test trials, either response was randomly reinforced 50% of the time. Unfortunately, because the test trials were the first choice trials the pigeons had received, they all showed strong position biases and were indifferent to the colors.

In a follow-up study (Clement, Feltus, Kaiser, & Zentall, 2000), during training, each of the two response requirements (high effort, 20 responses; low effort, 1 response) was followed by a simple simultaneous discrimination (e.g., red positive/yellow negative and green positive/blue negative, respectively) that appeared on the left and right response keys. Giving the pigeons a simple simultaneous discrimination in training forced them to look for the positive (S+) stimulus on each trial and prepared them to make a choice on test trials. The design of this experiment is presented in figure 33.1. On test trials involving a choice between the S+ stimuli, the pigeons showed a significant tendency to prefer the S+ that in training had been preceded by 20 pecks over the S+ that in training had been preceded by only 1 peck (figure 33.2). Interestingly, when the pigeons were given a choice between the S– stimuli, they also showed a strong tendency to prefer the S– that in training had been preceded by 20 pecks over the S– that in training had been preceded by only one peck.

To determine whether the differential response requirement experienced during training had an effect when it preceded the choice on test trials, three kinds of S+ and S– test trials were used: test trials preceded by only 1 peck to the circle, test trials preceded by 20 pecks to the circle, and test trials with no circle presented prior to presentation of the discriminative stimuli. Clement et al. (2000) found

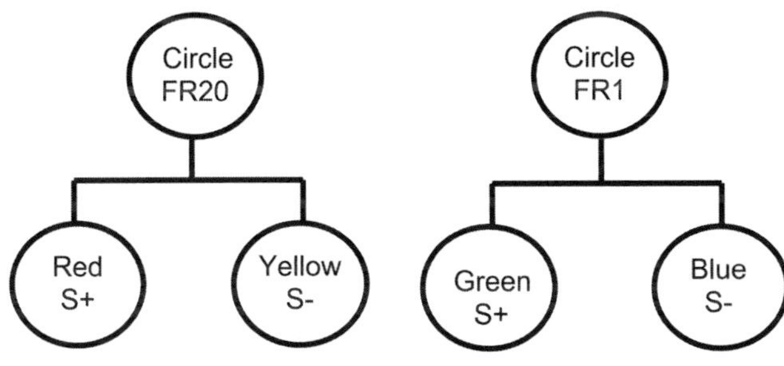

Figure 33.1. Design of experiment by Clement et al. (2000), in which one pair of discriminative stimuli followed 20 pecks and the other pair of discriminative stimuli followed 1 peck.

that the number of pecks that preceded choice of the two S+ or S– stimuli (0, 1, or 20) on test trials had little effect on stimulus choice (see figure 33.2). Thus, the pigeons did not learn to use the response requirement as a conditional cue to anticipate choice of the appropriate stimulus. Instead, it appeared that the color that had followed the greater effort had taken on added value relative to the color that had followed less effort.

In the next experiment, we asked if pigeons would show a similar preference for a more direct measure of food preference: the location of food that followed greater effort over a different location of the same food that followed less effort. To answer this question, we conducted an experiment in which we used two feeders: one that provided food on trials in which 30 pecks were required to the center response key, and another that provided the same food on trials in which 1 peck was required to the center response key (Friedrich & Zentall, 2004). Prior to the start of training, we obtained a baseline feeder preference score for each bird. Feeder preference was obtained by providing forced- and free-choice trials. On half of the forced trials, the left key was illuminated (white) and pecks to the left key raised the left feeder. On the remaining trials, the right key was illuminated and pecks to the right key raised the right feeder. On interspersed choice trials, both the right and left keys were lit and the pigeons could choose which feeder would be raised. In the training that followed, the nonpreferred feeder was associated with the high-effort response and the preferred feeder was associated with the low-effort response.

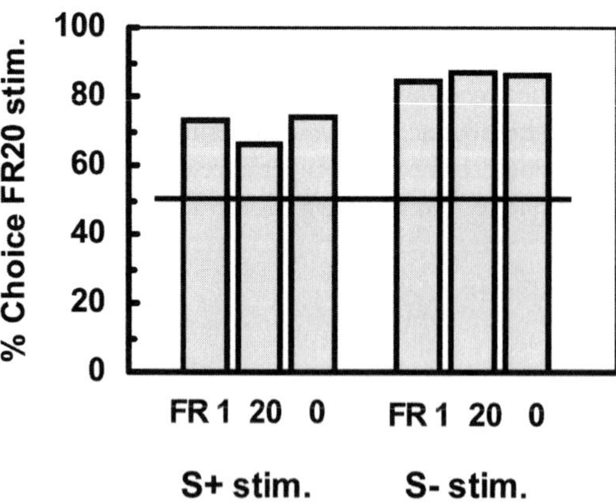

Figure 33.2. Results obtained by Clement et al. (2000). Pigeons preferred the S+ and the S– that in training followed 20 pecks over the S+ and S– that followed 1 peck.

On training trials, the center key was illuminated (yellow) and either 1 peck or 30 pecks were required to turn off the key and raise one of the two feeders. Forced- and free-choice feeder trials continued through training to monitor changes in feeder preference. On those free-choice trials, we found that there was a significant increase in preference for the originally nonpreferred feeder (the feeder associated with the high-effort response) (figure 33.3, filled circles). A control group was included to assess changes in feeder preference associated with the added sessions of experience; for this group, each of the two response requirements was equally often followed by each feeder. The control group showed no systematic increase in preference for the nonpreferred feeder from baseline, as a function of training (figure 33.3, open circles). Thus, it appears that the value of the location of food can be enhanced by being preceded by a high-effort response compared with being preceded by a low-effort response.

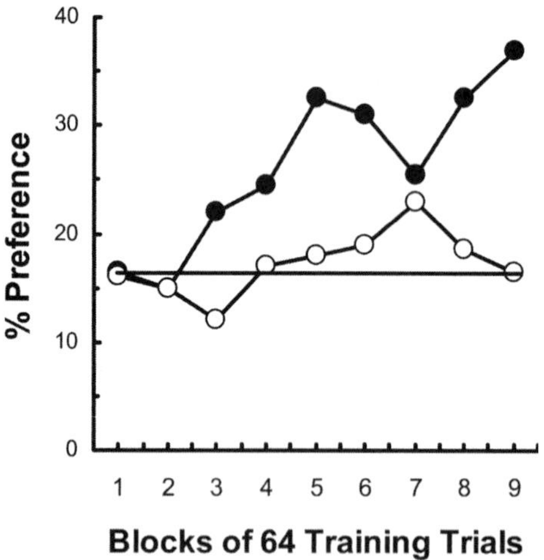

Figure 33.3. Results obtained by Friedrich & Zentall (2004). Graph shows the increase in preference for the originally nonpreferred feeder as a function of being associated with the high-effort (30-peck) response (*filled circles*). The preferred feeder was associated with the low-effort (1-peck) response. For the control group, both feeders were equally often associated with the high-effort response and the low-effort response (*open circles*). The *solid line* indicates the baseline preference for the originally nonpreferred feeder.

A MODEL OF JUSTIFICATION OF EFFORT IN ANIMALS

Had the two experiments described above been conducted with human participants, the results would probably have been attributed to cognitive dissonance. It is unlikely, however, that cognitive dissonance is responsible for the added value given to outcomes that follow greater effort in pigeons; instead, this phenomenon is more parsimoniously described as a form of contrast.

To model this contrast account, it is assumed that the relative hedonic state of the pigeon at the start of each trial at zero. Next, it is assumed that keypecking (or the delay of reinforcement resulting from the time to make those pecks) is a relatively aversive event that results in a negative change in the animal's hedonic state. It is also assumed that obtaining the reinforcer causes a shift to a positive hedonic state (relative to the pigeon's hedonic state at the start of the trial). The final assumption is that the value of the reinforcer depends on the *change* in hedonic state from the end of the response requirement to the appearance of the reinforcer or the appearance of the S+—in the case of the second experiment, the feeder location—that signals reinforcement (figure 33.4). Thus, because the change in hedonic state following a high-effort response is larger than the change in hedonic state following a low-effort response, the relative value of the reinforcer following a high-effort response should be greater than that following a low-effort response.

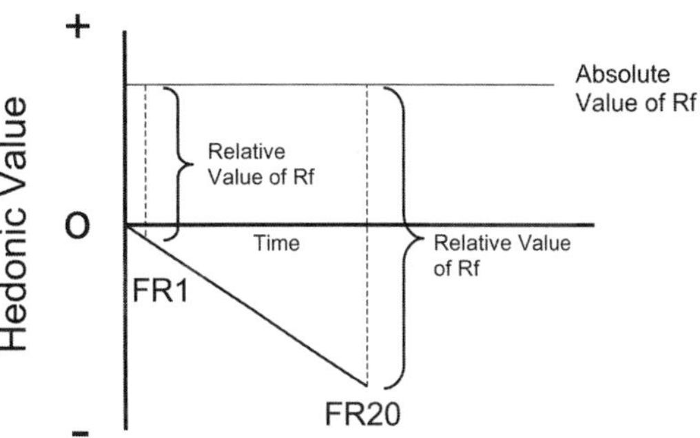

Figure 33.4. A model based on change in hedonic state, proposed to account for contrast effects of the kind presented in this chapter.

RELATIVE AVERSIVENESS OF THE PRIOR EVENT

Delay to Reinforcement as an Aversive Event

If the interpretation of these experiments that is presented in figure 33.4 is correct, then any prior event that is relatively aversive (compared with the comparable event on alternative trials) should result in a similar enhanced preference for the stimuli that follow. For example, given that pigeons should prefer a shorter delay to reinforcement over a longer delay to reinforcement, they should also prefer discriminative stimuli that follow a delay over those that follow no delay.

To test this hypothesis, we trained pigeons to peck the center response key to produce a pair of discriminative stimuli (as in Clement et al., 2000). On some trials, pecking the response key was followed immediately by one pair of discriminative stimuli (no delay), whereas on the remaining trials, pecking the response key the same number of times was followed by a different pair of discriminative stimuli, but only after a delay of 6 s (figure 33.5, top). On test trials, when the pigeons were given a choice between the S+ stimuli, they showed no preference (DiGian, Friedrich, & Zentall, 2004, Unsignaled Delay Condition).

One difference between the manipulation of effort used in the first two experiments and the manipulation of delay used by DiGian et al. (2004) was in the effort manipulation. In the first two experiments, once the pigeon had made a single peck to the initial stimulus and the discriminative stimuli failed to appear, the pigeon could anticipate that 19 (or, in some cases, 29) additional pecks would be required. Thus, whatever frustration might be produced by encountering a high-effort trial would have to be experienced in the context of having to make additional responses. In the case of the delay manipulation, however, the pigeon could not anticipate whether a delay would occur or not; at the time the delay occurred, no further responding was required. Thus, with the delay manipulation, the pigeon would not have to experience a comparable degree of presumed frustration in the context of responding. Would the results be different if the pigeon could anticipate the delay at a time when responding was required?

To test this hypothesis, the delay to reinforcement manipulation was repeated, but this time the initial stimulus was predictive of the delay (DiGian

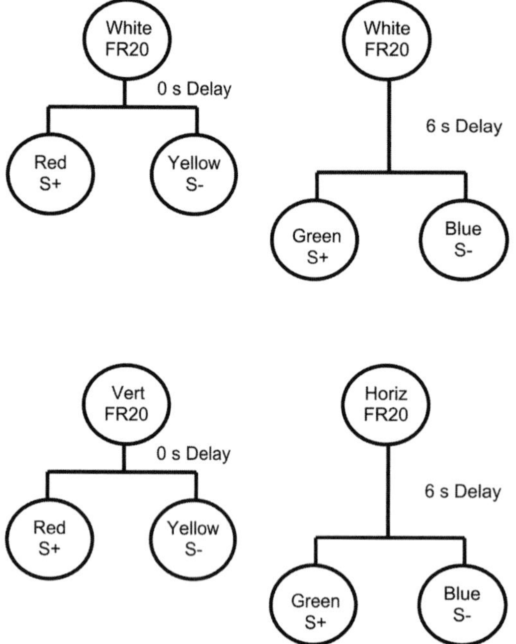

Figure 33.5. Design of experiments by DiGian et al. (2004), in which one pair of discriminative stimuli followed a delay and the other pair of discriminative stimuli followed the absence of a delay. *Top,* The delay and absence of a delay were unsignaled. *Bottom,* The delay and absence of a delay were signaled.

et al., 2004, Signaled Delay Condition). Thus, on half of the trials, a vertical line appeared on the response key and pecking resulted in the immediate appearance of a pair of discriminative stimuli (e.g., red and yellow). On the remaining trials, a horizontal line appeared on the response key and pecking resulted in the appearance of the other pair of discriminative stimuli (e.g., green and blue) but only after a 6-s delay (figure 33.5, bottom). In this condition, the pigeons could anticipate whether pecking would result in a delay or not, so they had to peck in the context of presumed frustration. When pigeons in this condition were tested, as in the effort manipulation experiments, they showed a significant preference for the S+ that in training had followed the delay. Once again, the experience of an aversive event produced an increase in the value of the positive discriminative stimulus that followed. Furthermore, the results of this experiment demonstrated that it may be necessary for the animals to anticipate the aversive event for contrast to be found.

The Absence of Reinforcement as an Aversive Event

A related form of relatively aversive event is the absence of reinforcement in the context of reinforcement (on other trials). Could reinforcement versus its absence result in a preference for discriminative stimuli that follow the absence of reinforcement? To test this hypothesis, pigeons were once again trained to peck a response key to produce a pair of discriminative stimuli. On some trials, pecking the response key was followed immediately by 2-s access to food from the central feeder and then immediately by the presentation of one pair of discriminative stimuli. On the remaining trials, pecking the response key was followed by the absence of food (for 2 s) and then by the presentation of a different pair of discriminative stimuli (figure 33.6, top). On test trials, when the pigeons were given a choice between the S+ stimuli, again they showed no preference (Friedrich, Clement, & Zentall, 2005).

Once again, however, for this group, the aversive event, which consisted of the absence of reinforcement, could not be anticipated prior to its occurrence. To test the hypothesis that the contrast effect depends on the anticipation of the aversive event, the absence of reinforcement manipulation was repeated, but this time the initial stimulus was predictive of the reinforcement condition that followed (Friedrich et al., 2005). As in the experiment that assessed the effect of delay to reinforcement on preference for the stimuli that followed, on half of the trials, a vertical line appeared on the response key and pecking resulted in the presentation of food followed by the appearance of a pair of discriminative stimuli. On the remaining trials, a horizontal line appeared on the response key and pecking resulted in the absence of food followed by the appearance of the other pair of discriminative stimuli (figure 33.6, bottom). In this condition, the pigeons could anticipate whether pecking would result in reinforcement. When pigeons in this condition were tested, they showed a significant preference for the S+ that in training had followed the absence of reinforcement. Once again, the experience of a relatively aversive event produced an increase in the value of the positive discriminative stimulus that followed, but only when the relatively aversive event could be anticipated.

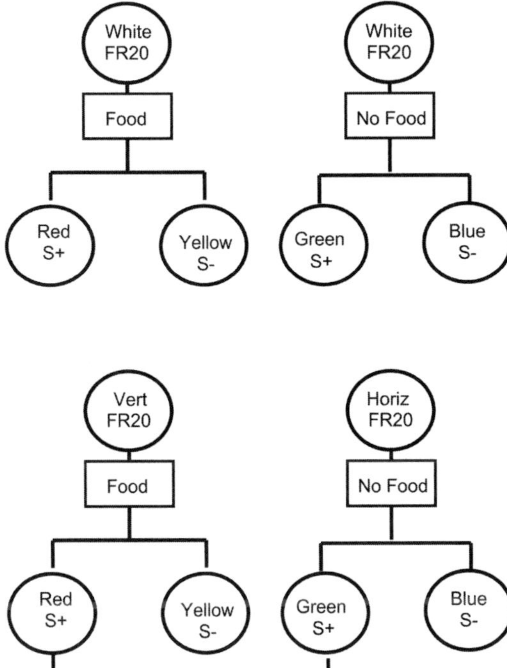

Figure 33.6. Design of experiments by Friedrich et al. (2005), in which one pair of discriminative stimuli followed reinforcement and the other pair of discriminative stimuli followed the absence of reinforcement. *Top*, The reinforcement and absence of reinforcement were unsignaled. *Bottom*, The delay and absence of reinforcement were signaled.

The Anticipation of Effort as the Aversive Event

Can anticipated effort that does not actually occur serve as the aversive event that increases the value of stimuli signaling reinforcement that follows? This question addresses the issue of whether the contrast between the initial aversive event and the conditioned reinforcer depends on actually experiencing the relatively aversive event. One account of the added value that accrues to stimuli that follow greater effort is that during training, the greater effort experienced produces a heightened state of arousal; in that heightened state of arousal, the pigeons learn more about the discriminative stimuli that follow than about the discriminative stimuli that follow the lower state of arousal produced by lesser effort. Although over the various experiments that we have conducted, there has been no tendency for the simultaneous discrimination that followed greater effort, longer delays, or the absence of reinforcement, to have been acquired faster than the discrimination that followed less effort, shorter delays, or reinforcement, those discriminations were acquired very rapidly, and it is possible that we failed to observe a small difference in the rate of discrimination acquisition sufficient to produce a preference for the S+ stimulus that follows the more aversive event.

Thus, the purpose of the next experiment was to ask if we could obtain a preference for the discriminative stimuli that followed a signal that more effort might be required but actually was not required on that trial. More specifically, at the start of half of the training trials, pigeons were presented with a vertical line on the center response key. On half of these trials, pecking the vertical line replaced it with a white key and one peck to the white key resulted in reinforcement. On the remaining vertical-line trials, pecking the vertical line replaced it with a simultaneous discrimination $S+_{FR1}S-_{FR1}$ on the left and right response keys and choice of the S+ was reinforced. A schematic presentation of the design of this experiment appears in figure 33.7.

On the remaining training trials, the pigeons were presented with a horizontal line on the center response key. On half of these trials, pecking the horizontal line replaced it with a white key and 30 pecks to the white key resulted in reinforcement. On the remaining horizontal-line trials, pecking the horizontal line replaced it with a different simultaneous discrimination $S+_{FR30}S-_{FR30}$ on the left and right response keys and again choice of the S+ was reinforced. On test trials when the pigeons were given a choice between $S+_{FR30}$ and $S+_{FR1}$, they once again showed a significant preference for $S+_{FR30}$.

In this experiment, it is important to note that the events that occurred in training on trials involving the two pairs of discriminative stimuli were essentially the same. It was only on the other half of the trials—those trials in which the discriminative stimuli did not appear—that differential responding was required. Thus, the expectation of differential effort, rather than actual differential effort itself, appears to be sufficient to produce a differential preference for the stimuli that follow. These results extend the findings of the earlier research to include the effect of anticipated effort.

Figure 33.7. Design of experiment by Clement and Zentall (2002, Experiment 1), in which they studied the effect of the anticipation of effort (rather than actual effort) on the preference for the discriminative stimuli that followed. FR1 = 1 peck, FR5 = 5 pecks, FR10 = 10 pecks, FR30 = 30 pecks, Rf = reinforcement, $S+_{FR1}$ and $S-_{FR1}$ = positive stimulus and negative stimulus, respectively, that on other vertical-line trials was associated with FR1. $S+_{FR30}$ and $S-_{FR30}$ = positive stimulus and negative stimulus, respectively, that on other horizontal-line trials was associated with FR30.

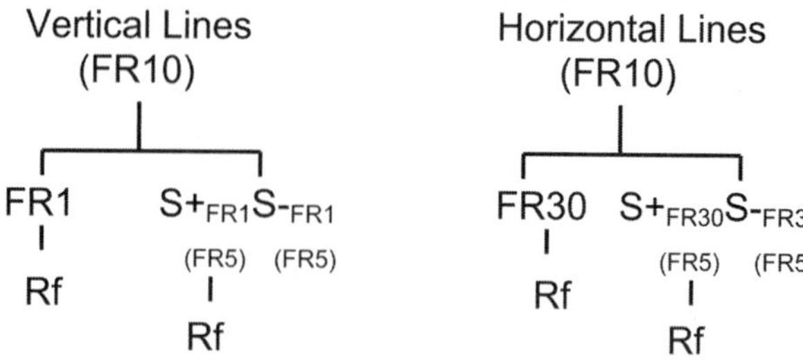

The Anticipation of the Absence of Reinforcement as the Aversive Event

If anticipated effort can function as a relative conditioned aversive event, then can the expected absence of reinforcement also serve the same function? Using a design similar to that employed to examine differential anticipated effort, we evaluated the effect of differential anticipated reinforcement (Clement & Zentall, 2002, Experiment 2). At the start of half of the training trials, pigeons were presented with a vertical line on the center response key. On half of these trials, pecking the vertical line was followed immediately by reinforcement. On the remaining vertical-line trials, pecking the vertical line replaced it with a simultaneous discrimination $S+_{Rf}S-_{Rf}$ and choice of the S+ was reinforced, but only on a random 50% of the trials. On the remaining training trials, the pigeons were presented with a horizontal line on the center response key. On half of these trials, pecking the horizontal line was followed immediately by the intertrial interval (the absence of reinforcement). On the remaining horizontal-line trials, pecking the horizontal line replaced it with a different simultaneous discrimination $S+_{NRf}S-_{NRf}$. Again, choice of the S+ was reinforced but, again, only on a random 50% of the trials. A schematic presentation of the design of this experiment appears in figure 33.8. On test trials when the pigeons were given a choice between $S+_{Rf}$ and $S+_{NRf}$, they showed a significant preference for $S+_{NRf}$. Thus, the anticipation of an aversive absence-of-food event appears to produce a preference for the S+ that follows it that is similar to the anticipation of a high-effort response.

In a follow-up experiment (Clement & Zentall, 2002, Experiment 3), we tried to determine whether preference for the discriminative stimuli associated with the anticipation of the absence of food was produced by the anticipation of positive contrast between the certain absence of food and a 50% chance of food (on discriminative stimulus trials) or negative contrast between the certain anticipation of food and a 50% chance of food (on the other set of discriminative stimulus trials). For Group Positive, on vertical-line trials, the conditions of reinforcement were essentially nondifferential (i.e., reinforcement always followed vertical-line trials whether or not the discriminative stimuli were presented). On half of the vertical-line trials, reinforcement was presented immediately for responding to the vertical line. On the remaining vertical-line trials reinforcement was presented for responding to the S+. Thus, there should have been little contrast established between these kinds of trials. A schematic presentation of the design of this portion of the experiment appears in figure 33.9, top left.

On horizontal-line trials, however, on half of the trials, no reinforcement always followed responses to the horizontal line. On the remaining horizontal-line trials, reinforcement was presented for responding to the S+. Thus, for this group, on horizontal-line trials, there was the opportunity for positive contrast to develop on discriminative stimulus trials (i.e., the pigeons should expect that reinforcement might not occur on those trials and they might experience positive contrast when it does occur).

For Group Negative, on horizontal-line trials, the conditions of reinforcement were essentially nondifferential (i.e., the probability of reinforce-

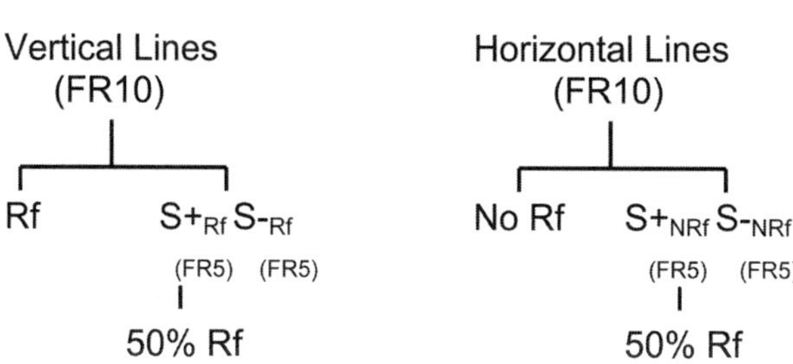

Figure 33.8. Design of experiment by Clement and Zentall (2002, Experiment 2), in which they studied the effect of the anticipation of reinforcement (rather than actual reinforcement) on the preference for the discriminative stimuli that followed. FR5 = 5 pecks, FR10 = 10 pecks, Rf = reinforcement, NRf = nonreinforcement. $S+_{Rf}$ and $S-_{Rf}$ = positive stimulus and negative stimulus, respectively, that on other vertical-line trials was associated with reinforcement. $S+_{NRf}$ and $S-_{NRf}$ = positive stimulus and negative stimulus, respectively, that on other horizontal-line trails was associated with nonreinforcement.

ment on horizontal-line trials was always 50% whether the trials involved discriminative stimuli or not). Thus, on half of the horizontal-line trials reinforcement was provided immediately with a probability of .50 for responding to the horizontal line. On the remaining horizontal-line trials reinforcement was presented for choices of the S+ but only on half of the trials. Thus, there should have been little contrast established between these kinds of trial (see figure 33.9, bottom right).

On vertical-line trials, however, on half of the trials, reinforcement was presented immediately (with a probability of 1.00) for responding to the horizontal line. On the remaining vertical-line trials, reinforcement was provided for choice of the S+ with a probability of only 0.50. Thus, for this

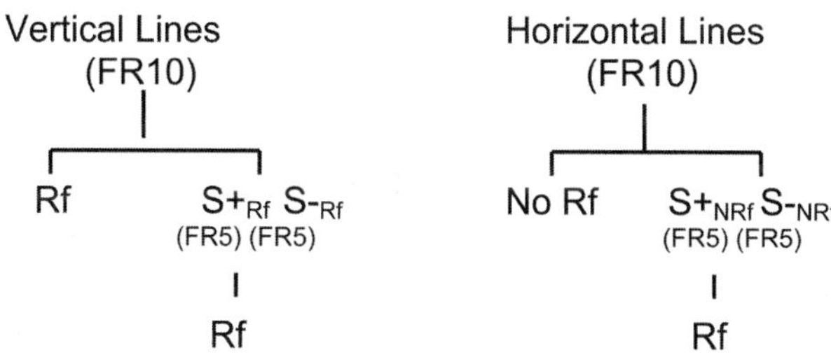

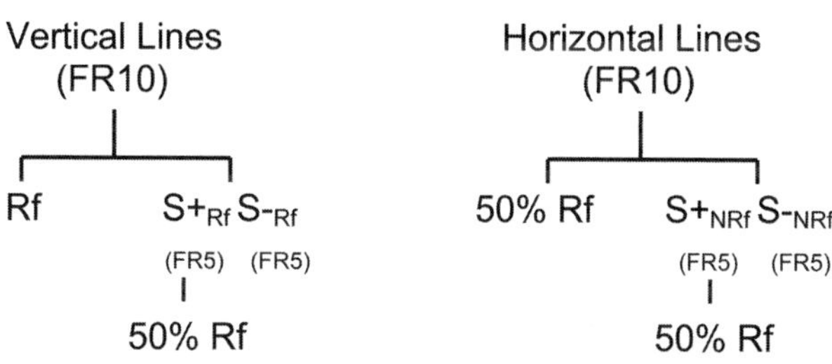

Figure 33.9. Design of experiment by Clement and Zentall (2002, Experiment 3), in which they studied the effect of the anticipation of reinforcement (rather than actual reinforcement) on the preference for the discriminative stimuli that followed and attempted to distinguish between positive contrast and negative contrast. FR5 = five pecks, FR10 = 10 pecks, Rf = reinforcement, NRf = nonreinforcement. $S+_{Rf}$ and $S-_{Rf}$ = positive stimulus and negative stimulus, respectively, that on other vertical-line trials was associated with reinforcement. $S+_{NRf}$ and $S-_{NRf}$ = positive stimulus and negative stimulus, respectively, that on other horizontal-line trials was associated with no reinforcement (*top*) or 50% reinforcement (*bottom*).

group, on vertical-line trials, there was the opportunity for negative contrast to develop on discriminative stimulus trials (i.e., the pigeons should expect that reinforcement is quite likely and they might experience negative contrast when it does not occur).

On test trials, when pigeons in Group Positive were given a choice between the S+ stimuli, they showed a significant preference for the positive discriminative stimulus that in training was preceded by a horizontal line (the initial stimulus that on other trials was followed by the absence of reinforcement). Thus, Group Positive showed evidence of positive contrast.

When pigeons in Group Negative were given a choice between the S+ stimuli, they also showed a significant preference for the positive discriminative stimulus that in training was preceded by a horizontal line (the initial stimulus that on other trials was followed by a lower probability of reinforcement than on comparable trials involving the vertical line). Thus, Group Negative showed evidence of negative contrast. In this case, the contrast should be described as a reduced preference for the positive discriminative stimulus preceded by the vertical line which on other trials was associated with a higher probability of reinforcement (1.00).

CONTRAST OR RELATIVE DELAY REDUCTION?

To this point, we have described the stimulus (and location) preference in terms of a contrast effect. However, one could also interpret this phenomenon in terms of the delay reduction hypothesis (Fantino & Abarca, 1985). The delay reduction hypothesis proposes that any stimulus that predicts reinforcement sooner in its presence than in its absence will become a conditioned reinforcer. In the present experiments, the relation between the discriminative stimuli and the reinforcers is constant, so one could argue that neither S+ serves to reduce the delay to reinforcement. But, the delay reduction hypothesis can also be applied in a relative sense; that is, one can consider the predictive value of the discriminative stimuli relative to the total duration of the trial. If one considers delay reduction in terms of its duration relative to the duration of the whole trial, then the delay reduction hypothesis can be applied to the present designs. For example, in the case of the differential effort manipulation, because it takes longer to produce 20 responses than to produce 1 response, 20-response trials would be longer than 1-response trials. Thus, the appearance of the discriminative stimuli occurs relatively later in a 20-response trial than in a 1-response trial. The later in a trial that the discriminative stimuli appear, the closer their onset would be to reinforcement, relative to the start of the trial; thus, the greater relative reduction in delay that they would represent.

The relative delay reduction hypothesis can account for the effect seen with 1 versus 20 pecks because 20 pecks take longer to produce than 1 peck. Similarly, a trial with a delay is longer than a trial without a delay. But, what about reinforcement versus the absence of reinforcement? In this case, the duration of the trial is the same with and without reinforcement prior to the appearance of the discriminative stimuli; however, delay reduction theory considers the critical time to be the interval between reinforcements. On trials in which the discriminative stimuli are preceded by reinforcement, the time between reinforcements is short, so the discriminative stimuli are associated with little delay reduction. On trials in which the discriminative stimuli are preceded by the absence of reinforcement, however, the time between reinforcements is long (the time between reinforcement on the preceding trial and reinforcement on the current trial), so the discriminative stimuli on the current trial are associated with a relatively large reduction in delay.

Relative delay reduction theory has a more difficult time accounting for the effects of differential anticipated effort because trials with both sets of discriminative stimuli were not differentiated by number of responses, delay, or reinforcement; thus, all trials with discriminative stimuli should have been of comparable duration. The same is true for the effects of differential anticipated reinforcement because that manipulation occurred on trials separate from the trials with the discriminative stimuli.

The different results found with signaled versus unsignaled delay (DiGian et al., 2004) and the absence of food (Friedrich et al., 2005) also present problems for delay reduction theory. According to delay reduction theory, it should not matter whether the delay or the absence of food is signaled; comparable preferences should have been found. However, preferences for stimuli that followed a delay and the absence of food were found only when those events were signaled. Taken as a whole, the contrast account appears to offer a more parsimonious account of the data than relative delay reduction theory.

Still, it should be possible to distinguish between

the delay reduction and contrast accounts with the use of a design similar to that used in the first experiment. However, instead of requiring that the pigeons peck many times on half of the trials and a few times on the remaining trials, one could use two schedules that accomplish the same thing while holding the duration of the event constant. This objective could be accomplished by using a fixed-interval schedule (the first response after a fixed duration would present one pair of discriminative stimuli) on half of the trials and a differential reinforcement of other behavior schedule (the absence of key pecking for the same fixed duration would present the other pair of discriminative stimuli) on the remaining trials. For each bird, an independent test would be conducted to determine which of the two schedules was preferred. According to the contrast account, the pigeons should prefer the discriminative stimuli that follow the differential reinforcement of other behavior schedule over the discriminative stimuli that follow the fixed-interval schedule. According to the delay reduction hypothesis, if trial duration is held constant and the two pairs of discriminative stimuli occupy the same relative proportion of the two kinds of trials, then the pigeons should not differentially prefer either pair of discriminative stimuli.

WHAT KIND OF CONTRAST IS THIS?

The contrast effects found in the present research appear to be somewhat different from other forms of contrast that have been reported in the literature (see Flaherty, 1996). Flaherty distinguishes among three kinds of contrast: incentive contrast, anticipatory contrast, and differential or behavioral contrast.

Incentive Contrast

In incentive contrast, the magnitude of reward that has been experienced for many trials suddenly changes. The change in behavior that follows the sudden change in reward is compared with the behavior of a comparison group that has experienced the final magnitude of reinforcement from the outset. Early examples of incentive contrast were reported by Tinklepaugh (1928), who found that if monkeys were trained for a number of trials with a preferred reward (e.g., fruit), then when they encountered a less-preferred reward (e.g., lettuce, a reward for which they would normally work), they often would refuse to eat it.

Incentive contrast was more systematically studied by Crespi (1942, see also Mellgren, 1972). Rats trained to run for a large amount of food and shifted to a small amount of food typically run slower than rats trained to run for the smaller amount of food from the start (negative incentive contrast). Conversely, rats trained to run for a small amount of food and shifted to a large amount of food may run faster than rats trained to run for the larger amount of food from the outset (positive incentive contrast). By its nature, incentive contrast must be assessed following the shift in reward magnitude rather than in anticipation of the change because, in general, only a single shift is experienced.

Incentive contrast would seem to be an adaptive mechanism by which animals can increase their sensitivity to changes in reinforcement density. Just as animals use lateral inhibition in vision to help them discriminate spatial changes in light intensity resulting in enhanced detection of edges (or to provide better figure-ground detection), so too may incentive contrast help the animal detect changes in reinforcement magnitude which are important to its survival. Thus, incentive contrast may be a perceptually mediated detection process.

Anticipatory Contrast

In a second form of contrast, anticipatory contrast, there are repeated (typically one a day) experiences with the shift, and the measure of contrast involves behavior that occurs prior to the anticipated change in reward value. Furthermore, the behavior assessed is typically consummatory behavior rather than nonconsummatory behavior like running speed. For example, rats often drink less of a weak saccharin solution if they have learned that it will be followed by a strong sucrose solution, relative to a control group for which saccharin is followed by more saccharin (Flaherty, 1982).

Behavioral Contrast

A third form of contrast involves the random alternation of two signaled outcomes. When used in a discrete-trials procedure with rats, the procedure has been referred to as simultaneous incentive contrast. Bower (1961), for example, reported that rats trained to run to both large and small signaled magnitudes of reward ran slower to the small magnitude of reward than rats that ran only to the small magnitude of reward.

The more-often-studied, free-operant analog of this task is called behavioral contrast. To observe behavioral contrast, pigeons are typically trained on an operant task involving a multiple schedule of reinforcement. In a multiple schedule, two (or more) schedules, each signaled by a distinctive stimulus, are randomly alternated. Positive behavioral contrast can be demonstrated by training pigeons initially with schedules involving equal probabilities of reinforcement schedules (e.g., two variable-interval 60-s schedules) and then reducing the probability of reinforcement in one schedule (e.g., from variable-interval 60-s to extinction) and noting an increase in the response rate in the other, unaltered schedule (Halliday & Boakes, 1971; Reynolds, 1961). Similar results can be demonstrated in a between-groups design (Mackintosh, Little, & Lord, 1972), in which pigeons are trained on the multiple variable-interval 60-s and extinction schedules from the start, and their rate of pecking during the variable-interval 60-s schedule is compared with other pigeons that have been trained on two variable-interval 60-s schedules.

The problem with classifying behavioral contrast according to whether it involves a response to entering the richer schedule (as with incentive contrast) or the anticipation of entering the poorer schedule (as with anticipatory contrast) is that, during each session, there are multiple transitions from the richer to the poorer schedule and vice versa. Thus, when one observes an increase in responding in the richer schedule resulting from the presence of the poorer schedule at other times, it is not clear whether the pigeons are reacting to the fact that the preceding schedule was poorer than the current schedule or they are anticipating that the next schedule may be poorer than the current schedule.

Williams (1981) attempted to distinguish between these mechanisms by presenting pigeons with triplets of trials in an ABA design (with the richer schedule designated as A) and comparing their behavior with that of pigeons trained with an AAA design. Williams found very different kinds of contrast in the first and last A components. In the first A component, Williams found a generally higher level of responding that was maintained over training sessions (see also Williams, 1983). In the final A component, however, he found a higher level of responding primarily at the start of the component, an effect known as local contrast, and the level of responding was not maintained over training sessions (see also Cleary, 1992). Thus, there is evidence that behavioral contrast may be attributable primarily to the higher rate of responding by pigeons in anticipation of the poorer schedule, rather than in response to the appearance of the richer schedule (Williams, 1981; see also Williams & Wixted, 1986).

It is generally accepted that the higher rate of responding to the stimulus associated with the richer schedule of reinforcement occurs because, in the context of the poorer schedule, that stimulus is a better relative predictor of reinforcement (Keller, 1974). Or, in more cognitive terms, the richer schedule seems even better in the context of a poorer schedule.

There is evidence, however, that it is not that the richer schedule appears better but that the richer schedule will soon get worse. In support of this distinction, although pigeons peck at a higher rate to stimuli that are followed by other stimuli that signal a worsening in the probability of reinforcement, it has been found that when given a choice, pigeons prefer stimuli to which they respond less but that are followed by other stimuli that signal no worsening in the probability of reinforcement (Williams, 1992). Thus, under these conditions, response rate has been found to be negatively correlated with choice.

The implication of this finding is that the increased responding associated with the richer schedule does not reflect its greater value to the pigeon but rather its function as a signal that conditions will soon get worse because the opportunity to obtain reinforcement will soon diminish. This analysis suggests that the mechanism responsible for anticipatory contrast (Flaherty, 1982), and, in the case of behavioral contrast, responding in anticipation of a worsening schedule (Williams, 1981), is likely to be a compensatory or learned response. In this sense, these two forms of contrast are probably quite different from the perception-like detection process involved in incentive contrast.

The Present Within-Subject Contrast Effect

What all contrast effects have in common is the presence, at other times, of a second condition that is either better or worse than the target condition. Often, the effect of the second condition is to exaggerate the difference between the conditions. Although there have been attempts to account for these various contrast effects, Mackintosh (1974) concluded that no single principle will suffice (see also Flaherty, 1996). Thus, even before the contrast effect reported here (Clement et al., 2000) was added to the list, contrast effects stubbornly resisted a comprehensive explanation.

Procedurally, the contrast effect reported by Clement et al. (2000) appears to be most similar to that involved in anticipatory contrast (Flaherty, 1982), because, in each case, there is a series of paired events, the second of which is better than the first. High effort is followed by discriminative stimuli in the case of the Clement et al. procedure, and a low concentration of saccharin is followed by a higher concentration of sucrose in the case of anticipatory contrast. However, the effect reported by Clement et al. is seen in a choice response made in the presence of the second event (i.e., preference for one S+ over the other) rather than the first (i.e., differential consumption of the saccharin solution).

Alternatively, although successive incentive contrast and the contrast effect reported by Clement et al. (2000) both involve a change in behavior during the second component of the task, the mechanisms responsible for these effects must be quite different. In the case of the Clement et al. procedure, the pigeons experienced the two-event sequences many hundreds of times prior to test and thus, they certainly could have learned to anticipate the appearance of the discriminative stimuli and the reinforcers that followed. However, in the case of successive incentive contrast, the second component of the task could not be anticipated.

The temporal relations involved in the within-trial contrast effect reported by Clement et al. (2000) would seem more closely related to those that have been referred to as local contrast (Terrace, 1966). As already noted, local contrast refers to the temporary change in response rate that occurs following a stimulus change that signals a change in reinforcement schedule. But, local contrast effects tend to occur early in training and they generally disappear with extended training. Furthermore, if local contrast were responsible for the contrast effect reported by Clement et al., then a higher response rate should have been found to the positive stimulus that followed the higher-effort response than to the positive stimulus that followed the lower-effort response. But, differences in response *rate* were not found, only differences in *choice*.

Thus, the form of contrast that is characteristic of the research described in this chapter appears to be different from the various contrast effects that have been described in the literature. First, it is a within-subject effect that is measured as a preference score. Second, in a conceptual sense, it is the reverse of what one might expect based on more typical contrast effects. Typically, a relatively aversive event (e.g., delay to reinforcement) is judged to be more aversive (as measured by increased latency of response or decreased choice) when it occurs in the context of a less-aversive event that occurs on alternative trials (i.e., it is a between-trials effect). The contrast effect described here is assumed to occur within trials and the effect is to make the events that follow the relatively aversive event more preferred than similar events that follow less-aversive events. Thus, referring to this effect as a contrast effect is descriptive, but it is really quite different from the contrast effects described by Flaherty (1996).

RELATED PHENOMENA

Contrafreeloading

A form of contrast that is similar to that found in the present experiment may be operating in the case of the contrafreeloading effect (e.g., Carder & Berkowitz, 1970; Jensen, 1963; Neuringer, 1969). Pigeons trained to peck a lit response key for food will often obtain food by pecking the key even when they are presented with a dish of "free" food. Although it is possible that other factors contribute to the contrafreeloading effect (e.g., reduced familiarity with the free food in the context of the operant chamber [Taylor, 1975] or perhaps preference for small portions of food spaced over time), it is also possible that the pigeons value the food obtained following the effort of key pecking more than the free food; if the effort required is relatively small, then the added value of food for which they have to work may at times be greater than the cost of the effort required to obtain it.

Justification of Effort

As mentioned earlier, justification of effort in humans has been attributed to the discrepancy between one's beliefs and one's behavior (Aronson & Mills, 1959). The present research suggests that contrast may be a more parsimonious interpretation of this effect not only in pigeons but also perhaps in humans. In fact, the present results may have implications for a number of related phenomena that have been studied in humans.

The term *work ethic* has been used in the human literature to describe a value or a trait that varies among members of a population as an individual difference (e.g., Greenberg, 1977). But, it also can be thought of as a typically human characteristic that appears to be in conflict with traditional learning theory (Hull, 1943). Work (effort) is generally viewed as at least somewhat aversive and as behavior to be reduced, especially if less-effortful alternatives are provided to obtain reward. Other things being equal, less work should be preferred to more work—and in general, it is. Yet, it is also the case that work, per se, is often valued in our culture. Students are often praised for their effort independent of their success. Furthermore, the judged value of a reward may depend on the effort that preceded it. For example, students generally value a high grade that they have received in a course not only for its absolute value but also in proportion to the effort required to obtain it. Consider the greater pride that a student might feel about an A grade in organic chemistry compared with a similar A grade in a physical education class (say, bowling).

Although, in the case of such human examples, cultural factors, including social rewards, may be implicated, a more fundamental, nonsocial mechanism may also be involved. In the absence of social factors, it generally may be the case (as in the research presented here) that the contrast between the hedonic state of the individual immediately prior to reward and at the time of reward may be greater following greater effort than following lesser effort. Contrast effects of the kind found in the present research may also be implicated in other social psychological phenomena.

Cognitive Dissonance Revisited

When humans experience a tedious task, their evaluation of the aversiveness of the task is sometimes negatively correlated with the size of the reward that is provided for agreeing to describe the task to others as pleasurable (Festinger & Carlsmith, 1959). As discussed before, the explanation that has been given for the cognitive dissonance effect is that the conflict between attitude (the task was tedious) and behavior (participants had agreed to describe the task to another person as enjoyable) was more easily resolved when a large reward was given ("I did it for the large reward") and, thus, a more honest evaluation of the task could be provided.

However, in light of the results of the pigeon experiments presented here, one could also view the contrast between effort and reward to be greater in the large reward condition than in the small reward condition. Thus, the subjective aversiveness of the prior task might be judged to be greater (negative contrast) when it is followed by the larger reward than when it is followed by the smaller reward. That is, the relative change in value from the aversive task to the larger reward may be deemed to be greater than the relative change in value from the aversive task to the smaller reward.

Intrinsic Versus Extrinsic Reinforcement

Contrast effects of the kind reported here may also be responsible for the well-known capacity of extrinsic reinforcement to reduce intrinsic motivation (Deci, 1975; but see also Eisenberger & Cameron, 1996). If rewards are given for activities that may be intrinsically rewarding (e.g., puzzle solving), then providing extrinsic rewards for such an activity may lead to a subsequent reduction in that behavior when extrinsic rewards are no longer provided. This effect has been interpreted as a shift in self-determination or locus of control (Deci & Ryan, 1985; Lepper, 1981).

But, such effects can also be viewed as examples of contrast. In this case, it may be the contrast between extrinsic reinforcement and its sudden removal that is at least partly responsible for the decline in performance (Flora, 1990). Such contrast effects are likely to be quite different from those responsible for the results of the within-trial contrast experiments, however, because the removal of extrinsic reinforcement results in a change in actual reward value, relative to the reward value that is expected (i.e., the shift from a combination of both extrinsic and intrinsic reward to intrinsic reward alone). Thus, the effect of extrinsic reinforcement on intrinsic motivation is probably more similar to incentive contrast due to reward shifts of the kind reported by Crespi (1942, i.e., rats run slower after they have been shifted from a large to a small magnitude of reward than rats that have always experienced the small magnitude of reward).

Learned Industriousness

Finally, contrast effects may also be involved in a somewhat different phenomenon that Eisenberger (1992) has called learned industriousness. If one is rewarded for putting a large amount of effort (rather than a small amount of effort) into a task, then it may increase one's general readiness to expend effort in other goal-directed tasks. Eisenberger has attributed this effect to the conditioned reward value of effort, a reasonable explanation for the phenomenon, but contrast may also be involved.

The contrast explanation is as follows: If the original task is difficult and the second task is also difficult, there should be little contrast between the two tasks. However, if the original task is easy and the second task is difficult, there should be negative contrast between the originally easy task and the second task; the negative contrast should result in a decrease in persistence. Alternatively, if the original task is easy and the second task is also easy, there should be little contrast between the two tasks. However, if the original task is difficult and the second task is easy, there should be positive contrast between the originally difficult task and the later easy task; that positive contrast should result in an increase in persistence. Thus, in either case, a contrast interpretation of these data suggests that pretraining on a difficult task should result in better transfer than pretraining on an easy task.

CONCLUSIONS

From the preceding discussion, it should be clear that contrast effects of the kind reported here in pigeons may contribute to a number of experimental findings that have been reported with humans but that traditionally have been explained using more complex cognitive and social accounts. Further examination of these phenomena from the perspective of simpler contrast effects may lead to more parsimonious explanations of what have previously been interpreted to be uniquely human phenomena.

Of course, even if contrast is involved in these more complex phenomena, it does not rule out the additional involvement of more cognitive factors, of the type originally proposed. It would be informative, however, to determine the extent to which contrast effects contribute to these phenomena.

Finally, our description of the various complex social phenomena as possible examples of contrast may give the mistaken impression that such effects are simple and are well understood. As prevalent as contrast effects appear to be, the mechanisms that account for them remain quite speculative. Consider the prevalence of the opposite effect, generalization, in which experience in one context (or with one stimulus value) spreads to other contexts (or stimulus values) in direct proportion to their similarity (Hull, 1943). According to a generalization account, generalization between values of reinforcement should tend to make the values more similar to each other, rather than more different. An important goal of future research should be to identify the conditions that produce contrast and differentiate them from those than produce generalization.

Whatever mechanisms are found to distinguish contrast from generalization effects, the contrast effects imply a form of relational learning that cannot easily be accounted for by means of traditional behavioral theories. That is, the large body of research on contrast suggests that the value of a reinforcer depends not only on its absolute value compared with the value of other available reinforcers but also on the relative state of the organism immediately preceding that reinforcer. This is not a radical idea. For example, food is certainly more valued if it is preceded by greater rather than lesser hunger. What is perhaps surprising, however, is the implication from our research that if a particular food A is always presented at a time of greater hunger and a different food B is always presented at a time of lesser hunger, then given a choice between the two different kinds of food, A should be preferred over B, regardless of the level of hunger of the animal at the time of that choice. This prediction has yet to be tested.

Acknowledgments The research reported in this chapter was supported by Grants MH59194 and MH63726 from the National Institute of Mental Health.

References

Akins, C. K., & Zentall, T. R. (1996). Imitative learning in male Japanese quail (*Coturnix japonica*) involving the two-action method. *Journal of Comparative Psychology, 110*, 316–320.

Akins, C. K., & Zentall, T. R. (1998). Imitation in Japanese quail: The role of reinforcement of demonstrator responding. *Psychonomic Bulletin & Review, 5*, 694–697.

Amsel, A. (1958). The role of frustrative nonreward in noncontinuous reward situations. *Psychological Bulletin, 55*, 102–119.

Aronson, E., & Mills, J. (1959). The effect of severity of initiation on liking for a group. *Journal of Abnormal and Social Psychology, 59*, 177–181.

Boice, R. (1973). Domestication. *Psychological Bulletin, 80*, 215–230.

Bower, G. H. (1961). A contrast effect in differential conditioning. *Journal of Experimental Psychology, 62*, 196–199.

Carder, B., & Berkowitz, K. (1970). Rats preference for earned in comparison with free food. *Science, 167*, 1273–1274.

Capaldi, E. J. (1967). A sequential hypothesis of instrumental learning. In K. W. Spence & J. T. Spence (Eds.), *The psychology of learning and motivation* (Vol. 1, pp. 67–156). New York: Academic Press.

Cleary, T. L. (1992). The relationship of local to overall behavioral contrast. *Bulletin of the Psychonomic Society, 30*, 58–60.

Clement, T. S., Feltus, J., Kaiser, D. H., & Zentall, T. R. (2000). "Work ethic" in pigeons: Reward value is directly related to the effort or time required to obtain the reward *Psychonomic Bulletin & Review, 7*, 100–106.

Clement, T. S., & Zentall, T. R (2002). Second-order contrast based on the expectation of effort and reinforcement. *Journal of Experimental Psychology: Animal Behavior Processes, 28*, 64–74.

Crespi, L. P. (1942). Quantitative variation in incentive and performance in the white rat. *American Journal of Psychology, 40*, 467–517.

Deci, E. (1975). *Intrinsic motivation*. New York: Plenum.

Deci, E., & Ryan, R. M. (1985). *Intrinsic motivation and self-determination in human behavior*. New York: Plenum Press.

DiGian, K. A., Friedrich, A. M., & Zentall, T. R. (2004). Reinforcers that follow a delay have added value for pigeons. *Psychonomic Bulletin & Review, 11*, 889–895.

Eisenberger, R. (1992). Learned industriousness. *Psychological Review, 99*, 248–267.

Eisenberger, R., & Cameron, J. (1996). Detrimental effects of reward. *American Psychologist, 51*, 1153–1166.

Fantino, E., & Abarca, N. (1985). Choice, optimal foraging, and the delay-reduction hypothesis. *Behavioral and Brain Sciences, 8*, 315–330.

Festinger, L. (1957). *A theory of cognitive dissonance*. Stanford, CA: Stanford University Press.

Festinger L., & Carlsmith, J. M. (1959). Cognitive consequences of forced compliance. *Journal of Abnormal and Social Psychology. 58*, 203–210.

Flaherty, C. F. (1982). Incentive contrast. A review of behavioral changes following shifts in reward. *Animal Learning & Behavior, 10*, 409–440.

Flaherty, C. F. (1996). *Incentive relativity*. New York: Cambridge University Press.

Flora, S. R. (1990). Undermining intrinsic interest from the standpoint of a behaviorist. *Psychological Record, 40*, 323–346.

Friedrich, A. M., & Zentall, T. R. (2004). Pigeons shift their preference toward locations of food that take more effort to obtain. *Behavioural Processes, 67*, 405–415.

Friedrich, A. M., Clement, T. S., & Zentall, T. R. (2005). Functional equivalence in pigeons involving a four-member class. *Behavioural Processes, 33*, 337–342.

Gallese, V., Fadiga, L., Fogassi, L., & Rizzolatti, G. (1996). Action recognition in the premotor cortex. *Brain, 119*, 593–609.

Greenberg, J. (1977). The Protestant work ethic and reactions to negative performance evaluations on a laboratory task. *Journal of Applied Psychology, 62*, 682–690.

Halliday, M. S., & Boakes, R. A. (1971). Behavioral contrast and response independent reinforcement. *Journal of the Experimental Analysis of Behavior, 16*, 429–434.

Hull, C. L. (1943). *Principles of behavior*. New York: Appleton-Century-Crofts.

Jensen, G. D. (1963). Preference of bar pressing over "freeloading" as a function of number of rewarded presses. *Journal of Experimental Psychology, 65*, 451–454.

Keller, K. (1974). The role of elicited responding in behavioral contrast. *Journal of the Experimental Analysis of Behavior, 21*, 249–257.

Lawrence, D. H., & Festinger, L. (1962). *Deterrents and reinforcement: The psychology of insufficient reward*. Stanford, CA: Stanford University Press.

Lepper, M. R. (1981). Intrinsic and extrinsic motivation in children: Detrimental effects of superfluous social controls. In W. A. Collins (Ed.), *Aspects of the development of competence: The Minnesota Symposium on Child*

Psychology (Vol. 14, pp. 155–214). Hillsdale, NJ: Lawrence Erlbaum.

Mackintosh, N. J. (1974) *The psychology of animal learning*. London: Academic Press.

Mackintosh, N. J., Little, L., & Lord, J. (1972). Some determinants of behavioral contrast in pigeons and rats. *Learning and Motivation, 3*, 148–161.

Mellgren, R. L. (1972). Positive and negative contrast effects using delayed reinforcement. *Learning and Motivation, 3*, 185–193.

Meltzoff, A. N. (1988). The human infant as *homo imitans*. In T. R. Zentall & B. G. Galef, Jr. (Eds.), *Social learning; Psychological and biological perspectives* (pp. 319–341). Hillsdale, NJ: Lawrence Erlbaum.

Mitchell, R. W. (2002). Kinesthetic-visual matching, imitation, and self-recognition. In M. Bekoff, C. Allen, & G. M. Burghardt (Eds.), *The cognitive animal* (pp. 345–351). Cambridge, MA: MIT Press.

Neuringer, A. J. (1969). Animals respond for food in the presence of free food. *Science, 166*, 399–401.

Piaget, J. (1962). *Play, dreams, and imitation in childhood*. New York: Norton.

Reynolds, R. S. (1961). Behavioral contrast. *Journal of the Experimental Analysis of Behavior, 4*, 57–71.

Taylor, G. T. (1975). Discriminability and the contrafreeloading phenomenon. *Journal of Comparative and Physiological Psychology, 88*, 104–109.

Terrace, H. S. (1966). Stimulus control. In W. K. Honig (Ed.), *Operant behavior: Areas of research and application*. New York: Appleton-Century-Crofts.

Tinklepaugh, O. L. (1928). An experiment study of representative factors in monkeys. *Journal of Comparative Psychology*, 8, 197–236.

Williams, B. A. (1981). The following schedule of reinforcement as a fundamental determinant of steady state contrast in multiple schedules. *Journal of the Experimental Analysis of Behavior, 35*, 293–310.

Williams, B. A. (1983). Another look at contrast in multiple schedules. *Journal of the Experimental Analysis of Behavior, 39*, 345–384.

Williams, B. A. (1992). Inverse relations between preference and contrast. *Journal of the Experimental Analysis of Behavior, 58*, 303–312.

Williams, B. A., & Wixted, J. T. (1986). An equation for behavioral contrast. *Journal of the Experimental Analysis of Behavior, 45*, 47–62.

Zentall, T. R., Sutton, J. E., & Sherburne, L. M. (1996). True imitative learning in pigeons. *Psychological Science, 7*, 343–346.

Postscript: An Essay on the Study of Cognition in Animals

STEWART H. HULSE

Let me say at the outset that I write this essay from a very personal perspective; those looking for annotated comments concerning facts and theories in animal learning and cognition will not find many of them here. Instead, I want to take a glance backward through my own experiences—and to make some guesses about what the years ahead may bring. The present day speaks clearly and well for itself—in particular through the earlier chapters in this book—although I will venture a few words about the current scene in due course.[1]

SOME HISTORY

Early Events

To set the stage for the appearance of the experimental study of animal cognition in the 1970s, let us go back a few decades to sketch the scene from which the new enterprise emerged. When I started graduate work at Brown University in 1953, I found the experimental psychology of learning to be rampantly behavioristic and expressed almost exclusively in S-R terms of stimulus-response association. This situation was true for experiments and theories aimed at both human and nonhuman behavior. My textbooks were, for example, Skinner's *The Behavior of Organisms* (1938) and some of his other contemporary books and papers, Hull's *Principles of Behavior* (1943) and *A Behavior System* (1952), and Hilgard's *Theories of Learning* (1956)—in an up-to-date second edition. Then, there were Spence's *Behavior Theory and Conditioning* (1956), Hilgard and Marquis's *Conditioning and Learning* (1940), and Tolman's *Purposive Behavior in Animals and Men* (1932).

Of course, there were many papers by these men (few women!) and others, but all were cast in the mold of strict definition by operations: that is, concepts were defined by the procedures (operations) used to study them. Furthermore, Behaviorism (with a capital B), and the philosophy of logical positivism (borrowed from the Vienna Circle of philosophers by way of physics) that lay behind it, were legitimate topics for discussion in the psychological literature. Thus, for example, Kenneth Spence (e.g., 1944) published papers on the philosophy of logical positivism and its application to experimental psychology in general. So did Skinner. And, for a specific instance, Garner, Hake, and Eriksen (1956) wrote an elegant discussion of the application of operational principles to the study of perception (the paper is still very much worth reading).

Tolman's work deserves a special comment because of some of the language that he used. Take his book, *Purposive Behavior in Animals and Men* (1932), for example. Tolman said behavior reeked of purpose. What? *Purpose*? By the attitudes of the day (at universities such as Brown, Yale, or Harvard on the East Coast, anyway—compared with Berkeley on the West Coast), *purpose* was a tainted word for a concept that was impossible to define or to measure in operational terms. This appraisal, of course, was unfair. Tolman and his colleagues at Berkeley did experiments that were just as strictly operational in their execution and interpretation as those done elsewhere. But, his choice of terms like *purpose, goals, means-ends readiness,* and the like smacked of forbidden, unseen (and unseeable) processes that begged definition. Perhaps Tolman wrote with tongue in cheek (maybe not!), but that passed right over the heads of those of us who should have known better. After all, California was a long way from New England in those days—both in distance and in time and expense to communicate. But Tolman's work presaged many things that are now at least a part of comparative cognition (what? *cognition*!?) as we know it today.

I want to move now to some parts of the study of animal learning that were notable for their absence well into the 1960s. I mention them here because, in my judgment, they had substantial impact on the later development of comparative cognition.

Memory

Remarkably, the word *memory* does not appear in either the text or the index of Hull's *Principles of Behavior* (1943) nor does it appear in the text or index of Skinner's *The Behavior of Organisms* (1938). The term is hard to find in articles on animal learning in either the *Journal of Comparative and Physiological Psychology* or the *Journal of Experimental Psychology* before and throughout the 1950s and into the 1960s. In fairness, memory was, of course, part of the lexicon and the curriculum in experimental psychology, and it was a subject of study since the time of Ebbinghaus (1885). But, the studies (e.g., the prolific work of B. J. Underwood and others in the 1950s) were couched, as usual, in the language of stimulus, response, and associative learning—and no one at all was addressing the issue from a comparative perspective. Today, it is hard to imagine a discussion of either animal or human behavior without the concept of memory playing a paramount role. But in the 1930s, 1940s, and 1950s, memory as such was not assigned a role in the comprehensive theoretical approaches to behavior of the day; indeed, Hull did not choose to treat memory as part of the theorems and postulates of his behavior system.

Interestingly, there was one notable person who speculated about the physiological and theoretical underpinnings of memory (and purpose, too!), and that was D. O. Hebb, whose book, *The Organization of Behavior* (1949) treated both concepts, although not at length. It is ironic, perhaps, that Hebb's contributions have had far greater impact on modern-day experimental psychology and neuroscience, in my opinion, than most of the books on learning and behavior of the time (Skinner's work is an important exception).

Ethology

Ethology and the study of behavior in natural settings was mostly ignored prior to the 1960s in American experimental psychology—certainly in the psychology to which I was exposed at Brown.[2] My only exposures as a student to ethology (my teachers and the *Zeitgeist* in America encouraged me no further) were, first, a colloquium given to the Psychology Department by William Verplanck (in 1952, I think) who had just returned from spending some time with ethologists in England, and, second, a lecture by Nikolaas Tinbergen—presented in the Biology Department, of course. Most of us, at our peril and to our subsequent misfortune, had begun to neglect Tinbergen's lecture by the time we returned to the psychology laboratories. We had no S-R hooks on which to hang his message. It is ironic, to say the least, that Lorenz and Tinbergen (along with Karl Von Frisch) were to win the Nobel Prize in 1973 for their work in ethology, or, as the Nobel committee put it in its citation, "for their discoveries concerning organization and elicitation of individual and social behaviour patterns."

It was not until the late 1960s and early 1970s that the ethological approach had much impact on the study of animal learning and comparative cognition in America. As a matter of fact, the first laboratory experiments on imprinting in this country, so far as I can tell, were done in 1956 with neonate chicks by Julian Jaynes at Yale University as his doctoral dissertation (e.g., Jaynes, 1956). The work was innovative and brilliant in my judgment, but it had little contemporary influence on either animal learning in America or ethology in Europe.

HARBINGERS OF COMPARATIVE COGNITION

Although the experimental psychology of animal learning was content to enter the 1960s with the theories and experimental approaches of behavioral psychology and S-R associationism, there were events in human learning and memory that were eventually to find their way into the study of animal learning. These events were to lead to the first hints of a science of comparative cognition in the late 1960s and 1970s.

Lashley and the Problem of Serial Order in Behavior

In my view, one of the most important papers ever published in psychology was Lashley's contribution to the published proceedings of the Hixon Conference at Princeton University, "The Problem of Serial Order in Behavior" (Lashley, 1951). In that paper, Lashley provided a concise description of the shortcomings of associative stimulus-response chains as a model for many aspects of human behavior.

There are two of his observations that are relevant here. First, he described how skilled serial movements, such as those of a concert pianist, could never be described by the then-current S-R models based on feedback from successive movements; there simply was not time for physiological feedback from one finger movement to modulate the production of the next. Instead, Lashley proposed that such complicated skills as the playing of a multinote arpeggio must rely on the afferent outflow of some preprogrammed central representation of the entire motor sequence. Upon this representation, there could then be others stacked in *hierarchical* fashion to produce the more complicated serial structure of an entire musical composition. For those wedded to linear, associative S-R approaches, this idea was heresy; most chose to ignore it. Not so for others who were beginning an interest in the psychology of language.

Lashley's second major contribution, akin to the first, was that language production defied the principles of S-R chains. To illustrate this point, he gives an example based on the use of the word "right" in a sentence. He says, and I quote (and paraphrase slightly), "The word right, for example, is noun, adjective, adverb and verb and has four spellings and at least ten meanings. In such a sentence 'The millwright on my right thinks that some conventional rite . . . symbolizes the right of every man to write as he pleases,' [. . . the proper . . .] arrangement is obviously not due to any direct association of the word *right* itself to other words but to meanings which are determined by some broader relations. . . ." "From such considerations, it is certain that any grammatical form which ascribes [. . . the arrangement . . .] to associative linkage of the words of the sentence overlooks the essential structure of speech. . . . The order is imposed by some other agent."[3]

As I have said elsewhere (Hulse, 2002), Lashley discusses virtually every topic that might appear in a book on comparative cognition—not only the problem of serial order, but also timing and temporal coordination, spatial organization, and the numerous ways in which we remember and recall information. His article remains seminal.

If Lashley's work helped mark the beginnings of modern linguistics and our contemporary understanding of language in both psychological and linguistic terms, then the appearance of Chomsky's work in the 1960s further secured the coffin of a purely associative approach to the structure of language. For an example of this work, see Chomsky (1957, 1965) and his review of Skinner's attempt to treat language in behavioral terms (Chomsky, 1959; Skinner, 1957).

The Computer Metaphor

The first hints of what we now call cognitive psychology began to appear in the late 1950s and early 1960s with the introduction of the digital computer as a model for psychological processes. Miller, Galanter, and Pribram were among the first psychologists to write on the topic with their publication of *Plans and the Structure of Behavior* in 1960. In that book, they conceived of human plans for action as a simple computer program. Their idea was that human action could be expressed in formal, logical *representations* of information. Thus began the use of the digital computer as a metaphor for human behavior. We now have *memory, storage, information processing, retrieval, attention*, and so on, as everyday parts of our psychological lexicon. In 1960, however, these terms and the ideas behind them were simply not part of animal learning.

The Demise of Responses as Arbitrary Events

For Skinner and others, responses were events that could be *arbitrarily* selected for instrumental (or operant) conditioning. It didn't matter whether the rat pressed the lever with its nose, its paws, or (on one occasion that I observed) its rear end. All these responses were functionally equivalent in that they got the lever pressed; each was presumed to be as typical of a Response (with a capital R) as any other.

Near the end of the 1960s, however, ethology and the idea that behavior was sometimes *not* arbitrarily selected began to have an impact on the study of animal learning in America. Among the first work was that of Garcia and his associates (e.g., Garcia & Koelling, 1966) on the specificity of cue to consequence, Bolles's (1970) idea of species-specific defense reactions, Seligman's (1970) rather circular idea of response preparedness as measured by the facility with which a certain type of response could be learned, Hinde and Stevenson-Hinde's (1973) notion of ethologically-based constraints on learning, and so on.

I think one of the major results of this work was to make us realize, on the one hand, that behavior was tied to a biological system that had evolved uniquely for the functional needs of each species, and that in the natural world some responses were *not* as effective as others in getting the job done. On the other hand, I think these discoveries and insights helped to free animal learning from the constraints of the behavioral tradition with its dogma of stimulus-response association, thus opening the way for us to contemplate alternative pathways for studying animal learning and behavior.

The Rise of Representation

One of the major legacies of the computer-as-metaphor revolution in the 1960s was the idea that behavior could be *represented* by systems that were not directly observable. Terms such as *image*, *attention*, even *memory* began to enter the lexicon of what was now called cognitive psychology. These terms were reflected in representational systems—often computer programs—and cognitive psychology became the study of the processes that worked on the representations. Once again, theorizing about human behavior had set the stage for important changes in the study of animal learning.

GLIMMERINGS

It would be a mistake to assume that animal cognition arose—de novo—from the events of the 1950s and 1960s. The idea of animal "mind" had been around since Darwin's time. Plus, there was a continuous debate over whether or not animals had minds, and if so, the manner in which "mind" was expressed in what animals could do. Similarly, there was debate over whether or not animals had "consciousness," and how that, too, might be expressed. In my view, the great contributions of behaviorism were (a) to see how far we could go in explaining behavior *without* the concepts of mind and consciousness and (b) to develop the behavioral tools and theory to do so.[4]

Memory

As I observed earlier, memory as a concept was notable in the study of animal learning mostly for its absence as either an everyday concept or something to study experimentally. Perhaps the first glimmers of animal cognition as we know it today were initial studies on animals' ability to remember things. Again, there were a few historical antecedents, notable in their own right, but not part of the *Zeitgeist* at the time. Walter Hunter's (1912) famous experiment on the delayed reaction in the early part of the twentieth century is a case in point. In order to solve a discrimination problem after a delay, the animal had to retain some representation of the items to be acted on after the delay. So is the example of Harlow's work on *learning sets* in the late 1940s and early 1950s. Here, representations (memories) of individual discrimination problems became combined into a single, organized memory—a categorical representation, if you will—that encoded features common to each of the individual problems. To be sure, Harlow (e.g., 1949) did not use this terminology (notice that he spoke of sets to learn, not to remember), but his experiments and others like them are easily interpreted this way.

But it was not until the late 1960s and early 1970s that the experimental study of memory in animals really began in earnest. One of the techniques that became widely used was that of delayed matching to sample. Here, you will recall, a stimulus is presented to an animal during an observation period, and later the initial stimulus, together with a comparison are presented simultaneously. The animal gains reward only by responding to the sample stimulus that was presented earlier. The variable of interest is the length of the delay period between presentation of the sample and presentation of the comparisons.

Werner Honig, Michael D'Amato, and William Roberts, among many others, researched this paradigm vigorously. One of the early consequences of this endeavor was the first (to my knowledge) conference on animal memory held at Dalhousie University in 1969. The book that resulted from that conference (Honig & James, 1971) was the first that really dealt with memory as representation and as such marks the true beginning of the study of animal cognition.

Developments

Through the 1970s, the field of comparative cognition began to plant deep roots. As evidence of this growth, consider some volumes that appeared during the decade. Medin, Roberts, and Davis published *Processes of Animal Memory* in 1976. Premack (1976) published *Intelligence in Ape and Man* in the same year. I, together with Harry Fowler and Werner Honig, published *Cognitive Processes in Animal Behavior* in 1978. With both pride and humility, I think we were the first actually to use the term *cognitive* in a title for a book reporting experimental work with animals. In the early 1980s, Roitblat, Bever, and Terrace (1984) published a large book (based on a conference at Columbia University) entitled *Animal Cognition* that contained chapters by the leaders in the new field.

And so it goes. I recently checked the Eisenhower Library book holdings at Johns Hopkins using the keywords *animal cognition*. The search generated 80 titles, the newest published in 2004. Without doubt, animal cognition is very much a part of the current scene in experimental psychology (and in parts of biology, evolutionary psychology, and ethology).

What Has Happened to S-R Associationism and Skinner's Behavioral Psychology?

A complete answer to the question of what has happened to S-R associationism and Skinner's behavioral psychology would no doubt require many essays, if not books. But I would like to make a few personal observations.

First, current studies of association as expressed in the language of Pavlovian conditioning are numerous and continue to make significant contributions to knowledge. Robert Rescorla, Allan Wagner, N. R. Mackintosh, John Pearce, and Peter Holland (now at Johns Hopkins, I'm delighted to say), among many others, both defined the modern field in the 1970s and continue to develop it today. There is no doubt that the study of simple associations (which are not so simple at all!) remains a fruitful and important enterprise. That is true not only for the information gained about associative learning per se but more recently because the associative model and the knowledge we have acquired about it in the last 30 years or so provide important tools for studying the mediation of learning and memory by the central nervous system. Besides, representation, memory, and the retrieval of memory remain important topics; they certainly fall within the general realm of cognitive processes.

I believe that Skinner's continuing influence lies not so much in the experimental analysis of behavior that was so important in the 1950s and 1960s, but rather in the practical application of behavioral control. Let me quote from the last sentence of *The Behavior of Organisms* (1938): "We must cast our lot with a non-statistical investigation of the individual and achieve whatever degree of reliability or reproducibility we may through the techniques of measurement and control" (p. 444).

Skinner was drawing a contrast between the statistical approach to the study of behavior in which one uses research to describe the behavior of groups of individuals in terms of measures of central tendency and variability, and the study of behavior in which one examines the variables that control behavior, one individual at a time. This single-organism approach has proven to be very powerful, especially in arenas where the goal is to help individuals manage themselves (e.g., in institutional settings where feedback, shaping, tokens, and so on, are important therapeutic tools). The approach that Skinner espoused has even contributed to our everyday lexicon. For example, although I did not use the term in raising my own children (not many did so then), my grandchildren are very familiar with "time out" for bad behavior; they are not alone, I'm sure. In any case, I suspect that few recognize that the term was originally used in the study of pigeon behavior at Harvard.

COMPARATIVE COGNITION TODAY

I started this essay with the observation that this book defines, per se, the current scene in comparative cognition as well as anything could. However, I want to make a few observations that may be handy.

Cognitive Processes in 1978 and in 2005

First, I think that the main contribution of animal cognition as it appeared in the 1970s was to legitimize certain topics for experimental study with nonhuman animals, and second to develop the techniques to do so. To illustrate this idea, let us compare the topics that were covered by the contributors to Hulse, Fowler, and Honig (1978) with those that are covered here. In 1978, the 14 chapters in Hulse, Fowler, and Honig touched on the following general topics using either rats or pigeons as subjects: representations and expectancies in Pavlovian conditioning, avoidance learning (especially cue-to-consequence effects), working and spatial memory, "surprise" in Pavlovian blocking, selective attention, timing, and serial learning. One chapter touched on nonhuman primate behavior: cognitive mapping in chimpanzees. A final chapter discussed the abstractness of human concepts and how that idea impinges potentially on a search for abstract concepts in nonhuman behavior; comparisons were made between the capacities of pigeons, nonhuman primates, and dolphins. Premack (who wrote the last chapter) could have talked about "language" in nonhuman primates, but he did not, at least directly. In fact, nonhuman primates were noteworthy for their limited appearance on stage—the platform was dominated mostly by rats and pigeons.

By 2005, approximately a quarter century later, the present book contains chapters covering the following topics (broadly defined): perceptual grouping; visual illusions, visual and spatial cognition; pitch perception; reaction time; search images and attention; spatial learning and mapping as used per se and in foraging; spatial, prospective, and retrospective memory, and memory for lists in both the auditory and visual domain. Then there is timing and the interaction of time and event/place learning; numerical ability; categorization and conceptualization (in many forms); sequential learning; tool use; cognitive development, and "intelligence" more generally defined. The field has certainly expanded!

Similarly, let us look at the species studied. They include the usual suspects, pigeons and rats, but also rhesus monkeys, capuchin monkeys, baboons, chickens, several species of songbirds (including scrub jays, ravens, crows, and chickadees), honeybees, humans, chimpanzees, dolphins, and quail (I hope I haven't missed any!). So, we have primates, both human and nonhuman, birds of several taxa, insects, and rodents; this contingent represents a substantial expansion of the animals studied since the 1970s.

What generalizations can we draw from these facts? First, the range of topics that are now included in the study of comparative cognition has broadened substantially. I am particularly impressed by the sensory and perceptual processes that are under scrutiny when they were not before, by the various guises in which research on memory now appears, by the growing body of literature concerning how animals find their way in the world through maps, landmarks, and the like, and by the various forms of research on concept and category formation.

The study of language or language-like behavior in nonhuman animals is not a major part of the discussion in this book, although several chapters do touch on the subject. My impression of this literature is that it has taught us more about human language than animal "language" in the sense that we have learned what people can do that animals cannot. But, maybe we have mined the best of what was to be learned about the topic and moved on.

In any case, it is clear that comparative cognition is alive and well today, attracting new students, and enjoying increasing international interest. What of the future?

COMPARATIVE COGNITION TOMORROW

In this section I want to speculate. That is an enterprise, of course, that is fraught with hazard because there is a good chance that some of my speculations (I hope not all!) will be wrong. But, prognostication can be useful, so I am going to take the plunge. I will take credit for any wisdom that proves prophetic in the times ahead; please indulge me any mistakes.

Will We Have a Truly Comparative Cognition?

In the previous section, I noted that the species that were studied in the 1970s were very limited in number, a fact that was first lamented by Frank Beach (1950) decades before the 1970s ever arrived. Substantial progress has been made in the last quarter century, as I also noted. But there is still room to grow.

I believe that it is especially important to emphasize an ethological tradition in choosing both species, topics, and experimental paradigms as we plan our research. That is why I lamented early on in my remarks about the relative absence of ethological influences in American studies of animal learning. My comment here is also in the spirit of the recent emphasis on evolutionary psychology and on the perspective that an evolutionary approach has to offer.

For example, with a few important exceptions, we rarely choose species as a *tool* in our experimentation. Sara Shettleworth has adopted this technique in some important work of her own (well summarized in her 1998 book), and several of the authors in the present book have also used this tool to good effect. For example, we can learn interesting things when we compare the behavior of closely related species on some common task, such as the food-storing ability of corvid birds. That is especially so when we are interested in the neurological substrate of the behavior in question.

In a related sense, we rarely—as experimentalists—select a species for its own sake and then work out methods to study whatever cognitive capacities that species may possess. We are still overly wedded, in my opinion, to a general-process theory of learning in which we cling to the faith that there are "typical" animals from which broad generalizations can be drawn about behavior in many species. We are getting better, as many of the chapters in this book demonstrate. I foresee less and less research on an existence proof, that is, whether or not a given species has the same cognitive capacity as we, or some other species, do (usually, the species is us). But, we are still stuck sometimes on an anthropocentric approach to the problems that we choose to study in nonhuman animals. Here is where ethology and a keen sensitivity to evolutionary principles can help us.

Going Into the Field

I believe that there is much to be gained by doing research on cognitive processes as they are used in animals' natural habitats—or as close to natural habitats as we can devise. Cheney and Seyfarth's (1990) field work in Africa is an excellent case in point. Although there are many obvious advantages to the controlled environment of the laboratory, who knows what we lose when we measure cognitive processes under such restricted and unnatural (for the animal) conditions? Although field work is expensive and difficult to do, we should do more of it. I think we, or our colleagues in ethology and evolutionary biology, will do so.

The Development of Cognitive Processes

It is striking how little work has been done on the *development* of cognitive processes in nonhuman animals. There is much to be learned, I think, from watching cognitively based behavior, such as memory, begin to take hold as an animal begins to grow. On the other end of the spectrum, we know little about the loss (or lack of it!) of cognitive capacity at the end of life. Developmental psychology has always been popular and important, and we should bring it into our field more than we have.

For example, what happens to the memory for food locations in food-caching birds as they age? Offhand, from a general-process point of view, we would suspect memory loss. But what if that were not so? Is food caching somehow a privileged capacity in these species such that it is highly resistant to forgetting even as the animal ages?

Applied Work

It is important to bring what we know about cognitive behavior in the abstract into situations of practical significance. Years ago, that was not so; there was something "pure" about basic research. For many, basic research was not to be sullied by bringing it to applied problems. That is certainly no longer true nor should it be.

Perhaps studies on the interaction between behavior and pharmacology provide one of the better examples. Given the surge in research on new drugs in the last decades, comparative cognition has a major role to play in the enterprise. For example, most of us who focus on behavior are distressed at the simple (if not simple-minded) use of such prosaic tasks as passive avoidance to assess the effects on behavior of psychotropic drugs. Passive avoidance tasks are cheap to develop and easy to administer, but they hardly provide a representative sample of the behavior for which the item in question may be used eventually. Comparative cognition can bring psychopharmacology the wealth of knowledge and the sophisticated techniques that can make the field far more realistic and fruitful. Besides, I am under the impression that research funds are far more readily available for applied work with animals than they are for basic research. We should go for it!

Neurobiology and Systems Neuroscience

I have two points to make here—beyond the obvious fact that neurobiology and the study of the interaction between brain and behavior are here to stay. The first is, in a way, related to what I have just had to say about the naive and rather simple-minded application of behavioral techniques in fields such as behavioral pharmacology. In commenting on this problem earlier, I had this to say (Hulse, 2002):

> I urge that instead of many complicated neurobiological manipulations measured by just one behavioral assay, we strive to use one neurobiological manipulation measured by many behavioral assays. An altered brain state creates, in effect, an entirely new animal for comparative study, and who knows how the alteration may manifest itself in behavior? (p. 16)

Psychologists and systems neuroscientists are following this tenet more and more, but it is an important thing to keep in mind.

My second point, also mentioned earlier, is the steady decline of the study of behavior for its own sake in animal psychology, in general, and in comparative cognition, in particular. I have the sense—this is certainly the case in biopsychology in my department at Johns Hopkins—that behavior is used primarily as an assay in the service of studying brain function. That is a slight overstatement, of course, but I am continually struck by how little graduate students know about the fundamentals of associative learning, for example, to say nothing of the principles of comparative cognition. Nonetheless, the brain is a fascinating structure; with the new tools that we now have to study it, it is going to remain a primary focus of attention.

I am not sure what to do about this. It is not a bad thing in principle. Students are trained to go where the funding is these days—they have to find jobs—and neuroscience is far richer at the moment than behavioral psychology, and likely to stay that way. I can certainly understand the need for training that leads to jobs, and I wish I knew how to increase funding for the study of behavior itself (but write your congressman!). Perhaps we should strive for a balance between the fields; after all, neuroscience is presumably in the service of explaining behavior, and it should better appreciate and understand what it is trying to explain. There are pendulums here, swinging back and forth in time, and it would be a pity if they did not come to rest somewhere in the middle.

Comparative Pseudo-Cognition

Since Darwin (and probably long before), we have always been fascinated by the concepts of mind and consciousness. There are some, I think, who have taken the growth of comparative cognition (as described by the topics in this book) as an opportunity to return to such fuzzy concepts. Here are some illustrative titles that I noted in Hulse (2002). I have added some others here:

The Question of Animal Awareness: Evolutionary Continuity of Mental Experience (Griffin, 1976)
How Monkeys See the World: Inside the Mind of Another Species (Cheney & Seyfarth, 1990)
Cognitive Ethology: The Minds of Other Animals: Essays in Honor of Donald R. Griffin (Ristau, 1991)
Wild Minds: What Animals Really Think (Hauser, 2000)
Animal Cognition: The Mental Lives of Animals (Wynne, 2001)
Animal Minds: Beyond Cognition to Consciousness (Griffin, 2001)

Now, in most cases, I have little question that these titles label books that describe perfectly sound and reasonable research and, once again, in most cases, perfectly sound and reasonable interpretations of that research. But, the titles are conducive—certainly as the public eye sees them—to interpretations of animal behavior that we have struggled for more than a hundred years to discredit. If behaviorism went to one extreme, then I believe these titles represent a view of comparative cognition that goes to another, a view we had best avoid. Perhaps I tilt at windmills here; I hope so.

There Be Dragons Here

Ancient mapmakers used the phrase, "there be dragons here," to describe unexplored parts of the world. That was a fair warning at the time. Today, other dragons lurk in comparative cognition, and unfortunately, the beasts are all too present in the current landscape. I refer to organizations such as People for the Ethical Treatment of Animals and a number of even more militant groups that are single-mindedly set against the use of animals for, among other things, any experimental purpose whatsoever. This whole issue is worth another essay at least, and many do exist, so I will not go further. However, as we all know, the future of our science is in jeopardy. This is especially so when we are working on problems in comparative psychology that easily lend themselves to anthropomorphic interpretations. These just ask for trouble. Fortunately, there are many organizations, such as the American Psychological Association, for example, that work diligently on behalf of science's point of view. But, this is a problem for which no clear end is in sight, and we would do well to climb the ramparts and remain dragon fighters.[5]

CONCLUSIONS

Before I began this essay, I asked the editors for some suggestions regarding the contents of a "postscript" chapter. The response was that I should describe comparative cognition as it grew over the past 25 years and then speculate what the field might look like 25 years from now. Neither I nor anyone can make valid guesses about what is going to happen to comparative psychology in the *near* future—much less 25 years from now. However, I have used my 50-year allotment by going back farther into history than the editors suggested. I thought it was necessary, and illuminating, to examine more distant roots of our field.

I also began this essay with some early personal experiences in order to describe the state of the field of animal learning as I (and many others) experienced it when we were students. Without doubt, we have all become wiser in the interim. Still, I lament that it took so long for comparative cognition to adopt some of the science that underpins it now. Behaviorism held such sway that animal psychology in America took years to return to its evolutionary roots and recognize the importance of ethology and related disciplines. Perhaps modern ethology and evolutionary ecology have benefited in return—at least from the disciplined thought about animal behavior that behaviorism required.

In any case, I see a bright future for our field, and I look forward to being part of it—maybe even for 25 years. My thanks to the editors for the chance to prepare this essay.

Notes

1. I have commented in other places on some of the ideas I discuss here, especially in a book edited by Fountain, Bunsey, Danks, and McBeath (2002). In that volume, I was especially concerned about the problem of sequential order in behavior (the topic of the conference from which the book originated), but I ventured some

thoughts about animal cognition more generally that are also relevant here. The reader will forgive me if I borrow briefly from myself on one or two occasions.

2. There were exceptions, of course, although all were couched not in ethological terms but in those of comparative psychology. N. R. F. Maier and T. C. Schneirla wrote *Principles of Animal Psychology* in 1935 from a comparative perspective. Some of us read this book. Then there was Margaret Washburn's *The Animal Mind* (which was published initially in 1908 and revised through a fourth edition in 1936). So far as I know, none of us read this one—for perhaps obvious reasons.

3. I have paraphrased some of this paragraph from Hulse (2002).

4. *Consciousness* is once again a topic for discussion and research—at least in human psychology. I would maintain that the term remains of dubious value in animal psychology. However, this is another example of psychology rediscovering old issues and looking at them afresh.

5. The dragon's breath, of course, flames over a much wider expanse of medicine and science than comparative cognition. Perhaps, too, I beat a dead reptile here.

References

Beach, F. (1950). The snark was a boojum. *American Psychologist, 5,* 115–124.

Bolles, R. C. (1970). Species-specific defense reactions and avoidance learning. *Psychological Review, 77,* 32, 48.

Cheney, D. L., & Seyfarth, R. M. (1990). *How monkeys see the world: Inside the mind of another species.* Chicago: University of Chicago Press.

Chomsky, N. (1957). *Syntactic structures.* The Hague: Mounton.

Chomsky, N. (1959). A review of B. F. Skinner's *Verbal Behavior. Language, 35,* 26–58.

Chomsky, N. (1965). *Aspects of the theory of syntax.* Cambridge, MA: MIT Press.

Ebbinghaus, H. (1885). *Über das Gedachtness.* Leipzig: Duncker and Humboldt.

Fountain, S. B., Bunsey, M. D., Danks, J. H., & McBeath, M. K. (Eds.). (2002). *Animal cognition and sequential behavior.* Norwell, MA: Kluwer Academic Publishers.

Garcia J., & Koelling, R. A. (1966). Relation of cue to consequence in avoidance learning. *Psychonomic Science, 4,* 123–124.

Garner, W. R., Hake, H. W., & Eriksen, C. W. (1956). Operationism and the concept of perception. *Psychological Review, 63,* 149–159.

Griffin, D. R. (1976). *The question of animal awareness: Evolutionary continuity of mental experience.* New York: Rockefeller University Press.

Griffin, D. R. (2001). *Animal minds: Beyond cognition to consciousness.* Chicago: University of Chicago Press.

Harlow, H. F. (1949). The formation of learning sets. *Psychological Review, 56,* 51–65.

Hauser, M. (2000). *Wild minds: What animals really think.* New York: Holt.

Hebb, D. O. (1949). *The organization of behavior: A neuropsychological theory.* New York: Wiley.

Hilgard, E. R. (1956). *Theories of learning* (2nd ed.). New York: Appleton-Century-Crofts.

Hilgard, E. R., & Marquis, D. M. (1940). *Conditioning and learning.* New York: Appleton-Century-Crofts.

Hinde, R. A., & Stevenson-Hinde, J. (Eds.) (1973). *Constraints on learning.* London: Academic Press.

Honig, W. K., & James, P. H. R. (Eds.). (1971). *Animal memory.* New York: Academic Press.

Hull, C. L. (1943). *Principles of behavior.* New York: Appleton-Century-Crofts.

Hull, C. L. (1952). *A behavior system.* New Haven: Yale University Press:

Hulse, S. H. (2002). Perspectives on comparative cognition, past, present, and future. In S. B. Fountain, M. D. Bunsey, J. H. Danks, & M. K., McBeath (Eds.), *Animal cognition and sequential behavior* (pp. 3–19). Boston: Kluwer.

Hulse, S. H., Fowler, H., & Honig, W. K. (Eds.) (1978). *Cognitive processes in animal behavior.* Hillsdale, NJ: Erlbaum.

Hunter, W. S. (1912). *Delayed reactions in animals and children.* Unpublished doctoral dissertation, University of Chicago.

Jaynes, J. (1956). Imprinting: the interaction of learned and innate behavior: I. Development and generalization. *Journal of Comparative and Physiological Psychology, 49,* 201–206.

Lashley, K. S. (1951). The problem of serial order in behavior. In L. A. Jeffress (Ed.), *Cerebral mechanisms in behavior* (pp. 112–146). New York: Wiley.

Maier, N. R. F., & Schneirla, T. C. (1935). *Principles of animal psychology.* New York: McGraw-Hill.

Medin, D. L., Roberts, W. A., & Davis, R. T. (Eds.) (1976). *Processes of animal memory.* Hillsdale, NJ: Erlbaum.

Miller, G. A., Galanter, E., & Pribram, K. (1960). *Plans and the structure of behavior.* New York: Holt, Rinehart, and Winston.

Premack, D. (1976). *Intelligence in ape and man.* Hillsdale, NJ: Erlbaum.

Ristau, C. A. (Ed.). (1991). *Cognitive ethology: The minds of other animals.* Hillsdale, NJ: Erlbaum.

Roitblat, H. L., Bever, T. G., & Terrace, H. S. (Eds.) (1984). *Animal cognition.* Hillsdale, NJ: Erlbaum.

Seligman, M. E. P. (1970). On the generality of the laws of learning. *Psychological Review, 77,* 406–418.

Shettleworth, S. (1998). *Cognition, evolution, and behavior.* New York: Oxford University Press.

Skinner, B. F. (1938). *The behavior of organisms.* New York: Appleton-Century-Crofts.

Skinner, B. F. (1957). *Verbal behavior.* New York: Appleton-Century-Crofts.

Spence, K. W. (1944). The nature of theory construction in contemporary psychology. *Psychological Review, 51,* 47–68.

Spence, K. W. (1956). *Behavior theory and conditioning.* New Haven, CT: Yale University Press.

Tolman, E. C. (1932). *Purposive behavior in animals and men.* New York: Appleton-Century-Crofts.

Washburn, M. F. (1908). *The animal mind: A textbook of comparative psychology.* New York: Macmillan.

Wynne, C. D. L. (2001). *Animal cognition: The mental lives of animals.* London: Palgrave Macmillan.

Author Index

Abarca, N., 660
Abroms, B., 151, 152
Adams-Curtis, L. E., 531, 546
Adamson, L. B., 639
Affuso, J., 429, 435
Agnetta, B., 372
Agostini, I., 546
Agrawal, N., 570
Agster, K. L., 441, 454
Ahluwalia, J., 643
Aitken, K. J., 643
Akins, C. K., 652
Albert, M., 59
Albert, M. K., 38
Albert, W. S., 222
Aldavert-Vera, L., 565
Alexander, J. R. M., 568
Alkire, M. T., 569
Allain, A. D., 590
Allan, L. G., 270, 276, 290
Allan, S. E., 92
Allen, C. K., 168
Allen, J., 49
Allen, J. A., 107–9, 113, 119
Alonso, C., 535, 547
Alonso, P. D., 565
Alsop, B., 285, 352, 626
Altman, J., 16
Altman, S. A., 16
Altmann, E., 376
Altwein, M., 192
Amelang, M., 571
Ameling, M., 557
Amsel, A., 653
Anderson, B., 556
Anderson, J., 531, 533
Anderson, J. R., 372, 375, 533, 540, 588
Anderson, K. C., 569
Anderson, L., 378
Anderson, M., 568
Andersson, M., 603, 606
Andreasen, N. C., 565
Andrew, R., 200
Andrew, R. J., 58, 66
Angarella, R., 366
Anger, D., 252
Angleitner, A., 569
Annau, Z., 445
Antinucci, F., 531, 533, 547
Antoniadis, E., 218
Antonsen, P., 190, 197
Aoki, N., 66
Arbas, E. A., 563
Arimatsu, K., 556
Armstrong, G. D., 153
Arndt, S., 565
Arnold, A. P., 628
Arolfo, M. P., 240
Aronson, E., 652, 653, 664
Arterberry, M. E., 56–57
Artugas, A. A., 214
Asai, S., 376, 536
Ashby, F. G., 388–89, 391, 398
Ashby, J., 135
Ashman, A. F., 569
Asselin, J., 376
Astley, S. L., 6, 326, 412, 558
Atkinson, R. C., 170, 174, 180
Atsumi, T., 627
Attneave, F., 136, 425, 504
Attwell, D., 117
Attygalle, A. B., 536
Aucella, A. F., 287
Audinat, E., 565
Augerinos, G., 426
Aust, U., 326–29, 331–32, 335–38
Avin, E., 258
Axelsen, B. E., 590
Aydin, A., 214, 326, 346, 433
Aznar-Casnova, J. A., 214

Bäck, T., 120
Backhaus, W., 191
Baddeley, A. D., 132, 136, 170, 468, 475, 569
Baer, D. M., 468
Bagnoli, P., 626, 627
Baird, J. A., 381
Bakan, R. J., 72
Baker, J. E., 477
Baker, J. G., 568
Baker, M., 536
Baker, M. C., 610
Baker, R. R., 242
Balda, R. P., 6, 117, 123, 160, 167, 566, 603–6, 608, 610, 611, 613, 614
Baldwin, C. D., 570
Baldwin, D. A., 381
Baldwin, J. D., 375
Ball, G. F., 72
Ballard, J. C., 131
Balsam, P., 307, 470
Baptista, L. F., 81

Barba, L. S., 460
Barbet, I., 22, 24, 39
Barcelo, F., 629
Bard, K. A., 130, 588, 639–42
Barenbatt, L., 571
Barfield, R. J., 83
Barnes, W. J. P., 193, 194
Baron, J., 196–99, 201, 204, 580, 594, 597
Baron-Cohen, S., 477, 639, 643, 645, 647
Barrett, P. M., 565
Barry, B., 566
Barsalou, L. W., 310, 366
Barth, A., 570
Barth, J., 373
Basil, J. A., 611, 614
Basso, G., 569
Basu, P., 631
Bateman, G. C., 605
Bates, M. E., 240, 241
Bateson, M., 268
Batki, A., 643
Baum, W. M., 8
Baxley, N., 410
Bayne, K. A. L., 30
Beach, F. A., 363, 615, 674
Beatty, W. W., 434
Beck, B. B., 520, 529, 532, 536
Becker, L., 202
Bedell, B. T., 566
Bednekoff, P. A., 610
Bekoff, M., 594
Belik, M., 115–17, 123
Beller, H. K., 111
Benhamou, S., 201
Benhar, E., 29
Bennett, A. T. D., 158
Bennett, R. W., 168
Benowitz, L., 624, 626
Benson, A. M., 426
Benson, D. M., Jr., 445
Berg, M., 629
Berggren, P., 591
Bering, J., 375
Berkowitz, K., 663
Berlie, J., 156
Berlin, B., 344
Berlyne, D. E., 128
Bernard, G. D., 193
Berry, D. C., 568
Berthelet, A., 581
Berthold, P., 156
Bessette, B. B., 32, 58
Beugnon, G., 240
Beusmans, J. M., 222
Bever, T. G., 445, 482, 672
Beveridge, W. I. B., 477
Bhatt, R. S., 49, 326, 405, 619
Bichot, N. P., 135
Bidder, T. G., 72
Bidwell, N. J., 192
Biebach, H., 146, 237
Biederman, I., 55, 337
Biegler, R., 214, 433
Bierley, C. M., 166
Bierschwale, D. T., 372, 590
Bindra, D., 149
Bingham, H. C., 596
Bingman, B. P., 626
Bingman, V. P., 53, 156, 242, 626, 627
Bird, L. R., 151, 152, 156
Birdsall, T. G., 314
Birge, J. S., 412
Biro, D., 132
Bisazza, A., 64, 210, 219
Bisch, S., 195, 196, 427
Bitgood, S. C., 257
Bizo, L. A., 293
Bjork, R. A., 181
Black, A. H., 426
Blaisdell, A. P., 213
Blake, R., 57
Blakemore, C., 4, 33
Blakers, M., 193
Blanke, J., 563
Bleckley, M. K., 127
Bleuler, S., 202
Blitzer, R. D., 426
Bloch, S., 58
Blodgett, H. C., 157
Blomqvist, D., 520
Blough, D. S., 30, 31, 90–93, 95, 96, 98–103, 114, 127, 129, 132–33, 135, 285, 316, 460, 461, 467, 471
Blough, P. M., 30, 31, 90–94, 110–13, 132–33, 135, 398
Blumenthal, A. L., 127
Boakes, R. A., 363, 521, 560, 662
Bobrow, D. G., 129
Boesch, C., 376, 546, 597
Boesch, H., 376, 597
Boesch-Achermann, H., 546
Boice, R., 651
Boinski, S., 532, 535, 546, 547
Boire, D., 631
Bolhuis, J. J., 174, 559, 611, 614, 631
Bolles, R. C., 671
Bonardi, C., 133
Bond, A. B., 93, 107–8, 110, 112–15, 118–23, 566
Bonnel, A., 72
Bonner, J. T., 563
Booth, M. Z., 571
Boothe, R. G., 130
Borchert, K., 557
Boring, E. G., 497
Borkenau, P., 569
Born, D. G., 168
Borys, R. H., 586
Bossema, I., 604–6, 608
Botto-Mahan, C., 376, 590
Bouchard, T. J., 570
Boulos, Z., 240, 241
Bouton, M. E., 204, 242, 455
Bovet, D., 371, 410, 418, 620
Bower, G. H., 129, 165, 661
Bowers, R. L., 287
Boyd, R., 520
Boyes-Braem, P., 344
Boysen, S. T., 369, 372, 376, 377, 523, 542, 588
Braaten, R. F., 73
Bradley, M. M., 169
Bradshaw, J. L., 581
Brady, J. H., 287
Brady, J. V., 131
Brady, P. M., 367
Braggio, J. T., 174
Braithwaite, V., 611
Brakefield, P. M., 119
Brandstätter, H., 566
Brandt, R., 202
Brannick, N., 583, 586
Brannon, E. M., 483, 490, 491, 493–508, 509n1, 509n8
Braver, T. S., 629
Bravo, M., 57
Breinlinger, K., 526–27
Bressan, P., 59
Brislin, R. W., 31
Broadbent, D. E., 112, 128, 133, 568, 626
Broadbent, H. A., 230, 265, 266, 272–75, 278, 280, 286
Broadbent, N., 626
Brockbank, M., 643
Brodbeck, D. R., 212, 300
Brodin, A., 603, 610, 611, 614, 627
Brooks, R. J., 73
Brown, 548n2
Brown, B. B., 583
Brown, B. L., 233
Brown, D. H., 595
Brown, E., 535
Brown, E. R., 441
Brown, J., 165
Brown, L., 570
Brown, M. F., 6, 127, 153, 427–36, 468
Brownson, R. H., 582
Bruce, V., 106
Brugger, P., 467, 468
Brunner, D., 275–76, 301
Brunswik, E., 301
Brush, E. I., 250
Brush, F. R., 250

Bshary, R., 523, 561
Buchanan, J. P., 174
Bucik, V., 568
Buckley, P. B., 508
Bugnyar, T., 606–7, 610
Bullemer, P., 440, 441
Bullock, T. H., 563
Bülthoff, H. H., 201, 330
Bunch, K. G., 607, 610
Bunsey, M. D., 676
Burgdorf, J., 83
Burger, R., 136, 137
Burgess, P., 569
Burke, D., 21, 26
Burke, M. W., 147
Burns, E. M., 83
Burns, J. E., 192
Burns, R. A., 440
Busby, J., 615
Buschio, S., 557
Bushnell, I. W., 640, 641
Bushnell, P. J., 131
Bussey, T. J., 149, 609, 615
Butcher, L. L., 628
Butler, A. B., 565
Butler, T. W., 91
Butters, N., 441
Butterworth, G. E., 644
Bylin, A., 603
Byrne, R. W., 566, 639

Cabeza de Vaca, S., 233
Cable, C., 285, 325, 359
Cacchione, T., 376, 377
Caldwell, D. K., 595
Caldwell, M. C., 595
Call, J., 372, 375, 530, 531, 566, 588–89, 639, 640, 645, 647, 648
Cameron, J., 307, 664
Campbell, C. B. G., 363, 364
Campbell, C. E., 439
Campbell, D., 61
Campbell, D. T., 477
Campbell, R., 178
Campos, J. J., 646
Cantero, M., 589
Cantlon, J., 483
Capaldi, E. A., 202
Capaldi, E. J., 426, 433, 439–40, 445–46, 653
Caputi, P., 567
Car, J. A. R., 229–32, 234, 238, 239, 241
Caraco, T., 109
Carder, B., 663
Carey, S., 379, 505
Carlin, M. T., 322
Carlsmith, J. M., 652, 664
Carlson, J., 33
Carman, H. M., 446
Carnap, R., 249
Carnathan, J., 252, 253
Carpenter, A. F., 509, 571
Carpenter, M., 645
Carpenter, P. A., 556
Carr, D. B., 583
Carr, J. A. R., 233, 236, 237
Carr, J. H., 570
Carroll, S. B., 119
Carruthers, P., 567
Carter, D. E., 286, 287
Cartwright, B. A., 201, 203, 211, 218
Caruso, D., 567
Case, R., 594
Casini, G., 242, 626
Casseday, J. H., 395
Castro, C. A., 174
Catania, A. C., 401
Catano, V. M., 567
Catchpole, C. K., 476
Cattell, J., 90
Cavoto, B. R., 308, 309, 315, 368
Cavoto, K. K., 308, 368
Cawley, S., 626
Cech, C. G., 372
Ceci, S. J., 568
Celli, M. L., 640, 647
Cerella, J., 23, 42, 49, 55, 326–27, 337, 345
Chahl, J. S., 201
Chalmers, M., 439, 486, 559
Chameron, S., 194
Chamizo, V. D., 214
Chan, A. Y. C., 567
Channon, S., 477
Chappell, J., 517, 521–23, 525, 547, 560, 630
Chapuis, N., 158
Charnov, E. L., 109
Chase, S., 331
Chase, W. G., 475
Chatlosh, D. L., 127, 128
Chavaillon, J., 581
Chavanne, T. J., 379, 534
Chaves, L. M., 624
Chelonis, J. J., 154
Chen, J. R., 120
Chen, Q. C., 396
Chen, S., 148, 440, 485, 487, 490–93
Chenevert, T., 509
Cheney, D. L., 371, 372, 674, 676
Cheng, K., 63–64, 66, 123, 189, 193, 195–99, 201, 204, 205, 210, 211, 214–15, 217–19, 222, 230, 233, 272, 298, 433
Chevalier-Skolnikoff, S., 532–33, 535
Cheverud, J. M., 564
Chiang, C., 32
Childers, L. J., 401
Chittka, L., 192, 193, 199, 204
Choate, L. S., 135
Chomsky, N., 396, 583, 670
Christensson, K., 83
Chun, J., 565
Church, R. M., 79, 147, 230, 233, 249–67, 270, 272–75, 278, 280, 281, 285–86, 288, 290, 293, 296, 300, 426, 482
Ciarrochi, J. V., 567
Cibois, A., 614
Cink, C., 113–14
Clark, C. W., 131
Clark, D. A., 566
Clark, E., 509n9
Clark, K., 629
Clarke, B. C., 107, 109
Clarkson, K., 607
Clayton, N. S., 53, 62, 146, 149, 155, 160, 170, 242, 372, 560, 602–9, 611, 615
Cleary, J., 412
Cleary, T. L., 662
Cleaveland, J. M., 476
Clement, T. S., 49, 411, 653, 654, 656, 658, 659, 663
Clements, K. C., 296
Clifton, C., Jr., 135
Clohessy, A. B., 135
Cohen, J. D., 629
Cohen, J. S., 71, 233, 298
Cohen, L., 460
Cohen, L. R., 287
Cohen, N. J., 624
Collett, M., 189, 193–96, 198, 201, 205, 427
Collett, T. S., 189, 192–99, 201, 203–5, 211, 215, 218, 427
Collins, S. L., 109
Colombo, M., 147, 486, 487, 508, 626
Colwill, R. M., 415, 425–26
Compostela, C., 23, 49, 55
Compton, B. J., 132
Connellan, J., 643
Connolly, K. J., 477
Connor, R., 590, 591
Conte, S., 23, 49, 55
Contos, J. J. A., 565
Conway, A. R. A., 127
Cook, B. R., 368
Cook, R. G., 20, 21, 58, 127, 153, 174, 176, 285, 307–11, 313–17, 319, 322, 332, 336–37, 397, 468, 561
Cookson, M. J., 565
Cools, A. R., 441

Cooper, J. M., 108, 113, 119
Cooper, R., 131, 132
Cooper, R. W., 532
Coppage, D. J., 408, 620
Corbalis, P. M., 59
Corballis, M. C., 146
Corcoran, R., 629
Coren, S., 32
Cosmides, L., 363, 566
Costa-Miserachs, D., 565
Cott, H. B., 121
Cotter, V. W., 410
Covey, E., 395
Cowan, N., 133
Cozzutti, C., 58, 62
Crabbe, S., 53
Craton, L. G., 39
Creelman, C. D., 101, 276
Crespi, L. P., 661, 665
Cribb, D., 440
Croft, D. B., 327, 594
Croft, H., 174
Croft, K., 372
Cronin-Golomb, A., 629
Crowder, R. G., 165, 174, 176, 181
Croze, H. J., 107–8
Crupi, C., 151, 152
Crystal, J. D., 235, 239, 241, 265, 266, 272–78, 280, 282
Cummins, S. E., 543
Cummins-Sebree, S. E., 544
Cunitz, A. R., 174
Cunningham, M., Jr., 409, 410
Cynx, J., 73, 79

Daan, S., 146, 229, 233
da Cunha, R. G. T., 532
D'Addetta, J., 158, 159, 427, 431
Dagnon, J., 624
Dale, C. L., 275, 279
Dale, K., 189, 197, 199
Dallal, N. L., 158, 160, 427, 440
Dally, J. M., 606, 607
Dalrymple, R. M., 311, 317, 368
Dalrymple-Alford, J. C., 174
Damasio, A. R., 236, 571
D'Amato, M. R., 79, 147, 164, 173, 326, 327, 332, 367, 486, 487, 508, 531
Dampier, W., 532
Danks, J. H., 676
Danthiir, V., 557
Dark, V. J., 128, 132, 133
Darwin, C., 3, 5, 73, 83–84, 307, 364, 532, 556
Dasser, V., 369
Davidson, T. L., 426, 440
Davies, D. R., 106, 131
Davies, N. B., 232
Davis, H., 493
Davis, J. D., 410, 412
Davis, R. T., 30, 672
Davison, M., 461
Dawkins, M. S., 107, 108, 111–13
Dawkins, R., 109, 562
Day, A., 567
Deary, I. J., 564
de Brabander, J. M., 236
de Bruin, J. P., 236, 624
Deci, E., 664
DeCoteau, W. E., 441
De Fries, J. C., 570
DeGange, A. R., 607
DeGutis, J., 509
Dehaene, S., 493
Deich, J., 307
Deipolyi, A., 64
Deiss, C., 460
de Kort, S. R., 610, 611
Delacour, J., 169
de Lillo, C., 20, 531
Delius, J. D., 272, 307, 316, 325, 327, 331, 335, 557–63, 565–67, 571, 582
Della Sala, S., 569
Deluty, M. Z., 257–58, 285, 288, 290
DeMarse, T., 411, 414, 415
Dember, W. N., 131
Demello, L. R., 62
Deng, C., 58
Denney, J., 460, 471
Dennis, N. A., 322
Denniston, J. C., 213
Dent, M. L., 83
de Oliveira, M. G., 519
de Oviedo, F. G., 532
Dépy, D., 22, 26, 39
Deringis, P., 107
Deruelle, C., 17, 22, 24, 39, 42, 49
Descartes, R., 8
D'Esposito, M., 569
Detterman, D. K., 568
Detweiler, J. B., 566
Deutsch, D., 72, 79
de Valois, K. K., 16
de Valois, R. L., 16
Devenport, L., 148, 149
Devine, J. B., 167, 168
Devine, J. V., 147
DeVolder, C. L., 408, 410, 414, 620
de Waal, F., 382, 566, 588, 646
Dewey, G. I., 328
Dews, P. B., 270, 288
Diamond, A., 62
Diamond, J. M., 515–16
Dickens, W. T., 570
Dickinson, A., 425
Dickinson, A. D., 62, 146, 149, 170, 242, 604, 605, 609, 615
Diekamp, B., 62, 557
DiGello, E., 429, 435
DiGian, K. A., 433, 434, 655, 656, 660
DiLisi, R., 594, 596
Dimitrov, M., 629
Dinsmoor, J. A., 415
DiPietro, N., 49, 57, 58
Divac, I., 62, 565
Dodd, B., 178
Dodd, P. W. D., 147
Dollard, J., 405–6, 411, 414, 418
Dolson, M., 72, 79
Dominguez, K. E., 29
Donaldson, W., 173
Donker, A., 624
D'Onofrio, B., 570
Dooling, R. J., 81–83
Dörner, D., 567
Dorris, M. C., 135
Dorsky, N. P., 426, 439, 446
dos Reis, N. R., 532, 536
Doty, R. W., 164–67
Dougherty, D. H., 301
Drew, J., 154
Dreyfus, L. R., 290, 298
Driver, P. M., 476
Dubbeldam, J. J., 565
Dube, W. V., 415
Dubois, M., 534
Dukas, R., 110, 112, 116, 118, 131
Dunbar, R. I. M., 566, 589
Duncan, J., 569
Duncan, L. M. J., 193, 194
Dunham, P. J., 644
Dunphy-Lelii, S., 365, 372, 380
Durier, V., 201
Durstewitz, D., 62, 564
Dusek, J. A., 560
Dvorak, M., 519
Dwyer, D. M., 611
Dyer, F. C., 158, 192, 202
Dykens, E. M., 570

Ebbinghaus, H. E., 174, 491, 669
Ebenholtz, S. M., 491
Eddy, D. R., 167, 168
Eddy, T. J., 372–74, 589
Eden, S. F., 607
Edwards, C. A., 212, 213, 223, 316
Edwards, C. E., 166
Edwards, E., 201
Egeth, H. E., 128
Ehrsson, H. H., 571
Eichenbaum, H. B., 441, 560, 624
Eikeseth, S., 406
Eisenberger, R., 307, 664, 665
Eisler, H., 270
Eisner, T., 536
Ekman, J., 603

Ekstrom, A. D., 559
Ell, S. W., 389
Emde, R. N., 646
Emery, N. J., 155, 372, 560, 603, 605–7, 609, 610, 615, 632, 643–45
Emmerton, J., 558, 560, 562
Emslie, H., 569
Enard, W., 570
Endler, J. A., 120, 121
Engle, R. A., 127
Enns, J. T., 18, 23
Epstein, R., 630
Ericcson, K. A., 475
Erichsen, J. T., 109, 626
Ericson, B., 376
Eriksen, C. W., 111, 668
Esch, H. E., 192
Etienne, A. S., 60, 156, 190
Etkin, M., 164
Evans, D., 566
Evans, F. J., 463
Evensen, J. C., 426, 439
Everett, B. A., 372
Everingham, P., 21
Everling, S., 135
Eysenck, H. J., 561

Fabian, S. A., 433, 434
Fachinelli, C. C., 316
Fadiga, L., 652
Fagan, A., 624
Fagot, J., 16–17, 20–22, 26, 27n1, 39, 42, 212, 335, 367–70
Fairhurst, S., 281, 282
Falk, H., 237
Fallgatter, A. J., 629
Falls, J. B., 72–73
Fan, J., 135
Fantino, E., 109, 660
Farabaugh, S. F., 81
Farroni, T., 643
Fauria, K., 189, 199
Fedigan, L., 530–33, 535, 536, 541
Feduccia, A., 565
Feigl, H., 8
Feinman, S., 646
Felsenstein, J., 614
Feltus, J., 653
Fendrich, R., 59
Fernandes, E. B. M., 532, 535, 547
Fernandez-Duque, D., 133
Ferno, A., 590
Ferry, A., 624, 628
Fertl, D., 590
Feruglio, M., 64
Fessl, B., 519, 520
Festinger, L., 652, 653, 664
Fetterman, J. G., 271, 275, 285–98, 300, 301, 414–16
Fibiger, H. C., 290
Fieder, M., 332
Fineman, M. B., 33
Finlestein, A., 631
Fischer, Q. S., 16
Fisher, R. A., 72
Fiske, D. W., 477
Fitch, M. D., 325
Fitch, W. T., 397, 571, 583
Fite, K. V., 611
Fitzpatrick, J. W., 607
Flaherty, C. F., 661–63
Flavell, E. R., 372
Flavell, J. H., 372
Fletcher, 62
Flora, S. R., 664
Floresco, S. B., 236, 237
Flynn, J. R., 570
Fobes, J. L., 16
Fodor, J. A., 64, 507, 631
Fogassi, L., 652
Fogel, A., 642
Fogleman, T., 644
Forkman, B., 23–25, 57, 59–62
Förster, B., 562
Forster, L., 200
Fortin, N. J., 441
Foss, D. J., 410
Foster, T. M., 62
Foucault, M., 176
Fountain, S. B., 426, 439–46, 448, 449, 451, 454, 676
Fouts, R. S., 588
Fowler, H., 673
Fox, E. A., 546
Fragaszy, D. M., 379, 519, 530–33, 535, 536, 538, 541, 544, 546
Frahm, H. D., 564
Frank, A. J., 311
Frank, J., 557
Franks, N. R., 563
Franz, M. O., 201
Fraser, J., 176
Freedman, D. J., 498
Frei, C., 195
Freire, F., 61
Fremouw, T., 20, 314, 388–90, 392–95, 400, 627
French, R. M., 321
Frensch, P. A., 322
Fricke, H., 561
Friedman, R. A., 566
Friedman, W. J., 146
Friedrich, A. M., 415, 416, 654, 655–57, 660
Friedrich, F. J., 401
Frier, H. J., 201
Friesel, M., 562
Frost, N., 508
Fujimori, M., 560
Fujita, I., 20, 21
Fujita, K., 23, 30, 31, 33–39, 42, 43, 49, 55, 58, 376, 379, 530, 534, 536, 544
Funahashi, S., 569
Funk, M. S., 57
Furuya, I., 42, 43, 49
Fussell, C., 214, 433
Fuster, J. M., 62, 236, 564, 569
Futuyma, D. J., 562

Gaffan, D., 167–69
Gaffan, E. A., 426
Gagliardo, A., 53, 66
Gagne, F., 571
Galanter, E., 670
Galef, B. G., Jr., 621
Gallagher, S., 626
Gallese, V., 652
Gallistel, C. R., 63, 64, 201, 203–5, 229, 234, 240, 241, 243, 270, 275, 278, 279, 363, 426, 433, 493
Gallizzi, K., 193, 195
Galloway, J., 233
Gandhi, C. C., 563
Gao, E., 395
Garber, P. A., 535
Garcia, J., 580, 671
Gardiner, J. M., 170
Gardner, B. T., 639
Gardner, H., 53, 266, 400
Gardner, R. A., 639
Garner, K. L., 311, 368
Garner, W. R., 668
Garver, A., 591
Gaulin, S. J. C., 363
Gawley, D. J., 154
Gazzaniga, M., 59
Gebhardt, R.-P., 562
Geiger, K., 192, 199, 204
Gelade, G., 19, 92, 97, 106, 127, 335
Gelman, R., 493
Gendron, R. P., 112
Georgakopoulos, J., 156
Georgeson, M. A., 33
Georgopolous, A. P., 509
Gerrans, P., 568
Getty, D. J., 256, 257, 275
Getty, T., 109, 112–13
Giambrone, S., 375, 381, 566
Gibbon, J., 79, 103, 147, 193, 204, 205, 230, 234, 261–64, 270, 272, 274–76, 279–82, 285, 286, 288, 290, 293, 301
Gibson, B. M., 311, 319
Gibson, E. J., 536
Gibson, J. J., 285, 295, 298, 536
Gibson, K. R., 532, 547, 581

Gigerenzer, G., 566, 567
Gilbert, D. B., 627
Gilinsky, S. A., 176
Gill, T. V., 174, 482
Gillam, B., 32
Gillan, D. J., 369
Gillman, C. B., 508
Gillund, G., 180
Ginn, S. R., 240
Giovagnoli, A. R., 629
Gisiner, R. C., 583, 586
Gisolfi, C. V., 565
Giurfa, M., 563
Gladen, B. C., 570
Glanzer, M., 174
Glenberg, A. M., 169, 178, 181
Glimcher, P. W., 462
Glover, J. A., 568
Godfrey, L. R., 381
Godin, J. G. J., 118
Goel, N., 108
Goetz, E. M., 468
Goldberg, B., 281
Goldiamond, I., 405, 407, 411
Goldin-Meadow, S., 567
Goldman-Rakic, P. S., 62
Goldstone, R. L., 310, 366, 410, 414
Goleman, D., 566
Goller, F., 72
Gomes de Oliveira, M., 532, 541
Good, M. A., 133, 214, 433, 626, 627
Goodall, J., 567, 588
Goodman, I. J., 628
Goodwin, D., 607
Gordijn, M., 146, 237
Gordon, D., 240
Gordon, W. U., 440
Gorfein, D. S., 181
Görner, P., 190
Gory, J. D., 586, 589, 591, 593
Gossette, M. F., 557
Gossette, R. L., 557
Gott, R. E., 389
Gottesman, I. I., 570
Gottselig, J. M., 129
Gould, J. L., 158, 192, 202, 203, 426
Gould, S. J., 123, 398
Gould-Beierle, K., 608, 613, 614
Gouteux, S., 64, 221
Graefe, T. M., 176
Grafman, J., 569, 629
Grafton, S. T., 509
Graham, C., 463
Graham, P., 199–201
Graham, S., 418
Grant, D. S., 164, 166–68, 173, 300, 301, 414
Grant, P. R., 519
Grass, D., 332
Grau, J. W., 130
Gray, E., 66, 224, 225
Gray, R. D., 517, 519, 520, 526
Gray, W. D., 344
Graybiel, A. M., 628
Green, C., 415, 416
Green, D. M., 101
Green, L., 154
Greenberg, J., 664
Greene, A. J., 560
Greene, S. L., 329, 331, 332
Greenfield, P. M., 547, 548n1
Greenfield, S., 4
Greenlee, M. W., 571
Gregory, R. L., 32
Grice, G. R., 410, 412, 414
Griffin, D. R., 3, 266, 571, 582, 676
Griffiths, D., 146, 149
Grigorenko, E. L., 568, 570
Grondin, S., 235
Grossberg, S., 53
Grover, D. E., 409, 410
Groves, C. P., 540
Grubb, T. C., Jr., 602
Grunow, A., 461
Guerani, L., 23, 49, 55
Guilford, T., 111–13
Guilhardi, P., 235
Gumbert, A., 202
Gunderson, V. M., 62
Güntürkün, O., 57–58, 62, 557, 563–65, 624, 625
Guyla, M., 508
Gygax, L., 530

Haag, R., 460, 595
Haarman, H., 180
Habers, G., 335
Hahmann, U., 58
Haier, R. J., 569
Hake, D. T., 410, 412
Hake, H. W., 668
Halasz, F., 622
Haley, A., 570
Hall, G., 133, 412, 414, 418, 628
Hall, S., 298
Hall-Aspland, S., 21
Halliday, M. S., 662
Halpern, A. R., 72
Hamilton, J. M. E., 497, 498, 504, 508
Hamm, J., 561
Hampton, R. R., 171, 611
Hanford, L., 557
Hannécart, F., 517
Hardy, O., 565
Hare, B., 372, 375, 588, 644
Harkness, R. D., 200
Harland, D., 193
Harley, H. E., 445, 582
Harley, N., 530
Harlow, H. F., 129, 487, 556, 624, 671
Harper, D., 626
Harper, D. N., 174
Harris, A. V., 29
Harris, F. D. A., 406
Harris, G., 589
Harris, P. L., 542
Harrison, H. M., 477
Harrison, S. N., 337, 345, 620, 621
Hartman, M., 441
Hartmann, B., 625
Hartmann, G., 204
Harvey, P. H., 614
Hasher, L., 133
Haskell, M., 61
Hauser, M. D., 64, 376–79, 397, 536, 548n2, 571, 582, 583, 590, 591, 615, 676
Hayashi, M., 645, 647
Hayes, A., 93
Hayes, C., 639
Hayward, A., 214, 220
Head, K., 569
Healy, S. D., 610–11, 614, 627
Hearst, E., 77, 316
Heaton, P., 569
Hebb, D. O., 594, 669
Heindel, W. C., 441
Heinemann, E. G., 258, 331
Heinrich, B., 107, 109, 560, 571, 580, 597, 606, 607
Heinsbroek, R. P., 624
Heller, R., 118
Hellmann, B., 58, 565
Hellwig, K. A., 178
Helson, H., 292
Helweg, D. A., 445
Hemmes, N. S., 233
Hemmi, J. M., 193–94
Hempel, C. G., 249
Henne, D. R., 440
Henneman, M. C., 533, 540
Hennessy, R., 31
Henthorn, T., 72, 79
Henty, C. J., 604
Herbranson, W. T., 20, 314, 388–94, 396–98, 400, 403n1, 585
Herman, E. Y. K., 582
Herman, L. M., 168, 582–83, 585, 586, 589
Hermann, B. P., 629
Hermelin, B., 569
Hermer, L., 64, 210, 211, 219
Hermer-Vasquez, L., 64

Hernández-Camacho, J., 532
Herrnstein, R. J., 26, 49, 109, 285, 325, 327, 328, 332, 335, 337, 338, 343, 359, 360, 391, 405, 461, 497, 558, 619
Hersh, H. M., 445
Herz, M., 53
Heschl, A., 563
Hespos, S. J., 567
Heth, C. D., 63, 211, 219, 221
Hetherington, M. M., 62
Heyes, C. M., 372, 581
Hickok, G., 72
Higa, J. J., 272, 286, 294, 401, 426
Higashijima, J., 569
Higgins, C. M., 565
Highfill, L. E., 594
Hightower, F. A., 401
Hihara, S., 530
Hile, A. G., 604
Hilfers, M. A., 311, 317, 368
Hilgard, E. R., 668
Hill, C. R., 626
Hill, T., 148
Hill, W. C. O., 532
Hilton, J., 565
Hinde, R. A., 671
Hinton, M., 21
Hirata, S., 640, 646–48
Hitchcock, C. L., 160, 610
Hobson, S. L., 296
Hochstein, S., 509n7
Hodapp, R. M., 570
Hodges, J. R., 628
Hodos, W., 32, 58, 363, 364, 557, 565, 622, 624, 626
Hoffman, D., 59
Hoffmann, J. E., 111
Hofmann, M. I., 201
Hogan, D. E., 166, 168, 316
Holder, M. D., 583, 585
Holland, J. H., 597
Hollard, V. D., 561–62
Holling, C. S., 107
Holloway, F. A., 242
Holloway, R., 483, 570
Holman, J., 468
Holman, J. G., 325
Holyoak, K. J., 502, 580, 590, 594, 597
Homborg, L., 631
Honey, R. C., 133, 627
Hong, N. S., 242
Honig, W. K., 6–7, 285, 287, 325, 412, 415, 417, 418, 672, 673
Honzik, C. H., 157
Hood, B. M., 378
Hope, S., 614
Hopkins, W. D., 17, 20, 21, 128, 130, 588, 589
Hopkinson, J., 477
Horel, J. A., 17
Horn, G., 66
Horne, P. J., 406
Horridge, G. A., 193
Horton, D. L., 409, 410
Hostetter, A. B., 589
Houdé, O., 568
Hough, G. E., 53, 626
Houston, A. I., 603, 607
Houston, A. L., 232
Howe, S. R., 131
Huber, L., 326–29, 331–38, 343, 346, 350, 355, 632
Hugart, J. A., 308, 335, 368
Huggins, C. K., 436
Hulbert, L. G., 440
Hull, C. L., 176, 406, 411, 412, 414, 418, 481, 581, 664, 665, 668, 669
Hulse, S. H., 71–73, 79, 426, 439–40, 446, 670, 673, 675–76, 677n3
Humpal, J., 73, 79
Humphrey, N. K., 7, 33
Humphreys, G. W., 106
Humphries, D. A., 476
Hunt, E., 555, 631
Hunt, G. R., 517, 519, 520, 526, 547
Hunter, J. E., 571
Hunter, M. W., 624
Hunter, W. S., 62, 439, 671
Huntley, R., 460
Hunziker, M. H., 460
Husband, S., 109, 627

Ianazzi, R., 109
Ingold, T., 581
Inhelder, B., 596
Innis, N. K., 272
Inoue, S., 337
Inoue-Nakamura, N., 541, 547, 647
Intraub, H., 176
Ioalé, P., 53, 627
Iriki, A., 530
Ito, S., 73, 77
Ito, Y., 55, 337
Ivancic, M., 582
Iverson, I., 418
Izar, P., 519, 532, 535, 536, 541
Izawa, E.-I., 66, 627

Jackendoff, R., 481
Jackson, A., 605
Jackson, R. R., 200, 581
Jackson-Smith, P., 153, 407, 627
Jacobs, W. J., 178
Jacobson, K., 526–27
Jacoby, L. L., 170, 171, 181
Jalles-Filho, E., 532, 534, 538
James, C. T., 410, 412
James, P. C., 604, 606–8
James, P. H. R., 672
James, W., 106, 127, 133–34, 136, 307, 586
Janson, C. H., 546
Janssen, R., 565
Jarrett, N. L. M., 644
Jarvis, E., 565
Jaspers, R., 441
Jassik Gerschenfeld, D., 565
Jawor, J., 477
Jaynes, J., 669
Jeeves, M. A., 624
Jeffery, K. J., 190
Jeffrey, J., 461
Jeffrey, W. E., 412, 413
Jen, P. H. S., 395, 396
Jenkins, J. J., 410, 411
Jenkins, P. F., 526
Jenkins, S. H., 606
Jenness, J. W., 91
Jennings, H. S., 9
Jensen, A. R., 568–70, 663
Jensen, G., 472
Jensen, G. D., 663
Jerison, H. J., 564
Jitsumori, M., 325, 327, 337, 345, 346, 349, 350, 352–55, 366, 367, 558
Joerges, J., 204
John, A., 430–32
Johnson, D. L., 570
Johnson, D. M., 344
Johnson, M. H., 641, 643
Johnson, M. L., 133
Johnson-Frey, S., 382
Johnston, W. A., 128, 132, 133
Jolly, A., 4
Jones, J. E., 218, 426, 557, 609
Jones, K. E., 577
Jones, L. C., 167, 168
Jones, M. R., 446
Jones, T.-J., 242, 626
Jonides, J., 135, 509
Joseph, J. P., 590
Judd, S. P. D., 199
Juhasz, B., 135
Jung, R. E., 569
Juola, J. F., 170
Just, M. A., 556

Kabela, E., 154
Kacelnik, A., 275–76, 301, 517, 521–23, 525, 527n2, 547, 560, 630
Kaessmann, H., 570
Kahn, M. C., 53, 626

Kahneman, D., 112, 133, 398
Kail, R., 561
Kaiser, D. H., 233, 653
Kako, E., 583
Kalish, D., 157, 483
Kalt, T., 62
Kamil, A. C., 3, 5–6, 10, 93, 109–10, 112–23, 160, 167, 218, 287, 296, 363, 426, 548, 557, 566, 603, 608, 609, 611, 613–14, 624
Kamin, L. J., 128, 213, 250, 296
Kanazawa, S., 38, 39, 640
Kane, M. J., 127, 133
Kanizsa, G., 23, 29, 38, 43, 44, 49, 55, 59
Kaplan, B., 588
Kaplan, G., 372
Karin-D'Arcy, R., 373
Karten, H. J., 622, 626
Kaschube, M., 564
Kassen, R., 118–20
Kassubek, J., 571
Kastak, C. R., 415
Kastak, D., 415
Katsnelson, A. S., 64
Katz, H. M., 557
Katz, J. S., 308, 309, 311, 315, 368
Kaufman, A. S., 555
Kaufman, L., 120
Kawai, N., 642, 645
Kawashima, T., 415
Keane, M. T., 335
Keele, S. W., 326, 352
Keen, R., 235
Keller, K., 662
Kellman, P. J., 25, 38, 39, 41, 45, 48, 56–57, 59
Kellogg, L. A., 639
Kellogg, W. N., 582, 639
Kelly, D. M., 63, 64, 66, 211, 214, 217, 219–25, 308, 311
Kelly, J. B., 82, 83
Kelly, W., 630
Kendrick, D. F., 174
Kennedy, J. S., 7, 8
Kennett, D. J., 621
Kenward, B., 517, 527n2
Keppel, G., 168, 489
Kesner, R. P., 174, 439, 441, 627
Ketcham, R. A., 565
Khanna, H., 81
Kiedinger, R. E., 326, 405, 619
Killeen, P. R., 271, 275, 280, 281, 286, 288–95, 298
Kinchla, R. A., 128, 132
King, A. P., 426
King, G. R., 154
King, J. E., 16
Kingsbury, M. A., 565
Kingstone, A., 18
Kirby, M. A., 16
Kirk, K. M., 570
Kirkpatrick, K., 55, 265, 267, 337
Kirkpatrick, V. M., 582
Kirkpatrick-Steger, K., 55, 308, 335, 337, 368
Kirshnit, C. E., 630
Kit, K. A., 151, 152
Klein, R. M., 135
Klimes-Dougan, B., 566
Klinnert, M. D., 646
Klüver, H., 532
Knauff, M., 571
Knauss, K. S., 326, 405
Knepper, B., 21
Knight, R. T., 17
Knoedler, A. J., 176, 178, 181
Knopman, D. S., 440–41
Knott, C. D., 547
Knowlton, B. J., 585
Knutson, B., 83
Kobayashi, H., 16
Kobayashi, K., 628
Koechlin, E., 569
Koehler, O., 53
Koelling, R. A., 580, 671
Koene, P., 146, 229, 233
Koffka, K., 26
Köhler, M., 563, 596
Kohler, W., 365, 376, 377, 381
Kolb, B., 236
Kolesaric, V., 571
Komarova, N. L., 567
Komischke, B., 202
Königstein, M., 566
Kono, H., 109, 114, 116
Kopp, C. B., 566
Koppenaal, R. J., 176
Kornell, N., 461, 483, 509
Korsnes, M. S., 176
Koshima, S., 16
Kosslyn, S. M., 26, 507, 619
Kosugi, D., 645
Kotovsky, K., 446
Kotrschal, K., 606–7, 610
Kozak, M., 435
Kraemer, P. J., 174
Kralik, J. D., 376, 377, 590
Krasnegor, N. A., 131
Krauchunas, S. M., 439
Kraus, T. A., 169
Krause, J., 118
Krause, M. A., 588
Krebs, J. R., 108–9, 146, 237, 559, 603, 604, 606, 608, 610–11, 614, 626, 627
Krist, H., 376, 377
Krizmanic, M., 571
Krumhansl, C. L., 71, 79
Kruschke, J. K., 326, 348
Kubota, K., 569
Kuch, D. O., 257
Kuczaj, S. A., II, 581–83, 586, 589, 591, 593–95
Kuhn, H. E., 538
Kummer, H., 530
Kundey, S. M. A., 441
Kunze, J., 199, 202
Kuroshima, H., 376, 536
Kurylo, D. D., 21, 26
Kuwahata, H., 641
Kyllonen, P. C., 555

Laasko, A., 8–9
LaBarbera, J. D., 254
Labhart, T., 191
Lachaud, J. P., 240
Lacinak, C. T., 591
Lacourse, D. M., 111, 112, 272, 426
Laland, K. N., 630
Lamb, M. R., 17, 127, 392, 395
Land, M. F., 200
Landauer, T. K., 497, 508
Lander, D. G., 325, 327
Langen, T. A., 604
Langer, J., 547
Langguth, A., 535, 547
Langley, C. M., 107, 108, 110, 112–14
Lanza, R. P., 630
Larew, M. B., 147
Larsen, O. N., 72
Larsen, T., 174
Lascaris, E., 631
Lashley, K. S., 439, 481, 670
Latham, P. E., 426
Lattal, K. M., 556
Laughlin, S. B., 117
Lauwereyns, J., 132
Lavallee, A. C., 535, 538
LaVelli, M., 642
Lavis, Y., 418
Lawrence, A. D., 628
Lawrence, D. H., 653
Lawson, J., 370
Layard, E. L., 517
Layard, E. L. C., 517
Layne, J. E., 193, 194
Layne, J. N., 607
Lea, S. E. G., 23, 44, 49, 57, 325–27, 337, 345, 346, 348–51, 359, 405, 557, 620, 621
Leavens, D. A., 588
Lebowitz, B. K., 428, 434
Leckman, J. F., 570
Ledoux, J., 567
Lee, A., 230

Lee, J. A. J., 23, 42, 55
Lee, P. C., 519
Lee, R., 477
Lee, T. D., 477
Lee-Teng, E., 624
Lefebvre, L., 381, 631
Lehr, M., 558
Lehrer, M., 192, 193
Leibowitz, H., 31, 32
Leighton, J. P., 560
Leith, C. R., 106, 127
Lejeune, H., 276, 298
Lenhoff, H. M., 72
Lenz, P., 556
Lenz, R., 326, 328, 346, 350, 355
Leonard, B., 156
Lepper, M. R., 664
Lerner, N. D., 256, 257, 275
Lesniak-Karpiak, K. B., 436
Lester, B. M., 640–41
Létocart, Y., 517
Levine, M., 570
Levitin, D., 72
Levy, W. B., 560
Lewandowsky, S., 481
Lewis, J. W., 628
Lewontin, R. C., 123, 398
Libby, M. E., 254–56
Liker, J. K., 568
Limongelli, L., 377, 379, 523, 533, 540, 542, 544
Lindauer, M., 191, 205
Lindbergh, J., 590
Lindbergh, S., 590
Lindlar, K., 562
Lindstrom, F., 109
Lionello, K. M., 418
Lionello-DeNolf, K. M., 408–13, 415–18
Lippa, Y., 410, 414
Little, L., 662
Liv, C., 379
Lloyd, J., 571
Lockhead, G. R., 425
Lockman, J. J., 536
Logan, F. A., 252
Logan, G., 132
Logie, R. H., 569
Logothetis, D. E., 240, 241
Logue, A. W., 154
Lohman, D. F., 568
Lohmann, A., 562
Lohr, B., 83
Loidolt, M., 328, 330–32
LoLordo, V. M., 178
Lombardi, C. M., 316, 561
London, B., 395
Looney, R. A., 287
Lord, J., 662
Lorincz, E. N., 372
Lougee, M., 557
Lovelace, E. A., 504
Loveland, D. H., 49, 109, 285, 325, 327, 328, 337, 343, 359, 391, 405, 619
Lowe, C. F., 406, 418
Lu, T., 624
Lubinski, D., 8
Lubow, R. E., 325, 326
Lucas, G. A., 154, 567
Luce, R. D., 89, 99, 100, 102
Lüer, G., 568
Lundborg, K., 611, 614, 627
Lundquist, A. L., 534, 538
Lydersen, T., 296
Lynn, R., 570

Ma, X., 395
Macarthur, R. H., 109
MacDonald, M. C., 397
MacDonald, S. E., 66, 147, 215, 217, 344, 367
MacDougall-Shackleton, S. A., 73
MacEwen, D., 286–88, 300, 301, 414
Machado, A., 235, 460, 461, 463, 467
Mack, R., 135, 287
Mackay, H. A., 322, 415
Mackenzie, B. D., 6
MacKenzie, C., 62
Mackintosh, N. J., 94, 111, 113, 127, 169, 214, 309–10, 317, 335, 350–52, 521, 560, 571, 624, 662, 663
Macko, K. A., 32, 58
Macmillan, N. A., 101, 276
Macomber, J., 526–27
Macphail, E. M., 160, 171, 363, 559, 561, 611, 614, 624, 626
Macuda, T., 300, 440
MacWhinney, B., 64
Maddi, S. R., 477
Maddox, W. T., 388–89, 391, 398
Maguire, E. A., 559
Maguire, R. W., 415
Maier, N. R. F., 477, 596, 677n2
Makecha, R. N., 594
Maki, W. S., 127, 166
Makino, H., 355
Malapani, C., 275, 279
Mallot, H. A., 201
Malloy, T. E., 390
Malott, M. K., 30
Malott, R. W., 30, 325, 327
Manabe, K., 415, 416, 418, 476
Mandler, G., 170
Mann, J., 591
Mann, M. D., 564
Manns, M., 565
Mannu, M., 532, 535, 540, 541, 547
Manoel, E. J., 477
Manser, K. L., 133
Mantanus, H., 298
Maratsos, M. P., 583, 586
March, J., 214
Marchant, L. F., 519
Marconato, F., 58
Margules, J., 201
Marino, L., 582, 594
Mark, T. A., 426
Markman, A. B., 556
Markus, N., 594
Marler, P., 72
Marquis, D. M., 668
Mars, P., 120
Marshalek, B., 555
Marshuetz, C., 509
Marslen-Wilson, W. D., 583
Martin, M., 17
Martindale, S., 109
Martin-Iverson, M. T., 290
Martinoya, C., 58
Mason, J. R., 621
Mason, W. A., 3
Masterton, B., 82, 83
Matell, M. S., 233
Matheson, W. R., 561
Mathevon, N., 566
Matlin, M. W., 556
Matsukawa, A., 337
Matsumoto, E., 560
Matsushima, T., 66, 627
Matsuzawa, T., 132, 367, 376, 541, 547, 640, 641, 643, 645–48
Matus, D. S., 582
Matzel, L. D., 556, 563
Mauldin, J. E., 557
Maurer, R., 156, 204
May, C. P., 133
Mayer, J. D., 566, 567
Mazmanian, D. S., 344, 345, 367
Mazur, J. E., 154
Mazza, M. P., 372
McAnulty, H., 568
McBeath, M. K., 676
McBride, A. F., 594
McCandliss, B. D., 135
McCarthy, D., 461
McCartney, K., 570
McClearn, G. E., 570
McCleery, R. H., 242
McComas, J. J., 477
McCormick, D. D., 570
McCowan, B., 594, 595
McCrary, C., 130
McDermott, J., 615
McDonald, R. J., 242, 626
McElroy, E., 469

McGonigle, B., 439, 483, 486, 559
McGregor, A., 214
McGrew, W. C., 519
McIlvane, W. J., 415
McIntire, K. D., 412
McKinney, M. L., 547
McLaren, I. P. L., 214
McLean, A. P., 174
McLeod, C. M., 131
McNamara, J. M., 603
McNaughton, B. L., 156
McQuoid, L. M., 621
Means, L. W., 240
Mechner, F., 477
Meck, W. H., 147, 158, 160, 233, 260–61, 263, 264, 272, 274, 285, 286, 289, 290, 296, 300, 427, 440
Medin, D. L., 325, 327–28, 330, 331, 343, 348, 397, 556, 672
Medina, L., 628
Meinertzhagen, I. A., 563
Mellgren, R. L., 661
Mellor, R., 605
Meltzoff, A. N., 652
Mendes, F. D. C., 534
Menzel, R., 193, 202–4, 563
Meran, I., 328
Mercado, E. I., 582, 585, 590
Merkel, F., 128
Mervis, C. B., 343, 344, 355
Messamer, J., 566
Mewhort, D., 73
Meyer, D. B. C., 109
Miall, R. C., 566
Michel, B., 190, 197
Michel, G. F., 7, 9
Michelsson, K., 83
Michotte, A., 53, 59
Milano, R., 590
Milbrath, C., 596, 597
Miles, R. C., 164
Milewski, M., 435
Milinski, M., 118
Miller, B. J., 235
Miller, C., 463
Miller, C. T., 376, 536
Miller, D. J., 440, 445, 446
Miller, E. K., 498, 569
Miller, G. A., 396, 481, 670
Miller, N., 307, 477
Miller, N. E., 405–6, 411, 414, 418
Mills, J., 652, 653, 664
Milner, A. C., 565
Milner, B., 629
Minda, J. P., 351
Miner, C. L., 441
Mingolla, E., 53
Mirskly, A. F., 131
Mishkin, M., 169
Mistlberger, R. E., 241, 277
Mitani, J. C., 72
Mitchell, C., 418
Mitchell, D. J., 569
Mitchell, J. A., 628
Mitchell, R. W., 372, 381, 588, 652
Mitra, P. P., 566
Mittermeier, R. A., 540
Miyazaki, K., 71, 72, 82
Mizuno, Y., 640–42
Moe, J. C., 166
Mogensen, J., 62
Moise, S. L., 164
Molina, P., 426, 440
Möller, A., 604, 609
Moller, P., 190
Möller, R., 201
Monroe, B. L., Jr., 72
Mook, D. M., 461
Moore, C., 644
Mora, F., 565
Morgan, C. L., 581, 586
Morgan, C. T., 149, 326–27, 337
Morgan, L., 293
Morgan, M. J., 33, 325
Mori, E., 560
Morimura, N., 646–47
Morris, R. D., 127
Morris, R. G. M., 214, 433
Morrison, S., 57
Morton, J., 641
Mostofsky, D., 325
Mottin, S., 566
Moura, A. C. de A., 519
Moyà-Solà, S., 563
Moyer, R. S., 497, 508
Mudge, P., 107
Mulack, T., 571
Müller, M., 204
Müller, U., 204
Mullin, J. T., 640
Mumford, D. B., 26, 619
Munakata, Y., 376
Munoz, D. P., 135
Murdoch, W. W., 107
Murdock, B. B., 481
Murphy, G. L., 558, 568
Murphy, T. D., 328
Murray, T. K., 626
Murton, R. K., 107
Mushiake, H., 509
Muzzio, I. A., 563
Myowa, M., 640
Myowa-Yamakoshi, M., 640, 641, 643, 647

Nachtigall, P. E., 582
Nadel, L., 156, 213, 426, 432
Nagasaka, Y., 39, 49
Nagell, K., 645
Nakajima, S., 556, 560
Nakamura, T., 327
Nakashima, N., 645
Namibar, R., 120
Napier, J. R., 16
Napier, P. H., 16
Natale, F., 532–33
Navon, D., 17, 26, 392
Nawrocki, T. M., 440, 446
Neal, S., 201
Nealis, P. M., 129
Neath, I., 170, 176, 178, 181, 433
Néel, C., 544
Neiss, M., 570
Neisser, U., 133, 134, 570
Nelson, D. A., 72, 73
Nelson, K. E., 372, 588
Neubauer, A. C., 568, 569
Neumann, P. G., 349
Neuringer, A. J., 285, 307, 459–61, 463, 466, 467, 469–72, 475, 477, 663
Newberry, R. C., 594
Newman, B. M., 33
Newman, C. V., 33
Newman, F., 296
Newsome, S., 567
Nguyen, A., 66, 224, 225
Nichols, H., 270
Nickerson, R. A., 467
Nickerson, R. S., 307
Nicol, C. J., 61
Nieder, A., 57, 498, 507, 509
Nievergelt, C., 202
Nightingale, N. N., 568
Nijhout, H. F., 119
Nims, P., 611
Ninokura, Y., 509
Nipher, F. E., 174
Nisbett, R. E., 597
Nissen, M. J., 440–41
Niyogi, P., 567
Njegovan, M., 71, 73, 75, 77, 81
Nocjar, C., 242, 626
Noelle, D. C., 629
Nolan, B. C., 311
Nolte, A., 532
Norman, D. A., 129, 132, 174
Norvig, P., 567
Nosofsky, R. M., 348, 351
Nottestad, L., 590
Novak, J. M., 174
Novak, M. A., 372
Nowak, B., 335
Nowak, M. A., 567
Nowicki, S., 72

Oaten, A., 107
Obayashi, S., 530
Oden, D. L., 335, 369

Ogden, E., 148
Ohgami, H., 645
Ohigashi, Y., 560
Ohyama, T., 307
Okamoto, S., 640, 642, 644–45
Okano, T., 639
Okanoya, K., 49, 82, 83, 628
O'Keefe, J., 156, 213, 426, 432
O'Leary, D. S., 565
Olsen, J. F., 395
Olson, D. J., 611
Olson, G., 460
Olthof, A., 158, 159, 217, 427, 431
Olton, D. S., 128, 149, 168, 237, 260, 261, 427, 428, 483, 626
Olufs, M., 461
Oppenheim, P., 249
Oram, M. W., 372
O'Reilly, J., 460, 595
O'Reilly, R. C., 376, 629
Orlov, T., 509n7
Osada, Y., 39, 49
O'Sullivan, J., 335
Ottoni, E. B., 519, 532, 535, 540, 541, 547
Overman, W. H., 164–67
Oxford, P., 532, 535

Pääbo, S., 570
Pace, D. S., 594, 595
Paciulli, L., 535
Pack, A. A., 582, 585
Page, S., 460–61, 463, 469, 470, 472
Page, S. C., 73
Pagel, M., 614
Pagni, P., 64
Palermo, D. S., 411
Pallier, G., 557
Palmer, S. E., 21, 23, 25, 58, 335
Pang, K., 128
Panger, M. A., 546, 547
Panksepp, J., 83
Panzer, S., 569
Papadimitriou, A., 626
Papini, M. R., 611, 615
Paradiso, S., 565
Parasuraman, R., 106, 131
Parker, B. K., 147
Parker, K. J., 233
Parker, S. T., 532, 533, 547, 596, 597
Parks, K. A., 372
Parr, L. A., 370
Parron, C., 24
Pashler, H. E., 106, 132
Pasquet, E., 614
Passingham, R. E., 571
Pasti, G., 58, 63, 219
Pastuovic, N., 571
Patterson, K. K., 502
Patterson, T. A., 627
Paulos, R. D., 581, 594
Pavlick, B., 604
Pavlov, I. P., 7–8, 148
Paz-y-Miño, C. G., 123
Pearce, J. M., 66, 156, 204, 214, 220, 326–28, 332, 346, 352, 366, 433, 455
Pearson, H. E., 376, 591
Pearson, H. M., 376, 378–79
Pellegrino, J. W., 561
Pellizzer, G., 509
Pena-Correal, T. E., 154
Pence, J. D., 240
Pepper, J. W., 606
Pepperberg, I. M., 57, 117, 560, 567, 632
Perales, O., 72
Perkins, D., 296
Perlmutter, L., 31
Perner, J., 639
Perrett, D. I., 372
Perry, V. H., 627
Perusse, R., 493
Peterhans, E., 57
Peters, J., 109
Peterson, G. B., 153, 411
Peterson, I., 477
Peterson, L. R., 165
Peterson, M. J., 165
Petitto, L. A., 482
Petrill, S. A., 568
Petrovic, V., 233, 234
Petter, G., 59
Phillips, K. A., 535
Phillips, L., 174
Phillmore, L. S., 81
Piaget, J., 60, 580, 594, 596, 597, 652
Pianka, E. R., 109
Pick, A. D., 536
Pierce, J. N., 415, 416
Pietrewicz, A. T., 93, 109, 110, 114
Pietrini, P., 569
Pitrewicz, A. M., 557
Pizzo, M. J., 239, 241
Plaisted, K. C., 111, 113, 395
Platt, J. R., 257
Platzman, K. A., 640–41
Plomin, R., 570
Plooij, F. X., 588
Plotnik, R. J., 557
Plous, S., 388
Pokrzywinski, J., 30
Poling, A., 62
Pollard, S. D., 200
Polli, C., 222, 223
Pollitt, E., 570
Pollok, B., 57
Pologe, B., 439, 440
Pomerantz, J. R., 425
Pond, H. M., 395
Poole, J., 325, 327
Porter, D., 285
Posner, M. I., 111, 128, 131, 133, 135, 138, 326, 352, 507
Postman, L., 174, 176, 489
Postmes, P., 624
Potì, P., 532, 533, 547
Poucet, B., 156
Poulton, E. B., 121
Povar, M. L., 366
Povinelli, D. J., 7, 363–65, 372–82, 521, 523, 536, 542, 547, 548n2, 566, 588–90
Powell, D. G., 235, 276
Powell, R. W., 50, 630
Powers, A. S., 622, 624
Pravosudov, V. V., 602, 603
Premack, A. J., 169
Premack, D., 7, 26, 169, 322, 335, 367, 369, 371, 372, 375–76, 482, 567, 571, 588, 639, 672
Preuss, T. M., 363
Pribram, K., 670
Pribram, K. H., 6
Price, J. L., 624
Prince, C. G., 586
Pring, L., 569
Prior, H., 57, 557
Proctor, R. W., 176
Procyk, E., 590
Profita, J., 72
Pryor, K. W., 460, 468, 590, 595
Pulliam, H. R., 109, 112–13
Putney, R. T., 138
Putz-Osterloh, W., 568
Pylyshyn, Z. W., 507

Quatrone, R. P., 546

Räber, F., 201
Rachlin, H., 4, 154
Rae, G., 568
Rafal, R. D., 135
Raffaele, K. C., 626
Rahhal, T., 133
Raichle, M. E., 131, 138
Rajalakshmi, R., 624
Rakowski, A., 79
Ralph, M. R., 242
Ramnani, N., 566
Ramos, J. A., 581, 594
Randle, V. R. L., 406
Ratcliff, R., 103
Rath, G. J., 469
Ray, C., 242
Rayner, K., 135
Raz, A., 135

Reader, S. M., 630
Real, P. G., 109, 113
Reaux, J. E., 372–73, 542, 566, 589, 590
Reber, A. S., 396, 400, 441
Rechberger, S., 632
Reebs, S. G., 240
Reed, P., 174, 348, 351
Reed, S. K., 328
Reed, T. E., 569
Rees, J. A., 196, 197, 199
Reeves, A., 133
Regolin, L., 44, 49, 55–56, 58, 60–62, 66
Rehen, S. K., 565
Rehkämper, G., 564
Reid, P. J., 109, 112, 113
Reidinger, R. F., 621
Reilly, S., 171, 624, 626
Reiner, A., 628
Reiss, D., 594
Reither, F., 567
Rensink, R. A., 23, 222
Renzaglia, G. J., 169
Renzi, P., 23, 49, 55
Rescorla, R. A., 213, 256, 425–26
Resende, B. D., 540, 547
Restle, F., 328, 331, 441
Reynolds, C. R., 568
Reynolds, R. S., 662
Reynolds, W. F., Jr., 326, 405
Rhodes, D., 460
Rice, C. E., 582
Richards, A., 590, 591
Richards, D. G., 582
Richards, J. E., 106
Richards, R. W., 287
Richardson, W. K., 128
Richardson-Klavehn, A., 170
Richelle, M., 298
Richerson, P. J., 520
Richey, E. T., 629
Ridgway, S. H., 582
Ridley, R. M., 626, 628
Riemann, R., 569
Riggio, R. E., 566
Rigoni, M., 62
Riley, D. A., 6, 106–8, 110, 113, 114, 127–29, 153, 468
Rilling, M., 296, 298
Rips, L. J., 558
Ristau, C. A., 8, 676
Ritchie, B. F., 157, 483
Ritchie, B. G., 533, 538
Rivaud, S., 58
Rizzolatti, G., 652
Robbins, T. W., 628
Roberts, A. D. L., 214
Roberts, R. C., 603
Roberts, R. D., 557
Roberts, S., 129, 147, 149, 150, 154, 155, 230, 233, 259, 260, 274
Roberts, W. A., 145–47, 149–52, 154–56, 158, 159, 164, 166–68, 173, 174, 217, 230, 233, 242, 286, 289, 296, 298, 300, 301, 344, 345, 367, 427, 431, 432, 439, 440, 615, 672
Robertson, L. C., 17, 392
Robinson, J. G., 536
Robinson, M. H., 121
Robinson, R., 119
Robinson, R. G., 565
Rocha, J. V., 532, 535, 536, 540
Rochat, P., 645
Rodet, L., 327
Rodrigo, T., 213–14
Rodriguez, M. L., 154
Rodriguez-Luna, E., 540
Roediger, H. L., III, 178, 179
Rogan, W. J., 570
Rogers, L. J., 58, 66, 372, 581
Rogers, R. D., 628
Rogers, T., 21
Rohack, J. J., 147
Rohlf, F. J., 80
Roitblat, H. L., 106, 127–29, 168, 270, 439–40, 445, 446, 559, 582, 672
Rolls, B. J., 62
Romanes, G. J., 4, 7, 9, 532, 581
Ronacher, B., 193
Ronning, R. R., 568
Roper, K. L., 6
Rosch, E., 343–45, 347, 351, 352, 355
Rose, S. P. R., 66, 627
Rosenbaum, D. A., 280
Ross, B. H., 366, 556
Ross, C., 461
Rossel, S., 191
Roth, G., 563
Rothbart, M. K., 135
Rothganger, H., 83
Rousseeuw, P. J., 120
Rovee-Collier, C., 367
Rowan, J. D., 439–45, 454
Rowe, D. C., 570
Rowe, T. B., 565
Royama, T., 107–9
Ruben, J., 565
Rubin, L. C., 630
Rubin, N., 25
Rudy, J. W., 626
Rulf, A. B., 372
Rumbaugh, D. M., 128, 130–32, 136, 370, 376, 482, 597
Rundus, D., 176
Rusak, B., 300
Ruskin, R. S., 628
Russel, S. J., 567
Russell, C. L., 639, 645
Russon, A. E., 381, 580
Rust, T. B., 218
Rutter, M., 570
Rutz, C., 517, 527n2
Ryan, C. M. E., 23, 44, 57, 348
Ryan, J. C., 109
Ryan, M. J., 615
Ryan, R. M., 664
Ryan, S. M., 628
Rylands, A. B., 540
Ryle, G., 343, 398

Saarinen, J., 18
Saayman, G., 595
Sackett, G. P., 62
Sacks, R. A., 287
Saffran, J. R., 397
Sahakian, B. J., 628
Sai, F., 640
Sakamoto, J., 619
Saksida, L. M., 146, 230, 237, 238
Sakuma, F., 517
Salih, H. R., 571
Salm, R. A., 532
Salmon, D. P., 79, 441, 531
Salovey, P., 566, 567
Samson, P., 230
Samuel, D., 29
Samuels, C. A., 643
Samuelson, R. J., 149, 427, 483
Sánchez-Moreno, J., 214
Sanchez-Santed, F., 624
Sanders, R. J., 482
Sands, S. F., 167, 168, 174, 176, 407, 439
Sanford, A. J., 497, 498, 504, 508
Santiago, H. C., 174
Santos, L. R., 64, 376–79, 536, 591
Sargent, T. D., 109, 116
Sartor, J. J., 81
Sato, A., 38–39, 49
Sato, M., 560
Saunders, K. J., 416
Saunders, R. R., 418
Savage-Rumbaugh, E. S., 128, 370, 376, 379, 588
Savastano, H. I., 213
Scarpuzzi, M., 591
Scarr, S., 570
Schacter, D. L., 230, 440
Schaffer, M. M., 327, 328, 348, 397
Schall, J. D., 135
Schatz, B., 240
Schmahmann, J. D., 565
Schmid-Hempel, P., 200
Schmidt, F. L., 571

Schmidt, R. A., 477
Schneider, B. A., 272
Schneider, H., 540
Schneider, W., 134
Schneirla, T. C., 677n2
Schofield, N. J., 569
Schölkopf, B., 201
Schrier, A. M., 366, 367
Schulman, R. J., 557
Schultz, W. J., 624
Schusterman, R. J., 415, 557, 583, 586
Schwarz, M., 441
Schyns, P., 327
Scopatz, R. A., 168, 439, 440, 445
Scott, P., 563
Searcy, W. A., 476
See, J. E., 131
Seelig, D., 376
Séguinot, V., 204
Seidenberg, M. S., 397
Sekiama, M. L., 532, 536
Sekuler, A. B., 23, 24, 42, 49, 55, 58
Self, R., 426
Seligman, M. E. P., 671
Sellen, K., 196
Seward, J. P., 157
Seyfarth, R. M., 371, 372, 674, 676
Seymour, K. H., 477
Shah, D., 202
Shallice, T., 131–32
Shapiro, K. L., 178
Shapley, R., 59
Shaw, S. R., 563
Shell, P., 556
Shepard, R. N., 101
Sherburne, L. M., 408, 409, 414, 652
Sherry, D. F., 160, 230, 610, 627
Shettleworth, S. J., 23, 42, 53, 55, 112, 113, 156, 201, 218, 559, 608, 611, 674
Shibata, Y., 517
Shields, W. E., 388
Shiffrin, R. M., 134, 174, 180
Shimizu, T., 42, 44, 49, 109, 624, 627
Shimp, C. P., 20, 314, 388–90, 392–94, 396–402, 403n1, 585
Shinohara, T., 621
Shipley, T. F., 25, 41, 45, 48, 57, 59
Shipley, W. C., 405
Sholl, M. J., 222
Shulman, G. L., 395
Shultz, T. R., 376
Si, A., 192
Sibley, C. G., 72
Sibly, R. M., 242
Siddall, J. W., 325, 327
Sidman, M., 415, 417, 418, 559
Siegel, J. J., 53
Siegler, R. S., 477, 594
Siemann, M., 325, 557–60, 562, 571
Silk, J. B., 371
Similä, T., 590
Simmelhag, V. L., 298, 299
Simmon, F., 643
Simon, B. B., 590
Simon, H. A., 446
Singh, M., 59
Sinha, S. N., 570
Sitompul, A. F., 546
Skinner, B. F., 7, 439, 445, 477, 481, 581, 668–70, 672–73
Sklepkovych, B., 603
Slater, A. M., 23, 44, 57
Slater, P. J., 476
Sloman, S. A., 558
Slotnick, B. M., 557
Slovic, P., 398
Slumskie, S. V., 158, 159, 427, 431
Smales, S., 568
Smith, B. A., 211
Smith, C., 201, 379
Smith, D. J., 388
Smith, E. E., 327, 328, 343, 509
Smith, J. D., 351
Smith, J. M., 459
Smith, J. N. M., 109
Smith, S. T., 370
Smith, T., 406
Smith, W., 433, 434
Smith Churchland, P., 571
Smolker, R., 590, 591
Smyth, B., 335
Snodgrass, R. D., 504
Snow, R. E., 555
Snyder, A. W., 569
Snyder, C. R. R., 111
Soares, A. H., 629
Sokal, R. R., 80
Sol, D., 631
Solomon, R. L., 250
Sommer, T., 135
Son, L., 483, 490, 501–3, 506, 507, 509, 509n1
Sontag, K. H., 441
Soraci, S. A., 322
Sorce, J. F., 646
Sousa, C., 640, 647
Sovrano, V. A., 64, 210, 219
Spaepen, G. M., 376, 591
Spalding, D. A., 66
Spalding, T. L., 366
Speck, G. B., 571
Spelke, E. S., 38, 56, 64, 130, 210, 211, 219, 376, 526–27, 567
Spellman, B. A., 560
Spence, C., 571
Spence, K. W., 350, 668
Sperling, G., 133
Spetch, M. L., 63, 66, 201, 210–25, 298–300, 414
Spinath, F. M., 569
Spinka, M., 594
Spinozzi, G., 20, 21, 369
Spradlin, J. E., 410, 418
Squire, L. R., 585
Srinivasan, M. V., 189, 190, 192–93, 205, 426
Staddon, J. E. R., 112, 272, 286, 294, 298, 299, 401, 415, 426, 476, 557, 559
Stadler, M. A., 322
Stankow, L., 557
Stanton, R., 348, 351
Stark, K., 176
Stebbins, W. C., 90
Steirn, J. N., 153, 407
Stempowski, N. K., 446, 447, 453
Stephens, D. W., 109
Sterio, D., 214
Sternberg, R. J., 556, 560, 568
Sternberg, S., 89, 507
Stettner, L. J., 624
Stevens, S. S., 270
Stevens, T. A., 604
Stevenson-Hinde, J., 671
Stoddard, L. T., 415
Stokes, P. D., 307, 463, 470, 477
St. Père, F., 571
Straub, R. O., 482, 486
Strawbridge, C. P., 322
Strecker, U., 117
Street, E. A., 130
Stretch, V., 173
Strik, W. K., 629
Stroop, J. R., 131
Stubbs, A., 285, 288, 290, 291
Stubbs, D. A., 290, 298
Sturdy, C. B., 71, 81
Stuss, D. T., 629
Subiaul, F., 483, 509
Suddendorf, T., 146, 372, 615
Suga, N., 395
Sugita, Y., 39, 44
Sun, X. D., 396
Suomi, S. J., 129, 379, 533, 534, 538, 640–41
Surprenant, A. M., 170, 178
Sutherland, R. J., 626
Sutherland, W. J., 607
Sutton, J. E., 158, 159, 217, 218, 427, 431, 652
Suzuki, S., 426
Swain, N., 626
Swank, P. R., 570
Swartz, H., 546

Swartz, K. B., 148, 440, 485, 487, 490–93
Sweatman, H. P. A., 109
Swets, J. A., 101, 314
Szostek, S., 570

Taborsky, M., 519, 520, 632
Taffe, M. A., 133
Tailby, W., 418
Takahashi, M., 49
Takeshita, H., 641
Takeuchi, A. H., 71
Tallarico, R. B., 557
Tan, A. O., 231, 232
Tanaka, H., 20, 21
Tanaka, M., 367, 369, 530, 640, 641, 643, 644
Tanji, J., 509
Tanner, W. P., 314
Tarsitano, M. S., 200
Tarvin, K. A., 109
Tautz, J., 192, 193
Tavolga, M. C., 594
Taylor, C. K., 595
Taylor, G. T., 663
Taylor, J. R., 343, 354–55
Taylor, T. J., 280, 281
Tebbich, S., 519, 520, 523, 526
Temple, W., 62
ten Cate, C., 610
Ten Eyck, G. R., 626
Terrace, H. S., 147–48, 439–40, 445, 447, 449, 482–83, 485–87, 490–508, 509n1, 509n8, 672
Terrinoni, M., 427, 429, 430
Thagard, P. R., 597
Theall, L. A., 372, 566, 589
Theeuwes, J., 136, 137
Thines, G., 53
Thinus-Blanc, C., 64, 221, 426
Thomas, D. R., 129
Thompson, C. R., 482
Thompson, R. K. R., 168, 335, 369, 412, 415
Thompson, T., 8, 412
Thorndike, E. L., 581
Thorpe, C. M., 231–37, 240, 241
Throckmorton, B., 566
Timberlake, W., 154, 240, 241, 567
Timmermans, S., 631
Tinbergen, L., 94, 107, 109, 110, 123, 398
Tinbergen, N., 210, 669
Tinklepaugh, O. L., 661
Titchener, E. B., 127
Tjian, R., 570
Tobin, H., 154
Todd, I. A., 301
Tolman, E. C., 4, 8, 156–58, 213, 426, 432, 483, 581, 590, 596–97, 668
Tomasello, M., 365, 372, 375, 376–77, 381, 520, 530, 531, 547, 566, 581, 588, 589, 639–40, 644–45, 647, 648
Tomback, D. F., 607, 610
Tommasi, L., 58–60, 64–66, 211, 222–24, 226
Tomonaga, M., 17, 20–21, 42, 135, 640–41, 643, 644, 647
Tonooka, R., 647
Tooby, J., 363
Toth, J. P., 171
Towe, A. L., 55
Towse, J. N., 469
Trabasso, T., 129
Treisman, A. M., 19, 92, 93, 97, 106, 127, 133, 335
Trevarthen, C., 643
Trinca, L., 377, 533, 538
Troje, N. F., 330, 332, 333, 336, 338, 339
Trone, M., 594
Truppa, V., 20
Tschudin, A., 589
Tulving, E., 146, 165, 170, 171, 173, 242, 445
Tune, G. S., 131
Turkheimer, E., 570
Tversky, A., 95, 333
Tversky, B., 381
Tversky, S., 398
Tyack, P. L., 582
Tyler, L. K., 583
Tzourio-Mazoyer, N., 568

Ueno, Y., 530
Ugarte, F., 590
Ullman, J. R., 326
Underwood, B. J., 168, 176
Uno, H., 628
Upton, D., 629
Urbani, B., 534
Urcuioli, P. J., 168, 287, 325, 407–18
Usher, M., 180
Ushitani, T., 39, 42, 43, 49
Uttal, W. R., 425
Uyeyama, R. K., 582, 585, 586

Vaccarino, A. L., 627
Valderrama, X., 536
Valentine, J. D., 469
Vallortigara, G., 23–25, 44, 49, 55–56, 58–66, 210, 211, 219, 223, 224, 226
Vance, E., 594
van der Elst, C., 589
Vander Wall, S. B., 149, 170, 603–8
van Dongen, P. A. M., 564
van Eden, C. G., 236
Van Hamme, L. J., 55, 337
van Kampen, H. S., 174
van Nest, J., 21
Van Sant, P., 326, 327, 332, 367
van Schaik, C. P., 519, 520, 546, 547
Van Zandt, T., 89, 100, 102
Varlet, C., 158
Vauclair, J., 16, 17, 26, 64, 221, 367, 410, 418, 620
Vaughan, J., 135
Vaughan, W., Jr., 26, 406, 619
Vaughan, W. J., 329, 331, 357, 432
Vecera, S. P., 135, 643
Veenman, C. L., 565, 628
Verbeek, N. A. M., 604, 606–8
Verin, M., 629
Vernon, P. A., 569
Verry, D. R., 426, 440, 446
Vesely, M., 195
Vetter, T., 330, 332
Vick, S., 375
Vickrey, C., 470
Vieira, A., 93
Vignal, C., 566
Visalberghi, E., 376–77, 379, 519, 523, 530–35, 538–42, 544, 546, 547
Viswanathan, G. M., 477
Vitale, A. F., 538, 546
Volman, S. F., 81, 563
von der Heydt, R., 57
von Fersen, L., 331, 346, 349–51, 558–60, 565, 582
von Frisch, K., 190–92, 205
von Glaserfeld, E. C., 482
Vonk, J., 344, 367, 370, 372, 375, 380
von Selzam, A., 557
Voss, C., 467, 475
Vreven, D., 111

Wagenaar, W. A., 468–69
Wagner, A. R., 213
Wagner, H., 57
Wahl, O., 240
Wake, D. B., 563
Wakita, M., 619
Waldron, M., 570
Walke, L., 594
Wallace, D. G., 426, 440
Wallace, R. J., 149
Wallis, J. D., 569
Wang, S. S.-H., 566
Wansley, R., 242

Want, S., 542
Ward, W. D., 72, 82, 83
Ward-Robinson, J., 214, 412, 433
Warm, J. S., 131
Warren, J. M., 557
Washburn, D. A., 20, 21, 128, 130–34, 138, 371, 388, 597
Washburn, M. F., 266, 581, 590, 677n2
Wasserman, E. A., 4, 6, 26, 49, 55, 57, 127–29, 147, 307, 308, 310–12, 314, 315, 317, 319–22, 326, 328, 330, 335, 337, 367–69, 405, 408, 410, 412, 414, 476, 558, 561, 615, 619, 620
Watanabe, S., 42, 43, 49, 55, 327, 337, 351, 352, 619–23, 626–29
Wathen, C. N., 432, 439
Watkins, M. J., 176, 181
Watson, J. B., 266, 532, 581
Watson, N. P., 240
Waugh, N. C., 174
Wearden, J. H., 276
Weaver, J. E., 411
Webber, M. I., 109
Wehner, R., 189–97, 200–202, 204, 205, 426, 427
Wehner, S., 189, 190
Weir, A. A. S., 517, 525, 526, 527n2, 547, 560, 630
Weiskrantz, L., 169
Weisman, R. G., 71–74, 77, 79–81, 83, 147
Weiss, R. L., 468
Weissenbach, J., 570
Wellman, H. M., 639
Werner, H., 588
Werner, T. J., 286, 287
Wesp, R., 628
West, R. E., 130
Westbrook, R. F., 327
Westergaard, G. C., 379, 530, 533–34, 538, 541, 546
Westwood, R., 272
Wheeler, M. A., 176
Wheeler, R. L., 153
Wheelwright, S., 643
Whiskin, E. E., 621
White, K. G., 293, 352
White, N. R., 83
Whiten, A., 372, 381, 519, 520, 566, 639, 646
Whitham, T. S., 109
Whitt, K. A., 395
Whittle, P., 631
Wickens, D. D., 168
Wickler, W., 561
Widman, D. R., 240–41
Wiens, J. J., 610
Wigmore, S. W., 621
Wilcox, R. S., 200, 581
Wild, J. M., 565
Wilde, J., 17
Wilkens, H., 117
Wilkie, D. M., 146, 229–43, 290, 298, 299
Wilkinson, G. S., 563
Williams, B. A., 662
Williams, D. C., 416
Williams, L., 352
Williams, M. N., 565
Williams, M. T., 71
Williams, S., 622
Willingham, D. B., 441
Willson, R. J., 230
Wilson, B., 521, 560, 590
Wilson, E. O., 567
Wilson, J., 395
Wilson, M., 148, 435, 597
Wiltschko, R., 565
Wiltschko, W., 565
Wimmer, H., 639
Winberg, J., 83
Winograd, E., 169, 178
Wintersteen, J., 436
Wiser, M., 379
Wittgenstein, L., 9, 343, 355, 398–400, 402
Wixted, J. T., 173, 301, 311, 314, 662
Wohlgemuth, S., 193
Wohlschläger, A., 571
Wolfe, J. M., 92
Wolz, J. P., 582
Woodruff, G., 7, 369, 371, 372, 375–76, 588, 639
Woodruff, R. S., 127
Woolfenden, G. E., 109, 607
Wooten, B. R., 91
Wright, A. A., 167, 168, 174, 176–79, 398, 407, 439, 569
Wu, H. M., 62
Wyler, A. R., 629
Wynne, C. D. L., 272, 559, 626, 676

Xia, L., 560, 562
Xi-Chun, M., 624
Xitco, M. J., 586, 589, 596

Yakovlev, B., 509n7
Yamaguchi, M. K., 640, 641
Yamakoshi, G., 546
Yamamoto, A., 233
Yamanaka, R., 42, 49
Yamazaki, Y., 621, 624
Yan, J., 395
Yanagihara, S., 66, 627
Yang, S. Y., 433
Yantis, S., 128
Yasukawa, K., 476
Yeo, R. A., 569
Yeomans, M., 174
Yerkes, R. M., 581, 596
Yoerg, S. I., 3, 5–6, 10, 296
Yonelinas, A. P., 170, 171, 173
Young, M. E., 26, 49, 57, 129, 307, 310–12, 314–17, 319–22, 335, 368–69, 476, 561
Young, R. J., 130
Yu, K. S., 146, 604, 615
Yund, E. W., 395

Zacks, J. M., 381
Zajonc, R. B., 570
Zaki, S. R., 348
Zanforlin, M., 57, 58, 60–64, 211, 219
Zatorre, R. J., 568
Zavortink, B., 489
Zawilinska, B., 570
Zeil, J., 189, 190, 193–94, 201
Zeiler, C., 430–32
Zeiler, M. D., 235, 276, 290
Zentall, T. R., 6, 49, 153, 166, 233, 301, 316, 407–9, 411, 414, 418, 558, 581, 652–54, 655–60
Zgorniaknowosielska, I., 570
Zhang, S. W., 192, 193
Zhang, Y., 395
Zhou, X., 395
Zhou, Z., 565
Zohary, E., 509n7
Zuberbühler, K., 530
Zuriff, G. E., 6, 9

Subject Index

absolute pitch (AP), 71
  across avian and mammalian species, 73–74
    discriminating among 27 individual tones, 74–76
    discriminating among 27 two-tone sequences, 77, 79
    easy and more difficult three-range discriminations, 74, 75
    eight-range discriminations, 76–77
  across avian species, 79–81
  and continuity of species, 83–84
  defined, 71
  discrimination of S+ from S– tones, 80, 81
  and experience, 81, 82
  gender and, 81
  in humans and songbirds, 71–73
  musical *vs.* general, 71, 72
  what avian auditory psychophysics tells us about, 83
absolute pitch (AP) tasks, laboratory
  comparative evidence from, 73–82
abstraction, 376, 401, 558. *See also* features
  of feature distributions, 352–54
  levels of, 335, 344–45, 366–67
    animal studies on, 344
acquired equivalence, 405–6, 417–18. *See also under* responses
active selection bias, 107
adaptive specialization, 612–13
adaptive specialization hypothesis, 604, 610–12, 614
ambiguity
  abstract rule learning in the face of, 389–92
  Gestalt reversible images and, 398
amodal completion, 25, 38, 45, 49, 54, 57. *See also* depth perception; occluded objects
  perception of object unity in nonhuman primates, 38–43
  pigeon problem, 42–44
  stimulus display inducing, 23
  what determines completion by monkeys, 41–42
anticipation of future events. *See also* aversive event
  evidence concerning animals', 153–56
anticipatory contrast, 661
anticipatory mediated generalization. *See* generalization, mediated
apostatic selection, 107, 118, 119
arthropod navigation. *See* navigation; route following
artificial grammar, 396
artificial grammar learning, rule learning and memorization strategies in, 396–97
attention, 93–95, 127–28. *See also* dolphin pointing; perceptual grouping; searching image; selective attention; stimuli
  aspects/dimensions of and metaphors for, 138
  attempts to manipulate another's, 607
  as controlled by environmental, experiential, and executive constraints, 136–38
  defined, 112
  as effect and cause of selection for processing, 133–36
  flexibility of, 391–92
    in local/global task, 391–96
  flexible allocation of, 398
  generalization across species regarding, 128–38
  is inhibited in the absence of change, 130–31
  research on, 106
  role in other cognitive abilities, 127–28
  shared, 645–46
  shifting focus of, 332–33
  stimuli eliciting, 131–33
  theories of, 127–28
    cause *vs.* effect theories, 133
  types of, 134, 135, 138

attraction, 476
attribute frequency model, 349
auditory list memory, interference processes in, 178–81
auditory list-memory processing, 177–78
automaticity, 132. *See also under* list-memory processing
averaging mechanism, 203–4
aversive event. *See also* anticipation of future events
  absence of reinforcement as, 656
  anticipation of absence of reinforcement as, 658–60
  anticipation of effort as, 657
  delay to reinforcement as, 655–56
aversiveness, relative
  of prior event, 655–60
avoidance learning, 249–51
avoidance procedure, Sidman, 254

background matching, 116–17
basal ganglion, 627–28. *See also* medial lobus parolfactorius
beacons and beaconing behavior, 199
behaving theory, 401
behavior, purpose of, 668–69
behavioral contrast, 661–62
behavioral mediation hypothesis, 298–99
behavioral theory of timing (BeT), 286, 293, 298
behaviorism
  and behavioral psychology of Skinner, 672–73
  operational, 9
biased forgetting, 300–301
birdsong, 72
bisection point, 290, 291
blocking, 214
blue jay (*Cyanocitta cristata*), 109–10
brain. *See also* neural tissue
  and intelligence, 563–65 (*see also* intelligence)
broadcast theory of timing, 280

cache recovery
  cognition in, 607–11
  social aspects of, 609–11
caching, 615
  to cache or not to cache, 603–4
  evolution and, 611–15
  role of cognition in, 604–7
  seasonal patterns in intensity of, 605
  social aspects of, 606–7
  what, when, and where to cache, 604–6
caching events, remembering the "what-where-and-when" of, 607–9
card sorting task, 629
categories, 343, 389. *See also* features
  basic objects in natural, 344–45
  m-out-of-n polymorphous, 345–51, 621
  nonlinearly separable, 355
  prototype, 345, 351–52
  superordinate, 344
    prototypicality in, 345
    structured by family resemblance, 355–56
categorization, 325–27, 343, 558. *See also* abstraction; concept formation
  avian visual, 402
    empirical research on, 388–98, 401–2
    Wittgensteinian evaluative perspectives on, 399–400
  flexibility in use of strategies for, 332–37
  item-specific/nonanalytic strategy of, 328
  perspectives on, from Wittgenstein's two philosophies, 398–400
  remaining questions regarding, 401–2
  theories of, 401 (*see also* modified feature theory of categorization)
category members, superordinate
  functional equivalence of, 357–60
category membership, gradient of, 346
category-specific features and information, 328–31. *See also* features
causality, physical
  conception of, 376–80
causal role of unobservables in behavior, 381–82
chaining paradigms, 483. *See also* simultaneous chaining paradigm
chaining theory, 481–83, 502, 507. *See also* simultaneous chaining paradigm
  Lashley's critique of, 481
change. *See* same/different (S/D) discrimination
"chimpanzee politics," 566
choose-short effect, 300
choose-small effect, 300
chunk boundaries, rats' use of compound cues to anticipate, 447–49
chunk formation. *See also under* sequences
  independent of associative demands, 447
chunking patterns by overshadowing, phrasing cues as discriminative stimuli for, 446–47
circadian and short-interval timing research, integration of, 281
circadian rhythms and internal clocks, 146, 237, 242, 300. *See also* timing
classification schemes. *See also* categorization
  second-order, 369
classification theories, 347–51. *See also* categorization
Clayton experiments, 149, 151
clock, internal. *See* circadian rhythms and internal clocks; timing, explanations of
cognition. *See also specific topics*
  animal, 53, 672 (*see also* comparative cognition)
    history of, 668–70, 672
  "higher-order," 365
  interest in the study of primate, 15
  studying the generality of, 5
cognitive abilities, 568. *See also specific topics*
  metabolic costs of, 117
cognitive adaptations, generalized *vs.* specialized, 526–27
cognitive control, 132
cognitive dissonance, 664. *See also* aversiveness; justification of effort
  in humans, 652
cognitive ethology, 3, 8–9
cognitive flexibility. *See* flexibility, cognitive
cognitive mapping, 213. *See also* mapping

cognitive maps, 156–57, 204, 426
cognitive processes
  development of, 674–75
  distinguishing other mental processes from, 4–5
  literature on, in 1978 and 2005, 673–74
cognitive processing, limits of, 128–29, 131
cognitive revolution, 400, 481
cognitive spatial displacement, 156–60
cognitive spatial travel, 145
cognitive time travel, 145, 146
common coding, 408
communication strategy, spontaneous
  dolphin pointing as, 586–90
communication systems of dolphins, 582
comparative cognition, 4, 5, 674. *See also* cognition; *specific topics*
  agenda of, 9–10
  central issues in, 5–9
    definitional and observational concerns, 4–5
    experimental locale, 6
  developments in the field of, 672
  future study of, 674–76
    applied work, 675
    going into the field, 674
  harbingers of, 670
    computer metaphor, 670–71
    demise of responses as arbitrary events, 671
    Lashley and the problem of serial order in behavior, 670
    rise of representation, 671
  natural science approach to, 5
  present study of, 673–74
  resolving methodological issues in, 82–83
  today, 673–74
comparative pseudo-cognition, 675–76
comparative psychology, 364
competition, 477
complementarity, principle of, 129
completion processes/perceptual completion, 25, 44–45. *See also* depth perception
  induced by visual depth cues, 25
  modal *vs.* amodal, 38 (*see also* amodal completion)
complex naturalistic behavior, 402
compound cues
  used to anticipate chunk boundaries, 447–49
  used to anticipate violation elements, 449–50
concept discrimination, 619
concept discrimination tasks, ways of solving, 326
concept formation, 365–71, 558–59
  according to functional equivalencies in pigeons, 558, 559
concept(s). *See also* features
  animal, 367
  artificial, 622
  natural, 622–23
  negative, 621–22
  notion of, 326
  social, 370–71
conceptual cognition, neural basis of
  as visual agnosia *vs.* learning deficit, 622–23
conceptualization, 405–6. *See also* acquired equivalence
conditional emotional response procedure, 254–56
configural perception, 337
connectionist model of timing, 286
consciousness, 671, 677n4
consistent mapping, 134
contention scheduling, 131, 132
context theory (classification), 348–49
contours
  occluded, 41 (*see also* occlusion)
  subjective, 57–58 (*see also* Kanizsa's triangle)
contrafreeloading, 663
contrast, 660–61
  types of, 661–63
contrast effect, 660–61
  within-subject, 662–63
controlled memory, 170
control system. *See* servomechanisms
corridor illusion, 22–23
corvids. *See* caching
counting hypothesis, 298
count *vs.* time mode, 286
crows. *See* New Caledonian crows

dead reckoning, 156
deception/deceptive strategies, 606, 607
delayed matching-to-sample (DMTS), 173
  single-item memory in, 164–67
delayed reduction theory, 660
delayed response problem, 62–63
depth perception, 21
  in baboons *vs.* humans, 15–16, 21–26
detour behavior, 60–61
Dickinson experiments, 149, 151
diet selection theory, 109
difference. *See* same/different (S/D) concepts; same/different (S/D) discrimination; similarity, and difference
differential-outcomes effect, 153
direction, telling, 191–92
discrimination
  simple pattern, 622
  two-dimensional (2D) *vs.* three-dimensional (3D), 623
discrimination learning, 286
discriminative cues, 460–61
discriminative processes, what reaction time (RT) distributions show about, 97–103
distance and magnitude effects, 497–98
  with arbitrary list items, 499, 501–4
  in humans *vs.* monkeys, 504–8
  obtained with numerical stimuli, 498–500
  in rhesus macaques, 498
distance-from-category-boundary peak-shift, 350–52
distance traveled, computing, 192–93
diversity. *See also* same/different (S/D) concepts; same/different (S/D) discrimination
  two faces of, 363–64
  without hierarchy, 380
dolphin play, and ontogeny of problem solving, 594–96

dolphin pointing, as spontaneous communication strategy, 586–90
dolphins
 ability to consider the other's perspective, 589
 communication systems of, 582
 gestural sequence processing in, 582–86
 planning their behavior, 590–94
 problem solving in, 580–82, 596–97
dominance, concept of, 371
duration, memory of, 259–60. *See also* timing, explanations of
duration discrimination. *See* temporal and numerosity discrimination

ectostriatum, 622–23, 626
edge-sensitive processes, 39
"education by master-apprenticeship," 646–47
effect, law of, 251–53
emotional intelligence, 566–67
emotions, 370–71
empathy. *See* dolphins, ability to consider the other's perspective
encoding information, 64–66
enculturation, 639
entopallium. *See* ectostriatum
entropy, 314–22
episodic-like memory and caching, 607–9
episodic memory(ies)
 in animals, evidence for, 146–53
 defined, 145, 146, 242
 familiarity, identity, and, 169–71
 in rats, search for, 149–53
 time-place learning and, 242
ethology, history of, 669–70
events, number of
 as time marker, 146
evolution
 caching and, 611–15
 of cognitive abilities, implications of cognition research for, 117–22
exemplar models of categorization, 328, 354–55
exemplars
 dynamic, 391–92
 static, 389–91
expectancy theory. *See* scalar expectancy theory
expectation, 95
 hunting by, 108–9, 111
exploration, 477

face recognition. *See* gaze recognition
familiarity
 vs. identity, 169–71
 vs. other forms of memory processing, 170
 proactive interference (PI) and, 169–73
family resemblance, superordinate categories structured by, 343, 355–56, 397
feature distributions, abstraction of, 352–54
feature frequency model, 349
feature learning, 332
feature lists, internal, 339
feature-positive effect, 330
features, 325–26. *See also* abstraction
 abstraction of category-specific, 328–31
 distinctive, 92
 as distinctive aspects of forms, 92
 dynamic, 333
 flexibility in creation and selection of, 327
 global *vs.* local, 335–36
 role in identification of objects, 92
 shifting focus of attention between various, 332–33
 "simple" *vs.* "higher," 337–38
feature theories of categorization, 328, 339. *See also* modified feature theory (MFT) of categorization
"fixed pacemaker" assumption, 293
flexibility, cognitive. *See also* attention, flexibility of; learned behavior, changing
 in creation and selection of features, 327
 origin of, 632
 in use of strategies for categorization, 332–37
food-caching. *See* caching
foraging behavior, 107, 149
 operant techniques and, 109–11
 selective attention and, 106–9
forgetting, biased, 300–301
forgetting model, 113
functional response, Type II *vs.* Type III, 107

gap procedure, 259
gaze, mutual, 642–43
gaze following, 643–45
 defined, 643
gaze recognition, 642–43
 recognition of mother's face, 640–42
generalization, 203–4, 619, 665. *See also* responses, as source of acquired equivalence; temporal generalization procedure
 across species regarding attention, 128–38
 averaging mechanism and, 203–4
 concept discrimination and, 619
 mediated, 406, 411–15
geometrical module, 64, 218–19
geometrical representation, nature of, 222–23
geometric sense of space, 63
geometry, making "natural," 63–66
gestural sequence processing in dolphins, 582–86
global advantage, 17, 18
global precedence effect, 17–18. *See also* perceptual grouping
global precedence hypothesis, 17
global-to-local inference, 17, 18
global vector, 190, 195–96
global *vs.* local properties, 335–36
goals, 668–69
grammar. *See* artificial grammar; dolphins, gestural sequence processing

habituation, 476
 and dishabituation, 56–57, 130
hemispheric specialization, 224–25
hippocampus, 454, 611–14, 626–27, 631–32

homology and homoplasy, 611–12
hunting. *See also* foraging behavior
  by expectation, 108–9, 111

ideal list learners, 488, 489
ideational behavior, 596
identity judgments, 169–70
illusions. *See also* Ponzo illusion
  types of, 29–30
image matching, 201
  landmark-based, 201
imprinting, 55
incentive contrast, 661
"incompleteness." *See* occlusion
independent cue models (classification), 347–48
information processing, limited capacity for, 128–29, 131
information-processing components of timing system, 285–86
information processing model of timing, 274
information-processing strategies, 582–86
inhibition of delay, 249–51
inhibition of return, 135
innovation, 630–31
  brain and, 631–32
  defined, 630
intelligence(s), 307–8, 555–56, 570–71
  animal, 556–62
  developing, 569–70
  evolving, 562–63
  general, 568–69
  genetics, biology, and, 569–70
  human, 567–70
  origins of, 562–67
  types of, 307, 565–69
intelligence tests, 555, 556, 568–71
intelligent brains, 563–65
intersubjectivity, primary, 643
interval time-place learning (TPL). *See also* time-place learning
  advances in, 231–37
  background information on, 230, 231
interval time-place (TP) task, unequal, 234–35
interval timing, 146–47, 229, 230, 281, 282. *See also* timing
invalid cues, costs of, 135–36
inverse hypothesis, 129
item-specific features and information, 328–31. *See also* categorization
item variability. *See* entropy

jays, 109–10
junction cues and reliability, role in depth perception of, 25–26
justification of effort, 663–64
  in humans, 652–53
  in pigeons, 653–55

Kanizsa's illusion, 43
Kanizsa's triangle, 30, 38, 57
knowing, 170. *See also* familiarity
knowledge acquisition, 477

Lana's "linguistic" sequences, analysis of, 482
landmark-based image matching, 201
landmark-based search, 212–14, 226
  open-field and touch-screen tasks, 211–12
  transformational approach to, 210–11
landmark configurations, learning relative relationships about, 218
landmarks, 191–92, 201. *See also* navigation; route following
  arrays of identical, absolute *vs.* relative relationships in, 214–18
  encoding locations from surfaces *vs.* discrete, 223–26
  interactions among multiple, 212
language, 15, 673. *See also* dolphins
latent learning experiments, 157
learned behavior, changing, 623–29
  neural structure of, 630
learned equivalence, 405. *See also* acquired equivalence
learned industriousness, 665
learning. *See also specific topics*
  of discriminations, 286
  reversal, 557, 624–25
  as spatial pattern detection, 425–26
learning sets, 556–58, 624, 671
lexigrams, 482, 483
linear feature model, 348
linear optimal decision bounds, 390, 391
linear timing (hypothesis), 270–75. *See also* nonlinear sensitivity to timing
  timing theories and, 279–81
line-drawn perspective, and Ponzo illusion, 32–33
"linguistic" sequences, Lana's
  analysis of, 482
list memory, interference processes in auditory, 178–81
list-memory processing, 168–69, 181
  auditory, 177–81
  automatic processes and, 174, 181
  visual, 174–76, 181
locale system, 157
local precedence effect, 17–20, 26. *See also* perceptual grouping
local vectors, 196
  desert ants', 196
local-view hypothesis, 156
local views, 156
local *vs.* global properties, 335–36
logical errors, 488

Machiavellian-intelligence hypothesis, 639
magnitude effects. *See* distance and magnitude effects
mapping
  cognitive, 213 (*see also* cognitive maps)
  consistent, 134
  varied, 134
marginal value theorem, 109
matching-to-sample (MTS) tasks, 322, 366, 369–70
mathematical abilities, 493. *See also* serial expertise

medial lobus parolfactorius, 625, 627–31
mediated generalization. *See* generalization, mediated
memories, 609
  delaying, 62–63
memorization strategies
  ability to switch, 398
  in artificial grammar learning, 396–97, 400
memory, 6, 164, 165, 671–72. *See also* forgetting
  historical perspective on, 669
  for the order of events, 147–49
  types of, 146, 147, 170, 242 (*see also* spatial memory; working memory)
memory decay, 165
memory load, 469
memory model of timing, 286
memory processing, in same/different (S/D) and list-memory tasks, 167–73
memory retrieval, 205
mental continuity between humans and nonhuman animals, 5
mentalism
  and cognition, 7–8
  and cognitive ethology, 3, 8–9
mental states. *See also* emotions; mind
  nonhuman primates' reasoning about, 372–76
metric encoding, 204–5
mind
  theory of, 371–72, 375, 376, 589, 639, 647–48 (*see also* mental states)
    unobservability hypothesis and research on, 371–76
  "windows" into the other's, 9
mind-reading system model, 647–48
modal completion, 38
modified feature theory (MFT) of categorization, 326–28, 338–39
  vs. other feature theories, 339
motivation, intrinsic
  vs. extrinsic reinforcement, 664–65
multiple control hypothesis, 297
multiple-oscillator theory of timing, 265, 266, 280
mutual gaze. *See* gaze, mutual

naturalistic visual concepts, 391
navigation. *See also* path integration; route following
  map-like, 201–4
  map- *vs.* route-based, 202–4
  memories used in, 205
negative concepts, 621–22
neostriatum caudolaterale (NCL), 62–63, 625
neural basis of visual concepts, 619–23
neural structure of changing learned behavior, 630
neural tissue. *See also* brain
  high metabolic cost of, 117
neurobiology, 675. *See also under* timing, explanations of
neuroscience, systems, 675
New Caledonian crows (*Corvus moneduloides*), tool use of, 515–16, 630, 631
  ecological explanations for, 525
  generalized *vs.* specialized cognitive adaptations and, 526–27
  in the laboratory, 520–21
    specific associations *vs.* general principles, 521–23
    tool selectivity, 521–23
  natural history and, 517
  social learning and, 525–26
  in the wild, 517–20
    comparison with other animals, 519–20
    natural history, 517
9-month revolution, 645
nonlinear optimal decision bounds, 390, 391
nonlinear sensitivity to timing, 275–79. *See also* linear timing (hypothesis); timing theories
nonlinear timing hypothesis, 270, 271. *See also* linear timing (hypothesis); timing theories
number discrimination. *See* temporal and numerosity discrimination
numerical abilities, 493. *See also* serial expertise
numerical categories, memory of, 494

object permanence, 57, 62
  development of, 60–61
object relations
  understanding first-order, 367–68
  understanding second-order, 368–70
object unity, perception of
  in nonhuman primates, 38–43
occluded objects
  recognizing partly, 54–59
  representing completely, 60–62
occlusion, visual, 41, 49
  as a cue to depth, 23–24
  establishing the direction of, 59–60
  is not inferred from junction cues, 24
oddity, stimulus, 319, 321, 322
odometry, 192–93
open hopper test (OHT), 231–32, 236
operant nature of variability, evidence for, 460–66
operant variability, 459, 460
  memory-based, 467–75
    reasons to respond unpredictably, 476–78
optimal decision bounds, linear *vs.* nonlinear, 390, 391
optimal decision rules, 390–92
optimality
  of behavior, 398
  in categorizing multidimensional stimuli, 390–92
order, memory for, 147–49
ordinal timing, 229
overselection by predators, 118
overshadowing, 212–14, 219–20
  phrasing cues as discriminative stimuli that chunk patterns by, 446–47
oystercatcher memory, 242–43

pacemaker-counter framework, 293
pacemaker countermechanisms, 293
packet theory, 265–66
paleostriatal complex, 627
paleostriatum augmentatum (PA), 627, 628

Pandanus leaf tools, 517–19
path integration, 189–93
  in fiddler crabs, 193–94
  learning and, 194–95
  metric coding required for, 204–5
pathogenesis, 204, 205
pattern discrimination, simple, 622
pattern elements, rats' use of different cues to anticipate different, 447–49
pattern learning. *See* spatial pattern learning
patterns. *See* spatial patterns
peak procedure, 263–64
peak-shift effects, 350–51, 355
people-present/people-absent discrimination studies, 328–38
perception, 29. *See also specific topics*
  elemental and configural, 337
perception-action routines, 536
perception-action theory of tool use, 536, 547, 548
perceptual grouping, in baboons *vs.* humans, 15, 26
  and attention to global and local stimulus levels, 20–21
    attention to global and local stimulus properties, 18–19
    global/local precedence effects, 17–18
    local precedence *vs.* global disadvantage, 19–20
perseverative errors, 488
phase timing, 229
phenotypic diversity, generation and maintenance of, 118–22
photographic perspective, and Ponzo illusion, 33–35
physical causality, conception of, 376–80
physical events, observable *vs.* unobservable features used to describe, 376, 377
pictorial depth. *See* depth perception
piloting, 210
Plaisted hypothesis, 113
planning, 590–94
  defined, 591
  route, 199–201
pointing, 586–90
point of subjective equality (PSE), 290, 291
polarized light, 191
pole box task, 432–35
  learning and performance in, 427–31
  separate systems for avoiding revisits and coding pole contents, 436
polymorphous categories
  m-out-of-n, 345–51, 621
  2-out-of-3, 345–46, 349
polymorphous stimuli, 343
Ponzo illusion, 29–30, 36–38, 48–49
  illusory perception by nonhuman primates, 31–32
  illusory perception by pigeons, 30–31
  line-drawn perspective and, 32–33
  photographic perspective and, 33–35
  short *vs.* converging lines and, 34, 36
"pop out," 92
practical intelligence, 567–68
predators. *See also* foraging behavior
  free-ranging, 107, 108
  overselection by, 118
prefrontal cortex, 62, 236
prey sequences, nonrandom, 107–9
primacy effect, visual, 176–77
primate cognition, interest in the study of, 15
primates
  illusory perception by, 31–32
  perception of object unity in, 38–43
  reasoning about mental states in, 372–76
priming, 132
  sequential and associative/symbolic, 111–12
    interactions between, 114–17
priming effects, negative, 133
proactive interference (PI), 166–70
  in auditory list memory, 178–81
  familiarity and, 169–73
  serial position function (SPF) and, 174–81
proactive interference (PI) function, testing familiarity and the, 171–73
problem solving, 580–81. *See also* dolphins
  types of, 596–97
protection, 476
prototype categories, 351–52
prototype effects, 346–49, 353, 355, 356, 361
prototype models, 351, 354–55
prototypes, defined, 351–52
prototype theory, 326
prototypicality
  in linearly separable categories, 352–55
  in superordinate categories, 345
prototypical *vs.* nonprototypical members of categories, 343
purpose of behavior, 668–69

ramped interval procedure, 265, 266
random, defined, 459–60
random operant responding, 459–60. *See also* operant nature of variability; operant variability
Raven intelligence scales, 555, 556
reaction time (RT), 102–3
  attention, expectation, and, 93–95
  contributions from visual search experiments, 91–97
  defined, 89
  as function of stimulus luminance, 90
  mathematical functions useful in modeling, 99–100
  visual processes and, 90–91
reaction time (RT)/display size functions, 91–93
reaction time (RT) distributions
  and control by incentive value, 101–3
  and control by stimulus onset, 98–99
  and control by target-distractor similarity, 99–101
  discriminative processes and, 97–103
reciprocity, 645–46. *See also* gaze, mutual
recognition, 95
  gaze, 642–43
  of mother's face, 640–42
recollection, 170
reference memory. *See* semantic/reference memory
reflection, 580–81

regularity rule, overall, 42
rehearsal, and visual primacy effect, 176–77
reinforcement, 460. *See also under* aversive event; temporal and numerosity discrimination; timing, explanations of
  intrinsic *vs.* extrinsic, 664–65
  of stochastic distributions, 461–66
reinterpretation hypothesis, 375–76
relatability rule, 41
relational discrimination learning, 307. *See also* same/different (S/D) discrimination
relational frequency models (classification), 349–50
relational representations, multifaceted nature of, 321–22
relations between objects. *See* object relations
relative delayed reduction theory, 660
relative delay reduction, 660–61
relative pitch (RP), 73
  defined, 73
remembering, 170
repeated acquisition, lesions and, 626
repeated acquisition procedure, 625–28
response dimensions, 461
response latency. *See* reaction time (RT)
response-mediated generalization. *See* generalization, mediated
responses
  as arbitrary events, 671
  as mediators of C-D transfer, 411–15
  as members of acquired equivalence classes, 415–18
  as source of acquired equivalence, 406–11, 417–18
response sets, 461
retroactive interference (RI), 176–81
reversal learning, 624–25
  serial, 557
rigidity concept experiment, 523–24
risk-sensitive foraging theory, 109
robots, 515, 516
rotation invariance, 561–62
route following, 196–201, 205
route planning in jumping spiders (*Portia*), 199–201
rule learning, 397–98
rule-learning theory of sequential behavior, 439–40

same/different (S/D) behavior
  approaches to, 321
  stimulus control of human, 319–21
same/different (S/D) concepts, 367, 368. *See also* concept formation; similarity, and difference
  convergent findings regarding, 308–13
  divergent and conflicting findings regarding, 313–18
  simultaneous, 308–11
  successive, 311–13
  uni- *vs.* multidimensional model of, 314
    dialectic and reconciliation, 318–19
same/different (S/D) discrimination, 308, 321–23
same/different (S/D) discrimination procedures, basic, 308–13
same/different (S/D) tasks, memory processing in, 167–69
scalar expectancy theory, 285
scalar timing theory, 261–64, 280
search asymmetry, 92–93
"search-image," nature of the, 94–97
searching behavior, 65–66
searching image
  attention, priming, and, 111–14
searching image hypothesis, 107–10
searching in enclosed spaces
  abstracting geometry from models and two-dimensional schemata, 221–22
  features that do not appear to overshadow, 219–20
  geometric module, 218–19
  nature of geometrical representation and, 222–23
  training experience and, 220–21
search systems, 190–91, 195
selection, apostatic, 107, 118, 119
selection bias, active, 107
selective attention, 106
  costs of, 117–18
  priming and, 112–14
self-control experiments, 153–54
semantic/reference memory, 146
sensorimotor vectors, 196
  bees' and wasps', 196–99
sequences
  Lana's "linguistic," 482
  resilience of within-chunk response, 453–54
sequential behavior, 439, 455. *See also* compound cues; serial patterns
  deconstructing, by probe methods, 447
  models of, 439–41
  neurobehavioral studies of, in rats, 454–55
sequential learning. *See also* serial patterns
  identification and study of concurrently active behavioral processes in, 441
sequential patterns, role of pattern elements as cues in, 452–53
sequential processors, animals as multimodality, 455
serial expertise, 486–87
  accuracy on partially completed trials, 489–90
  conditional probabilities that provide evidence of, 489–90
  derived lists, 491–92
  development of, 488–89
  difficulty of simultaneous chain as function of list length, 487–88
  ideal list learner, 488
  knowledge of ordinal position, 490–91
  memory of particular stimuli *vs.* numerical categories, 494
  numerical sequences, 492–94
    representation of, 494–96
serial learning, 481
serially organized behavior, 481. *See also* sequential behavior
  influence of "ape language" studies, 482
serial order in behavior, problem of, 670
serial-pattern learning method for rats, 441–42

serial patterns. *See also* sequential behavior
hierarchically-organized, 442–44
interleaved, 445–46
rats' sensitivity to structure and violations of structure in, 442–46
serial position (SP), 440. *See also* serial patterns
serial position function (SPF), 490, 491
and interference among list items, 174–81
serial probe recognition (SPR) task, 167
serial reversal learning, 557
servomechanisms, place-finding, 189, 190, 196, 205
shared (joint) engagement, 645–46
shortcut experiments, 157–58
Sidman avoidance procedure, 254
sigmoid diet functions, 107–9
signal detection theory, 314
similarity, 333, 363. *See also* categorization
and difference, 363–64 (*see also* same/different (S/D) concepts)
treated equally, 382
simultaneous chaining paradigm, 482, 484–85, 507, 509
simultaneous chain(s), 482–83, 489
as function of list length, difficulty of, 487–88
S-R chains *vs.* cognitive maps, 483
vs. successive chains, 483, 485
single-item memory, 180
in delayed matching-to-sample (DMTS), 164–67
skill acquisition, 477
sky-compass, 191
smooth interpolation, 39
social aspects of cache recovery, 609–11
social aspects of caching, 606–7
social cognition. *See also specific topics*
chimpanzee, 639–48
social concepts, 370–71
social intelligence, 565–67
social intelligence hypothesis, 639
social learning, 525–26
social transmission of cognitive skills, 647
songbirds, 72. *See also* absolute pitch
space, concept of. *See* cognitive spatial displacement; stuck-in-space hypothesis
spatial cognition, 210, 226. *See also* landmarks; searching
spatial cognitive displacement. *See* cognitive spatial displacement
spatial cues, hierarchal use of redundant, 212–13
spatial learning
cue competition in, 213–14
absence of cue-competition effects, 214
and spatial performance, 426–27
spatial memory, 611–14. *See also* adaptive specialization hypothesis
spatial pattern detection, learning as, 425–26
spatial pattern exemplar, use of positive and negative information about location of, 435–36
spatial pattern learning, 434–37. *See also* pole box task
as module separate from other spatial control mechanisms, 433
as part of more general pattern learning process, 433–34
spatial pattern representation *vs.* response learning, 431–33
spatial patterns, 437
conditional control by two, 435
as represented by figure and ground, 436
what is learned about, 431–34
spatial relations, static and dynamic, 538
spatial search, how the learned pattern influences, 434–36
spatial theory, 502
spatiotemporal boundary formation, 45–50
schematic representation of, 45
spontaneous recovery, 148
stimuli
can come to elicit attention via experience, 131–33
how many can be processed into behavior, 128–29
that can't be ignored and automatically influence behavior, 129–30
stimulus control, 132, 314
stimulus generalization, 619. *See also* generalization
stimulus "oddity," 319
stimulus-response (S-R) associationism, 670–73
stochastic-counting-cascades model of timing, 280–81
stochastic distributions, reinforcement of, 461–66
stochastic-generator hypothesis, 467, 469–70
stochasticity, 459–60, 476
evaluation of, 463–64
stochastic variability. *See also* operant variability
reasons for, 478
Stroop task, 131–32
stuck-in-space hypothesis, 145, 156, 160. *See also* cognitive spatial displacement
stuck-in-time hypothesis, 145, 148, 160. *See also* temporal displacement
subjective contours. *See* contours, subjective
subjective shortening, 300
successive chaining paradigm, 483
successive *vs.* simultaneous chains, 483, 485
superposition, 288–90
surface-based search
open-field and touch-screen tasks, 211–12
transformational approach to, 211
surfaces *vs.* discrete landmarks, encoding locations from, 223–26
syntactic abilities of dolphins, 582–86
systems neuroscience, 675

taxon system, 157
telencephalon, function of avian, 630
temporal and numerosity discrimination, 259–60, 285, 301–2
changing rates of reinforcement and, 293–95
stimulus control (analysis), 295–99
delayed discriminations, 299–301
history of attempts to understand, 285–86
learning, 286–88
psychophysics of, 288, 293
bisection, 290, 291
contextual, 290–93
superposition, 288–90

single mechanism underlying, 295–96, 301–2
stimulus duration and, 256–57
temporal bisection, 290, 291
temporal discrimination procedure, retention interval in, 259–60
temporal displacement, 146–56, 160
temporal generalization procedure, 262–63
temporal order of events, memory for, 147–49
temporal processing procedure, simultaneous, 263
thalamofugal visual system, 58
time, animals' sensitivity to, 146
timed performance, 249
time-horizon experiments, 154
time keeping. *See* temporal displacement
time left procedure, 261–62
time perception, 249, 281. *See also* timing
time-place (TP) behavior
distraction and, 232–34
prefrontal lesions and, 235–37
time-place-event codes, 240, 241, 242
time-place learning (TPL), 229, 242–43. *See also* interval time-place learning
daily, 237–41
memory theories and, 241–43
time *vs.* count mode, 286
timing. *See also* linear timing (hypothesis); nonlinear sensitivity to timing
types of, 229
timing, explanations of, 266, 274. *See also* timing theories
by characteristics of internal clock (cognitive), 253–54, 267–68, 300
characteristics of internal clock, criterion, and response rule, 257–58
control of internal clock: gap procedure, 259
expected time to reinforcement, 254–56
proportional timing, 254
temporal memory, 259–60
variability of internal clock: titration procedure, 256–57
by general principles (behavioristic), 249, 266–67
inhibition of delay: avoidance learning, 249–51
law of effect: competition, 251–52
stimulus control: differential reinforcement of short-latency responses, 252–53
by mathematical models (quantitative), 261, 268
multiple oscillator theory, 265, 266, 280
packet theory, 265–66
scalar timing theory, 261–64, 280
by neural mechanisms (biological), 260–61, 268
timing mechanism, 286
timing theories, 279–81, 288. *See also* temporal and numerosity discrimination; timing, explanations of
Gibbon and Church's model, 285–86
titration procedure, 256–57
tool use, 515–16, 529–30, 547–48, 646–47
in capuchin monkeys (*Cebus apella*), 530, 531, 536–38, 547–48
behavioral and environmental factors promoting and constraining, 546–47
for first-order problems (single relations), 537–40
historical overview of tool use reports, 531–36
for moving across irregular surfaces, 542–46
for second-order problems (two relations), 537–42
studies of, 532–36
cognition and, 516
complexity of, 519–20
cumulative cultural evolution and, 520
defined, 532
diversity of, 519
frequency of, 519
innovation, 524–25
perception-action view of, 536, 547, 548
relations produced through action with an object evident in, 537–42
theoretical perspectives on, 547
tool making and, 630–31
topological maps, 158–60
trace conditioning, 250
transformational approach to landmark- and surface-based search, 210–11
transitive responding, 559–61
in pigeons, squirrel monkeys, and humans, 559–60
triadic interactions, 645–46
lack of, 646–47
trial-and-error learning, 580–81
typicality effects. *See* prototypicality

unequal interval time-place (TP) task, 234–35
unobservability hypothesis, 364–65, 380, 382
concept formation research and, 365–71
physical causality research and, 376–80
theory of mind research and, 371–76
unobservables, 366, 376, 377, 380
causal role in behavior, 381–82
cognition and, 6–7
as homogeneous *vs.* heterogeneous class, 380–81

variability. *See also* operant nature of variability; operant variability
definitions and meanings of, 459
levels of, 461–66
sources of, 460
varied mapping, 134
vector(s), 203
generalization and averaging mechanism, 203–4
global, 190, 195–96
local, 196
sensorimotor, 196–99
view-based, 203
vigilance, 130–31
visual cognition research, 16–17. *See also specific topics*
visual concepts
negative concepts as going beyond polymorphous concepts, 620–22
neural basis of, 619–23
with and without explicit rules, 619–20
visual primacy effect, rehearsal and, 176–77
visual search experiments, and reaction times (RTs), 91–97

visual search paradigm, 134–35
volition, 477–78

Weber's law in animal timing, 285, 290–91
weight, brain and body, 564
"windows" into others' minds, 9
Wisconsin Card Sorting Test (WCST), 629
Wittgenstein, Ludwig
  Philosophical Investigations, *Tractatus Logico-Philosophicus*, and categorization, 398–402
Wittgensteinian evaluative perspectives on avian visual categorization, 399–400
work ethic, 664
working memory, 62, 132, 147, 151, 569
  for location of visited poles, 427–31
Wulst, 624, 628